Essays on Time in Buddhism

By the Same Author

(1) ***Amalā Prajñā : Aspects of Buddhist Studies***
(Co-edited with N. H. Samtani, 1989)

(2) ***The Uttaratantra of Maitreya***

(3) ***Time in Indian Philosophy*** (Edited)

(4) ***The Buddhist Philosophy of Time***

Bibliotheca Indo-Buddhica No. 78

Essays on Time in Buddhism

Edited by

H.S. Prasad
MA (BHU), PhD (ANU)
Department of Philosophy
University of Delhi

Sri Satguru Publications
A Division of
Indian Books Centre
Delhi

Published by
© Sri Satguru Publications
Indological and Oriental Publishers
a Division of
Indian Books Centre
40/5, Shakti Nagar,
Delhi-110007
India

First Edition, Delhi, 1991

ISBN—81-7030-262-5

Printed in India

Laser set at : **Sita Composers Pvt. Ltd.**, H-135 Ashok Vihar, Phase-I, Delhi-110052.

Printed at
Chawla Offset Printers
Delhi

Contents

Acknowledgements

I am most grateful to the concerned authors/ editors/ publishers for permission, where necessary, to reprint their works in this Volume. This has been shown within brackets against these works contained in the bibliography.

My sincerest thanks are due to the staff of the Menzies Library of the Australian National University, Canberra, for making available to me some of the materials for this Volume from other libraries abroad.

I am greatly indebted to Professor J.W. de Jong for his help in getting me the Australian National University scholarship and ensuring my fruitful stay in Canberra for three years, 1979 - 1982. Without the scholarship grant all this would not have been possible.

I am also grateful to my colleague Dr. V.K. Bharadwaja for his comments on an earlier draft of the *Introduction*.

H.S. Prasad

Introduction

H. S. Prasad

The idea of this Volume was conceived in the early 1979 during my stay at the Australian National University, Canberra, for my Ph.D. under Professor J.W. de Jong. At the end of 1981 I found that I had collected almost all those important materials, dealing with the Indian conceptions of time and temporality, which were already published in some journals or books. I classified them into two groups : (1) *Essays on Time in Buddhism*, and (2) *Time in Indian Philosophy*, representing non-Buddhist schools.

The aim of this enterprize is to present a picture of the modern studies of time and temporality based on Indian philosophical literature. As we can see, some of these studies are pursued by great savants like Th. Stcherbatsky, Louis de la Vallée Poussin, Stanislaw Schayer, A.B. Keith, O. Schrader and M. Walleser. In the absence of a comprehensive and systematic book on this subject it became imperative to collect and reprint them together. My own forthcoming book on time, *The Buddhist Philosophy of Time*[1], which is an outgrowth of my Ph.D. dissertation, will be a supplement to these collections. I hope these three works will arouse interest in the scholars to undertake further studies of the concept of time in Indian philosophy.

The ordering of the articles, although not strictly, is in accordance with the historical development of the Buddhist schools. In some more than one schools are discussed. But I prefer to begin with the Theravāda school, i.e. Pali Buddhism[2], through the Sarvāstivāda-Vaibhāṣika and Sautrāntika schools to the Mādhyamika and Yogācāra-Vijñānavāda schools. Naturally, there is parallel development of the thoughts of time and temporality to the historical development of these schools.

But one thing is very clear that no Buddhist School holds time as a substantive reality, except at one place in the *Vibhāṣā* where time is considered as a receptacle of everything. This view is called an erroneous view (*mithyādṛṣṭi*) by the Buddhists in general.

André Bareau's opening remark is true when he says : "Ever since its origin the Buddhist doctrine is concerned with the problem"(p. 1) of time so much so that Schayer could not resist himself from reacting enthusiastically on this issue that "As a matter of course, India is indebted for real progress in the critical analysis of the Time-problem ... to Buddhism. This progress was so essential that, if the history of Indian Time Philosophy is ever written, it will be in a large measure a history of Buddhist thought."(p. 322)

In Buddhism, the time-concept evolved from the experience of the fact of change which led to accepting it as the basic assumption of the Buddhist schools. The full implications of this is reflected in the Yogācāra- Vijñānavāda school of Vasubandhu and Diṅnāga. This has been intelligently discussed by Stcherbatsky and Satkari Mookerjee. Further, Bareau's treatment of time in early Buddhism (i.e. Hīnayāna Buddhism comprising Theravāda as well as Sarvāstivāda-Sautrāntika schools is based on the *Kathāvatthu*, Vasumitra's *Treatise of Sects*, the *Abhidharmakośa* and the *Mahāvibhāṣā*, which mentions some of the least known schools such as Kāśyapikas, Andhakas, Pūrvaśailas, Aparaśailas, Vātsīputrīyas and Bahuśrutiyas. His discussion of the three time-expressions : past, present and future according to these schools and his conclusion that one of the Buddhist views "sees in time a mere modal expression of things" (p. 12) and "the notion of time, as conceived by early Buddhism, is all the more important as it is closely related to the notion of ontology, the master conception of Buddhist Philosophy, whose fundamental notion is that of unsubstantiality" (ibid.), are interesting and to be further investigated.

Genjun H. Sasaki deals with the notion of time discussed mainly in the *Dhammasaṅgaṇi* together with its commentary *Aṭṭhasālinī* and the *Nyāyānusāraśāstra* of Saṃghabhadra which makes an attempt to counter the Sautrāntika criticism of the Sarvāstivāda on *traikālyavāda*. The latter discussion is also found in La Vallée Poussin's articles reprinted in this volume. Sasaki's approach is textual lacking critical analysis, but one can gather from it some ideas of time and temporality in early Buddhism. He tries to show (p. 26) that both the aspects of time, subjective as well as objective, have their psychological origin, i.e., they are consciousness-based. Time as a substantive reality, he rightly says, is denied throughout Buddhism. Another word which is used somewhat in place of time *(kāla)* is *'samaya'* having various connotations (pp. 25-26). Although the title of his paper is - "The Time Concept in Abhidharma", he fails to develop a clear concept of time in Abhidharma.

Louis de la Vallée Poussin's three articles are unique in the sense that they are exclusively based on the Chinese sources, the Sanskrit counterparts of which are now lost. He has done a commendable service to fill the serious lacunae created by this loss in the history of the Buddhist notion of time. His "Documents d'Abhidharma" is a restoration into French from the Chinese version of the *Vibhāṣā* and Saṃghabhara's *Nyāyānusāraśāstra* which is also a Vaibhāṣika text. The latter is one of the two texts, the other being the *Abhidharmadīpa,* which counter the Sautrāntika polemics against the Vaibhāṣika notion of temporality or the three time-epochs *(traikālyavāda)* contained in Vasubandhu's *Abhidharmakośa* and its *Bhāṣya.*

In April 1974, *Philosophy East and West* brought out a special issue containing verious articles on 'Time and Temporality'. Some of its articles are being reprinted here. One of them is D.J. Kalupahana's "The Buddhist Conception of time and temporality" in which he maintains that "early Buddhism considered both time and causation as parts of our experience, not as mere inferences based primarily on the succession of momentary ideas. Thus, it is possible to maintain that early Buddhism presents us with an empiricist analysis of time" (p. 483). He makes a controversial claim that "the Buddha seems to have considered time as an essential feature of the universe and the experience of it". (*Ibid.*). What I think is that it is change which is an essential feature of the universe in Buddhism and time is a derived notion from it. The Buddha's statement regarding time should be understood not at its face value, rather through the interpretation of the contexts in which he held an empiricist view of time. Kalupahana's own observations are based on such interpretations. He himself realises that in due course after the Buddha's passing away, the empiricist view of time and temporality changed completely. Such a shift was a logical implication of the Buddha's certain statements about the nature of the universe. His article, after all, makes an important contribution to the understanding of the notions of time and temporality in early Buddhism. But one of his final conclusions is very objectionable that "the Abhidharma scholasticism produces an absolutistic conception mainly because of its speculative approach" (p.486). What I find is that even in the Abhidharma, time as an absolute substantive reality is clearly denied. Some of these issues are discussed in one of my articles on the concept of time in Pali Buddhism mentioned earlier.

I agree with Kenneth K. Inada that :

> The Buddhist would have no problem at all in accepting or incorporating the conventional way in which we speak of time, that is, in terms of the three temporal periods - past, present, and future *(atīta, paccupanna, anāgata)*. It is the function of the mind, after all, to conceive of time in that order or indeed to give order to the nature of things. Thus, whether it is simple clock time, physical time (measurements of movements), or psychological time, the mind knows or senses time because of the abstractive quality. And to this extent, time is conventional *(papañca/ prapañca)* but very useful. (p. 470)

He very well summarises the Mādhyamika approach to time and temporality. Time is nothing more than temporality in terms of past, present and future at conventional level. This means that even from the empirical point of view time is not a reality, and temporality of the sequence of events (or entities) shows their relational origination and thus the voidness of their own nature *(niḥsvabhāvatā, śūnyatā)* from the ultimate point of view. He rightly maintains that temporality is "lived time" (p. 475).

A. Charlene McDermott's article mainly discusses in the light of contemporary Western thinking the Sautrāntika polemic against the four Sarvāstivādins: Dharmatrāta, Ghoṣaka, Buddhadeva and Vasumitra, found in the *Abhidharmakośabhāṣya* and the *Tattvasaṃgrahapañjikā*. Her such endevour cannot go unchallenged. Her observation that there is "an undeniable kinship between Dharmatrāta and the detensers for whom reality is at bottom a beginningless neo-Eleatic whole" (p. 410) is true in the case of other Sarvāstivādins also, namely, Ghoṣaka, Vasumitra and Buddhadeva. All the four Sarvāstivāda theories bear such kinship. Further, Ghoṣaka-type modification of *dharma* is basic and common in all the remaining three, who too admit the underlying becomingless substance, a position held by detensers. In Dharmatrāta, change is not only epistemic in Bradleyan sense, but they are very much real in the Sarvāstivāda realism. Hence it is wrong to say that in Dharmatrāta temporal evolution is not solved but dissolved.

In Ghoṣaka, *lakṣaṇa-anyathātva* is not without Dharmatrāta-type change on which are based the *lakṣaṇas* or the characteristics of pastness, presentness and futuritty. Change cannot be explained in Ghoṣaka in terms of a *dharma*'s adjuncts. The so-called adjuncts which, according to McDermott, belong to a *dharma* are not real but only psychological. The perceptual state of a *dharma* gives rise to the notion of present time; its earlier or preceding state, which is now a content of memory, to past time and its succeeding state or would-be state, which is a mere expectation at the present moment, to future time. In the case of a non-temporally characterized "content" (i.e. *dravya* of the Sarvāstivāda), this is the only way of conceiving temporality in terms of past, present and future. But the Sarvāstivāda postulation of *'prāpti'*, a new metaphysical category *(dravya)* as an external force which causes modification in *dharma* and thus gives rise to the notion of temporality, leads to an infinite regress. That is why the Sautrāntikas maintain that a *dharma* is inherently potential *(samartha, śaktirūpa)*[3] in changing itself from one state to another. McDermott is right when she, following A.N. Prior, says that "one cannot form a tensed utterance by attaining "some sort of modifier to ... a non- temporally characterized 'content'", seems to me to sum up neatly the Sautrāntika case against Ghoṣaka." (p. 410)

From a careful reading of the *Abhidharmakośa* together with its *Bhāṣya* and *Vyākhyā*, it will be clear that the Sautrāntikas do accept change of the states *(anyathātva)*[4] of an enduring substratum *(āśraya)*. The notions of sempiternal substratum and its modification or change are not mutually incompatible. The non-temporality of substratum and the temporality of its states are co-extensive. I have discussed in detail the Sautrāntika *āśraya* theory together with their *bīja* theory in my *Introduction* to *The Uttaratantra of Maitreya.*[5]

Further, McDermott's comparison of Ghoṣaka with McTaggart is not warranted. McTaggart shows the impossibility of A-series (past, present and future) and thus the reality of time, whereas Ghoṣaka at least admits the possibility of A-series. Moreover, from the above discussion it is obvious that the Sautrāntikas will not reject the theory that "becoming is a species of qualitative change" (p. 411).

McDermott seems to be very fond of tense logic, but her treatment of the Buddhist notion of temporality is questionable. She interprets the Sautrāntikas as P- tensers (p. 414), for which 'real' means 'what now exists' (n.2). I think they are also at the same time C-tensers, for which 'real' means 'what has existed, exists now, or will exist', if we take into account their theories of substratum *(āśraya)*, seed *(bīja)* and change *(anyathātva)* where the underlying substance is timeless or atemporal (=detensed). This means that the Sautrāntikas are all together P-tensers, C- tensers and de- tensers. But the significance of McDermott's article lies in the fact that it shows the relevance of the Sautrāntika view of time and temporality in the light of Western contemporary thinking and this initiates a discussion which should be pursued further.

Paul M. William's article - "Buddhadeva and Temporality" is similar to that of McDermott. He analyses the Sautrāntika arguments against Buddhadeva's theory of temporality on the line of McTaggart's analysis of temporal events in the light of A-Series (past, present and future) and B-series (earlier than, simultaneous with and later than). He has consulted the same Buddhist sources as done by McDermott, but for McTaggart he has heavily used R.M. Gale's edited book: *The Philosophy of Time*[6] which comprises editor's own illuminating introductions to all of its five sections.

Paul M. Williams makes a fanciful conjecture that the occurrence of the words *apekṣā* and *apekṣya* both in the Sanskrit sources quoting Buddhadeva's view on the past, present and future, and in the *Madhyamakakārikā* of Nāgārjuna, chapter XIX, suggests that

> Nāgārjuna's approach in constructing his refutation of time took as its starting point an approach to time which he knew already existed among philosophers of the school he was combatting. It could therefore be conjectured that perhaps Buddhadeva's view was the most firmly established one at the time, or it is even possible that it was the only Sarvāstivādin view on the subject that Nāgārjuna knew about. There would, after all, be little point in constructing a refutation of time based on a view nobody held. (p. 419)

Even if this is true, it serves no philosophic purpose, and secondly, Nāgārjuna uses these words extensively to show the relational dependence of the concepts of the entities. This is his characteristic style of refuting philosophic views. Williams' conjecture is based on certain historicity calculated by Louis de la Vallée Poussin which proves that Buddhadeva was earlier than Nāgārjuna. Still his article is worth-reading, but his following remarks are untenable :

> It is interesting to note in passing just what the metaphysical elements in Buddhadeva's theories were. It is clear that his explanations of the distinctions between the temporal stages of events is logico-linguistic and not metaphysical in the sense that the theories of Dharmatrāta, Ghoṣaka and Vasumitra were. (p. 426)

Nowhere do these three Sarvāstivādins maintain time or the past, present and future as metaphysical entities. They do, of course, take the *dharmas* as an eternal substantive reality (*dravya*).[7] But their talk of temporality is always with respect to the modes of existence of a *dharma*. This is evident from their use of such terms as *adhvan, atīta, pratyutpanna* and *anāgata* instead of *kāla*. The similar is the case, as Lewis R. Lancaster rightly says, with the early Mahāyāna *Sūtras* in which "the discussion of time *(adhvan)* does not mention the term in the singular, only in the plural : the three times of past, future and present", (p. 499). He quotes a Chinese source, according to which, a Buddhist school called Dārṣṭāntika (perhaps not the same which is identified with the Sautrāntika school) proposes that

> the three times exist and are permanent while the conditioned entities which move through them are impermanent. They described their view by giving the analogy of three houses one beside the other. From the first house a man emerges and goes to the second, that is, he leaves the future and enters the present, then he moves from the second house to the third, thereby going from the present to the past. Man is the impermanent and fleeting one while the three houses of time are fixed and stand always ready to receive the constant flow of impermanent things. (*Ibid.*)

Lancaster thinks that the Mahāyāna literature, particularly the Mādhyamika, gives contradictory accounts of the concept of time. Kumārajīva's Chinese commentary on the *Prajñāpāramitā* treats time in direct opposition to that of Nāgārjuna in his *Madhyamaka-kārikā*, chapter XIX:

> If the triple times have not even a single distinguishing characteristic, does this means that the Mahāyāna taught the nonexistence of time? It is never said that time is lacking existence, but only that time is empty *(śūnyatā)* and that it is suchness *(tathatā)*, for since it lacks any marks, it is the whole reality, the truly universal. But this is not only true for time, it is true of everything, for example, form, *skandhas*, *dharmas* all conditioned things. (p. 500)

I think the contradictory account of the concept of time in the Mādhyamika is superficial. The *Madhyamaka- kārikā* of Nāgārjuna does not represent the whole Mādhyamika tradition. As I have argued in my *Introduction* to *The Uttaratantra of Maitreya*, this text prepares the background only by rejecting all philosophic views including those about time, to pave the way for creating a universal spiritual culture. Maitreya's *Uttaratantra* (or the *Ratnagotravibhāga*) is one of those texts which establish the oneness of ultimate reality on this line. At this level, the maniness of phenomena is shown to be only epistemic lacking independent ontological status.

The concept of time can be formed only when change in reality or succession of events representing past, present and future are experienced. In the absence of such change in terms of temporality, etc., there will be no concept of time. Time is in this sense a derived notion. At the level of suchness (*tathatā*) or ultimate reality, no such change is admitted whether in Kumārajīva's commentary on the *Prajñāpāramitā* or in the *Uttaratantra* of Maitreya. Thus, if time lacks any marks, how can we say that there is time. When Lancaster says that "it is the whole reality, the truly universal", he takes time as the durational whole of the reality.

The four Sarvāstivādins, mentioned earlier, tried to explain the temporal becoming in terms of different modes (or states or temporal characteristics or temporal relations) of a *dharma* whose underlying substance remains unchanged during its transition (*adhvan*) from one mode to another. These are inessential attributes of a *dharma*. Change *in* (not *of*) sempiternal essence of a *dharma* should be analysed into a series or a succession of events which are modes, etc., and change *of* time of events again into a succession of events. If this is so, then John M. Koller's charge against the Sarvāstivādins that they commit a mistake by admitting apparent changes in the changeless substance is baseless. He says :

> having made this mistake they - as exemplified by Dharmatrātra try to account for temporal becoming in terms of changing *appearances*. But having already effectively denied change by postulating unchanging being as the basic reality, they get not real, but only apparent, becoming. In effect, they have denied temporal becoming. (pp. 491-92)

Koller (pp. 494-95), supporting D.J. Kalupahana, wrongly maintains that Nāgārjuna's "analysis of time in chapter 19 of the *Mūlamadhyamaka-kārikā* is...directed primarily at the Sarvāstivādin, who took time to be an ontological container of change and divided the container into three segments: past, present, and future." I do not find even a single reference from the Sarvāstivāda sources which substantiates Koller's contention. But his articles together with the ones by Inada and Lancaster certainly contribute to our understanding of the notions of time and temporality in the Mādhyamika school.

Two of the most important items of the present collection are the translation by Stanislaw Schayer of *Traikālyaparīkṣā* of Śāntarakṣita's *Tattvasaṃgraha* with Kamalaśīla's commentary on it supplemented with preface, two introductory chapters and an appendix containing the translation of Prajñākaramati's refutation of the *traikālyavāda* found in his commentary on Śāntideva's *Bodhicaryāvatāra*, and La Vallée Poussin's "Documents d'Abhidharma".

Both Śāntarakṣita and Kamalaśīla are known for their Sautrāntika-Yogācāra leanings, whereas Prajñākaramati is a Prāsaṅgika-Mādhyamika, a follower of Nāgārjuna's *śūnyavāda*. Schayer's method of translation here is a model for us to imitate. Its footnotes and references from Chinese version of the *Vibhāṣā* enhance its importance in understanding the Sarvāstivāda (Vaibhāṣika)- Sautrāntika controversy on time and temporality. It also presents the gist of the central doctrines of the two schools. Those who are interested in understanding the twin concepts of time and temporality in Buddhism, for them Schayer's *Contributions to the Problem of Time in Indian Philosophy* is an indispensable and invaluable guide and source. Had Kalupahana and Koller consulted this work, and the above cited Sarvāstivāda literature, they would not have committed the mistake of interpreting the Sarvāstivāda notion of time as an ontological container of change. Schayer writes,

> The [Sarvāstivāda] doctrine of the *traikālyavāda* is an interesting and original attempt at replacing the hypostasis of a substantial Time by another hypostasis, *viz.* that of real future and past elements of being. Each *dharma* exists through the three phases of the future, present and past. The future has no beginning but it has an end, the present has both a beginning and an end; the past has a beginning but no end. In this sense it is said that a *dharma* exists always (=*sarvam asti* = *sadāsti* = *sarvadāsti*) and that it is only its "mode of existence" (*bhāva, avasthā*) which is changing. (p. 310).

The past, present and future are not independent entities or segments of ontological or substantive time, as Kalupahana and Koller think. As a matter of fact, they are derived notions from various modes of a *dharma*. Their status is purely psychological.[8] They are nothing but tensed ways of expressions by a speaker. The speaker's intentionality or his state of belief causes these expressions, as and when he remembers an event (in the case of past), perceives it (as in the case of present) and anticipates it (as in the case of future). In every case, there is reference to consciousness. But remembering, perceiving or anticipating the events in the history of a *dharma* does not in any sense show that they are ontological entities independent of the *dharma* and consciousness. Their empirical applicability is only in our tensed ways of talking. But the properties of tensed expressions do not refer to the corresponding properties of the time-segments. A Buddhist will never talk of time other than temporality. Time (*kāla*) subjected to criticism by Nāgārjuna in his *Madhyamaka-kārikā*, therefore, does not belong to the Sarvāstivāda school, rather to a non-Buddhist school, such as Nyāya-Vaiśeṣika. It so happens that sometimes in the absence of an actual propounder, Nāgārjuna conceives of a view and crticises it. For him, Buddhist as well as non-Buddhist or for that matter any philosophic view on any topic is equally contradictory in itself or conflicts with other views.

Schayer's calling of the Time-notion in some of the non-Buddhist schools as "physicalism" (p. 309) is disturbing. Time is not a physical entity in any system of Indian philosophy. In certain myths, time (*kāla*) is personified or deified, but this does not mean that time is a physical entity. Some philosophers in the West do talk of "spatialised time", but then this time would require a hyper-time to endure through. The physical or spatialised time is conceived only when we think of "space-time as four-dimensional space in the geometrical sense of the word 'space' ".[9] But the traditional concept of time as impersonal substance will not accept time in this sense. Schayer's "physicalism" seems to be different from the sense in which a contemporary philosopher takes it as "The doctrine that all propositions asserting "matters of fact and real existence" can be formulated as statements about publicly observable physical objects and activities."[10]

Further, Schayer, I think, has misunderstood Vasumitra when he says,

> in reality, Vasumitra does not deny that there is an 'increase' of the past *dharmas* and a 'decrease' of the future *dharmas*. He means only that, in comparison with the immensity of the future and of the past, the saying that *dharmas* either 'increase' or 'decrease' has no practical

> significance. We can guess the intention of such a point of view: it was probably the wish to retain the old Buddhist conception of the future pouring itself into the past, and to avoid at the same time the necessarily arising consequence that the whole world automatically strives after extinction. (p. 325)

Vasumitra, a Sarvāstivādin as he is, is a realist and substantialist for whom *dharmas* are everlasting (*sarvadā asti*) and substantive reality (*dravya*)[11]. A *dharma*, according to him, is activated by certain forces (viz. *prāpti*; cf. the four *saṃskṛtalakṣaṇas: jāti, sthiti, jarā* and *vināśa*)[12]. This activity is called its causal efficiency (*arthakriyākāritva*). Its potent state before it becomes causally efficient is said to belong to the future time; its actualised state, i.e. when it is causally efficient, the time connected with it is called present time; and the time connected with that state of a *dharma* when it has become quiescent after having performed its causal efficiency is called past time. There is nothing like the flow of time from future, through present, to past, and thus no gradual increasing of the quantity of the past or decreasing of that of future. It is ridiculous to say that Vasumitra wishes to take care of such a myth prevalent in the pre-systematic era of Buddhism. In the exhaustive list of the 75 elements of existence (*dharma*), time appears nowhere.

Schayer (p. 327) thinks that parallel to the three non-contingent *dharmas* and 72 contingent (*dharmas*), there are respectively absolute time and empirical time present in the Vaibhāṣika doctine, though in disguise. Such an interpretation is entirely against the Vaibhāṣika contention. Contingency or non-contingency is the characteristic feature of certain *dharmas*. The two types of times are derived notions from them to satisfy our psychology. Further, as I have said, certain forces work on the contingent *dharmas* to make them causally efficient. The transition (*adhvan*) of the *dharmas* from one state to another gives rise to the psychological notion of temporality, i.e. past, present and future, which are not ontologically independent time-phases through which a *dharma* passes one by one. They should be understood in colloquial or metaphorical sense only as Schayer (p. 328) himself admits by correcting or contradicting his earlier statement. All this is the negative side of his monograph. But its positive side as already pointed out deserves serious attention and should be emphasized more.

Th. Stcherbatsky's "Vasubandhu on the Fundamental Principle of the Sarvāstivāda School" is an English translation of the *Abhidharmakośa-bhāṣya*, V. 24-26, which deals with the Sarvāstivāda-Sautrāntika controversy on time and temporality. This has already been discussed above. His "The Theory of Instantaneous Being" and those by Satkari Mookerjee, Rita Gupta and Jwala Prasad dwell on the Buddhist doctrine of momentariness and its metaphysical and epistemological implications. The ever-changing character of the state of a *dharma* has its bearings on the Buddhist notions of time and temporality. In this sense they are significant and hence included in the present Volume.

M. Walleser's analysis of the *Milindapañha* on time and temporality supports the general Buddhist view of them. The text rightly says that the root cause of the view of time as a reality lies in our ignorance about the nature of reality.

Alex Wayman's article explores some new materials including the *Madhyānta-vibhāga*, a Yogācāra text. He has, on the basis of some Indo-Tibeten materials, added another category of "No Time" to Mircea Eliade's two categories of "Great Time" and "Profane Time", without attributing, unlike Eliade, any ontological status to them. He takes "No Time" as the source of religion, "Great Time" as the source of myth, and "Profane Time" as the source of reason. In the system philosophy of the Buddhists, according to him, either there is no time or if there is any discussion of it, it is profane.

Stcherbatsky's third contribution, "Le tempts (kāla)", is taken from his book : *La théorie de la connaissance et la logique chez les buddhistes tardifs*. It deals with the concept of time in Buddhist as well as non-Buddhist systems. He discusses the Buddhist denial of time as a substance, Nāgārjuna's critique of time and temporality, and other related concepts such as space, moment and causality in usual manner.

Notes and References

1. To be published soon by Indian Books Centre, Delhi.
2. See my article, 'The Concept of Time in Pali Buddhism', *East and West*, Vol. 38, Nos 1-4 (December 1988), pp. 107-136.
3 A *dharma* is impregnated with *vāsanā*, which is a motive force (*śaktirūpa*) causing evolution in it. In this sense, I have called a *dharma* to be inherently potential (*śaktirūpa*). Cf. *Pramāṇavārtikabhāṣya* of Prajñākaragupta (quoted in A.K. Chatterjee, *Yogācāra Idealism*, Delhi, Motilal Banarsidass, 1975, p. 88, fn. 5) : *iṣyate vāsanāvidbhiḥ śaktirūpā hi vāsanā; Nyāyaratnākara* on Kumārila's *Ślokavārtika, Śūnyavāda, śloka* 17; Yaśomitra's *Vyākhyā* on the *Abhidharmakośa-bhāṣya* (ed. by D.D. Shastri, Varanasi, 4 volumes, 1970-73), p. 218.16: *śaktiviśeṣalakṣaṇaṃ bījabhāvam; Abhidharmakośa-bhāṣya, ibid., p. 217.3-4: kiṃ punar idaṃ bījaṃ nāma. yan nāmarūpaṃ phalotpattau samarthaṃ sākṣāt pāramparyeṇa vā. saṃtatipariṇāmaviśeṣāt;* and *Vyākhyā*, p. 990.22: *bījaṃ sāmarthyaṃ cetaso gotram.*
4. Cf. *Abhidharmakośa- bhāṣya, ibid.*, p. 217.5: *ko 'yaṃ pariṇāmo nāma. saṃtater anyathātvam.*
5. Published by Indian Books Centre, Delhi, 1990, notes 16-23.
6. Macmillan, London, 1968.
7. Cf. *Abhidharmakośa- bhāṣya, op. cit.*, on V. 25, and *supra*, n. 5.
8. For discussion on this issue by the Western schol ars, see *supra*, n.6, pp. 70ff.
9. J.J.C. Smart, 'Spatialising Time' in Gale, *op. cit.*, p. 166
10. Antony Flew, *A Dictionary of Philosophy*, Pan Books, London, 1981, p. 249.
11. See *supra*, n. 7.
12. See my article, 'A Critique of the Saṃskṛtalakṣaṇas' in *Śramaṇa Vidyā : Studies in Buddhism* (Professor Jagannath Upadhyaya Commemoration Volume), ed. by N. H. Samtani, Varanasi, Central Institute of Higher Tibetan Studies, 1987, pp. 151- 59.

The notion of time in early Buddhism

Ever since its origin the Buddhist doctrine is concerned with the problem of time. Indeed, does not the first of the Noble Truths teach us that all is suffering and impermanence, or rather that all is suffering in as much as all is impermanence? This idea is developed in the common doctrine of the Sutra and we are taught that all things are impermanent (*anitya*) because they are composite (*saṃskṛta*) and thus possess different characteristics, to wit production (*uppāda*) or birth (*jati*), duration (*sthiti*) and old age (*jarā*) or the change of condition (*thitassa aññathatta*) and disappearance (*vaya*) or cessation (*nirodha*). Such is the common basis on which rest all the speculations of early Buddhism (1) relating to time and the problems to which it gives rise. From this starting point a whole series of discussions spread out in several directions, some of which interfere with each other and of which it is difficult to determine the chronology.

One of these series refers to the instant (*kṣaṇa*). Indeed, all things are impermanent, all are of limited duration, and in some cases this duration is the briefest that can be conceived, *i.e.* the instant. Let us leave aside the several attempts made towards defining with precision this duration, and let us only bear in mind the intention that lies behind it: the instant is the minimum duration, the atom of time. Although among the characteristic features of composites are duration or change of condition, most schools soon come to explain the change of things as a succession of momentary states (*kṣaṇika*). The origin of this notion is certainly to be looked for in the axiom accepted by some Buddhist schools and found also outside Buddhism, which holds that two psychic conditions cannot co-exist in thought because the field of conscience is unique. Consequently, psychic phenomena should be considered as a series of momentary states. This once granted, it was all the easier to extend this explanation to the whole field of the phenomena of the outer world, as no clear distinction was drawn between the nature of material things and of spiritual ones. Thus most of the early Buddhist sects, the Sarvāstivādin, the Mahīśāsaka, the Kāśyapiva, the Vātsiputria, the Pūrvaśaila, and the Apasaśaila, maintained that all things are momentary. As all composite things are impermanent, the Pūrvaśaila declared, they only last a single instant of thought (*ekcittakkhaṇika*), for, being impermanent, what difference is there between a thing which is rapidly destroyed and another which lasts for a long time? (2).

The reasoning of Vasubandhu is more elaborated: « Destruction is not dependent on a cause: therefore the conditioned perishes as soon as it is born; should it not perish at once it will not perish later on, for it remains the same. Now, as you admit that it perishes, you must admit that it perishes at once. Would you say that a conditioned thing changes; that consequently it will later on be subject to destruction? To maintain that a certain thing changes, becomes another thing, while yet remaining that same thing whose features you say you see modified, is absurd » (3). Other schools refused to accept the theory of the momentariness of all things. Among others, the Theravādin called attention to the fact that the great earth, the great ocean, the king of mountains Sumeru, water, fire, wind, the grass, the woods, the trees, last much longer than a single instant of thought (4). If all things, they went on to say, had only momentary duration, it would be impossible to explain sensorial knowledge, for its several elements are not produced at the same time. Not only was this opinion more in keeping with observation, but it had also remained nearer to the basic doctrine which assumed as we have seen, a certain duration in phenomena, and a certain development. On the other hand, the other schools, having carried the idea of impermanence to its utmost limit, which is instantaneity, were soon to find themselves faced with difficulties when endeavouring to harmonise this notion with the theory of the time characteristics of composites.

Indeed, how could a phenomenon of momentary duration possess production, duration, change of state and cessation? The Sarvāstivādin tried to achieve the impossible by reconciling momentariness, total realism (*sarvāstivāda*), and the letter of the *Sūtra*. They taught that a single instant possesses the three characteristics of production, decline and cessation, whose times of action are different: at the moment when a thing is produced, production comes into play; at the moment when a thing ceases, decline and cessation, come into play. Although the substance only exists one single moment, activity has a before and an afterwards. Things were still further complicated by the fact that they admitted secondary features (*anulakṣana*) as the production of production and also because in keeping with their panrealism they held them to be substantial realities (5).

The Sautrāntika and the Dārṣṭāntika, whose doctrine was more elastic, got round these difficulties more adroitly. The Dārṣṭāntika affirmed, on the one hand, that the characteristic features of composites are not substances (*drayva*) for they are included in the disjointed composites of thought (*cittaviprayuktasaṃskāra*), i.e. abstractions possessing no intrinsic reality (6). Moreover, the moment, they said, is devoid of the three characteristics of birth, decline and cessation, for, did it possess them, it would have to be born, decline and cease all at the same time, which is obviously impossible (7).

On their side, the Sautrāntika did not recognise the characteristic of duration (*sthiti*) — but like the Theravādin — only that of modification (*sthityanythātva*) (8). There was in their theories a certain amount of evolutionism, in opposition to the pure Instantaneousness of the Sarvāstivādin. This trend is found again in the theory attributed to them by the *Vijñaptimātratāsiddhi* according to which these characteristics may be attributed not only to the moment but also to a certain prolonged condition (9). It would thus seem that they adopted on this point a compromise between the opinion of the Sarvāstivādin, for whom the characteristics are proper to the instant, and that of the Sammatīya, according to whom they are, on the contrary, proper to a prolonged condition (10). It seems indeed that the Dārṣṭāntika, who gave to the moment its real value, *i.e.* the nullity of duration, were also evolutionists. They maintained, in opposition to the Sarvāstivādin, that things arise gradually and not all at once (11). Nevertheless, the same source attributes to them a theory which it is rather difficult to interpret, but which seems to contradict the previous one, as it claims that there is neither a precise moment of production nor a precise moment of cessation, so that, in the case of composites, there are only two times, that in which they have not yet been produced, and that in which they have already been produced; or that in which they have not yet ceased, and that in which they have already ceased (12).

The only two schools whose speculations on the nature of the moment have come down to us, the Sarvāstivādin and the Dārṣṭāntika, therefore held diametrically opposite opinions. The former, having inconsiderately made of radical momentarism one of the bases of their doctrine, had been led to introduce far too many elements into the moment, swelling, thickening and weighting this atom of time with all the potentialities, the efficiency of duration. As a reaction to this the Dārṣṭāntika laid down *a priori* the equation « moment = zero », and stuck to it stolidly, refusing to see in the moment anything but its nullity, and this drove them back to the evolutionary stand which is more orthodox and more in keeping with common sense.

Another series of speculations, which are much more important for the doctrine as a whole, forced the Buddhist doctors of the several schools, as early, it would seem, as the 3rd century B.C., to take into account other problems relating to time. Instead of breaking time up into its ultimate elements, and scrutinising their nature, the discussions con-

Relief symbolising the Hinâyâna. Gandhâra, 2nd-4th cent. A.D.

ducted along these lines examined time as the bearer of events and more especially of knowledge and causality.

It would seem that it was the eponymic theory of the Sarvāstivādin that gave rise to this series of controversial debates. All exists (*sarvam asti*), they declared, the past (*atīta*) and the future (*anāgata*) exist with the same right as the present exists [*pratyutpanna* (13)] The Blessed One indeed has said in his *Sūtra* « Oh monks, if the past matter (*rūpa*) did not exist, the holy instructed auditor would not exist. If you do not take past matter into consideration... If future matter did not exist, the holy instructed auditor would not be « denying consideration » to past matter... If future matter did not exist the holy instructed auditor would not be, « not complacent » in the future matter. It is because future matter exists that the holy auditor instructs... » We deduce from this *Sūtra* — evidently forged to meet the needs of the cause, and which the other schools do not recognise, — that the Sarvāstivādin drew no distinction between things in themselves, such as past and future matter, and the representations one can have of them and which serve as subjects for meditation. Thus we find here a first sign of that

Bodhisattva Maitreya, Wei Art (6th cent. A.D.)

coarse and even puerile realism on which their doctrine down the centuries has been based and which was often to give rise to grave difficulties for them.

They also noted that the Buddha had said: « Knowledge (*vijñāna*) is produced by two things. What are they? The organ of sight (*cakṣurindriya*) and what is visible (*rūpa*), mind (*manas*) and things (*dharma*) ». On the other hand, they noted, it is impossible that in the same persons (*pudgala*) two thoughts (*citta*) should exist at the same time, more especially that of the object to be known (*alambana*) and that of the means of knowing it. This led them to the conclusion that one of these thoughts will still be in the future at the time when the first is born. So, they concluded, if things past and future did not exist, there could be no meeting between the agent of knowledge and its object, and all knowledge would be impossible. And here we find the opinion that had already been at the basis of momentariness which holds that two psychic conditions cannot coexist in the same person because in him the field of consciousness is only one.

The Sarvāstivādin based their theory on yet another consideration which concerned more closely the very doctrine of Buddhism. The same person — they contended — cannot simultaneously accomplish an act (*karman*) and receive the fruit to which it has given rise (*vipākaphala*). When an act is performed, the fruit to which it gives rise is a future thing, and when the agent picks that fruit the act which engendered it is a thing of the past. If therefore things past and future did not exist, past acts, being non-existent, could not engender fruits. It must be confessed that bold as this thought was, in this particular case it was very ingenious, since Buddhism rejected all personal substances which, like the *ātman* of the *Upaniṣads* or the *jīva* of the Jains, might have acted as a support for the mechanism of retribution for deeds committed.

But this panrealism soon came up against difficulties within the Sarvāstivādin themselves, when they tried to go deeper into it. Four principal interpretations are offered by the partisans of *sarvāstivāda*. According to Dharmatrāta, durable objects preserve the substance (*dravya*) but the state (*bhava*), that is to say figure (*ākṛti*), qualities (*guṇa*) and above all the past, future or present state, changes. Thus the thing abandons the future state for the present one, and then that for the past. In the opinion of Ghosaka the past, the present and the future are features (*lakṣaṇa*) and not states. According to Vasumitra they are positions (*avasthā*) similar to the boxes in which one places the counters and which assure them their different values of units, tens, hundreds. This interpretation was held to be the best. Lastly, according to Buddhadeva the past, the future and the present are based on reciprocal relations (*anyonya*) one and the same thing being past in relation to what will follow it, and future in relation to what has preceded it. As we can see, the past, the present and the future were not considered by the Sarvāstivādin as things in themselves, but as modes of being, states, features, positions, reciprocal relations. Indeed these explanations reflect notions that disagree with other points of the doctrine. On the one hand they consider things as realities possessing a substance, which runs counter to the Buddhist conception of unsubstantiality, and durability, which runs counter to the momentarism professed by the school. On the other hand, the interpretation given by Vasumitra, which is considered as the only orthodox one, is dangerously near to the theory we shall examine further on, according to which time exists independently of things and is permanent.

Let us now examine the objections the other sects opposed to the Sarvāstivādin. Space does not allow us to take up again in detail the debate between Sautrāntika and Sarvāstivādin on the panrealism that is outlined in the *Abhidharmakosa* of Vasubandhu and to which the reader will kindly refer (14); here we will only quote the more important attacks: « The Sautrāntika criticises: If the past, if the future exist as things, then they are present: why describe them as past and future? » (15) This objection, at least in our opinion, is decisive, and shows that in the circles nearest to the Sarvāstivādin, people were not dupes to the subterfuge which consisted in calling past or future those things which possessed all the efficiency and all the reality of the present. Moreover, « if they are said to exist really, then one admits that conditioned things (*saṃskṛta*) exist always, and are therefore eternal » (16). Thus the panrealism of the Sarvāstivādin tended to restore a substantialism that original Buddhism had condemned.

The objections of the Theravadin are rather different (17). They claimed that according to their very definitions things past and future cannot exist: What has ceased (*niruddha*) has passed (*vigata*), is transformed (*vipariṇata*), has disappeared (*atthaṅgata*), is exterminated (*abbhatthaṅgata*), and can no more exist than can things that are not yet born (*ajāta*), have not yet become (*abhūta*), nor are created (*asañjata*), nor reborn (*anibbata*), nor completely reborn (*anabhinibbata*), nor appeared (*apātubhūta*).

And here we find again, expressed in another form, the objection of the Sautrāntika, who claim that only that which is present can be said to exist. Moreover, the Theravādin declared, one should not mix up the present, the past and the future with the things which they affect, as the Sarvāstivādin seem to do. For when present matter (*rūpa*) ceases (*nirujjhamāna*) it leaves (*jahati*) its condition of being present (*paccuppannabhāva*) but it does not abandon its condition of matter (*rū-*

The expression of contemplative repose on the face of the Buddha. Gandhāra, 8th cent. A.D.

pabhāva). One cannot, therefore, say of present matter that in it « matter » and « present » are identical (*ekaṭṭha*) similar (*sama*), equal (*samabhāga*), alike (*tajja*). This does not mean that matter never changes its state of matter, for, were it so, it would be, like the *nibbāna*, permanent (*nicca*), solid (*dhuva*), eternal (*sassata*) and not subject to the law of transformation (*avipariṇāma-dhamma*).

This objection deserves our attention. In the first place it shows that the Theravādin drew a clear distinction between things and their temporal qualifications. Their theory is much like that of Dharmatrāta, which we examined above and which was accused by the other Sarvāstivādin of transformism. Now this theory was accepted by the Theravādin. as is shown by their comment on matter which, as it is not eternal, must sooner or later lose its condition of matter. An objection comes at once to mind: when matter gives up its state of being matter what remains of it? Unfortunately no answer is given to this question, and in spite of its importance we may set it aside, for it relates to the nature of being and not to the nature of time. The Theravādin went on analysing the three epochs. If indeed the present and the future must relinquish their state of present or of future, this does not hold good for the past, for what is past remains for ever past, although it is not, like the *nibbāna*, permanent, solid, eternal etc. They then rejected the argument that the Sarvāstivādin drew from the process of cognition. The perception or cognition of an object, they said, is only possible if the several factors of this perception or this cognition — and more especially of the organ and the object — are present and therefore simultaneous.

They therefore rejected the famous theory, accepted by the Sarvāstivādin and by other schools, which holds that two thoughts cannot exist simultaneously on the same plane of consciousness. The Theravādin added other arguments to their rejection, which seem to have been peculiar to them. If things past were to exist, they declared, then past passions (*rāga*), hatreds (*doṣa*), and errors (*moha*) would exist in the Arahant and would continue to afflict him as they did in the past; and this is incompatible with his nature of Arahant. Likewise, one could make use of past hands, feet, water, fire, etc., which is contrary to current experience. Lastly, there would be three series of aggregates (*khandha*), of domains (*āyatana*), of elements (*dhātu*), etc., one present, another past, and the last future, a theory which cannot be upheld.

Although the eponymic theory of the Sarvāstivādin was difficult to defend, it can claim the merit of calling attention to certain important sides of the Buddhist doctrine. While it was fairly easy to find a solution to the problem of the process of cognition by admitting, as the Theravādin did, the simultaneous existence of several thoughts in the same individual, it was much more difficult to explain the mechanism of the retribution for actions performed. Indeed, the only real halfway theory between the *sarvāstivāda* and their opponents which has been upheld, that of the Kasyapīya, represents one more attempt to solve this last question. The case is the same — they explain — as with plants. Until the sprout has appeared what exists is the seed. but as soon as the sprout appears the seed ceases to exist (18). But in spite of this nice analogy, their theory was as difficult to uphold as that of the Sarvāstivādin. Attached both by them and by their adversaries, it never played an important part. The Theravādin not unreasonably saw in it a variation of the *sarvāstivāda* and refuted it with the help of the same arguments they used against the *sarvāstivāda;* while the Sarvāstivādin looked upon it as a kind of mutilated *sarvāstivāda* which failed to recognise the existence of all the past.

The ontological theory of the Ardhaka can be looked upon as a middle course, for it admits that one can say of a thing that it both exists and does not exist at the same time. Thus the past exists as the past but does not exist as present and future (19). This was a position of relativity which was nothing but an emanation of the deeply unsubstantialist doctrines adopted by most of the sects of the Mahāsāṅghika group. Against these views the Theravādin objected that existence (*atthibhāva*) and inexistence (*natthibhāva*) are not identical (*ekaṭṭha*), alike (*sama*), equal (*samabhāga*) and similar (*tajja*), and that consequently the same thing cannot both exist and not exist. There would certainly be much to say on these two ontological positions, both alike interesting, but this would lead us far from our subject. We will only say that they contributed nothing to the solution of the problem posited by the Sarvastivadin.

But both the Andhaka and the Theravādin resided in regions far removed from those where the Sarvāstivādin dwelt, and this probably accounts for the fact, that, as far as we know, they never tried to explain the mechanism of the retribution of deeds. On the other hand, the Sautrāntika, near neighbours of the Sarvāstivādin, were forced by the attacks of the latter, to express their views on this matter. For this purpose they elaborated the theory of seeds which they expressed as follows: « By seed (*bija*) we mean the *nāmarūpa*, that is to say the complex of the five *skandha*, which can generate a fruit either immediately or mediately, by means of the *pariṇāmaviśeṣa* of the series. The series (*saṃtati*) is the *saṃskara* of the past, the present, and the future in their causal relation, which forms an uninterrupted series. The *pariṇāma*, or evolution of the series, is the modification (*anythātva*) of the series, for the series is born different from itself at each moment. The *viśeṣa*, or culminating term of this evolution, is the moment of the series which possesses the capacity of generating fruit at once (20). And here we find again the evolutionism of the Santrāntika, to which we referred above when speaking of the moment, and which, in view of the fundamental unsubstantiality of Buddhism, alone enabled one to explain satisfactorily the mechanism of the retribution of deeds.

Several schools seem to have studied more closely the nature of time. It should be noted that the word time (*kāla*) is practically absent from the Buddhist vocabulary and above all from its technical vocabulary. The Sarvāstivādin held the opinion that there is no distinction between the nature of time and that of composites (*saṃskāra*). In other words, time consists of composites and composites are time, or else time is that the growth of which reveals the composites (21). In the light of what has been said above we may interpret this theory by considering time as a mere modality of the composites which could not exist apart from them. As we have seen, in the opinion of the Sarvāstivādin, time is closely linked to the activity of things, to causation, and has for them an essentially functional value.

The Darṣtantika and the Vibhapyavādin had reached, as far back as the beginning of our Era — for it is mentioned several times in the *Mahābibhāṣā* — a quite different notion of time. In their opinion the substance (*dravya*) of time is distinct from that of the composites. The substance of the composites is impermanent (*anitya*) while that of time is permanent (*nitya*). The composites are placed within time, like a fruit in a pot. And just as a fruit can be removed from one pot and placed in another, or just as many men come out of a house and enter another, so the composites come out of the future and enter the present, then come out of the present and enter the past (22). And here at last we have time conceived of as a thing in itself, independent of phenomena. And at once, as is generally the case, it is thought of on the same plane as space, as an analogous environment in which events move. Like space it is also conceived of as permanent, and we may therefore deduce from this that it is thought of as uncomposed (*asaṃskṛta*), that is to say as an absolute, like space itself and the *nirvāṇa*. Indeed, we may consider Vasumitra's interpretation of the *sarvāstivāda*, held to be orthodox, as a stage on the path leading to this conception. The analogy he draws between things and counters, which take different names according to the boxes in which they are placed, is quite near to that of the fruit placed in a pot, and of the men in the house, chosen by the Vibhajyavādin and the Dārṣṭāntika. The only difference, but it is an essential one, is in the point of view of the thinkers. Vasumitra sees things only, and pays no attention to the space in which they are situated, whereas his opponents consider both, and draw between them the comparisons and the relations which force themselves on their minds.

This theory should be approached and perhaps identified with the anonymous one brought forward in the *Kathāvatthu*, which holds that the three epochs (*addha*) *i.e.* the past, the future and the present, are completed (*parinipphanna*) realities, that is to say things in themselves (23). This theory was founded, so it seems, on the following passage of a Sutra: « Three, oh monks, are the subjects of narratives (*kathavatthu*) — which three? — Oh' monks, one can tell a story (*kathā*) relating (*ārabbha*) to past time (*addhana atita*): « So it was in time past », — or one can tell, oh monks, a story relating to future time (*anāgata*): « So it will be in future time »; or else, oh monks, one can tell now (*etarahi*) a story relating to the present time (*paccuppanna*): « it is thus now (*hoti*), therefore in the present ». Such, oh monks, are in truth the three subjects of narratives ».

The refutation of this opinion by the Theravādin is based on the fact that, if it were so, there would be three distinct series of each thing, one past, the other future, and the last present, and this is not so. Its only interest is that it shows us that the Theravādin did not consider the three epochs, and certainly not time, as completed realities. The fact that they almost always used the terms past, future and present as adjectives, enables us to conclude that in their case also periods were but simple modes of things.

One may compare with these opinions, which hold that the time or the epoch are things *per se*, those which relate more especially to the present. There is first of all the anonymous theory, frequently refuted in the *Mahāribhāṣā* (24) which states it as follows: the future and the past do not exist, but the present exists and is not composite (*asaṃskṛta*), *i.e.* it is absolute like *nirvāna* and like space (*ākāsa*).

In the absence of data we cannot, unfortunately, know exactly the meaning that should be given to this opinion which seems, in its simplicity, rich in philosophic content; and we can only have recourse to hypotheses. If the present is uncompounded, then it is permanent (*nitya*), which means that it possesses the eternity of that which being situated outside the past, the future, and the present, is unaffected by the vicissitudes of becoming. Consequently, time resolves itself into an eternal present, thus acquiring a plenitude and an efficiency which come very near to those the Sarvāstivādin assigned to the past and to the future. We can see in this theory a reaction of a special kind against the *sarvāstivāda*, which might be formulated as follows: it is because they emerge into the present, because they are carried by the eternal present, that past and future events exist and are endowed with efficiency.

Two theories attributed to the mysterious school of the late Mahīśāsaka would seem to support this interpretation. According to that school, the real nature (*svabhāva*) of tendencies (*anuśaya*) remains perpetually (*sadā*) present (*pratyutpanna*) because it gives birth (*utpadyati*) to all things (*dharma*) and so, although it is past, it does not relinquish the present (25). Likewise, the aggregates (*skandha*), the domains (*āyatana*) and the elements (*dhātu*) are perpetually present (26). Indeed, only the seeds (*bija*) which are perpetually present, can give birth to things, and this is why the aggregates, the domains, and the elements are perpetually present. It should be noted that Vasumitra, who is here our only source of information, attributes to these same late Mahīśāsaka the *sarvāstivāda* itself, which shows that the theories relating to the eternal present were, after all, near to the great eponymic theory of the Sarvāstivādin.

The passage from the above conceptions to the evolutions of the late Mahāsāṅghika and of the Mahīśāsaka is easy. The former consider that act (*karman*) and its maturation (*vipāka*) develop at the same time (27). As the past does not exist as a substance (*dravya*) and as the deed and its fruit (*phala*) are produced at different times, so, they argued, as long as the act is not completed, it exists in a perpetual present, and as the maturation of the fruit is likewise present, it exists at the same time as the act. In the case of the act which has fructified, it is completed, it has entered into the past, and can therefore no longer exist at the same time. This confirms what we were saying above on the subject of the eternal present. We may also note that this theory is near to that of the Kāśyapīya, just as the previous one was related to that of the Sarvāstivādin. The essential difference between them is that they consider as of the present what the Sarvāstivādin and the Kāśyapīya called past or future.

The evolutionism of the late Mahāsāṅghika is most clearly expressed in another of their theories, which they formulated as follows: the seeds (*bija*) themselves are sprouts (*aṅkura*) (28). Matter (*rūpa*) — they explained — lasts a long time. As it has production (*utpāda*) and cessation (*nirodha*), the substance (*dravya*) of the seeds turns into sprouts and ceases to exist. As soon as the seeds have ceased to exist the sprouts are produced.

The late Mahāsāṅghika (29) and the Mahīśāsaka (30) concluded from this that the great elements (*mahābhuta*) or the material (*rūpin*) faculties (*indriya*) evolve (*pariṇamanti*). Material things last long, the former said. Thus because it possesses production and cessation, the substance of milk (*kṣīra*), turns into curds (*dadhi*). On the other hand the Mahīśāsaka explained that in the interval between conception and death the main elements of the faculties change, as milk changes into curds. As their nature (*bhāva*) is not born and does not die instantaneously (*kṣaṇaṃ*), evolution takes place. They differ however on one point. While the Mahīśāsaka admitted that thought (*citta*) and mental phenomena (*caitta*)

The Dream of Māyā (Surga Period from Bharhut, 2nd cent. B.C.)

develop like material things, the late Mahāsāṅghika were of the opinion that as thought and mental phenomena arise and cease instantaneously (*kṣaṇika*), their duration is too short to allow of development. Thus while these two sects agreed in recognising the duration and evolution of material things — a duration and evolution which were matters of current observation, — they differed on the subject of psychic phenomena whose characteristic features cannot be so easily observed. And here we find again the controversies on the instant and on duration which we examined in our earlier pages.

The opinion of the Mahīśasaka on this subject must moreover be considered with caution. Thus Vasumitra ascribes to them both the above theory, which is definitely an evolutionary one, and which K'ueichi confirms and comments, and also that which holds that all compounds (*saṃskṛta*) are completely destroyed at each instant and lack duration (*sthiti*); and this is confirmed by Bhavya (31). Moreover, the *Vijñaptimatratasiddhi* complicates the matter by declaring that in the opinion, of the Mahīśasaka there are three kinds of aggregates (*skandha*): those that only last an instant (*kṣaṇaskandha*); those that last a whole existence (*ekajanmāvadhiskandha*) like the organs of the senses (*indriya*) etc.; and those that last until the transmigration e.. s (*saṃsārakoṭiniṣṭaskandha*) (32). Should these differences be explained by an error in the sources at our disposal, or by different opinions

held by different branches of the same sect, or by different stages in the evolution of the sect's doctrine, this is what we do not know. And after all it matters but little by whom or when these theories were enounced, as it clearly appears that they were really held. and that is what matters to us.

We have still to examine some minor controversies which will enable us to define certain notions of time and to show how complex they were in the early Buddhist doctrines.

One of the fundamental tenets of the *sarvāstivāda*, as we have seen, was based on the fact that one can think of the past and of the future, and one can even know certain events that do not belong to the present. The Sarvāstivādin, as well as some of their adversaries, the Theravādin (33), insisted that as thought had for its object (*alambana*) the past or the future, it is provided with an object (*sālambana*), for, the latter said, such thought produces an appeal to attention (*āvajjanā*). ideation (*ābhoga*), reflection (*samannāhāra*), observation (*manasikāra*), volition (*cetanā*), aspiration (*patthanā*), and resolution (*paṇidhi*). But the Theravādin drew a distinction between the object of thought and the thing in itself, which thought represents. Other sects, such as the Uttarāpathaka (34) and that of the *Śāriputrābhidharma* (35) declared, on the other hand, that thought which has for its object the past or the future, lacks an object as neither the past nor the future exist.

Several sects such as the Andhaka (36), the school of the *Śāriputrābhidharma* (37) and the Sarvāstivādin, admitted a certain knowledge (*jñāna*) of the future. Mention is indeed made in certain *Sutra* of the power possessed by the Buddha to foresee the future. The Theravādin (38) replied that no mode of knowledge enables us to know the future.

According to the Andhaka, one is provided (*samannāgata*) with the past and with the future as one is with the present. Indeed, he who knows the eight liberations (*aṭṭhavimokkhañayī*), who possesses according to his desire (*nikāmalābhī*) the four meditations (*jhāna*), is in possession (*labhī*) of the nine concentrations of successive regions (*anupubbavihārasamāpatti*). He is therefore in possession both of past and of future stages of meditation. The Theravādin did not agree to this (39). Since the past no longer exists and the future does not yet exist — they argued — it is impossible to possess them. It is not easy here to interpret the views of the Andhaka, which may be due only to their mode of expressing themselves, or else to confusion between an event and its effects or its possibilities. Taken literally, their theory would be a corollary of the *sarvastivada*, and this we cannot admit.

Certain Uttarāpathaka (40), in which we must recognise the Sarvāstivādin (41), asserted that we abandon (*jahati*) the past, future and present defilements (*kilesa*). But according to the Theravādin, one cannot abandon past or future defilements because they do not exist.

As all this shows, the study of time led to very different conceptions in early Buddhism, conceptions that often arose from passionate controversies. Here we find again that diversity and that doctrinal wealth that characterised this great movement of ancient Indian thought. Some schools considered time as an empty frame, similar to space, while others refused to see in it something other than simple modes. Some conceived it as a perpetual present full of the reality and efficiency of existence and being the very substance of existence, while others maintained that past and future exist as does the present. For some there was nothing but a succession of separate instants; for others everything is evolving. Mention should also be made of the intermediate opinions, of conciliating, synthetic and varied shades of meaning.

Here as elsewhere in Buddhism, this variety is the result of the attempts made to reconcile contradictory data, or, to say the least, data that it is very difficult to harmonise, pertaining as they do to the fundamental doctrine. In the case of time, it arises from the efforts made to reconcile the non-substantiality and impermanence of things considered as mere phenomena, with the mechanism of knowledge, and above all of retribution for acts. The disagreement between these two groups of theories was accentuated by the fact that in most of the schools they were studied separately, without perceiving their incompatibility. It would certainly have been wiser to keep to the strict teaching of the Buddha, and to follow faithfully his advice to avoid philosophical speculations, but the nature of man is such that all mysteries only intensify his thirst for knowledge.

Following in the direction of impermanence, the notion of momentariness was reached, and when that had been reached, it was impossible to avoid discussions on the nature of the instant, on which a wealth of meaning was sometimes conferred which pertains only to duration. But the instant, like the atom, can be conceived only by inference, and the schools which gave more importance to observation than to reasoning — and it was often this that created opposition between the Theravādin and the Saravāstivādin — avoided the complications to which momentariness leads, and adhered to an evolutionism whose nature they were careful not to try to fathom. Between these two extremes we meet with the intermediate theories which consider that things, according to their respective natures, vary in duration, some being instantaneous, which is generally considered to be the case with psychic phenomena, down to the *kalpa*, which is that of atoms of matter.

But if nothing has substance, if everything is but a succession of instants, then how can events become apparent at very different times as is the case with the act and its consequence? Are they perhaps related by a causal relation? The first solution offered was that of the Vātsīputrīyas, who boldly reintroduced a substance known as « personality » (*pudgala*) which continues through all the vicissitudes of transmigrations. They drew a careful distinction — though at the cost of what difficulties! — between the *pudgala* and the *ātman* and *jīva*, which the Buddha had declared to be fictitious; but this distinction was rejected by all the other sects as heretical. The problem, however, was not solved, and this is why the Sarvāstivādin soon offered another solution, yet more daring. As no substance exists that assures the causal relation between the act and its result, this relation is supplied, in their opinion, by the very nature of the temporal limitations of things, and thus past and future things exist as well as present ones. It was easy for the other schools to prove that this explanation, the product of speculation, encountered even greater difficulties than those it claimed to solve, and was in flagrant contrast with the data of current observation. The Sarvāstivādin themselves perceived this when they endeavoured to investigate their theory; hence the four different interpretations they gave of it. Are the present, the past and the future, states, features, positions; or are they nothing but reciprocal relations? Whatever explanation was offered, it postulated the thing *per se*, considered, at least provisionally, as a substance (*dravya*).

It was to the credit of the *sarvāstivāda* that it drew attention to this essential problem and that, as a reaction, it gave rise to a great variety of solutions and opinions. Some schools were thus led to consider the three stages as independent realities, or even to see in time, taken as a whole, a substance not only independent but eternal and consequently absolute; making of it a kind of temporal empty medium similar to space, thus linking up ideas which many centuries later were to appear in the West.

But if this theory was related to the great Buddhist theory of universal void, it could hardly be of use in settling the problem enunciated by the Sarvastivādin. What was needed, indeed, was not a time conceived as void and inert, similar to the conception of space, but, as had been clearly shown by the *sarvastivada*, a time full and active. Now, if this plenitude and this activity could not be attributed to the past and to the future, which no longer have existence, one could, nay one had to seek them in the present, hence arose the theories which centre their notion of time on the present, considered as an absolute, and therefore as eternal.

This idea is found again in those entertained by the later Mahīśāsakas, in whose opinion the tendencies and the several elements of which personality is built up are eternally present, for only present things are endowed with efficiency. Nevertheless, it does not seem that one can find here, in the present, a substance, but rather, as with the Sarvāstivādin and the Theravādin, a mere mode. Fundamentally, this theory was closely related to the *Sarvāstivāda* for it was satisfied to name eternal present, what the Sarvāstivādin called past and future. Again, it thus reintroduced into Buddhism the notion of substance, for what but substances are these things eternally present?

Most of the other sects avoided this shoal by turning to the evolutionist solution, more in conformity with their fundamental doctrine. Based on analogy with certain phenomena such as the conversion of milk into curds, or of a seed into a sprout, they admitted that things continue to be present until such time as they have produced their effects, thus taking up again and improving the theory of the Kāśyapīya; or else, as was the case with the Sautrāntika, they considered the series of momentary facts, or facts of limited duration, ascribing to it greater importance than to those timate elements which had claimed too much attention from the Sarvāstivādin.

If one wishes to set forth the main features of the notion of time held by early Buddhism, one should first call attention to its diversity and its amplitude, which have led to the elaboration of theories which deserve the attention of the historian of philosophy and even of the philosopher himself, for their daring and the reflections they assume and suggest. These several theories cover practically all the points of view from which time can be considered, and, taken as a whole, they supply an almost complete theory on the subject, whether time be viewed as substance or mood, absolute or relative, void or full, active or inert, as moment or duration, invariability or transformation, etc. Of all these opinions, that which met with most favor was the evolutionary one, which sees in time a mere modal expression of things.

In conclusion, it should be noted that the notion of time, as conceived by early Buddhism, is all the more important as it is closely related to the notion of ontology, the master conception of Buddhist philosophy, whose fundamental notion is that of unsubstantiality (42).

André Bareau

NOTES

(1) I use the term « early Buddhism » for what is generally referred to as Hinayana, without reflecting on the humiliating implications of this term for the Theravadin of today.

(2) *Katharatthu*, XXII, 8.

(3) La Vallée-Poussin: *L'Abhidharmakośa de Vasubandhu*, IV, p. 5.

(4) *Katharatthu*, XXII, 8.

(5) La Vallée-Poussin, *Abhidharmakośa*, II, pp. 224, 234.

(6) *Maharibhaṣā*, T. S., 1545, pp. 108a, 977b.

(7) Ibid., p. 200a.

(8) La Vallée-Poussin, *Abhidharmakośa*, II, pp. 223, 224.

(9) Id.: *Vijñaptimatratāsiddhi*, p. 67.

(10) Ibid.

(11) *Maharibhaṣa*, T. S. 1545, pp. 270a and 463a.

(12) Ibid., pp. 141b and 919b.

(13) La Vallée-Poussin: *Abhidharmakoṣa*, V, pp. 49-65; *Mahāribhasa*, T. S. 1545, pp. 393-396b; T. S. 1539, pp. 531-537; *Katharatthu*, I, 6.

(14) La Vallée-Poussin, op. cit., V, pp. 49-65.

(15) Ibid., p. 55.

(16) Ibid., p. 50.

(17) *Katharatthu*, I, 6 & 7.

(18) *Katharatthu*, I, 8; *Maharibhaṣa*, T. S. 1545, pp. 96b, 263c, 741b; *Abhidharmakośa*, V, p. 52.

(19) *Katharatthu*, I, 10.

(20) La Vallée-Poussin: *Abhidharmakośa*, II, p. 185.

(21) *Mahāribhaṣa*, T. S. 1545, pp. 393a, 700a.

(22) Ibid., pp. 393a, 700a.

(23) *Katāratthu*, XV, 3.

(24) T. S. 1545a, pp. 65b, 74b, 85b; 190a, 393a, 479a, 684a, 919bc.

(25) Vasumitra: *Treatise of Sects*, 9th theory of this school.

(26) Ibid., 10th theory of this school.

(27) Ibid., 5th theory of this school).

(28) Ibid., 6th theory of this school.

(29) Ibid., 7th theory of this school.

(30) Ibid., 18th theory of this school.

(31) Ibid., 21st theory of this school; Bhavya, 15th and 17th theories of this school.

(32) La Vallée-Poussin: *Vijñaptimātratāsiḍdhi*, p. 180.

(33) *Katharatthu*, IX, 6 and 7.

(34) *Katharatthu*, IX, 6 and 7.

(35) T. S. 1518, p. 593c and 717ab.

(36) *Katharatthu*, V, 8.

(37) T. S. 1518, p. 594c.

(38) *Kathāratthu*, IX, 12.

(39) *Katharatthu*, IX, 12.

(40) Ibid., XIX, 1.

(41) *Abhidharmakośa*, V, pp. 48-50.

(42) This article was already finished when I became acquainted with Mlle. Silburn's beautiful book: *Instant et Cause*, just recently published. The conclusions reached by the Author differ considerably from mine. This is due to the fact that we start from different points and entertain different views, and also because Mlle. Silburn was unfortunately unable to have access to the Chinese sources, which in this matter are the most important.

Die Zeit.

M. Walleser

Dies alles steht durchaus im Einklang mit der prinzipiellen Tendenz des Buddhismus, sich auf die positive Erfahrung zu beschränken und transzendente Faktoren auszuschalten. Es ist nun von Interesse, zu sehen, wie dieser Grundsatz jetzt auch auf die Zeit, die, wie ich an anderer Stelle[2] ausgeführt habe, für die Beurteilung und Lösung des Ichproblems wichtigste formale Kategorie, ausgedehnt wird. Weder im Sutta- noch im Abhidhammapiṭaka scheint die Tragweite und erkenntnistheoretische Bedeutung der Zeit besonders gewürdigt oder auch nur beachtet zu sein. Das läßt sich allerdings nur mutmaßen, solange der Abhidhamma nicht genauer bekannt ist, aber an und für sich wäre es leicht zu verstehen, daß erst die nach-kanonische Periode auf das Zeitproblem aufmerksam geworden wäre.

Es werden (II. 2. 9.) zunächst drei Arten oder Zustände von Zeit unterschieden: Vergangenheit, Zukunft, Gegenwart. Es gibt Zeit, welche existiert, und solche, die nicht existiert (koci addhā atthi koci na-tthīti). „Mit Hinsicht auf Vorstellungen (saṅkhārā), die vergangen, verflossen, entschwunden, von Grund aus verändert sind, ist keine Zeit. Mit Hinsicht auf Zustände (dhammā), die zur Reife gelangt sind (d. i. als Frucht früheren karmas), und auf solche, denen noch die Fähigkeit des Reifens innewohnt, und solche, die anderweitig zur Wiedergeburt führen, ist Zeit. Auch mit Bezug auf Wesen (sattā), die nach dem Tode anderswo wiedergeboren werden, ist Zeit. Mit Bezug auf Wesen, die nach dem Tode nicht wiedergeboren werden, gibt es keine Zeit. Ebenso gibt es für völlig erlöste Wesen (d. i. für diejenigen, welche das parinirvāṇa erlangt haben) keine Zeit — wegen ihres völligen Erlöstseins".[1]

Wenn hier von Zeit, addhā (ssk. adhvan), die Rede ist, so ist es nicht die reale, von dem Standpunkt des erkenntnistheoretischen Realismus transzendente, die offenbar unter kāla zu verstehen ist, sondern die subjektive Kategorie der Zeitlichkeit, vielleicht noch genauer die bewußte Zeitlichkeit oder die Vorstellung der Zeit. Der Buddhist ist so sehr Empirist, daß er die Realität des Seins und der Zeit davon abhängig macht, ob das Individuum sich ihrer bewußt wird. Er versteht eben unter ihr nur die Erscheinung derselben für ein Bewußtsein, und es ist daher nicht sinnlos, wenn er sagt: koci addhā atthi koci na-tthi. Das atthi („ist") fällt eben hier mit „bewußt sein" zusammen, während das gemeinsame grammatische Subjekt beider Sätze die transzendental bezogene Zeit bezeichnet, deren Fraglichkeit durch das gleichzeitige Bejahen und Verneinen besonders hervortritt. Die Zeit als subjektive Erscheinung wird nun abhängig gedacht von den saṅkhārā. Diese bringen demnach das Zeitbewußtsein hervor, stehen daher über demselben und sind nicht, wie die Zeit, bloß ideal, sondern relativ real. Wie sind nun aber diese saṅkhārā zu denken, zeitlich oder unzeitlich? Sie können jedenfalls nicht selbst als von dem addhā, d. i. der ideellen Zeit, umschlossen gedacht werden. Es bleibt also nur die Möglichkeit übrig, den kāla

[1] ed. Trenckner, p. 50.

die transzendente Zeit — falls diese Interpretation überhaupt richtig ist — für ihr reales fundamentum in Anspruch zu nehmen. Davon ist aber keine Rede, und wir werden wohl annehmen dürfen, daß das Problem gar nicht so weit fortgesponnen wurde. Man blieb bei den saṅkhārā stehen, betrachtet diese als die Bedingung der wahrgenommenen Zeit, ohne sich die Frage vorzulegen, in welcher realen Beziehung die saṅkhārā zur Zeit, als dem anscheinend umspannenden Prinzip stehen.

Es käme also für eine genauere Untersuchung vor allem darauf an, festzustellen, in welcher besonderen erkenntnistheoretischen Bedeutung die Ausdrücke addhā und atthi jeweils gebraucht werden. Da es aber zu weit führen würde, den vorliegenden Abschnitt von diesem Gesichtspunkt aus detaillieren und analysieren zu wollen, möchte ich nur diejenige Auffassung hervorheben, welche sich mir aus einer solchen Analyse ergeben zu müssen scheint.

Die transzendentale Beziehung der subjektiven Zeit, d. h. die transzendente Zeit, wird nicht bestritten. Nur hat diese an und für sich für uns keine Bedeutung, da sie nicht ins Bewußtsein fällt. Sie existiert also für mich und andere meinesgleichen nur dadurch, daß sie mir bewußt wird, und insofern, als sie mir bewußt wird. Diese ihre Gegenwart (die eine subjektiv-ideale ist) wird abhängig gedacht von Zuständen des Individuums (saṅkhārā) als ihren Bedingungen; mit diesen steht und fällt sie.

Nach bekannter buddhistischer Anschauung sind nun aber diese saṅkhārā unmittelbar abhängig von der in beständigem Kreislauf ins Unendlich zurückgehenden, aber nicht auch in die Zukunft hinein unendlichen avijjā — sie hören mit der Überwindung des „Nichtwissens" durch das Wissen oder das nirvāṇa auf. Eine Erörterung dieser Entstehungsgeschichte und genetischen Zusammenhänge der saṅkhārā gehört aber nicht hierher, sie bildet ein Kapitel des pratītya-samutpāda, den wir an dieser Stelle füglich beiseite lassen, und wird nur erwähnt, um zu zeigen, daß das Aufhören des Bewußtseins und damit der Zeit selbst ein tatsächlicher, aktueller Vorgang ist, über den man keinenfalls hinwegkommt.

Die bezügliche Darstellung des Milinda-pañha läßt demgemäß nur die eine Deutung zu, daß die Zeit im gewöhnlichen Sinne (kāla) etwas Transzendentes ist, daß sie aber, als subjektiv-ideale Form betrachtet, ebensowohl sein wie nicht sein kann, wobei ihr Sein und

Nichtsein von den das Bewußtsein ermöglichenden Voraussetzungen abhängt.

Es ist übrigens leicht begreiflich, wie diese und ähnliche Stellen zu der sicher irrtümlichen Ansicht führen konnten, der Buddhismus habe die Realität der Zeit geradezu geleugnet. Man fand hier die Zeitlichkeit als subjektive Anschauungsform stark betont und glaubte damit ohne weiteres die Zeit als eine transzendente Kategorie ausgeschaltet. Tatsächlich liegt aber die Sache so, daß eine Leugnung der Existentialität der Zeit gar nicht ins Auge gefaßt wurde. Ich möchte nun zwar nicht annehmen, daß eine derartige extrem-idealistische Auffassung der Zeitlichkeit ohne innere Wahrscheinlichkeit wäre, und ich habe selbst (Problem des Ich, p. 52) zu zeigen gesucht, wie sich auch ohne die Annahme einer transzendenten Zeit das Dasein widerspruchslos konstruieren ließe. Aber jedenfalls können Stellen, wie die angeführten, höchstens das eine beweisen, daß man schon zur Zeit des Milinda-pañha die ideale Zeit (addhā) von der existentialen (kāla) unterschied und die subjektive Zeit nicht schlechthin als seiend annahm, aber nicht, daß man die Zeit als transzendente schlankweg bestritt, wie die extrem-idealistische Auffassung einzelner Forscher behauptet.

Für die Beurteilung der in Frage kommenden buddhistischen Theorie ist nun aber die sich anschließende Erörterung[1] von entscheidender Wichtigkeit. Es wird da nach dem Grunde (mūlaṃ) der vergangenen, zukünftigen und gegenwärtigen Zeit gefragt. Nāgasena antwortet damit, daß er das Nichtwissen als mūlaṃ angibt. Im Anschluß an die avijja werden dann die übrigen elf Glieder des paticcasamuppāda aufgeführt, und zwar in der üblichen Weise, wie z. B. auch im Mahā-Nidāna-Sutta (ed. Grimblot, p. 246) und Saṃyutta Nikāya XXII, p. 90. Die Aufzählung geschieht aber hier nur, um die Undenkbarkeit eines Anfangs zu zeigen. Milinda kann es nicht verstehen, daß ein Anfangspunkt undenkbar sei, worauf ihm der Weise bedeutet, daß die vergangene Zeit eben der Anfangspunkt sei.

Auf die Frage, ob sich denn über diesen Anfang gar nichts ausmachen lasse, erwidert Nāgasena, in gewisser Hinsicht sei es schon angängig, in anderer nicht. Aufgefordert, sich genauer zu erklären,

[1] II. 3. 1 ff. Trenckners ed. p. 50.

sagt der Weise: „Früher, o König, war in jeder Hinsicht jedes einzelne [Gegenstand unseres] Nichtwissens. Es ist uns, als wäre es nicht gewesen. In anbetracht dessen ist der erste Anfang unbekannt. Was aber nicht war, das wird; sobald es begonnen hat zu werden, löst es sich wieder auf. Mit Bezug hierauf ist der erste Anfang bekannt".[1]

Der Sinn dieser Stelle ist der, daß ein beliebiger Zustand sich bis zu einem gewissen Zeitpunkt, einer Grenze zurückverfolgen läßt, d. h. also, daß eine jede Individualität einen bestimmten Anfangspunkt hat. Dieser selbst ist aber eine Folge von etwas, von dem wir sagen müssen, „es war nicht" (nāhosīti); demgemäß war ursprünglich alles, mag es sich in einer Form darstellen, in welcher es wolle — avijjā, Nichtwissen.

Wie könnte hier avijjā anders gedeutet werden, als in dem Sinne von unserem individuell-zufälligen Nichtwissen des früheren Zustandes. Denn wenn wir sagen: „Das und das war nicht", so heißt dies nicht: „Es war ganz und gar nicht" — denn dann müßte etwas aus nichts entstehen können, was dem Inder als ein Unding vorkam, wenn auch gerade der spätere systematische Buddhismus das Prinzip einer Entstehung aus dem Nichts verfocht[2]; sondern es bedeutet, daß es nicht so, daß seine „Form" oder „Gestalt" eine absolut verschiedene war. Nur dann hat jener Satz einen Sinn, wenn avijja, Unwissenheit, so viel ist wie: von uns ungewußt und unbegriffen.

Man könnte nun versucht sein zu glauben, daß an der angegebenen Stelle statt der aus dem Zusammenhang sich ergebenden nächstliegenden Bedeutung von „Unkenntnis der ferneren Vergangenheit" jene andere Bedeutung von avijjā unversehens Platz greift, die diesem Terminus in dem paṭicca-samuppāda zukommt. Da kann er aber verschiedenes bedeuten, und die Glossen der späteren Scholastiker tragen eher dazu bei, das Urteil zu verwirren, als die Einsicht in den ursprünglichen, naiven Sinn zu fördern. Aber jedenfalls drückt er nicht unsere subjektive Unwissenheit und Unkenntnis des Anfangs aller Dinge aus. Denn diese wäre doch — von anderen Argumenten, nach denen man nicht lange zu suchen braucht, abgesehen — eine

[1] ed. Trenckner, S. 51.

[2] „asataḥ saj jāyate" wird von Vācaspati Miçra in der Sāṅkhya-Tattva-Kaumudī (Einleitung zu Kārikā 9) als buddhistischer Grundsatz angegeben. — Vgl. auch Garbe, Sāṅkhya-Philosophie, p. 228 ff.

bewußte Vorstellung, ein Gedanke, und käme zu viññāna zu stehen, wenn die Reihe überhaupt logisch-konsequent wäre, aber interessant ist es immerhin, daß zwei so disparate Dinge, wie unsere augenblickliche Unwissenheit und das den saṃsāra aus sich erzeugende Prinzip ohne Anstoß zu erregen gleich benamt wurden — benamt werden konnten. Es läßt sich gerade hieraus vielleicht entnehmen, daß die Vieldeutigkeit des Wortes ein Grund seiner Verwendung hinsichtlich eines Verhältnisses war, welches das dunkelste und unfaßbarste seiner ganzen Natur nach sein muß — des Ursprungs von Sein und Bewußtsein.

Für die Feststellung der in dem Milinda-pañha vertretenen Auffassung der Zeitkategorie kommt nun aber noch besonders die sich an den zuletzt erörterten Passus unmittelbar anschließende Diskussion in Betracht:

„Ehrwürdiger Nāgasena, was, ohne gewesen zu sein, wird, und nachdem es geworden ist, vergeht, das geht beiderseitig begrenzt (eigentlich abgeschnitten) unter". — „[Ja] o König, wenn das beiderseitig Begrenzte untergeht". — „Kann das beiderseitig Begrenzte sich weiterentwickeln (eig. wachsen)?" — „Ja, es kann sich weiterentwickeln". — „Nicht hiernach frage ich, sondern ob es von dem Punkte der Gegenwart aus (koṭito) [nach einer Seite hin] sich entwickeln kann?" — „Ja, es kann sich entwickeln". — „Gib ein Beispiel!" — Der Weise verglich es mit einem Baume: „Die skandhas sind nur die Samen des Leides". — „Lehrreich bist Du, ehrwürdiger Nāgasena." [1]

---

[1] Trenckners Ausg., p. 52.

Bhante Nāgasena, yam ahutvā sambhoti hutvā paṭivigacchati, nanu taṃ ubhato chinnam atthaṃ gacchatīti. — Yadi mahārāja ubhato chinnā attham (A. chinnam attham) gacchati ubhato chinnā sakkā vaḍḍhetun-ti. Āma, sā pi sakkā vaḍḍhetun-ti. Nāham bhante etam pucchāmi, koṭito sakkā vaḍḍhetun-ti. — Āma, sakkā vaḍḍhetun-ti. — Nāham bhante etam pucchāmi, koṭito sakkā vaḍḍhetun-ti. — Āma sakka vaḍḍhetun-ti. — Opammam karohīti. — Thero tassa rukkhūpamam akāsi: khandhā ca kevalassa dukkhakkhandhassa bījanīti. — kallo si bhante Nāgasenāti.

Rhys Davids Übs. ib. p. 61. „But, reverend Sir, if that which was not, becomes, and as soon as it has begun to become passes again away, then surely being thus cut off at both ends, it must be entirely destroyed?" „Nay, surely, o king, if it be thus cut off at both ends, can it not at both

Diese Auseinandersetzung läuft darauf hinaus, daß die Wirklichkeit nach den zwei Dimensionen der Vergangenheit und Zukunft hin auf einen Punkt reduziert ist. Also auch hier haben wir es mit der Frage nach dem Wesen der Zeit zu tun. Um aber der an dieser Stelle vertretenen Anschauung möglichst gerecht zu werden, sehen wir uns veranlaßt, einen geschichtlichen Rückblick auf die früheren Begriffsbestimmungen der Zeitkategorie zu werfen.

---

ends be made to grow again?" „Yes, it might. But that is not my question. Could it grow again from the point at which it was cut off?" „Certainly." „Give me an illustration." Then the elder repeated the simile of the tree and the seed, and said that the skandhas (the constituent elements of all life, organic and inorganic) were so many seeds, and the king confessed himself satisfied.

Die Stelle ist im Pālitexte ohne Zweifel verderbt. Rhys Davids bemerkt zu dem Wechsel des Geschlechts chinnaṃ — chinnā (p. 82, Anm. 2): „possibly the word ignorance has been dropped out. Trenckner says the passage is corrupt, and the Siṃhalese is so involved as to be unintelligible". Der Vorschlag Rhys Davids ist unannehmbar. Eine Reinigung des Textes ist nur durch Vergleichung der Handschriften möglich. Ich möchte indessen auf folgendes hinweisen. Zunächst deutet das erste „Āma, sā pi etc." darauf hin, daß eine Frage des Milinda unmittelbar vorausgeht. Ich interpungiere also in dem vorangehenden Satze zwischen gacchati und ubhato und betrachte den ersten Satzzusammenhang als Antwort des Nāgasena auf die vorangehende Frage des Königs, den zweiten als die sich weiter anschließende Frage desselben. Diese letztere lautet demnach: Ubhato chinnā sakkā vaḍḍhetum?, worauf die genau entsprechende Antwort erfolgt: Āma, sā pi sakkā vaḍḍhetum. Nun bleibt aber immer noch der Wechsel des Geschlechtes von chinnaṃ zu chinnā zu erklären. Man könnte entweder mit Rhys Davids ein feminines Substantiv zu chinnā ergänzen (aber jedenfalls nicht avijjā); oder einen maskulinen nom. plur. — etwa khandhā entsprechend der endgültigen Entscheidung „khandā ca kevalassa dukkhakkhandassa bījānīti" — allerdings müßte dann auch das verbum finitum in den Plural gesetzt werden; oder aber chinnā ist ein subst. fem. und bedeutet „etwas Begrenztes", eine Gebrauchsweise, die aber erst anderweitig belegt werden müßte, ehe man sie zur Erklärung heranzieht. Einstweilen, d. h. bis eine genauere Feststellung auf Grund von Handschriften erfolgt, neige ich noch am ebesten zu der Annahme, daß man es hier mit einer, bei laxer Ausdrucksweise ja recht wohl denkbarer Metabasis aus dem sächlichen ins weibliche Geschlecht zu tun habe, und lege daher auf den Geschlechtsunterschied kein weiteres Gewicht.

Wenn man den Begriff der Zeit in die Vergangenheit zurückverfolgt, so stellt sich heraus, daß derselbe erst verhältnismäßig junger Entstehung ist. Im Ṛgveda kommt das Wort kāla nur an einer Stelle vor, und zwar in einem der spätesten Teile (X, 42, 9), und überdies mit der Bedeutung der bestimmten Zeit (= ved. ṛtu). Selbst in der älteren Brāhmaṇa-Literatur, in welcher das Wort anfängt häufiger zu werden, herrscht noch die Anschauung einer bestimmten Zeitspanne vor, so daß auch in jener Periode die Zeit als Begriff offenbar noch nicht in das Bewußtsein getreten war.[1] Von da an tritt aber die Zeit als der urgewaltige Schöpfer, als das eigentliche Prinzip des Seins immer mehr in den Vordergrund; im Atharvaveda wird sie an einer Stelle (XIX, 54) als der Ursprung der Gewässer (kālād āpaḥ samabhavan), an einer anderen (XIX, 53) als Vater Prajāpatis, Träger des Brahman und Parameshṭhin, als Erzeuger des Svayambhū bezeichnet.[2] Über die Bedeutung des kāla-vāda, jener Lehre, welche die Zeit als das Absolute betrachtet und alles aus ihr ableiten möchte, im Mahābhārata, hat Schrader a. a. O. eingehender gehandelt: auch damals noch war man sich weder der Naivität bewußt, die darin liegt, die Zeit als eine reale Größe von allerdings unbestimmten Umfang sich vorzustellen, noch dachte man daran, zwischen einer bewußtseins-immanenten und -transzendenten Zeit zu unterscheiden; denn die Stelle, welche Schrader in entsprechendem Sinne aufzufassen versucht (XII, 227, 29): kālaḥ kāle nayati mām, „Die Zeit führt mich in der Zeit", läßt andere, jedenfalls näher liegende Deutungen zu, wenn sie überhaupt ernst zu nehmen ist. Es liegt also hier noch nichts vor, was man eine systematische Theorie nennen könnte; es sind Spekulationen von dem jener Epoche eigenen teils pantheistischen, teils materialistischen, teils animistischen Charakter, die, von dem genetischen Gesichtspunkt aus betrachtet, sehr beachtenswert sind, aber doch nur von geringem Interesse, soweit philosophische Probleme in Frage kommen. Zu einer systematischen Form hat es auch in der Folgezeit der kāla-vāda nicht gebracht, obwohl Schrader (p. 27) darauf hinweist, daß aus den durch Malayagiri im Kommentar zur Nandī überlieferten Zitaten auf das derzeitige Vorhandensein eines speziellen Lehrbuches des kāla-vāda zu schließen sei. Der Ausdruck

---

[1] Vgl. Schrader, „Über den Stand der ind. Phil. etc.", p. 19.
[2] Vgl. Deussen, Allgem. Gesch. der Philos. I, p. 210 f.

„Lehrbuch“ dürfte hier eben schwerlich am Platze sein; denn die abfällige und ins Lächerliche ziehende Beurteilung Malayagiris deutet darauf hin, daß man jene kālavādins überhaupt nicht ernst nahm. Auch Gauḍapāda, der Verfasser der Kārikā zur Māṇḍūkyā-Upanishad, welcher so ziemlich am Anfang der eigentlich systematischen Philosophie steht, erwähnt die „Kāla-Theoretiker“ (Kāla-cintakā I, 8) und „Kāla-Kenner“ (kāla-vido II, 24) in einer Weise, die nur den Schluß auf die völlige Bedeutungslosigkeit dieser Schule zuläßt; Çaṅkara erwähnt sie in seinem Kommentar überhaupt nicht, und Ānandagiri identifiziert in der zugehörigen Glosse jene kāla-vādins mit den jyotirvidaḥ, d. h. den Astronomen[1], und dazu stimmt vorzüglich, daß der Astronom Varāhamihira († 587 A. D.) im Eingang seiner Bṛhat-Saṃhitā[2] den Kālavāda unmittelbar dem Sāṅkhya- und Vaiçeshika-Systeme zur Seite stellt: der Astronom machte es da gerade so wie der Grammatiker, wenn dieser das Pāṇini-darçaṇam zur Philosophie rechnet[3] und behauptet, die Grammatik (vyākaraṇa-çāstram) müsse wegen ihrer Zweckdienlichkeit zur Erreichung des höchsten Zieles studiert werden (l. c. p. 147).

Sehen wir nun von dieser Lehre des kāla-vāda, von dem uns aber nichts weiter berichtet wird, und der naturgemäß nur eine untergeordnete Rolle spielen konnte, ab, so enthält, wie es ja auch bei dem metaphysik-feindlichen Charakter des ursprünglichen Buddhismus zu erwarten ist, das Sutta-Piṭaka nichts, was irgendwie auf die Auffassung und den Begriff der Zeit einen Schluß gestattete. Das Māluṅkyāputta-Sutta, das 63ste des Majjhima-Nikāya (I, 426 ff.), und Aggi-Vacchagotta-Sutta, das 72ste derselben Sammlung (I, 483 ff.), lassen die völlige Gleichgültigkeit Buddhas gegenüber Fragen, wie die nach der Dauer der Welt, nach einem zeitlichen Leben im Jenseits, deutlich erkennen. Diese Indifferenz gegenüber einer theoretischen Naturbetrachtung, die wir an anderer Stelle ausführlicher charakterisiert haben, hinderte aber auch noch zur Zeit der Entstehung des Abhidharma eine ernstliche Beschäftigung mit derartigen spekulativ-naturwissenschaftlichen Problemen, und erst im Milinda-pañha, welcher

[1] Zu I, 8: jyotirvidāṃ kalpanāprakāram āha | kālād iti |
Zu II, 24: kālaḥ paramārtha iti jyotirvidaḥ |

[2] Hsg. von Kern, Calc. Bibl. Ind. 1865. Vgl. Thibauts Einl. zu seiner Ausg. der Pañca-siddhāntikā. Ben. 1889.

[3] Vgl. Sarva-darçana-saṅgraha (Kalk. 1858), p. 135 ff.

noch in enger Beziehung zu dem Tripiṭaka steht, aber doch schon den Geist der kommenden Systematik spüren läßt, begegnen uns, wenn auch keine streng-dialektischen Erörterungen, so doch Begriffe und Definitionen, welche eine lange Schulung des begrifflichen Denkens und in gewissem Sinne auch eine systematische Gründlichkeit der logischen Entwicklung erkennen lassen. Man wird sich dessen recht wohl bewußt, wenn man jene eigentümliche Stelle des Milinda-pañha näher ins Auge faßt, welche uns zu dieser rückschauenden Betrachtung über die Zeitvorstellung der vorbuddhistischen Literaturepochen veranlaßte.

Verschiedenes läßt sich jener Stelle entnehmen. Zunächst, daß die Zeit schon auf die momentane Gegenwart reduziert war. Diese selbst war nach den zwei Seiten der Vergangenheit und Zukunft hin „abgeschnitten" (chinnā) — also die Beschränkung der realen Zeitlichkeit auf den unteilbaren Punkt des Jetzt wurde schon damals als eine notwendige Konsequenz des positivistischen Denkens erkannt.

Ferner läßt jenes Gespräch erkennen, daß man mit der Subjektivierung der Zeit Ernst machte, daß man sich darüber klar war, der Zeit nur als eines ideellen Phänomens bewußt zu sein — eine Annahme, die ja nur die Konsequenz jener anderen ist, daß nur die Gegenwart auf aktuelle Bedeutung Anspruch erheben kann. Denn wenn Vergangenheit und Zukunft nicht real sind, so sind sie entweder absolut nicht oder nur phänomenal. Da das erstere zu behaupten nicht angeht, insofern die Vergangenheit und Zukunft doch in einer unbezweifelbaren Beziehung zu einander wie zur Gegenwart stehen, so bleibt nur übrig, sie ideell aufzufassen, und diesen Schritt hatten die Buddhisten schon um Christi Geburt getan. Die hiermit eng zusammenhängende, in seiner endgültigen Antwort zum Ausdruck kommende Ablehnung des Ausdrucks koṭito „von der punktuellen Gegenwart aus" (d. h. nach der Zukunft hin) durch Nāgasena läßt sich so leicht erklären: er will eben jeden Anlaß vermeiden, die Vermutung aufkommen zu lassen, als ob die Zukunft etwas Reales, etwas Seiendes, etwas Existentes wäre. Er behauptet auch nicht das Gegenteil davon, nämlich daß sie etwas Irreales oder Nicht-Seiendes wäre, denn er fürchtet mit Recht, dadurch nur wieder eine nicht minder verwerfliche und gefährliche Anschauung wachzurufen, insofern er selbst von jeder Dogmatik hinsichtlich seines erkenntnistheoretischen Standpunktes frei ist. Indem er also eine Veränderung, eigentlich

Wachstum (vaḍḍhetuṃ), zugibt, hält er doch indirekt an der punktuellen Gegenwart fest, indem er jene auf die khandhas, die psychischen Zustände, bezieht, die letzteren aber auf das Leiden, das dukkhaṃ, das immer da ist, solange psychisches Sein in zeitlicher Form existiert.

Man wird aber vielleicht einwenden, diese ganze Erörterung über das Zeitproblem habe doch herzlich wenig mit der Frage des Ich zu tun und passe überhaupt nicht in die vorliegende Abhandlung hinein. Ich möchte indessen einer solchen Annahme entgegenhalten, daß philosophische Probleme ohne Berücksichtigung der Zeitkategorie sich überhaupt nicht auch nur einigermaßen befriedigend beantworten lassen. Gerade deshalb, weil in dem besprochenen Passus der „Fragen des Milinda" eine präzisierte Auffassung der Zeitlichkeit vorliegt, ist derselbe für die buddhistische Weltanschauung von so außerordentlicher Wichtigkeit, und es wird unsere nächste Aufgabe sein, die jener Darlegung zu Grunde liegenden Ansichten mit besonderer Beachtung ihrer Beziehung zum Erkenntnisproblem zu analysieren.

GENJUN H. SASAKI, KYOTO

THE TIME CONCEPT IN ABHIDHARMA

In Early Buddhism, the concept of time did not hold great significance, but later in Abhidharma it became increasingly important and was frequently discussed in relation to its psychological aspect. The time concept in Buddhism is also suggestive for the problem of human relations. Buddhism in its experimental sense is the investigation of the entirety of human relations and the human organism for coherence and meaning in all phases of being, human and non-human. Man is made for wholeness, rather than for fragmentation. Human beings are interrelated with each other in the form of the reciprocal relationship (*pratyaya*) of lives and they are not content merely with uni-directional relationships (*hetu-phala anubandha*) having no real coherence.

Theravāda School

Time is represented in the Theravāda school by the term *samaya*, meaning both 'condition' and 'time'. Among the many commentaries, the one referring most often to the problem of time is Buddhaghoṣa's *Atthasālinī*, the commentary on *Dhammasaṅgani*, in which *samaya* is divided into the following five classifications :—

1. *Kāla* (time) represents the continuity of a situation, such as the time of coldness or of an illness, etc. This term is again classified into nine sub-divisions : (a) momentary (mental) time (*citta-kara*); (b) the *dhamma* of beings, memory of *dhamma*, or *dhamma* in the past, present and future; (c) the orderly process of things (*dhammapatti*), i. e., the time when seeds sprout; (d) the appearance of things (*dhamma-lakkhaṇa*), i. e., the time of being born or of old age; (e) the time of reception or intimation (*dhammakicca*); (f) the action of human beings (*sattakicca*), i. e., the time of taking a bath or of eating; (g) the postures of movement (*iriyāpatha*), i. e., walking, standing, sitting and lying; (h) the proceedings of natural phenomena (*candimāsuriyādi, parivattana*) i. e.;, the progress of the morning, evening or night and the day's evolution; and (i) the divisions of time (*kālasaṁdaya*)[1], i. e., half-month, month and year.

2. *Samūha* (the group). A group in the sense of accumulation (*puñja*) of *dhamma* such as *phassa* (touch, feeling), utilized to deny the notion of an individual entity, and the single cause and effect theory since Buddhism maintains everything exists by means of conditions or causes and effects. This classification was directed against the incorrect view that one existence can arise independently of others, therefore it demonstrates mutual interdependence.

3. *Hetu* (cause) represents the mutual interdependence of existence. For example, in order to see, the eye consciousness is required as a sufficing condition.

4. *Khaṇa* (momentariness) refers to the connected situation of consciousness from the past to the present and pertains only to the meritorious mind and not to the non-meritorious. As momentariness is constantly flowing from moment to moment into the past, it is difficult to attempt to catch the moment itself. The mind itself is considered to exist in the manner of momentariness. Just as momentariness is difficult to grasp, so it is difficult for the meritorious mind to arise and remain static. This classification refers to Buddhist morality or practice, because momentariness is considered only in relation to the meritorious mind. The ethical stress is to utilize the moment in the practice of good deeds.

1. *The Atthasālinī* (ed., by P. V. Bapat, Bhandarkar Oriental Research Institute, Poona, 1942) reads '*kālasaṁcaya*', while the Pāli Text Society Edition (London, 1897) reads '*kālasamaya*'. The former is preferable to the latter, for the concept of *samaya* is in this passage defined by other terms.

5. *Samavāya* (combination refers to a concord among the conditions (*paccaya-sāmaggī*) and is intended to demonstrate that the consciousnesses have a mutual coordination in the present. In other words, it shows that time is dependent and interrelated (*aññamaññ'upekkhā*). Time is shown to have no reality and the existence of a Creator is denied. These five above-mentioned classifications can be reduced into following two aspects in the nature of time.

(i) *The objective aspect of time.*—What we designate to be time divisions such as day, night and other phenomena exist apart from our consciousness but what we consider to be objective time actually arises in relation to our attitude. It is only by means of counting the changes in natural phenomena and accumulating these changes into designated groups that we arrive at a notion of time. The sub-human level also experiences the change of natural phenomena but there is no concept of time. We can say that without any relationship to our consciousness none of the apparently objective aspects can exist as such, for their categorization as time concepts are a product of the human reason. Or as the *Atthasālinī* (p. 49) reads:

> 'Time may be clearly shown as an intimation abstracted by mere conventional usage from this or that [event].'

(ii) *The subjective aspect of time*:— Since time is created by the subjective mind, lacking its own reality or an independent creator, time is therefore dependent upon the psychological factors. The dependency of time corresponds to the dependency of consciousness, which consists of many different psychological factors. Buddhaghosa quotes in one passage of the *Atthasālinī* that Buddha said, 'time is intimated by consciousness' (*tam tam upādāya paññatto kālo, Asl.* p. 48). Time is considered objectively as a category. It is due to the following three processes: arising (*uppāda*), preservation (*thiti*) and decay (*bhaṅga*).[1] Even if we consider time as existing separately from our consciousness, still time belongs to these three categories. Time exists only momentarily, which means 'to connect' (*candahana*) one conscious moment with the next conscious moment.

We can find a similarity to this Pāli concept in Mahāyāna Buddhism; The *Mahāprajñāpāramitāśāstra* (Chap. 16. T. 25, 65c-66a) refers to two concepts of time, *kāla* and *samaya*. They call the former concrete time (*dravya*) and the latter intimated time (*prajñapti*). In Pāli, *samaya* is a concept which includes *kāla* and refers to the process of consciousness but not to concrete time (*dravya*).

The Theravāda school drew attention to the subjective aspect. According to this school time is shown as being dependent on other things and interrelated to them. The dependency of time corresponds to the dependency of consciousness, which is based upon the Dependent Origination Theory (*paṭiccasamuppāda*). The *paṭiccasamuppāda* formulates the uni-directional relatedness. On the other hand, the Twenty-Four Conditions Theory[2] formulates in this school the reciprocal relatedness.

The Sarvāstivāda School deals with two aspects of relationship, uni-directional and reciprocal, in relation to time. The time concept has according to this school, also two aspects, one the causality and the

1. It is interesting to note that these three processes, *uppāda*, *thiti* and *bhaṅga*, are analogous to the three principles of *trimurti*: arising (*Brahmā*), preservation (*Viṣṇu*) and decay (*Śiva*). These three also correspond with *catvāri lakṣaṇāni* or the four characteristics of the created (*saṁskṛta*) in the Sarvāstivāda School, namely, *jāti*, *sthiti*, *jarā* and *anityatā*. The Pāli concept *thiti* includes *anyathā* (*jarā* in the Sarvāstivāda school) in a compound term *thiti-anyathā*. This implication is exemplified by the Sarvāstivāda, which takes *sthiti* (*thiti* in Pāli) as a synonym for *jarā*, i.e., '*tathā jarāyā sthity-anyathātvaṁ paryāya iti*', (*Yaśomitra's Abhidharmakośavyākhyā*, ed., by Wogihara. p. 171-172; *Abhidharmakośa*, Chinese version, V. verse 46cd).

2. The fundamental treatises in Pāli Abhidhamma are enumerated as seven, of which two, the *Vibhaṅga* and *Paṭṭhāna*, mention about the twenty four modes of causality: *hetu-paccaya*, *ārammaṇa*°, *adhipati*°, *anantara*°, *samanantara*°, *sahajāta*°, *aññamañña*°, *nissaya*°, *upanissaya*°, *purejāta*°, *pacchājāta*°, *āsevana*°, *kamma*°, *vipāka*°, *āhāra*°, *indriya*°, *jhāna*°, *magga*°, *sampayutta*°, *vippayutta*°, *atthi*°, *natthi*°, *vigata*° and *avigata*°. (*Paṭṭhāna, paccaya-vibhaṅgavāra; Vism.*, pp. 532-541; also cf. L. Sadaw, 'On the Philosophy of Relations', *JPTS.* 1915-1916. pp. 21-53; U. K. Bhagawat, *The Buddhist Philosophy of Theravāda School, as embodied in the Pāli Abhidhamma*, Patna 1924-25; G. H. Sasaki, *A Study of Abhidharma Philosophy*, pp. 46-61, Kobundo, Tokyo, 1958).

other the actuality. The former aspect is represented by the Dependent Origination (*pratītyasamutpāda*), which according to Saṁghabhadra, is confined merely to the transmigration of the body. It thus refers to the uni-directional relationship. The latter is represented by the Six-Causes-and-Four Conditions theory, which is based upon the concept *kāritra* (actuality) of time. It thus refers to the reciprocal relationship.

The causality of time denotes the cause and effect relationship between the past, present and future. According to this conception, chronological time is considered to flow from past to present and into the future. The concept of causality is static, a uni-directional relatedness between past and present in which case the flow does not return to the source.

The activity (*kāritra*) of time, on the other hand, refers to a simultaneous relationship among the time divisions, and concerns the activity of living things in mutual relationship. These two extensive aspects of time underlie Saṁghabhadra's interpretation of the systematic view of human life, which is expounded by two theories : the Dependent Origination and the concept of the relativity of phenomena (the Six-Causes-and -Four Conditions theory).

The formula of *pratītya-samutpāda* (the Dependent) Origination is generally summarized in the following manner[1] : when this (cause) exists, then that (effect) disappears. Based upon this logical formula the twelve links of Dependent Origination are enumerated as follows : upon ignorance (*avidyā*) depend the *karma*-formations (*saṁskāra*); thereon consciousness (*vijñāna*), thereon mentality and corporeality (*nāma-rūpa*); thereon the six sense-bases (*ṣaḍāyatana*); thereon sense (or mind) impression (*phassa*); thereon feeling (*vedanā*); thereon craving (*tṛṣṇā*) thereon clinging (*upādāna*); thereon the process of becoming (*bhava*; here *karma-bhava*); thereon rebirth (*jāti*); thereon old age and death (*jarā-maraṇa*).

Traditionally, the process of these twelve links is interpreted by Abhidharmika according to the three time divisions as follows. Ignorance (*avidyā*) and the *karma*-formations (*saṁskāra*) exist in the past; consciousness (*vijñāna*) through to the process of becoming (*bhava*) is in the present; rebirth (*jāti*), old age (*jarā*) and death (*maraṇa*) are in the future. This is termed the three lives' interpretation.

In Early Buddhism this interpretation applied to the human structure alone and was not yet extended to include the relativity of phenomena. Saṁghabhadra, an exponent of the orthodox doctrine of Sarvāsti-vāda school, followed the traditional phycho-physiological interpretation (the three lives' interpretation) on the one hand. Namely, he interprets it according to the three time divisions as noted above. On the other hand, he expounded the theory from the view point of time. In his own exposition the psycho-physiological interpretation of the Dependent Origination is based upon the causality of time. He also proposed a new interpretation, which is based upon the actuality of time. In regards to the latter, he divided the aphorism ' when this exists .. when this occurs ' into two distinct aspects for analysis. First he defines the meaning of exist (*asti*) and secondly the meaning of occurs (*utpadyati*).

First ' exist ', to Saṁghabhadra, has a dual connotation which in one sense is applicable to the past and in another to the present. ' Something exists now because something existed in the past. ' In this case the present and past are connected by chronological time or causality, and we can say that chronological time or causality belongs to the domain of conventional truth.

1. In Mahāyāna this formula is dealt with from the view-point of *śūnya-vāda* (*Madhyamaka-kārikā* XXIV. *kr*.18), which does not distinguish this formula, ' *imāsmiṁ sati, idaṁ hoti* ...... ' from the passage: ' Upon ignorance depend the karma-formations ...... '. Mādhyamika's interpretation of the twelve links is transformed into examinations of *pratyaya* (*ibid.*, I.) and *Dvāsaṅga* (*ibid.*, XXVI). Nāgārjuna's interpretation reduced the twelve links into *pratyaya* (the Relativity) in the light of *śūnya* idea. It is experimental. It concerns merely the notion of relativity (*parasparāpekṣā* or *anyonyāpekṣā*).

In other words, in Mahāyāna Buddhism '*pratītyasamutpāda* ' denotes *saṁvṛti*, a state convered by ignorance, as opposed to *paramārtha*. Candrakīrti criticizes the Sarvāstivāda view that *pratītyasamutpāda* means creation (*utpāda*) by one cause or with no cause (*Prasannapadā*, *Bibl. Bud.* IV, ed., L. Vallè Poussin, pp. 10-11). Later Mahāyāna Buddhism interprets this formula ' When this exists, that exists...... ' as the ' dependence of things ' confining the concrete application of the formula ' upon ignorance depend the karma-formation......' only to the Hinayānistic idea. Saṁghabhadra's analysis of *Pratītyasamutpāda* is worthy of note.

Secondly the term 'occurs' concerns the relationship between the present and the future, for only if there is a present potentiality, can there be a future occurrence. If conditions (*pratyaya*) gather together in the present, then they can give birth to things in the future. This explanation alludes to potentiality and can be termed Absolute Truth (*paramârtha-satya*).

We can say that the first portion of the aphorism 'when this exists' relates to the realm of conventional truth (*saṁvṛti-satya*) which does not include potentiality. The latter part of the aphorism 'when this occurs' represents Absolute Truth (*paramârtha-satya*) because potentiality is present. Thus, in his interpretation of pratītyasamutpāda, Saṁghabhadra followed the traditional Abhidharmika's view from the standpoint of causality on the one hand. But he also drew attention to the potentiality of time on the other. It is a feature of the time aspect, namely the actuality. In regards to the actuality he entitled it *parārtha* and gave it prime emphasis. Existents in terms of conventional truth are the opposite of actuality, in so far as all existents exist without conditions (*pratyaya*). Existents in terms of Absolute Truth are the actuality which occurs from conditions. In other words, nothing new occurs without conditions and all entities possess actuality. Saṁghabhadra's emphasis on the actuality of time as superceding the causality of time can also be found in his interpretation of *ādi* (the beginning), which refers to *avidyā* (ignorance), one of the Twelve Links of Dependent Origination. We can summarize his view of *avidyā* as found in the *Nyāyānusāraśāstra* (fascil. 28, T. 29, 499a ^{22} – 502^{3}) as follows.

1. *Avidyā* is derived from the prefix *a* and *vidyā*, the negation of *vidyā*, but we cannot confine, its connotation merely to a negation *vidyā* (knowledge). In the Orthodox (*āgama*) *sūtras* we find sufferings such as *samyojana, sambandha, anuśaya*, etc., used as synonym for *avidyā*. These synonyms are defined as real (*dravya-sat*), therefore, *avidyā* also must be considered as real.

2. *Avidyā* in its nature is impossible to discern. It is a reality from which we must be emancipated in order to attain Enlightenment, thus as a positive obstacle to Enlightenment *avidyā* is not merely the logical negation of *vidyā*.

3. *Avidyā* is a reality which is clearly perceived and comprehended (*upalabdhyate*) in that it is analogous to the comparison between darkness and light. Darkness is not merely a logical negation of light, but rather a positive affirmation of the object of the eye consciousness since we are capable of perceiving darkness as well as light. In the same way *avidyā* is the positive affirmation of the object of consciousness as far as it relates to the sufferings in consciousness. It is in this sense that *avidyā* can be considered as real.

4. *Avidyā* is said to be a cause (*hetu*) in so far as it produces suffering. Both cause and effect are considered real since the product of suffering is apparent, thus *avidyā* is real.[1]

5. *Avidyā* is that which is to be destroyed by the arising of *vidyā*, just as wrong view (*midhyādṛṣṭi*) will be destroyed by right view (*sammādṛṣṭi*).

6. *Avidyā* is said to be a real thing (*eka-dharma*) as Saṁghabhadra gave a quotation from the *Āgama* reading: 'If a Bhikkhu destroys a thing (*ekadharma*), he is declared by me to be a man who has completed all his Buddhist obligations'. This thing (*dharma*) is called *avidyā*.

This explanation of *avidyā* demonstrates that it is a real element producing suffering. It is not a simple negation of the real for it is considered as an independent actual *dharma* just as *vidyā* is an actual independent *dharma*. Thus the two terms *vidyā* and *avidyā* exist separately and in opposition. *Avidyā*

1. This idea can be found also in the Theravāda's interpretation. '*Na-yidaṁ ādimattakathanaṁ; paṭṭhānadhammakathanaṁ pan'etaṁ.' Tiṇṇan hi vaṭṭānaṁ avijjā paṭṭhānā; avijjāggahaṇena hi avasesa-kilesavaṭṭañ ca kammādīni ca bālaṁ paṭibedhenti......Iti yaṁ gaṇhato bandho muccato ca mokkho hoti, tassa paṭṭhānadhammassakathanam idaṁ, na ādimattakathanan ti. Evam idam bhavacakkaṁ avidātādi ti veditabbaṁ*' (*Vism*, p. 577). *Avijjā* as *ādi* is distinguished from *pakati* (*prakṛti*) in Sāṁkhya: '*kasmā pan'ettha avijjā ādito vuttā. Kim, pakativādinaṁ pakati viya, avijjā pi akāraṇaṁ mūlakāraṇaṁ lokassā ti. Na akāraṇam; āsavasamudayā avijjā samudayo ti hi avijjāya kāraṇam vuttaṁ*' (*Vism*, p. 525).

possesses a specific function as the cause of suffering and it is in this capacity that *avidyā* is termed *ādi*, meaning 'from the beginning' since it represents the beginning of the Twelve Links.

The theory of Dependent Origination (*pratītyasamutpāda*) is commonly divided into the three divisions of past, present and future. This interpretation is based upon the causality of time. This conventional truth Saṁghabhadra termed 'acceptable agreement' (*dharmasaṅketa*) to distinguish it from *paramārtha* (absolute truth). In the *NY.*, he says 'it is said in the Paramārthaśūnyatāsūtra (T. 2. 920c) that *dharmasaṅketa* means the causal chain of the Twelve Links, namely, *saṁskāra* originates from *avidyā* .... *jarāmaraṇa* from *jāti*. In other words, *dharmasaṅketa* denotes the causal relationship between cause and effect (*hetu-phala-anubandha*).' (*Ny.* T. 29, 428c). This causal relationship Saṁghabhadra also termed 'intimation' (*prajñapti*) since it relates to the domain of conventional truth.

Since Early Buddhism the things are considered to arise by means of *pratītyasamutpāda*, depending upon conditions. We cannot actually determine which is the beginning and which is the end. The mutuality and conditionality of these things are, according to Saṁghabhadra, based upon the actuality of time. From this standpoint there can be no beginning and no end. This conception can be properly termed by him *paramārtha* (the absolute truth). Saṁghabhadra stated that the Twelve Links had a beginning (*ādi*) and were also beginningless. The former statement is due to the time aspect of causality, which is termed *dharmasaṅketa*, while the latter to another aspect of actuality, which is termed *paramārtha*. In his philosophy the latter, namely, *paramārtha*, receives prime importance. We will not find any inconsistency in his double statements that the Twelve Links had a beginning and that they are also beginningless.[1]

From these two view points we can realize also that *ādi* does not mean a *causa prima* nor is it equivalent to the *prakṛti* of Sāṁkhya philosophy. The idea of *causa prima* is held up by the cause and effect relatedness in progression or causality. We normally are inclined to consider the regressive causes until we finally arrive at the last cause which we term 'the first cause'. *Avidyā* was placed at the beginning of *pratītyasamutpāda* merely because it is considered to be the most effective and mighty among the other defilements producing suffering, not because it is the last cause where we arrive by inference. It does not refer to the origin or beginning of life in the cosmic sense, but rather refers to the fundamental principle from which all the other links of *pratītyasamutpāda* come into existence. As it is the principle of defilement in actual existence, so it is real and actual in its existence although negative in form (*a-vidyā*). In Saṁghabhadra's[2] interpretation the beginning of the psycho-physiological process still remains, but it is merely *dharmasaṅketa* in lieu of the Absolute Truth. When he considers *avidyā* to be the most important factor in the psycho-

1. The application of the two concepts (*paramārtha* and *dharmasaṅketa*) to *ādित्व* is a product of the genium of Saṁghabhadra. It is possibly due to the critical attitude of the Sarvāstivāda school against heretic views. We can not overlook that the Sarvāstivāda views have been systematized and formulated to meet the heretic ones. (Cf. Chatterjee '*Problems of Knowledge* and the Four Schools of later Buddhism', *Annals of the Bhandarkar Oriental Research Institute*, Vol. XXII, part iii.) In contrast, the Theravāda school faithfully followed the early Buddhist tradition, interpreting it from the point of view of psychology rather than epistemology.

2. Saṁghabhadra (5th Century A. D.) composed two *śāstras*: *Abhidharma-nyāyānusāra* and *Samayapradīpikā*, which are extant both in Chinese and Tibetan. The former has also the French translation for the three chapters (50-52 chapters) out of 80 chapters (translated by La Vallée Poussin, *Mélanges chinois et Bouddhique*, 1936-1937). Poussin's translation corresponds to the Chinese 'Shun-Caṇ-li-lun' (*Nyāyānusāraśāstra*), but not to the Chinese 'Choen-tcheng-luen' (*Samayapradīpikā*), which he himself wrongly identified. In these texts and commentaries the author's name is differently described. The texts mentioning the name 'Saṁghabhadra' are Yaśomitra's *Abhidharmakośavyākhyā*, and possibly the original Sanskrit *śāstras* of the Chinese *Pradīpa* and *Nyāyānusāra*; the texts mentioning '*Sahantabhadra*' are Śāntirakṣita's *Tattvasaṁgraha* (*Gaekwad Series*. No. XXX. 1926, Baroda) and possibly the Sanskrit original of the Tibetan *Pradīpa*; the Tibetan translation of the *Abhidharmakośavyākhyā* mentions both Saṁghabhadra (*ḥdus bz'aṅ*) and Sahantabhadra (*ḥdul bz'aṅ*). The former is found in three chapters, *dhātunirdeśa*, *indriya* and *loka*, while the latter in two chapters, *karmanirdeśa* and *Samādhi*'. Cordier's Catalogue (*mdo-ḥgrel* 64) gives two Tibetan names to the author of *Pradīpa*: *ḥdus-bz'aṅ* and *ḥdul-bz'aṅ*; the latter is considered to stand for the Sanskrit name *Vinītabhadra*, which perferably stands for *Sahantabhadra*. It would not be unfair to consider the original Mongolian name as an equivalent to the Sanskrit *Sahantabhadra*. Cordier gives *Binayabhadra* to the Original Mongolian.

physiological process, he takes it as the actuality beyond the causality of time. He further suggested in his writings that actuality (*kāritra*) is the conditions (*pratyaya*) through which all things should be observed for no existent can exist as such without conditions.

Kāritra and Pratyaya.—The Buddhist Sanskrit term *kāritra* (actuality) plays an important role in Saṁghabhadra's epistemology. *Kāritra* is used as synonym for such words as *karma, kriyā* and *puruṣakāra.* Saṁghabhadra also distinguishes *kāritra* from *vyāpāra* (an efficient function) which means the ability concerning a definite object or the ability arising for a definite object, i.e., the eyes have *vyāpāra* only when they have contact with the object, the ears have it only when they encounter the sound. *Kāritra*, however, is used only in reference to the time divisions. Saṁghabhadra designated *kāritra* as the 'ability to draw forth' (*ākṣepaśakti*) the effect but not to 'produce' (*janana*) it. (*Ny.* 51. T. 29, 631c; *Tattvasaṁgraha* p. 506. *Gaekwad Oriental Series*, no. xxx. 1926, Baroda). This means that when the effect comes into existence, *kāritra* is not the direct cause but rather an indirect or helping cause (*Ny.* 52. T. 29, 631d).[1]

According to this concept of *kāritra* in reference to the time divisions, the future means the situation in which *kāritra* has not yet arisen, the present signifies that *kāritra* has just arisen and the past denotes a situation in which *kāritra* has arisen and passed away (*Ny.* 52, T. 29,633a). The three time divisions are dependent upon the rise of *kāritra* and are not a category of reason since the time concept in the category of reason excludes experience while the time concept of *kāritra* includes it. In other words, the time divisions express *kāritra* as experienced in concrete form. It is not time as a category of reason that gives us the conception of phenomena but rather time as *kāritra*. Buddhist time in this sense is experimental.

The arising of any single existent requires the grouping of conditions (*pratyaya*). Without the necessary conditions no existent can come into being. *kāritra*, as we have noted, is also an auxiliary cause in its function as 'drawing forth'. The question then arises as to the difference between these two types of auxiliary causes, *pratyaya* and *kāritra*.

Regarding this distinction, Saṁghabhadra said in his *Ny.*, 'Even if both do not completely differ, nevertheless, *kāritra* comes into existence relying upon *pratyaya* because the *dharma* itself does not come into

1. *Kāritra* apparently is based on Skt. *cāritra* blended with forms of *ka r–, kār–* (Edgerton, *Hybrid Sanskrit Dictionary*, p. 179, Yale University Press, 1953). The Pāli *cāritta* stands for the Skt., cāritra, '*yāvad antaśo mālogunaparikṣiptā api tadrūpa* (*su ha sahasa*) *cāritraṁsāpadya*(*nte*) (Waldschmidt, 51). —*Das Mahāparinirvāṇasūtra*, Teil II, S. 112, Akademie-Verlag, 1951). The change of a single consonent, $c > k$ can be found in numerous cases : *ci–ciketa* (aor.); *keta* (derivative), *cāru–kālu* (Aśoka edict. Queens Edict no. I. line 5), *katābhi* (i) = *kāresu* = *kṛtābhicāreṣu* (Girnar Rock Edict V), a queen *kāluvāki* = cāruvāki (C. D. Chatterjee, 'Studies in the Inscriptions of Aśoka' no. 1 (c). *Annals of the Bhandarkar Oriental Research Institute*, XXXVII, 1956, p. 232) etc. The Pāli *cāritta*, derived from *car*, to move, to proceed, means *cāritta–vāritta* (the manner of acting and avoiding. J. iii. 195; Th. 591. etc.). *Cāritta* denotes merely 'to move' and is not a positive term such as 'to produce', or 'to create'. Saṁghabhadra designated *kāritra* as the 'ability to draw forth' (*ākṣepaśaktiḥ*) the effect but not to 'produce' (*janana*) it. (*Ny.* 51. T. 29, 631c; also see *Tattvasaṁgraha*, p. 506, Gaekwad's Oriental Series, no. XXX, 1926, Baroda). This means that when the effect comes into existence, *kāritra* is not the direct cause but rather an indirect or helping cause, (*ibid.*, 52. T. 29, 631d). *Kāritra* is used as synonym for *puruṣakāra; puruṣa* is used as a compound *puruṣakāra-phala*, one of the six causes. (A. K. V., p. 201). The meaning of *puruṣa* is considered as a difficult word, but it does not denote 'strong power' as is commonly believed. It means 'human effort, manly virility (M. Williams, *SED*) or manly performance' (Edgerton, *BHD.*, p. 348b). The meaning of the Pāli *purisakāra* also is the same as the Skt. *puruṣakāra*. (D. I. 53; Miln. 96). *Puruṣakāra* denotes merely the conventional usage to express the humanly performance just like the foot of crow, the medicinal herb, the drunken elephant and the general, (*Abhidharmakośa*, 19 T. 29, 35b). Thus, *puruṣakāra* represents the manner of moving, which is the original significance of *kāritra*.

Dīpakāra (450–550. *A. D.*), the disciple of Saṁghabhadra, discusses about *kāritra* in his Abhidharmadīpa, pp. 261–296. He interprets it as 'present state' or '*dharma* having the actuality', i.e., '... *labdhasāmarthyasya dharmasya yaḥ phalākṣepastatkāritramityucyate. sā ca vartamānakālā vṛttiḥ kāritramityākhyāyate.*' (*Abhidharmadīpa*, p. 281, ed. by P. S. Jaini, Kashi Jayaswal Research Institute, Patna, 1959; on the author and his text see G. H. Sasaki's article 'Abhidharmadīpa, ed. by Jaini'...*Bulletin of the School of Oriental and African Studies. University of London*, XXV; part 2, 1962).

Kārya mimāṁsā, Rājaśekhara, gives a suggestion; *kārayitri* ...... *pratibhā* (creative), *bhāvayitri*...... *pratibhā* (reflective; *kārayitā – kāritra*, meaning 'to draw forth' (thanks to Dr. Chatterjee, Calcutta, who gave this suggestion on the occasion of the XXVI International Congress of Orientalists, New Delhi, 1964).

existence depending upon *pratyaya* (*Ny.* 52. T. 29, 633a). *Kāritra* comes into existence depending upon conditions, therefore, conditions are the basis of the arising of *kāritra*. Even if there are many conditions present, *kāritra* does not necessarily come into existence. It is analogous to the relationship between the eye-consciousness and the conditions. Namely, even though there are such existing conditions as the eyes, object of the eye and so on, the eye consciousness does not necessarily come into existence. The reverse, however, is not true, for when *kāritra* arises, the necessary conditions must be present. *Pratyaya* as such is not equivalent to *kāritra* but rather a requirement for the arising of *kāritra*. *Pratyaya* can be called *kāritra* only when it has an efficient function (*vyāpāra*). Saṁghabhadra says, 'where *kāritra* exists, *pratyaya* exists' (*ibid.*, 633a). He also attempted to relate the *kāritra* concept in combination with *pratyaya*. He applied *kāritra* in combination with *pratyaya* in his explanation of the relativity of the phenomenal world. This latter theory is represented in Abhidharma philosophy by the Six-Causes-and-Four-Conditions theory, which will be discussed later.

In the distinction between both concepts there is an apparent difference between the Sarvāstivāda and Sautrāntika schools. Saṁghabhadra maintained that *pratyaya* is related to *kāritra* but not equivalent. He gave both terms a separate reality. This attitude demonstrates the character of his realism. The Sarvāstivāda position was inclined towards an analysis of reality while the Sautrāntika held a contrary position, negating and denying reality to stress the momentariness of existence. With regard to *pratyaya*, the Sautrāntika gave precedence to *pratyaya* over *dravya-sat*. Saṁghabhadra in protest against the Sautrāntika's equivalency of *kāritra* and *pratyaya* stated: 'If [Sautrāntika] says that conditions (*pratyaya*) are considered[1] to exist, hence, *kāritra* as arising can be said to exist, this notion is false' (*ibid.*, 632a). He also quoted the Sautrāntika standpoint: 'Our school [Sautrāntika] admits that continuity (*saṁtati, skandha*) is transposed and relies upon *pratyaya*, hence, *saṁtati* will give rise to effect. If so [because *pratyaya* exists] we must admit that *kāritra* also exists,' (*ibid.*, 632d). This means that wherever *pratyaya* exists there *kāritra* also exists. In other words *pratyaya* and *kāritra* are one and the same thing. Thus Sautrāntikas considered *kāritra* and *pratyaya* to be equivalent while Saṁghabhadra merely considered the two terms as related in the sense that *pratyaya* is the basis of *kāritra*. The former does not have actuality (*kāritra*) but when the former functions, then at that moment the latter comes into existence. *Kāritra* cannot come into existence merely through the grouping of conditions alone.

The Predominance of Pratyaya.— Even in Saṁghabhadra's psycho-physical interpretation of *pratītyasamutpāda* he gave predominance to *pratyaya*.[2] This direction was assimilated and extended by Abhidharmika in the Six-Causes-and-Four-Conditions theory. Principally this theory dealt with the predominance of *pratyaya*. The predominance of *pratyaya* over *hetu* in line with Early Buddhist thought can be demonstrated by an analysis of this theory. In terms of time, the theory concerns simultaneity and continuity as can be seen in the following diagram.

1. About the Sautrāntika's equivalency of *Kāritra* and *pratyaya* see *Ny.* T. 29.632b [10-12]. This idea is based upon the theory of momentariness. According to this theory all dharmas have the ability to interrelate with each other in a form of *pratyaya*; all of them have *sarūpya* (conformity). This notion of the relatedness has been expounded by Dharmakirti, who established a presupposition: '*Sambandha* is help up by *paratantrya*'. (Frauwallner, 'Dharmakirti's Saṁbandhaparikṣā', *Wiener Zeitschrift für die Kunde des Morgenlandes*, XLI Bd. 265–300 SS.). Tibetan version, of Peking Ed. 95. 357 a-358b; 358–364b and also *Pramāṇavārtikabhāṣyam*, Patna, 1953.

According to the Sarvāstivāda school *Dharmas* are interrelated with each other by means of *sabhāga-hetu* and *niṣyanda-phala*.

2. The Theravādas gave predominance to *pratyaya* since the beginning of this tradition, which concerned merely the human relationship. Hence they did not have to distinguish between *hetu* and *pratyaya*. A psychological attitude was applied to the concept of *paṭiccasamuppāda*; each of psychological factors arising is related to the twelve lines of dependence: 'When [the unwholesome mind] arises, *saṅkhāra* depends upon *avijjā*, etc, (*Vibh.* p. 165). Buddhaghoṣa terms this aspect as *ekacittakkhanika-paṭiccasamuppāda* (momentary dependent origination, *Sammohavinodanī*, p. 203).

Six causes (*ṣaḍhetavaḥ*)	Simultaneity	*kāraṇahetu* (active cause)
		sahabhūhetu (accompanied cause)
		sabhāgahetu (corresponding cause)
		samprayuktahetu (associated cause)
	Continuity	*sarvatragahetu* (common cause)
		vipākahetu (resultant cause)
Four-conditions (*caturpratyaya*)	Simultaneity and Continuity	*hetupratyaya* (effective condition)
		samantarapratyaya (immediate conditions)
		ālambanapratyaya (the object as conditions)
		adhipatipratyaya (eminent conditions)

In this diagram we can observe that *hetupratyaya* of the Four-Conditions can embody in its contents all the Six-Causes with the exception of *kāraṇahetu.* The other three *pratyayas (samanantara, ālambana* and *adhipati)* are a diffusion of *kāraṇahetu.* In reference to time, these three *pratyayas* are based upon simultaneity as well as continuity. The former can be considered as equivalent to the actuality of time, while continuity is equivalent to the causality of time. The other five kinds of causes in the diagram (*sahabhū, sabhāga, samprayukta, sarvatraga* and *vipāka*) illustrate the reciprocal relationship from A to B and *vice versa.* They also represent the relationship of *pratyaya (hetu-pratyaya).*[1]

The above explanation shows us that the cause-effect relationship is included in the category of *pratyaya,* and reveals a predominance of the *pratyaya*-relationship over *hetu*-relationship. It has been a primary characteristic of Buddhist philosophy from the beginning, and continues to influence present Buddhist thought. In Early Buddhism, *hetupratyaya* was inseparable in definition and connoted a mutual relationship (*sahakāra*). In the Abhidharma period, however, Buddhist thought concerned itself with the concept of *hetupratyaya* not merely as a combined term, but also established a distinction between the two. Thus the distinguished *hetupratyaya* were represented in the theory, namely, the Six-Causes-and-Four-Conditions of the Sarvāstivāda school.

In Early Buddhism intellectual thought was concerned only with the human structure and not with the phenomenal world. Abhidharma,[2] in broadening this concept to include the latter, subsequently reduced *hetu* into *pratyaya,* or cause into condition. In the process of historical development *pratyaya* has come to include *hetu.* In other words, the reciprocal relationship has come to assimilate the uni-directional one. We can notice here that the concept of *pratyaya* in the Buddhist sense is much more important than the concept of *hetu.* The idea of assimilation is extremely important and cannot be overlooked in analysing the time concept in Buddhism. From the point of view of time the diagram can be summarized as the relationship between the actuality and causality of time, and a demonstration of how the uni-directional relationship has been included in the reciprocal one.

1. The Vaibhāsikas hold the view that the four *pratyayas* have their own natures, which correspond to *svabhāva* or *bhāva.* (*Pradīpa,* T. 29. 822a). The Vaibhāsika's equivalency of *svabhāva* to *bhāva* sometimes gives rise to the controversy between the Sarvāstivāda and the Sautrāntika. According to the Vasubandhu's interpretation, approximating the Sautrāntika, the concept *hetu-pratyaya* is considered to be *bīja,* which is based upon *ālayavijñāna. Ālayavijñāna,* in its turn, has a double aspect: *phalabhāva* and *hetubhāva. Bhāva* in this sense implies *śakti* or function. Nevertheless, Saṃghabhadra interprets it as a reality or entity, for *Bhāva* in his sense is equivalent to *svabhāva* (reality), (*Ny.* T. 29, $440b^{10-11}$; $440b^{3-4}$).

2. Both schools, Theravāda and Sarvāstivāda, call the syllogism '*imasmin sati idaṁ hoti......*' *idappaccayatā* (*idapratyayatā*), and the formula 'upon ignorance depend the karma-formations......' *paṭiccasamuppanna-dhamma* (*pratītyasamutpādadharma*). But the Theravādin does not discuss the syllogism separated from the formula, taking both of these as two different aspects of the one and same thing. Namely, the former refers to *paṭiccasamuppāda* in view of *karaṇa* (causing), while the latter in view of *dhamma* (the caused). *Sammohavinodani* reads, *idappaccayatā ti saṅkhārādinaṁ kāraṇāni avijjādini aṅgāni. Paṭiccasamuppannadhammā ti avijjādihi nibbattā saṅkhārādayo dhammā* (*Sammohavinodani,* p. 139).

Dravya and Time.—According to the Sarvāstivāda school, all existing things, both material and non-material, possess a permanent entity (*svabhāva*) and are termed real (*dravya*). Sarvāstivāda philosophy is usually designated as Buddhist realism. When they consider time, however, they did not include time in the category of reality as is evinced in the *Mahāvaibhāsikā-śāstra.* The question then arises, why time is not included in the *dravya* category as an entity ?[1]

If we examine this realism[2] from the view point of time, we will discover that reality is based upon the relationship between cause and effect, for it comes into existence by the law or causality from future to present, and from present to past. Causality can be possible only when cause and effect may exist in a degree of reality. The permanent reality of existents (*svabhāva*) and causality (*hetuphala-anubandha*) are inter-related on a mutual basis and this is one of the characteristics of existents as *svabhāva.* In terms of time existents (*svabhāva, dravya*) are considered as existing ' at all times ' (*sarvasmin kāle*). ' At all times ' differs from ' permanency ' (*nitya*), whicb usually means eternal existence passing through the three divisions of time.[3] The concept *nitya* can be possible only when *dravya* exists passing through the three divisions of time. Namely *dravya* can be considered as *nitya,* when it is observed from the view point of chronological time or the causality of time. ' At all times ', however, means the absolute at this moment because existents in this respect are in the present moment which includes the past and future. Only in this sense existents are said to exist at all times (*sarvasmin kāle* or *sarvadā*). Namely *dravya* (*svabhāva*) can be considered as existent at all times, when it is observed from the view point of the actuality of time, but not from the causality of time. The concept *nitya* can be said to refer to horizontal time while *sarvasmin kāle* refers to vertical time.

Existents (*dravya, svabhāva*) are in Abhidharma considered permanent or impermanent. The difference of terminology is not a discrepancy, but merely related to the aspects of time as viewed from different phases. Saṁghabhadra in his *Ny.* explains these two view points as follows.

> ' The reason is this : Even though created things (*saṅskṛtadharma*) exist permanently, nevertheless, they have variations according to their own situations (*avasthā*). These different situations come into existence according to conditions (*pratyaya*). After one moment no existent can remain (*sthiti*). For this reason *dharma-svabhāva* are impermanent for their *svabhāvas* do not differ (*vyatirikta*) from the variations of [the situations] ' (*Ny.* 52. T. 29, 633a).

Dharma as such is considered as permanent, but in view of its variety of situations, it is impermanent. *Dharma* depends in its nature upon the variation and changeability of situations (*avasthā*) in terms of time, these situations (*avasthā*) imply the actuality of time. Here we can note that it is in view of the actuality of time that permanent *dharma* can be termed impermanent. Therefore, the two expressions '*dharma* is permanent ' and ' *dharma* is impermanent ' are not inconsistent as they are based upon two different standpoints. When

1. The time concept is not considered as *dravya* (*Mahāvaibhāṣyaśāstra.* T. 27. 141b ; 183 ; 919b. etc. also cf. the Chinese commentary on the *Mādhyamaka-kārikā,* T. 42. 130c).

2. The A. K. V. mentions three kinds of *sat : trividhaṁ hi yogācārāṇāṁ sat. paramārtha saṁvṛti-satdravya-sacca. dravyataḥ sva-lakṣaṇataḥ sad dravyasad iti.* (A. K. V., p. 524; L. de la Vallée Poussin, *L' Abhidharmakośa de Vasubandhu* VI. 4. p. 141, note 1; IV, p. 18, n. 1.) The concept *svalakṣaṇena sat* (the being its own nature) is the characteristics common to these three *sat.* Buddhist realism distinguishes between *svalakṣaṇa* (abstraction and generality), placing the emphasis upon the former (cf. Arnold Kunst, '*Probleme der Buddhistischen Logik in der Darstellung des des Tattrasaṅgraha,* Kroków, 1939. p. 33).

3. Yaśomitra mentions the distinction between *sarvāsmin kāle* and *nitya : svabhāvaḥ sarvadā cāstiti. yad rūp'ādeḥ svalakṣaṇaṁ. tat sarvasmin kāle vidyata itiṣyate. yadi rūp'ādeḥ sarvadā'sti tena rūp'ādi-bhāvo nityaḥ prāpnoti. ata āha. bhāvo nityaś ca neṣyate.* (A. K. V., p. 472). The fundamental standpoint of the Sarvāstivāda school is clearly shown in the principles : *svabhāvaḥ sarvadā cāsti* as well as *sarvadharmāḥ nityāḥ santi.* To understand these apparently inconsistent principles we must deeply investigate the two aspects of time : actuality and causality. I have got an opportunity to discuss about two modes of time with Professors Lousi and Margaret Chandler, Illinois University, U. S. A. who gave me kind suggestions.

dharma (*svabhàva*) is considered from the causality of time it is believed to exist at all times (*sarvadà, sarvasmin kàle)*, while when it is considered from the actuality of time, it is impermanent (*anitya*). This logical construction of *dharma-svabhàva* is the concept upon which Buddhist realism is based.

Practically speaking, we can consider that in the future there exist multitudes of existents receiving their causes and conditions to those which momentarily arise in the present. The existents which now appear in the present will disappear momentarily and flow to the past. This type of realism demonstrates that all existing things are based upon the present moment which includes both the future and the past.[1] All existent creatures have the past behind them and future potentiality before them.

1. The Theravāda also came to the same conclusion as the Sarvāstivāda through a different approach toward
the time. The present (*paccuppanna*) in the Pāli sense, derived from *prati–uppanna*, refers to the potential future.
Uppanna is classified into the four divisions : *vattamāna*, *bhūtāpagata*, *okāsakata* and *bhūmiladdha* (*Vism.*, p. 687).
Beginning with *vattamān'uppanna* (' things presently arisen '), the other three divisions follow in an order of a decreasing
degree of actuality (Nyanaponika, *Abhidhamma Studies*, p. 83). We would like to consider it as the transformation of
reality from the objective to the subjective; *vattamān'uppanna* refers to things objectively existing, while the last division
bhūmiladdh'uppanna to the human defilement existing in our mind, which may be conquered and overcome, or more
accurately speaking, may be changed in conformity with the world of immediate phenomena. The Pāli concept of the
present implies momentary actuality representing the Early Buddhist tradition. It implies also the effort to attain
Nirvāṇa in the present. The *Dīgha Nikāya* reads : *khīnā jāti, vusitam brahmacariyam, katam̆ karaṇiyam̆, nāparam*
itthattāyāti abbhaññāsi (*D.* i. p. 203). This passage corresponds to the *Suttanipāta* 729. Buddhaghosa interpreted *itthabhāva*
in the *Suttanipāta* as the hunan state (*SN. Com.*, II. 2. p. 505) meaning the Arahat attaining complete Enlightenment will
not again return to this present state to remove remaining defilements because he has already removed himself from all
defilements. *Nāparam itthattāya* in the *Dīgha Nikāya* is translated in the Chinese version as ' not to enter another birth ',
This translation easily misleads us to the notion of a transmigration of life after death. Buddhaghosa points out two cases
the dative and the ablative. In both cases it means there no longer exists a state in which we must do further practices
(*DN. Com.* I. p. 226). The usage of the concept *nāpāram itthattāya* in the ablative case can be found also in the
Samyutta Nikāya (*S. II.* p. 104); *paccudāvattati kho idam̆ viññāṇam nāmarūpamhā nāparam̆ gacchati*. We can amend the
former sentence into *itthattāya nāparam̆ gacchati*. The *PTSD.* gives *idha* as an equivalent to *ittha*. However, this
could also be an equivalent to *etta*. We like to take it as *iha*, derived from the *i–tra*, meaning ' just now ' or ' present
state '. *Nāparm itthattāya* refers to the present state and can similarly be applied to *Nirvāṇa* in the present, but not to
the life after death.

LA NOTION DE TEMPS RÉVERSIBLE DANS LA MYTHOLOGIE BOUDDHIQUE

Paul Mus

Le bouddhisme ancien a établi sa doctrine du salut sur le contraste de deux eschatologies, entre lesquelles est interdite toute communication de nature. D'une part, c'est le cercle vicieux de la transmigration, parcouru suivant un enchaînement de causes dont la dernière ramènera la première, et c'est, d'autre part, le saut dans le Nirvāna — donc par delà toute notion logiquement constructible. Le Nirvāna, enseigne en effet le bouddhisme, n'est ni à définir par l'existence, ni par le néant, ni par une combinaison des deux, ni par leur négation simultanée. Autant dire qu'il est irrationnel. Réel cependant, quoique les premiers interprètes s'y soient trompés, en ce sens que, découvert par le Buddha et par lui seul révélé, qualifié par ailleurs d'Incréé, de Refuge, de Béatitude, d'Ile sortie des eaux de l'existence, qui sont toutes Douleur, il accueillait les Saints à la façon d'une « autre rive ». De par la défense canonique d'en rien énoncer de positif, en dehors de sa vertu libérative, on se le figurait surtout par contraste avec le spectacle de la transmigration. Pour percevoir, — on serait tenté de dire complémentairement — le Nirvāna, les bouddhistes commençaient par contempler en esprit la masse sans nombre et sans repos des êtres: passant d'état en état, de monde en monde, du plus profond enfer au plus haut des cieux, et du ciel en enfer, à travers toutes les conditions intermédiaires, avec d'incessants retours; de tout temps et à jamais; sans Création initiale ni Destruction finale; inévitablement reproduits, au delà de la mort (param maranāt), en de nouveaux corps créés par leur attachement à l'existence et leurs actes passés (karman); donc sans autre origine qu'eux-mêmes, dans la nuit du passé, et sans autre avenir qu'eux-mêmes, dans les profondeurs du futur. Le Nirvāna, c'est l'« Issue ».

On observera que, chacune à sa manière, ces deux eschatologies — celle de la reproduction indéfinie et celle de la rupture— échappent également à notre habituelle représentation d'un temps «évolutif», qui se développerait, sous la loi de l'homogénéité absolue de ses parties comme la condition formelle et, en dernière analyse, linéaire d'un complexe cosmique de causalités liant les uns aux autres les instants du monde. Le Nirvāna, par définition, brise cette série cosmique. Quoi qu'il soit de lui, où qu'il soit, il n'est plus dans le cours du temps. Quant au cycle des renaissances, le temps qu'il suppose de son côté est essentiellement hétérogène. Il est alternativement forme d'évolution et forme d'involution. Non seulement parce qu'une série causale très élaborée explique, sous sa loi, la succession compensée des morts et des retours à l'être (1), mais surtout parce qu'il soumet l'ensemble du cosmos à un rythme que ponctuent des créations et des destructions périodiques. Les premiers âges sont ceux de la vertu, de la félicité et d'une fabuleuse longévité. Après quoi la part du vice et de la souffrance croît, jusqu'aux suprêmes convulsions, tandis que la durée normale de la vie humaine tombe à 100, à 50, à 10 ans. Toutes les mesures, toutes les conditions de l'existence s'altèrent de façon systématique au rythme de ces alternances. Du temps du Buddha Çākyamuni la taille des hommes était encore de 8 pieds. Elle descendra au-dessous de ce qu'on la voit être. Mais elle sera redevenue colossale au temps où le Buddha futur, Maitreya, commencera sa prédication. On voit sans peine comment le bouddhisme adapte cette théorie des Ages du monde (empruntée au fonds commun des croyances asiatiques) au plan rétributif de la transmigration. Des enfers aux cieux, une inégalité du milieu rétributif différencie les rétributions, conformément aux actes passés. Il en sera de même de cette autre inégalité de milieu qu'établit, dans le temps, la succession des Ages cosmiques. On naît non seulement à l'endroit mais à la date que vous assignent telles ou telles séries d'actes.

(1) H. Oldenberg, trad. A. Foucher, *Le Bouddha*, p. 250 sq, sur la théorie des Douzes Causes. D'autres énumérations sont parfois proposées : Dix Causes, p. ex., dans Digha nikāya II p. 30 sq. — Contrairement à l'avis d'Oldenberg la série dénaire a quelque apparence d'être la plus ancienne.

Toutefois, et bien que l'épigraphie d'Açoka (IIIᵉ siècle av. J.-C.) implique déjà toute la théorie des Ages cosmiques par sa mention des « Périls de l'Avenir » (anāgata bhayāni), il est de fait que le bouddhisme canonique, tant dans les recensions sanskrites (passées en chinois) que pāli, s'inquiète bien plutôt de la causalité elle-même, avec ses douze articles, que des formes temporelles où elle s'intègre. Une certaine notion du temps est condition du système rétributif. Mais elle n'est pas, en soi, l'objet de méditations ou de développements particulièrement fréquents ou poussés. Il faut attendre les débuts du bouddhisme mythologique dit du Grand-Véhicule (Mahāyāna) pour que s'amorce, avec Amitāyus, « Buddha à l'Age infini » (1), un « primat chronologique », déifié à plus basse époque encore par le bouddhisme magique des Tantra sous les traits de Mahākāla, le Temps Universel.

Etranger à ces généralisations, le bouddhisme ancien concentre tout son intérêt chronologique sur le point où l'application cyclique de la causalité rompt la continuité dans le temps, c'est-à-dire la durée des êtres, en les faisant basculer à tour de rôle dans une impermanence érigée en loi suprême du cosmos. Chronologie, si l'on veut, mais chronologie croulante.

La mythologie des temps postérieurs est cependant en germe dans cette conception. On en trouvera auprès de textes relativement anciens une preuve d'autant plus frappante qu'elle se fixe en images. Il était réservé au bouddhisme magique de représenter le Temps cosmique (Mahākāla) comme un ogre gigantesque embrassant le monde qui transmigre et y plantant griffes et dents. Mais voici déjà comment le code de discipline (Vinaya) d'une ancienne école de langue sanskrite, les Mūla Sarvāstivādin, peignait la « Roue » de la transmigration et, par contraste, le « refuge » du Nirvāna. Le Buddha dit à ses disciples :

« Il vous faut, suivant la dimension (que vous adopterez), faire avec un cercle l'image d'une roue. Au centre vous placerez le moyeu,

---

(1) Āyus, « âge, individuel et cosmique, puissance vitale, quantité de vie, etc. » Notions aussi difficiles qu'importantes, désormais tirées au clair par la vigoureuse étude de M. E. Benveniste, *Les expressions indo-européennes de l'éternité*.

puis vous disposerez cinq rayons (= secteurs) qui représenteront les cinq séjours des êtres (gati = Voies de l'existence). Audessous du moyeu vous dessinerez les enfers (naraka = Purgatoires : le séjour n'en est pas plus définitif que celui des autres secteurs). Des deux côtés vous dessinerez les animaux et les preta (revenants, âmes affamées, esprits des arbres, des lieux, etc.). Puis au-dessus vous dessinerez les hommes et les dieux (deva). A l'emplacement du moyeu vous ferez un cercle de couleur blanche. Au centre vous dessinerez l'image du Buddha. Vous dessinerez tout autour (sur la jante de la roue) les douze conditions (nidāna), signes de la naissance et de la suppression de la naissance, savoir : l'ignorance (avidyā), etc., (ce sont les douze nidāna, « conditions » qui ramènent de la mort à la vie, prolongent celle-ci jusqu'à une mort nouvelle, puis, toujours pareilles à elles-mêmes, la projettent par delà cette mort en une vie de plus, et ainsi de suite. Sur la jante de la roue, une vignette correspond à chacun de ces nidāna). A l'emplacement de la jante vous représenterez une roue à irrigation (ghaṭīyantra, litt. roue à seaux, « noria »). Vous y placerez un grand nombre de seaux d'eau et vous dessinerez l'image de créatures qui naissent et qui meurent. Celles qui naissent auront la tête hors du seau; celles qui meurent auront les pieds hors du seau.

« Au-dessus de la roue il faudra faire le grand spectre (yaksha) de l'Impermanence, les cheveux épars et la bouche ouverte, écartant largement ses deux bras pour tenir la roue de la naissance et de la mort. Des deux côtés de la tête du spectre vous écrirez ces deux stances (gatha) :

Mettez-vous en quête ! Sortez !
Dans la doctrine du Buddha montrez-vous zélé !
Terrassez l'armée de la naissance et de la mort
Comme un éléphant brise une hutte d'herbages !

Si dans cette Loi (dharma) et dans cette Discipline (vinaya)
On pratique sans cesse, sans relâchement,
On pourra épuiser la mer des souillures (kleça)
Et on abordera à la rive de cet océan qu'est la douleur.

« En outre, au-dessus du spectre de l'Impermanence, vous devrez faire un tertre rond et blanc symbolisant la pureté parfaite du Nirvana » (1).

Le Yaksha — spectre ou génie — de l'Impermanence préside par conséquent à la destruction incessante de toutes les existences produites à l'intérieur du cercle. Il annonce ainsi le Mahakala des écoles postérieures, lointain héritier, à travers lui peut-être, des antiques représentations du Temps dévorant (2).

Mais si l'on rapporte la description qu'on vient de lire à l'ensemble des documents canoniques, ce grand Yaksha apparaît plutôt comme une image expressive que comme la traduction d'une croyance réelle. Il est l'interprétation de la structure causale en douze articles, raison directe de l'impermanence. Il personnifie celle-ci (sans nullement encore la diviniser) d'une façon en quelque sorte supplémentaire. C'est là un de ces endroits où il semble que l'imagination des artistes aille plus loin que la stricte dogmatique. Pour celle-ci, en effet, les nidāna sont tout ce qui compte : c'est le temps dans lequel rien ne dure, saisi non pas en soi (comme semblerait le peindre le Yaksha de l'imagerie édifiante) mais *per causas*.

***

On aura remarqué que le Vinaya des Mūla Sarvāstivādin définit la série causale à la fois comme la condition de la

(1) J. Przyluski, *La Roue de la Vie à Ajantā*, Journ. Asiatique 1920, II, p. 316-18, d'après le Vinaya des Mūla Sarvāstivadin. M. Przyluski est, on le sait, le grand expert pour ce traité fondamental, de dimensions imposantes et qui malheureusement ne s'est conservé qu'en chinois et en tibétain.

(2) L'article auquel nous nous référons met déjà en lumière la probabilité d'un rapport historique entre la description de la Roue de la naissance et de la mort fournie par le Vinaya des Mūla Sarvāstivādin et la grande floraison de l'art bouddhique, dans le Nord-Ouest de l'Inde, au contact des traditions hellénistiques. Mais celles-ci, mêlées aux traditions iranisantes, ont amené vers l'Inde une masse singulièrement riche et féconde de croyances et de pratiques de provenance en partie asianique. Le symbolisme chronologique de la Roue ici décrite leur doit peut-être quelque chose. On souhaiterait que M. Przyluski reprît la question : elle bénéficierait de ses actuelles recherches sur la divinité du Temps, — divinité ambiguë, tantôt masculine, tantôt féminine : alternance qui a son écho jusque dans le panthéon tantrique auquel appartient Mahakāla.

naissance indéfiniment répétée et comme celle de l'arrêt de la naissance. C'est dire que le même enchaînement, selon la façon de le prendre, asservit ou libère. Renversement de valeurs dont le sens courant, dans le bouddhisme canonique, est bien fixé. La délivrance s'obtient en arrêtant, par la cessation du désir, tout ce qui procédait, de proche en proche, du terme initial, savoir : ignorance, formations (samskāra), connaissance, nom et corps..., attachement à l'existence, existence, naissance, vieillesse et mort, et ainsi de suite in aeternum (1). Il y a alors arrêt du processus. Les textes toutefois envisagent, comme une condition préalable, son inversion : l'esprit doit s'exercer à le parcourir non seulement dans l'ordre direct (anulomam) mais encore à rebours (patilomam, skr : pratilomam, « à rebrousse poil »). Est-ce là une simple indication pédagogique, tendant à l'acquisition d'une parfaite maîtrise de la liste, ou bien est-il permis de lui attribuer une portée philosophique? Dénote-t-elle une réversibilité du temps?

Sans poser cette question, M. P. Masson-Oursel a noté le renversement du processus dans un travail où il s'est attaché à éclaircir un des aspects (l'un des plus anciens sans doute) du symbolisme si touffu de la Roue des Existences :

« Le terme de samsāra évoque par son étymologie la notion d'un flux torrentiel qui charrie les existences (sam : « ensemble, continûment, en interdépendance » + sarati : « couler, courir »)... (ou bien c'est) un milieu dans lequel se trouve l'existence humaine, un ensemble de conditions physiques ou métaphysiques desquelles dépend cette existence. Il se compose, ce milieu, de l'ensemble des mouvements constitutifs du monde. D'où l'expression upanishadique ā samsārāt« depuis le début du monde » et cette théorie de la Çvetāçvatara upanishad, VI. 16 (la plus ancienne mention brāhmanique du samsāra): à sthiti, la permanence, s'oppose samsāra, le changement. Un immense mécanisme produit tout le devenir et les Hindous se le représentent comme une machine cosmique aux mouvements rotatifs. Çvetāçvatara I. 6 nous apprend avec précision

(1) H. Oldenberg, op. cit. pp. 252—53.

qu'une seule rotation, mais effectuée en des sens différents, explique les deux processus (asservissement et libération). Il nous révèle du même coup quel engin de l'industrie humaine servait de prototype à l'idée de mécanisme universel : c'est la noria des rizières, si répandue dans l'Inde et l'Indochine, cette roue aux tubes de bambou qui fait passer l'eau alternativement de l'un à l'autre des deux biefs qu'elle met en rapport » (1).

Un point est hors de doute : pour le brahmanisme, comme pour le bouddhisme, le mouvement de la machine est le cours même du temps cosmique. La succession en interdépendance de la naissance et de la mort (pratītyasamutpada, selon l'expression bouddhique), quel qu'en soit l'ultime moteur, se développe suivant une durée brisant sans fin ce qu'elle vient de poser. Pour celui de qui cela n'est plus vrai, pour celui qui renverse le processus, se libère et se dirige vers le Vrai, l'Immortel, l'Incréé, vers l'Ile émergeant des eaux de la Douleur et de l'Impermanence, n'y a-t-il pas non seulement arrêt, mais réversibilité de ce flux (sāra) du temps ? Ne revient-on pas en arrière, de quelque façon, pour échapper à ses conséquences ? C'est ce que paraît bien impliquer l'allusion à une double rotation, effectuée dans des sens différents. Asservissement dans le sens que nous savons que suit le cours naturel du temps ; libération, dans un sens formellement donné comme inverse du précédent.

Tenons compte cependant du fait que les textes bouddhiques les plus anciens et les plus considérables s'accordent à définir le salut par la destruction et non par la prise à rebours du samsara ; il suffit d'ouvrir le Dhammapada :

« Arrête avec vigueur le cours du torrent de l'existence ; proscris loin de toi tout plaisir : quiconque a reconnu la fin de tout ce qui est périssable, celui-là connaît l'Incréé » (383).

« J'errais sur le chemin de bien des renaissances, vainement, cherchant le bâtisseur de l'existence ; c'est une grande douleur que de toujours renaître. A présent je t'ai découvert, bâtis-

(1) P. Masson-Oursel, *La noria, prototype du Samsara*, Mélanges Linossier II, pp. 419-20.

seur de la maison; tu ne dois plus rebâtir la maison. Tes poutres sont toutes brisées, le faîte de la maison est détruit. L'âme, échappée à l'instabilité du monde, a atteint le terme du désir » (153 sq.).

Indication qui commande toute recherche concernant la part éventuellement faite par le bouddhisme à la notion d'une réversibilité du temps. Ce n'est point vers l'absorption du Saint dans le Nirvāna qu'il faut s'orienter: cet état est l'arrêt de l'« écoulement » dans le samsāra, ou la destruction de celui-ci (1) — mais par contre, si l'idée entrevue à travers le témoignage de la Çvetāçvatara upanishad a une relation avec le système bouddhique, il faut s'attendre à ce que soit à propos de l'état ambigu, intermédiaire entre la transmigration de plein exercice (d'où cet état provient, mais où il ne rentrera pas) et l'absolue Délivrance (dont le bénéficiaire n'est plus perçu en ce monde), qui est celui des Buddha durant leur dernière existence terrestre. En fait, ils y accèdent non par l'Illumination, mais dès leur miraculeuse naissance. Dès cet instant une suite de prodiges proclament qu'ils ont définitivement échappé au monde de la naissance et de la mort. Ils ne sont plus des créatures de la transmigration. Sans doute ne sont-ils pas encore

(1) Destruction qui, à ce niveau de texte, ne doit pas s'entendre du samsāra cosmique. L'idée spécifiquement mahāyāniste que tous les êtres obtiendront un jour le nirvāna n'est pas demeurée absolument étrangère au canon pāli (Oldenberg, op. cit. p. 369); mais elle est loin d'en exprimer la position ordinaire. Le salut, selon la grande majorité des textes canoniques, est affaire proprement individuelle. S'ils ont l'air par endroits de s'exprimer en termes cosmologiques (comme dans Dhammapada, 153 sq. cité ci-dessus), ces témoignages spécieux sont faciles à réduire en reconnaissant que la cessation de toute renaissance dans le cycle transmigratoire détruit celui-ci pour le délivré, mais pour lui seul. Pour lui, dès l'instant où il s'est abîmé dans le Nirvāna, le monde n'a plus lieu. *Identité de suppression* du monde et du corps, du macrocosme et du microcosme, qui est l'adaptation bouddhique d'une des idées fondamentales de la spéculation indienne: l'équivalence de l'homme et de l'univers. Cf. Samyutta nikāya I. p. 62. « Je ne connais pas (dit le Buddha) de fin de la douleur, si l'on n'a pas atteint la fin du monde. Mais je vous le dis, dans ce corps animé, qui n'est grand que d'une toise, le monde habite et l'origine du monde et la suppression du monde et le chemin vers la suppression du monde. » (cf. Bau, II. 3. 20; 4. 13; *infra*, p. 26).

matériellement retranchés du samsāra aussi absolument qu'une fois passés à l'« autre rive ». Mais ils ne sont déjà plus comptés parmi ses ressortissants. Si le samsāra, dogmatiquement comme étymologiquement, est la propulsion par soi-même du cercle vicieux de l'existence, ils ne lui appartiennent plus que par leur passé. Il leur reste une certaine provision d'existence, mais ne projetant plus d'avenir. L'impulsion renouvelée, essence du samsāra, y fait défaut. Ils courent sur leur erre. La légende, d'ailleurs, les transporte symboliquement au-dessus du niveau qu'ils ont à jamais dépassé.

Le texte pāli fondamental se trouve dans le Majjhima nikāya:

« Aussitôt né, le Bodhisattva, les deux pieds posant à plat à terre, fait sept enjambées vers le Nord (litt. la région supérieure, où est le sommet du Mont cosmique), un parasol blanc tenu derrière lui au-dessus de sa tête. Il examine tous les points de l'espace et pousse ce mugissement de taureau: « C'est moi qui suis le plus haut du monde (aggo'mhi lokassa).... Voici la dernière naissance! Il n'y aura plus pour moi de retour! » (1).

Une version plus récente développe ainsi ce thème :

« [Le Bodhisattva fut reçu à sa naissance par quatre dieux ; une fois posé sur le sol], il se tint debout sur la terre, face à l'Est. Des milliers d'univers autour de lui furent comme une place découverte et unie... Il passa en revue les quatre directions collatérales, le nadir et le zénith. Dans ces dix régions, il ne vit personne qui fût pareil à lui. « Voici le Nord », se dit-il, et il fit sept enjambées (dans cette direction)... et c'est alors que, s'arrêtant debout à son septième pas (sattamapade thito) (2), il lança ce mugissement de taureau (3), ce rugissement de lion : « C'est moi qui suis le plus haut du monde etc. » (4).

(1) Ed. Pts, III, p. 123.

(2) Ces pas, liés à la conception d'un cosmos à sept étages, dénotent l'accès à la cime de l'étagement.

(3) « Taureau du monde » signifie Chef du Monde, Guide du troupeau des créatures.

(4) Jātaka, éd. Fausböll, I, p. 53.

Images qui toutes illustrent mythiquement le passage du nouveau-né au delà du domaine de la transmigration. Le motif des « pas » miraculeux, qui n'est pas sans affinités avec la légende védique des Pas de Vishnu, l'emporte à la cime du monde. S'y trouvant « le plus haut » (agga, skr. agra), il contemple à ses pieds les étages où transmigrent les autres créatures. L'inspection cosmique à laquelle il a procédé l'assure qu'il n'appartient plus à aucune des catégories, terrestres ou supra-terrestres, entre lesquelles elles se répartissent. C'est la condition préalable de sa retentissante affirmation : « Il n'y aura plus pour moi de retour ! » Le thème du nivellement, complété, dans certaines versions, par l'apparition magique d'un lotus ou de lotus, s'apparente à ces idées : le saṃsāra, avec les mondes dont il se fait un théâtre, sera comme effacé sous les pas de l'Être en qui, dès cet instant, est présente la certitude du Nirvāna (1). Entre toutes les traditions bouddhiques, il n'en est aucune à laquelle on puisse demander plus naturellement qu'à cette Nativité un témoignage sur l'éventuelle notion d'un renversement du samsāra, autrement dit du cours des choses, préparant et réalisant déjà à demi l'absolue Délivrance.

Or, le témoignage existe, concis et formel. Au moment où il annonce qu'il est quitte de la Transmigration, le Bodhisattva établit, en effet, sa transcendance non seulement à l'égard de l'étendue cosmique (aggo'mhi lokassa), mais tout aussi clairement à l'égard du Temps du Monde : « Je suis l'Aîné du Monde », ajoute-t-il (jettho'mhi lokassa, skr. jyeshtho'smi lokasya). Ces expressions ne signifient-elles pas que le Maître s'est libéré des règles de la durée cosmique, aussi bien que de l'asservissement à celles de l'espace, et cela récurrentiellement, vers le passé, aussi bien que vers l'avenir, dont il tranche les liens? Né au parc de Lumbinī, près de Kapilavastu, du sein de Mahāmāyā, épouse de Çuddhodana, lointain rejeton des rois

(1) Ce motif du nivellement est, dans le bouddhisme ancien, l'antécédent le plus direct du bouddhisme mythologique des Terres Pures. Cf. *Barabudur, Esquisse d'une histoire du bouddhisme*, pp. 475-576, 662 sq, 798-802.

fabuleux de l'Inde, le petit Siddhārtha de cette légende — le futur Çākyamuni — ne saurait se poser en Premier-né (jyeshtha) de l'univers sans rompre, au moins allégoriquement, avec la manière dont les hommes comptent le temps « au dedans » du samsāra.

Il est vrai qu'auprès de cette acceptation, jyeshtha admet aussi le sens plus général de « le meilleur, excellent » (1). Mais la valeur d'« Aîné » ou de « Premier né » est imposée par la parabole cosmique commentant l'expression :

« Tout de même, dit le Buddha (2) lorsqu'une poule a pondu des œufs, huit ou dix ou douze et que la poule s'est couchée sur eux et les a tenus au chaud et les a couvés suffisamment : lors donc qu'un des poussins, le premier, avec la pointe de sa griffe ou son bec brise la coquille et sort heureusement de l'œuf, comment nommera-t-on ce poussin, l'aîné ou le plus jeune ? — On le nommera l'aîné, vénérable Gotama, car il est le plus âgé d'entre eux. — De même aussi, ô brāhmane, entre les êtres qui vivent dans l'ignorance et sont comme enfermés et emprisonnés dans un œuf, je l'ai brisée, la coquille de l'ignorance, et seul dans le monde j'ai obtenu la bienheureuse. l'universelle dignité de Buddha. Ainsi je suis, ô Brāhmane, l'aîné, le plus noble d'entre les êtres ».

Imagerie d'une simplicité trompeuse. Pour bien l'entendre, il faut se rappeler que l'initiation brahmanique était considérée comme une seconde naissance (3). Le nom le plus courant des initiés était dvija : « deux fois né, twice-born ». Or, les oiseaux, les serpents, etc, recevaient eux aussi ce nom, en tant que nés d'un œuf. La ponte de celui-ci était assimilée à la « première naissance », c'est-à-dire à la naissance naturelle de l'homme. Son

(1) E. G. Manu II, 155 : « l'aînesse (jyaishthya) procède du savoir, chez les prêtres; de la puissance, chez les princes; de la richesse chez les agriculteurs et commerçants (de sang āryen : Les Vaiçya); et chez les gens de la caste servile (çūdra), de la (date de) naissance (seulement) ». Kulluka glose : « aînesse » (jyaishthya, qualité de celui qui est jyeshtha) par « excellence » ou « supériorité » (çreshthatva, çreshtha), « le meilleur ».

(2) Suttavibhanga, Pārājika I, 1. 4, cf H. Oldenberg, op. cit. pp. 364-65.

(3) Fort comparable en cela à ce qu'est l'initiation dite « primitive » auprès de nombreuses tribus échappant à toute culture classique.

éclosion correspondait à la naissance surnaturelle de l'initiation. Par ailleurs, les codes brāhmaniques ne manquent pas d'établir en principe que l'initié est socialement le supérieur, l'*aîné* du non-initié, quelles que soient leurs relations d'âge physique ou de parenté.

Voilà d'où l'allégorie du Suttavibhanga tire tout son sens: elle joue indirectement sur les mots que suggèrent les images. C'est l'interprétation bouddhique des vues brāhmaniques sur le dvija, aîné de ses aînés de par la seconde naissance, symbolisée par le bris de la coquille de l'œuf. L'allégorie appartient donc au cycle fort étendu des métaphores empruntées par le bouddhisme au brāhmanisme pour définir la condition de ses Saints. Le Buddha et ceux qui se délivrent à sa suite sont les « vrais » brāhmanes, les seuls brāhmanes: ils sont, dirons-nous, avec le Suttavibhanga, les vrais dvija; le Buddha l'est *kat'exokhên*.

Mais, du même coup, l'allégorie ainsi orientée vers les valeurs brāhmaniques ne pouvait manquer d'évoquer, dans le contexte de l'Inde ancienne, une seconde correspondance, celle-ci plus franchement mythique. Comment eût-on décrit, même métaphoriquement, la naissance surnaturelle du Buddha en l'égalant à la rupture de l'œuf où est enclos, en puissance, le « Premier-né » (jyeshtha) de l'Univers, sans que vînt naturellement à la pensée des auditeurs l'« œuf cosmique » des traditions brāhmaniques (1) d'où sort, à l'aube des temps, le Dieu primordial de la création, diversement dénommé l'Embryon d'Or (Hiranyagarbha). le Père ou le Maître des Créatures (Prajāpati), Agni (Dieu du feu, et Feu rituel) ou le *brahman* (principe sacrificiel, « prière », texte des hymnes, etc., divinisé)?

Nulle part l'accord partiel mais formel du bouddhisme et du brāhmanisme n'est mieux documenté philologiquement. Agni, pour la spéculation védique, est à la fois le plus jeune des dieux, puisqu'on l'allume chaque matin, et le dieu premier

(1) Qui, d'ailleurs, est formellement identifié à l'Année, expression symbolique du Temps cosmique: le samsāra, autre image de la durée cyclique, ramenée à ses causes, correspond donc exactement à l'œuf mythique. Or, c'est évidemment du samsāra que ce Buddha du Suttavibhanga détruit symboliquement l' « enveloppe ».

né, aux sources du temps cosmique. L'Upanishad a donné à ce motif le plus grand développement, et il est très notable que ses expressions soient, identiquement, celles dont use aussi le cycle bouddhique de la Nativité.

Le Buddha, marchant sur un univers nivelé et qui n'offre plus d'inégalités sous son pied, est miraculeusement l'Aîné du monde (jyeshtha) et la plus noble des créatures (çreshtha). Mais, dans la Brhadāranyaka upanishad, Agni, diversement identifié au *brahman* (principe sacrificiel, etc.), au Soleil, au Souffle, au Feu sacré, premier-né du cosmos, est déjà comme le Buddha « le lotus unique » parmi les hommes (1) et, comme lui, il ne rencontre sous ses pas aucun sol qui leur soit inégal : il prend partout un appui égal (2), et, passant ainsi plus haut que tout, il est célébré sous les appellations fondamentales de jyeshtha « l'Aîné » et çreshtha « le plus Noble » (3).

Où qu'il soit, à quelque moment qu'il croisse, Agni, ou le *brahman*, sous ses diverses formes, doit être reconnu comme le

(1) Sur la comparaison de la naissance du Buddha avec celle d'un lotus, se reporter à A. Foucher, *Iconography of the Buddha's Nativity* et à A.K. Coomaraswamy, *Early Buddhist Iconography*. Le thème du Lotus unique est fourni notamment par Brhadāranyaka up. VI, 3, 6.

(2) Nous avons montré ailleurs que ce thème, d'où provient le cycle mahāyāniste des Terres Pures, répond à l'idée d'un déluge symbolique : les eaux célestes nivellent toutes les inégalités où se joue la transmigration et il ne subsiste, par delà celle-ci et par delà toute durée assignable, qu'une surface glorieuse où l'on naît porté par un lotus. Tel est le séjour du Buddha à l'Âge infini, Amitāyus. Le Buddha de la Nativité, qui lui aussi domine le Temps cosmique en s'intitulant « Premier-né du Cosmos », et que la légende place sur un lotus au-dessus du monde « nivelé », fait transition, historiquement, entre ces développements (aux abords de l'ère chrétienne) et l'ancien mythe védique d'Agni, porté par un lotus ou une feuille de lotus, au début du temps du monde, et au-dessus des Eaux Cosmiques, symbole de l'éternité. Il est bon d'observer d'ailleurs que le symbolisme même des Eaux Cosmiques a été conservé par les traditions bouddhiques, qui se bornent à l'adapter : au début de chaque période cosmique, avant que rien ne soit créé et par conséquent ne dure, les Eaux Cosmiques sont là. La force des actes passés, en les ramenant, en tirera l'univers, prison des créatures qui transmigrent. Mais le Buddha ne transmigre plus. Venu au monde par un miracle, il n'est plus du ressort de ce monde. Sa place est donc symboliquement sur les Eaux qui transcendent le Samsāra et la Durée. D'où le lotus, jailli d'une *planities* allégorique.

(3) Bau, VI. 1. 1-3 ; *cf.* Chāndogya upanishad, V, 1, 1 sq.

Premier-né du Cosmos : à peine né, il s'identifie, en effet, *à lui-même*, c'est-à-dire à sa forme immortelle, présente à la naissance de l'Univers et archétype de toutes les spécifications ultérieures. Mythes dont on hésiterait à admettre l'application au Buddha, à date ancienne : cela supposerait une divinisation déjà très accentuée de sa personne; mais l'Upanishad elle-même prépare l'adaptation bouddhique en reportant le pouvoir de récurrence du Dieu aux simples sages. Par dessus le monde et le temps « nivelés », ceux-ci vont rejoindre Agni, tout comme il se rejoint lui-même, aux origines du monde et de la durée, dans l'essence métaphysique et rituelle du sacrifice (le *brahman*) :

« En vérité, à l'origine, le *brahman* seul existait. Il ne connaissait donc que lui-même : Je suis *brahman*. Et il était le Tout. Puis chacun des dieux le fut, au fur et à mesure qu'ils s'éveillèrent à la pensée. De même des rshi (sages inspirés), de même des hommes. (Par exemple), c'est ce que voyant le rshi Vāmadeva a déclaré : J'ai été Manu (père des hommes, l'un des Démiurges) et Sūrya (le Soleil). De même aujourd'hui celui qui sait ainsi ».

« Qui connaît ce grand génie (yaksha) premier-né (prathamaja), qui sait que *brahman* est toute réalité, celui-là est maître des mondes...»

« Celui-là en vérité qui connaît le premier et le meilleur... est le premier et le meilleur (jyeshthaç ca çreshthaç ca) entre les siens et aussi parmi tous ceux entre lesquels il désire l'être...»

« Celui qui a trouvé, qui a conquis l'Être en soi (ātman)
Engagé dans les ténébreuses complexités du corps,
Celui-là est le Créateur, il est l'auteur du tout.
Le monde lui appartient, il est le monde lui-même. » (1)

On entrevoit le mécanisme de cette réversibilité du temps, ou de cette réversibilité dans le temps, qui reporte les sages au point du temps où le cosmos est à l'état naissant, et comment elle a pu être acceptée par le bouddhisme, non comme un dogme étranger auquel il se fût rendu, mais comme l'illustration

(1) Bau. I. 4. 10; V, 4. 1; VI, 1, 1; IV, 4; 3e éd. et trad. Senart, pp. 12, 93, 102, 82.

limitative d'une partie de sa propre dogmatique. Pour l'Upanishad, le retour, contre le temps, des Sages au Dieu, des êtres (nés à une époque plus ou moins tardive) à l'Etre qui rayonne à l'origine des temps, se présente essentiellement comme un retour logique, celui de la partie au tout. Il n'est, à travers le monde, qu'un seul sujet réel, le Tout, donné en une fois, avant que des différences s'y fussent marquées. En vérité relative, celles-ci sont les êtres, elles sont nous. Dans l'absolu, elles sont tout au plus les attributs du Tout. Il est le sujet de toute proposition, sous son aspect concentré, aussi bien qu'il en est l'objet, la modalité et les circonstances, sous son aspect dispersé. De cette métaphysique tautologique, à laquelle le génie de l'Inde s'est complu (1), trois conséquences principales se dégagent pour notre étude. Si le Grand Tout primordial est éminemment tout, tout être est subsidiairement lui : donc, retour logique à l'origine (contre le temps). Mais, de par la commune réduction à ce sujet unique, toute chose sera aussi bien toute autre chose (contre la division des êtres, laquelle, dans son ensemble, forme l'étendue). Enfin, cette double relativité, vue à la fois en profondeur et transversalement, tend à ne faire du monde qu'une vaste illusion cosmique au sein de l'Un immuable. Le retour mythique à l'origine signifie donc, en dernière analyse, l'accès à un Absolu, par rapport auquel (si l'on peut dire) le monde perceptible n'a plus lieu.

⁂

Il est inutile de faire observer que cette dialectique de l'être plein (2) était, pour le bouddhisme, radicalement irrecevable : il

(1) Elle démarque la spéculation rituelle sur l'universalité du sacrifice et de son principe (le *brahman*), identifiés à toutes choses, parce qu'ils les «produisent». Le passage du *brahman*, en ce sens ancien, au *brahman* de l'Upanishad est celui d'une production allégorique, mais réelle par ses effets, à une production logique, réelle en soi, mais dont l'effet, i. e. le cosmos, n'est plus, par compensation, qu'une vaste allégorie.

(2) cf. Bau, V, 1, 1 :

Cela est plein, ceci est plein.
Le plein sort du plein.
Même le plein une fois tiré du plein,
Ce plein reste plein.

1*

n'est venu que de l'avoir contredite. En fait son plus grand effort a porté contre la proposition II : convertibilité des êtres entre eux, qui risquait de ruiner la morale en supprimant la responsabilité personnelle (1). Sur ce point, il n'y a, pour l'école ancienne,

---

(« *Cela* est le *brāhman* qui échappe aux sens; *ceci* le *brāhman*, tel qu'il apparaît dans la création; celui-ci émane de celui-là, lequel n'en est pas diminué » — note de E. SENART, loc. cit. p. 92)

(1) cf. BAU, IV, 3, 20-22 «... il imagine: Je suis cet univers, je suis tout. C'est pour lui le monde suprême... la condition bienheureuse où tout désir est comblé, où il n'est de désir que de l'*ātman* (l'être en soi)... Là le père n'est pas père, la mère n'est pas mère, les mondes ne sont pas mondes, les dieux ne sont pas dieux, les Veda ne sont pas Veda. Là le voleur n'est pas voleur, l'avorteur n'est pas avorteur, le cāndāla n'est pas cāndāla, le paulkasa n'est pas paulkasa (c. et p. sont des hommes de basse caste) le çramana (moine, etc) n'est pas çramana, l'ascète n'est pas ascète; ni bien ni mal ne le lie aux actions; car il est alors par delà toutes les souffrances du cœur.» Ou encore ibid. IV. 4. 22-23 «.. ni crainte pour le mal qu'il a commis ni espoir pour le bien qu'il a fait (car « c'est d'un autre qu'on a peur » ibid , I. 4 2. aussi bien que c'est d'un autre seulement qu'on espère: or il est tout, invariablement)... c'est cela même qu'exprime le vers :

Telle est la grandeur éternelle du brāhmane.
Les actes ne peuvent ni l'augmenter ni la diminuer.
Il faut en connaître les voies; qui les connaît
Ne peut être souillé par les mauvaises actions »

Il ne faut pas se méprendre sur cet enseignement ésotérique. Pour atteindre à cette vue générale de l'univers, le sage doit d'abord se dégager des souillures, s'armer de vertu ; en même temps, et de façon réciproque, la doctrine a une efficacité cathartique, par laquelle l'adepte est confirmé dans la vertu : « C'est pourquoi celui qui sait ainsi, étant calme, dompté, détaché, patient, recueilli, se voit lui-même dans l'*ātman* (l'être en soi, identifié avec le *brahman*, principe premier tant métaphysique que rituel), voit l'*ātman* en tout; le mal ne le souille pas, il domine tout mal» (ibid. IV. 4. 23). Il commet cependant de mauvaises actions, voire même tous les crimes. Mais uniquement par les voies détournées de la *grammaire de l'être* que nous venons d'esquisser. Ayant rejoint le brahman-ātman, il est, en lui, le sujet de toute proposition. Il est substantiellement, tout voleur, tout avorteur, aussi bien que tout ascète. Toutefois, par une nouvelle conversion logique, à peine ces attributs posés, il les reprend en lui, les égalise et les fond Ils sont sa modification passagère. Ils ne sont rien, en fin de compte, en tant qu'il tire tout l'être à lui. Seul avec lui-même, il n'a rien à craindre, ni à attendre. D'où les formules au premier abord énigmatiques: « Quelque souffrance qu'aient à endurer les créatures, elles la gardent pour elles; seul le bien va à lui » (I. 5. 20) et « C'est cet *ātman* à toi qui est en tout. Tout ce qui n'est pas lui est voué à la souffrance » (III. 4. 2; c'est l'assertion fameuse de Chāndogya up. VI, 8, 7 etc: tat tvam asi « Tu es (aussi tout) ce (monde) là »). Mais à certaines écoles ces spéculations éthérées n'ont point paru assez en

aucun accommodement possible, aucun compromis. La distinction des individus, bien que ne reposant plus sur la notion d'une personnalité absolue (mais nous venons de voir que cette notion, poussée à ses dernières conséquences, détruisait les

garde contre un cynisme symbolique (endémique dans l'Inde) qui retrancherait de la loi commune le «délivré vivant», jīvanmukta), lui permettant tout. L'Upanishad elle-même envisage par instants sans scandale le cas où le sage agirait mal et cela non plus, comme tout à l'heure, en devenant l'auteur symbolique du bien et du mal fait par toutes les créatures dont il a capté les personnalités (aussi illusoires que ces actes, en vérité absolue, c'est-à-dire en lui) à travers l'ātman originel — mais bel et bien de sa personne: «.... celui qui sait ainsi, quelque péché qu'il paraisse commettre, dévore tout et est pur, net, sans vieillesse, immortel» (BAU, V, 14, 18). Non pas certes en son être apparent, qui a commis la faute, mais par delà le développement symbolique du monde dans l'étendue et la durée: au sein du *brahman*, rejoint «à l'origine». Le brāhmane (*brāhmana*), homme, s'identifiant rétroactivement au *brahman*, principe, devient, comme lui, le «plein». En effaçant ainsi les individualités, la dialectique intempérante de l'être risquait d'effacer et compromettait en tout cas à coup sûr la notion de responsabilité. Et voilà justement contre quoi le bouddhisme s'est élevé avec la dernière vigueur. Pour sauver la responsabilité, âme de ses vues sur le monde, il n'a pas hésité à faire le sacrifice de la personnalité métaphysique, telle que le brāhmanisme l'avait élaborée. Renversant la position, il n'a rien trouvé de mieux que de définir les créatures par cette responsabilité même, prolongée d'existence en existence par l'héritage des actes passés. Une sorte de personnalité court tout le long de cette chaîne d'héritages, à la fois toujours autre et toujours la même. Les êtres sont dits «héritiers du Karman» (karmadāyāda). Mais cet héritage, en bonne doctrine, c'est tout eux-mêmes: trait dont on n'eût pas méconnu la portée, si l'on avait mieux analysé les théories indiennes du droit sucessoral (*Barabudur*, p.*119 sq). On serrera la conception bouddhique de plus près que de toute autre manière en y reconnaissant la transposition d'une définition quasi juridique de la personne (disons de la personne morale, plutôt que de la personne physique, celle-ci devenant la conséquence de celle-là). Le résultat en est que les individualités sont posées *empiriquement* avec une rigueur et une nécessité exceptionnelles. Trait essentiel, auquel le refus de poser le problème de la nature ultime de l'existence donne toute sa portée dogmatique: et son sens historique, en le réintégrant dans la suite des faits indiens, est de s'inscrire en réaction contre la désintégration de cette notion empirique d'individualité et de responsabilité par le prétendu *personnalisme* brāhmanique. C'est en négligeant ces retours de l'histoire que les premiers interprètes européens ont pris pour une négation pure et simple de la personnalité du bouddhisme canonique, où nous pensons qu'il faut reconnaître le moment de la pensée indienne où la notion empirique de personnalité, fondée sur le thème proprement juridique de la responsabilité, s'est posée avec la force la plus pressante (cf *Barabudur*, pp.*170-*188, etc.).

différenciations individuelles — pour comprendre historiquement le bouddhisme il faut donc dire: *parce que* ne reposant plus sur cette notion d'une personnalité absolue), devient le fait majeur. Pour toute l'infinie durée du Samsara, qui embrasse toute existence, les séquences rétributrices, au long desquelles sont suscitées les apparentes personnalités des créatures, jamais ne se confondent, jamais ne se mélangent. La proposition I: réductibilité des êtres à un Grand Tout primordial qui les a émis et qui les réabsorbera, n'a pas davantage d'application directe. C'est un autre aspect — en profondeur — de la métaphysique de l'Absolu, contre laquelle le bouddhisme s'est inscrit en faux. Il en résulte, si l'on passe au troisième point, que le monde empirique a, à son niveau et en un certain sens, plus de réalité dans le bouddhisme qu'auprès de l'idéalisme brāhmanique: précisément le même degré de réalité que les individualités « en série » auxquelles il donne la réplique, en établissant autour d'elles les conditions de leur rétribution. Il n'est pas d'« être en soi » qui affaiblisse les couleurs empiriques de ce tableau cosmique, en en tirant à lui la substance. Le samsāra, tel qu'il est, voilà le dernier mot, au moins pour toute cette partie de la révélation bouddhique. Si l'on n'en part point, il n'est pas de salut et le Buddha lui-même n'a acquis la suprême illumination qu'en gardant ce spectacle devant les yeux, jusqu'à complète maîtrise de la vérité sur lui.

C'est cependant sur ce dernier point qu'en un sens le système bouddhiste se trouvait le moins éloigné du brahamanisme. En effet, tout en se refusant à rien énoncer de positif à l'endroit de ses dernières fins — savoir si le nirvāna est existence, non existence, etc. — et tout en ne représentant ses vérités que comme la vérité *sur* le samsāra, le bouddhisme affirme sans ambiguïté que cette vérité n'est pas *dans* le samsāra. Le monde tel qu'il est, ou se fait (yathā bhūtam), c'est-à-dire complété par son passé et son avenir, et contenant à jamais la masse des créatures, n'est vraiment tel qu'aux yeux de celui qu'il ne tient plus. Le Buddha, à l'instant où il le domine, n'est déjà plus, de plein droit, une créature de la transmigration. Le nirvāna, ultime accomplissement de cette libération, n'a pas de lieu, si on le considère du niveau du samsāra : ni chez les hommes, ni au plus haut de la « voie » des Dieux il n'y a de place pour le Saint sur la roue de la Naissance et de la Mort. Mais n'est-ce pas dire, réciproquement, que pour les Délivrés, parvenus au repos définitif, le samsāra n'a plus lieu? Il n'a été suscité que par l'erreur, la nescience (avidyā). Comme pour le brāhmanisme, qui l'adoptera de son côté, ce schéma transmigratoire résulte d'une mauvaise manière de poser le problème de l'existence. Dans les deux cas, il faut qu'à un certain moment de la marche vers le vrai le monde se dissolve devant le sage. Quoique de part et d'autre le procédé diffère (1), un même mouvement est discernable et l'on parlera également dans les deux cas de « libération » (moksa).

La troisième des propositions résumant les vues brāhmaniques : absence de réalité dernière dans les mondes, en face du plein de l'être absolu, inacceptable, sous cette forme, par le bouddhisme ancien, pourra donc cependant être prise comme symbole du manque de réalité dernière par lequel cette doctrine caractérisait le samsāra, *considéré du point de vue du nirvāna*. Saisissons bien l'agencement des deux eschatologies sur lesquelles nous avons reconnu que se joue le dogme bouddhique. Elles n'ont entre elles aucune communi-

(1) Les deux différences principales sont : 1° au niveau de la libération : que le procès du samsāra se résout, pour le brāhmanisme, dans l'être immuable dont il était sorti, à l'origine des choses, tandis que, pour le bouddhisme, il n'y a pas d'origine des choses, ni d'être antérieur, mais seulement la possibilité de couper le samsāra, à un certain moment, et d'en sortir, hors de l'être comme du non-être ; 2° au niveau du samsāra : qu'il est pour le brāhmanisme le résultat direct d'une erreur — le pur esprit s'obnubile (pourquoi, comment, c'est une question qui ne reçoit pas de réponse très satisfaisante) et lui, l'immuable, rêve le monde et se rêve dans le monde, fantasmagorie qui vient à quiescence dans le sommeil sans rêve, image de l'absolu ; et qu'il n'est, au contraire, pour le bouddhisme, le résultat de l'erreur qu'au second degré — l'erreur, principe de l'attachement à l'existence, produit celle-ci non comme un rêve, mais comme une grave réalité empirique dont aucun « être en soi » ne permet plus d'opérer la sublation brusque. Il ne reste, pour le bouddhisme ancien, que la voie suivie de millénaire en millénaire par les Buddha : celle d'une lente « purification » de ces liens empiriques, qui tombent pour l'être parvenu à la perfection.

cation de nature ; il le faut, pour que la seconde échappe à l'impermanence, concept contagieux, matérialisée par la première : mais peut-être n'en sont-elles que plus inséparables dans l'économie de la révélation.

De l'une, celle du nirvāna, ou de la rupture, qui est tout le but des bouddhistes, ceux-ci n'ont rien à dire. L'autre, qu'ils rejettent, est riche en couleurs et emplie de toutes les formes de la vie. Chacun des deux termes possède ainsi en propre ce qui manque à l'autre. Tout en respectant leur incompatibilité, voire même en l'accusant, cette opposition fonde le mouvement de celui-ci à celui-là, i. e. l'échappée vers la libération. Connaître la matière transmigrante non point telle qu'elle s'apparaît à elle-même, avec ses fausses perspectives d'éternité vers le haut des mondes divins, mais en sachant lui imposer la forme circulaire de l'éternel retour, c'est déjà plus qu'à moitié avoir donné à sa propre pensée la forme du nirvāna.

La description du samsāra est, en effet, une révélation propre au bouddhisme, au même titre que celle du Salut, qu'elle conditionne. Voir le cercle de l'erreur, en toute vérité, et lui échapper, c'est un seul et même fait (1). Il est exact que l'image bouddhique de l'eschatologie *descriptible* s'incorpore, avec leurs cieux, les divinités du panthéon indien : Indra, Brahmā, d'autres encore. Mais le cycle interprétatif où l'on introduit ces dieux, qui les explique, les régit, les limite et les fait basculer, l'heure venue, dans l'universelle impermanence, procède spécialement de la dogmatique bouddhique et c'est en cela qu'il est permis d'y rechercher la contrepartie du nirvāna.

La forme circulaire imposée au dessin que détaille notamment le Vinaya des Mūla Sarvāstivādin n'est point cosmologique, au sens spatial. Car l'univers se présente à l'imagination de l'Inde entière — et de l'Inde bouddhique aussi bien — comme une superposition de mondes, étagés le long d'un axe marqué, soit à notre niveau, soit au niveau immédiatement supérieur, par le Mont Mythique, le Meru (2).

(1) Cf. H. Oldenberg, op. cit., pp. 136, 140 et 153.
(2) E. g., Bau. IV. 3. 33 ; VI. 2. 15.

Telle est la commune croyance. La roue du Samsara la brise. Elle en recueillera les éléments, du plus profond enfer au plus élevé des cieux. Mais elle bouleverse l'étagement en le remplaçant, dans l'ensemble, par une permutation circulaire, sous la loi des douze causes. Cosmologie encore, si l'on veut, mais interprétée, et non plus descriptive. Le cercle n'est pas dans les choses. Il est la vérité sur elles. Quant au sens de cette « vérité », il est assez clair : c'est la durée « dévorante », rompant ce qui est sous sa loi et ramenée aux douze causes de cette impermanence indéfiniment reproduite.

Le résultat direct de cette manière « correcte » de prendre le monde est de projeter le Nirvāna hors série — c'est-à-dire, matériellement, hors du cercle. Pour l'Upanishad, qui s'en tient d'habitude à la cosmologie étagée, la félicité suprême, l'« Immortel » se trouve au sommet d'une hiérarchie de cieux où l'on conçoit que la vie est de plus en plus longue (mais non plus désormais éternelle : l'idée de transmigration s'est étendue à eux) jusqu'au monde du *brahman* lequel est au-dessus de tout et échappe, seul, au devenir. A ce tableau, l'imagerie bouddhique s'oppose en un contraste significatif. Au delà des mondes les plus transcendants et où la durée de la vie acquiert des proportions inconcevables, il n'y a pas l'infini, l'éternel, le Nirvāna, mais le cercle des douze causes, égal à lui-même, là comme ailleurs. Le Nirvāna ne fait donc pas suite à ces durées fabuleuses, qui ne sont encore rien, à l'égard de l'absolu de nature qui le tient hors de toutes spécifications. Une tache blanche, hors du cercle, en sera la seule représentation symbolique.

Mais on ne s'y trompera pas : ce vide de caractéristiques, ce blanc tire sa valeur à la fois de la présence, au-dessous de lui, des images spécifiques du samsāra et de la position qui lui est faite, de l'autre côté du cercle, au-dessus du spectre de l'Impermanence. On ne peindrait pas le blanc tout seul. Comme le dit très bien M. Przyluski, commentant ces vieilles dispositions picturales, « il s'agissait beaucoup moins d'orner les temples que d'offrir un sujet de méditation aux fidèles. Les symboles employés étaient simples, facilement intelligibles, car on s'adressait à la masse des laïques ; on s'efforçait de vulgariser la doctrine, de la rendre accessible à tous » (1) : appoint inappréciable, aujourd'hui encore, pour l'interprétation de passages fréquemment et volontairement obscurs, tout au moins quand on les aborde à la seule lumière du dogme strict.

Le Nirvāna est-il plutôt existence ineffable ou plutôt annihilation ? Ne reprenons pas cette vaine discussion. Le Vinaya sanskrit est à présent, en ce qui le concerne, suffisamment clair : le « tertre blanc » du Nirvāna, pareil à une île au-dessus des eaux bariolées de l'Impermanence et de la transmigration, forme un refuge, un asile. Bien que ce soit sur un autre plan, il n'est pas moins réel, mais plus réel que les « couleurs » caractéristiques des diverses catégories d'êtres. Il subsiste, en blanc, lorsque ces couleurs s'effacent, pour le Délivré, avec les conditions d'existence qu'elles dessinaient. De toutes ces figures tracées par le mal et l'erreur, le tertre blanc est nettoyé. Mais pour que cette purification soit possible, il faut que l'image complète ait d'abord été peinte. Peut-être, en fin de compte, n'y a-t-il rien de plus à dire du Nirvāna de l'ancienne école.

On entendra mieux la valeur du symbole en se reportant à son sujet à un autre texte du Petit Véhicule sanskrit, le Saddharmasmrtyupasthāna sūtra, vaste somme cosmologique conservée en chinois et en tibétain. A la différence du Vinaya, le S. S. U. ne prescrit aux moines qu'une production imaginaire de la Roue des Existences. Il emprunte cependant couleurs et précisions techniques à l'art pictural réel, tout en prétendant l'abandonner aux laïques :

« [L'esprit du méditant] se peint à lui-même... les cinq gati, avec les couleurs propres aux différentes sortes d'actes (karman) qui caractérisent les différents êtres dans chacune

(1) « A cet effet la roue était peinte sous le porche [des couvents], là où devaient nécessairement passer les visiteurs, et un moine disert et intelligent était spécialement chargé d'en donner l'explication » J Przyluski, loc. cit., p. 320. cf. Waddell *A Buddhist Pictorial Wheel*, Journ. Asiat. Soc. of Bengal., 1892 p. 334, S. Z. Aung — Caf Rhys Davids., *A Compendium of Philosophy*, trad. de Abhidhamma Attha - Samgaha, Pts, 1910, p. 260 sq.

de ces gati (Voies de l'existence, secteurs de la Roue). » Le blanc, couleur des actes méritoires, prédomine chez les dieux. Chez les hommes, les couleurs sombres et violentes de la souffrance et du mal seront comparativement plus fréquentes et plus variées. « Les hommes riches (par l'effet de précédents actes méritoires) et immoraux (donc en puissance de rétributions mauvaises) sont « peints » en couleurs karmiques blanches et noires ; les hommes pauvres et moraux (i. e. qui subissent une punition et se préparent une récompense) en rouge et en blanc ; les hommes pauvres et immoraux, en noir (méchants punis et qui le seront encore) ; les hommes adonnés à la mauvaise volonté et au désir, en noir et en jaune, etc. » (1).

Si l'on tient compte des textes décrivant les conditions divines (2), on observe aisément que ce blanc, croissant à mesure qu'on gravit la hiérarchie des êtres, n'est pas exactement une couleur comme les autres. Il dénote moins l'imprégnation des êtres par les forces pernicieuses liant à l'existence que la purification au moins temporaire de ces imprégnations. C'est moins une teinte qu'un effacement. On constate à mesure que l'on s'élève d'étage en étage un détachement progressif de l'existence concrète : non seulement de ses objets, mais de ses éléments constitutifs (passions, mais aussi caractères physiques, organes des sens, etc. : tact, goût, odorat cessent de s'exercer).

Les dieux inférieurs sont loin d'être exempts des couleurs de la violence. Ils luttent contre les Démons (ou « Titans », Asura). Ils ne sont pas toujours vainqueurs. Mais, plus haut, toute querelle, tout bruit, tout dissentiment, toute espèce d'agitation cessent. L'existence se décante de ce qui la troublait. On arrive au domaine de l'infini de l'espace, à celui de l'infini de la connaissance, à celui où il n'y a plus rien et pour finir, à celui où il n'y a plus ni conscience, ni absence de

(1) [J. Takakusu, S. Lévi,] P. Demiéville, *Hôbôgirin*, supplément au IIIe fascicule (feuille volante non paginée).

(2) *Abhidharmakoça*, ou encore le cycle des textes sanskrit traduits en pali par des Birmans : *Cha Pancagatidipani*, *Lokapannatti*, etc. ; ou encore le *Saddharmasmrtyupasthana*.

conscience (naivasaṃjñānāsaṃjñāyatana) : négations croisées qui sembleraient préparer la définition suspensive du nirvāna.

Il subsiste cependant une différence capitale : sur le tableau bouddhique, le cercle des douze causes enserre encore la voie divine. Si fabuleuse que soit la durée de l'existence dans les domaines les plus élevés, elle est une durée. Il est clair qu'aucune représentation picturale n'est possible d'un monde « où il n'y a plus rien », pour ne rien dire du monde où la conscience même (toute autre qualification physique ou morale supprimée) s'évanouit, sans s'anéantir, par delà l'être et le non-être. Mais cet état reste spécifié par sa position : il est dans la « gati » des Dieux. Le peintre reportera au contraire le « tertre blanc » du Nirvāna hors de celle-ci, par delà l'impermanence. C'est dire qu'en dernier ressort, le Vinaya des Mūla Sarvāstivādin ne fait consister le salut, en bonne orthodoxie, que dans la destruction, *pour le sage*, de la prison du samsāra. La localisation attribuée au Nirvāna devra évoquer les stances citées au début de cette étude : « . . . . bâtisseur de la maison, tu ne dois plus rebâtir la maison. Tes poutres sont toutes brisées... » On n'en doit attacher que plus d'importance à la manière dont ce texte ancien traite figurativement l'état intermédiaire que la légende et le dogme insèrent entre les parties les plus purifiées du Samsāra et le Nirvāna : savoir, la vie et la condition du « délivré vivant » qu'est le Buddha, dès l'instant de sa dernière naissance.

Les textes, nous l'avons déjà fait observer, annoncent catégoriquement la « fin du monde », i. e. la cessation de la transmigration. Mais ce n'est, canoniquement, qu'une métaphore. Elle évoque non l'absolue suppression du samsara, qui n'a pas de fin, mais son anéantissement autour du Délivré, en même temps que celui-ci cesse d'avoir un corps — c'est-à-dire un ensemble présent de conditions rétributrices figurées en une personne sortie du passé et grosse d'un avenir, la structure du samsāra soutenant et complétant du dehors ces trois temps de la rétribution et n'ayant pas d'autre sens.

« Je ne connais pas de fin de la douleur si l'on n'a pas atteint la fin du monde. Mais je vous le dis, dans ce corps animé qui n'est grand que d'une toise, habitent et l'origine du monde et la suppression du monde et le chemin vers la suppression du monde ».

L'origine et la suppression du monde sont ainsi symboliques de ce qui, pour les bouddhistes, est l'essentiel : l'attachement à un corps et la délivrance du corps, non point par un suicide religieux qui renverrait dans le samsara, mais par la destruction de l'impulsion transmigratrice. Qu'est-ce à dire, sinon que pour définir un Nirvana dont il n'y a justement rien à dire ni rien à peindre, les textes et les monuments figurés se sont ingéniés à faire apparaître, en termes de samsara, la *direction* du Nirvana ? C'est en ce sens, et en ce sens seulement, qu'Agni, Aîné du Monde, reporté mythiquement au bord du temps qui va se créer sous sa loi pour contenir le monde, a pu s'identifier, métaphoriquement, avec un Buddha remontant lui aussi à l'« origine » du monde (comme Agni, il en sera le plus haut placé, agra, et l'Aîné, jyeshtha) pour signifier — et c'est là la différence radicale — non point qu'il va le créer, mais qu'il est passé par delà son origine et sa fin, en se délivrant des liens transmigratoires avec un corps, lieu unique de la « création » et de la « destruction » du monde *pour chacun*.

On aperçoit mieux, sous cet angle, la nature de l'emprunt fait par le bouddhisme au brāhmanisme : la tradition bouddhique ne s'est point, par ce contact, enrichie de dogmes, mais de thèmes expressifs. Le dogme, bien fixé, n'était à aucun moment remis en question. Nulle éternité concrète n'est amenée sur la tête du Buddha, contre l'orthodoxie, par l'application des images et de la terminologie où s'exprime l'éternité du *brahman*. Il est trop clair, en effet, que cette application vaut uniquement pour l'état intermédiaire où se prépare le Nirvana définitif, avec lequel tout retombera à quiescence, non point seulement le monde et ses composantes, mais la personne même en laquelle le Maître, délivré de ce monde, s'y est manifesté comme en suspens entre la transmigration d'où il émergeait et l'insondable salut où il allait se plonger. Comme l'apparente éternité des plus grands Dieux est vaincue par le samsāra, l'apparente éternité du *brahman* peut sans inconvénient se projeter sur Çakyamuni, aux heures glorieuses de sa carrière terrestre. Ces métaphores à leur tour seront vaincues par le Nirvāna : chacun est assez bien informé de la nécessité, absolue à cette époque, par où, en donnant le spectacle de sa mort, le Buddha lui-même devra canoniquement illustrer, ultime enseignement, la règle que « tout ce qui a commencé finira ».

Le Vinaya sanskrit fait apparaître avec ingéniosité, par ses prescriptions picturales, cet état ambigu, où deux ordres radicalement étrangers — celui de la servitude et celui de la libération — se confondent momentanément dans le corps symbolique du Buddha. La tache blanche du Nirvāna, où il faut comprendre que les Buddha et les Saints trouvent asile, n'offre naturellement aucun signe perceptible de leur présence. D'autre part, la figure du Saint ne saurait être placée ni dans la « gati » des hommes, ni au plus haut de la voie divine. On a imaginé de l'introduire cependant dans le système, en la dessinant au moyeu de la Roue. Là donc, comme l'observe fort à propos M. Przyluski, « où la roue ne tourne pas ». Hors du compte des temps. Hors du mouvement produit par les douze causes, et cependant tout au bord de ce mouvement, auquel le Maître ne participe plus entièrement.

Cette image illustre la même idée que l'attribution au Buddha des qualifications récurrentielles d'Agni « premier-né » du cosmos : savoir que le Buddha, en son corps transitoire, a déjà pris pied sur l'autre rive du temps et voit celui-ci s'écouler sous lui. Le cycle légendaire et brāhmanisant de l'Aînesse (jyaishthya) lui faisait remonter le courant jusqu'à sa source. Les peintures de la Roue (telles que les décrit le Vinaya) l'ont logé au moyeu, dans cette cavité (kha) sans participation au mouvement du système, qui fournissait par ailleurs à l'étymologie philosophante l'image concrète du vide, du zéro, de l'éther, etc. (toutes valeurs du même mot kha). Ce sont donc là deux manières presque équivalentes de dire que le Buddha, en son ultime incarnation, est « sorti » de la mobilité perpétuelle sur laquelle il ne projette plus l'ombre d'un avenir. Mais par là-dessus le symbolisme pictural des Mūla Sarvāstivādin, bien conforme à la stricte orthodoxie, achève son « enseignement par l'image » en plaçant à l'extérieur de la roue complète, jante, rayons et moyeu, le spectre de l'impermanence — de cette impermanence à laquelle il n'est pas jusqu'au corps quasi divin (et mieux que divin) du Buddha, qui ne soit asservi. Ce grand tableau qu'on nous décrit proclame donc que la vérité dernière n'est pas en ce corps, mais dans l'« arrêt » du Nirvāna (1).

---

(1) Est-ce aux progrès de la piété à l'endroit de cette personne du Buddha enrichie de caractères de plus en plus surnaturels qu'est dû le fait, signalé par M. Przyluski, de sa disparition du moyeu de la Roue, sur les images plus tardives que nous conservons, et où le Buddha est soit omis, soit peint à l'extérieur de la Roue que tient le temps? Le défaut de documents archéologiques anciens (à l'exception de la peinture très incomplètement préservée d'Ajantā) rend difficile d'interpréter cette évolution. On observera aussi que la noria, mentionnée par le Vinaya, et d'application déjà restreinte dans le passage correspondant du Divyāvadāna, tombe définitivement des compositions postérieures. Les deux mouvements relevés par M. Masson-Oursel dans la Çvetāçvatara up. ne jouent donc pas un rôle appréciable dans la documentation bouddhique actuellement accessible. Il est vrai que le Vinaya des Mūla S. parle d'êtres qui naissent la tête hors du seau, et d'êtres qui meurent les pieds hors du seau, i. e. la tête dans le seau. Mais ces deux mouvements contraires sont impliqués par un seul et même mouvement de la roue : sur une partie de leur course les seaux de la noria puisent l'eau qu'ils déverseront ensuite. On conçoit d'ailleurs assez clairement que la Roue bouddhique, à la différence de la Roue brāhmanique, ne met pas en communication deux « biefs » conjugués, dont l'un soit servitude et l'autre libération, avec passage alternant de l'un à l'autre. Dans le système brāhmanique, les êtres sortent d'un Absolu antérieur à la transmigration, demeurent quelque temps (peu de temps, au regard de l'Absolu) dans celle-ci, puis rejoignent l'être divin dont ils se sont détachés sans jamais, en vérité absolue, être sorti de son sein. Les deux tours de la roue les jettent donc dans le samsāra, puis les en retirent. Mais les seaux de la roue bouddhique ne peuvent en aucune circonstance porter au nirvāna. Ils puisent les êtres (la tête dans le seau) dans le tourbillon du monde et ils les y rejettent (la tête hors du seau). Si l'on voulait presser la comparaison technique, peut-être pourrait-on alléguer qu'un système fréquent de noria reçoit au moyeu, dans un « canal » (ou tube de bambou) déférent, l'eau puisée par les seaux périphériques : or c'est par le moyeu que l'image du Buddha semble échapper au samsāra. Mais nous avons vu, avec M. Przyluski, que ce motif ne s'est point finalement imposé. Ces remarques confirment les conclusions qui se sont

Un exemple parallèle au motif de la Nativité élucidera définitivement la portée cosmologique de la « réversibilité du temps » et son rapport à la Délivrance : c'est celui des dieux dits Akanishtha. On vient de voir que le Bodhisattva, lors de sa dernière naissance, domine le samsara en gagnant, à sa limite, simultanément le haut et l'origine du monde. Mais il existe une catégorie d'êtres que la cosmologie bouddhique place eux aussi au sommet du monde : ce sont les dieux dénommés Akanishtha. Comme Siddhartha nouveau-né, ils se tiennent à la pointe (agra) de l'étendue cosmique (1). Vont-ils, comme le Buddha, toucher aux limites du temps aussi bien qu'à celles de l'espace?

Leur nom est obscur et plusieurs interprétations en ont été proposées. Le dictionnaire de la Pali Text Society, s. v. [a] Kanittha, propose : « qui n'est pas le plus petit », c'est-à-dire « le plus grand, le plus haut ». Le récent *Dictionary of Pali Proper Names* édité par M. G. P. Malasekhara (1937) se contente de renvoyer au commentaire pali : « Buddhaghosa déclare qu'ils reçoivent ce nom en raison de leur suprématie en vertu et béatitude, et parce qu'il n'y a pas, parmi eux, de cadets » (s. v. Akanittha deva). La Vibhanga attha-

dégagées de la première partie de cette étude : la réversibilité du temps et ses divers symboles, admis par instants dans le bouddhisme n'y ont point valeur de dogme, mais d'images. On s'est servi de ce symbolisme pour souligner certains aspects de la doctrine. Mais il a été traité, canoniquement, avec beaucoup de circonspection. Sa valeur est restée celle de ces éléments d'emprunt que nous proposons de nommer des thèmes expressifs.

(1) Comme le montrent les tables comparatives établies par M. W. Kirfel dans sa monumentale *Kosmographie der Inder*, 1920, maintes traditions bouddhiques s'arrêtent, dans la hiérarchie divine, au ciel des Akanishtha. Par contraste avec l'enfer Avici, point le plus bas du cosmos, il est le point le plus haut de celui-ci, la pointe de l'existence (bhav'agga, cf l'affirmation du Buddha, dès sa naissance : aggo'mhi lokassa). D'autres traditions ajoutent des cieux encore plus abstraits et reportent la pointe de l'être (bhūtakoti) au monde « sans conscience ni absence de conscience ». L'Abhidharmakoça parait concilier les deux données en tirant argument de ce que les dieux et les cieux venant après les Akanishtha (lesquels sont à l'extrême limite des mondes de la Forme pure), n'étant pas « étendus », ne sont pas réellement, mais seulement idéalement « au-dessus » d'eux.

kathā, 521, glose a-kanittha « non cadet » par jettha (skr. jyeshtha) « l'aîné, le meilleur » — c'est-à-dire par le terme même dont use le cycle de la Nativité : « Par l'âge (āyus) comme par la connaissance, ils sont les dieux *à nuls autres inférieurs* (a-kanittha), autrement dit *supérieurs à tous* (jetthaka), en d'autres termes, les dieux, entre tous les dieux, *les plus accomplis* (panītatara) ». Vasubandhu consacre à ces dieux, dans son Abhidharmakoça, la notice suivante : « Au-dessus des Akanishtha, il n'y a plus de résidences (sthāna). C'est pourquoi, leur résidence étant supérieure aux autres, aucune résidence ne lui étant supérieure, on la nomme akanishtha » (1). Voici pour finir le commentaire sur le Dīgha nikāya. « Tous pré-excellents (jettha) tant par les vertus personnelles que par la naissance [bhavasampatti; skr. samprāpti], [par] l'obtention (i. e. « la date de l'obtention d'une naissance [en ce lieu] » cf. pali bhav'uppatti), on en conclut qu'il n'y a pas, dans ce monde là, de cadets (ou d'inférieurs : kanittha), d'où le nom d'Akanittha » (2).

Mêmes alternances, par conséquent, que tout à l'heure pour l'interprétation de jyeshtha : s'agit-il d'excellence ou d'aînesse ? La comparaison avec le cycle de la Nativité inciterait déjà à préférer le second sens. Mais, dans le cas des dieux Akanishtha, il s'impose directement. A l'époque où ont été rédigés les Commentaires, la tradition pāli énumérait, en effet, d'autres dieux encore, à la suite des Akanishtha. Dieux non point matériellement supérieurs ni antérieurs à ceux-ci, lesquels touchent déjà de quelque manière aux limites de l'étendue et de la durée spécifiées, mais assurément supérieurs en « excellence ». Hors de l'espace et du temps tels que les mesurent les hommes, ils l'emportent en quintessence d'abstraction, donc, pour les bouddhistes, en félicité, culminant au ciel où il n'y a plus ni conscience ni absence de conscience, cette préfiguration du Nirvāna. L'autre interprétation, chronologique, a-kanishtha : « non-cadets », demeure ainsi la plus indiquée.

(1) Trad. L. de La Vallée-Poussin, III, p. 168.
(2) II, p. 480.

Reste à déterminer le sens du composé négatif : « [les dieux] à nuls autres cadets », avec Vasubandhu, ou : « entre lesquels il n'est pas de cadets », avec Buddhaghosa ? Cosmologiquement moins compliquée que la première traduction, la seconde paraît grammaticalement aussi bonne ; toutefois, que sont au juste ces dieux « sans cadets » ? Représentent-ils une classe d'« Aînés du monde » prenant naissance tous ensemble à l'origine des choses ? Hypothèse que condamnent tous les textes canoniques : d'une part, la vie chez les Akanishtha, pour longue qu'elle soit, vient naturellement à terme, et, d'autre part, il est constant qu'à tout moment des créatures s'en vont renaître auprès d'eux. C'est le cas de la classe de Saints techniquement dénommés les Anāgāmin « ceux qui ne reviendront pas » : ils obtiennent le Nirvāna « au ciel », à la fin de leur existence divine. A l'instant où ils apparaissent dans la communauté des Akanishtha, des myriades de siècles se sont ainsi écoulées depuis le début des temps (1) : comment donc ces nouveaux venus ne seraient-ils pas les « cadets » des dieux d'origine?

Mais l'analyse de la réversibilité symbolique du temps, établie à propos de la naissance du Buddha comme Aîné du monde, éclaire suffisamment, ici encore, et la doctrine et l'expression. Passant au point à partir duquel est mesuré le monde perceptible, les Akanishtha, et aussi les êtres qui se réunissent à eux en cours de période cosmique (2), tout en restant soumis à la loi d'impermanence, semblent échapper déjà à certaines manières de compter la durée. L'exclamation de Siddhārtha : aggo'mhi lokassa, jettho'mhi lokassa, « je suis du monde le plus haut et l'Aîné », démarquée du mythe védique, en la serrant de plus près, nous a paru signifier un événement moins cosmique que personnel, l'échappée hors de la servitude transmigratoire, en ce qui a trait au

(1) Début relatif, comme de juste, seulement à une phase de la périodicité cosmique.

(2) E. Senart a cru apercevoir dans Brhadār. up. IV, 3, 33 une distinction entre « les dieux de nature » et ceux qui accèdent au statut divin par le karman (p. 77, n. 1).

passé comme à l'avenir, l'accès à ce que le Samyutta nikaya nommera l'origine et la destruction du monde, *localisées toutes deux dans le corps* (1). Les Akanishtha, eux aussi au sommet du monde perceptible (bhav'agga, skr. bhavāgra), paraissent y accéder à un état partiellement analogue. Ils échappent, vers le passé de la période cosmique, à la servitude du temps; ils en remontent le cours et se perdent dans une Aînesse collective. Ils ne sont cependant pas, sauf les Anāgāmin, affranchis de l'avenir. Ils finiront, pour renaître ailleurs. La certitude du Nirvāna n'est point enclose dans leur naissance.

Mais même ainsi leur mythologie chronologique réfléchit quelque chose de l'ambiguité qui nous a paru caractériser la nature du Buddha au cours de sa dernière existence. Il reste donc très remarquable, à cet égard, que les Anāgāmin, ceux pour qui, comme dans le cas de Siddhārtha, debout au haut du monde, « il n'est pas de retour », aillent gagner le Nirvāna au ciel des Akanishtha, i. e. des « sans-cadets » (2).

---

(1) Supra, p. 26.

(2) En pāli, antarā parinibbāyin « celui qui atteindra le nirvāna dans un autre monde » est techniquement synonyme de akanitthagamin « celui qui se rend chez les Akanishtha » ; il est qualifié d'uddhamsota (skr. ūrdhvasrota) « celui qui remonte le courant, i. e. le cours de la transmigration [par les douze causes] », expression fort significative de la réversibilité, objet de la présente étude. L'Abhidharmakoça situe, en outre, des Saints « allant au Nirvāna » dans le monde suprême où il n'y a plus ni conscience ni absence de conscience, c'est-à-dire « au-dessus » du monde des Akanishtha — mais, « au-dessus », nous l'avons vu, en un sens tout spirituel.

Si l'on compare la condition des Akanishtha, spécialement de ceux qui sont aussi des Anagamin, avec le cycle de la Nativité du Buddha, deux remarques s'imposent :

1° Le Buddha, qui est le modèle des Saints Moines (Arhat) destinés à acquérir le Nirvāna sur terre au terme de leur actuelle existence terrestre, devient en même temps, par le double miracle d'un passage symbolique au-dessus du monde et aux origines du temps, le modèle des Anāgāmin, destinés à obtenir le salut « au ciel ». Tous les miracles subsidiaires, qui font reposer les pieds du Buddha sur un lotus ou sur une floraison de lotus sortis sous ses pas, ou encore qui nivellent les mondes sous ses pieds, sont une traduction matérielle de cette nouvelle qualification. A l'instar des Rois, qui ne doivent pas fouler la terre,

Ces analogies et ces légendes rentrent, en fin de compte, dans le cycle des illustrations « par anticipation » du Nirvāna. De ce qu'il est ou n'est pas, rien n'est exprimable directement. On ne le connaît que par ses accès. La plus proche figuration sensible qu'on en puisse proposer sera donc naturellement en deçà de l'ultime rupture, dans les parties du samsāra qui touchent aux limites de la purification « mondaine » (Akanishtha, ou Naivasamjnānasamjnāyatana), ou déjà à demi hors du samsara, dans la personnalité ambiguë du Délivré vivant qu'est le Buddha dès l'instant de sa dernière naissance (jyeshtha, agra, etc.).

C'est bien dans cet esprit que le bouddhisme a librement emprunté au brāhmanisme une séquence de termes propres à identifier, à première vue, le Buddha au *brāhman* (ou à Brahmā, personnification de ce principe rituel). Le corps suprême du Buddha est un corps de Brahmā (brahmakaya : expression amphibologique que l'on peut traduire aussi « corps de *brahman* »), sa voix est une voix de Brahma, la Roue de sa Loi, une Roue de Brahmā, etc. Il ne faut voir là cependant aucune contamination dogmatique directe. Ces termes et les idées qu'ils convoient ont aidé les bouddhistes

---

l'ingéniosité des conteurs et des artistes mènera le Buddha jusqu'au Nirvāna sans l'avoir laissé remettre le pied sur le sol réel, avec ses aspérités, symbolisant les servitudes de la condition humaine. Toutes données qui accuseraient le caractère secondaire du thème, déjà canonique cependant, dont nous avons esquissé l'étude.

2° Le miracle de la terre aplanie, celui des lotus, etc., où E. Senart reconnaissait des emprunts aux mythes solaires (*Légende du Buddha*, p. 144 : « expression imagée des rayons lumineux qui sans peine et sans effort se posent également dans les profondeurs et sur les cimes » ; cf. Rgveda I, 35, 3, ; VI, 24, 8, etc.) sont peut-être cela très indirectement. Mais, en leur application immédiate à la légende bouddhique, ils font seulement de Çakyamuni un hôte du ciel des Akanishtha, ou de quelque ciel plus transcendant encore ; porté par sa nature au delà de tous les temps assignables, une succession de prodiges, annonciateurs du bouddhisme des Terres Pures, lui évitent de poser ses pas sur une terre à laquelle son avenir n'appartient plus, et à peine son présent. Pour arriver au Buddha « surnaturel » (lokottara) des écoles postérieures, il aura suffi de prendre au pied de la lettre ces métaphores, ce à quoi a dû contribuer leur réalisation artistique.

à se représenter *les abords* du suprême mystère. Ils ont, en dernière analyse, laissée intacte la transcendance de celui-ci. Ultimes images que le samsara tire de lui-même pour représenter, mais encore inadéquatement, un état qui ne lui appartiendra plus, ils sont en tout et pour tout, comme nous le disions, des thèmes expressifs.

Le motif de la naissance miraculeuse de Siddhârtha, avec les affinités qui le rapprochent de la classe mythique des dieux Akanishtha n'a point d'autre portée. Il naturalise dans le bouddhisme le mythe de la naissance d'Agni, dieu qui renverse le temps en se reportant à sa source. Mais, pour le bouddhisme, ce n'est qu'illustration conventionnelle ; on aperçoit sous la métaphore soutenue qui en procède, dans l'art comme dans la légende, la donnée rigoureusement canonique de la Délivrance des liens transmigratoires, fait personnel et non cosmique, logé dans le dernier corps assumé par le Buddha : c'est elle qui s'exprime à l'aide des équivalences cosmologiques que nous venons d'indiquer.

Cet emploi conventionnel des idées et des figures du brahmanisme suppose historiquement deux conditions, dont il n'est guère douteux qu'elles n'aient été pleinement réalisées dans les milieux où se sont fixées les traditions canoniques : une connaissance étendue des légendes et des pratiques védiques ou sub-védiques (Brahmana, Upanishad, débuts de l'Epopée) et une stricte fidélité à l'orthodoxie bouddhique, assez assurée d'elle-même pour s'adjoindre, sur les points les plus critiques, une ample provision d'images empruntées à l'hérésie mais détournées de leur sens primitif au service de la Bonne Loi. On peignait le Buddha sortant du temps ou en remontant le cours, comme Agni. Nul ne s'y trompait. Ce n'était pas diviniser le Maître au delà du Nirvana, mais en deçà du Nirvana, et par une simple allégorie : dernier mirage des couleurs multiples propres à la transmigration, avant le complet effacement, hors de toutes prises d'entendement et hors de toute représentation figurée.

Il était réservé à certaines écoles postérieures de « réaliser » ces métaphores et de les changer éventuellement en dogmes, rompant avec la vieille école, précisément là où celle-ci s'était surchargée d'emprunts, intégrés désormais de plein droit au système. L'aplanissement du sol sous les pas du Maître suscitera, de proche en proche, la doctrine des Terres Pures. La naissance au-dessus de l'étendue et hors des limites du temps, métaphoriquement attribuée à Çākyamuni, se multipliera autant de fois qu'il y aura d'êtres accédant à ces nouveaux Paradis, où prolifèrent les Buddha surnaturels, imitant Amitāyus, « Buddha de l'Age infini », par qui l'éternité du *brahman* et d'Agni, enrichie d'apports iranisants, prend droit de cité dans la doctrine. De même, la notion de temps réversible, utilisée avec tant de précaution dans les traditions anciennes, aboutit finalement à la figure toute mythologique de l'Ādibuddha, ou Buddha primordial (1), origine de tous les autres Buddha, comme Agni l'était des dieux dans l'élaboration brāhmanique authentique.

Peut-être, au terme de ces analyses sommaires, nous est-il possible d'entrevoir le cours et les causes de cette révolution : transportés historiquement et géographiquement dans des milieux nouveaux, hors des conditions d'équilibre — entre le brāhmanisme classique et le bouddhisme orthodoxe — qui en avaient déterminé et limité l'emploi, les thèmes expressifs du bouddhisme canonique sont devenus des thèmes productifs et, reçus comme tels, ont foisonné en mythes.

(1) La meilleure étude publiée en une langue européenne sur ce personnage demeure l'article de L. de La Vallée-Poussin, Ādi-Buddha, dans la *Hastings Encyclopædia of Religion and Ethics*.

1939. MELUN. — IMPRIMERIE ADMINISTRATIVE. — 689 I.

LOUIS DE LA VALLÉE POUSSIN

Notes sur le 'moment' ou *ksana* des bouddhistes [1].

a. Les sources pâlies sont pauvres ou peu techniques. On peut citer *Aṅguttara* IV, p. 137 et I, p. 10: „La rivière ne s'arrête pas: il n'y a pas de *khaṇa*, de *laya*, de *muhutta* où la rivière s'arrête: de même le flux des pensées…"

„Seize moments de pensée naissent et périssent pendant que dure un Dharma matériel [2]. Aucun exemple ne peut donner une idée de la brièveté de leur temps. Aussi Bhagavat a dit qu'il ne voit aucun Dharma de 'révolution' aussi brève (*laghuparivatta*) que la pensée.

b. Les sources Sarvāstivādins sont le mystérieux *Śārdūlakarṇāvadāna* (ou *Mātaṅgasūtra, Divyāvadāna*, p. 642—643. où on a: 120 *tatkṣaṇa* = 1 *lava*), la *Lokaprajñapti* (fol. 556, sommaire dans *Cosmologie bouddhique*, 1918, p. 309). *Vibhāṣā*, cahier 136; *Abhidharmakośa* III, 88, trad. III p. 179, II 45—46

[1]) *Notes Bouddhiques*, 19 et 20. Voir *Bulletin Académie Belgique*. Sur le problème du temps, STCHERBATSKY. *Théorie de la connaissance*… Musée Guimet, 1926: WESENDONK. *Kālavāda and Zervanite system*, *JRAS*. 1931, 57—67. Pour les Sarvāstivādins, le temps, c'est les cinq *skandhas*, c'est-à-dire les choses mêmes qui sont passées, présentes, futures; non pas *viprayuktasaṃskāra*, une certaine entité inconsciente associée à la série mentale, *Kośa*. I. 12, III. 188, IV. 62, V. 52; mais certaines écoles (Darṣṭantikas et Vibhajyavādins) font du temps une chose en soi et éternelle, *Vibhāṣā*, cahier 135, éd. Taisho, p. 701, col. 1.

[2]) *Dharma* se traduit assez bien 'chose'. Les *dharmas* sont les petites entités matérielles dont l'ensemble constitue le 'monde réceptacle', les petites entités matérielles et immatérielles qui constituent les êtres vivants. Un moment de couleur, de son…, une pensée, une sensation … autant de *dharmas*. L'espace et le Nirvāṇa sont aussi des *dharmas*.

(théorie des *lakṣaṇas*), trad. p. 232; IV, 2—3, trad. p. 4, et SAṂGHABHADRA aux mêmes endroits; *Nyāyavārttika*, 418; *Tattvasaṃgraha*, 142.

1. Le *kṣaṇa*, mesure du temps.

Chez les Sarvāstivādins, on a:

120 *kṣaṇas* = 1 *tatkṣaṇa*; 60 *tatkṣaṇas* = 1 *lava*; 30 *lavas* = 1 *muhūrta*, heure; 30 *muhūrtas* = 1 *ahorātra*, jour et nuit; 30 *ahorātras* = 1 *māsa*, mois; 12 *māsas*, plus les *ūnarātras*, ou jours à omettre pour faire concorder les mois lunaires avec les mois de trente jours = 1 *saṃvatsara*, année. Donc:

kṣaṇa = 0,013333 seconde;
tatkṣaṇa = 1,6 seconde;
lava = 96 secondes = 1,6 minute;
muhūrta = 48 minutes.

A voir les nombreux systèmes, MANU, *Viṣṇupurāṇa*, *Kauṭilīya*, *Sūryasiddhānta*, MAHĀVĪRA, SŪDHARA, BHĀSKARA (Tableau dans BARNETT, *Antiquities of India*, 1913, p. 218 et *Bakhshālī Manuscript* by G. R. KAYE, *Arch. Sur. India*, New Imp. Ser., vol. 43, 1927, p. 59), on constate que la définition: „*muhūrta* = 48 minutes" est générale. La *kalā* de *Manu-Viṣṇupurāṇa* est de 96 secondes et correspond à notre *lava* (le *lava* de *Kauṭilīya* est de 0.12 seconde). Pour le reste, grande diversité.

2. Le *kṣaṇa*, temps minimum. — Explications de la *Vibhāṣā*.

On essaie de définir le *kṣaṇa*, non plus en partant de l'heure (*muhūrta*) ou de la minute (*laya*, *lava*), mais en le considérant comme la limite (*paryanta*) du temps, le temps minimum, comme l'atome (*paramāṇu*) est la limite de la matière, l'élément matériel indivisible.

Vibhāṣā, 136, p. 700.

Quelle est la mesure du *kṣaṇa*?

Il y en a qui disent que, d'après la *Prajñāpti*, une fileuse d'âge moyen, quand elle tord les fils, touche (*teou-seou*, 64 et 4, 64 et 15) le fil ni long ni court: le temps de cette manoeuvre, c'est la mesure du *tatkṣaṇa* [3]). Ce texte ne veut pas dire que le fil soit court ou long; mais seulement que, le fil sortant d'entre les doigts, le temps du contact (ou de la sortie) est un *tatkṣaṇa*.

Mais, dira-t-on, nous interrogeons sur le *kṣaṇa*; pourquoi citer la *Prajñāpti* sur le *tatkṣaṇa*?

Parce que, au moyen du grossier, on donne une idée du subtil. Le subtil est difficile à connaître. On dit donc: „120 *kṣaṇas* font un *tatkṣaṇa*; 60 *tatkṣaṇas* font un *lava* qui vaut donc 7200 *kṣaṇas*; 30 *lavas* font un *muhūrta* qui vaut donc 216,000 *kṣaṇas*; 30 *muhūrtas* font un jour-nuit, qui vaut donc 6,480,000 (soit 6,500,000 moins 20,000). Le corps formé des cinq *skandhas* n'arrête pas de naître et de périr pendant ce jour-nuit".

Il y en a qui disent: „Ceci est un calcul grossier; ce n'est pas la mesure du *kṣaṇa*. Voici mon opinion: 64 *kṣaṇas* passent dans le temps qu'un homme fort fait claquer les doigts" [4]).

Il y en a qui disent: „Non; d'après moi, deux hommes forts tirent et rompent des fils de Bénarès: le temps de la rupture, c'est le *kṣaṇa*".

Il y en a qui disent: „Non; d'après moi, deux hommes tiennent tendus des fils de Bénarès et l'un d'eux les tranche avec un dur couteau de Chine bien affilé: le temps de la rupture, c'est le *kṣaṇa*".

Il y en a qui disent: „Ceci encore est grossier. Telle n'est pas la mesure du *kṣaṇa*. La vraie mesure du *kṣaṇa*, Bha-

[3]) Cette définition de la *Prajñāpti* nous est connue dans l'original, Śardūlakarṇa, *Divya*, p. 644: *tadyathā striyā nātidīrghanātihrasvakartinyāḥ sūtrodyāma evaṃ dīrghas tatkṣaṇaḥ*. Ni le chinois ni le sanscrit ne sont faciles à comprendre.

[4]) L'original est connu par *Mādhyamakavṛtti*, p. 547: *balavatpuruṣāccha ṭāmātreṇa pañcaṣaṣṭiḥ kṣaṇā atikrāmantītipāṭhāt*.

La *Vibhāṣā* a 64, SAMGHABHADRA (ci-dessous p. l. 6) a 65.

VASUBANDHU (*Kośa*, III, p. 178) cite cette définition comme celle des Vaibhāṣikas; il a 65.

Mahāvyutpatti, 253, 10, *acchaṭāsaṃghātamātra*; de même *Divya*, p. 142, 11: „Qui pensera au Bouddha, ne fût-ce que la durée d'une...". Ibid. p. 555, 21: „Eveillé par le bruit d'une *acchaṭā*".

Même emploi de *accharā*, *accharāsaṃghāta*, références RHYS DAVIDS-STEDE, dont les explications étymologiques n'emportent pas la conviction.

gavat ne l'a pas dite. Comment savons-nous cela? Par le Sūtra qui dit: Un certain bhikṣu vint auprès de Bhagavat, le salua, se tint de côté et demanda: „Combien vite naissent et périssent les 'facteurs vitaux' (*āyuḥsaṃskāra*, *Kośa*, II, p. 122)?" Bhagavat répondit: „Je pourrais l'enseigner; mais vous ne pourriez comprendre". Le bhikṣu dit: „N'y a-t-il pas une comparaison qui en donne une idée?" Bhagavat répondit: „Je vais vous la dire. Supposez quatre bons archers placés à côté l'un de l'autre et faisant face aux quatre points cardinaux [5]). Vient un homme alerte qui leur dit: „Tirez en même temps: je suis capable d'arrêter les quatre flèches, qui ne tomberont pas sur le sol". Qu'en pensez-vous, cet homme serait-il vraiment rapide pour faire cela?" Le bhikṣu répondit: „Il serait très rapide". Bhagavat reprit: „Sa rapidité n'approche pas de celle des Yakṣas terrestres; la rapidité de ces Yakṣas n'approche pas de la rapidité des Yakṣas de l'atmosphère (*vihāyasagāmin*); la rapidité de ces Yakṣas n'approche pas de celle des dieux des Quatre Grands Rois; la rapidité de ces dieux n'approche pas de celle des roues du soleil et de la lune; la rapidité de ces roues n'approche pas de celle des *devaputras* dits *dṛḍhagāmin*, les dieux qui conduisent les chars de ces roues. La vitesse toujours accrue des dieux en succession au delà de ceux-ci, la vitesse de la naissance et de la destruction des facteurs vitaux est encore plus vite. Le flux des *kṣaṇas* ne s'arrête pas". — Nous savons par ce texte que Bhagavat n'a pas dit la vraie mesure du *kṣaṇa*. — Pourquoi n'a-t-il pas dit aux autres la vraie mesure du *kṣaṇa*? — Parce qu'aucun être n'est capable de la comprendre. — Śāriputra n'est-il pas capable de

[5]) C'est une recension du Sutta de Saṃyutta, II, p. 265: *cattāro daḷhadhammā dhanuggahā*... — On a: „vitesse (*java*) de l'homme qui arrête les flèches; vitesse des lune-soleil: vitesse des *devatās* qui courent devant les lune-soleil". Dans la citation d'*Atthasālini*, p. 60: „vitesse du dieu Yama qui court devant les lune-soleil".

Dans notre texte: 1. Yakṣas terrestres, *li-hing* (clef 32 et 3, clef 144) = *pṛthivicara*, *bhūmicara*, *bhūmigāmin* (?), sans doute les *bhaumas* de *Vyutpatti*, 156; 2. Yakṣas de l'atmosphère, *kong-hing* (clef 116 et 3), traduit par *vihāyasagāmin*, *Vyutpatti* 126, 54; sans doute les *antarikṣavāsin* de *Vyutpatti*, 156; 3. Devaputra *kien-hing* (clef 32 et 8), peut-être *dṛḍhagāmin*. — „Conduire" = *tao-in* (clef 41 et 13, 57 et 1), conduire-guider: *puro dhāvati*.

la comprendre ? — Il en est capable. Mais cette connaissance est sans utilité. C'est pourquoi Bhagavat ne l'a pas enseignée; car le Bouddha n'enseigne pas en vain.

3. Le *kṣaṇa*, temps minimum. — Sautrantikas.

a. Vasubandhu, *Kośa*, III. 85 (trad. p. 177), suivant ici l'opinion des Sautrāntikas, du moins c'est probable, donne deux définitions du *kṣaṇa*: „Les conditions étant réunies, l'instant dans lequel un Dharma obtient son être ou sa „nature propre" (*ātmalābha*)", et: „Le temps dans lequel un Dharma en mouvement se déplace de la mesure d'un atome".

Pour la seconde explication, qui décrit l'infiniment petit de la durée en fonction de l'infiniment petit de l'étendue — „Le *kṣaṇa* n'a pas une partie antérieure et une partie postérieure, comme l'atome n'a pas de parties spatiales" — comparer la définition toute pareille que les sources jaïnas (*Tattvārthādhigama*, J. de Soc. Or. Allemande, t. 40 (Jacobi), et *Gaṇitasāra-saṃgraha*, Madras 1912, I. 32, cités *Abhidharmakośa*, III, p. 178, note) donnent du *samaya* qui est le *kṣaṇa* des Jaïnas: il faut un nombre infini de *samayas* pour faire une *āvali* ou *āvalikā* qui est la plus petite durée appréciable. Pour le *samaya*, on a: *paramasūkṣmakriyasya sarvajaghanyagatipariṇatasya paramāṇoḥ svāvagāhanakṣetravyatikramakālaḥ samaya iti*: „Die Zeit, die ein Atom in langsamster Bewegung gebraucht, um sich um seine eigene Körperlänge weiter zu bewegen" (Jacobi); et: *aṇur aṇvantaraṃ kāle vyatikrāmati yāvati sa kālaḥ samayo 'saṃkhyaiḥ samayair āvalir bhavet:* „The time in which an atom (moving) goes beyond another atom (immediately next to it) is a *samaya*..." (M. Rangācārya). On doute si *aṇvantara* signifie „un autre atome"; plutôt „l'intervalle, l'étendue d'un atome".

La première explication est réfutée par Saṃghabhadra (32, p. 521) qui, après avoir cité le „Sautrāntika" (=Vasubandhu) dit: „Il faut considérer si un Dharma, avant de naître, possède ou ne possède pas sa „nature propre" (*ātmabhāva*)[6]). D'après

---

[6]) Les Sarvastivadins, „qui affirment l'existence de tout", croient à l'existence du passé et du futur. Si notre acte ancien n'existait plus,

les Ābhidhārmikas, le concours des conditions fait que le Dharma obtient la naissance, non pas qu'il obtient sa nature propre, qu'il possède en effet avant que de naître. — Mais alors à quoi bon la naissance? Au moment du concours des conditions, la nature propre existe déjà; mais les conditions font que le Dharma [qui est cette nature propre] arrive à l'état où il devient „cause projetant son fruit“; où, en d'autres termes, il produit une éminente activité. Quand cette activité productrice du fruit a cessé, le Dharma est nommé „passé“. — Pourquoi, dira-t on, le Dharma futur n'a-t-il pas cette activité? — L'objection est futile. C'est comme si on objectait: Pourquoi le Dharma futur n'est-il pas nommé „présent“? Je dis que le Dharma qui est actif est „présent.“ — Pourquoi adopter cette doctrine de l'existence de la nature propre des Dharmas dans le passé et le futur? Parce que les autres doctrines se heurtent à d'innombrables textes et arguments. Nous expliquerons ce problème lorsque nous traiterons du temps (V. 25). Donc la mesure du *kṣaṇa* proposée par le Sautrāntika n'est pas admissible... D'après les Ābhidhārmikas, du point de vue de la vérité vraie, la mesure du *kṣaṇa* que durent tous les Dharmas peut être indiquée par des exemples. Mais le Bouddha Bhagavat ne l'a point définie, parce qu'il ne voyait personne qui pût la comprendre. Toutefois, dans le but d'instruire les étudiants, on peut avoir recours à des comparaisons; par exemple: „Soixante-cinq *kṣaṇas* passent dans le temps qu'un homme fort fait claquer les doigts“.

b. Vasubandhu signale une troisième explication (*Kośa*, IV, p. 14): *ātmalābhānantaravināśī kṣaṇaḥ | sa yasyāsti sa kṣaṇika iti.* — Comme *kṣaṇa* s'explique souvent par *kṣaya*, on pense à corriger *vināśaḥ* et à traduire: „Le *kṣaṇa* est la destruction qui se produit immédiatement après l'acquisition de l'être. Est dit *kṣaṇika*, instantané, ce à quoi on attribue le *kṣaṇa*.“ — Mais la formule Sautrāntika est citée *Tattvasaṃgraha*, p. 142, et commentée: *utpādānantaravināśisvabhāvo vastunaḥ kṣaṇaḥ*: „Le *kṣaṇa*, c'est la nature de la chose, nature qui est de pé-

---

comment pourrait-il fructifier au cours de notre vie actuelle? D'ailleurs la pensée ne peut penser que de l'existant. — Sur cette doctrine, qui n'est pas simple, *Kośa*, chap. V, p. 50—65.

rir immédiatement après être née. La chose qui a cette nature est dite *kṣaṇika*, instantanée".

D'après les Sautrāntikas, la destruction est spontanée, ne dépend pas d'une cause — de même que la flèche tombe (*Vibhāṣā*, 20, p. 103, 21, p. 105), de même qu'une motte de terre tombe (*Madhyamakavṛtti*, 222). Elle est donc immédiate. Aussi bien Bhagavat a dit que les choses ne duraient pas. (*Vibhāṣā*, 39, p. 201).

La durée du Dharma sera nulle, puisqu'il périt aussitôt né.

4. Le *kṣaṇa* des Sarvāstivādins.

D'après Vasumitra, Bhagavat n'a pas voulu dire que les choses ne duraient absolument pas, mais seulement qu'elles ne duraient pas longtemps, qu'elles ne duraient pas au delà d'un *kṣaṇa* (*Vibhāṣā*, ibid.).

Le *kṣaṇa* est ainsi nommé parce qu'il est le temps le plus réduit (*paramanikṛṣṭa kāla*; *sarvāntyo hi kālaḥ kṣaṇaḥ*); la période pendant laquelle, après un long futur et avant un long passé, le Dharma est actif (*sakāritra*), c'est-à-dire présent. Les Dharmas présents, ayant cette mesure d'état de durée, sont nommés *kṣaṇika*, momentanés [7]).

Le *kṣaṇa*, qui est donc le moment présent, ne se divise pas en une partie antérieure, une partie postérieure. Cependant il n'est pas simple. Tout Dharma a naissance, durée, modification ou vieillesse, destruction.

Les Sarvāstivādins n'entendent donc pas le terme *kṣaṇika*, momentané, dans le même sens que les Sautrāntikas.

Non seulement ceux-ci nient l'existence du Dharma passé et du Dharma futur, et aussi l'existence des Asaṃskṛtas (espace, etc.); il nient encore que le Dharma momentané ait naissance, durée-modification, destruction, c'est-à-dire les trois ou quatre caractères que le Bouddha dit être les caractéristiques de tout Dharma produit par les causes. D'après eux, quand le Bouddha dit que le Dharma dure (*sthiti*, *avatiṣṭhate*),

---

[7]) *Tattvasaṃgraha*, p. 142: *atha kṣaṇasthitikālāḥ kṣaṇikāḥ* | *sarvāntyo kālaḥ kṣaṇaḥ* | *taṃ ye 'vatiṣṭhante te kṣaṇikāḥ* |.
Kośa, III, p. 177: *kālaparyantaḥ kṣaṇaḥ*.

il entend que, le moment (*kṣaṇa*) postérieur ressemblant au moment antérieur, on peut dire que celui-ci „est comme s'il durait" (*avatiṣṭhata iva*): le moment postérieur est, pour ainsi dire, la durée (*sthiti*) du moment antérieur. Et il y a aussi „modification", parce que, dans la durée ainsi comprise, se produit une dissimilitude de plus en plus accusée.

Les Sarvāstivādins, fidèles à la lettre du vieux Sūtra, reconnaissent au Dharma momentané „naissance, durée-modification ou vieillesse, disparition". Ils renchérissent, divisant le deuxième caractère „durée-modification" en deux, durée et modification. — La naissance, c'est ce qui fait naître le Dharma; la durée (*sthiti*), ce qui le stabilise ou fait durer (*sthāpayati*); la vieillesse (*jarā* ou *sthityanyathātva*), ce qui le détériore; la disparition ou impermanence (*anityatā*), ce qui le détruit.

Ces quatre ne sont pas conçus comme des états du Dharma; ce sont quatre entités, des *saṃskāras*, qu'on nomme les caractères (*lakṣaṇas*) du Dharma, et qui entrent en activité quand les conditions sont présentes. La naissance, plus les causes et conditions extérieures, fait naître le Dharma; la durée le fait durer... l'impermanence le fait périr. Il est faux que, comme l'enseignent les Sautrāntikas, le Dharma périsse sans cause, par le fait même qu'il est né, immédiatement. Il périt par la vertu de l'entité „impermanence", après que l'entité „durée" l'a fait durer.

Aussi les Sautrāntikas disent aux Sarvāstivadins: „Vous direz peut-être que, pour vous, le *kṣaṇa* c'est le temps où les quatre caractères (naissance, durée, vieillesse, impermanence) du Dharma ont achevé leur action (*caturlakṣaṇakriyāparisamāpti*)" (*Kośa*, II, p. 232). Saṃghabhadra ignore cette ligne du *Kośa* dans sa réfutation du *Kośa*; mais on a l'impression qu'elle donne une idée assez exacte du *kṣaṇa* des Sarvastivadins-Vaibhāṣikas.

La discussion des trois ou quatre „caractères" occupe plusieurs pages dans le *Kośa* (II, p. 222—237), et dans Saṃghabhadra (p. 405—412). — Voir aussi la critique de Candrakīrti dans *Madhyamakavṛtti*, p. 544, et *Madhyamakāvatāra*, p. 193. Tout n'est pas simple dans ces longues controverses.

Mais on ne peut douter que, pour les Sautrāntikas, le *kṣaṇa*, durée du Dharma, soit une grandeur de temps se rapprochant de zéro à l'infini: le Dharma périt immédiatement après être né; le Dharma-cause produit le Dharma-effet comme un fléau de la balance monte quand l'autre descend; tandis que, pour les Sarvāstivādins-Vaibhāṣikas, encore que le Dharma périsse aussitôt né, il ne laisse pas de durer: ses naissance-durée-vieillesse-mort ne font qu'un *kṣaṇa* et on ne peut pas dire: *catuḥ kṣaṇikaṃ vastu* „la chose dure quatre *kṣaṇas*"; mais ces quatre ne sont pas simultanés bien que le *kṣaṇa* ne soit pas divisible, n'ait pas un avant et un après. En d'autres termes, le temps est discontinu et fait de *kṣaṇas*, comme le corps étendu (*rūpa*) est fait d'atomes.

Bruxelles, février 1931.

LA CONTROVERSE

DU TEMPS ET DU PUDGALA

DANS LE VIJÑĀNAKĀYA,

PAR

LOUIS DE LA VALLÉE POUSSIN,

PROFESSEUR À L'UNIVERSITÉ DE GAND.

Le Vijñānakāya de Devaśarman [1], quatrième Abhidharma des Sarvāstivādins, se divise en six chapitres : 1. Maudgalyāyanaskandhaka [2]; 2. Pudgalaskandhaka; 3. Hetupratyayaskandhaka; 4. Ālambanaskandhaka; 5. «Mélanges» [3]; 6. Samanvāgamaskandhaka [4].

Le chapitre Ier établit, contre Maudgalyāyana, l'existence du passé et du futur.

Dans le IIe, le partisan de la «vacuité» (*śūnyatāvādin*) réfute le partisan du «moi» ou Pudgala (*pudgalavādiṇ*).

(1) NANJIO, 1281, Tokio, XXIII, 9, fol. 1-72. — WATTERS, *Yuan Chwang*, I, 373, discute l'affirmation de Hiuan-tsang (*Vie*, p. 123) — que Devaśarman composa ce traité pour nier «l'existence du *moi* et du *non-moi*» — et, n'ayant pas lu le chapitre II, déclare qu'elle est inexacte. — L'analyse de Takakusu (*On the Abhidharma Literature of the Sarvāstivādins*, *J.P.T.S.*, 1905, p. 107) est aussi décevante.

(2) La restitution °*skandhaka* paraît certaine.

Le chapitre VI du Jñānaprasthāna est nommé, dans la Kośavyākhyā, indriyaskandhaka.

(3) 雜蘊. — Peut-être *saṃkīrṇa-skandhaka*, d'après Mahāvyutpatti, 127, 33.

(4) Restitution de Takakusu. Mais *samanvāgama* ne signifie ni «completion» ni «consequence».

Le IIIe (16 *a* - 25 *b*) examine les causes (passées, futures, présentes), des six *vijñānakāyas* ou catégories de connaissance (connaissance de l'œil, etc.).

Le IVe (26 *a* - 45 *a*) examine l'objet (*ālambana*) des six *vijñānakāyas*, lequel diffère quand la connaissance est passée, future, présente; quand elle appartient à l'œil, etc.; quand elle est du domaine du Kāmadhātu, etc.; quand elle est bonne, etc.

Le Ve (45 *a* - 54 *a*) pose de nombreuses questions, les unes relatives aux *vijñānakāyas*, les autres relatives à la couleur et à la figure (*rūpa*), à l'acte et au fruit, à la sensation détruite sans être passée, aux diverses sortes de pensée, aux *dharmas* propres aux Āryas, etc.

Le VIe établit le tableau de l'association des pensées : «Si quelqu'un est muni (*samanvāgata*) de la pensée bonne du Kāmadhātu peut-il aussi être muni de la pensée mauvaise de la même sphère?... peut-il aussi être muni de la pensée d'Arhat?...»

Les chapitres III-VI intéressent l'histoire de l'Abhidharma, car Vasubandhu, pour ne nommer que lui, s'en est servi. D'ailleurs ils ne sont pas sans présenter avec les sources palies des parallélismes et des contrastes. Mais nous nous occuperons ici des deux premiers chapitres qui illustrent deux des controverses notables de l'ancien Bouddhisme.

1. Maudgalyāyana — Mŏu kān liên ou simplement Mŏu liên — rappelle le Sapurisa mogaliputa de Sānchi, l'illustre Tissa, fils de Moggalī, président du Concile d'Aśoka, rédacteur du Kathāvatthu. Dans ce livre (I, 6-7), le docteur orthodoxe qui prétend représenter les Anciens (Theravādin)[1] et qui, d'après la tradition, est Tissa, combat les partisans de l'existence du passé et du futur (Sarvāstivādin) : il occupe la position que Devaśarman attribue à Maudgalyāyana. — D'ailleurs peu ou point de relations entre les deux

[1] A en juger d'après Majjhima, I, 164, *Theravāda* = doctrine traditionnelle, non pas doctrine des Sthaviras.

discussions. Le Kathāvatthu et le Vijñānakāya représentent et font triompher deux doctrines contradictoires; ils ne se rencontrent pas[1].

2. Au contraire le deuxième chapitre, *pudgalaskandhaka*, présente avec Kathāvatthu, I, 1, des analogies qui vont jusqu'à l'identité de certaines formules[2]. Pour réfuter le «partisan du Pudgala», le «partisan de la vacuité» — «vacuité», *śūnyatā*, s'entendant ici de l'inexistence du «moi» et du mien — emploie des arguments utilisés par le Theravādin contre les Vajjiputtakas et les Sammitīyas[3].

(1) La comparaison est cependant instructive. On verra aussi Milinda, p. 50-54. Le Vijñānakāya est ici une des sources de Vasubandhu, Kośa, V, 25, traduit dans Stcherbatski, *Central conception of Buddhism*, 1923, Appendice. — On sait que, d'après Tissa Moggalīputta, le Bouddha fut «partisan de la distinction» (*vibhajjavādin*). Bhavya (Rockhill, *Life of Buddha*, 184) dit que la «doctrine de la distinction» est la théorie qui reconnaît l'existence de certain passé (la cause qui n'a pas encore porté son fruit) et l'existence de certain futur (le fruit «projeté» par une cause mais non encore réalisé). Aucune allusion à cette théorie dans le chapitre Maudgalyāyana de notre livre. — Les deux passages de l'Écriture où, à ma connaissance, le Bouddha s'est déclaré *vibhajjavāda* (Majjhima, II, 197, Aṅguttara, V, 190), concernent l'attitude du Bouddha au sujet de la vie-à-la-maison et au sujet de la mortification (*tapas*). D'après le commentaire de Kathāvatthu, XIX, 2, les Andhakas se trompent faute de distinguer les emplois du mot «vide»; XI, 5, les Mahāsāṃghikas devraient distinguer entre les *kalpas*. — Il semble bien que toutes les écoles ont admis que certaines questions comportaient une «réponse en distinguant» (*vibhajyavyākaraṇa*, Kośa, V, 22). — Les Vibhajyavādins ont peut-être dû leur nom aux distinctions qu'ils établissaient dans l'examen d'un problème déterminé. La tradition est extrêmement confuse sur les thèses des Vibhajyavādins : quelques-uns les identifient avec les Mahīśāsakas; d'autres entendent par Vibhajyavādins un ensemble de sectes, etc. (Sources citées par Saeki Kiokuga, *ad* Hiuan-tsang, trad. du Kośa, Kioto, 1888, XIX, fol. 14 *a*; Abhidharmakośa, I, p. 69, II, 215, IV, 33, 40, 212, V, 23, 29, 52, VI, 123.)

(2) Voir ci-dessous, p. 358, note 2, et p. 359, note 1.

(3) Voir p. 358, note 1. — Sur les Vātsīputrīyas, leur fondateur Vatsīputra, et les autres sectes (au nombre de quatre) qui croient au *pudgala*, voir Rockhill, *Life of Buddha*, 184 (traduction de Bhavya); Tāranātha, p. 44; nos notes dans l'article *Councils* de *Hastings*, IV, p. 183;

CHAPITRE PREMIER.

Maudgalyayanaskandhaka [1].

I

1 (2 *b* 2-15). Le śramaṇa Maudgalyāyana dit : Le passé et le futur n'existent pas; le présent et l'inconditionné (*asaṃskṛta*) existent.

On lui demandera : Oui ou non, ce que Bhagavat a dit dans le Sūtra, à savoir : «Il y a trois racines de mal, l'attachement (*lobha*) racine de mal, la haine racine de mal, l'aberration racine de mal», cela est-il bien dit, bien expliqué, bien déclaré?

Il répond : Oui, c'est bien dit.

On lui demandera : Oui ou non, y a-t-il des hommes qui ont vu, qui voient, qui verront que l'attachement, racine de mal, est mauvais?

Il répond : Oui.

L'attachement, objet de cette vue, est-il passé, futur, présent?

S'il répond que l'attachement, objet de cette vue, est passé, on doit lui dire : Le passé existe; il ne faut pas dire que le passé n'existe pas; soutenir que le passé n'existe pas est illogique. — S'il répond que l'attachement est futur, on doit lui dire : Le futur existe; il ne faut pas dire que le futur n'existe pas; soutenir que le futur n'existe pas est illogique. — S'il répond que l'attachement, objet de cette vue, est présent, on doit lui dire : Il y a donc, dans

Nanjio 1169 cité dans Przyluski, *Empereur Açoka*, p. 20; Mrs Rhys Davids, *Introd. à la traduction du Kathāvatthu*.

[1] Le chapitre de Maudgalyāyana est divisé en quatre parties précédées chacune d'un *uddāna* ou sommaire (quatre *pādas* de sept syllabes). — Premier *uddāna* (2 *b* 1) : 1. Racines (*mūla*), 2. mauvaise action (*duścarita*), 3. notion (*saṃjñā*), 4. *vitarka*, 5. *dhātus*, 6. *āsravas*, 7. feux (*agni*), 8. soif (*tṛṣṇā*), 9. toute souillure (*mala*), tout lien, tout cela est triple (c'est-à-dire des trois époques). — Deuxième *uddāna* (3 *a* 5) : *oghas*, *yogas*, *upādānas*, *granthas*, *nīvaraṇas* .... — Troisième *uddāna* (3 *b* 20) : 1. *saṃyojanas*, 2. *nīvaraṇas*, 3. *bodhyaṅgas*, 4. *citta*, 5. *vedanā*, 6. *manas*, 7. dompter ou exercer, 8. fermeté (陀堅 ou 持堅). — Quatrième *uddāna* (5 *b* 8) : 1. Sans objet, 2. *dhyānas*, 3. *pṛthagjana*, 4. *mahāpuruṣa*, 5. pudeur, 6. *sattvāvāsas*, 7. aliment, 8. *āryasatyas*, 9. abandon des *āsravas*.

une personne (*pudgala*), deux pensées simultanées; la pensée objet de la vue [à savoir la pensée d'attachement] et la pensée sujet de la vue [à savoir la pensée qui voit l'attachement]; ce qui est inadmissible. — S'il n'admet pas que, dans une personne, deux pensées soient simultanées, celle qui est vue et celle qui voit, alors il ne doit pas dire qu'on voit le présent : soutenir qu'on voit le présent est illogique. — S'il dit : «On ne voit pas l'attachement passé, futur, présent», alors il n'y a pas quelqu'un qui a vu, voit ou verra que l'attachement, racine de mal, est mauvais. S'il n'y a pas quelqu'un qui a vu, voit ou verra cela, il n'y a pas quelqu'un qui s'est dégoûté, qui se dégoûte, qui se dégoûtera de l'attachement. S'il n'y a pas quelqu'un qui se dégoûte, il n'y a pas quelqu'un qui se soit détaché (*viraj*), qui se détache, qui se détachera. S'il n'y a pas quelqu'un qui se détache, il n'y a pas quelqu'un qui se soit délivré (*vimuc*), qui se délivre, qui se délivrera. S'il n'y a pas quelqu'un qui se délivre, il n'y a pas quelqu'un qui a obtenu, qui obtient ou qui obtiendra le Nirvāṇa.

Comme nous avons examiné la manière dont on peut voir que l'attachement est mauvais (*akuśala*), de même on examinera la manière dont on peut voir que l'attachement est *saṃyojana*, *bandhana*, *anuśaya*, *upakleśa*, *paryavasthāna*, à rejeter, à laisser, à abandonner, à connaître (*tyaj*, *prahā*, *parijñā*).

On demande encore à Maudgalyāyana : Oui ou non, y a-t-il des hommes qui ont vu, voient ou verront que l'attachement, racine de mal, produit dans le futur une rétribution pénible?

Il répond : Oui.

Ce qui est l'objet de cette vue, est-ce l'attachement passé? est-ce l'attachement futur? est-ce l'attachement présent?

S'il répond que c'est l'attachement passé, on doit lui dire : Le passé existe; il ne faut pas dire que le passé n'existe pas; soutenir que le passé n'existe pas est illogique. — S'il répond que c'est l'attachement futur, on doit lui dire : Le futur existe; il ne faut pas dire que le futur n'existe pas; soutenir que le futur n'existe pas est illogique. — S'il répond que c'est l'attachement présent, on doit lui dire : Il y a donc une personne qui, en même temps, accomplit l'acte et éprouve la rétribution de cet acte : c'est inadmissible. — S'il n'admet pas qu'une même personne, en même temps, accomplisse l'acte et éprouve la rétribution de cet acte, alors il ne doit pas dire qu'on voit le présent; dire qu'on voit le présent est illogique. — S'il dit qu'on ne voit pas l'attachement passé, futur, présent, il n'y a donc pas quelqu'un qui, de l'attachement racine de mal, a vu, voit ou verra qu'il produit, dans le futur, une rétribution pénible. Si personne ne voit ainsi l'attachement, personne qui s'en soit dégoûté, détaché, délivré; personne donc qui ait obtenu, obtienne ou doive obtenir le Nirvāṇa.

Comme pour l'attachement, racine de mal, même examen de la haine (*dveṣa*), racine de mal, de l'aberration (*moha*), racine de mal.

2 (2*b* 15-17). Pour la mauvaise action corporelle (*kāyaduścarita*) et la mauvaise action vocale, elles sont mauvaises (*akuśala*); elles ne sont pas *saṃyojana, bandhana, anuśaya, upakleśa, paryavasthāna*; elles doivent être rejetées, laissées, abandonnées, connues; elles produisent, dans le futur, une rétribution pénible.

La mauvaise action mentale (*manoduścarita*) est mauvaise; est *saṃyojana, bandhana, anuśaya, upakleśa, paryavasthāna*; doit être rejetée, laissée, abandonnée, connue; produit, dans le futur, une rétribution pénible.

3 (2*b* 17). Les *kāmasaṃjñā, vyāpādasaṃjñā* et *vihiṃsāsamjñā* sont mauvaises; ne sont pas *saṃyojana, bandhana, anuśaya, upakleśa, paryavasthāna*; doivent être rejetées, laissées, abandonnées, connues; produisent, dans le futur, une rétribution pénible.

4 (2*b* 18). Les *kāmavitarka, vyāpādavitarka* et *vihiṃsāvitarka* sont mauvais; ne sont pas *saṃyojana, bandhana, anuśaya*; sont *upakleśa*; ne sont pas *paryavasthāna*; doivent être rejetés, laissés, abandonnés, connus; produisent, dans le futur, une rétribution pénible.

5 (2*b* 18-20). Le *kāmadhātu* et le *vyāpādadhātu* sont mauvais; sont *saṃyojana, bandhana, anuśaya, upakleśa, paryavasthāna*; doivent être rejetés, laissés, abandonnés, connus; produisent, dans le futur, une rétribution pénible.

Le *vihiṃsādhātu* est mauvais; n'est pas *saṃyojana, bandhana, anuśaya*; est *upakleśa*; n'est pas *paryavasthāna*; doit être rejeté, abandonné, connu; produit, dans le futur, une rétribution pénible.

6 (2*b* 20-3*a* 1). Le *kāmāsrava* et l'*avidyāsrava* sont mauvais; sont *saṃyojana, bandhana, anuśaya, upakleśa, paryavasthāna*; doivent être rejetés, laissés, abandonnés, connus; produisent, dans le futur, une rétribution pénible.

Le *bhavāsrava* n'est pas mauvais; est *saṃyojana, bandhana, anuśaya, upakleśa, paryavasthāna*; doit être rejeté, laissé, abandonné, connu; ne produit pas, dans le futur, une rétribution pénible.

7 (3*a* 1-2). Les *lobhāgni, dveṣāgni, mohāgni* et la *kāmatṛṣṇā* sont mauvais; sont *saṃyojana, bandhana, anuśaya, upakleśa, paryavasthāna*; doivent être re-

jetés, laissés, abandonnés, connus; produisent, dans le futur, une rétribution pénible.

8 (3 *a* 2-3). La *rūpatṛṣṇā* n'est pas mauvaise; est *saṃyojana, bandhana, anuśaya, upakleśa, paryavasthāna*; doit être rejetée, laissée, abandonnée, connue; ne produit pas, dans le futur, une rétribution pénible.

9 (3 *a* 3-4). Tout ce qui est *lobha*, tout ce qui est *dveṣa*, tout ce qui est *moha*, le *lobhamala*, le *dveṣamala*, le *mohamala*, le *lobhabandhana*, le *dveṣabandhana*, le *mohabandhana*, sont mauvais; sont *saṃyojana, bandhana, anuśaya, upakleśa, paryavasthāna;* doivent être rejetés, laissés, abandonnés, connus; produisent, dans le futur, une rétribution pénible (3 *a* 4).

II (3 *a* 7-3 *b* 18).

Le śramaṇa Maudgalyāyana dit : Le passé et le futur n'existent pas, le présent et l'inconditionné existent.

On lui demandera : Oui ou non, ce que Bhagavat dit dans le Sūtra, à savoir : «Il y a quatre *oghas*, kāmaugha, bhavaugha, dṛṣṭyogha, avidyaugha», cela est-il bien dit ?

Il répond : Oui.

Quelqu'un a-t-il vu, voit-il, verra-t-il que les *oghas* sont mauvais?...

[La discussion se poursuit comme ci-dessus, et reprend dans les mêmes termes pour les *yogas*, les *upādānas* (*kāma, dṛṣṭi, śīlavrata* et *ātmavāda*), les *granthas*, les *nīvaraṇas* (*kāmacchanda, vyāpāda, vicikitsā, styānamiddha, auddhatyakaukṛtya*), les *avarabhāgīyas* et les *ūrdhvabhāgīyas*, les cinq *sin-kēn-tsāi*, les cinq *sin-kiū-ngāi* [1], les *dṛṣṭis* (*satkāya*, etc.), l'*ātmabhāvacchanda* (?) [2], les *anuśayas*, les *mithyāṅgas* (?) [3], les *saṃyojanas*, les *karmapathas*.]

(1) Il semble que les cinq 心拘礙 doivent être les cinq 心貢結 du Daśottara (Tokio, 9, 44 *b* 11) qui sont certainement les *cetokhila* de Saṃgītisuttanta, Dīgha, III, 238. — D'autre part, il y a cinq «clous» du *manas* 心貢釘 (Tokio, 10, 70 *b* 3); ce qui donne *cetaḥkīla*, peut être une variante pour *khila-khīla*. — Mais les 根栽 de notre texte diffèrent-ils des 根裁 qui sont aussi des *khila* ?

(2) «Corps-soif.»

(3) Lire probablement *mithyātvāṅgas*. L'homme qui commet un *ānantaryakarman* est *mithyātvaniyata* «voué à la perdition».

III

1 (*4 a* 1-8). Le śramaṇa Maudgalyāyana dit : Le passé et le futur n'existent pas...

On lui demandera : Oui ou non, ce que Bhagavat dit dans le Sūtra, à savoir : Lorsqu'il a lien de l'œil[1], il sait en vérité : «J'ai lien de l'œil»; lorsqu'il n'a pas lien de l'œil, il sait en vérité : «Je n'ai pas lien de l'œil», et il sait aussi en vérité : «Le lien de l'œil d'abord n'est pas né, ensuite naît; étant né, il faut le couper; une fois coupé, il ne renaîtra plus» — ce Sūtra est-il bien dit ?

Il répond : Oui.

On doit lui demander : Ce qui est ainsi objet d'un savoir exact, est-ce passé, futur ou présent? — S'il répond que c'est passé, on doit lui dire : Alors le passé existe; il ne faut pas dire que le passé n'existe pas; soutenir que le passé n'existe pas est illogique. — S'il répond que c'est futur...

[Argumentation comme ci-dessus jusque :]

S'il dit : On ne voit pas le lien-de-l'œil passé, futur ou présent, alors ce que Bhagavat a bien dit, expliqué et déclaré dans le Sūtra : «Lorsqu'il y a en lui un lien-de-l'œil...» cette parole de Bhagavat dans le Sūtra, tu la nies, tu la contredis, tu la rejettes. Nier, contredire, rejeter le Sūtra proclamé par le Bhagavat est inacceptable.

Même argumentation pour les liens de l'ouïe, de l'odorat, du goût, du tact et du sens interne.

2 (*4 a* 9-12). La śramaṇa Maudgalyāyana dit : Le passé et le futur n'existent pas...

On doit lui demander : Oui ou non, ce que Bhagavat dit dans le Sūtra, à savoir : «Lorsqu'il y a en lui *kāmacchandanīvaraṇa*, il sait en vérité : j'ai *kāmacchandanīvaraṇa*...», cela est-il bien dit, bien expliqué, bien déclaré?

[Le reste comme ci-dessus, en terminant par :]

Même argumentation en ce qui concerne le *vyāpāda*, le *styānamiddha*, l'*auddhatyakaukṛtya*, le *vicikitsānīvaraṇa*.

3 (*4 a* 18-*4 b* 6). On doit lui demander : Oui ou non, ce que dit Bhagavat dans le Sūtra : «Lorsqu'il y a en lui le membre de la Bodhi nommé mémoire

[1] 若有內眼結 = lorsqu'il y a en lui lien de l'œil : *asty adhyātmaṃ cakṣuḥsaṃyojanam*... (Comp. Saṃyutta, IV, 89.)

(*smṛtisaṃbodhyaṅga*), il sait en vérité : j'ai le *smṛtisaṃbodhyaṅga*. Lorsque ce membre lui manque, il sait en vérité qu'il n'a pas ce membre. Et il sait en vérité : Ce membre qui n'est pas né, il faut qu'il naisse; étant né, il faut qu'il dure, qu'il ne se perde pas, qu'il soit cultivé, qu'il soit rempli, qu'il se développe de plus en plus, qu'il soit réalisé (*sākṣātkar*)» — cela est-il bien dit, bien expliqué, bien déclaré?

[La discussion se poursuit comme ci-dessus : «L'objet de ce savoir est-il passé?»]

Même argumentation en ce qui regarde les six autres *saṃbodhyaṅgas*.

4 (4 *b* 7-14) ...On doit lui demander : Oui ou non, ce que dit Bhagavat dans le Sūtra, à savoir : «Lorsque sa pensée est associée au désir (*sarāga*), il le sait en vérité; lorsque sa pensée est dissociée du désir (*vigatarāga*), il le sait en vérité», cela est-il bien dit?...

Même argumentation en ce qui regarde la pensée *sadveṣa*, *vigatadveṣa*, *samoha*, *vigatamoha*, *saṃkṣipta*, *vikṣipta*, *līna*, *pragṛhīta*, *uddhata*, *anuddhata*, *avyupaśānta*, *upaśānta*, *asamāhita*, *samāhita*, *abhāvita*, *bhāvita*, *avimukta*, *vimukta* (voir Abhidharmakośa, VII, 11 *d*).

5 (4 *b* 14-5 *a* 7). ...On doit lui demander : Oui ou non, ce que dit Bhagavat dans le Sūtra, à savoir : «La sensation est de deux sortes, corporelle, mentale», cela est-il bien dit?

Il répond : Oui.

Lorsqu'on sent la sensation corporelle et la sensation mentale, dis-moi à quelle époque appartient alors la sensation? Est-elle passée, future, présente? — S'il répond qu'elle est passée, c'est donc que le passé existe; il ne doit pas dire que le passé n'existe pas : soutenir que le passé n'existe pas est illogique; s'il répond qu'elle est future, même critique. S'il répond qu'elle est présente, c'est donc qu'une personne sent en même temps deux sensations, la corporelle et la mentale — hypothèse inadmissible. S'il admet que cette hypothèse est inadmissible, il ne doit pas dire qu'on sent la sensation présente. S'il répond enfin que la sensation n'est ni passée, ni future, ni présente, il contredit le Sūtra.

Le śramaṇa Maudgalyāyana dit : Le passé et le futur n'existent pas...
[Discussion du texte sur les trois sortes de sensation, l'agréable, la désagréable, l'indifférente.]

6 (5 *a* 8-13). Discussion du texte : «En raison de l'organe mental (*manas*) et des *dharmas* naît la connaissance mentale (*manovijñāna*).»

Au moment où naît le *manovijñāna*, de quelle époque est le *manas?* est-il passé, futur, présent ?... S'il répond que le *manas* est présent, il admet que dans une personne il y a rencontre de deux pensées simultanées... (*apūrvam acarimam cittadvayasaṃnipātaḥ*)[1].

7 (5 *a* 13-19). Discussion du texte : «Les dents contre les dents, la langue contre le palais, par la pensée il dompte, discipline, exerce la pensée»[2].

La pensée qu'il dompte est-elle passée, future, présente ?... S'il répond qu'elle est présente, il s'ensuit que la pensée qui dompte et celle qui est domptée sont simultanées...

8 (5 *a* 20-5 *b* 6). Discussion du texte : «Bhagavat dit au Bhikṣu Puṣkarasārin : L'homme comporte dix-huit considérations par l'esprit» (*manopavicāras*)[3].

Lorsque, l'œil ayant vu le visible, on considère (*upavicarati*) le visible agréable, les autres dix-sept *manopavicāras* sont-ils passés, futurs, présents ?

IV

1 (5 *b* 9-20). Le śramaṇa Maudgalyāyana dit : Il y a une pensée dont l'objet est inexistant[4].

On lui demandera : Oui ou non, ce que Bhagavat dit dans le Sūtra, à savoir : «Bhikṣus, il est appelé *vijñāna* parce qu'il discerne, parce qu'il discerne (*vijānāti vijānātīti vijñānam*). Et que discerne-t-il ? Il discerne le visible; il discerne le son, l'odeur, la saveur, le tangible, les *dharmas*», cela est-il bien dit...?

Il répond : Oui.

Reconnais la position illogique où tu tombes! Si tu dis qu'il y a une pensée dont l'objet est inexistant, alors tu ne dois pas approuver ce que Bhagavat dit dans le Sūtra : «Bhikṣus, il est appelé *vijñāna* parce qu'il discerne, parce qu'il

(1) En effet, par *manas* ou *mana-indriya* «organe mental», il faut entendre la pensée qui vient de disparaître, non pas le «cœur» (*hṛdaya*) comme on pense à Ceylan (Kośa, I, 17).

(2) Majjhima, I, 242 : *yan nūnāhaṃ dantehi dantam ādhāya jivhāya tālum āhacca cetasā cittam abhiniggaṇheyyam abhinippīleyyam abhisaṃtāpeyyam.*

(3) 補穡揭羅娑利. C'est le Pukkusāti de Majjhima, III, 239.

(4) *Asty abhāvālambanaṃ cittam* — Voir Kośa, V, 25; Kathāvatthu, IX, 6-7.

discerne. Et que discerne-t-il ? Le visible, le son, l'odeur, la saveur, le tangible, les *dharmas*.» — Si maintenant tu approuves ce que Bhagavat dit dans le Sūtra : «Bhikṣus, il est appelé *vijñāna*... », alors tu ne dois pas dire qu'il y a une pensée dont l'objet est inexistant : dire qu'il y a semblable pensée est illogique.

Il dit : Il y a certainement une pensée dont l'objet est inexistant. Quelle pensée ? Celle qui porte sur le passé, celle qui porte sur le futur.

On lui demandera : Oui ou non, cela est-il bien dit ce que Bhagavat dit dans le Sūtra à l'ancien pêcheur (*kaivartapūrva*) le Bhikṣu Svāti : «Bhikṣu, suivant que le *vijñāna* naît en raison de telle ou telle cause, de telle ou telle condition, étant né il prend tel ou tel nom. En raison de l'œil et du visible naît un *vijñāna* : ce *vijñāna* prend le nom de *vijñāna* de l'œil. De même pour les *vijñānas* de l'oreille, de l'odorat, de la langue, du corps et du *manas*». (Majjhima, I, 259.)

Il répond : Oui, cela est bien dit.

Reconnais la position illogique où tu tombes. Si tu dis qu'il y a certainement une pensée ayant un objet inexistant, tu ne dois pas approuver ce que dit Bhagavat à Svāti...

2 (6 *a* 1-7). Le śramaṇa Maudgalyāyana dit : Le passé et le futur n'existent pas; le présent et l'inconditionné existent.

On lui demandera : Oui ou non, un homme muni de honte, de pudeur, de repentir, de discipline, prenant plaisir dans la règle, obtiendra-t-il les quatre espèces de *dhyāna* mondain[1] ?

Il répond : Oui.

Alors, à la fin de la méditation de cet Āyuṣman, ses compagnons en vie religieuse viennent et lui demandent : Āyuṣman, il faut déclarer ce que tu as réalisé et obtenu. Il répond : J'ai obtenu les quatre espèces de *dhyāna* mondain.

On doit demander à Maudgalyāyana : Ce que cet homme déclare avoir réalisé, est-ce passé, futur ou présent?... S'il répond que c'est présent, alors il y aura, dans une personne, deux modes de pensée, ce qui est déclaré et ce qui déclare; en outre, il faut que cet homme, tout en étant recueilli, parle (*vācībheda*)[2]. S'il admet que les deux pensées ne sont pas simultanées et qu'on ne parle pas dans le recueillement, alors il ne doit pas dire que l'objet de la déclaration est présent : dire que l'objet de la déclaration est présent, est

[1] C'est-à-dire les quatre *dhyānas* non associés à la connaissance pure (*anāsrava*) des vérités. Ce sont les «extases du monde profane» de J. Przyluski, *Légende d'Açoka*, p. 390.

[2] Comparer Kathāvatthu, II, 5.

illogique. S'il dit que les *dhyānas* déclarés ne sont ni futurs, ni passés, ni présents, alors cet homme s'attribue faussement des qualités surnaturelles et il mérite d'être expulsé.

3 (6 *a* 8-17). Le śramaṇa Maudgalyāyana dit : Le passé et le futur n'existent pas; le présent et l'inconditionné existent.

On doit lui demander : Oui ou non, est-ce bien dit, bien expliqué, bien promulgué, ce que Bhagavat dit dans le Sūtra : «Bhikṣus, il y a cinq facultés (*indriyas*) : foi, énergie, mémoire, recueillement, discernement. En raison de l'excellence (*adhimātra*), de la vivacité (*tīkṣṇatva*), de la perfection(?), de la plénitude de ces cinq *indriyas*, on est Arhat de la classe *ubhayatobhāgavimukta*. Par les mêmes *indriyas* plus petits (*tanu*), plus faibles (*mṛdu*), on est *prajñāvimukta;* par les mêmes *indriyas* plus petits, plus faibles, on est *kāyasākṣin;* ...on est *dṛṣṭiprāpta;* ...on est *śraddhādhimukta;* ...on est *dharmānusārin;* par les mêmes *indriyas* plus petits, plus faibles, on est *śraddhānusārin.* C'est ainsi, ô Bhikṣus, qu'à l'excellence ou hiérarchie (*pāramitā*) des *indriyas* correspond la hiérarchie des fruits; qu'à la hiérarchie des fruits correspond la hiérarchie des saints (*pudgalapāramitā*). Les cinq *indriyas* ne sont pas inefficaces. Si ces cinq *indriyas* manquent complètement à quelqu'un, je déclare qu'il est homme du dehors, appartenant à la classe des Pṛthagjanas» (comparer Saṃyutta, V, 202; Kośa, II, 9).

Il répond : Oui, c'est bien dit.

Lorsque le saint de la classe *śaikṣa* (non Arhat) produit une pensée souillée (*paryavasthita*), à quelle époque appartiennent les cinq *indriyas?* Sont-ils passés, futurs, présents? S'il répond qu'ils sont passés, alors le passé existe. S'il répond qu'ils sont futurs, alors le futur existe. S'il répond qu'ils sont présents, c'est donc que, dans une même personne, en même temps, il y a deux pensées, la pensée de Śaikṣa et la pensée souillée : ce qui est impossible. S'il admet en effet que cela est impossible, il ne doit pas dire que les *indriyas* sont présents. S'il dit que les *indriyas* ne sont ni passés, ni futurs, ni présents, alors le Śaikṣa, lorsqu'il produit une pensée souillée, est un homme du dehors, est un Pṛthagjana, est à ranger dans la catégorie des Pṛthagjanas du dehors.

4 (6 *a* 17-6 *b* 2). Le śramaṇa Maudgalyāyana dit : Le passé et le futur n'existent pas; le présent et l'inconditionné existent.

On doit lui demander : Oui ou non, est-ce bien dit ce que Bhagavat dit dans le Sūtra lorsque, parlant à Aniruddha dans le Mahāpuruṣavitarka, il déclare : « Le peu-de-désir (*alpecchatā*) est Dharma, le beaucoup-de-désir est Adharma »[1] ?

Il répond : Oui.

Le peu-de-désir, quelle sorte de *dharma* est-ce là?

Il répond : C'est un *dharma* mental (*caitta*), associé à la pensée (*cittasaṃprayukta*).

Si un Arhat, qui se trouve dans le kāmadhātu[2], entre dans la *nirodhasamāpatti*, ou recueillement de l'arrêt de la pensée (*saṃjñāvedita*) (Abhidharmakośa, II, 43), à quelle époque appartient son peu-de-désir? est-il passé, futur, présent? S'il répond qu'il est passé, c'est donc que le passé existe. S'il répond qu'il est futur, c'est donc que le futur existe. S'il répond qu'il est présent, alors l'Arhat en question n'est pas entré dans la *nirodhasamāpatti*. S'il répond qu'il n'est ni passé, ni futur, ni présent, c'est donc qu'un Arhat, qui se trouve dans le kāmadhātu, une fois entré dans la *nirodhasamāpatti*, ne possède pas le peu-de-désir.

5 (6 *b* 3-7). Le śramaṇa Maudgalyāyana dit : Le passé et le futur n'existent pas...

On lui demandera : Approuves-tu ce que dit Bhagavat dans le Sūtra? Bhagavat dit à l'Āyuṣman Rāhula : « Celui qui, le sachant, dit un mensonge, et n'a ni honte, ni respect, ni repentir, je dis qu'il n'y a pas de péché qu'il ne fasse[3]. »

Oui, répond-il, cela est bien dit.

Honte, respect, quelle sorte de *dharma* est-ce là?

C'est un *dharma* mental, répond-il, un *dharma* associé à la pensée.

Si un Arhat né dans le kāmadhātu[4] entre dans la *nirodhasamāpatti* « recueillement de l'arrêt des notions et des sensations », de quelle époque sont sa honte et son respect? sont-elles passées, futures, présentes? Si Maudgalyāyana

(1) 少欲是法大欲非法. Voir Aṅguttara, IV, 228, et Dīgha, III, 287, qui énumèrent les huit *mahāpurisavitakkas*. Le texte pāli diffère : *appicchassāyaṃ dhammo nāyaṃ dhammo mahicchassa*...

(2) C'est-à-dire un Arhat qui est un homme. Certains saints acquièrent la qualité d'Arhat après être devenus des dieux.

(3) Majjhima, I, 415 : *yassa kassa ci sampajānamusāvādā natthi lajjā nāhaṃ tassa kiṃ ci pāpam akaraṇīyam ti vadāmi*. C'est pourquoi le renoncement au mensonge est un « membre » de toutes les disciplines religieuses, Kośa, IV, 34 *a-b*, Senart, *Piyadasi*, II, 208, 213, S. Lévi, *J. As.*, 1896, I, 475.

(4) Dans l'Ārūpyadhātu la *hrī* et l'*apatrāpya* n'existent pas. Kośa, II, 32.

répond : «passées», il confesse que le passé existe; s'il répond : «futures», il confesse que le futur existe; s'il répond «présentes», comment l'Arhat en question peut-il se trouver dans la *nirodhasamāpatti?*; s'il répond : ni passées, ni futures, ni présentes», c'est donc que l'Arhat, né dans le kāmadhatu, est privé de honte et de respect une fois entré dans la *nirodhasamāpatti*.

6 (6 *b* 7-7 *a* 4). Le śramaṇa Maudgalyāyana dit : Le passé et le futur n'existent pas...

On lui demandera : Oui ou non, est-ce bien dit ce que Bhagavat dit dans le Sūtra? — «Il y a neuf demeures des êtres (*sattvāvāsa*) : il y a des êtres matériels divers de corps, divers de notions, à savoir les hommes et certains dieux : tel est le premier *sattvāvāsa*... [1]»

Il répond : Oui, c'est bien dit.

Si un Arhat qui se trouve dans le kāmadhātu entre dans la *nirodhasamāpatti*, dans quel *sattvāvāsa* réside-t-il?

Il répond : Parmi les êtres divers de corps, divers de notion (*nānātvakāyā nānātvasaṃjñinaḥ*) (premier *sattvāvāsa*).

A quelle époque appartient la notion en raison de laquelle tu dis que cet Arhat possède notion? est-elle passée, future ou présente? — S'il répond qu'elle est passée, alors le passé existe; s'il répond qu'elle est future, alors le futur existe; s'il répond qu'elle est présente, alors cet Arhat n'est pas entré dans la *nirodhasamāpatti*, recueillement où la notion (*saṃjñā*) disparaît. S'il répond que la notion n'est ni passée, ni future, ni présente, on admettra qu'un Arhat se trouvant dans le kāmadhātu, entré dans la *nirodhasamāpatti*, étant exempt de notion, est un dieu de la classe nommée «Êtres sans notion» ou «Inconscients» (*asaṃjñisattva*) : donc il est un *asaṃjñisattvopaga* (cinquième *sattvāvāsa*).

7 (7 *a* 5-10). [Même début; discussion du texte : «Tous les êtres durent par l'aliment» (Abhidharmakośa, III, 38 *d*; Dīgha, III, 211, etc.).]

Quel est l'aliment des dieux inconscients (*asaṃjñisattvadeva*)?

Il répond : C'est *sparśa*, *manaḥsaṃcetanā* et *vijñāna*.

A quelle époque appartient cet aliment? est-il passé, futur ou présent?

S'il répond qu'il est passé... S'il répond qu'il est présent, alors ces dieux ne sont pas des *asaṃjñisattvas*. S'il répond qu'il n'est ni passé, ni futur, ni

[1] Voir Abhidharmakośa, III, 5 et suiv.; Dīgha, III, 263; Mahāvyutpatti, 119, etc. Les sources palies portent : «à savoir les hommes, certains dieux, certains *vinipātikas*».

présent, alors il rejette le Sūtra d'après lequel tous les êtres durent par l'aliment...

8 (7 *a* 11-20). [Même début; discussion du texte : «Il y a six corps de connaissances, connaissance de l'œil..., connaissance mentale».]

Y a-t-il quelqu'un qui, en ce qui regarde la connaissance de l'œil, a vu, voit ou verra que cette connaissance est impermanente, douloureuse, vide, non substantielle? qui a vu, voit ou verra la cause (*hetu*) de cette connaissance (*hetu, samudaya, prabhava, pratyaya*)? qui a vu, voit ou verra la destruction de cette connaissance (*nirodha, śānta, praṇīta, niḥsaraṇa*)? qui a vu, voit ou verra le chemin par lequel on abandonne cette connaissance (*mārga, nyāya, pratipatti, nairyāṇika*)[1]?

Il répond : Oui.

Ce qui est l'objet de la vue, est-ce passé, futur, présent?... S'il répond que cet objet est présent, alors, dans une seule personne, il y a rencontre de deux pensées : l'objet de la vue et le sujet de la vue...

Si l'objet n'est ni passé, ni futur, ni présent, personne ne verra que la connaissance de la vue est impermanente...; personne n'a obtenu, n'obtient, n'obtiendra le Nirvāṇa. — Même argumentation en ce qui regarde les cinq autres connaissances.

9 (7 *b* 1-5). Le śramaṇa Maudgalyāyana dit : Le passé et le futur n'existent pas...

On doit lui demander : Oui ou non, est-ce bien dit ce que Bhagavat dit dans le Sūtra? — à savoir : «Bhikṣus, il faut abandonner les «passions» ou *āsravas*.»

Il répond : Oui, c'est bien dit.

L'*āsrava* qu'il faut abandonner, est-il passé, futur ou présent?

S'il répond : «On abandonne l'*āsrava* passé», il doit dire que le passé existe, il ne doit pas dire que le passé n'existe pas; dire que le passé n'existe pas est contradictoire. S'il répond : «On abandonne l'*āsrava* futur», il doit dire que le futur existe; il ne doit pas dire que le futur n'existe pas; dire que le futur n'existe pas est contradictoire. S'il répond : «On abandonne l'*āsrava* présent», alors, dans une même personne, il y a en même temps deux modes ou complexes de pensée, ce qui est abandonné et ce qui abandonne : supposition inadmissible. S'il dit que, en effet, deux pensées ne peuvent être simul-

(1) L'auteur énumère les quatre «aspects» (*ākāras*) de chaque vérité, Mahāvyutpatti, 54; Kośa, VII, 13.

tanées, alors il ne doit pas dire qu'on abandonne l'*āsrava* présent; dire qu'on abandonne l'*āsrava* présent est contradictoire. S'il dit qu'on n'abandonne pas l'*āsrava* passé, ni le futur, ni le présent, alors ce que Bhagavat a bien dit, expliqué, déclaré dans le Sūtra : «Bhikṣus, il faut abandonner les *āsravas*», ce Sūtra dit par Bhagavat, tu le rejettes, tu le contredis, tu le repousses.

CHAPITRE II.

Pudgalaskandhaka[1].

I

1 *a* (7 *b* 9-8 *a* 5). Le Pudgalavādin dit : En vérité, en réalité, le Pudgala est constaté, est connu, est, existe. Donc il y a certainement un Pudgala[2].

Le Śūnyatāvādin lui demande : Oui ou non, est-ce bien dit, bien défini, bien déclaré[3] ce que Bhagavat dit dans le Sūtra? Il dit : «les cinq destinées (*gati*) sont déterminées et ne se confondent pas, à savoir les destinées d'être

(1) Ce chapitre, à tenir compte des Uddānas, se divise en trois paragraphes : Premier *uddāna* (7 *b* 8) : 1. destinées (*gati*), 2. *pudgalas* de huit espèces, 3. trois catégories (*rāśi*), 4. trois espèces, 5. fait par soi, 6. vu-entendu-senti-connu en dernier lieu. — Deuxième *uddāna* (12 *b* 18) : 1. dire quel est l'objet de la bienveillance, 2. catégories de connaissance (*vijñānakāya*), 3. *smṛtyupasthāna*, 4. membres de la Bodhi, 5. conditionné (*saṃskṛta*) et inconditionné. — Troisième *uddāna* (14 à 19) : 1. le Pudgala est inexistant, vide : le concours des *dharmas*, 2. chacun son effet, 3. par combien connaît-on?, 4. naissance ensemble, 5. nature de la pensée impermanente, 6. clair, 7. ayant la soif pour cause. — I, 1 correspond à Kathāvatthu, 1, 1, 158-161; I, 2 à 1, 1, 221; I, 5 à 1, 1, 212; II, 5 à 1, 1, 225-227.

(2) 補特伽羅論者作如是言諦義勝義補特伽羅可得可證現有等有是故定有補特伽羅. — Kathāvatthu : *saccikaṭṭhaparamaṭṭhena puggala upalabbhati.* — *K'o tě* correspond probablement à *upalabhyate*, bien qu'on ait couramment *tě* =*prāp.*, mais *tě*=*upalabdhi; k'o tchéng* =*prāpyate* (d'après Kośa, trad. Hiuan-tsang, VI, 14 *b* 3, *nêng tchéng*=*prāpaka*) plutôt que *sākṣātkriyate; tèng yeòu* =*saṃvidyate; hién yeòu* fait difficulté, *hién* correspond normalement à *abhi*.

(3) 善語善詞善説 = *sūktam, suniruktam* (?), *subhāṣitam* ou *sunirdiṣṭam.*

infernal, d'animal, de preta, de dieu et d'homme. A part, la destinée d'être infernal... à part, la destinée d'homme».

Le Pudgalavādin répond : Oui, c'est bien dit (*om ity āha*).

Le Śūnyatāvādin demande encore : Oui ou non, arrive-t-il que [le Pudgala], tombant par la mort de la destinée d'être infernal, renaisse dans la destinée d'animal.

Le Pudgalavādin répond : Oui.

Reconnais que tu tombes dans une position contradictoire[1]. S'il y a cinq destinées déterminées et distinctes, destinées d'être infernal, d'animal, etc.; si la destinée d'être infernal est à part, si la destinée d'animal est à part, alors il ne faut pas dire que [le Pudgala], tombant par la mort de la destinée d'être infernal, renaît dans la destinée d'animal : ta seconde réponse n'est pas logique. Si tu soutiens maintenant que [le Pudgala], tombant par la mort de la destinée d'être infernal, renaît dans la destinée d'animal, alors il ne faut pas dire que les cinq destinées sont déterminées et distinctes et que chacune est à part. Dire que ces destinées sont déterminées, distinctes, existant à part, c'est illogique.

Le Pudgalavādin dit : Certainement il arrive que [le Pudgala], tombant par la mort de la destinée d'être infernal, renaisse dans la destinée d'animal.

On doit lui demander : Oui ou non, est-ce le même [*sa eva saḥ*]?

Le Pudgalavādin répond : Non (7 *b* 16).

Reconnais que tu tombes dans une position contradictoire. Si certainement il arrive que [le Pudgala], tombant par la mort de la destinée d'être infernal, renaisse dans la destinée d'animal, alors il faut dire que c'est le même : ta réponse négative est illogique. Si tu n'admets pas que ce soit le même, alors il ne faut pas dire qu'il arrive certainement que [le Pudgala], tombant par la mort de la destinée d'être infernal, renaisse dans la destinée d'animal. Dire qu'il tombe d'une destinée et renaît dans une autre, c'est illogique.

Si le Pudgalavādin répond : C'est le même [= celui qui meurt est le même qui naît], il faut lui demander : Oui ou non, l'être infernal [qui meurt] est-il l'animal [qui renaît]?

Le Pudgalavādin répond : Non.

Reconnais que tu tombes dans une position contradictoire. Si c'est le même [qui meurt et qui renaît], alors il faut dire que l'être infernal est

[1] 汝聽墮負. Les deux derniers caractères (dans Bukkyō Daijiten, p. 1181) = *nigraha*. — Kathāvatthu : *ājānāhi niggaham*.

l'animal : ta réponse est illogique. Si tu n'admets pas que l'être infernal soit l'animal, alors il ne faut pas dire que c'est le même [qui meurt et renaît]. Dire que le même meurt et renaît, c'est illogique.

Si le Pudgalavādin dit : Il est différent [=ce n'est pas le même qui meurt et qui renaît] (*ayaṃ tasmād anyaḥ?*). On doit lui demander : Oui ou non, l'être infernal est-il anéanti et un autre être naît-il dans la matrice animale?

Le Pudgalavādin répond : Non.

Reconnais que tu tombes dans une position contradictoire. Si celui qui meurt est différent de celui qui naît, alors il faut dire que l'être infernal est anéanti et qu'un autre être naît dans la matrice animale : ta réponse est illogique. Si tu n'admets pas que l'être infernal soit anéanti et qu'un autre être naisse dans la matrice animale [8 *a*], alors il ne faut pas dire que l'être qui renaît diffère de celui qui meurt : dire qu'il est différent est illogique.

Si le Pudgalavādin dit : « Que [l'animal] soit le même [que l'être infernal] ou en soit différent, il est impossible de le dire », — on doit lui demander : Oui ou non, quant à ce que vous avez dit : « Certainement il arrive que [le Pudgala], tombant par la mort de la destinée d'être infernal, renaisse dans la destinée d'animal », est-il aussi impossible de dire que [le Pudgala] soit le même ou différent? (8 *a* 2.)

Le Pudgalavādin répond : Non.

Reconnais que tu tombes dans une position contradictoire. S'il est impossible de dire que [l'animal] soit le même que [l'être infernal] ou qu'il en soit différent, alors il faut aussi reconnaître qu'il est impossible de dire que [le Pudgala], tombant par la mort de la destinée d'être infernal et renaissant comme animal, soit identique ou différent. Ta réponse est illogique. Si, au contraire, tu n'admets pas l'impossibilité de décrire comme identique ou différent [le Pudgala] qui, mourant comme être infernal, renaît comme animal, alors il ne faut pas dire qu'il est impossible de dire que [l'animal] soit le même que [l'être infernal] ou qu'il en soit différent.

b. [Même argumentation lorsqu'on examine l'être infernal rené en qualité de *preta.*]

c (8 *a* 5-8 *b* 5). [On examine le cas de l'être infernal rené en qualité d'homme.]

...Si tu n'admets pas que l'être infernal soit l'homme, alors il ne faut pas dire que c'est le même [qui meurt et qui renaît]. Dire que c'est le même est illogique.

En outre, si le Pudgalavādin dit que c'est le même, il faut lui demander : Oui ou non, n'est-il pas vrai que dans la destinée d'être infernal manque la capacité de produire les *indriyas* purs (foi, énergie, etc.), les forces, les membres de la Bodhi, tandis que cette capacité existe dans la destinée d'homme?

Le Pudgalavādin répond : Oui.

On doit lui demander : Oui ou non, celui qui ne possède pas cette capacité est-il celui qui possède cette capacité?

Le Pudgalavādin répond : Non.

Reconnais la contradiction. Si c'est le même [qui meurt et qui renaît], alors il faut dire que celui qui ne possède pas cette capacité est celui qui la possède : ta réponse est illogique. Si tu n'admets pas que celui qui ne possède pas cette capacité est celui qui la possède, alors il ne faut pas dire que c'est le même [qui meurt et renaît].

Si le Pudgalavādin dit : Il est différent [= ce n'est pas le même qui meurt et renaît], on doit lui demander : Oui ou non, l'être infernal est-il anéanti et un autre être naît-il dans la destinée d'homme?...

d. [Même argumentation lorsqu'on examine l'être infernal rené en qualité de dieu. Même argumentation au sujet des destinées d'animal, de preta, de dieu et d'homme. Il faut, le cas échéant, omettre le paragraphe relatif à la capacité et à l'incapacité des *indriyas* purs, etc.]

2 *a* (8 *b* 5-9 *a* 10). Le Pudgalavādin dit : En vérité, en réalité, le Pudgala est constaté...

Le Śūnyatāvādin lui demande : Oui ou non, est-ce bien dit, bien défini, bien déclaré ce que Bhagavat dit dans le Sūtra? Il dit : Il y a huit *pudgalas* déterminés, ne se confondant pas : le *srotaāpannaphalapratipannaka*... l'Arhat; autre et à part le *srotaāpannaphalapratipannaka*... autre et à part l'Arhat.

Le Pudgalavādin répond : Oui, c'est bien dit.

On lui demande : Oui ou non, le Pudgala qu'on nomme *srotaāpannaphalapratipannaka* obtient-il le fruit de *srotaāpanna?*

Le Pudgalavādin répond : Oui.

Reconnais la contradiction. S'il y a huit *pudgalas* déterminés, distincts, à part, à savoir le *srotaāpannaphalapratipannaka*... l'Arhat, alors il ne faut pas dire que le *srotaāpannaphalapratipannaka* obtient le fruit de *srotaāpanna :* ta réponse est illogique. Si maintenant tu admets que le *srotaāpannaphalapratipannaka* obtient le fruit de *srotaāpanna,* alors il ne faut pas dire que les huit *pud-*

galas sont déterminés... Dire que les huit *pudgalas* sont déterminés..., c'est illogique (8 *b* 16).

Le Pudgalavādin dit : Certainement le Pudgala nommé *srotaāpannaphalapratipannaka* obtient le fruit de *srotaāpanna.*

On doit lui demander : Oui ou non, est-ce le même (*sa eva saḥ*)?

Le Pudgalavādin répond : Non.

Reconnais la contradiction. Si le Pudgala nommé *srotaāpannaphalapratipannaka* obtient le fruit de *srotaāpanna*, alors il faut dire que c'est le même [qui est *srotaāpannaphalapratipannaka* et *srotaāpanna*] : ta réponse est donc illogique. Si tu n'admets pas que ce soit le même, alors il ne faut pas dire que le *srotaāpannaphalapratipannaka* obtient le fruit de *srotaāpanna* : dire qu'il l'obtient est illogique (8 *b* 19),

Si le Pudgalavādin dit que c'est le même, on doit lui demander : Oui ou non, le candidat à un fruit (*pratipannaka*) est-il le résident dans un fruit (*phalastha*)?

Le Pudgalavādin répond : Non.

Reconnais la contradiction. Si c'est le même [qui est *srotaāpannaphalapratipannaka* et *srotaāpanna*], alors tu dois dire que le candidat est le résident. Si tu n'admets pas que le candidat soit le résident, alors tu ne dois pas dire que c'est le même [qui est *srotaāpannaphalapratipannaka* et *srotaāpanna*]. Dire que c'est le même est illogique (9 *a* 1).

En outre, si le Pudgalavādin dit que c'est le même [qui est *srotaāpannaphalapratipannaka* et *srotaāpanna*], il faut lui demander : Oui ou non, n'est-il pas vrai que le Pudgala nommé *srotaāpannaphalapratipannaka* n'est pas en possession d'un fruit, tandis que le *srotaāpanna* est en possession d'un fruit?

Le Pusgalavādin répond : Oui.

On lui demandera : Oui ou non, celui qui est en possession est-il celui qui n'est pas en possession ?

Le Pudgalavādin répond : Non.

Reconnais la contradiction. Si le Pudgala nommé *srotaāpannaphalapratipannaka*, qui n'est pas en possession d'un fruit, est ce même *srotaāpanna*, lequel est en possession d'un fruit, alors il faut dire que celui qui n'est pas en possession est celui qui est en possession : ta réponse est illogique. Si tu n'admets pas que celui qui n'est pas en possession soit celui qui est en possession, alors il ne faut pas dire que c'est le même [qui est *srotaāpannaphalapratipannaka* et *srotaāpanna*]. Dire que c'est le même, c'est illogique.

Si le Pudgalavādin dit que ce n'est pas le même, il faut lui demander : le *srotaāpannaphalapratipannaka* est-il anéanti ? naît-il un autre qui est le *srotaāpanna?* (9 *a* 4).

Le Pudgalavādin répond : Non.

Reconnais la contradiction. Si ce n'est pas le même [qui est *srotaāpannaphalapratipannaka* et *srotaāpanna*], alors il faut dire que le *srotaāpannaphalapratipannaka* est anéanti et qu'un autre naît qui est le *srotaāpanna* : ta réponse est illogique. Si tu n'admets pas l'anéantissement du *srotaāpannaphalapratipannaka* et la naissance d'un autre, du *srotaāpanna*, alors il ne faut pas dire que ce n'est pas le même [qui est *srotaāpannaphalapratipannaka* et *srotaāpanna*]. Dire cela, c'est illogique (9 *a* 6).

Si le Pudgalavādin dit : Il est impossible de dire que c'est le même [*srotaāpannaphalapratipannaka* qui est *srotaāpanna*], que c'est un autre, — alors on doit lui demander : Quant à ce que tu as dit, à savoir que le *srotaāpannaphalapratipannaka* obtient le fruit de *srotaāpanna*, est-il aussi impossible de dire que c'est le même, que c'est un autre ?

Le Pudgalavādin répond : Non.

Reconnais la contradiction. S'il est impossible de dire que c'est le même [*srotaāpannaphalapratipannaka* qui est *srotaāpanna*], de dire que c'est un autre, alors aussi il est impossible de dire que c'est le même, de dire que c'est un autre en ce qui concerne le *srotaāpannaphalapratipannaka* obtenant le fruit de *srotaāpanna* : ta réponse est illogique. Si tu n'admets pas ce second point, alors tu ne dois pas dire que le *srotaāpannaphalapratipannaka* ne peut être défini ni comme identique au *srotaāpanna*, ni comme différent du *srotaāpanna* : en disant cela, tu es illogique.

La relation qui existe entre le *srotaāpannaphalapratipannaka* et le *srotaāpanna*, existe entre le *sakṛdāgāmiphalapratipannaka* et le *sakṛdāgāmin*. Même argumentation, avec cette différence que le *sakṛdāgāmiphalapratipannaka* n'est pas nécessairement non-possesseur d'un fruit. [Il peut posséder le fruit de *srotaāpanna*] (9 *a* 10).

b (9 *a* 11 - 9 *b* 14). Le Pudgalavādin dit : En vérité, en réalité, le Pudgala est constaté...

Discussion du même texte que ci-dessus, les huit *pudgalas* : on examine si l'*anāgāmiphalapratipannaka* obtient le fruit d'*anāgāmin*.

c (9 *b* 14 - 10 *a* 18). Le Pudgalavādin dit : En vérité, en réalité, le Pudgala est constaté...

On examine si l'*arhatphalapratipannaka* obtient le fruit d'Arhat.

3 (10 *a* 19 - 11 *a* 19). Le Pudgalavādin dit : En vérité, en réalité, le Pudgala est constaté...

Oui ou non, est-ce bien dit ce que dit Bhagavat, à savoir «Il y a trois catégories (*rāśi*) déterminées, distinctes, à part : *samyaktvaniyatarāśi, mithyātvaniyatarāśi, aniyatarāśi*»[1] ?

On examine si un homme, un *pudgala*, peut passer de la catégorie des êtres «voués à la perte» dans la catégorie des êtres «non prédestinés», dans la catégorie des êtres «prédestinés au salut», etc. La discussion, qui se poursuit parallèlement aux précédentes, comporte plusieurs paragraphes introduits comme ci-dessus : «Le Pudgalavādin dit : Le Pudgala est constaté...» L'auteur signale quelques caractères des diverses «catégories» : par exemple, la personne qui se trouve dans la catégorie non prédestinée n'est qu'un champ de mérite limité; celle qui se trouve dans la catégorie prédestinée est un champ de mérite infini. Dire que la première, restant identique à elle-même (*sa eva saḥ*), passe dans la catégorie prédestinée au salut, c'est dire qu'un champ de mérite limité est un champ de mérite infini.

4 (11 *b* 5 - 11 *b* 13). Même argumentation, portant cette fois sur la distinction du Śaikṣa, de l'Aśaikṣa, du Naivaśaikṣanāśaikṣa : quelqu'un qui est Śaikṣa (un saint non-Arhat) peut-il, restant identique, devenir Aśaikṣa ou Arhat?

5 *a.* (11 *b* 14 - 12 *a* 11). Le Pudgalavādin dit : Il y a un moi (*ātman*), un être (*sattva*), un vivant (*jīva*), un être qui naît (*jantu*), un être qui se nourrit (*poṣa*), un mâle (*puruṣa*), un *pudgala*. Parce qu'il y a un *pudgala*, on fait des actions ou agréables à sentir [dans leur rétribution] (*sukhavedanīya*), ou désagréables à sentir, ou ni-désagréables-ni-agréables à sentir. Ayant fait des actions agréables à sentir, on éprouve des sensations agréables; ayant fait des actions désagréables à sentir, on éprouve des sensations désagréables; ayant fait des actions ni-désagréables-ni-agréables à sentir, on éprouve des sensations ni-désagréables-ni-agréables.

Le Śūnyatāvādin lui demande : Oui ou non, la peine et le plaisir sont-ils faits par soi?

Le Pudgalavādin répond : Non.

Reconnais la contradiction. S'il y a un moi, un être, un vivant... *et le reste jusque :* on éprouve des sensations ni-désagréables, ni-agréables, alors il faut dire que la peine et le plaisir sont faits par soi : ta réponse est illogique.

[1] Mahāvastu, I, 175, III, 318; Hoernle, *Mss. Remains,* I, 23; Mahāvyutpatti, 95, 11-13; Abhidharmakośa, III, 44 *c-d;* IV, 80; Dīgha, III, 217; Puggalapaññatti, p. 13; Dhammasaṅgaṇi, 1028, Nettippakaraṇa, 96, 99.

Mais si tu n'admets pas que la peine et le plaisir sont faits par soi, alors il ne faut pas dire : «Il y a un moi, un être vivant» *et le reste*. Dire que : «Il y a un moi» *et le reste*, c'est illogique (11 *b* 14 - 12 *a* 2).

Si le Pudgalavādin dit : La peine et le plaisir sont faits par soi[1], — il faut lui demander : Est-ce bien dit ce que Bhagavat dit dans le Sūtra ? Bhagavat dit au Tīrthika parivrājaka Timburu[1] : «Timburu, la sensation est la même chose que celui qui sent, [ainsi disent] ceux qui soutiennent que la peine et le plaisir sont faits par soi : mais ce n'est pas, Timburu, ce que je dis»[2].

Le Pudgalavādin répond : Oui.

Reconnais la contradiction. Si la peine et le plaisir sont faits par soi, alors il ne faut pas dire que ce que Bhagavat à Timburu est bien dit : ta réponse est illogique. Si maintenant tu soutiens que ce que Bhagavat dit à Timburu est bien dit, alors il ne faut pas dire que la peine et le plaisir sont faits par soi : dire cela, c'est illogique.

Si le Pudgalavādin dit : La peine et le plaisir sont faits par un autre, — alors il faut lui demander s'il approuve ce que Bhagavat dit aussitôt après à Timburu : «Autre la sensation, autre celui qui sent. Si on veut que la peine et le plaisir soient faits par un autre, ce n'est pas ce que je dis»...

b (12 *a* 12 - 12 *b* 7). Même début que ci-dessus : Le Pudgalavādin dit : Il y a un moi, un être... il éprouve des sensations ni-désagréables-ni-agréables.

Le Śūnyatāvādin lui demande : Oui ou non, celui qui fait l'action est-il le même qui sent la sensation (*sa karoti sa vedayati*) ?

Le Pudgalavādin répond : Non.

Reconnais la contradiction. S'il y a un moi ... qui éprouve des sensations ni-désagréables-ni-agréables, alors il faut dire que celui qui fait l'action est le même qui sent la sensation : ta réponse est illogique. Si maintenant tu n'admets pas que celui qui fait l'action soit le même que celui qui sent, alors il ne faut pas dire : Il y a un moi... Dire : Il y a un moi..., cela est illogique (12 20).

Si le Pudgalavādin dit : «Celui qui fait l'action est le même qui sent la sensation», — alors il faut lui demander s'il approuve ce que Bhagavat dit dans le Sūtra à un Brâhmane : «Brâhmane, dire que celui qui fait l'action est le

[1] Saṃyutta, II, 19 : kiṃ nu kho bho gotama sayaṃkataṃ dukkham... — Sur le problème du *svayaṃkṛta duḥkha*, Madhyamakavṛtti, XII, 1; Udāna, VI, 5; Kathāvatthu, I, 1, 212; VII, 6, 1.

[2] Saṃyutta, II, 23, Sūtra de Timbaruka 鈷部盧 (...*sā vedanā so vediyati*...).

même qui sent la sensation, c'est tomber dans la vue extrême de la permanence (*śāśvatānta*).»

Le Pudgalavādin répond : Oui.

Reconnais la contradiction. Si celui qui fait l'action est le même qui sent la sensation, alors il ne faut pas dire que ce que dit Bhagavat au Brâhmane est bien dit. Si tu te refuses à condamner le Sūtra, il ne faut pas soutenir l'identité de l'agent et du mangeur du fruit.

Si le Pudgalavādin répond : Autre celui qui fait l'action, autre celui qui sent la sensation, on lui oppose la déclaration de Bhagavat : «Brâhmane, dire que celui qui fait l'action est autre, que celui qui sent la sensation est autre, c'est tomber dans la vue extrême de l'anéantissement» (*ucchedānta*).

6. (12 *b* 8-16). Le Pudgalavādin dit : Il y a un *ātman*, un *sattva*, un *jīva*, un *jantu*, un *poṣa*, un *puruṣa*, un *pudgala*. Parce qu'il y a un Pudgala, relativement aux *dharmas* vus, entendus, sentis, connus, il y a acquisition, recherche, considération mentale.

Le Śūnyatāvādin demande : Considères-tu comme bien dit ce que Bhagavat, dans le Sūtra, dit au Bhikṣu Ariṣtha l'ancien ânier? Bhagavat lui dit : «L'acquisition, la recherche, la considération mentale relativement aux *dharmas* vus, entendus, sentis, connus, tout cela il reconnaît en vérité que ce n'est pas *ātman*, n'est pas «mien», n'est pas mon *ātman* [1]».

Le Pudgalavādin reconnait que c'est bien dit.

Reconnais donc la contradiction ! Si tu dis . . . il ne faut pas dire que le Sūtra est bien dit . . .

II

1 (12 *b* 18-13 *a* 18). Le Śūnyatāvādin dit : En vérité, en réalité, le Pudgala n'est pas constaté, n'est pas perçu, n'est pas, n'existe pas. Donc il n'y a pas de Pudgala.

Le Pudgalavādin demande : Quel est donc l'objet de la bienveillance (*maitryālambana*)?

[1] Le Sūtra visé est une recension de Majjhima, I, 135, où l'interlocuteur de Bhagavat est l'ancien «tourmenteur de vautour», *gaddhabādhipubba* (comp. Cullavagga, I, 32). Notre Ariṣtha est un ancien ânier 本牧驢 (*gardabha*...). — Il semble que les deux textes diffèrent. Le Majjhima donne : *yaṃ pidaṃ diṭṭhaṃ sutaṃ mutaṃ viññātaṃ pattaṃ pariyesitaṃ manasā taṃ pi netaṃ mama neso ham asmi na meso attā ti samanupassati*. D'après la version chinoise : *dṛṣṭaśrutamatavijñātadharmeṣu* (於所見聞覺知法中) *prāptam*... — Pour la nomenclature *dṛṣṭa*, *śruta*, etc., voir Abhidharmakośa, IV, 75.

Le Śūnyatāvādin répond : Les *dharmas* ont une nature propre [1], sont existants; ils reçoivent par métaphore le nom de *sattva* [2], être vivant : dans ce sens, la bienveillance a pour objet la série des *skandhas* «assumés» (*upātta*) [3].

Le Pudgalavādin demande : Dis-tu vraiment que la bienveillance a pour objet la série des *skandhas* assumés? [13 *a*.]

Le Śūnyatāvādin répond : Oui.

Le Pudgalavādin reprend et demande : Ce que Bhagavat dit dans le Sūtra [1] : «L'ascète entre dans le recueillement de bienveillance en pensant : Puissent les êtres vivants (*sattva*) être revêtus de bonheur !» cela est-il bien dit, défini, déclaré?

Le Śūnyatāvādin répond : Oui, c'est bien dit.

Le Pudgalavādin dit : Reconnais la contradiction où tu tombes! Si la bienveillance a pour objet la série des *skandhas* assumés, tu ne dois pas dire que le Sūtra s'exprime bien lorsqu'il dit : ... en pensant : «Puissent les êtres être heureux!...» Ta réponse affirmative à ma seconde question est contradictoire. Si maintenant tu dis que le Sūtra s'exprime bien, tu ne dois pas dire que la bienveillance a pour objet les *skandhas*. Dire que la bienveillance a pour objet les *skandhas* est contradictoire.

2. Le Śūnyatāvādin doit demander : Admets-tu que Bhagavat, dans le Sūtra, s'exprime bien lorsqu'il dit : «Il y a six catégories ou corps de connaissances (*vijñānakāya*), connaissance de la vue, de l'ouïe, de l'odorat, du goût, du tact, et connaissance mentale»?

Le Pudgalavādin répond : Oui.

Le Śūnyatāvādin demande : Avec laquelle de ces connaissances la bienveillance est-elle associée (*saṃprayukta*)? Avec la visuelle ou avec l'auditive...? — Si le Pudgalavādin répond : «Avec la connaissance visuelle», il est acquis que la bienveillance n'a pas pour objet les êtres, car la connaissance visuelle porte exclusivement sur les choses visibles, la couleur et la figure. Si le Pudgalavādin répond : «Avec la connaissance auditive», il est acquis que la bienveillance n'a pas pour objet les êtres, car cette connaissance porte exclusivement

(1) 性有等有 *svabhāvataḥ saṃvidyante?*

(2) 由想等想假說有情. Je ne sais que faire des mots *yeóu siang tèng siàng*. A traduire littéralement, on a : *saṃjñādisaṃjñayā sattvā iti prajñapyante.*

(3) Les *skandhas* «assumés» sont les «éléments» qui servent de support à la pensée et aux mentaux. La matière subtile qui constitue les organes des sens est assumée... (voir Abhidharmakośa, I, 34 *c-d*, p. 63 de ma traduction).

sur les sons... Si le Pudgalavādin répond : «Avec la connaissance mentale», il est acquis que la bienveillance n'a pas pour objet les êtres, car cette connaissance porte exclusivement sur les *dharmas*. Si le Pudgalavādin répond : «La bienveillance n'est associée à aucune des six connaissances», c'est donc qu'il y a une septième connaissance, la «connaissance des êtres» (*sattvavijñāna*), avec laquelle la bienveillance sera associée. Or Bhagavat n'a pas connu de son savoir de Bouddha (*abhisaṃbudh*) cette septième connaissance. Or Bhagavat, décrivant les «absences de crainte» (*vaiśāradya*, Aṅguttara, II, 8, Kośa, VII, 32), s'exprime en ces termes : «Je connais tous les *dharmas* de mon savoir de Bouddha. Qu'un religieux, un brâhmane, un dieu, Māra ou Brahmā, avec raison, me critique ou m'avertisse, disant que moi, le Bouddha, je ne connais pas du savoir de Bouddha un *dharma* quelconque, je n'en vois pas la possibilité et n'en voyant pas la possibilité, j'obtiens le calme, la sérénité, l'absence de crainte.» — Si tu affirmes l'existence d'une septième connaissance, en fait, tu accuses le Bouddha d'ignorance.

Le Pudgalavādin répond : Je n'accuse pas le Bouddha d'ignorance; le Bouddha connaît de son savoir de Bouddha la septième connaissance; mais il ne la proclame pas. (13 *a* 12.)

Mais, réplique le Śūnyatāvadin, il y a un texte : «Ānanda, en ce qui concerne les *dharmas*, je les proclame sans omission, à savoir les 4 *smṛtyupasthānas*, les 4 *samyakpradhānas*, les 4 *ṛddhipādas*, les 5 *indriyas*, les 5 *balas*, les 7 *saṃbodhyaṅgas*, les 8 *āryamārgāṅgas*. Ānanda, en ce qui concerne les *dharmas*, le Tathāgata ne fait pas le maître qui ferme la main, qui cache, qui, dans la crainte que d'autres ne sachent, n'explique pas ce qu'il connaît[1].» — Si tu dis que le Bouddha sait et ne proclame pas tu accuses le Bouddha de faire le maître qui ferme la main.

[1] 我於諸法無間宣傳..... 如來於法無有師拳謂自覆藏恐他知我無所識解. — Dīgha, II, 100 = Saṃyutta, V, 153 : *desito Ananda mayā dhammo anantaram abāhiraṃ katvā/natthānanda tathāgatassa dhammesu ācariyamuṭṭhi* : «I have preached the truth without making any distinction between exoteric and esoteric doctrine...» (Rhys Davids, O. Franke). — Notre texte omet *ahāhiraṃ* et traduit *anantaram* = sans intervalle (無間). Dans Mahāparinirvāṇa (Tokio, 9, 13 *a* 9) on a 我所說法內外已訖終不自稱所見通達 : Les *dharmas* que j'ai enseignés, tant intérieurs qu'extérieurs, sont au complet...; (car) je suis vieux. — Wogihara (Bodhisattvabhūmi) signale Jātaka, II, 221, 250, Milinda, p. 144. Ajouter Mahāvyutpatti, 245, 123, ROCKHILL, *Life*, p. 131 : «I am not one of those teachers unwilling to lend his books». — D'après Buddhaghosa cité *S.B.E.*, XI, p. 36, le maître qui ne livre son secret que sur le lit de mort.

Le Pudgalavādin répond : Je n'accuse pas Bhagavat d'ignorance, je ne l'accuse pas de faire le maître qui ferme la main. Bhagavat connaît de son savoir de Bouddha, mais il ne proclame pas. En effet, il a dit dans le Sūtra de la forêt des Śiṃśapās (Saṃyutta, V, 437) : «Bhiksus, jusqu'au nombre complet des feuilles des forêts de Śiṃśapās de cette grande terre, j'ai directement connaissance de ces *dharmas* (1). Quoique je les sache de mon savoir de Bouddha, je ne les dis pas aux autres.» C'est ainsi que Bhagavat, connaissant la septième connaissance, ne la proclame pas.

Le Śūnyatāvādin doit demander : Le Sūtra de la forêt de Śiṃśapās ne contient-il pas une conclusion? Bhagavat, en fait, continue et dit : «Les *dharmas* [que je n'enseigne pas] ne sont pas utiles au salut, au bien, au dharma, à la vie religieuse (*brahmacarya*), ils ne produisent pas l'intelligence (*abhijñā*), la Bodhi, le Nirvāṇa.» A supposer qu'existe votre Pudgala (2), il n'est pas utile au salut, au bien, au dharma, à la vie religieuse, il ne produit pas l'intelligence, la Bodhi, le Nirvāṇa : il est sans emploi. Donc le Pudgala n'existe pas.

3 (13 *a* 18-13 *b* 16). Même argumentation en remplaçant les six *vijñānas* par les quatre *smṛtyupasthānas*. Si la *maitrī* est associée au *kāyasmṛtyupasthāna*, c'est donc qu'elle a pour objet le corps... Il n'y a pas un cinquième *smṛtyupasthāna*, un *sattvasmṛtyupasthāna* auquel serait associée la *maitrī*.

4 (13 *b* 16-14 *a* 1). Même argumentation en remplaçant les six *vijñānas* par les sept membres de la Bodhi (*saṃbodhyaṅgas*)..... «Si la *maitrī* est associée au *smṛtisaṃbodhyaṅga*, c'est donc qu'elle a pour objet les *dharmas*.....»

5 (14 *a* 15-17). Le Pudgalavādin dit : «Le Pudgala existe...» Le Śūnyatāvādin demande : Le Pudgala, faut-il dire qu'il est *saṃskṛta*, qu'il est *asaṃskṛta*? S'il est *saṃskṛta*, on peut dire du Pudgala, comme des autres *saṃskṛtas*, qu'il naît, dure, se transforme, périt; s'il est *asaṃskṛta*, on peut dire du Pudgala, comme des autres *asaṃskṛtas* qu'il ne naît pas... — Bhagavat a dit : «Bhikṣu, je dis qu'il y a deux choses, le *saṃskṛtā*, l'*asaṃskṛta*; en dehors du *saṃskṛta* et de l'*asaṃskṛta*, il n'y a pas une autre chose». Donc il n'y a pas de Pudgala.

(1) ...我於彼法自然了知. — (2) ...設有如是補特伽羅.

III

1 *a* (14 *a* 20-14 *b* 8)[1]. Il y a six collections de connaissance (*vijñānakāya*), connaissance de l'œil ou de la vue (*cakṣurvijñāna*), de l'ouïe, de l'odorat, du goût, du tact, et connaissance mentale (*manovijñāna*).

En raison de l'œil et du visible (*rūpa*), naît la connaissance de l'œil. De la sorte (*evam*) la connaissance de l'œil connaît le visible, non pas le Pudgala[2]. Le Pudgala n'est pas connaissable (*vijñeya*) par la connaissance de l'œil : c'est seulement le visible qui est connaissable par la connaissance de l'œil. Donc la connaissance de l'œil n'est pas connaissance du Pudgala.

En outre, en raison de l'œil et du visible naît la connaissance de l'œil; par la rencontre des trois, contact. De la sorte, le contact de l'œil touche le visible, non pas le Pudgala. Le Pudgala n'est pas «touchable» par le contact de l'œil; c'est seulement le visible qui est touchable par le contact de l'œil. Donc le contact de l'œil n'est pas contact du Pudgala.

En outre, en raison de l'œil et du visible naît la connaissance de l'œil; par la rencontre des trois, contact (*sparśa*)[3]; en raison du contact naît la sensation. De la sorte, la sensation née du contact de l'œil sent le visible, non pas le Pudgala. Le Pudgala n'est pas «éprouvé» (*vedya*) par une sensation née du contact de l'œil : c'est seulement le visible qui est éprouvé par une sensation née du contact de l'œil. Donc la sensation qui naît du contact de l'œil n'est pas une sensation née du contact du Pudgala (*pudgalasparśajā vedanā*).

En outre, en raison de l'œil et du visible naît la connaissance de l'œil: par

(1) Le texte utilisé ici par Devaśarman est l'Ajitasūtra (jen king) : *cakṣuḥ pratītya rūpāṇi cotpadyate cakṣurvijñānam / trayāṇāṃ saṃnipātaḥ sparśaḥ / sahajā vedanā saṃjñā cetanā ca.* — Voir Abhidharmakośa, III, 32 et trad. de Hiuan-tsang, XXIX, 14 *b*.

(2) 如是眼識唯識諸色非補特伽羅. On peut traduire *evaṃ cakṣurvijñānaṃ rūpam eva vijānāti na pudgalam.*

(3) Saṃyutta, II, 72 : *cakkhuṃ ca paticca rūpa ca uppajjati cakkhuviññāṇam / tiṇṇaṃ saṃgati phasso. . .* — Sur le *sparśa* et les faits psychologiques auxquels le *sparśa* donne naissance (*vedanā, saṃjñā, cetanā*), voir Stcherbatski, *Central conception of Buddhism*, 1923, p. 15, 17, 55, dont on hésite à admettre les ingénieuses explications peu en harmonie avec Abhidharmakośa II, 24, III, 30, 32; les explications de Buddhaghosa, Atthasālinī (p. 142) prêtent aussi à la critique. Mais Milinda-Nāgasena (p. 87) ont reconnu la difficulté du problème et dans les mêmes termes que Vasubandhu, interprète du Vaibhāṣika (Kośa, II, 24).

la rencontre des trois, contact; en raison du contact naît la «notion» (*saṃjñā*). De la sorte, la notion née du contact de l'œil prend notion (*saṃjānāti*) du visible, non pas du Pudgala. Le Pudgala n'est pas «objet dénotable» (*saṃjñeya*) de la notion née du contact de l'œil; c'est seulement le visible qui est «dénotable» par la notion née du contact de l'œil. Donc la notion qui naît du contact de l'œil n'est pas une notion née du contact du Pudgala.

En outre, en raison de l'œil et du visible naît la connaissance de l'œil; par la rencontre des trois, contact; en raison du contact naît la «volition» (*cetanā*). La volition née du contact de l'œil «veut» le visible, et non pas le Pudgala. Le Pudgala n'est pas «voulu» par une «volition» née du contact de l'œil : c'est seulement le visible qui est ainsi «voulu». Donc la *cetanā* née du contact de l'œil n'est pas une *cetanā* née du contact du Pudgala.

En raison d'aucun des *dharmas* dont le *sparśa* est le cinquième[1] (vision ... contact) le Pudgala n'est atteint, perçu, étant, existant. Donc il n'y a pas de Pudgala.

Même argumentation en ce qui regarde la connaissance de l'ouïe, etc.

b (14 *b* 9-14 *b* 16). Il y a six *vijñānakāyas : cakṣurvijñāna... manovijñāna*. «En raison de l'œil et des visibles naît la connaissance de l'œil.» Or œil, visibles et connaissance de l'œil ne sont pas le Pudgala : nous avons seulement connaissance de l'œil naissant en raison de l'œil et des visibles.

En outre, «en raison de l'œil et des visibles naît la connaissance de l'œil; par la rencontre des trois, contact (*sparśa*)». Or œil, visibles, connaissance de l'œil, contact de l'œil ne sont pas le Pudgala : nous avons seulement naissance de la connaissance de l'œil en raison de l'œil et des visibles; par la rencontre des trois, contact.

En outre, «en raison de l'œil et des visibles naît la connaissance de l'œil; par la rencontre des trois, contact; en raison du contact naît la sensation (*vedanā*)». Or œil, visibles, connaissance de l'œil, contact de l'œil, sensation née du contact de l'œil ne sont pas le Pudgala : nous avons seulement...

En outre «en raison de l'œil et des visibles naît la connaissance de l'œil; par la rencontre des trois, contact; en raison du contact de l'œil naît la notion (*saṃjñā*)». Or œil, visibles, connaissance de l'œil, contact de l'œil, notion née du contact de l'œil ne sont pas le Pudgala.

En outre, «en raison de l'œil et des visibles naît la connaissance de l'œil, par la rencontre des trois, contact; en raison du contact naît la volition (*ceta-*

[1] 由此諸法觸爲第五. Même expression, *phassapañcamā*, dans Visuddhimagga, p. 595.

nā)». Or œil, visibles, connaissance de l'œil, contact de l'œil, volition née du contact de l'œil ne sont pas le Pudgala : nous avons seulement naissance de la connaissance de l'œil en raison de l'œil et des visibles; par la rencontre des trois, contact; en raison du contact de l'œil naissance de la volition. En raison d'aucun des *dharmas* dont le contact est le cinquième, le Pudgala n'est constaté . . . donc il n'y a pas de Pudgala. . . . .

Même raisonnement en ce qui concerne la connaissance de l'ouïe, etc. (14 *b* 9-16).

c (14 *b* 17-15 *a* 9). Il y a six *vijñānakāyas* . . . En raison de l'œil et des visibles naît la connaissance de l'œil. Que l'œil naisse, que le visible naisse et que la connaissance de l'œil ne naisse pas, c'est ce qu'on ne constate pas. Que l'œil naisse, que le visible naisse et que la connaissance de l'œil naisse, c'est ce qu'on constate. Que l'œil périsse, que le visible périsse et que la connaissance de l'œil ne périsse pas, c'est ce qu'on ne constate pas. Que l'œil périsse, que le visible périsse et que la connaissance de l'œil périsse, c'est ce qu'on constate.

On continue par l'examen du contact, de la sensation, de la notion, de la volition (14 *b* 18-15 *a* 7).

De la sorte ces *dharmas*, dont le contact est le cinquième, naissent ensemble, durent ensemble, périssent ensemble. Lorsque l'un d'eux naît, tous naissent; lorsque l'un d'eux périt, tous périssent. En raison d'aucun de ces *dharmas*, dont le contact est le cinquième, le Pudgala n'est constaté, n'est perçu, n'est étant, n'est existant. Par conséquent il n'y a pas de Pudgala.

Même raisonnement en ce qui concerne la connaissance de l'ouïe, etc.

2 (15 *a* 10-17). Il y a six *vijñānakāyas* . . . «En raison de l'œil et des visibles naît la connaissance de l'œil». Cette connaissance (*vijñāna*) discerne (*vijānāti*) le visible; elle ne le touche pas (*saṃspṛśati*), ne le sent pas comme agréable, etc. (*vedayati*), n'en prend pas notion (*saṃjānāti*), ne le veut pas (*cetayati*), car la connaissance a pour caractère de discerner (*vijānanālakṣaṇa*).

«En raison de l'œil et des visibles naît la connaissance de l'œil; par la rencontre des trois, contact.» Le contact de l'œil touche le visible, ne le discerne pas, ne le sent pas, n'en prend pas notion, ne le veut pas, car son caractère est de toucher . . .

De la sorte ces *dharmas*, dont le contact est le cinquième, naissent ensemble. . . Puisque, étant né, chacun d'eux fait sa propre besogne (*kārya*) et non celle des autres, en raison d'aucun de ces *dharmas*... le Pudgala n'est constaté...

Même raisonnement en ce qui concerne la connaissance de l'ouïe.

3 *a* (15 *a* 18-15 *b* 2). Il y a six *vijñānakāyas* : *cakṣurvijñāna* ... *manovijñāna*.

Question : Que discerne la connaissance de l'œil (*cakṣurvijñāna*)? — Réponse : Le visible (*rūpa*). — Question : Qu'est-ce qu'il ne discerne pas? — Réponse : Onze *āyatanas* (l'œil, le son, etc.)... — Question : Que discerne la connaissance mentale (*manovijñāna*)? — Réponse : les dix-huit *dhātus* : œil, visible, connaissance visuelle ... *manas*, *dharmas* et connaissance mentale.

Donc ces six *vijñānakāyas* discernent (*vijānanti*), ont pour nature de discerner non pas de ne pas discerner. Or le Pudgala n'est pas tel : donc il n'y a pas de Pudgala.

b (15 *b* 2-5). Il y a douze *āyatanas* ou sources de la connaissance : l'œil et les visibles... le *manas* et les *dharmas* (*cakṣurāyatana*, *rūpāyatana* ... *manaāyatana*, *dharmāyatana*).

Question : Par combien de connaissances est connu le *rūpāyatana*? Réponse : Par la connaissance de l'œil et la connaissance mentale... Le *śabdāyatana* est connu par la connaissance de l'oreille et la connaissance mentale... Les sept autres *āyatanas* sont connus par la seule connaissance mentale.

Les douze *āyatanas* ont pour nature d'être connus par la connaissance, non pas de ne pas être connus. Le Pudgala n'est pas tel.

4 *a* (15 *b* 6-7). Il y a six *vijñānakāyas*... En raison de l'œil et des visibles naît la connaissance de l'œil. De la rencontre des trois, contact; avec le contact nées ensemble la sensation, la notion, la volition. En raison d'aucun de ces *dharmas*, dont le contact est le cinquième, le Pudgala n'est constaté.

b (15 *b* 8-12). A l'égard de l'objet désirable (*rañjanīya vastu*), en raison de l'ignorance (*ajñāna*) naît la concupiscence (*saṃrāga*) : l'ignorance est l'*avidyā*, la concupiscence est *saṃskāra*; le discernement du caractère de l'objet est le *vijñāna*. Le *vijñāna* avec les quatre autres *skandhas*, c'est le *nāmarūpa*; les *indriyas* qui s'appuient sur le *nāmarūpa*, c'est le *ṣaḍāyatana*; la rencontre (*saṃnipāta*) du *ṣaḍāyatana*, c'est le *sparśa*; l'impression (*anubhava*) y relative (*tatra*), c'est la *vedanā*; l'attachement (*adhyavasāna*) né de la *vedanā*, c'est la *tṛṣṇā*; le développement (*vaipulya*) de la *tṛṣṇā*, c'est *upādāna*; l'acte qui produit une nouvelle existence, c'est *bhava;* l'apparition des *skandhas*, c'est la naissance; la maturation (*paripāka*) des *skandhas*, c'est la vieillesse; la destruction (*vināśa*) des *skandhas*, c'est la mort; la brûlure intérieure (*antardāha*), c'est le chagrin (*śoka*); la lamentation, c'est le *parideva;* la sensation désagréable (*asāta*) associée (*saṃprayukta*) aux cinq connaissances, c'est le *duḥkha;* la sensation désagréable associée à la connaissance mentale, c'est le *daurmanasya;* les brûlure, torture et tourment de la pensée sont les *upāyāsas*[1]. — L'expression *sambhavanti* signifie «naissent». — Le mot *evam* exprime «indication, explication, éclaircissement». — Ce qui est produit est appelé *samudaya.* — *kevala*, c'est-à-dire «extrême» (*vṛddhikāṣṭhāgata*), complet (*paripūrṇa?*)[2]. — «grande masse de souffrance» (*mahato duḥkhaskandhasya*), c'est-à-dire grand malheur (*ādinava, vipatti*), grande peine (*viṣama?*), grande infortune, grand tourment (*upāyāsa*), accumulation de tous les *dharmas* pénibles[3].

c (15*b* 13-18). Avec, pour cause et condition, l'ignorance (*avidyā*) non abandonnée (*aprahīṇa*), non connue (*aparijñāta*), naissent les *saṃskāras*, de trois catégories : *puṇyasaṃskāras, apuṇyasaṃskāras, āneñjyasaṃskāras.*

Avec, pour cause et condition, les *saṃskāras* non abandonnés, non connus, naît le *vijñāna*, qui se rend dans une bonne destinée (*sugatyupaga?*), qui se rend dans une mauvaise destinée

Avec, pour cause et condition, le *vijñāna* non abandonné, non connu, naît le *nāmarūpa*, soit dans cette vie, soit dans la vie à venir (*ihalokastha* [?], *paraloka* ou *paścāllokastha*).

Avec, pour cause et condition, le *nāmarūpa* non abandonné, non connu, naît le *ṣaḍāyatana*, ou complet ou incomplet.

En vue de la rencontre (*saṃnipāta*) du *ṣaḍāyatana* a lieu le contact (*sparśa*)[4];

[1] Le Sūtra qu'analyse Devaśarman porte : *jātipratyayā jarāmaranaśokaparidevaduḥkhadaurmanasyopāyāsāḥ sambhavanti | evam asya kevalasya mahato duḥkhaskandhasya samudayo bhavati* || — Saṃyutta, II, 2; Mahāvastu, III, 448, Śālistamba (*Douze causes*, p. 71), Vibhaṅga, p. 135, 145, etc.

[2] *Kevala* est expliqué (Kośa, III, 28 *a-b*) *ātmātmīyarahita.* — «grande masse» = «masse sans commencement ni fin». — Comparer Madhyamakavṛtti, p. 558.

[3] 大惱順大世分衆苦法聚 = *mahopāyāsamahālokabhāgīyasarvaduḥkhadharmaraśeḥ* (?).

[4] Je traduis 故 par *arthena*, d'après Śālistamba (*Douze causes*, p. 81) : *sparśanārthena sparśaḥ. . . :* «en vue du contact, le *sparśa*». — Le *sparśa* est le *dharma* en vertu duquel l'organe (ṣaḍāyatana) est «comme s'il touchait l'objet», de telle sorte que la connaissance naît semblable à l'objet. — Il ne saurait être question de «contact» au sens propre du mot, car, pour ne donner que cette raison,

en vue de la sensation (*anubhava*) du contact a lieu la *vedanā;* en vue de l'attachement né de la *vedanā* a lieu la *tṛṣṇā*. L'excès (*vaipulya*) de la soif s'appelle *upādāna*...

[Le reste comme ci-dessus.]

5 (15*b* 19-20). En raison de quatorze causes, il faut savoir que la pensée, de sa nature, est impermanente. En raison de 1. *prayoga* (*abhisaṃskāra?*), 2. *saṃprayoga*, 3. *īryāpatha*, 4. *śilpasthāna*, 5. *kāyakarman*, 6. *vākkarman*, 7. *manaḥkarman*, 8. *hetu*, 9. *samanantara*, 10. *ālambana*, 11. *adhipati*, 12. *kliṣta*, *akliṣta*, 13. *vedanāviśeṣa*, 14. *kāryavastukarmaparamparānyathātva*.

6 (16*a* 1-2). Lorsqu'une pensée est née elle est clairement (*sphuṭam*) connue (*gamyate*, *prajñāyate*) comme actuelle ou d'une autre époque. Ce dont on se souvient est ce qui a été éprouvé. De la sorte la pensée, de sa nature, n'existe pas indépendamment d'une pensée antérieure. De ce raisonnement, il résulte que la série (*paramparā*) des pensées n'a pas eu d'origine. La succession (*krama*) des pensées est ainsi nommée «vérité de la douleur» *duḥkham āryasatyam* [c'est-à-dire la succession des pensées est douleur, comme le voient exactement les Āryas]. De même il faut y reconnaître la vérité de l'origine.

Voir ainsi, c'est ce qu'on appelle «vue correcte» (*samyagdṛṣṭi?*).

Voir autrement, c'est ce qu'on appelle «faux savoir» (*mithyājñāna*).

7 (16*a* 3-6). Si la soif n'est pas abandonnée et connue, avec la soif comme cause et condition naîtra, dans le futur, la douleur. Si la soif est abandonnée et connue, il n'y a pas cause et condition de la naissance, dans le futur, de la douleur. A supposer que la soif [ne soit pas] abandonnée et connue, il y a cause et condition de la naissance, dans le futur, de la douleur. Par conséquent on peut voir, on peut entendre qu'un tel, [non] détaché de la soif, naisse dans ce monde. Mais, ayant abandonné et connu la soif, il n'y a pas cause et condition de la naissance, dans le futur, de la douleur. Par conséquent on ne voit pas, on n'entend pas qu'un tel, détaché de la soif, naisse dans ce monde. C'est là ce qu'on appelle la vérité de la destruction de la douleur. C'est ainsi qu'il faut voir la vérité de la destruction de la douleur. Voir ainsi, c'est ce qu'on appelle «vue correcte», voir autrement, c'est ce qu'on appelle «faux savoir».

l'organe mental et les *dharmas* ne sont pas matériels. Mais Stcherbatski s'aventure un peu en faisant du *sparśa* un donné psychologique inconscient; nous savons que c'est un *dharma* mental (*caitasika*) associé à toute pensée (*citta* ou *vijñāna*).

(16 *a* 7-11). Il y a six *vijñānakāyas*, *cakṣurvijñāna* . . . *manovijñāna*. Le *cakṣurvijñāna* a quatre conditions (Kośa, II, 61) : *hetupratyaya*, *samanantarapratyaya*, *ālambanapratyaya*, *adhipatipratyaya*. Quel est son *hetupratyaya?* Les *dharmas* coexistants (*sahabhū*) et associés (*samprayukta*). Quel est son *samanantarapratyaya?* La pensée (*citta*) et les mentaux (*caittas*) qui lui sont pareils (*sama*) et immédiats (*anantara*) : le *cakṣurvijñāna* déjà né et naissant. Quel est son *ālambanapratyaya?* Les visibles. Quel est son *adhipatipratyaya?* Tous les autres *dharmas*, lui-même excepté.

De même, de quoi le *cakṣurvijñāna* est-il le *hetupratyaya?* Des *dharmas* qui lui sont coexistants et associés. De quoi est-il le *samanantarapratyaya?* De la pensée et des mentaux déjà nés et naissants qui lui sont pareils et immédiats. De quoi est-il l'*ālambanapratyaya?* De la pensée et des mentaux qui l'ont pour objet. De quoi est-il l'*adhipatipratyaya?* De tous les autres *dharmas*, lui-même excepté.

Pour le *śrotravijñāna*, etc., comme pour le *cakṣurvijñāna* [1].

[1] Ces derniers paragraphes devraient, semble-t-il, être rattachés au chapitre III, « causes et conditions ». Toutefois ils montrent que le jeu des causes fonctionne sans qu'un *pudgala* soit nécessaire.

Vasubandhu on the Fundamental Principle of the Sarvāstivāda School

Th. Stcherbatsky

The fifth chapter (*koça-sthāna*) of the *Abhidharma-koça* (v, 24-6) contains a detailed exposition of the argument between the Sarvāstivādins or Vaibhāṣikas and the Sautrāntikas upon the question of the reality of future and past elements (*dharmas*), written according to the method of later dialectics. It is divided in two parts, *pūrvapakṣa* and *uttarapakṣa*. In the first the Vaibhāṣika makes a statement of his case, and he is attacked by the Sautrāntika; he answers the questions and triumphs over the opponent. In the second the parts are reversed: the Vaibhāṣika puts the questions and the Sautrāntika answers them and secures the final victory. As a conclusion the Vaibhāṣika gives voice to his despair at the impossibility of conceiving the transcendentally deep essence of the elements of existence. The translation is made from the Tibetan text of the Peking edition of the Bstan-hgyur. Mdo, vol. 64, fol. 279, b. 5–285, a. 2. Some explanations have been introduced from Yaçomitra's Commentary, and the Tibetan commentary of Mchims-pa, which is the standard work for *abhidharma* throughout Mongolia and Tibet.

An Episodical Investigation into the Possibility of Past and Future Efficiency

(*Abhidharma-koça, Kārikās V*, 24–6)

(The author establishes that some passions exist only at the time when the corresponding objects are present, such are love or disgust towards sense-objects. But there are other passions of a general scope, such as preconceived dogmatical ideas, delusion, a doubting turn of mind, etc.; these have a bearing towards all objects whether past, present, or future. The following question is then raised.)

Bstan-hgyur, 64, f. 279, b. 5. But are this past and this future really existent or not? If they are, it would follow that the elementary forces (*saṃskāra*) (which are active in the process of life) must be permanent (i.e. immovable), since they exist through all time. If they are not, how is it to be explained that a man is attracted to (objects past and future) by such (passion as he experienced formerly, or will be subject to in future) ?

The *Vaibhāṣikas* do not admit those elements (which combine in the process of life) to be permanent, since they are subject (to the action of four energies which are) the characteristic appurtenance of such elements (viz. the forces of origination, decay, existence, and destruction). But, on the other hand, they emphatically declare that " the times " (i.e. everyone of the three times) are existent in reality.

The *Sautrāntika* asks, for what reason ?

(Part I.—*The case for Everlasting Elements*)

The *Vaibhāṣika* answers: The times are always existent Kārikā, v, 2
(1) because this has been declared in Scripture, (2) because of the double (cause of perception), (3) because of the existence of the perception's object, (4) because of the production of a result (by previous deeds). Since we maintain that all this exists, we profess the theory that everything exists (*Sarvāstivāda*).

(1) *Because this has been declared in Scripture.*—Our Sublime 279, b. 7.
Lord has declared: (" the elements of matter, O Brethren, the Yaçom.
past and the future ones, are impermanent, not to speak of the present ones. This is perceived by the perfect saint, endowed, as he is, with wisdom. Therefore, he is regardless of past sense-objects, he does not rejoice at future enjoyments, he entertains disgust and aversion in regard to the present ones, he is engaged in keeping them off). O Brethren ! if some kind of past matter 279, b. 7
did not exist, the perfect saint endowed with wisdom could not be regardless of past sense-objects, but, since they are existent, he (enjoys the privilege of) disregarding them. If some kind of future matter were not existent, the wise and perfect saint could not be free from rejoicing at future enjoyments (since his independence would have no object). But future sense-objects do exist, etc."

(2) *Because of the double (cause of perception).*—It is declared 280, a. 2.
in Scripture : " consciousness, when operating, is conditioned by (elements) of a double kind." What are they ? The sense of vision and colour (for a visual consciousness), and so on (an organ of perception and its respective object for each of the six kinds

of consciousness, the last being) the intellect itself and its non-sensuous objects [1] (for consciousness purely mental).

Thus these first two reasons for admitting the existence of the past and the future are taken from Scripture, but there are others, too, which are founded on argument.

280, a. 4. (3) *Because of the existence of an object.*—If there is an object, its cognition can arise; if there is none, neither can its cognition be produced. If the past and the future were not existent, the objects (of the corresponding cognition) would be non-existent, and, as non-existent, they could not be cognized.

(4) *Because of the production of a result* (*by former deeds*).—If the past did not exist, how could a deed, good or bad, attain, after some lapse of time, its fruition, since, at the time when the
Yaçom. latter appears, the cause which has produced retribution is gone. (A former deed, good or bad, does exist in reality, because, when it becomes ripe, it produces fruition, just as a present one does.)

280, a. 6. For these reasons we *Vaibhāṣikas* maintain that the past and the future necessarily exist. This leads to the theory that everything is existent, and our school is known by emphatically adhering to the principle of such universal existence (*Sarvāstivāda*). Accordingly (it is said above in the mnemonic verse): "since we maintain that all this exists, we profess the theory that everything exists." Those who maintain that everything, past, future, and present, exists are advocates of universal existence (*Sarvāstivādins*). On the other hand, those who make a distinction, partly admitting and partly denying this theory, are termed the Distinguishing School (*Vibhajyavādins*). They maintain that the present elements, and those among the past that have not yet produced their fruitions, are existent, but they deny the existence of the future ones and of those among the past that have already produced fruition.[2]

280, b. 2. *Sautrāntika.*—And how many branches are there among these advocates of universal existence?

Kārikā, v, 25. *Vaibhāṣika.*—There are four branches, inasmuch as they maintain (1) a change of existence (*bhāva-pariṇāma*), (2) a change of aspect (*lakṣaṇa-pariṇāma*), (3) a change of condition (*avasthā-pariṇāma*), or (4) contingency (*apekṣā-pariṇāma*). The third is

[1] *Manaḥ* and *dharmāḥ*.
[2] Cf. above, p. 43, n. 3.

all right. The difference in time reposes on a difference of condition (i.e. function of the elements).

(1) It was the venerable Dharmatrūta who maintained the 280, b. 3.
view that existence (*bhāva*) changes in the course of time, not substance (*dravya*). He is known to have been arguing thus: when an element enters different times, its existence changes, but not its essence, just as when a golden vessel is broken, its form changes, but not its colour. And when milk is turned into curds, its taste, consistency, and digestive value are gone, but not its colour.[1] In the same manner, when an element, after having been future, enters into a present time, it gets rid of its future existence, but not of the existence of its essence, and when from present it becomes past, it casts away its present existence, but not the existence of its substance.

(2) It was the venerable Ghoṣa who assumed a change in the 280, b. 6.
aspect of the elements (*lakṣaṇa*). He is known to have professed the theory that, when an element appears at different times, the past one retains its past aspect, without being severed from its future and present aspects, the future has its future aspect, without being altogether deprived of its past and present aspects, the present likewise retains its present aspect, without completely losing its past and future aspects. Just as, when a man falls into passionate love with a female, he is not altogether deprived of his capacity of love towards other females (but this capacity is not prominent).

(3) A change of condition (*avasthā*) is advocated by the 281, a. 1.
venerable Vasumitra. He is known to have maintained that, when one element manifests itself at different times, it changes in condition, and receives different designations according to the condition which it has reached, without changing in substance. (When an element is in a condition in which it does not yet Yaçom.
produce its function, it is called future; when it produces it, it is called present; when, having produced it, it ceases to work, it is past, its substance remaining the same.) Just as in an abacus the same ball receives different significations according to the place it is thrown in. If it is thrown in the place for units it means one, if in the place for hundreds it means a hundred, if in the place for thousands it means one thousand.

[1] Or, if *rūpa* stands for *svarūpa*, "its essence."

281, a. 3. (4) An advocate of contingency (*apekṣā*) is the venerable Buddhadeva. He is known to have maintained the principle that an element in the course of time receives this or that denomination on account of its relation to the former and the

Yaçom. next moment. (An element is future with respect to the former one, be it past or present, it is present with respect to a former, i.e. past one or with respect to the next one, i.e. future one, it is past with respect to the next one, be it present or future.) Just as the same female may be called a mother (with respect to her children) and a daughter (with respect to her own mother).

Thus it is that all these four (lines of thought) are so many varieties of the theory which maintains Universal Existence. As regards the first of them, it is nothing else than the doctrine of the changing manifestations (of one eternal matter). Therefore it must be included in the Sānkhya system (which has already been rejected). As to the second, it is a confusion of all times, since it implies co-existence of all the aspects (of an element) at the same time. The passion of a man may be prominent towards one female, and merely existent (imperceptibly) towards another one, but what has this fact to do with the theory it is supposed to illustrate? According to the fourth explanation, it would follow that all the three times are found together, included in one of them. Thus in the scope of the past time we can distinguish a former and a following moment. They will represent a past and a future time. Between them the inter-

281, a. 7. mediate moment will correspond to a present time. Thus it is that among all proposed explanations the (remaining one alone), the third in number, is right, that which maintains a change of condition (or function). According thereto the difference in time reposes on the difference in function: at the time when an element does not yet actually perform its function it is future; when performing it, it becomes present; when, after having performed it, it stops, it becomes past.

281, b. 1. *Sautrāntika.*—Although I perfectly understand all this, I do not see my way to admit that it implies a real existence of the past and of the future. For, if the past is really existent and the future likewise, what induces us (to make a distinction between them and) to call them past and future?

Vaibhāṣika.—But have we not already explained it: the time of an element is settled in accordance with the time of its function.

Sautrāntika.—If this be the case, an eye which does not look at the present moment will not be present, because it does not perform its function?

Vaibhāṣika.—It is present (because it performs its other functions): it is the immediate cause (of the next moment of its existence and the remote cause) determining (its future character).

(Although an eye that does not look is not performing its function, it, nevertheless, is efficient in immediately producing and forecasting the homogeneousness of its future with its past and in producing its, so-called, co-operative result.[1] In that sense it is present.) Mchims-pa, ii, 166, a. 4.

Sautrāntika.—In that case the past will be the same as the present, since the past likewise produces such results—the past viewed as a cause of homogeneousness in consecutive moments,[2] as a general moral cause,[3] and as a cause requiring retribution [4]—all these causes would be present since they may perform their actual functions at the present moment.

Vaibhāṣika.—I call present a cause which exhibits at the present moment a double function—that of giving an immediate result

[1] The Sarvāstivādins establish several kinds of causal relations between the elements. If e.g. a moment of the sense of vision produces in the next moment a visual sensation, it is termed *kāraṇa-hetu* and its result *adhipati-phala*. This relation will be absent in the case of an inefficient condition of the organ of vision. But there are other relations between the moments of this organ. When the next moment is just the same as the foregoing one, thus evoking in the observer the idea of duration, this relation is termed *sabhāga-hetu* as to a *niṣyanda-phala*. If this moment appears in a stream (*santāna*) which is defiled by the presence of passions (*kleça*), this defiling character is inherited by the next moments, if no stopping of it is produced. Such a relation is called *sarvatraga-hetu* as to *niṣyanda-phala*. Finally every moment in a stream is under the influence of former deeds (*karma*) and may, in its turn, have an influence on future events. This relation is termed *vipāka-hetu* as to *vipāka-phala*. The simultaneity of the inseparable elements of matter will produce a co-operative result (*puruṣakāra-phala*). These last three relations must be existent even in the case of a non-operative moment of the sense of vision. Cf. *Ab. K.*, ii, 50 ff.; O. Rosenberg, *Problems*, chap. xv.

[2] *Sabhāga-hetu*.

[3] *Sarvatraga-hetu*.

[4] *Vipāka-hetu*.

and that of determining the character of its remote future. A past cause, although it may produce a result at the present moment, does not, at present, determine its general character (which has been previously determined). Therefore the past is not the same as the present.

Sautrāntika.—If the time is settled according to efficiency, an element may be past inasmuch as its power of determining the general character of a remote result belongs to the past, and it may be present nevertheless, since it produces the result of the present moment. Thus a confusion of the characteristic signs of all the three times will arise, and I maintain that you are guilty
41, b. 3. of such confusion. Your standpoint leads to the absurdity of assuming actual or semi-actual past causes (i.e. semi-present elements), since the cause of homogeneousness and other past causes may produce a (present) result. A confusion of the essential natures of the three times is the consequence.

1, b. 4. (PART II.—*The case against Everlasting Elements*)

ārikā, v. 25. *Sautrāntika.*—To this we must make the following reply:—

What is it that keeps (an element from exhibiting its action)? And how is (the time of this action to be determined)? If it, the time of an element's existence, does not differ from the essence of the element itself, there will altogether be no time. If the element in the future and in the past exists just in the same sense as in the present, why is it future and past? The essence of the elements of existence (*dharmatā*) is deep!

1. b. 4. If the essence alone of the elements of existence persists throughout all the three times, but not their function, what is it that constitutes an impediment to this function? What is it that sometimes induces them to perform and sometimes keeps them back from performing their function?

Vaibhāṣika.—The function is performed when all the necessary conditions are present.

Sautrāntika.—This won't do! because (according to your theory) these conditions are always present. Again, as to the functions themselves, they likewise may be past, future, and present. They then require an explanation in their turn.

281, b. 6. Will you admit the existence of a second function (which will determine the time of the first)? or will you suppose that it neither is past, nor future, nor present, but that it, nevertheless, does exist? In this case this function will not be subject to the elementary forces of life (*saṃskṛta*) and will represent an immovable eternal entity (*asaṃskṛta*). For this reason you cannot maintain that, as long as an element does not yet perform its function, it is future.

Vaibhāṣika.—If the function of an element were something different from the element itself, your objections would be right. But since it is not different, they do not hold good. 281, b. 7.

Sautrāntika.—Then there is no time at all! If the function is the same as the substance, the elements will always remain identical. For what reason are they sometimes called past, sometimes future, and sometimes present?

Vaibhāṣika.—An element that has not yet appeared is future, one which has appeared and not yet disappeared is present, one which has disappeared is past. What is it you find unfounded in this explanation?

Sautrāntika.—The following point needs here to be established:—if the past and the future exist in the same sense as the present, as realities, why is it, then, that, being existent in the same sense, they are future and past? If the substance of the same element is alone (permanently) existent, what is the reason that it is spoken of as "having not yet appeared" or "gone"? What is it that does not appear later on and whose absence makes us call it "past"?

Thus it is that the notion of three times will altogether have no real foundation, as long as you don't accept the view that the elements appear into life out of non-existence and return again into non-existence after having been existing. (Your theory implies eternal existence of the elements.)

Vaibhāṣika.—It is absurd to maintain that it implies eternal existence! There are the four forces (of origination, decay, maintenance, and destruction) to which every element is subject, and the combination (of the permanent essence of an element with these forces produces its impermanent manifestations in life).

Sautrāntika.—Mere words! They cannot explain the origination and decay (which are going on in the process of life). An element, according to this view, is permanent and impermanent at the same time. This, indeed, is something quite new! It has been said on this occasion :—

a. 7. Maintained eternal essence ;
Denied eternal being !
And yet no difference between
This essence and this being.
'Tis clearly a caprice
Of the Almighty !
'Tis spoken by His order !

(*Vaibhāṣika*.—But Buddha has said that there "is" a past and there "is" a future.)

Sautrāntika.—We, likewise, maintain that there "is" a past and there "is" a future. But this means that what has been formerly "is" past, and what, in the (presence of its causes), will happen "is" future. They exist in this sense only, not in reality.

b. 1. *Vaibhāṣika*.—Who has ever maintained that they exist just in the same sense in which the present exists?

Sautrāntika.—How can one exist otherwise?

Vaibhāṣika.—The essence of the past and of the future is (always) existent.

Sautrāntika.—If they are always existent, how is the (remarkable result) brought about that they are called past or future? Therefore the words of our Sublime Lord, "there *is* a past, there *is* a future," must be understood in another sense. He proffered them when discussing with the Ājīvikas (who denied moral responsibility for past deeds). He strongly opposed their doctrine, which denied the connexion between a past cause and a future result. In order to make it known that a former cause and a future result are something which happened formerly and will happen in future, he categorically declared: "There *is* a past, there *is* a future." For the word "is" acts as a particle (which may refer to something existent and to non-existence as well). As e.g. people will say: "there *is* absence of light" (before it has been kindled), "there *is* absence of light after (it has been put out)," or the "light *is* put out, but I did not put it out". When Buddha declared that there "is" a past and there "is" a future, he used the word "is" in that sense.

Had it been otherwise, it would be absolutely impossible to account for (the notions of) a past and a future.

Vaibhāṣika.—But, then, how are we to understand the words of our Sublime Lord when addressing the Lāguḍaçikhīyaka wandering ascetics (the bearers of a tress on the head and a stick in the hand)? Why did he declare: "a deed (which requires immediate retribution) is past, is accomplished, is finished, is gone, has disappeared, but, nevertheless, it does exist." What did these ascetics really deny? Not that the accomplished deed was past, (but that it could have some actual existence, i.e. some efficiency. Hence the words of Buddha imply an actual existence of the past). 282, b. 5.

Sautrāntika.—(No!) He meant that a force to produce retribution is driven by a past deed into the run (of combined elements which constitute an individual). Were it existent in reality, it would not be past. This is the only way in which this passage needs be understood, because on another occasion, in the sermon about "Non-substantiality as the Ultimate Truth",[1] the Sublime Lord has spoken thus: "when the organ of vision appears into life, there is absolutely nothing from which it proceeds, and when it vanishes, nought there is to which it retires. Therefore, O Brethren, this organ of vision has no former existence. Then it appears, and after having been existent it vanishes again." If a future organ of vision were existent, Buddha would never have declared that it appeared out of non-existence (out of nothing). 282, b. 7.

Vaibhāṣika.—(This passage means that), as far as the present time is concerned, it did not exist, and then appeared (in the scope of this time). 283, a. 2.

Sautrāntika.—Impossible! Time is not something different from the object (existing in it).

Vaibhāṣika.—But may not its essence have not been present and then have appeared?

Sautrāntika.—This would only prove that it had no (real) future existence.

(*The second argument of the Sarvāstivādins refuted*)

Sautrāntika.—Now your second argument is drawn from the circumstance that cognition, when arising, reposes on two factors: 283, a. 3.

[1] *Paramārtha-çūnyatā-sūtra*, Saṃyuktāgama, xiii, 22 (McGovern).

a perceptive faculty and a corresponding object. Here we must at first (consider the instance) of mental cognition reposing on the operation of the intellect and on a mental (not sensuous) object.[1] Is this object a real cause in the same sense as the intellect ? or is it a mere (passive) object realized by the intellect ? If it were a real active cause, how could events which must happen after the lapse of a thousand æons, or those which never will happen, possibly constitute an active cause of the corresponding cognition ? And the Final Deliverance, which is synonymous with the total cessation of every operation of all the elements of existence, how can it constitute a really active cause of its own conception ? But if, on the other hand, such objects are mere passive objects of the operating mind, then I maintain that they may be future and may be past.

a. 7. *Vaibhāṣika.*—If they altogether do not exist, how can they possibly be objects ?

Sautrāntika.—Their existence I admit, (understanding by existence) that very form in which they are conceived by us at the present moment in the present place.

a. 8. *Vaibhāṣika.*—And how are they conceived ?

Sautrāntika.—As past and as future. If somebody remembers a past object or a former feeling, he has never been observed to say " it exists ", but only " it did exist ".

(*The third argument of the Sarvāstivādins examined*)

b. 1. *Sautrāntika.*—As (to the cognition of past and future) sense objects, the past ones are remembered in that very form in which they were experienced when they were present, and the future ones are known to Buddhas just in that form in which they will appear at the time when they will be present.

Vaibhāṣika.—And if it be just the same existence (as the present one) ?

Sautrāntika.—Then it is present.

Vaibhāṣika.—If not ?

Sautrāntika.—(It is absent : and thus) it is proved that absence can be cognized just as well (as presence).

Vaibhāṣika.—But (will you not admit that the past and the future) are fragments of the present itself ?

[1] *dharmāḥ*, i.e. 64 *dharmas*, *āyatana* No. 12.

Sautrāntika.—No, because we are not conscious of apprehending fragments.

Vaibhāṣika.—But, then, it may represent the same stuff, with the mere (difference that in the past and the future) its atoms may be disjoined?

Sautrāntika.—In that case, atoms will be eternally existent, and (all the process of life) will consist in their either combining or disjoining. There will altogether be no new origination, no real extinction, and thus you will become guilty of adhering to the (heretical) doctrine of the Ājīvikas.

Moreover, you will be contradicted by the scriptural passage (referred to above): "when the organ of vision is produced, it does not come from some other place; when it disappears, it is not going to be stored up in another place, etc." 283, b. 4.

On the other hand, it is impossible that feelings and other (mental phenomena), which have no atomic structure, should be divided into fragments. If remembered, they likewise are remembered in that very form in which they did appear and were experienced. And, if you suppose that they continue to exist in the same form, they must be eternal. If they do not, it will be proved that (a non-existent feeling) may be apprehended (by memory) just as well (as an existent one is apprehended by self-perception).

Vaibhāṣika.—If non-existence is capable of being apprehended, you must add to (the list of all things cognizable, i.e.) to the twelve bases of cognition (*āyatana*), a new category, the thirteenth, non-existence. 283, b. 6.

Sautrāntika.—Supposing I think about the absence of a thirteenth category, what will be then the object corresponding to my thought?

Vaibhāṣika.—It will be this very (category, i.e. its) name.

Sautrāntika.—And what is it (generally speaking) that we apprehend, when we are expecting to hear a word which as yet is not pronounced?

Vaibhāṣika.—It is nothing else than this very word.

Sautrāntika.—Then a person who desires not to hear this word, will be obliged to pronounce it!

Vaibhāṣika.—It may be the future condition of this word?

Sautrāntika.—If it is something existent, why does it produce an idea of absence?

Vaibhāṣika.—Then it may be its present absence?

Sautrāntika.—No! it is the same. (If this present absence is something existent, why does it produce an idea of non-existence?)

Vaibhāṣika.—Then it may be the characteristic sign of a future; (this sign is absent at present, and gives rise to the idea of non-existence).

Sautrāntika.—This sign consists (in the fact that the future) will appear into existence out of a previous non-existence. Thus it is that both existence and non-existence may be objects of cognition.

84, a. 2. *Vaibhāṣika.*—And how do you explain the words of the future Buddha, who has spoken thus: "that these persons know or perceive things which do not exist in the world—this is impossible!"?

Sautrāntika.—These words (do not mean that non-existence cannot be an object of cognition, but they) have the following meaning:—"there are other, manifestly deluded, persons (who have not yet attained the divine power of vision: they) perceive things that never did exist. I perceive only existing (remote) things." If, on the contrary, every possible thought had only existing things for its object, what reason could there have been for doubting (the accuracy of the assertion of such people about what they were perceiving by their power of divine vision)? or what would have been the difference (between the *bodhisattva's* real power of vision and the incomplete power of these men)?

84, a. 5. It is inevitable that we should understand the passage in this sense, because it is confirmed by another scriptural passage, which begins with the words: "come unto me, ye monks, my pupils!" and goes on until the following words are spoken: "what I am telling him in the morning becomes clearer at night, what I am conversing about at night becomes clearer to him next morning. He will cognize the existence of what does exist, the non-existence of what does not exist. Where something still higher exists, he will know that there is something still higher; and where nothing higher exists, he will know that (it is the Final Deliverance, that) there is nothing higher than that!" Therefore the argument (in favour of a real existence of the past, that you have drawn from the supposed fact that) our intellect can have only existent things for its object—this argument is wrong.

(*The fourth argument of the Sarvāstivādins examined*)

Sautrāntika.—As to your next argument (in favour of the real existence of the past, viz. because it has a real) result—we must observe that we, the Sautrāntikas, never did maintain that a result can be produced from a past deed (directly). 284, a. 7.

Vaibhāṣika.—How is it produced, then?

Sautrāntika.—(This deed) is the beginning of a peculiar chain of events (in the course of which the result appears sooner or later). A more detailed explanation of this point will be given later on, when we will refute the theory (of the Vātsīputrīyas, who) maintain the existence of an individual.[1] (As to your view, it is manifestly inconsistent.) What result can a past deed produce according to this view? If the past and the future are actually existent, the result will necessarily be pre-existent from all eternity.

Vaibhāṣika.—(But we assume the existence of the force of generation?)

Sautrāntika.—Well, then, it will be established that this force 284, b. 1.
itself appears after having previously been non-existent! In fact, if everything without any exception is pre-existent, there can be nothing that could have a force to produce anything! In the end it comes to the same as the theory of the followers of Varṣaganya. According to them there is neither production of something new nor extinction of something existent: what exists is always existent, what does not exist will never become existent.

Vaibhāṣika.—But the force (of a past deed) may consist in "making present" (some already existing element)?

Sautrāntika.—How is this "making present" to be understood? 284, b. 3

Vaibhāṣika.—It consists in removing (the result from one) place to another.

Sautrāntika.—Then the result would be eternally pre-existent. And, as to non-existent elements, how can they (be made to change place)? Moreover, such "removing" means production (of a motion, i.e. of something) which previously did not exist.

[1] *Ab. K.*, ix, translated in my *Soul Theory.*

84, b. 5. *Vaibhāṣika.*—It may consist in a "specification" of the (everlasting) essence of an element?

Sautrāntika.—This, again, would prove that there is production of what previously did not exist. To conclude: the principle of Universal Existence, as far as exegetical literature is concerned, where it implies an actual existence of the past and of the future, does not hold good. On the contrary, it is all right if we strictly conform to the words of Scripture, where it is declared that "everything exists".

Vaibhāṣika.—And in what sense has it been declared in Scripture that "everything exists"?

Sautrāntika.—O Brahmins! it has been declared, "everything exists": that means no more than "the elements included in the twelve categories (*āyatana*) are existent".

Vaibhāṣika.—And the three times (are they not included among these elements)?

Sautrāntika.—(No, they are not!). How their existence is to be understood we have already explained.

(The Sarvāstivādin reverts to his first argument)

84, b. 7. *Vaibhāṣika.*—If the past and the future did not exist, how could it be possible that a man should be attracted by (a past and future passion) to a (past or future object of enjoyment)?

Sautrāntika.—This becomes possible because past passions leave residues (or produce seeds), which are the causes of new passions; these seeds are existent (and the saint has the capacity of keeping them down, of being independent of them). Therefore, a man can be bound by (past accesses of) passion. And it is in this sense that he can be allured by (future or past) objects, because the seeds of these passions, which are directed towards (past and future enjoyments), are always present in him.

Conclusion

Cf. Mchims-pa, ii, 167, b. 7. *Vaibhāṣika* (does not feel discountenanced by this series of arguments, and says:) We Vaibhāṣikas, nevertheless, maintain
85, a. 1. that the past and the future certainly do exist. But (regarding the everlasting essence of the elements of existence, we confess) that this is something we do not succeed in explaining, their essence is deep (it is transcendental), since its existence cannot

be established by rational methods.[1] (And as to the use we make of the notion of time in common life, it is contradictory. We use) the expression: "what appears vanishes" (implying that the same element appears and disappears, e.g.) "some matter appears and disappears". But we, likewise, say "one thing appears, another disappears", implying that one element, the future one, enters into life, and another one (the present one), stops. We also speak of the appearing of time (itself "the time is come"), because the element which enters into life is included in the notion of time. And we speak about being born "from time", since the future includes many moments (and only one of them actually enters into life).

End of the Episodical Investigation

[1] The Peking and Narthang Bstan-ḥgyur read here *drañ-bar mi nus-so.* This may mean that the remark of the Vaibhāṣika applies to the elements of mind alone, i.e. the elements that cannot be carried from one place to another. But Saṅghabhadra's text points to a reading *bçad-par mi nus-so,* which undoubtedly is the correct one, since it is supported by the translation of Hiuen-Tsang. The corruption must be very old, since the block-print of the Aga monastery, which is founded on old sources coming from Dergo, repeats it and it is retained by Mchims-pa.

L'Abhidharmakośa de Vasubandhu (V. 25-27)

Louis de la Vallée Poussin

25 a-b. Les *dharmas* existent aux trois époques, parce que Bhagavat l'a dit, parce que la connaissance mentale procède de deux, parce qu'elle a un objet, parce que le passé porte un fruit. [2]

1. Bhagavat a enseigné en propres termes *(kaṇṭhatas)* l'existence du passé et de l'avenir : « Moines, si le *rūpa* passé n'existait pas, le saint Śrāvaka instruit ne serait pas ' ne prenant pas en considéra-

le chapitre du Vijñānakāya de Devaśarman qui traite de l'existence du passé et du futur.

Voir Kośa, i. 7 c-d, 34 d, iv. 35 a-b, v. 62 ; trad. i. p. 25.

Kathāvatthu, i. 7-8, note de Shwe Zan Aung, p. 375, 392 de la traduction ; ix. 6-7 ; Milinda, 50-54 ; Visuddhimagga, 686 (Si on abandonne les passions présentes, passées, futures ; comp. Kathāvatthu, xix. 1).

Āryadeva, Catuḥśatikā, 256-8 (Memoirs As. Soc. Bengal, iii. n° 8, 1914, p. 491) ; Bodhicaryāvatārapañjikā, 579-580 (Traikālyavādin) ; Madhyamaka, xvii. 14, xxii. 11, xxv. 5 ; Wassilieff (sur les Prāsaṅgikas), 363 (= 331).

Remarques de A. B. Keith, Buddhist Philosophy, 163-5.

Voir aussi la bibliographie ci-dessous p. 52, 53.

1. *saṃskṛtalakṣaṇayogān na śāśvatatvaprasaṅgaḥ.*

2. dus rnams kun tu yod gsuṅs phyir / gñis phyir yul yod phyir ḥbras phyir. — On a certainement : .... [*ukter*] *dvayāt* [*sadviṣayāt*] *phalāt* /. — Il est plus malaisé de transcrire en sanscrit les premiers mots : *dus rnams kun tu yod* : peut-être *sarveṣu adhvasu santi.* — Les versions chinoises donnent : « Les trois époques (littéralement ' mondes ', *loka*) existent » ; mais d'après le tibétain : « Les Vaibhāṣikas ne soutiennent pas que les conditionnés *(saṃkṛtas)*, lesquels ont les caractères des conditionnés, sont éternels ; mais ces docteurs soutiennent que : ils existent à toutes les époques » *(dus rnams kun tu yod par ni gsal bar dam ḥchaḥo).*

tion ' le *rūpa* passé ... Si le *rūpa* futur n'existait pas, le saint Śrāvaka instruit [2 b] ne serait pas ' ne se complaisant pas ' dans le *rūpa* futur. C'est parce que le *rūpa* futur existe que le saint Śrāvaka instruit.... ». [1]

2. Bhagavat enseigne la même doctrine implicitement *(arthatas)* lorsqu'il dit : « La connaissance *(vijñāna)* est produite en raison de deux. — Quels sont ces deux ? — L'organe de la vue et le visible..... le *manas* et les *dharmas* ». [2] Or si les *dharmas* passés et futurs n'existaient pas, la connaissance mentale *(manovijñāna)* qui les a pour objet ne naîtrait pas en raison de deux.

Voilà pour les preuves tirées de l'Écriture. Quant aux preuves rationnelles :

3. Étant donné l'objet *(ālambana)*, la connaissance peut naître ; non pas, si l'objet n'est pas donné. Si les choses passées et futures n'existaient pas, il y aurait connaissance sans objet ; donc, faute d'objet, il n'y aurait pas de connaissance.

4. Si le passé n'existe pas, comment l'acte bon et mauvais peut-il, dans l'avenir, donner un fruit ? En effet, au moment où le fruit est produit, la cause de rétribution *(vipākahetu)* (ii. 54 c-d) est passée.

C'est ainsi que, pour des raisons tirées de l'Écriture et du raisonnement, les Vaibhāṣikas affirment l'existence du passé et du futur.

Les docteurs qui se proclament *Sarvāstivādin*, ' partisans de l'existence de tout ', soutiennent que le passé et le futur existent comme choses *(dravya)*.

25 c-d. Celui qui affirme l'existence des *dharmas* des trois époques est tenu pour Sarvāstivādin. [3]

1. Saṃyuktakāgama, iii. 14 : ***rūpam anityam atītam anāgatam / kaḥ punar vādaḥ pratyutpannasya / evaṃdarśī śrutavān āryaśrāvako 'tīte rūpe 'napekṣo bhavati / anāgataṃ rūpaṃ nābhinandati / pratyutpannasya rūpasya nirvide virāgāya nirodhāya pratipanno bhavati / atītaṃ ced bhikṣavo rūpaṃ nābhaviṣyan na śrutavān āryaśrāvako .....***

Comparer la citation du même Sūtra, Madhyamakavṛtti, xxii. 11 ; Majjhima, iii. 188.

2. Saṃyutta ii. 72, etc. ; Kośa, iii. 32.

3. de yod smra baḥi phyir thams cad / yod par smra bar ḥdod = [***tadastivādāt sarvāstivādī mataḥ***]

Le docteur qui affirme l'existence de tout, passé, présent, futur, est tenu pour Sarvāstivādin. Celui qui affirme l'existence du présent et d'une partie du passé, à savoir de l'acte qui n'a pas donné son fruit ; et l'inexistence du futur et d'une partie du passé, à savoir de l'acte qui a donné son fruit, il est tenu pour Vibhajyavādin ; il n'appartient pas à l'école Sarvāstivādin.[1]

Combien de systèmes dans cette école ? Combien de manières d'entendre la doctrine de l'existence de tout *(sarvāstivāda)* ? Et quelle est la meilleure ?

25 d-26. Les Sarvāstivādins sont de quatre espèces suivant qu'ils enseignent la différence de *bhāva*, la différence de caractère *(lakṣaṇa)*, la différence de condition *(avasthā)*, la différence mutuelle. Le troisième est le meilleur : les trois époques sont établies en raison de l'activité.[2]

1. Paramārtha : « Si un homme dit que tout existe, passé, futur, présent, espace, *pratisaṃkhyānirodha* (= Nirvāṇa), *apratisaṃkhyānirodha*, on dit que cet homme est de l'école Sarvāstivādin. Il y a d'autres hommes qui disent : « Les *dharmas* présents existent ; les actes passés, s'ils n'ont pas donné leur fruit, existent ; quand ils ont donné leur fruit et les *dharmas* futurs qui ne sont pas fruits [d'un acte passé ou présent] n'existent pas ». Ces hommes qui disent que les trois époques existent mais font ces distinctions, on ne dit pas qu'ils sont Sarvāstivādins, mais qu'ils sont Vibhajyavādins ».

Vasumitra, sur les Kāśyapīyas (Wassiliev, 283, fol. 176 b) : « L'acte dont la rétribution a mûri, n'existe pas ; l'acte dont la rétribution n'a pas mûri, existe ; les *saṃskāras* naissant de causes passées et non pas de causes futures ». — C'est la thèse des Kassapikas, Kathāvatthu, i. 8.

Sur les Vibhajyāvādins, ci-dessus p. 23-24.

2. de dag / rnam bzhi dṅos daṅ mthsan ñid daṅ / gnas skabs gzhan gzhan ḥgyur zhes bya / gsum pa bzaṅ ste bya ba yis / dus rnams rnam bzhag.

La Vyākhyā donne les termes *bhāvānyathika, lakṣaṇānyathika, avasthānyathika, anyathānyathika.*

[*caturvidhāḥ / ete bhāvalakṣaṇāvasthānyathānyathikāhvayāḥ /*] *tṛtīyaḥ śobhano 'dhvānaḥ kāritreṇa vyavasthitāḥ /*

bhāvānyathika = « qui maintient que les époques diffèrent *(anyathā)* par le fait du *bhāva* ». Mais *anyathānyathika* est traduit *gzhan daṅ gzhan du gyur pa pa ;* et on a la glose *pūrvāparam apekṣyānyonya ucyate :* « l'époque est dite réciproquement distincte *(anyonya)* en raison de ce qui suit et précède ». *gzhan daṅ gzhan* = *anyonya.* — Les sources chinoises traduisent le nom

1. Le Bhadanta Dharmatrāta défend le *bhāvānyathātva*, c'est-à-dire il affirme que les trois époques, passé, présent et futur, sont différenciées par la non identité du *bhāva*.

Quand un *dharma* chemine d'une époque à une autre époque, sa nature *(dravya)* n'est pas modifiée, mais le *bhāva* est modifié. Exemple qui montre la différence de figure *(ākṛti)* : un vase d'or qu'on brise et qu'on transforme : la figure *(saṃsthāna*, i. 10 a) est modifiée, non pas la couleur *(varṇa)*. Exemple qui montre la différence des qualités *(guṇa)* : le lait devient petit lait ; la saveur [3 b], la force, la digestibilité sont abandonnées, mais non pas la couleur. De même, lorsque le *dharma* futur passe du futur dans le présent, le *bhāva* futur *(anāgatabhāva)* est abandonné, le *bhāva* présent est acquis ; mais la nature *(dravya)* reste identique ; lorsqu'il passe du présent dans le passé, le *bhāva* présent est abandonné, le *bhāva* passé est acquis ; mais la nature reste identique.

2. Le Bhadanta Ghoṣaka défend le *lakṣaṇānyathātva*.

Le *dharma* chemine à travers les époques. Quand il est passé, il est muni *(yukta)* du caractère *(lakṣaṇa)* de passé, mais il n'est pas démuni *(aviyukta)* des caractères de présent et de futur ; futur, il est muni du caractère de futur, mais il n'est pas démuni des caractères de présent et de passé ; présent, il est muni du caractère de présent, mais il n'est pas démuni des caractères de passé et de futur.[1] Exemple : un homme attaché *(rakta)* à une femme n'est pas détaché *(avirakta)* à l'égard des autres femmes.

3. Le Bhadanta Vasumitra défend l'*avasthānyathātva* ; les époques diffèrent par la différence de condition *(avasthā)*. Le *dharma*, che-

du quatrième docteur : « qui affirme que la différence des époques tient à la relation *(apekṣā)* ».

Voir Rockhill, Life of the Buddha, p. 196 (traduction de l'ouvrage de Bhavya sur les sectes) ; Watters, Yuan Chwang, i. 274. – L'auteur des Yogasūtras, iii. 13, iv. 12, etc., dépend des sources Sarvāstivādins, voir Notes bouddhiques, Bull. Acad. de Belgique, 1922, p. 522.

1. Quand un caractère est en activité *(labdhavṛtti)*, le *dharma* est muni de ce caractère, mais il n'est pas démuni des autres caractères, car, dans cette hypothèse, un certain *dharma* futur ne pourrait pas être, plus tard, ce même *dharma* présent et passé.

minant à travers les époques, ayant pris *(prāpya)* telle ou telle condition, devient différent par la différence de la condition, non par une différence de nature *(dravya)*. Exemple : le jeton *(vartikā, gulikā)* placé dans la case des unités, s'appelle un ; placé dans la case des dizaines, dix ; placé dans la case des centaines, cent.

4. Le Bhadanta Buddhadeva défend l'*anyonyathātva* : les époques s'établissent par relation.

Le *dharma*, cheminant à travers les époques [4 a], prend différents noms par relation, c'est-à-dire, il est appelé passé, futur, présent, par rapport à ce qui précède et à ce qui suit. Exemple : une même femme est fille et mère.[1]

C'est ainsi que ces quatre docteurs soutiennent l'existence de tout.[2]

Le premier, professant la « transformation » *(pariṇāma)* est à réfuter avec les Sāṃkhyas.[3]

1. Les deux commentateurs de Hiuan-tsang diffèrent. D'après Fa-pao, le futur est établi relativement *(apekṣya)* au passé et au présent ; le passé, relativement au présent et au futur; le présent, relativement au passé et au futur. C'est l'opinion de Saṃghabhadra. D'après P'ou-kouang, le futur, relativement à l'antérieur ; le passé, relativement au postérieur ; le présent, relativement à l'un et à l'autre : c'est le système de la Vibhāṣā, 77, 2.

2. Vibhāṣā, 77, 1. — « Les Sarvāstivādins ont quatre grands maîtres qui établissent différemment la différence des trois époques ..... 1. Vasumitra qui dit qu'elles diffèrent par l'état *(avasthā)* ; 2. Buddhadeva qui dit qu'elles diffèrent par le point de vue *(apekṣā)* ; 3. le partisan de la différence quant au *bhāva*, qui dit : le *dharma*, changeant d'époque, diffère par le *bhāva* non pas par la nature ... ; le *dharma*, passant du futur dans le présent, quoiqu'il abandonne le *bhāva* futur et acquière le *bhāva* présent, cependant ~~ni ne~~ perd ni n'acquiert sa nature .... ; 4. le partisan de la différence quant au *lakṣaṇa* ».

L'école Ekavyavahārika (i-chouo-pou) dit que les trois époques ne sont que parole, que leur nature n'existe pas.

Les Lokottaravādins établissent l'époque en raison (?) du *dharma* : donc ce qui est mondain *(laukika)* existe relativement ; ce qui est supra-mondain *(lokottara)* existe réellement.

Pour l'école des Sūtras, pour l'école des Mahāsāṃghikas (king-pou ; ta-tchong-pou), le passé et le futur n'existent pas ; le présent existe.

3. La Vibhāṣā, 77, 1, réfute la théorie de la différence du *bhāva* : « En dehors du caractère *(lakṣaṇa)* d'un *dharma*, quel peut bien être son *bhāva* ? » Mais un commentaire dit : La nature du *dharma* dans les trois époques n'est pas transformée ; il y a seulement différence dans le fait de l'activité *(kāritra)*, de la

Dans l'hypothèse du second, les époques, passé, présent, futur, sont confondues *(adhvasaṃkara)*, puisque les trois caractères se trouvent partout. L'exemple d'ailleurs manque de ressemblance, car, chez l'homme en question, il y a concupiscence en activité à l'égard d'une femme *(rāgasamudācāra, rāgaparyavasthāna)* ; à l'égard des autres, il y a seulement ' possession de la concupiscence ' *(rāgaprāpti)* (ii. 36).

Dans l'hypothèse du quatrième, les trois époques existent en même temps : un *dharma* passé, par exemple, est passé par rapport à ce qui précède ; futur, par rapport à ce qui suit ; présent, par rapport à ce qui précède et à ce qui suit.

Par conséquent le bon système est celui de Vasumitra, d'après lequel les époques et les conditions sont établies *(vyavasthāpita)* par l'opération ou activité *(kāritra)* : quand le *dharma* n'accomplit pas son opération, il est futur ; quand il l'accomplit, il est présent ; quand l'opération a pris fin, il est passé.[1]

Le Sautrāntika critique : Si le passé, si le futur existent comme choses, ils sont présents [4 b] : pourquoi les qualifier passé et futur ?

Réponse : Nous l'avons dit. C'est l'opération, non faite, en train d'être faite, déjà faite, qui détermine l'époque du *dharma.*[2]

Fort bien. Mais quelle opération assignerez-vous à l'œil *tatsabhāga ?* L'opération d'un œil est de voir et l'œil *tatsabhāga* ne voit pas (i. 42). Direz-vous que son opération est de projeter et de donner

non-activité, etc. : c'est là le *bhāva* du *dharma.* Et cette transformation *(pariṇāma)* n'est pas pareille à celle des Sāṃkhyas : ceux-ci disent que la nature des *dharmas* est éternelle et qu'elle se transforme en les vingt-trois *tattvas.* Or la nature du *dharma* conditionné *(saṃskṛta)* n'est pas éternelle. C'est en raison de cette modification, activité, non-activité, etc., que nous parlons de transformation. Les théories établies par Ghoṣaka et par Buddhadeva sont aussi irréprochables : elles ne présentent pas grande différence avec celle de Vasumitra. Seulement Vasumitra donne une explication solide et simple. Aussi le maître du Śāstra (Vasubandhu), d'accord avec la Vibhāṣā, la préfère ....

1. *uparatakāritram atītam / aprāptakāritram anāgatam / prāptānuparatakāritraṃ vartamānam /*

2. Vibhāṣā, 76, 11 : La sensation non encore éprouvée est future ; pendant qu'on l'éprouve, présente ; éprouvée, passée .....

un fruit *(phaladānaparigraha*, ii. 59) ? Mais alors, si donner le fruit est ' opération ', les causes *sabhāgahetu*, etc. (ii. 59 c) donnant leur fruit quand elles sont passées, on arrive à cette conclusion que, passées, elles accompliront leur opération et seront par conséquent présentes. Ou si l'opération, pour être complète, exige la projection et le don du fruit, ces causes passées seront du moins à demi-présentes. Les époques se trouvent donc confondues.

Poursuivons cet examen.

27 a. Qu'est-ce qui s'oppose à l'activité du *dharma ?*[1]

Pourquoi, existant toujours, le *dharma* n'exerce-t-il pas toujours son activité ? Quel obstacle fait que tantôt il produit et tantôt ne produit pas son opération ? On ne peut pas dire que son inaction résulte de la non-présence de certaines causes, puisque ces causes aussi existent toujours.

27 a. Comment l'activité peut-elle être passée, etc. ?[2]

Comment l'activité elle-même sera-t-elle passée, etc. ? Imaginerez-vous, de l'activité, une seconde activité ? Ce serait absurde. Mais si l'activité, en elle-même, par elle-même *(svarūpasattāpekṣayā)*, est passée, etc., pourquoi ne pas admettre qu'il en va de même du *dharma ?* Et à quoi bon dire que l'époque dépend de l'activité passée, etc. ?

Direz-vous que l'activité n'est ni passée [5 a], ni future, ni présente, et que, cependant, elle est ? Alors, étant *asaṃskṛta*, elle est éternelle *(nitya)*, et comment pouvez-vous dire que le *dharma* est futur quand il n'exerce pas son activité, passé quand il ne l'exerce plus ?

Ces objections porteraient, réplique le Sarvāstivādin, si l'activité était autre que le *dharma*.[3]

1. *kiṃvighnam* = gegs su byed. — Entendre : *kiṃvighnaṃ [kāritram]*, ou lire *kiṃ vighnam* = *ko vibandhaḥ*.

2. de yaṅ ji ltar = [*tad api katham*]

3. Vibhāṣā, 76, 14 : L'activité est-elle la même chose que la nature du *dharma* ? Est-elle différente ? — Il n'est pas possible de dire qu'elle est la même chose ou qu'elle est différente ....,

27 b. Mais, si elle n'est pas autre que le *dharma*, les époques ne sont plus justifiées.[1]

Si l'activité est la nature même du *dharma*, le *dharma* existant toujours, l'activité aussi existera toujours. Pourquoi et comment dit-on tantôt qu'elle est passée, tantôt qu'elle est future ? La distinction des époques n'est plus justifiée.

Le Sarvāstivādin réplique : En quoi n'est-elle pas justifiée ? En effet le *dharma* conditionné qui n'est pas né est appelé futur ; celui qui, étant né, n'est pas détruit, est appelé présent ; celui qui est détruit est appelé passé.

Le Sautrāntika répond : Si, passé et futur, le *dharma* existe avec la même nature *(tenaivātmanā)* que lorsqu'il est présent,

27 b-c. Existant de même, comment peut-il être non-né ou détruit ?[2]

La nature propre *(svabhāva)* de ce *dharma* continuant d'être, comment ce *dharma* serait-il non-né ou détruit ? Qu'est-ce qui lui manquait d'abord, par l'absence de quoi on le qualifiait non-né ? Qu'est-ce qui lui manquera après, par l'absence de quoi on le qualifiera détruit ? Par conséquent, si on n'admet pas que le *dharma* existe après avoir été inexistant *(abhūtvā bhāvaḥ)* [5 b] et n'existe plus après avoir existé *(bhūtvā abhāvaḥ)*, les trois époques ne peuvent être établies.[3]

Il convient d'examiner les raisonnements du Sarvāstivādin.

1. Pour cet argument que, possédant les caractères du conditionné (naissance, etc., ii. 45 c), les conditionnés ne sont pas éternels bien qu'ils existent et dans le passé et dans le futur, c'est pur verbiage, car, existant toujours, le *dharma* n'est susceptible ni de naitre ni de périr : « le *dharma* est éternel, et le *dharma* n'est pas éternel ». Parler ainsi, c'est se contredire dans les termes *(apūrvaiṣā vāco yuktiḥ)*.

1. gzhan ma yin / dus su mi ruṅ = *nānyad* [*adhvā na yujyate* /]

2. de bzhin du / yod na ci phyir ma skyes śig = [*tathā san kim ajo naṣṭaḥ*]

3. Sur la définition *abhūtvā bhāvaḥ*, voir les sources citées Madhyamakavṛtti, p. 263, Majjhima, iii. 25, Śikṣāsamuccaya, 248, Milinda, 52, etc.

C'est ce qu'explique la stance : « La nature propre existe toujours, et on ne veut pas que l'être soit éternel, ni que l'être soit différent de la nature propre : c'est clairement fait du prince. »[1]

2. Quant à cet argument que Bhagavat a enseigné l'existence du passé et du futur — puisqu'il a dit : « l'acte passé est, le fruit futur est »[2] — nous aussi nous disons que le passé est, que le futur est *(astiti)*. Passé, ce qui fut existant *(yad bhūtapūrvam)* ; futur, ce qui, la cause étant donnée, sera existant *(yad bhaviṣyati)* : c'est dans ce sens que nous disons que le passé est, que le futur est. Mais ils n'existent pas en fait *(dravyatas)* comme le présent.

Le Sarvāstivādin proteste : Qui dit qu'ils existent comme le présent ?

S'ils n'existent pas comme le présent, comment existent-ils ?

Le Sarvāstivādin répond : Ils existent avec la nature de passé et de futur. [6 a]

Mais, s'ils existent, comment peut-on leur attribuer nature de passé et de futur ? — Par le fait, Bhagavat, dans le texte invoqué par le Sarvāstivādin, a pour but de condamner la vue de la négation de la cause et de l'effet (iv. 79, v. 7). Il dit : « le passé est », dans le sens de : « le passé fut » ; il dit : « le futur est », dans le sens de : « le futur sera ». Le mot ' est ' *(asti)* est un *nipāta*[3], ainsi qu'on voit dans les expressions : « Il y a *(asti)* inexistence antérieure de la lampe », « il y a inexistence postérieure de la lampe », et comme on dit encore : « Elle est éteinte cette lampe, mais ce n'est pas moi qui

1. *svabhāvaḥ sarvadā cāsti bhāvo nityaś ca neṣyate /*
na ca svabhāvād bhāvo 'nyo vyaktam īśvaraceṣṭitam //

Cité par Prajñākaramati, Bodhicaryāvatāra, p. 581, qui utilise (p. 579-582) le Kośa sans citer sa source.

C'est-à-dire : La nature propre *(svabhāva, svalakṣaṇa)* du *rūpa*, etc. existe toujours ; mais l'être, *rūpa*, etc. *(rūpādibhāva)*, on ne veut pas qu'il soit éternel. Il sera donc différent de la nature propre ? Non, il n'est pas différent de la nature propre. Purement arbitraire, cette théorie est un fait du prince, qui ne comporte pas de justification *(nātra yuktir asti)*.

2. Saṃyukta, 13, 21.

3. D'après Hiuan-tsang : « le mot ' est ' s'applique à ce qui existe et à ce qui n'existe pas ». — Bodhicaryāvatāra, 581, 17 : *astiśabdasya nipātatvāt kālatrayavṛttitvam*. — Voir ii. 55 d, p. 232 de notre traduction.

l'ai éteinte ».[1] C'est de la même manière que le texte dit : « le passé est », « le futur est ». A comprendre autrement, le passé, ' étant ', ne serait pas passé.

Le Sarvāstivādin répond. — Nous voyons que Bhagavat, s'adressant aux ascètes *(parivrājakas)* Laguḍaśikhīyakas [2], s'exprime ainsi : « L'acte passé, détruit, qui a péri, qui a cessé, cet acte est ». D'après l'explication proposée, le sens sera : « Cet acte fut ». Or pouvons-nous supposer que les Parivrājakas n'admissent pas que l'acte passé eût été jadis ?

Le Sautrāntika réplique. — Lorsque Bhagavat dit que l'acte passé est, il a en vue le pouvoir de donner un fruit, pouvoir qui fut placé dans la série de l'agent par l'acte qui a été jadis. A comprendre autrement, si l'acte passé existe actuellement en soi *(svena bhāvena vidyamānam)*, comment peut-on le considérer comme passé ?

Du reste, l'Écriture contient une déclaration formelle. Bhagavat a dit dans le Paramārthaśūnyatāsūtra : « L'œil, ô Bhikṣus, naissant, ne vient de nulle part [6 b] ; périssant, il ne va s'accumuler nulle part. De la sorte, ô Bhikṣus, l'œil existe après avoir été inexistant et, après avoir existé, il disparaît ». [3] Si l'œil futur existait, Bhagavat ne dirait pas que l'œil existe après avoir été inexistant.

1. *asti niruddhaḥ sa eva dīpo na tu mayā nirodhitaḥ.*

2. Ou, d'après une variante : « au sujet des Parivrājakas .... ». Il s'agit des religieux qui firent assassiner Maudgalyāyana et qui affirmaient l'inexistence de l'acte passé : *yat karmābhyatītam tan nāsti.*

D'après la glose de l'éditeur japonais, ce Sūtra se trouve dans Madhyama 4, 10; d'après la Vyākhyā dans Saṃyuktakāgama.

Ni le Jātaka 522, ni le commentaire du Dhammapada (x. 7) qui racontent la mort de Maudgalyāyana, ne donnent le nom des Parivrājakas.

3. Citation (Saṃyukta, 13, 22) reproduite dans Bodhicaryāvatāra ad ix. 142 (p. 581) : *cakṣur bhikṣava utpadyamānaṃ na kutaś cid āgacchati / nirudhyamānaṃ ca na kvacit saṃnicayaṃ gacchati / iti hi bhikṣavaḥ cakṣur abhūtvā bhavati bhūtvā ca prativigacchati.*

Un autre fragment du Paramārthaśūnyatāsūtra est cité ad ix. 73 (p. 474) : *iti hi bhikṣavo 'sti karma / asti phalam / kārakas tu nopalabhyate ya imān skandhān vijahāti anyāṃś ca skandhān upādatte;* citation reproduite Madhyamakāvatāra (p. 262, trad. tibétaine), Sūtrālaṃkāra, xviii. 101 (texte p. 158, trad. p. 264) et utilisée par Vasubandhu (version d'Hiuan-tsang xxix. 16 a, xxx. 2 a) dans le supplément du Kośa.

Le Sarvāstivādin dira peut-être : L'expression : « il existe après avoir été inexistant » signifie : « après avoir été inexistant dans le présent » *(vartamāne 'dhvany abhūtvā)*, c'est-à-dire « après avoir été inexistant en tant que présent » *(vartamānabhāvena abhūtvā)*. — Inadmissible. Car l'époque ne diffère pas de l'œil.

Dira-t-il qu'on doit comprendre : « après avoir été inexistant en sa nature propre *(svalakṣaṇatas)* » ? [1] — C'est avouer en propres termes que l'œil futur n'existe pas.

3. Quant à l'argument que « le passé et le futur existent, puisque la connaissance naît en raison de deux choses », faut-il entendre que — la connaissance mentale naissant en raison de l'organe mental *(manas)* et des *dharmas* passés, futurs et présents — ces *dharmas* sont condition de la connaissance mentale au même titre que l'organe mental, c'est-à-dire en qualité de « cause génératrice » *(janakapratyaya)* ? Ou sont-ils seulement « condition en qualité d'objet » *(ālambanamātra*, ii. 62 c) ? — Evidemment des *dharmas* futurs, qui se produiront après des milliers d'années ou qui ne se produiront jamais, ne sont pas cause génératrice de la connaissance mentale actuelle. Evidemment le Nirvāṇa, qui est contradictoire à toute naissance, ne peut être cause génératrice. Reste que les *dharmas* soient condition de la connaissance en qualité d'objet : nous admettons qu'il en est ainsi des *dharmas* futurs et passés.

Le Sarvāstivādin demande : Si les *dharmas* passés et futurs n'existent pas, comment peuvent-ils être objets de la connaissance ? — Ils existent de la manière dont ils sont pris comme objets. [2] Et de quelle manière sont-ils pris comme objets ? Ils sont pris comme objets avec la note de passé et de futur [3] comme ayant existé, comme devant exister. En effet, l'homme qui se souvient d'un visible *(rūpa)* ou d'une sensation passés, ne voit pas : « cela est » ; mais il se souvient : « cela fut » ; l'homme qui prévoit le futur ne voit pas le futur comme existant, mais il le prévoit comme devant exister *(bhaviṣyat)*.

1. *svātmani cakṣuṣi cakṣur abhūtvā bhavati.*
2. *yathālambyante yathā gṛhyante.*
3. *abhūd bhaviṣyati ca* : ce qui, dans la condition de présent, a été ou sera « visible », cela est l'objet.

Autre point. La mémoire (qui est une certaine connaissance mentale) saisit le visible *(rūpa)* tel qu'il a été vu, la sensation *(vedanā)* telle qu'elle a été sentie, c'est-à-dire le visible et la sensation à l'état de présent. Si le *dharma* dont on se souvient est, de fait, tel qu'on le saisit par la mémoire, il est manifestement présent ; s'il n'est pas tel qu'on le saisit par la mémoire, la connaissance de mémoire a certainement un objet inexistant.

Dira-t-on que le visible passé ou futur existe sans être présent, parce que le visible passé ou futur n'est autre chose que les atomes *(paramāṇu)* à l'état de dispersion *(viprakīrṇa)* ? — Mais nous dirons : (1) lorsque la connaissance prend comme objet, par la mémoire ou la prévision, le visible passé ou futur, elle ne le prend pas comme objet à l'état de dispersion, mais bien au contraire aggluting *(saṃcita)* ; (2) si le visible passé ou futur est le visible du présent à cette différence près que les atomes sont dispersés *(paramāṇuśo vibhaktam)*, les atomes sont donc éternels ; il n'y a jamais ni production *(utpāda)* ni destruction ; il y a seulement association et dispersion des atomes. Soutenir semblable thèse, c'est adopter la doctrine des Ājīvikas et rejeter le Sūtra du Sugata : « L'œil, ô Bhikṣus, naissant, ne vient de nulle part... » [7 b] ; (3) l'argument ne vaut pas pour la sensation et les autres *dharmas* ' non-massifs ' *(amūrta)* : n'étant pas des agglutinations d'atomes *(aparamāṇusaṃcita)*, on ne voit pas comment ils seraient, dans le passé et le futur, des atomes à l'état de dispersion. En fait, d'ailleurs, on se souvient de la sensation telle qu'elle a été sentie lorsqu'elle était présente ; on la prévoit telle qu'elle sera sentie lorsqu'elle sera présente. Si, passée et future, elle est telle qu'on la saisit par la mémoire ou la prévision, elle est éternelle. Donc la connaissance mentale nommée « mémoire » a un objet inexistant, à savoir la sensation telle qu'elle n'est pas actuellement.

Le Vaibhāṣika dit : Si ce qui n'existe absolument pas peut être objet de la connaissance, un treizième *āyatana* (i. 14) pourra être objet de la connaissance.

L'auteur répond : Quel est donc, d'après vous, l'objet de la connaissance qui consiste à dire : « Il n'y a pas de treizième *āyatana* »? Direz-vous que c'est son nom, ' treizième *āyatana* ' ? Alors cet objet n'est qu'un nom ; la chose désignée, l'objet, n'existe pas. — En outre, quel sera l'objet existant sur lequel porte la connaissance de l'inexistence antérieure du son *(prāgabhāva)* ?

Le Vaibhāṣika répond : L'objet de cette connaissance est le son même et non pas son inexistence.

Alors, celui qui est en quête *(prārthayate)* d'inexistence du son, devra faire du bruit !

Le Vaibhāṣika répond : Non, car le son dont il y a inexistence antérieure, existe à l'état futur, et c'est ce son à l'état futur qui est l'objet de la connaissance d'inexistence antérieure.

Mais si le son futur, dont il y a inexistence antérieure, existe de fait, comment a-t-on la notion qu'il n'existe pas *(nāsti)* ?

Le Vaibhāṣika répond : Il n'existe pas en tant que présent *(vartamāno nāsti)* ; d'où la notion : « il n'existe pas ».

Vous n'avez pas le droit de parler ainsi, car c'est le même *dharma* qui est passé, présent, futur. Ou, s'il y a différence entre le son futur et le son présent, et que la notion : « il n'existe pas » porte sur cette différence, reconnaissez que le caractère distinctif du présent existe après ne pas avoir existé. — Nous tiendrons donc pour établi que l'existant et l'inexistant *(bhāva, abhāva)* peuvent être l'objet de la connaissance.

Le Vaibhāṣika dit : Si l'inexistant *(abhāva)* peut être objet *(ālambana)* de la connaissance, comment le Bodhisattva à sa dernière existence *(caramabhavika)* a-t-il dit : « Il est impossible que je connaisse [8 a], que je voie ce qui n'existe pas dans ce monde » ? [1]

Disons que le sens de ce texte est clair : « Je ne suis pas comme d'autres ascètes orgueilleux *(ābhimānika*, v. 10 a) qui s'attribuent une ' illumination ' *(avabhāsa)* [2] inexistante : moi, je ne vois comme étant que ce qui est. » D'ailleurs, à admettre votre thèse, l'objet de

1. *yat loke nāsti taj jñāsyāmi ... eṣa sambhavo nāsti.*
2. *divyacakṣuravabhāsa*, vii. 42.

toute idée *(buddhi)* sera réel *(sadviṣayā)* : si tout ce qu'on pense est réel, il n'y a plus place pour doute ou examen *(vimarśa, vicāra)* ; il n'y a pas de différence entre le Bodhisattva et les autres.

. Ajoutons que les idées *(buddhi)* ont certainement pour objet l'existant et l'inexistant *(sadasadālambana)*, car Bhagavat dit ailleurs en propres termes : « A partir du moment où je lui ai dit « Viens, Bhikṣu ! » (iv. 26 c), mon Śrāvaka, instruit par moi le matin progresse le soir, instruit le soir progresse le matin : il connaîtra ce qui est comme étant *(sac ca satto jñāsyati)* et ce qui n'est pas comme n'étant pas, ce qui n'est pas le plus élevé *(sa-uttara)* comme n'étant pas le plus élevé, et ce qui est le plus élevé *(anuttara* = Nirvāṇa) comme étant le plus élevé. » (iv. 127 d)[1]

Par conséquent la raison ne vaut pas que le Sarvāstivādin a donnée en faveur de l'existence du passé et du futur : « parce que l'objet de la connaissance est existant. »

4. Le Sarvāstivādin tire aussi argument du fruit de l'acte. Mais les Sautrāntikas n'admettent pas que le fruit naisse directement de l'acte passé. Le fruit naît d'un état spécial de la série *(cittasaṃtānaviśeṣāt)*, état qui procède de l'acte *(tatpūrvakāt)*, ainsi qu'on verra à la fin de cet ouvrage à l'endroit où nous réfutons la doctrine des Vātsīputrīyas *(ātmavādapratiṣedha* ; voir iv. 85 a).

Mais les docteurs qui affirment l'existence réelle *(dravyatas)* du passé et du futur [8 b], doivent admettre l'éternité du fruit : quelle efficace *(sāmarthya)* pourront-ils attribuer à l'acte ? efficace quant à la production *(utpāda)* ? efficace quant au fait de rendre présent *(vartamānīkaraṇa)* ?

a. C'est admettre que la production existe après avoir été inexistante *(abhūtvā bhavati)*. Si vous dites que la production elle-même préexiste, comment pouvez-vous attribuer à quoi que ce soit efficace à l'endroit de quoi que ce soit ? Vous n'avez plus qu'à joindre l'école des Vārṣagaṇyas : « Ce qui est, seulement est ; ce qui n'est pas, seule-

1. Saṃyukta, 26, 25. — « progresse » = khyad par du ḥgro. — Saṃghabhadra (xxiii. 5, 44 a 3) cite une rédaction plus développée.

ment n'est pas ; ce qui n'est pas ne naît pas ; ce qui est n'est pas détruit. »[1]

b. Que faut-il entendre par ' le fait de rendre présent ' ?

Serait-ce le fait de tirer vers un autre lieu *(deśāntarākarṣaṇa)* ? Nous y voyons trois difficultés : (1) le fruit ainsi attiré sera éternel ; (2) comment le fruit, quand il est immatériel *(arūpin)*, pourra-t-il être attiré ? (3) quant à la translation, elle existe après avoir été inexistante.

Serait-ce le fait de modifier la nature propre du fruit préexistant *(svabhāvaviśeṣaṇa)* ? Mais n'y a-t-il pas, dans cette hypothèse, apparition *(bhavana, prādurbhāva)* d'une modification antérieurement inexistante ?

Par conséquent le *sarvāstivāda*, ' la doctrine de l'existence de tout ', des Sarvāstivādins qui affirment l'existence réelle du passé et du futur, n'est pas bonne dans le Bouddhisme *(na śāsane sādhuḥ)*. Ce n'est pas dans ce sens qu'il faut entendre le *sarvāstivāda*. Le bon *sarvāstivāda* consiste à affirmer l'existence de *tout* en comprenant le terme *tout* comme le comprend l'Écriture. Comment le Sūtra affirme-t-il que tout existe ? — « Quand on dit : ' tout existe ', ô brāhmane [9 a], il s'agit des douze *āyatanas* : ce sont des termes équivalents. »[2] Ou bien, le tout qui existe, c'est les trois époques. Et comment elles existent, cela a été dit : « Ce qui a été auparavant, c'est le passé ..... » (ci-dessus p. 58).

Mais si le passé et le futur n'existent pas, comment peut-on être lié *(saṃyukta)* par un *kleśa* passé ou futur à une chose *(vastu)* passée ou future ?

On est lié par le *kleśa* passé en raison de l'existence, dans la série, d'un *anuśaya* qui est né du *kleśa* passé ; on est lié par le *kleśa* futur

1. *Lo rtsi ba pa rnams* — La troupe de la pluie. — Il faut ajouter cette citation aux deux passages signalés par Garbe, Sāṃkhya-Philosophie, p. 36, Yogabhāṣya, iii. 52 et Sāṃkhyatattvakaumudī, *ad* 47. — Saṃghabhadra, 53 a 15.

2. Mahāniddesa, p. 133 : *sabbaṃ vuccati dvādasāyatanāni* ; Saṃyutta, iv. 13 : *kiñ ca bhikkhave sabbam ? — cakkhuṃ ceva rūpā ca* ... — Majjhima, i. 3. — Saṃyukta, 13, 16. — Mon « Nirvāṇa » (1924) chap. iii. § 1er.

en raison de l'existence d'un *anuśaya* qui est la cause du *kleśa* futur. On est lié à une chose passée ou future en raison de l'*anuśaya* d'un *kleśa* qui a eu ou aura cette chose pour objet.

Le Vaibhāṣika dit : « Le passé et le futur existent vraiment. [1] Quant à ce qui ne peut pas être expliqué, il faut savoir que

27 d. La nature des choses est profonde ; [2]

certainement, elle ne peut pas être établie par le raisonnement. » [3]

[Donc il ne faut pas nier le passé et le futur] [4]

On peut dire *(asti paryāyaḥ)* que cela même qui naît périt : par exemple le visible naît, le visible périt [: le *dravya*, l'essence reste la même]. [5] On peut dire que ce qui naît diffère de ce qui périt : en effet, ce qui naît, c'est le futur ; ce qui périt, c'est le présent. Le temps aussi naît, car ce qui est naissant est compris dans le temps, a pour nature le temps [6] ; et le *dharma* naît du temps, en raison de la multiplicité des moments du temps futur. [7]

1. *santy evātītānāgatāḥ (dharmāḥ).*

2. chos ñid dag ni zab pa yin = [*gambhīrā jātu dharmatā* //]

3. gaṅ zhig draṅ bar mi nus pa de la ni ḥdi ltar / chos ñid dag ni zab pa yin de gdon mi za bar rtogs pas sgrub pa ma yin no zhes bya bar rig par byaḥo zhes zer ro

Hiuan-tsang : « Le passé et le futur existent vraiment, comme le présent. Tous ceux qui, ici, ne sont pas capables d'expliquer [les objections des Sautrāntikas : *glose de l'éditeur japonais*] et qui désirent leur propre bien (Mahāvyutpatti, 245, 1201), doivent savoir que : « La nature des choses est très profonde » ; elle n'est pas du domaine du raisonnement. Est-ce que ceux qui ne sont pas capables d'expliquer ont le droit de nier ? (k'i pou nêng chē pién poūo wéi oû) ».

Saṃghabhadra (xxiii. 5, 54 a 2) proteste avec vivacité : « N'attribuez pas aux Vaibhāṣikas des opinions qui ne sont pas les leurs !... Quelles sont les difficultés que je n'ai pas expliquées ? »

Je ne crois pas que la version de Stcherbatskoi, p. 91, soit correcte. — *draṅ ba* = *t'ōng-che* = *nī* = expliquer. Il n'y a pas lieu de corriger « undoubtedly » en *bçad pa* qui n'est suggéré ni par Hiuan-tsang ni par Saṃghabhadra, quoi qu'en pense M. Mac Govern.

4. Addition de Paramārtha.

5. *dravyānanyatvāt.*

6. *adhvasaṃgṛhītatvāt* = *adhvasvabhāvatvāt*, i. 7 c.

7. *adhvano 'py upādānarūpād utpadyate dharmaḥ / kasmād ity āha /*

Nous en avons fini avec ce problème que la théorie des *anuśayas* nous a fait rencontrer.

Quand un homme abandonne un objet[1] *(yad vastu prahīṇam)* [9 b] par la disparition de la possession qu'il avait de cet objet *(prāptivigamāt)*, y a-t-il pour lui « disconnexion » d'avec cet objet *(tadvisaṃyoga)* par la rupture de la possession de la passion qui porte sur cet objet *(tadālambakakleśaprahāṇāt)* ? Et inversement, quand il y a disconnexion, y a-t-il abandon ?

Quand il y a disconnexion d'avec un objet, il y a toujours abandon de cet objet ; il peut y avoir abandon sans disconnexion.

anekakṣaṇatvād anāgatasyādhvana iti / tasmād anekeṣāṃ kṣaṇānām anāgatānāṃ rāśirūpāṇāṃ kaś cid eva kṣaṇa utpadyate.

Vibhāṣā, 66, 13 : « Lorsque les conditionnés *(saṃskṛta)* futurs naissent, doit-on dire qu'ils naissent étant déjà nés, ou qu'ils naissent n'étant pas encore nés ? — Quel mal à admettre l'une ou l'autre hypothèse ? — Les deux sont mauvaises ..... — Réponse : On doit dire que le *dharma*, déjà né, naît en raison des causes et conditions *(hetupratyaya)* ; c'est-à-dire que tous les *dharmas* possèdent déjà leur nature propre *(svabhāva)* ; chacun d'eux se tient dans sa nature et, possédant déjà cette nature, on dit qu'il est déjà né. Mais il n'est pas né des causes et conditions : bien que sa nature soit déjà née, on dit qu'il naît parce qu'il est produit par le complexe des causes et conditions. D'autre part le *dharma*, non né, naît en raison des causes et des conditions : c'est-à-dire que le *dharma* futur est qualifié non-né parce qu'il naît présentement des causes et conditions .... »

1. Ci-dessous n. 3 et p. 67 ; l'éditeur japonais glose *vastu* par : « ayant la nature d'*anuśaya*, etc. »

DOCUMENTS D'ABHIDHARMA[1]

TRADUITS ET ANNOTÉS

LOUIS DE LA VALLÉE POUSSIN

LA CONTROVERSE DU TEMPS

On trouvera ici la traduction de quelques textes relatifs à un des problèmes qui divisa les écoles du Hīnayāna : 1. Fragments de la Vibhāṣā ; 2. Commentaire de Kośa, v, 25-27, par Saṃghabhadra ; 3. Notes sur le « moment » des Vaibhāṣikas et des Sautrāntikas.

Voir « Controverse du Temps dans le Vijñānakāya » (Études Asiatiques, 1925, 343-376) et Kośa, v, 25-27 (trad. française, 1925 ; trad. anglaise de Th. Stcherbatsky, 1923, Appendice à « Central Conception of Buddhism and meaning of the word Dharma »).

Sources sanscrites : Tattvasiddhi de Harivarman ; Bodhisattvabhūmi, 277 (Hiuan-tsang 544) ; Yogaśāstra, 6, p. 304, 2 — 305, 2 (réfutation de l'existence réelle du passé et de l'avenir, un des seize systèmes vicieux, 303, 3, 1) ; Karmasiddhiśāstra, 783, 1-2 ; Vasumitra et Bhavya, Traités sur les Sectes ; Madhyamaka, chap. 19 (Kālaparīkṣā) ; Prajñāptiśāstra ; Tattvasamgraha (Gaekwad, 1926) : Sthirabhāvaparīkṣā (pp. 131-166) et Traikālyaparīkṣā (503-519).

Harivarman est fort intéressant. Voir notamment les chapitres 32 : Les Kāśyapīyas disent que « l'acte qui n'a pas donné son fruit existe »; 29 : Définition de l'existant (conçu à tort comme « ce qui est l'objet de la pensée... ») ; 20 : Définition de l'inexistant ; 21 : Existence du passé et du futur ; 22 : Inexistence du passé et du futur (thèse correcte) ; 23 : Existence et inexistence de tout ; 73 : Le Vijñāna dure un petit temps (sinon, il ne connaîtrait pas) ; 74 : Le Vijñāna ne dure pas. — Harivarman, en ce qui concerne la controverse des époques,

[1] La controverse du Temps et du Pudgala dans le Vijñānakāya, Études Asiatiques, 1925 (École française d'Extrême-Orient), p. 343-376.

Textes relatifs au Nirvāṇa et aux Asaṃskṛtas, Bulletin de l'École française d'Extrême-Orient, t. 30, 1930, pp. 1-28, 29-80.

La doctrine des Refuges, Mélanges chinois et bouddhiques, i, 1932, pp. 65-70.

Le corps de l'Arhat, ibid., pp. 110-125.

J. Rahder, La Satkāyadṛṣṭi d'après Vibhāṣā, 8, ibid., pp. 227-240.

partage l'opinion des Sautrāntikas ; il se sépare des Sautrāntikas en niant les « traces », les *anuśayas* distincts des *kleśas ;* il se distingue des Sarvāstivādins en niant, non seulement le passé et le futur, et la durée, mais encore les *viprayuktas* (*prāpti*, etc.) et les *caittas* qui ne sont que des *cittas* spéciaux.

Th. Stcherbatsky (Sources bouddhiques et brahmaniques), Central Conception ; Théorie de la connaissance et la logique (trad. française, 1926), chap. 2 ; Buddhist Logic, 1932, pp. 79-118 (The theory of the instantaneous being, kṣaṇikavāda).

Sources pâlies, notamment : 1. Kathāvatthu,[1] i, 6-8 (*sabbam atthi :* Sabbatthivāda ; *avipakkavipākam atītam atthi :* Kassapika) ; ix, 12 (Qu'on possède, *samannāgama, paṭilābha*, les extases passées et futures : Andhaka) ; xv, 3-4 (*kālasaṃkhāto addhā nāma parinipphanno*...). — 2. Note sur « Time and Space », d'après un traité du XIIe siècle, Points of Controversy, p. 392. — 3. Milinda p. 49 avec les précieuses notes de Paul Demiéville, Bulletin, XXIV, p. 129. — 4. Visuddhimagga, p. 472, quatre définitions du passé, présent, futur (ci-dessous, p. 157). — 5. Compendium of Philosophy, p. 25 : les trois « instants » d'un seul instant de pensée (ci-dessous, p. 157).

I

VIBHĀṢĀ, 76, Pages 393-396

Il y a encore trois sortes de *dharmas*, les passés, les futurs et les présents.

L'auteur, en traitant ce sujet, veut réfuter les doctrines erronées et montrer la vraie doctrine.

1. D'après une opinion, le temps (*adhvan*) est autre chose que les *saṃskāras*.[2] En effet, les Dārṣṭāntikas et les Vibhajyavādins disent : « Le temps, de sa nature, est éternel (*nitya*), les *saṃskāras* sont non-éternels (*anitya*). Les *saṃskāras* circulent dans le temps,

[1] Mrs Rhys Davids, Points of Controversy, 1915. — P. 296, 10 *khaṇas* = 1 *laya*.

[2] On ne traduirait pas mal : « autre chose que les choses » — *saṃskāra*, au sens étroit, un autre nom pour « acte » (deuxième terme du Pratītyasamutpāda) ; au sens large, que nous avons ici, presque synonyme de *saṃskṛta*, « produit par les conditions, conditionné » ; le « conditionnant », *saṃskāra*, est toujours « conditionné ». — De même *pratītyasamutpāda* = *pratītyasamutpanna*, Kośa, iii. p. 74.

comme des fruits dans des corbeilles, sortant de cette corbeille-ci pour entrer dans cette corbeille-là, ou comme plusieurs hommes sortent de cette maison-ci pour entrer dans cette maison-là. De même les *saṃskāras*, du futur, entrent dans le présent, du présent, entrent dans le passé. » L'auteur veut arrêter cette opinion, montrer que le temps ne diffère pas de nature des *saṃskāras* : le temps est les *saṃskāras* ; les *saṃskāras* sont le temps. Comme il dit dans le Mahābhūtaskandhaka [1] : « Quels *dharmas* sont nommés par le mot de temps ? — Les *saṃskāras* sont désignés par cette expression (*adhivacana*). » [P. 393, col. 1, l. 18.]

2. Il y a aussi des fous qui, parmi les trois temps (*tryadhva-svabhāva*), nient l'existence du passé et du futur, et affirment que le présent est inconditionné (*asaṃskṛtadharma*). L'auteur veut montrer que la « nature propre » [2] du passé et du futur est réelle (*dravyasat*) et que le présent est conditionné (*saṃskṛta*).

a. Si le passé et le futur n'étaient pas réels, il ne pourrait y avoir possession et non-possession (*samanvāgama*...) du passé..., [3] pas plus que d'une deuxième tête, d'une troisième main, d'un sixième *skandha*, d'un treizième *āyatana*, d'un dix-neuvième *dhātu*. Or il y a possession du passé... ; donc nous savons que le passé est réel.

b. Interrogeons le négateur de la « nature propre » (*t'i*) du passé-futur. — Quand existe une cause de rétribution (*vipākahetu*) présente, le fruit obtenu par cette cause est-il présent, passé ou futur ? Si vous dites qu'il est passé, nous concluons que le passé doit exister ; si vous dites qu'il est futur, nous concluons que le futur doit exister ; si vous dites qu'il est présent, nous concluons que la cause de rétribution et son fruit doivent être simultanés. Contradiction, car la stance dit :

[1] Cinquième livre du Jñāna prasthāna, Takakusu, On the Abhidharma Literature, JPTS., 1905, p. 92.

[2] *t'i siang ; t'i* est *svabhāva, dravya*. — On aurait *svabhāvalakṣaṇa*.

[3] Sur la *prāpti* ou *samanvāgama*, Kośa, ii, p. 179. — Aussi longtemps qu'on ne l'a pas abandonnée par le Chemin, on est en possession de la passion passée...

« Celui qui fait le mal ne le sent pas aussitôt, à la manière dont le lait devient du lait fermenté ; mais, comme le fou qui marche sur un feu couvert de cendre, il est longuement brûlé.[1] »

Si vous dites que le fruit de cette cause ne se trouve dans aucune des trois époques, nous concluons que cette cause n'a pas de fruit, car le fruit de rétribution n'est pas inconditionné : si elle n'a pas de fruit, la cause aussi n'existe pas, comme une deuxième tête ou une troisième main.

De même nous demandons à quelle époque appartient la cause qui correspond au fruit de rétribution (*vipākaphala*) présent... [P. 393, col. 2, l. 13.]

c. Si le passé et le futur ne sont pas réels, il ne peut y avoir sortie du monde et profession réligieuse (*pravrajyā* et *upasaṃpad*). Il y a une stance :

« Si on soutient que le passé n'existe pas, le Bouddha passé n'existe pas : donc manqueront sortie du monde et profession. »

Encore, si le passé et le futur ne sont pas réels, il faut que les religieux (*pravrajita*), qui possèdent le savoir exact, tiennent des discours de mensonge. Il y a une stance :

« S'il soutient que le passé n'existe pas et si, cependant, il parle d'années peu nombreuses ou nombreuses [depuis la profession], il doit, de jour en jour, accroître son savoir exact (*samyagjñāna*) et ses discours faux et trompeurs. »

d. Si le passé et le futur ne sont pas réels, le présent aussi n'existe pas. Car le présent « est désigné » (*prajñapyate*) en considération (*apekṣya*) du passé et du futur. Si les trois époques manquent, manquent les *dharmas* conditionnés. Donc manquent aussi les inconditionnés qui sont établis en considération des conditionnés. Les uns et les autres manquant, manquent tous les *dharmas*. Donc manque aussi la délivrance, la sortie, le Nirvāṇa.

[1] Comparer Dhammapada, 74.

Admettre cette négation, c'est grande « vue fausse »[1]. Par conséquent... [P. 393, col. 2, l. 27.]

e. D'autre part, le présent n'est pas un *dharma* inconditionné, car il naît des causes et conditions, car il possède activité (*kāritra*, *tso yong*) : tel n'est pas l'inconditionné.

C'est ainsi que l'auteur a fait ce traité pour réfuter les opinions des autres systèmes et manifester la vraie doctrine. [P. 393, col. 2, l. 29.]

3. Quels sont les *dharmas* passés ? Une partie des cinq *skandhas*, des douze *āyatanas*, des dix-huit *dhātus*. — Même réponse pour les présents et les futurs.

En quoi ont leur nature propre (*tse sing*, *svabhāva*) les trois époques ? — En tous les *dharmas* conditionnés.[2] Comme elles y ont leur nature propre, elles y ont leur soi (*ātman*), leur être (*dravya*), leur propre substance (*svarūpa*), leur *siang fen*, leur nature radicale (*mūlabhāva*).[3] [P. 393, col. 3, l. 6.]

4. Nous avons dit leur nature propre ; c'est pourquoi il faut maintenant se demander pourquoi les [*dharmas* en question, tous les conditionnés,] reçoivent le nom d'*adhvan* (« chemin », époque »), et quel est le sens de ce mot.

Le sens est « marche » (*gamana*, *hing*). — Les *saṃskāras* (*hing*) ni n'arrivent ni ne partent : comment le sens d'*adhvan* [, lequel *adhvan* est défini comme étant les *saṃskāras*,] peut-il être « marche » ? — Pourquoi cette question ? — Si les *saṃskāras* arrivent, ils ne partent pas, car ils sont munis du caractère d'arrivée ;

[1] *mithyādṛṣṭi*, Kośa, v, p. 18.

[2] Définition des conditionnés, Kośa, i, 7, trad. pp. 11-12 : « Les *dharmas* conditionnés, c'est les cinq *skandhas* ; ils sont le chemin... (*adhvan* = temps) ». Bhāṣya : « Ils sont le chemin (*che-lou*), parce qu'ils ont pour nature d'être allés, d'aller, de devoir aller.

[3] *ngo ou tse-t'i siang-fen pen-sing.*

Comparer, p. 290, col. 2, l. 21, où on a *tse-t'i*, qui doit être *svarūpa*, *tse-ngo*, *svātman*, *tse-ou*, *svadravya*, *tse-sing*, *svabhāva*, *tse-siang*, *svalakṣaṇa*.

siang-fen, dans les lexiques, est un des quatre *fen* (ou *bhāga*, *aṃśa*) des mentaux (*caittadharma*).

s'ils partent, ils n'arrivent pas, car ils sont munis du caractère de départ. En outre, s'ils arrivent, le lieu d'où ils arrivent se videra ; s'ils partent, le lieu où ils se rendent se remplira.

C'est pourquoi le Bhadanta Vasumitra dit : « Les *saṃskāras* ni n'arrivent ni ne partent. Comme ils sont momentanés, l'idée de durée (*sthiti*) aussi est exclue. Les *saṃskāras* étant exempts des caractères d'arrivée, départ, etc., comment établir la distinction des trois époques (ou « chemins », *adhvan*) ? — C'est en fonction de l'activité (*kāritra*) que les époques sont distinguées, et, de ce point de vue, le sens d'époque (ou chemin) est : « marche ».

C'est-à-dire : les « conditionnés » (*saṃskṛtadharmas*), quand ils n'ont pas encore d'activité, sont dits « futurs » ; « présents », quand ils ont activité ; « passés », quand leur activité est détruite. [P. 393, col. 3, l. 16.]

D'après ce principe, le *rūpa* qui n'a pas encore *rūpaṇa* (Kośa, i, p. 24) est dit futur ; présent quand il a *rūpaṇa ;* passé, quand le *rūpaṇa* est détruit. — De même pour les quatre autres *skandhas*. La *vedanā* ne sent pas encore, sent, ne sent plus (*anubhava*) ; la *saṃjñā* ne saisit pas encore, saisit, ne saisit plus les « marques » (*nimittodgrahaṇa*) ; les *saṃskāras* ne « modèlent » pas encore (*abhisaṃskāra*) ... ; le *vijñāna* ne distingue pas encore (*prativijñapti*) ...

Encore, l'œil qui ne voit pas encore les visibles (*rūpa*) est dit « futur » ; « présent », quand il voit les visibles; « passé », quand la vision des visibles est détruite. — De même pour les autres *āyatanas* jusqu'au *manas* (organe mental) : le *manas* qui ne connaît pas encore les *dharmas*... [P. 393, col. 3, l. 26]

Mais, dira-t-on, lorsque l'œil présent appartient à la catégorie *tatsabhāga* (Kośa, i, p. 75, Vibhāṣā, 71, p. 368), il n'a pas l'activité de vision (*darśanakāritra*). Donc, aux termes de la définition, il ne sera pas présent ?

Cette activité lui manque ; mais ne lui manque pas l'activité qui consiste à « prendre un fruit » (ou à « projeter », *ākṣepa, grahaṇa*, Kośa, ii, p. 293), car il est « cause semblable » de *dharmas* futurs (*sabhāgahetu*, ii, p. 255) ; les conditionnés, résidant dans le présent, sont tous « cause qui prend un fruit d'écoulement » (*niṣyandaphala*, ii, p. 289). Cette activité de « prendre le fruit » s'étendant à tous les « présents », pour éviter la confusion des époques, c'est de ce point de vue qu'on établit la distinction des passé, présent et futur. [P. 394, col. 1, l. 2.]

5. Quand les trois *saṃskṛtalakṣaṇas* (Kośa, ii, p. 222) du conditionné n'ont pas encore d'activité, le conditionné est dit « futur » ...

Les conditionnés qui n'ont pas encore la quadruple activité conditionnante (*catuḥpratyayakāritra*, ii, p. 299), la sextuple activité causale (*ṣaḍhetukāritra*, ii, p. 245), sont dits « futurs » ...

Les conditionnés qui ne prennent pas encore, qui ne donnent pas encore le *puruṣakāraphala*, le *niṣyandaphala* (ii, p. 225, p. 289), sont dits « futurs » ...

Les *dharmas* mauvais (*akuśala*) et bons-impurs (*kuśalasāsrava*) qui ne prennent pas encore, qui ne donnent pas encore le fruit de rétribution (*vipākaphala*, ii, p. 271) sont dits « futurs » ; « présents », quand ils prennent ce fruit, mais ne le donnent pas encore ; « passés », quand ils ont pris ce fruit. [P. 394, col. 1, l. 15.]

Les conditionnés, quand ils ne répondent (*tch'eou*, 104 et 6) pas encore au *saṃprayuktaka* et au *sahabhūhetu* (ii, pp. 267, 248), sont dits « futurs » ; « présents », quand ils y répondent ; « passés », quand ils n'y répondent plus.

Les conditionnés, quand ils n'ont pas encore répondu au *sabhāga* et au *sarvatragahetu* (ii, pp. 255, 268), sont dits « futurs » ; « présents », quand ils y ont répondu et ne sont pas détruits ; « passés », quand ils y ont répondu et sont détruits. — De même, les conditionnés non-définis de rétribution, quand ils n'ont pas encore répondu au *vipākahetu*.

Les conditionnés qui ne sont encore ni produits, ni détruits, sont dits « futurs »; « présents », ceux qui sont produits, non encore détruits ; « passés », ceux qui sont produits et détruits. — De même, en remplaçant « détruit » (*niruddha*) par « endommagé » (*hoai*, 32 et 16, *vipariṇata*), par « abandonné » (*li*, 172, *vyatīta*, *vigata*...). — De même en remplaçant « produit » (*utpanna*) par « né » (*jāta*). [P. 394, col. 1, l. 27.]

6. Cependant le Sūtra dit des futurs qu'ils sont nés (*jāta*), etc. Il s'exprime ainsi en considérant leur nature (*tchong-lei*, *jāti*, *prakāra*).

Comme il est dit : Les *dharmas* réels (*saddharma*, *yeou-fa*), nés (*jāta*), existants (*yeou*, *bhūta*), faits (*tso*, *kṛta?*), modelés (*saṃskṛta*), ayant un effet (*sakaraṇīya*), produits en dépendance (*yuen i cheng*, *pratītya-utpanna*), sont de leur nature périssables (*kṣayadharman*), voués à la disparition (*vyayadharman*), objets de détachement (*virāgadharman*), voués à la destruction (*nirodhadharman*), voués à la détérioration (*naśyanadharmaka*). Que ces *dharmas* ne soient pas détériorés, c'est hors de cause. [1]

Par « né », le Sutra entend seulement « *dharma* engendré par la naissance » (Kośa, ii, p. 222) ; « existant » (*bhūta*) montre qu'il possède une nature propre (*sasvabhāva*), « fait » (*kṛta?*), qu'il est malheureux (*sādīnava*) ; « modelé » (*saṃskṛta*), qu'il est « achevé » (*abhisaṃskṛta*); « ayant un effet », que l'acte a un fruit; « produit en dépendance » montre le concours des causes et conditions. Les termes « périssable », etc., montrent qu'on désirera certainement qu'il ne se détériore pas. « C'est hors de cause » montre la nécessité (*asvātantrya*).

7. Le conditionné qui a deux époques avant lui, est dit « passé » ; qui a deux époques après lui, « futur » ; qui est entre deux époques, « présent ».

[1] Comparer Aṅguttara, iii, 54 : *maraṇadhammaṃ mā mīyīti... khayadhammaṃ mā khīyīti... nassanadhammaṃ mā nassīti alabbhanīyaṃ ṭhānaṃ samaṇena vā...* Paṭisambhidā, i, 53 : *rūpaṃ atītam... aniccaṃ saṃkhaṭaṃ paticcasamuppannaṃ khayadhammaṃ vayadhammaṃ virāgadhammaṃ nirodhadhammaṃ...*

Le conditionné qui a pour cause [des *dharmas*] des trois époques, est dit « passé »; qui a pour cause [des *dharmas*] de deux époques, « présent » [car il y a des causes simultanées] ; qui a pour cause [des *dharmas*] d'une époque, « futur ».

Le conditionné qui a pour fruits [des *dharmas*] des trois époques, est dit « futur »...

8. Le conditionné, relativement au passé et au présent, est désigné (*prajñapyate*) comme « futur » ; non pas relativement au futur, parce qu'une quatrième époque manque. Relativement au futur et au présent, il est désigné comme « passé », non pas relativement au passé, parce qu'une quatrième époque manque. Relativement au passé et au futur, il est désigné comme « présent », non pas relativement au présent, parce qu'une quatrième époque manque.

Telle est la distinction des trois époques. De la sorte, on établit que les *saṃskāras* marchent (*hing*). Par là il est démontré que le sens de *adhvan* est « marche ». [P. 394, col. 2, l. 18.]

9a. Lorsque naissent les conditionnés futurs, naissent-ils étant déjà nés, naissent-ils n'étant pas encore nés ? Les deux hypothèses font difficulté. Comment ? Dans la première hypothèse pourquoi ne continuent-ils pas à revenir ? Dans la seconde, comment nierez-vous que les *saṃskāras* existent (ou commencent d'exister) après inexistence (*abhūtvā bhāvaḥ, abhūtvā bhavanam*) ?

Voici la réponse. — On peut dire (*asti paryāyaḥ*)[1] : Parce qu'il y a causes et conditions, étant déjà nés, ils naissent. C'est-à-dire : tous les *dharmas* possèdent déjà leur nature propre, car chaque futur réside dans son caractère essentiel (*svabhāvalakṣaṇa*). Possédant déjà une nature propre, ils sont dits déjà nés : ce n'est pas que leur nature propre soit née des causes et conditions. Étant [ensuite] produits par le concours des causes et des conditions, ils sont dits naître.

[1] La formule *asti paryāyaḥ*, glosée par *asti vacanakramaḥ*, est traduite par Hiuan-tsang : « Il faut dire ».

Parce qu'il y a causes et conditions, n'étant pas encore nés, ils naissent. C'est-à-dire : les *dharmas* futurs sont dits non-nés, car c'est par le fait des causes et conditions qu'ils obtiennent actuellement de naître [P. 394, 2, 27.]

9b. Lorsque naissent les conditionnés futurs, naissent-ils existant déjà ou n'existant pas ? Les deux hypothèses font difficulté. Dans la première, à quoi bon naître, puisque leur être (*tse t'i, svarūpa*) existe déjà ? Dans la seconde, on dira que les *dharmas*, après inexistence, existent : la doctrine du Sarvāstivāda tombe.

Voici la réponse. — On peut dire que les *dharmas* naissent existant déjà.

Vous écartez la deuxième objection, mais comment résoudre la première ?

Comme il suit. — La nature propre (*t'i, svabhāva*) du *dharma* existe, mais non pas son activité. Rencontrant causes et conditions, le *dharma* engendre l'activité. Demandez-vous si l'activité et la nature propre sont une même chose ou des choses différentes ? Il est impossible d'affirmer l'identité ou la différence. De même que, « sur » la nature propre de chaque *dharma* impur (*sāsrava*) se trouve la foule des caractères (*i-siang, artha-lakṣaṇa*) comme impermanence, etc.; et on ne peut pas dire qu'il y ait identité ou différence. De même ici : la critique n'est donc pas justifiée. [P. 394, col. 3, l. 9.]

9c. Est-ce le même *dharma* qui naît et qui périt ? Faut-il penser qu'un autre *dharma* naît, qu'un autre *dharma* périt ? — Les deux hypothèses font difficulté. Dans la première, le futur naît, le futur périt. Dans la seconde, le *rūpa* naît, et c'est autre chose, sensation, etc., qui périt.

On peut dire [1] : Parce qu'il y a causes et conditions, on dit que

[1] Des fragments de ces deux paragraphes sont cités Kośa, v, p. 69, et la Vyākhyā (Wogihara, 477) fournit des parties de l'original et une ṭīkā.

le même *dharma* naît et périt : le *rūpaskandha* naît, le *rūpaskandha* périt... le *vijñānaskandha* naît, le *vijñānaskandha* périt. Parce qu'il y a causes et conditions, on dit qu'un autre *dharma* naît, qu'un autre *dharma* périt : le temps futur naît, le temps présent périt. [P. 394, col. 3, l. 16.]

9d. Lorsque naissent les conditionnés futurs, est-ce le temps même (le *t'i*, le *svabhāva* du temps) qui naît ? ou naissent-ils du temps ? [1] Les deux hypothèses font difficulté. Dans la première, lorsque naît un *dharma*, tous les *dharmas* du temps futur doivent naître ; et, quand il sera né, on n'aura plus de futur ; et, quand il aura péri, on n'aura plus de présent : c'est la ruine du Sarvāstivāda. Dans la seconde, comment les *saṃskāras* ne différeraient-ils pas du temps ?

On peut dire : Parce qu'il y a causes et conditions, on dit que le temps même naît, car, quand naît un *saṃskāra* momentané, c'est bien le temps futur qui naît. Parce qu'il y a causes et conditions on dit que le *saṃskāra* naît du temps, car les *saṃskāras* du temps futur comportent beaucoup de moments et, parmi ces moments, c'est un seul qui naît. [P. 394, col. 3, l. 24.]

9e. Lorsque naît le conditionné futur, faut-il penser que naît sa nature propre (*svabhāva*) ou que naît une autre nature (*parabhāva*) ? Les deux hypothèses font difficulté. Dans la première, comment éviter la conclusion que la nature propre existe après inexistence ? D'abord la chose (*bhūtadravya*, *che-ou*) n'existe pas, maintenant elle existe. Dans la seconde, comment éviter la conclusion que [le *dharma*] abandonne sa nature propre et se trouve sans le caractère d'être (*sing-siang*, *bhāvalakṣaṇa*) ?

Voici la réponse. — On peut dire que la nature propre ne naît pas, ni non plus une autre nature. Mais, dans la nature propre, tel *dharma* (*evaṃdharma*), après être né, périt. [P. 395, col. 1, l. 1.]

[1] Le chinois traduit par le locatif, « dans le temps

10. Le *dharma* qui est du *rūpa* (*yo rūpabhāvo dharmaḥ*) est-il passé (*asti so 'tītabhāvaḥ*)? Quatre alternatives : 1. *rūpa*, sans être passé : à savoir le *rūpa* présent et futur ; 2. passé, sans être *rūpa* : à savoir les quatre autres éléments (*skandha*) passés ; 3. *rūpa* et passé : à savoir le *rūpa* passé ; 4. ni *rūpa* ni passé : à savoir les quatre autres éléments présents et futurs, et les inconditionnés.

De même, quatre alternatives pour les relations du *rūpa* et du futur, du *rūpa* et du présent : donc trois fois quatre alternatives pour le *rūpa*. De même pour les quatre autres éléments. En tout quinze fois quatre alternatives. [P. 395, col. 1, l. 10.]

11a. Le *dharma* qui est du *rūpa* est-il « étendu » (*fang-tch'ou*)? [1] — Tout *dharma* qui est étendu est *rūpa ;* mais il y a du *rūpa* qui n'est pas étendu, à savoir le *rūpa* passé et futur, les atomes présents, l'*avijñaptirūpa* présent.

Le *dharma* qui est *vedanā* est-il étendu ? — Non. Il y a des *dharmas* qui ne sont ni *vedanā*, ni étendus : à savoir les *saṃjñā*, *samskāras*, *vijñānaskandha*, les atomes, l'*avijñaptirūpa*, les inconditionnés.

De même pour le *saṃjñāskandha*, etc. [P. 395, col. 1, l. 17.]

b. Le *dharma* qui est *rūpa* est-il impénétrable ? [2] — Tout ce qui est impénétrable est *rūpa ;* mais il existe du *rūpa* exempt d'impénétrabilité, à savoir le *rūpa* passé et futur, les atomes présents, l'*avijñapti* présente.

Le *dharma* qui est sensation (*vedanā*) sent-il (*anubhava*)? — Tout ce qui sent est sensation ; mais il y a de la sensation qui ne sent pas, à savoir la sensation passée et la future.

[1] Même expression dans Saṃgraha, Upanibandhana, p. 394. — *deśastha?* — Le terme ordinaire est *mūrta*.

[2] « impénétrabilité », traduction approximative de *rūpaṇa*, Kośa, i, p. 24, l'obstacle qu'un *rūpa* (matière) oppose à ce que son lieu soit occupé par un autre *rūpa*. — Le *rūpa* étant caractérisé par le *rūpaṇa*, il s'ensuit que le *rūpa* passé n'est pas *rūpa?* Objection discutée Vibhāṣa, 75, p. 389, Kośa, i, p. 25, 28, 45 Saṃghabhadra, p. 636, col. 1 l. 8.

Mêmes questions et réponses pour les autres « éléments » : il y a de la « perception » (*saṃjñā*) qui ne saisit pas les marques (*nimittodgrahaṇa*), des « activités volontaires » (*saṃskāras*) qui ne « modèlent » pas (*abhisaṃskaraṇa*), de la connaissance (*vijñāna*) qui ne « distingue » pas (*prativijñapti*). [P. 395, col. 1, l. 28.]

12. Les *dharmas* futurs sortent et n'entrent pas ;[1] les passés entrent et ne sortent pas. Comment les futurs ne sont-ils pas décrits (ou conçus, *prajñapyate*) comme diminuant et les passés comme s'accroissant ?

Vasumitra dit : « S'ils étaient comptés, dirait-on (*eul yen*) que les futurs ne sont pas décrits comme diminuant ? » Et encore : « N'est-il pas vrai que les passés ne sont pas décrits comme s'accroissant ? Puisqu'ils ne sont pas comptés,[2] comment peut-on dire qu'ils ne peuvent être décrits, les futurs comme diminuant, les passés comme s'accroissant ? A la vérité, les passés et les futurs, étant sans mesure, ne peuvent être décrits comme s'accroissant, comme diminuant. De même l'eau de la grande mer, étant sans mesure et sans limite, on peut y prendre ou y verser cent mille cruches, et on ne sait pas qu'elle diminue ou s'accroît. » Et encore : « Les *dharmas* futurs, n'étant pas encore produits (*utpanna*), détruits (*niruddha*), ne sont pas décrits comme diminuant ; les *dharmas* passés, étant produits, détruits, ne sont pas décrits comme s'accroissant. » Et encore : « Les *dharmas* futurs, n'étant pas encore produits, détériorés... » [Avec substitution à *niruddha* de *hoai* et de *li*, avec substitution à *utpanna* de *jāta*, comme ci-dessus, p. 14.] [P. 395, col. 1, l. 14.]

Bhadanta dit : « S'il s'agissait de choses solides (*sapratigha*) cheminant à travers les époques, on pourrait les décrire comme diminuant, comme s'accroissant ; mais les conditionnés naissent

[1] C'est-à-dire : les *dharmas* futurs sortent du futur ; aucun *dharma* n'entre dans le futur.

[2] J'entends : « Comment le fait de n'être pas comptés empêche-t-il de les considérer comme s'accroissant... ? »

en raison du concours des conditions et, nés, périssent. Comment décrire les passés comme s'accroissant, les futurs comme diminuant ? »

Pārśva dit : « Les passés et les futurs sont dépourvus d'activité. Comment les décrire comme s'accroissant, comme diminuant ? » [P. 395, col. 2, l. 18.]

13. Les passés et les futurs sont-ils « agglomérés » (*saṃcita*, Kośa, i, p. 25, iii, p. 210) comme les murs et autres objets (*vastu*) du temps présent, ou ne sont-ils pas agglomérés, chaque [*dharma*] étant « dispersé » (*viprakīrṇa*) ? Les deux hypothèses font difficulté.

Dans la première : 1. le travail de l'aumônier (*dānapati*) pour préparer la chose à donner ne sera-t-il pas sans utilité ?[1] 2. pourquoi le futur n'occupe-t-il pas un lieu (*deśa*, *fang souo*) ; 3. comment les murs, etc., ne sont-ils pas éternels ? 4. comment les passés et les futurs ne sont-ils pas manifestes ?[2]

Dans la seconde, 1. comment dire qu'existent les choses passées ? Comme dit le Sūtra : « Jadis il y eut un roi nommé Mahāsudarśana ; sa capitale fut Kuśāvatī ; il habita le palais Sudharma » (Dīgha, ii, p. 170). Les textes analogues sont sans mesure, sans limite ; 2. comment dire qu'existent les choses futures ? Comme dit le Sūtra « Dans l'avenir, il y aura un Bouddha nommé Maitreya ; dans ce temps-là, il y aura un roi nommé Śaṅkha ; sa capitale sera Ketumatī » (Dīgha, iii, p. 75) ; 3. comment le savoir du souvenir des anciens séjours (*pūrvanivāsānusmṛtijñāna*) voit-il les choses passées ? 4. comment le savoir des morts et des naissances (*cyutyupapādajñāna*) voit-il les choses futures ? 5. comment le « savoir d'application » (*praṇidhijñāna*, Kośa, vii, 88) voit-il les choses passées et futures ? 6. enfin, quand les *dharmas*

[1] *t'ang-kiuen* 30 et 7, 64 et 7, vantard-rejeter. *vyartha* Kośa, iv 19 *b* 5, xxix, 11 *b* 6.

[2] *hien-kien*, 96 et 7, 147, n'est pas dans Rosenberg ; Vibhāṣā, 93, 1, 8 ; Siddhi, ii, 9 *b* 7.

futurs viennent se réunir [pour être] présents, n'est-il pas clair que la chose agglomérée (*saṃcitavastu*), d'abord inexistante, existe maintenant ? Et quand les *dharmas* se dispersent et vont au passé n'est-il pas clair que la chose agglomérée, après avoir existé, retourne à l'inexistence ? [P. 395, col. 3, l. 4.]

D'après une opinion, les passés et les futurs sont aussi des agglomérés comme les murs et autres objets du temps présent. De la sorte, les secondes difficultés sont expliquées, mais comment expliquer les premières ? — Dans l'ordre : 1. l'effort de l'aumônier fait que l'objet soit manifeste. Avant que l'aumônier prépare l'objet, celui-ci, quoiqu'existant, n'est pas manifeste ; quand il l'a préparé, l'objet est manifeste. L'effort n'est donc pas inutile ; 2. quel défaut à admettre que le passé et le futur occupent une place ? 3. les murs, etc., ne sont pas éternels, parce que l'impermanence momentanée (?) (*kṣaṇa-anitya*) leur est jointe ; 4. le passé et le futur ne sont pas manifestes parce qu'ils ne sont pas objet des cinq connaissances (visuelle, etc.) présentes. Pour être manifeste une chose doit être objet des cinq connaissances présentes. [P. 395, col. 3, l. 13.]

P'ing [1] dit : « Les passés et les futurs ne sont pas des agglomérés comme sont les objets présents ; ils sont dans l'état de dispersion. »

C'est éviter les premières difficultés, mais comment expliquer les secondes ? — Dans l'ordre : 1-2. à dire que les choses passées [existent] comme ayant été présentes, que les choses futures [existent] comme devant être présentes, il n'y a pas défaut ; 3-5. on demande comment les trois savoirs en question voient-réalisent les choses passées et futures : ils les voient-réalisent comme ayant été, comme devant être « expérimentées ». Quel défaut ici que je n'explique pas ? — Quelques-uns disent : De même, quand on prononce les syllabes, leur succession sériale révèle (*sākṣātkaroti*)[2] les noms et les phrases, et manifeste le sens :

[1] P'ing-kia, Kośa, Index, vi, p. 124; ci dessous p. 156.

[2] *in-cheng*, guider-naître, Siddhi, ii, 22 *a* 2, iv, 21 *b* 6. Sur les syllabes, noms, phrases, Kośa, ii, p. 238.

les syllabes ne sont pas agglomérées ; elles n'en sont pas moins capables de révéler les noms et les phrases, et de manifester le sens. De même les *dharmas* passés et futurs, quoique non agglomérés, sont capables d'engendrer le savoir : l'objet à connaître est connu comme il convient dans chaque cas (*yathāyogam*). — Quelques-uns disent : Au moyen des choses présentes, on déduit (*lei-koan*, *anvaya* — voir) les passées et les futures ; comme le cultivateur au moyen des actuelles récolte et semence déduit (*lei-tche*, *anvaya-jñāna*) l'antérieur et le postérieur (Kośa, ii, p. 303, vii, p. 89) ; 6. les *dharmas* des trois époques ont en succession, comme il convient, la nature de cause et de fruit. En soi, ils restent tels sans accroissement ou diminution. C'est du point de vue de l'activité qu'on dit tantôt qu'ils existent, tantôt qu'ils n'existent pas. Pour les « choses agglomérées », elles s'appuient sur les entités réelles (*dravyasadvastu*) : c'est par métaphore qu'on leur attribue l'existence ; tantôt elles existent, tantôt n'existent pas. — C'est ainsi que ce système [du Sarvāstivāda] conçoit l'existence et la non-existence. De quelle difficulté ne rend-il pas compte ? Car il admet l'existence et la non-existence des [divers] états [du *dharma*]. [P. 396, col. 1, l. 4.]

Les quatre Maîtres

L'école Sarvastivādin a quatre grands maîtres [1] qui établissent différemment l'existence des trois époques. [2] Pour Dharmatrāta, différence de *bhāva* [3] ; pour Ghoṣaka, différence de *lakṣaṇa* ; pour Vasumitra, différence d'*avasthā* ; pour Buddhadeva, différence *d'apekṣā*.

Le partisan de la différence de *bhāva* ou de « manière d'être »

[1] Maître = *ācārya* ; chinois, *śāstrācārya*.

[2] Var. « des deux époques ».

[3] Mieux peut-être : différence [des époques] en raison du *bhāva*... — Pour les théories des quatre maîtres, ci-dessous Saṃghabhadra, p. 89.

(*bhāvānyathika*) dit : Les *dharmas*, circulant dans les époques, se différencient par le *bhāva*, ou manière d'être, sans qu'il y ait différence dans la chose même (*dravya*). C'est ainsi qu'un vase en or peut être brisé, qu'on en fait d'autres objets : la figure est différenciée, mais la couleur (*varṇarūpa*) n'est pas différenciée. Ou encore, quand le lait évolue en petit lait, il perd sa saveur, sa force, etc., mais il ne perd pas sa couleur. De même les *dharmas* : quand ils arrivent du futur dans le présent ils abandonnent leur *bhāva* de futur, acquièrent le *bhāva* de présent ; toutefois leur être (*dharmadravya*) n'est ni acquis, ni abandonné. Quand ils arrivent du présent au passé, de même. [P. 396, vol. 1, l. 23].

Le partisan de la différence de *lakṣaṇa* ou « caractère » (*lakṣaṇānyathika*) dit : « Les *dharmas*, circulant dans les époques, se différencient par le caractère, mais non pas par la chose. Le *dharma* de chaque époque possède les caractères des trois époques : il est actuellement revêtu du caractère d'une époque, mais n'est pas étranger aux caractères des deux autres. De même on ne considère pas qu'un homme, actuellement épris d'une femme, soit détaché des autres femmes. De même le *dharma* qui réside dans le passé est actuellement revêtu du caractère du passé, mais on ne peut pas dire qu'il soit étranger aux caractères des deux autres époques. De même le *dharma* qui réside dans le futur... » [P. 396, 2, 1.]

Le partisan de la différence d'*avasthā* ou « état » (*avasthānyathika*) dit : « Les *dharmas*, circulant dans les époques, se différencient par l'état, mais non pas par la chose. De même, quand on prend un bâtonnet et qu'on le place dans la case des unités, on le nomme « un » ; quand on le place dans la case des dizaines, on le nomme « dix », et ainsi de suite : il y a sans doute différence dans les positions successives, mais il n'y a pas différence dans le bâtonnet. De même le *dharma* passe dans les états des trois époques : il prend différents noms sans que la chose change. »

Dans le système de ce maître les époques sont établies de telle sorte qu'elles ne se confondent pas : c'est en raison de l'activité qu'il établit la différence des trois époques. Le *dharma* conditionné qui n'a pas encore d'activité est nommé « futur »; il est nommé « présent » quand l'activité est actuelle ; il est nommé « passé » quand l'activité a pris fin. [P. 396, 2, 8.]

Le partisan de la différence d'*apekṣā* ou « relation » (*apekṣānyathika*) dit : « Les *dharmas*, circulant dans les époques, prennent différents noms en raison des relations mutuelles d'antériorité et de postériorité. De même qu'une femme est nommé « fille » relativement à sa mère, et « mère » relativement à sa fille ; son essence n'est pas changée, mais, vu la différence des relations, elle reçoit le nom de fille et de mère. De même le *dharma* est dit « passé » relativement à ce qui suit, « futur » relativement à ce qui précède ; « présent » relativement à l'un et à l'autre. »

Les époques, comme ce maître les établit, se confondent. — Pourquoi ? — Les trois époques se trouveront dans une même époque, puisque l'antérieur et le postérieur sont relatifs. Les moments antérieur et postérieur du passé seront dits « passé » et « futur » ; le moment intermédiaire sera dit « présent ».[1] Le futur sera de même tritemporel. Le *dharma* présent, bien qu'il soit instantané, sera des trois époques, relativement à l'antérieur, au postérieur, à l'un et à l'autre. Est-ce admissible ? [P. 396, 2, 17.]

Les époques, comme les établit le partisan des caractères, sont aussi confondues, puisqu'il attribue au *dharma* de chaque époque les caractères des trois époques.

Quant au partisan de la différence de « manière d'être » (*bhāva*), on demande ce qu'est la manière d'être (*bhāva*) à part (*vyatirikta*) de la nature propre (*svabhāva*, *tse-sing*) ? Le système est donc mauvais. — Lorsque le *dharma* conditionné, du futur arrive au présent, il faut que sa première manière d'être périsse ; lorsque, du présent, le *dharma* arrive au passé il faut que sa

[1] Tattvasaṃgraha, p. 505 : *caturthasyāpy ekasminn evādhvani trayo 'dhvānaḥ prāpnuvanti | tathā hy atīte 'dhvani pūrvapaścimau kṣaṇāv atītānāgatau madhyamaḥ kṣaṇaḥ pratyutpanna iti.*

dernière manière d'être naisse : par conséquent le passé naît, le futur périt : est-ce admissible ?

Seul le troisième maître établit bien les époques, parce que les *saṃskāras* ont une période d'activité. [P. 396, 2, 23.]

II

SAMGHABHADRA

Choen-tcheng-luen, 50-52, pp. 621-636

SOMMAIRE

I. — Introduction

Avant-Propos, 621, 3, 5-14.

1. Définition de l'existant : « ce qui engendre l'idée » (Ce qui existe comme chose, ce qui existe comme désignation), 621, 3, 14.

2. Critique du Dārṣṭāntika, 622, 1, 16.

Sept arguments (pour établir que le non-existant est objet de connaissance). Arguments pour l'existence de l'objet de la pensée : de raison, 622, 1, 27, scripturaires (trois textes), 622, 2, 7.

Textes allégués par le Sautrāntika, 622, 3, 28.

Refutation des sept arguments, 623, 2, 8 — 624, 3, 6. — 1. Le cercle du tison et l'ātman ; 2. la connaissance d'*adhimukti* ; 3. le Māyājāla ; 4. savoir qu'on ne désire pas ; 5. connaissance du rêve, du taimirika, de deux lunes ; 6. connaître le non-existant comme non-existant : étude des expressions négatives ; 7. non-existence antérieure du son.

3. Si le passé-futur n'a qu'une existence « de désignation » ? 624, 3, 6 — 625, 1, 9.

4. Quelle sorte d'existence attribuer au passé-futur ? — Le *svabhāva* et le *bhāva*, 625, 1, 9.

II. — Preuves de l'existence du passé et du futur d'après la kārikā, v, 25

1. Preuve scripturaire (625, 3, 1 — 627, 3, 16). — Sūtra du détachement a l'endroit du passé... ; Sūtra des Lāguḍaśikhīyakas.

Discussion si ces Sūtras sont de sens définitif : Sūtras qui paraissent nier le passé... (Paramārthaśūnyatā ; vue de l'absence du lien de l'œil ; ceci n'étant pas, ceci n'est pas...), 626, 2, 20.

Interprétation Sautrāntika des textes sur l'existence du passé... (Le passé = ce qui a été) ; emploi de *asti* relativement au passé ; d'une partie du passé, on peut dire qu'elle a été ; Lāguḍaśikhīyakas... 627, 2, 11.

Le Sthavira explique à sa façon les textes sur le détachement du passé, sur les Lāguḍaśikhīyakas..., 627, 3, 16.

2. « Parce que la connaissance naît de deux, de l'organe et de l'objet », 627, 3, 16 — 628, 2, 27. — Explications du Sautrāntika. Connaît-on le passé comme ayant été ?

3. « Parce que la connaissance a un objet existant », 628, 2, 27 — 629, 1, 26. — Le Sthavira croit que l'objet peut être inexistant ; comment on connaît le passé par l'étude des causes et des fruits ; le *purātana-anu-dhātu* (?).

4. « Parce que l'acte passé donne un fruit », 629, 1, 26 — 630, 1, 11. — Théorie Sautrāntika sur la génération du fruit (évolution de la série ; série de la graine et série « karmique »).

5. Divers arguments pour l'existence du passé-futur (630, 1, 11 — 630, 3, 6) : 1. le passé-futur est impermanent ; comment l'impermanence est conciliable avec la pérennité du *dharma* ; remarques du Sthavira; 2. Pūrṇasūtra ; 3. meurtre.

III. — La doctrine de l'activité (kāritra)

1. Définition du Sarvāstivāda, 630, 3, 6 — 631, 1, 3.

2. Les quatre maîtres du Sarvāstivāda ; approbation du système de Dharmatrāta ; préférence pour celui de Vasumitra (631, 3, 1).

3. Étude de l'activité (*kāritra*), une sorte déterminée de la puissance (*śakti*), objections du Sautrāntika, en court (— 631, 3, 17), en détail d'après la kārikā v, 27.

a) Quel obstacle rencontre l'activité dans le passé et le futur ? 631, 3, 19

b) Comment l'activité est-elle passée, future ? 632, 2, 24.

c) L'activité diffère-t-elle du *dharma* ? 632, 3, 7.

d) Si le *dharma* reste le même, comment naît-il ? 633, 2, 7. — Le *svabhāva* et le *bhāva* ; théorie des Vārṣagaṇyas ; l'acte et le fruit ; théorie des *anuśayas* : critique des vues du Sautrāntika.

e. Aveu d'impuissance faussement attribué au Sarvāstivādin par le Sautrāntika 634, 3, 19 — 635, 1, 9.

IV. — Remarques finales, 635, 1, 11 — 636, 2, 16

1. Adoptons-nous les opinions de Kapila ?

2. Le Sūtra : « a été, sera », 635, 1, 18.

3. Coexistence de la pensée pure et de la pensée souillée, 635, 1, 29.

4. Dans le système du Sarvāstivāda, le passé n'est pas « conditionné », la délivrance est impossible.

5. Caractère « conditionné » du passé et du futur.

6. La « coupure ».

7. Le Sūtra : « Ceci n'étant pas... », et l'existence du passé et du futur.
8. Le futur et la « fruition ».
9. La « résistance » de la matière passée ; la lampe future ; la visibilité du « visible » futur.
10. Le caractère « conditionné » du passé et du futur.

Note sur le Sarvāstivāda.

Nous devons maintenant examiner si le passé et le futur existent, ou n'existent pas, « en soi » (*dravyasat*) [1] ; dans la première hypothèse, ils peuvent être objet d'attachement. [2] En fait, les maitres, depuis longtemps, embrassent des thèses de partisans sur ce problème, se réfutent les uns les autres, établissent en concurrence des plaidoyers, [3] exposent des arguments scripturaires et des arguments de raison pour établir leur opinion ; et semblables controverses (*vivāda*) sont devenues partout traditionnelles. [4] Les tenants de l'existence en soi citent abondamment textes et raisons et, de toute manière, réfutent la non-existence et démontrent l'existence; de même les tenants de la non-existence en soi réfutent l'existence et démontrent la non-existence. Ils produisent ainsi, les uns et les autres, une grande masse de calamité (*ādīnava*) (P. 621, col. 3, l. 10.)

C'est pourquoi je produis grandement bonne résolution (*samyak-prahāṇa*) : en conformité avec une saine considération des choses, j'établis que le passé-futur, quoique différent du présent, n'est

[1] *dravyasat* (*che*, 40 et 11, et *yeou*), en contraste avec *prajñaptisat*, « existant comme désignation ». On a aussi pour *che-yeou*, *bhūtasat*, « réel ». — Par « passé », entendre « le *dharma* passé... »

[2] La controverse du temps, dans le Kośa, « s'accroche » à la théorie des passions (*kleśa*). L'homme est-il lié par le désir qu'il a eu pour une chose passée ?

[3] Ou simplement des « textes » (voir 627, 3, 25) ; *luen-tao*, des « chemins de *śāstra* ou de *vāda* ». On a le choix entre *vādamārga* (*vādamagga*, Kathāvatthu, Commentaire, p. 7) et *vādapatha* (Pali Text Dictionary). — Vibhāṣā, p. 1, col. 2, l. 6 : Bhagavat en divers endroits, s'adressant à diverses personnes, a enseigné l'Abhidharma au moyen de divers *luen-tao*.

[4] *tch'ou-tch'ou tchoan-wen jou-se tcheng-luen* = « çà et là traditionnellement entendre comme cela traités-de-dispute ».

tcheng-luen, *vivāda* dans Vyutpatti, une des sept sortes de *vāda*, Tsa-tsi ; Taisho 1606, p. 771, col. 1.

pas absolument inexistant. Le passé-futur n'est pas existant à l'instar du présent, mais il n'est pas inexistant à l'instar d'une corne de cheval : j'établis que le passé et le futur existent en leur « nature propre » (*t'i*). — Seules ces vues sont conformes au système correct de l'Abhidharma. [P. 621, col. 3, l. 14.]

1. *Définition de l'existant.*

Nous devons, pour commencer, voir ce qu'il faut entendre par « existence » [: donner la définition de l'existant, *sat-lakṣaṇa*]. [1] Avec cette définition présente à l'esprit, on pourra savoir si le passé et le futur existent. Par la définition bien élucidée, le problème deviendra facile, et ceux-là même qui ont des vues obstinées seront capables d'adhérer à la vérité. [P. 621, col. 3, l. 16.]

D'après certains maîtres, « est existant » ce qui est né et n'est pas détruit ». Cette définition de l'existence n'est pas admissible, car, par le fait, « être né et ne pas être détruit », c'est le caractère spécifique du présent (*vartamāna*). Si vous dites que l'existence se définit par la « présence » (*vartamānatā*), vous dites implicitement que le passé-futur n'existe pas : et nous demanderons : « Pour quelle raison le seul présent est-il défini comme existant, et non pas les autres époques ? » Donc cette définition de l'existence est mauvaise. [P. 621, col. 3, l. 20.]

Voici ma définition : « Le véritable caractère de l'existant est d'engendrer l'idée (*buddhi*) en qualité d'objet ». L'existant est de deux sortes : *dravyasat* (*che-yeou*), ce qui existe comme chose, (ce qui existe en soi) ; *prajñaptisat*, [2] ce qui existe au titre de désignation : ces deux catégories, en effet, correspondent à la vérité absolue (*paramārthasatya*) et à la vérité d'expérience (*saṃvṛtisatya*). Lorsque l'idée naît à l'endroit d'une chose sans

[1] Nous aurons l'occasion d'analyser les chapitres de Harivarman signalés ci-dessus p. 7.

[2] *kia-yeou*, faux-être. — L'expression usuelle est *che-che* (70 et 5, 149 et 4). Pour les deux vérités, voir ci-dessous p. 159.

dépendre [d'autres choses], cette chose est *dravyasat* : par exemple la couleur, la sensation. Lorsqu'elle naît à l'endroit d'une chose en dépendance [d'autres choses], cette chose est *prajñaptisat*, par exemple la cruche, l'armée. [L'idée de couleur se réfère à une entité, à une certaine chose ; l'armée n'existe que comme désignation des soldats, etc.] [P. 621, col. 3, l. 25.]

D'autres docteurs admettent une troisième catégorie, l'existence relative,[1] par exemple cette rive-ci, cette rive-là. Cette catégorie rentre dans les catégories qui précèdent : le nom diffère, mais ne désigne pas une chose différente. En outre, cette thèse « sort » du Sūtra[2] qui ne connaît que deux sortes d'existence. [P. 621, col. 3, l. 27.]

L'existant en soi (*dravyasat*) est de deux sortes : « ce qui possède seulement nature propre (*t'i*) » (*sasvabhāvamātra*), « ce qui possède activité » (*sakāritra*). Ce second existant est de deux sortes, « ce qui possède pouvoir », « ce qui est dépourvu de pouvoir »[3]. Ainsi avons-nous déjà expliqué ce qui possède seulement nature propre. [P. 622, col. 1, l. 1.]

L'existant par désignation (*prajñaptisat*) est aussi de deux sortes : ce qui dépend de choses existantes en soi, ce qui dépend de choses existantes par désignation. Exemples, dans l'ordre, cruche (désignation d'atomes), armée (désignation d'hommes, qui sont des désignations des cinq *skandhas*). [P. 622, col. 1, l. 2.]

L'enseignement sacré, considérant ensemble toutes ces catégories, dit qu'elles sont. En résumé, quatre sortes d'existence : le mot *asti* marque l'existence comme chose, comme condition, comme possédé, comme cause.

a) Des textes comme : *asti rūpaṃ anityam aham atra samanujānāmi samanupaśyāmi...* ou *yal loke nāsti taj jñāsyāmi... eṣa saṃbhavo nāsti* (Kośa, v, p. 62), visent la chose existante en soi.

[1] *āpekṣika*, *siang-tai-yeou*.
[2] *wei-yue k'i king*, « contredit - excède le Sūtra », ne peut être que *utsūtra*.
[3] *kāritra* = *tso-yong* (9 et 5, 101), « activité » ; *kong-neng* (19 et 3, 130 et 6), pouvoir ; voir ci-dessous, p. 631, col. 3.

b) Des textes comme : « Quand il y a arbre, il y a ombre » ou : « Bhikṣus, s'il y a concorde [entre vous], point de maître qui me soit semblable », visent la chose existante en tant que condition.

c) Des textes comme : *santy anucchinnāni anusahagatakuśalamūlāni* [1] ou *asty ādhyātmikaṃ cakṣuḥsaṃyojanam* ou *tayor nāsty uṣmagatam* [2] ou *yasya nāsti tṛṣṇā sa cakṣuṣmān ucyate*, visent la chose existante en tant que possédée.

d) Des textes comme *imasmiṃ sati idaṃ hoti, imasmiṃ asati idaṃ na hoti* (Kośa, iii, p. 81) visent la chose existante en tant que cause.

e) Des textes comme : « Il n'y a pas de torrent boueux comparable au désir. Quand il y a désir, je déclare qu'il n'y a pas de salut », visent l'absolue inexistence.

Les docteurs qui n'admettent que l'existence du présent sont incapables d'expliquer ces emplois de *asti*, « il y a », dans l'Écriture... [P. 622, col. 1, l. 16.]

2. *Critique du Dārṣṭāntika.*

Le Dārṣṭāntika n'admet pas la définition de l'existence que donne notre système. Que l'existant soit ce qui engendre l'idée, c'est inexact, car, dit-il, nous maintenons que l'inexistant aussi peut, en qualité d'objet, engendrer l'idée [3] : 1. lorsque naissent l'idée de cercle formé par le tison (*alātacakra*) et l'idée de « soi » (*ātman*), l'objet (*viṣaya*) est inexistant [4]; 2. l'acte d'attention dans les Kṛstnāyatanas, [5] etc., est un *adhimukti-manaskāra* [6] : si toute idée a pour objet un existant (*sadālambana*), l'*adhimuktimanaskāra*

[1] Kośa, iv, p. 172, Saṃyutta, iii, p. 130, Kathāvatthu, p. 215, Atthasālinī, p. 244.
[2] *pei eul ou noan*, traduction conjecturale; exemple repris ci-dessous, p. 59.
[3] « idée » = *buddhi* ; ces textes seront discutés ci-dessous, p. 37.
[4] *asadviṣayā buddhiḥ*, l'idée a pour objet un inexistant.
[5] Kośa, viii, p. 213.
[6] Kośa, ii, p. 325 : « un acte d'attention » qui ne porte pas sur une chose réelle, *bhūtārthe*, mais qui résulte de la volonté de l'ascète. Quand, par exemple, celui-ci voit une femme comme une cage d'os décharnés.

est impossible ; 3. dans le Māyājāla, il est dit qu'il y a vision portant sur un non-existant ; 4. le Sūtra dit qu'on connaît le non-existant : « Quand le désir (*kāmacchanda*) est absent, il connait en vérité son inexistence » ; 5. l'objet de la connaissance est non-existant dans le rêve, quand l'œil a une taie, quand on voit deux lunes ; 6. quand on sait du non-existant qu'il est non-existant, qu'est-ce que l'idée a pour objet (*kiṃviṣayeyaṃ buddhiḥ*)? 7. quel est l'objet (*ālambana*) de l'idée qu'on a de « l'inexistence antérieure du son (*prāgabhāva*)? — Concluons que l'existant et le non-existant peuvent tous deux engendrer l'idée. Donc la définition de l'existence : « ce qui engendre l'idée », est mauvaise [P. 622, col. 1, l. 27.]

D'après les Ābhidhārmikas, il n'y a pas d'idée ayant un objet non-existant (*asadviṣayā buddhiḥ*), car l'Écriture enseigne que les idées ont deux causes. Le Sūtra dit qu'il y a six sortes d'idées qui toutes ont un support (*āśraya*) et un objet (*ālambana*) : « L'idée visuelle a pour support l'organe de l'œil et pour objet la couleur », et ainsi de suite jusque : « L'idée mentale a pour support le *manas* et pour objet les *dharmas*. » Il n'existe pas une septième sorte d'idée qui naisse sans objet (*aviṣaya*) et dont on puisse dire qu'elle est une idée portant sur un objet non-existant (*asadviṣayālambaka*). [P. 622, col. 2, l. 2.] (Voir ci-dessous, p. 35.)

Si vous admettez que certaines idées naissent sans objet, vous devez aussi bien admettre que certaines idées n'ont pas de support — les aveugles-nés auront des idées visuelles — car l'objet et le support sont également causes de l'idée qui ne peut pas plus se passer de l'un que de l'autre.

En outre, les choses inexistantes[1] ne sont comprises dans aucune des six catégories d'objet.

Soutenir qu'il y a des idées portant sur le non-existant (*asadālambaka*) est donc déraisonnable, opposé à l'Écriture et tout à fait téméraire (*sāhasika*)[2]. [P. 622, col. 2, l. 6.]

[1] ou fa, *abhāvadharma? asaddharma?*

[2] *Chou* (103 et 7 ou 157 et 7) — ye, divergent-sauvage ; *chou-lio* = *sahasā* dans Vyutpatti.

D'autres docteurs objectent. — L'expérience montre que certaines idées ont pour objet de l'existant (*sadālambana*) : vous concluez qu'il en va de même de toutes les idées. De même, du fait avéré que certaines idées portent sur le passé-futur, on pourra conclure que les idées visuelles, etc., portent aussi sur le passé-futur. Or vous n'admettez pas cette conclusion [car les idées visuelles se réfèrent au seul présent] : donc vous ne devez pas non plus conclure du caractère « existant » de l'objet de certaines idées au caractère « existant » de l'objet de toutes les idées. Votre raisonnement doit être abandonné; si vous le maintenez, il présente le défaut d'*anaikāntikatā*. [1] Donc il est acquis que certaines idées sont « ayant pour objet du non-existant ». [P. 622, col. 2, l. 11.]

Ce ne sont là que des mots dénués de toute valeur.

Les choses existantes constituent divers objets (*ālambana*) : d'où résulte la variété des idées ; exemple : les idées visuelles, etc. De même que les idées visuelles, etc., naissent à l'endroit des choses présentes, diverses, sans que, pour cela, toutes aient pour objet toutes les choses présentes ; de même toutes les idées naissent à l'endroit des diverses choses existantes, sans que, pour cela, toutes aient pour objet tous les *dharmas* existants.

En outre, que certaines idées aient un objet existant, c'est évident et nous l'admettons l'un et l'autre. Que, de même, toutes les idées aient un objet existant, la conclusion est irréprochable.

Que certaines idées aient un objet non-existant (*asadālambana*), ce n'est pas évident, nous sommes aussi d'accord. Comment donc votre argument en faveur de l'idée à objet inexistant serait-il irréprochable ? [P. 622, col. 2, l. 18.]

Les Dārṣṭāntikas disent que l'existant et le non-existant, tous deux, sont objet qui engendre l'idée. Cela n'est pas exact, car la *buddhi*, idée [ou représentation ou *cogitatio*], correspond (*toei*) à un *bodhya*, objet [ou représenté ou *cogitandum*] : un *bodhya*

[1] « undistributed middle », Vyutpatti, 199, 24.

est nécessaire pour qu'il y ait une *buddhi*. On donne le nom de *buddhi* à ce qui atteint (*prāpnoti*) un objet (*viṣaya*) : si le « à atteindre » manque, quel sera l'atteignant ? La nature propre (*svabhāva*) de la connaissance (*vijñāna*) est de « saisir »[1] l'objet (*viṣaya*) ; si le « à connaître » (*vijñeya*) manque, que connaîtra la connaissance ? Donc la connaissance « à objet non-existant » de notre adversaire ne peut être nommée « connaissance » puisqu'elle n'a pas de « connaissable ». [P. 622, col. 2, l. 23.]

L'expression « non-existant » (*asat*) signifie absence absolue de nature propre (ou d'être) (*svabhāvātyantābhāva*). Le non-existant est étranger à tout caractère général, à tout caractère propre *(sva sāmānyalakṣaṇa)*. Comment lui donnerez-vous le nom de *bodhya* ou de *vijñeya*, représentable, connaissable ?

Si vous répondez que le non-existant est *bodhya*, est *vijñeya* : c'est faux, car l'idée et la connaissance doivent avoir un objet existant (*sadviṣayā buddhiḥ*). Les pensées, les mentaux (*citta caittadharma*) ne peuvent porter que sur les caractères généraux ou propres ; ils ne peuvent naître en prenant pour objet des *dharmas* qui ne sont absolument pas. Ce point a déjà été mis, sommairement, en lumière dans l'explication du Nirvāṇa.[2] [P. 622, col. 2, l. 27.]

1. Les idées qui auraient pour objet le non-existant seraient manifestement trompeuses[3] de leur nature. Bhagavat a dit en effet : « Ce qui n'existe pas dans le monde, si je le vois, il faut que je me trompe.[4] » Or Bhagavat ne peut se tromper. Donc il n'y a certainement pas d'idée qui prenne pour objet le non-existant. Manifestement, il n'y a pas d'objet (*āyatana*) capable de produire la pensée qui ne soit du domaine du savoir du Bouddha. [P. 622, col. 3, l. 3.]

[1] *neng liao*. — *upalabdhi*, Siddhi, v, 6 a 3. — *liao-pien* = *vijñapti*.

[2] Saṃghabhadra, p. 432, col. 1 ; voir Documents d'Abhidharma, Textes relatifs au Nirvāṇa..., p. 63.

[3] *k'oang-loan*, « enragé - désordre

[4] *loke yan nāsti tat paśyāmi...*

2. Il n'y a pas d'idée qui prenne pour objet le non-existant. car les textes disent qu'il ne peut pas être connu, ne peut pas être perçu (ou atteint)[1] : « Le commencement (*pūrvā koṭi*) du Saṃsāra n'est pas connu (*na prajñāyate*) », « Aucun agent n'est perçu (*kartā nopalabhyate*). » Ces textes montrent que l'objet de l'idée existe. Comme le commencement du Saṃsāra et l'agent n'existent pas, ils ne sont pas connus, perçus. — Celui qui admet que l'idée nait en prenant pour objet le non-existant, doit admettre que le commencement du Saṃsāra est connaissable, que l'agent est percevable, car il ne peut y avoir obstacle [à la connaissance] dans ce qui n'existe absolument pas.[2] Ira-t-on dire que, parmi les non-existants, quelques-uns sont objet de l'idée tandis que d'autres ne sont pas objet ? Impossible : on ne peut dire que celui-ci et celui-là sont respectivement fort et faible. [P. 622, col. 3, l. 10.]

3. Le Sūtra dit que le non-existant ne peut être connu : « Ce qui n'existe pas dans le monde, que je le connaisse, que je le voie, c'est impossible.[3] » — Le Sautrāntika explique ce Sūtra dans le sens que voici.

Le Bouddha veut dire que d'autres hommes, dans leur présomption, voient qu'elle existe d'une illumination qui n'existe pas (*asantam avabhāsaṃ santaṃ paśyanti*) : mais moi, dit-il, c'est seulement ce qui existe que je vois comme existant. A comprendre le Sūtra comme vous faites, poursuit le Sautrāntika, toutes les idées prenant pour objet de l'existant (*sadviṣayatva*), comment pourrait-il y avoir doute-examen[4] quant à l'objet (Existe-t-il... ?) ? Comment y a-t-il différence entre le Bouddha et les autres ?

[1] *na jñāyate nopalabhyate.*

[2] *akiṃcitkc* (*ou souo yeou tchong*) *na pratibandhaḥ* (*na vighnaḥ*).

[3] *yal loke...* ci-dessus, p. 6 ; le Sautrāntika est Vasubandhu, Kośa, v, p. 62, Vyākhyā, éd. Wogihara, p. 476.

hien-siang, *avabhāsa*, correspondance non signalée dans Rosenberg qui a *naimittikatva* (Vyut. 127, 54) et *upādhi* (?). — *divyacakṣuravabhāsa.*

[4] *vimarśa* glosé par *vicāro saṃdeho vā.*

On a *asadālambanatva*, *abhāvālambanatva.*

Cette explication est fantaisiste.[1] — Rien de non-existant ne peut être l'objet d'une illumination (*avabhāsa*). Comment dire que des présomptueux voient comme existante une illumination qui n'existe pas ? Si on obtient illumination à l'endroit du non-existant, on pourra aussi bien obtenir illumination à l'endroit d'un treizième *āyatana*. Le caractère de ce qui n'existe pas, étant par delà les douze *āyatanas* (organes et objets des connaissances), personne n'est capable de le voir, faute de tout moyen d'investigation.[2] [P. 622, col. 3, l. 19.]

Tel n'est pas le sens du Sūtra. Il faut entendre que des présomptueux disent qu'ils ont vu par illumination ce qu'ils n'ont pas vu. Le Bouddha, au contraire, ne s'attribue que l'illumination qu'il a. — Point de doute en effet qu'il y ait des savoirs d'objet erroné (*viparīta*) ; mais il n'est pas de savoir dont l'objet soit non-existant. Toutes les idées (*buddhi*) portent donc sur un objet existant. [P. 622, col. 3, l. 22.]

Et c'est ainsi que s'explique l'examen-doute à l'endroit de l'objet : « Mon savoir, à l'endroit de ce visible, est-il correct ou erroné ? » Et aussi la différence, parce que, à l'endroit du même existant, il y a différence dans la vision.

Le non-existant ne présente avec l'existant aucun caractère commun : comment y aurait-il différence [entre l'idée qui porte sur l'existant et celle qui porte sur le non-existant, *sadasadālambanabuddhi*] ? C'est seulement relativement à l'existant qu'il y a différence ; c'est seulement dans l'idée d'un objet existant qu'il y a différence. Seule l'idée qui porte sur l'existant se différencie. Aucune [comparaison et] différence entre l'existant et le non-existant. [P. 622, col. 3, l. 28.]

Le Sautrāntika reprend. — Il en est bien comme je le dis (*sadasadālambanā buddhayaḥ*), car, dans un autre Sūtra, Bhagavat dit : « Viens, Bhikṣu ; si tu es mon disciple, sincère, loyal, croyant,

[1] *tan choai ki ts'ing.* — *ts'ing* = *ruci.*
[2] *li-ts'iu.*

zélé (*asaṭha amāyāvin*), je t'enseignerai le matin de manière à ce que tu obtiennes des « distinctions » (*viśeṣa*) le soir ; je t'enseignerai le soir de manière à ce que tu obtiennes des distinctions le matin ; tu connaîtras le *sat* comme *sat*, l'*asat* comme *asat*, l'existant comme existant, le non-existant comme non-existant. » Ce texte dit formellement que l'on connaît l'existant et le non-existant.[1] [P. 623, col. 1, l. 3.]

Cette explication du Sautrāntika procède du manque de réflexion : car le mot *sat* signifie ici *praṇīta* « bon »; le mot *asat* signifie ici *apraṇīta*, « mauvais ». Dans ce monde, par la force d'un faux enseignement, les disciples forment des jugements erronés ; ils considèrent le mauvais comme bon et inversement. Non pas les disciples du Bouddha : la force de son bon enseignement fait que ses disciples jugent correctement du bon et du mauvais.

Tel est certainement le sens de ce passage du Sūtra, car le Sūtra continue : « Tu connaîtras l'inférieur (*sa-uttara*) comme inférieur, le supérieur (*anuttara*), comme supérieur » (Kośa, iv, p. 255), pour qu'on n'entende pas *sat* et *asat* dans le sens d'existant-non-existant, mais bien dans le sens de bon-mauvais. Bon, mauvais, c'est-à-dire « sans défaut », « avec défaut » : le « sans défaut » est « supérieur », le « avec défaut » est inférieur. Les mots « inférieur-supérieur » signifient donc « mauvais-bon ». Ou bien, dans le bon-mauvais, il y a du fort et du faible, et c'est pour indiquer cette différence que le Sūtra ajoute : « Tu connaîtras l'inférieur et le supérieur. »

A comprendre ainsi le Sūtra, on voit que l'enseignement du Dharma est de grande utilité : le disciple, dans tous les *dharmas*, voit ce qui est bon, mauvais, fort, faible ; il peut réaliser un grand effort à l'endroit des *dharmas* qu'il faut couper ou cultiver, et

[1] Cité Kośa, v, p. 63, avec variantes ; d'après S. Kiokuga, Saṃyukta, 26 à la fin. — *chan-lai*, *svāgata*, *sugata* ; mais aussi *ehi*, Kośa, xiv, 9 a 9, xx, 3 a 4. — Le tibétain diffère : ṅaḥi ñan thos kyi dge sloṅ thsur śog ces bya ba nas | de nas naṅ btams na nub khyad par du ḥgro | nub gtams na naṅ khyad par du ḥgro ste.

sat est transcrit *sa*, 140 et 13.

obtenir des *dharmas* « distingués ». Si l'enseignement allait seulement à faire connaître l'existant et le non-existant, on ne pourrait lui attribuer cette souveraine utilité. [P. 623, col. 1, l. 18.]

Saṃghabhadra poursuit en montrant que le contexte justifie son interprétation du Sūtra cité par le Sautrāntika. Il s'agit des *vaiśāradyas*. Bhagavat connaît les *antarāyikadharmas* et la *nairyāṇikapratipad :* « Si on doute de mon rugissement de lion, mon disciple, instruit le matin... ». Donc l'argument du Sautrāntika est sans valeur... Il est donc acquis qu'aucun savoir ne connaît le non-existant ; il n'y a pas d'idée qui ait pour condition objective du non-existant. [P. 623, col. 2, l. 2.]

D'ailleurs ce que dit le Sautrāntika, que l'idée prend pour objet du non-existant, est contradictoire. Si l'idée a un objet, ne dites pas que cet objet est non-existant ; si l'objet est non-existant, ne dites pas que l'idée a un objet, car ce qui n'existe pas manque absolument. Si vous soutenez que l'être (nature propre) de cet objet manque absolument, dites donc franchement que l'idée n'a pas d'objet. Pourquoi cette timidité, ces détours astucieux qui vous font dire qu'il y a une idée qui a pour objet le non-existant ? Tenons donc pour avéré qu'aucune idée ne porte sur le non-existant. [P. 623, col. 2, l. 8.]

1. Notre adversaire pense que l'idée du cercle formé par le tison, l'idée de « soi », sont des idées ayant pour objet du non-existant. Nous maintenons que l'objet de ces deux idées existe, comme l'objet de l'idée d'homme à l'endroit du poteau.

Les gens, dans l'obscurité, à distance, ayant vu la couleur-figure (*rūpa*) d'un poteau, produisent à son endroit l'idée d'homme, et disent, au présent : « Je vois un homme ». Dans l'homme qu'ils voient, il n'y a aucune nature propre d'homme ; mais l'idée d'homme ne naît pas relativement à un objet non-existant : car elle a pour objet la couleur-figure du poteau. En effet, elle ne naît pas relativement à l'endroit où il n'y a pas de poteau. [P. 623, col. 2, l. 13.]

De même en va-t-il de l'idée du cercle formé par le tison mû circulairement [1]. Cette idée ne manque pas d'un objet existant. La couleur-figure du feu naît rapidement en des endroits formant cercle : cette couleur est l'objet de l'idée de cercle. Certes, il n'y a rien de circulaire dans la « nature propre » de cette couleur-figure : cependant, quand l'idée naît, elle naît sous l'aspect de cercle. L'idée, relativement à l'objet, est « d'aspect erroné » [2] ; mais l'idée de cercle ne naît pas visant un non-objet.

De même pour l'idée d'*ātman* (« je »). L'objet de cette idée est les « éléments » (*skandha*), couleur-figure, etc. : mais son aspect est erroné, qui consiste à nommer *ātman* ce qui n'est pas *ātman*. L'objet, pour cela, n'est pas erroné [ou inexistant ?]. C'est pourquoi Bhagavat a dit : « Bhikṣus, tous les brahmanes et religieux qui admettent un *ātman*, ce qu'ils considèrent, c'est seulement les cinq « éléments d'assomption ». [3] — La vue d'*ātman* (*satkāyadṛṣṭi*, etc.) a pour objet les « éléments », car, quant on voit ceux-ci en vérité, cette vue est absolument coupée. [P. 623, col. 2, l. 23.]

2. Jugeons de l'*adhimuktimanasikāra* [4] d'après les mêmes principes. L'ascète (*yogācāra*) [5] voit une petite image (*parīttanimitta*) ; par la force de sa « décision » (*adhimukti*), il produit, à l'endroit de ce qu'il voit, un « aspect grand » (*mahadgata ākāra*), et engendre une idée (*buddhi*) correspondante. Cette idée a pour objet les « éléments ».

Les Forestiers [6] disent : « La naissance de ce grand aspect est le

[1] *alātacakra*, Kośa, iii, p. 212, Index sub. voc.

[2] *viparītākāra*.

[3] *upādānaskandha*, Saṃyutta, iii, p. 46 ; Kośa, iii, p. 87, ix, p. 253 ; Rahder, Mélanges, i, sur la *satkāyadṛṣṭi*.

[4] Kośa, vi, p. 49, et Index sub voc. — Abhibhvāyatanas, Kośa, xiii, p. 211.

[5] *yoga-ācārya*, Kośa, vi, p. 150 ; voir Index, p. 129.

[6] *tch'ou-k'ong-hien-tche* ; *k'ong-hien-tch'ou* = *araṇya*, donc *araṇyavihārin* ou *āraṇyaka*.

La doctrine attribuée ici aux Forestiers est voisine de celle attribuée aux Yogācāras, Kośa, iv, 18. Il s'agit de spéculations sur l'extase propres aux religieux qui, professionnellement, s'attachent à l'extase : habitants de cimetière, de la forêt.

fruit du recueillement.[1] La force du recueillement dans l'état de concentration (*samāhitāvasthā*) tire-engendre cet aspect, comme elle fait la création magique (*nirmāṇa*). » [P. 623, col. 2, l. 27.]

3. Quant à l'argument : « Il est dit dans le Māyājāla[2] que la vision porte sur le non-existant », cela est faux. Ce Sūtra-là dit en effet qu'elle porte sur de l'existant. Il dit que, quand on voit un spectacle magique (*māyāvastu*), bien que [les choses] supposées n'existent pas, l'image magique (*māyānimitta*)[3] ne manque pas. S'il n'en est pas ainsi, l'image magique manque donc. Qu'est-ce que l'image magique ? C'est le fruit de la magie ; comme les formes (*rūpa*) créées (*nirmita*) par le possesseur des pouvoirs mystiques (*abhijñā*), elle est réelle couleur-figure. Née de la magie, elle peut être objet de vision. Mais les choses réelles (*bhūtavastu*) supposées [qu'on voit dans l'exhibition magique] sont absolument inexistantes : c'est pourquoi ce Sūtra-là dit que le [spectacle magique] est non-existant. Il comporte des aspects irréels ; il trompe et confond autrui ; il est nommé « trompe-l'œil. ».[4] [P. 623, col. 3, l. 4.]

4. Notre adversaire cite un Sūtra disant [à son avis] qu'on connaît le non-existant : « Quand il n'y a pas désir sensuel[5] l'ascète connaît en vérité qu'il n'y a pas désir sensuel. » — Non ! Ce que connaît l'ascète, c'est [non pas la non-existence, mais] le contre-carrant (***pratipakṣa***) du désir sensuel.

Le Sūtra dit encore, de ce qui est « coupé » (***ucchinna***),[6] que cela est non-existant : ***tatprahāṇam***[7] ***tadabhāvaḥ***, « abandon de

[1] *samāpatti*, *cheng-ting*, Kośa, xv, 8 b 7, xxviii, 8 a 7.

[2] Il semble bien que ce soit le nom d'un Sūtra. — Pour *māyā*, nous avons dans ce paragraphe *hoan* et *hoan-chou*.

[3] *hoan-siang*.

[4] *neng loan yen*.

[5] *kāmacchanda*, *yu-yu* ; peut-être *kāmaguṇeṣu chandarāgaḥ*, Majjh. ii, 114, Kośa, v, 84.

[6] *ucchinna*, *toan-mie*, Kośa, v, 5 a 2, xxx, 4 a 7.

[7] *yong toan*, absolument coupé.

cela, non-existence de cela ». Mais ce mot « non-existence (*ou*) » n'indique pas absence de nature propre (*ou-t'i-sing*, *niḥsvabhāvatā*). [P. 623, col. 3, l. 8.]

5. Nous n'admettons pas que la connaissance du rêve, la connaissance de l'homme dont l'œil a une taie, la connaissance qui voit deux lunes, soient des connaissances à objet non-existant.

Il n'est pas prouvé que la connaissance du rêve porte sur un objet non-existant. Soit en raison des pensées [1] qui précèdent le sommeil, soit par l'influence des dieux durant le sommeil, soit par le conflit des éléments du corps, [2] se produisent, dans l'état de sommeil, des idées de souvenir relatives aux choses du passé : c'est ce qu'on appelle rêve. Or il n'est pas établi que le passé soit non-existant. On ne peut donc pas citer le rêve comme preuve de la connaissance à objet non-existant. Les objets vus en rêve ont été auparavant expérimentés. [3] Ces objets ne sont pas seulement des visibles, comme dans le rêve [de la mère] du Bodhisattva ; on rêve aussi des sons entendus. — Il est vrai que, dans le rêve, on voit une corne de lièvre : c'est que, en des endroits différents, on a vu lièvre et corne ; dans le rêve, en raison de l'hébétement-confusion (*styāna-viparyāsa*) de la pensée, on se souvient de lièvre et corne en les plaçant ensemble. Ou bien on a vu ou entendu parler de semblables bêtes vivant dans le Grand Océan. — Il faut juger des autres rêves d'après les mêmes principes. Donc l'argument tiré du rêve est inopérant. [P. 623, col. 3, l. 18.]

[1] Le Madhyāntavibhāga, p. 25, démontre que la connaissance du rêve, etc., n'a pas d'objet. On croit à tort que son objet (*ālambana*) est un *nimitta*, à savoir un *viprayuktasaṃskāra*, reflet de la chose (*arthapratibimba*).

parikalpa-cintanā, *ki-touo* (Kośa, xiii, 3 b 7 ; aussi *nirūpaṇa*), *se-wei* (aussi *anuvitarka*, etc.).

[2] Littéralement : *kāya-abhyantara-dhātu-parasparavirodha* ; les *dhātus* sont trois *mahābhūtas* à l'exclusion du *pṛthivīdhātu* ; du moins voir Kośa, iii, p. 136, iv, p. 127.

[3] *anubhūta*, *souo-keng*, 73 et 3 ; voir Siddhi, vii, 6 b 7.

Quant à la connaissance qui a pour support l'œil malade [1], il est faux que son objet soit non-existant. Cette connaissance porte sur figure-couleur. Mais, l'organe ayant une taie, la prise de l'objet n'est pas claire. Il en résulte, à l'endroit de l'objet, une « interprétation » [2] erronée. L'aspect (*ākāra*) de la connaissance peut être erroné, l'objet en fait ne manque pas. C'est dans un lieu où il y a du visible (*rupa*) [3] que l'homme aux yeux malades voit ces multiples choses (*nimitta*). Le visible ne manque pas complètement : dans l'hypothèse contraire, il y aurait vision dans un endroit où il n'y a pas de visible. [4]

L'objet ne manque pas non plus à la connaissance qui porte sur plusieurs lunes : la connaissance visuelle (*cakṣurvijñāna*), naissant, ne voit qu'une lune ; mais l'altération (*vikāra*) de l'organe produit une connaissance peu claire, et l'idée naît, confuse-trouble, qu'il y a plusieurs lunes. Il est faux que cette idée naisse en visant du non-existant : en fait, elle a pour objet le disque lunaire. Dans l'hypothèse contraire, on verrait [plusieurs lunes] dans l'endroit où il n'y a pas [de lune] [5] : puisque la connaissance visuelle ne naît pas à l'endroit où il n'y a pas de lune, [6] cette connaissance prend bien pour objet le disque lunaire.

La connaissance du rêve, etc., naît bien en portant sur un objet réel, car il y a diversité dans l'aspect et la clarté de cette connaissance, comme, à l'état de veille, [pour] la pensée qui porte sur le bleu, etc. [P. 623, col. 3, l. 28.]

6. Est-ce qu'on ne cite pas un texte qui démontre que la connaissance (*vijñāna*) porte [7] sur le non-existant : « Il connaît le

[1] *i-mou ; i*, 109 et 11, « taie ». On a plus souvent *i*, *timira*, 124 et 12.
[2] *kiai*, 148 et 6, *buddhi*.
[3] « Il faut il-y-a-visible lieu ». (Écarter la traduction : « Il faut qu'il y ait du visible », du *rūpāyatana* ».)
[4] « Il faudrait pas-visible-lieu voir. »
[5] « Pas-[lune]-lieu devrait voir. »
[6] « Pas-lune-lieu cette connaissance ne naît pas. »
[7] *yuen*, *pratyaya*, *ālambaka*.

non-existant comme non-existant (*asad asattaḥ*) [1] ? Quel est l'objet (*ālambana*) de cette idée ?

Elle naît en portant sur un « signifiant » qui nie l'existence [2] ; elle n'a pas pour objet le non-existant (*asadviṣaya, abhūtaviṣaya*). Nous voulons parler d'une expression (*abhilāpa*) [3] qui signifie la négation de l'existence, c'est-à-dire un certain signifiant qui affirme la non-existence. Lorsque, relativement à cette expression signifiant la non-existence, vient à naître une idée, elle l'interprète en non-existence [bien que cette expression soit très réelle]. Par conséquent on ne peut pas dire que l'idée naisse en portant sur le non-existant. [P. 624, col. 1, l. 3.]

Mais le signifiant qui affirme la non-existence n'existe-t-il pas ? Comment l'idée [que vous dites qui vise le signifiant,] le nierait-elle ? [4]

L'idée ne nie pas l'expression ; elle comprend seulement que ce qui est signifié (*abhidheya*) n'existe pas. Expliquons-nous. L'idée, naissant, a pour objet la négation de l'existence, mais elle ne naît point avec le non-existant pour objet. Qu'entendons-nous en disant que « [l'idée a pour objet] la négation de l'existence » ? Nous voulons dire [qu'elle a pour objet] un signifiant de forme

[1] *fei-yeou* et *ou*.

[2] *bhāvapratiṣedhakam* (*tche yeou*) *abhidhānam* (*neng-tsiuen*).

[3] nom-parole, *ming-yen*, qui paraît bien être *abhilāpa*; en effet, on rencontre l'équivalence *mṅon-brjod*. — On aurait *bhāvapratiṣedhābhidhāyako 'bhilāpaḥ*.

[4] Comparer Kośa, v. p. 61, au bas (où la traduction est inexacte), Wogihara, 475.

Le Vaibhāṣika. — Si ce qui n'existe absolument pas peut être l'objet de la connaissance, un treizième *āyatana* sera donc objet de la connaissance.

L'auteur. — La connaissance qui connaît la non-existence d'un treizième *āyatana*, quel sera donc son objet ? Si vous dites qu'elle a pour objet ce nom même [: « treizième *āyatana* »], c'est donc que l'on nie l'existence de ce nom, [puisque c'est le nom qui est l'objet de la connaissance en question, et non pas l'existence du treizième *āyatana*].

Vyākhyā : *trayodaśam apy ālambanaṃ syād* iti ; trayodaśānām āyatanānāṃ pūraṇaṃ trayodaśam āyatanam tad vijñānasya ālambanaṃ syāt asadālambanatva iṣyamāṇe... *atha trayodaśam* iti vistaraḥ *atha trayodaśam nāstīti vijñānasya kim ālambanam*] *etad eva nāma* iti vaibhāṣikaḥ yad etan nāma trayodaśam āyatanam iti tad ālambanam *evaṃ tarhi nāmaiva nāstīti* pratīyate nābhidheyaṃ trayodaśāyatanābhāvalakṣaṇam.

négative.[1] Puisqu'elle a pour objet un signifiant, il est faux qu'elle ait pour objet un non-existant. [P. 624, col. 1, l. 8.]

Comme on dit dans le monde : non-brahmane, non-permanent, etc.[2] Quoique ces [signifiants] nient un autre existant, la chose [signifiée] n'est pas non-existante. En effet naît à leur endroit un savoir qui a pour objet le signifié du signifiant qui nie les natures de brahmane, de permanent, etc. En d'autres termes, le signifiant qui nie ces natures se réfère à son signifié qui est le *kṣatriya*, les *saṃskāras*, etc. [P. 624, col. 1, l. 12.]

Par le fait, toutes les expressions négatives rentrent dans deux catégories. Ou bien elles ont un « signifié » (*abhidheya*) existant, ou bien elles ont un « signifié » non-existant. Première catégorie, par exemple les mots « non-brahmane », « non-permanent ». Deuxième catégorie, comme lorsqu'on dit les mots « non-existence », « non-chose » (*abhāva*, *avastu*).

Quant au savoir qui naît en raison des premières, au moment où il est produit, il a seulement pour objet le « signifiant » ; ensuite, il connaît la non-existence de ce qui est nié ; enfin, il porte sur le « signifié » : on sait que, dans la nature de telle chose, la [marque] niée n'existe pas.

Quant au savoir qui naît en raison des secondes, d'abord comme après, il porte seulement sur le « signifiant »; il sait que, là, n'existe pas ce qui est nié. — Que des expressions signifiantes comme « non-existence » (*abhāva*), etc., n'aient absolument pas de « signifié », cela ne fait point faute, car les « non-existence », etc., n'ont absolument pas de nature propre. Si ce qui n'a absolument pas de nature propre était « signifié », le monde n'aurait pas de parole (*vāc*) exempte de signification (*anarthaka*). [P. 624, col. 1, l. 20.]

D'après quelques-uns, toutes les expressions (*abhilāpa*) ont un signifié (*abhidheya*) puisqu'on leur donne le nom de « signifiant » (*abhidhāna*). Dans cette hypothèse, quel pourra bien être le signifié

[1] Littéralement : *abhāve utpannam abhidhānam*.

[2] Ce sont des *paryudāsapratiṣedhas* opposés aux *prasajyapratiṣedhas*.

de toutes les expressions qui désignent (*prajñap*) des choses irréelles (*abhāva-dharma*), de tous les mots comme « non-existence » (*abhāva*), « non-chose » (*avastu*), ou encore « deuxième tête », « troisième main »? Ces mots existent cependant : en manière de signifié, ils visent leur propre signification.[1] [P. 624, col. 1, l. 24.)

Objection. — S'il y a « signifiant » sans « signifié », il y aura de même connaissance (*buddhi*, *bodhi*) sans connaissable (*bodhya*). Vous niez ceci, pourquoi admettez-vous cela?

Le cas n'est pas le même. L'idée (*buddhi*) ne peut naître qu'en s'appuyant sur un objet (*ālambana*), comme un infirme sur un bâton. La nature (*dharmatā*) des pensées et mentaux (*cittacaitta*) est de naître en raison de quatre conditions [parmi lesquelles la condition-en-qualité-d'objet, *ālambanapratyaya*][2] : telle n'est pas la nature des *rūpas* (choses matérielles), etc. Le « signifiant » [qui est un mot, donc du *rūpa*] est produit sans dépendre d'un signifié ; il est réalisé par la force du *hetusamutthāna* et du *tatkṣaṇasamutthāna*[3]; il naît en conformité avec le caprice individuel[4]; il ne doit pas, pour naître, s'appuyer sur un signifié. C'est pourquoi le Sūtra dit qu'il y a des sons vocaux dépourvus de signification (ou d'objet). — Au contraire, les pensées et mentaux doivent pour naître s'appuyer sur un objet (*viṣaya*) : le Sūtra les nomme donc *sālambana ;* l'inexistant ne peut être dit *sa-*.[5]

Lorsque naît la correcte intellection (*samyagavabodha*) qui comprend l'absence-de-soi (*nairātmya*), elle a pour objet toutes les choses (*dharma*). Comme dit le Sūtra : « Alors il contemplera par la sapience l'absence-de-soi de toutes choses. » [P. 624, col. 2, l. 4.]

[1] Traduction douteuse : *i yuen* (*ālambante*) *ts'e siang* (*saṃjñā*) *wei ts'e souo tsiuen* (*abhidheya*) : parce qu'ils visent cette *saṃjñā* comme cet *abhidheya*.

[2] Kośa, ii, p. 299.

[3] Le texte a *hetukṣaṇasamutthānabala*, voir Kośa, iv, p. 36-37, qui explique l'origine de la *vijñapti*.

[4] Littéralement : *sva-citta-saṃjñā-abhilaṣita*.

[5] *sa-ālambana* (*sa-ālamba*, *ālambaka*), « avec un objet » ; la pensée ne peut « être avec » avec un non-existant, et réciproquement. — Kośa, i, 62, ii, 177.

7. Le Sautrāntika (c'est-à-dire Vasubandhu) expose l'objection établie par le [Sthavira Śrīlāta]. [1]

L'idée (ou connaissance) qui prend pour objet la non-existence antérieure du son, quel est son objet? — Le Vaibhāṣika dira que c'est le son même : mais alors [l'objet est le son, non pas la non-existence du son, et] celui qui veut avoir « non-existence du son » devra d'abord faire du son. — Non, réplique le Vaibhāṣika, car l'objet de cette connaissance, la non-existence antérieure du son, c'est le son à l'état futur. — Mais, d'après le Vaibhāṣika, le son à l'état futur existe réellement ; comment dire qu'il n'existe pas et parler de sa non-existence? Que le Vaibhāṣika réponde : « Le son futur ou passé n'est pas présent : par conséquent, la connaissance qui vise le son non-présent est une connaissance de non-existence », il se contredit. Car, pour lui, il y a identité : c'est le même son qui est passé, présent, futur. S'il reconnaît quelque différence de nature entre le son futur et le son présent — différence qui justifie la notion de la non-existence du son futur — il reconnaît que cette différence existe après avoir ne pas existé. Concluons que la connaissance a pour objet l'existant et le non-existant (*sat* et *asat*). » [P. 624, col. 2, l. 9.]

Cette argumentation n'est pas bonne comme nous l'avons expliqué ci-dessus [2] dans la discussion du Pratisaṃkhyānirodha. Le Sautrāntika prétendait que l'Écriture dit : « Il y a un non-né... un Nirvāṇa », à la manière dont on dit : « Il y a non-existence antérieure du son ». [3] Nous avons répondu en demandant si cette expression : « Il y a non-existence... » est employée à l'endroit d'une chose absolument non-existante, ou si elle n'est pas employée à l'endroit d'une chose existante dans le but de nier une autre chose. S'il y a une chose réelle, distincte du son, qui se trouve avant et après le son, il est licite, en vue de nier le son, d'affirmer la

[1] Kośa, v, p. 62 ; Vyākhyā, Wogihara, p. 475.

[2] Page 431, col. 2 ; voir Documents d'Abhidharma, Bulletin, 1900, 3-4, pp. 59-60.

[3] *asti śabdasya prāgabhāvaḥ.*

non-existence du son : le sens est que « dans cette chose, il y a non-existence du son. » Quand on parle « de non-existence mutuelle » (*anyonyābhāva* : le cheval n'est pas le bœuf), il s'agit évidemment d'existants. — Mais, d'une chose complètement non-existante, dire « il y a » (*astīti*), n'est-ce pas contradictoire ? [P. 624, col. 2, l. 16.]

Par conséquent le Sautrāntika n'a pas le droit d'égrener toutes ces objections : « Le Vaibhāṣika dira que l'objet est le son même... » (Ci-dessus, p. 45, l. 4).

D'après l'explication que nous venons de répéter du sens de l'expression « Il y a non-existence », on voit bien que la connaissance qui porte sur la non-existence antérieure du son [1] ne porte pas sur le son mais sur l'*adhiṣṭhāna* [2] du son : c'est-à-dire sur l'ensemble des facteurs [3] qui servent de support au son. Ces facteurs, dans l'état (*avasthā*) où ils n'ont pas encore produit le son, voilà ce qu'on désigne par l'expression « non-existence [antérieure] du son ». De même, le savoir qui connaît le non-existant comme non-existant (*asad asattaḥ*) naît en ayant pour objet des choses (*dharma*) existantes et en niant d'autres choses. — Il doit en être ici de même [que dans l'exemple du son]. Aurait-on ici une autre explication ? [P. 624, col. 2, l. 22.]

Même à admettre que [la connaissance de la non-existence du son] ait pour objet le son même, l'objection est sans valeur. Nous disons en effet que le passé-futur, bien que sa nature propre (*t'i*) soit, n'a pas le même mode d'être [4] que le présent. Cependant il n'y a pas « existence après non-existence » (*abhūtvā bhāvaḥ*), car l'être (*t'i*) et l'activité (*tso-yong*) ne sont ni identiques ni différents. C'est ce que nous expliquerons plus loin (p. 102). [P. 624, col. 2, l. 25.]

[1] *śabdaprāgabhāvālambaka.*

[2] *i-tch'ou*, s'appuyer-lieu, *āyatana*, *adhiṣṭhāna* (Kośa, ii, 367.)

[3] *upakaraṇa*, *kiu* (12 et 6); voir Trentaine, définition de l'*alobha* (Lévi, p. 27, l. 3).

[4] *yeou-i*, *bhāva-artha*. — Quand on parle du passé-futur comme « existant », on ne donne pas au mot « exister » le sens qu'on lui donne quand on parle, de même, du présent.

Comment d'ailleurs sait-on que le son n'existe pas antérieurement (*prāgabhāva*) ? — Parce qu'il n'est pas né, répondra-t-on.

Cette réponse présente la même difficulté, car la question se pose si le son, dans l'état non-né, existe ou n'existe pas. Par conséquent, quand je demande : « Comment sait-on que le son n'existe pas antérieurement ? », on ne peut répondre : « Parce qu'il n'est pas né », car les termes « antérieurement » et « non-né » ont le même sens. [P. 624, col. 2, l. 28.]

Puisque l'argument : « Parce qu'il n'est pas né » n'est pas un argument capable d'établir que le son non-né n'existe absolument pas, on ne peut évidemment pas, par l'inexistence du son non-né [qui n'est pas prouvée], établir que la connaissance (*vijñāna*) prend pour objet le non-existant. [P. 624, col. 3, l. 1.]

Nous établirons plus loin que toutes les connaissances naissent en ayant pour objet un existant. Il n'y a pas d'idée qui ait pour objet un non-existant : ce qui précède le démontre.

Semblable idée manquant, la définition que nous avons proposée de l'existant (*sallakṣaṇa*) est démontrée : « la chose qui engendre l'idée ». Tous les maîtres qui acceptent cette définition doivent admettre l'existence du passé et du futur puisque le passé et le futur engendrent l'idée en qualité d'objets. [P. 624, col. 3, l. 6.]

3. — *Existence de désignation.*

Nous avons vu, p. 28, que les deux sortes d'existants, ce qui existe comme chose (*dravyasat*), ce qui existe par désignation (*prajñaptisat*), peuvent engendrer l'idée. L'idée naît relativement au passé et au futur : faut-il penser que le passé et le futur sont *dravyasat* ou *prajñaptisat* ?

D'après une opinion, ils sont seulement *prajñaptisat*. Opinion incorrecte, puisque n'existerait pas un passé-futur *dravyasat* qui serait le point d'appui du passé-futur considéré comme *prajñaptisat*. Si on dit que le présent est ce point d'appui, c'est aussi inadmissible, parce que la relation de dépendance (*apekṣā*) manque : ce n'est pas en dépendance du présent qu'ont lieu (ou « procèdent », *pravart*) les savoirs portant sur le passé-futur. Or nous avons défini le *prajñaptisat* : « Si l'idée naît à l'endroit d'une chose en dépendance [d'autres choses], cette chose est *prajñaptisat.* » [P. 624, col. 3, l. 12.]

Dans le monde, lorsque le point d'appui de la désignation (*prajñapti*) a disparu, la désignation arrête de « procéder ». Tous les *dharmas* qui existent par désignation, *pudgala*, cruche, vêtement, chariot, lorsque le point d'appui de la désignation (*skandhas*, terre cuite, fils, timon) a disparu, arrêtent de « procéder ». Mais, quand les *dharmas* présents ont disparu, le passé-futur continue néanmoins d'être désigné. Donc il est faux que le passé-futur soit seulement *prajñaptisat*. [P. 624, col. 3, l. 15.]

Le point d'appui de la désignation (*prajñapti*) et la désignation qui s'appuie, ne peuvent être disparates. Les « choses conditionnées » (*saṃskṛta dharma*) voyagent à travers les époques : le passé-futur ne se trouve pas avec le présent. Comment les désignations de passé-futur auraient-elles le présent pour point d'appui ? [P. 624, col. 3, l. 18.]

Il est d'ailleurs inouï (*apūrvadṛṣṭa*) que, dans des états successifs, « ce qui existe comme désignation » devienne « existant comme chose », et inversement. Si le futur existe seulement comme désignation, admettez donc que le présent, lui aussi, existe comme désignation et non pas comme chose. Ou, bien plutôt, reconnaissant que le présent existe comme chose, reconnaissez la même existence au passé et au futur. — La thèse de notre adversaire est contradictoire. Qu'on la rejette ! Qu'on ne s'y opiniâtre pas ! [P. 624, col. 3, l. 22.]

Ajoutons que les choses de désignation (*prajñaptisat*), *pudgala*, cruche, vêtement, et autres choses semblables, ne sont pas l'objet du Chemin (*āryamārgaviṣaya*).[1] Or le Chemin a pour objet, [outre les présents], les conditionnés (*saṃskṛtadharma*) passés

[1] On entend par Chemin, *āryamārga*, la collection des « patiences » et « savoirs » par lesquels le futur saint comprend les Vérités, Kośa, vi. — Sur *abhisamaya*, « compréhension », vi, p. 122 ; sur la *parijñā* et le *parijñeya*, v, pp. 110-118.

et futurs : s'il n'en était pas ainsi, les passés et les futurs ne seraient pas « à pénétrer » (*parijñeya*) par les patiences et les savoirs de la Compréhension.

En outre, si les sensations, etc., passées et futures, ne sont pas prises comme objet au moment de la Compréhension, il s'ensuit que les choses (*dharmas*) internes, sensations, etc., ne sont pas l'objet de la Compréhension : puisque, d'une part, on ne veut pas que celle-ci porte sur le passé-futur ; puisque, d'autre part, deux sensations, etc., ne sont pas simultanées. [P. 624, col. 3, l. 29.]

Que le Chemin ne pénètre pas tous les conditionnés, c'est en contradiction avec le Sūtra : « Si un seul *dharma* reste non pénétré, je dis qu'on ne peut réaliser la fin de la douleur.[1] » Donc le Chemin porte sur le passé et le futur. [P. 625, col. 1, l. 3.]

De même que le passé-futur n'est pas d'existence de désignation parce qu'il est « à pénétrer », de même parce qu'il est « à abandonner », « à cultiver »[2] : un *dharma* de désignation n'est pas à abandonner... [P. 625, col. 1, l. 5.]

Ajoutons que, de la *prajñapti* et du *dravya*, de ce qui existe par désignation et de ce qui existe comme chose, on ne peut affirmer l'identité ou la différence. Comme, de la lettre *i*, qu'on écrit [en brāhmī] au moyen de trois points, on ne peut dire qu'elle soit une ou multiple.

Le passé, le présent, le futur, ce sont trois états successifs [des *dharmas*]. Peut-on supposer que le passé et le futur, existant par désignation, aient le présent comme support de cette désignation ? — Ce système est illogique, n'est pas conforme à l'Écriture, ne peut donc être accepté. [P. 625, col. 1, l. 9.]

4. — *Comment existent le passé et le futur.*

Nous disons que le passé-futur existe. Quel genre d'existence

[1] Kośavyākhyā, Kośa, i, p. 4 au bas, Wogihara, p. 4, l. 16 : *nāham ekadharmam apy anabhijñāya aparijñāya duḥkhasyāntakriyāṃ vadāmi.*

[2] Le *duḥkha* est « à connaître » ; le *samudaya* (cause de *duḥkha*) est « à abandonner » ; le chemin (nobles savoirs) est « à cultiver ».

faut-il lui attribuer ?[1] Celui que disent les Ābhidhārmikas.

Comment existe le passé-futur d'après les Ābhidhārmikas ?

Comme il est cause et fruit, chose de souillure et de purification, sa « nature propre » (*svabhāva, tse-sing*) n'est pas fausse : on dit qu'il est *dravyasat* (*che yeou*), « existant comme chose ». Mais il ne reçoit pas le nom de *dravyasat* au même titre que le présent.[2] C'est-à-dire : le passé-futur n'est pas absolument non-existant (*atyantābhāva*), comme une corne de cheval, comme une fleur du ciel ; il n'est pas « existant seulement par désignation », comme cruche, vêtement, armée, forêt, chariot, maison, nombre, prise, allée et venue,[3] etc. ; il n'est pas « existant comme chose »[4] au même titre que le présent. — Comment cela ? — N'étant ni absolument non-existant, ni d'existence de désignation, à l'instar de la corne de cheval ou de la cruche, on peut dire qu'il possède la nature de cause, fruit, etc. (*hetuphalādibhāva*) ; mais, de ce qui a péri et de ce qui n'est pas né [c'est-à-dire du passé-futur], on ne peut dire qu'il soit *dravyasat* également au présent.[5] — Ayant ces considérations présentes à l'esprit,[6] nous affirmons fermement que le passé-futur existe. [P. 625, col. 1, l. 19.]

Les conditionnés (*saṃskṛtadharma*) traversent les trois époques ; leur caractère essentiel (*svabhāvalakṣaṇa, t'i-siang*) n'est pas modifié [au cours de ce voyage]. Dira-t-on [sans contradiction] que leur manière d'être (*yeou-sing, sattā*) devient différente ?

[Répondons à cette objection.][7]

[1] « Comment faut-il connaître leur caractère d'existant ?

[2] *vartamānavat, jou hien tsai.*

[3] *ts'iu*, 156 et 8.

[4] On a *che yeou sing.*

[5] *t'ong hien che yeou.*

[6] *ts'ang tsai sin tchong.*

[7] Le sens général de ce paragraphe n'est pas douteux. Saṃghabhadra rencontre l'objection du Sautrāntika : « Vous soutenez que le *svabhāva* existe toujours et que le *bhāva* est transitoire. » (Kośa, v, p. 58.)

Saṃghabhadra pense qu'il n'y a pas contradiction. — Toute sensation est « expérience », « sentir » : c'est là son *svabhāva*, son essence ; mais la sensation agréable et la pénible diffèrent quant au *bhāva*, espèce. [De même une sensation agréable, passant du futur dans le présent, perd le *bhāva* de futur pour prendre

Nous constatons l'existence simultanée de choses (*dharma*) qui, essentiellement identiques (non différentes quant au *svabhāvalakṣaṇa*), diffèrent quant à la manière d'être [1] : l'élément-terre [qui est toujours, de son essence, solidité], a diverses natures, [2] étant interne (*ādhyātmikabhāva*), externe ; la sensation (*vedanā*) [qui est toujours, de son essence, « expérience »,] a diverses natures, étant personnelle, d'autrui, agréable, pénible.

Or il n'y a pas lieu de distinguer la nature (*sing*) d'avec l'être (*yeou, sat*) ; la première étant différenciée, la seconde doit l'être aussi. Par conséquent bien que le caractère essentiel de l'élément-terre soit constant (*t'ong*), on peut dire qu'il a variété de nature (*sing*), interne et externe ; la sensation, etc., est « expérience », etc., de son caractère essentiel : on peut cependant dire qu'elle a variété de nature, agréable, désagréable. Les [divers organes,] œil, etc., résidant dans une série, ont tous le même caractère essentiel d'être de la « matière secondaire épurée » (*upādāyarūpaprasāda*, Kośa, i, p. 15); mais ils présentent variété de nature [3] (*sing-lei*), car leur pouvoir (*kong-neng*, voir p. 93), voir, entendre, etc., diffère. Or le pouvoir ne se distingue pas de l'être (*yeou*) de telle manière que la manière d'être (*yeou sing*, *sattā*) pourrait être la même (*teng*) malgré la diversité du pouvoir. En fait le pouvoir de voir, etc., est l'être (*yeou*) de l'œil, etc. Le pouvoir étant divers, la manière d'être (*yeou-sing*, *sattā*) l'est aussi. [P. 625, col. 1, l. 28.]

Nous savons donc pertinemment que, à un moment donné,

bhāva de présent : elle reste, essentiellement, la même : on s'attache à la sensation agréable future comme à la sensation agréable présente...]

[1] Le détail de la traduction présente quelque difficulté. Nos sources sanscrites (Kośa, v, p. 52, 58) opposent le *svabhāva* (*tse-sing*, *t'i*, *fa-t'i*) au *bhāva* (*sing* ou *lei*). Saṃghabhadra, ici, outre *sing* (*bhāva*, « nature ») a *yeou*, *yeou-sing* ; et *sing-lei*. Cette dernière expression équivaut à *sing* ou *lei* tout court. J'ai calqué *sat* (« être »), *sattā* (« manière d'être ») sur *yeou*, *yeou-sing*. On peut penser que *yeou-sing*, abrégé parfois en *sing*, équivaut à *bhāva* (comme on voit par l'emploi des deux termes, notes 2 et 3).

[2] *Yeou sing*.

[3] *Sing*; voir p. 97.

Mais en eux il y a (*yeou*) *sing-lei* (bhāva) *pie* (bheda). »

la « nature propre » de [certains] *dharmas*, malgré l'identité du caractère essentiel (*svabhāvalakṣaṇa, t'i-siang*), a (*yeou*) diversité de manière d'être (*sing-lei pie*). Nous pouvons, de ce fait, conclure que les *dharmas*, traversant les trois époques, ne se différencient pas en ce qui regarde leur caractère essentiel, mais ont diversité de manière d'être. Ainsi est bien établie la doctrine de l'Abhidharma. [P. 625, col. 2, l. 2.]

Le Sautrāntika (Vasubandhu) prend ici parti pour les théories du Sthavira (Śrīlāta) et dit : « Si le passé et le futur, l'un et l'autre, sont, comment dire qu'ils ont la nature (*sing*) de passé et de futur (*atītabhāva, anāgatabhāva*) ? »

Cette critique n'est pas pertinente, car il est logique d'admettre que la même chose réelle (*dravyasat*) a (*yeou*) diversité de manière d'être (*yeou-sing*).[1] [P. 625, col. 2, l. 6.]

Aussi bien les partisans de l'existence des trois époques (*adhvatrayāstitvavādin*) pourraient à leur tour demander : « Si le passé et le futur sont tous deux non-existants, comment peut-on dire que ceci est passé, ceci futur ? » Celui qui professe le système de l'éternelle existence (*nityāstitva*), s'appuyant sur un *dharma* « substantiel » (*yeou-t'i, sasvabhāva* ou *satsvabhāva*), en raison de la diversité de « nature propre » (*tse sing, svabhāva*) [qui fait que les diverses choses passées sont différentes], de la non-identité des causes-conditions [qui fait que la même chose est présente, passée, future], peuvent établir qu'il y a distinction des « natures »[2] (*bhāva, sing lei*) [de passé, etc.]. Mais ceux qui enseignent la « non-substance » (absence de *t'i, niḥsvabhāvatā*) du passé et du futur, puisque la « substance » (*t'i*) du passé et du futur manque, ne peut parler de la diversité de la nature propre et des causes-conditions : comment pourrait-il distinguer le passé et le futur ?

De même que celui qui s'appuie sur [un *dharma*] de substance réellement non-existante (*che ou t'i*) établit faussement cette

[1] « diversité » : *tchong-tchong yeou-sing tch'a pie ; nānāsattāviśeṣa, nānābhāvaviśeṣa.*

[2] *yong* (20 et 7) *k'o li yeou sing lei tch'a pie.*

déclaration qu'il est capable d'enseigner la différence du passé et du futur ; tant s'en faut que celui qui s'appuie sur [un *dharma*] de substance réellement existante (*che yeou t'i*) soit, en bonne logique, incapable d'enseigner la diversité du passé et du futur. [P. 625, col. 2, l. 13 : Fin du cahier 15.]

II. — Preuves de l'existence du passé et du futur, Kārikā, V, 25

Nous avons expliqué sommairement la différence des doctrines correcte et incorrecte, celle qui affirme et celle qui nie l'existence des trois époques. Nous allons maintenant, en suivant le texte de la stance [de Vasubandhu], expliquer ce problème tout au long et avec une claire précision. La stance [1] dit :

« Les trois époques existent, [2] parce que Bhagavat l'a dit, parce que la connaissance mentale procède de deux conditions, parce qu'elle a un objet, parce que l'acte a un fruit. Celui qui affirme l'existence des trois époques est considéré comme Sarvāstivādin. »

Existent réellement le passé, le futur, le présent : cela est prouvé par l'Écriture et par le raisonnement à la fois. — S'il en est ainsi, quelle est la différence des trois époques ? — Pourquoi faire cette objection hors de place ? La question qu'il faut poser est la suivante : « Quels textes de l'Écriture, quels raisonnements ? » Je vais citer textes et arguments logiques pour établir ma thèse de l'existence des trois époques : une fois leur existence mise en lumière il sera facile d'expliquer leurs différences.

L'existence réelle du présent ne fait pas de doute. Quels textes,

[1] Les trois premiers pādas et la première partie du quatrième pāda de la kārikā, v, 25 ; voir v, pp. 50 et 51. — Voir Wassilieff, p. 270, note.
[*sarveṣv adhvasu santy ukter*] *dvayāt* [*sadviṣayāt*] *phalāt* |
[*tadastivādāt sarvāstivādī mataḥ*]

[2] C'est-à-dire : le *dharma* passé, futur, présent, existe.

quels arguments logiques en ce qui concerne le passé et le futur ? [P. 625, col. 3, l. 1.]

1. — *Parce que Bhagavat l'a dit dans le Sūtra.*

Bhagavat a dit[3] : « Le *rūpa* (couleur et figure) passé, le *rūpa* futur sont impermanents ; à plus forte raison le *rūpa* présent. S'il est capable de voir ainsi l'impermanence du *rūpa*, le disciple instruit s'applique à rejeter le *rūpa* passé ; s'applique à couper la complaisance à l'endroit du *rūpa* futur ; s'applique au dégoût, au détachement, à la destruction du *rūpa* présent. Si le *rūpa* passé n'existait pas, le disciple ne s'appliquerait pas à rejeter le *rūpa* passé ; mais, parce que le *rūpa* passé existe, le disciple doit s'appliquer à le rejeter. Si le *rūpa* futur n'existait pas, le disciple ne s'appliquerait pas à couper la complaisance à l'endroit du *rūpa* futur ; mais, parce que le *rūpa* futur existe, le disciple doit s'appliquer à couper la complaisance à l'endroit du *rūpa* futur. » [P. 625, col. 1, l. 10.]

Et Bhagavat, s'adressant à Śāriputra, dit : « Les religieux Lāguḍaśikhīyakas,[1] troublés d'esprit, profèrent des paroles mal examinées, non réfléchies. Dans leur folie, ignorants, mauvais,

[1] Le texte donné par la Vyākhyā (v, p. 51, Wogihara, 468 au bas ; Saṃyuktāgama, iii, fol. 14) : *rūpam anityam atītānāgataṃ kaḥ punarvādaḥ pratyutpannasya evaṃdarśī śrutavān āryaśrāvako 'tīte rūpe 'napekṣo bhavati anāgataṃ rūpaṃ nābhinandati pratyutpannasya rūpasya nirvide virāgāya nirodhāya pratipanno bhavati | atītaṃ ced bhikṣavo rūpaṃ nābhaviṣyan na...* — Tattvasaṃgraha, 505 au bas : *uktaṃ hi bhagavatā | atītaṃ ced...* — Madhyamakavṛtti, 444 : *atītaṃ ced bhikṣavo rūpaṃ nābhaviṣyan na śrutavān āryaśrāvako 'tītaṃ rūpam abhyanandiṣyat...*

Le texte que nous avons ici : *atītasya rūpasya vinodāya pratipanno bhavati | anāgatarūpe 'bhinandanocchedāya pratipanno...*

L'équivalence *yen-che*, dégoût-rejet = *vinoda*, paraît établie par Kośa, iv, 16 b 6 et xx, 2 a 10 ; toutefois *che* = *upekṣā*.

pratipanna = *k'in-sieou.*

abhinand. = *hin-k'ieou.*

[2] Voir Kośa, v, p. 59, et Index, p. 130 (Rockhill, 109, traduit Cūlekasataka). — D'après Kiokuga Saeki, éditeur du Kośa : Madhyamāgama, iv, fol. 10 ; d'après la Vyākhyā : un *sūtra* prononcé à Nālandā et Saṃyuktakāgama. — Les sources pâlies (Jātaka, 522, Dhammapada, 135) ne donnent pas le nom des religieux (*parivrājakas*) assassins de Maudgalyāyana. — Ci-dessous, p.

ils disent que l'acte, quand il est passé, épuisé, détruit, aboli, [1] n'existe absolument plus. Pourquoi [est-ce là propos fou] ? L'acte passé, épuisé, détruit, aboli, n'en existe pas moins. » [P. 625, col. 3, l. 14.]

Comment savons-nous que ces Sūtras qui enseignent l'existence du passé et du futur sont des Sūtras de sens exprès (*nītārtha*) ? [2]

Parce qu'il n'y a pas de textes qui les démente. Comparez les textes relatifs au Pudgala. [3] Il y a plusieurs textes qui affirment l'existence du Pudgala : cependant on peut dire que le Pudgala n'a pas réellement d'existence en soi, parce que le « Sūtra de l'homme », [4] clairement, dément ces textes. Nous savons ainsi que les Sūtras qui affirment l'existence du Pudgala ne sont pas de sens exprès (*anītārtha*). — De même n'est pas de sens exprès le Sūtra qui dit qu'on doit tuer son père et sa mère, parce que d'autres Sūtras disent que c'est là un « péché mortel » [5] et que le coupable tombe nécessairement en enfer. — De même n'est pas de sens exprès le Sūtra qui dit : « Il n'y a pas de mauvais acte que ne puisse faire l'homme soumis au désir », car d'autres Sūtras nient que l'Ārya puisse faire volontairement de mauvais actes. [6]

Il faut juger des textes analogues d'après les mêmes principes. [P. 625, col. 3, l. 23.]

[Si] les [Sūtras que nous avons cités] ne disaient pas clairement et catégoriquement l'existence du passé-futur, [si] ailleurs [Bhagavat] niait clairement et catégoriquement l'existence du passé-futur, on pourrait conclure que ces [Sūtras] ne sont pas

[1] *atīta, kṣīṇa, niruddha, vipariṇata.* — Tattvasaṃgraha, p. 517 : *yady evaṃ kathaṃ uktaṃ bhagavatā : asti tat karma yat kṣīṇaṃ niruddhaṃ vipariṇatam iti.*

[2] Voir Kośa, ix, p. 246 (et Index, p. 58).

[3] Voir Kośa, chap. ix. — Pourquoi Bhagavat enseigne le *pudgala*, Sūtrālaṃkāra, xviii, 102.

[4] Voir Kośa, ix, pp. 245, 257.

[5] Dhammapada, 295 ; sur le péché mortel, *ānantarya*, Kośa, iv, p. 201. — Enseignement « intentionnel », voir notamment Sūtrālaṃkāra, xii, 16.

[6] Sur l'*akaraṇasaṃvara* du Srotaāpanna, voir par exemple Kośa, vi, p. 218 ; iv, p. 201, n. 3 (Index, p. 16), du Bodhisattva, Sūtrālaṃkāra, iv, 23. — *si-yu* ; *a*, 124 et 6, *sevanā, bhāvanā, samudācāra.*

de sens exprès. Mais ils sont certainement de sens exprès, car ils « dépassent » le caractère non-exprès d'autres Sūtras [qui les contredisent].[1]

Pourquoi ces « docteurs de confusion »[2] parlent-ils avec si grand mépris, se bornant à rejeter comme de sens non-exprès les Sūtras qui contredisent leur système ? [P. 625, col. 3, l. 27.]

Mais n'y a-t-il pas un Sūtra qui nie le passé et le futur, à savoir le Paramārthaśūnyatāsūtra ? On y lit : « L'organe-œil, à l'état de naissance, pas de lieu d'où il vienne ; l'organe-œil, au temps où il périt, pas de lieu où il aille s'accumuler. D'abord il n'existe pas, maintenant il existe ; après avoir existé, il s'en va. » Si dans le futur préalablement existait l'organe-œil, le texte ne dirait pas : « D'abord il n'existait pas, maintenant il existe. »[3] [P. 626, col. 1, l. 1.]

Stupidité ! Opiniâtreté ! Incapacité de comprendre les choses les plus simples ! Exposons notre commentaire de ce texte.

Comment savez-vous qu'il faut, à la lumière du Paramārthaśūnyatāsūtra, considérer les premiers Sūtras comme de sens non-exprès, et non pas, au contraire, à la lumière des premiers Sūtras, considérer le Paramārthaśūnyatāsūtra comme de sens non-exprès ?

D'ailleurs, à s'en tenir au Paramārthaśūnyatāsūtra que notre adversaire allègue, on ne peut établir la non-existence du passé et du futur : car ce texte, dont le but est d'établir qu'il n'existe pas d'agent (*kartar*) à part des « opérants » (*saṃskāra*), ne peut réfuter l'existence réelle du passé et du futur. [P. 626, col. 1, l. 6.]

Examinons le sens de cette phrase : « L'organe-œil, à l'état de naissance, pas de lieu d'où il vienne. » Si l'œil, à l'état naissant,

[1] *yue* (156 et 5) *yu* (autre) *king* (sūtra) *pou-liao* (anīta) *siang* (lakṣaṇa).

[2] *hoang-hou-luen-tche* — trouble-trouble-śāstrin.

[3] *cakṣur bhikṣava utpadyamānaṃ na kutaścid āgacchati | nirudhyamānaṃ na kvacit saṃnicayaṃ gacchatīti hi bhikṣavaḥ cakṣur abhūtvā bhavati bhūtvā ca prativigacchati.* — Kośa, v, p. 59; Wogihara, p. 474 au bas ; Saṃyukta, xiii, 22 ; Bodhicaryāvatāra, ix, 142 (p. 581).

est une chose réelle, l'existence du futur est acquise. Si on soutient que l'œil [avant de naître] n'existe pas, pourquoi ce doute et cette enquête qui fait dire : « A l'état naissant, pas de lieu d'où il vienne » ? Car, visiblement, il n'y a pas de lieu d'où puisse venir une chose qui n'existe pas : on ne doit pas se donner la peine de nier qu'elle vienne de n'importe où ; on doit simplement dire : Quand elle naît, elle n'existe pas. » Puisque Bhagavat nie qu'il y ait un endroit d'où vienne cet œil, nous savons que, d'après le Grand Maître, il n'y a pas, à part, un certain lieu de dépôt d'où l'œil vienne : car le texte dit ensuite : « Au moment où il périt, pas de lieu où il aille s'accumuler. » [P. 626, col. 1, l. 12.]

Il y a dans le monde des docteurs d'erreur (*mithyāvādin?*) d'après lesquels l'œil, quand il naît, vient du cercle de feu [1] où il retourne s'accumuler quand il périt : c'est pour écarter cette théorie que le Sūtra dit les deux phrases ci-dessus. Ou bien pour écarter la théorie que l'œil sort de sa nature propre et, périssant, y retourne. [2] Ou encore pour nier que l'œil soit fait par le Seigneur (*īśvara*) : le Sūtra nie que l'œil ait un Fabricant et montre qu'il dépend seulement de l'enchaînement des causes et des fruits. [P. 626, col. 1, l. 27.]

Ayant réfuté l'opinion adverse, pour mettre en lumière son opinion, Bhagavat dit ensuite deux autres phrases : « D'abord il n'existe pas, maintenant il existe ; ayant existé, il s'en va. »

« D'abord il n'existe pas, maintenant il existe (*abhūtvā bhavati*) [3] » : ceci montre que l'œil n'avait pas, avant, un lieu de dépôt, et qu'il naît de ses causes et conditions. Ou bien quelques-uns pensent que la cause contient le fruit (*phalabhājanībhūta*) [4] : c'est pourquoi Bhagavat dit que le fruit n'existait pas antérieure-

[1] *houo-luen.* — *tejaścakra, tejomaṇḍala?* — Voir Harivarman, chap. 47, sur la nature ignée et solaire de l'œil : « Les Tīrthikas disent que, quand l'homme meurt, l'œil retourne au soleil, l'oreille à l'espace... »

[2] Théorie des Svabhāvavādins.

[3] Madhyamakavṛtti, p. 263, xxi, 4, xxvii, 12 ; Kośa, ii, 228-229, 237, 260, v, 57 ; Majjhima, III, 25 ; Milinda, 51-52 ; Saundarananda, xvii, 18, etc.

[4] Théorie Sāṃkhya.

ment dans la cause (*hetāv abhūtvā*) : en raison de la cause naît un fruit qui en est distinct. Ou bien encore, l'œil, quand il naît, arrive à un état où il n'était encore, de tout temps, jamais arrivé, à savoir l'état de présent. — C'est ainsi qu'il faut comprendre la phrase : *abhūtvā bhavati*. [P. 626, col. 1, l. 22.]

Tel doit être le sens de ce Sūtra. Aussi Bhagavat continue-t-il en disant : « Après avoir existé, il s'en va (*bhūtvā prativigacchati*). [1] » Ceci montre que l'œil, après avoir produit son activité (*kāritra*), projeté son fruit, s'en va et arrive à un état de non-activité semblable à celui qui précède la naissance. Si Bhagavat disait : « D'abord il n'existe pas... » avec l'intention de nier l'existence du passé et du futur, de même qu'il dit « D'abord il n'existe pas, maintenant il existe », et dirait, dans la seconde phrase : « Ayant existé, il retourne à la non-existence ». Puisque Bhagavat ne parle pas de cette non-existence et dit seulement : « Il s'en va », nous sommes assurés qu'il n'admet pas la non-existence du passé... — Comment peut-on alléguer ce Sūtra contre l'existence du passé et du futur ? [P. 626, col. 1, l. 28.]

Après avoir dit : « L'œil, quand il naît... après avoir existé, il s'en va », voyant qu'il y aura des hommes qui, se méprenant sur le sens du Sūtra, diront : « Le passé et le futur n'existent pas » et développeront la vue fausse de la négation de la cause, de la négation du fruit, — voulant écarter cette vue fausse, — Bhagavat poursuit en disant : « Il y a acte ; il y a rétribution ; mais on ne constate pas l'existence d'un agent ». Ceci montre que, pour que naisse le futur fruit de rétribution, une cause est nécessaire, à savoir l'acte passé ; mais n'existe pas à part l'activité d'un agent. Donc, si le Tathāgata enseigne ce Paramārthaśūnyatāsūtra, c'est pour montrer que n'existe pas un réel *ātman*, qu'il y a seulement enchaînement des causes et des fruits ; ce n'est pas pour nier l'existence réelle du passé et du futur.

Donc le Sūtra allégué par notre adversaire ne contredit pas

[1] *hoan-k'iu* (162 et 13, 28 et 3).

ceux que nous avons cités. Donc ceux-ci sont de sens exprès. [P. 626, col. 2, l. 7.]

On dit qu'il y a des Sūtras qui nient l'existence du passé et du futur.

Le Sūtra dit : « Quand [lui] manque le « lien de l'œil » (*ādhyātmika cakṣuḥsaṃyojana*), [le saint] sait en vérité : Je n'ai pas le lien de l'œil. [1] » — Le Sūtra dit : « Ceci n'étant pas, cela n'est pas. [2] » — Le Sūtra dit : « Ces deux-là n'ont pas la chaleur. [3] » [P. 626, col. 2, l. 9.]

Ces Sūtras ne sont pas démonstratifs, car, dans ces mêmes Sūtras, nous lisons des phrases qui établissent l'existence du passé et du futur. Ils disent en effet : « Quand il y a lien de l'œil, il sait en vérité : J'ai le lien de l'œil », or, lorsque la pensée est bonne (*kuśalacittāvasthāyām :* et il y a ici pensée bonne, puisqu'il y a « savoir en vérité »), il n'y a pas, en activité, lien de l'œil : Ce Sūtra enseigne donc l'existence du passé et du futur. — « Les *saṃskāras* étant, le *vijñāna* est » : or le fruit de rétribution (*vipākaphala*, dans l'espèce, le *vijñāna*) n'est pas simultané à la cause de rétribution (*vipākahetu*, à savoir les *saṃskāras*). Ce Sūtra enseigne donc l'existence du passé et du futur. — Le Bouddha dit aux deux bhikṣus : « Il est un sermon (*dharmaparyāya*) en quatre phrases (*cātuḥpādaka*) que je vais vous dire. » Ceci prouve que... [4] existent en soi (*t'i*) les futures syllabes, etc., qui seront prononcées. Ce Sūtra enseigne donc l'existence du passé et du futur. — Sans doute, il est dit que le lien n'existe pas : mais la pensée est que telle personne n'est pas munie (*asamanvāgata*) du lien, ne crée pas le lien, ne le possède pas (*prāpti*).

Concluons qu'on ne rencontre pas de Sūtras qui nient

[1] Variante : le lien de l'œil de chair. — Voir ci-dessous, p. 85, le Pūrṇasūtra.

[2] Pratītyasamutpādasūtra.

[3] *pei cul ou noan* (?). — Si j'entends bien, les deux bhikṣus ci-dessous ne possèdent pas encore les *uṣmagatas* (Kośa, vi, p. 163) : donc ceux-ci, futurs, n'existent pas.

[4] On a ici : *chen nei* = *kāyāntare, śarīrāntare* (?).

certainement le passé-futur comme on a des Sūtras qui l'affirment certainement. Donc les Sūtras affirmatifs que nous avons cités doivent raisonnablement être regardés comme vraiment de sens exprès. Ils réfutent l'opinion que les Sūtras de sens exprès cités d'abord ne sont pas de sens exprès, car ils sont en contradiction avec la thèse de notre adversaire. [P. 626, col. 2, l. 20.]

Le Sautrāntika, voulant par tous moyens établir que nos Sūtras ne sont pas de sens exprès, dit [1] : « Moi aussi je dis que le passé et le futur sont. Le passé, c'est ce qui a été : on dit donc qu'il est. Le futur, c'est ce qui sera, la cause étant. [2] C'est dans ce sens que l'on dit que le passé et l'avenir sont ; on n'entend pas dire que le passé et le futur, comme le présent, existent « comme choses » (*dravyatas*). [3] Aussi, quand on dit qu'ils sont, c'est en visant la nature de cause du passé, la nature de fruit du futur, non pas en les considérant comme des choses réelles. Bhagavat, pour condamner la vue fausse qui nie la cause et la vue fausse qui nie le fruit, dit que le passé et le futur sont, pour dire que le passé (= la cause) fut, que le futur (= le fruit) sera ; car on peut employer le mot « est » (*astiśabda*) au sujet de choses qui sont et de choses qui ne sont pas. [4] Comme, par exemple, on dit dans le monde : « Il y a (*asti*) non-existence antérieure de la lampe ; il y a non-existence postérieure de la lampe » et encore « Cette lampe est (*asti*) éteinte, elle n'a pas été éteinte par moi. [5] » C'est dans ce sens qu'on dit que le passé et le futur sont. Si on écarte cette explication, les notions de passé et de futur ne seront pas établies. [P. 626, col. 2, l. 27.]

[1] Vasubandhu, dans Kośa, v, p. 58.
Dans le Kathāvatthu, i, 6, l'adversaire du Sarvāstivāda cite le Sūtra Saṃyutta, iii, 71 : *yaṃ hi bhikkhave rūpam atītaṃ niruddhaṃ vipariṇataṃ ahosīti tassa saṅkhā... na tassa saṃkhā atthīti na tassa saṅkhā bhavissatīti.*

[2] *atītaṃ tu yad bhūtapūrvam | anāgataṃ yat sati hetau bhaviṣyati.*

[3] Saṃghabhadra saute ici deux lignes de Vasubandhu.

[4] Sur la valeur du mot *asti*, Kośa, v, 58, ii, 282.

[5] *asti niruddhaḥ so 'tra dīpo* (Wogihara, p. 473, 9 : *sa pradīpo*) *na ca mayā nirodhita iti vaktāro bhavanti.*

L'explication que le Sautrāntika donne du verbe « être » (« je dis que le passé et le futur sont ») n'est pas bonne, car le Sautrāntika n'admet pas qu'il s'agisse d'une existence réelle (*dravyasat*) et nous avons montré qu'il ne s'agit pas d'une existence de désignation (*prajñaptisat*). Or le verbe « être » ne peut s'appliquer qu'à ces deux modes d'existence, qui sont les seuls. — Pourquoi limiter »[1] le mot « sont » du Sūtra (« Le passé et le futur sont »), en disant : « Moi aussi je dis que le passé et le futur sont », avec la glose : « Du passé, qui a été, on dit qu'il est ; le futur, c'est, la cause étant, ce qui sera » ? En fait cette phrase n'est qu'une manière artificieuse de dire, en d'autres termes, que le présent est, et ne concerne pas le passé ou le futur. — Par conséquent la déclaration du Sautrāntika : « Moi aussi je dis que le passé et le futur sont », n'est que parole vide ; il est tout à fait incapable d'expliquer comment [pour l'auteur du Sūtra] le passé et le futur sont. [P. 626, col. 3, l. 6.]

Si le passé est seulement ce qui fut, si le futur est seulement ce qui sera, toute réalité manque au *dharma* passé et futur, et on ne peut pas dire qu'il est. Ou, si on veut qu'il soit, on ne doit pas dire que le passé et le futur sont seulement ce qui fut et ce qui sera. — Si on dit du passé qu'il existe réellement, quoique réellement inexistant, parce qu'il a été, on pourra aussi bien dire du présent qu'il n'est pas, quoique réellement existant, parce qu'il n'est pas « ayant été ». Le passé est à la fois « ayant été » et n'étant pas ». D'après les mêmes principes on parlera du futur : celui-ci est à la fois « devant être » et « n'étant pas ». [P. 626, col. 3, l. 11.)

A la vérité, dans le réellement existant qu'est le *t'i* du passé, il y a une partie dont on doit dire qu'elle « a été ». C'est par là que le passé a la nature (*yeou sing*) de passé. De même, dans ce réellement existant qu'est le *t'i* du futur, il y a une partie dont on doit dire qu'elle « sera ». C'est par là que le futur a la nature de futur. (Ci-dessous p. 93.)

[1] *kiue-p'an*, décider-juger, *paricchedda* (Vyutpatti), *niyama*, Kośa, xvii, 5 a 10.

On voit bien que, dans la vie vulgaire, on dit d'un *dharma* d'existence réelle, qu'il a été et qu'il sera. Au contraire, il est inouï qu'on dise d'un *dharma* qui n'existe pas réellement, qu'il a été et qu'il sera. C'est ainsi que Śāriputra dit à Bhagavat : « Chanda le bhikṣu alla, dans un village de brahmanes, quêter dans une maison. » Or, à ce moment, cette maison existait présentement. Et Bhagavat dit : « Ānanda le bhikṣu sera un Sthavira » Or, à ce moment, Ānanda existait présentement. — Donc il est bien établi que le passé et le futur, quoique réellement existants, ont été et seront. [P. 626, col. 3, l. 19.]

Si le passé et le futur ne sont pas des choses réelles, on ne peut condamner l'hérésie qui nie la cause et le fruit. En effet, si réellement existe le passé, cause, capable de produire le futur, réellement existant, qui est le fruit, on peut nommer « hérésie qui nie la cause et le fruit » la doctrine qui affirme l'inexistence de ce passé et de ce futur. Mais si le passé et le futur, la cause et le fruit, n'existent pas réellement, peut-on considérer comme hérésie la doctrine qui considère comme inexistant ce qui, en fait, n'existe pas ? Mieux vaut, pour réfuter cette hérésie, affirmer l'existence du passé et du futur. [P. 626, col. 3, l. 23.]

Mais, réplique le Sautrāntika, n'ai-je pas dit que ce qui a été et ce qui sera, tous deux sont ?

Mais j'ai dit moi aussi, que [ces deux époques] sont et ne sont pas. Et pour quelle raison dites-vous que le passé et le futur sont, en considérant ce qui a été et ce qui sera, alors que, de ce qui n'a pas été et ne sera pas, vous ne dites pas qu'il n'est pas présent ? A s'exprimer ainsi on pourrait condamner la doctrine de la permanence (*śāśvatadṛṣṭi*). — Donc les discours du Sautrāntika sont illogiques.

D'ailleurs, j'ai fait remarquer que les mots « ce qui a été », « ce qui sera », ce n'est qu'une manière de dire en d'autres termes que le présent est. Cela ne concerne pas le passé et le futur. Comment cela réfutera-t-il [l'existence du passé et du futur] ? [P. 626, col. 3, l. 27.]

Que le verbe « être » s'entende [dans nos textes] de ce qui est et de ce qui n'est pas (p. 60, l. 20), cela est faux, car semblable emploi n'est pas admis. Celui qui prétend que ce verbe a ce double sens doit parler avec sincérité : l'usage mondain est que « est » s'entend seulement de ce qui est ; il est inouï que « est » désigne la non-existence. Pourquoi soutenir que ce verbe a les deux sens ? Je sais bien qu'on parle, en disant qu'elle est, de la non-existence antérieure et de la non-existence postérieure de la lampe. Nous avons parlé de cela en expliquant l'inexistence du son et nous y reviendrons (p. 45). [P. 627, col. 1, l. 3.]

Le Sautrāntika dit : « S'il en est autrement, [si le passé et le futur existent], la nature de passé et de futur n'est pas établie ». Ceci aussi est incorrect, parce que son [passé-futur] n'est pas établi Son passé n'a pas la nature de passé ; son futur n'a pas la nature de futur ; car on ne peut attribuer une nature (*bhāva*) à ce qui n'existe pas réellement.[1] Ou bien il doit faire effort, de quelque façon que ce soit, pour établir l'existence réelle du passé et du futur : à ce prix seulement ces deux époques sont établies.

Dans le système du Sautrāntika, il est impossible de rendre compte des Sūtras qui enseignent l'existence du passé et du futur. Que ce système soit incapable de rendre compte de ces Sūtras, ce n'est pas une raison suffisante pour rejeter les Sūtras proclamés par le Sugata. Donc il faut croire et savoir que le passé et le futur existent. [P. 627, col. 1, l. 10.]

Le Sautrāntika explique le Lāgudaśikhīyakasūtra (p. 54).

Bien que l'acte soit passé, le Bouddha dit qu'il est ; mais, ce que le Bouddha a en vue, c'est le pouvoir de donner le fruit, pouvoir qui se trouve dans la série projetée par cet acte. S'il en était autrement, l'acte passé, existant actuellement, ne serait pas passé. On ne peut en douter, car Bhagavat, dans le Paramārtha-śūnyatāsūtra dit : « L'œil, dans l'état de naissance, ne vient de nulle part... »

[1] *ou tse t'i, niḥsvabhāva ; sing, bhāva.*

Il faut comparer le Sautrāntika à l'homme dans un bateau entraîné par un courant rapide... ; pas de raison pour que le bateau s'arrête. Le Sautrāntika suppose qu'il y a dans la série actuelle un certain pouvoir de donner le fruit : ce pouvoir, le docte, scrutant la vérité, cherche quel est son caractère et est impuissant à le découvrir. Comment Bhagavat pourrait-il dire que l'acte passé, qui n'a plus d'être propre, existe, en visant ce pouvoir de donner un fruit ? Nous avons déjà maintes fois réfute les hypothèses de cet artificieux hypocrite, *anudhātu*, *śakti*, *vāsanā*, *bīja*, *upacaya*, *avipraṇāśadharma*, etc.[1] Toutes ces hypothèses peuvent-elles réfuter l'affirmation de l'existence du passé-futur que contiennent des Sūtras de sens exprès, et montrer que ces Sūtras ne sont pas de sens exprès ? [P. 627, col. 1, l. 21.]

Même à admettre la réalité du pouvoir projeté par l'acte, ce n'est pas une raison pour dire, d'une chose qui n'existe pas (à savoir de l'acte passé, dans l'hypothèse Sautrāntika), qu'elle existe. Car on pourra, vu la non-existence (supposée) de sa cause (à savoir l'acte passé), dire que le pouvoir aussi n'existe pas. Il n'y a aucune raison pour admettre l'existence du pouvoir si on nie l'acte passé.

D'ailleurs ce que dit Bhagavat n'a rien de commun avec la théorie du « pouvoir ». Il dit clairement que l'acte, bien que passé, épuisé, détruit, aboli, existe cependant. Et le pouvoir de donner le fruit projeté par l'acte, pouvoir qui réside dans la série, le Sautrāntika le tient pour actuel : son être n'est pas passé, épuisé, détruit, aboli. Comment donc Bhagavat pourrait-il parler comme il fait en ayant en vue ce pouvoir ? Si Bhagavat voulait dire ce qu'on lui fait dire, il dirait clairement : « Quoique l'acte soit passé,

[1] Voir ci-dessous, p. 66, 76; dans le commentaire de Saṃghabhadra, pp. 397, 440. — Tous ces termes sont à peu près synonymes et se réfèrent au pouvoir, à la trace, aux semences que la pensée (et l'acte) placent dans la série. — On distingue le *karman* et le *karma-upacaya* (cp. Kathāvatthu). — Sur l'*avipraṇāśa*, voir Karmasiddhiprakaraṇa. — Le terme le plus difficile est *soei-kiai*, exactement *kieou-soei-kiai*, *anu-dhātu* ?, *purāṇa-anu-dhātu ?* Voir *anusahagata*, *aṇusahagata*, Kośa, ii, 245, iv, 172. — Voir des « Notes sur la série des Sautrāntikas » qui continueront ces Études d'Abhidharma; ci-dessous 99, 100, 103-105, 114.

aboli, cependant le pouvoir projeté par l'acte réside dans la série. » Or il dit seulement : « Cet acte existe cependant. » Donc nous savons que l'acte passé existe réellement. [P. 627, col. 1, l. 28.]

D'ailleurs Bhagavat dit seulement que l'acte passé est ; comment s'assurer qu'il parle du pouvoir qui donne le fruit ? — Ne l'avons-nous pas expliqué ? Si on écarte cette explication, il reste que l'acte passé, existant actuellement comme chose, n'est pas passé. — Mais j'ai répondu à cette objection.[1] — Comment cela ? — J'ai dit que, quoique le caractère de la chose[2] reste sans différences, cependant on y constate des différences dans la manière d'être.[3] Les manières d'être ne sont pas les mêmes. Quel défaut voyez-vous dans cette explication. Il y a, là-dessus, une stance :

« Le caractère essentiel du *dharma*[4] est unique; les pouvoirs, les manières d'être sont multiples. Celui qui ne connaît pas [cela] en vérité est dit résider en dehors du Bouddhisme (*buddhaśāsana*). » [P. 627, col. 2, l. 7.]

Le Paramārthaśūnyatāsūtra doit s'expliquer comme nous avons dit, et ne démontre pas la thèse Sautrāntika. Cette thèse n'admet pas l'existence réelle de l'acte passé : mais ce Sūtra ne dit pas : « Après avoir existé, il retourne à l'inexistence.[5] » Notre adversaire n'a donc pas le droit de le citer comme preuve. Au gré de sa fantaisie, il en donne une exégèse erronée, et reste incapable de détruire la doctrine de l'existence réelle du passé et du futur. [P. 627, col 2, l. 11.]

Le Sthavira explique les Sūtras qui affirment l'existence du passé et du futur.

a) « Si le *rūpa* passé n'existait pas, le disciple instruit ne s'appliquerait pas à se dégoûter du *rūpa* passé...[6] »

[1] Voir p. 51.
[2] *t'i-siang*, ou « caractère essentiel ».
[3] Manière d'être, *yeou-sing*, *sattā*, *bhāva*.
[4] *fa t'i-siang*.
[5] Ci-dessus, p. 58.
[6] Ci-dessus, p. 54.

Ce texte signifie, d'après le Sthavira : « Si le *rūpa* passé n'était pas passé, le disciple instruit ne s'appliquerait pas à rejeter le *rūpa* passé, mais, comme du *rūpa* présent, il s'appliquerait à s'en dégoûter, à s'en détacher, à le détruire (*nirvide virāgāya nirodhāya*) », ou bien : « Si le *rūpa* passé, de la série personnelle ou d'une autre série, n'avait pas été expérimenté, le disciple instruit ne s'appliquerait pas à le rejeter ; il faut que ce *rūpa* ait été expérimenté pour qu'on puisse le rejeter, car comment rejeter ce qui n'a pas été expérimenté ? C'est parce que ce *rūpa* est passé et, étant passé, a été expérimenté, que le disciple instruit s'applique à rejeter le *rūpa* passé. » [P. 627, col. 2, l. 19.]

b) Quant au Lāguḍaśikhīyakasūtra. [1]

« On peut dire que l'acte passé existe, parce qu'il est condition en qualité de cause (*hetupratyaya*) [2] ; parce qu'il est *anudhātu* [3] ; parce que sa série ne peut être arrêtée ; parce que son fruit de rétribution n'a pas encore mûri ; parce que, à la fin, il sera capable d'amener la rétribution. Mais ce qui est passé n'existe pas comme chose réelle. » [P. 627, col. 2, l. 22.]

Ces explications prêtent à rire ! Réussissent-elles à réfuter l'existence du passé et du futur ? Interpréter de la sorte les Sūtras de l'Omniscient, est-ce orner le pays d'Inde ?

a) Quant à la première explication du premier Sūtra. — « Si le *rūpa* passé n'était pas passé, le disciple ne le rejetterait pas, mais, comme du *rūpa* présent, il s'appliquerait à s'en dégoûter, à s'en détacher, à le détruire » : tel ne peut pas, quelque effort que fasse le Sthavira, être le sens du Sūtra. Car, si ce *rūpa* n'était pas passé, il serait ou actuel ou futur, par conséquent le disciple ne prendrait pas seulement à son endroit l'attitude qu'il prend à l'endroit du *rūpa* actuel. — Ces confuses et forcées explications peuvent-elles être considérées comme un commentaire de l'inten-

[1] Ci-dessus, pp. 54, 63.
[2] Kośa, ii, p. 299.
[3] *soei-kiai*, abréviation de *kieou-soei-kiai*, ci-dessus p. 64.

tion du Sūtra ? — Si le sens était ce que vous prétendez, le Sūtra dirait : « Si le *rūpa* passé n'était pas passé » ; il ne dirait pas : « Si le *rūpa* passé n'existait pas. » Et, plus loin, il dirait : « Parce que le *rūpa* passé est passé » ; il ne dirait pas : « Parce que le *rūpa* passé existe. » Donc, la première explication ne vaut rien. [P. 627, col. 3, l. 4.]

Cependant le Sthavira expliquera peut-être : « Si le *rūpa* passé n'existait pas, passé, le disciple ne le rejetterait pas. Car on ne peut rejeter une chose non-existante (*asaddharma*, *ou fa*). Il faut que le *rūpa* passé ait la nature de passé pour qu'on puisse le rejeter ; de même que le *rūpa* présent, ayant la nature de présent, on peut s'efforcer à s'en dégoûter... » — A comprendre ainsi, pas de différence avec mon système. On achève de prouver l'existence réelle du passé. — Concluons que, à quelque prix que ce soit, le Sthavira n'aboutit pas à prouver la non-existence. [P. 627, col. 3, l. 9.]

b) Quant à la deuxième explication du premier Sūtra, elle rend compte d'une partie du sens du Sūtra : en effet, on rejette ce qui a été expérimenté ; ce qui n'a pas été expérimenté ne donne pas lieu à rejet. Mais nous ne voyons pas comment, en présentant cette explication, le Sthavira entend réfuter l'existence du passé. Si le passé n'est pas réel, le rejet à son endroit est inexplicable et disparaît.

c) L'explication du Lāguḍaśikhīyaka n'est pas non plus satisfaisante. En effet un *dharma* non-existant ne peut pas avoir la nature de condition en qualité de cause (*hetupratyaya*) ; l'expression *anudhātu* n'a pas de « signifié » (*abhidheya*) ; dans la doctrine de l'*ekakṣaṇa*[4], la série est impossible ; un *dharma* qui n'existe pas ne peut produire un fruit de rétribution : autrement, le Saṃsāra n'aurait pas de fin. Je dis donc que le passé et le futur existent. [P. 627, col. 3, l. 16.]

[4] Doctrine suivant laquelle n'existe que le *dharma* présent qui dure un instant, doctrine du Sautrāntika. — Voir ci-dessous, § iii, Notes sur le moment des Vaibhāṣikas et des Sautrāntikas.

2. — *Parce que la connaissance naît de deux*, dvayāt.

« Parce que la connaissance (*vijñāna*) naît en raison de deux conditions (*pratyaya*).[1] »

Le Sūtra dit : « La connaissance visuelle naît en raison de l'œil et du visible (*rūpa*) », et ainsi de suite jusque : « La connaissance mentale (*manovijñāna*) naît en raison de l'esprit (*manas*, *manaindriya*, organe mental) et des *dharmas*. »

Si le passé et le futur n'existent pas, la connaissance [mentale] qui les vise (*ālambate*) n'aura pas deux conditions [: car elle visera des *dharmas* non-existants]. [P. 627, col. 3, l. 19.]

Le Sautrāntika dit là-dessus : « Il convient d'examiner : la connaissance mentale naissant avec le *manas* et les *dharmas* pour condition, les *dharmas* sont-ils condition au même titre que le *manas*, à savoir condition génératrice (*janakapratyaya*), ou sont-ils seulement « condition en qualité d'objet » (*ālambanamātra*) ? — Dites-vous qu'ils sont condition génératrice ? Comment des *dharmas* futurs qui ne se produiront qu'après des centaines de milliers de millénaires (*kalpas*), ou qui ne se produiront jamais, peuvent-ils être la condition génératrice qui engendre la connaissance mentale actuelle ? Et le Nirvāṇa ? Contradictoire à la naissance, c'est une absurdité d'en faire une condition génératrice. — Mais si les *dharmas* sont seulement condition en qualité d'objet, je dis que le passé et le futur sont, en effet, objet de la connaissance mentale. [P. 627, col. 3, l. 25.]

Ce discours tourne le dos au texte.[2] En effet, les Ābhidhārmikas

[1] C'est le deuxième argument de la *kārikā*, v, 25. — Ci-dessus, p. 53. — Kośa, v, pp. 60-63 ; Tattvasaṃgraha, p. 504 : *dvayāśrayaṃ ca vijñānaṃ tāyinā kathitaṃ katham... — dvayaṃ pratītya vijñānam utpadyata iti bhagavatoktam | katamad dvayam | cakṣū rūpāṇi yāvan mano dharmā iti | asati cātītānāgate tadālambanaṃ vijñānaṃ dvayaṃ pratītya na syād ity āgamavirodhaḥ.* — Réfutation, p. 517 : *dvayaṃ pratītya vijñānaṃ yad uktaṃ tattvadarśinā | seṣṭā saviṣayaṃ cittam abhisaṃdhāya deśanā || dvividhaṃ hi vijñānaṃ sālambanam anālambanaṃ ca :* « Quand le Voyeur de la vérité dit que la connaissance dépend de deux conditions, nous croyons que cet enseignement vise la pensée qui a un objet. Car la connaissance est de deux sortes, ayant un objet, n'ayant pas d'objet. | — Comparer Harivarman, chap. 191.

[2] Ci-dessus, 621, 3, 8 ; *luen-tao.*

disent : « Le Bouddha enseigne que deux conditions engendrent la connaissance. » Et le [Sautrāntika] parle seulement de supports (*āśraya*) réel et fictif.[1] L'organe, plus l'objet, engendre la connaissance, car le couple [de conditions génératrices du Sūtra] ne peut être obtenu qu'au moyen de [l'objet]. Un non-existant ne peut figurer parmi les deux conditions. Donc le Bouddha a implicitement condamné la doctrine que la connaissance puisse naître avec un non-existant pour objet. Puisqu'elle naît en visant le passé et le futur, nous savons que le passé et le futur existent réellement (*dravyasat*). [P. 628, col. 1, l. 1.]

Telle est la doctrine traditionnelle [ou reçue][2]. Le Sautrāntika dit cependant : « Comme l'existant, le non-existant est condition en qualité d'objet. » C'est au Bouddha qu'il s'attaque, non pas à la doctrine de l'Abhidharma. Les Ābhidhārmikas reçoivent l'intention du Bouddha, la placent dans leur pensée,[3] et disent : « Le passé et le futur existent réellement. » [P. 628, col. 1, l. 4.]

Le Sautrāntika dit : « Il convient d'examiner... » — Que faut-il examiner ? Le *manas* est condition génératrice de la connaissance mentale au titre de support ; les *dharmas* engendrent la connaissance mentale au titre d'objet. Le support et l'objet sont pareillement des conditions génératrices, puisque le Bouddha dit que deux conditions engendrent la connaissance. De même que la connaissance ne naît pas faute de support, de même, si l'objet manque, elle ne naît pas ; puisque ces deux sont ensemble les conditions génératrices de la connaissance. Qu'y a-t-il à examiner dans un texte de sens si clair ? [P. 628, col. 1, l. 9.]

Mais le Sautrāntika dira : « L'organe *manas* fait partie d'une même série (*ekajātīyasaṃtāna*) avec la connaissance à engendrer, et il amène immédiatement cette connaissance à la naissance[4] :

[1] Le *dharma* passé est un support irréel de la connaissance.

[2] *tsong tch'eng ki eul*, doctrine-recevoir-puisque-ainsi.

[3] *sin-cheou*, pensée-tête.

[4] En effet, le *manas* est le moment de pensée qui précède immédiatement le moment de pensée, ou de connaissance (*vijñāna*), dont il est le support et le générateur.

il est donc nommé « générateur ». Mais il n'en va pas de même des *dharmas.* » — Dans ce cas, ni l'organe-œil ni le visible ne seront générateurs de la connaissance visuelle. Car ils ne font pas partie d'une même série avec cette connaissance, et ne l'amènent pas immédiatement. [P. 628, col. 1, l. 12.]

Le *dharma* futur qui va naître tout de suite ne sera pas générateur de la connaissance mentale ; car il ne fait pas partie d'une même série avec la connaissance à engendrer, et ne l'amène pas immédiatement. Or le Sautrāntika croit que ce *dharma* engendre, puisqu'il dit : « Comment ce qui arrivera dans cent mille millénaires, ou n'arrivera pas, comment le Nirvāṇa pourraient-ils être la condition génératrice de la connaissance actuelle ? » (Voir p. 68, l. 15.) Que si le *dharma* futur qui va naître n'est pas générateur de la connaissance mentale actuelle, pourquoi le Sautrāntika parle-t-il seulement de ce qui arrivera dans cent mille millénaires, ou n'arrivera pas, et du Nirvāṇa, pour demander comment ces choses peuvent engendrer la connaissance actuelle ? — Cela encore prête à la critique. [P. 628, col. 1, l. 18.]

Le Sugata a nettement décidé que le support et l'objet engendrent la connaissance. Il n'est pas nécessaire qu'ils fassent partie de la même série : car on sait bien que la mère engendre. [P. 628, col. 1, l. 20.]

Quant à la question que pose le Sautrāntika : « Comment les *dharmas* qui ne seront qu'après cent mille millénaires peuvent-ils être la condition génératrice qui engendre la connaissance actuelle ? », il faut répondre en demandant : « Comment le *dharma* futur qui va naître tout de suite peut-il engendrer la connaissance actuelle ? » Car en tant que causes, fruits, choses de souillure, choses de purification, les *dharmas* proches ou lointains sont de même nature. [P. 628, col. 1, l. 24.]

Autre point. [Pour le Sautrāntika], aucun *dharma*, de sa nature, n'est agent, n'est actif.[1] Il n'y a pas lieu d'établir la distinction « qui engendre », « qui est engendré ». Donc tous les *dharmas*

[1] Voir Kośa, ix, 280.

qui ont une nature propre sont seulement support et objet de la connaissance. Ce mot « seulement » n'indique pas [que l'objet doit avoir nature propre pour qu'il y ait] existence de la connaissance, puisque des *dharmas* exempts de nature propre peuvent être objets. [P. 628, col. 1, l. 27.]

Ici le Sautrāntika se fait une objection et l'explique.[1] « Si [le passé et le futur n'existent] pas, comment sont-ils l'objet de la connaissance ?[2] Je dis qu'ils existent de la manière dont ils sont l'objet de la connaissance. De quelle manière ? Comme ayant été, comme devant être.[3] Quand on se souvient du *rūpa* passé, de la *vedanā* passée, on ne les voit pas [clairement] exister comme de l'actuel ; on s'en souvient seulement comme ayant été.[4] Inversement on voit le futur comme devant être. On se souvient (de l'existence) du *rūpa* tel qu'il a été éprouvé lorsqu'il était présent, et on prévoit l'existence du *rūpa* futur tel qu'il sera éprouvé lorsqu'il sera présent.[5] Si [le *rūpa* passé-futur] existe comme le présent, il est présent. Si son être (*t'i*) n'est pas [tel] actuellement, il faut reconnaître que la connaissance peut prendre le non-existant pour objet.[6] » [P. 628, col. 2, l. 5.]

Le disciple du Dārṣṭāntika se méprend sur la vérité mondaine (*saṃvṛti*) parce que son intelligence (*prajñā, hoei-kiai*) est grossière et peu profonde. Dans cette épaisse forêt du connaissable, le savoir peu profond du monde ne peut servir de mesure ; car ce sont choses que seul atteint l'excellent savoir, correspondant

[1] Kośa, v, p. 60 ; Wogihara, p. 474.

[2] *katham ālambyante* ou *gṛhyante*.

[3] *yathā gṛhyante | katham | abhūd bhaviṣyati ceti.*

[4] « On ne le voit pas en disant : C'est, mais on s'en souvient en disant : Ce fut. » — Le mot « clairement » manque dans l'original.

[5] L'intention (*abhiprāya*) est : « Ce qui fut et ce qui sera est saisi comme du *rūpa* présent (*vartamānarūpam iva*). »

[6] *yathā ca tat tathaiva astīti | atha nāsti tat tathaiva asad apy ālambanam bhavatīti siddham.* — Je suis le commentaire qui explique *yathā* par *yathā vartamānam.* — Le sens doit être : « Si le passé est comme il est perçu (*yathā gṛhyate*), il est présent : on dit *asti ;* s'il n'est point tel... »

Deux arguments, semble-t-il : 1. la mémoire ne saisit pas son objet clairement

à l'objet, de ceux qui sont munis d'une pure intelligence. [P. 628, col. 2, l. 8.]

Pour ceux dont l'intelligence mondaine n'est pas pure, il faut que l'objet ait été éprouvé pour que la mémoire soit possible. C'est pourquoi ce qu'ils arrivent à déduire sur le passé et le futur diffère [de la connaissance du présent]. Leur vue relative au futur est extrêmement obscure parce que le futur n'a pas été éprouvé. Mais les hommes d'intelligence pure, contemplant le passé et le futur, et à défaut de toute perception antérieure, voient avec une clarté parfaite. [P. 628, col. 2, l. 11.]

Le passé n'existe pas à la manière dont il est perçu. Quand on voit un homme dans un poteau, un oiseau dans une motte de terre, la chose existe-t-elle comme elle est perçue ? Par conséquent, en ce qui regarde le passé et le futur, autre la manière dont ils sont perçus, autre la manière dont ils existent. On ne peut pas dire qu'ils existent de la manière dont ils sont perçus : car, leur existence étant passée ou future, on les perçoit comme s'ils étaient présents. [P. 628, col. 2, l. 14.]

Le Sautrāntika se contredit en effet. -- Il dit d'abord : « Celui qui se souvient d'un visible (*rūpa*) passé, d'une sensation passée, ne voit pas clairement comme il fait l'actuel : Cela est, — mais seulement il se souvient : Cela fut ». — Il ne devrait donc pas dire ensuite : « On se souvient du visible tel qu'il a été éprouvé lorsqu'il était présent. » Car, quand on éprouve actuellement le visible, on ne l'éprouve pas comme ayant été, mais bien comme étant. Et quand on se souvient du visible passé, on ne s'en souvient pas comme étant, mais bien comme ayant été.

comme la connaissance actuelle saisit l'objet actuel. Encore faut-il que l'objet ait été « éprouvé » antérieurement. Saṃghabhadra répondra que certains hommes voient clairement le passé, qu'ils voient des choses passées qu'ils n'ont pas éprouvées ; 2. la note de passé n'est pas liée à l'image que donne la mémoire : on se souvient de la chose « comme présente » (*vartamānavat*). Si je me souvenais d'une chose passée avec le caractère de passé, on pourrait dire que cette chose passée existe. Mais l'image que j'en ai est l'image d'une chose présente : or la chose passée ne peut pas correspondre à semblable image. Donc la mémoire saisit une chose non-existante, a pour objet une chose non-existante.

Admettre qu'on se souvient de l'objet passé sous l'aspect de « étant », et dire que « le passé existe à la manière dont il est perçu », c'est admettre l'existence réelle du passé : car, comme actuellement on éprouve le caractère d'une chose réelle (*dravyasallakṣaṇa*), de même on se souvient du passé comme existant. Puisque le Sautrāntika pense que le passé existe de la manière dont on s'en souvient, comment l'être (*svabhāva, t'i*) du passé ne serait-il pas réel (*dravyasat*) ? Par conséquent la seconde remarque du Sautrāntika contredit sa première opinion. [P. 628, col. 2, l. 24.]

Le Sautrāntika a encore dit : « S'il existe comme le présent, il est présent ; si sa nature propre (*t'i*) actuellement n'existe pas, on doit admettre que la connaissance a pour objet du non-existant. »

Ceci a été expliqué. — Comment cela ? — J'ai dit que le passé-futur n'existe pas comme le présent, car j'admets qu'il y a différentes manières d'être (*yeou-sing*) de tous les êtres réels (*dravyasat*) [d'ailleurs] constants [dans leur nature propre]. [P. 628, col. 2, l. 27.]

3. — *Parce que la connaissance a un objet existant*, sadviṣayāt. [1]

Parce que toutes les connaissances ont un objet existant.

On voit que, lorsqu'existe un objet, la connaissance naît. Bhagavat dit en effet : « Qu'est la connaissance ? [2] C'est la discrimination du caractère des objets. — De quels objets ? — Du visible (*rūpa*) ... de la connaissance. [3] »

Le Sūtra ne dit pas qu'il y ait une connaissance à objet non-existant. Par conséquent la connaissance qui porte sur le passé et le futur ayant un objet existant, le passé et le futur sont des choses réelles.

[1] Troisième argument de la kārikā, ci-dessus p. 53.

[2] Littéralement le *vijñāna upādānaskandha*.

[3] Voir Kośa, i, 16 a, p. 30. — Tattvasaṃgraha, p. 505 : *prati vastu vijñaptyātmakaṃ vijñānam | asati ca jñeye na kiṃ cid anena jñeyam ity avijñānam eva syāt.*

Les points où nous sommes en conflit avec le Sautrāntika ont été expliqués ci-dessus et nous n'y reviendrons pas. [P. 628, col. 3, l. 3.]

Le Sthavira dit : « Le savoir qui porte sur le non-existant ne laisse pas d'avoir les deux conditions requises (il a objet comme il a support, *ālambana* et *āśraya*), en vertu de l'examen de la succession des causes et des fruits (*hetuphalaparamparā*). »

Qu'est-ce à dire ?

C'est après avoir « pris » le présent qu'on peut rapidement examiner dans le passé et l'avenir (*pūrvāparāntakoṭi*). On examine : « Tel fruit présent naît de telle cause passée ; cette cause à son tour est produite par telle cause », et ainsi de suite longtemps et loin, dans chaque cas comme il convient (*yathāyogam*). Ces [savoirs] déductifs atteignent (*adhigacchante*) [leur objet] comme présent. Ou bien on examine : « Telle cause présente engendre tel fruit futur ; ce fruit à son tour amène à naître tel fruit », et ainsi de suite, longtemps et loin, dans chaque cas comme il convient. Ces [savoirs] déductifs atteignent [leur objet] comme présent. De la sorte, en succession, on voit les causes passées, dans chaque cas comme il convient, en remontant longtemps et loin : atteignant [leur objet] comme présent, ces [savoirs] ne sont pas erronés. Quoique leur objet n'existe pas comme chose, ces savoirs ne laissent pas d'avoir objet et support. [P. 628, col. 3, l. 13.]

Le [Sthavira] dit : Lorsque naît le savoir de telle cause, c'est en raison des causes-conditions qui se trouvent dans la série : tel savoir qui s'est produit jadis est la cause médiate qui fait que naisse tel savoir actuel. Puisque le savoir actuel a pour cause le savoir ancien, il s'ensuit que le savoir actuel naît et connaît (*kiai*) comme l'ancien, c'est-à-dire qu'il a pour objet (*ālambana*) l'ancienne chose (*viṣaya*, objet de l'ancien savoir). L'objet de cet ancien savoir, actuellement, n'existe pas : cependant, quoiqu'il n'existe pas, il est l'objet [du nouveau savoir]. Par conséquent on ne peut pas dire que la double condition requise manque. — De même en va-t-il en ce qui concerne le futur. [P. 628, col. 3, l. 18.]

Ici le Sthavira soulève une difficulté et l'explique.

Lorsque le savoir porte (*ālambate*) sur une chose (*viṣaya*) prise antérieurement, on peut dire qu'il a pour objet actuel (*ālambana*) l'ancienne chose. Mais quand il porte sur une chose passée qui n'a pas été prise, ou quand on pense à des choses futures, le savoir aura-t-il pour objet une ancienne chose ? Dans la série, se trouvent nécessairement des savoirs qui portent sur les causes et sur les fruits (*hetujñāna*, *phalajñāna*) ; l'antérieur étant né, le savoir actuel, naissant, a nécessairement pour objet la chose qui a été l'objet du savoir précédent, puisque ce savoir est la cause qui engendre le savoir actuel. Le savoir actuel, comme l'antérieur, examine : « De telle cause naît tel fruit », ou bien : « Tel fruit vient de telle cause. » Tous atteignent comme il convient dans chaque cas (*yathāyogam*) ; atteignant conformément à ce qui est à atteindre, ils ne sont pas erronés. Leur objet n'existe pas comme chose et cependant ils ne manquent pas des deux conditions requises (d'objet et de support). [P. 628, col. 3, l. 27.]

Tout ce que dit là le Sthavira est semblable au discours en rêve d'un muet. Nous avons déjà réfuté le Sthavira en étudiant les quatre conditions (*pratyaya*) (ad ii, 61). Mais il convient de discuter le texte ici proposé.

Le discours ne peut tromper que des sots. L'homme éclairé voit bien qu'il n'a aucun sens... [P. 629, col. 1, l. 2.]

Le Sthavira dit : « Dans la série, se trouvent nécessairement des savoirs qui portent sur les causes ou sur les fruits ; l'antérieur étant né, le savoir actuel, naissant, a nécessairement pour objet (*ālambana*) la chose (*viṣaya*) qui a été l'objet du savoir antérieur. » — Nous demandons : Quel est ce savoir antérieur déjà né, savoir de cause ou de fruit, dont vous dites que l'objet est visé (atteint) par le savoir actuel ? Direz-vous que ce savoir antérieur a déjà visé l'objet du savoir actuel ? Ou bien, qu'il est un savoir visant un autre objet ? — Dans la première hypothèse, puisque la chose a déjà été l'objet d'un savoir antérieur, comment pouvez-vous dire que cette chose n'a pas été prise antérieurement ? Dans la seconde hypothèse, puisque vous soutenez que l'objet du savoir antérieur est l'objet du savoir actuel, comment le savoir actuel peut-il être dit avoir pour objet une chose passée ou future non encore prise ? En d'autres termes, la cause ou le fruit qui est l'objet du savoir antérieur portant sur cause ou fruit, est l'objet du savoir actuel. Cet objet a déjà été pris par un savoir. Comment pouvez-vous dire qu'il n'a pas été déjà pris ? Il y a contradiction dans les termes. [P. 629, col. 1, l. 11.]

En outre, à admettre l'existence du *pūrva-anu-dhātu*,[1] il n'est pas absurde de dire que, par la force de la série de la succession des causes et des fruits, une chose qui a péri depuis des milliers de millénaires est actuellement saisie. Mais comment un objet futur qui doit être dans des milliers de millénaires sera-t-il actuellement saisi ? Car il n'est pas permis de dire que c'est par la force de la série de la succession des causes et des fruits ; car, comme une corne de cheval, le futur à saisir n'a pas de réalité ; car ne se trouve pas, dans la série [mentale], un *anu-dhātu* [relatif au futur]. — En outre, si la connaissance naît relativement à l'objet saisi jadis, en raison de l'enquête régressive sur le passé, le temps de la prise sera rapide ou lent suivant que l'objet saisi jadis se trouve proche ou éloigné. [P. 629, col. 1, l. 18.] Celui qui réside actuellement à Pāṭaliputra, se souvenant des choses de gouvernement expérimentées jadis,[2] ne doit pas examiner la succession des causes pour que la connaissance naisse, car c'est soudainement que naît la connaissance qui a ces choses pour objet.

[1] Ci-dessus, p. 64.

[2] *chen* (corps) *hien tchou* (actuellement habitant) *pa-ta-li-tch'eng i* (se souvenant : cherchant à se souvenir) *si* (autrefois) *souo-keng* (éprouvées) *fou-ho* (lier-réprimander)-*kouo* (royaume) *-che* (affaires), cherchant causes-succession, alors il y a connaissance naître...

— Encore, de la connaissance auditive naît immédiatement une connaissance qui porte sur ce qui a été pris antérieurement : en raison de quelle cause est produite cette connaissance ? Ce n'est pas en raison du futur *anudhātu*, car la connaissance auditive ne porte pas sur cet objet-là. Ce n'est pas non plus en raison d'une connaissance qui a jadis pris cet objet-là, car actuellement semblable connaissance n'existe pas. Ce n'est pas avec une chose non-existante (*asaddharma*) comme cause qu'elle naît,[1] car une corne de cheval aussi bien naîtrait.

Nous avons déjà longuement réfuté en étudiant les quatre conditions (*pratyayas*). Par conséquent, pour ceux qui n'admettent que l'existence du seul moment (*ekakṣaṇamātrāstitvavādin*),[2] la connaissance qui porte sur le passé et le futur naît sans avoir les deux conditions requises [support et objet]. Pour ceux qui croient à la réelle existence du passé et du futur, les deux conditions sont acquises. [P. 629, col. 1, l. 26.]

4. — *Le passé-futur existe, parce que l'acte passé a un fruit futur*, phalāt.[3]

L'acte bon ou mauvais fait antérieurement, en dépendance des conditions nécessaires, produit un fruit agréable ou désagréable, ainsi que nous l'avons exposé en traitant de l'acte. — Or le fruit de rétribution ne naît pas immédiatement après l'acte et, lorsque naît le futur fruit, la cause de rétribution n'est plus actuelle. Si le *dharma* passé n'existe plus en réalité, il faut que le fruit naisse sans cause ou ne naisse absolument pas. Par conséquent le passé existe réellement. [P. 629, col. 2, l. 2.]

Cependant le Sautrāntika[4] dit à ce sujet ce qui suit :

[1] *pou k'o* (pas possible) *ou-fa-wei-in* (*asad-dharma-hetuka :* ayant pour cause un *dharma* inexistant) *cheng* (elle naisse) *ou.* — Je ne sais que faire de ce *ou.*

[2] Ci-dessus p. 67, les Sautrāntikas.

[3] Quatrième argument de la Kārikā, v, 25 ; ci-dessus, p. 53. — Tattvasaṃgraha, 505 : *api cātītaṃ karma phaladaṃ na syād yadi tan niḥsattvaṃ sattāśūnyaṃ bhavet phalotpattikāle vipākahetor abhāvāt | na cāsataḥ kāryotpādanaśaktir asti sarvasāmarthyavirahalakṣaṇatvād asattvasya.*

[4] Vasubandhu dans Kośa, ix, p. 295 ; voir aussi, ii, p. 185.

Les maîtres de l'école des Sūtras ne disent pas que l'acte passé engendre le fruit futur : ce qui fait que le fruit futur naît, c'est le moment suprême (*viśeṣa*) de l'évolution (*pariṇāma*) d'une série projetée par l'acte comme premier terme. Comme, dans le monde, la graine engendre le fruit futur : c'est-à-dire, de même que le fruit futur naît de la graine ; ce n'est pas qu'il naisse de la graine détruite ; ce n'est pas qu'il naisse immédiatement après la graine ; mais, ce qui engendre le fruit, c'est un moment suprême de l'évolution d'une série projetée par la graine comme premier terme. D'abord de la graine naît la pousse (*aṅkura*) ; naissent ensuite en série[1] successive la feuille, etc., jusqu'à la fleur. De la fleur enfin naîtra le fruit. On dit cependant que le fruit naît de la graine : parce que le pouvoir d'engendrer le fruit a été projeté (*ākṣipta*) par la graine, et est arrivé par intermédiaires (*paramparāyāta*) dans la fleur. Car si la fleur ne possédait pas un pouvoir projeté par la graine, elle ne pourrait pas engendrer telle sorte de fruit. [P. 629, col. 2, l. 11.] — De la même manière le fruit futur naît de l'acte : ce n'est pas que le fruit naisse de l'acte détruit ; ce n'est pas que le fruit naisse immédiatement après l'acte ; ce qui fait que le fruit naît, c'est le moment suprême de l'évolution d'une série projetée par l'acte comme premier terme. Par « série de l'acte » (*karmasaṃtāna*), on entend la série de pensées, moments successifs qui ont l'acte pour principe ; par évolution (*pariṇāma*), le fait que cette série est différente de moment en moment. Cette « évolution », au dernier moment, possède le pouvoir souverain d'engendrer immédiatement le fruit : ce moment étant, de ce chef, différent du reste [de la série] évolutive, est nommé « moment suprême » (*pariṇāma-viśeṣa*). [P. 629, col. 2, l. 17.]

Il faut juger de cette théorie d'après ce qui précède. Nous l'avons déjà réfutée lorsque nous avons examiné l'acte. Mais le sujet n'est pas épuisé, et il convient de discuter le problème tout au long. [P. 629, col. 2, l. 19.]

[1] *upajāyante, siu-k'i* (continuer-surgir), voir Kośa, xiii, 7 a 6, xvii, 4 a 6.

a) On ne peut définir la « série de l'acte » comme étant la naissance en série de pensees (*citta*) ayant l'acte pour premier terme. Car l'acte présente des différences avec la pensée. Différences de nature propre (*svabhāva*), de manière d'être (*lei*, *jāti*, *bhāva*), de causalité. — La nature propre diffère puisque les caractères (*lakṣaṇa*) sont distincts.[1] La manière d'être diffère, car la pensée et les mentaux (*caittadharma*) ont des manières d'être distinctes. La causalité diffère, puisque la pensée naît de deux causes et les mentaux de trois. Étant données ces différences, comment dire que la procession[2] des pensées postérieures constitue la « série de l'acte » ?

Encore, la pensée naît en même temps que l'acte. Nous avons établi ce point lorsque nous avons étudié la « cause simultanée » (*sahabhūhetu*)[3] et ailleurs. Il est donc acquis que l'acte et la pensée ne forment pas une seule série, et il est inadmissible (« non-vu ») que, avec la série des *cetanās* (ou des *caittas* ou des actes) et la série des *vijñānas* (ou des *cittas*, pensées), se produise simultanément une série de son espèce.[4] [P. 629, col. 2, l. 27.]

b) Encore, dans votre système, le « recueillement de cessation » (*nirodhasamāpatti*) comporte la pensée. Le Bouddha a dit que, dans ce recueillement, les *manaḥsaṃskāras* (parmi lesquels est la *cetanā* qui est « volition » ou « acte ») sont détruits. Comment pensée et l'acte feraient-ils une série ? — Si on admet qu'ils font une série, alors, si la pensée n'est pas détruite dans le recueillement, les *manaḥsaṃskāras* ne peuvent y être détruits. Et si ceux-ci sont détruits, celle-là doit aussi être détruite. [P. 629, col. 2, l. 29.]

En fait, la pensée manque dans ce recueillement ; nous l'avons expliqué en traitant des *viprayuktasaṃskāras* (Kośa, ii, p. 211).

[1] L'acte est par définition *cetanā*, volition, un *caitta* ou mental.

[2] *siu-cheng*, probablement *anusaṃdhi*. On a aussi *pratisaṃdhi*, Kośa, iii, 13 b 6, vii, 9 b 2, xvii, 4 a 3, xxvi, 11 a 5. L'expression *neng-siu* correspond à *pratisaṃdadhāti*, xxx, 2 a 9.

[3] Voir Kośa, ii, 248.

[4] *tsé lei siang siu* svajātīyaḥ saṃtānaḥ. — Le texte porte *cetanāsaṃtānavijñānasaṃtānamadhye* (*tchong*).

La série de l'acte est donc coupée : donc le fruit ne naîtra pas [si le fruit est engendré par le terme ultime de la série]. On ne voit pas en effet que le fruit puisse naître quand la série graine, pousse, etc., est interrompue.

Donc les explications du Sautrāntika ne sont que vaines suppositions. [P. 629, col. 3, l. 3.]

c) Autre point. Il n'est pas établi, comme le croit le Sautrāntika, que le fruit naisse de la fleur. Car, d'après notre théorie, la « nature propre » de la graine détruite reste cependant réellement existante.

d) Mais, même à admettre la thèse du Sautrāntika, il n'est pas logique d'admettre que la série de l'acte soit semblable à la série graine, fleur, graine: nous avons ci-dessus expliqué les différences. [P. 629, col. 3, l. 7.]

La cause des fruits agréables et désagréables est déterminée.[1] C'est-à-dire : la mauvaise action (*duścarita*) est la cause propre qui produit un fruit désagréable ; tout fruit agréable a nécessairement pour cause une bonne action. — Or, si on admet que le fruit de l'acte naît de la même manière que le fruit de la graine, lequel naît de la fleur qui est le moment suprême de l'évolution de la série de la graine, où trouver le principe de la règle que la bonne et la mauvaise action produisent respectivement un fruit agréable ou désagréable, que la mauvaise action n'a pas le pouvoir de produire un fruit agréable, que la bonne action n'est pas capable de produire un fruit désagréable, que l'action non-définie manque de l'un et de l'autre pouvoir ? En effet, les trois sortes de pouvoir [de production de fruit agréable, etc.] ne sont pas, quant à la nature propre (*t'i*), distincts de la pensée [à laquelle on les attribue]. Et on ne peut pas dire qu'ils en sont distingués quant à l'espèce.[2]

[1] Voici comment on peut entendre l'argument développé dans ce paragraphe. — Il y a entre la graine, la fleur avant-dernier terme de la série végétale, et le fruit, des relations constantes : telle fleur produit tel fruit. Dans la série « karmique », un acte bon est suivi d'une série de pensées dont la dernière (qui peut être mauvaise) est supposée posséder la force (projetée par l'acte) de produire une sensation agréable.

[2] *tchong-lei*, semence-genre, *prakāra*, *jāti*, *bhāva* (voir, pp. 89, 103, 109, 110).

Différence d'espèce, non-différence de nature propre, ce serait inouï. [P. 629, col. 3, l. 14.]

On peut admettre que la fleur, en raison de la série pousse, tige, etc., possède le pouvoir de la graine, car ce pouvoir n'a pas une nature propre distincte de celle de la fleur. Mais le bon et le mauvais ne peuvent pas ne pas différer de nature propre. Cela mènerait très loin ! [P. 629, col. 3, l. 17.]

e) La graine, la pousse, etc., constituent une seule série. La fleur qui, d'après vous, possède le pouvoir de la graine, doit aussi posséder le pouvoir de la pousse, etc. : pourquoi y aurait-il différence quant à ces pouvoirs ? Les pouvoirs de la pousse, etc., et de la graine n'ont pas une autre nature propre que la fleur. Par conséquent puisque le pouvoir [de la graine] intégré à la fleur, avec la fleur comme condition auxiliaire (*sahakāripratyaya*), engendre le fruit, la pousse, etc., aussi devrait naître de la fleur. Or la fleur engendre le fruit, non la pousse, etc. On demande pourquoi ? — Il est impossible qu'il y ait dans la fleur des parties subtiles occupées par les divers pouvoirs projetés par la graine, etc., de telle sorte que, à ce moment, c'est seulement le pouvoir projeté par la graine qui, avec la fleur comme condition auxiliaire, amène le fruit à la naissance. Il n'y a pas dans la fleur [de pouvoir] projeté par la pousse, etc. [P. 629, col. 3, l. 24.]

f) Mais on peut dire : « Le pouvoir projeté par la pousse, etc., réside dans la fleur ; mais, il faut que le fruit, la pousse, etc., soient produits pour que naissent la pousse, la tige, etc. »

S'il en est ainsi, de même que le pouvoir projeté par l'ancienne graine, après avoir engendré le fruit, est à nouveau la cause qui engendre une postérieure série végétale (*bījasaṃtāna*), pousse, tige, etc., de même il faudra que le pouvoir projeté par l'ancien acte, après avoir engendré le fruit de rétribution (*vipākaphala*) que l'acte doit produire, soit à nouveau une cause qui produise une postérieure série karmique (*karmasaṃtāna*). [P. 629, col. 3, l. 27.]

Mais, d'après votre système, la rétribution est la fin [de la série karmique], et c'est un autre acte qui est la cause qui projette une [nouvelle] série karmique. L'ancienne graine d'acte (*karmabīja*) n'a pas le pouvoir de projeter un nouvel acte. Par conséquent l'exemple de la série végétale (*bījasaṃtāna*) n'explique pas comment la série karmique engendre un fruit. [P. 630, col. 1, l. 2.]

g) Autre point. — Les graine, pousse, etc., depuis toujours (*anādikāla*), constituent des séries distinctes suivant leur espèce (*jāti*). On n'a jamais vu que les graine, pousse, etc., de riz, aboutissent à la production du fruit de l'ivraie. Tandis que, d'après votre système, une seule et même série karmique projette et engendre des fruits agréables et désagréables. Donc l'exemple de la série végétale n'est pas un « exemple pareil ». [P. 630, col. 1, l. 5.] Encore. Si le pouvoir propre à la *cetanā* (volition, acte) est intégré à la nature propre (*t'i*, *svabhāva*) du *vijñāna* (ou *citta*, pensée)[1] ; si le pouvoir propre au *vijñāna* est intégré à la *cetanā*, comme le pouvoir et le *dharma* même n'ont pas une nature propre à part, comment les caractères (*lakṣaṇa*) sont-ils distingués : « Ce *vijñāna*, cette *cetanā* »?

h) Encore. Dans ce système, confusion des diverses sortes d'actes, actes rétribués dans cette vie, etc. [P. 630, col. 1, l. 8.]

Tels sont, parmi d'autres, les défauts que je ne me lasse pas de signaler en divers endroits de cet ouvrage, parce que ce philosophe, haïssant l'existence du passé et du futur, n'arrive pas à établir la théorie des relations de la cause et du fruit. Cet homme déraisonnable, « destructeur des Sūtras »,[2] prétend que le fruit est produit par le moment suprême de l'évolution de la série : mais sa doctrine ne tient pas. [P. 630, col. 1, l. 11.]

5. — *Divers arguments.*

Le Sautrāntika objecte. — Si le passé et le futur existent réelle-

[1] « Si le *t'i* du *vijñāna* embrasse (*tai*, 50 et 8) le pouvoir de la *cetanā*... ». — Dans Kośa, xxx, 9 a 5, *tai* signifie « reproduire », « imiter » ; mais, dans Siddhi, i, 21 a 5, vii, 30 b 2, le même emploi qu'ici.

[2] *in* (170 et 14) *-mie-king*. — *pradūṣaka ?*

ment (*dravyatas*), de tout temps (*sarvadā*) la nature propre du fruit (*phalasvabhāva*) existe éternellement (*nitya*) : quel est, à l'endroit de ce fruit, le pouvoir de l'acte ?[1]

Nous examinerons cette objection au moment convenable. Mais, dirons-nous, chez vous, la relation de l'acte et du fruit n'est pas établie. [P. 630, col. 1, l. 14.]

1. *a*) Et il faut bien que le passé et le futur existent réellement, car on leur attribue des caractères (*lakṣaṇa*), comme au présent. Le Sūtra dit : « Le *rūpa* passé et le *rūpa* futur sont impermanents (*anitya*) ; à plus forte raison, le *rūpa* présent est impermanent.[2] » Or l'impermanence (*anityatā* = *nirodha*) est un des caractères des choses conditionnées (*saṃskṛta*). Le présent, qui possède ce caractère, existe réellement : tout le monde est d'accord. Si le passé et le futur n'existent pas réellement, on ne doit pas dire qu'ils possèdent, ainsi que le présent, le caractère des choses conditionnées. Car, ce qui n'existe absolument pas, fleur du ciel, corne de cheval, on ne peut dire que cela soit impermanent. Il est donc acquis que le passé et le futur existent réellement. [P. 630, col. 1, l. 19.]

On dira peut-être que la définition du Sūtra, attribuant le caractère (*lakṣaṇa*) d'impermanence au passé et au futur, doit s'entendre au passé et au futur. Le sens serait : « Le *rūpa* passé a été impermanent, le *rūpa* futur sera impermanent. » Cette explication, imaginée pour les besoins de la cause, n'est pas admissible. Le Sūtra ne s'exprime pas dans ces termes. Il attribue l'impermanence, dans la même formule, au passé-futur et au présent.

Cependant ce que le Sautrāntika veut faire dire au Sūtra : « Le *rūpa* passé a été impermanent », ne serait qu'une manière de dire que le *rūpa* présent est impermanent, puisqu'il serait

[1] Tattvasaṃgraha, p. 516 : *yasyātītānāgataṃ dravyato 'sti tasya phalam api nityam astīti* ; p. 513 : *yady atītānāgataṃ dravyato 'sti tadā sarvasaṃskārāṇāṃ śāśvatatvaprasaṅgaḥ*. — Kośa, v, p. 63 ; Wogihara, p. 476.

[2] Ci-dessus, p. 54.

question de l'impermanence passée, future, présente. — Dès lors comment expliquer que le Sūtra, ayant déjà dit que le *rūpa* présent est impermanent [en disant que le *rūpa* passé a été impermanent], ajoute : « A plus forte raison le *rūpa* présent est-il impermanent »? Le Sūtra devrait dire simplement que le *rūpa* présent est impermanent : on saurait par là que le passé et le futur le sont aussi puisqu'ils ne sont que le présent dans l'état de détruit et dans l'état de non-né. [P. 630, col. 1, l. 25.]

b) Objection. — Si de tout temps la « nature propre » (*t'i*) existe constamment (*sadā asti*), l'impermanence n'est pas établie.

Nous expliquerons ce point en traitant de la différence des trois époques. Remarquons-le, on ne peut pas dire qu'une « chose d'inexistence » (*abhāva-dharma*) soit impermanente.

Le Sthavira explique : « [Une chose] est dite impermanente en raison du manque de nature propre (*t'i*). Si la nature propre ne manque pas, [la chose] n'est pas impermanente. »

Dans cette hypothèse, le présent, il faut que sa nature propre soit éternelle (*śāśvata*).[1] Si, [quoique] l'existence ne lui manque pas (*fei ou*), le présent est impermanent, ne dites pas [qu'une chose] est impermanente en raison de la non-existence (*abhāvād anityam*). [P. 630, col. 2, l. 1.]

c) Le Sthavira objecte encore : « Si, durant à travers les trois époques, la nature propre (*tse sing*) demeure constamment, on doit dire qu'elle est éternelle. » — La critique n'est pas justifiée. [Elle est éternelle] comme quoi? Il n'y a pas d'autre *dharma* dont, à travers les époques, la nature propre demeure constamment et qu'on doive supposer éternel. Rien de ce qui est éternel ne dure à travers les époques. [P. 630, col. 2, l. 4.]

Et il ne faut pas dire que la manière d'être (*bhāva*) demeure constamment, car nous soutenons que les passé, futur, présent, diffèrent par la manière d'être. — Par conséquent le défaut indiqué par le Sthavira n'est pas prouvé.

[1] *jo eul hien-tsai ing ti che tch'ang*. — On attend : « Le présent, qui a certainement nature propre, sera éternel. »

d) Le Sūtra dit que le *rūpa* passé et futur est impermanent. Le Sthavira l'explique en disant : « Impermanent, parce que sans *t'i* (nature propre) actuellement. » — Mauvaise explication. Car le Sūtra ajoute : « A plus forte raison, le *rūpa* présent est-il impermanent. » Par là, il est prouvé que les passé-futur ne sont pas impermanents parce que manquant actuellement de nature propre, car chacun admet que le présent a une nature propre et est cependant impermanent. Le Sūtra dit en effet : « Tous les *saṃskāras* sont impermanents, sujets à la naissance et à la destruction. » Le Bouddha ne dit pas, des choses non-existantes, qu'elles sont impermanentes. [P. 630, col. 2, l. 10.]

La nature propre des passé-futur est réelle ; on peut dire cependant qu'ils sont sujets à la naissance et à la destruction (*jātinirodhadharmaka*). Nous nous expliquerons plus loin là-dessus. — Mais, de ce qui n'a pas de nature propre, on ne peut dire que cela possède le caractère d'impermanence. Par conséquent le passé et le futur existent réellement. [P. 630, col. 2, l. 13.]

2. Cela est encore démontré par le Pūrṇasūtra. [1] On lit dans ce Sūtra : « Ce bhikṣu Pūrṇa, ayant vu le visible par l'œil, connaît le visible, connaît l'attachement (*rāga*) au visible ; quand il a attachement pour le visible que distingue l'œil (*cakṣurvijñeya-rūparāga*), il connaît en vérité (*yathābhūtam*) : J'ai attachement pour le visible que distingue l'œil », et le reste.

Or la vue en vérité (*yathābhūtadarśana*) ne peut naître en même temps que l'attachement. — Incorrect aussi de dire que Pūrṇa voit que dans sa série se trouvent des traces d'attachement (*rāgānuśaya*), car l'existence des traces n'est pas établie. [2] Fût-elle établie, la vue de la trace n'est pas établie : car la nature propre

[1] Ci-dessus 626, 2, 9. — Manque dans les recensions pâlie, Saṃyutta, iv, 60, Majjhima, iii, 267, dans Divya, 30 ; mais Divya, 37 au bas, le point d'attache du développement que nous avons ici.

[2] Saṃghabhadra n'admet pas l'*anuśaya* du Sautrāntika-Sthavira qui est la « trace » de la passion en exercice (*kleśa*) ; pour lui *anuśaya* = *kleśa* (voir Kośa, v, 5 et suiv., où Vasubandhu expose et accepte la théorie Sautrāntika).

de la vue et celle de la trace ne sont pas distinctes,[1] et on n'admet pas qu'un savoir puisse se prendre soi-même pour objet. Comment pourrait-on dire que Pūrṇa voit la trace ? Dira-t-on qu'il sait qu'il n'a pas cultivé l'antidote de l'attachement (*rāgapratipakṣa*), et croit, par conséquent, qu'il est muni d'attachement ? Ceci aussi n'est pas possible, car on doit nous dire dans quel état se trouve cet attachement. En d'autres termes, à supposer que Pūrṇa croie-sache qu'il est muni d'attachement, dans quel état croit-il que se trouve cet attachement ? Si on répond que l'attachement est, non pas passé, futur ou présent, qu'on nous dise comment Pūrṇa peut croire qu'il a attachement, car un *dharma* éternel ne peut recevoir le nom d'attachement. — Par conséquent on doit admettre l'existence du passé et du futur. [P. 630, col. 2, l. 25.]

Le Sūtra dit : « [L'ascète] passe son temps (*viharati*) à examiner la sensation », et le reste. Il y a de la sorte beaucoup de textes (*āgamas*) qui établissent l'existence certaine du passé et du futur.

3. Il y a un autre argument en faveur de cette thèse. — Faute du passé-futur, le meurtre (*prāṇātipāta*) ne s'explique pas. Car le moment actuel de l'organe vital (*jīvitendriyakṣaṇa*), sans qu'aucun effort soit nécessaire, est détruit par le caractère « destruction »[2]. Si le futur n'existe pas réellement, qu'on nous dise ce qui constitue le meurtre ? Quels sont les *dharmas* que le meurtre « empêche » en faisant qu'ils ne soient pas, des *dharmas* déjà nés ou des *dharmas* qui doivent naître ? Les *dharmas* déjà nés ne peuvent pas être empêchés, comme nous l'avons dit ci-dessus. Les *dharmas* qui doivent naître ne peuvent être empêchés, puisqu'ils n'existent absolument pas. Les *dharmas* passés sont détruits. Il ne reste pas matière à meurtre. — Donc, si les passé-futur n'existent pas, le meurtre est impossible. [P. 630, col. 3, l. 4.]

[1] Pour l'adversaire de Saṃghabhadra, la même pensée qui est « vue en vérité » porte l'*anuśaya*. — Pūrṇa ne pourrait voir les « traces » que par une pensée à laquelle sont « intégrées » les traces : donc la pensée se connaîtrait elle-même, ce qui est impossible.

[2] *nirodhalakṣaṇa*; Kośa, ii, p. 222. — Définition du meurtre, iv, p. 153 : « Comment peut-il y avoir meurtre puisque les *skandhas* sont momentanés ? »

Autre point. Les passé-futur ne sont pas sans réalité, car les idées qui les ont pour objet sont différenciées, comme celles qui visent les actuelles forme-figure, etc. Or les choses non-existantes ne présentent pas de différences : on ne peut produire des idées différentes à leur endroit. [P. 630, col. 3, l. 6.]

III. — *Doctrine de l'activité* (kāritra)

1. — *Définition du Sarvāstivāda.* [1]

Tous ceux, laïcs ou religieux, [2] qui croient à l'existence des trois époques comme expliquée ci-dessus, et à l'existence réelle des trois sortes d'inconditionné (*asaṃskṛta :* les deux « destructions » et l'espace) peuvent se proclamer Sarvāstivādins ; parce qu'ils affirment l'existence de ces seuls *dharmas.* Nous disons qu'ils sont l'école Sarvāstivādin, non pas les autres qui ajoutent ou retranchent.

A savoir, les Ajouteurs, [3] qui admettent l'existence réelle d'un *pudgala* et celle des *dharmas* mentionnés ci-dessus ; les Vibhajyavādins, qui admettent seulement l'existence du présent, et celle de l'acte passé qui n'a pas encore donné son fruit [4] ; les Kṣaṇavādins, [5] qui admettent seulement l'existence des douze *āyatanas* présents pour un seul instant ; les Prajñaptivādins, [6] qui disent que les *dharmas* présents aussi n'ont qu'une « existence de désignation » ; les Nihilistes, [7] qui disent que tous les *dharmas*

[1] Commentaire de la dernière partie de la kārikā, v, 25 : *tadastivādāt sarvāstivādī mataḥ ;* ci-dessus, p. 53.

[2] « laïcs » : aux religieux (*pravrajita*) s'opposent les *yeou tch'ou sou* (être-lieu-vulgaire), qui doivent être les laïcs ?

[3] *ādhyāropika.*

[4] Comparer les Kassapikas de Kathāvatthu, i, 8, et de Harivarman, chap. 32 ; voir Kośa v, p. 24, note. — Sur les Vibhajyavādins, Paramārtha cité par P. Demiéville, Mélanges, i, p. 50.

[5] Ci-dessus, p. 67, Ekakṣaṇavādin ; les Sautrāntikas.

[6] Littéralement : *prajñapti-sad-vādin ;* Kośa, v, p. 24, ii, p. 219.

[7] *tou-ou-luen-tche.* — Le *sarvanāstigrāha* de Kośa, ix, p. 273.

sont absolument sans « nature propre » (*svabhāva*), telles des fleurs de l'espace. Tous ces gens-là ne sont pas des Sarvāstivādins. [P. 630, col. 3, l. 15.]

Le Sautrāntika critique. — Affirmer l'existence réelle du passé et de l'avenir, ce n'est pas bien comprendre la doctrine bouddhique. Si on veut bien « affirmer l'existence de tout » (*sarvāstivāda*), il faut l'affirmer comme l'affirme le Sūtra. — Que dit le Sūtra ? — Le Sūtra dit : « Brahmane, il faut savoir que « tout [ce qui] est », c'est seulement les douze *āyatanas* [1] », — ou bien, tout, c'est les trois époques : comment elles existent, nous l'avons dit. [2]

Ce Sūtra dit-il qu'existent seulement les douze *āyatanas* présents, non pas les passés ou futurs ? Non. Voit-on ailleurs un enseignement clair qui nie les passés et futurs *āyatanas?* On ne le voit pas. Lisons-nous (*śru*) d'autres Sūtras qui affirment l'existence des deux époques, la passée et la future ? Je les lis. Pourquoi tourner le dos à l'enseignement sacré, et critiquer les Astivādins en disant que leur doctrine n'est pas bien dite (*sādhu*) ? [3] [P. 630, col. 3, l. 22.]

Encore vous dites que, parmi les douze *āyatanas* présents, les uns sont réels, les autres pas, comme dans le système du Sthavira, des *rūpas*, *śabdas*, *spraṣṭavyadharmas*. [4] Comment serait-ce là du Sarvāstivāda ? [P. 630, col. 3, l. 24.]

Il y a d'autres maîtres qui, sous l'empire de la « passion »

[1] Mahāniddesa, p. 133 : *sabbaṃ vuccati dvādasāyatanāni cakkhu ceva...* — Saṃyutta, iv, p. 45 : *sabbaṃ vo bhikkhave dessissāmi... kiṃ ca bhikkhave sabbam | cakkhuṃ ceva...* — Kathāvatthu, i, 5, trad. p. 84. — Tattvasaṃgraha, p. 507 au bas : *sarvaṃ sarvam iti brāhmana yad uta pañca skandhā dvādaśāyatanāny aṣṭādaśa dhātava iti.* — Harivarman, chap. 23. — Paramārtha cité par P. Demiéville, Mélanges, i, 56.

[2] Kośa, Vyākhyā, Wogihara, p. 477 en haut : *adhvatrayam vā* | kim | sarvam astīty adhikṛtam | *yathātra tad asti tathoktam* | yad bhūtapūrvam tad atītam...

L'existence des trois époques doit s'entendre : « Ce qui fut, c'est le passé... » (Ci-dessus, p. 60.) Hiuan-tsang paraît comprendre « Comme elles existent, nous disons qu'elles sont » (*jou k'i souo yeou eul chouo yeou yen*).

[3] Compris comme nous le faisons, dit le Sautrāntika, *sarvāstivādaḥ śāsane sādhuḥ*.

[4] Voir les paragraphes sur les deux vérités, Saṃghabhadra, cahier 58. (Cidessous, p. 174.)

(*kleśādhipatyena*), disent que tous les *dharmas* n'ont qu'une existence de désignation. Serait-ce là du Sarvāstivāda ?

D'autres, sous l'empire de la vue fausse (*mithyādṛṣṭi*), disent que tous les *dharmas* sont absolument sans nature propre (*niḥsvabhāva*)[1] ; ils disent que les choses présentes ont une existence fausse et de magie. Peuvent-ils dire qu'elles existent de choses existant ainsi ? Méritent-ils le nom de Sarvāstivādins ? [P. 630, col. 3, l. 29.]

C'est donc pour réfuter l'existence du *pudgala* et pour expliquer, en général, l'existence des *dharmas* objets de connaissance (*jñeyadharmāstitva*), que Bhagavat a dit au Brahmane le Sūtra en question. Non pas pour montrer qu'existent seulement les actuels instantanés (*ekakṣaṇika*) douze *āyatanas*.

Donc ceux qui haïssent l'existence réelle du passé et du futur n'ont pas le droit de se dire Sarvāstivādins, parce que leur doctrine diffère de celle des Nihilistes en ceci seulement qu'elle admet l'existence instantanée. [P. 631, col. 1, l. 3 ; fin du 51e cahier.]

2. — *Les quatre maîtres.*

Le système de l'existence universelle (*sarvāstisamaya*), combien de variétés présente-t-il reçues des anciens maîtres ? Et, parmi ces maîtres, lequel établit le mieux les époques ? La kārikā dit :

« Il y a quatre variétés, partisans de la différence de manière d'être (*bhāva*), de caractère (*lakṣaṇa*), d'état ou de situation (*avasthā*), de relation (*apekṣā*). Le troisième est bon, qui établit les époques par l'activité.[2] » [P. 631, col. 1, l. 12.]

[1] Il me semble que le docteur en cause est Harivarman, partisan du « vide des *dharmas* ». Saṃghabhadra ignore le Grand Véhicule.

[2] Kośa, fin de la kārikā, v, 25 et kārikā 26, trad. v, p. 52 ; Vyākhyā, Wogihara, p. 469.

[*caturvidhāḥ* ||
te bhāvalakṣaṇāvasthānyathānyathikasaṃjñitāḥ ||]
tṛtīyaḥ śobhano 'dhvānaḥ kāritreṇa vyavasthitāḥ ||

bhāva est traduit par *lei* ; ci-dessous, p. 633, col. 3, l. 17, on a *sing*.

Les théories des quatre maîtres ont été signalées pour la première fois par Rockhill, Life of the Buddha, p. 195 (traduction de l'ouvrage de Bhavya sur les sectes). La mention la plus ancienne est dans Vibhāṣā, ci-dessus, p. 22.

D'après le Bhadanta Dharmatrāta, les époques sont distinctes par la différence de la manière d'être (*bhāva*) du *dharma*. Le *dharma*, circulant (*pravartamāna*) par les époques, se différencie par la manière d'être sans qu'il y ait modification de la « chose » (*t'i*, *dravya*). De même, si on brise un vase d'or pour en faire d'autres objets, la forme est différenciée sans qu'il y ait modification de la chose. De même, quand le lait tourne à petit lait, la chose abandonne son goût, sa force, etc., mais n'abandonne pas sa couleur. De même le *dharma*, circulant par les époques, arrive du futur au présent, arrive du présent au passé ; il abandonne

Il paraît probable que Yogasūtra, iii, 13, dépend des sources bouddhiques. Les quatre théories sont expliquées en détail dans Tattvasaṃgraha, p. 504.

tatra bhāvānyathāvādī bhadantadharmatrātaḥ | sa kilāha | dharmasyādhvasu vartamānasya bhāvānyathātvam eva kevalam na tu dravyasyeti | yathā suvarṇadravyasya kaṭakakeyūrakuṇḍalādyabhidhānanimittasya guṇasyānyathātvaṃ na suvarṇasya | tathā dharmasyānāgatādibhāvād anyathātvam | tathā hi | anāgatabhāvaparityāgena vartamānabhāvaṃ pratipadyate dharmo vartamānabhāvaparityāgena cātītabhavam | na tu dravyānyathātvaṃ sarvatra dravyasyāvyabhicārāt | anyathānya evānāgato 'nyo vartamāno 'nyo 'tīta iti prasajyeta[a] | kaḥ punar bhāvas teneṣṭaḥ | guṇaviśeṣo yato 'tītādyabhidhānajñānapravṛttiḥ |

lakṣaṇānyathāvādī bhadantaghoṣakaḥ | sa kilāha | dharmo 'dhvasu vartamāno 'tīto 'tītalakṣaṇayukto 'nāgatapratyutpannābhyāṃ lakṣaṇābhyām aviyuktaḥ | yathā puruṣa ekasyāṃ striyāṃ raktaḥ śeṣāsv aviraktaḥ / evam anāgatapratyutpannāv api vācyau | asya hy atītādilakṣaṇapravṛttilābhāpekṣo vyavahāra iti pūrvakād bhedaḥ |

avasthānyathāvādī bhadantavasumitraḥ | sa kilāha | dharmo 'dhvasu vartamāno 'vasthām avasthāṃ prāpyānyo 'nyo nirdiśyate | avasthāntarato na dravyataḥ | dravyasya triṣv api kāleṣv api kāleṣv abhinnatvāt | yathā mṛdguḍikā ekāṅke prakṣiptā ekam ity ucyate śatāṅke śataṃ sahasrāṅke sahasram | tathā kāritre 'vasthito bhāvo vartamānas tataḥ pracyuto 'tītas tadaprāpto 'nāgata iti | asya hy avasthāpekṣayā vyavahāro yathā mṛdguḍikāyām | na hi tasyāh svabhāvānyathātvam bhavati kiṃ tārhi sthānaviśeṣasaṃbandhāt saṃkhyābhidyotakaṃ saṃjñāntaram utpadyate |

anyathānyathiko [bhadanta]buddhadevaḥ | sa kilāha | dharmo 'dhvasu vartamānaḥ pūrvāparam apekṣyānyonya ucyate | yathaikā strī mātā cocyate duhitā ceti | asya pūrvāparāpekṣo vyavahāraḥ | yasya pūrvam evāsti nāparaḥ so 'nāgataḥ | yasya pūrvam asty aparam ca so vartamānaḥ | yasya aparam eva na pūrvaṃ so 'tītaḥ |

iti catvāraḥ sarvāstivādā [c] bhāvalakṣaṇāvasthānyathānyathikasaṃjñitāḥ.

a. Édition : ... anāgate... prasajyate.
b. Édition : asya vyavasthāpekṣayā.
c. Édition : sarve astivādā.

une certaine manière d'être, acquiert une autre manière d'être, mais il n'abandonne pas un « être », il n'acquiert pas un « être » (*t'i*).

D'après le Bhadanta Ghoṣaka, les époques sont distinctes par la différence du caractere (*lakṣaṇa*). Le *dharma* circule par les époques : passé, il est éminemment muni (*yukta*) du caractère de passé, mais on ne peut pas dire qu'il soit démuni (*viyukta*) des caractères de présent et de futur. De même, présent ou futur, il est muni du caractère de présent ou de futur, sans être démuni des caractères des autres époques. Comme un homme épris d'une certaine femme n'est pas détaché des autres femmes.

D'après le Bhadanta Vasumitra, les époques sont distinctes par la différence de l'état (*avasthā*). Le *dharma* circule par les époques ; il prend tel et tel nom en arrivant à tel et tel état, en raison de la différence de l'état et sans que la chose soit modifiée. De même le bâtonnet placé dans la case des unités se nomme 1 ; il se nomme 100 et 1000 quand il est placé dans la case des centaines ou des milliers.[1] [P. 631, col. 1, l. 26.]

D'après le Bhadanta Buddhadeva, les époques sont distinctes par la différence de la relation (*apekṣā*). Le *dharma* circule par les époques ; on lui donne différents noms par rapport à ce qui précède et à ce qui suit, sans qu'il y ait modification de la chose, de la manière d'être ou du caractère. Comme la même femme, relativement à ce qui précède et à ce qui suit, reçoit le nom de fille ou de mère, de même le *dharma*, circulant par les époques,

[1] Yogabhāṣya, Ānandāśrama, p. 130 : *yathaikā rekhā śatasthāne śataṃ daśasthāne dasa ekā (ekam?) caikasthāne.* — Woods, p. 216 : The same stroke is termed one in the unit-place and ten in the ten's place and a hundred in the hundred's place. — La même *rekhā* dans Saṃkara, Thibaut, i, p. 397. (D'après W. E. Clark, Hindu-Arabic Numerals, Mélanges Lanman, p. 236).

Vasubandhu parle d'une *vartikā* placée dans la place des unités... La Vyākhyā donne *gulikā*, « boule », « pilule » pour *vartikā : yathaikā vartikā yathaikā gulikā ekāṅke nikṣiptā ekasthāne sthāpitā ekam ity ucyate...*

Hiuan-tsang, pour *vartikā*, a *tch'eou* (118 et 14), « bâtonnets qui servent à marquer le nombre des personnes... »

gulikā, vartikā se rapportent au système de l'abaque : *rekhā* suppose l'écriture. — Voir Dynasties, Appendice, 298.

est nommé passé par rapport au présent et au futur, futur par rapport au passé et au présent, présent par rapport au passé et au futur. [P. 631, col. 2, l. 5.)

Parmi ces quatre sortes de Sarvāstivādin, l'opinion traditionnelle [1] est que le premier, affirmant la transformation (*pariṇāma*) du *dharma*, doit être rangé parmi les partisans du système Sāṃkhya. — Cela n'est pas exact. En effet, le Bhadanta ne dit pas que le *t'i* du *dharma* conditionné soit éternel : en traversant les trois époques, le *dharma* disparaît, le *dharma* apparaît ; il dit seulement que, le *dharma* circulant par les époques, encore que le *t'i-siang* [2] reste identique, la manière d'être (*sing-lei*) diffère. — Cette théorie est partiellement semblable à celle de Vasumitra : comment pourrait-on la considérer comme semblable à celle des infidèles Sāṃkhyas ? [P. 631, col. 2, l. 10.]

Dans le deuxième et le quatrième système, les caractères des époques sont mêlés. Par conséquent, parmi les quatre systèmes, le troisième est le meilleur : en raison de l'activité (*kāritra*) les états (*avasthā*) du *dharma* sont différents, et la différence des époques résulte de la différence des états.

Comme je l'ai expliqué, le passé et le futur existent réellement. Ceci ne contredit pas la « nature des choses » (*dharmatā*) ; ceci est la doctrine (*iṣṭa*) de l'Écriture. Mais, au contraire, nier le passé et le futur, c'est contredire la nature des choses ; c'est s'opposer à l'Écriture.

Par conséquent il faut savoir que la réalité du passé et du futur, comme l'établit Vasumitra, est d'accord avec le raisonnement, conforme au Sūtra et irréfutable. [P. 631, col. 2, l. 15.]

3. — ***Étude de l'activité ; objections ; commentaire de la Kārikā*, v, 27.**

Ce Bhadanta dit : « Le Bouddha enseigne dans le Sūtra l'existence

[1] C'est en effet l'opinion de la Vibhāṣā, p. 396, col. 2 (ci-dessus, p. 24), que répète Vasubandhu, v, p. 54.
[2] *t'i* = *dravya*, *t'i-siang* = *dravyalakṣaṇa*.

des trois époques. Comment est établie la différence des trois époques ? La différence des trois époques est établie par l'activité. Les *saṃskāras*[1] qui n'ont pas encore d'activité sont dits « futurs » ; au temps où ils ont activité, ils sont dits « présents » ; quand leur activité est détruite, ils sont dits « passés ». Mais il n'y a pas de distinction dans la chose (*dravya*). »

Que faut-il entendre par « activité » (*tso yong*) ? Le « pouvoir » (*kong neng*) qu'a le *dharma* conditionné de projeter le fruit, la capacité d'être cause (*hetutā*) de la naissance d'une autre chose.[2] [P. 631, col. 2, l. 21.]

Celui qui sait, en s'appuyant sur cette doctrine, établir la distinction des trois époques, ou construire une autre explication irréprochable de l'existence des trois époques, les doctes penseront qu'on doit le nommer un « homme qui reflète la logique ».[3] Mais celui qui, établissant d'une manière trouble la théorie de la différence des époques et craignant les objections, en vient à rejeter les textes sacrés ou à déclarer de sens non-exprès les Sūtras de sens exprès, accepte l'existence du présent tout en déclarant que le passé et le futur n'existent pas, ou n'accepte que le présent en lui reconnaissant une existence de désignation[4] ; ou, d'une manière générale, nie l'existence des trois époques — toutes opinions en contradiction avec l'Écriture et le raisonnement — les doctes le blâment comme un homme de confusion logique. [P. 631, col. 2, l. 25.]

Tous ceux qui nient l'existence réelle des trois époques se souillent d'innombrables sortes de défauts ; quels que soient leurs efforts, la délivrance[5] leur est difficile. Mais les docteurs qui

[1] *saṃskāra* ne se distingue pas ici de *saṃskṛta*, « *dharma* conditionné ».

[2] Nous ne lisons pas cette définition dans la Vibhāṣā ; d'ailleurs les anciens Sarvāstivādins ne distinguent pas le *tso-yong* et le *kong-neng*, ci-dessous, p. 94. — La *anyabhāvajanane hetutā* n'est pas de l'activité (*tso-yong*), ci-dessous, p. 95.

[3] *kien-li-jen :* miroir-logique-homme, s'oppose à *mi-li-jen* qui suit.

[4] Ci-dessus, p. 87.

[5] On a bien *kiai-t'ouo, vimukti*, « délivrance »; mais on attend « explication ».

affirment l'existence réelle des trois époques, encore qu'il y ait quelques difficultés (*virodha*), la délivrance leur est facile. Par conséquent les doctes se garderont de nier l'existence des trois époques. [P. 631, col. 2, l. 29.]

Je vais, en m'appuyant sur Vasumitra, établir la distinction des trois époques en fonction de l'activité et, dans la mesure de mes forces, réfuter les objections. [P. 631, col. 3, l. 1.]

Le Sautrāntika dit : « Si les trois époques sont établies en fonction de l'activité [non encore née, née non détruite, détruite], les présents organes, œil, etc., de la classe *tatsabhāga* [qui ne voient pas...] [1], quelle est, bien qu'ils soient présents, leur activité? Si vous répondez que l'activité consiste à prendre et à donner le fruit [2] [et que, par conséquent, l'œil qui ne voit pas est actif], nous observerons que certaines causes (*sabhāgahetu*, etc.] donnent leur fruit quand elles sont passées [3] [donc, passées, elles posséderont demi-activité, et seront demi-présentes]. Donc, dans ce système, les époques sont mêlées. » [P. 631, col. 3, l. 5.] [4]

Cette objection montre que le Sautrāntika ne connaît pas la « nature des choses » (*dharmatā*). La force (*che-li, śakti*) des *dharmas* est de deux sortes : activité (*tso-yong, kāritra*), pouvoir (*kong-neng*,

[1] Kośa, i, p. 75, v, p. 55 ; Vibhāṣā, 71, p. 368 : L'œil qui, pour une raison quelconque, ne voit pas, est dit *tatsabhāga*.

[2] Kośa, ii, p. 294. — Prendre (*grah*) un fruit, c'est en être la semence, c'est le projeter (*ākṣip*). Donner (*prayacch, dā*) le fruit : le *dharma* donne le fruit au moment où le fruit entre dans la condition de présent. — Pour les causes *sahabhū* (« simultanée »), etc., les deux opérations sont simultanées.

[3] Kośa, ii pp. 294 297. — Le meurtre, cause d'enfer (rétribution), projette ou « prend » l'enfer au moment où il est accompli ; il ne donne l'enfer que plus tard.

[4] Tattvasaṃgraha, p. 506 : adhvānaḥ kāritreṇa vyavasthitāḥ | kiṃ punar atra kāritram abhipretam | yadi darśanādiko vyāpāraḥ... evaṃ sati pratyutpannasya tatsabhāgasya cakṣuṣo nidrādyavasthāyāṃ kāritrābhāvād vartamānatā na syāt | atha phaladānagrahaṇalakṣaṇaṃ kāritram... evaṃ tarhy atītānām api sabhāgasarvatragavipākahetūnāṃ phaladānābhyupagamād vartamānatvaprasaṅgaḥ | atha samastam eva phaladānagrahaṇalakṣaṇaṃ kāritram iṣyate | evam atītasya sabhāgahetvāder ardhavartamānatvaprasaṅga iti.

vṛtti, sāmarthya, vyāpāra?).[1] Le pouvoir de projeter le fruit (*phalākṣepa*) est ce qu'on nomme activité ; l'activité ne comprend pas tout le pouvoir ; il y a pouvoir en dehors de l'activité. C'est ainsi que, dans l'obscurité, le pouvoir [qu'a l'œil] de voir les visibles est contredit par l'obscurité,[2] mais non pas son activité. En d'autres termes, l'obscurité empêche le pouvoir de vision (*darśanavyāpāra*), mais l'activité de projection du fruit n'est pas empêchée par l'obscurité : c'est pourquoi l'œil, dans l'obscurité, projette son fruit [qui est un nouveau moment de l'œil]. Dans l'état de présent, l'activité ne manque pas, car c'est l'activité qui établit cet état. La cessation de l'activité n'entraîne pas l'inexistence.[3] Quant au fait d'être cause de la naissance d'un *dharma* différent,[4] cela n'est pas activité, mais seulement pouvoir, car c'est le seul présent qui projette le fruit, car l'inconditionné [qui est en dehors du temps] ne projette pas de fruit, car c'est la seule projection du fruit que l'on nomme activité. — C'est donc par insuffisante connaissance de la doctrine d'Abhidharma que le Sautrāntika, dans l'exégèse qu'il propose, considère le pouvoir de donner le fruit comme étant de l'activité. La cause passée, quoiqu'elle donne le fruit, est dépourvue d'activité. — Conclusion :

[1] Dans la kārikā, ii, 46*a-b*, *vṛtti* est traduit par *neng* que l'éditeur Kiokuga Saeki, explique *kong-neng*.

Les anciens Sarvāstivādins (Vibhāṣā) ne distinguaient pas *tso-yong* et *kong-neng*. [Mais, faute de cette distinction, on ne peut répondre à l'objection : « La bonne action, passée, donne un agréable fruit de rétribution ; donc elle a *kāritra*, activité ; donc, d'après la définition, elle doit être présente », ci-dessus, p. 93.] Les nouveaux Sarvāstivādins distinguent, Saṃghabhadra, cahier 14 (p. 409, vol. 3) : Les conditionnés qui sont cause (*hetu*) et amènent leur « propre fruit », c'est leur *kāritra ;* quand ils sont condition (*pratyaya*) et aident autre chose, c'est leur pouvoir (*vṛtti, sāmarthya, vyāpāra*) : tous les présents sont cause, tout œil présent amène à l'existence le futur œil ; tous les présents ne sont pas condition qui aide autre chose : par exemple, dans l'obscurité, le pouvoir de l'œil est endommagé ; il ne fait pas naître la connaissance visuelle... Le présent seul a *kāritra*, le pouvoir de prendre (ou de projeter) le fruit ; le passé ne peut avoir que pouvoir, le *phaladāna-kong-neng*, le pouvoir de « donner » le fruit, de faire naître autre chose.

[2] Au lieu de *an*, obscurité, on a *che*, 169 et 9.

[3] Douteux. — *pou tche ou wei :* « ne parvient pas *asaṃskrta* » ? ?

[4] D'un autre *sing*, d'un autre *bhāva*, d'un autre être.

les caractères des époques ne sont pas mêlés.[1] [P. 631, col. 3, l. 17.]

Cependant le Sautrāntika développe de longues objections[2] :

« Qu'est-ce qui s'oppose à l'activité ? Comment est-elle passée, etc. ? Si elle ne diffère pas du *dharma*, les époques disparaissent. Si le *dharma* existe toujours de la même manière, comment est-il non-né ou détruit ? En vérité, la nature des choses est profonde ! »[3]

A. — *kiṃvighnam.*[4]

a) « Si la nature propre (*svabhāva*, *tse-sing*) du *dharma* existe toujours, elle doit en tout temps produire l'activité. Quel obstacle fait que l'activité produite par cette nature propre (*t'i*) du *dharma* quelquefois existe, quelquefois n'existe pas ?[5] »

Le sens de cette objection est comme il suit : « Puisque le caractère (*lakṣaṇa*) de la nature propre (*t'i*) du *dharma* est sans changement, quelle force fait obstacle [de telle sorte que le *dharma*] n'a pas toujours la même manière d'être ? (*sing-lei*) ? »

Cette objection n'est pas justifiée. L'identité du caractère de la nature propre n'est pas un argument qui démontre l'unité (ou identité) de la manière d'être. On voit en effet dans le monde que, le caractère de la nature propre ne présentant pas de différence,

[1] Le Tattvasaṃgraha, p. 506, cite Saṃghabhadra (édition : Sahantabhadra) : dharmāṇāṃ kāritram ucyate phalākṣepaśaktiḥ | na tu phalajananam | na cātītānāṃ sabhāgahetvādīnāṃ phalākṣepo 'sti vartamānāvasthāyām evākṣiptatvāt | na cākṣiptasyākṣepo yukto 'navasthāprasaṅgāt | tasmād atītānāṃ na kāritrasaṃbhava iti nāsti lakṣaṇasaṃkara iti.

[2] Je ne comprends pas les lignes 17 et 18.

[3] Kārikā, v, 27 (omise dans le petit traité de Saṃghabhadra, p. 901, puisqu'elle est la critique, non l'exposé, du système Vaibhāṣika) ; Kośa, v, pp. 56-65.

kiṃvighnaṃ [*tad api kathaṃ*] *nānyad* [*adhvā na yujyate*] |
[*tathā san kim ajo naṣṭo*] *gambhīrā jātu dharmatā* ||

[4] *kiṃvighnaṃ kāritram* : « Qu'est-ce que l'activité a comme obstacle ? »

[5] *t'i* = *tse-sing* = *svabhāva* ; ailleurs *t'i* = *dravya*. — Ci-dessous *t'i-siang*, que nous lisons *svabhāvalakṣaṇa*, « caractère de la nature propre ». — On peut traduire *dravyalakṣaṇa* ; mais *fa-t'i-siang* donnerait *dharmadravyalakṣaṇa*. — Ci-dessous, 623, 3, 23 : « Le caractère de la nature propre et la manière d'être... » Le sens exige : « La nature propre (*svabhāva*) et la manière d'être (*bhāva*) ... »

la manière d'être diffère. Nous l'avons remarqué (p. 51) : l'élément-terre (*pṛthivīdhātu*), etc., la sensation (*vedanā*), etc., l'œil, etc., [diffèrent de manière d'être tout en étant le même élément-terre, etc.]. [P. 631, col. 3, l. 28.]

b) Ou bien l'objection peut se formuler comme il suit : « Dans mon système les *saṃskāras* (ou « conditionnés »), les conditions, le concours [des conditions] existent après inexistence. Les conditions sont de diverses sortes. Quelquefois elles concourent quelquefois elles ne concourent pas. On comprend que les *dharmas* ne naissent pas toujours. Mais vous soutenez que les *saṃskāras* et leurs conditions, de tout temps, sont perpétuellement munis de nature propre (*yeou-t'i, sasvabhāvāḥ*) : car vous ne voulez pas que les *dharmas* existent après inexistence. Ils doivent donc être toujours présents. Quelle force peut s'y opposer ? » [P. 632, col. 1, l. 3.]

Cette remarque aussi n'est pas justifiée, car le problème a été élucidé. Nous avons dit que le caractère de la nature propre (*t'i-siang*) restant le même, la manière d'être (*lei-sing*) varie. Cette notion étant établie, on nous dit cependant : « Vous soutenez que, de tout temps, sont perpétuellement munis de nature propre (*sasvabhāva*, *yeou-t'i*) les *saṃskāras* et leurs conditions.[1] Qu'est-ce qui fait que leur activité n'existe pas toujours, qu'ils ne soient pas de tout temps perpétuellement présents ? » L'objection tombe quand on comprend la doctrine exposée ci-dessus : la nature propre est constante, mais les manières d'être (*sing-lei*) sont différentes. [P. 632, col. 1, l. 9.]

Si toutefois notre adversaire s'obstine, il faut lui répliquer : Dans votre système, les conditions (*pratyaya*) et la chose (*saṃskāra*) à engendrer présentent aussi non-modification (*viśeṣa*) du caractère de la nature propre (*t'i-siang*) dans leur succession (*pūrvāpara*, *ts'ien-heou*) ; et cependant vous admettez que, d'instant en instant,

[1] On a : *tchou-hing* (saṃskārāḥ) *tse-t'i* (sva-svabhāvāḥ) *tchong-yuen* (pratyayāḥ) *i-ts'ie-che* (sarvadā) *hiu* (iṣṭāḥ) *tch'ang* (nityaṃ) *yeou-t'i* (sasvabhāvāḥ) ... — Je lis *tchou-hing ki pei tchong-yuen*... comme ci-dessus.

il y a graduelle (*ts'ien ts'ien*, *anupūrveṇa*) différenciation (*i*, 102 et 6, *anyathātva*). Puisque les conditions ne sont pas modifiées du moment antérieur au postérieur, quel obstacle fait qu'elles ne se produisent pas non-différenciées ? Cependant vous soutenez que, de proche en proche (*heou heou*, *uttarottaram*), changeant-changeant (*tch'oan-tch'oan?*), il y a différenciation. En d'autres termes, le *saṃskāra* du moment antérieur naît en même temps que les conditions et, sans que le caractère de sa nature propre soit altéré (*k'oei*, 141 et 11), il périt en même temps que les conditions. Or c'est par la force de cette cause que, au moment postérieur, naît le fruit : il ne peut différer (*viśeṣa*) en espèce de la cause antérieure, car les deux sortes de conditions génératrices, de même espèce ou non, ne sont pas modifiées (*viśeṣa*) du moment antérieur au postérieur. Quelle condition fait obstacle [de telle sorte] que le postérieur se différencie de l'antérieur ? Direz-vous que telle est la loi (*dharmatā*) des conditionnés ? Pourquoi ne pas admettre qu'il en va de même de l'activité ? [P. 632, col. 1, l. 16.]

La sensation, bien que les conditions soient diverses, ne présente pas de différence quant au caractère de nuisible ou d'avantageux. De même en ce qui concerne les autres pensée-et-mentaux. En dépit de la différence de ses conditions, combustibles de diverses sortes, on constate que le feu ne diffère pas quant à son caractère de brûlant.

Concluons que les conditionnés, quant à leur nature propre (*t'i*) et à leur manière d'être (*bhāva*), ont plusieurs chemins. On ne peut arguer que, l'ensemble se devant accorder avec un terme,[1] la manière d'être doit être la même dans tous les états (*avasthā*). [P. 632, col. 1, l. 19.] [P. 632, col. 1, l. 20.]

c) « Puisque vous soutenez que les conditions sont permanentes, l'activité engendrée par les conditions doit être permanente » ; cette objection aussi est sans valeur.

N'arrive-t-il pas en effet que, les conditions étant permanentes,

[1] *tsong* (120 et 11) *wei i li* (9 et 6) : *sāmānyasya ekādhīnatve ?*

le fruit des conditions n'existe pas? Par exemple votre *vāsanā*,[1] par exemple l'œil. 1. Vous ne croyez pas que le fruit naisse de la cause détruite et à distance. Mais sont en même temps actuellement présentes dans la série toutes sortes de graines projetées par de nombreuses causes : les fruits de ces graines ne naissent pas toujours et ensemble. Il arrive que la graine projetée par une cause, après de nombreux millénaires, donne enfin son fruit. A supposer que le fruit naisse dans l'intervalle, ni le temps de la naissance, ni le fruit ne sont déterminés. Puisque toutes les causes existent en tout temps, qu'est-ce qui s'oppose à ce que les fruits naissent toujours et ensemble? Une cause, à tel moment, engendre un fruit, à tel moment, n'engendre pas ; à tel moment, telle cause engendre un fruit, et telle cause n'engendre pas. Comment expliquer? — 2. Les conditions de la connaissance visuelle, œil, etc., étant toujours présentes, il se fait que la connaissance visuelle ne naît pas toujours. — Par conséquent l'objection n'est pas bien venue que formule le Sautrāntika : « Puisque vous soutenez que les conditions sont permanentes, l'activité du *dharma* doit être permanente. » [P. 632, col. 2, l. 2.]

Le Sautrāntika dira : « Dans mon système, l'évolution (*pariṇāma*) de la série, en dépendance de conditions extérieures, engendre le fruit. »

Le Sautrāntika doit admettre qu'il en va de même de l'activité. Les conditions qui projettent le fruit sont de deux sortes, simultanées (*sahaja*) et antérieures (*pūrvaja*). Les simultanées sont de deux sortes, nées du même tas (*samakalāpaja*),[2] nées d'un autre tas (*bhinnakalāpaja*). Ces dernières ou appartiennent à des êtres vivants (*sattvākhya*), ou n'appartiennent pas à des êtres vivants (*asattvākhya*). Les antérieures sont de deux sortes, de la même série (*sāmasaṃtānika ; svāsaṃtānika?*), d'une autre série

[1] Ci-dessus, p. 64.

[2] *tsiu* (128 et 8) = *kalāpa, rāśi, saṃcaya*. — Le sens de *kalāpa* dans Siddhi de Hiuan-tsang ne vaut pas ici. — Pour *sattvākhya*, Kośa, i, p. 17. — Je n'ai pas rencontré ailleurs la classification que nous avons ici.

(*para*, *bhinna*) ; ces dernières sont de deux sortes : nées d'un tas faisant partie d'une même série (*sāmasaṃtānika-kalāpa-ja*), nées d'un tas faisant partie d'une autre série ; ces dernières appartiennent ou n'appartiennent pas à des êtres vivants. — En dépendance de ces conditions de diverses sortes, de même époque ou d'époques différentes, de la série ou d'une autre série, le *dharma* a le pouvoir de projeter le fruit : ce pouvoir est ce qu'on nomme « activité ». — Donc ne dites pas que, à admettre la perpétuelle existence des conditions, l'activité doit aussi exister toujours : car les conditions ne peuvent pas perpétuellement concourir. [P. 632, col. 2, l. 13.]

Cependant je ne comprends pas comment le Vénérable (*āyusmat*), après s'être enquis de ce que j'entends par activité, n'hésite pas à demander maintenant quel obstacle fait que l'activité manque au *dharma* passé ou futur.

Le *dharma* futur, au moment du concours des conditions, produit un pouvoir éminent que l'on nomme activité ; le *dharma* muni de l'activité est dit « présent » ; quand l'activité a pris fin, le *dharma* est dit « passé ». Cependant sa nature propre ne change pas d'avant à après. — On ne peut objecter : « Quelle force fait que le passé et le futur n'ont pas d'activité ? »

Voici ce que nous voulons dire : pour le *dharma* futur, dans l'état du concours des conditions, l'activité se produit ; une fois l'activité produite, il n'est plus nommé « futur » (*anāgata*, non-arrivé), puisque, à ce moment, il est nommé « arrivé » (*āgata*) ; dans l'état où l'activité a pris fin, il n'est plus nommé « présent », car, à ce moment, il est « passé » (*atīta*, allé au delà); quand l'activité dure, il ne reçoit pas le nom de « passé », puisque, à ce moment, il est nommé « présent ».

C'est ainsi que nous expliquons la différence des trois époques en fonction de l'activité. Si le Sautrāntika critique, c'est qu'il ne connaît pas ma doctrine. Celle-ci est parfaitement cohérente et démontrée ; mais il ne la connaît pas. [P. 632, col. 2, l. 24.]

B. — *tad api katham.* [1]

Nouvelle critique : « Comment peut-on dire que l'activité est passée, future, présente ? »

C'est-à-dire : « Que le *dharma* soit passé, futur, présent, en raison de l'activité [passée, future, présente], soit ; mais l'activité elle-même en vertu de quoi présente-t-elle la distinction des trois époques ? En vertu d'une activité de l'activité ? [Alors défaut de regrès à l'infini, *anavasthā*]. Si l'activité n'est ni passée, ni future, ni présente ; si on prétend cependant qu'elle existe : alors elle est donc « inconditionnée » (*asaṃskṛta*) et ne cessera jamais d'exister. Ne dites donc pas que le *dharma* est nommé « passé », « futur », quand l'activité n'est pas née, quand l'activité est détruite. » [P. 632, col. 2, l. 28.]

Est-il jamais arrivé aux Ābhidhārmikas de donner l'activité comme passée ou future ? Pouvez-vous maintenant critiquer-nier [en disant que c'est] illogique ? — Le *dharma* futur, quand l'activité est née, est nommé « présent » ; le *dharma* présent, quand l'activité a pris fin, est nommé « passé » : l'objection est-elle justifiée ? Je ne dis pas que le passé et le futur aient aussi activité : on ne peut donc me critiquer [en disant que, d'après moi,] l'activité est passée, future. — Mais, direz-vous, si le passé et le futur n'ont pas d'activité, c'est donc que l'activité existe après inexistence et retourne à inexistence après existence ? Ce que vous dites, je le dis en effet : l'activité existe après inexistence et retourne à inexistence après existence, car l'activité existe seulement dans le présent. [P. 632, col. 3, l. 7.]

C. — *nānyad adhvā na yujyate.* [2]

Le Sautrāntika dira : « S'il en est ainsi, l'activité spécifie le

[1] Ci-dessus, p. 96. — *tat* = *kāritram* ; sous-entendre *atītādi* : *kāritram api katham atītādi.*

[2] Ci-dessus, p. 96. — « Si l'activité n'est pas autre que le *dharma*, les époques ne sont pas établies. » — Comparer Tattvasaṃgraha, p. 508 : *kāritraṃ sarvadā nāsti sadā dharmaś ca varṇyate dharmān nānyat kāritraṃ vyaktaṃ devaceṣṭitam* ||

dharma (*svabhāvaviśeṣaṇa*). Dites-nous si l'activité est oui ou non différente du *dharma*. Si oui, elle doit avoir une nature propre à part [du *dharma*] : celle-ci existera après inexistence et, après existence, retournera à non-existence. Et il en doit être de tous les conditionnés comme de l'activité. Si non, dites-nous comment, sans être différente de la nature propre du *dharma*, elle peut le spécifier. L'activité qui existe après inexistence et, après existence, retourne à non-existence, n'est-elle pas de la nature propre même du *dharma* ? » [P. 632, col. 3, l. 11.] [1]

Je prétends que l'activité spécifie le *dharma* ; que, cependant, on ne peut dire qu'elle soit différente du *dharma*.

Comment cela est-il possible ?

Comme, dans votre système, on voit que, dans une bonne pensée, résident des graines (des pouvoirs de diverses espèces projetés par des *dharmas* de diverses espèces, mauvais, etc.) qui ne sont pas différentes de la bonne pensée et qui, cependant, la spécifient. Comment ces graines ne sont-elles pas de la même espèce [que la pensée] ?

Le Sthavira admet que la douleur (*duḥkha*) est la nature propre de la sensation. Comment peut-il dire que celle-ci est spécifiée en « réconfortante » ? [2] — De même, les sensations ont pour

[1] Voir ci-dessus p. 16. — Comparer Tattvasaṃgraha, p. 508 :
yad uktam ananyatve 'pi kāritraṃ sārvakālikaṃ prāpnoti dharmasvarūpād aviśeṣād iti | atra bhadantasaṃghabhadra (Éd. Sahantabhadra) āha : svarūpād vyatirikto 'pi dṛṣṭaḥ sapratighatvavat | viśeṣaś ced... | svarūpād vyatirikto 'pi viśeṣako dharmo dṛṣṭo yathā sapratighatvādiḥ pṛthivyādīnām | te hi padārthatvenāviśiṣṭā api sapratighā apratighāḥ sanidarśanā anidarśanā iti

On dit : « Si l'activité n'est pas autre chose que le *dharma*, elle sera comme lui éternelle n'étant pas distincte de la nature propre (*svarūpa*) du *dharma*. » — Saṃghabhadra répond : A part (*vyatirikta*) de la nature même (*svarūpa*), on constate l'existence d'un *dharma* spécificateur (ou d'une qualité spécificatrice), comme par exemple les qualités d'impénétrabilité (résister), etc., de la terre, etc. : en effet [les choses], quoique non différenciées dans leur qualité de choses (*padārtha*), sont impénétrables, non-impénétrables, localisables, non-localisables, etc.

[2] Kośa, vi, p. 129 : « Certains maîtres nient la sensation agréable, affirment que toute sensation est douloureuse ; la sensation dite agréable est la sensation d'une douleur diminuée ou modifiée... » — Vibhāṣā, 78, p. 402, col. 3 ; dans Saṃghabhadra, 58 début, p. 663, col. 2, l. 7, après avoir examiné « l'opinion d'autres écoles », on a : « Le Sthavira dit : Quoique ne manque pas la sensation réconfortante,

commun caractère d'être « expérience » (*anubhava*) : cependant les spécifications d'agréable, etc., ne manquent pas. — De même encore la doctrine de la « durée de la série » (*saṃtānasthiti*) que vous enseignez [1] : le caractère des *dharmas* ne se modifie pas du moment antérieur au moment postérieur (*pūrvāparakṣaṇe*), les conditions extérieures restant les mêmes ; et cependant le postérieur diffère de l'antérieur ; s'il en était autrement, le caractère de « transformation » (*anyathātva*) manquerait. — Supposons un objet en relation avec le feu : le caractère grossier de la série [qui est cet objet] reste le même du moment antérieur au moment postérieur ; cependant, à chaque moment, a lieu une transformation subtile. [P. 632, col. 3, l. 20.]

De même dans ma doctrine : la nature propre du *dharma* dure (*tiṣṭhati*) ; cependant, soit par la rencontre de conditions différentes, soit par la force de la nature des choses, [2] « sur » cette nature propre se produit une activité spécificatrice qui d'abord n'existe pas, ensuite existe, retourne enfin à la non-existence après avoir existé ; cependant que la nature propre reste, comme devant, immuable en son caractère propre. — Rien, dans cette théorie, qui contredise l'Écriture ou la raison. [P. 632, col. 3, l. 23.]

Nous avons ci-dessus établi que le caractère de la nature propre (*t'i-siang*) ne subit pas de modification ; que la manière d'être (*bhāva*, *sing-lei*) du *dharma* n'est pas sans différenciations ; que

elle ne sort pas de la catégorie « douleur », parce que tous les *dharmas* impurs sont cause de douleur ; par conséquent, dans le saṃsāra, la sensation est seulement douloureuse. » — D'après la Vyākhyā, opinion du Bhadanta Śrīlāta. — La même doctrine dans Harivarman, chap. 78, et dans Saundarananda, xvii, 19 (voir Johnston, Acts of the Buddha p. xxxii). — Comparer Kathāvatthu ii, 8 (le Gokulika, Kukkulika, Keith, Buddhist Philosophy, 151).

[1] Kośa, ii, 227, où est discutée l'interprétation Sautrāntika du caractère durée-transformation (*sthity-anyathātva*) ; Vyākhyā, Wogihara, 173 ; Saṃghabhadra, 13, p. 407, col. 3, l. 9 : « Le Sthavira, partisan (*p'ong*) du Sautrāntika, dit : ... dans l'intervalle [entre la naissance et la fin], la continuation (*anuvart.*) de la série, c'est la durée (*sthiti*) ; la différenciation (*bheda*, *pie ?*) de l'antérieur au postérieur, c'est la transformation (*sthityanyathātva*) ... »

[2] *dharmatābala*, *fa eul li*, Kośa, v, 18 *b* 5, xxvi, 6 *a* 1.

le caractère de la nature propre et la manière d'être[1] ne sont ni différents ni identiques (*eka*, *anya*). Le caractère propre des conditionnés est permanent, mais le pouvoir éminent [qu'on nomme activité] a commencement et fin [P. 632, col. 3, l. 25.]

Notre adversaire dira : « Je pense que, durant le temps de la série des *dharmas* (*dharmasaṃtānakāla*), le caractère propre (*svalakṣaṇa*) est modifié (*viśiṣyate*) d'instant en instant : il n'existe pas d'abord, puis existe, puis retourne à non-existence après existence. Vous dites que le caractère propre du conditionné (*saṃskṛta*) dure toujours (*sadā tiṣṭhati*) : seule la spécification (*viśeṣaṇa*) [du conditionné] n'existe pas d'abord, puis existe, puis retourne à non-existence après existence. Comment la comparaison est-elle possible entre nos théories ? » [P. 632, col. 3, l. 27.]

Nos théories seraient identiques si je disais que le caractère propre n'existe pas d'abord, ou si vous disiez qu'il existe d'abord. La comparaison serait impossible. Pour que celle-ci soit possible, il faut qu'on ait partielle différence, partielle identité. [P. 633, col. 1, l. 1.]

Voici comment s'institue la comparaison en cause.

Le caractère propre (*svalakṣaṇa*) de la série des *dharmas* reste pareil (*t'ong*) et cependant les spécifications (*viśeṣaṇa*, *tch'a pie*) n'y manquent pas : le caractère propre est spécifié, la nature propre (*dravya*, *t'i*) ne change pas. Nous prétendons que la série du caractère propre est constante ; nous ne déclarons pas que la nature propre du *dharma* (*fa-t'i*) dure et ne dure pas. Les spécifications s'y produisent en dépendance des conditions. Par conséquent nous n'admettons pas que les spécifications existent toujours. — Pour vous, quoique vous admettiez que le *dharma*, d'abord inexistant, naisse ensuite, vous n'admettez pas que d'autres caractères se produisent d'instant en instant. —

[1] Il n'est pas impossible que Hiuan-tsang ajoute des *siang*, *lakṣaṇa*, à l'original : « La nature propre (ou le *dravya*, ou la chose) ... ne change pas ; elle n'est pas identique à la manière d'être (*bhāva*) ... »

Comment donc n'aurions-nous pas ici un « exemple pareil »?

A la vérité, d'après vous, le caractère propre du *dharma* est pareil du moment antérieur au postérieur, et cependant [la série] se différencie. Et moi, je pense que, au cours de ses états successifs, le caractère propre du *dharma* est pareil, et que cependant [le *dharma*] se différencie. Il est donc établi que nous avons ici un « exemple pareil ». [P. 633, col. 1, l. 8.]

Nous avons donc établi que, bien que l'activité (*kāritra*) ne soit pas autre chose que la chose (*t'i*, *dravya*), elle naît en raison des conditions ; et il est faux que le *dharma* en soi (*dharmasya svarūpa*, *fa tse t'i*), parce qu'il naîtrait des conditions, d'abord n'existe pas, existe maintenant, retourne à la non-existence après existence. [P. 633, col. 1, l. 11.]

Ainsi se trouve aussi bien expliquée la phrase du Sūtra : « D'abord n'existe pas, existe maintenant » (*abhūtvā bhavati*) ; aussi nous conformons-nous bien au Sūtra qui enseigne l'existence du passé et du futur ; aussi est bien réfutée l'objection que le *dharma* serait éternel (*nityastha*), car, quoique la nature propre (*t'i*) du conditionné existe toujours (*sadā asti*), il y a différenciation des états (*avasthā*), il y a transformation (*pariṇāma*).

La différenciation des états naît des conditions. Il n'y a pas durée (*sthiti*) au delà d'un moment[1] : par conséquent la nature propre du *dharma* est aussi impermanente, car cette nature propre n'est pas distincte (*vyatirikta*) de la différenciation (ou spécification). La transformation n'est possible que si on pose un *dharma* existant (*saddharma*, *bhūtasaddharma*) ; la transformation d'un non-existant est inadmissible.

La notion des époques ainsi établie est bien prouvée. [P. 633, col. 1, l. 16.]

Le Sautrāntika dit encore : « Cette théorie des époques est ruineuse. Si l'activité est la nature propre (*t'i*) du *dharma*, cette nature existant toujours, l'activité existera toujours. Comment

[1] Voir ci-dessous, p. 152.

se fait-il qu'elle soit nommée tantôt passée, tantôt future ? Les époques ne sont pas établies. »

Cette objection n'atteint pas ma théorie. En effet, je ne dis pas que l'activité soit la nature propre du *dharma* : pourquoi l'activité existerait-elle toujours avec le *dharma?* Et je ne dis pas que la nature propre du *dharma*, sur laquelle s'appuie l'activité[1] et qui existe toujours, puisse être nommée passée ou future. — Pourquoi les époques ne seraient-elles pas établies ? [P. 633, col. 1, l. 22.]

Comment sont-elles établies ?

Comme mon système l'enseigne. Le conditionné (*saṃskṛtadharma*), dans l'état où n'est pas encore née l'activité qui le spécifie (*ajātaviśeṣakakāritrāvasthāyām*), est nommé « futur ». Aussitôt qu'elle naît, il est nommé « présent ». Quand elle a pris fin (*uparata*), il est nommé « passé ».

On ne peut pas dire que l'activité spécificatrice soit autre chose que la nature propre sur laquelle elle s'appuie ; exemple : la série des *dharmas* (*dharmasaṃtati*, *saṃtāna*).[2] — De même que les conditionnés, naissant d'instant en instant sans intervalles, reçoivent le nom de « série » : et la série n'est pas autre chose que les *dharmas*, n'ayant pas une nature propre à part ; et la série n'est pas les *dharmas*, car chaque *dharma* serait la série ; et on ne peut pas dire que la série n'existe pas, car on voit que la série a un emploi (*kārya*). De même l'activité qui spécifie le présent n'est pas autre chose que le *dharma*, n'ayant pas une nature

[1] *souo fou* (170 et 5); dans Siddhi, viii, 25 *b* 5, on a *i-fou ; āśrita* est donc un bon équivalent.

[2] Tattvasaṃgraha, p. 509, cite Saṃghabhadra :

punaḥ sa evāha | na kāritraṃ dharmād anyat | tadvyatirekeṇa svabhāvānupalabdheḥ | nāpi dharmamātram | svabhāvāstitve 'pi kadācid abhāvāt | na ca na viśeṣaḥ | kāritrasya prāgabhāvāt || saṃtānavat | yathā dharmanairantaryotpattiḥ saṃtāna ity ucyate | na cāsau dharmavyatiriktas tadavibhāgena gṛhyamāṇatvāt | na ca dharmamātram ekakṣaṇasyāpi saṃtānatvaprasaṅgāt | na ca nāsti tatkāryasadbhāvad iti | āha ca

saṃtatikāryaṃ ceṣṭaṃ na vidyate sāpi saṃtatiḥ kā cit |
tadvad avagaccha yuktyā kāritreṇādhvasaṃsiddhim ||

propre à part ; elle n'est pas le *dharma*, car elle manque à une époque où le *dharma* existe ; on ne peut pas dire qu'elle n'existe pas, car, quand elle est produite, elle projette le fruit. Là-dessus une stance :

« La série n'a pas une nature propre à part ; mais on admet qu'elle a son emploi. De même pour l'activité. La notion des époques est donc établie. » [P. 633, col. 2, l. 4.]

Il y a d'autres exemples : relation de la cause et du fruit (*hetuphalasambandha*), concours (*sāmagrī*, *saṃnipāta*...), association (*saṃprayoga*), pureté de la pensée, etc. [1]

Donc, passé, présent, futur, le caractère de la nature propre [2] reste le même : cependant la manière d'être (*bhāva*) est différenciée. Les trois époques sont donc établies. [P. 633, col. 2, l. 7.]

D. — *tathā san kim ajo naṣṭaḥ.* [3]

« Il faut vous expliquer : si, de même que la nature propre (*t'i*) du *dharma* présent existe réellement (*dravyatas*), de même [pour] les *dharmas* passé et futur, qu'est-ce qui n'est pas né, qu'est-ce qui est détruit ? Si la nature propre existe réellement toujours, comment le *dharma* pourrait-il être non-né ou détruit ? Qu'est-ce qui lui manquait d'abord, par l'absence de quoi on le nommait non-né ? Plus tard que lui manquera-t-il, par l'absence de quoi on le nommera détruit ? Par conséquent, si on nie que le *dharma* d'abord n'existe pas, ensuite existe et retourne à non-existence après avoir existé, les trois époques ne peuvent d'aucune façon être établies. » [P. 633, col. 2, l. 13.]

Holà ! C'est un petit mérite qui produit semblables fruits ! L'intelligence que manifeste notre adversaire est très obtuse !

[1] La cause n'est ni identique au fruit ni différente. Même relation entre le concours et les *dharmas* qui concourent, la pensée et les mentaux qui lui sont associés, la pureté de la pensée et la pensée.

[2] *t'i siang* que je traduis *svabhāvalakṣaṇa*, mais qui sera aussi bien ou mieux *dravyalakṣaṇa*.

[3] Ci-dessus, p. 96 ; Kośa, v, p. 57 (xx, 5 *a* 7).

Incapable de voir en vérité, il accumule des paroles dépourvues de sens ! Serait-ce qu'il n'a pas pris la peine de considérer et de discerner la Vérité et l'Écriture ? Il s'attache au pervers, nourrit de l'hostilité contre la Vérité, indique et garde le contradictoire. Fréquemment ai-je pratiqué la logique ; je n'ai rien entendu de semblable. Je vais encore m'animer à parler, à ouvrir ce destructeur des Sūtras.

Le Bhadanta entend une thèse qui n'est pas de mon système, à savoir que « le passé et le futur existent comme existe le présent », car, [d'après moi,] si les trois époques existent réellement, elles ont une manière d'être distincte. Le Bhadanta ne doit pas, en suivant son explication personnelle, calomnier les maîtres qui expliquent correctement l'enseignement du Bouddha.

Les anciens grands Riṣis [1] étaient tous omniscients (*sarvajña*). La lumière qui tombe d'eux explique bien le Sūtra, brise l'obscurité de l'erreur (*mohāndhakāra*) de telle sorte que l'omniscient est nommé « parfaitement instruit ». [2] Pourquoi le Bhadanta fait-il une méchante alliance avec les gens qui mettent la confusion dans l'Écriture et dans la logique ? Il calomnie les saints disciples du Bouddha de hautes qualités et d'éminent savoir ; il fait tomber d'innombrables communautés dans le trou des mauvaises vues.

J'espère que désormais il coupera ces discours vides de sens. S'il ne coupe pas, c'est très nocif : allant contre l'enseignement du Muni et contre la logique, il est certainement incapable de réaliser la vraie réalité des *dharmas*. [3] [P. 633, col. 2, l. 25.]

D'ailleurs je ne comprends pas comment vous exposez notre doctrine sur le « présent » en nous faisant dire que, à la manière dont la nature propre du *dharma* présent est réelle, de cette manière aussi le passé et le futur sont réels. En vérité, dans notre système, les *dharmas* conditionnés sont dits présents, lorsqu'ils

[1] Sans doute les rédacteurs-auteurs des Abhidharmas.

[2] *p'ou-wen, sarvaśruta, samantaśruta ?* — *bahuśruta* est bien connu. — Probablement : « De telle sorte que ces omniscients sont nommés... » — Voir p. 117.

[3] *tchen-che*, vrai-vrai, *bhūta, satya, sāra, paramārtha*.

sont dans l'état où ils projettent leur fruit. Cet état de projection du fruit, avant, n'existe pas encore, après, n'existe plus. C'est ainsi que nous avons expliqué les trois époques. Avons-nous dit que le passé et le futur sont réels à la manière du présent? [P. 633, col. 2, l. 28.]

En résumé, de même que les *dharmas* conditionnés, quoique constants en leur vraie nature,[1] sont diversifiés par le pouvoir, de même les trois époques, quoique constantes en leur vraie nature, ne sont pas sans être diversifiées quant à l'activité, car il y a un nombre infini de sortes de manières d'être (*bhāva*).[2] Donc les objections formulées sont sans valeur. — Il y a une stance où est énoncé ce point de vue :

« Les *rūpas*, etc., sont tous « douleur »; mais on pense qu'il y a de nombreuses différentes manières d'être[3] de la douleur (*duḥkhabhāva*). De même pour les trois époques qui présentent les différences de non-né, etc.» [P. 633, col. 3, l. 5.]

Par conséquent les trois sortes de modes d'existence,[4] présent, passé, futur, sont distinctes. Disons-nous que le passé et le futur sont comme le présent?

On ne peut parler de « non-né » et de « détruit » que par rapport à un existant (*sat*). La non-naissance et la destruction s'entendent de quelque chose qui manque [à cet existant]. A cet existant fait d'abord défaut l'activité : celle-ci n'existant pas encore, [le *dharma*] est dit « non-né ». Au *dharma* existant (*saddharma*) fait défaut plus tard, et à nouveau, l'activité : celle-ci n'existant plus, [le *dharma*] est dit « détruit ». — Par conséquent c'est seulement l'existant qui peut être non-né et détruit. Ainsi sont établies les trois époques.

Mais pour le non-existant? Si le passé et le futur n'ont absolument aucun être (*t'i*), qu'est-ce qui est non-né, qu'est-ce qui est

[1] *che t'i*. — *che* (40 et 11), *dravya, tathya, bhūta* (dans l'expression *yathābhūta*).
[2] *sing-lei*.
[3] *sing*.
[4] *yeou sing, sattā*.

détruit ? On ne peut donc établir les trois époques relativement au non-existant. [P. 633, col. 3, l. 13.]

Autre point. Le non-existant ne peut recevoir le nom de « matière du discours ». [1] Or le Sūtra dit que les trois époques sont matière du discours. Donc le passé et le futur sont réellement munis d'une nature propre (*sasvabhāva*).

Cependant ce contempteur de l'Abhidharma [2] dit : « Soutenir que le *svabhāva* existe toujours, dire que le *bhāva* n'est pas éternel, c'est une combinaison-de-mots inouïe. [3] Là-dessus une stance :

« On tient que le *svabhāva* des *dharmas* existe toujours, et on dit que le *bhāva* n'est pas éternel : cependant le *svabhāva* et le *bhāva* ne sont pas à part. — C'est vraiment là décision de roi. [4] » [P. 633, col. 3, l. 18.]

Ceci est du mépris hors de place, car le Bouddha Bhagavat

[1] *kathāvastu*; Kośa, i, p. 12 : « Les conditionnés sont kathāvastu »; Aṅguttara, i, p. 197.

[2] Le « Sautrāntika », Vasubandhu, Kośa, v, p. 58, Vyākhyā, p. 472, que Saṃghabhadra cite ici, prose et stance (*saṃgrahaśloka*).

[3] *apūrvaiṣā vacoyuktiḥ*. — *vacoyuktiḥ* = *i-yen*, « sens-mot ».

[4] *svabhāvaḥ sarvadā cāsti bhāvo nityaś ca neṣyate* |
na ca svabhāvād bhāvo 'nyo vyaktam īśvaraceṣṭitam ||

Cité dans Bodhicaryāvatāra, ix, 142, comm. p. 581.

Comparer la stance Tattvasaṃgraha, p. 508, citée ci-dessus, p. 101.

J'ai traduit (Kośa, v, p. 58) : « La nature propre existe toujours, et on ne veut pas que l'être soit éternel, ni que l'être soit différent de la nature propre ». — Stcherbatsky, Central conception, p. 84 : « Maintained eternal essence, denied eternal being ! And yet no difference between this essence and this being. »

Vyākhyā : *svabhāvaḥ sarvadā cāstīti* yad rūpādeḥ svalakṣaṇam tat sarvasmin kāle vidyata itīṣyate | yadi rūpādeḥ svabhāvaḥ sarvadāsti tena rūpādibhāvo nityaḥ prapnoty ata āha | *bhāvo nityaś ca neṣyate...* : « Le caractère propre du visible existe toujours. Donc la chose qu'est le visible (*rūpādibhāva*) est éternelle ? — Non. — Alors la chose est autre que le caractère propre ? — Non. »

[Notons que *svabhāva* = *svalakṣaṇa*. Donc *t'i-siang* = *dravyasvalakṣaṇa*, *padārthasvalakṣaṇa*, et non pas *svabhāvasvalakṣaṇa*.]

Le Sautrāntika et le Vaibhāṣika n'entendent pas de même *svabhāva* et *bhāva*. Traduisant avec Stcherbatsky, avec la Vyākhyā, avec le Sautrāntika, *svabhāva* par « essence » et *bhāva* par « being », la doctrine Vaibhāṣika est absurde. Mais, pour le Vaibhāṣika, *svabhāva* = « being », la chose, et *bhāva* = la chose spécifiée, un mode d'être. Toute sensation, comme chose, en son être (*svabhāva*), est « expérience » ; mais les sensations diffèrent par le *bhāva*, « expérience spécifiée, expérience agréable, etc. »

a dit : « Qu'apparaissent ou n'apparaissent pas des Tathāgatas, la nature de la production en raison des causes est perpétuellement constante »[1], et, ailleurs : « La production en raison des causes est impermanente (*anitya*). » Le Bouddha Bhagavat est-il lui aussi digne de mépris, qui affirme que le *dharma* est perpétuel (*nityastha*) et le déclare ensuite impermanent ? Direz-vous qu'il tient un langage inouï ? [P. 633, col. 2, l. 22.]

Mais, dira-t-on, le Bouddha échappe à toute critique parce qu'il n'affirme pas la permanence et l'impermanence en visant le même objet.

Fort bien ; mais il en va de même de nos thèses : la nature propre du *dharma* est toujours la même, mais la manière d'être se transforme. Le *dharma* conditionné, cheminant par les époques, n'abandonne pas sa nature propre, mais, en raison des conditions, produit une activité, et, aussitôt, l'activité produite prend fin. C'est pourquoi on dit que la nature propre du *dharma* existe toujours (*sarvadā asti*) sans être toutefois éternelle, parce que la manière d'être se transforme (*bhāvaḥ pariṇamati*). Qu'on ne se moque pas en disant que c'est arbitraire. [P. 633, col. 3, l. 27.]

C'est à l'Ābhidhārmika qu'il appartient de reprendre le Sautrāntika. — Affirmer l'existence des trois époques et nier l'existence du passé et du futur, c'est une attitude inouïe. Quoique vous disiez que le passé et le futur sont dans le passé et le futur (en tant que « ayant été » et « devant être »), ce n'est là qu'une manière de dire que le présent est ; cette définition ne concerne pas le passé et le futur, comme nous l'avons remarqué ci-dessus (pp. 60, et suiv.). Voici sur ce point, une stance :

« On affirme l'existence des trois époques, et cependant on nie le détruit et le non-né : dès lors inexistence de la troisième. N'est-ce pas là une fantasmagorie divine ? » [P. 634, col. 1, l. 3.]

[1] *utpādād vā tathāgatānām anutpādād vā sthitaiva pratītyasamutpādadharmatā* (Douze Causes, pp. 109-113). — Voir Kośa, iii, p. 77, où est examinée l'opinion que le Pratītyasamutpāda est « inconditionné ».

Là-dessus, le Sautrāntika objecte encore : « Il faut donc professer la fausse doctrine patronnée par les infidèles Vārṣagaṇyas, [1] qui disent : Ce qui est, nécessairement, est toujours ; ce qui n'est pas, nécessairement, n'est jamais ; ce qui n'est pas ne peut pas naître ; ce qui est ne peut périr. »

Le Sautrāntika critique à tort. Nous parlons de non-né et de détruit d'une manière amphibologique (*paryāyeṇa*), [2] car nous soutenons que le non-né et le détruit sont à la fois existants et non-existants. Expliquons-nous. Les *dharmas* passés et futurs, visibles (*rūpa*) et autres, ont la nature de choses soumises à la naissance et à la destruction, d'objets du savoir [3] ; ils ont la nature de *pūrvaja-sahacara-phala* [4] ; mais ils n'ont pas actuellement la nature de projeter le fruit. Ce qui a le pouvoir de projeter le fruit est nommé présent ; le passé et le futur ne sont pas tels. — Est-ce là une doctrine semblable à celle des Vārṣagaṇyas? [P. 634, col. 1, l. 11.]

En fait, ce sont les partisans de l'existence du seul moment présent qui se défendront mal du reproche de ressembler aux Vārṣagaṇyas. Pour eux, le présent seulement existe (*asty eva*), le passé et le futur seulement n'existent pas; ils n'admettent pas que le passé et le futur puissent être, que le présent puisse ne pas être.

[1] *lo rtsi ba pa rnams*, « les gens qui comptent les années », *yu-tchong*, « troupe de la pluie ». — Kośa, v, p. 63. — Sur cette école, Vindhyavāsin (dont le maître est Vṛṣagaṇa), Vārṣagaṇya, Bhagavat Vārṣagaṇya, voir Takakusu, BEFEO., 1904, JRAS., 1905, 47, 162 ; Col. Jacob, ibid., 355 ; Garbe, Sāṃkhya-Philosophie, 36, et Grundriss, 4. — Sāṃkhyatattvakaumudī, ad 47 ; Bhāmatī, 2, 1, 3 ; Yogabhāṣya iii 52, iv, 47 (Woods, p. xx et 99). — Johnston, Acts of the Buddha, p. xlvi, lvii, et 12, 33. — Pour le Col. Jacob, Vindhyavāsin, élève de Vṛṣagaṇa, est un Vārṣagaṇya.

Hiuan-tsang s'écarte du tibétain (et de l'original) : *gaṅ yod pa de ni yod pa kho naḥo* | *gaṅ med pa de ni med pa kho naḥo.*

[2] *yo i men*, « d'après une autre porte » ; comp. Kośa, xiii, 15 *b* 6 (*niḥparyāyeṇa*).

[3] Littéralement : *sajātinirodha-jñeya-dharmaka.*

[4] Version probable de : ts'ien cheng (*pūrvaja*) kiu hing (*sahacara, sahagata*) kouo sing (*phalabhāva*) : « Ils sont des fruits nés d'une cause antérieure (par exemple *vipākahetu*, cause de rétribution) ou simultanés à leur cause (par exemple *sahabhūhetu*, cause simultanée) ».

Donc ils ressemblent aux Vārṣagaṇyas. [P. 634, col. 1, l. 14.]

Si le Sautrāntika répond : « Le présent, existant, tourne à être passé, non-existant; le futur, non-existant, tourne à être présent, existant », cela n'est pas correct, en raison de la différence de l'existant et du non-existant. L'existant et le non-existant ne peuvent tourner et s'identifier. En effet, votre présent n'est pas à la fois existant et non-existant; votre passé-futur n'est pas à la fois non-existant et existant. Le présent est seulement existant, le passé-futur seulement non-existant. L'existant et le non-existant peuvent-ils soudainement s'interchanger? Donc c'est votre système qui se classe avec celui des Vārṣagaṇyas.

D'après nous, ce qui est seulement existant, comme ce qui est seulement non-existant, ne peut pas naître : une corne de cheval ne peut pas naître. Dira-t-on que, si la corne de cheval ne peut pas naître, c'est faute de cause? La réponse est mauvaise, car l'acte qui a pour fruit le cheval pourrait être la cause de la corne, puisque vous soutenez que corne et corps du cheval sont tous deux non-existants avant de naître. On ne voit pas que des non-existants puissent différer. Pourquoi tel non-existant ne naîtrait-il pas si tel autre naît? [P. 634, col. 1, l. 23.]

Le Sautrāntika dit encore : « Pour celui qui admet l'existence réelle (*dravyatas*) du passé et du futur, le fruit existe de tout temps en sa nature propre. Quel pouvoir attribuer à l'acte relativement au fruit? »[1]

Cette objection est sans valeur. — Encore que la nature propre [du fruit] soit permanente, [l'acte] a pouvoir relativement à la différence d'état [du fruit]. L'acte fait que le fruit produise l'éminente activité : amener l'activité du fruit, tel est le pouvoir de l'acte. Le fruit, quand l'activité est née, est nommé présent. L'acte a donc pouvoir relativement à la différence d'état du fruit. — Si l'acte pouvait faire que le non-existant tournât à existant, pourquoi l'acte qui crée comme fruit le cheval ne serait-il pas

[1] Kośa, v, p. 63.

une cause qui ferait exister une corne de cheval ? La corne de cheval est non-existante au même titre que le cheval futur.

Là-dessus des stances :

« Si le non-existant peut devenir existant et l'existant non-existant : vous admettez que le visible (*rūpa*) naît du visible, pourquoi la sensation ne naîtrait-elle pas d'une corne de cheval ? Il n'y a pas, entre corne de cheval et sensation, relation de cause à fruit (*hetuphalasaṃbandha*) : de même, cette relation manque entre [votre] visible-cause et [votre] visible-fruit.[1] L'absence de relation causale est identique dans les deux cas. Si vous admettez que le visible naît du visible, et niez que la sensation naisse de la corne de cheval, c'est évidemment parce que c'est votre bon plaisir (*vyaktam īśvaraceṣṭitam*) ».

Par consequent un *dharma* démuni de nature propre ne peut avoir une cause, ne peut pas naître. Comment le philosophe qui hait la doctrine de l'existence du passé et du futur pourra-t-il établir la relation de la cause et du fruit ? [P. 634, col. 2, l. 10.]

Si le passé et le futur n'existent pas réellement, comment établir le *saṃyojana*, « ce qui lie », et le *saṃyojanīya*,[2] « ce à quoi on est lié » ?

Le Sautrāntika a là-dessus une théorie.[3] — Existent actuellement les *anuśayas*[4] qui sont engendrés par les passions (*kleśa*) ou qui en sont la cause ; par conséquent nous disons qu'existent les passions passées et futures qui lient (*saṃyojana*). Existent les *anuśayas* des passions portant sur des objets passés ou futurs, par conséquent nous disons qu'existent les objets auxquels on est lié (*saṃyojanīyavastu*), passés et futurs. [P. 634, col. 2, l. 13.]

[1] *heturūpa, phalarūpa.*

[2] *souo hi fou, saṃyojanīya*, Kośa, xxii, 6 *b* 10, Siddhi, v, 2 *b* 5. — Aṅguttara, i, 50, etc.

[3] Kośa, v, p. 64.

[4] *anuśaya*, passion à l'état de sommeil, trace et semence de la passion à l'état de veille ; un cas particulier de la *vāsanā* (ci-dessus, p. 64). — Étymologie, Kośa, v, p. 78. — Pour le Vaibhāṣika, *anuśaya* = *kleśa* (Kośa, v, Introduction) ; même doctrine chez Harivarman ; mais Aśvaghoṣa (Saundarananda) est, sur ce point, Sautrāntika.

En d'autres termes. Les *anuśayas* engendrés par les passions passées existant actuellement, on dit que les passions qui lient, passées, existent. Les *anuśayas* qui seront cause des passions futures existant actuellement, on dit que les passions qui lient, futures, existent. Les *anuśayas* des passions qui visent des choses passées et futures existant actuellement, on dit qu'existent, passés et futurs, les objets auxquels on est lié. [P. 634, col. 2, l. 16.]

Tout cela n'est que paroles vides de signification. Parce que les actuels *anuśayas*, engendrés par les passions passées, n'ont aucune existence réelle dans la série. Nous avons expliqué ce point. Comment dire que, en raison de ces *anuśayas*, on est muni des passions passées qui lient ? A admettre l'existence actuelle de ces *anuśayas*, comment dire que, en raison d'un existant (*saddharma*) [à savoir l'*anuśaya*], on est muni d'un non-existant [à savoir la passion passée] ? En effet, il n'y a pas de relation possible de l'existant avec le non-existant. [P. 634, col. 2, l. 21.]

Si celui qui a le fruit (*anuśaya*) est muni de la cause (passion), il faut que l'on soit muni de la cause du fruit de rétribution quand celui-ci naît. Ce que [le Sautrāntika] n'admet pas, car, dans son système, le pouvoir de donner le fruit de rétribution, pouvoir projeté par la cause de rétribution, est détruit, non-existant, quand naît la rétribution.

Si l'on n'est pas muni de cette cause (« du fruit... ») parce qu'elle est sans emploi, de même, évidemment, dans le cas qui nous occupe. Comment serait-on muni de la passion passée ? Ne dites pas que la passion passée, qui n'existe plus, a cependant maintenant un emploi : ce qui a maintenant un emploi, c'est l'*anuśaya ;* à quoi sert d'être muni de la passion passée ? [P. 634, col. 2, l. 26.]

A supposer que soit présent l'*anuśaya* qui peut être cause de la passion future, on ne peut pas dire qu'on soit muni de la future passion qui lie. Car cette proposition entraîne des conséquences non admises. Si celui qui a la cause est muni du fruit, l'être qui a coupé les racines de bien, ayant la cause qui produira les racines de bien, sera muni des racines de bien.[1] Donc, en même temps, il est « ayant coupé les racines de bien », il est « muni des racines de bien ». Dites avec précision quelle sorte d'être c'est, cet être de racines coupées et de racines non-coupées. [P. 634, col. 3, l. 3.]

Le Śaikṣa (c'est-à-dire l'Ārya qui n'est pas encore Arhat) porte des causes de l'état d'Aśaikṣa (ou Arhat) ; il faut donc dire qu'il est en possession du fruit d'Arhat : le Śaikṣa sera donc Arhat. Dira-t-on qu'il est en possession du fruit d'Arhat et n'est pas, cependant, nommé Arhat ? Alors l'Arhat, qui est en possession du fruit d'Aśaikṣa, ne sera pas non plus nommé Arhat ; ou bien il n'est pas en possession du fruit d'Arhat. — Toute l'Écriture, tout le raisonnement sont contredits par la théorie du Sautrāntika. Donc celui qui nie le passé et le futur est incapable d'établir les passions passées et futures, et dit vainement qu'on est lié par les passions passées et futures. [P. 634, col. 3, l. 9.]

Le Sautrāntika a dit : « Parce qu'existent les *anuśayas* des passions qui les visent, nous disons qu'existent les objets (*vastu*) auxquels on est lié, passés et futurs. »

Ceci aussi est en contradiction avec son système. Il soutient en effet que le passé et le futur n'ont pas d'existence réelle ; donc les objets passés et futurs manquent. Il est inouï que des non-existants, des passés et des futurs, reçoivent le nom de *vastu*. — Le Sautrāntika dira qu'existent dans la série les *anuśayas* des passions visant ces *vastus* : ces *anuśayas* doivent être différents des passions, car les passions qui les ont projetés sont détruites depuis longtemps tandis que les *anuśayas* qui sont projetés existent actuellement. Étant donnée la différence des passions et des *anuśayas*, comment peut-on dire que, en raison des actuels *anuśayas*, on est lié aux *vastus* passés et futurs ? Comment peut-on dire que les *anuśayas* actuels visent les *vastus* passés et futurs ? Ce

[1] Les racines de bien (*kuśalamūla*) ne sont jamais détruites définitivement ; après leur coupure (*samuccheda*, Kośa, iv, p. 170) a lieu leur renaissance (*pratisaṃdhāna*, p. 175). Donc l'homme qui les a coupées possède la cause qui les fera renaître.

qui est né autrefois et ce qui n'est pas encore né, ne peut lier. [P. 634, col. 3, l. 19.]

E. — gambhīrā jātu dharmatā. [1]

Ici le Sautrāntika attaque artificieusement. D'après lui, [2], « Les Vaibhāṣikas disent : Comme le présent (*vartamānavat*), [3] réellement existent le passé et le futur. Tous ceux qui, ici, ne sont pas capables d'expliquer [4] et qui s'aiment eux-mêmes, doivent savoir que « la nature des choses est profonde » (*gambhīrā dharmatā*) et n'est pas du domaine de la dialectique. Ce qu'on n'est pas capable d'expliquer, ira-t-on le nier ? » [5] [P. 634, col. 3, l. 22.]

Nous lui dirons qu'il s'arroge le droit de mettre sous le nom des Vaibhāṣikas un texte de sa fabrication ! A la vérité, les Vaibhāṣikas ne disent rien de semblable. Il est faux que, comme le Sautrāntika le prétend en suivant sa fantaisie, nous disions que le passé et le futur sont des choses réelles comme le présent, puisque, d'après nous, les trois époques, toutes trois réelles, diffèrent de manière d'être (*bhāva*). On dirait qu'il aspire à ravager l'enseignement sacré [6] ; il a des paroles insidieuses et fausses pour attaquer les bien-pensants. [7] Espère-t-il que semblables attaques porteront dommage à mon système ? Est-ce un fait que les grands maîtres de mon école, qui ont examiné partout et sérieusement compris l'Écriture et le raisonnement, qui sont revêtus de toutes les qualités et justement nommés des « totalement instruits », [8] sont incapables d'expliquer quelque petite

[1] Dernier pāda de la kārikā 27.

[2] Extrait de Kośa, v, p. 65. — Je m'écarte de l'interprétation de Th. Stcherbatsky, Central Conception, p. 90.

[3] « Comme le présent », manque semble-t-il dans le tibétain (Stcherbatsky, Central Conception, p. 90) et dans la version de Paramārtha.

[4] D'après Kiokuga Saeki : « capables d'expliquer les objections du Sautrāntika ».

[5] Même source : « Ce que je ne suis pas capable d'expliquer, irez-vous, Sautrāntika, le nier, à savoir le passé et le futur ? »

[6] *śāsana*, le Bouddhisme.

[7] *tcheng luen tche*, peut-être *samyagvādin* ; ailleurs *tcheng li luen choai*, les maîtres du Śāstra de correct principe, les Ābhidhārmikas opposés aux Sautrāntikas.

[8] *p'ou wen*, ci-dessus, p. 108.

difficulté que ce soit ? Par conséquent, son attaque est hors de place. Puisque, suivant sa fantaisie, il nous attribue à tort ces opinions, il est semblable à quelqu'un qui n'aurait jamais ouvert l'œil sur la vraie Vibhāṣā. [P. 635, col. 1, l. 1.]

Toutes les difficultés formulées, je les ai comprises et résolues. Quelle est la difficulté qu'on dit que je n'ai pas comprise ? Dans les pages qui précèdent, j'ai envisagé la théorie du passé et du futur du Sautrāntika : je l'ai complètement réfutée jusqu'à épuisement des forces de mon adversaire, et mot à mot. Du même coup, j'ai sommairement réfuté ce que dit le Sthavira. Car ce qu'il dit ressemble partiellement à la thèse du Sautrāntika, et est réfuté par ce que nous avons dit ; ou bien une réfutation détaillée n'est pas nécessaire, car il y a des choses si superficielles qu'elles ne méritent pas l'examen ; ou bien encore, le Sthavira se borne à attaquer les Āryas et à se vanter lui-même faussement. Si on répondait point par point en suivant son discours, quel est l'homme intelligent [1] qui, entendant, ne le réprouverait ? [2] [P. 635, col. 1, l. 9.]

IV. — Remarques finales

1. Il y a une espèce de disciple aveugle [3] qui dit que mon système est semblable à la thèse de Kapila-le-Ṛṣi.

Cela n'est pas exact. En effet, Kapila pense que la cause se

[1] *yeou-tche, vijña, prajñāvat,* etc.

[2] Ici deux lignes difficiles : « A supposer (*che*, 149 et 4) pas-miroir-homme (*pou-kien-tche*) à nouveau, s'appuyant sur ce système-là, faussement orner textes-paroles, faussement élever objections ; les comprenant-miroir (*tchou yeou-ta-kien*) bien-voir-traité doivent maintenant détailler-juger garder pensée vérité intelligence. Moi désormais je retourne m'appuyer sur le vieux système (*kieou-tsong*), suivant ce qu'il dit, expliquer et réfuter. »

[3] *yeou i lei kien tche mong t'ou,* « miroir-savoir aveugle disciple ». On a des *kien li jen*, des hommes qui reflètent (ou se règlent sur) la logique. — Ci-dessus, n. 2, des *yeou ta kien* et l'expression : « à supposer pas miroir » (*pou kien*). — [Kien-tche est le nom d'un maître de l'école de Dhyāna, Tch'an-Zen.]

disparaît ensuite en rentrant dans la Prakṛti ; donc le passé, transforme et devient la nature propre (*t'i*) du fruit : le fruit le futur et le présent sont identiques de nature propre (*t'i*). Dans mon système, les époques ne sont pas mêlées. Ce qui possède activité, c'est le seul moment présent : cet état n'est pas compris dans les deux époques [passée et future] ; la cause et le fruit ne se « font » pas mutuellement[1] ; le *dharma*, une fois détruit, ne revient pas naître ; le fruit ne disparaît pas en entrant dans la Prakṛti ; la cause n'est pas primordiale ; [le fruit] naît de plusieurs causes ; la cause et le fruit ne sont pas supportés par un soi (*ātman*). Les différences entre les deux systèmes sont infinies : dira-t-on que mon système est semblable à celui de Kapila-le-Rṣi ? [P. 635, col. 1, l. 18.]

2. D'autres disent : « Le passé et le futur n'existent pas, car le Sūtra dit que le passé a existé, que le futur existera. Bhagavat dit : « Les hommes intelligents (*manasvin*), quand ils sont pris de doute sur le passé, doivent se dire avec certitude : « Le passé a existé » ; quand ils sont pris de doute sur le futur, doivent se dire avec certitude : « Le futur existera ». — Il ne dit pas du passé et du futur qu'ils soient existant réellement. Donc nous tenons pour acquis que le passé et le futur n'existent pas réellement.[2] »

Ceci n'est pas exact, car on voit que les expressions « a été », « sera », sont quelquefois employées relativement à des choses présentes, et, assurément, on ne peut pas dire que celles-ci n'existent pas. — L'éminent pouvoir [que nous nommons « activité »] a été dans le passé ; dans le seul présent, il y a activité. De telle sorte que le passé peut être désigné de deux manières : il existe réellement quant au caractère propre ; il a existé, quant à l'activité. Parallèlement, le futur. Pour le présent, il est existant réellement [comme le passé et le futur], et, en outre présent :

[1] *pou siang tso.*
[2] Ci-dessus, p. 60.

parce que, au moment présent, le réel *t'i* est muni d'activité. [P. 635, col. 1, l. 27.]

Cependant les choses des trois époques sont ensemble la matière du discours (*kathāvastu*).[1] On exprime un sens différent à l'endroit du passé et du futur[2] ; pour éviter la confusion, on dit [: « a été », « sera »]. Ce n'est pas dire que le passé et le futur ne sont pas existant réellement. [P. 635, col. 1, l. 29.]

3. D'autres disent : « Si le passé et le futur existent réellement, pourquoi ne pas admettre qu'une pensée (*vijñāna*) pure et une pensée souillée naissent en même temps ? Puisque les causes de ces deux pensées sont réelles. »

Non ! Car quand naît une pensée, c'est parce que le support et l'objet (*āśraya, ālambana*) concourent. A supposer que les supports et les objets de toutes les pensées concourent, ce n'est pas une raison pour admettre que les pensées visuelles, etc., naissent ensemble. De même en va-t-il pour la pensée relative au passé, etc. — Remarquez que votre système donne prise à la même objection. Il admet que la chose, d'abord non-existante, naît : pourquoi le souillé et le pur, contradictoires, ne naîtraient-ils pas ensemble ? Direz-vous que cela seul naît qui a une cause ? Mais vous nous affirmez que le souillé et le pur, l'un et l'autre, sont non-existants d'abord : comment dire que ceci a une cause, que cela n'en a pas ? Vous ne nous avez pas expliqué où serait la raison d'une distinction. Encore, les partisans de la non-existence-réelle du passé et du futur pensent que toujours existent actuellement dans la série les causes du souillé et du pur, *anudhātu*, *bījas*, etc. De telle sorte que l'objection porte contre leur système, non pas contre le mien, puisque je n'admets pas que les causes soient toujours présentes. [P. 635, col. 2, l. 10.]

[1] Ci-dessus, p. 110.

[2] « Relativement à passé-futur *chouo pou kong i* ». — Le sens de *pou kong i* (*asādhāraṇārtha ?*) est fixé par Vibhāṣā, p. 183, col. 2, l. 10 : « Ici il y a encore un *pou kong i* : ces choses sont-elles... ou sont-elles... ? »

4. On dit : « Le passé n'est certainement pas une chose réelle, car il a abandonné le caractère propre de *saṃskāra* présent (*vartamāna saṃskāra svalakṣaṇa*). Autrement la nature propre (*t'i, svabhāva*) des *saṃskāras* serait éternelle ; la délivrance serait impossible. »

Non ! Si le passé, comme vous le dites, a abandonné le caractère propre de *saṃskāra*, il n'est plus compris parmi les *saṃskāras*. Ce qui n'a absolument pas de nature propre ne peut être nommé *saṃskāra*. Puisque vous considérez le [passé] comme un *saṃskāra*, ne dites pas qu'il a abandonné le caractère propre de *saṃskāra*. Car il n'y a pas une autre nature propre de *saṃskāra* à part du caractère propre, de telle sorte qu'on puisse dire qu'il [reste] seulement une nature propre de *saṃskāra* qui a abandonné son caractère propre.

Pensez aussi à ce que nous avons dit. — Qu'avez-vous dit ? — Que « ce qui est totalement non-existant ne peut avoir la nature d'impermanent. » Le passé, s'il n'a pas de nature propre, ne sera pas impermanent. [P. 635, col. 2, l. 17.]

5. Pourquoi la délivrance ne serait-elle pas justifiée dans notre système [et bien que le passé conserve son caractère de *saṃskāra*] ? Le Sūtra dit seulement : « destruction de la douleur présente, non-recommencement (*apratisaṃdhāna*) d'une autre douleur, sans-prise Nirvāṇa »[1] ; il ne dit pas que, [pour] le Nirvāṇa, il faille que les *dharmas* abandonnent leur caractère. Sans qu'ils l'abandonnent, il y a destruction des *saṃskāras*, ce qu'on nomme Nirvāṇa,[2] ainsi que nous l'avons expliqué plus haut. [P. 635, col. 2, l. 20.]

On dit encore : « Si le passé existe réellement, il n'y a pas Nirvāṇa, car, pour l'Arhat, à l'époque où existent les *skandhas* (« éléments de l'existence »), il n'y a pas Nirvāṇa. Si la douleur passée existe éternellement, les êtres ne seront pas délivrés. »

[1] *sien ts'iu ni-pan*, var. *ou-ts'iu*, *anupādāya nirvāṇa*.

[2] « ... il faut (*yao*) abandon *dharmalakṣaṇa* ; pas (*pou*) abandon *dharmalakṣaṇa*, cependant (*eul*) il y a *saṃskāranirodha*, nommé Nirvāṇa ».

Non ! Il n'y a pas Nirvāṇa, dites-vous, dans l'hypothèse où la douleur (*duḥkhaskandha*) passée existe : nous dirons que, dans votre système, le passé et le futur étant sans nature propre, il y aura toujours Nirvāṇa, vu l'inexistence de la douleur ; ou bien nous dirons que les êtres sont, d'origine, délivrés, vu l'inexistence de la douleur passée.

Si vous répondez : « Le Nirvāṇa dépend uniquement de la destruction de la douleur présente et du non-recommencement d'une autre douleur », alors ne dites pas que l'existence de la douleur (*duḥkhaskandha*) passée rend le Nirvāṇa impossible. [P. 635, col. 2, l. 27.]

6. On dit encore : « Le passé et le futur n'existent pas réellement, car le caractère de *saṃskāra* leur manque. Quel est le caractère des *saṃskāras?* D'avoir début et fin. Les deux époques, passé et futur, respectivement, n'ont pas l'un ou l'autre. Donc le caractère de *saṃskāra* leur manque. »

L'observation n'est pas justifiée. Comparez le Saṃsāra, à qui fait défaut un des deux, et dont le caractère de *saṃskāra* est certain. Le Saṃsāra des êtres n'a pas de début, et on ne peut cependant lui refuser le caractère de *saṃskāra*.

D'autre part, le présent, comme l'entend notre contradicteur, tombe sous sa critique : le présent de ceux qui nient la réalité du passé et du futur, n'a pas de début et n'a pas de fin.

Enfin, dans notre système, le passé a début et fin : le début, c'est le moment où l'activité a pris naissance ; la fin, c'est le temps postérieur depuis ce moment. Le futur aussi a début et fin. Telle étant la nature des choses (*dharma-sing-lei*), il n'y a pas lieu à critique. [P. 635, col. 3, l. 5.]

7. On dit encore : « Si le passé et le futur existent réellement, la « coupure » ne fait pas différence[1]. Dans l'hypothèse contraire,

[1] *prahāṇa*, « abandon », *toan*, « coupure ». — Si la passion passée existe, le fait de se détacher, le fait de « couper » la passion, n'amène aucun changement. — Sur l'abandon du présent, Kośa, ii, p. 281.

il en irait de même du présent. Pour le présent, coupure ou pas coupure, il n'y a pas différence : de même il n'y aura pas [différence pour le passé et le futur]. »

A la vérité, *dharmas* souillés et partie des *dharmas* non-souillés, quand ils sont coupés, on n'en est plus muni ; partie des *dharmas* non-souillés, quand ils sont coupés, on en reste muni, mais le lien de l'erreur (*mohabandhana*) a disparu : cela fait la différence entre coupure et pas coupure.[1] [P. 635, col. 3, l. 9.]

8. On dit encore : « L'existence du passé et du futur est contredite par l'Écriture, car il est dit dans l'Écriture : « Ceci étant, cela est; ceci n'étant pas, cela n'est pas.[2] » [Pour vous,] il est faux que le futur soit parce que le présent est, que le présent ne soit pas parce que le passé n'est pas, puisque vous affirmez la perpétuelle réalité du passé et du futur. On aura seulement le présent est, le présent n'est pas. — Donc le passé et le futur n'existent pas réellement. » [P. 635, col. 3, l. 13.]

Examinons si le mot « est » du Sūtra (« ceci est... ») indique l'existence d'une nature propre ou le fait de la naissance.

Dans la première alternative, votre système est en faute. — Le Sūtra dit d'abord : « Ceci étant, cela est » : or, pour vous, le présent existe bien que le passé n'existe pas ; en effet, vous soutenez que le *vijñāna* présent existe bien que les *saṃskāras* détruits n'existent pas.[3] Le Sūtra dit ensuite : « Ceci n'étant pas, cela n'est pas » : or, pour vous, le futur n'existe pas bien que le présent existe ; en effet, vous soutenez que le *vijñāna*

[1] On coupe tous les *dharmas* dits *sāsrava*, c'est-à-dire favorisant l'existence : tout, à l'exception des inconditionnés et du Chemin. Les *sāsravas* sont ou souillés (*kliṣṭa*, *nivṛta*) ou non-souillés. Quand on coupe un *dharma* souillé (concupiscence, etc.), on n'en est pas muni ; mais le saint qui coupe la connaissance visuelle (*dharma* non-souillé) continue à voir : la différence produite par la coupure, c'est que les objets visibles lui apparaissent comme ils sont (douloureux, etc.). Le lien de l'erreur est rompu.

[2] Théorie de la « production en raison des causes », *pratītyasamutpāda*.

[3] On a : « L'ignorance étant, les *saṃskāras* sont ; les *saṃskāras* étant, le *vijñāna* est... »

futur n'existe pas bien que les *saṃskāras* présents existent. — Le texte que vous citez pour détruire mon système détruit le vôtre, comme une formule homicide [détruit le sorcier]. [P. 635, col. 3, l. 18.]

Dans la seconde alternative, on aura : « Parce qu'il y a cette cause-ci, il y a naissance de ce fruit-là. » Par exemple on dit : « Cette cause-ci [étant], il y a ce riz-là. » Le mot « est » (« il y a ») n'indique pas l'existence d'une nature propre, mais le fait de la naissance. — Ceci ne fait pas difficulté dans mon système. Par conséquent la réalité du passé et du futur est logiquement établie.

Les Ābhidhārmikas expliquent le mot « est » en disant : « Parce que ceci est, il se fait que cela ait naissance. » La cause n'est pas capable de faire que la nature propre du *dharma* soit ; elle fait seulement que l'activité du *dharma* naisse. [P. 635, col. 3, l. 23.]

On objectera : « Ce que les conditions font être, c'est là le fruit ; la nature propre du *dharma* ne tombe pas dans cette définition. [1] »

L'objection ne vaut pas. En effet, [ce que les conditions font être] n'est pas autre que la nature propre. — Dans ce cas, la nature propre et l'activité sont toutes deux produites par la cause ? — Non, comme nous l'avons expliqué. — Qu'avez-vous dit ? — L'activité et la nature propre ne sont pas des choses (*t'i*) à part ; elles sont cependant différentes. Le concours des conditions fait que la nature propre du *dharma* ait un autre état, qu'une spécification (*viśeṣa*) naisse. Cette spécification, naissant, n'est pas autre que la nature propre. C'est pourquoi on peut dire par métaphore que la nature propre naît. — Là-dessus il y a une stance :

« Qu'elle existe en raison des conditions [2] ; c'est le point de vue vulgaire (*saṃvṛti*) ; quoiqu'elle naisse, la nature propre reste

[1] *fa t'i ing fei :* « *dharma*-nature-propre il faut pas [être faite être par les conditions] ». — Ou bien : « La nature propre n'est certainement pas fruit. » Niant que le *dharma* procède des conditions, le Sarvāstivādin contredit la formule : « Ceci étant, cela est. »

[2] Ou bien : « Que l'existence ou l'existant (*yeou*) vienne des causes... »

identique ; c'est la vérité absolue (*paramārthasatya*). » [P. 636, col. 1, l. 2.]

9. On dit encore : « Pas de futur [existant réellement], parce que sa « fruition »[1] ne s'épuise pas. La fruition du futur est inépuisable. »

Ceci aussi n'est pas bon (*ayukta*). En effet, chacun admet qu'il n'y a pas de limite à la fruition des *dharmas* du Saṃsāra. Il n'apparaît pas d'être nouveaux,[2] d'innombrables êtres sont déjà passés dans le Nirvāṇa : cependant la fruition des *dharmas* du Saṃsāra ne s'épuise pas. De ce [fait] actuel, nous déduisons que le futur, bien qu'il n'ait pas une limite d'épuisement, n'est pas sans exister. [P. 636, col. 1, l. 7.]

10. On dit encore : *a*) « Le passé et le futur [n'existent pas réellement] parce que leur manque le caractère de l'existant (*vidyamānalakṣaṇa*). Par exemple « le *rūpa* (matière) est nommé *rūpa* parce qu'il est endommagé (*rūpaṇāt*) »,[3] or le *rūpa* passé et futur n'est pas endommagé ; donc il n'existe pas réellement. »

Ceci aussi n'est pas bon. En effet, [la susdite définition du *rūpa*] ne vise qu'une partie du *rūpa :* tous les *rūpas* présents ne sont pas endommagés,[4] et ne sont pas pour cela sans exister.

Ou bien nous dirons que le passé et le présent existent comme [vous faites] exister le *vijñāna* (connaissance). Le Sūtra dit : « Parce qu'il discrimine (*prativijñapti prativijñapti*), on le nomme *vijñāna.*[5] — Que discrimine-t-il ? — Les visibles, les audibles... les *dharmas* (qui sont l'objet de la connaissance mentale) ». Or, dans votre système, la connaissance [présente] qui porte sur le passé et le futur n'a rien qu'elle puisse discriminer [, puisque le passé et le futur n'existent pas] ; toutefois vous soutenez que

[1] *cheou-yong, anubhava, bhoga, saṃbhoga, upabhoga, yāpanā.*
[2] Certains hérétiques prétendent que de nouveaux êtres apparaissent.
[3] Voir Kośa, i, pp. 24-25.
[4] Cette partie du *rūpa* qui est l'*avijñapti.*
[5] Kośa, i, 16 (p. 30) : *vijñānaṃ prativijñaptiḥ.*

la nature propre de cette connaissance existe, non pas n'existe pas, puisque le présent existe.

Donc ce nouvel argument contre l'existence [du passé et du futur] n'est pas établi (*asiddha*). [P. 636, col. 1, l. 13.]

b) On dit encore : « Le passé et le futur n'existent pas réellement en nature propre. S'ils existaient réellement, ils feraient obstacle. Les choses matérielles (*rūpīṇi dravyāṇi*) se font mutuellement obstacle, ne pouvant résider dans le même lieu. Si les choses matérielles passées ou futures existaient réellement, elles se feraient obstacle : ce n'est pas le cas ; donc elles ne sont pas des choses matérielles (*rūpa*). — Cette objection montre que [le passé et le futur] n'existent pas réellement. »

Ceci aussi n'est pas bon. — Dans votre système : « Il est faux que l'existant naisse ; [mais certain non-existant ne naît pas] en raison du manque de ses conditions.[1] » C'est-à-dire : vous dites que l'existant ne naît pas, mais [parmi les non-existants] c'est le futur qui naît et certainement pas le passé. — De même dans mon système : les *dharmas* existants font obstacle, mais seulement les présents, non pas les passés et les futurs, car, dans l'état de présent, le *dharma* a un pouvoir spécial. [P. 636, col. 1, l. 20.]

c) D'autres maîtres disent : « La lampe future brûle-t-elle ou non ? Si oui, elle ne diffère pas de la lampe présente ; si non, elle n'a pas la nature propre d'une lampe. »

Cette critique n'est pas bonne, car [la lampe future] a seulement « nature propre ». C'est-à-dire : du passé et du futur, il y a « nature propre », il n'y a pas activité. Par nature propre, on entend la cognoscibilité (*jñeyadharmatā*) du passé et du futur ; comme ils sont munis de cognoscibilité, nous disons qu'ils existent ; nous ne disons pas qu'ils aient le pouvoir de brûler.

Ou bien, cette lampe existe réellement comme votre *vijñāna* (connaissance) : vous admettez une connaissance sans objet,

[1] *fei yeou eul cheng pei fa* (var. *yuen*) *k'iue kou :* na saj jāyate tatpratyayavaikalyāt.

qui n'a rien à connaître, à laquelle ne manque pas cependant la nature propre [de connaissance]. De même, pour moi, la lampe passée ou future : elle n'a pas l'activité de brûler, mais la nature propre [de lampe] ne lui fait pas défaut. [P. 636, col. 1, l. 27.]

d) On dit encore : « Le visible (*rūpa*) passé et futur [n'existe pas réellement], car il n'est pas saisi par l'œil. S'il existait réellement, pourquoi ne serait-il pas saisi par l'œil ? »

Ceci aussi n'est pas bon, car l'organe-œil (*cakṣurindriya*) n'a pour domaine (*viṣaya*) que le visible muni de l'activité éminente [qui caractérise le présent]. — Les *dharmas* des trois époques ont le même caractère essentiel (*t'i-siang*), mais différent de manière d'être (*bhāva*, *yeou-sing*), comme nous l'avons expliqué. De ce que l'œil a pour domaine le visible, on ne peut conclure qu'il doit saisir tous les visibles, car il ne saisit pas la matière atomique (*paramāṇurūpa*). Par conséquent, si l'œil saisit le présent, ne saisit pas le passé et le futur, cela tient à la variété de l'état, au caractère spécifique de l'activité. — Point de difficulté. [P. 636, col. 2, l. 3.]

11. On dit encore : « [Le passé et le futur n'existent pas réellement], car ils n'ont pas les caractères du conditionné (*saṃskṛta*). Ils n'ont pas les caractères du conditionné ; ils ne sont pas inconditionnés ; donc ils n'existent pas réellement. »

Ceci aussi n'est pas bon, car ils sont de la nature du conditionné[1] : le futur sera périssable, le présent est actuellement périssable, le passé a été périssable.[2] Par conséquent [les *dharmas* des trois époques] ne sont pas démunis des caractères du conditionné.[3] — Le *dharma* destiné à naître[4] naît par la force des

[1] Le texte porte : *taddharmakatvāt*, *pei fa sing kou.*

[2] *anāgatasya nirutsyamānadharmakatvāt, vartamānasya nirudhyamānadharmakatvāt, atītasya niruddhadharmakatvāt.* — Les temps sont marqués par *k'o*, *tcheng*, *i* : *k'o mye fa sing kou.*

[3] *li yeou-wei siang.*

[4] « destiné à naître », « non destiné à naître » : parmi les futurs, quelques-uns naîtront, d'autres ne naîtront pas ; voir la théorie de l'*apratisaṃkhyānirodha*. — Kośa, i, 10 (texte chinois, i, 4 b 1) a *cheng-fa*, *utpattidharman*, *pou-cheng-fa*,

causes : nous avons expliqué (pp. 15, 106) ce qu'il faut entendre par « naissance du *dharma* ». Le *dharma* qui n'est pas destiné à naître est de la même espèce que le *dharma* destiné à naître[1] : par conséquent il reçoit le nom de « ayant la nature du destiné à naître ». S'il ne naît pas, c'est par déficience des conditions. Cette déficience a été expliquée plus haut. [P. 636, col. 2, l. 10.]

Ou bien la connaissance (*vijñāna*) [comme vous l'entendez] nous servira encore d'exemple « pareil ». Vous admettez une connaissance prenant pour objet le non-existant et qui n'a pas de connaissable : dont pourtant la nature de connaissance n'est pas non-existante. — De ce point de vue, comment le fait qu'ils n'ont pas les caractères du conditionné pourrait-il empêcher le passé et le futur d'exister ? [P. 636, col. 2, l. 13.]

Ajoutons que votre présent n'a pas [le caractère de] naissance (*utpāda*), car il est déjà né ; il n'a pas [le caractère de] durée-transformation (*sthityanyathātva*), car il périt aussitôt né ; il n'a pas [le caractère de] destruction (*nirodha*), car, dans votre système, la destruction est nommée « non-existence » (*abhāva*), et la « présence » (*vartamānatā*) est « existence ».

Encore les caractères du conditionné, dans votre système, s'entendent de la série et non pas du « moment » (*kṣaṇa*)[2] : donc vos moments n'existeront pas [puisqu'ils n'ont pas les caractères du conditionné]. [P. 636, col. 2, l. 16 : fin du cahier 52 et de la discussion du Sarvāstivāda].

Note sur le Sarvāstivāda

I. Le Sarvāstivāda distingue parmi les *dharmas*, « êtres » ou « entités » ou « choses », les êtres réels (*dravyasat*), les entités existant en soi, existant au sens absolu (*paramārthatas*), et les

anutpattidharman ; notre texte a *cheng-fa* et *k'o-cheng-fa*, expressions synonymes comme le dit l'éditeur japonais du Kośa.

[1] *k'o cheng fa sing.*

[2] Kośa, ii, p. 227.

êtres que nous nommerions des « êtres de raison », en sanscrit des « êtres de désignation » (*prajñaptisat*), lesquels n'existent que du point de vue de l'expérience (*saṃvṛti*), sans que pour cela l'activité leur soit refusée.

a) Sont des « êtres réels » (*dravyasad dharma*) les « conditionnés » présents. « Conditionné » (*saṃskṛta*) : qui est produit par les causes et conditions, qui est causé. Tout ce qui est produit par les causes est, à son tour, cause : *saṃskāra* est donc à peu près l'équivalent de *saṃskṛta*.

Les conditionnés présents sont des « instantanés » (*kṣaṇika*) ; des unités indivisibles au point de vue du temps (conditionnés matériels ou mentaux) ; des « atomiques » (*paramāṇu*), unités indivisibles au point de vue spatial (conditionnés matériels). — Ils sont les éléments ou « moments » (*kṣaṇa*) des « séries » ou des « blocs » (*saṃtāna*, *piṇḍa*) psychologiques, somatiques, physiques que l'opinion vulgaire accepte comme des êtres simples ou de durée, l'âme, le corps, la flamme ou la montagne. Les séries et les blocs n'existent pas en dehors de leurs éléments : l'âme n'est qu'une succession de moments mentaux ; la forêt n'est que des arbres. Séries et blocs n'existent que comme « désignations » (*prajñapti*) de *dharmas* réels, quoiqu'étant quelque chose à part (p. 106).

b) Sont aussi des êtres réels les trois « inconditionnés », entités éternelles : l'espace, le Nirvāṇa et la « non-production à nouveau en raison de l'absence des causes. »

c) Sont des êtres réels les conditionnés passés et futurs. — On a bien défini ci-dessus le *dharma* conditionné présent en le définissant comme une entité instantanée : le *dharma* conditionné naît, dure un instant, périt.

Cependant, avant de naître par la force des causes, il existe, et il continue d'exister après avoir péri. En d'autres termes, il traverse les trois époques ; est successivement futur, présent, passé ; successivement sera, est, fut : toujours réel, toujours la même entité de caractère constant. Avant de naître, il est lui-même ; il reste lui-même après avoir péri.

On ne doit pas dire que le *dharma* conditionné « existe après ne pas avoir existé » et « retourne à la non-existence après avoir existé ».[1]

[1] L'école Sautrāntika n'admet que les *dharmas* conditionnés présents ; elle nie les *dharmas* éternels; elle nie la réalité des *dharmas* conditionnés futurs et passés : d'où le nom de *ekakṣaṇavāda*, « doctrine de l'existence du seul *kṣaṇa* ou instant présent ». — Elle nie aussi un certain nombre de *dharmas* conditionnés inventés par le Sarvāstivādin (*viprayuktasaṃskāra*). — Noter aussi

2. Le *dharma* futur, présent, passé, est toujours le même *dravya*, *vastu*, *artha*, *ātman*, *ātmabhāva*, *ātmalābha*, *svalakṣaṇa*, *svarūpa*, *svabhāva*.

Les trois premiers termes [1] se traduisent assez bien par « chose » et tendent vers la notion de substance. Les termes *ātman*, *ātmabhāva*, « soi », donnent l'idée d'individualité. Les trois derniers termes, « caractère propre », « forme propre », « être ou nature propre », semblent exprimer la notion d'essence. Mais le bouddhiste du Petit Véhicule ne parle pas de substance ou d'essence ; il ignore le substrat, plus ou moins métaphysique, des qualités ou activités ; il nie le *dharmin*, « ce qui possède les qualités ou activités ». Le *dharma* tout entier réside dans sa nature ou caractère (*svalakṣaṇa*). Une connaissance visuelle n'est pas un complexe, avec un je ne sais quoi qui connaît, mais une connaissance, une image visuelle sans plus.

3. A plusieurs points de vue, le *dharma* futur ou passé ne diffère pas du *dharma* présent.

Il est, comme lui, exactement comme lui, « cognoscible », *jñeya*. Supposer que le *dharma* futur n'est pas, en sa nature cognoscible, identique au *dharma* présent, c'est admettre que la connaissance mentale que nous avons, que le Bouddha a, du futur est une connaissance sans objet. En bonne philosophie, le non-être ne peut être connu : l'objet de l'idée ne peut être que réel, actuellement existant.

Connu, le futur ou le passé est désiré, possédé. L'homme qui a éprouvé une passion, aussi longtemps qu'il n'a pas coupé cette passion par le chemin bouddhique, reste « en possession » de cette passion, reste souillé par cette passion, reste attaché à ce qui fut l'objet de cette passion. — L'homme qui, à grand'peine, s'est élevé à une extase, « possède » la même extase à l'état futur : il pourra, sans peine, amener une extase semblable à celle qu'il a jadis conquise.

Certains *dharmas*, à savoir les actes bons ou mauvais, ne donnent leur fruit de rétribution (ciel ou enfer) que lorsqu'ils sont passés, parfois dans la prochaine période cosmique.

Les preuves scripturaires et logiques abondent qui obligent à admettre la pré-existence et la post-existence du *dharma* présent

que le Sarvāstivāda, quoiqu'il confesse le caractère instantané du *dharma* conditionné présent, reconnaît cependant à ce *dharma* une durée (*sthiti*) minima que le Sautrāntika nie.

[1] Monier Williams : substance, thing, object ; any really existing substance or essence ; thing, object.

et instantané. — C'est une folie de penser que « les causes et conditions » créent le *dharma* : leur seul rôle est de faire passer le *dharma* de la condition future dans la condition présente ; de lui donner, ou de l'aider à produire, une certaine activité qui caractérise la condition présente.

4. Quelle est cette « certaine activité » ?

Ce n'est pas, comme on pourrait croire, l'activité (*śakti*, *sāmarthya*) qui consiste à produire un effet extérieur, un fruit différent du *dharma* même. Seul l'œil présent produit la connaissance visuelle, mais l'œil présent ne produit pas nécessairement cette connaissance : par exemple dans l'obscurité. — Si l'œil présent, pour ne pas voir, n'en est pas moins œil, il s'ensuit que la vision n'est pas essentielle à l'œil, que l'œil futur et passé est aussi bien un œil.

L'activité caractéristique du *dharma* présent, qu'on nomme *kāritra* (pour la distinguer de l'activité en général, *śakti*, *sāmarthya*), résulte du fait qu'il est inséré dans la série. Le *dharma* futur entre dans la série (et dans le présent) en qualité d'effet ou de « fruit ». Dans cette série, il devient en même temps cause : il projette un fruit — quelquefois un fruit dissemblable de lui-même — toujours, et c'est le point, un fruit semblable à lui-même. L'œil, dans l'obscurité, est une succession de *dharmas*-œil, passant tour à tour du futur dans le présent, chacun engendrant le suivant.

5. Ces remarques, assurément, ne font pas disparaître toutes les difficultés.

Le Sarvāstivāda pose un feu futur, qui est chaleur comme le feu présent, mais qui, en fait, ne brûlera qu'à l'époque où les causes le feront entrer dans une série ignée ; une connaissance visuelle qui connaîtra la couleur à l'époque où elle entrera dans la série mentale, par la coïncidence d'un certain moment de la série mentale, de la série de l'organe-œil, de la série d'une chose coloriée : cette connaissance, avant de connaître et après avoir connu, est, dans sa nature propre, la même connaissance.

Le souci majeur des docteurs du Sarvāstivāda n'est pas d'expliquer, mais de montrer que leur théorie du *dharma* n'est pas en contradiction avec la définition scripturaire, à savoir que le *dharma* est impermanent.

Le caractère (*lakṣaṇa*) du *dharma* est constant.[1] Cependant le *dharma* n'est pas éternel, il naît et périt. En effet, en raison

[1] Saṃghabhadra, 625, 1, 20; 632, 1, 9; 633, 1, 7.

des causes et conditions, le *dharma* devient présent, c'est-à-dire développe [1] une activité qui s'appuie [2] sur le *dharma*, qui « spécifie » le *dharma*. Cette activité n'est pas autre chose que le *dharma* : donc du *dharma*, bien que son caractère soit constant, on peut dire qu'il naît et périt, puisque l'activité, qui lui est « intégrée », commence et finit.

Cependant si l'activité n'est pas autre chose que le *dharma*, elle n'est pas non plus la même chose. Aussi l'école enseigne que le *dharma* a deux états (*avasthā*) ; celui où il est seulement son caractère constant (futur et passé), celui où il est, par surcroît, activité (présent).

Le caractère constant du *dharma* est la même chose que le *dharma* (*svalakṣaṇa* = *dharma*) ; ce caractère est momentanément spécifié par l'activité caractéristique du présent ; cette activité est intégrée au caractère, au *dharma*.

Dharma, c'est-à-dire *svabhāva*, nature propre ou essentielle du *dharma*, auquel on attribue un caractère constant (qui est le *dharma* même) par opposition au caractère momentané et supplémentaire que le *dharma* prend, ou qui devient le *dharma*, lorsque le *dharma* est présent.

Dharma, c'est-à-dire *bhāva*, l'être qui existe actuellement : c'est le *svabhāva* auquel est intégrée l'activité du présent. D'après la version chinoise, *bhāva* équivaut à « mode », « espèce », donc une manière d'être du *dharma*, et le *dharma* même. — Donc *bhāva* et *svabhāva* ne sont ni identiques ni différents. [3]

8. Nous entendrions mal la réalité du *dharma* futur, et l'individualité du *dharma*, si nous ne tenions pas compte de la doctrine du *dharma* « non destiné à naître ».

La réalité du *dharma* futur est indépendante du fait qu'il sera présent.

Les *dharmas* futurs forment en effet deux catégories : ceux qui naîtront, ceux qui ne naîtront pas ; non seulement les futurs, comme nous entendons ce mot, mais encore les « possibles », ou mieux « mes possibles ». Existent, de tout temps, tous les *dharmas* nécessaires à ma transmigration continuée. J'entre dans le chemin du Nirvāṇa : je coupe en moi le désir qui est le principe des renaissances ; je coupe, par le fait même, les renaissances : en termes techniques et exactement, les désirs qui devaient faire

[1] Ou « produit », 631, 3, 28.
[2] 633, 1, 22.
[3] 632, 3, 11. — Comparaison (terre, sensation), 625, 1, 19; 631, 3, 28.

procéder ma transmigration, et les multiples états d'âme ou états somatiques qui devaient constituer ma transmigration, deviennent « non destinés à naître ».

Nous concluons que les *dharmas* futurs ne forment pas un tas indiscriminé ; ils n'entrent pas, indifféremment, dans la série de n'importe quel homme chez lequel existe, à certain moment, le complexe des causes qui « actualise » un *dharma* futur de telle ou telle sorte. Tout *dharma* futur est comme marqué, parmi les *dharmas* identiques, pour entrer dans la série de telle personne. Il constitue une individualité. — Cependant il n'y a pas, parmi les *dharmas* futurs, antériorité et postériorité : fait qui complique la connaissance du futur.

9. Le *dharma* futur, s'il possède « en puissance » certaine activité (*kāritra ;* « extériorisation de sa nature propre » : pour le feu, brûler), existe déjà « en acte » à certain point de vue.

Le *dharma* est une qualité ou caractère propre (*svalakṣaṇa*), la « nature propre » (*svabhāva*) qui est un être en soi, une individualité (*dravya*, *vastu*, *artha*, *ātman*) : le feu est chaleur, non pas une chose chaude ; une connaissance, discrimination ; une sensation, expérience. Le « caractère » tient par soi et constitue tout le « caractérisé » (*lakṣya*), ou, plus exactement, il n'y a pas un être caractérisé par le caractère propre. Le *dharma* est éternellement et réellement le caractère propre, car, futur ou présent, il est connu comme tel. Le feu futur est du feu puisqu'il est connu comme feu. Du point de vue de l'idée, du point de vue de la « cognoscibilité », le *dharma* est identique et éternel ; et la cognoscibilité entraîne l'être, non pas l'être potentiel, mais l'être réalisé. Cependant il est évident que, dans l'ordre du réel, rien ne correspond à cette éternelle cognoscibilité, à cette éternelle essence, à cette éternelle existence.

10. L'Abhidharma et Saṃghabhadra ne conçoivent pas le *dharma* comme une substance qui possèderait, depuis toujours et en puissance, certaines qualités ou activités, et qui les manifesterait, à certain moment, « en raison des causes et des conditions » — conception qui s'entend bien et qu'on est tenté d'attribuer à « ceux qui affirment l'existence du passé et du futur ».

Je ne suivrai pas les maîtres éminents qui pensent pouvoir tirer parti des vues du Grand Véhicule dans l'explication du Sarvāstivāda. D'après un savant dont la mort précoce fut une grande perte pour nos études — pourquoi faut-il que nous ayons aujourd'hui à déplorer la disparition d'Obermiller ? — d'après

Rosenberg (*Probleme*, pp. 231-233 de la traduction allemande), le *dharma* du Sarvāstivāda est une entité supra-empirique, inconnaissable, résidant dans une sorte d'*Uebersein*, le vraiment étant ; l'empirique, c'est-à-dire le phénomène présent, est la réflexion et comme une sorte d'émanation du *dharma* transcendant.

Ceci est presque la définition de la « nature des *dharmas* » (*dharmatā*) ou *tathatā* du Grand Véhicule, l'unique et inconnaissable (hormis par le Bouddha) « matière » des *dharmas* dont la « forme » est illusoire.

Mais je ne peux pas croire que le *dharma* du Sarvāstivāda soit une sorte de *tathatā* atomique : ce *dharma*, en son éternité, se définit en fonction du *dharma* présent ; il est le *dharma* présent, moins une certaine activité qui lui sera ou lui fut momentanément associée, mais qui n'intéresse pas son être. Inconnaissable? Saṃghabhadra dit que la « cognoscibilité » (*jñeyadharmatā*) est sa nature propre.

Et si on affirme l'existence éternelle du *dharma*, c'est parce que le Bouddha, qui parle souvent du passé et du futur, a dit : « Que je connaisse une chose qui n'existe pas, c'est impossible », et encore « L'acte passé existe ». C'est parce que, étrange confusion de l'idéal et du réel, curieuse survivance d'une « psychologie primitive », on affirme l'existence « objective » de tous les objets (*ālambana*) de la pensée.

III

NOTES SUR LE MOMENT (*KṢAṆA*) DES VAIBHĀṢIKAS ET DES SAUTRĀNTIKAS

1. Le temps et les *saṃskāras* : le temps n'est pas une chose à part des choses qui naissent et périssent. — 2. Les grandes écoles enseignent que tous les « conditionnés », matériels et spirituels, sont « instantanés » (*kṣaṇika*), mais plusieurs sectes n'admettent pas le caractère instantané des choses matérielles. — 3. Mesure du moment ; comparaisons. — 4. Conflit Vaibhāṣika-Sautrāntika. — 5. Définitions du Sautrāntika. — 6. La destruction n'a pas de cause. — 7. Doctrine du Vaibhāṣika.

I. — Le temps et les saṃskāras

1. Vibhāṣā, 136, p. 700, col. 1, l. 25.

Quel *dharma* est nommé « temps » ? — C'est là une désignation (*adhivacana*) des *saṃskāras*.

Pourquoi fait-il ce traité ? [1] — Pour arrêter la doctrine des autres et manifester la sienne. En effet les Dārṣṭāntikas [et les] Vibhajyavādins [2] prétendent que le temps est autre chose que les *saṃskāras*. L'être (*t'i*) du temps est éternel : les *saṃskāras*, qui ne sont pas éternels, quand ils circulent dans le temps éternel, comme des fruits dans des vases, tournent-changent ; ou comme des hommes qui entrent dans des maisons. Pour réfuter cette opinion et montrer que les trois époques ne sont pas autre chose que les *saṃskāras ;* que, ceux-ci n'étant pas éternels, le temps n'est pas éternel, pour cette raison, il fait ce traité. Les trois époques sont comme il est expliqué dans le Saṃyojanaskandhaka. [3]

2. Kośa, iv, p. 62. — Quel est le *dharma* que nous appelons « temps » ?

[Ce n'est pas un *padārtha* éternel comme le croient quelques-uns. Le mot « temps » est] une expression par laquelle sont désignés les *saṃskāras* [en tant que passés, futurs, actuels].

Saṃghabhadra, 37, p. 551, col. 3, l. 2. — Quel *dharma* est nommé « temps » ? — Pas à part des *saṃskāras*.

Kośa, i, 7 ; trad. i, p. 12 : « Les conditionnés sont le chemin. »

Kośa, iii, p. 187 : « Le *kalpa* consiste dans les cinq *skandhas* », *pañcaskandhasvabhāvaḥ kalpaḥ*. [4]

[1] La Vibhāṣā nomme *luen*, *śāstra*, les nombreux paragraphes du Jñānaprasthāna.

[2] La relation du Dārṣṭāntika et du Vibhajyavādin, et l'identité du Vibhajyavādin, ne sont pas claires, Abhidharmakośa, vol. vi, pp. 116-118 et 133-134.

[3] Deuxième livre du Jñānaprasthāna. — Suivent des observations sur le *kalpa* (période cosmique), qui n'est pas exclusivement *rūpa* mais encore les quatre autres *skandhas ;* sur les trois sortes de *kalpa*, etc.

[4] Yuan-houei (Enki), cité Kośa, xii, 7 *b*, par Kiokuga Saeki (voir la trad. iii,

3. Dans la liste des « Cent dharmas » du Lakṣaṇasamaya (Vasubandhu ; P. Kimura, Original and developed doctrines, 1920 ; Muséon, 1906), le temps (*adhvan*, *kāla*) est un *viprayuktasaṃskāra*, le 90e *dharma*. — Mais il est bien entendu que ce qu'on nomme *kāla* (*che*, 1 et 3), c'est la pensée (*vijñāna*) se manifestant sous l'apparence des trois époques (*adhvan*, *che*, 72 et 6), Siddhi, 30, 524.

II. — Dharmas impermanents (anitya) *mais non-instantanés*

1. Le Theravādin (Kathāvatthu, xxii, 8) condamne les Pubbaseliyas et les Aparaseliyas qui disent : « Tous les conditionnés sont impermanents (*anitya*), donc ils sont tous de la durée d'un instant de pensée (*ekacittakṣaṇika*). Leur impermanence étant identique (*samāna*), d'après quelle règle l'un périrait-il vite et l'autre après un long temps ? »

2. Opinion des Saṃmitīyas, Kośa, Vyākhyā, 179. — Le *rūpa* dure (*kālāntarāvasthāyin*), tandis que la pensée et les « mentaux » (*cittacaitta*) sont instantanés (*kṣaṇika*).

3. Vasumitra, Traité des Sectes, thèse 45 des Mahāsāṃghikas : « Les organes matériels (c'est-à-dire la « matière secondaire ») et les grands éléments (c'est-à-dire la « matière primaire ») « évoluent » (*pariṇamati*) ; la pensée et les *dharmas* mentaux n'évoluent pas. » — Commentaire de K'ouei-ki : « Les *dharmas* matériels longtemps continuent, se produisant et périssant : on admet que l'être (*t'i*) du lait évolue en petit lait. La pensée et les *dharmas* mentaux « naissant-périssant en un instant »

139, 187) observe que le temps dans l'*ārūpyadhātu* (sphère immatérielle) n'est que quatre éléments (*skandha*) ; que durant le *kalpa* vide (quand tout l'univers a disparu), le temps n'est que deux éléments, à savoir *rūpa* (l'*ākāśadhātu* ?) et *saṃskāras*. — Sur l'origine du « cercle du vent », Kośa, iii, 139, 210, et Vibhāṣā, 133, p. 691, 2.

(= *kṣaṅabhaṅgura*), l'antérieur ne se change pas en le postérieur. » — Le commentaire de K. Oyama (Kyoto, 1891) cite la Vibhāṣā, 194, p. 996, col. 3, 11 (Étude des opinions fausses du Brahmajāla) : « Les partisans de l'évolution (*pariṇāmavādin*) prétendent que le lait se transforme en petit lait, la graine en pousse, le combustible en cendre. Ce qui existe en continuation de cela est l'évolution de cela : il est faux que ce *dharma*-là périsse et que ce *dharma*-ci naisse. Tous les *dharmas* de leur nature propre (*svabhāva*) tiennent toujours (*nityasthāyin*). » L'opinion des Saṃmitīyas est semblable à celle des Mahāsāṃghikas.

4. Opinion des Vātsīputrīyas, etc., Tattvasaṃgraha, p. 132. — « A leur avis, la pensée (*buddhi*), la flamme, le son, etc., sont instantanés ; mais la terre, le ciel (*vyoman*), etc. ne le sont pas. »

Les « autres » de Kośa, iv, p. 4, qui croient au déplacement, et par conséquent à la non-instantanéité du corps, sont les Vātsīputriyas d'après la Vyākhyā, les Saṃmitīyas d'après Saeki. [1]

5. Saṃghabhadra, 34 début.

Dans la Bonne Loi, il y a des gens qui disent que le corps, la montagne, [2] etc., durent longtemps (*ciraṭṭhitika*) sans périr. Le Sūtra dit : « Il arrive qu'un corps dure dix ans... [3] » Et encore :

[1] Les Saṃmitīyas soutiennent que les combustibles, etc., durent longtemps. Lorsqu'ils périssent c'est en raison de deux causes : le caractère « destruction » qui est interne, le feu, etc., qui est externe. — La durée et la destruction ne sont pas simultanées. — Quant à la pensée et aux mentaux, etc., ils périssent en raison du caractère « destruction » et non pas en raison de causes externes... Le commentaire du Samayabheda (Nanjio 1286) dit : Les *saṃskāras* durent un certain temps ; ils périssent aussi au moment même (*kṣaṇanirodha*). Les Saṃmitīyas concluent de ce Sūtra que la pensée, les mentaux, la flamme, le son périssent aussitôt. Parmi les *dharmas* matériels, les montagnes par exemple, durent un *kalpa*.

[2] Éternité des montagnes ! Les générations passent, vivant quarante mille ans, vivant cent ans ; les Bouddhas se succèdent ; la montagne ne fait que changer de nom. (Saṃyutta, ii, p. 190).

[3] Saṃyutta, ii, p. 94 : « Mieux vaut considérer comme un Soi ce corps fait

« Le *kalala* dure sept jours. [1] » Et encore : « [Les Nāgas] porteurs de la terre (*dharaṇīṃdhara*) durent pendant un demi-*kalpa*. [2] » Ces textes nous enseignent que le corps peut durer longtemps. Par conséquent le mouvement est possible, et le mouvement constitue l'acte corporel. [P. 534, col. 2, l. 17.]

Faux ! Car ces docteurs admettent que la pensée et les mentaux (*cittacaitta*) périssent immédiatement (*kṣaṇanirodha*). Et, de cette donnée, nous pouvons démontrer le *kṣaṇanirodha* du corps et de la montagne qu'ils n'admettent pas. Voici le raisonnement. [P. 534, col. 3.]

Il y a *kṣaṇanirodha* du corps, car on constate que le corps se modifie (*pariṇam*) en fonction des pensée-mentaux. On constate que les caractères (*lakṣaṇa*) du corps, quand se produisent douleur, plaisir, désir, haine, etc., se modifient en fonction des pensées-mentaux. Puisque le corps se modifie en fonction des pensées-mentaux qui sont des *dharmas* qui périssent de moment en moment, il faut que le corps ait *kṣaṇanirodha*. [P. 534, col. 3, l. 3.]

En outre, le corps suit la condition, aise ou malaise, de la pensée. Le corps étant « assumé » (*upātta*) par la pensée qui périt d'instant en instant, sa condition doit être celle de la pensée. Le corps, quand il est muni de pensée (*savijñānaka*), dure longtemps en série ; mais quand la pensée (*vijñāna*) quitte le corps, celui-ci pourrit. Puisque le corps suit la condition de la pensée qui périt d'instant en instant, il faut bien que lui aussi ait *kṣaṇanirodha*. [P. 534, col. 3, l. 7.]

En outre, les textes parlent du corps comme ils parlent de la pensée (*vijñāna*). Le Sūtra dit : « Pensée, esprit, connaissance (*citta* = *manas* = *vijñāna*), à chaque seconde (*kṣaṇa*), à chaque

des quatre grands éléments que non pas la pensée. On voit ce corps durer un an... cent ans, davantage. Mais ce qui porte le nom de pensée (*citta*), esprit (*manas*), connaissance (*vijñāna*), de nuit et de jour, naît autre, périt autre. De même qu'un singe prend une branche, la lâche, en prend une autre... »

[1] Sur le *kalala*, premier stade de l'embryon, Kośa, Index.

[2] Kośa, iii, 275.

minute (*lava*), à chaque heure (*muhūrta*), naît autre, périt autre.[1] » Mais aussi : « Le corps, de moment en moment (? *tattatkṣaṇāvakāśe*) dépérit, vieillit, pourrit, s'épuise.» Et encore : « Bhikṣus, les *saṃskāras* ne s'arrêtent pas ; vite, ils vont à la destruction. » Et encore : « Bhikṣus, les *saṃskāras*, comme une magie, s'accroissent, diminuent, durent un peu et périssent. » Et encore : « Māṇavaka, de la nuit de la conception et jusqu'à la vieillesse, il va vite sans s'arrêter, sans revenir en arrière ». Ces textes et plusieurs autres montrent que tous les *saṃskāras* périssent instantanément et ne durent pas longtemps. [P. 534, col. 2, l. 14.]

Cependant il y a des textes qui parlent de la durée [des *saṃskāras* matériels, montagne, etc.] : parce que ces textes ont en vue les séries homogènes que forment les *saṃskāras*. Ils s'expriment métaphoriquement. Donc il n'y a pas contradiction. [P. 534, col. 3, l. 15.]

Aussi bien plusieurs textes attribuent la durée à la pensée même : « Cette pensée est fixée et ne change pas » ; « La pensée, de la première extase (*dhyāna*), change et entre dans la deuxième » ; « La pensée, une fois domptée, est capable de se fixer ».

En outre, en raison de la longue durée de la douleur, etc., une fois que la douleur, etc., est née, on parle métaphoriquement de sensation prolongée.[2] Aussi bien notre adversaire, qui pense que la lune dure un millénaire, parle métaphoriquement de la nouvelle lune. Il n'est pas permis de prendre pour exactes et réelles des expressions métaphoriques. [P. 534, col. 3, l. 20.]

Autre considération. Quand le caractère (*lakṣaṇa*) est différent, la chose (*dravya*, *lakṣya*) est différente ; la même chose ne peut avoir des caractères différents, car on constate que, quand la chose diffère, le caractère diffère : comme le bœuf et le cheval n'ont pas les mêmes poils. Or, dans une série, les caractères

[1] Comparer Saṃyutta, ii, p. 94-95 ; aussi Aṅguttara, iv, 137 : « Comme une rivière de montagne... il n'y a pas *khaṇa*, *laya*, *muhutta*, où elle se repose, mais elle va... ; la vie des hommes est petite... Ce qui est né ne peut pas ne pas mourir. »

[2] Voir Bukkio Daijiten, 457, 1.

diffèrent : ce qui démontre que la chose aussi diffère. Soient le lait et le petit lait : la couleur est pareille, mais les caractères qui l'accompagnent sont différents ; les choses diffèrent par conséquent. Il y a deux couleurs avec goût doux et goût acide. C'est donc que, [dans la série], d'avant à après, la chose n'est pas la même. De même en va-t-il du corps : d'avant à après, le caractère change : de là nous concluons que, en ce qui concerne la masse des éléments du corps, l'antérieur et le postérieur sont différents. — Le *kṣaṇanirodha* est donc établi. [P. 534, col. 3, l. 27.]

III. — Mesure du kṣaṇa ; *comparaisons*

1. Les bouddhistes, comme tout le monde, font du *kṣaṇa* un temps très court qui est une partie déterminée du jour-nuit ou de l'heure (*muhūrta*). Ainsi compris le *kṣaṇa* vaut un peu plus d'un centième de seconde.

D'après les sources Sarvāstivādin, on a 120 *kṣaṇas* = 1 *tatkṣaṇa*, 60 *tatkṣaṇas* = 1 *lava* ; 30 *lavas* = 1 *muhūrta*. — Dans tous les systèmes, le *muhūrta* est le trentième du jour-nuit. — On a donc : *kṣaṇa* = 0,013333 seconde.

Dans Śārdūlakarṇa (Divya, p. 645), 16 *nimeṣas* (« clin d'œil ») = 1 *kāṣṭhā*, 16 *kāṣṭhās* = 1 *kalā*, 64 *kalās* = 1 *muhūrta*. — Manu a 18 *nimeṣas* = 1 *kāṣṭhā*, 30 *kāṣṭhās* = 1 *kalā*, 30 *kalās* = 1 *muhūrta*. — Nombreuses variantes dans les Purāṇas, Kauṭilīya, Bhāskara qui a 100 *truṭis* = 1 *tatpara*, 30 *tatparas* = 1 *nimeṣa*, 18 *nimeṣas* = 1 *kāṣṭhā*...

Voir G. Thibaut, Astronomie..., 1899, p. 12 ; L. D. Barnett, Antiquities of India, p. 218 ; G. R. Kaye, Arch. Sur. India, vol. 43, 1927, p. 59 (Bakhshālī MS.) ; Cosmologie bouddhique, 1914-1919, p. 309 ; Kośa, iii, 88, 179.

Khaṇa, « instant », dans Aṅguttara, IV, p. 137 : « Il n'y a pas d'instant, de minute (*laya*), d'heure (*muhutta*) où la rivière s'arrête.»

Kṣaṇa, *khaṇa* est le moment favorable, en opposition avec les *akṣaṇas* (Naître dans une période vide de Bouddhas, etc.). C'est le sens du mot dans Dhammapada, 315, où le Pali Text Dict. traduit à tort : « Let not the slightest time be wasted », pour : « Ne laissons pas passer le bon moment. »

2. — Vibhāṣā, 136, p. 701, col. 2, l. 2.

Quelle est la mesure du *kṣaṇa?*

Quelques-uns se réfèrent à la Prajñāpti qui dit : « Une femme, d'âge moyen, quand elle file, touche le fil, ni long, ni court : on dit que cela est la mesure du *tatkṣaṇa.* » Cela ne veut pas dire que le fil soit court ou long. On veut dire que, le fil sortant d'entre les doigts, le temps de sa sortie est le *tatkṣaṇa.*[1]

Nous interrogeons sur le *kṣaṇa.* Pourquoi citer la Prajñāpti[2] et parler du *tatkṣaṇa?*

Parce que, au moyen du grossier, on donne une idée du subtil. Le subtil est difficile à connaître et ne peut être expliqué directement : 120 *kṣaṇas* font 1 *tatkṣaṇa*; 60 *tatkṣaṇas* font 1 *lava* qui vaut donc 7.200 *kṣaṇas*; 30 *lavas* font 1 *muhūrta* qui vaut donc 216.000 *kṣaṇas*; 30 *muhūrtas* font 1 *ahorātra* (jour-nuit) qui vaut donc 6.500.000 moins 20.000 *kṣaṇas.* — Le corps formé des cinq éléments (*skandhas*), un jour et une nuit, durant cette période, naît, périt, est impermanent. [P. 701, col. 2, l. 13.]

Il y en a qui disent : « Ceci est grossier. Ce n'est pas la mesure du *kṣaṇa.* Mon opinion est que 64 *kṣaṇas* passent dans le temps qu'un homme fort fait claquer les doigts. »

[1] Je comprends mal la version chinoise. L'original, qui nous a été conservé dans le Śārdūlakarṇa, Divyāvadāna, p. 644, est obscur : *tadyathā striyā nātidīrghanātihrasvakartinyāḥ sūtrodyāma evaṃdīrghas tatkṣaṇaḥ.* — *udyāma*, the act of erecting or stretching out. — Voir Kośa, iii, p. 179, note.

[2] Le Prajñāptiśāstra est un des Abhidharmas des Sarvāstivādins ; voir les notes de Takakusu et Stcherbatsky dans JPTS., 1905, pp. 75, 116, et P. Cordier, Catalogue du Tandjour, p. 392. — Une analyse de la première et de la deuxième partie, Lokaprajñāpti, Kāraṇaprajñāpti, dans l'Appendice de Cosmologie bouddhique, 1914-1919, pp. 263, 309, *kṣaṇa*, *tatkṣaṇa* (*de yi skad cig*).

Il y en a qui disent : « Non. D'après moi, deux hommes forts rompent en les tirant des fils de Bénarès. Le temps de la rupture, c'est la durée du *kṣaṇa.* »

Il y en a qui disent : « Non. D'après moi, deux hommes tiennent tendus des fils de Bénarès, et un homme, au moyen d'un dur couteau de Chine bien affilé, alertement les tranche : le temps de la rupture, c'est la durée du kṣaṇa. »

Il y en a qui disent : « Ceci encore est grossier. Ce n'est pas la mesure du *kṣaṇa :* la vraie mesure, Bhagavat ne l'a point dite. — Comment savons-nous cela ? — Par le Sūtra [1] qui dit : « Un certain bhikṣu vint auprès de Bhagavat, le salua, se tint de côté et demanda combien vite naissent et périssent les facteurs vitaux (*āyuḥsaṃskāras*). Le Bouddha dit : « Je peux le dire, mais tu ne peux comprendre. » Le bhikṣu demanda s'il y a, ou non, une comparaison qui en donne une idée. Le Bouddha dit : « Oui et je vais te la dire. Supposons quatre bons archers placés dos à dos et faisant face aux quatre points cardinaux. Vient un homme alerte qui leur dit : « Tirez en même temps ; je suis capable de prendre les flèches, et aucune ne tombera à terre. » D'après toi, cet homme serait-il, oui ou non, rapide ? » Le bhikṣu répondit que cet homme serait très rapide. Bhagavat reprit : « Sa rapidité n'approche pas de celle des Yakṣas terrestres [2] ; la rapidité des Yakṣas terrestres n'approche pas de celle des Yakṣas de l'atmosphère ; la rapidité des Yakṣas de l'atmosphère n'approche pas de celle des dieux de la suite des Quatre-Grands-Rois ; la rapidité de ces dieux n'approche pas de celle des roues du soleil

[1] Recension allongée du Dhanuggaha de Saṃyutta, ii, 265, avec la morale : « Les facteurs vitaux périssent encore plus vite. Par conséquent, ô bhikkhus, soyez attentifs ! »

On a les archers, et l'homme alerte ; puis la vitesse (*java*) de lune-soleil, puis celle des *devatās* qui courent devant les lune-soleil (*purato dhāvanti*).

[2] Yakṣas terrestres, *ti-hing*, *pṛthivīcara*, *bhūmicara ?* Sans doute les *bhaumas* de Vyutpatti, 156.

Yakṣas de l'atmosphère, *kong-hing*, *vihāyasagāmin*, Vyutpatti, 126, 154, *antarikṣavāsin* de 156.

Les *kien-hing* peuvent être des *dṛḍhagāmin* (?).

et de la lune ; la rapidité de ces roues n'approche pas de celle des *devaputras kien-hing* qui courent devant le char des roues du soleil et de la lune.[1] La vitesse [toujours accrue] de la série des dieux en commençant par ceux-ci, la vitesse de la naissance et de la destruction des facteurs vitaux est encore plus grande. Le flux des *kṣaṇas* n'a pas d'arrêt. » Nous savons, par ce texte que Bhagavat n'a pas dit la vraie mesure du *kṣaṇa*. — Pourquoi ne l'a-t-il pas dite ? — Parce que personne n'est capable de la comprendre. — Śāriputra n'est-il pas capable de la comprendre ? — Oui. Mais cette connaissance est sans utilité. C'est pourquoi le Bouddha, qui n'enseigne pas en vain, n'a pas expliqué. [P. 701, col. 3, l. 8.]

IV. — Conflit Vaibhāṣika-Sautrāntika

Mais il ne s'agit pas ici d'un *kṣaṇa* mesurable, mais du *kṣaṇa* philosophique, de l'instant. Que veut-on dire quand on dit que les choses sont « instantanées » ?

Kośa, iii, 177 (kārikā 85) : « L'instant est la limite du temps, comme l'atome est la limite de la matière et la syllabe la limite du nom. »[2]

Les Sautrāntikas acceptent cette définition des Sarvāstivādins-Vaibhāṣikas. Mais ils l'entendent à leur manière.

Pour les Sarvāstivādins, le temps — exactement l'existence des choses ou *dharmas* — est un discontinu : il est formé de points ou d'atomes temporels dont la durée extrêmement courte est cependant appréciable. On peut dire, pour se faire une idée de leur idée, que l'instant est le temps requis pour l'apparition

[1] « qui courent devant » d'après le pāli ; nous avons *tao-in*, conduire-guider, montrer le chemin. — Variante dans la citation d'Atthasālinī, 60 (Expositor, 80) : « ... greater is the speed of the Yama God (var. Yāma) who runs before the sun and the moon. »

[2] Voir Bhojarāja ad Yogasūtra, iii, 52 ; Ṣaḍdarśana-samuccaya, éd. Suali, p. 28.

et la disparition d'un phénomène psychique, de la sensation par exemple.

Pour les Sautrāntikas, l'existence est un continu : l'instant est une coupe arbitraire et idéale dans la durée d'une « série » (*saṃtāna* ou « continu ») ; les instants, postulats imaginaires, sont en nombre infini dans la durée la plus courte.

Tandis que le Sarvāstivādin accorde une certaine durée à la chose instantanée, la durée nécessaire à l'activité, le Sautrāntika enseigne qu'il n'y a que des instants de naissance (*utpattikṣaṇa*) ; on ne peut pas dire que la naissance (*utpattibhāva*) soit différente de la destruction (*vināśabhāva*).[1] L'activité (*kriyā*) de la chose instantanée réside toute dans son existence même, existence causée et causante.[2]

Le Sautrāntika admet naissance, durée, etc. en ce qui regarde la série, et aussi, en manière de dire, en ce qui concerne les moments de la série : le moment ultérieur ressemble au moment antérieur, donc le moment antérieur dure ; le moment ultérieur diffère du moment antérieur, donc le moment antérieur vieillit ou change. Mais, à parler franc, le moment ne dure pas, il périt immédiatement après être né (*utpattyanantaranirodha*).

V. — Diverses définitions du Sautrāntika

Vasubandhu, commentant la kārikā, iii, 85, p. 177, donne deux définitions : « Quelle est la dimension de l'instant ? — 1. Les conditions étant présentes, le temps qu'il faut pour qu'un *dharma* prenne son être (*yāvad dharmasya ātmalābhaḥ*) ; ou bien 2. un

[1] Voir le Siddhānta analysé par Wassilieff, p. 305 (278). On a fol. 160 *a* 6 de l'édition tibétaine : *skye baḥi skad cig tsam kho na yin paḥi phyir* | *de yaṅ skye baḥi ṅo bo yaṅ gzhan la ḥjig paḥi ṅo bo yaṅ gzhan zhes brjod par mi nus paḥi phyir.*

[2] *kṣaṇikāḥ sarvasaṃskārā asthirāṇāṃ kutaḥ kriyā* | *bhūtir yaisāṃ kriyā saiva.* Cité Tattvasaṃgraha, p. 11, avec la mauvaise lecture *yeṣām.*

dharma étant en marche, le temps qu'il faut (*yāvat*) pour qu'il aille d'un atome à un autre atome.[1] »

a) Première définition.

1. Saṃghabhadra, 32 début, p. 521, col. 2, approuve et commente la définition de la kārikā, que l'instant est la limite du temps, le plus petit temps (*paramanikṛṣṭa kāla*) : « Si on coupe la matière (*rūpa*) par l'esprit, on arrive à l'atome, qui est la plus petite matière parce qu'il ne peut être coupé. De même, si on coupe le nom (*nāman*) et le temps, on arrive à la syllabe (*vyañjana*), à l'instant. » — Mais il condamne la glose du Sautrāntika (Vasubandhu) : « Le moment (*k'ing*, 181 et 2), les conditions étant réunies, le *dharma* obtient son être (*t'i : ātman*). »

« Il faut examiner si, avant la naissance [que produisent les conditions], l'être du *dharma* existe oui ou non. Les Ābhidharmikas disent que, quand les conditions concourent, le *dharma* obtient naissance : ce n'est pas [que naisse] sa « nature propre » (*svabhāva* = *t'i* = *ātman*). Mais, dira-t-on, dans cette hypothèse à quoi bon la naissance ?... »

Suit l'explication que nous connaissons : la naissance, pour le *dharma*, ce n'est pas « l'acquisition de son soi » (*ātmalābha*), mais l'arrivée à l'état de présent de ce soi.

Cependant « Le Sautrāntika ne précise pas quel est le temps de cette acquisition de son soi. A la question : « Quelle est la dimension de l'instant ? », on devrait répondre : « L'instant est tel... » Les docteurs de la Vibhāṣā disent que la dimension de l'instant n'a pas été dite par le Bouddha, car il ne vit personne capable de le comprendre, mais qu'on a des comparaisons, que 65 instants passent dans le temps qu'un homme fort fait claquer les doigts. »

Saṃghabhadra écarte l'explication Sautrāntika ; il ne dit pas : « Le temps qu'il faut pour qu'un *dharma* arrive à l'état de présent » ; il définit l'instant par le présent (ci-dessous p. 152).

[1] La Vyākhyā est muette, mais la version tibétaine est claire : ***rkyen rnams thsogs na ji srid du chos kyi bdag ñid thob pa am | chos ḥgro ba na ji srid du rdul phra rab nas rdul phra rab gzham du ḥgro ba yin no.***

2. — Vasubandhu, Kośa, iv, 4.

Les Vātsīputrīyas définissent l'acte corporel (*kāyavijñapti*) comme un mouvement ou un déplacement (*gati*). Vasubandhu répond : « Non; car les conditionnés (*saṃskṛta*), parmi lesquels les parties matérielles, sont instantanés, *kṣaṇika*, et par conséquent périssent à l'endroit où ils naissent». — « Qu'est-ce que le *kṣaṇa?* L'*ātmalābha* périssant immédiatement.[1] Ce qui a le *kṣaṇa* est nommé *kṣaṇika*, comme l'homme qui a un bâton (*daṇḍa*) est nommé *daṇḍika*. »

Saṃghabhadra (p. 533, col. 2, l. 21) cite la définition de Vasubandhu, et dit : « Cette explication est mauvaise, car on ne peut dire [que le *kṣaṇika*, la chose instantanée, diffère du *kṣaṇa*, instant] comme l'homme diffère du bâton. La comparaison manque de similitude. Il n'y a pas de *dharma* qui diffère de l'*ātmalābha* (« prise de son être ») qui par nature périt immédiatement. Comment dire que [le *dharma*] a *kṣaṇa* comme l'homme a bâton ? »

Le Tattvasaṃgraha, p. 142, cite Uddyotakara (Nyāyavārttika, 418) et le réfute. Uddyotakara dit : « La notion de possession que comporte le mot *kṣaṇika* (« muni du *kṣaṇa* », « de qui est le *kṣaṇa* ») est inadmissible. Si on comprend *kṣaṇa* dans le sens de *kṣaya*, destruction : « Celui qui a *kṣaṇa* est dit *kṣaṇika* », cela ne va pas, vu la différence des temps. Quand il y a destruction, la chose n'est pas périssante (*kṣayin*). Si *kṣaṇa* est défini comme un existant (*bhāva*) caractérisé par la destruction (*vināśa*) immédiate[2], cela ne va pas non plus... Si enfin on définit *kṣaṇika* comme « ce qui dure le temps d'un *kṣaṇa* ; le *kṣaṇa*

[1] *ātmalābho 'nantaravināśī kṣaṇaḥ | sa yasyāsti sa kṣanikaḥ |*. — Les MSS. de Paris ont *ātmalābho 'nantaravināśī*. [Et j'ai jadis corrigé *ātmalābhād anantaravināśī* ou *°vināśo :* « Le *kṣaṇa* est la destruction immédiatement consécutive à l'acquisition de l'être », « ce qui périt immédiatement après l'acquisition de son être ».] — Le Tattvasaṃgraha, p. 143, qui cite Vasubandhu : *ātmalābhānantaravināśī*. — Mais Wogihara, Vyākhyā, 345, a la bonne lecture, comme le prouvent les gloses de Saṃghabhadra qui clairement fait de *ātmalābha* le sujet de la phrase.

L'*ātmalābha*, — « acquisition de l'être », « prise de l'existence », « coming into existence, birth » (Monier Williams), — n'est pas autre chose que le *dharma* instantané lui-même ; équivalents : *svabhāva, svarūpa* (Tattvasaṃgraha).

On a donc : *kṣaṇa*, instant, « c'est l'être périssant immédiatement ».

« Ce qui a le *kṣaṇa* », *kṣaṇikaḥ kṣaṇe bhavaḥ kṣaṇo 'syāsti vā.* (Vyākhyā.)

[2] Lire : *atha punar bhāvo 'nantaravināśeṇa viśiṣyamāṇaḥ ;* au lieu de *atha punar bhāvānantara°*

est le temps le plus réduit ; ce qui dure ce temps est dit *kṣaṇika*[1] », cela ne va pas non plus, car il est admis que le temps (*kāla*) n'est que « désignation » (*saṃjñāmātra*) et une pure désignation ne peut caractériser une chose (*vastu*). — Là-dessus la kārikā 377 :

« L'être (*svarūpa*) de la chose ne dure pas (= périt) immédiatement après la production : c'est ce qu'on nomme *kṣaṇa*. Est *kṣaṇika* ce qui a le *kṣaṇa*. »

On nomme *kṣaṇa* l'être (*svabhāva* = *svarūpa*) de la chose (*vastu*) ; est *kṣaṇika* ce qui a le *kṣaṇa*. Comme dit Vasubandhu : « La prise du soi (*ātmalābha* = *svabhāva*) périssant immédiatement, c'est le *kṣaṇa*... » — Mais, dira-t-on, la chose (le *kṣaṇika*) n'est pas distincte du *svabhāva* (ou *ātmalābha*, qui est le *kṣaṇa*). Et l'idée : « Ceci a cela » suppose la distinction. — Là-dessus la kārikā 378 : « Même s'il n'y a pas distinction en fait (*arthabheda*), on peut dire que l'un a l'autre, car les mots reposent sur la convention arbitraire. »

Même quand il n'y a pas distinction réelle (*vāstava bheda*) — par exemple : le corps du buste — on emploie le génitif en raison d'une distinction imaginaire. Car les mots ne sont pas conformes à la nature des choses : ils sont soumis au désir de celui qui parle... Les savants ont fixé le mot *kṣaṇika* pour désigner la chose (*vastumātra*) qui ne dure pas au delà de sa production. Qu'il corresponde ou non à une idée, cela n'a pas d'importance.

b) Seconde définition.

Cette définition, qui explique l'infiniment petit de la durée en fonction de l'infiniment petit de l'étendue, est connue par des sources jaïnas.

Le *kṣaṇa* des Jaïnas se nomme *samaya*. Il faut un nombre incalculable de *samayas* pour faire une *āvali* ou *āvalikā* qui est la plus petite durée appréciable. On a une définition du *samaya* dans le Tattvārthādhigama d'Umāsvāti, iv, 15, éd. de la Bibl. Ind., p. 103, trad. de Jacobi, ZDMG., 40, p. 320 : Das Zeitatom, wenn man so sagen darf, ist der *samaya*, die Zeit, die ein Atom in langsamster Bewegung gebraucht, um sich um seine eigene Körperlänge weiterzubewegen (*tatra paramasūkṣmakriyasya sarvajaghanyagatipariṇatasya paramāṇoḥ svāvagāhanakṣetravyatikramakālaḥ samaya iti*) : « Le *samaya* est très difficile à comprendre, indescriptible. Les Jinas le savent mais ne l'enseignent pas. » Même notion dans le Gaṇitasārasaṃgraha, I, 32 (Traité de mathématiques publié et traduit par M. Rangācārya, Madras, 1912) : « The time in which an atom (moving) goes beyond another atom (immediately next to it) is a *samaya* » (*aṇur aṇvantaraṃ kāle vyatikrāmati yāvati | sa kālaḥ samayaḥ...*)

[1] Comparer Ṣaḍdarśanasamuccaya, p. 28 : ... *paramanikṛṣṭaḥ kālaḥ kṣaṇaḥ tatrabhavāḥ kṣaṇikāḥ kṣaṇamātrāvasthitaya ity arthaḥ* |

VI. — La destruction n'a pas de cause

La destruction immédiate s'ensuit logiquement du principe : « La destruction n'a pas de cause », *ākasmiko bhāvānāṃ vināśaḥ, ahetuko vināśaḥ, akasmādbhavo vināśaḥ*. On nous dit que ce principe est le bien propre du Sautrāntika, et le Sarvāstivādin, en effet, dit que la destruction a une cause. Mais cette cause est une cause intime, constitutionnelle, contemporaine à la naissance : c'est un des « caractères » (*lakṣaṇa*) du conditionné ; la cause de la destruction est la naissance même.

a) Les sources relatives à la destruction spontanée, immédiate, sont nombreuses.

Vedāntasūtra, 2, 2, 23 ; Nyāyavārttika, 3, 2, 14 ; Nyāyavārttika-tātparyaṭīkā (Viz. S. S.), p. 383 ; Mimāṃsāślokavārttika, p. 736. Un Sūtra des Sautrāntikas cité Ṣaḍdarśanasamuccaya, éd. Suali, p. 46.[1] — Yogaśāstra, 34, p. 433 ; Karmasiddhiśāstra, pp. 781-782.

Kośa, ii, 234 ; iv, 5-8 (discussion de la théorie du mouvement du Vātsīputrīya).

Tattvasaṃgraha, p. 140.

Nyāyabindu, trad. et commentaire de Stcherbatsky, Buddhist Logic, II, 93.

Madhyamakavṛtti, 173, 412 (Contre le Vaibhāṣika : « Celui qui prétend que la destruction a une cause, parce que la destruction est un des caractères du conditionné... »)

b) Vibhāṣā, p. 105, col. 1.

Le *dharma* obtient naissance parce qu'il y a des causes-conditions. Doit-on dire que, de même, le *dharma* périt parce qu'il y a des causes-conditions ?

Le Dārṣṭāntika Bhadanta dit : « La naissance dépend des causes-conditions, non pas la destruction. Comme, quand un

[1] pañcemāni bhikṣavaḥ saṃjñāmātraṃ pratijñāmātraṃ saṃvṛtimātraṃ vyavahāramātram | katamāni pañca | atīto 'dhvā anāgato 'dhvā sahetukavināśaḥ ākāśaṃ pudgala iti.

homme tire à l'arc, pour lancer la flèche, il faut de la force ; mais la chute de la flèche n'est pas telle.[1] Comme, pour mettre en mouvement la roue du potier, il faut de la force, mais l'arrêt de la roue n'est pas tel. »

Les maîtres de l'Abhidharma disent : « Naissance et destruction du *dharma* dépendent, l'une et l'autre, des causes-conditions. Car la destruction, comme la naissance, a un emploi (activité, œuvre : *kārya*). »

[Le Bhadanta] a cité des comparaisons (flèche, roue du potier) : comment les expliquer ?

Pas n'est besoin de les expliquer, car elles ne se trouvent pas dans l'Écriture (Tripiṭaka). Les choses (*dharma*) vulgaires et philosophiques (*ārya*) sont différentes : on ne peut décider des secondes d'après les premières. D'ailleurs, c'est en raison de causes que la flèche tombe, que la roue s'arrête. — Causes de la chute de la flèche : heurt (?),[2] cuirasse, but, etc. ; s'il n'y a pas d'autres causes,[3] la courbure de l'arc ; si on ne tirait pas d'abord à l'arc, comment y aurait-il chute ? — Causes de l'arrêt de la roue : la main, le bâton, etc. ; s'il n'y a pas d'autres causes, ce qui met la roue en mouvement ; si d'abord elle ne tournait pas, comment y aurait-il arrêt ?...

c) Saṃghabhadra, p. 533, col. 3, l. 4.

Comment savons-nous que les conditionnés sont tous « périssant instantanément » (*kṣaṇabhaṅgura*) ?

[1] La Madhyamakavṛtti, p. 222, cite une stance prâcrite que Kumārila (Mīmāṃsātantravārttika, Ben. S. S., p. 171) donne comme un exemple de jargon (voir JRAS., 1902, p. 370) : « De même que, une motte de terre étant jetée en haut, il y a une cause de sa projection en haut ; mais il n'y a pas de cause de sa chute en dehors de la cause de sa projection. » La projection est la cause de la chute ; pas d'autre cause. De même ici, c'est la naissance que nous décrivons comme la cause de la destruction. Il est donc faux que la destruction soit sans cause.

Sur le problème, si compliqué, de la chute plus ou moins rapide de la flèche, de la motte de terre, Kośa, ii, 200, 217, iv, 102 ; Nyāyavārttika, 420.

[2] *p'ai*, 64 et 8 ou 75 et 8.

[3] *hetvantara*, c'est-à-dire une cause extérieure.

Le Sautrāntika (Vasubandhu) dit[1] : « La destruction des conditionnés ne dépend pas d'une cause (*hetvanapekṣa*). Pourquoi ? Ce qui dépend d'une cause est un fruit (*phala*). La destruction est « non-existence » (*abhāva*) et n'est donc pas un fruit. Donc elle ne dépend pas d'une cause. Ceci posé, il s'ensuit que, aussitôt né, le *dharma* périt. S'il ne périt pas d'abord (ou tout de suite), il ne périra pas plus tard, puisque, avant et après, il est le même. [2] » [P. 533, col. 3, l. 10.]

Cette explication ne vaut rien... Il est faux que la destruction ne dépende pas d'une cause. Je donne donc l'explication suivante. [P. 533, col. 3, l. 29.]

La destruction du *dharma* ne dépend pas d'une cause adventice (*āgantuka*). Puisqu'elle ne dépend pas d'une cause adventice, aussitôt né, le *dharma* périt. S'il ne périssait pas d'abord (*ādau*), il ne périrait pas ensuite ; parce que, ensuite et d'abord, la cause intime[3] reste la même. Puisque nous constatons qu'ensuite il y a destruction, nous savons que, antérieurement, le *dharma* périt d'instant en instant. — On répond : « Non, parce que le monde constate : il constate que le bois existe antérieurement ; que, rencontrant ensuite une cause adventice, le feu, il va à la destruction, va à l'inexistence, n'est plus visible. Or il n'y a pas de moyen de connaissance supérieure à l'évidence (*pratyakṣa*). Il est donc faux que la destruction du *dharma* ne dépende pas d'une cause adventice. » — Ne doit-il pas en être [du bois et de tous les *dharmas*] comme du son de la cloche et de la flamme de la lampe ? Indépendamment de la main ou du vent, le son et la flamme périssent d'instant en instant en raison d'une cause intime : la rencontre de la main et du vent fait qu'un nouveau son, une nouvelle flamme ne naît pas : après, son et flamme n'existent pas et ne peuvent être perçus. De même, le combustible périt

[1] Kośa, iv, p. 5.

[2] La *yeou-sing* (*sat-tā*) est pareille.

[3] Je traduis *tchou-in*, « cause royale », par opposition à *k'o-in*, cause étrangère, extérieure.

d'instant en instant en raison d'une cause intime; sa rencontre postérieure avec le feu, alors qu'il est dans la « condition détruite », n'est pas une autre cause [de destruction] : si on ne le perçoit plus, c'est parce qu'il ne naît plus à nouveau. Donc ce problème relève du raisonnement, non de l'évidence. — Quel raisonnement? — Comme la naissance, la destruction n'est pas sans cause. On ne voit pas que les *dharmas* conditionnés naissent sans dépendre de deux causes, l'intime et l'adventice : l'embryon (*kalala*), le bourgeon, le mur, la connaissance (*vijñāna*), etc. ne naissent qu'en dépendance du concours de conditions extérieures, semence, sang, eau, terre, organe, etc. Si la destruction du combustible avait lieu en dépendance de causes adventices, il faudrait que les *dharmas* conditionnés ne périssent que postérieurement, en dépendance de causes adventices, comme c'est le cas pour la naissance. Or le monde constate que la pensée, la flamme, le son périssent, indépendamment de causes adventices, en raison d'une cause intime. Donc tous les *dharmas* conditionnés périssent indépendamment d'une cause adventice ; donc ils périssent aussitôt nés parce que la cause de destruction est toujours là. Donc la destruction instantanée (*kṣaṇanirodha*) est démontrée. [P. 534, col. 1, l. 18.]

VII. — Doctrine du Vaibhāṣika

1. L'instant du Sautrāntika — c'est-à-dire le *dharma*, puisque le temps n'existe pas en soi — est un infiniment petit. La chose, exactement, périt en naissant.

L'instant du Sarvāstivādin — c'est-à-dire le *dharma* du Sarvāstivādin — diffère. Le *dharma*, une fois né, dure pendant un temps très réduit avant de disparaître. Cependant le *dharma* est instantané.

Le Sūtra, rédigé à une époque où l'on considérait les choses comme impermanentes (*anitya*) et non pas comme instantanées (*kṣaṇika*), dit que « le conditionné (*saṃskṛta*) a trois caractères (*lakṣaṇa*) conditionnés, à savoir la naissance, la durée-transformation (*sthiti-anyathātva*), l'impermanence (*anityatā*) ou destruction (*nirodha*).[1]

L'école du Sarvāstivāda enseigne que le deuxième caractère se divise en deux : durée et transformation (Le Majjhima ne parle-t-il pas d'*upaṭṭhiti?*). Et elle considère les caractères comme des entités (*dharma*) qui font naître, durer, dépérir, périr le *dharma*. C'est-à-dire : la naissance fait passer le *dharma* du futur dans le présent ; la durée l'y maintient...

Est-ce à dire que le *dharma* soit « de quatre instants »? Telle est la doctrine qu'une source jaïna attribue au Sāṃmitīya[2] et nous savons que les docteurs de Ceylan mettent trois instants dans un instant de pensée. Mais la doctrine du Sarvāstivāda, qui distingue naissance, durée, vieillesse, veut que ces trois ne forment qu'un présent indivisible, un présent où on ne peut distinguer l'antérieur et le postérieur.

2. — Saṃghabhadra, p. 533, col. 2, l. 7.

Qu'est-ce que le *kṣaṇa?* — Le plus petit temps (*kāla*), qui ne peut plus être divisé en une partie antérieure et postérieure. — Qu'est-ce que le temps? — Les conditions (*avasthā*) différentes de passé, futur, présent. Nous savons par là que le temps est une spécification (*viśeṣa*) des *saṃskāras* (ou « conditionnés »). Et la plus petite condition des *saṃskāras* est nommée *kṣaṇa*.

Il est donc dit : « C'est nommé *kṣaṇa* parce que c'est le temps

[1] Sources dans Kośa, ii, 223, Vyākhyā, 223. — Dans Aṅguttara, I, 152 : production, disparition (*vaya* = *vyaya*), changement de ce qui dure (*ṭhitassa aññathattam*) ; mais dans Majjhima, III, 25 : *uppajjanti, upaṭṭhahanti, abbhattham gacchanti*. — Saṃyutta, II, 274, v, 180. — Kathāvatthu, trad. 55. — Madhyamakavṛtti, 145.

[2] Le Ṣaḍdarśanasamuccaya (de Haribhadra, éd. L. Suali, p. 46) fait dire au Sāṃmitīya : « La chose est de quatre instants (*catuḥkṣaṇikaṃ vastu*) : la naissance l'engendre, la durée le fait durer, la vieillesse le fait vieillir, la destruction (*vināśa*) le détruit. » — On sait que, dans ce texte, les Sāṃmitīyas représentent le Petit Véhicule à l'exclusion des Sautrāntikas.

le plus réduit (*paramanikṛṣṭa*). » Le [mot] *kṣaṇa* désigne seulement la condition du *dharma* munie d'activité (*sakāritrāvasthā*) : donc le présent. Le *dharma* présent, ayant cette mesure de durée (? *sthitibhāgapramāṇa*), est nommé *kṣaṇika*, instantané, comme « un fils d'un mois » (*māsikaputravat*).

Ou bien il est nommé *kṣaṇa* parce que détruisant. Il est la cause qui fait périr les *dharmas* : c'est le caractère « impermanence » (*anityatālakṣaṇa*) qui détruit le *dharma*. Le *dharma*, qui en est accompagné (*tatsahacara*), est nommé *kṣaṇika*.

Ou bien le monde dit *kṣaṇika* dans le sens de *śūnyaka* (qui a des vides, qui manque de). La condition présente, il n'y a rien qui la tienne pour qu'elle ne périsse pas ; elle ne peut durer ; elle est donc dite *kṣaṇika*.

Ou bien le monde dit *akṣaṇa* dans le sens de « manque de loisir ». On nomme *akṣaṇika* celui qui, occupé par d'autres affaires, n'a pas le loisir de s'attacher à soi-même. C'est seulement le temps présent qui doit avoir quelque loisir puisqu'il prend son fruit. Donc *kṣaṇika*.

A la vérité toutes les conditions de la série du conditionné ont les divers temps, minutes (*lava*), etc. De tous les temps, le *kṣaṇa* est le plus réduit. Le *dharma* l'a : il est donc nommé *kṣaṇika*. [P. 533, col. 2, l. 21.]

Mais le Sautrāntika dit... (Ci-dessus, p. 145.)

3. Vasubandhu (Kośa, ii, p. 232) prête au Sarvāstivādin une définition du *kṣaṇa* que Saṃghabhadra, qui relève soigneusement toutes les erreurs du Kośa, passe sous silence (voir p. 409, col. 3). D'après le texte original, cité dans la Vyākhyā (p. 178, l. 18) : *eṣa eva hi naḥ kṣaṇa iti kāryaparisamāptilakṣaṇaḥ*, avec la glose : *na tūtpattyanantaravināśalakṣaṇa ity arthaḥ* : « Voilà pour vous le *kṣaṇa* : il a pour définition l'achèvement de l'œuvre [du *dharma* : c'est-à-dire la projection du fruit], non pas la destruction immédiatement consécutive à la naissance. » — Mais, d'après la version

de Hiuan-tsang [1] : *lakṣaṇakāryaparisamāptir eṣa eva hi naḥ kṣaṇaḥ*, et d'après Paramārtha : *caturlakṣaṇakāryaparisamāptir*... : « Notre *kṣaṇa*, c'est l'achèvement de l'œuvre des caractères » ou « des quatre caractères ». Ce qui donne : « L'instant, c'est le *dharma* dont la naissance, la durée, la vieillesse, la disparition sont achevées. »

4. — Saṃghabhadra, p. 409, col. 2, fin.

« [Quand] les quatre caractères [naissance, durée, vieillesse, destruction ou impermanence] produisent leur activité [ou accomplissent leur opération], la condition (*avasthā*) [du *dharma*] n'est pas la même. Dans le temps [où le *dharma* est] « naissant » (*jāyamāna*), le caractère « naissance » produit son activité. Quand il est arrivé à la condition « né », les trois, durée, vieillesse, destruction, ensemble, simultanément, chacune produit une activité différente. Donc les quatre diffèrent quant à l'époque et quant à l'activité. On ne peut objecter que le *dharma*, un, aura simultanément naissance, durée, vieillesse, destruction. Au temps où le *dharma* est « périssant » (*nirudhyamānakāle*), en raison d'un autre caractère, la durée, cause prépondérante, le *dharma* (*lakṣyadharma*) dure pendant un petit temps et peut projeter son fruit. Et dans le même temps, en raison d'un autre caractère, la vieillesse, cause prépondérante, il se fait que le *dharma* dépérit. Et dans le même temps, en raison d'un autre caractère, la destruction, cause prépondérante, il se fait que le *dharma* périt. Donc il n'y a pas contradiction à ce que ces trois [produisent] en même temps [leur activité]. » [P. 409, col. 3, l. 8.]

Le vice de ce système est évident. « De deux choses l'une, dit Vasubandhu. [2] Ou bien ces trois, durée, vieillesse, destruction,

[1] Le contexte est en faveur de la version chinoise.

[2] Je résume Kośa, ii, pp. 231-233. — Kośa, ii, p. 226, l. 5, réfuté par Saṃghabhadra, p. 406, col. 2, l. 16 ; ii, 227, 3, Saṃghabhadra, 407, 2, 12 ; ii, 228, 1, Saṃghabhadra, 407, 3, 9 ; ii, 229, 15, Saṃghabhadra, 408, 3, 7. — Voir aussi 409, 3.

exercent leur opération successivement, et, dans cette hypothèse, comment pouvez-vous professer la doctrine du *kṣaṇanirodha*, de la destruction instantanée ? Le *dharma* passe par trois états, durant, dépérissant, périssant : il dure donc trois *kṣaṇas*. Ou bien ces trois exercent leur opération simultanément : il faudra nous expliquer comment le *dharma*, en même temps, dure, dépérit, disparaît. Direz-vous que votre instant n'a pas pour définition « destruction immédiatement consécutive à la naissance », mais « achèvement de l'opération [des durée, vieillesse, destruction] », nous demanderons pourquoi, naissant simultanément à vieillesse-destruction, la durée exerce son opération de faire durer avant que la vieillesse fasse vieillir et la destruction périr... »

5. — La durée d'après la Vibhāṣā.

[Si on reconnaît aux conditionnés (*saṃskṛta*) le caractère de « durée » (*sthitilakṣaṇa*)], comment expliquer le Sūtra : « Bhikṣus, les conditionnés (*saṃskāras*) ne durent pas » ?

Le Sūtra dit qu'ils ne durent pas parce qu'ils ne durent pas longtemps ; il ne veut pas dire que le caractère de durée pendant un « instant » (*kṣaṇasthitilakṣaṇa*) leur manque complètement. [P. 201, col. 2, l. 26.]

Le Bhadanta Vasumitra dit : « Le Sūtra dit qu'ils ne durent pas pour écarter la durée au delà d'un instant. Il ne veut pas dire que les conditionnés n'ont pas la durée d'un instant. S'ils ne duraient absolument pas, Bhagavat n'aurait pas établi les désignations de temps (*adhvan*) et d'instant (*kṣaṇa*). »

Il dit encore : « Le caractère de durée pendant un instant est subtil, difficile à connaître, difficile à concevoir (*prajñapyate*). C'est pourquoi le Sūtra dit que les conditionnés ne durent pas : la mesure d'un instant est connue du Bouddha, elle n'est pas du domaine des Śrāvakas et des Pratyekabuddhas. Dans le temps où on étend le bras, l'homme à locomotion magique va d'ici jusqu'au sommet de la sphère du Rūpa : dans cet intervalle de temps, si cet homme n'était pas une série [d'instants], il ne pourrait aller d'ici jusque-là. Il est inadmissible qu'un *dharma* unique (dont la durée est d'un instant) « change et tourne » jusque-là ; ou d'ici, (sans changer), franchisse et aille jusque-là. Par conséquent, c'est une série, naissant et périssant d'instant en instant [et de lieu en lieu] qui va d'ici jusque-là. Dans cet intervalle, la mesure de l'instant est extrêmement subtile : le Bouddha seul la connaît. C'est pourquoi il est dit que les conditionnés ne durent pas. » [P. 201, col. 3, l. 7.]

Le Bhadanta dit : « Les conditionnés, après être nés, durent un petit temps ; cependant la vieillesse et l'impermanence (*iarā*, *anityatā*) vite les détériore-détruit (*upahan*, *nirudh*). C'est pourquoi il est dit qu'ils ne durent pas. »

Il en est qui disent : « Les *dharmas* conditionnés n'ont pas le caractère de durée. » — Comment alors expliquer ce qui est dit ci-dessus ? A savoir : « Les naissance-durée-vieillesse-impermanence des *rūpas* [sont-elles autre chose ou la même chose que les *rūpas ?*] » Il faut dire : « Les naissance-vieillesse-impermanence des *rūpas...* » — On ne devrait pas dire « durée » ; on dit toutefois « durée » : il faut savoir que « durée » est un autre nom de « vieillesse ». Comme la naissance (*jāti*) est nommée « production » (*utpāda*), et l'impermanence (*anityatā*) « destruction » (*nirodha*), de même la vieillesse (*jarā*) est nommée « durée » (*sthiti*). C'est pourquoi, dans l'énumération des trois caractères, la vieillesse reçoit le nom de « durée-transformation » (*sthityanyathātva*). — Comment alors s'explique [1] ce que dit le Prakaraṇapāda ? [2] Il dit : « Qu'est-ce que la durée ? Le non-dépérissement des conditionnés déjà nés. » — Ce que dit ce Traité, je ne peux l'expliquer. [P. 201, col. 3, l. 15.]

P'ink [3] dit : « Puisqu'on ne peut expliquer ce texte, on doit

[1] *kathaṃ nīyate* (t'ong, 162 et 7). — C'est-à-dire : « Comment interpréter le texte de telle manière qu'il soit d'accord avec votre thèse ? » Le docteur qui nie la durée doit être un Ābhidhārmika puisqu'il reconnaît l'autorité du Prakaraṇa.

[2] Le troisième Abhidharma de Vasumitra, Nanjio 1292 et 1277 ; Takakusu, On the Abhidharma Literature, JPTS., 1905 ; Kośa, vol. VI, p. xxxii.

[3] *P'ing* ou *P'ing-kia,* « le critique », formule l'opinion orthodoxe de la Vibhāṣā. — On lit parfois dans la Vibhāṣā après un exposé des opinions divergentes : « Il n'y a pas de *p'ing-kia.* » — K'ouei-ki emploie la même expression à propos d'une doctrine du Vijñānavāda (les 10 *samatās*) : « Il y a trois opinions (*vāda*) : la troisième est le *p'ing-kia-i* » c'est-à-dire « le sens (*artha*) admis, orthodoxe ».

croire qu'il y a durée. C'est par la force du caractère « durée » que les conditionnés, après être nés, « prennent » leur fruit, saisissent leur objet. Par la force de la transformation-destruction, après un instant, ils n'ont plus d'activité. Si le caractère « durée » manquait, les conditionnés ne pourraient former une série de causes et fruits. La pensée et les mentaux n'auraient pas d'objet. Par conséquent, il faut qu'il y ait durée. [P. 201, col. 3, l. 19.]

6. — Les docteurs de langue pâlie, admettant, comme les textes scripturaires y invitent, la durée du *dharma*, n'hésitent pas à dire qu'un instant de pensée (*eka cittakkhaṇa*) comporte trois instants.

a) Visuddhimagga, 431, 473 : Le présent (*paccuppanna*) comporte trois instants : *uppāda, ṭhiti, bhaṅga.* [1]

b) Compendium of Philosophy (Abhidhammasangaha), 1910, p. 25.

To every separate state of consciousness (*cittuppāda*) ..., there are three phases — genesis (*uppāda*), development (*ṭhiti*), and dissolution (*bhaṅga*). Each of these phases occupies an infinitesimal division of time — an instant (*khaṇa*) — so that to every state of consciousness there are three instants, in which successively it becomes, exists, and disappears. These three instants — nascent, static, and cessant (or arrested) — together form one mental moment

[1] Visuddhimagga, p. 472.

Les présent, passé, futur, s'entendent différemment du point de vue de l'*addha*, de la *saṃtati*, du *samaya*, du *khaṇa*, chemin, série, époque, instant.

1. La vie actuelle, de la naissance à la mort, c'est le chemin présent.

2. Le *rūpa* qui procède actuellement d'un aliment homogène..., c'est la série (*saṃtati*) présente du dit *rūpa*. — Les choses mentales qui procèdent actuellement d'un seul « état de conscience » (*vīthi*), d'une seule « aperception » (*javana*), d'une seule « concentration » (*samāpatti*), c'est la série mentale présente.

3. Du point de vue du *samaya*, époque, on considère comme présentes l'heure, la matinée, la soirée, la nuit-jour actuelles.

4. L'instant présent, c'est les trois instants actuels : production, durée, destruction. — Ou bien le passé, ce dont l'activité de cause (*hetu*) et de condition (*paccaya*) a passé ; le présent, ce dont l'activité de cause est achevée, non pas l'activité de condition ; le futur, ce qui n'a obtenu aucune des deux activités. — Ou bien l'instant présent, c'est l'instant actif (*sakicca-*).

(*cittakkhaṇa*), the period occupied by any single state of consciousness, or any separate act of mind or thought. And it pleases commentators to say that there are more than one billion of such thought-moments in the time that would be occupied by the shortest flash of lightning.

7. Harivarman, comme les Sautrāntikas, — la tradition lui donne pour maître Kumāralāta, — nie la durée de la pensée. Dans les chapitres 73 et 74, il expose les raisons pour et contre. La traduction du chapitre 74 présente de sérieuses difficultés.

73. Le *citta* périt-il à chaque instant ou dure-t-il un petit temps ?

Le *citta* dure un petit temps, car il connaît le *rūpa ;* s'il périssait à chaque instant, il ne pourrait le connaître ; donc il est faux qu'il ne dure pas. Encore, le *rūpa* ne serait pas connaissable : l'éclair, qui dure un peu de temps, n'est pas connaissable, à plus forte raison [le *citta*], périssant d'instant en instant, ne pourra connaître... — Si vous dites que le *manas* connaît parce qu'il fait série : non ; car chaque *citta* ne connaissant pas, comment la série connaîtra-t-elle ? De même une bande d'aveugles. Si vous dites qu'une corde ne suffit pas à lier un éléphant, que des cordes réunies le peuvent lier ; que, de même, un *citta* ne connaît pas, que la série peut connaître : non ; car chaque corde possède une petite force.. — Si la pensée périt d'instant en instant, les actes passé, futur, etc., n'auront pas d'efficace ; ils doivent durer pour avoir efficace.

Donc le *citta* ne périt pas d'instant en instant ; bien qu'il soit impermanent (*anitya*), il dure un peu.

74. Vous dites que la pensée ne périt pas d'instant en instant, puisqu'elle connaît. L'argument n'est pas bon. Si la pensée connaît, ce n'est pas parce qu'elle dure, mais parce que la marque (*nimitta*, la marque de l'objet) se trouve [placée] dans la pensée. Si la durée était nécessaire à la connaissance, le son ne pourrait être connu, puisqu'on admet qu'il périt d'instant en instant...

Comme la lampe, bien qu'elle périsse d'instant en instant, éclaire... prend, de même la pensée...

The Nature of Time

Though the Canon recognizes the impermanent character of existence it is devoid of any serious consideration of the meaning of impermanency. Any effective handling of the question of time is certainly missing from the Upaniṣads; the indivisible non-time of the *Maitrāyaṇī Upaniṣad* is merely a time before the actual normal time, and in the *Atharvaveda* and the *Mahābhārata*, where time appears in the light of a creator, we have nothing seriously philosophical. The explanation of the doctrine is simple enough; in the Brāhmaṇa speculation Prajāpati, the creator, is also regarded as the year; creation in time leads to the simple conception of creation by time, and there is certainly no trace even in the more advanced speculation of the *Mahābhārata* of any distinction between time as real or transcendent and time as subjective. It is hardly surprising, therefore, that early Buddhism with its clear dislike for problems not immediately tending to salvation should have left the issue severely alone; the eternity or other condition of the world is expressly included among the indeterminates.[1]

The *Milindapañha* [2] shows us a clear advance of interest in the question of time. Milinda questions Nāgasena in detail on this point, and is informed that there is past, present, and future time; time which exists and time which does not exist. This is explained in the sense that there are dispositions (*saṁkhāra*), which are past in the sense of having ceased to be, or having been dissolved, or altogether changed; to them time is not. But there are also conditions which are now producing their effect, or have in them the potentiality of producing effect, or which will otherwise lead to re-individualization; to them time is. When there

[1] Walleser, PGAB., pp. 123 ff.; Schrader, *Über den Stand der ind. Phil.*, pp. 19 f.; AV. xix. 53, 54; MBh. xii. 227. 29.

[2] pp. 50 ff. Cf. KV. i. 8, doctrine of Kassapikas.

are beings who when dead will be reborn, there is time; when there are beings who when dead will not be reborn, there is no time; and, when beings have been altogether set free by the attainment of Nirvana and bodily death, there time is essentially not. The king inquires also as to the root of past, present, and future time, and is informed that it is in ignorance; the meaning of the reply is clear when the answer proceeds to enumerate the chain of causation beginning with the dispositions, for we have seen that the idea of time is illustrated by the condition of the dispositions. Were it not for ignorance, there would be no dispositions, and therefore no time; the enlightened one is exempt from connexion with time. Further, it is made clear that there is no possibility of finding a beginning to time, or ultimate point in the past; the position is made clear by the analogy of the seed, fruit, seed; egg, hen, egg; and the circle of eye, colours, sight, contact, feeling, longing, action, and, as the outcome of action, an eye in a future birth. Finally, the sage insists as against the suggestion of the king that there may be discontinuity between the present and the past and the future that there is constant continuity. That which has not been becomes, that which has begun to become vanishes away; past, that is to say, passes over to the present, and the present passes over to the future.

Prof. Walleser has deduced from these passages the conclusion that, while the existence of transcendent time is not denied, it is made clear that time is reduced to the momentary present, and that time is an ideal phenomenon, a result which follows necessarily from the reduction of time to the momentary present; past and future time, if not real, must either be absolutely nothing or phenomenal, and the latter decision is the natural one to adopt to accord with the facts. These conclusions, however, seem rather to over-estimate the degree of philosophical competence of the composer of the *Milindapañha*. There is, it must be added, no clear or probable understanding in the text of a true momentary present; indeed the true version rather emphasizes the continuity of time; the idea that the present is sharply cut off from the past and future, which appeals to the king, is rebuked by Nāgasena. A distinction between phenomenal and transcendental time is not present to the composer; his point is different, but quite clear and satisfactory; time is essentially a thing of the world of experience alone; the world exists in it, and the time is ever in motion; but in true enlightenment there is as little room for time as for anything else empirical. Of time as a mental creation of any sort there is no suggestion; the text takes it as it is found in experience, and makes no effort to analyse or explain its nature.

The ideas of the *Milindapañha* appear in a varied form in the *Abhidharmakoça*.[1] The Sarvāstivādins are there credited with maintaining the existence of everything past, present or future, while the Vibhajyavādins distinguish in their usual mode between (1) the present elements and those among the past which have not yet produced their fruition, which are existent and (2) future elements and those among the past which have produced their fruition, which are non-existent. Of the first view there are variant aspects. Dharmatrāta maintained that the essence of an element remains unchanged throughout various times, its existence alone altering, an idea made intelligible by the change of milk into curds or the breaking of a vessel of gold. The view is obviously closely akin to the Sāṁkhya in which all change is merely alteration of an existent without fundamental change of substance, and is rejected by the Vaibhāṣikas on that account, for it implies a permanent substance. In Ghoṣaka's view, when an element appears at different times, the past element retains its past aspects without being severed from its present and future aspects, and the present retains its present aspect without completely losing its past and future aspects, a view which the Vaibhāṣikas very sensibly reject on the ground that it simply destroys distinctions of time, since all the aspects are to coexist. Buddhadeva adopts the view that, just as a woman can be regarded as mother, wife, or daughter, so the same entity may be described as present, future, or past in accordance with its relation to the preceding or succeeding moment; this view also the Vaibhāṣikas reject on the ground that it treats all three times as found together in one.

[1] Cf. Poussin, TDC., pp. 57 f.; AK. v. 24 ff.; Stcherbatskoi in Dasgupta, *Ind. Phil.* i. 115 f. For Sāṁkhya views, see SS., p. 73.

The view of Vasumitra, on the other hand, is accepted by the Vaibhāṣika school. It holds that difference in time is dependent on difference in efficiency; when an entity has performed its function and has ceased to act, it is past; when it is producing it, it is present; when it has not yet produced it, it is future. In all three cases there is real existence; this is obvious as regards present and future, and can be proved as regards the past by the considerations that, if the past were not real, i. e. did not exercise efficiency—this being the crucial test of reality—it could not be the object of knowledge nor could deeds done in the past produce effects in the present.

The Vaibhāṣika position is not approved by the Sautrāntika on the decidedly legitimate ground that all forms of this view really involve belief in the existence of a permanent substance persisting throughout time, the time distinctions appearing in it. If, it is pointed out, the past exercises efficiency at present, it clearly cannot be distinguished from the present, an objection which no attempt to distinguish between efficiencies will enable us to remove. Secondly, we can as experience shows know non-existing entities just as well as we can know existing entities; now non-existing entities have *ex hypothesi* no efficiency, so that it is not necessary that the past should have efficiency to be known. Again, if a distinction is drawn between an efficiency and an entity, there is immediately raised the insoluble problem why the efficiency started at any particular time and stopped at another. The true doctrine is that there is no distinction between the entity, the efficiency, and the time of its appearance;[1] entities appear from non-existence;[2] they exist for a moment; then they cease to exist. Their existence activity and action are all one. This harmonizes with the fact that, when we remember a thing as the past we do not and cannot know it as existing in the past; we know it in the same way as we knew it when it was present;

[1] Cf. the verse in BCAP. ix. 6; TV., p. 170; *Bhāmatī*, p. 361; *Upadeçasāhasrī*, p. 369; *Vedāntakalpataru*, p. 278; and see Çañkara, BS. ii. 2. 20: Poussin, JA. 1903, ii. 377: *Kṣaṇikāḥ sarvasaṁskārā; asthirāṇāṁ kutaḥ kriyā? bhūtir yaiṣāṁ kriyā saiva kārakaṁ saiva cocyate.*

[2] cf. Vācaspati on SK. 9. Past and future time are mere names, TRD., p. 46; MKV., p. 389; all are mere void; MK. xix; Ui. VP., p. 46. So as regards space; ibid., pp. 46 f.

similarly it is not true, as on the Vaibhāsika theory, that our past passions exercise causal efficiency upon us; in point of fact they have left residues impressed which become the antecedents of the passion of the present.

The Vaibhāṣikas in their doctrine of time made a distinct change on the canonical simplicity, which recognizes merely origin and passing away [1] or the three stages of coming into being, decay, and annihilation; [2] it interpolates the moment of existence (*sthiti*), which, it asserts, was suppressed by the Buddha because of the danger which it involved to the doctrine of impermanence, but which is implicitly included in the last stage (*sthityanyathātva*).[3] What is more obvious is that the discrimination is hardly exact. These four moments of existence were evidently taken by the school as four kinds of forces, which by coming into combination with the essence of an entity produced its impermanent manifestations in life. The idea is curious and interesting; it shows how deeply rooted was the realism which converted time into a potency possessing causative force of its own.

In the *Kathāvatthu*[4] we find an elaborate, but as [illegible]al not very profitable, refutation of the Sarvāstivādin view that everything exists, understood in the sense that past, present, and future equally exist; the passages of the Suttas in favour of the former view are refuted effectively enough by other passages, without anything more than dialectical ingenuity. The conclusion arrived at is that the present alone exists, and the same doctrine is stoutly maintained against the Kassapikas, who are credited with

[1] Defended in KV. ii. 7 which denies duration of consciousness. That the Buddha accepted some duration is possible; cf. MKV., p. 283, n. 1, MK. vii. discusses origination (*utpāda*), existence (*sthiti*) and destruction (*bhaṅga*).

[2] Defended in KV. xxii. 8 against the momentary doctrine of Pubba-and Apara-seliyas. Continuity appears also in xv. 8. See AN. i. 152; KV. i, p. 61; *Compendium*, pp. 25 f., 125; the attempt to explain it away in *Points of Discourse*, pp. 374 f. is absurd. See MKV., pp. 145, 545 f., BSB. I. xvii. 15 (the characters apply to each moment; to the series, acc. AKV.) Momentariness is true of consciousness, however; KV. ii. 7; x. 1 (against the Andhakas). The Vaibhāṣikas (acc. to Wassilieff, *Bouddhisme*, p. 277) divide things as eternal and non-eternal, and ascribe all compounds to the latter category, but do not make them momentary. The Sautrāntikas reduce all to a series of moments of coming to be.

[3] The four are given in TRD., p. 46 as *jāti, sthiti, jarā, vināça*. Cf. DS., § 596.

[4] i 6 ff.

asserting that some of the past, i.e. that which is to bear fruition exists, as well as some of the future, i.e. that which is inevitably to be, as distinct from that which is only contingent. The fact is extremely interesting and raises an obvious difficulty in the face of the doctrine which is attributed elsewhere to the Vibhajyavādins[1] and which certainly appears in the *Milindapañha*; that text certainly admits the existence of past potentialities of future action, though it denies the existence of the future and the past that has performed its activity. We have in fact in this point a suggestion that the *Kathāvatthu* as we have it cannot be regarded as representing always Vibhajyavādin views, and with this concurs the obvious consideration that in not a few cases the argument is very obviously much the better in the case of the opponent than of the Vibhajyavādin, and, for example in the case of the discussion of time itself, we find in the work two distinct doctrines. The true momentariness of all consciousness is on the one hand asserted, while on the other hand it is denounced as a heresy to hold that all existence is to be reduced to conscious moments, the case of the elements, trees, &c., being adduced against such an idea, and stress is laid on the fact that the Canon assumes the more or less permanent existence of external sense matter, of the sense organs as material, and objects to any attempt to identify either with actual consciousness.[2] We may derive from these views the conception that for the *Kathāvatthu* consciousness was momentary—this is asserted even of the consciousness of a god—but that material things had some endurance, though they were not permanent, and this view is in accord with the relative permanence of body admitted in the Canon. But the *Kathāvatthu* certainly does not make explicit the doctrine.

Abbreviations

(Prepared by the editor)

AK - Abhidharmakośa. Book iii, ed. Poussin, London, 1918 : other citations from Paris (Asiatic Society) or Burnouf MSS.

AKV - Abhidharmakośavyākhyā of Yaśomitra.

AN - Aṅguttara Nikāya, ed. PTS, 1885-1900.

AV - Atharva Veda.

BCAP - Bodhicaryāvatārapañjikā of Prajñākaramati, ed. BI.; ix also in Poussin, Bouddhisme, Études et Materiaux, London, 1898.

BI - Bibliotheca Indica, Calcutta.

BS - Brahma Sūtra of Bādarāyaṇa, ed. BI, 1854-63.

BSB - Bodhisattvabhūmi, summary in Le Muséon, vi and vii.

Compendium - Trs. of Abhidhammatthasamgaha, PTS, 1910.

DS - Dhammasaṅgaṇi, ed. PTS, 1885; trs. PTS, 1901.

JA - Journal Asiatique.

KV - Kathāvatthu, ed. PTS, 1894-7; trs. as Points of Controversy, PTS, 1915; commentary ed. Journal of the Pali Text Society, 1889.

MBh - Mahābhārata.

MK - Mūlamadhyamakakārikās, ed. Poussin, Bibliotheca Buddhica, Petrograd, 1913.

MKV - Prasannapadā of Candrakīrti on MK, ibid.

MN - Majjhima Nikāya, ed. PTS, 1888-1902.

PGAB - Walleser, M., Die philosophische Grundlage des älteren Buddhismus, Heidelberg, 1925.

PTS - Pali Text Society publications.

SK - Sāṁkhyakārikā of Īśvarakriṣṇa.

SS - Sāṁkhya Sūtra, ed. BI, 1888.
TDC - Poussin, L.de la Vallée, Théorie des douze causes, Ghent, 19
TRD - Tarkarahasyadīpikā of Guṇaratna, ed. BI (with Ṣaḍdarśanasamuccaya), 1905.

Ui, VP- Ui, H., Vaiśeṣika Philosophy according to the Daśapadārthaśāstra, London, 1917.

Contributions to the Problem of Time in Indian Philosophy

By

Stanislaw Schayer

Kraków
1938

Contents

Preface

To any historian studying philosophy as a phenomenon of human civilization the views of old Indian thinkers on Time are an exceptionally attractive as well as instructive subject. We learn, not without surprise, that this notion, which seems so abstract, already appears in the oldest pre-systematical records, not however as an empty *Anschauungsform*, but as a concrete mythological hypostasis. We meet it later on in a number of developed scholastic systems, as an impersonal substance, as a subtle Time-stuff. This very »physicalism« of the Indian Time-notion is its most striking feature. I am devoting to it the first chapter of the present study, without trying however to sketch the history of its development as reflected in the oldest mythological speculations. I shall confine myself to giving the main points and arguments of the philosophy of Time-substance as represented by Vaiśeṣikas and Mīmāṃsakas, the two classical representatives of the *kālavāda*.

The second chapter is devoted to the problem of Time in early Buddhism and in the system of the Vibhāṣā. The first subject to be discussed here is the reconstruction of the pre-canonical Buddhist Time-theories. My observations concerning this problem are evidently only provisional and hypothetical, nevertheless, the fact that the old Buddhism diverged, on this point as well, from the constructions of the Abhidharma is beyond doubt.

The next and the most important problem is the Vaibhāṣika doctrine of the three Time-epochs, the *traikālyavāda*. We are now relatively well informed on this doctrine by the Abhidharmakośa, and the work of interpretation carried on by Rosenberg, de La Vallée Poussin and Stcherbatsky helped us to understand its most substantial points. Nevertheless some questions remained unexplained, as for instance the problem of the »activity« *(kāritra)* of an element and its relation to »essence« *(svabhāva)*. I have tried to ascertain the standpoint of the Vaibhāṣikas in this matter on the basis of some evidences from Mahāvibhāṣā and Nyāyānusārāśāstra.

The doctrine of the *traikālya* is an interesting and original attempt at replacing the hypostasis of a substantial Time by another hypostasis, *viz.* that of real future and past elements of being. Each *dharma* exists through the three phases of the future, present and past. The future has no beginning but it has an end, the present has both a beginning and an end; the past has a beginning but no end. In this sense it is said that a *dharma* exists always *(= sarvam asti = sadāsti = sarvadāsti)* and that it is only its »mode of existence« *(bhāva, avasthā)* which is changing.

This theory has been criticised by the Sautrāntikas, a school which has a long history not yet sufficiently explored. But the arguments against the *traikālyavāda* seem to have been stereotyped in all epochs, from the old Dārṣṭāntikas till the school of Sautrāntika-Yogācāras. I have refrained from giving an exposition of these arguments, but I have given instead a complete translation of the *traikālyaparīkṣā* in the Tattvasaṃgraha of Śāntarakṣita and Kamalaśīla. Both these authors are Sautrāntika-Yogācāras.

The main idea of the Sautrāntika doctrine is the negation of the reality of the future and past elements: the only one to be real is the dynamical moment of efficacious activity *(artha-kriyā-kāritra)* and this is essentially »present«. The distinction of the three times is only a construction of the mind, a pure imagination. In the place of the Time-substance and also in the place of real future and past elements, Buddhism in its ripest form puts the theory of moments, the *kṣaṇavāda*, thus closing an important chapter in the history of the Time-problem on Indian soil.

Between the Indian and Western speculations on Time many parallelisms can be pointed out. The notion of Time existing independently as a substance was not unknown to Greek philosophers (Epicurus?, Iamblichus, Proclus), and it survives even in Newton's philosophy. His *tempus absolutum, verum et mathematicum* which flows evenly and exists *in se et natura sua absque relatione ad externum quodvis*, differs however from the Indian Time-substance which is conceived principally as an immovable stuff containing movable, contingent phenomena. It may consequently be compared rather with the *dharma* of the Jainas, the fine, ubiquitous substance which makes motion possible, like water to a moving fish.

A thorough analysis of the Indian and Western coincidences in Time speculation is however not possible as long as the history of Time notion in Western thought is not sufficiently examined. In this regard — in spite of a recent study by Z. Zawirski, *L' évolution de la notion du temps*, Cracovie 1936 — much remains to be done by historians of ancient as well as of modern philosophy.

Another problem which can also only be pointed out is the influence of Indian Time-theories on the philosophy of Islam. Unfortunately, it is a subject as important as it is obscure. The informations of Horten, *Die philosophischen Probleme der spekulativen Theologie im Islam*, Bonn 1910, p. 72, taken from the treatise »The roaring Sea« (al-Baḥr az-zaḫḫār) of 'Aḥmad ibn Jaḥjā ibn al-Murtaḍā show an unquestionable influence of the Buddhist *traikālyavāda*, but the details as to whence and by which routes these influences travelled remain to be examined.

In a word: more is left to be done than what has already been achieved in this line and so this study is really only a modest contribution to a vast and complicated question.

I can only cherish the hope that I shall be able to continue my researches in a further series of similar contributions.

I. The philosophy of Time-Substance

Indian philosophy arose out of mythology not in a roundabout way through protest and scepticism, as Deussen imagined, but directly through a rationalization of mythological hypostases. It is often said that mythology is a symbolical philosophy. This formulation is not wrong, provided that the term »symbol« is taken in its proper meaning. »Myth« is a »symbol« in the sense that it describes a real, primeval miracle which happened once upon a time and created a holy precedent, a holy paradigm which is since repeated and reconstructed in rituals, acts of cult and ceremonies [1]. When told in words it is a holy story, when considered as a precedent it is a norm for the explanation of life and the world, hence a »doctrine«. The transition from mythology to philosophy is imperceptible: wherever philosophy was created, it sprang from the same faith which formed myths.

The starting point of the evolution of Indian philosophy is the sacred story about the creation of the world by the Cosmical Anthropos, an asexual or rather bisexual supreme god who, through a series of hypostases, emanates the empirical plurality out of himself. The Iranian variant of this divine androgyne is Zurvān, the parent of the inimical twins, Ahuramazda and Angramanyu. In Vedic lore he appears as Puruṣa, as Prajāpati, as Brahman and Ātman; in Buddhism he can be easily discovered in the person of the Great Male, the Mahāpuruṣa Tathāgata; in Hinduism his attributes are inherited by Viṣṇu and Śiva [2].

---

[1] For this definition of the myth cf. B. Malinowski, *The Foundations of Faith and Morals*, Riddel Memorial Lectures, London 1936.

[2] We are indebted for the detailed reconstruction of the old-Indian myth about Anthropos to the remarkable work of Dr Maryla Falk, *Il mito psicologico nell' India antica*, Memorie

Unfortunately, we can build only suppositions about the genesis of this conception. According to a well known and undoubtedly ancient version, the differentiation of the Anthropos consists in its »disintegration«: the divine androgyne was dismembered in sacrifice and out of his parts arose the Sun, the Moon, the Earth, etc. It is easy to suppose some relation between this version and the myths about the dismemberment of Osiris, Attis, Tiamat, etc., but it is very difficult to prove that relation in detail. We can only quote as an hypothesis the supposition of Professor Przyluski, *La Grande Déesse*, Muséon XLIX p. 303, that the god-androgyne is as a rule a substitute for the Great Mother Goddess, and that the Indo-Iranian Anthropos is the result of an amalgamation between the old Asiatic Great Goddess and the Indo-European masculine Father-God of the type of Dyaus-Zeus. At any rate, the non-Indo-European and also non-Aryan origin both of Zurvān and of Puruṣa is beyond all reasonable doubts. The bisexual androgyne is somehow or other connected with the pre-Aryan substratum of Iranian and Indian civilizations. In the Brahmanical literary tradition it appears, in spite of all retouching, as an adaptation of a ready-made doctrine, developed outside Brahminism.

Among the substances emanated by the Anthropos out of himself in the creative process there appears, already in the oldest records, Time, or rather »Year« *(saṃvatsara)* as the texts say, at an epoch when the word *kāla*, originally a pastoral term denoting the driving of the cattle,[1] had not yet acquired its later, abstract meaning. According to RV X 190, 2 the »Year« originated as the first product out of Cosmic Waters. According to Bṛh. Ār. Up. I 2, 4 the Anthropos at first emanates the female hypostasis Speech (Vāc), and subsequently he himself, through his mind *(manasā)*, unites with her in the sexual act as Death (Mṛtyu) and Hunger. The sperm then poured out, was the Year. For — as the text adds — before there was no Year.

---

dell' Accademia dei Lincei, Rome 1938. In this study the connection between the anthropological myth and *yoga* has been for the first time fully elucidated and the whole complicated evolution from the Xth Mandala of the Ṛg-Veda till the beginnings of Buddhism subtly disentangled.

[1] Cf. W. Wüst, ZII Bd. V p. 165 ff.

Time created as a child of Death is itself Death. Therefore that part of the Cosmos which is permeated by it is mortal and impermanent. All mythological personifications of Kāla as a god of destruction and of inexorable fate, the identification of Time with Yama, as well as his connection with the later belief in the power of *daiva* and *viddhi*, the Indian Heimarmene, have their source in this conception. Hellenistic astrology, when introduced into India, might have made use of, but did not give birth to it.

Beyond the created Time lies the infinite, unlimited and indivisible substance of immortality, the *amṛta*. It permeates the upper part of the Cosmos, but apart from that, being homogeneous and without limits, it reaches beyond the cupola of the world into the sphere of the acosmic Absolute. It is identical with the true essence of the Supreme Being, with that condition which existed before the act of *sṛṣṭi*. And this very substance of eternity is also identified with Time in some later texts. The paradox is only apparent: the divisible changeable and flowing Time can be only an accident of the eternal Time; change, impermanence and death can be but a disturbance in the womb of Eternity. The same god who as Hunger and Death impregnates Speech is, at the same time, beyond death by his true nature. He is Eternity, Unlimited Life without dying. In one word: he is the Absolute Time. In this sense, according to a stereotyped formula of the Brāhmaṇas, the god Prajāpati is the Year[1]. The Buddhist hypostasis of Unlimited Life is Amitāyus, in

[1] If we take into account the fact that Prajāpati just as Zurvān is androgyne and that, just as Zurvān, he is the father of *devas* and *asuras*, the Indo-Iranian parallelism should be considered as complete in this matter. Between Zurvānism and the Indian identifications of the Supreme Being with Time there is, undoubtedly, a very ancient connection. In opposition to Scheftelowitz, *Die Zeit als Schicksalsgottheit in der indischen und iranischen Religion*, Stuttgart 1929, who finds here later influences of Hellenistic astrology, I accept, along with Professor J. Przyluski, rather the unity of Indian and Iranian civilizations based, not only on the common pre-Aryan substratum, but also on historical interactions. About the date of Zurvānism cf. now A. Christensen, *L' Iran sous les Sassanides*, Copenhague 1936, p. 143 ff., 430 ff. and of the same author *Études sur le Zoroastrisme de la Perse antique*, Copenhague 1928.

Hinduism it is Kāla as identified with Śiva (= Mahākāla) or with Viṣṇu. This type of divinity is quite different from Kāla = Mṛtyu in the same degree as Absolute Time is different from Created Time. As behoves a being who is the ultimate source of all antitheses, itself remaining far beyond and high above them, this universal God-Time is absolutely »impartial«. It is He who speaks through the mouth of Kṛṣṇa in Bhagavad-Gītā IX 29: *samo 'haṃ sarvabhūteṣu, na me dveṣyo 'sti na priyaḥ.*

This identification of the Absolute with Time has played no great part as a philosophical motive; it has however shown great vitality, beginning from the well known hymns of Atharva-Veda up to the latest scholastic treatises which do not omit the *kālavāda* when enumerating the possible metaphysical views[1].

As I have already pointed out, the characteristic trait of these oldest conceptions of Time is their »physicalism« or better »somatism«: Time, empirical as well as absolute, is conceived of as a kind of body, a subtle stuff filling space. The principal difference between the created and the eternal Time lies only in the fact that the former is divisible and limited while the latter is one, homogeneous, indivisible and unlimited. The empirical Time fills the lower part of the Cosmos which is built up of coarse-matter and which lies under the Sun; the eternal Time occupies the spiritual spheres on the other side. The three following passages may be quoted as an illustration. 1) Jaiminīya-Br. I 11: »All that is on the other side of the Sun is immortal, but what is on this side is perpetually destroyed by Day and by Night (= by the empirical Time, by Mṛtyu) just as a storm uprooting [trees etc.]. There are many worlds on the other side of the Sun«. — 2) Bṛh. Ār. Up. IV 4, 16: »Below which the Year with its day rotates, upon that immortal Light of Lights the gods meditate[2] as longevity«. — 3) Maitr. Up. VI 15: »There

---

[1] On *kālavāda* cf. F. O. Schrader, *Über den Stand der indischen Philosophie zur Zeit Mahāvīras und Buddhas*, Leipzig 1902. — It may be noted that in later treatises (as *e. g.* in Tattvasaṃgraha) the term *kālavāda* means not only the doctrine which identifies the Absolute with Time, but also the opinions of all philosophers who hold Time to be a real substance.

[2] *upāsate.* On the meaning of the term *upās* cf. the article of Dr Maryla Falk in Rocznik Orientalistyczny XIII 1938.

are two forms of Brahman: Time and Not-Time. What is before the Sun [1] is the indivisible Not-Time (*akālo 'kalo*), and what begins with the Sun is the divisible Time (*kālaḥ sakalaḥ*)«. In other words: the limit between the eternal, spiritual and the impermanent, material worlds is the cupola of the heavens on which the Sun wanders [2].

The conception of Time as a subtle substance clearly survives in the majority of later scholastical systems. According to the Vaiśeṣikas, *kāla* is one of the nine *padārthas* side by side with four coarse-material elements, the ether, space, the mind and the soul. Time appears also in the list of substances accepted by Mīmāṃsakas. The stand-point of the Jainas is semi-realistic: Time is not an *astikāya*, because it is without spatial localization (*pradeśa*); nevertheless it is a *dravya*, a real substance [3]. According to Rāmānuja it belongs together with the *mūlaprakṛti* to the categories of insentient substances [4].

The foundation of all these realistic Time-theories is nearly the same in all the schools and can be reduced principally to two arguments.

1) Language possesses a number of expressions denoting Time-relations: simultaneity, subsequence, precedence etc. Moreover, with the help of suffixes, it can express times and time-aspects of action: *kriyate, kṛtam, kariṣyati* [5]. We make efficacious use of all these terms in our every day experience, there exists consequently an empirical applicability (= *vyavahāra*) of these terms which would not be possible were it based only on fiction, *i. e.* if to all expressions denoting Time-relations and to all concepts connected with them no separate reality, nor special element would correspond. In other words: real Time must be postulated as

---

[1] *prāg ādityād* = 'before the Sun' is meant here spatially not temporally *i. e.* before the creation of the Sun.

[2] The obscure stanza of AV X 8, 12 is probably concerned with this very limit: »Far extends what is unlimited; mutually separating the Unlimited and the Limited, which touch each other, the Guard of the Heavens (= the Sun), the Knower of the future and of the past, wanders«.

[3] Cf. Glasenapp, *Der Jainismus*, p. 154.

[4] Cf. the classification of substances in Veṅkanātha's Tattvamuktākalāpa, quoted in Sarva-darśana-saṃgraha, p. 112.

[5] Cf. TSP p. 206.

a necessary objective correlate of Time-terms and Time-notions. This is the meaning of the definition in Vaiśeṣika-Sūtra II 2, 6: »[concepts such as] 'earlier', 'later', 'simultaneous', 'not simultaneous', 'slow' and 'quick' are symptoms *(liṅga)* of Time'. The same argument is formulated concisely and clearly by Baladeva Vidyābhūṣana, the author of the Govindabhāṣya: *kālaś ca bhūta-bhaviṣyad-varttamāna-yugapac-cira-kṣiprādi-vyavahāra-hetuḥ* [1].

2) The second argument refers to the fact of the changeability and impermanence of all that belongs to empirical existence. There are specific causes *(asādhāraṇakāraṇa)* which decide that in the given *hic et nunc* there arises a determined effect *p* and not *q* or *r* or *s*. But, side by side with this specific determination there exists another, general determination owing to which all effects originate, endure and disappear. The passage through these three phases of existence is a universal feature characterising everything that is »contingent«. Specific causes are not sufficient for its explanation. On the other hand, it can be explained by Time as a general cause *(sādhāraṇakāraṇa)*, hence the definition of Praśastapāda: Time is »the cause of the origination, duration and disappearance of all effects« [2].

The Time-substance is, by its very nature, inaccessible to sensuous perception. Its existence can be inferred only indirectly *(sāmarthyād)*, just as we infer the existence of *manas*, *ātman*, or *ākāśa*. The school of Prabhākara which holds that Time, contrarily to *ākāśa* and *manas*, is *ṣad-indriya-grāhya* and must not be inferred from conceptions such as simultaneity etc. [3] is the only one to differ from this *siddhānta* generally accepted by all *kālavādins*.

Independently from this difference of opinion concerning the origin of our knowledge of the reality of Time, the Mīmāṃsakas, as well as Vaiśeṣikas and partly also the Vedāntins unanimously ascribe to the Time-substance the four following characteristic marks: 1) subtlety *(sūkṣmatva)*; 2) omnipenetrability or

---

[1] Quoted in *Bedānta Darshaner Itihas* by Swami Prajñānanda Sarasvati, vol. III p. 844 (Calcutta, Bangabda 1934).

[2] According to Vaiśeṣikas such »general causes« are, apart from Time, the will of Īśvara, space *(dig)* and *karman*.

[3] Mānameyodaya ed. Kunhan Raja and Suryanarayana Sastri, Madras 1933, p. 189 gives a formal demonstration of this theory.

omnipresence *(vibhutva)*; 3) eternity *(nityatva)* and 4) unity and indivisibility *(ekatva, anavayatva)*. The same qualities are characteristic of *ākāśa* as well. Thus, in Indian philosophy, Time and Space stand in the middle of the scale between spiritual and coarsely material substances, having in common with the former subtlety, unity and eternity, and, with the latter, lack of consciousness *(acetanatva)* and insensibility *(jāḍatva)*. Consequently, between Time and Space there is, from the Indian stand-point, also some analogy and some parallelism, though in a quite different sense than in Kantian philosophy: they are not two *Anschauungsformen* but two objective, substantial fluids in which are merged all contingent beings. They are moreover two »elements« differing from earth, water, air and light[1] only by a higher degree of subtlety This is why they can permeate coarse bodies without offering resistance.

As subtle and eternal substance Time is, for the majority of schools, an indivisible, homogeneous, never-ending mass. We can express it in other terms by stating that Time exists in only one, unique example just as the moon, ether and similar »descriptions« which do not form a »class«. In a word: there is no *jāti* of Time to which could be subordinated several, individual »Times«. Nevertheless we speak of moments, hours etc. How are they to be understood? — The difficulty is solved by the theory of *upādhis*: just as the unique Space is divided in appearance by pots etc. into several compartments, so also is Time, one and the same, differentiated only in appearance into greater and smaller »Time-portions«, beginning with moments up to astronomical periods *(parārdha)*, by a projection on the background of empirical plurality. Thus all measures of Time have only a metaphorical significance because, in reality, we do not measure Time itself but only coarse

[1] On account of its subtlety light, more than other material elements, is akin to Time, Space and Consciousness. Hence the repeated attempts of a mystical *adaequatio (= upāsana)* of the spiritual Absolute not only with Time, Space and Consciousness, but also with Light. We must not forget, however, that Indian optics are based on the stand-point of the »corpuscular theory«: light is composed of atomic »photons« *(kiraṇa, marīci)* and is not a unique continuous substance.

bodies existing in Time. — *kālasyāpi vibhutve 'py upādhivaśād aupādhiko bhedavyavahāro 'sti*[1].

The Mīmāṃsakas refer also to the following analogy: just as the one, uncreated Word manifests itself in empirical sounds with a definite articulation, accent, length etc., so also Time, though one, eternal and omnipresent, manifests itself as divided in coordination with the motion of the Sun: *yathā hi varṇo nityaḥ sarvayato 'pi dīrghādirūpeṇa vibhakto bhāsate dhvanyupādhivāśāt, tathā kālo 'pi svayam abhinno 'py ādityasya gatikriyopādhivaśād bhinno bhāsate*[2]. To sum up: the factor which differentiates the omnipresent, subtle Time is coarse matter, its movements and its accidents.

The problem of the divisibility of Time has, however, another, more complicated aspect in connection with the problem of impermanence. Whatever is merged in the fluid of Time is impermanent and changeable. Time as a mythological hypostasis of Life and Death gives birth to beings, makes them »ripen« *(pacayati)* and, just as the Greek Chronos, devours its own offspring. In the philosophical, rationalised version, this myth is reduced to the already mentioned conception of Time as the »general cause« determining the origination, duration and disappearance of all empirical beings. To the distinction of these three phases of existence corresponds the differentiation of Time into three »portions«, acting consecutively, the first by »originating«, the second by »stabilizing« and »making ripen«, the third by »annihilating«. These three »portions« are identical with the »three Times«, the Future, the Present and the Past: *kālas tūtpatti-sthiti-vināśa-lakṣaṇas trividhaḥ*[3]. And this division is also only

---

[1] Mānameyodaya, p. 191. — The real divisibility of Time-substance is taught by Madhva. Cf. Glasenapp, *Madhva's Philosophie des Vishnu-Glaubens*, Bonn 1923, p. 53: »Die Zeit besitzt in sich selbst Unterschiede und erhält diese nicht erst durch die Vorfälle, die sich zufällig in ihr abspielen«.

[2] Pārthasārathi ad Ślokavārttika, Śabdanityatādhikaraṇa, 301—2 = TS 2299. Cf. TSP p. 633: *yathaiko 'pi nityo gakārādivārṇo yadā kenacid dhvaniviśeṣeṇa kvacitpradeśe vā vyajate, tadā deśādivibhāgena pravibhakto gamyate, tathā kālo 'pi yady api cāsau sarvapadārthavyāpī, tathāpī yadā kvacit kriyāviśeṣeṇa kvacitpadārthe vyajyate.*

[3] Saptapadārthī, § 14. Mitabhāṣinī (ed. Amarendra Mohan

an »imposition« of accidental *upādhis* on the unique, indivisible Time-substance. In other words: Time is itself motionless, but the empirical things which it permeates arise and disappear, and this change is reflected on the screen of Time as its apparent tripartition.

Bhattacharya, Calcutta 1934, p. 21) explains: *kālasyau 'pādhikaṃ vibhāgam āha: utpattīti. padārthānām utpatti-sthiti-vināśair lakṣyata ity utpatti-sthiti-vināśa-lakṣaṇaḥ. utpattyā bhaviṣyan, sthityā vartamānaḥ, vināśena bhūtakālo lakṣyata iti trividhaḥ.*

II. Time in Early Buddhism and in the System of the Vibhāṣā

Passing on to systems which blankly rejected the conception of a real Time-substance, we shall mention at first the Sāṃkhya in its classical form. — »Time which is accepted by Vaiśeṣikas — says Vācaspatimiśra [1] — cannot originate alone the terminological distinction of the future etc. Hence there exist only the *upādhi*, the differentiation of which effects the differentiation of the future etc. Time is therefore considered by the Masters of Sāṃkhya as redundant and that is why we do not admit the reality of Time as a seperate entity *(na kālarūpatattvāntarābhyupagama iti)*«.

In spite of this decided protest against the hypostatizing of a real Time, the Sāṃkhya, as a matter of fact, does not go beyond the problems and constructions of the »Substantialists«, Vaiśesikas, Mīmāṃsakas etc. The distinction of eternal and created Time is retained in the form that the former becomes an attribute *(guṇaviśeṣa)* of the *prakṛti*, while the latter is reduced to *ākāśa* as the motion of the Sun and of the planets. The Sāṃkhyas also do not dismiss the conception of Time as the general cause. — *»nanv ātmā svabhāvato na baddhaḥ, kiṃ tu kālavāśād baddho bhaviṣyatīty āha: 'na kālayogato vyāpino nityasya sarvasaṃbandhāt'. bhavatv ayam, yadi tasya kadāpi kālayogaḥ syāt, na syāt vā. nityasya vyāpinaḥ sarvakālasaṃbandhopādhitvāt«* [2]. Therefore I can hardly agree with Garbe, *Die Sāṃkhya Philosophie*,

---

[1] Sāṃkhyatattvakaumudī, ad Sāṃkhyakārikā 33.

[2] Aniruddha ad Sāṃkhyasūtra I 12; Sāṃkhyapravacanabhāṣya, p. 25. It is not denied that Time (just as Space, *karma* etc.) possesses *paraṃ kāraṇatvaṃ sāmānyarūpeṇa*; what is denied is only that it is a special cause, an *asādhāraṇakāraṇa*.

1917, p. 168, that the views on Time in the Sāṃkhya system are »ein höherer philosophischer Standpunkt« and that, in the philosophical analysis of the problem, the Sāṃkhya is »am weitesten vorgedrungen, da es Zeit und Raum für zwei Qualitäten der ewigen als Einheit betrachteten Materie erklärt«. A true estimate would rather be just the opposite, *i. e.* that the classical Sāṃkhya manifested strikingly little interest in the Time-problem and that, apart from the negation of Time as a separate substance, it confined itself to copying the views of the rejected *kālavāda.*

As a matter of course, India is indebted for real progress in the critical analysis of the Time-problem not to Sāṃkhya but to Buddhism. This progress was so essential that, if the history of the Indian Time philosophy is ever written, it will be in a large measure a history of Buddhist thought. Since sources are only partly opened, it is difficult to attempt an exhaustive exposition just now. But some facts can be ascertained.

I shall begin with the statement that there is no general Buddhist theory of Time accepted by all schools and sects. If therefore we characterize Buddhists as antagonists of the *kālavāda*, then even this characterization will be correct only in reference to some schools belonging, it is true, to the most representative ones. Moreover we should take into account the relative chronology and the very complicated stratification of Buddhist scholastics. The origin of Buddhism and its oldest pre-hīnayānistic phase lies, at any rate, in the pre-systematical epoch which is directly connected with the Anthropological Myth and its problems. Hence it would have been surprising if we could not find any traces whatsoever of Time speculations in the style of the old Indian »substantialism«. Indeed, in the list of the Hundred Dharmas of the Yogācāras[1], among the *viprayuktasaṃskāras*, there appears *kāla* side by side with empirical space *(dig)*. The fact that we come across this conception in relatively recent records has evidently no importance. In Mahāyāna, much more then in the Hīnayāna, old and original elements have been preserved. Besides, I am sure that with a better and more exact acquaintance with the sources,

[1] Cf. Rosenberg, *Problemy*, p. 319; de La Vallée Poussin, *L'Abhidharmakośa*, III p. 188.

support for hypostases of Time will also be found in hīnayānistic literature.

Meanwhile we can only form suppositions as to how Time was conceived in the pre-hinayānistic Buddhism. The starting point must be the fact that in the oldest Buddhism, just as in the Upanishads, impermanence was confined to the sphere of coarse materiality *(rūpa)*, while all other, subtle, spiritual elements *(citta, vijñāna)* lay beyond its reach. It is possible that in Buddhism as well this conception was connected with the distinction of two Times: one transcendental, indivisible and identical with eternity and immortality, the other contingent, divisible and determining the origination of impermanent beings. It may also be that eternal Time did not form a separate »sphere« *(āyatana)* as *ākāśa* or *vijñāna* but was only a fluid permeating or containing in itself the subtle as well as the coarse material substances. These suppositions however are not so strongly founded as to constitute a basis for further constructions. Nevertheless, we can state that the idea of Time as the real reservoir of contingent beings is not without support in Buddhist literature. Mvbh. p. 393a quotes the following erroneous view: »the *svabhāva* of Time is *nitya*, but the *svabhāva* of the *saṃskṛtadharmas* is *anitya*. The *saṃskṛtadharma* wander across the times just as a fruit from one pot to another, or as a man from one house into another. This is also the case with the *saṃskṛtadharmas*: going out of the future they enter into the present, and they go out of the present and enter into the past«. We are allowed to suppose that this theory of three reservoirs is only a later development of the more primitive conception of Time as a unique, universal reservoir in which future, present and past entities are placed in layers, one upon another.

When speaking of the traces of the »somatistic« Time-conception preserved in Buddhist literature, we may mention another point. In Abhidharmakośa[1] we hear of such a version of the *traikālyavāda*, according to which the »actualization« *(vartamānīkāraṇa)* of a future effect consists in »dislocation« *(deśāntarakarṣaṇa)*. The Sautrāntika rightly objects that this theory is unable to explain the origination of spiritual phenomena *(arūpiṇo dharmāḥ = citta-*

[1] T p. 106a 18—22 = de La Vallée Poussin, *L'Abhidharmakośa*, III p. 63. Cf. also TSP p. 516$_{15}$.

caittāḥ) since they are principally without spatial localization *(adeśastha)*[1]. But this objection holds good only in connection with later scholastics which extends impermanence also to the psychical sphere. In the pre-hīnayānistic doctrine, connecting Time and impermanence only with coarse materiality, the theory of spatial dislocation totally fulfils its object, thus corroborating its archaic character.

There is still another problem connected with the theory of Time as a reservoir containing future, present and past things. If the process of life consists in a pouring out of the future through the present into the past then, sooner or later, there must come a moment when the entire future will be exhausted to its dregs, and the whole world will be only the past. So far as I can see, such a formulation does not accur *verbatim* in any text. I can however point out an interesting discussion in Mvbh. p. 395a which indirectly presupposes the existence of such conceptions: »All future *dharmas* are [connected] with 'going out' and all past *dharmas* are [connected] with 'entering into' (= the *dharma* goes out of the future and enters into the past). Why is it said that in the future there cannot be imagined *(prajñapyate)* any 'decrease', and why is it said that in the past there cannot be imagined any 'increase'?« — The Bhadanta Vasumitra gives the following answer: the future *dharmas* are not yet countable (= *chu shu)* and the past *dharma* are no more countable. They are both without measure and without limits. Just as the Great Ocean which does not undergo any decrease even if 100.000 pots of water are taken away and which does not undergo any increase even if 100.000 pots are added«. — What is the meaning of this *dṛṣṭānta*? To ∞ we can add whatever finite number, and from ∞ we can substract whatever finite number: the result will always be the same, *i. e.* ∞. But the Great Ocean is not an infinity strictly speaking: on the contrary, its drops are uncountable only from the empirical stand-point just as the particles of sand of the Ganges which represent a very high ($= 10^{52}$) but, nevertheless,

[1] Cf. Mvbh. p. 395a: »If a *dharma* has the nature of *vedanā*, it is necessarily not *deśastha*; there exist however, *dharmas* which are not *deśastha* and which do not possess the nature of *vedanā*, *viz.* the *saṃjñās*, the *saṃskāras*, the *vijñānas*, the *paramāṇus*, the *avijñapti* and the *asaṃskṛtas*.

a finite number. Thus in reality, Vasumitra does not deny that there is an 'increase' of the past *dharmas* and a 'decrease' of the future *dharmas*. He means only that, in comparison with the immensity of the future and of the past, the saying that *dharmas* either 'increase' or 'decrease' has no practical significance. We can guess the intention of such a point of view: it was probably the wish to retain the old Buddhist conception of the future pouring itself into the past, and to avoid at the same time the necessarily arising consequence that the whole world automatically strives after extinction. This idea was not alien to Mahāyāna and probably also to old Buddhism, but for the Hīnayānists it was not acceptable because it rendered useless, or at any rate diminished the value of individual, ascetic efforts.

Finally let me quote from Saṃghabhadra's, Nyāyānusāra-śāstra p. 636 a 14 the following argumentation of an opponent who denies the reality of the three Times: »Past and future do not really exist because, if they existed, they would resist one another. Indeed, the elements of *rūpa* must occupy a definite place. If the already destroyed elements and the elements not yet born existed really, then they would resist one another. All *rūpa*-elements, if they exist, possess impenetrability *(apratighatva)* and whatever does not possess impenetrability is not a *rūpa*«. This argument also presupposes that past and future are two receptacles of a finite volume. The canonical theory removes this difficulty by stating that impenetrability is attributed to the present *rūpadharmas* alone [1]. Hence only these present *rūpadharmas* are *deśastha*, spatially localised, while all past and future elements are lacking in 'localization'. It is an obvious correction of the more primitive theory according to which the difference between the future, present and past elements was due literally to the difference of *avasthā*, of spatial »position« in one of the three Time-spheres.

Now, coming to the system of the Vaibhāṣikas, we may

---

[1] Cf. Mvbh. p. 395 a: »Question: If a *dharma* has the nature of *rūpa*, is it *deśastha*? — Answer: If a *dharma* is *deśastha*, it has necessarily the nature of *rūpa*; there exist, however, *dharmas* which have the nature of *rūpa* and which are not *deśastha*, *viz*. the past and the future *rūpas*, the present *paramāṇus* and the *avijñapti*«.

begin with a short review of the most important innovations introduced into Buddhism by the hīnayānistic Abhidharma.

1) The most strinking feature of the primitive doctrine was the dualism of the impermanent coarse matter *(rūpa)* and the permanent, subtle soul-stuff *(citta)*. In the Hīnayāna a new thesis of universal impermanence, which extends also to the psychic phenomena, gets the upperhand [1].

2) In the *saṃsāra* there no more wanders a subsisting soul (a *gandharva*, a *pudgala*), and what is called personality is now changed into a continuum of appearing and disappearing psychophysical elements.

3) These separate elements are called *dharmas*, by the same term which, in the old Buddhism, designated the permanent, spiritual and suprasensuous reality. This new significance of the term *dharma* (always in the plural) can be explained as a differentiation of one universal Dharma, the true essence of Tathāgata and synonymous with Brahma, just as all *rūpa*-elements are differentiations of the one cosmic Rūpa, the body of the Makranthropos [2]. The Hīnayānists interpret this new notion by the learned etymology: *svalakṣaṇadhāraṇād* (or: *svabhāvadhāraṇād*) *iti dharmaḥ*, thus giving to the term *dharma* the meaning of a bearer of phenomena manifesting themselves in the continuum.

4) In pre-hīnayānistic Buddhism salvation was the deliverance of the pure and radiant soul-stuff *(ādiśuddha, prabhāsvara citta)* from stains and defilements *(kleśa, āsrava)* caused by coarse materiality. This purification was at the same time a going out from the mortal, coarsely material world to the higher, spiritual sphere *(ārūpyadhātu)* which was the element of immortality *(= amṛtadhātu)* on the other side of the sun. A saint who made his way to this upper sphere, reaching the 'top of existence' *(= bhūtakoṭi)*, acquired the 'place from which there was no fall' *(acyutapada)*. He became an Anāgamin — 'One who does not return' and this was probably the final goal of a Saint's career. But as a consequence of extending impermanence to the spiritual sphere this old soteriological conception has also been re-interpreted: in order to reach salvation one should go beyond

[1] Cf. my *Precanonical Buddhism*, Archiv Orientální VII 1935 and Keith, IHQ XII 1936.

[2] Cf. M. Falk, *Nāma-Rūpa and Dharma-Rūpa*, Cracow 1938.

the element of consciousness. True eternity and true immortality became a transmundane *(lokottara)* element of fully extinguished empirical existence. Higher than Anāgamin, who has been changed into an individual not returning to birth in the lower, material worlds, now stays the Arahan, the Saint who is perfectly released from all forms of existence.

5) In relation with these new views the old conception of Time must also have undergone a change. The limit between the eternal and created Times has been shifted so far as to embrace the whole Cosmos within mortality. The sun ceased to be the Gate of Immortality and the many worlds beyond became victims of Māra the Papimān just as the lower, material world.

This is however only a general frame for the treatment of the problem of Time. In connection with the new Abhidharmic philosophy, the first question to be asked was whether Time is a *dharma* or not.

According to the Vaibhāṣikas, there exist not only *dharmas* participating in the continuum of life, but also some which always remain beyond contingency and never manifest themselves in the empirical world. Hence they cannot be positively defined. These are the three *asamskṛtas*, *viz.* the two *nirodhas* and *ākāśa*. As a homogeneous, universal fluid of space, the *asaṃskṛta-ākāśa's* mark is »non-resistance«. Besides this absolute space there exists also empirical, finite and divisible space, the *ākāśa-dhātu*, which is considered by Vaibhāṣikas not as an *upādhi* of the *asaṃskṛta-ākāśa*, but as a derivative of the *rūpadhātu*. By analogy we could have expected the same distinction between the absolute and empirical Times as two different kinds of *dharmas*. But, in reality, there is in the list of 75 *dharmas* of Vaibhāṣikas no Time, either absolute or empirical. Nevertheless, we find both notions also in Vaibhāṣika doctrine, though in disguise. The absolute Time, Eternity is identical with the *amṛtadhātu* which is another name for the *nirvāṇadhātu*. And the empirical Time hides in the *saṃskṛtalakṣaṇas*, the *jāti*, *sthiti*, *jarā* and *anityatā* which together form the Vaibhāṣika correlative of the *sādhāraṇakāraṇa* of the Vaiśeṣikas etc. Their function is to drive each *saṃskṛtadharma* through the three Time-phases: the *jāti* forces the *dharma* to go out of the future and enter into the present, the *sthiti* stabilizes the *dharma* for a moment, the *jarā* and *anityatā* make it go out of the present and enter into the past [1]. I am refraining from analysing the theory of the *saṃskṛtalakṣaṇas* and shall confine myself to point out that we have here a doctrine corresponding to the Nyāya-Vaiśeṣika distinction of the two *abhāvas*: the antecedent non-existence *(prag-abhāva = paṭo bhaviṣyati)* and the non-existence after destruction *(pradhvaṃsābhāva = paṭo naṣṭaḥ)*. Between these two *abhāvas* — which are however *padārthas* — is squeezed in the present *bhāva*, just as is the manifestation of the *dharma* of the Vaibhāṣikas between its future and past phases. It may also be supposed that, originally, *anityatā* alone acted as a substitute for empirical Time (a reduction of Mṛtyu), that it has subsequently been developed into the triad of *jāti*, *sthiti* and *nirodha* and that the classical tetrad is but a later synthesis.

By introducing the theory of the *saṃskṛtalakṣaṇas* as special factors cooperating with all *saṃskṛtadharmas*, the Vaibhāṣikas dismissed the older theory of Time as a receptacle containing empirical beings. There exists only one universal fluid in which the *dharmas* are merged, *viz.* the *ākāśa*. But Time is not thus conceived. and the parallelism between Time and Space is given up. It is true, the Vaibhāṣikas further say in a colloquial sense that the *dharmas* wander across the three Times, that *nirvāṇa* lies beyond the three Times, that there exists a Future and a Past etc., but all these expressions are meant only metaphorically and not literally: each *dharma* exists in the three Times as future, present and past and the term »three Times« is consequently only a synonymous denomination *(adhivacana)* for *saṃskṛtadharmas* [2].

We can try to guess the motive of this new view. It may be that the difficulty of spatial localization of the three Times has played some part here. Accepting that *ākāśa* as a unique and homogeneous fluid filling up the whole Cosmos, one should have to admit that this Space-fluid is itself permeated by another fluid of Time. Such a conception would not have been

[1] Cf. Mvbh. 394 a: »If all the three *saṃskṛtalakṣaṇas* have not yet been active, the *dharma* is called future. If one of them has already finished its activity and two are just active, then the *dharma* is called present. If they all have already finished their activity, the *dharma* is called past«.

[2] Cf. AbhK I, *kārikā* 7: *ta evādhvāḥ*.

unheared of in India[1], but it did not solve the other difficulty, that of assigning place to the three Times of future, present and past, within one Cosmos. The conception of Time-layers would have come into conflict with an analogous spatial dislocation of the worlds and the dodge of the fourth dimension was unfortunately not yet known. Nothing remained but the theory, which was accepted as a matter of fact, *viz.* that all future and past *dharmas* are without spatial localization *(adeśatha)*.

This was however only a partial solution and the main question, *viz.* the difference between the future, present and past *dharmas* remained to be answered.

The simplest interpretation which can be deduced from the Vaibhāṣika stand-point is the following. Each *dharma* is the bearer of its specific mark *(svalakṣaṇa)*, which is at the same time its special function *(svakriyā, vṛtti, kāritra, svabhāga)*. On this relation are based the definitions of the Abhidharma: the essence of a *dharma*, its ***svabhāva*** as ***definiendum*** *(=lakṣya)* is defined by its ***kāritra*** *(=svakriyā* or *svalakṣaṇa)* as ***definiens***[2]. Now, although

---

[1] Cf. Bṛh. Ār. Up. III 8, 7: *yad urdhvaṃ divaḥ, yad avāk pṛthivyāḥ, yad antarā dyāvāpṛthivī ime, yad bhūtaṃ ca bhavac ca bhaviṣyac cety ācakṣate, ākāśa eva tad otaṃ ca protaṃ ceti.*

[2] This double logical and ontological meaning has been pointed out by the present author in *Ausgewählte Kapitel aus der Prasannapadā*, p. 2 in a remark on Chapter V of the Madhyamakakārikā where the problem of *lakṣya* and *lakṣaṇa* is discussed by Nāgārjuna on the example of *ākāśa*, and its *svalakṣaṇa*, the *anāvaraṇatva*. But Professor Stcherbatsky, RO X p. 35 holds that this discussion is without any connection with the problem of *dharmasvabhāva* and *kāritra*, and as a result accuses me, in the plainest terms, of not distinguishing between *lakṣaṇa = svalakṣaṇa* and *lakṣaṇa = saṃskṛtalaksaṇa* and of having overlooked that *ākāśa* is not a *saṃskṛtadharma!* These are indeed *pārājika* sins which I have, however, not commited; hence I need not atone for them. I wish only to add that the *asaṃskṛtadharmas*, as *e. g. ākāśa*, have also their *svakāritra* from the standpoint of the Vaibhāṣikas. Cf. de La Vallée Poussin, *Documents d'Abhidharma* (BEFEO XXX), p. 43: »L'Ākāśa inconditionné, bien qu'il n'ait point d'appui, a cependant un effet *(kārya)*: à savoir, il donne place à toute lumière; par le fruit est manifestée la cause qui a donc réels nature et caractère«. Ibid. p. 50, 54: »Les organes, l'organe de l'oeil, etc. ne sont pas connus par évidence; néanmoins nous savons qu'ils existent parce qu'ils possèdent une

each *dharma* always possesses its *kāritra*, yet it manifests the *kāritra* only at a given moment, and having thus discharged its function, becomes sterile once for all. Just this moment of discharging is called the present, and we can thus say that the future *dharmas* are those which have not yet manifested their *kāritra* and the past ones are those which have already manifested their activity. In my *Ausgewählte Kapitel aus der Prasannapadā* I have given this very interpretation and it was not mistaken in so far as we really come across such a conception in Mvbh. p. 393 c: »Question. On what is based the distinction of Time-epochs? — Answer. On the *kāritra*. The *saṃskṛtadharmas* which do not yet possess the *kāritra* are called 'future', the *saṃskṛtadharmas* which just now possess the *kāritra* are called 'present', the *saṃskṛtadharmas* whose *kāritra* is already destroyed, are called 'past'. Or: the *rūpa*, when it does not offer any resistance *(pratighatva)* is called 'future', when it offers resistance just now, is called 'present', when it has already ceased to offer resistance, is called 'past' etc.«

This apparently simple theory leads in reality to great complications. If we admit as present only such *dharmas* as are just now manifesting their special function, then what should we do with the elements of an eye which sleeps or is obstructed by darkness? These elements are obviously present, nevertheless they do not perform their *kāritra*, they do not give sight. Hence the necessity of another definition of the term *kāritra*.

Indeed, we can take another stand-point according to which the manifestation of the specific function of the *dharma a* is the activity not of this very *dharma*, but of other preceding *dharmas* *p*, *q*, *r* etc. by which the function of the *dharma a* is causally determined. The true activity of a *dharma* is consequently its faculty of determining other *dharmas*, *i. e.* of compelling future *dharmas* to manifest their special functions. The Hīnayānistic scholastics admit, as we know, six different types of such a determination by 1) simultaneous cause *(sahabhūkāraṇa)*, 2) an im-

---

certaine activité *(kāritra)*. De même l'Ākāśa possède une certaine activité«. In one word: it is true that »die *samskṛtalakṣaṇas* begleiten bloss die *saṃskṛtadharmas*«, but the problem of *kāritra* of the *asaṃskṛtadharmas* has nothing in common with it.

mediate cause (*samanantarakāraṇa*), 3) homogeneous cause (*sabhāgakāraṇa*), 4) a moral omnipenetrant cause (*sarvatragakāraṇa*), 5) a moral specific cause (*vipākakāraṇa*) and 6) a general negative cause (*adhipatikāraṇa*)[1]. If, in the stream of life, there appears a *dharma* of sight (*cakṣurindriya*), it is 1) the simultaneous cause for the *saṃskṛtalakṣaṇas*, 2) the homogeneous cause for all next *dharmas* of sight which form the illusionary unity of the same eye and, 3) the general negative cause for all other *dharmas* whose origination it does not hinder. In brief: in this conception the *kāritra* of a *dharma* is no more its *svakāritra*, *svabhāga* etc., but its *hetubhāvāvasthāna*, its *phalotpadanasāmarthya*: its causal function and its faculty of producing effects.

In order to fulfil the purpose of establishing the distinction of the three Times, this new definition of *kāritra* needs however some further supplementary restrictions as well. There exist cases where a given *dharma a* determines the effect *p* at a longer distance, *e. g.* the karmic retribution becomes ripe only some time after the act has been committed[2]. In the moment *t*, when the karmic cause has already ceased and the »fruit« has not yet begun to exist, the determination lasts. Should we consequently accept that a past act is present as long as it has not produced its effect?

To avoid these difficulties the Vaibhāṣikas construct the following definite theory: the mechanism of the functioning of the six causes is different according as to whether the effect is realized in the same moment or in an immediately subsequent moment or in some more remote moment in the *saṃtāna*. The simultaneous and the immediate causes belong exclusively to the first category, the homogeneous and the omnipenetrant causes to the second or to the third and the specific moral cause exclusively to the third[3]. The determination of the effect by a cause can consequently be compared with the throwing of a projectile in which two phases can be distinguished: 1) the phase of »pro-

---

[1] Cf. Stcherbatsky, *Central Conception*, p. 81 and de La Vallée Poussin, *L'Abhidharmakośa*, II p. 244 ff.

[2] Cf. Yaśomitra, ed. Wogihara p. 178: *atītasyāpi hi phaladānakāritram iṣyate.*

[3] Cf. de La Vallée Poussin, *L'Abhidharmakośa*, II p. 293 ff.

jection« *(ākṣepa)* which is otherwise called »the grasping« *(grahaṇa)* of the effect and 2) the phase of »giving« *(dāna)* the effect, its actual realization. Each *dharma*, in the moment in which it becomes present and »discharges« its activity, as it were grasps and throws its future effect. When the course of the projected effect has the form of a parabola, both the phases of »projecting« and »giving« are distinctly separated. But when a *dharma* projects and gives its effect in the same or in two immediately subsequent moments, then »throwing« and »giving« coalesce. Nevertheless the distinction of both these moments is indispensable because only the »throwing« decides of the passing of a *dharma* from the future into the present[1]. This is just the definition of the *kāritra* advocated by Saṃghabhadra[2]: *kāritra* = *phalākṣepaśakti*, the potency of projecting effects. Acts already done, even if they have not yet produced their effect, are not present because they have already performed the act of projecting[3].

Now we come to the last but the most controversial point: what is the relation between the activity thus conceived and the element itself, between the *phalākṣepaśakti* and the *svabhāva* or *svarūpa* of the *dharma*? All theories which accept the reality of the three Times emphasise unanimously that a *dharma*, when passing through the Time-epochs, does not change its essence and that it is only its empirical aspect, the *bhāva* in the terminology of Dharmatrāta, the *avasthā* in the terminology of Vasumitra, which undergoes transformation. But both these terms do not mean much as they are unfortunately not explained in details, but only *modo indico* illustrated by *dṛṣṭāntas* which should not be taken literally. Vasumitra appeals to the example of an abacus where the same ball according to its »position« *(avasthā)* receives

---

[1] Ibid. p. 293, note 3: »Le *dharma* existe toujours, qu'il soit futur, présent ou passé. Nous disons qu'il prend ou projette un fruit au moment où, devenant présent, il devient cause ou semence d'un fruit«. Cf. also E. Lamotte, *Le traité de l'acte de Vasubandhu Karmasiddhiprakaraṇa*, 1936, p. 80 ff.

[2] N p. 631 b. cf. infra p. 36.

[3] On the contrary, the function of »giving« effects is characteristic of past as well as present *dharmas*; it is absent only from future and from all *asaṃskṛtas*.

the significance of 1, 100 or 1000. In this case we are dealing with changes in the spatial positions, with *avasthās* in the literal sense of the word, and this was possibly also the meaning of the Time-*avasthā* in pre-Abhidharmic speculation. But for Vasumitra, as we know, the Time-*avasthās* of a *dharma* are not spatial positions and the term is used only *upacāreṇa*. Similarly, it is quite difficult to say something more definite about the *bhāva* of Dharmatrāta: whether a kind of quality is meant or rather a »mode of existence«, something in the kind of *guṇas* of the Sāṃkhya as Dr Johnston [1] supposes. All these difficulties were probably felt by the Vaibhāṣika themselves and thus as a result the theory of »impredicability« *(anirvacanīyatva)* of the *kāritra* was adopted as the correct view.

In the Mvbh. p. 394 c we come across the following discussion: »Are *kāritra* and *svabhāva* the same or are they different? — Answer: It cannot be said categorically whether they are the same or different. Just as the *svabhāva* of each *sāsrava-dharma* possesses many *lakṣaṇas* as *anitya* etc., and it cannot be said categorically whether they are identical with or different from [these *lakṣaṇas*], such is the case here. Therefore [the relation between *kāritra* and *svabhāva*] is not predicable«.

Saṃghabhadra, N 633 a adduces another instance: the relation between *kāritra* and *svabhāva* is, just in the same manner, not accessible to determination as is the case with the relation between the *dharmas* and the *saṃtāna*. In one word: *kāritra* and *svabhāva* are and are not identical.

The statement of the Vaibhāṣikas that, when a *dharma* wanders across the Times, only the *kāritra* not the *svabhāva* changes, and that, nevertheless, it cannot be said that *kāritra* is *svabhāva* nor that *kāritra* exists independently of *svabhāva*, is ridiculed by the Sautrāntikas who call such a theory »a caprice of the Īśvara«:

kāritram sarvadā nāsti, sadā dharmaś ca varṇyate
dharmān nānyac ca kāritraṃ vyaktaṃ devaviceṣṭitam [2]

---

[1] *Early Sāṃkhya*, 1937, p. 31.
[2] Cf. AbhK V p. 57. = TS 1802.

But Saṃghabhadra N 633 c vehemently protests: »This irony is improper! Because Buddha Bhagavān himself also teaches: 'Tathāgata is and is not *lokottara*'; 'the *dharmatā* of the *pratītyasamutpāda* is and is not *nitya*'. Should the Buddha Bhagavān also be made ridiculous for that? We accept that *dharma* exists always and, at the same time, we teach that *dharma* is not eternal. Your criticism [of this theory] is unfounded because the terms 'eternal' and 'not eternal' are used here in two different senses. Therefore one should not deride Buddha! Is it not so in this case as well? The *dharma* lasts eternally but the *dharmabhāva* changes. When the *saṃskṛtadharmas* wander across the Times, they do not lose their *svabhāva* and the *kāritra* which arises depends on *pratyayas*. Immediately after its origination, *kāritra* disappears. Therefore we teach: the *dharma* is eternal, but the *dharmabhāva* is not eternal. Wherefore Your irony in saying that it is a caprice of the Iśvara?«

And this is the summary of the Vaibhāṣika doctrine given by Saṃghabhadra, N 633 b: »All *samskṛtadharmas* in the state *(avasthā)* of *phalākṣepa* are called present. This state of *phalākṣepa* is »previously« and »subsequently« inexistent. In accordance [with this previous and subsequent inexistence] the distinction of the three Times is established. Past and Future exist just as the Present. In brief: although the *svabhāva* of all *saṃskṛtadharmas* remains always the same, yet the »potencies« are different. In this manner although the *svabhāva* of the three Times is always the same, yet, their *kāritra* is not without differentiation«.

From the evidences quoted above it becomes clear that the Vaibhāṣika teach a »duality of aspects« of the *dharma*, which is however not a duality »of two different planes« or of »two sets of elements« as Professor Stcherbatsky accepted it till recently[1]. *kāritra* is no »supplement« to the *svabhāva*, it is not the second element neither the second nature of the element; neither is it the element itself, the *svalakṣaṇa*. As we learn from TS[2], this view was explicitly rejected by Saṃghabhadra. The

---

[1] *Central Conception* p. 42, *Nirvāṇa* p. 27; cf. also Mookerjee, *The Buddhist Philosophy of Universal Flux*, Calcutta 193, p. 250: »duality of nature«. [2] Cf. infra p. 45.

difference between *kāritra* = *phalākṣepaśakti* and *svakāritra* = *svalakṣaṇa* is indeed very fundamental: the *svalakṣaṇas* as *sapratighatva* etc. express the whole essence of the *dharma* and that is why a *dharma* possessing *sapratighatva* can never become *apratigha*. On the contrary, the *phalakṣepaśakti* is an accidental, temporary characteristic of a *dharma*, it is only *kādācitka*.

In other terms, the Vaibhāṣika doctrine teaches a kind of *bhedābhedavāda*, a theory according to which the relation between the true essence of reality and its phenomenal manifestation is one of identity in difference.

III. Śāntaraksita's Analysis of the Three Times with the Commentary of Kamalaśīla

Table of contents:

§ 1. The theories of Dharmatrāta, Ghoṣaka, Vasumitra and Buddhadeva.

Now, in order to demonstrate that [the absolute reality as conceived by the shool of Sautrāntika-Yogācāras is characterised] by the absence of duration *(asaṃkrānti)* [1], [Śāntarakṣita opens the discussion by quoting the following objection]:

> Then, following the analogy of gold, the permanence *(sthiratvam)* [of the being] is assumed. There are even certain Buddhists who accept that the being *(bhāva)* possesses different states *(avasthābhedavān)*. [1786]

[Our teaching:] 'nothing has duration' *(avasthāna)* is assailed [by the opponent who says:] How can it be asserted that nothing persists as long as there are even certain Buddhists, as Dharmatrāta and others, who pretend that the being persists through the three Times. The reason [adduced by those Buddhists] is the differentiation of states *(avasthābheda)*. The homogeneous instance *(sādharmya)* [of this syllogism] is gold.

The [meaning of this comparison is explained by the next *kārikā*:

> Just as gold, even when its states are changed, does not lose its colour during the Time-epochs, in the same manner elements of being (= *bhāva*) do not lose their substance *(dravya)*. [1787]

1. The venerable Dharmatrāta [2] is the author of a theory, according to which there is a differentiation of the *bhāva*. He states: when a *dharma* is wandering through the Times, only its *bhāva* changes, not its substance *(dravya)*. Just as gold itself is not changed, but only this quality (= *guṇa*) of the substance of gold,

---

[1] Cf. TS 4: *asaṃkrāntim anādyantam* etc. P 13: *saṃkrāntivādinaḥ* = *sarvāstivādinaḥ*. They teach that *skandhas* etc. exist in three Time-epochs without changing and without abandoning their essence (= *asaṃkīrṇasvabhāvāḥ, ajahatsvabhāvāḥ*). This is denied by Sautrāntikas, the advocates of the doctrine *abhūtva bhavati*, who may be consequently designed as Asaṃkrāntivādins. The term *saṃkrānti*, however, denotes also 'transmigration of the *sūkṣmacitta* from one world to the other' and in this sense the Sarvāstivādins (= the Vaibhāṣikas) are Asaṃkrāntivādins, the Sautrāntikas — Saṃkrāntivādins. Cf. J. Masuda, ***Origin and Doctrines of Early Indian Buddhist Schools***, p. 66., note 3 and E. Lamotte, *Karmasiddhiprakaraṇa*, MBC IV 1936, p. 24—26.

[2] The exposition of the four doctrines of the *sarvāstivāda*, as given by Kamalaśila, is a quite accurate reproduction of Mahāvibhāṣā, T 1545, p. 396; Abhidharmakośa V p. 52—56, Nyāyānusāra, T 1562, p. 631.

which is the cause *(nimitta)* of terminological distinction *(abhidhāna)* such as »bracelets«, »armlets« »ear-rings« etc. The *dharma* is differentiated in respect to the *bhāvas* of the future, present and past in the same manner *i. e*: by discarding its future *bhāva* it attains the present *bhāva* and by discarding its present *bhāva* it attains the past *bhāva*. The *dravya* does not change because it is never missing *(= sarvatra 'vyabhicārāt)*. Otherwise we shall arrive at the *prasaṅga* that the *dravya* is one in the future, another one in the present and still another one in the past. Now what is the *bhāva* postulated by this theory? The answer is: the *bhāva* is a special quality[1] *(= guṇaviśeṣa)* to which are related cognitive processes *(jñānapravṛtti)*, expressed in distinction of terms *(abhidhāna)*: »future«, »present« and »past«.

2. The venerable Ghoṣaka is the author of a theory according to which there is a differentiation of the *lakṣaṇa*. He states that when a *dharma* is wandering through the Times then, as a past one, it is connected with the *lakṣaṇa* of the past without however being, at the same time, free from the connection with the remaining two *lakṣaṇas* of the present and of the past. Just as a man, although devoted to one wife, is not free from passion for other wives[2]. The future and the present [Times] are to be explained in the same way. The empirical applicableness *(vyava-*

---

[1] As pointed out by Dr. E. H. Johnston, *Early Sāṃkhya*, 1937, p. 31, there is an old connection between *bhāva* — 'state of being' and the *guṇas* of the Sāṃkhyas. I am however not quite convinced that, in the expression *guṇaviśeṣa* used by Kamalaśīla as definition of the *bhāva* of Dharmatrāta, we are concerned with the Sāṃkhyan *guṇas*. I entirely agree that the *guṇapariṇāma* is a later theory, unknown to the early Sāṃkhya, but Sāṃkhya was known to Kamalaśīla only in its later form, and it is hardly probable that he, when commenting Dharmatrāta, is likely to refer to a meaning which the word *guṇa* possessed in the Epic Age. I should also like to refrain from drawing any far reaching conclusions from the fact that Dharmatrāta and Vaibhāṣikas are accused of affinity with the Sāṃkhya. These accusations are made by the Sautrāntikas for polemical purposes and, as it seems, not necessarily *bona fide*. Cf. note 5.

[2] The Chinese translations of this comparison distinguish *ch'i shih* = 'a legitimate wife' from *chi yin* = 'a concubine'. — »A man who feels passion for his legitimate wife is not free from passions for concubines«.

hāra) [of the terms denoting the three Times] is based on the fact that the *lakṣaṇas* of the past etc. attain (in succession) their activity *(= vṛtti)*. This is the difference between the present theory and the preceding one.

3. The venerable Vasumitra is the author of a theory, according to which there is a differentiation of the *avasthā*. He states: when a *dharma* is wandering through the Times, having reached this or an other *avasthā*, it receives different designations with reference to different *avasthās*, but not with reference to its substance *(dravya)*. Because its substance remains unchanged in all the three Times. Just as, in an abacus, the same ball, when thrown in the place of units, means »one«, in the place of hundreds, »hundred«; in the place of thousands, »thousand«. In the same manner a *dharma (= bhāva)*, when staying in its *kāritra*, is called »present«, when fallen down from it — it is called »past«, when it had not yet reached it, it is called »future«. The applicableness of [different Time-designations] depends on *avasthā*, just as in an abacus. Indeed, [when counting on it], the *svabhāva* [of the ball] remains unchanged, only as a result of [its] being connected with different positions *(sthānaviśeṣa)* there arise different numeral notions.

4. The venerable Buddhadeva is the author of a theory, according to which there is [only] a differentiation of the *anyathā*[-relation]. He says: when a *dharma* is wandering through the Times, it is called in each case 'another one' in a different sense in accordance with its relation to the antecedent and subsequent [moments]. Just as the same woman is called 'mother' and 'daughter'. Thus a *dharma* which [at a given moment] has its antecedent but no subsequent moments is called 'future'; that which has its antecedent as well as its subsequent moments is called 'present'; that which has only its subsequent but no antecedent moments is called 'past'.

Thus we have, in all, these four schools of the *sarvāstivāda*, designed as the theories of the *bhāva-anyathātva, lakṣaṇa-anyathātva, avasthā-anyathātva* and *anyathā-anyathātva*.

The first of them does not differ from the Sāṃkhya doctrine[1]

---

[1] We find the same objection in AbhK V p. 54, but Saṃghabhadra N p. 631 b, 6—10, protests: »There is no analogy!

which teaches the transformation *(pariṇāma)* [of the permanent substance]. The refutation of this [variant of the *sarvāstivāda*] is consequently identical with the refutation of the [*pariṇāmavāda*]. [The main line of argumentation is as follows:] transformation is possible either by abandoning the previous *svabhāva*, or without abandoning the previous *svabhāva*. If there is no abandoning, then a confusion *(saṃkara)* of Time-epochs will be the consequence; if so, we have a contradiction with [the fundamental thesis of your school] that [entities] exist always *(sadāstitva)*.

Neither are the advocates of the second theory free from the consequence of Time-confusion, because [accepting the *lakṣaṇa-anyathātva* they must admit that] each *dharma* is connected [simultaneously] with each [of the three] Time-*lakṣaṇas*. Moreover there is no analogy at all between the *dṛṣṭānta* of a 'man in passion' and [the *dharma* wandering through the Times] as the subject to be illustrated by this *dṛṣṭānta*. Indeed, a man is called 'in passion' *(=rakta)* with reference to the actual operation *(samudācāra)* of passion towards an external object; and he is called 'not without passion' *(avirakta)* with reference to the fact of possessing *(=samanvāgamamātreṇa)* [passion as a potential disposition][1]. But the acquisition *(prāpti)* of Time-*lakṣaṇas* by a *dharma* is not in this sense [sometimes] an actual operation *(samudācāra)*, and [sometimes] a [mere] possession *(samanvāgama)*.

The refutation of the third theory, teaching that the distinction of Time-epochs is based on *kāritra*, will be given later in detail.

Finally, according to the fourth theory, in each Time-epoch we should have simultaneously all three Times together, *e. g.*: in the past Time the subsequent and the antecedent moments would represent the past and the future, and the middle moment would be the present. The refutation of this theory is self evident.

This Bhadanta does not teach that the *svabhāva* of the *saṃskṛta-dharmas* is *nitya* and that, during the Time-epochs, the *dharma* becomes sometimes invisible *(tirobhūta)* and sometimes manifest *(āvirbhūta)*. On the contrary he teaches: the *dharmas* wander through the Time-epochs. Although their *svabhāva* remains the same, theis *bhāva* changes. [This standpoint] is identical with the view of the Bhadanta Vasumitra. How can it be held as identical with the heresy of the Sāṃkhyas?«

[1] Cf. Y p. 470: *kevalaṃ samanvāgamaḥ*.

A more detailed critical analysis of the *traikālya*-doctrine, will be undertaken later.

The example of gold [in the *kārikā* 1787] is mentioned only in order to give a [generally accepted] *siddhānta*, not in order to give a special illustration of the first theory of Dharmatrāta. Also when it is said [in the *kārikā* 1791]: »the distinction of Time-epochs is established by the *kāritra*«, [the theory of Dharmatrāta is not alluded to by these words]. The thesis that the Time-epochs are established by the *kāritra* is, indeed, the doctrine of Vasumitra and not that of Dharmatrāta.

§ 2. Five arguments of the Vaibhāṣikas demonstrating the reality of the past and of the future.

[Now let us expound the main arguments by which the Vaibhāṣikas try to demonstrate the reality of past and future things].

Otherwise the cognition of the past and of the future would be without any object. Moreover, how could Buddha have then said that consciousness *(vijñāna)* is supported by two factors?

And how would it be possible to assume that an unreal past *karma* could give a moral retribution? And how could the Yogins possess a distinctly differentiated knowledge of the past and of the future?

Past and future *[dharmas]* are therefore not deprived of substantial reality because under the heading 'Time-epoch' *(adhvan)*, just like the present, [past and future] *rūpas* etc. are comprehended. [1788—1790]

1) If past and future things are not real, then the consciousness *(vijñāna)* of such [judgments] referring to the past and to the future, as *e. g.*: 'there was once [a king] Mahāsammata', or: 'there will be once the Cakravartin Śaṃkha' would be objectless *(nirālambana)*. And then there would be no consciousness at all, just because of the inexistence of the objective correlate *(ālambana)*. Indeed it is said: 'consciousness is essentially awareness of the corresponding object *(=prativastu vijñaptyātmakaṃ vijñānaṃ)* and if there was no cognizable object *(jñeya)*, nothing could be known by it'. Hence there would be no consciousness at all.

2) Moreover [it has been said by Buddha]: 'consciousness originates in a correlative dependence from two factors, *viz.* in correlative dependence from eye and visual forms etc. up to mind *(manas)* and mental objects *(dharmāḥ)*'. Hence, if there was no past and no future, consciousness which has them as objective correlates could not originate in a correlative dependence from those two factors. And thus a contradiction with the Āgama would result therefrom [1].

3) The past *karma* would give no moral retribution *(vipāka)*, if it were inexistent and devoid of all reality, because then the m oment moral retribution would arise, the moral cause *(vipākah etu)* would be inexistent; and what is inexistent does not possess the potency of producing effects *(kāryotpādana-śakti)*. Indeed, 'inexistence' is defined as a total absence of all potencies *(= sarvas āmārthya-viraha)*.

4) The distinctly differentiated consciousness of Yogins, h aving as its object past and future [events]: 'there was once [a king] Māndhātar' [2], 'there was once [a king] Brahmadatta', or: 'th ere will be once the Cakravartin Śaṃkha', 'there will be once t he Tathāgata Maitreya', would be impossible. Indeed, there can b e no distinct differentiation *(vibhāga)* of what does not exist. An d, therefore, past as well as future [events], as Śriharṣa etc. c annot be deprived of substantial reality *(= dravyapratiṣedharūpa)*.

5) Past and future things are real, because it has been taught th at, just like the present, the [three] Time-epochs are comprehended under the headings of *rūpa* etc. Indeed, it has been said by the Bhagavān [3]: »If, o monks, there were no past *rūpa*, a learned Śrāvaka could not become disgusted with a past *rūpa*. But as there exist past *rūpas*, therefore a learned Śrāvaka is disgusted with a past *rūpa* etc.« In this manner whatever past and future *rūpas* may exist, they all must be put together in order to get the complete class of the *rūpaskandha*.

The explanation of the expression *a dhva-saṃgraha-rūpādibhāvāder* is as follows: *adhvanā saṃgraho yeṣām, te 'dhva-saṃgrahā*

---

[1] The arguments 2—5 are enumerated in AbhK V 51.

[2] G.: Māndhāna(sic!); Tib. has only *rgyal po.* On the Cakravartin Māndhātar cf. the references by de La Vallée Poussin, AbhK III 28.

[3] Saṃyukta III 14. Cf. AbhK V 51; Prasannapadā p. 444.

rūpādayaḥ. *ādi* [in *rūpādi*] indicates that other *skandhas*, as *vedanā* etc. are understood. *teṣām* = *adhva-saṃgrahānāṃ rūpādīnāṃ bhāvaḥ* = *adhva-saṃgraha-rūpāditvam* = the fact that under 'Time-epochs' *rūpa* etc. is comprehended. *adhva-saṃgraha-rūpādi-bhāvādi*: here again the word *ādi* is added in order to indicate that [under 'Time-epochs' not only the *skandhas*, but also] other [synonyms] as *duḥkha-samudaya*, *anitya*, *anātma* etc. are included [1].

§ 3. Saṃghabhadra's definition of the *kāritra*.

It may be so. But if [the *svabhāva* of the *dharma*] is everlasting *(sadāvasthita)* like *ākāśa*, how is the distinction of past etc. possible?

[The answer of the Vaibhāṣika is given in the following *kārikā*:]

> One must not think that the distinction of Times is groundless; because this distinction is established by the *kāritra*. What is just manifesting its *kāritra* is called present, past — when it has abandoned its *kāritra*, and future — when it has not yet reached its *kāritra*.
>
> The *kāritra* of the *dharmas* is projecting a *kārya*, not producing it. The past *[dharmas]* do not possess this potency of projection and therefore they cannot possess a *kāritra*. [1791—1793]

[The Vaibhāṣika] defines as »present« [a *dharma*] which has just fully attained its *kāritra*; as »past« — [a *dharma*] whose *kāritra* has already ceased, as »future« — [a *dharma*] which has not yet attained its *kāritra*. In this way the distinction of Times is based on *kāritra* [2].

Now the question arises: what is the meaning of the term *kāritra*?

The Vaibhāṣika answers: *kāritra* means *vyāpāra*, activity or operation, as seeing etc.; [in another words:] it is [the special potency] by which the eye is seeing, the ear is hearing, the nose is smelling, the tongue is tasting etc.; it is [further the special

---

[1] There exists no separate *dharma* of Time. *adhvan* is only a synonymous denomination of *saṃskāra*. Cf. Jñānaprasthāna, T 1544, p. 987 b. 4.

[2] Cf. Mvbh. p. 393 c 18—26.

potency] by which consciousness *(vijñāna)* is active as cognizing; [and finally] it is [the special potency] by which visual forms *(rūpa)* etc. are made objects of the corresponding sense-organs *(svendriya gocaratva)* [1].

[This theory is rejected by Sautrāntikas].

[First objection:] [2] if it were so, then an actually given *tatsabhāga* eye (= an actually given *dharma* of the homogeneous series forming the so called eye) would possess no presence in the state of sleep owing to the lack of its *kāritra*.

[Vaibhāṣika formulates a new definition:] *kāritra* means [not the special potency of a *dharma*, but the capacity of] giving and of grasping a result *(phala-dāna-grahaṇa)*. So *e. g.* the *saṃskṛta-lakṣaṇas* (= *jāti* etc.) which are co-existent *(sahabhū)* with a given element A of the] *cakṣur-indriya* constitute its anthropomorphic result *(puruṣakāra-phala)*. [Another] immediately succeeding [element B of the] *cakṣur-indriya* is [with reference to the element A at the same time:] its result of the type *puruṣakāra*, of the type *adhipati* and of the type *niṣyanda*. When the eye (= an element of the *cakṣur-indriya*) produces all these effects, it is 'giving'; when it becomes the cause of these effects *(hetubhāvāvasthānād)*, it is 'grasping'. In this sense it is called present.

[Second objection:] if so, the consequence would be that past causes *sabhāga*. *sarvatraga* and *vipāka* are present, because it is admitted that they are also 'giving an effect'.

Vaibhāṣika. [This objection does not hold good]. We accept that *kāritra* = *phala-dāna* + *phala-grahaṇa* (jointly). [The past *sabhāga* although »giving«, is not »grasping«].

Sautrāntika. In this case the consequence will be the semi-presence [3] *(arddha-varttamānatva)* of the past causes *sabhāga* etc.

Anxious to avoid these drawbacks the Master Saṃghabhadra declares [4]: »the *kāritra* of the *dharmas* means potency *(śakti)* only

---

[1] Cf. Y p. 17. [2] Cf. supra p. 22.

[3] The past causes can be *saphala*, consequently they possess, as it were, one half of *kāritra*.

[4] This is not a quotation but a résumé of a longer passage from N p. 631 b 15 – c 14 which sounds as follows: »As I have explained, past and future exist. This is not contradicted by the *dharmasvabhāva* and agrees with the Āgamas. Should one deny the past and the future, then there would be a contradiction with the

of projecting results *(phalākṣepa = grahaṇa)*, not the [actual] generation *(janana = dāna)*. Past causes *sabhāga* etc. do not possess the potency of projecting results because the projecting takes

---

dharmasvabhāva, the Āgamas would be disregarded and many difficulties would arise. Therefore let it be known: the past and the future, as it has been stated by Bhadanta Vasumitra, exist really. In accordance with sound logic and the testimony of the Āgamas it cannot be altered. And this is what Bhadanta Vasumitra teaches: Buddha has said in the Sūtra that the three Times exist. — With regard to what are they differentiated? — Answer: the differentiation of the three Times is established by the *kāritra*. All *saṃskṛtadharmas* whose *kāritra* is not yet manifested are called 'future', all *saṃskṛtadharmas* whose *kāritra* is just now manifesting itself are called 'present'; all *saṃskṛtadharmas* whose *kāritra* is already destroyed are called 'past'. On the contrary in the substance of the *saṃskṛtadharmas* there is no change«.

»Now what is *kāritra*? — Answer: it is the potency [inherent] in the *saṃskṛtadharmas* to produce a result *(= saṃskṛtadharmāṇām phalākṣepaśaktiḥ)*. It means that they can become a determining cause of other *svabhāva* in the moment of their origination. He who, in accordance with this, establishes the differentiation of the three Times and who explains the [unexplained] remainder without trespassing into contradictory theories, should be called by wise men an individual with a clear understanding. But if one erroneously establishes the principle of differentiation of the three Times, or from fear of difficulties, directly rejects the Āgamas, or makes an easily understandable meaning of the Sūtra difficult to understand, or teaches that there is only present and no past and no future, or even that the present is equally fictitious as the past and the future, or if he rejects altogether the three Times and teaches that they are all unreal, then he falls into a contradiction with the Truth of the Āgamas and wise men should denounce him as an person with a confused understanding«.

»Moreover, he who shows disrespect to the Āgamas by teaching that the Times do not exist really, is covered with immeasurable faults, meets with many hindrances and attains salvation with difficulty. On the contrary, he who teaches that the three Times exist really is a true Master of the Śāstras, he meets with little hindrances and attains salvation easily. This is why a wise man does not show disrespect to the Āgamas by teaching that there are no Times. As for myself, I am relying on Bhadanta Vasumitra who teaches that the differentiation of the three Times is established by the *kāritra*. And as far as I am capable of it, I am solving difficulties«.

place only in the state of presence. An [already] projected result is not, on its part, connected with [new potency of] projection, because otherwise a regressus in infinitum would result. Therefore no past *dharmas* can possess a *kāritra* and hence there is no confusion of Time-marks«.

§ 4. A *prasaṅga* argument showing that *kāritra* is neither different from nor identical with the *dharmasvabhāva*.

Sautrāntika replies:

These [advocates of the *sarvāstivāda* doctrine] must concede, that the *kāritra* is either different or identical with the *dharma*, the third possibility being altogether unreal.

»The Sautrāntika raises the following objection: If the distinction of the three Times is established by the *kāritra*, then what is the *kāritra* of the *tatsabhāgacakṣuḥ* and of other *tatsabhāga-indriyas* which are present? If you say [that although without *svakarma*] they are grasping an effect and giving an effect *(=phalaṁ gṛhṇanti phalaṃ ca dadanti)*, then the *sabhāgahetus* etc., as they are also giving an effect *(phaladānāt)*, would possess their *kāritra*. Or they would possess a half-*kāritra*. And a confusion of the Time-marks would result *(adhvalakṣaṇānāṃ saṃkaro bhavet)*«.

»[We answer:] all these difficulties have their origin in the lack of understanding of the *dharmasvabhāva*. The *śaktis* of a *dharma* are of two kinds: one is called *kāritra*, the other is called *sāmarthya*. *kāritra* has been defined as a *phalākṣepasāmarthya*, but *kāritra* is not always identical with *sāmarthya*. There exists also a *sāmarthya* which is different from *kāritra*. If. *e. g.*, in darkness, the eye sees the *rūpas*, its *sāmarthya* is obstructed by an *āvaraṇa*, but not its *kāritra*. The *darśanasāmarthya* is obstructed by the *tamas* and it is why, in darkness, the eye is not able to perceive the *rūpas*. But its *kāritra* [which is identical with] 'projecting an effect' *(phalākṣepa)* is not obstructed by darkness. Therefore the eye is able to project an effect also in darkness«.

»Apart from the present condition *(avasthā)*, *kāritra* is absent, because it arises only in dependence with the present. [A *dharma*] the *kāritra* of which is destroyed, is not absolutely inactive *(niṣkriya?)*: when an other *svabhāva* originates, it may become its determining cause. But this [determination] is not *kāritra*, it is only *sāmarthya*. Because [a *dharma*] can project an effect only

In case of difference, the antecedent and subsequent unreality of present *[dharmas]* would arise on account of [their] being a cause, being contingent, etc., just as is the case with the *kāritra*. In the opposite case permanence would follow on account of the uninterrupted duration of essence. Indeed, besides substantial identity there is no other essential mark of permanence. [1794—1796]

[Saṃghabhadra and his adherents] must concede that the *kāritra* is alternatively either different or not different from the *dharma*, because these two theses are mutually exclusive, so that when denying the one we affirm the other and *vice versa*. A third possibility does not exist.

[Now it will be shown that both alternatives imply consequences which are not acceptable by Sarvāstivādin].

A. [We begin with the *prasaṅga* deduction from the supposition that the *kāritra* is different from the *dharma*]. If *kāritra* is different from the *dharma*, then we would arrive at the conclusion that *dharmas* existing in the present are unreal in their antecedent and subsequent states. [This inference can be formulated in the following syllogism:]

Probandum: *dharmas* existing in the present are unreal in their antecedent and subsequent states.

Reason: because they are causes *(= hetutvād)*, or because they are contingent *(= saṃskṛtatvād)*.

Example: just as is the case with *kāritra*.

The same probandum can be proved also by other reasons, as *e. g.* 'reality' *(vastutva)*. All these remaining reasons are alluded to by the addition of the word 'etc.' [in the *kārikā* 1795:] »being a cause, being contingent, etc.«.

In the opposite case, if there were no antecedent and no subsequent unreality, then the permanence *(nityatā)* of all which is contingent *(saṃskṛta)* would arise, because the essence *(svabhāva)* [of a *dharma*] would continue to exist in all Times *(= sarvadā)*. Indeed, besides everlasting existence *(sadāsattva)*, there is no other essential mark of permanence.

---

when it is present. What is [absolutely] inactive cannot project its special effect *(na svaphalam ākṣipati)*, and only the projection of a special effect is called *kāritra*«.

As it is said:

»Wise men call permanent a thing the essence of which is never destroyed«.

[Now our opponent may object that the *kāritra (= śakti)* is [also] inherent to permanent substances *(= nityasya śaktiḥ)*[1]. Consequently [in our syllogism] there is no exclusion of the reasons: *hetutva* (being a cause) or *saṃskṛtatva* (being contingent), etc. from the class of negative instances *(= hetoḥ sādhyavipakṣeṇa virodhaḥ)*, [*i. e.* in our case from the class of permanent entities].

[In order to reject this objection, the author says:]

The causal determination of something which is permanent has been previously rejected by showing its impossibility in both alternative cases of a successive and of a simultaneous [manifestation of all the effects]. Indeed, it is obvious that in the permanent there is no place for contingency. [1797]

»Previously« means: »in Chapter [VIII of this treatise, devoted to the] Analysis of permanent Substance«. As it is generally admitted that whatever is contingent *(saṃskṛta)* is also impermanent *(anitya)*, the statement: »no contingency is possible in the permanent« *(saṃskṛtatvaṃ nitye na saṃbhavati)* is self-evident.

[In other words: it can be shown by the way of logical argumentation that the assumption of a *kāritra*, as different from the *dharma* itself, is not compatible with the *traikālya* doctrine].

[The same result can be drawn from the testimony of the Scripture:]

By admitting *kāritra* along with *skandhas, āyatanas* etc. there would arise [for the Sarvāstivādin] an unavoidable contradiction with the fundamental theses of [his] own system. [1798]

By admitting the *kāritra* as something different from the *skandhas*, *āyatanas* etc., there would arise a contradiction with the fundamental thesis of [Buddhist] doctrine. Indeed, the Blessed

---

[1] G. *nityatā śaktiḥ*. T. *gal te rtag pa daṅ nus pa daṅ*. — According to Mahāvibhāṣā, cf. supra p. 21², the *asaṃskṛtas* do not possess any *hetutva*, but nevertheless they have a *sui generis* negative *kāritra*.

One said[1]: »The people are saying 'all': o Brahman! by 'all' are meant the five *skandhas*, the twelve *āyatanas*, the eighteen *dhātus*«. [= The reality of a *kāritra* of the *dharma* apart from the *dharmas* themselves is implicitly denied by this saying of Buddha].

B. [We analyze next the second alternative, *viz.* the supposition that the *kāritra* of a *dharma* and the *dharma* itself are identical. The author says:]

Also when assuming its identity, *kāritra*, because of its non-difference from the *dharma*, would be perpetually existing, just as the essence of the *dharma*. And therefore the distinction of Times could not be based on it, as, indeed, there would be no possibility of distinction between the loss, the attaining and the non-attaining of the *kāritra* [by *dharma*]. [1799—1800]

We may admit that *kāritra* is identical with the *dharma*. Then in its quality of being not different from the *dharma* itself, the *kāritra*, just as the *dharmasvabhāva* would also become 'perpetually existing'. And consequently there would be no distinction of Times based on *kāritra* as in the aforesaid definition: »What has lost its *kāritra* is past, what has attained its *kāritra* is present, what has not yet attained its *kāritra* is future«.

[Indeed this distinction of Times is possible only when

---

[1] *sarvam asti* belongs to those canonical formulae, which are accepted by all schools, but the interpretation of which was by no means settled. In the sense of the Sūtra quoted in the text (Saṃy. Nik. IV, 15), the Sautrāntikas too are »Sarvāstivādins«. But Vaibhāṣikas take *sarvam asti* to mean *sarvadā asti* = *trikāleṣv asti.* Neither one explanation nor the other seem, however, to convey the original meaning which was probably the totality of the differentiated, mortal, world as opposed to the primeval unity of the undifferentiated absolute. Cf. de La Vallée Poussin, *Nirvāṇa*, p. 139, n. 2: »quand l'Écriture parle de »tout« elle entend tout ce qui est l'objet de la connaissance vulgaire: elle fait abstraction d'une chose plus subtile, plus difficile à connaître, à savoir le Nirvāṇa. Ceci résulte de Majjhima, I, 3, où sont séparés et distingués, d'une part »tout«, d'autre part le Nirvāṇa«. In other words: *sarvam* = *sarve [saṃskṛta] dharmāḥ* = *nāmarūpa* as opposed to the one, absolute and transcendental Dharma = *dharmakāya* = *nirvāṇadhātu.*

attaining and not attaining [of the present] are understood as [two real and] distinctly differentiated [states] of the *kāritra* and precisely those two [states] cannot be distinctly differentiated because there is no such a differentiation for [entities] which perpetually persist in the same unique essence (= *sadāvasthitaikarūpa).*

[Another consequence of the identity of *kāritra* and *dharma* is the following one:]

> Or in consequence of its being not different from the *kāritra*, the *dharma* may be just as *kāritra*: cut off before and after and condensing its whole existence in the instantaneous middlepoint (= *madhyamātrakasarva).* [1801]

In consequence of its being not different from the *kāritra*, the *dharma* would be just as *kāritra*, lacking past and future and possessing its whole existence only in the middle [point-instant]. [This view is actually accepted by the Sautrāntikas, it stands however in direct opposition to the theory of *sarvāstivāda*].

§ 5. The third possibility of a *kāritra* which is and is not identical with the *dharmasvabhāva* is rejected.

[The Vaibhāṣika rejoinders: Your two *prasaṅgas* do not exhaust all possibilities of the problem. Indeed, besides difference and identity of *kāritra* and *dharma* a third theory is possible according to which *kāritra* and *dharma* are and are not identical. This is just our stand-point. We teach that the *kāritra* does not exist independently, as something different from the *dharma*, but we deny that the *kāritra* is simply identical with the *dharma* and that it lasts permanently just as does the *dharma*].

[Alluding to this theory the Sautrāntika states:] The assertion that *kāritra* and *dharma* are and are not identical includes a mutual contradiction. It is therefore justly turned into ridicule by the following stanza:

> The *kāritra* does not exist permanently, the *dharma* is characterised as existing permanently, but nevertheless the *kāritra* is not different from the *dharma*! Indeed, it is a caprice of the Īśvara in its arbitrariness [1]. [1802]

---

[1] Cf. AbhK V, 58; N p. 6; Bodhicaryāvatārapañjikā, p. 5.

As a consequence of the non-difference from the *kāritra* it follows that the *dharmas* of *rūpa* etc. do not exist permanently. Therefore the Vaibhāṣika admits: »the *kāritra* does not exist permanently«. In the same way as a consequence of non-difference] it follows that *kāritra* is not different from *dharma* and it is just this which is [also] admitted [by the Vaibhāṣika]. [And nevertheless the Vaibhāṣika assumes that the *dharma* exist permanently!] This attitude has been characterized as a caprice of the Īśvara. Just as the Īśvara and similar almighty persons, without troubling themselves about what is rationally founded or not, act arbitrarily, such is exactly the attitude of these Vaibhāṣikas: arbitrary and disregarding all logical consistency.

§ 6. *kāritra* of *kāritra*, rejected.

[Besides this *prasaṅga*-deduction there is another argument against the thesis of Vaibhāṣikas, *viz.* that the distinction of Times is based on the *kāritra*:]

> If the Time-epochs [of the *kāritra*] are established also with reference to another *kāritra*, we must repeat the same method of arguing ad infinitum. [1803]

According to Vaibhāṣikas the *kāritra* is not different from the *dharmas*. Consequently it lasts also during the three Times and has its future, present and past states[1], *viz.*: the *kāritra* which has not yet attained its existence is a future *kāritra*; the *kāritra* which has just attained its existence is the present *kāritra*; the *kāritra* which has already ceased to be is a past *kāritra*].

[Now we state:] If you claim the possession of three Times, future etc. by the *kāritra* [of a *dharma*], without however admitting the existence of a second *kāritra* of this *kāritra*, then you cannot say that the distinction of Times is [always] based on the *kāritra*, because you admit an exception to this rule. You teach namely that the *kāritra* possesses the three Times, future etc.

---

[1] This tacit supposition is necessary for deducing the *prasaṅga* formulated by the Sautrāntika. This very starting point is, however, erroneous. The Vaibhāṣika do not teach that *kāritra* possesses the three Times; *kāritra* is momentary and the *dharmasvabhāva* only lasts through the three Times.

only with reference to its own essence (= *svarūpasattā*), [not with reference to its *kāritra*] and you should also treat the *dharmas* (= *bhāvas*) precisely in the same manner. Hence what is the use of inventing a *kāritra*?

Now, if in order to avoid the objection that there are exceptions from the rule accepted, the Vaibhāṣika admits the *kāritra* of the *kāritra* of a *dharma*, then the whole *prasaṅga*-deduction: [difference or not difference] must be repeated. And moreover there would arise the error of a regressus in infinitum.

§ 7. Śāntarakṣita's criticism of the theory according to which the *kāritra* is a quality differentiating the essence of a *dharma*.

If one holds that *kāritra* is a *viśeṣa* like *sapratighatva* etc., which is not different[1] from the *svarūpa*, we reply: this theory is useless against the argument in question.

sapratighatva etc. is not conceived as an occasional [quality] of an unvariably concomitant substance because it expresses the being as such. [1804]

Let us return to the syllogism: assuming the identity [of *kāritra* with the *dharma*], the *kāritra* would be everlasting because, in that case, no differentiation (*viśeṣa*), just as in the case of the *dharmasvarūpa*, would be possible. Referring to this argument Saṃghabhadra says: there exist determining qualities (*viśeṣaka dharma*) which are not different from the *svarūpa* (= *svabhāva*) [of the *dharma*], as *e. g.* the *sapratighatva* of the earth etc. Indeed, the [*dharmas*], although not differentiated by their *padārthatva* [which they posses in common], are differentiated as *sapratigha* and *apratigha*, *sanidarśana* and *anidarśana* by qualities (= *dharma*) which are not different from their *svarūpa*. In the same manner, a *dharma* may be determined by a *kāritra* [which is itself not different from the *svarūpa* of the *dharma*].

[1] G has *svarūpād vyatirikto*, but. Tib. reads °*tha mi dad* = *svarūpāvyatirikto*.

[Master Śāntarakṣita rejects this theory, because] it is useless against the argument in question which is as follows: having admitted that *kāritra* is not different from the *svarūpa*, no differentiation (=*viśeṣa*) of the *padārtha*, which has been identified with the *kāritra*, is possible; hence the necessary conclusion that no distinction of Times can be established by *kāritra*.

[Between special qualities and *kāritra* there is of course no analogy]. The *dharmas* of the earth etc. are different because they are differentiated by their mutually exclusive *svalakṣaṇas* Hence some are *sapratigha*, and some *apratigha*, as *e.g.* the *vedanā* etc. But these [*dharmas*] which are *apratigha* can never become *sapratigha*, because there is no unique unvariably concomitant substance (= *eko 'nugamī padārthātmā*) to which the *sapratighatva*) of the earth etc. could be attributed as a temporary, occasional quality (*kādācitka dharma*). Special qualities as *sapratighatva* etc. express the whole being as such, *i.e.* as determined by the exclusion of all remaining homogeneous (*sajātīya*) as well as heterogeneous (*vijātīya*) qualities. Hence, although not differing from the *svarūpa*, they cannot be [in opposition to the *kāritra*], the principle of differentiation of the same [unchangeable substance].

[Objection:] if there is no *sapratighatva* as a principle of differentiation existing independently of the *svarūpa* itself, why is the expression *rūpasya sapratighatvam* used as if we were concerned with a real entity differentiating the *rūpa* into *sapratigha* and *aprātigha*?

The author answers:

> Without rejecting other differences, the *dharma* (= *bhāva*) is thus characterized by the expression *rūpasya sapratighatva* just as we say also *cetaso vāsanā*. [1806]

anakṣiptānyabhedena = *bhedāntarāpratikṣepena* [1] = without rejecting other differences. — »Is thus characterized« = as if it were an [independently existing] principle of differentiation (= *vyatirekī*). »Just as the *vāsanā* of the mind« is the example [2].

---

[1] T. *mi ḥphen yin*. G. has *bhedāntarapratikṣepeṇa*.

[2] The *vāsanās* (= *bījas*) are *upatta* by the *citta*: »'appropriés' — embrassés (*parigrah*, 'intégrés') dans son être, partageant son destin bon ou mauvais (*ekayogakṣemeṇa*)«. De La Vallée Poussin, *Siddhi*, p. 124.

§ 8. The impredicability of *kāritra.*

Again Master [Saṃghabhadra] says[1]: the *kāritra* is not different from the *dharma*, because we do not perceive it independently of the *svabhāva* [of the *dharma*]; neither is it simply the *dharma*, because, even when the *svabhāva* [of the *dharma*] exists, *kāritra* may sometimes be absent. It can neither [be said, that] *kāritra* does not exist at all, only because there is no difference [between *kāritra* and *dharma*], or because *kāritra* is antecedently inexistent. [In one word:] *kāritra* is just as *saṃtāna* which is defined as the immediate succession of *dharmas*. Indeed, it is not different from the *dharmas*, because it is not perceived independently of them. Moreover, it is also not simply the *dharmas*, because, in that case a single *dharma* would still be a *saṃtāna*. Finally, it cannot be said that *saṃtāna* does not exist at all, because its effects are real. It is said therefore:

> We postulate the effects of *saṃtāna* [as existing really], but the *saṃtāna* itself can nowhere be found; our thesis that the distinction of Times is based on *kāritra* may be also understood by analogy to this.

[The author now criticizes this theory]. He says:

> *kāritra* is described [by you] as being exactly like *saṃtāna* etc.: impredicable with reference to both alternatives of identity and non-identity [with the *dharmaṣ*]. In this case would it not possess [only] a *saṃvṛti*-reality?
>
> And hence being only a construction of the mind *(= kalpita)*, it will not be able [to produce] any effect *(kārya)*, exactly like the *saṃtāna*, because only real entities possess the potency of efficacious action *(= arthakriyā)*.
>
> Its existence is not real and therefore the distinction of Times which is based upon it is not *tāttvika* either (= is also without foundation in absolute reality). [1807—1809]

In the *kārika* it is said: »*saṃtāna* etc.« — by the word »etc.« other similar entities as collection *(samūha)* etc. are included. As regards the *saṃtāna*, neither its identity nor its non-identity with elements constituting it can be predicated. Therefore the *saṃtāna*

[1] Cf. N p. 633 a 25.

[for us Sautrāntikas] is *niḥsvabhāva.* Just as the *pudgala* [which is also impredicable], and, in the same sense the *kāritra* is *niḥsvabhāva* as well. Indeed, if there is any *svabhāva* [in a thing], it is necessarily either identical or not identical. And hence, because it is [only] a construction of the mind *(=kalpitatvāt)*, the *kāritra* of the *dharma* is not capable to produce any effect, exactly like the *saṃtāna.* Indeed, the *saṃtāna*, being only a construction of the mind, possesses no capacity of producing effects in consequence of its *niḥsvabhāvatva*, and because the production of effects is intimately bound with the *svabhāva.* Therefore only real elements of the *saṃtāna* are capable of efficacious action, and not the constructed *(kalpita) saṃtāna.*

[A further consequence of all these statements is that] *kāritra*, because it exists only as a *prajñapti*, does not exist *paramārthatas* neither before nor after [its manifestation]. And, therefore, the distinction of Times as well which is [according to your doctrine] based upon it, is only a construction of the mind and nothing real *(na bhāvikam = na tāttvikam).*

§ 9. *kāritra* as *prajñapti* is rejected

[Our opponent asks:] It may be granted that *kāritra*, and consequently the distinction of Times which is based upon it as well, are only *prajñaptisat.* What is wrong in this assumption?

[The author answers:]

The *kāritra*, which has been defined [by you] as a potency of projecting effects, has only a nominal existence *(= śabdagocara)*. But potency means reality, therefore how can it be only *prajñaptisat*?

Can the *rūpa*-[elements of fire], which are postulated as effecting the action of burning, ripening etc., be accepted as identical in their past and future states?

If so, how can such mutually exclusive aspects as [precedent] non-activity, actual activity and [subsequent] loss of activity coexist in the same undifferentiated *(nirviśiṣṭa)* thing? Now [our opponent] may admit that the thing existing during the [three] Times is postulated, not as being the same and undifferentiated, because it attains its next [Time-] condition after having abandoned the [previous one]. In this case we must ask: are the conditions *(= avasthā)* different from the being itself? [The answer cannot be but:] No. Because [otherwise] inactivity would be the consequence.

Indeed [only] because those [three Time-conditions] are really existing, the existence of effects is perceived. [1810—1815]

[Sautrāntika:] You have defined the *kāritra* of the *dharmas* as the potency of projecting results *(phalākṣepa)*. [The potency of projecting results, however, is just the definition of the *svabhāva*, consequently it can be only *tāttvika,* having its foundation in absolute reality, and not *śabdagocara*, belonging only to the domain of verbal conventions. Indeed, the *svabhāvalakṣaṇa*, because it does not belong to wordly experience *(= avyavahārikam)*, cannot be attained by words. And thus, being not different from the being itself] [1], how can potency possess [only] a *prajñapti*-existence? [The answer is:] it cannot. And therefore the Time-distinction, which depends on it, must be also accepted as »based upon absolute reality« *(tāttvika)*.

Moreover: we perceive *rūpa*-elements constituting fire etc., which possess [the potency of] effecting such purposive actions [= which are *arthakriyākāri*] as burning, ripening etc. [Concerning such] potencies [there arises the question:] are they in their past and future conditions the same or different [potencies]? If they are the same, how can the three mutually exclusive qualities, *viz.* the [antecedent] inactivity etc., by which the distinction of succeeding conditions of future, past and present is established, be coexistent in one and the same, undifferentiated thing? Indeed, if, notwithstanding the attribution of contradictory qualities, the identity [of a thing] could be preserved, then all differentiations would disappear and the whole world would become one. And the consequence of identity would be the simultaneous origination [of all effects].

Now, [to avoid all these *prasaṅgas* another theory may be taken into consideration:] the thing [existing] during [the three] Times is not postulated as being without differentiation *(nirviśiṣṭa)*, because [in reality] it is differentiated by the difference of aban-

[1] The whole passage is wanting in G. My translation follows the T.

doning [the one] and of grasping [the another] condition. If it is so, we must ask: of what sort are those conditions? — Are they different *(bhinna)* or not different from the being itself *(bhāva = svabhāva)*?

Our opponent answers: they are not different *(abheda)*. — Why? [For two reasons:] 1° because the inactivity of the being would be the consequence, and 2° because the potency of producing effects would be realized in the case of presence as well in the case of absence *(= anvaya-vyatirekābhyām)* of those conditions.

§ 10. The 'thing' and its 'conditions'.

Now [Śāntarakṣita] criticizes [also these views. He says:]

How can those [three conditions] be proved not to be different from the thing itself during the Time-epochs? As they exist and disappear after having been previously inexistent, how can they be 'essentially identical' *(= tādātmika)*?

If in the middle (= present) condition a thing is active by its own essence *(svabhāvena = svarūpeṇa)*, then the same essence exists also in both remaining conditions [of future and of past] and [consequently] how can you imagine the previous lack and the subsequent loss of activity in this thing's own essence, in those two conditions?

On the other hand, if [the thing] is active through the essence of some other being *(pararūpeṇa = parabhāvena)*, then its own inactivity would result.

[But] if we admit that [things as] fire etc. are not the same in the conditions of past and future, this thesis would give no support to the objection of intermingling activity [and non-activity]. [The consequence would be the doctrine, that] the capacity of producing effects *(= kāryayogya)* arises in the present moment *(= idānīm)*, after having been previously inexistent, and that it does not last, after its having gained existence. In this manner the absence of invariable coexistence of the thing [with its Time-conditions] would be proved. [1816—1820]

[We ask:] how can it be demonstrated that the conditions *(avasthā)* are not different from the thing itself *(vastu)*? [And we answer:] it is not possible at all. Indeed, the *avasthās* come into existence after having been inexistent and they disappear after having been existent; but the *vastu* is not postulated thus, for it is granted [by all schools] that it exists permanently. Consequently, how can the *avasthās*, which come into existence after having been inexistent and which [afterwards] cease to be existent, be 'essentially identical' *(tādātmika)* [with the *vastu*]? [We reply again:] it is quite impossible! The *yogakṣema* [1] [of these two notions: *avasthā* and *vastu*] is [essentially] different.

[Now we are giving a formal demonstration of our denial of the Vaibhāṣika doctrine by the way of the *prasaṅga* method:]

[First alternative (I):] the *avasthās* and the *vastu* are not different [2]. Then two following *prasaṅga* syllogisms could be formulated:

a) the *avasthās* exist permanently because they are not different from the *vastu*; just as it is the case with the *svabhāva* of the *vastu*;

b) the *vastu* comes into existence after having been inexistent, because it is not different from the *avasthās*, just as the *svabhāvas* of the *avasthās*.

[Second alternative (II):] the *avasthās* and the *vastu* are different. [In this thesis two further alternatives may be distinguished: a) in all *avasthās* the *vastu* is the same, identical *vastu*, b) in each *avasthā* there is a different *vastu*.]

a. Admitting that there is a difference between the *avasthās* and the *vastu*, [which is the same in all *avasthās*], the attribution of contradictory qualities [to the same subject] will again be unavoidable.

[Indeed, let us consider in this connection the following *prasaṅga*:] the *vastu* displays its *kāritra* in the middle (= present) *avasthā* either through its *svabhāva* (= through its own essence), or through the *parabhāva* (= through the essence of another *vastu*). [Both suppositions lead to unacceptable consequences:]

---

[1] *bhinnayogakṣema* = 'different destiny' = »a different connotation«: as opposed to *ekayogakṣema*; cf. Triṃśikā p. 19, Jacobi p. 13: »als etwas durchaus Gleichartiges«; TSP p. 134: *ekayogakṣemalakṣaṇatvād abhedasya* and supra, p. 45 note 2.

[2] *bhavatu cāvasthābhedaparikalpanā*, Tib.: *gnas skabs tha dad pa yoṅs su brtags pa yin du chug mod.* G. has *parakalpanā*.

α) First alternative: the *vastu* displays its *kāritra* (= the *vastu* is *kāraka*) in the middle-*avasthā* through its *svabhāva*; then the same *svabhāva* also exists in the remaining two *avasthās* of the past and of the future, and, consequently, in the very *svabhāva* which is just displaying its *kāritra*, the absence of the not yet manifested and of the still vanished *kāritra* would be coexistent. How it is possible?

β) Second alternative: the *vastu* displays its *kāritra* in the middle-*avasthā* through the *svabhāva* of another *vastu* (= through the *parabhāva*): then the *vastu* itself is without its own *kāritra*; it is hence a non-*vastu*.

In this way the alternative (II a) that *vastus*, as fire etc. are the same in all *avasthās*, [is shown] to be impossible.

b. [Now let us analize the alternative (II b), that there is a different *vastu* [in each *avasthā*]. When accepting this thesis we would be free from the objection of intermingling in the same subject (= *ekatra*) mutually exclusive qualities as *kāritra* and non-*kāritra*, just because the *vastu* would not be the same. But [on the other hand a new difficulty would arise, *viz.*] that the *vastu* as fire etc. which possesses its *kāritra* as burning, ripening etc. would come into existence after having been inexistent, and that it would cease to exist after having been existent. Thus the contradiction with the accepted definition of the *vastu* as possessing a permanent existence (= *sadāstitva*) would arise as consequence of the absence of coexistence (= *anvaya*) [of the *vastu* with its *avasthās*].

§ 11. Two *prasaṅga* arguments shoving the impossibility of a thing without *kāritra*.

[Vaibhāṣika objects:] the *vastu*, as possessing the *kāritra*, may indeed come into existence after having been inexistent, and it may cease to exist after having been existent. [But this does not exclude that the *vastu* exists in the past and in the future *avasthās* [as the same *vastu*], possessing however no *kāritra*. Consequently, there is no contradiction with the permanent existence accepted [by our school].

[To this we reply:]

Only a *vastu* (= *bhāva*) which possesses *kāritra* (= *kriyā*) is really existent. And precisely this kind of *vastu* does not exist in both *avasthās* [of the past and of the future]. From the *vastu* which exists [in these *avasthās* without *kāritra*] no effect *(kārya)* can originate. [1821]

[Vaibhāṣika again protests:] the past *sabhāga-hetus* possess the *kāritra (= kāryayogya)*. Your argument: 'no *kārya* can originate from the *vastu*, which exists [in these *avasthās* without the *kāritra*]' is not right.

[In reply to this objection Śāntarakṣita adduces further *prasaṅga* deductions showing the impossibility of the Vaibhāṣika doctrine. He says:]

That past *vastu* [without *kāritra*] would be evidently a present one because, in consequence of its occasionalness *(kādācitkatayā)*, it is coming into existence after having been [previously] inexistent, exactly like other [present *vastus*].

What is free from causal determination *(ahetutva)* can only be either always existent or always inexistent. A thing the existence of which is necessarily determined by causal factors is called 'present'.

Our opponents teach, that there is a substantial difference *(vailakṣaṇya)* with the *pratisaṃkhyānirodha* etc., because the *saṃskṛtatva* of *rūpa* etc. is due to association with *jāti*, *sthiti* etc.

Concerning this [theory] we must ask: what is the *viśeṣa* produced [by the *jāti*] and with reference to which [the *jāti*] is called 'the parent of the [*rūpa*]'? — Is it different or not different from the not yet born *rūpa*?

To begin with [the first alternative:] if this *viśeṣa (= atiśaya)* is not different, then it has no potency of producing, because, just like after the realization [of the *jāti*], it exists also before [its] realization.

This *viśeṣa (= atiśaya)* does not exist as a different one, because, owing to this difference, there is no possibility [of any real relation] [1]. Moreover, the *asatkārya* would then be the consequence, because it was previously inexistent.

---

[1] A similar argumentation is to be found in TSP 146, ad TS 402 where the impossibility of cooperation of the *sahakārins* with a *sthirapadārtha* is discussed: *teneti = atiśayena, tasyāpīti = nityasya kaḥ saṃbandha ityādinottaram āha. kaḥ saṃbandhaḥ =*

[When analysing] disintegration, stabilization and destruction in both alternatives of difference and identity, precisely the same logical errors concerning [the remaining *saṃskṛtalakṣaṇas*], *jarā* etc. will arise. [1822—1828]

[First *prasaṅga* (I): the past *vastu* without *kāritra*, which you admit, would be a present one,] because in consequence of its occasionalness [it comes into existence after having been previously inexistent]. Example: other present *vastus* which do not constitute the subjects of our discussion (= which are not the *dharmin* of the present syllogism).

[This argument] is valid, because the invariable concomitance *(anvaya)* [between occasional existence and presence is not missing]: everything which is produced by causal determinants *(hetupratyaya)*, is called 'present', and everything which exists occasionally *(kādācitka)* is necessarily produced by causal determinants. Indeed, for an entity which is not produced by causal determinants *(= ahetuka)* only two alternatives are possible: to be always existent or to be always inexistent, for only in these two cases complete independence from any other entity is guaranteed. [Hence, the third possibility, that of being sometimes existent and sometimes inexistent is reserved to entities which are causally determined = whose existence is limited by causal determinants]. Therefore [we may fairly conclude:] whatever exists occasionally, is necessarily produced by causal determinants, and whatever is produced by causal determinants is necessarily in the present. [In one word:] 'to exist occasionally *(kādācitkatva)*' implies: 'to be present *(varttamānatva)*' [and our *prasaṅga* deduction is precisely based on this *vyāpti*].

[Second *prasaṅga* (II):] if past and future things exist as real entities *(dravyatas)*, then the consequence would be the permanent existence *(śāśvata)* of all *saṃskṛta*-elements *(= saṃskāra)*, and hence the special quality *(viśeṣa = atiśaya)* which distinguishes

---

naiva kaścid ity arthaḥ. dvividha eva hi saṃbandhas: tādātmyaṃ tadutpattiś ca. tatra na tāvat tādātmyalakṣaṇo bhedasyā 'ṅgīkṛtatvāt. nāpi tadutpattilakṣaṇaḥ sahakāribhya eva tasyotpatteḥ. tatas tasyotpattir aṅgīkriyate, tadā tanmātrabhāvitvād atiśayānāṃ yugapad evotpattiḥ syāt. tataś ca sarvakāryāṇām yugapad utpattiprasaṅgaḥ. atiśayavataḥ kāraṇasya sarvadā 'vasthitatvāt.

the *saṃskṛta* elements, such as *rūpa* etc., from the *asaṃskṛta* elements, such as *pratisaṃkhyānirodha* etc., would not be possible.

The Vaibhāṣika protests: the *saṃskṛtatva* of *rūpa* etc. is due to the association of these elements with the four *saṃskṛtalakṣaṇas*; *asaṃskṛta* elements, as infinite space etc. are not associated with them. There is therefore an essential difference (*=vailakṣaṇya*) between *rūpa* etc. and *pratisaṃkhyānirodha* etc.

We reply: Your theory is wrong. [In order to demonstrate it, let us consider your distinction of] the four *saṃskṛtalakṣaṇas*, *viz. jāti, jarā, sthiti* and *anityatā*, and their special potencies (*= kāritra, vyāpara*) causing birth, disintegrating, stabilizing and destroying.

We may start with the analysis of the *jāti*. [According to your doctrine] it gives birth to a supplementation (*viśeṣa*) [*i. e.* to a special quality [1] owing to which future *saṃskṛta*-elements acquire

---

[1] 1. According to the Nyāya-Vaiśeṣika, etc. the origination of an effect is due to the cooperation of many special causes (*asādhāraṇa-kāraṇa*) which can be divided into the 3 following categories: a) basal instrumental cause (*sādhakatama, atiśayaśaktimat-kāraṇa, karaṇa*), b) subsidiary or assisting causes (*sahakāri*), c) material cause (*samavāyi, upādāna-kāraṇa*). To this may be added the fourth variety of general or universal causes (*sādhāraṇa*), as Space, Time, the will of God etc. The »collocation« of all these factors destroys a given whole (*avayavin*) and produces a new »collocation«, a new whole out of the same material. This transition is what is called the *asatkāryavāda*: it does not obviously teach the creation of a new substance, but only an increment, an outgrowth of immanent potencies (*atiśaya-ādhana*, 'Steigerung der Kräfte') owing to which the clay is supplanted by a pot, a seed by a sprout etc. The basal cause is the *sādhakatamam kāraṇam* because it contributes pre-eminently to the production of the *atiśaya*.

2. The theory of causation elaborated by the Buddhist Abhidharma shares with the Naiyāyikas the view that no effect arises from a single cause. There is also — in spite of the essentially different interpretation of causal interdependence as *pratītyasamutpāda* — some analogy and correspondence between the Buddhist and the Nyāya-Vaiśeṣika classifications; so *e.g.* the *adhipati-pratyaya* can be compared with the *atiśayaśaktimat = sādhakatamaṃ kāraṇaṃ*, the *samanantara-pratyaya* with the *upādāna* or *samāvayikāraṇa*. Cf. Th. Stcherbatsky, *Central Conception*, p. 106, *Buddhist Logic* II, p. 311. There is also an obvious analogy between the

their *kāritra* and produce their effects]. In this sense *jāti* is called 'the parent of the *saṃskṛtadharmas*'. [It does not produce the *saṃskṛta*-elements themselves, but it makes them present.]

We ask: of what kind is this *viśeṣa?* — Does it differ or not from the element itself?

1. First alternative: the *viśeṣa* is not different from the element itself. This thesis is impossible, because then this *viśeṣa*, being realized *(niṣpanna)* before the *jāti* had displayed its *kāritra*, would be fully ineffective just like after [its] realization. Indeed, what is [already] realized, is without *kāritra*, otherwise everything would possess its *kāritra (= atiprasaṅgāt)* [1].

2. Second alternative: the *viśeṣa* is different from the element. This cannot be admitted either, because then the relation expressed by [the Genetive case:] 'the *viśeṣa* of this *rūpa*' would be without real fundation. [Indeed, what kind of a relation would in this case be possible?] The relation of substantial identity *(tādātmya)* is excluded by the very supposition that there is a difference, or because the aforesaid consequences would arise. Causal relation *(tadutpatti)* is also out of question, because the *jāti*, [not the element itself] is the producing cause of this

---

sādhāraṇa-kāraṇas of Nyāya-Vaiśeṣikas, Sāṃkhyas etc. and the *saṃskṛtalakṣaṇas* of the Vaibhāṣikas. Thus the effect is produced by the cooperation of two sets of causal determinants: by the totality of special causes and conditions *(hetu-pratyaya-sāmagrya)* and by the four (or three) universal forces of contingency *(saṃskṛtalakṣaṇa)*. Cf. AbhK II 234. The essence of the *saṃskṛta-dharma* always exists but only at a given moment, when a definite constellation of *hetu* and *pratyayas* arises, *jāti* and the remaining *saṃskṛtalakṣaṇas* associate with the *dharma* and compel it to manifest the momentary *kāritra.* The eternal elements as *ākāśa* are never associated with the *saṃskṛtalakṣaṇas* and are therefore beyond the reach of contingency and causality.

3. This doctrine is rejected by Sautrāntikas. The *saṃskṛtalakṣaṇas* taught by Buddha refer to the whole personal series *(saṃtāna)*, not to the separate elements. Moreover, the hypostasis of the *saṃskṛtalakṣaṇas*, as independent forces cooperating with all *saṃskṛtadharmas*, is quite superfluous: it is the totality of causes and conditions *(sāmagrya)* which makes the *dharma* present, not the *jāti.* Cf. AbhK II 228, 235.

[1] According to T., G. has *anavasthāprasaṅgāt.*

viśeṣa (= jāter eva tadutpatteḥ)[1]. Other relations, as *ādhāra*, *ādheya* etc. cannot be admitted either, because they are only special cases of causal dependence.

Now [let us again consider] the assumption of causal dependence. [Then two following *prasaṅgas* may be taken into account:]

1) [The element] is a *tanmātra-kāraṇa* (= a basal, main cause)[2]. Then the *viśeṣa*, as produced exclusively by it, would always arise and *jāti* would be of no use.

2) The element produces the *viśeṣa* in correlation with the *jāti*. This assumption is possible only when the *jāti* is the *saha-kāri-kāraṇa*. But then, by analysing the two alternatives of identity and not-identity in the same manner as the *viśeṣa* analysed before, we shall have a *regressus ad infinitum*.

Therefore [we conclude]: admitting the difference of the element and its *viśeṣa*, we are unable to establish logically any relation between them.

Another [argument against the theory of difference]: the *viśeṣa* of the element is previously inexistent; the consequence therefore is the *asatkārya*, the inexistence of the effect before its creation by the cause.

In the same manner, when the disintegration (= *anyathātva*) is accomplished by *jarā*, the stabilization by *sthiti* and the annihilation by *anityatā* two alternatives [must be taken into consideration, *viz.* the alternative] of identity and of non-identity [between the element itself and the *viśeṣa* produced by the special potencies] of these [three remaining *saṃskṛtalakṣaṇas*], disintegration etc. The criticism which applies to *jarā* etc. is just the same as in the case of the *jāti*.

§ 12. *kāritra* and the momentariness of past and future *dharmas*.

[Now we come to another argument:]

Those [*saṃskṛtalakṣaṇaṣ*] *jāti* etc. are executing their special effects by an essential determination of their potency (= *sāmarthya-niyamātmanā*) and their essence exists before

---

[1] Lit: »because it arises out of *jāti*«.

[2] *tanmātra-kāraṇa* = *atiśaya-śaktimat, sādhakatamaṃ kāraṇaṃ*, cf. TSP p. 407, 413.

and after; therefore why do they not always[1] display the activity which is [produced] by their [everlasting] essential potency? But if they do, the indefiniteness of Time-epochs [is the consequence]. [1830]

Moreover, the fact that *jāti* etc. each display their special effect is due to the determination of their *sāmarthya-svabhāva*. Now [as you teach] that *sāmarthya-svabhāva* (= essential potency) is always existent, hence [you are obliged to allow that the *saṃskṛtalakṣaṇas* must] always display their special effects[2]. [And if you object that this consequence would not arise, because the displaying of special effects *(svakārya)* of *jāti* etc. depends on cooperation with auxiliary causes and conditions *(hetu-pratyaya)*, then we answer:] the lack of [auxiliary] causes and conditions is no [argument], because these causes and conditions [again according to your own theory] are always present.

We conclude that *jāti* etc. produce their special effects as origination etc. [not only in the present, but also] in their past and future conditions. Hence the indefiniteness (= *aparimitatva* = non-discrimination) of Time-epochs in each single Time-epoch is the inevitable consequence [of your stand-point]

Moreover of what nature are past [and future] things? Are they momentary or not? If we admit the first, the indefiniteness of Time-epochs would arise again. [Indeed] a moment which just originates is present, when it is annihilated after having arisen, then it is past; that which will arise is a future one. [1831—1832]

There are two alternatives: past and future things may be either momentary or not momentary. If we admit the first alternative, *viz.* that they are momentary, then we shall have just the same indefiniteness of Time-epochs, [as before]. By the words 'a moment which just originates etc.' the author explains this [indefiniteness].

---

[1] G. has *prārabhante na kiṃ tadā svānurūpaṃ kriyāṃ* and *tadā* is also confirmed by the Tib. version *(de tshe)*. The sense, however, requires clearly *sadā*.

[2] The same argument AbhK II, 56.

Or they are not momentary. Then we shall have a contradiction with the fundamental tenet. Indeed, the doctrine that all *saṃskāras* are momentary has been taught as a fundamental thesis [of Buddhism]. [1833]

The second alternative is: past and future things are not momentary. If we admit this, we will be in contradiction with the fundamental tenet *(siddhānta, kṛtānta)* which proclaims that all *saṃskāras* are momentary.

We shall also have a contradiction with sound logic: whatever exists is necessarily momentary [1], just as is the present. We have already demonstrated before the implication-relationship between these two predications *(= atra)*. [1834]

Moreover, this thesis, [*viz.* the non-momentariness of past things] would be not only in contradiction with the fundamental, [generally admitted] tenet [of Buddhist philosophy], but also it would be in contradiction with logical arguments, namely with the following syllogism:

Whatever is existing is momentary.
Example: present things.
Reason: past and future things are existing.
Conclusion: they are necessarily momentary.

In a previous Chapter, that on Momentariness [2] *(kṣaṇabhaṅgādhikāre)*, we have proved the implication-relationship *(=pratibandha)* of this *hetu (= sattva)* [with the *sādhya* '*kṣaṇikatva*']. This syllogism is therefore not *anaikāntika.* Indeed the potency of producing effects *(arthakriyākāritva)* is the essence of existence, because non-momentary entities exclude simultaneous as well as successive *arthakriyākāritva*: therefore, when excluding the *arthakriyākāritva*, we also exclude existence *(= sattva)* which is identical with it. The predicate 'existence' *(= sattva)* is excluded from all *dharmins* which are predicated by the negation of the *sādhya* (= from all *sādhya-vipakṣas*) [and thus the validity of our syllogism is ascertained].

---

[1] G. *santaś cen niyamāt kṣaṇabhaṅginaḥ*; but *santaś ca* (as in Tib.) would be a better reading.

[2] TS 391—394, TSP p. 143.

§ 13. *kāritra* and *saṃskṛtatva.*

[A further argument proceeds as follows]:

Those past and future [elements] may be either able or unable to produce an *arthakriyā.* If this ability is really existent [in past and future elements], then [past and future elements] are present just as other [present elements].

On the other hand, in the case of being not present, the already destroyed and the not yet born elements would become deprived of all potencies, just like sky flowers etc.

All non-contingent *(= akṛta = asaṃskṛta)* elements, as space *(ākāśa)* etc. fall under the same rule; they are [consequently] not arguments for the assumption of the *anaikāntikatva* [of our syllogism deducing momentariness from existence].

The potency of elements to produce a determined *arthakriyā* is identical with origination from *pratyayas.* If there were no causal determination, all would arise out of all in the same manner.

The origination of the potency of a determined *arthakriyā* is produced by *pratyayas* and there is no other definition of a present element.

And precisely this [characteristic of the present] entirely fits in with your past and future elements. Therefore why is the nature of being present not ascribed to them?

We consider two alternatives: past and future elements are either capable to produce an *arthakriyā* or not.

1. If they are capable to do it then, this capacity being really existent, they become present, just as [other] present elements which are not subjects of this discussion.

Whatever is able to produce an *arthakriyā*, is present.

Example: present elements, which are not the subject of this discussion *(avivādāspadībhūta).*

Reason: past and future elements are able to produce an *arthakriyā.*

[Conclusion: they are present].

This syllogism is based on the relation of substantial identity between the *hetu* and the *sādhya.* And it is not *anaikāntika,* because it denies the predication '*varttamānatva*' for elements which are already destroyed or which are not yet born. The privation of all potencies *(=sarva-sāmarthya-viyogitva)* would be the consequence, just like in the case of sky flowers and other unreal things.

prayoga:

Whatever is not present does not possess any potency.
Example: just like a sky flower etc.
Past and future things are not present.
Consequently they do not possess any potency.

This syllogism is based on the non-apprehension (=negation) of the implicans *(=vyāpakānupalabdhi)*. [And it is not true that] it is made uncertain *(anaikāntika)* by the *asaṃskṛta*-elements, as *ākāśa* and the two *nirodhas*, because they can also be present as *dharmin (=pakṣikāraṇāt)* in the same syllogism. They are therefore no arguments for the assumption that [our syllogism] is uncertain.

Indeed you must concede that the potency of the *dharmas (=bhāvas)* to produce determined *arthakriyās* is identical with their origination from *pratyayas* (=with their *hetutva*). Otherwise if this [potency] were without *hetu* then, owing to the absence of determining *hetus*, there would be no determined potency of *dharmas (=bhāvas)* at all. And then it would be possible to assume any cause for any effect. Therefore [the attribution of] the determined potency to the non-contingent *(=akṛta)* entities as *ākāśa* etc. is not possible and thus there is no reason for the assumption that our syllogism is made uncertain by these non-contingent entities.

Neither is it true that our first syllogism is invalidated by the error of the *saṃdigdha-vipakṣa-vṛttikā* (=uncertainty of absence in contrary cases), because the origination of the potency of determined *arthakriyās* is produced by *hetu-pratyayas* and precisely the fact of being produced by *hetu-pratyayas* is the essential mark of the 'present'. Now this very essential mark of presence is found wholly in past and future [*dharmas*]. As there are no other reasons [for designing a *dharma* as present], why will you not admit that [your past and future *dharmas* are in reality] present?

§ 14. The reality of the past and of the future renders the striving for salvation useless. The theory of 'displacement' rejected.

[Another argument:]

The efforts directed towards the acquisition of heaven and salvation would therefore by useless, and no religious result to be realized by striving could be pointed out. [1841]

[In Abhidharmakośavyākhya[1] it is said:]

»The result *(phala)* of a thing, the past and the future of which exist really (= a thing which exists really in its past and future state), must also be permanent (= *nitya*, existing always)«. Hence all efforts directed towards the acquisition of heaven and final salvation would be useless, because there would be no result at all to be striven for[2]. Indeed what kind of a *sāmarthya* could be attributed in this case to striving, as the making a vow etc.? Indeed it is said in the Abhidharmakośavyākhya: If *sāmarthya* is taken in the sense of producing *(utpādana)* then our thesis: 'emergence into existence after having been previously inexistent' is proved. And if you say that this *sāmarthya* is 'a potency of making a thing present'? *(vartlamānīkaraṇa)*, then we ask: what does this 'making present' mean? If only 'a displacing' *(deśāntarākarṣaṇa)*, then [again] we have as consequence that the result is permanent, because it exists in all [three] Times. Besides,

---

[1] Cf. AbhK V p. 63.

[2] This objection is quoted as *pūrvapakṣa* in Saṃghabhadra's Nyāyānusāra, p. 635 b, 20: »If the past were really *(dravyatas)* existent, then there would be no *nirvāṇa*, because an Arhant is not extinguished as long as the *skandhas* exist. And if the past *duḥkha* did exist permanently *(nityam)*, then all *sattvas* would be unreleased *(avimukta)*«. It is obviously a *male fide* argument. Saṃghabhadra replies in the same way, l. c. p. 635 b, : »Your doctrine is that the past does not exist really. Hence, on account of the inexistence of the *duḥkhaskandha, nirvāṇa* would be permanently [realized] and all *sattvas* would already be released«. The Vaibhāṣika does not teach »that *atītaduḥkhaskandha* exists«; he teaches only: »*nirvāṇa* is the state when the present *duḥkha* is already destroyed and a new *duḥkha* does not succed it«. »It is therefore not admissible to say: 'as the totality of the past *dharmas* constituting the *duḥkhaskandha* exist, therefore the *nirvāṇa* is not possible'«.

how would it be possible to displace the *arūpiṇo dharmāḥ*, as *vedanā* etc., as they are without localisation in space[1]. 'Displacing' can be understood only in the sense of our formula: emerging into existence after having been previously inexistent.

The explanation of the terms: 'heaven', 'salvation' etc.: 'heaven' *(svarga)* are the paradises on the back of Meru etc.; 'salvation' is [final] deliverance [from *saṃsāra*]; *saṃsarga* = *prāpti* is the acquisition of them; 'efforts' means making a vow etc.

And if we now concede that they do not possess any potency of *arthakriyā*, then they are inexistent just like a sky-flower. [1842]

Now let us admit the seconde alternative, *viz.* that those past and future *dharmas* do not possess the *arthakriyākāritva*. Then as the consequence of being deprived of *arthakriyā* their inexistence, just as in the case of a sky-flower, would arise because 'inexistence' is just defined as a total lack of any potency *(sāmarthya)*.

§ 15. The refutation of the five arguments of the Vaibhāṣikas.

Having at first given [our own] arguments showing the inexistence of past and future [*dharmas*], we now come to the refutation of arguments by which [the Vaibhāṣikas] try to prove the existence of the past and of the future:

Even as predicates predicating existence (= even as *bhāvadharmas*) these arguments are not [conclusive], because their [*dharmin*] is unreal. Or [their *dharmin*] possesses reality, and then [these arguments] are contradictory because, as a consequence of the reality of the present, they are contradicted by the *dharmin*. [1843]

---

[1] The thesis, that the *arūpiṇo dharmāḥ* could not be »displaced« is explained by Y. p. 476: *arūpiṇām ca vedanādīnām. katham taddeśāntarākarṣaṇā? — amūrtatvenādeśasthatvān na tad yujyata ity abhiprāyaḥ.* G. has instead of '*adeśasthatvād*' '*niṣkriyatvād*' and this misreading must be an old one because it occurs also in the T. version: *byed pa med paḥi phyir.*

The arguments [of the Vaibhāṣika] which have been enumerated above *viz. adhvasaṃgṛhītatva* (= the fact that all *rūpas* etc. are included under the heading 'Time-epoch') etc., are lacking in a real subject *(= āśrayāsiddha)* because the *dharmin* [of these syllogisms] the past etc. is not ascertained *(asiddha)*. Indeed it has been said [by Dharmakīrti in his Pramāṇavārttika I 192 c]: »'Existence' as predicate [to be proved] *(=bhāvadharma)* is not [possible] because [the *dharmin*] is not ascertained« [1].

Now let us suppose that past and future things are ascertained *(siddha)*. Then the arguments [of the Vaibhāṣikas] are contradictory [*viruddha*] because accepting [as homogeneous instance] the reality of the present, we would prove just the contrary of what is the essence *(svarūpa)* of the probandum *(dharma = sādhya-dharma)*.

[There is a further objection *viz.*:] how is it possible to teach that past and future *rūpas* are included under the heading 'Time-epoch'? Indeed, no such [distinctions] as 'past' or 'future' can be established about the horn of a hare, which is absolutely inexisting.

[The author summarizes again the standpoint of the Sautrāntikas:]

A *rūpa* which already disappeared after having come into existence, is called 'past'; that which will appear, when the totality of conditions *(pratyaya-sākalya)* is given, is called 'future'.

But, assuming real existence for them, the presence [of the past and of the future] would be the consequence. This is established because 'existence' is the only definition of the present. [1844—1845]

These *kārikās* are clear in themselves.

What is consequently [the real meaning of] the statement, that *rūpas, vedanās* etc. are included [under 'Time-epoch']? — The answer is:

That *rūpa* etc. is included under 'past etc.', has been said [by the Buddha] in the sense of an imputed *(adhyā-*

---

[1] *nāsiddhe bhāvadharmo 'sti.* Cf. TSP 412 25 and the Sanskrit text of the Pramāṇavārttika edited by Rāhula Sāṅkṛtyāyana in Appendix to Journal of the Bihar and Orissa Research Society, Vol. XXIV, Pts. I—II, p. 16.

ropya), not in the sense of a real distinction of the past and of the future conditions. [1846]

Now what is the true meaning of the doctrine that consciousness depends on two factors?

> The Seer of Truth has said that consciousness depends on two factors. This teaching refers to the mind *(citta)* connected with an object *(saviṣaya)* and was meant as [a doctrine] of provisory sense *(abhisaṃdhāya).* [1447]

Consciousness *(vijñāna)* is of two kinds: having an objective correlate *(sālaṃbana)* and without one *(anālaṃbana).* The teaching of the Bhagavān about consciousness depending on two factors refers to the first category of consciousness having an objective correlate. It was meant as a doctrine of provisory sense. [Next question:] how is the existence of consciousness without an objective correlate to be ascertained? The answer is:

> Indeed there is no objective correlate for such notions *(buddhi)* as Eternal Being, Almighty God *(īśvara)* etc. because [in this case] the *dharmas* of words, names etc. are not connected with a corresponding [objective] aspect *(ākāra).* [1448]

In »etc.« [after »Almighty God] are comprised other [kinds of absolute entities] as *pradhāna, kāla,* etc., which are hypostasized by different philosophers. We must not think that all these notions *(buddhi)* possess words etc. as their objective correlate *(ālaṃbana)* [1] In order to emphasize it the author says: »the *dharmas.*

---

[1] This is perhaps an allusion to the theory of the eternal Word, as expounded by Bhartṛhari in his Vākyapadīya. According to that theory, each true cognition is necessarily supported by words which possess their own, objective validity and which are emanations of a unique, transcendental Logos *(brahma śabdatattvam).* From the Buddhist view-point, metaphysical verbal hypostases as *īśvara, kāla,* etc. are pure »constructions« *(kalpanā)* without any corresponding reality; not only without an external object, but even without the support of pure, unutterable sensation. In acts of empirical sense perception, however, »words« do not likewise play any substantial rôle: cognition arises through the coordination *(sārūpya)* of the moment of pure self-conscious sensation with a mental reflex *(ābhāsa)* and this reflex is »capable of coalescing with a verbal designation«, but the association

of words, names etc. are not connected with a corresponding [objective] aspect«. The [objective] aspect of [the notion] God etc. is eternity, totality of causal determinants etc., and this very aspect, which is ascertained by these notions, is not connected with words, names and other *viprayuktasaṃskāras*.

By »etc.« in »*dharmas* of words, names etc.« are meant other determinants *(nimitta)* which may be accepted by our opponents as having potencies *(svabhāva = sāmarthya)* producing the mental reflex of an external object etc. *(arthapratibimbakādi)*.

Objection: if consciousness even without an object is possible, how can it be called cognition *(jnāna)*? Consciousness *(vijñāna)* has been defined as 'what cognizes' *(vijānātīti vijñānam)* and, if there is no object to be cognized *(vijñeya)*, how can consciousness [as cognition] exist?

We answer:

> Consciousness [as cognition] is admitted only in the sense of a 'conscious accompaniment'. And this 'conscious accompaniment' of the consciousness is assumed *(parikalpita)* to be identical with its immateriality *(ajaḍarūpatva)* on account of its 'luminousness' *(prākāśya)*. [1849]

If our opponent thinks that there is no 'conscious accompaniment' *(bodhānugama)* possible without an object to be made conscious *(bodhya)*, we answer: This conscious accompaniment of consciousness *(vijñāna)* is only another expression for its 'immateriality' *(ajāḍarūpatva)*[1]. As there is no external object to be illuminated *(prakāśyavastvantarābhāvāt)* [by the light of consciousness] and as there is no separate illumination either, just as in the case of light in the sky [which is only one and indivisible], therefore, with regard to this luminous essence, consciousness is called 'having cognition as its essence'[2].

---

with a word is by no means a *conditio sine qua non* of perception. Cf. Stcherbatsky, *Buddhist Logic*, II p. 19 ff.

[1] Cf. TS 2000:

> *vijñānaṃ jaḍarūpebhyo vyāvṛttam upajāyate*
> *iyam evā 'tmasaṃvittir yā 'jaḍarūpatā.*

[2] According to the epistemology of the Vijñānavādins the act of cognition presupposes a tripartition of the unique and homogenous mind-stuff into: a) a subject-portion *(grāhaka = pramāṇa = darśanabhāga)*, b) an object-portion *(grāhya = prameya =*

Refering to the question how can past *karma* give a moral retribution *(phala)*, the author says:

We do not admit that a past moral cause *(vipākahetu)* gives a retribution *(phala)*. The retribution is granted only as an effect of a whole series of conscious moments *(vijñāna-prabandha)*, so far as it became permeated *(vāsita)* by [the moral character of] this[1] [past cause]. [1450]

[The whole *saṃtāna*] having been permeated *(vāsita)* [by the past *karma*] becomes capable of producing retribution[2].

Opponent: But Bhagavān has said: »A *karma* which is annihilated, reduced to nought and destroyed does not, nevertheless, cease to exist«. How is this to be understood?

Answer:

Alluding to the *vāsanā* [permeating the whole] stream of consciousness *(cetaḥsaṃtāna)* [Bhagavān] has taught in metaphorical sense *(bhaktyā = upacāreṇa)* that the [past] *karma* exists. In the same manner we are speaking of the non-destruction of the [already annihilated] basic-element *(mūla)*. [1851]

As long as a series of effects *(phalaprabandha)* which form [the illusory unity of one permanent material thing], a piece of

---

nimittabhāga), and c) the self-conscious portion *(svasaṃvittibhāga)*, by which both the preceding portions are »supported«.

According to some Yogācaras, this process of division is real, and the *bhāgas* exist as independent »parts«; but, according to the school of Dignāga, *citta* is one and indivisible and the separation of the *darśana* and *nimittabhāga* from their »support« *(āśraya)* which is self-consciousness, is only illusory. Cf. Trikālaparīkṣā, śl. 31—32, Mdo XCV № 6, 179 a 4—180 b, 1, restored by Dr. E. Frauwallner, *Festschrift Winternitz*, p. 237 ff., Pramāṇavārttika, III 354 and Pramāṇasamuccaya, quoted by de La Vallée Poussin, *Siddhi*, p. 131.

[1] *tad-vāsitāt*, according T.; G. has *sad-vāsitāt*.

[2] Cf. the stanza quoted in Bodhicaryāvatārapañjikā, p. 473 and Sarvadarśanasaṃgraha, Poona 1924, p. 49:

yasminn eva hi saṃtāne āhitā karmavāsanā
phalaṃ tatraiva badhnāti kārpase raktatā yathā.

For the problem of moral retribution in Buddhist philosophy one may now consult the study of Professor E. Lamotte, *Le Traité de l'acte de Vasubandhu, Karmasiddhiprakaraṇa*, Mél. Chin. et Bouddh., vol. IV 1936.

gold etc., and which is produced by a basic element[1] *(mūladravya)* continues to exist, this basic element, [although it is in reality already destroyed,] is spoken of as 'not yet destroyed'. In the same manner the [past and already annihilated] *karma* is called 'existing'.

The author explains what is the aim of such metaphorical teachings *(upacāreṇa deśanā)*:

> This doctrine has been revealed by the Teacher in order to destroy the *ucchedadṛṣṭi.* [There is no other sense of this doctrine.] Otherwise how could the teaching given in the Śūnyatāsūtra be explained? [1852]

Had it been said that the past *karma* does not exist, then people might believe that the potency of producing effects indirectly *(paramparyeṇa phalotpādanasāmarthya)* which has been created by the past *karma* [and which as a *vāsanā* permeates the whole *saṃtāna*] does not exist either. And individuals to be guided *(vineyajana)* would fall into the heresy of the *ucchedadṛṣṭi.* Therefore, in order to prevent these false conclusions, Bhagavān has said: »The past *karma* exists«. [And this teaching is to be understood only in this sense]. Otherwise, if the past did really exist, how could the teaching of the Paramārthaśūnyatāsūtra be explained[2]: »When the eye originates it comes from nowhere and when it disappears, it goes nowhere. Therefore the eye exists after having been inexistent, and it ceases to exist after having been existent«.

And if the Vaibhāṣika thinks that the meaning of this Sūtra is that the *dharma* exists after having been previously inexistent as present (= in the present Time-epoch = *varttamāne 'dhvany abhūtvā*[3]), then this view is also to be rejected, because Time-epochs and elements *(= bhāva)* are not different things. Indeed [in the Abhidharmakośa I, 7] it is stated [explicitly], that *saṃskṛtadharmas* are [otherwise called] *adhvan* and *kathāvastu*[4].

---

[1] *mūladravya* = 'the basic element' = the first element of a homogeneous series *(pravāha)*.

[2] Saṃyukta 13 12. Cf. AbhK. V p. 59, note 3.

[3] Cf. AbhK. V p. 60.

[4] *ta evādhvā kathāvastu.* G. has: *ta evādhvānas tathā 'vasthivacanāt* (sic!).

[There is another subterfuge of the Vaibhāṣika according to which the formula *abhūtvā bhavati* is to be interpreted as *svātmany abhūtvā*[1]:] 'a *dharma* exists after having been previously inexistent in its essence'. This [interpretation] is obviously nothing short of an acknowledgment that [just as we are teaching] the past eye does not exist.

Moreover: if the contingent elements *(=saṃskāra=saṃskṛtadharma)* exist permanently, then there are no causes *(hetu)* and no effects *(phala)*; hence the origination of painful existence *(=duḥkhasamudaya)* would be unreal, and, as a consequence of its unreality, the non-existence of the suppression [of painful existence] and of the path [leading to it] *(nirodhamārgayor)* would result. In this way, if the four Aryan Truths are unreal, neither the *parijñā*, nor the *prahāna*, nor the *sākṣātkriyā*, nor the *bhāvanā* would be possible[2]. These being unreal, neither candidates [for the attainment of *nirvāṇa*] *(pratipannaka pudgala)* nor individuals enjoying the fruition of the Path *(phalastha pudgala)* would exist. Thus [as conclusion] the whole doctrine of the Buddha would be contradicted. Therefore we state: the conception of real thing which is past etc. does not possess any objective correlate *(= nātītādivastujātakalpanā sādhvī)*.

Finally we come to the problem, of how Yogins can possess a distinct knowledge of past and future [events]. It is explained by the author in the following *kārikās*:

---

[1] Cf. AbhK V p. 60: *svātmani cakṣusi cakṣur abhūtvā bhavati.* Y. p. 474: *atha svātmani cakṣuṣi caksur abhūtvā bhavati siddham idām anāgatam cakṣur nāstīti.*

[2] This seems to be an antistrophe of Mvbh p. 393b, 21: »Moreover, if the past and the future did not exist really, then the present would also be inexistent, because the present is established [only] by the [right] discernment of the past and of the future. If the three Times were inexistent then the *samṣkṛta* would be inexistent. If the *saṃskṛta* were inexistent then the *asaṃṣkṛta* would also be inexistent, because the *asaṃskṛta* is established [only] by a [right] discernment of the *saṃskṛtadharmas*. If the *saṃskṛta* as well as the *asaṃskṛta* were inexistent, then all *dharmas* would be inexistent. If all *dharmas* were inexistent, then salvation and the reaching of *nirvāṇa* would be inexistent. Great heresies would thus arise. In order to avoid these mistakes it must be known that the past and the future exist really«.

The Yogins cognize this aspect of the present which, indirectly or directly, is an effect [of the past causes] or a cause [of future effects].

And thereupon they associate it with conscious moments which, although belonging to the empirical sphere, are nevertheless purified; in their true essence they are objectless but, nevertheless, they are connected with conceptual hypostases *(vikalpa)*.

Therefore, supported by this past and future stream of causes and effects, statements in verbal form (= teachings, *deśanā*) about the past and the future arise.

But the teachings of the Tathāgata, whose stream of consciousness is entirely free from the net of all discursive notions, emanate even without any conscious volitional effort *(anābhogena)*. [1853—1856]

kārya-kāraṇatāṃ gatam = atītārthāpekṣayā kāryatām gatam, anāgatāpekṣayā kāraṇatām = [the present] is recognized as an effect with reference to a past thing and as a cause with reference to a future one.

[The moments of] consciousness 'which are objectless in their real essence' *(= tattvato 'viṣayair)* means: 'which are connected with a [purely] verbal designation' *(āviṣṭābhilāpa)*, because they do not possess as their substratum a *svalakṣaṇa*, a moment of pure sensation (= because they do not objectify a pure sensation = *svalakṣaṇasyā 'viṣayīkaraṇāt)*. Therefore with Yogins who are not completely purified [instructions], concerning past and future events could arise, supported by the past and the future chain of causes and effects *(hetuphalayoḥ saṃtatiṃ bhūtaṃ bhāvinīṃ āśritya)*. But the Bhagavān Tathāgata does not possess any mundane consciousness *(laukikaṃ jñānam)*, even purified *(śuddha)*, because he is permanently in a state of a deep trance *(samāhita)* as he discarded all ignorance *(avidyā)* while discursive notions *(vikalpa)* are by their essence identical with ignorance. As it is said:

Those discursive notions are themselves essentially identical with ignorance. Because they possess [only] an imputed reality *(= āropya vartate)*, in the form of an external object which is only a reflex of consciousness itself[1].

The teaching of the Tathāgata whose nature is similar to the nature of the miraculous gem Cintāmaṇi, arises even without any conscious volitional effort *(anābhogena)* out of the potency acquired by the accumulation of former vows *(praṇidhāna)*, meritorious deeds *(puṇya)* and wisdom *(jñāna)*[2].

End of the Analysis of the three Times.

---

[1] The equation *kalpanā = avidyā* is a *locus communis* of the Mahāyānistic philosophy, cf. *e. g.* Madhyamakāvatāra, p. 230 6:

pṛthagjanāḥ kalpanayaiva baddhā |
akalpayan muktim upaiti yogī ||
yā kalpanānām vinivṛttir etad |
phalam vicārasya budhā vadanti ||

[2] A more detailed exposition of this docetic doctrine which is common to all Mahāyāna schools is given in Madhyamakāvatāra, p. 360 19: The Buddhas display for the benefit of all living beings an activity which consists in applying the methods of conversion according to the need of individuals. Now the question arises: since on the *buddhabhūmi* there is no *kalpanā* any longer, how is this activity possible? — Answer: Buddhas do not think in *vikalpas*; nevertheless, just as a magical jewel *(cintāmaṇi)* or the »Wish-three« *(kalpataru)*, they are devoted to the realization of human happiness without disturbing even for one moment the *dharmadhātu*. While converting beings, they are free from *karma* and they manifest the Dharma [automatically] through the power of vows taken previously. Moreover [this manifestation of the Dharma] takes place also owing to the fact, that the *karma* of listening to such a Dharma by the *vineyajanas* becomes ripe. Therefore one should know that the *tattvadeśanā* and the *sattvārthakriyā* follow even when no conscious effort *(prayatna)* is made for their production.

Appendix

Prajñākaramati's Refutation of the *traikālyavāda*

(Bodhicaryāvatārapañjikā, p. 579—582)

[Vaibhāṣika:] phenomena *(bhāva)* are not absolutely unreal. They are »coming« from the future Time-epoch to the present Time-epoch owing to the force of causal determinants *(hetupratyaya)*, and again, they go away from the present Time-epoch into the past Time-epoch owing to the force of impermanence *(anityatā)*. [The »three marks of contingency« *saṃskṛtalakṣaṇa)*], *viz.* origination, duration and destruction have been taught in this sense. In this sense too, »dependent origination« *(pratītyasamutpāda)* is quite acceptable.

Refering to this doctrine of the *traikālyavāda*, the Master Śāntideva says: »Nothing is coming from elsewhere, nor does it stay, nor does it go away« (IX 143 a).

Commentary: »nothing is coming from elsewhere« = from any other place or Time; nor having come does it go away out of the present to any place whatsoever; nor does it stay anywhere in its own essence *(svabhāvena)* as the same, identical being.

Indeed, if it came from the future Time-epoch to the present and went away from the present to the past, then even a contingent element *(saṃskṛta)* would be permanent *(nitya)*. As existing always, it could not be impermanent. And it would be impossible to prove that such a *dharma* is not permanent.

Now [the Vaibhāṣika teaches that] the differentiation of the *dharma* [wandering] through the Time-epochs consists in the fact that its *kāritra* is absent 'previously' and 'subsequently'; *i. e.*, as long as the *dharma* has not yet acquired its *kāritra* and is unable to perform its function *(kṛtya)*, it is called 'future'; as soon it performs its function, it is 'present'; when it has accomplished its function it is 'past', these are the differences [between the Time-epochs].

We answer: This theory is also of no value. Indeed we must ask: if the *dharma* exists permanently in its own, identical essence, why does not the *kāritra* also [always] exist?

[If you say that the occasional existence and inexistence of the *kāritra* depends on special external conditions, we must reject this explanation because] dependence on external conditions is not possible for a substance which permanently exists by its own essence.

And if you accept that a substance can exist even if it has no *kāritra*, then the reality of such unreal things as horns of horses, etc. would be the consequence of this theory.

Or you admit that *kāritra* [being not different from the *dharma*] is also future, present and past. But how can it be possible? Is it due to the presence of another *kāritra* [of the first *kāritra*] or does [this first] *kāritra* exist [as future, present and past] by its own nature? Accepting the former we shall fall into *regressus ad infinitum*, accepting the latter we are not allowed to deny for a *dharma* the same possibility of existing as past etc. by its own nature [and without the help of a *kāritra*].

Moreover, the Vaibhāṣika teaches that past and future *dharmas* exist *substantialiter* just as present ones. This is however quite impossible. Indeed, how can a *dharma* which exists [always] by its own essence be at the same time essentially connected with origination and destruction? What does it miss in its previous state owing to the lack of which it is called 'not yet born'? And what does it miss in its later state, owing to the lack of which it is called 'already destroyed'? The consequence is that [the *dharma*], in the condition of the antecedent and of the subsequent Time-epochs, is existing by its own nature just in the same manner as in the present state. [There is no difference at all between your 'future' 'present' and 'past' *dharma*]. Therefore, on account of inexistence [of Time-distinctions], the triad of Time-epochs is absolutely impossible. For one who accepts the essential reality *(= tattva = svātmanā, ekasvabhāvenā 'stitva)* the past etc. cannot be existent. This is summarized in the following stanza [AbhK V p. 57 = TS 1802]:

kāritra does not exist permanently, *dharma* is characterized as existing permanently, but nevertheless the *kāritra* is not different from the *dharma!* Indeed, it is a caprice of the Īśvara in its arbitrariness.

Now [the Vaibhāṣika quotes a scriptural evidence. He says:] The past etc. must be really existent, because it is said in the Sūtra: 'past *karma* exists, future retribution exists'.

We answer: Only in order to refute the heresy denying [moral] causality *(hetuphalāpavāda)*, has the Bhagavān said: 'past *karma* exists, future retribution exists'. But 'past' means: 'previously inexistent, which originated and has been already destroyed', and 'future' means: 'that which will be when the cause is given'. In this sense it has been said that causes etc. exist. The word 'exist' being a *nipāta* can have the meaning of all three tenses.

And this is [the true doctrine taught] by the Bhagavān in the Paramārthaśūnyatāsūtra: »When the eye originates it comes from nowhere and when it disappears, it goes nowhere. Therefore the eye exists after having been inexistent, and it ceases to exist after having been existent«. Were the future eye really existent, it would not have been said that 'it exists after having been inexistent'. Therefore there is no 'transgression' *(saṃkrānti)* from one Time-epoch into another. And thus as there is no coming from anywhere nor going away, and as the present *rūpa* which is only an unreal appearance does not possess duration in any sense, therefore the Master Śāntideva asks: »what is the difference between the *māyā* and the phenomena [produced by causes] which are considered by ignorant individuals as existing really? — [Evidently there is no difference at all].

Abbreviations

AbhK *L'Abhidharmakośa de Vasubandhu*, by L. de La Vallée Poussin, 1923—1931 (quoted by volume and page number).
G. Gaekwad edition of the TS.
Mvbh. Mahāvibhāṣā, Taishô Nr 1545.
N Nyāyānusāra, Taishô Nr 1562.
P Kamalaśīla's Pañjikā to the Tattvasaṃgraha (quoted by page number of the Gaekwad edition).
T Taishô edition of the Chinese Tripitaka.
TS Tattvasaṃgraha of Śāntarakṣita (quoted by kārikā number of the Gaekwad edition).
Tib., T. Tibetan Version of the TS and of the P. [Narthang].
Y Yaśomitra's Sphūtartha, ed. Wogihara.

Addenda

p. 40. »Wise men call permanent etc.« — This is a quotation from Pramāṇavārttika, II 204.

Examination of the 'Traikālyavāda'— Things Continuing to Exist During Three Points of Time

G. N. Jha

COMMENTARY.

Under Text 4, the True Doctrine has been called 'Immobile'; the Author proceeds to support that idea.

TEXT (1786).

ON THE GROUND OF THE GOLD CONTINUING TO BE THE SAME, WHEN IT COMES TO BE REGARDED AS SOMETHING PERMANENT,—SOME BUDDHISTS ALSO HOLD (ON THE BASIS OF THIS) THAT THE THING (BY ITSELF PERMANENT) PASSES THROUGH DIVERSE STATES.—(1786)

COMMENTARY.

The Buddhist Doctrine is that 'there is nothing that has continued existence'; against this, the following objection is urged:—"How can it be said that 'there is nothing that has continued existence'—when as a matter of fact, some Buddhists (of the Vaibhāṣika-Realistic-School) also,—like *Dharmatrāta* and others—have accepted the view that an object continues to exist at three points of time, through its diverse states;—this view is held on the analogy of the *Gold* (discussed above) continuing to exist (in the state of the Pot and that of the Dish)?"

This same idea is further expounded in the following *texts*:—

TEXTS (1787–1790).

"JUST AS GOLD DOES NOT ABANDON ITS COLOUR, EVEN WHEN THERE ARE DIFFERENCES IN ITS STATE,—SIMILARLY UNDER ALL ITS STATES, THE ENTITY DOES NOT ABANDON ITS CHARACTER OF 'SUBSTANCE'.—IF IT WERE NOT SO, THEN THE COGNITION OF PAST AND FUTURE THINGS WOULD BE OBJECT-LESS.—HOW AGAIN, IS IT THAT IT HAS BEEN ASSERTED BY *Tāyin* THAT COGNITION RESTS UPON THESE TWO?—HOW AGAIN IS ACTION, WHICH IS PAST AND HAS NO FURTHER EXISTENCE, HELD TO BE PRODUCTIVE OF RESULTS? HOW TOO COULD MYSTICS HAVE THE DISTINCT COGNITION OF PAST AND FUTURE

THINGS?—FROM ALL THIS IT FOLLOWS THAT PAST AND FUTURE THINGS ARE NOT THE OBJECTS OF MERE 'NEGATION OF SUBSTANCE',—BECAUSE THEY ARE INCLUDED UNDER THE CHARACTER OF THE 'STATES', ETC.,—JUST LIKE THE PRESENT THING."—(1787–1790)

COMMENTARY.

Among the Buddhist writers (referred to under Text 1786) are the following:—

(1) *Bhadanta-Dharmatrāta*—the upholder of the view that while the thing undergoes changes, it remains substantially the same. He argues as follows:—When a certain thing has entered into its course of existence, there is change only in its *mode* of existence, not in the *substance*; for instance, the substance Gold undergoes several changes through which it comes to be called the 'armlet', 'necklet', 'ear-ring' and so forth,—but there is no change in the Gold itself. In the same way, the object is something different from the Future, and other 'modes'. For instance, when a certain object abandons its 'future' Mode and reaches the 'present' Mode;—and when it renounces its 'present' Mode, it reaches the 'past' Mode,—and yet the Object itself does not change; as throughout the three Modes, the same character of the 'substance' continues. If it were not so, the 'future', 'present' and 'past' objects would be entirely different from one another.—What is it that is meant by the term '*bhāva*', 'Mode', here?—It is a particular quality on which the notions of 'Past,' etc. are based."

(2) *Bhadanta-Ghoṣaka*—holds that the changes undergone by the Object are in its *character*. He argues as follows:—"When the Object has entered into its course of existence, it is said to be 'past', when it has the character of the 'past', but is not entirely deprived of the character of the 'future' and the 'present': for example, a man may be attached to one woman, but he need not be disgusted with other women. Similarly when the Object is 'future' or 'present' [it has these characters, but is not entirely devoid of the other two characters]."—The difference between this view and the previous one is that under this view things are spoken of as 'past' on account of the actual presence of a particular character.

(3) *Bhadanta-Vasumitra*—holds the view that the changes undergone by things is in their *aspects* or states. He argues as follows:—"When a thing has entered the course of existence, it is spoken of variously, according to its varying *aspects* (or conditions); and these variations relate to the *aspect*, not to the *substance*; as the Substance remains the same at all three points of time. For example, when the clay counting-piece is placed in the place of *Units*, it is denominated 'one', when placed in the place of *Hundreds*, it is denominated 'hundred', and in place of *Thousands*, it is denominated a 'thousand'. Similarly when the thing is in the state of activity, it is called 'present'; and when it has ceased from activity, it is 'past', and while it has not become active at all, it is 'future'. So that things are spoken of in accordance with their *states*, as in the case of the clay counting-piece, where there is no change in the nature of the Substance;

only different denominations are assigned to it in accordance with its varying position, which makes it indicative of varying numbers ".

(4) *Buddha-deva* (a writer of the second century A.D.)—holds the view that the changes are due to changes in 'Relativity'.—He argues as follows :—" When an object has entered its course of existence, it is called one or the other in relation to what has gone before and what is to come. For instance, the same woman is called 'mother' as well as 'daughter'; and the usage in question is also dependent upon the *past* and the *future*; when a thing has something before it, but nothing after it, it is called 'future'; when it has something before it and also something after it, it is called 'present'; and when it has something after it, but nothing before it, it is called 'past'."

All these four Buddhists are *Asti-vādins*, Realists (upholding the view that things have real and permanent existence).—called respectively: (1) 'Mode-changers', *Bhāva-vādin*, (2) *Lakṣaṇavādin*, 'Character-changers', (3) *Avasthāvādin*, 'Aspect-changers' and (4) *Anyathānyathika*, 'Relative changers'.

(1) Of these, the first (Dharmatrāta—the *Mode-changer*) does not differ from the *Sāṅkhya*, who holds the 'Modification' theory. So that the refutation that has been put forward against the *Sāṅkhya* is applicable to this Buddhist Realist. For instance, would the 'modification' come about without the abandoning of the previous mode or after its abandonment? If the former, then there would be comingling and confusion of the Modes. If the latter, then that would be incompatible with the permanent existence of things.

(2) As regards the second view (that of *Ghoṣaka*),—here also there would be the same comingling and confusion; as all things may have all characters. As regards the *man* (falling in love with one woman, which has been cited as an example), he is spoken of as 'attached' (or 'in love') on account of the appearance of *Attachment*, which is a totally different thing; and he is said to be 'not disgusted', when there is mere association (meeting together); in the case of the ordinary thing however, there is no *appearance* of the 'character', nor the mere association of 'character',—which would constitute the 'attainment' of it by the thing; as, if it were, then like 'attainment', the 'character' also would become something different from the thing. Thus there is no analogy between the two cases—the case in question and that of the example cited.

(3) As regards the third view (of *Vasumitra*),—that the changes in things are due to variations in their ***aspects or states of activity***,—its refutation is going to be set forth in detail below.

(4) As regards the fourth view (that of *Buddhadeva*), it involves the incongruity of three ***states*** occurring under the same ***state***. For instance, under the 'Past' state, the preceding and the succeeding moments would be 'past' and 'future' and the 'middle' moment would be the 'present'. This criticism against this is quite clear.

The Examination of the 'Idea of things continuing to exist during the Three Points of Time' proceeds in the Text, only with reference to the *third* among the above views—[i.e. the view of *Vasumitra*, that the changes in things are due to the variations in their *states of* activity].—What has been stated in connection with the example of Gold (under *Texts* 1786-1787) is only an indication of the thesis of all these writers,—and it is not in strict reference to the view of *Dharmatrāta* only (the first of the views described). This is clear from what is going to be said (under *Text* 1791)—'As regards the distinction among things due to their states of activity, etc. etc.' ;—and under the view of *Dharmatrāta* the distinction is not based upon states of *activity* ; it is only under *Vasumitra's* view that it is so.

This view (*Vasumitra's*) is as follows :—

"If the 'Past' and the 'Future' were not there, then such notions as 'There lived *Mahāsammata*', '*Shaṅkha* is going to be an all-world sovereign' and so forth,—which involve the idea of what is *past* and what is *going to be*—would be entirely baseless ; in fact, the Object not being there, the Idea also could not be there ; because in regard to the case of everything, the Idea is in the form in which the Object is cognised ; so that if the cognised Object is not there, there is nothing that could be apprehended by the Cognition ; hence there would be no Cognition (or Idea) at all.

"Further, the Blessed One has declared that 'Every cognition is produced on the basis of two things.—Which *two things* ?—The Eye and the Colours and the Mental Function'. If then the Past and the Future are not there, the cognition based upon these would not be *on the basis of two things* ; so that there would be incompatibility with the scriptures.

"Further, a past act could not bring about its fruit, if it were devoid of essence and devoid of existence, at the time of the appearance of the fruit, as the cause of that fruit would not be there ; what is non-existent cannot have the capacity to produce an effect ; as 'non-existence' consists in the *absence of all capacity*.

"Then again, such ideas as 'Māndhāna Devadatta lived', 'the world-sovereign Shaṅkha shall be Maitreya Tathāgata',—which appear distinctly and severally in the minds of Mystics, in regard to the Past and the Future, could not be possible ; as there can be no distinction among things that are *non-existent*.

"From all this it follows that *past* and *future* entities, like *Shriharṣa* and others, cannot be regarded as mere 'negations of substance',—because they have been declared as '*to be included under the states*'.—The Blessed Lord has declared as follows :—'O *Bhikṣus*, if the Past form had not existed, then the noble *Shrāvaka* would not have heard and been entirely indifferent regarding past forms ; hence, because there is a Past form of things, therefore the noble *Shrāvaka* has heard and has thus become indifferent to the Past. All this severally would be much too detailed ; hence thus whatever form has been *past* or is in *future*,—all this is spoken of briefly as *Colour-phase*'."

In the compound (in the text)—'*Adhvasaṅgraha, etc. etc.*',—the term '*adhvasaṅgraha*' stands for Colour, etc., in the sense that they are 'included under the *states*'.

The 'Etc.' includes 'Sensation' and other Phases.

The second '*ādi*' implies the further reason that all these have been taught as consisting of suffering, transitory as a whole, devoid of the Soul, and so forth.—(1787-1790)

The following might be urged :—' Like *Ākāsha*, all things are always existent ; hence there can be no idea of the *Past*, etc.'

The answer to this is as follows :—

TEXTS (1791–1793).

"IN THIS CONNECTION, THERE SHOULD BE NO SUCH COGITATION AS TO HOW THIS DIVERSITY IN THE *states* COMES ABOUT. BECAUSE THIS DISTINCTION AMONG THE STATES IS CONCEIVED ON THE BASIS OF *activity*. THAT WHICH IS ENGAGED IN ACTIVITY IS CALLED 'PRESENT' ; THAT WHICH HAS CEASED FROM ACTIVITY IS CALLED 'PAST' ; AND THAT WHICH HAS NOT YET ATTAINED ACTIVITY IS CALLED 'FUTURE'.—THE 'ACTIVITY' OF THINGS SERVES ONLY TO 'PROJECT' THE RESULT, NOT TO PRODUCE IT. AS THERE CAN BE NO SUCH 'PROJECTING' IN THE CASE OF PAST THINGS, THERE IS NO POSSIBILITY OF ACTIVITY IN THEM."—(1791-1793)

COMMENTARY.

The various states are determined through activity ; that which is engaged in activity is 'Present' ; that of which the activity has ceased is 'Past' and that which has not yet attained Activity is 'future'.

Objection :—" What is it that is meant by '*Kāritra*', '*Activity*', in this connection ?—If it is *operation*, in the shape of *seeing* and the rest,—e.g. *seeing* and the rest are the 'activity' of the Eye and other organs,—since the Eye *sees*, the Ear *hears*, the Nose *smells*, the Tongue *tastes*,—and Cognition also is the Cogniser, as it is that which cognises things ; and thus Colour, etc. become perceptible by the Senses ;—if this is what is meant by 'activity', then, even when the Man has been born, if the Eye, which shares the fate of the body, has no activity, the man (or the Eye)—could not be regarded as 'present'.—Secondly, *activity* may be held to consist in the giving (producing) and receiving of the fruit,—for instance, the *caste* and other properties of man, which are born along with the Eye, are the result (fruit) of human effort ; the Visual organ (Eye) or the supervising Deity, or Vibration brings about human effort ; and it is by reason of bringing about this result that the Eye becomes a cause, and hence comes to be spoken of as 'present'.—Under this definition of 'activity', even Past things, being held to be productive of all-embracing results sharing the same fate, would have to be regarded as 'Present'.—Thirdly, it may be held that the 'Activity' meant here is that which gives and takes all sorts of results.—In that case, the Past, being the cause of some part of such results, would have to be regarded as 'Half-present'."

In view of this objection, *Āchārya Sahantabhadra* has offered the following explanation :—What is called the 'activity' of things is the potency of *projecting* the Result,—not of *producing* it ; the Past and other things, which are only partial causes, do not *project* the result ; it is only in the 'present' state that the Result is *projected* (thrown out) by its cause. Nor can there be 'projection' of what has been already projected, as that would lead to an infinite regress. Thus there being no 'activity' possible in what is 'past', there can be no confusion in the character of these (Past, Future and Present).—(1791–1793)

The following *Texts* answer the above arguments (of the Realist Buddhist):—

TEXTS (1794–1796).

THESE PEOPLE WILL HAVE TO ADMIT THAT THIS 'ACTIVITY' IS EITHER DIFFERENT FROM, OR THE SAME AS, THE OBJECT CONCERNED ; AS THERE CAN BE NO OTHER WAY IN WHICH IT CAN REALLY EXIST.—IF IT IS SOMETHING DIFFERENT FROM THE OBJECT, THEN THE PAST AND FUTURE STATES OF 'PRESENT' THINGS WOULD HAVE TO BE REGARDED AS FORMLESS,—BECAUSE THEY ARE 'CAUSES' AND ARE 'EMBELLISHED', AND SO FORTH,—LIKE THE ACTIVITY. OTHERWISE, THE THINGS WOULD BE EVERLASTING ; AS THE 'FORM' WOULD BE THERE ALL THE TIME ; AND APART FROM THIS, THERE IS NO OTHER CHARACTERISTIC OF THE 'EVERLASTING'.—(1794–1796)

COMMENTARY.

The said Activity will have to be regarded by these people either as different from, or the same as, the Entity ; as there can be nothing apart from both 'difference' and 'non-difference', as these are mutually exclusive ; the affirmation of one being invariably concomitant with the denial of the other ; and there is no other way in which the thing can exist.

If then the Activity is something *different* from the Entity, then the Past and Future states of Present things would have to be regarded as 'formless',—because of their being *causes* and being *embellished*,—like the Activity.—The term '*and so forth*' is meant to include 'being an entity' and so forth.—*Otherwise*—that is, if, they were not formless in the Past and in the Future,—then, all 'embellished' things would have to be regarded as eternal ; as the 'form' (or Nature) would be always there ; and the 'eternality' of a thing is nothing more than *being always there* ; as declared in the following words—'The learned men regard that Form as *eternal* which is never destroyed'.—(1794–1796)

The following might be urged :—"If *eternality* is a potency,—then how can the two Reasons—'being cause' and 'being embellished'—escape from being not incompatible with the contrary of the Probandum ?"

This is answered in the following—

TEXTS (1797-1798).

THE IDEA OF THE ETERNAL THING *being a cause* HAS ALREADY BEEN REJECTED BEFORE—ON THE GROUND OF THE IMPOSSIBILITY OF ITS EFFECTS APPEARING EITHER SUCCESSIVELY OR SIMULTANEOUSLY. AS FOR *being embellished*, THIS IS CLEARLY IMPOSSIBLE IN AN ETERNAL THING.—WHEN 'ACTIVITY' IS DESCRIBED AS SOMETHING DIFFERENT FROM THE 'PHASES' AND OTHER THINGS (POSTULATED BY BUDDHISTS), THERE IS THE IRRESISTIBLE CONTRADICTION OF YOUR OWN DOCTRINES.—(1797-1798)

COMMENTARY.

'*Before*'—i.e. under the chapter on the 'Permanence of Things'.

All that is 'embellished' has been held to be non-eternal, hence the character of *being embellished* cannot belong to an eternal entity;—this is clearly understood.

Further, when the 'Activity' is described as something different from the 'Phases' (*Skandhas*) and the 'Inner Receptacles' (*Āyatanas*),—there is clear contradiction of your own (Buddhist) doctrine; as the Blessed Lord has declared as follows—"All things, O Brāhmaṇa, are included in the Five 'Phases' and the Twelve 'Receptacles' and the Eighteen 'Substances'."—(1797-1798)

TEXTS (1799-1800).

IF, ON THE OTHER HAND, THE 'ACTIVITY' IS *not different* FROM THE ENTITY, THEN, BEING INSEPARABLE FROM THE ENTITY, IT WOULD BE THERE AT ALL TIMES, JUST LIKE THE NATURE OF THE ENTITY; AND IN THAT CASE, THE DIVISION AMONG THE STATES COULD NOT BE MADE ON THE BASIS OF THIS ACTIVITY; AS THERE COULD BE NO SUCH DISTINCTION AS THAT BETWEEN *cessation*, AND *non-attainment*, OF THE SAID ACTIVITY.—(1799-1800)

COMMENTARY.

If the Activity is held to be non-different from the Entity, then like the nature of things, it would be inseparable from the Entity; the Activity also would be something existing at all times; and in that case there could be no such distinction among states as that—that which has ceased from activity is 'Past', that which is still active is 'Present', and that which has not yet attained Activity is 'Future'. Because if the Activity were distinguishable into 'attained' and 'not attained',—then alone could the said distinction be possible ; the said distinguishing however is not possible ; because there can be no such distinction in the case of what is always present in the same form —(1799-1800)

TEXT (1801).

OR (CONVERSELY), BECAUSE IT WOULD BE NON-DIFFERENT FROM THE ACTIVITY—THE ENTITY, LIKE THE ACTIVITY, WOULD BE DEVOID OF THE 'PREVIOUS' AND 'LATER' CONDITIONS, AND WOULD HAVE ITS SOLE EXISTENCE IN THE *middle* (PRESENT).—(1801)

COMMENTARY.

Further, being non-different from Activity, the Entity also would have only such existence as is devoid of the previous and later ends,—like Activity itself.

The compound '*Pūrvāpara, etc.*' is to be explained as 'that which has its all—sole existence—in the middle,—being devoid of the two ends of the 'previous' and the 'later'.—(1801)

In the following *Texts* the Author laughs at the other party for expounding mutually contradictory doctrines :—

TEXTS (1802-1803).

ACTIVITY IS NOT THERE ALWAYS,—AND THE ENTITY IS DESCRIBED AS BEING THERE AT ALL TIMES,—AND YET THE ACTIVITY IS SAID TO BE NON-DIFFERENT FROM THE ENTITY ;—CERTAINLY THIS IS CONDUCT WORTHY OF A DIVINE BEING !—EVEN IF IT BE HELD THAT THE EXISTENCE OF THE STATES (IN THE ACTIVITY ITSELF) IS DEPENDENT UPON OTHER ACTIVITIES,—THE SAME QUESTION WOULD BE EQUALLY WELL RAISED AGAINST THAT VIEW ALSO.—(1802-1803)

COMMENTARY.

Under the circumstances, it comes to this that the Entities, Colour and the rest, do not exist at all times, as they are non-different from Activity. This is shown in the Text—'*The Entity, etc. etc.*'

For the following reason also the Activity must be something different from the Entity—'*And the Activity is non-different, etc. etc.*'.

'Divine Beings'—God and the like ; who act and live independently, not minding what is proper and what is improper ; and just as their behaviour is unreasonable, so also is the conduct of the philosopher under review.

Then again, if the Activity itself is regarded as 'future', without another Activity, then it should not be said that the states are determined by Activity; as that would not be true; inasmuch as in the case of Activity itself its 'future' and other states are determined on the basis of its own existence; and in the same manner the 'future' and other states of Entities also could be determined on the basis of their own existence.

In order to avoid this objection it might be held that, in the case of Activity also, there would be another Activity, which would be the determining factor.—But in that case also the same question—as to its being different or non-different from the former Activity,—would arise. And this would be open to the further defect that it would involve an infinite regress.—(1802-1803)

It has been pointed out that if the Activity is non-different from the Entity, it must be there at all times,—like the form or nature of the Entity itself.—*Bhadanta-Sahantabhadra* has offered an answer to that, which is anticipated and answered in the following—

TEXTS (1804-1805).

"PROPERTIES DISTINCT FROM THE ENTITY HAVE ALSO BEEN FOUND TO QUALIFY IT; FOR INSTANCE, THE QUALITY OF 'RESISTANCE'",—IF THIS IS URGED, THIS CANNOT HELP THE MATTER UNDER DISCUSSION; SUCH CHARACTERS AS THAT OF RESISTANCE AND THE LIKE ARE NOT PRESENT IN THE ENTITY AT ALL TIMES; THEY HAVE BEEN REGARDED AS OCCASIONAL; BECAUSE THE ENTITY ITSELF IS PRODUCED IN THAT WAY.—(1804-1805)

COMMENTARY.

"As a matter of fact, Properties distinct from the Entity and yet qualifying it have been found; for example, the character of *Resistance* and the like found in Earth and other things. These things—Earth, etc.—as *Categories*,—are all the same; and yet these are found to be 'resistant' and 'non-resistant', 'similar' and 'dissimilar',—thus being qualified by properties which are distinct from the form of the things themselves. In the same manner, the Entity could be qualified by Activity, which may be different from the Entity itself."

This explanation will not help the present topic. The topic under consideration is this—If the Activity is regarded as non-different from the Thing,—then there can be no distinction in the Activity which, being of the same nature as the Entity, could not serve to determine the distinction among the states (as 'Past', etc.).—As regards Earth and the other things (that have been cited by *Bhadanta-Sahantabhadra*),—they are distinct from

9

one another by reason of their being associated with mutually divergent characters,—and hence it is that while some are 'resistant', others are 'non-resistant'; as is found in the case of 'Sensation', etc.; but it is not that those same are 'non-resistant' which are 'resistant'; and this for the same reason that there is no comprehensive entity in the form of 'Category', by virtue of which the qualities of 'Resistance', etc. could be occasional. In fact, what happens is that the Entity itself, which is impartite, and is 'excluded from like and unlike things',—*is produced in that way.* For these reasons it is not right that any property, other than the form of the Entity itself, should distinguish any single Entity.—(1804-1805)

Question :—" How then is it that there is such an expression as '*Rūpasya sapratighatvam*', 'Resistance of the Form', where the two appear as different from one another,—if a property non-different from a thing cannot serve to distinguish it ?"

Answer :—

TEXT (1806).

IT IS THE ENTITY ITSELF, WHEN IT DOES NOT INDICATE 'DIFFERENCE FROM OTHER THINGS', THAT IS SPOKEN OF BY THE WORDS 'IT IS OF THE FORM'; JUST AS 'DISPOSITION' IS SPOKEN OF AS 'OF THE MIND'.—(1806)

COMMENTARY.

'*When it does not, etc. etc.*';—that is, when it ignores the difference from other things.

'*Spoken of as, etc.*'—i.e. as if it were something different.

'*It is of the form, etc.*'—'It' stands for 'Resistance'.

'*By the words*',—i.e. by the expression 'Resistance *of* the Form'.

An example is cited—'*As Disposition, etc. etc.*'.

The term '*api cha*' should be understood in the cumulative sense.—(1806)

The same writer (*Bhadanta-Sahantabhadra*) has argued as follows :—" Activity is not something different from the Entity,—as it is not found to have any nature apart from that.—Nor is it the *Entity* only; because even though it forms its very nature, yet it is non-existent at times.—Nor is it a particular (form of it), as the Activity has had no previous existence. In fact, the 'Activity' is like the 'Chain' (Series): the consecutive birth of the Entity is called the 'Chain' (or Series),—and yet it is not something different from the Entity, as it is always apprehended as not-separate from it; nor is it the Entity only, as in that case even a single 'Moment' would have to be regarded as the 'Chain';—and yet with all this, it cannot be said that the Chain does not exist; because its effects are found to exist.—[Similar is the case with 'Activity'].—All this has been thus asserted—'It is admitted that there are effects of the Chain,—and yet the *Chain*, as such, is nowhere existent (by itself, apart from the Entity); similar should be understood to be the case with '*Activity* as bringing about the *states*'."

The answer to this is as follows:—

TEXTS (1807–1809).

IF THE 'ACTIVITY' IS DESCRIBED AS 'NEITHER SAME NOR DIFFERENT', LIKE THE 'CHAIN', ETC.,—THEN IT BECOMES PURELY 'ILLUSORY'; AND THUS BEING PURELY IMAGINARY, LIKE THE 'CHAIN', IT COULD SERVE NO USEFUL PURPOSE IN REGARD TO ANY EFFECT; AS IT IS ONLY A REAL ENTITY THAT IS CAPABLE OF EFFECTIVE ACTION. THUS THEN, AS THE PRESENCE OF THE 'ACTIVITY' WOULD NOT BE REAL, ANY DETERMINING OF THE STATES BASED UPON THAT 'ACTIVITY' COULD NOT BE *real*.—(1807–1809)

COMMENTARY.

'*Like the Chain, etc.*'—the 'etc.' is meant to include the 'Aggregate' and such things.—

The 'Chain' is incapable of being spoken of as either different or non-different from the links of the chain; hence, like the 'Pudgala' (Body) it is featureless, devoid of form;—in the same way the 'Activity' in question also would be featureless;—when there is some feature (or form), it is necessary that it should be either different or non-different. Thus then, the Activity in question being purely imaginary, it could not serve any useful purpose in the bringing about of any effect; just like the 'Chain'. The 'Chain', which is purely a creature of fancy, does not serve any useful purpose towards any effect, because it is featureless; and the appearance of an effect is inseparably connected with some feature (or character). Hence it is only an *entity*, which has the form of a 'link in the chain' that is capable of effective action, —not the imaginary 'Chain'. From this it follows that the 'Activity' in question having a purely imaginary existence,—there can be no real presence of it, either before or after anything, and consequently any notions of the distinct 'states' determined upon the basis of such Activity must also be *imaginary*, not *real*.—(1807–1809)

Says the other party—"It may be that the Activity has a purely *imaginary* existence; and hence the distinction of the *states* based thereupon may also be only *imaginary*;—what is the harm in that?"—This is the view taken up in the following—

TEXTS (1810-1815).

Firstly, THE ACTIVITY IN QUESTION CONSISTS IN 'THE CAPACITY TO THROW OUT RESULTS' AND IS CAPABLE OF BEING SPOKEN OF; HOW CAN IT BE SAID TO HAVE AN IMAGINARY EXISTENCE, WHEN THE CAPACITY OF THINGS IS AN ENTITY ?—*Secondly*, THE FORM THAT IS ADMITTED TO BE BRINGING ABOUT SUCH EFFECTS AS *burning*, *cooking* AND THE LIKE,—IS THIS SAME FORM HELD TO BE IN THE 'PAST', 'PRESENT' AND 'FUTURE' STATES ?—IF IT IS THE SAME, HOW CAN *activity*, *inactivity* AND *cessation of activity* BELONG TO THE ENTITY THAT HAS A SINGLE FORM ?—HOW CAN THESE MUTUALLY CONTRADICTORY MODES BE PRESENT IN WHAT IS ONLY *one and undifferentiated* ?—IF IT IS ARGUED THAT—" BECAUSE IT ABANDONS ONE 'STATE' AND THEN TAKES UP ANOTHER, THAT ENTITY CANNOT BE UNDIFFERENTIATED, WHICH PASSES THROUGH THE STATES ",—THEN THE QUESTION ARISES—ARE THESE 'STATES' DIFFERENT FROM THE ENTITY ?—[THE OTHER PARTY ANSWERS]—" NO; AS IN THAT CASE, THE ENTITY WOULD NOT BE AN ACTIVE AGENT. BECAUSE IT IS ONLY THROUGH THE EXISTENCE OF THE 'STATES' THAT THE EXISTENCE OF THE EFFECTS IS APPREHENDED."—(1810-1815)

COMMENTARY.

You (Sahantabhadra) have explained that the capacity of entities to throw up their effects is what is meant by 'Activity';—now, how can *this capacity to throw up effects* have a merely imaginary existence ? That is, it can never be so. Consequently the distinction of the 'states' based thereupon should also be accepted as *real*.

Further, the Form of Fire is found to be one that is capable of such efficient actions as those of Burning, Cooking, etc. ;—is this the same that continues in the 'Past' and other states ? Or is it different ? If it remains the same,—then how can such contradictory properties as 'activity', 'inactivity' and 'cessation from activity' belong to the said form which is one and the same, totally undifferentiated ?—And it is only through the presence of these properties that the Entity could have such states as the 'Future', 'Present' and 'Past' respectively. If, even in the presence of contradictory properties, the entity remained the same, then all ideas of Difference would become uprooted, and the entire universe would have to be regarded as *one* only. And such *one-ness* would mean that all things should be produced together at one and the same time.

It might be argued that—" By virtue of the variations undergone in the process of abandoning one state and taking up another,—the Entity in the three states is *not* entirely *undifferentiated* ".

But even so, are these states different or non-different (from the Entity) ? This has got to be explained.

Says the other Party—" They are not different ;—i.e. they do not differ from the Entities.—'Why ?'—Because, in that case the Entity could not be an active agent; i.e. it would be inactive; as through positive and negative concomitance, it has been ascertained that efficient activity (causal efficiency) to produce effects belongs to the *states* only. [Hence by being different from the States, the Entity could not be an active agent]".—(1810–1815)

The objections against this last view [that "the States are *not different* from the Entity"] are pointed out in the following—

TEXTS (1816–1820).

HOW DO THESE PEOPLE ACCEPT THE VIEW THAT THERE IS NON-DIFFERENCE BETWEEN THE ENTITY AND THE STATES?—THEY (THE STATES), NOT HAVING BEEN IN EXISTENCE, COME INTO EXISTENCE AND THEN BECOME DESTROYED:—HOW THEN COULD THEY BE THE SAME AS THE ENTITY?—IN THE MIDDLE 'STATE', THE ENTITY IS 'ACTIVE' IN ITS OWN FORM,—THEN, AS THE SAME FORM PERSISTS IN OTHER TWO STATES ALSO, HOW COULD 'ACTIVITY' AND 'CESSATION OF ACTIVITY' BE THERE IN THESE TWO STATES?—IF IT IS 'ACTIVE', IN THE FORM OF SOMETHING ELSE, THEN IT CEASES TO BE ACTIVE AGAIN.—IF, LASTLY, IT BE HELD THAT THE FIRE AND OTHER THINGS, IN THE PAST AND FUTURE STATES, ARE DIFFERENT FROM THE SAME IN THE PRESENT STATE,—THEN IT IS TRUE THAT THERE WOULD BE NO ROOM FOR THE OBJECTION THAT COMINGLING AND CONFUSION WOULD BE INVOLVED; BUT EVEN SO, AS THE ENTITY IN THE MIDDLE (PRESENT) STATE BECOMES CAPABLE OF FRUITFUL ACTION ONLY WHEN IT COMES INTO EXISTENCE AFTER THE TIME DURING WHICH IT WAS NOT IN EXISTENCE, AND AFTER HAVING COME INTO EXISTENCE, IT DOES NOT CONTINUE TO EXIST,—THERE WOULD BE NO CONTINUITY OF EXISTENCE FOR THE ENTITY.—(1816–1820)

COMMENTARY.

How can any one accept the view that the states are non-different from the Entity?—No one can accept it.—Because the States come into existence after having been non-existent, and after having come into existence, they become destroyed;—while nothing like this happens to the Entity; because it has been held to be existent at all times. Under the circumstances, having been non-existent, then coming into existence and then ceasing to exist,—how could the States be the same in essence as the Entity?—They can never be so; because, they stand upon entirely different footings.—Otherwise, being the same as the Entity, the States also would have to be regarded as existing at all times,—just like the nature of the Entity; because they are non-different from the Entity; or (conversely) the Entity itself would have to be regarded as subject to *non-existence before existence* and so forth,—like the form of the States.

Even granting the assumption that the States are non-different from the Entity,—the objection based upon the attributing to them of mutually contradictory properties still remains unanswered. For instance, when the Entity is in the 'middle' (Present) state,—is it active in its own form? Or in the form of something else?

If it is active in its own form, then, as that same form would be there in the Past and Future states also,—how could this form of the active entity become active and inactive?

If it is active in the form of something else, then it ceases to be active; and hence becomes a non-entity.

Thus it is clear that it is not right to say that the same form is there in the Past and Future states also.

If then there is some other form (of the Entity) in these States,—then, under this view, there would be no room for the objection that it involves the confusion and comingling in the same thing of mutually contradictory properties of Activity and Inactivity,—because the Entity would not be the same. But (the other difficulty will remain, that) if the Entity, Fire, which is capable of such action as *Burning* and *Cooking*, comes into existence after having been *non-existent*, and having come into existence, it disappears,—this is incompatible with the doctrine of the permanent existence ot the Entity; because there is no continuity of existence.—(1816–1820)

The following might be urged—"It is true that the Entity, not being capable of action before it becomes capable of action, and having become capable of action, it ceases to be so; but even so, in these Past and Future states also the Entity is there all the same, though not capable of action; so that our theory is not incompatible with the idea of the Entity being there at all times".

The answer to this is as follows:—

TEXT (1821).

AS A MATTER OF FACT, THAT ENTITY ALONE IS REAL WHICH IS *capable of action*; HENCE FROM THAT WHICH IS NOT SO IN THE TWO STATES,—NO EFFECT CAN PROCEED.—(1821)

COMMENTARY.

'*That alone*'—which is capable of action.

'*In the two states*'—in the Past and Future states.

'*That which is not so*'—i.e. not capable of action.—(1821)

The following might be urged:—"In the case of such 'Past' entities as the 'Partial (or divided) cause', *capacity for action* is actually held to be there; hence the conclusion that 'no effect can be produced' cannot be admitted".

The answer to this is as follows:—

TEXTS (1822–1828).

SUCH A PAST ENTITY WOULD BE ONE THAT HAS COME INTO EXISTENCE, NOT HAVING BEEN THERE BEFORE, AND AS SUCH IT WOULD CLEARLY BE 'PRESENT', —JUST LIKE ANY OTHER 'PRESENT' ENTITY; ALSO BECAUSE IT WOULD BE OCCASIONAL.—IF AN ENTITY HAS NO CAUSE, IT CAN BE EITHER ETERNALLY EXISTENT OR NON-EXISTENT, BECAUSE IT WOULD NOT BE DEPENDENT UPON ANYTHING ELSE. THAT HOWEVER, WHICH HAS ITS EXISTENCE DEPENDENT UPON A CAUSE MUST BE CALLED 'PRESENT'.—THEN AGAIN, OTHER PEOPLE HAVE POSTULATED THAT 'MODIFICATION' OF FORM, ETC. IS DIFFERENT IN CHARACTER FROM 'PRATISAṄKHYĀNIRODHA' (DISSOCIATION FROM IMPURITIES BROUGHT ABOUT BY TRANSCENDENTAL KNOWLEDGE), AND OTHER 'ETERNAL VERITIES'; AND THIS 'MODIFICATION' OR EMBELLISHMENT OF FORM AND OTHER THINGS, COMES ABOUT THROUGH BIRTH, EXISTENCE, ETC.; NOW WHAT IS THAT PECULIARITY BY PRODUCING WHICH, BIRTH IS SAID TO BE 'PRODUCTIVE' OF THE THING? IS IT SOMETHING *non-different* FROM THE 'UNBORN' FORM? OR *different* FROM IT? IF THE PECULIARITY IS *non-different* FROM THE FORM, THEN THERE CAN BE NO 'PRODUCTION' OF IT; AS IT WOULD, IN THAT CASE, BE THERE EVEN BEFORE THE 'BIRTH', JUST AS AFTER IT. AS FOR A *different* PECULIARITY, THERE CAN BE NO SUCH,—BECAUSE BY REASON OF THIS DIFFERENCE, THERE CAN BE NO RELATION BETWEEN THEM. FURTHER, AS IT WOULD NOT BE EXISTENT BEFORE, IT WOULD INVOLVE THE NOTION THAT THE EFFECT WAS NOT EXISTENT (WHICH IS INCOMPATIBLE WITH THE OPPONENT'S DOCTRINES).—SIMILARLY IF THERE WERE 'REVERSAL OF CHARACTER', 'CONTINUANCE' AND 'DESTRUCTION' (BROUGHT ABOUT RESPECTIVELY BY THE EMBELLISHMENTS OF 'DECAY', 'STABILITY' AND 'NON-ETERNALITY'),—THE OBJECTIONS BASED UPON THEIR BEING 'DIFFERENT OR NON-DIFFERENT', 'DECAY' AND THE REST, WOULD BE APPLICABLE TO THESE ALSO.—(1822–1828)

COMMENTARY.

'*Just like any other present Entity*'—i.e. any other Entity whose 'present' character is not disputed.

'*Also because it would be occasional*';—this also goes with 'it would be *Present*'.

The Reason here put forward cannot be regarded as Irrelevant. Because as a matter of fact that thing is called 'Present' which has been produced by the Causal Link (or Factor); and what is *occasional* must owe its birth to a Causal Factor; because for that which has no cause, there are only two conditions possible—perpetual existence or non-existence; for the simple reason that its existence is not dependent upon anything else; hence what is occasional must have an existence that is brought about by a Causal Factor,—

and thus it becomes established that. that which has its existence brought about by a Causal Factor must be 'Present'; that is to say, 'Being Present' is invariably concomitant with 'being occasional'.

Further, if the Entity is really objectively 'Past' and 'Future', then all 'Embellishments' (or Modifications) would be everlasting; and in that case, there would be no difference between Form, etc. and the 'Dissociation from Impurities by transcendental knowledge' and other 'eternal verities'.

It might be argued that it is only the Form and such things as are actually found to be embellished (or modified) that can be regarded as 'modified'—not *Ākāsha* and the other Eternal Verities; so that there would be clear difference between Form, etc. and the said 'Eternal Verities'.

This is the view that has been held by other people.

This however cannot be right. Because there are four marks of *modification*—(1) Birth, (2) Decay, (3) Existence, and (4) Non-eternality. Among these, *Birth* produces things, *Existence* leads to their continuance, *Decay* leads to their decadence, and *Non-eternality* destroys them; hence among these, the functions of Producing and the rest have been held to be present.

Now the question arises—What is that Peculiarity which *Birth* produces by virtue of which it comes to be spoken of as 'productive' of the Form, etc. ?—Is this Peculiarity something different from the Form, etc. ? Or non-different from them ? These are the only two possible alternatives.

It cannot be *non-different* from Form, etc.; because the Peculiarity in question would, in that case, be an accomplished thing even before the functioning of 'Birth', and as such it would be incapable of being brought about,—just as after its accomplishment; what is already an accomplished entity cannot be brought about again; if it were, then there would be an infinite regress.

Nor can a Peculiarity be brought about which is different from the Form, etc.; because as it would be different from them, there could be nothing to determine that 'this Peculiarity belongs to that Form'. For instance, the relation between them cannot be that of Identity,—as they are held to be different; if they are not held to be different, then the above objections come in. Nor can the relation between them be that of one being produced by the other; as the production of the thing is due to Birth itself. No other kind of relation is possible;—those of *container and contained* being included under that of *being produced*. If then the relation of *being produced* from it is held to subsist between the said Peculiarity and Form, etc.—then, as the Peculiarity would be capable of being produced by the Form itself alone, it would be produced at all times from that alone; and under the circumstances, what would 'Birth' do to it ?—It might be argued that "the Form produces the Peculiarity, *through Birth*".—The answer to that is that it cannot be right that there should be any dependence upon the *Birth* which can render no help at all. Otherwise it would lead to an absurdity. If the Birth be held to actually render some help, then in regard to this Help, the question would arise as to its being different or non-different and so forth,—just as it arises in the case of the Peculiarity; and this would lead to an infinite regress.

From all this it follows that if there is difference, then there can be no relationship.

Further, if it be held that the said 'Peculiarity' did not exist before,—then it would mean the acceptance of the view that the effect has been non-existent (which is inconsistent with the opponent's doctrines).

Similarly, if Decay brings about a *reversal of character*,—and if Existence brings about *stability*,—and if Non-eternality brings about *destruction*,—then the question regarding these—'Reversal', etc.—being different or non-different, will arise, as it arose in connection with Birth; and all the objections then urged would be applicable in the case of these also.—(1822–1828)

TEXTS (1829-1830)

THESE, 'BIRTH' AND THE REST, ARE PRODUCTIVE OF THEIR EFFECTS, IN ACCORDANCE WITH THE LIMITATIONS OF THEIR NATURE; AND THIS CAPACITY OF THEIRS IS THERE BEFORE AS WELL AS AFTER; THIS POTENT FORM THUS BEING THERE AT ALL TIMES, WHY SHOULD THEY NOT PROCEED WITH THE ACTIVITY IN KEEPING WITH THEIR NATURE? AT THE STARTING OF SUCH ACTIVITY THERE CAN BE NO LIMITATION ON THE 'STATES'.—(1829-1830)

COMMENTARY.

Then again, the capacity of 'Birth' and the rest to produce their effects is limited to their respective capacity; and this capacity of theirs is there at all times; hence they should produce their effects at all times. It cannot be urged that there is absence of the 'Causal Factor' (which prevents the production). Because the Causal Factor also is there at all times. Thus then, as Birth and the rest would be producing their effects in the 'past' and 'future' states also,—one and the same 'state' should include all the States, of which thus there need be no division.—(1829-1830)

TEXTS (1831-1832).

FURTHER, WOULD THE 'PAST' AND OTHER ENTITIES BE MOMENTARY, OR NOT?—IF THE FORMER, THEN THERE IS THE SAME ABSENCE OF RESTRICTION.—THE 'MOMENT' THAT IS BORN BECOMES THE 'PRESENT',—THAT WHICH, ON BEING BORN, BECOMES DESTROYED, BECOMES THE 'PAST',—AND THAT WHICH IS YET TO BE BORN BECOMES THE 'FUTURE'.—(1831-1832)

COMMENTARY.

Again, are the Past, Present and Future things momentary or not? These are the two alternatives.—If the former,—if they are momentary,—

then there is the same absence of restriction.—The next sentence—'*The Moment, etc. etc.*' shows this same absence of restriction.—(1831-1832)

TEXT (1833).

IF, ON THE OTHER HAND, THE SAID THINGS ARE *not momentary*,—THEN THAT GOES AGAINST YOUR DOCTRINE ; UNDER YOUR DOCTRINE IT HAS BEEN SHOWN THAT ALL MODIFICATIONS ARE MOMENTARY.—(1833)

COMMENTARY.

If the other alternative is accepted—that the Past and the rest are not momentary—then it goes against your doctrine.—The term '*Kṛtānta*' stands for *Siddhānta*, accepted doctrine.—The doctrine referred to is that 'all modifications are momentary'.—(1833)

TEXT (1834).

THE VIEW IN QUESTION IS OPPOSED TO REASON ALSO : IF THE THINGS ARE EXISTENT, THEY MUST BE MOMENTARY, LIKE PRESENT THINGS. THE INVARIABLE CONCOMITANCE BETWEEN THESE TWO TERMS HAS BEEN ALREADY ESTABLISHED BEFORE.—(1834)

COMMENTARY.

Further, the view in question does not go against your own doctrine only, it is opposed to Reason also. For instance, whatever is existent must be momentary,—like the Present thing,—the Past and the Future are existent —hence they must be momentary. Previously—under the treatment of the Momentary Character of things (under Chapter VIII) the Invariable Concomitance of this Probans (*Being existent*, with the Probandum, *Being momentary*) has been established. Hence it cannot be said to be 'Inconclusive' (Doubtful). Further, 'existence' is characterised by *capacity for effective action* ;— what is not-*momentary* is not compatible with effective action, either successive or simultaneous ;—and when there is no *effective action*, there must be cessation of *existence* also, which is characterised by *effective action*. Thus *Existence* becomes excluded from where the Probandum (momentariness) is absent.—(1834)

TEXTS (1835-1840).

ARE THESE 'PAST' AND 'FUTURE' THINGS CAPABLE OF EFFECTIVE ACTION? OR NOT?—IF THEY HAVE THAT CAPACITY, THEN THEY MUST BE REGARDED AS 'PRESENT', LIKE OTHER 'PRESENT' THINGS.—IF THE 'PAST' AND THE 'FUTURE' ARE NOT REGARDED AS 'PRESENT', THEN THEY MUST BE DEVOID OF ALL CAPACITIES.—JUST LIKE THE 'SKY-LOTUS'.—THE *Ākāsha* AND OTHER 'NON-PRODUCED' (ETERNAL) THINGS ARE OPEN TO THE SAME OBJECTION; HENCE THESE CANNOT SERVE TO MAKE OUR REASON 'INCONCLUSIVE'.—IN THE CASE OF ALL ENTITIES, THEIR RESTRICTED CAPACITY FOR EFFECTIVE ACTION MUST BE DUE TO SOME CAUSE; IF IT WERE WITHOUT A CAUSE, EVERYTHING WOULD BE USED FOR EVERYTHING. IN FACT, THE RESTRICTED CAPACITY FOR EFFECTIVE ACTION MUST BE BROUGHT ABOUT BY A CAUSE; AND THERE IS NO OTHER CHARACTERISTIC FEATURE OF THE 'PRESENT' THING. IN THE CASE OF THE 'PAST' AND 'FUTURE' ALSO, THE SAID CAPACITY IS THERE FULLY COMPLETE, ACCORDING TO YOUR VIEW; WHEREFORE THEN SHOULD NOT THE CHARACTER OF THE 'PRESENT' BE ATTRIBUTED TO THEM?—(1835-1840)

COMMENTARY.

Further, there are the two alternatives—these Past and Future things are capable of effective action—or not capable.—If they are capable, then, the capacity being there, the things must be regarded as 'Present',—like those things whose 'present' character is not disputed. The argument may be thus formulated—Things that are capable of effective action must be regarded as Present,—as those things whose 'present' character is not disputed,—and the Past and Future things are capable of effective action; hence there is this Reason based upon the nature of things, which provides the *Reductio ad absurdum*.—The Probans cannot be said to be 'Inconclusive'; because the absence of the 'Present' character in the Past and Future things would imply the absence of all capacities,—just as in the 'sky-lotus'.—The argument may be thus formulated:—Things that are not-'Present' are also *not-efficient* for any action,—e.g. the 'sky-lotus',—and the Past and Future things are not 'Present'; hence there is perceived in them the absence of the wider character.

Nor can this argument be said to be 'Inconclusive', in view of the three 'eternal verities'—*Ākāsha*, *Pratisaṅkhyā-nirodha* and *Apratisaṅkhyā-nirodha*,—which do not undergo modifications;—because these also are included under the Minor Term (Subject of the Syllogism).

Thus there is no ground for the Reason being regarded as 'Inconclusive' (or Doubtful).

Then again, the restricted capacity for effective action that there is in entities, must be admitted to be due to some cause; otherwise, if it were without cause, then there could be nothing to restrict it ; and the capacity of things would, in that case, not be restricted (or limited) ; with the result that each and every thing would be utilised in bringing about each and every effect. Thus it cannot be right to restrict the efficiency of the eternal verities, *Ākāsha* and the rest. Consequently they do not supply the ground for regarding the Reason as 'Inconclusive'.

Nor can it be urged that the former Reason is one whose presence in the contrary of the Probandum is open to suspicion ; because the efficiency that pertains to a particular efficient activity,—the birth of which is due to causal factors,—is what characterises the 'Present' ; and this characteristic of the 'Present' is present intact in the Past and Future things also ; hence, there being no other basis for this, why should these be not regarded as 'Present' ?—(1835–1840)

TEXT (1841).

As a consequence of this, all attempt to attain Heaven and Final Beatitude would be futile ; as no fruit is found that could be attained by effort.—(1841)

COMMENTARY.

Then again, for the man for whom the Past and Future are actually present,—the fruit of acts also would be there at all times ; hence any effort to attain Heaven or Final Beatitude would be futile ; as there would be no fruit that could be attained by effort,—what would be the efficiency of the Austerities and Penances that constitute 'effort' ?—It might be said that "they would have the efficiency to produce the desired results".—That would mean that the said 'Production' of Results is something that was not there before and has come about now.—But even so, what is it that would be efficient ? And wherein would it be efficient ?—"The efficiency would lie in making the results 'present'".—What do you mean by 'making them *present*' ?—If it means 'bringing them to another place', then the thing becomes eternal, as it would remain for all time.—How too could there be any such 'bringing' in the case of Sensations, etc., which are immobile ? Even so, this 'bringing' would be something that did not exist before, but has now come into existence.

'*Heaven*' stands for the place on the summits of mount *Mēru*.—'*Apavarga*', 'Final Beatitude', stands for Deliverance ;—the '*Samsarga*' of these is their *attainment*.—The '*effort*' for this consists in Observances and Austerities.—(1841)

TEXT (1842).

IF, ON THE OTHER HAND, THE PAST AND FUTURE THINGS ARE HELD TO BE WITHOUT THE *capacity for effective action*,—THEN, ON THAT GROUND ALONE, THEY WOULD BE *non-existent*,—LIKE THE 'SKY-FLOWER'.—(1842)

COMMENTARY.

If then the second alternative view (proposed under *Text* 1835) is accepted —that the Past and Future things are devoid of capacity for effective action, —then, in that case, for that very reason,—of being devoid of *capacity for effective activity*,—they would have to be regarded as 'non-existent', like 'sky-flowers'; as the only characteristic of 'non-existence' consists in the *absence of all capacity*.—(1842)

Having thus adduced arguments in favour of the view that the 'Past' and the 'Future' do not exist, the author proceeds to refute the arguments that have been put forward in support of the view that they do exist :—

TEXT (1843).

AS REGARDS THE REASONS THAT HAVE BEEN ADDUCED, THEY MUST RESIDE IN THINGS; AND UNTIL THESE THINGS ARE ESTABLISHED, THE REASONS CANNOT BE ADMITTED.—OR ELSE, ON ACCOUNT OF THE 'PRESENT' CHARACTER BEING ESTABLISHED, THE SAID REASONS ARE 'CONTRADICTORY', —AS GOING AGAINST THE NATURE OF THE SUBJECT.—(1843)

COMMENTARY.

The 'Reasons' meant here are those adduced by the other party, under the *Text* 1790; these are 'Inadmissible in regard to their substratum'; because the things in which they are said to reside are the Past and Future things, and it has been shown that these do not exist; as has been said— 'if the thing is not there, its property cannot be there'.

Even if the said things existed, as they have been proved to have the 'Present' character, the Reasons in question would be proving something contrary to the very nature of the *Subject*; and as such, they would be 'Contradictory'.—(1843)

Question :—"If that is so, then how is it that Buddhist writers have declared the Past and Future Forms, etc. to be included among the 'states'? The Past and Future character of non-entities like the Hare's Horns is never tried to be determined".

Answer :—

TEXTS (1844-1845).

That form which, having come into existence, has ceased to exist, has been described as 'Past'; and that which is to come when the causal factors are complete has been described as 'Future'.—If the 'existence' of this were insisted upon, then they must be regarded as 'Present'; this is what has been just proved; as the only characteristic of the 'Present' is that it should be *existent*. —(1844-1845)

COMMENTARY.

This is easily understood.—(1844-1845)

Question :—" How is it that the presence of Form, Sensation and the rest has been attributed to these ? "

Answer :—

TEXT (1846).

When Form, etc. are attributed to the Past and Future things, it is through *imposing* upon them their past and future conditions ; and not in reality.—(1846)

COMMENTARY.

'*Tām dashām*'—that condition.—(1846)

Question :—" How is it then that Cognition has been declared to rest in two substrates ? "

Answer :—

TEXT (1847).

When the Seer of Truth declared that Cognition proceeds from two causes,—this teaching was in view of the Cognition with an object.—(1847)

COMMENTARY.

Cognition is of two kinds—with object (objective) and without object (purely subjective). It is in reference to the *Cognition with Object* that Cognition has been taught by the Blessed Lord, as being based upon two substrates.—(1847)

Question :—" How is it known that there is Cognition *without Object* also ? "

Answer :—

TEXT (1848).

IN THE CASE OF THE COGNITIONS OF 'ETERNAL THINGS', 'GOD' AND SO FORTH,—THERE IS NO OBJECTIVE BACKGROUND; AS WORDS AND NAMES ARE DEVOID OF THE FORMS OF THOSE.—(1848)

COMMENTARY.

'*And so forth*', includes such other assumed things as Primordial Matter, Time, etc.

No such idea should be entertained as that these cognitions have their objective background in the words; this is what is meant by the words—'*As Words and Names, etc. etc.*'—What is meant is that the 'form' of God—such as Eternality, Being the Cause of all things and so forth,—that is envisaged in the said cognitions,—of that form, the Word or the Name is entirely devoid,—which Word or Name does not undergo any modification.

The term '*ādi*' in '*shabdanāmādi*', is meant to include the contingent cause (of Cognition), postulated by other people, in the shape of the Reflected Image of things.—(1848)

Question:—"If then there is Cognition *without object* also, then how is it called 'Cognition'? Because 'Cognition' stands for *that which apprehends things*; and when there is nothing *to be apprehended*, how could the *cognition* be there?"

Answer:—

TEXT (1849).

IT IS CALLED 'COGNITION' ONLY BY VIRTUE OF THE PRESENCE OF THE NATURE OF 'CONSCIOUSNESS'; AND THIS 'CONSCIOUSNESS' ALSO CONSISTS IN THE COGNITION BEING *not-dark* WHICH IS DEDUCED FROM ITS *being luminous*.—(1849)

COMMENTARY.

"The presence of the nature of Consciousness also is not possible without cognition";—in answer to this it is added—'*And this Consciousness, etc. etc.*'—'*Sā*' stands for the presence of the nature of Consciousness;—'*asya*'—i.e. of the Cognition.—"What is it?"—It consists in the Cognition being *not-dark*; only, on account of there being nothing else to be illumined by it, and also of the absence of any other source of illumination, the Cognition is of the nature of Light itself,—like the Light diffused in the atmosphere; and it is by virtue of this *luminosity* that it is called 'Cognition'.—(1849)

Question:—"How does the *past act* bring about its fruit"?

Answer:—

TEXT (1850).

WHAT BRINGS ABOUT THE FRUIT IS THE CAUSE OF FRUITION,—NOT ANYTHING 'PAST'. IN FACT, THE FRUIT IS HELD TO PROCEED FROM THE 'CHAIN' OF COGNITIONS IMPRESSED BY THE ENTITY (WHEN PRESENT).—(1850)

COMMENTARY.

'*Impressed*'—i.e. rendered capable of producing the fruit, through the long series of 'causal factors'.—(1850)

Question:—"If that is so, then how is it that the Blessed Lord has declared that—'There is *Karma*, which decays, is obstructed and becomes modified'?"

Answer:—

TEXT (1851)

IN VIEW OF THE SAID IMPRESSION BEING ATTRIBUTED TO THE 'SERIES OF COGNITIONS', THE LORD HAS SAID THAT 'THERE IS *Karma*', WHICH ASSERTION IS FIGURATIVE; AS THE PRINCIPAL (OF THE DEBT) IS SAID TO BE 'NOT DESTROYED (LOST)'.—(1851)

COMMENTARY.

'*Bhaktyā*'—Figuratively.

When in the case of a Debt, when the accrued interest has become equal to the Principal, the Principal actually disappears; yet it is said to be 'not lost'. In the same way the *Karma*, Act, also, though past and gone, is spoken of as 'not gone and destroyed'.—(1851)

Question:—"What was the purpose for which the Teaching was given in figurative language?"

Answer:—

TEXT (1852).

THE MATTER HAS BEEN EXPLAINED IN THIS WAY BY THE TEACHER, FOR THE PURPOSE OF REMOVING THE NOTION OF THE UTTER ANNIHILATION (OF PAST ACTS). OTHERWISE, HOW COULD HE EXPLAIN THE TEACHING IMPARTED IN THE APHORISM DECLARING THE 'VOID'?—(1852)

COMMENTARY.

If it were declared that 'the Past act does not exist', it might be understood that there is non-existence of that *potency to produce the fruit* which had been set going by the past act; and the disciples would come to take up the view of the utter annihilation of the Past and its Effects; it is in view of this possibility that the Lord has said that 'the Act persists'.

'*Otherwise*'—if the Past really persisted,—then how could we explain the teaching in the aphorism where we are taught that '*in reality* all is *void*'?

As a matter of fact, when the Eye is produced, it does not come from anywhere; similarly when it is destroyed, it does not go away to any other place; what happens is that after having been not in existence, it comes into existence, and having come into existence, it again becomes non-existent.—It might be urged that—"in the Present state, it comes into existence, after having not been in existence"—That is not so; because the 'State' is not anything different from the entity (Eye); as is clear from the assertion that these same (things) are the 'States' and they exist as such.—If it be meant that—"not having been itself, it becomes itself";—then it would be established that there can be no 'future' Eye.—Further, if the Modifications are always there, the Cause and Effect would not be there; which would mean that there is no fixed Truth; and this would imply the absence of the two paths of Repression' (Purification) also; and thus the *four Truths* being non-existent, there would be no possibility of True Knowledge, Renunciation, Direct Intuition and Meditation. These being not there, there would be non-existence also of the *Pudgalas* (Bodies) which are near about the regions where the Fruit of Acts come about. This would put an end to all Teaching.—From all this it follows that the assumption of 'Past' and 'Future' things is not wholesome.—(1852)

It has been asked by the Opponent (under *Text* 1789)—"How have Mystics distinct cognitions of the Past and Future?"

The answer to this is as follows:—

TEXTS (1853-1856).

THE MYSTICS COGNISE THAT FORM OF THE 'PRESENT' THING WHICH, DIRECTLY OR INDIRECTLY, HAS BECOME EITHER AN EFFECT, OR A CAUSE; SUBSEQUENTLY, THEY FOLLOW IT UP WITH *conceptual cognitions*, WHICH ARE PURELY COMMON (SECULAR) IN CHARACTER, AND WHICH ARE REALLY WITHOUT OBJECTS (WITHOUT A REAL OBJECTIVE BACK-GROUND).—THUS IT IS THAT, ON THE BASIS OF THE SAID PAST AND FUTURE SERIES OF CAUSES AND EFFECTS, PROCEED ALL TEACHINGS REGARDING THE PAST AND THE FUTURE.—AS FOR THE *Tathāgata* HIMSELF, HIS TEACHINGS PROCEED WITHOUT CIRCUMLOCUTION; BECAUSE THE SERIES OF HIS COGNITIONS ARE ENTIRELY DEVOID OF THE WEBS OF CONCEPTUAL CONTENT.—(1853–1856)

COMMENTARY.

It has become the 'Effect' in relation to the 'Past',—and 'Cause' in relation to the 'Future'.

10

'*Vikalpānugatātmabhiḥ*'—i.e. with Conceptual (Determinate) Cognitions.

'*Really without objects*';—because the Specific Individuality of things cannot be envisaged by Cognitions associated with verbal expressions.

'*Tat*'—Thus, Therefore.

On the basis of the Past and Future series of Causes and Effects,—proceed all teachings regarding the Past and the Future,—from such Mystics as have not yet reached the Purest (Highest) stage.

As regards the Blessed Lord Himself, He does not even have the purely secular cognition,—because He is always calm and collected on account of the destruction of all Illusion and Ignorance; and all that is *Conceptual* is the product of Ignorance and Illusion. This has been thus declared—'Conceptual Content itself having assumed the form of Ignorance proceeds to impose its own form in the shape of the External world'.—So that, under the influence of the whole mass of His previous Meditations, Piety and Knowledge, His nature has become like that of the *Chintāmaṇi-gem*; hence His teachings proceed without circumlocution of any kind.—(1853-1856)

End of Chapter XXI.

A. Charlene McDermott The Sautrāntika arguments against the *traikālyavāda* in the light of the contemporary tense revolution

Many and many a grief ago (or so the pointer on a Buddhist chronometer might license one to express matters), the Sautrāntikas successfully countermanded a four-pronged resurgence of the eternalist heresy.[1] And, though the general dynamics of the Sautrāntika-Yogācāra critique of the Sarvāstivādin doctrines is by now widely disseminated and fairly well understood (thanks especially to the efforts of S. Schayer, T. Stcherbatsky and L. de la Vallée Poussin), there remains a cluster of difficulties surrounding the inadequately explicated technical notions of the Sarvāstivādins. Thus, still another rereading of the Sautrāntika-Sarvāstivādin dialogue would seem to be in order—this one in tandem with the writings of some of the so-called tense-revolutionaries and their philosophical predecessors,[2] for the reason that recent Western philosophical literature on time and change contains a partial replication of the various Buddhist positions and counterpositions. Registering several prima facie conceptual and methodological parallels between the two traditions therefore promises to be a step in the direction of further disambiguation of Sarvāstivādin terminology, a task which is nowhere near completion.

Having given a very sketchy indication of a few of these similarities below, I hope to exploit them in a subsequent study in the following manner: The more developed Western theories, as applied to their Buddhist counterparts, may not unreasonably be expected to provide an inventory of possible alternatives for filling in vague outlines and for deciding on the exact import of the illustrative examples which accompany discussions of such key words as, for example, *bhāva, prāpti, anyathā,* etc.[3] The emphasis is primarily, if not exclusively, epistemological,[4] amounting to a partial reconstruction of the positions of Dharmatrāta, Ghoṣaka, Buddhadeva, and Vasumitra, respectively, to each of which is adjoined the Śāntarakṣita-Kamalaśīla rebuttals.[5] One note of caution—none of what follows warrants imputing the status of a systematized tense logic to any structure disclosed in the several Buddhist proposals; any formal devices mentioned have a purely heuristic function.

I

The first view to be considered is that of Dharmatrāta, the view which reduces becoming to *bhāva-anyathātva* or alteration in the *bhāva* (manner of being, manifestation or appearance) of a substance (*dravya*) which itself does not undergo change; but this kind of reduction is better described as a *reductio ad absurdum* of becoming. One is tempted to baptize Dharmatrāta's interpretation "Buddhist-Sāṃkhya"[6] and the *Abhidharmakośa* expositor (see Louis de la Vallée Poussin, *L'Abhidharmakośa* V, p. 54) yields (doubtless due to pardonable eristic enthusiasm) to this temptation. No matter! There is also

A. Charlene McDermott is Associate Professor of Philosophy, University of New Mexico.

an undeniable kinship between Dharmatrāta and the above-cited detensers,[7] for whom reality is at bottom a becomingless neo-Eleatic whole.

A standard *dṛṣṭānta,* namely, that of the transformation of milk into curds (cf., A. B. Keith's résumé of this debate in *Buddhist Philosophy in India and Ceylon,* 1923, p. 165) is better replaced by the following less misleading (and more evocative) picture painted by F. H. Bradley:

> We seem to think that we sit in a boat and are carried down the stream of time, and that on the bank there is a row of houses with numbers on the door. And we get out of the boat and knock at the door of No. 19 and re-entering the boat suddenly find ourselves opposite No. 20, and having done the same we go on to No. 21. And all this while the firm fixed row of the past and future, stretches in a block behind us and before us.[8]

The changes rung on what is assumed to be a sempiternal substance are its mere epistemological precipitates,[9] its modes of *manifestation to consciousness.* The problem of temporal evolution is here not solved but dissolved.

II

Next, Kamalaśīla records his ramification of the Sautrāntika polemics against Ghoṣaka's *lakṣaṇa-anyathātva,* the mythos of a universe of peregrine *dharmas,* each affiliating itself in its wanderings with the diverse *lakṣaṇas* or characteristics of pastness, presentness, and futurity, respectively. Again, as in I, alteration is not attributed to the dharmic essence itself;[10] instead, according to hypothesis II, change is explained in terms of a *dharma's* adjuncts. It is not quite accurate to speak of the unseating of old *lakṣaṇas* in favor of new ones, for in some inscrutable way, the "soul" of a given *dharma* is never totally dissevered from any of the three *lakṣaṇas:* pastness, presentness, or futurity. The illustration of a man who "although devoted to one wife, is not free from passion from other wives" (Schayer, p. 30), far from clarifying this, merely dogmatically reasserts it. Yet, if all three aspects are alleged to be timelessly compresent in (or at least not entirely absent from) each *dharma,* what sense is to be attached to the key notion of the acquisition (*prāpti*) of *lakṣaṇas?* The upshot of A. N. Prior's (albeit semantically slanted) analysis of this matter—namely, that one cannot form a tensed utterance by attaching "some sort of modifier to . . . a non-temporally characterized 'content'" seems to me to sum up neatly the Sautrāntika case against Ghoṣaka.[11]

Too, C. D. Broad's objections of McTaggart's (Ghosaka-like) view are germane to the Sautrāntika attacks on both Ghoṣaka and Vasumitra (see footnote 21 below). Broad says:

> When I utter the sentence 'It will rain', I do *not* mean that in some mysterious non-temporal sense of 'is', there *is* a rainy event, which now possesses some determinate form of the quality of futurity and will in course of time lose futurity and acquire instead the quality of presentness. What I mean is that raininess will be, but is not now, being manifested in my neighborhood.[12]

[Moreover] Broad claims even to find a *logical* defect in talk of events, or as he puts it "event-particles," as "acquiring presentness" and then losing it. If this did happen, he says, "the acquisition and loss of presentness by this event-particle is itself an event-particle of the second-order, which happens to the first-order event-particle. Therefore every first-order event-particle has a history of indefinite length . . . Yet, by definition, the first-order event-particle . . . has no duration, and therefore can have no history in the time series along which presentness is supposed to move."[13]

In any case, Broad and the Sautrāntikas concur in their rejection of the theory that becoming is a species of qualitative change (however widely their paths may diverge beyond this point); rather, both regard it as an irreducible given. What then of the indictment levelled by one of his critics against Broad that, in the process of arriving at this rejection, Broad has succumbed to "the spell of Indo-European language, which bristles with time distinctions"?[14] Regretfully, a Mādhyamika-oriented critique of Sautrāntika stark-coming-into-being lies beyond the narrow limits of this article. We turn now to a consideration of the proposal of Buddhadeva.[15]

III

Buddhadeva's *anyathā-anyathātva* theory identifies change with the diverse orientational features or relationships of an invariant *dharma*. "When a *dharma* is wandering through the Times, it is called in each case 'another one' in a different sense in accordance with its relation to the antecedent and subsequent moments, just as the same woman is called 'mother' and 'daughter'" (Schayer, p. 31). Now, while one cannot be faulted for maintaining (a) that the present moment precedes the moment which will follow it and succeeds the moment which precedes it (except, perhaps, on grounds of insipidity or triteness), to go on therefrom to conclude (b) that the present moment *is* (in a timeless sense of the word 'is') past with respect to the subsequent moment and future with respect to the antecedent moment, is to overlook the *lexical* character of the terms 'past', 'present', and 'future', as it were, to demand the cake one has just eaten. To drive this point home, the referent of the term 'this' in the phrase 'this moment' (or of 'present' in the phrase 'is present') varies in such a manner that whenever one uses a sentence in which 'this moment' (or 'is present') figures in order to make a statement, one thereby refers to a time simultaneous with the time of utterance of that statement, that is, simultaneous with the tensed utterance token; similarly, with necessary adjustments, for the terms 'past' and 'future'. Hence, reducing disguised to obvious nonsense, it plainly will not do to say that this moment (where 'this' refers to the time of the utterance) is timelessly past (where 'past' refers to a time earlier than the time of the *same* utterance).

David Lewis' embroiderings on this are illuminating. On pages 186–187 of his "Anselm and Actuality,"[16] he remarks that: "although 'This time is present' is always true, 'All times are present' is never true. If we take a timeless point of view and ignore our own location in time, the big difference between the present time and other times vanishes. That is not because we regard all times as equally present, but rather because if we ignore our own location among the worlds we cannot use temporally indexical terms like 'present' at all."

Arguing in a similar vein, Broad refuses to concede that a description of events in terms of their "B-relations" (namely, the tenseless two-place predicates 'is earlier than', 'is at', 'is later than') can ever replace without loss an analysis in terms of the "A-determinants" ('pastness', 'presentness', 'futurity') of the events.[17] In a later study I intend to examine more fully the relevance of Broad's contention to the Sautrāntika rejoinder to Buddhadeva; for the present, I merely note the recurrence of theory III (and minor variations thereupon) as, dybbuklike, it takes possession of the fancies of any number of distinguished Eastern and Western philosophers. The locus classicus (in the latter tradition) of the hypothesis that past, present, and future, in some sense, exist, is Augustine's *Confessions,* book 9, chapters 17 and 18 (which hypothesis is later supplanted by Augustine's reflection that "neither past nor future is existent . . . the present of things past is in memory; the present of things present is in intuition; the present of things future is in expectation"[18]). An essentially similar view, albeit in modern dress, is espoused by the C-tensers. For all that, it is no less defeasible according to both the Sautrāntikas and A. N. Prior.[19]

IV

The same sort of emasculation of change occurs in the *avasthā-anyathātva* theory of Vasumitra-Saṃghabhadra, who also hold that *dharmas* are continuants, the applicability of the temporal predicates 'past', 'present', and 'future' being due, according to them, to fluctuations in each dharma's *kāritra* or potency to project results (*phalākṣepa*). Vasumitra maintains that: "a *dharma* . . . receives different designations due to different *avasthās* . . . . Just as, in an abacus, the same ball, when thrown in the place of units means *one,* in the place of hundreds, *hundred*; in the place of thousands, *thousand.* In the same manner a *dharma* (=*bhāva*), when staying in its *kāritra,* is called present, when fallen down from it is called past, when it has not yet reached it is called future."[20] But, in this context, the possibility of regarding a *dharma's* time-*avasthās* as its spatial positions having been ruled out,[21] the explanatory value of the abacus example is questionable.

There follow several unsuccessful attempts to define the notion of *kāritra,* which we cannot hope to detail here. But whether *kāritra* be defined as, for example, the capacity of giving or grasping a result (*phala-dāna-grahaṇa* (Schayer, p. 36) or, again, as the potency to project a result (*phalākṣepaśakti* (Schayer, p. 37), insofar as a *dharma's* functionality is thereby regarded as (1) an aspect of the *dharmasvabhāva*, *distinguishable* from the *dharma*, cogent reasons for that functionality's being held in abeyance at one time, and becoming productive at another, cannot be given.[22] (2) Neither is a halfway house, namely, the theory that the *dharmasvabhāva* and its *kāritra* or functionality both are and aren't identical, a congenial resting place. (3) Nor is there much solace to be derived from the evasive stance that the relationship between *svabhāva* and *kāritra* is ineffable. (4) If, finally, a *dharma's kāritra* is alleged to have a merely nominal existence (*prajñaptisat*), he will, ipso facto, have conceded the Sautrāntika's point.

In sum, the Sautrāntika critic would obliterate the (to him pseudo-) distinctions between a *dharma's* essence or intrinsic nature, its functionality, and the point of time at which that functionality manifests itself. (Cf., A. N. Prior, *Past, Present and Future*, pp. 187–188. "A world-state proposition in the tense-logical sense is simply an index of an instant; indeed, I would like to say that it *is* an instant, in the only sense in which 'instants' are not highly fictitious entities. To be the case *at* such-and-such an instant is simply to be the case *in* such-and-such a world; and that in turn is simply to be the case *when* such-and-such a world-proposition is the case." Such demystification cannot but have a salutary effect on the philosophy of, e.g., Veṅkaṭanātha who, claiming to have found inconsistencies in the Buddhist theory of momentariness, would replace it with a proliferation of ontological categories.)[23] An entity is no more and no less than its capacity to produce effects (*artha-kriyā-kāritva*), a thanatomanic, dimensionless chronon,[24] identical with the instantaneous dynamics of its own coming-into and passing-out-of being. An aggregate of such fluxions, each of which we regard as redolent with past traces and proleptic of future projections, is *fused* (via the primordial *con-fusion* that is endemic to our conceptual apparatus) into a continuum (*kṣaṇa-santāna*), a mere facade superimposed on an "overblotted series of intermittences."[25] But that is an old and well-known story.

V

Having undercut the "platonic" moorings of the four preceding views, it remains to ease the most significant of the mental cramps that accrue to the Sautrāntika's own posture: namely, that arising from their supposed inability to explain cognition of and discourse about "inexistent" past and future moments. Here the attentive reader of later Buddhist epistemology has only to cast a recapitulative glance at the adequately (and often) expounded Sautrāntika theory of reference to irrealia in general, wherein past and future virtualities emerge as a subset of possibilia and are to be dealt with accordingly. To my 1970 discussion of this matter,[26] I merely append the following remarks of Prior:

> Philosophers may be worried about the fact that certain undoubted truths appear to be about objects which, though not in the least abstract, are merely fictitious, or are mere has-beens or will be's (i.e. they have ceased to exist or have not yet begun to). Quantification, it seems to me, *is* relevant to this worry, but not quite in the way Quine says it is: indeed in almost exactly the opposite way. Quine says in effect that non-existents cannot figure as the values of bound variables; I would suggest that, on the contrary, this is the only way in which non-existents of this sort *can* figure. I cannot directly refer to what does not exist but is merely imagined to exist or is merely going to exist; but I can make purely *general* (i.e. quantified) statements about the imaginary or future denizens of the world. The quantification, however, must occur within a 'modality'. I may, indeed, imagine some real object to be a mermaid; but we can then say that there is an x such that x is imagined by me to be a mermaid; but if what is involved is as we say, a 'merely imaginary' mermaid, then we cannot say that *there is an x such that I imagine that x* is a mermaid, but only that *I imagine that there is an x such that x* is a mermaid. Analogously, it may be that some existing person is going to live so long as to rule England in A.D. 3000; more likely, however, the ruler of England at that date does not yet exist, in which case we cannot say that for *some x, it will be the case then that x* rules England, but only that *it will be the case then that for some x,* x rules England.[27]

In short (and here I think the Sautrāntikas would very likely go along with Prior the P-tenser, had they his refined tools), in analyzing 'It will be the case that something ϕs' ($F(\underline{\exists}x)\phi x$), we do not mean (or need) to say that some identifiable *already existing* x will *continue to exist* and will $\phi((\underline{\exists}x)F\phi x)$.[28]

The foregoing leads should be pursued further; in addition, the ordinary man's felt difference between the apprehension of anterior and posterior truths, as well as the status of that difference (and all other temporally rooted distinctions) to an enlightened being, ought to be investigated. In relentless disregard of these desiderata, *tempus loquendi* (my allotted time) yields its place to *tempus tacendi.*

1. More accurately, the Sautrāntikas unveiled a Nicodemian reversion to eternalism on the part of the Sarvāstivādins. For the Sarvāstivādins, having explicitly decried the view that time is an eternal substance, posit in its place real, perdurable *dharmas.* Cf. *Abhidharmakośa*, IV, 28, *Yaśomitra, Sphuṭārthā, Abhidharmakośa vyākhyā*, ed. Wogihara (Tokyo: The Publication Association of Abhidharmakośavyākhyā, 1932–1936), p. 375, line 4, *"kālo nityaḥ padārtho'stītyeke/ . . . /kālo nāma ka eṣa dharmaiti/kāla ity asyābhidhānāsya kim adhidheyam . . . saṃsāra paridīpanādhivacanam . . . ."*

2. In an article entitled "Tense Logic! Why Bother?" *Nous* III (Feb., 1969), pp. 17–32), G. J. Massey examines the programs of "a dedicated band of revolutionaries [who], under the aegis of Arthur Prior, impugn the legitimacy of certain central notions of modern logic and have begun to develop and explore alternative logics, so called *tense logics,* reminiscent of certain ancient and medieval logical developments" (p. 17). Massey goes on to subclassify twentieth-century logicians as follows: "Hereafter we shall refer to logicians who insist on de-tensed formalized languages as *de-tensers,* and to the revolutionaries who demand tensed ones as *tensers,* either P-tensers or C-tensers according to their style of tense logic" (pp. 18–19). "Tenser and de-tenser agree that one can refer only to what is real . . . but this agreement is more verbal than substantival. For the

P-tenser 'real' means 'what now exists'; for the de-tenser, 'real' means what exists (tenseless)'; and for the C-tenser, it means 'what has existed, exists now, or will exist'" (p. 21).

3. The need to unpack the equally refractory conception of *kāritra* is far less pressing, since Śāntarakṣita-Kamalaśīla have subjected it to a relatively thorough examination; hence I shall do little more than reiterate their comments.

4. For reasons of brevity and coherence, and not because I regard them as unimportant, I ignore ethically and/or eschatologically based critical rejoinders.

5. See chapter 3 of S. Schayer's monograph, *Contributions to the Problem of Time in Indian Philosophy* (Krakow: *Polski Builetyn Orientalistycany,* 1938) (hereafter cited as Schayer, *Contributions*).

6. See footnote 9.

7. See footnote 2. *Mutatis mutandis,* of course. A fully articulated model of a block universe comprising four-dimensional objects and time slices thereof, cannot be ascribed to Dharmatrāta. Buddhist sophistication does not extend to endowing empirical time with the status of a fourth dimension or to assigning loci to past and future *dharmas.* They are placeless (*adeśástha*). (See Schayer, *op. cit.*, p. 21.) For these and other reasons, it would be prochronistic (even were I competent to do so) to take up the question of the relationship between the Buddhist world-model and that proposed by quantum physics. However, it is interesting to note that M. Čapek ("Time in Relativity Theory: Arguments for a Philosophy of Becoming," pp. 434–454, J. Fraser, ed., in *The Voices of Time* (New York: G. Braziller, 1966) pp. 434–454) contends that a modern analogue of view I "not only does not follow from relativity theory, but is even incompatible with it" (p. 451). In this Čapek stands diametrically opposed to (among others) A. Grünbaum, *Philosophical Problems of Space and Time* (New York, Knopf, 1963), and to W. V. O. Quine, *Word and Object* (Cambridge: Massachusetts Institute of Technology Press, 1960), p. 170.

8. F. H. Bradley, *The Principles of Logic* (London: Oxford University Press, 1922), vol. I, pp. 54–55. Bradley, however, immediately discards this picture in favor of another.

9. On p. 30 of Schayer, *Contributions,* the *bhāva* is said to be "a special quality (=*guṇaviśeṣa*) to which are related cognitive processes (*jñānapravṛtti*), expressed in distinction of terms (*abhidhāna*): *future, present* and *past.*" Schayer also observes that it is not all certain that *'guṇa'* in *'guṇaviśeṣa'* ought to be equated with the *'guṇa'* of Sāṃkhya metaphysics.

10. However, in *contrast* to I, account II explicitly rules out the suggestion of an alternating current of manifestations and evanishments. (See Schayer, *Contributions,* p. 32, note.)

11. A. N. Prior, *Past, Present and Future* (Oxford: The Clarendon Press, 1967), p. 15.

12. C. D. Broad, *Examination of McTaggart's Philosophy,* vol. 2, Part I (Cambridge: Cambridge University Press, 1938), p. 316.

13. A. N. Prior, *Past, Present and Future,* pp. 7–8.

14. D. Williams, "The Sea Fight Tomorrow," in *Structure, Method and Meaning,* ed. by P. Henle, H. Kallen, and S. Langer (New York, Liberal Arts Press, 1951), p. 299. A propos, one feels that a *linguist's* approach to the problem might be very rich in results. (Zeno Vendler's distinction between achievements and processes is an example that comes immediately to mind. Vendler notes in *Linguistics and Philosophy* (Ithaca, New York, Cornell University Press, 1967, p. 114) that "running or crossing the street are processes going on in time and as such can't be broken down into indivisible time instants—their very notion indicates a time stretch; whereas spotting (an achievement) connotes a unique indivisible time instant."

15. In order to facilitate exposition, I have reversed the order in which Kamalaśīla reviews the last two theories.

16. *Nous* 4 (May, 1970).

17. That is, one cannot assimilate tensed to tenseless predicates. See C. D. Broad,

"Time and Change," in *Aristotelian Society Supplementary Volume* 8 (1928), p. 187. The "A-B" dichotomy derives from McTaggart's now famous distinction between two essentially different types of temporal series, the "A-series" which runs from past to present to future, and the "B-series" which runs from earlier to later than with a permanent generating relation of *earlier than.* For a fuller discussion, see chapters 1–4 of R. M. Gale, *The Language of Time* (London: Routledge & K. Paul), 1968.

18. Book 9, chapter 20 of Augustine's *Confessions,* p. 83; A. Hyman and J. Walsh, *Philosophy in the Middle Ages* (New York: Harper and Row, 1967).

19. See especially the last chapter of Prior's *Past, Present and Future.*

20. S. Schayer, *Contributions,* p. 31.

21. See footnote 7.

22. In this regard, the positing of *jati, jarā, sthiti,* and *anityatā* is both unwarranted and unhelpful, as is the assumption of second-order *kāritras* (namely, *kāritras* of *kāritras*), the latter giving rise to a vicious infinite regress.

23. See S. Dasgupta, *A History of Indian Philosophy,* vol. III (Cambridge: Cambridge University Press, 1940), pp. 273–274.

24. On the strict Sautrāntika notion of a *kṣaṇa* (directly intuitable, if at all, only via the transcendental intuition of a yogin) and its relationship to the impermanent but briefly persisting "moment" of earlier Buddhism, see E. Conze, *Buddhist Thought in India* (Ann Arbor: University of Michigan Press, 1962), pp. 134–137. (See also E. Sarathchandra, *Buddhist Psychology of Perception* (Colombo: Ceylon University Press, 1958), pp. 42–44.) Regarding the latter notion, compare A. Moles' remark in his *Information Theory and Esthetic Perception* (Urbana, Illinois: University of Illinois Press, 1966), p. 15: "The act of perception, being an electrochemical process, is carried on at a tremendously high speed. Nonetheless it does possess a measurable duration . . . . The threshold of perception could be described as the 'length of the present'. Its value is around .05 second."

25. For this well-turned phrase (as well as for the paper's subtitle), I am indebted, of course, to the poet Ezra Pound.

26. Cf., my *An Eleventh-Century Buddhist Logic of 'Exists'* (Reidel: Dordrecht, 1970).

27. A. N. Prior, Papers on *Time and Tense* (Oxford: The Clarendon Press, 1968), p. 143.

28. Or that a now existing x stands forever in a variety of relations to other denizens of a frozen universe.

PAUL M. WILLIAMS

BUDDHADEVA AND TEMPORALITY

Buddhadeva occupies the position of an enigmatic and at the same time intensely thought provoking Indian philosopher. Although we have access to none of his works in either Sanskrit or Chinese and Tibetan translations, and although he rarely receives more than a few lines of stereotyped exposition and refutation at the hands of fellow Sarvāstivādins and members of other schools alike, nevertheless it is possible to discern in his contributions to the problem of temporality considerably subtler analytic powers than are seen to be present in those of the other three Sarvāstivādin masters whose views are examined in the *Vibhāṣā*.[1] In fact, it will be shown that problems which arise out of the differences between Buddhadeva's views and those of the others lie at the very centre of the treatment of time in contemporary philosophy, and that correspondingly the old controversies in which Buddhadeva participated can only be appreciated when they are understood to be real, living problems and not just rather sterile phases in the history of ideas.

Apart from refutations in philosophical treatises, we have little independent knowledge of Buddhadeva's life or even of when he lived. Tāranātha places him just after Dharmatrāta, Ghoṣaka and Vasumitra, and immediately before Nāgārjuna.[2] The latter probably lived around A.D. 150, while the three former were more or less contemporaneous with Kaniṣka, who, in spite of considerable academic controversy can be dated as having reigned from roughly A.D. 78–102.[3] However, Warder gives Dharmatrāta the date "a little after 50 A.D." and describes Vasumitra as the nephew of Dharmatrāta and co-author with Pārśva of the *Mahāvibhāṣā*, which he dates at about A.D. 100. Since Buddhadeva is, of course, mentioned in the *Vibhāṣā* as an established Sarvāstivādin master, we could perhaps place him between A.D. 50 and A.D. 100, that is, as a junior contemporary of Dharmatrāta. This would agree with Warder's own estimate of Buddhadeva's chronological placing, and it would thus probably make him an older contemporary of Vasumitra. But this clearly doesn't tally with Tāranātha, who says that Buddhadeva lived after Vasumitra. If we accept that Vasumitra, or rather the same Vasumitra that Tāranātha refers to, was the co-author of the *Vibhāṣā* and thus supported his own views against those of

Journal of Indian Philosophy 4 (1977) 279–294. *All Rights Reserved*

Dharmatrāta, Ghoṣaka and Buddhadeva, then we would have to discard Tāranātha's testimony and deny the relative chronological placing of the four philosophers given by him. But once we decide to place Buddhadeva earlier than Tāranātha would suggest, we are really at liberty how much earlier we decide to place him. In particular, as Poussin has noticed,[4] this reopens the question of the exact relationship between Buddhadeva and the inscription on the Mathurā Lion Pillar which mentions a certain 'Buddhatreva'. The identification of these two personages was originally suggested by Sylvain Lévi, "L'inscription K est tracée en l'honneur de l'ācārya Buddhadeva. Un personnage de ce nom, qualifié de mahābhadanta, est compté parmi les quatre grands ācāryas de l'école Vaibhāṣika, avec Dharmatrāta, Ghoṣaka . . . et Vasumitra. Ghoṣaka et Vasumitra enseignent au temps de Kaniṣka et de son successeur; Buddhadeva est de la génération immédiatement postérieure à ces deux docteurs, immédiatement antérieure à Nāgārjuna."[5] Sten Konow, however, in his book on the inscriptions notes that it is impossible on this basis that the inscription could be referring to the philosopher Buddhadeva, since "the Lion Capital is at least a century older than Kaniṣka".[6] But of course since we can no longer accept the testimony of Tāranātha, we are perfectly free to place the date of Buddhadeva a good century before Kaniṣka. As Poussin says, "Aucun mal à ce que Buddhadeva soit très antérieur à la Vibhāṣā. Les Sarvāstivādins doivent leur nom au 'Tout existe', que Buddhadeva est probablement un des premiers à avoir expliqué."[7]

Some support for this can be gained from a source which has previously not been considered in this context. In the 'Kālaparīkṣā' of Nāgārjuna's *Madhyamakakārikās*, written 50 to 100 years after the probable dates of Dharmatrāta, Ghoṣaka and Vasumitra, there is absolutely no reference to the views of any of these philosophers in spite of the fact that Nāgārjuna, although a southerner, was educated according to Bu-ston at Nālandā and would surely have been acquainted with such views had they enjoyed a very widespread support.[8] Nāgārjuna's treatment of time in fact depends entirely upon a certain view which sees the temporal stages of past, present and future as having a mutually dependent existence. He says, for example, "(The present and future) are not able to be established without dependence on the past. Therefore the present and future do not exist . . . By this (method) the remaining two (categories) are dealt with, inverting their order."[9] Now, all authorities agree that the principal characteristic of Buddhadeva's view is that the categories of present, past and future are in some way relative, the disagreement occurring as to what exactly they are relative to. In the *Vibhāṣā*, for example Buddhadeva is called "Le partisan de la différence d'*apekṣā* ou 'relation'",[10] while Saṃghabhadra says in his *Choen-tcheng-luen* that "D'après le Bhadanta Buddhadeva, les époques sont distinctes par la différence de la relation (*apekṣā*)."[11] Fa-pao, one of the commentators on Hiuan-tsang, understood by such statements as this that according to Buddhadeva "le futur est établi relativement (*apekṣya*) au passé et au présent; le passé relativement au présent et au futur; le présent relativement au passé et au futur",[12] and this corresponds exactly with the analysis accepted by Nāgārjuna as the foundation upon which to build his refutation of temporality. It is perhaps no coincidence that the words used for 'relation' or 'in dependence on' were probably the same in all cases, since the words '*apekṣā*' and '*apekṣya*' are found in every one of our Sanskrit sources for Buddhadeva's views as well as in the passage quoted from Nāgārjuna. Thus it is possible at least to suggest that Nāgārjuna's approach in constructing his refutation of time took as its starting point an approach to time which he knew already existed among philosophers of the school he was combatting. It could therefore be conjectured that perhaps Buddhadeva's view was the most firmly established one at the time, or it is even possible that it was the only Sarvāstivādin view on the subject that Nāgārjuna knew about. There would, after all, be little point in constructing a refutation of time based on a view nobody held. But all this is, of course, pure supposition, having merit only in that it enables us to reflect more deeply on Poussin's suggestion that Buddhadeva be placed earlier than is generally done. Warder's statement that he was a junior contemporary of Dharmatrāta is given no evidence to support it and the best that can be said for it is that there is as little departure as possible from Tāranātha's chronology.

It is possible to view the status of an event in time in two different ways, corresponding to a distinction between the static and dynamic temporal.[13] The classic exposition of this distinction is provided by J. M. E. McTaggart in his book *The Nature of Existence*[14] in an argument first published in 1908 to prove the complete unreality of time and subsequently criticised, albeit always within the framework of McTaggart's distinctions, by many of the most important twentieth century philosophers from Russell and Broad through to Strawson and Findlay.[15]

Quite simply, temporal events can be seen as being past, present and future and as changing in respect of each determination from being far future to less future, then to present and subsequently to recent past and further past.

Alternatively, it is possible to view events not in relationship to their changing temporal status, but rather in their relationships to each other in terms of 'before', 'simultaneous with' and 'after'. Now, it might be considered that these two ways of looking at time are in fact the same, that one series is reducible to the other. But if this is so, and the history of the contributions to the problem of time by contemporary philosophers is largely a series of attempts to show just that, it is by no means the case in a nonproblematic sense. For whereas an event is continually changing its status in respect of past, present and future, an event's status as before, simultaneous with and after is for all times a fixed one. When one event is before another it is always before it, whatever the changing status of events in terms of the past, present, future series. To quote McTaggart's own words:

Positions in time, as time appears to us *primâ facie*, are distinguished in two ways. Each position is Earlier than some and Later than some of the other positions. To constitute such a series there is required a transitive asymmetrical relation, and a collection of terms such that, of any two of them, either the first is in this relation to the second, or the second is in this relation to the first . . . In the second place, each position is either Past, Present or Future. The distinctions of the former class are permanent, while those of the latter are not. If M is ever earlier than N, it is always earlier. But an event, which is now present, was future and will be past.[16]

The series which runs from future through present to past McTaggart calls the 'A-series', while the series of before, simultaneous with and after he calls the 'B-series'. The relations 'earlier than' or 'before' can correspondingly be called 'B-relations', while the pastness, etc. of an event can be called its 'A-determination'.[17]

It is worth noting briefly, because it does have some relevance to criticisms offered of Buddhadeva's position, exactly what use McTaggart made of the distinctions he had drawn in constructing his proof of the unreality of time. He argues firstly that the B-series, while different from the A-series is nevertheless subordinate to it, since events can only bear B-relations to each other because each event has a particular A-determination, "The B-series, however, cannot exist except as temporal, since earlier and later, which are the relations which connect its terms, are clearly time-relations. So it follows that there can be no B-series where there is no A-series, since without an A-series there is no time."[18] Thus it is clear that, from McTaggart's point of view, if the A-series can be shown to involve a contradiction, given that nothing which involves a contradiction can be true of reality the A-series and by implication the B-series can be shown to be impossible. This McTaggart does to his own satisfaction by arguing that granted that there is no first and last event, every single event in the A-series has all three mutually incompatible A-determinations:

Past, present, and future are incompatible determinations. Every event must be one or the other, but no event can be more than one . . . And this exclusiveness is essential to change, and therefore to time. For the only change we can get is from future to present, and from present to past. The characteristics, therefore are incompatible. But every event has them all. If M is past, it has been present and future. If it is future, it will be present and past. If it is present, it has been future and will be past. Thus all the three characteristics belong to each event. How is this consistent with their being incompatible?[19]

Lest it be objected that the very use of tensed verbs carries with it the implication that no one event has all these determinations at the same time but rather successively, this means, according to McTaggart, that to say M is present is to say it is future at a moment of past time, past at a moment of future time and present at a moment of present time. This, of course, does nothing more than introduce a second order time series to which the same problems apply. Thus there is generated a vicious infinite regress.[20]

For the purposes of this paper we are concerned specifically with two aspects of McTaggart's thesis. Firstly, there is the distinction between the A-series and the B-series and the point that whether or not the existence of one is dependent on that of the other they are nevertheless so different from each other as to constitute radically different ways of speaking about the phenomenon of time and the nature of events in time. Secondly, we are concerned with McTaggart's argument that the distinctions of past, present and future involve the coexistence in any one time stage of all three A-determinatic

The earliest statement we have available of Buddhadeva's views is in the *Vibhāṣā*:

Le partisan de la différence d'*apekṣā* ou 'relation' (*apekṣānyathika*) dit: "Les *dharmas*, circulant dans les époques, prennent différents noms en raison des relations mutuelles d'antériorité et de postériorité. De même qu'une femme est nommé 'fille' rélativement à sa mère, et 'mère' relativement à sa fille; son essence n'est pas changée, mais, vu la différence des relations, elle reçoit le nom de fille et de mère. De même le *dharma* est dit 'passé' relativement à ce qui suit, 'futur' relativement à ce qui précède; 'présent' relativement à l'un et à l'autre."[21]

Although we are unable to check with the Chinese text, this can be cross-checked with the Sanskrit sources we have for Buddhadeva's views and found to be quite accurate. For example, the *Tattvasaṃgraha* describes his ideas as follows, "A *dharma* circulating in the (three) times is named (present, etc.) in mutual dependence on (the moments) before and after. Just as the same woman is called 'mother' and 'daughter'. Thus with reference to before and after, when there is something previous (to a *dharma*) but nothing after it, that (*dharma*) is future, when there is both a before and after, that is present, (and) when there is an after (but) no before, that is past."[22] And in the *Abhidharmadīpa* we find, "A *dharma* circulating in (the three) times is said to be one or the other dependent on before and after. This (*dharma*) does not undergo change of condition or of essential nature. Just as one woman is called mother or daughter in dependence on before and after."[23] Yaśomitra, in the only extant Sanskrit commentary on the *Abhidharmakośa*, glosses the Kośa's own discussion of Buddhadeva (from which the sources quoted above almost certainly obtained their information) as follows, "It is named by mutual dependence on before and after. This means that it is called present, future and past as a result of dependence on before and after. It is called future in dependence on the fact that present and past are prior. It is called present in dependence on the fact that past is prior or future comes after. And it is called past in dependence on the fact that present or future comes after."[24] We can make use of the *Abhidharmakośa* itself by using Poussin's translation from the Chinese, "Le Bhadanta Buddhadeva défend l'*anyonyathātva*: les époques s'établissent par relation. Le *dharma*, cheminant à travers les époques, prend différents noms par relation, c'est-à-dire, il est appelé passé, futur, présent, par rapport à ce qui précède et à ce qui suit. Exemple: une même femme est fille et mère."[25]

Two questions immediately arise in considering what has been given. Firstly, what exactly is Buddhadeva trying to say, and secondly is what he is saying philosophically coherent? We can begin by noting something that has already been noticed briefly in another context, that two of the Chinese commentators of Hiuan-tsang had very different views as to what Buddhadeva meant by 'dependence'. Fa-pao[26] considered that it was a question of the mutual dependence of the three categories past, present and future, and this analysis corresponds to the way Nāgārjuna treats time. Support for the view of Fa-pao can be derived from Saṃghabhadra's *Choen-tcheng-luen*, probably the most important and influential orthodox Sarvāstivādin critical work after the *Vibhāṣā*, "D'après le Bhadanta Buddhadeva, les époques sont distinctes par la différence de la relation (*apekṣā*). Le *dharma* circule par les époques; on lui donne différents noms par rapport à ce qui précède et à ce qui suit, sans qu'il y ait modification de la chose, de la maniére d'être ou du caractère. Comme la même femme, relativement à ce qui précède et à ce qui suit, reçoit le nom de fille ou de mère, de même le *dharma*, circulant par les époques, est nommé passé par rapport au présent et au futur, futur par rapport au passé et au présent, présent par rapport au passé et au futur."[27] The last part of this, together with the view of Fa-pao, clearly doesn't fit with either the *Vibhāṣā*, which is our earliest source for Buddhadeva's views, or with the *Abhidharmakośa* and the other sources which depend on it for their information. Even more surprising, the *Abhidharmadīpa* says quite clearly, "A *dharma* circulating in (the three) times is said to be one or the other dependent on before and after."[28] This is surprising because the *Abhidharmadīpa* was probably written by Vimalamitra,[29] a disciple of Saṃghabhadra who shows no sign of wanting to disagree with his master, and who would have presumably discussed, and probably upheld Saṃghabhadra's teaching had the latter made it clear he was putting forward an unorthodox view of Buddhadeva's theories. Nevertheless, the orthodox interpretation is undoubtedly that put forward in China by P'ou-kouang, that Buddhadeva's doctrine is, "le futur, relativement à l'antérieur; le passé, relativement au postérieur; le présent, relativement à l'un et à l'autre".[30] How are we to view this disagreement between the commentators? It seems obvious that there is a disagreement, and yet it seems probable that at least among the Indian Buddhists the disagreement was not realised to be one. In one sense this is not really surprising, since Buddhadeva's theories were always expounded in an offhand, stereotype manner simply as a prelude to their refutation, and were never really examined as genuine philosophical positions. Perhaps a key to the difficulty is provided by remembering what Richard Robinson had to say about the dangers of misinterpretation in reading Plato, "Because you have abstracted Y from X, you assume your author did too. But such an assumption must not be made on general grounds, for no man has made or ever will make all the abstractions possible from any one object present to his consciousness."[31] The fact is that a distinction between the two views was simply not realised, Saṃghabhadra was not aware that he had unconsciously made an inference from what it seems Buddhadeva had probably held to what he assumed him to be holding. How this came about is quite easy to see.

Consider the series past, present and future as being represented by A, B, C, respectively; and the series before, simultaneous with and after by X, Y, Z, respectively. Now, the series X, Y, Z, corresponds to the B-series, and X, Y, and Z are B-relations that hold between events. The series A, B, C, corresponds to the A-series, and A, B, and C are A-determinations that an event has successively. What Buddhadeva appears to be proposing is to understand by the series A, B, C, the series X, Y, Z, that is, to say an event is past is equal in meaning to saying that it is before what comes after, and so on.[32] The two series are to be viewed as strictly identical both internally and externally, that is to say, (A, B, C,) equals (X, Y, Z,); and (A) equals (X); (B) equals (Y); and (C) equals (Z). On this basis, whenever the one series appears in a proposition, the other series can be substituted for it without a change of truth value to that proposition, provided that the rest of the proposition remains the same. Thus to say, as does the *Tattvasaṃgraha*, that "a *dharma* circulating in the (three) times is named (present, etc.) in mutual dependence on the (moments) before and after" is strictly equal in meaning to Saṃghabhadra's statement that "le *dharma*, circuiant par les époques, est nommé . . . présent par rapport au passé et au futur".

We can therefore see that Saṃghabhadra is in fact perfectly orthodox once we permit this inference which Buddhadeva himself would probably have permitted. But it is quite clear that while this is a valid inference, it nevertheless leads to a factually confused conclusion. The A-series is not the same as the B-series, and A-determinations and B-relations are completely different things. An event changes its A, B, C, status, but it keeps for ever X, Y, Z, relations. Thus for Saṃghabhadra to argue that Buddhadeva *meant* by each time stage that it was dependent on the other two as he does, is to falsify the latter's position. Buddhadeva's intention was to reduce statements about the A-series to statements about the B-series, to explain the B-series as the *meaning*, insofar as one process can be said to be the meaning of another, of the A-series. Thus to first of all accept his analysis and then to revert to talking in terms of A-determinations, that is, to use terms like 'past' and 'future' is to try to operate with both series at the same time and thus to cross incompatible categories. To be strictly logical and to avoid such confusions it would be necessary after accepting Buddhadeva's analysis to abandon altogether use of the words 'past', 'present' and 'future' in favour of the corresponding B-relation terms.

But it might be objected that all sources agree that what Buddhadeva was doing was offereing an explanation of how we use the words 'past' and so on. This is undoubtedly correct, since in reducing one series to the other terms used to convey the divisions in the one series can be made absolutely equal in meaning to the terms used to convey the corresponding divisions in the other series. But in that case, the connotative meanings that the terms of the reduced series possessed before the reduction are no longer possessed by them if the terms of the second series to which they have been reduced in meaning do not have them in the normal course of events. Thus to say that the word 'past' is equal in meaning to the word 'before' and so on for the rest of the series is to say that the A-series is equal to the B-series in the sense that all the statements that were true of the B-series are now true of the A-series for pure reasons of identity; but it is emphatically not the case that the reverse applies, and this, of course, ultimately signals that the reduction is a failure. This, basically, is the reason why it is both dangerous and confusing to continue to use terms as Saṃghabhadra does, which were part of the linguistic armoury of the now explained-away A-series, once the reduction has been completed.

A far more important objection to the argument that Buddhadeva was constructing a B-series explanation of temporal events is that, in spite of what we have said, he does not in fact think of the present in terms of the category 'simultaneous with' but rather in terms of the relations which a present event has to the preceding and posterior events. It is in fact by no means clear that 'simultaneous with' is a B-relation, but we have taken it as being so for the purposes of this paper on the basis of Richard M. Gale's argument, "We are counting 'simultaneous with' as a B-relation. Our justification for doing this is that 'simultaneous' (a) expresses a permanent temporal relation between events, as does 'earlier than', and (b) is needed for the construction of the B-series, since 'earlier than' relates classes of simultaneous events."[33] Now, what Buddhadeva has done is defined the A-determination 'present' in terms of a matrix provided by the two B-relationships 'before' and 'after'. It is that which comes before after and after before. This means, of course, that it holds two determinations at the same time, and we are reminded of the infinite regress in McTaggart's argument against the reality of A-determinations.[34] And this brings us to what is in fact the primary flaw in Buddhadeva's treatment of the present time – that he is using the terminology of B-relations while still containing in his mind the model supplied by an understanding of the A-series in terms of spatiality, that is, that the present time is somehow between past and future in the same way that the four inch mark is between the three and five inch marks on a ruler. This is clearly not the case, since 'between' is a relative term that takes as its points of reference the two independently established positions on either side, whereas 'before' and 'after' as relations are before and after *something*, which must itself be the independently established point. Thus the B-relation temporal determination of that something cannot itself be in terms of before and after, or else no temporal stages are established, as Nāgārjuna was well aware. In other words, to try to reduce present to a B-relation in terms of before and after is to put the cart before the horse. This conception of a spatial structure of time lies at the very root of the Sarvāstivādin difficulty over the real existence of past and future events, since to think of the present in terms of an analogy with the spatial position 'between' is to think that the two terms on either side must have existential reference in the same way that to be between necessitates the existence of those elements which the entity or event is said to occur between.

Thus we have to agree that Buddhadeva's explanation of time in terms of a B-series is deficient, but this can be explained by the pure novelty of the approach he was taking. The fact still remains that he did attempt to account for all three A-determinations solely in terms of B-relations; his mistake lay in thinking that it could be done with only two such relations. Nevertheless, his treatment of time constitutes as far as we can tell the only purely B-series explanation of time in Ancient India, and occupies a completely different level of philosophical subtlety from the metaphysical theories of temporality put forward by his Sarvāstivādin opponents.

It is interesting to note in passing just what the metaphysical elements in Buddhadeva's theories were. It is clear that his explanations of the distinctions between the temporal stages of events is logico-linguistic and not metaphysical in the sense that the theories of Dharmatrāta, Ghoṣaka and Vasumitra were. Nevertheless, Buddhadeva undoubtedly offered his account of temporality as a contribution to the clarification of the cardinal Sarvāstivādin doctrine of the real existence of events throughout the three times. One cannot avoid noticing that like his fellows he speaks of *dharmas* 'circulating' through time, and the *Abhidharmadīpa* says that he held that there is no change in either condition or essential nature. Of course, in one sense such statements serve only to mark Buddhadeva out as an orthodox Sarvāstivādin, eager to assert his adherence to the cardinal doctrine of the continued existence of the *svabhāva*. But in Buddhadeva's case this has more meaning than in the cases of the other Sarvāstivādin philosophers, since he did not hold a metaphysical view of temporal events, that is, that there were elements in addition to an event which gave it its temporal position. It is purely the relations between events, albeit real, objective and permanent relationships, that give events their temporal status, not something that an event does or is. And therein lay Buddhadeva's real originality.

We have explained the nature of Buddhadeva's theory, its originalities and

Abbreviations

(Prepared by the editor)

AK - Abhidharmakośa of Vasubandhu, Hsüan Tsang's translation. Nanjio No.1270 (verses only), N.1269, 1267. In such numbers as (2-7a), 2 refers to the number of the fascicle, the same in all editions; 7 refers to the number of the sheet, "a" means right side,"b" left side. The pagination of each edition, of course, differs.

DA - Dīrgha Āgama, Nanjio No.545.

FCh - Fa-chieh-an-li-t'u. Not in Nanjio or the Tripiṭaka, but consisting almost entirely of quotations from the Canonical works.The pagination (in notes) follows the edition in the School of Oriental Studies.

FT - Fo-tsu-t'ung-chi, Nanjio No.1661.

MB - Spence Hardy's Manual of Buddhism.

MVy - Mahāvyutpatti, Kyoto edition.

NA - Nanjic No.1265 quoted as N.A.

Le Temps (Kāla)

Th. Stcherbatsky

Parallélisme des idées de temps et d'espace. — *Kālavāda*, le temps dans les *Upaniṣads*. — La notion du temps dans les systèmes *Vedānta*, *Sāṅkhya* et *Vaiçeṣika*. — La polémique entre *Praçastapāda* et les Bouddhistes. — L'identification du temps avec le Dieu unique dans le système *Nyāya* ultérieur. — La négation de la substantialité du temps chez les Bouddhistes. — Critique de la notion du temps chez *Nāgārjuna*. — La preuve de la contradiction interne de l'idée de substance. — La doctrine des « moments ». — Théorie de la causalité.

Avant d'aborder l'analyse de la théorie bouddhique de la connaissance, nous voulons faire une revue historique des doctrines qui avaient cours aux Indes à différentes époques et dans divers milieux, au sujet du temps et de l'espace.

Les Bouddhistes, quelle que fût leur tendance, soit idéaliste, soit réaliste, avaient leur doctrine propre du temps et de l'espace, qu'ils opposaient à celle de la philosophie brahmanique *Çaṅkara*, *Mādhava* et d'autres placent cette doctrine en tête de leur exposition et de leur réfutation de la conception bouddhique du monde. Sans doute ni *Dignāga*, ni *Dharmakīrti*, ni *Dharmottara* n'exposent en détail cette doctrine, mais c'est parce qu'ils la supposent connue de tout le monde, comme impliquée à la base de tout le reste. Par contre, nous trouvons dans les sources brahmaniques de multiples expositions et réfutations de cette doctrine. Pour la doctrine de l'espace, nous n'avons jusqu'à présent que des renseignements fragmentaires, assez obscurs, sur l'idée que s'en faisaient les Bouddhistes de tendance réaliste. Selon les Bouddhistes de tendance idéaliste cette question n'avait pas d'importance, parce que l'idéalisme prenait son point de départ dans d'autres arguments, et non dans la doctrine de l'espace. De la preuve de l'inexistence du monde extérieur dérivait nécessairement l'irréalité de l'espace. Dans leur conception du temps et de l'espace, comme dans toutes leurs opinions philosophiques, les Bouddhistes furent dans une étroite dépendance à l'égard des spéculations antérieures répandues dans les milieux brahmaniques. Beaucoup d'entre elles survécurent au Bouddhisme et règnent aujourd'hui encore dans les écoles philosophiques modernes de l'Inde. Nous trouvons là des théories sur le temps considéré comme une substance à part, susceptible d'entrer en relation avec les objets, ou bien comme une propriété des objets ; nous rencontrons aussi la doctrine du temps absolu, cause première de toute existence, ainsi que la doctrine des temps séparés ; enfin la théorie bouddhique négative de la réalité du temps, théorie qui eut elle-même un précédent, semble-t-il, dans une thèse analogue énoncée dans les milieux non bouddhiques (1). La doctrine de l'espace un et absolu, ainsi que de son inexistence, se présentait d'une façon parallèle. Mais la compréhension de la doctrine primitive de l'espace qui s'est conservée dans plusieurs systèmes et à une époque tardive post-bouddhique est rendue difficile par la terminologie. En outre du terme *diç*, « espace », « partie du monde », nous avons le mot *ākāça*, l'espace infini, qui se comprend de manières très différentes. Tantôt il est le symbole de l'infini en général ; comme tel, il embrasse le temps et l'espace (2) ; tantôt il ne signifie que l'immutabilité, l'absence de changements (3) ; il arrive que les deux termes *diç* et *ākāça* se rencontrent côte à côte, pour désigner deux substances différentes dont la relation manque de clarté. Quelquefois *ākāça* désigne une substance particulière, l'« éther », véhicule du son. Le son passait pour une qualité, non pour une substance, il devait donc y avoir une substance spéciale qui fût le support de cette qualité. Cette substance était l'« éther » ; mais son existence se prouvait par le son ; nous serons amenés à en parler plus loin. Aussi n'y eut-il jamais, aux Indes, un parallélisme complet entre les manières de traiter de l'espace et du temps.

La doctrine du temps et de l'espace ne sert de point de départ à aucun des six systèmes principaux, quoique chacun effleure ces questions incidemment. Le système *vaiçeṣika* est celui qui

(1) Voir Schrader, *Die indische Philosophie zur Zeit Buddhas und Mahāvīras* (Strasbourg, 1902), p. 56, note 3.
(2) Voir plus bas, p. 46.
(3) Voir p. 41.

leur accorde le plus d'attention. Dans ce système le temps et l'espace figurent au nombre des neuf substances, c'est à ce titre qu'on les étudie (1).

Mais parmi de nombreux systèmes philosophiques qui ont cessé d'exister à une époque historique en raison de leur fusion graduelle avec d'autres systèmes, ou par le fait de l'oubli, il s'en trouve un cependant qui s'appelle proprement la philosophie du temps (*Kālavāda*). Certains motifs nous induisent à penser qu'il était assez répandu, car il est mentionné fréquemment dans dans les épopées comme dans la littérature la plus ancienne des *Bouddhistes* et des *Jainas*. En outre, nous savons qu'il se trouvait des manuels de ce système, où il était développé sous une forme systématique (2).

Il est difficile, à cause de la pauvreté des renseignements, de dire en quoi consistait cette doctrine. Dans les épopées, le temps est chanté comme une cause de tout ce qui existe, comme principe de la naissance et de la mort, comme facteur essentiel du cours de la vie. Dans les enseignements systématiques, ainsi que l'attestent les renseignements fournis par le compilateur jaina *Malayagiri* (3), le temps est considéré comme le commencement absolu de l'univers entier, comme la cause primordiale de l'être ; on examinait déjà la question de savoir si le temps a été l'origine immuable, universelle, éternelle, une, ou bien s'il comporte la division en temps séparés, en parties de temps. S'il est l'être éternel et immuable, on ne peut y voir la cause des phénomènes consécutifs dans le temps. Pour expliquer cette succession des phénomènes, on admettait l'existence d'un autre temps, changeant celui-là, qui accompagne le temps absolu et offre la cause complémentaire et annexe par laquelle sont conditionnés le changement des phénomènes et leur alternance dans le temps. Par ce renseignement nous pouvons constater que les contradictions logiques inhérentes à la conception du temps qui dure furent remarquées aux Indes dès une époque très ancienne. Nous rencontrerons plus tard d'autres tentatives pour expliquer la succession des phénomènes par des facteurs complémentaires, le temps

(1) Cf. V. D., I, 1, 5.
(2) Voir Schrader, *op. cit.*, p. 25.
(3) *Ibid.*, p. 27.

qui dure ou la substance douée d'une existence de durée étant reconnus pour des explications insuffisantes. Rien n'a subsisté de cette philosophie à l'époque historique, soit qu'elle eût été oubliée, soit, ce qui est plus probable, qu'elle eût fusionné avec l'astronomie. Son titre même de « *Kālavāda* » signifie aussi astronomie. *Çrīdhara* (1), lorsqu'il déclare que le temps se divise en moments, en secondes, et ainsi de suite jusqu'aux grandes périodes mondiales, fait un renvoi aux mathématiques et à l'astronomie où cette doctrine est développée en détail.

La conception du temps absolu, comme origine suprême de la création du monde, disparue de la philosophie générale, subsista dans la religion, habituelle compagne de la philosophie. L'une des formes sous laquelle *Çiva* est révéré porte le nom de *Mahākāla*, « le grand Temps » ; son épouse est la méchante déesse *Kālī*. Ces divinités apparaissent comme le symbole de la destruction et de la mort ; le mot même de *Kāla* signifie mort. Le dieu *Viṣṇu* est aussi assimilé au temps (2).

Nous trouvons comparativement peu de réflexions relatives au temps dans les *Upaniṣads*. Dans la *Maitrāyaṇa-Upaniṣad* figure le thème si ancien de la nature transitoire de tout ce qui est (3), thème qui devint plus tard la doctrine fondamentale du Bouddhisme. En effet, le temps est envisagé dans cet ouvrage, d'un côté comme divisé en parties infinies, de l'autre comme comportant des parties plus grandes : années, saisons, mois, etc. (4). Les réflexions sur la nature du temps s'unirent naturellement au calcul du temps d'après les révolutions des astres célestes ; la philosophie se muait ainsi en astronomie. Toutefois le même ouvrage identifie le temps avec la substance universelle, spirituelle, le *Brahman*. Il distingue aussi, vaguement il est vrai, le temps absolu et le temps fini, divisé en parties ; le premier comme le second sont assimilés à la substance spirituelle, essence du monde entier (5). Dans la *Bṛhadāraṇyaka-upaniṣad* une autre relation nous est décrite entre le temps et le *Brahman*. Le *Brahman* est l'essence et la cause primordiale de tout ce qui est, de lui

(1) Cf. *Çrīdhara ad Praçast.*, p. 65.
(2) Schrader, p. 29.
(3) *Sarvam kṣaiṣṇu*, cf. *Maitrāy. up.*, I, 4.
(4) *Maitrāy. up.*, VI, 14.
(5) *Ibid.*, VI, 15-16.

procède d'abord l'espace, puis de l'espace le temps (1). Ici le temps n'est pas identifié au *Brahman*, mais provient de lui, non pas même immédiatement, mais par l'*ākāça* ; il est aux pieds du *Brahman*, comme le dit poétiquement l'auteur de cette *Upaniṣad*. La production du temps par l'*ākāça* fut aussi acceptée, nous le verrons, par le système *sāṅkhya* (2). C'est dans cette théorie qu'on peut découvrir la raison pour laquelle le système *Vedānta*, sous sa forme ultérieure, ne s'occupe pas du tout du problème du temps. Ni chez *Bādarāyaṇa*, ni chez *Çaṅkarācārya* nous ne trouvons de dissertation sur le temps, alors que l'*ākāça* trouve sa place déterminée dans leur conception du monde, et que sa relation avec le *Brahman* y est décrite explicitement.

Quoique *Çaṅkara* attaque avec violence les Bouddhistes négateurs de la réalité du monde extérieur (3), lui-même n'admet cette réalité que du point de vue empirique (4). A cet égard, par suite, le temps n'existe pas du tout, puisqu'il n'y a ni succession des phénomènes psychiques,ni changement dans les objets extérieurs. Cette conception se rapproche donc de la négation bouddhique du temps.

Les idées du système *Sāṅkhya* sur le temps et l'espace dérivent directement des fondements mêmes de ce système. La matière primordiale éternelle (*pradhāna*) a deux attributs. le temps et l'espace. De même que la matière ces attributs sont coextensifs à tout et éternels (5). Tout le reste, en dehors de l'esprit et de la matière primordiale, est non éternel, disent les *Sāṅkhya sūtras* (6). Non éternels aussi, les produits de la matière, constitutifs du monde phénoménal. Au monde changeant des phénomènes ce temps et cet espace, qualités de la matière primordiale, ne suffisaient pas ; aussi a-t-on supposé l'existence d'un temps et d'un espace autres, ni éternels, ni extensifs à tout ; ils sont les produits de l'*ākāça*, c'est-à-dire de l'éther ou de l'espace cosmique. En tant que les espaces et les temps sont limités, ils procèdent de l'*ākāça*, par suite de sa fusion avec tels ou tels substrats (*upādhi*) ;

(1) Cf. *Bṛhadāraṇyaka-up.*, III, 8, 6-10.
(2) Voir plus bas, p. 56.
(3) Cf. *Çaṅkarabhāṣya, ad Brahmasūtra*, II, 2, 28.
(4) Cf. Deussen, *Das System des Vedānta*, p. 260.
(5) Garbe, *S. Phil.*, p. 276.
(6) S. S., p. 72.

ils ne sont pas autre chose que l'*ākāça* en tant que limité par un certain substrat (1). Si le substrat de l'*ākāça* est l'objet ou le monde extérieur, il en résulte l'espace limité ; si le substrat est le mouvement des corps sidéraux, il en résulte le temps. Les partisans du *Sāṅkhya* s'insurgent contre les *Vaiçeṣikas* qui affirment l'existence d'un temps infini, divisé en temps distincts sous l'influence de substrats (*upādhi*) qui constituent les mouvements des corps sidéraux. D'après eux le temps se compose de parties créées par le mouvement des astres ; hormis ce temps composé de parties il n'y a pas d'autre temps. Au contraire, d'après les *Vaiçeṣikas* (2), indépendamment des parties distinctes du temps il existe encore un temps indivisible. Si les partisans du *Sāṅkhya* avaient admis avec les *Vaiçeṣikas* l'existence d'un temps indivisible, ils auraient nécessairement dû admettre son éternité, mais ce serait incompatible avec leur théorie fondamentale des deux substances éternelles qui ne dépendent de rien, la matière éternelle et l'esprit éternel, tout le reste étant non éternel. A l'objection des *Vaiçeṣikas*, conçue en ce sens que le temps, l'espace et l'*ākāça* sont, eux aussi, éternels, les *sūtras* du *Sāṅkhya* répondent évasivement, répètent simplement l'affirmation que seule la matière est éternelle, parce qu'elle n'a pas de parties ; ils citent à l'appui l'*ultima ratio* des philosophes brahmaniques : les textes sacrés (3). Si l'on considère ainsi comme prouvé que seule la matière est éternelle, il s'ensuit que le temps ne peut l'être. Ici comme dans le *Kālavāda* nous nous heurtons à la même difficulté de trancher le problème du temps : est-ce une substance éternelle, ou quelque chose d'inhérent à la suite constante des phénomènes changeants ? En général, les questions relatives au temps et à l'espace ne sont touchées qu'en passant et d'une façon très superficielle dans le système *Sāṅkhya* ; les contradictions résultant de ces conceptions sont insolubles. La matière et l'esprit sont éternels et coextensifs à tout ; ils sont donc en rapport (*sambandha*) avec tous les temps et tous les lieux. Cependant ces mêmes temps et espace, comme produits de l'*ākāça*, ne paraissent être,

(1) S. S., I, 12 ; cf. Garbe, *op. cit.*, p. 287.
(2) Cf. *Sāṅkhyatattvakaumudī*, trad. du prof. Garbe, p. 79 ; sur la doctrine des *Vaiçeṣikas*, voir plus bas, p. 22 et autres.
(3) *Aniruddha ad S. S.*, VI, 79.

dans le monde, que des facteurs subordonnés et secondaires. Nous trouvons manifestement ici le mélange de deux conceptions non harmonisées. Que le temps et l'espace soient les produits de l'*ākāça*, c'est une opinion ancienne, issue des *Upaniṣads* (1). La conception du temps et de l'espace comme qualités de la matière primordiale (*prakṛtiguṇaviçeṣa*) est, au fond, la vraie conception *sānkhya*, qui n'a pas reçu de développement, parce qu'évidemment on n'attribuait qu'une médiocre importance à ce problème.

Le système *Vaiçeṣika* plaçait le temps parmi les substances (*dravya*). On en comptait neuf : la terre, l'eau, le feu, l'air, l'éther (*ākāça*), le temps, l'espace, l'âme et l'intellect (2). La substance se définit la cause essentielle (*samavāyikāraṇam*)des phénomènes, douée de qualités et d'activité (*kriyaguṇaval*) (3). Le temps se définit une substance non perçue immédiatement par les sens, mais dont nous concluons l'existence d'après ses propriétés. Ce sont : la succession, la simultanéité, la lenteur et la vitesse des phénomènes (4). A la question de savoir pourquoi le temps est considéré comme une substance, en particulier comme une substance éternelle, *Kanāda* répond en renvoyant aux arguments qu'il a fournis à propos d'une autre substance, l'air (5). Quoique l'air soit invisible on peut néanmoins le sentir. Ce sens du toucher est d'une nature spéciale, distincte de celui avec lequel nous sentons les substances perçues par la vue, la terre, l'eau et le feu (6). Cette sorte de toucher invisible est la qualité de l'air (7). Nous concluons donc de ses qualités invisibles à l'existence de l'air, de même que nous concluons de ses qualités invisibles à l'existence du temps. Tout ce qui a une qualité, une marque, est une substance, donc le temps qui a l'attribut mentionné, doit être compté parmi les substances. Le temps est aussi éternel que l'air, l'air étant lui-même considéré comme éternel, en ce sens qu'il continue à exister même après la destruction périodique du monde et sa reconstruction. Mais l'auteur des *sūtras* se rendait compte évidemment qu'en

(1) Cf. plus haut, p. 16.
(2) Cf. *V. D.*, I, 15.
(3) Cf. *V. D.*, I, 1, 15.
(4) *V. D.*, II, 2, 6.
(5) *Ibid.*, II, 2, 7.
(6) *Ibid.*, I, 1, 9.
(7) *Ibid.*, I, 1, 8.

reconnaissant l'existence d'une substance invisible il s'engageait dans une voie dangereuse ; aussi recourt-il, pour corroborer sa manière de voir, à l'habituelle *ultima ratio*, aux textes sacrés (1). Bien que, dans ses *sūtras*, *Kaṇāda* plaçât le temps parmi les substances matérielles, il se rend compte cependant des diverses difficultés qu'entraîne une pareille solution du problème. Les partisans ultérieurs du système parlent avec plus d'assurance à l'époque post-bouddhique. La réaction contre l'idéalisme bouddhique avait pour conséquence de souligner plus nettement les indécisions du réalisme, et d'inciter les auteurs à masquer les contradictions auxquelles il menait.

La philosophie des *Jainas* se place au même point de vue. Ils considèrent le temps comme une substance (*dravya*), quoique différente des autres substances (*astikāya*) par le fait de ne pas occuper d'espace (2). *Pracastapāda*, l'écrivain de l'école *vaiçeṣika*, qui vient ensuite, fait déjà partie de l'école post-bouddhique. En conservant, dans ses traits généraux, la définition de *Kaṇāda*, il la complète et la défend contre les Bouddhistes : « le temps, dit-il (3), est ce qui implique la représentation du loin et du près (4), du simultané et du non simultané, du lent ou du rapide, à titre de qualités. S'il est de la nature même de certains objets qu'à une première représentation succèdent d'autres représentations, différentes (de la première), c'est l'effet du temps. Il est à la fois, pour toute chose, le principe qui la fait être et ce qui constitue sa fin ; car ce sont là des notions de temps. Il est de même ce qui nous fait parler de moments, de minutes et autres divisions du temps ». *Praçastapāda* énumère ensuite les différentes qualités, propres au temps comme substance ; il en trouve cinq : le nombre, l'extension, l'isolement (*pṛthaktva*), la possibilité d'union et de

(1) *V. D.*, I, 1, 17.
(2) Voir *Sarvadarç.*, p. 29 (*Ānandaçrama Sk. Series*).
(3) *Praçast.* 63, 15.
(4) Littéralement : « le transfert (*vyatikara*) des représentations du loin et du près ». *Çrīdhara* l'explique ainsi : se représenter comme près ce qui est situé loin et comme loin ce qui est près, voilà le transfert ou le changement. Cf. *Çrīdhara* ad *Praçast*, 64, 6. Cf. cependant *Nyāyavārt.*, p. 254, et *Tātp.*, p. 280, où le temps est présenté comme ce qui fait qu'un proche, par exemple un vieillard, suscite la représentation de sa vieillesse, en connexion avec la représentation lointaine de sa jeunesse ; un objet tout proche dans le présent peut donc, grâce au temps, provoquer des représentations qui devraient être localisées très loin. Cf. aussi *Āthalye*, *Tarkasaṃgraha*, p. 130 et 167.

séparation en certains temps. La seconde partie de la définition est dirigée contre les Bouddhistes. Ces derniers, nous le verrons, niaient l'existence du temps non seulement comme substance, mais en général comme être de durée. D'après eux, dans chaque objet, le moment suivant n'a rien de commun avec le précédent. *Praçastapāda* objecte que la cause qui fait que dans l'objet le premier moment est suivi par d'autres — ou encore le principe qui rend possible l'être de durée — c'est le temps. Voici l'explication que donne *Çrīdhara* sur ce point (1). « Certains affirment que si nous distinguons un âge moindre et un plus grand, un vieillard d'un jeune homme, la cause n'en est pas (le temps), mais un nombre plus considérable ou plus petit de révolutions solaires. Maïs cela est inexact. Entre les révolutions du soleil et l'âge il n'y a aucune relation. Cependant la cause doit toujours être en relation avec le résultat. La simultanéité, au dire de quelques autres, est l'existence ensemble (indépendante du temps). C'est inexact, car, s'il n'y a pas de temps, l'existence ensemble est impossible. (On dit que) si pendant une action quelconque les objets se trouvent en corrélation, c'est là ce qui les fait être ensemble (2).

C'est faux, car ce qui n'a pas apparu, existé, puis disparu, ne peut être en corrélation réciproque, et encore la corrélation réciproque entre objets qui existent simultanément ne prouve pas l'absence du temps. De la même façon encore devra s'expliquer l'idée de la succession de l'existence, etc. Si l'on demande comment un temps indivisible suscite différentes représentations (de la simultanéité de la succession, etc.), cela s'explique chaque fois par une différence dans la totalité de toutes les conditions (du phénomène donné ; parmi elles, le temps a aussi une signification). Quand par un seul acte de connaissance nous voyons un phénomène surgir tandis qu'un autre existe déjà, c'est alors le temps, par l'intermédiaire de cet (acte de conscience), qui suscite la notion de leur succession (âge relatif) (3). Mais quand (ce

(1) *Çrīdhara* ad *Praçast.*, p. 64 et autres.

(2) *Çrīdhara* vise la théorie bouddhique qui admet la production simultanée de plusieurs moments ou choses (*nirāntarotpāda*) tout en niant l'existence d'un temps, cause substantielle de cette simultanéité.

(3) Par exemple, si nous voyons un jeune homme et un vieillard, nous prenons grâce au temps une idée de leur différence d'âge.

temps) contribue à faire percevoir, en un même acte de conscience, l'apparition de plusieurs objets (à la fois) ou de leurs actions, il provoque la notion de la simultanéité. Par contre lorsque (le temps) contribue à nous faire percevoir une plus ou moins grande quantité de moments contenus entre l'apparition et la disparition de quelque objet, il fait naître l'idée de vitesse ou de lenteur. Telles sont les explications qu'il faut en donner dans chaque cas différent ».

« Mais, objectera-t-on, si nous admettons que toutes ces représentations (de la succession et de la simultanéité) résultent de causes particulières, c'en est fait du temps (c'est-à-dire qu'il n'est pas nécessaire de supposer son existence). — Non ! s'il n'y avait pas de temps, aucun phénomène ne pourrait surgir ; car d'abord, ce qui existe éternellement, l'espace, par exemple, n'a pas de commencement ; et aussi ce qui n'existe pas du tout, n'en a pas non plus, par exemple, des cornes sur le corps humain ; cela seul a un commencement, qui n'existait pas auparavant (mais existe maintenant). Si le temps n'existait pas, le mot « avant », qui désigne le non-être antérieur (de chaque phénomène) n'aurait aucun sens ; on ne pourrait établir une différence (entre l'être et le non-être), donc rien ne pourrait apparaître dans le monde. Comment, dès lors, la représentation peut-elle se définir en fonction du temps, si ce dernier n'est pas perçu par les sens ? A cette question, quelques-uns (1) répondent ainsi : quand apparaît une représentation définie en fonction du temps, le temps est sa cause au sens où l'activité des organes sensoriels est cause de la représentation, mais non pas au sens où (un objet extérieur), par exemple un bâton, (est la cause de la représentation d'un bâton). Ce sont là des bagatelles. Notre connaissance, qui consiste dans l'élaboration de représentations claires (des objets du monde extérieur), ne peut avoir d'autres facteurs déterminants que ceux qui résultent du contact avec les objets du monde extérieur. C'est pourquoi nous répondons autrement à la question ci-dessus. Notant la différence entre l'aspect extérieur d'un vieillard et d'une personne jeune, nous inférons que la cause (de cette différence) doit résider dans leur rapport au temps ; alors survient leur représentation qui contient en elle-même la notion du temps ».

(1) Cela vise les Bouddhistes.

Contre cette conception réaliste que nous venons de mentionner, selon laquelle le temps est un facteur extérieur qui provoque en nous certaines représentations ou qui leur assigne des déterminations, l'objection qui est faite ici consiste à alléguer que le temps est transporté du monde extérieur dans le monde intérieur et devient un facteur subjectif dont dépend la localisation des représentations dans la succession temporelle. Les Bouddhistes, nous le verrons, niaient l'existence d'une substance extérieure, appelée le temps. Le temps n'existe pas (*kālo nāsti*), disaient-ils, faisant allusion à sa prétendue existence comme substance spéciale, agissant du dehors sur notre conscience. Pourtant, la critique bouddhique de la conception réaliste du temps a eu un effet contraire sur les *Vaiçeṣikas*. Dans les *sūtras* de *Kaṇāda* on distingue encore clairement que l'auteur se rendait compte de la difficulté, qu'il éprouvait comme de la gêne à placer le temps dans le même groupe où il range les autres substances. A l'époque du conflit avec le Bouddhisme, et en partie sous l'influence de la polémique soutenue contre cet adversaire, les *Vaiçeṣikas*, emportés par le désir de réagir contre l'idéalisme bouddhique, non seulement ne se bornèrent pas à leur ancien point de vue, mais devinrent encore plus hardis dans leur réalisme. Ils affirment dorénavant que le temps est une substance extérieure matérielle (*sthūlakāla, kālapiṇḍa*), invisible à nos yeux, mais dont nous pouvons inférer l'existence par les modifications qui ont lieu dans le corps et par cette corrélation qui résulte du contact de ce corps avec le temps. *Çrīdhara* dit nettement que le monde extérieur est la seule source de notre connaissance ; aussi tout ce qui se trouve dans la connaissance doit se trouver auparavant dans le monde extérieur ; le temps se trouvant dans la représentation, il faut qu'il se trouve aussi dans le monde extérieur. Peu assuré à ses débuts, chez *Kaṇāda*, le réalisme trouve chez *Praçastapāda* son expression rigoureuse.

La place assignée au temps dans les *sūtras* du système *Nyāya* n'est pas la même que dans le système voisin, le *Vaiçeṣika*. On ne compte que cinq substances, elles coïncident avec les cinq premières de *Kaṇāda*, mais possèdent une signification un peu différente, celle d'éléments de la matière (*bhūta*) (1). On men-

(1) Voir *N. D.*, I, 1, 13.

tionne en passant le temps et l'espace ; ce sont des substances éternelles, coextensives à tout et qui, comme l'éther (*ākāça*), pénètrent tout (1). Dans ce système, les substances sont aussi divisées en éternelles et non éternelles, coextensives à tout et non coextensives à tout ; or le temps et l'espace appartiennent au groupe des substances éternelles et coextensives à tout (2). *Vātsyāyana* n'a rien ajouté à ces indications fragmentaires de *Gotama*. L'écrivain de cette école qui vient ensuite, *Uddyotakara* appartient à l'époque où la logique est devenue le champ de bataille entre les *Naiyāyikas* et les Bouddhistes. Nous trouvons dans ses œuvres une polémique contre la conception bouddhique du temps et du même coup les démonstrations de sa propre théorie sur cette question, à titre d'argumentation dans la polémique contre le Bouddhisme. Il parvient exactement à la même définition du temps que donne *Praçastapāda* et fait usage d'arguments pareils aux siens. Comme il n'y a pas, chez *Gotama*, de *sūtra* spécialement consacré au problème du temps, *Uddyotakara* doit rattacher la polémique contre les Bouddhistes, en ces matières, aux *sūtras* qui traitent du raisonnement (3). Selon l'enseignement des *Naiyāyikas*, c'est à l'aide du raisonnement que l'on connaît l'existence de l'objet dans chacun des trois temps, alors que la perception ne peut être la source de la connaissance de l'objet que dans le temps présent. Citons cette curieuse polémique (4).

« Nous affirmons que l'objet du raisonnement se trouve dans chacun des trois temps, puisque nous pouvons raisonner sur l'objet présent, passé et futur. Là-dessus (les Bouddhistes) objectent que le temps, à proprement parler, n'existe pas. — Nous répondons : Non ! car cela n'est pas prouvé. On ne prouve pas directement l'inexistence du temps. »

(Le Bouddhiste.) « Le fait que nous ne percevons pas directement le temps ne prouve-t-il pas son inexistence ? »

(Le *Naiyāyika*.) « Non, puisque nous le percevons quelquefois (5). La non perception provenant de trois causes différentes (6),

(1) Voir *ibid.*, II, 1, 22.
(2) Cf. *Nyāyavārt.* ad II, 1, 22 : *dīgadinām nityatvād ujapakatvāça.*
(3) Cf. *N. D.*, II, 1, 35 et suiv.
(4) *Nyāyavārt.*, p. 254, 8 et suiv.
(5) Littéralement : à la suite du désaccord, c'est-à-dire de l'absence de la concomitance nécessaire entre le temps et sa non perception.
(6) La cause de la non perception peut être : 1° l'inexistence de l'objet ;

nous pouvons seulement, dans le cas présent, conclure, en nous appuyant sur la non-perception, à l'insuffisance des facteurs qui provoquent la perception, et non pas à l'absence de l'une et de l'autre (de la perception et de l'objet). Pourquoi dire alors qu'évidemment le temps n'existe pas ? »

(Le Bouddhiste.) « Cette non-perception résulte de l'inexistence de l'objet à percevoir ; tel est le sens de notre affirmation (que le temps n'existe pas). »

(Le *Naiyāyika.*) « Dans ce cas vous ne donnez aucune raison, car vous répétez seulement votre affirmation (il n'y a pas de temps parce qu'il n'y en a pas). La raison que vous invoquez ne fait qu'un avec votre affirmation même. (S'il existe, en outre, des déterminations du temps, il doit exister une substance substrat de ces déterminations). Les qualités ne peuvent exister sans substance, parce qu'elles n'auraient pas de substrat (et ne seraient pas des qualités). »

(Le Bouddhiste.) « Des qualités du genre de celles que vous invoquez n'existent pas. »

(Le *Naiyāyika.*) « Vos preuves ne signifient rien, puisque nous n'accordons aucune force probante à ce qui n'existe pas (c'est-à-dire : vous vous appuyez sur l'inexistence du temps prise comme preuve, mais on ne peut prouver quelque chose que par un fait, non par une inexistence)(1). On ne peut nier l'existence du temps : la succession des représentations doit avoir une cause ; celui qui nie le temps doit fournir une raison de la succession des représentations. De même que les représentations de la couleur et des autres (objets extérieurs) doivent avoir leur cause, nous ne pouvons nous imaginer que les représentations reçoivent leur détermination dans le temps sans aucune cause, puisqu'il faut que ces déterminations soient le résultat d'une cause quelconque. »

(Le Bouddhiste.) « Le temps est un (indivisible) : donc la diversité des représentations du temps est impossible. »

(Le *Naiyāyika.*) « Vous pensez que si le temps est un la succes-

2° son inaccessibilité aux sens quand il est hors de leur sphère d'activité ; 3° l'insuffisance des autres facteurs de la perception, et ainsi de suite. Cf. *N. b. ṭ.*, p. 23, 5 et suiv. ; trad. p. 48 ; et *Tātp.*, p. 280. *Kaṇāda, Praçastapāda* et *Çrīdhara* signalaient déjà l'invisibilité du temps.

(1) Cf. *Tātp.*, 280, 7 et suiv. : « L'inexistence admise par l'adversaire est une inexistence privée de toute efficacité, incapable de servir de preuve ».

sion des représentations dans le temps est impossible ; que la cause unique ne peut engendrer des résultats différents? Mais elle le peut. Cela dépend des circonstances. Un père, par exemple, peut être (non seulement père, mais aussi) pourvu d'un autre attribut (selon les circonstances). Chez le même individu, bien qu'il reste un seul et même homme, on peut avoir, sous différents rapports, un père, un fils, un frère. Le temps lui aussi, malgré son unité, parce qu'il est cause ou action, provoque les représentations d'antériorité, de succession, etc. Ainsi l'existence du temps est prouvée. »

Les *Naiyāyikas* examinent aussi la question de savoir si le mouvement des astres n'est pas, par lui-même, un facteur suffisant à expliquer le temps. Nous connaissons déjà sur ce point la solution des *Sāṅkhyas* et des *Vaiçeṣikas* (1). La réponse des *Naiyāyikas* est la même que celle des *Vaicesikas* ; elle consiste à dire qu'entre le mouvement des astres et la succession des phénomènes il n'y a pas de relation directe, tandis que la succession des phénomènes provient du rapport immédiat au temps matériel (*kālapiṇḍa saṃyoga*) (2). Ainsi les *Naiyāyikas* considéraient le temps exactement comme les *Vaiçeṣikas* : dans les traités postérieurs, où les deux systèmes sont fondus en un seul, la définition de *Kaṇāda* et de *Praçastapāda* (3) est répétée avec peu de changement. Quelques modifications y furent alors apportées, en ce sens que les substances matérielles furent divisées en substances occupant un espace défini (*mūrta*) et en substances illimitées n'occupant pas un espace défini (*vibhu*) (4). C'est parmi ces derniers que le temps est classé. L'identification du temps avec l'espace, que nous trouvons dans les *Upaniṣads* et dans le système *Sāṅkhya*, dérive justement de cette représentation du temps, conçu comme une substance matérielle, bien qu'invisible, n'occupant pas d'espace défini, mais coextensive à tout, omniprésente. Cette représentation incitait à conclure que l'espace et le temps ne font qu'un. Un écrivain aussi tardif que *Vācaspatimiçra* (5)

(1) Voir plus haut, p. 17.
(2) Cf. *Tātp.*, p. 281, 19.
(3) Cf., par exemple, la définition donnée dans le *Bhāṣaparicchéda*, p. 44, 5. Cf. *Āthalye*, p. 130.
(4) Cf. *Āthalye*, p. 128.
(5) *Tātp.*, p. 281.

se croit obligé de réfuter cette opinion. Mais les *Naiyāyikas* plus modernes y sont revenus indirectement, identifiant le temps, comme l'espace, avec Dieu (*Içvara*).

La conception du temps comme substance extérieure à notre connaissance et infinie conduisit naturellement à l'identifier avec Dieu, qui était considéré comme substance infinie. Nous trouvons cette représentation dès l'aurore de la philosophie indienne, dans l'ancien *kālavāda* ; dans le *çivaïsme* où *Îçvara* est révéré comme *Mahākāla*, et chez les *Naiyāyikas* modernes qui sont, pour la plupart, des *çivaïtes*. Nous la rencontrons de même dans la philosophie occidentale, depuis l'antiquité jusqu'à la dissertation de Kant inclusivement, où le temps comme substance est identifié à *aeternitas Dei phaenomenon*, et l'espace défini comme *omnipraesentia Dei phaenomenon*.

La différence essentielle entre l'ensemble des systèmes brahmaniques et la philosophie bouddhique se fait sentir très nettement à propos du temps. Pour tous les systèmes brahmaniques le temps est une substance ; pour les Bouddhistes il ne peut en être une, ne fût-ce que parce qu'ils n'admettent l'existence d'aucune substance. Par la critique de l'idée elle-même de substance active, ils arrivent à cette conclusion, qu'il n'y a pas de substances douées d'une existence de durée, qu'il n'y a ni des substances psychiques en nous, ni des substances matérielles dans le monde extérieur. Le Bouddhisme s'appropria cette idée dès les premiers jours de son existence et lui resta fidèle durant toute son histoire, malgré la diversité des écoles et des tendances qui y trouvèrent place. Il se peut fort bien que la doctrine de la nature transitoire de tout ce qui est soit plus ancienne que le Bouddhisme. Dans les *Upaniṣads* (1) ainsi que dans les épopées (2) se trouvent, par endroits, des remarques qui l'indiquent. Il y a une vague mention de l'existence de cette théorie avant le *Bouddha* (3). Dans le sys-

(1) Cf. *Maitr. Up.*, I, 4.

(2) Cf. Schrader, *op. cit.*, p. 25.

(3) *Ibid.*, p. 27, n. 3. Schrader discerne, dans certains traits de l'ancien *kālavāda*, les germes de cette critique de l'idée d'une substance active (*Denkunmöglichkeit einer actuellen Substanz*) qui prit plus tard une grande importance dans la philosophie bouddhique. Nous trouvons en outre, chez Schrader, la mention de l'existence d'un système spécial, *samucchedavāda*, qui, bien que distinct du Bouddhisme, part de cette idée, qu'une substance qui dure constitue une *contradictio in adjecto*, et qui conclut qu'il faut rem-

tème *Vaiçeṣika* se trouve une doctrine sinon identique, du moins analogue (1). En tout cas, eût-elle existé avant le Bouddhisme, ce dernier l'accepta et se l'assimila. Le Bouddha ne voyait dans le monde extérieur qu'une chaîne ininterrompue d'êtres, une apparition et une disparition illimitée de phénomènes, dont aucun ne se fixe, fût-ce un instant. Le processus de l'existence est comparé à celui de la combustion (2). Pareille à la flamme d'une lampe qui, bien qu'imperceptiblement, change et disparaît sans jamais être la même qu'au moment précédent, l'existence dans le monde extérieur comme dans le monde intérieur est un processus ininterrompu, une succession de phénomènes, sans aucune permanence sous-jacente, sans aucune substance. Pas de substance spirituelle au delà du flux continu des produits de la conscience ; pas de substance matérielle par delà le cours des phénomènes du monde extérieur. De cette conception dérive la notion correspondante du temps considéré comme un processus de destruction constante, renouvelée à chaque moment, irrémissible.

Mais le Bouddha ne s'exprime pas clairement sur la question de savoir si le flux des phénomènes évanescents n'est qu'un processus intérieur à la connaissance, ou bien si le monde extérieur, lui aussi, n'est que l'apparition et la disparition ininterrompue et sans cause des phénomènes. C'est pourquoi ce problème fut l'occasion d'un schisme dans la communauté des moines bouddhiques de la première époque. Au sein des Bouddhistes surgit la secte des *Sarvāstivādins*, c'est-à-dire des réalistes hardis d'après lesquels tout, dans le monde extérieur, était doué d'existence. Le fait même de la formation de cette secte et le nom qu'elle se choisit ou qu'elle reçut de ses adversaires, prouve que dès cette

placer la notion de la réalité d'une substance par la notion d'une activité (*arthakriyākaritva*). Cette activité se compose de moments d'existence séparés, non reliés par une commune inhérence à quelque substance durable. C'est pourquoi l'idée du lien causal doit être remplacée par l'idée d'une disparition sans cause, instantanée, continuelle. Ce *samucchedavāda*, vraisemblablement, n'est pas autre chose que le Bouddhisme, puisque ses thèses ont une ressemblance si prononcée avec les thèses générales du système bouddhique.

(1) Voir plus bas, p. 29 et suiv.

(2) Cf. *Dhammapadam*, XI, 1 ; *Milindapañha*, II, 2, 1 et autres ; la comparaison du processus universel avec la combustion et du temps avec le feu fut probablement en usage dès l'ancien *kālavāda*. Cf. Schrader, *op. cit.*, p. 25.

époque existait une conception opposée, l'interprétation idéaliste des discours du Bouddha. Malheureusement nous ne possédons là-dessus aucun document ; c'est à une date très tardive que l'idéalisme bouddhique a reçu sa rédaction littéraire.

Les réalistes distinguent deux espèces de destruction : celle dont on a, celle dont on n'a pas conscience. Par la première, on entend, par exemple, la destruction d'une cruche sous l'action d'un coup de marteau. Par la seconde, l'usure graduelle d'une cruche. Cette usure s'opère à chaque moment, sans jamais s'arrêter. Par la destruction insensible de la cruche, dit un philosophe (1), « on entend son anéantissement de chaque instant inaccessible à nos sens, incompréhensible au vulgaire et susceptible d'être prouvé par des arguments ». Ainsi, ce que nous appelons l'existence d'une chose est, au fond, une série de moments isolés dans chacun desquels nous obtenons un tout autre objet, distinct de celui du moment précédent et de celui du suivant. *Vācaspatimiçra* dit : « le moment est l'existence pendant une parcelle de temps sans parties (2) ». C'est donc l'atome du temps. De même que l'on admettait l'existence des atomes non extensifs à la base de la matière extensive, on admettait aussi que le temps qui dure fut composé de moments sans durée. Or le « moment » n'est pas seulement une parcelle du temps, mais encore l'existence elle-même, ou bien l'objet, qui alors et alors seulement existe, puisqu'une chose, fût-ce à notre insu, change constamment, de sorte qu'à chaque moment nous avons affaire à une chose différente. « Chez les Bouddhistes, dit *Brahmavidyābharaṇa* (3), le terme « moment » indique une chose, par exemple une cruche ; et en dehors d'elle n'existe aucun temps désigné par le terme : moment. » Aussi le monde apparaît-il au philosophe bouddhique de tendance réaliste comme analogue à un tableau cinématographique. En conséquence les Bouddhistes ne se contentèrent pas de nier le temps comme substance douée de durée, mais les « moments » eux-mêmes, dont ils admettaient l'existence, étaient en réalité non des parcelles du temps, mais des objets instantanés. Un

(1) *Brahmavidyābhāraṇa* ad *Vedāntasūtra*, II, 2, 22.
(2) Littéralement : une première et une autre partie : *kṣaṇikatvam pūrvāparabhāgavikālakalāvasthāyitvam* : voir *Tātp.*, p. 380.
(3) *Ibid.*, p. 407.

trait qui rappelle cette conception s'aperçoit aussi dans le système *Vaiçeṣika*. En examinant la question de la transformation des choses sous l'influence du feu, quand, par exemple, un pot de terre glaise, noir avant la cuisson, devient rouge sous l'action du feu, le *Vaiçeṣika* se posait ce problème : le pot qui a changé de couleur sous l'influence du feu, est-il le même qui était noir auparavant, ou bien est-ce un autre, tout nouveau ? La réponse était que c'est un pot nouveau qui, sauf les atomes, n'a rien de commun avec l'ancien. Les atomes se dissipent et se rassemblent à nouveau. Dans la cuisson, l'ancien pot se disperse, le feu crée la couleur rouge dans les atomes, puis, sous l'influence du feu, les atomes se rassemblent dans le nouveau pot rouge. Comme, selon les *Vaiçeṣikas*, le feu ne peut être à l'intérieur des parois du pot, la cuisson ne peut s'expliquer autrement. Le processus s'accomplit si vite, qu'il échappe à l'observation. De même, pendant que le fruit mûrit, que le corps animal grandit, le changement de volume consiste en un changement de matière : l'ancienne se détruit, la nouvelle renaît continuellement (1). La conception bouddhique est très analogue puisque, à chaque moment de l'existence d'une chose donnée, nous avons une chose particulière, toute neuve ; l'autre a disparu sans laisser de trace. *Çaṅkara* (2) appelle les *Vaiçeṣikas* des semi-nihilistes, *ardhavaināçika*, les prédicateurs de la destruction partielle, puisque les atomes, d'après eux, ne se détruisent pas, mais se rassemblent instantanément à nouveau. Il appelle les Bouddhistes des nihilistes radicaux prédicateurs d'une entière destruction (*pūrṇavaināçika*), parce que l'existence momentanée ne laisse rien subsister après sa destruction, même pas les atomes. Puisque dans chaque existence de durée le « moment » est la cause du suivant, il est clair que nier le lien intérieur entre les « moments » isolés équivaut au fond à la négation du lien intérieur entre la cause et son action. *Çaṅkara* (3) déclare à ce propos : « Ceux qui disent qu'un objet n'existe que pendant un moment, affirment que lorsqu'il entrera dans le second, l'objet qui existait dans le premier cessera d'exister. Dans ce cas, entre les deux objets il ne peut pas y avoir de lien causal puisque l'exis-

(1) Voir *Āthalye*, p. 137, et *Thibaut*, *Vedāntasūtra*, I, 401, note 1.
(2) *Ad Vedāntasūtra*, II, 2, 13.
(3) *Ad Vedāntasūtra*, II, 2, 20.

tence du moment antérieur de l'objet devient néant et ne peut être la cause du moment suivant. En supposant que le simple fait de l'existence du moment précédent est la cause du suivant, on fait une supposition fausse, puisque nous ne pouvons nous imaginer la production d'un résultat qui ne serait pas du même genre que sa cause. Mais (du point de vue bouddhique) on ne peut admettre que la cause, en son essence, continue à vivre dans le résultat ; cela équivaudrait à admettre une existence de durée de la cause, et conduirait à renoncer à la théorie de l'instantanéité de l'être. »

L'exposé systématique de cette théorie de l'instantanéité de l'existence ne nous est point parvenu dans la littérature bouddhique en sanscrit. Partout on la traite comme connue de tout le monde. Par contre, les auteurs brahmaniques l'exposent en détail et la réfutent, comme étant la thèse fondamentale de la philosophie bouddhique. Avant de procéder à l'exposé systématique de cette théorie, il y a lieu de s'arrêter à une école qui tient une place à part dans l'histoire de la philosophie bouddhique. L'école de *Nāgārjuna*, surnommée école nihiliste, comprend la doctrine de l'irréalité du monde dans ce sens, qu'aucune assertion touchant la réalité de quoi que ce soit n'est possible, toute notion renfermant une contradiction logique. Cette attitude de critique implacable rappelle de très près l'attitude des sophistes grecs. *Nāgārjuna* allait dans sa négation jusqu'à nier les notions les plus chères aux Bouddhistes, telle la notion de l'Illuminé (un bouddha), du salut suprême (nirvâṇa), etc. Fidèle à sa méthode, *Nāgārjuna* se garde bien d'établir la théorie de la momentanéité de l'être. Il se contente de critiquer et de réfuter comme contradictoire la notion vulgaire du temps, séparé en temps présent, passé et futur.

« On dit, déclare *Nāgārjuna* (1), que dans chaque être il y a une réelle existence de durée (substantialité), car ce serait là ce qui nous permettrait de parler (pour toute existence) des trois temps (le présent, le passé, l'avenir). Le seigneur Bouddha en-

(1) Nous citons les *Kārikās* de *Kālaparikṣā* avec l'énumération concordante et quelques fragments du Commentaire de *Candrakīrti*, indispensables à l'intelligence du texte. Cf. *Mūlamadhyamikakārikās*, éd. *de la Vallée Poussin*, p. 382 et suiv.

seigne que dans notre monde, il y a trois temps, le passé, l'avenir et le présent, qui ont pour substrat l'être. Ainsi l'être apparu et disparu est cet être de durée qu'on appelle passé. L'être apparu et non disparu est cet être de durée qu'on appelle présent. L'être encore non réalisé s'appelle futur. C'est ainsi qu'il enseigna les trois temps qui ont pour cause l'existence réelle (substantielle) de l'être, et ces (trois temps) existent. Voilà pourquoi l'être de durée des objets, qui en dépend, existe aussi. — A cela nous répondons : l'être de durée qui nous permet de parler des trois temps pourrait exister, si les trois temps, comme vous le supposez, existaient, mais ils n'existent pas. » Qu'ils n'existent pas, c'est ce que déclare *Nāgārjuna* dans les sentences suivantes :

1° « Si le présent et l'avenir dépendaient du passé, ils devraient déjà exister dans le passé. Si quelque chose n'existe pas du tout en autre chose, ce sont deux termes indépendants l'un de l'autre ; par exemple, une femme stérile et son fils.

2° Mais si le présent et l'avenir n'existaient pas déjà dans le passé, comment peuvent-ils alors n'exister que relativement à lui ?

3° Puisqu'on ne peut prouver l'existence du présent et de l'avenir en dehors de leur rapport avec le passé, il s'ensuit qu'il n'y a ni présent, ni avenir.

4° Pareillement le passé et l'avenir n'existent pas en eux-mêmes, puisqu'ils n'existent que relativement au présent. De même le passé et le présent n'existent pas, puisqu'ils n'existent que relativement à l'avenir. C'est tout comme lorsqu'on est obligé de déterminer les objets que l'on considère en fonction du haut, du milieu, du bas, ou encore comme unité et multiplicité (1). »

« Mais on pourrait objecter : (2) le temps existe sûrement, puisqu'il se mesure. Si une chose n'existe pas en tel endroit, elle n'a pas de mesure : par exemple, les cornes sur la tete d'un lièvre. Le temps se mesure, parce qu'il se divise en moments, minutes, heures, jours, nuits, vingt-quatre heures, demi-mois, mois, années, et ainsi de suite. Ayant des mesures, le temps existe certainement.

(1) « Si ce qui est plus haut n'existe qu'autant qu'il se distingue du milieu et du bas, il n'existe pas en lui-même. » Nous paraphrasons, nous détaillons davantage la 4e *kārikā*.

(2) *Candrakīrti, ibid.*, p. 235, 11.

A cela nous ripostons : si un temps existait, il pourrait comporter une mesure, mais il n'existe pas ; en effet :

5º Un temps immuable qui fût aperceptible n'existe pas ; et un temps variable ne saurait être aperçu. Comment peut-on alors parler d'un temps qui ne se perçoit pas ?

Si (1) ce qu'on appelle temps existait en ce monde, distinct et des moments et des autres mesures, il pourrait être perçu, car il se mesurerait par les moments, etc. Mais il n'existe aucun (objet) indépendant, immuable et perçu par les moments ou mesures analogues.

Peut-être dira-t-on qu'il y a un temps éternel, constitué d'immutabilité, ~~doué~~ seulement en ~~apparence de~~ moments et d'autres mesures de ce genre. Ne dit-on pas très justement : le temps amène à maturité tout ce qui existe, le temps anéantit les hommes, le temps veille quand tout le monde dort, personne n'échappe à l'empire du temps ? Ce temps a bien une existence réelle. — Mais, répliquons-nous, on ne perçoit pas davantage un tel temps immuable qui nous apparaît en moments ou en parties de ce genre et si l'on nous demande pourquoi il n'existe pas de temps immuable, nous répondrons : parce qu'en dehors des moments séparés nous n'en apercevons pas...»

« On dit encore (2) : Si nous admettons qu'il n'y a pas de temps éternel, existant par lui-même, indépendamment des objets visibles ou autres, nous pouvons cependant affirmer que par les expressions « moments », etc., nous désignons le temps, dont les objets, visibles ou autres, avec leurs qualités, apparaissent comme les substrats. »

A cela *Nāgārjuna* répond : 1º « Si le temps n'existe que relativement aux objets, d'où viendrait le temps ~~indépendant~~ des objets ? Or nous nions l'être des objets, *a fortiori* l'existence du temps. »

Les réflexions de *Nāgārjuna* sur le temps ne représentent aucune théorie. Ce n'est que l'application, au sujet du temps, d'une méthode dialectique négative, qui reste toujours la même, peu importe l'objet auquel elle est appliquée. Les Bouddhistes, quelle que fût leur tendance, croyaient au bien-fondé de l'idée

(1) *Candrakīrti*, *ibid.*, p. 386, 1.
(2) *Ibid.*, p. 387, 3.

de moment (*kṣaṇa*), conçu comme substrat réel des phénomènes de durée dans le monde soit extérieur, soit intérieur. Cette idée qui a un aspect tant soit peu positif, n'arrêta pas la critique radicale de *Nāgārjuna*, ni plus ni moins que n'importe quelle autre idée positive.

La démonstration systématique de la théorie des moments se trouve exposée dans plusieurs sources brahmaniques (1). Voici, en traduction libre, l'argument comme nous le trouvons chez *Mādhava*.

« La momentanéité des objets instantanés, de la couleur bleue, par exemple, ou d'autres, peut se déduire de l'idée de leur existence. Tout ce qui existe est fugitif, comme un nuage (2) ; les objets existent (donc ils sont fugitifs). Ce raisonnement ne peut être déclaré faux, car la perception nous révèle que l'existence, dont le trait distinctif est d'être productive de quelque chose, n'appartient qu'aux moments. En outre, cela résulte du fait que les objets non instantanés ne peuvent rien produire. L'idée d'activité dépend de celle ou bien de succession, ou bien de simultanéité. Si nous prouvons qu'il ne peut exister ni simultanéité, ni succession dans l'activité de l'être de durée, alors, d'après la règle selon laquelle tout ce qui est en contradiction avec l'idée générique est en contradiction aussi avec l'idée spécifique, nous prouvons du même coup que l'être de durée, lui non plus, ne peut exister. Tout acte doit, ou bien succéder, ou bien être simultané à la cause ; il ne peut être autrement. Ayant prouvé que ni la succession, ni la simultanéité de l'activité ne peuvent appartenir à l'être de durée, nous prouvons qu'il ne peut être actif et par conséquent qu'il ne peut exister. Commençons par (la succession). Si l'on demande pourquoi un être non momentané ne peut être actif, nous dirons que c'est inadmissible, en vertu du dilemme suivant : quand l'être de durée est actif dans le présent, garde-t-il, ou non, la faculté d'être actif dans le passé et dans l'avenir ? Dans le premier cas

(1) *Sarvadarç.*, p. 7-10 (*Anandacram.*) traduit par Cowell dans sa traduction complète de cette œuvre. *De la Vallée Poussin*, *Muséon*. 1901-2 et Deussen. *Allgemeine Geschichte der Philosophie*. I. 3. p. 207 et suiv. La traduction que nous donnons diffère quelque peu des précitées. La théorie est exposée avec encore plus de détails dans *Tātp.*, p. 380 et suiv. ; *Nyāyakaṇikā*, p. 126 et suiv.

(2) Le sens de cet exemple sera expliqué plus bas, voir p. 35.

(si l'on admet que l'être de durée garde toujours la faculté d'être actif), cela signifie qu'il ne peut en être privé, car si un objet est capable de quelque chose, il ne peut être séparé (de cette capacité). Ce qui, à un moment donné, est capable de quelque chose, l'exécute ; par exemple, l'ensemble des conditions (*sāmagrī*) de certains phénomènes produit toujours des résultats correspondants. L'être de durée donné possède cette faculté (d'accomplir des actes passés et futurs, donc il doit les accomplir). Dans ce second cas (si l'être de durée est privé de la faculté d'accomplir des actes passés et futurs), il ne les accomplira jamais, puisque chaque acte est indissolublement lié à la capacité qui le produit. Même conséquence pour le raisonnement contraire : ce qui, à un moment donné, n'accomplit pas une certaine chose, n'a pas la faculté de cet accomplissement ; par exemple, une pierre ne peut créer une plante. (Un être de durée) donné, pendant l'accomplissement de son acte, n'accomplit pas ses actes passés et futurs. (Donc il n'a pas la capacité de les accomplir, donc il ne les accomplira jamais.)

L'être de durée, pourrait-on dire, accomplit successivement ses actes passés et futurs, grâce à la coopération successive des causes concomitantes. Mais alors répondez, s'il vous plaît, à cette question : les causes concomitantes coopèrent-elles véritablement à constituer l'être de durée ? Si elles n'y contribuent pas, elles n'ont pas de signification, les (causes) qui ne produisent rien ne pouvant avoir aucune signification. Mais si elles y contribuent effectivement, il faut demander : ces facteurs coopérants se distinguent-ils de l'être même (auquel ils prêtent assistance), ou non ? S'ils s'en distinguent, ces causes supplémentaires seront les vraies causes, et non pas l'être de durée lui-même, puisque le résultat sera indissolublement lié à l'efficace des causes supplémentaires... Objecte-t-on à cela que chaque être n'accomplit son acte qu'en union avec les causes concomitantes, et que c'est en cela même que consiste son essence ? Nous répondrons : s'il en est ainsi, qu'il ne se sépare donc pas de ses associés ; si ceux-ci ont quelque velléité de se dérober, qu'il attache une corde à leur cou et les force à accomplir l'action qu'ils sont tenus d'accomplir. Personne ne peut échapper à son essence.

On fait, en outre, l'objection suivante : grâce aux causes

concomitantes (dans la substance de durée) il se produit quelque modification (intermédiaire entre la cause et l'acte). Cette modification, demanderons-nous, engendre-t-elle à son tour une modification, ou non ? Dans l'un et dans l'autre cas, l'adversaire est comme criblé d'une pluie de pierres par les objections mentionnées plus haut. En effet, si l'on admet que (chaque modification) engendre une autre modification, surgit une difficulté qui consiste en tout un ensemble de *regressus in infinitum*... Si l'on admet que la modification produite par les facteurs concomitants (1) ne diffère pas de l'être de durée, il s'ensuit que l'être passé, qui n'avait pas de modification a disparu, et qu'un nouvel être avec telle modification apparaît. Nous ne voulons pas dire autre chose, quand nous parlons des substances actives — c'est cela précisément que nous désirions prouver : l'arbre de nos désirs a porté son fruit. » (C'est-à-dire : puisque l'idée d'une substance de durée et active est contradictoire en soi, chaque moment d'être n'a aucun rapport avec le précédent, à chaque moment il y a un être distinct ; aussi n'existe-t-il ni un être de durée, ni un temps de durée.)

« L'activité d'un être de durée, par conséquent, est impossible à prouver (du point de vue de la succession). Il est aussi impossible à prouver si l'on suppose sa simultanéité, car alors se présente ce dilemme : l'être capable de créer d'un coup tous ses actes continue-t-il à exister au temps suivant ou non ? Si oui, la création de l'acte qui a lieu maintenant doit durer aussi au temps prochain. Sinon, espérer l'acte de l'être de durée, c'est comme vouloir faire pousser une plante au moyen de graines mangées par les souris.

« Tout ce qui est susceptible de changer de condition est différent en soi-même, comme le chaud et le froid (c'est-à-dire ce n'est pas le même objet qui change de température, mais l'objet froid est un autre objet, différent de celui qui était chaud). Ainsi se démontre le lien indivisible (entre l'objet et l'impermanence), par exemple, dans un nuage, etc. (Ne croyons pas que le susdit)

(1) L'auteur distingue les causes concomitantes (*sahakārin*) des facteurs coopérants (*apakārin*). Cf. *N. b. ṭ.*, p. 10, 12 où l'on cite la même différence. *Dharmottara* remarque qu'au point de vue bouddhique le *sahakārin* seul existe, et non pas le *upakārin*.

principe soit faux ; si l'on admet que l'être de durée peut tantôt être capable, tantôt non, de créer son acte, cela entraîne des conséquences fâcheuses.

Les conclusions qui prouvent l'incapacité (de l'être de durée à créer un acte) ont déjà été citées. Les raisonnements qui au contraire prouvent sa capacité sont les suivants : ce qui, à un moment donné, n'est pas capable de créer son acte, ne le crée pas ; par exemple, un caillou ne produit pas une plante (puisqu'il en est incapable. Pareil est l'objet qui, à un moment donné, crée son acte dans le présent, il est incapable de créer des actes passés et futurs. Tout ce qui, à un moment déterminé, crée un acte déterminé, en est capable, par exemple, l'ensemble des causes d'un phénomène (*sāmagrī*) est capable de créer son acte, l'être donné produit dans le passé et dans l'avenir ses actes passés et futurs ; (il en est donc capable) — telle est la conclusion contraire. (Ainsi l'être de durée est à la fois capable et incapable de créer ses actes passés et futurs ; il n'y a donc pas d'être de durée ; à chaque moment il y a un être particulier.)

« Il est établi, de la sorte, que l'être n'appartient qu'aux moments séparés, puisqu'il ne peut appartenir à la substance de durée ni au cas où elle créerait successivement ses actes, ni au cas où elle les créerait d'un seul coup. Le lien indissoluble de l'être et de l'instantanéité (non durabilité) se démontre négativement (tout ce qui n'est pas un moment ne saurait en aucune façon exister), en raison de l'inexistence de l'être de durée ; —et positivement (tout ce qui existe est un moment) en vertu des deux conclusions contraires qui résultent de la supposition d'un être de durée. »

En tant que ce raisonnement tend à démontrer les absurdités logiques, issues de la conception des objets comme êtres de durée et substances actives, il n'est pas difficile de reconnaître des idées rencontrées déjà dans l'histoire de la philosophie occidentale, quoique revêtues ici d'un costume proprement indien.

La critique de la notion d'une existence de durée part du fait que ce n'est que le dernier moment de l'existence d'un objet qui produit le résultat, ou plus exactement, c'est le dernier moment de la cause qui est lié au premier moment de l'effet ; il n'y a pas de lien entre les autres moments de la cause et de l'effet. Si l'être de durée était en état de produire quelque chose, il le produirait pendant toute la durée de son existence, c'est alors qu'il serait réellement un être de durée. Mais alors il devrait produire toujours et sans interruption. Ainsi donc chaque existence se résout en une série d'existences momentanées, une série qui jamais ne sera interrompue, les moments de l'objet-cause se continuant dans les moments de l'objet, qu'arbitrairement nous croyons être le produit de cette cause. Le dernier moment dans l'existence supposée de la cause est nommé « faiseur de forme » (*kurvadrūpa*), c'est le moment après lequel la série quoique ininterrompue nous apparaît sous une autre forme. Le dernier moment de la série, que nous appelons « semence », pour prendre un exemple, est le faiseur de forme par rapport à la série que nous allons appeler « plante ». En réalité les deux séries ne sont pas séparées, l'une glisse dans l'autre ; puisque c'est seulement le moment précédent qui est la cause du moment suivant, il ne peut y avoir de lien causal entre séries. C'est encore un caractère de ce que nous nommons cause ou effet, que c'est toujours un composé, jamais une existence simple. L'existence simple ne change jamais, c'est une existence éternelle, immuable. Ce qui n'est jamais cause est de deux catégories : l'éternel ou bien le néant (1). Jamais un être simple ne produit quelque chose, « l'unique ne provient pas de l'unique, tout provient d'un ensemble de causes », disent les Bouddhistes (2). Donc, l'effet est toujours un ensemble d'existences momentanées appartenant à des séries différentes. La série semence, par exemple, quoique un composé elle-même, ne produit la plante que concurremment avec d'autres séries d'existences : terre, eau, chaleur, air, etc. Chaque moment de l'existence « terre » est relié au moment précédent et au suivant, de même la série « eau », etc. Soudainement, par pure chance, ces séries se rencontrent, les moments de toutes ces séries surgissent en contiguïté les uns des autres, alors apparaît la plante que nous croyons être un effet de la semence, tandis que, en vérité, ce n'est qu'un complexus (*samagrī*) de moments disparates dont chacun appartient à sa série propre. Si nos sens étaient assez aigus pour pénétrer

(1) *Tātp.*, p. 91, 18.
(2) *Akāraṇam dvidhā nityam asacca.*

la composition de la plante, nous serions en état d'y apercevoir les différents éléments dont elle est composée : les éléments « terre » « eau », etc., et ceux qui proviennent de la semence. Le fait que nous apercevons une plante n'est que le résultat de notre ignorance, de l'insuffisance de nos sens. Après quelques moments d'existence ce complexus se disperse, les séries « eau », « terre », etc. s'en vont continuer leur existence à part. Ainsi tout être n'est qu'un composé factice, produit de notre ignorance. La réalité consiste dans les existences momentanées, qui forment un courant ininterrompu. La réalité ainsi comprise échappe à la distinction que nous faisons entre substance et qualité, comme nous le verrons plus tard. Elle échappe aussi à la difficulté qui se pose quand il s'agit de comprendre le lien entre le mouvement et les choses qui se meuvent. Le mouvement n'est qu'une production de moments qui surgissent en juxtaposition les uns des autres (*nirāntaraksanotpada*) (1). Il n'y a pas de substance, chose durable, qui se meut, il n'y a qu'une ligne de « moments », c'est-à-dire le mouvement lui-même.

Il est facile de voir que cette théorie du temps, qui est illustrée par l'exemple de la graine et de la plante, s'applique au monde phénoménal dans son ensemble. C'est en même temps une théorie de la causalité. Seul l'immuable, l'éternel ou bien le néant peut échapper à la loi de cette causalité. La vie consiste en un flux ininterrompu d'existences momentanées. L'origine de ce processus n'existe pas, il est sans commencement (*arcādi*), mais il aura une fin (*sānta*) dans l'absolu (*nirvāna*). Aussi cet absolu se définit comme production d'un « moment » dissemblable (*visabhāga-kṣaṇotpāda*) (2), un moment qui n'est pas relié aux moments-causes, un moment qui est libéré du lien causal, qui n'appartient plus au monde phénoménal.

Le germe de cette doctrine, nous l'avons déjà constaté, se trouve dans les discours du Bouddha, auquel on attribuait cette observation, que la flamme de la lampe apparaît à chaque moment comme une flamme nouvelle, puisque la combustion du moment précédent est achevée et a cessé quand celle du suivant

(1) Cf. *Nyayavārt.*
(2) Cf. *Ibid.*

se produit (1). Sur ce point, les adversaires des Bouddhistes, toutes les sectes Brahmaniques sans exception, attaquent et réfutent cette théorie. Mais parmi les Bouddhistes eux-mêmes, tous étaient loin d'être d'accord sur son aspect positif, c'est-à-dire sur la thèse selon laquelle l'objet n'existe réellement que pendant un seul moment, sans que le moment possède une connexion réelle avec les moments suivants. Voici comment s'exprime *Candrakīrti* (2) : « quel homme de bon sens croira qu'un objet peut, dans la durée d'un moment, apparaître, exister et disparaître ? » Au point de vue des « nihilistes » le moment existe aussi peu que la substance de durée.

Les idéalistes, conformément à leurs données premières, transportèrent les moments du monde extérieur dans le monde intérieur, et en firent des moments de la conscience.

Une position intermédiaire entre cet idéalisme rigoureux et le réalisme fut adoptée par l'école *sautrāntika yogācāra* à laquelle les deux grands philosophes indiens *Dignāga* et *Dharmakīrti* appartenaient. Tout notre exposé ultérieur servira à éclaircir ce point de vue.

(1) Voir plus haut, p. 27.
(2) *Mādh. vṛtti*, ch. VII, p. 131 (éd. *Bibl. Buddhica*).

Kenneth K. Inada
Time and temporality—A Buddhist approach

This article may create more problems rather than settling the question of time and temporality. And if it does, it only points to the fact that these concepts have not been systematically treated in Buddhism proper or have not been the central issues around which schools have developed. There is a tendency, to be sure, to downgrade these concepts as "not conducive to calm, to higher knowledge, enlightenment—*nirvāṇa*," or to treat them cursorily, in a very indirect way, which leaves the reader in suspense or puzzlement. I hope, of course, to present an approach which is consistent or coherent with the fundamental structure of Buddhist doctrines.[1] Thus I have come here to learn just as much as you have come to question.

I believe it is generally safe to say that Buddhism falls within the category of process philosophies since one of its cardinal principles is impermanence (*anicca/anitya*). Any and every item will have to be accounted for within this context. Yet, as we all know, explaining or describing the tenets of a process philosophy is nearly an impossible task, leaving so much unsaid or unattended that we are left in a general state of vagueness, if not doubt. It must be noted that in process philosophy the primary problem is to perceive the process and its elements in the proper order and relation. Methodologically speaking, although we can distinguish between the dynamic and the static aspects, in the final analysis (speaking from the standpoint of concrete actuality), the seemingly static elements must be viewed within the dynamic nature of things. This is the predicament we face over and over again.

Now, the concepts of time and temporality have come to us as a real challenge to view the dynamic nature of Buddhist reality, for they will show up that predicament very plainly and, hopefully, lead us the way to its resolution and to Buddhist reality.

The whole of Buddhist thought is permeated with the notion that life is transitory, not only in the fact that life terminates in death, but, more philosophically, that between birth and death we live in momentariness. This is the theory known as *khaṇa-vāda/kṣaṇa-vāda*. Life is a series of experiential moments, each one unique but each is so infinitesimally small that except by a method of abstraction and by hypostatization the ordinary mind is unable to conceive it. A Buddhist *sutta*, *Aṅguttara-Nikāya*, asserts as follows "Arising (*uppāda*) is revealed, duration (*ṭhita*) is revealed, and dissolution (*bhanga*) is revealed. These are the three marks of the compounding nature of things (*saṅkhāta*)."[2]

The assertion points at several things: (1) The experiential process is a compounding phenomenon. Many factors or elements are involved in the so-

Kenneth K. Inada is Professor of Philosophy, State University of New York at Buffalo.

called creative process. (2) The moment of existence or an experiential event can be referred to or inferred by way of the three characteristics. (3) The three characteristics are revealed after the moment has "transpired," that is, after the compounding phenomenon becomes a fact. They are characteristics or afterglows of the moment, so to speak. Thus they are not the moment per se but visible markers of the moment for our reference. (4) It points to the fact that a compounded phenomenon or a moment of existence is smaller than the conscious moment. Thus it would take more than the conscious mind to "grasp" the moment.

We are not normally oriented to this type of fractional dimension in the nature of a moment of existence. For the most part, we uncritically accept the condition that the mind, the conscious mind, can only function from the standpoint of temporal parallelism, that is, a parallelism that exists between a mental phenomenon and a perceptual phenomenon. An extension of this is, perhaps, the isomorphic theory of perception. When we become conscious of an object we tend to conclude that perception had been a simple and singular event. We normally do not consider the nature of continuity of the experiential process in ways which do justice to the manifold of overt as well as covert factors in function. The life process, after all, goes on incessantly whether or not we are conscious of an object. The process never takes a holiday although consciousness does. The Buddhist has a term for the basic life-continuum, *bhavaṅga*. It is the interminable force of being until physical dissolution occurs. Thus, consciousness rises and subsides in *bhavaṅga*, either when the doors of perception (five sense organs) are opened and various forms develop "internally" and continue on to the conscious mind or when the mind arouses itself in activity, for example, by recollection or by dreaming. In consequence, the mind is just another faculty, like other sense faculties, and it is never really aloof from or transcendent of the experiential process. Indeed, it plays a vital role in the whole process. Naturally, I do not mean to deny the mind its abstractive function and thereby to reject any so-called power over certain activities we are engaged in. We loosely call this power "transcendence."

The Buddhist would have no problem at all in accepting or incorporating the conventional way in which we speak of time, that is, in terms of the three temporal periods—past, present, and future (*atīta, paccuppanna, anāgata*). It is the function of the mind, after all, to conceive of time in that order or indeed to give order to the nature of things. Thus, whether it is simple clock time, physical time (measurement of movements), or psychological time, the mind knows or senses time because of the abstractive quality. And to this extent, time is conventional (*papañca/prapañca*) but very useful.

Now, the Buddhist would take the abstractive or conventional nature of time for what it is. It aids one to speak about or to analyze events that we assign to the past, present, or future. There is no difficulty here. However, the Buddhist would be quick to reply that a problem arises when one gives a strict topological nature to time and manipulates it as such in the experiential process. The neat division into past, present, and future (or earlier, simultaneous, and later) is a mental construction, a fiction as well as a hindrance, in the final analysis, when it comes to grasping the dynamic nature of being as *khaṇa-vāda*. The three periods are not distinct and different entities however hard one may try to make them out to be so. This is the argument used by Nāgārjuna (2–3 A.D.) to reject the opponent's stand on the hypostatization of the three temporal periods. For him the three moments or periods are mutually influencing terms both on the abstractive and concrete level of things—abstractive in the sense that all three are mental constructs which mutually supplement each other's descriptive nature and concrete in the sense that the experiential process involves a continuum of being which includes all three as a unique interlocking phenomenon. The past (immediate or remote in certain instances) is in the present, just as the future (immediate or remote in certain instances) will be in the present. But the present is not *simply* a transference of content from the past, nor is it *simply* a stepping stone to the future. The present does not only have a linear connection or relationship with the past and future but multiple factoral relations and conditions in its own making on the vertical scale.

Nāgārjuna spoke for all Buddhists, both Mahāyāna and Theravāda I believe, when he resolved all objectifiable elements in the unique experiential process termed *pratītyasamutpāda/paṭiccasamuppāda*, translated as dependent or relational-origination. The objectifiable elements refer to the abstract or concrete entities, as the case may be, which the mind creates and to which it assigns certain realities or objective contents. These are in the realm of conventional nature, as stated earlier, and thus rightly constitute the realm of relative truths (*saṃvṛti-satya*). But in truth, we do live greatly in the realm of relative truths because it is the realm of the visible, the tangible, the manipulatable, the empirical. Yet, the Buddhist would remind us not to rely too heavily on the relative, that the relative is not the only realm of existence; indeed, the relative must seek its raison d'etre in a wider, purer, nonobjectifiable realm. This is in reference to the supreme realm of truth (*paramārthasatya*), the goal of all Buddhists.

We shall have to concentrate on the concept of relational-origination, but before doing so let me pause to summarize that, from the Buddhist standpoint, experiential events do not take place or flow *in* time. Rather, it would be more accurate to say that events flow *as* time, thus denying any primacy to an absolute status of time. If time is understood in this way, we are able to appreciate the deeper dimensions of being because now we must focus on the process itself, the becomingness of being. Here the sister concept of temporality seems to appear almost naturally. Temporality at least moves us in the right direction and seems to permit us to have glimpses of what the Buddhist calls reality. It has a profound meaning in that it runs across but retains or contains the multiple set of conditions and factors at play in the experiential process. It is intimately tied up with the concept of relational-origination.

It is significant to note that relational-origination is a hyphenated term. It depicts a total arising or origination (*sam-uppāda*) within the matrix of a complex of relations or conditions (*paṭicca/pratītya*). The complex of relations, more specifically, refers to the term, *paccaya/pratyaya*, which may differ in numerical accounting with respect to the different Buddhist schools,[3] but, essentially, it describes the multifaceted, multirelational factors and conditions involved in the development of the experiential process. While these factors seem to be graphic structural descriptions of the process, it should be emphasized that they are vital factors in the "internal" ontological development of the process or even of consciousness itself. Again, we are dealing with a microscopic process, infinitely smaller than the process of conscious play. As a matter of fact, we are dealing with so-called preconscious units of movement. It is interesting to note that the Abhidhamma claims that the duration of thought is one-sixteenth of the duration of a moment of matter.[4] Yet, however fractional the thought duration is said to be, the conscious mind with thought as the goal takes seven units of movement to mature or fruit from the initial opening of the sense doors.[5] In these microscopic processes, the various *paccayas* are operative; for example, in a simple perception of an object, there are the objective relation (*ārammaṇa-paccaya*), the proximate relation (*anantara-p.*), contiguous relation (*samanantara-p.*), antecedent relation (*purejāta-p.*), consequent relation (*pacchājāta-p.*), resultant relation (*vipāka-p.*), etc.—all minutely describing the "internal" development that leads to consciousness or, as the case may be, it may not lead to consciousness. In other words, perceptual forms (*rūpa*) are involved from the moment the eye organ is in contact with the outside realm of object and on to the consciousness of the object. Although these factoral or relational movements take place very rapidly, still, it is possible to speak of preconscious (not particularly subconscious) developments. Incidentally, the relations are directed, ultimately, to the understanding and fulfillment of the way to the enlightened state. This would involve analysis of the elements within the meditative exercise or discipline, but that is another technical accounting for another time.

In sum, the *paccayas* amplify the conditions involved in the experiential process called relational-origination. As such, there is no simple causal analysis possible. Experiential events are not simple but are invariably complex occurrences. There are successive events, to be sure, but they do not follow one another in a trainlike procession. The events themselves cannot be broken up into separate or disparate entities simply because there is nothing that separates or isolates them into clear and distinct realms. In fact, the rapidity of the events in the nature of interlocking phenomenon prevents one from holding such a view, although it is common practice to look upon these events as separable for our own view, understanding, guidance, and anticipatory action. From the Buddhist standpoint, as seen earlier, any arbitrary separation is in the nature of abstraction and therefore relegated to the conventional nature of truth. Thus, the uniqueness of experiential events does not lie in the separable and independent nature but rather lies in the truly dynamically dependent nature of things.

To use an old metaphor, events are taking place like waves in the vast ocean. In mid-ocean the myriad waves are appearing and disappearing as if each is independent of each other but in truth there are many factors and conditions at play which make it possible for each wave to appear and disappear thus and so. Such is also the nature of the rise and subsidence of consciousness.

All this goes to show that relational-origination is a conditioning or compounding phenomenon; it is exhibiting the complex but unique way in which an experiential event transpires. Most of us fail to fathom its meaning, much the less its actual occurrence, because we are caught up in the elements of convention. We do not perceive the rise or subsidence of events properly because we are in a bind with the elements, though unconsciously for the most part. But it is heartening at least to know that despite the conventionality of things the life-continuum moves on as usual. Herein lies the truth of existence and perhaps the way out.

There is a famous Buddhist saying, "He who discerns relational-origination discerns the *Dhamma* (Buddhist Truth), and he who discerns the *Dhamma* discerns relational-origination."[6]

If I read the saying correctly, it is asserting that we who are conventionally caught up in the elements of the process of relational-origination, though unknowingly, can still perceive the Buddhist nature of reality within that self-same process. In other words, the path to the enlightened realm is always open; it is never closed. In fact, the closure is of one's own making. That is to say, various types of hindrances or obstacles are created over a period of time and these become parts of one's experiential process. For example, there are obstacles that arise based on the three basic "ills," that is, greed (*rāga*), hatred (*dosa*), and delusion (*moha*), or based on the four "overpowering forces," that is, forced being (*bhava*), wrong or dogmatic view (*diṭṭhi*), sensuality (*kāma*), and general ignorance (*avijjā*). One is usually influenced by any or all of the above grounds of forced living, from which it becomes increasingly difficult to disengage oneself as time goes on, if one remains unmindful. So, in the Socratic manner, the worst type of ignoramus is the one who does not admit his ignorance. Only the Buddhist would make certain that the nature of ignorance has another dimension, a dimension which has to do with the ontological nature of the experiential process, that is, so long as one's experiential process does not take into consideration all the factors involved the ignorant status remains. The experiential process is an inclusive total process, one that includes the epistemological realm. Thus even the domain of reason must be subsumed under the larger context of experience. We all readily admit this much, but our experiential data are by and large controlled and influenced by what reason assigns.

The concept of relational-origination depicts the dynamic coming together or a gathering of the factoral conditions into a whole, that is, a becoming of an event. It is the real concrete nature of the experiential process "seen" long enough before it moves on to the next coming together process. In a sense, we may say that a single relational-origination "takes time" for its fruition but not in the usual sense of the phrase. I believe the Buddhist would use the term, *samaya,* to describe the temporal nature of that single process.[7] This term presents a temporal dimension or temporality to the reality of experience. Perhaps, we may say that Buddhist temporality means a kind of "arresting to see" phenomenon of the experiential process. We are all in the process and yet we do not "see clearly" because we are in bind with the elements of the three basic "ills," the four "overpowering forces," general defilements (*kilesa/kleśa*), etc.—all of which compel us to repeat or engage ourselves in the conventional conditioned ("veiled") realm of existence. This is in general called *saṃsāra,* the famous spinning of the Wheel of Life or Birth-Death Cycle of Being. As long as we force the wheel to spin, we cannot see, much less realize, the enlightened path and realm. As all Buddhists know, the realms of *saṃsāra* and *nibbāna/nirvāṇa* are not mutually distinct and exclusive. Their realms of function are coterminous. We find this idea clearly expressed in the thoughts of such Buddhists as Nāgārjuna and Buddhaghosa (5 A.D.), that is, that relational-origination functions equally in both the samsāric and nibbānic realms. If it did not, then *nibbāna* would be a mysterious concept, a never to be realized realm of existence; it would be a fiction, a myth, a castle-in-the-sky concept. But as Buddhist doctrines are empirically grounded, at least the fundamental ones, the *nibbāna* content must find its source or basis accordingly.

At this point, the logical question is, what makes it possible for relational-origination to span both realms? Or, how could the two realms have the same basis of being? We have arrived at the crux of Buddhist experience or reality. Nāgārjuna, for example, says that it is because of *śūnyatā* (voidness) that everything is possible.[8] By this remark he means, if I read him correctly, that the experiential process with all its contents or elements is held together in virtue of *śūnyatā* as a kind of "voidal being," or, from another standpoint, that *śūnyatā* is the basis of the undifferentiated nature which gives substance to the differentiations. Thus, *śūnyatā* is a supreme experience of ontological togetherness. It holds our experiences together because it is not limited to the differentiated (conventionalized) realm. It is the "substance" with which one "ferries" oneself to the other shore, so to speak.

Buddhaghosa, coming a few centuries later, asserts in a similar vein that relational-origination ("The Wheel of Becoming") reveals no known beginning, no maker, no experiencer; it is void (*suñña*) with a twelvefold voidness (that is, reference to the sense faculties and the sense objects, including the mind and its objects) and spins on and on.[9] Again, we note the central role of *śūnyatā* ("voidness") in the ordinary experiential process. *Śūnyatā* is what makes the two realms coexistent, not side by side, but as two sides of the same reality. Thus relational-origination spans the saṃsāric and nibbānic realms, because it is in essence a voidal, undifferentiated process.[10]

I venture to say then that relational-origination, in its unique sense of voidness, refers to a Buddhist notion of temporality. In this sense, temporality is that experience which is coterminous with the reality of things as they are. It is to catch the Wheel of Becoming as it really is. Perhaps, Buddhist temporality is just another bridge-concept in amplifying the tenets of meditative discipline, for one of the most important steps in *samādhi* (concentration) is the development of the state of rest (*samatha*) or tranquillity (*passaddhi*). As I see it, rest or tranquillity must somehow be relatable to the concept of temporality. The achievement of rest is necessary for one to perceive things in their proper natures, that is, within the process of relational-origination. Temporality offers a dimension of rest, a coolness of being, to our experiential process. It is a way of being with the life-continuum, comprehending it in its natural flow, and living in the unhindered heightened sense. Temporality is "lived time" and from which the sense of the eternal issues forth.[11]

CONCLUSION

In the preceding brief discussion I have attempted to present a single approach in order to focus on the question of time and temporality. I have shown that the concept of time (*kāla*) is a general concept which is used in the ordinary conventional sense, such as, variations of clock time or the psychological nature of time. However, this usage is really an abstraction and a limitation, without the unsuspecting mind really knowing. Thus the Buddhist would not place much emphasis on this type of time since it is not conducive to the development of the path of enlightenment. As a consequence, in discussing the Buddhist concept of reality or experience, we turned to the concept of temporality to give us a fuller accounting of our experiential process. That process was analyzed to be relational-origination (*paṭiccasamuppāda*), which in its essential way reflects the nature of temporality (*samaya*), the coming together of an event. Temporality is, in a sense, the fruition of a wave in the ocean. It clearly describes a durational moment or rest to exhibit itself, but it also has the nature of voidness (*śūnyatā*), which permits a wave to rise and subside in the waters. The experiential events are then never separate or discrete for the experiencer always describes his own life-continuum, his own wheel of becoming, within the matrix of totality. Temporality becomes an important ingredient in the Wheel of Becoming because it expresses that capture of rest which not only gives an eternal flavor to becomingness but an overview on the course of things.

1. I view later Buddhist developments, especially in the Mahāyāna, as only expansions or extensions of the fundamental thought of Buddhism and not a deviation in any drastic sense. If some do appear deviant, for example, in tantric or esoteric types, they were so in terms of differing times and circumstances, but the basic thoughts were "secretly" guarded all along.

2. I, 152 (PTS trans., *Gradual Sayings*, I:135). It is interesting to note that the same paragraph goes on to say cryptically that the three marks are not revealed.

3. The Abhidhamma philosophy offers twenty-four types of *paccayas* which are later abstracted into four principal ones: *ārammaṇa-paccaya* (objective relation or condition), *upanissaya-p.* (sufficing relation), *kamma-p.* (actional relation), and *atthi-p.* (presence relation). The Sarvāstivāda, on the other hand, introduces the ten relational "causes," six of which are more causal in nature (*kāraṇa-hetu, sahabhū-h., sabhāga-h., samprayukta-h., sarvatraga-h.,* and *vipāka-h.*) and four more relational in nature (*hetu-pratyaya, samanantara-p., ālambana-p.,* and *adhipati-p.*). While the first six are new, the last four are identical with four of the Abhidhamma's *paccayas*.

4. E. R. Sarathchandra, *Buddhist Psychology of Perception* (Colombo: The Ceylon University Press, 1958), p. 43. Cf. also Nyanaponika Thera, *Abhidhamma Studies* (Kandy, Ceylon: Buddhist Publication Society, 1965), p. 112. Shwe Zan Aung, in his introductory essay to the *Compendium of Philosophy* (London: Luzac & Co., 1972), p. 26, says: "The Buddhists have come to speak of matter as lasting for seventeen thought moments."

5. *Op. cit., Compendium of Philosophy*, pp. 27–30.

6. *Majjhima-Nikāya*: I, 191. (PTS trans., *The Middle Length Sayings*, I:236–237.

7. *Samaya* is to be distinguished from the term, *kāla*, which describes the general or conventional nature of time. *Samaya* is closer to the actual becoming nature of being because it gives the sense of gathering, coming together, arising, a kind of "durational passage."

8. *Mūlamadhyamakakārikā*, XXIV, 14.

9. *Visuddhimagga*, XVII, 273.

10. This voidal undifferentiated process is "greater" and "wider" in dimension than the differentiated realm of existence. Therefore, it is accommodative or inclusive of the latter. In a sense, the undifferentiated is the unlimited or nonconfining realm. Time does not permit me to develop further the interplay or interfusion of the two realms, but suffice it to say that the Hua-yen School in China handled the situation beautifully in the concept of *dharmadhātu*. Its treatment of the nonobstructiveness of the ten periods of time is an extension of the above concept.

11. Dōgen Zenji (1200–1253), the great Sōtō Zen master, made the following observations: "Temporality (*uji*) means that time is existence and existence time." "As different entities do not obstruct one another, so do different moments not obstruct one another." "Passage (experiential process) is like spring with all its manifestations, i.e., spring

179

comes to pass without any external elements intervening." [*Shōbōgenzō*, Chapter on Uji (Temporality or Temporal Reality), passim. *Shōbōgenzō Chūkai Zensho*, II:1-66 (Tokyo: Muga Sanbō, 1912)]. Dōgen's thoughts seem to be a crystallization of Hua-yen philosophy which was touched upon lightly in footnote 10. However, to sum up and amplify his words, we might assert: "Flowers do not bloom in the spring. Flowers in bloom are spring!"

David J. Kalupahana The Buddhist conception of time and temporality

During the early period of Indian thought, time (*kāla*) baffled the Indian thinkers to such an extent that they came to look upon it not only as the cause of the universe but also as an all-pervading principle which governs everything in it.[1] But as speculation advanced, time came to be considered one of the causes which determines the course of natural phenomena. Thus, a later Jaina scholiast, Śīlāṅka, attempting to explain the nonabsolutism in Jaina thought, maintained that time can be recognized as one of the causal factors in the evolution of nature, because it is found that certain events like the flowering of trees, etc., occur at certain times only, not all the time.[2] In the thought of the Upaniṣads, with its emphasis on permanence and eternity and the resulting denial of change and causation as being illusory, the problem of causation received scant attention. But in early Buddhism, where there is a denial of permanence, the conceptions of change and causality, and, hence, of time, occupied prominent places.

Causality (Pāli, *Paṭiccasamuppāda*; Skt., *pratītyasamutpāda*) is the central philosophy of early Buddhism. With the insight he gained as he sat contemplating under the bodhi tree on the bank of the river Nerañjarā, the Buddha realized that everything in this world of experience is causally produced. It was this insight that enabled him to eliminate all the doubts (*kaṅkhā*) he had entertained regarding the nature of existence.[3] Thus, in early Buddhism, the recognition of the fact that everything is impermanent (*anicca*), conditioned (*saṅkhata*), and causally produced (*paṭiccasamup-panna*), along with the denial of anything permanent (*nicca*) or eternal (*dhuva, sassata*) led to fruitful speculation regarding time. But it must be emphasized that during this early period of Buddhist thought whatever reflections there were on the problem of time were invariably connected with speculation on the nature of things which are temporal (*kālika*).

Let us begin with the Buddha's conception of the universe. Unlike his later Mahāyāna disciples who maintained that there is no beginning (*ana-varāgra*) of the world process (*saṃsāra*),[4] the Buddha insisted that the beginning is totally inconceivable (*anamatagga*).[5] Although the beginning is inconceivable, yet it is possible to see periods of evolution (*vivaṭṭa*) and dissolution (*saṃvaṭṭa*) following one another.[6] These periods are reckoned in terms of aeons (*kappa*), each of which is said to be of such immense duration that it can only be illustrated by means of similes, and these became very popular in Indian thought later on. One such simile is as follows: "If there were to be a great mountain, one league in width, one league in length and one league in height, a solid mass without chasms or clefts, and a man at the end of every hundred years, were to strike it once each time with a silken cloth, that mountain will sooner be done away with than would an

David J. Kalupahana is Associate Professor of Philosophy, University of Hawaii.

aeon."[7] This passage, while emphasizing the immensity of time, also shows that we can observe events only and use processes based on these events to measure time.[8] Thus we derive time from events which are in time (*kālika*), but not vice versa.[9]

The processes of evolution and dissolution are said to take place in accordance with the causal principle which is stated as: "When this exists, that exists or comes to be; on the arising of this, that arises. When this does not exist, that does not exist or come to be; on the cessation of this, that ceases."[10] Since it has been pointed out that "there is a profound connection between the reality of time and the existence of an incalculable element in the universe,"[11] let us pause to consider the nature of the causal principle stated in the preceding formula. This causal principle was presented by the Buddha in the background of several theories, one of which was popular in the early Upaniṣadic tradition. In the early Buddhist texts, this is referred to as the theory of self-causation (*sayaṃkata-*[*vāda*])[12] and was based on the belief in a self (*attan*) considered to be the essence of everything (*sabbaṃ*). Thus, "everything exists" (Pāli, *sabbaṃ atthi*; Skt. *sarvam asti*)[13] means that this essence of everything exists. This leads to the view that the consequence preexists in the cause, the future in the present. Such a strictly determined causal principle would also mean that we can, by examining the present, predict with absolute certainty what will happen in the future, for the future is merely the hidden present. For this reason temporality becomes a mere illusion.

The Buddha's theory of causality differs from this in that it is not a form of strict determinism of this sort. The very use of the term 'when' (and this idea is expressed by the use of the locative absolute construction in Pāli), which in this context is equivalent to the conditional particle 'if', should be sufficient to show that the future events cannot be predicted with absolute certainty. For this reason, we find that none of the extrasensory perceptions recognized in early Buddhism refer to the future. As is well known, omniscience (*sabbaññutā*), as later understood, was not claimed by the Buddha. We come across only two instances when the Buddha made any kind of prediction into the future with much certainty. One is the prediction that a 'stream entrant' (*sotāpanna*) is certain (*niyata*) to attain enlightenment (*sambodhiparāyana*),[14] and the other is that a person who has eliminated craving and thus attained enlightenment will not be reborn (*khīṇa jāti, nâparaṃ itthattāya*).[15] Both these could be considered knowledge based on inductive inference (*anvaye ñāṇa*).[16] Depending on such inductive inferences the Buddha recognized the future validity of the causal principle. This prompted him to make such declarations as: "Whether the Tathāgatas were to arise in this world or were not to arise, this causal status, this causal pattern, this conditionality remains."[17] If this causal pattern is said to exist always in this world, and if "perceiving the *dhamma* means perceiving causality (*paṭiccasamuppāda*),"[18] then it is possible to say that his teachings will be valid at all times. It is only in this sense that the teaching (*dhamma*) was described as being timeless (*akālika*).[19] On the basis of this theory of causality, it is possible to define the three periods of time, past, present, and future, in the following manner: the past is the determined (=*bhūta*); the present is the moment of becoming (=*bhava*); and the future is the as yet undetermined (=*bhavya*).[20]

Thus, using the terminology of Whitrow on the problem of time, it is possible to say that according to Buddhism, "the future is hidden from us—not in the present, but in the future."[21] Time is the mediator between the past and the present. Hence for that which is born (*jātassa*), death is a matter of time. This may be the idea behind the use of the phrases *kālaṃ karoti*[22] (literally, "he does his time," "is fulfilling his time"), which means dying, and *kālaṃ kaṅkhati*[23] (literally, "awaiting time"), that is, awaiting death. For this reason, time assumes the position of Māra, the personification of death. The famous quatrain in the Jātaka runs:

> Time consumes all beings
> including oneself;
> the being who consumes time,
> cooks the cooker of beings.[24]

Although time is supposed to overwhelm ordinary human beings, yet the one who has attained enlightenment is able to bring time under his control. Just as he overwhelms Māra, the evil one, even so does he overcome time. He is said to overcome time, not because he attains to a state of permanent existence (as it was advocated in Mahāyāna),[25] but because of two important reasons. First, with the complete eradication of craving and attachment, he no longer has any longing for existence or anything associated with it. Hence, dying or 'fulfilling time' (*kālakiriyā*) never worries him, as it does the ordinary man. Secondly, he has put an end to continued becoming (*bhava*). Thus, immortality (Pāli, *amata*; Skt. *amṛta*) in early Buddhism becomes a synonym of no-rebirth (*a-punabbhava*).[26] He who has overcome the process of becoming also overcomes time, because there is no time apart from the process of becoming. As pointed out by Whitrow, ". . . the idea that time is ultimate and irreducible does not commit us to the unnecessary hypothesis that it is absolute, for moments do not exist in their own right but are mere classes of co-existent events."[27]

It was mentioned that during the pre-Buddhist period there was a theory which upheld that "everything exists." The foundation of this theory seems to be the view that an event can never cease to be an event.[28] Because of the popularity this theory enjoyed during this period, the Buddha seems to have taken much trouble to refute it. In addition to the argument from experience that he adduced to refute this theory, the Buddha also pointed out that it was the result of a linguistic fallacy.[29] His criticism runs thus:

> Monks, there are these three linguistic conventions or usages of words or terms which are distinct, have been distinct in the past, are distinct at present and will be distinct in the future and which are not ignored by the recluses and brahmans who are wise. Which three? Whatever form (*rūpa*) there has been, which has ceased to be, which is past and has changed is called, reckoned or termed "has been" (*ahosi*); it is not reckoned as "it exists" (*atthi*) nor as "it will be" (*bhavissati*). (The same is said about the other four aggregates—sensation, perception, dispositions and consciousness.) . . . Whatever form is not arisen, not come to be, is called, reckoned or termed "it will be" (*bhavissati*) and is not reckoned as "it exists" or as "it has been." . . . Whatever form has become and has manifested itself is called, reckoned or termed as "it exists" (*atthi*) and is not reckoned as "it has been" or as "it will be."[30]

It is very clear from this passage that the theory according to which the past and the future exist in the present or even the view that a thing exists during the past, the present, and the future are the results of unwarranted interpretation of linguistic usage. Here the temporal copulas "was," "is now," or "will be" in propositions which assert temporal relations between events are being confused with the timeless copulas of logic.

One of the arguments against the reality of time seems to be based on the view that it is not an object of the five types of sense experience. Hence it is nothing but a mysterious illusion of the intellect.[31] For early Buddhism, which not only recognized six senses but also held that the sixth sense (that is, the mind) could be developed to perceive, with the help of memory, a long period of one's past history, time was an important ingredient of experience.[32] As if rejecting the theory of atomic moments of time, which is recognized to be a logical abstraction,[33] the Buddha is represented as saying: "This physical body made up of the four primary existents is seen to exist for one, two, three, four, five, ten, twenty, thirty, forty, fifty, hundred or more years. That which is called the mind, thought or consciousness arises as one thing and ceases as another whether by night or by day."[34] This is a clear recognition of the two types of experience that we have. One is the experience of things which endure for some finite segment of time, and the other is the experience of momentary things. The latter experience is illustrated by the simile of the flowing river. According to the description in the early Buddhist texts, "there is no moment, no inkling, no particle of time that the river stops flowing."[35] These two types of experience of time can be compared to the experiences one has of the movement of the two hands of the clock, the hour hand and the second hand.[36] It is important to note that early Buddhism never reduced the experience of the former to the experience of the latter, although logical abstraction can always lead to such a hypothesis. In fact, a reduction of every form of experience into further indivisible moments (Pāli, *khaṇa*; Skt. *kṣaṇa*) was carried out during the period of scholasticism, and such a theory is conspicuous by its absence in the early discourses. Therefore, during the early period, although there were statements which could be interpreted to mean a theory of momentariness, the most dominant view was the one which recognized a finite segment of time as constituting our immediate experience. The recognition of this finite segment of time means that according to early Buddhism there is a duration of temporal experience with a certain unification of perspective. For this reason, unlike in the cases where a theory of moments dominated,[87] early Buddhism considered both time and causation as parts of our experience, not as mere inferences based primarily on the succession of momentary ideas. Thus, it is possible to maintain that early Buddhism presents us with an empiricist analysis of time.

With regard to the problem of time, early Buddhism seems to have followed the middle path, so famous in the history of Buddhist thought. It appears as if it considered absolute time as an extreme and an unnecessary hypothesis. The other extreme is the consideration of time as a mysterious illusion of the intellect. Avoiding both these extremes, the Buddha seems to have considered time as an essential feature of the universe and the experience of it.

With the development of scholasticism after the passing away of the Buddha, this empiricist philosophy of time and temporality changed completely. Unbridled speculation during the period of the Abhidharma led to the development of many theories which are more metaphysical than empirical.

In his desire to eliminate the pre-Buddhist conception of an eternal and immutable self (*attan*), the Buddha adopted the analytical method (*vibhajjavāda*) of reducing things to their components. Thus the human personality was analyzed sometimes into five aggregates (Pāli, *khandha*; Skt. *skandha*) and at other times into six elements (*dhātu*). Yet all these aggregates, as well as the elements, were the contents of experience, not of pure logical analysis. But with the development of scholasticism, this analytical approach was carried to its logical conclusion, and the result was the emergence not only of a theory of atoms (*paramāṇu*) but also a theory of moments (*khaṇa*), spatial analysis giving rise to temporal atomicity.[88] The development of these two theories occasioned several other doctrines which are not compatible with the basic teachings of the Buddha.

One of the immediate results of the analysis of time into atomic units or *chronons* was the view that time is fleeting or flowing from the future into the present and from the present into the past. Thus, in the commentarial literature, we come across expressions such as *gacchante gacchante kāle* meaning "as time passed by" or "with the passage of time."[39]

All these developments were summarized by Buddhaghosa in the *Atthasālinī*, his commentary on the *Dhammasaṅganī*, where he refers to the three varieties of the present (*paccuppanna*).[40] The first is the protensive present (*addhā paccuppanna*) or the finite segment of time constituting our immediate experience. This is said to be the kind of present recognized in the discourses (*sutta*). The second is the flowing or the continuing present (*santati paccuppanna*), which was then accepted in the commentarial tradition (*aṭṭhakathā*). The third is the momentary present (*khaṇa paccuppanna*), which is not identified with any tradition. Yet it was the conception mentioned last which dominated the scholastic tradition.

Buddhaghosa's commentary on the *Vibhaṅga*, the second book of the *Abhidhamma Piṭaka*, in introducing the theory of moments, says that it is a doctrine peculiar to the Abhidhamma and not to the Suttanta. According to this, *rūpa* (matter or form) is classified as past, future, or present (*atītānāgatapaccuppanna*) in the Suttanta and this division is made on the basis of becoming (*bhavena paricchinna*). In the Abhidhamma, however, the division is made on the basis of moments (*khaṇena paricchinna*).[41]

These are different versions of the theory of moments. The Sarvāstivādins recognized four moments, the nascent (*jāti*), the static (*sthiti*), the decaying (*jarā*), and the cessant (*nāśa*).[42] Post-Buddhaghosan Theravāda recognized three: the nascent (*uppāda*), the static (*ṭhiti*), and the cessant (*bhaṅga*).[43] The Sautrāntikas differed from all of them in accepting two moments only, the nascent (*utpāda*) and cessant (*vyaya*), and rejecting the static moment (*sthiti-kṣaṇa*).[44]

The difficulties posed by the analysis of time into atomic units are innumerable. Although a moment was considered to be the unanalyzable unit of time, it was found that a distinction had to be made between a moment of thought and a moment of matter, because, as pointed out earlier, thought changes more rapidly than physical bodies.[45] Therefore, in the Theravāda Abhidhamma it is said that during the lifetime of a single moment of matter sixteen moments of thought arise and pass away.[46]

The most difficult problem created by the theory of moments concerned the experienced continuity of temporal events. A moment was considered to be durationless, comparable to the dimensionless point of space, and hence, past, present, and future moments are utterly distinct from each other. They are discrete. To explain the problem of continuity arising as a result of the analysis of time into momentary and discrete units, the Buddhist schools offered various solutions. The most widely known and the most severely criticized of these different solutions was that proffered by the Sarvāstivādins who insisted that underlying the succession of momentary events is the substance or 'own-nature' (*dravya, svabhāva*) which remains unchanged.[47] Thus, a thing (*dharma*) has two aspects: the characteristic (*lakṣaṇa*) which is temporal (*kālika, kṣaṇika*) and the substance (*dravya*) which is eternal or timeless. The term *sarvāstivāda* means the "theory that everything exists" (*sarvam asti*). This everything (*sarvam*) was the substance of everything which, they held, exists during the three periods, past, present and future. This theory was examined by the Theravādins in their *Kathāvatthu* where they make the Sarvāstivādins admit that not only everything past, present, and future exists, but that past, present, and future themselves exist, that is, they are independently real.[48] While the basic theory of the Sarvāstivādins was not much different from the Upaniṣadic theory of "everything exists" referred to and criticized by the Buddha, there is also a significant difference. Unlike the thought of the Upaniṣads which is idealistic, the Sarvāstivāda represented a school of realism and therefore, as pointed out by the Theravādins, they upheld the independent reality not only of things, but also of time. It is interesting to note that in support of their rejection of this theory of "everything exists" (*sarvam asti*), the Theravādins are represented as quoting a discourse from the Buddha on the nature of linguistic conventions referred to earlier.[49]

The school of Buddhism known as the Sautrāntika rejected the Sarvāstivāda conception of substance (*svabhāva*) as being no different from the theory of self (*atman*).[50] But the rejection of this underlying substance compelled them to the view that there is no duration whatsoever and that what *appears* as duration is a series of fleeting moments, like the cinematograph. This continuum of durationless instants, no doubt, is the result of logical abstraction, a theoretical construction based on the empirical data of consciousness. Unlike the Theravādins who recognized two different types of moments, that is, a moment of thought and a moment of matter, the Sautrāntikas made no such distinctions. The most important consequence of this conception of time was the theory that there are no instantaneous connections between external events and the observer.[51] Hence there is no direct perception of an object; there is inferential knowledge (*anumāna*) only. Thus the Sautrāntikas were popularly known for their doctrine of "representationism," that is, the inferability of the external object (*bahyārthānumeyavāda*).[52]

In the *Mūlamadhyamakakārikā,* Nāgārjuna devotes one chapter to the examination of the problem of time.[53] It is indeed a very short but extremely important chapter. There is no doubt that it was the Sarvāstivāda conception of time which drew the criticism from Nāgārjuna. The theory, as explained by Candrakīrti, recognized the existence of the substance of things during the three periods. It was argued by the realist that since substance exists, time with which it is associated also exists.[54] It is this independent reality of time which Nāgārjuna takes up for criticism. His criticism was based on the fact that a thing (*bhāva*) or its substance (*bhāvasvabhāva*) and time (*kāla*) are relative to or dependent upon one another. Early Buddhism, as pointed out earlier, would have stopped at this point, but Nāgārjuna did not. He employed his dialectic to demonstrate the unreality or nonexistence of time.[55] Nāgārjuna's argument was based on the assumption that two things cannot be related unless they are coexistent. Hence, if present and future are held to be contingently related to the past, then both present and future should be in the past. Otherwise they cannot be contingently related. On the other hand, present and future could not exist without being contingent on the past. Hence, according to Nāgārjuna, there is no justification for the recognition of a present and a future time.[56] The selfsame argument was used to refute the reality of the past. Past, present, and future, which were comparable to such concepts as above, below and middle (*uttamādhamamadhyama*), or arising, enduring, and passing away (*utpādasthitibhaṅga*), etc., could not thus withstand the onslaught of Nāgārjuna's dialectic.

The opponents argued that time exists because it has dimension and is measured in terms of moments, days, fortnights, months, and years.[57] Nāgārjuna pointed out that it is not possible to measure time. He maintained that nonenduring or nonstatic time cannot be measured, because it cannot be manipulated, and that an enduring or static time, although manipulatable, does not exist.[58] By way of conclusion, Nāgārjuna points out that if time exists depending on existential structure, then it cannot be obtained without such structure. But no existential structure is to be found, for he has already refuted such a structure.[59] Hence, according to him, time does not exist.

Nāgārjuna claimed that his exposition of the doctrine is based on the recognition of the two truths, the conventional (*saṃvṛti-satya*) and the ultimate truth (*paramārtha-satya*).[60] According to Candrakīrti, the ultimate truth is the independent (*aparapratyaya*), peaceful (*śānta*), without conceptual proliferation (*prapañcātīta*), nonconceptual (*nirvikalpa*), and without plurality (*anekārtha*).[61] Hence, Nāgārjuna's, no doubt, was a transcendentalist criticism of phenomenal reality. This would become clear from a comparison of the standpoints adopted by the two schools, early Buddhism and Mādhyamika. When early Buddhism maintained that things are relatively real, Nāgārjuna insisted that things are unreal because they are relative, the real being the transcendental.

Summing up the whole discussion, I may say that (1) early Buddhism presented an empiricist and relativistic conception of time; (2) the Abhidharma scholasticism produced an absolutistic conception mainly because of its speculative approach, and (3) the Mādhyamikas, as a result of their transcendentalism, denied the reality of time.

1. *Atharvaveda Saṅhitā*, ed. R. Roth and W. D. Whitney (Berlin: F. Dümmler, 1924), 19.54; *Maitri Upaniṣad* 6.14 (see *The Principal Upaniṣads*, ed. and trans. S. Radhakrishnan (London: George Allen & Unwin, 1953)).

2. *Sūtrakṛtāṅga* with the commentary of Śīlāṅka, ed. A. S. Suri and C. Ganindra (Bhavanagara, Bombay, Vijayadeva Sura, 1950–1953), i.31–2, "Tathā kālo 'pi kartā, yato bakulacampakāśokapunnāganāgasahakārādīnāṃ viśiṣṭa eva kāle puṣpaphalādyudbhavo na sarvadeti."

3. *Udāna*, ed. P. Steinthal (London: PTS, 1948, reprint), p. 1: "Yadā have pātubhavanti dhammā/ātāpino jhāyato brāhmaṇassa/ath'assa kaṅkhā vapayanti sabbā/yato pajānāti sahetudhammaṃ."/

4. *Mūlamadhyamakakārikās* (hereafter cited as *MK*) des Nāgârjuna, avec la Prasannapadā commentaire de Candrakīrti (hereafter cited as *MKV*), publié par Louis de la Vallée Poussin (St. Petersburg: Academy of Sciences of USSR, 1903–1913), xi. 1.

5. *Samyutta Nikāya* (hereafter cited as *S*), ed. Leon Feer (London: PTS, 1884–1904), i.178 ff.; *Sāratthappakāsinī*, ed. F. L. Woodward (London: PTS, 1929–1937), ii.156, anamattaggo aviditaggo.

6. *Dīgha Nikāya* (hereafter cited as *D*) ed. T. W. Rhys Davids and J. E. Carpenter (London: PTS, 1890–1911), iii.84–5; *Taishō Shinshu Daizōkyō* (hereafter cited as *Taishō*), ed. J. Takakusu and K. Watanabe (Tokyo, The Taishō Shinshu Daizōkyō Kanko Kai, 1962, reprint), i.37b–c.

7. *S* ii.181–4; *Taishō* ii.242a–243b.

8. Whitrow, G. J., *The Natural Philosophy of Time* (London: Thomas Nelson & Sons, 1961), p. 34.

9. Cp. J. Alexander Gunn, *The Problem of Time* (London, 1929), p. 323 (quoted by Whitrow, *op. cit.* p. 36).

10. *Udāna*, p. 1; *Majjhima Nikāya* (hereafter cited as *M*), ed. V. Trenckner and R. Chalmers (London: PTS, 1948–1951), i.262–4; *S* ii.28, 70, 96; *MKV* 9; *Taishō* i.562c; ii.10a, 67a, 713c–714a.

11. Whitrow, *op. cit.*, p. 295.

12. *S* ii.18; *Taishō* i.76a; ii.81a, 86a–c.

13. *S* ii.17; *Taishō* ii. 85c.

14. *D* i.156; *Taishō* i.616c.

15. *M* i.184; *Taishō* i.658a. In fact, on one occasion it was anticipated that an outsider might point out that the Buddha has knowledge with regard to the past but not with regard to the future. The Buddha's reply was that, with regard to the past, his knowledge follows in the wake of memory (*satānusārī*) and that, with regard to the future, the knowledge is that gained with enlightenment (*bodhiñāṇa*), namely, the knowledge that there is no more future rebirth. See *D* iii.134; *Taishō* i.75.

16. *S* ii.58; cp. *Taishō* ii.99c–100a.

17. *S* ii.25; *Taishō* ii.84b; *MKV* 40.

18. *M* i.190–1; *Taishō* i.467a, "Yo paṭiccasamuppādaṃ passati so dhammaṃ passati."

19. *Aṅguttara Nikāya* (abbr. *A*), ed. R. Morris and E. Hardy (London: PTS, 1885–1900), iii.212, etc.; *Taishō* i.616c.

20. Cp., *op. cit.*, p. 295.

21. *The Natural Philosophy of Time*, p. 259.

22. *Vinaya Piṭaka*, ed. H. Oldenberg (London: PTS, 1879–1883), iii.80.

23. *S* i.187; *Sutta Nipāta*, ed. D. Anderson and H. Smith (London: PTS, 1948), 516.

24. *Jātaka*, ed. V. Fausboll (London, 1895–1907), ii.260.

25. Kālo ghasati bhūtāni sabbān'eva sahattanā,
yo ca kālaghaso bhūto so bhūtapacaniṃ paci.

Cp. *Maitri Upaniṣad*, 6.15. See also *Theragāthā*, ed. H. Oldenberg and R. Pischel (London: PTS 1883), 661; *MKV* 386.

Speaking of the Tathāgata, the *Saddharmapuṇḍarika-sūtra* (ed. H. Kern and B. Nanjio (St. Petersburg: Academy of Sciences of the USSR, 1912, p. 271)) says that he remains for ever (*sadā sthitaḥ*).

26. *S* 1.174; *Taishō* ii.27b.

27. Whitrow, *op. cit.*, p. 313.
28. See J. M. E. McTaggart, *Nature of Existence* (Cambridge: At The University Press, 1927), ii.10.
29. *S* ii.17; *Taishō* ii.85c.
30. Cp. C. D. Broad, *Examination of McTaggart's Philosophy* (Cambridge: At The University Press, 1938), ii.316, "When I utter the sentence 'It has rained', I do *not* mean that, in some mysterious non-temporal sense of 'is', there *is* a rainy event, which momentarily possessed the quality of presentness and has now lost it and acquired instead some determinate form of the quality of pastness. What I mean is that raininess has been, and no longer is being, manifested in my neighbourhood. When I utter the sentence 'It will rain', I do *not* mean that, in some mysterious non-temporal sense of 'is', there is a rainy event, which now possesses some determinate form of the quality of futurity and will in course of time lose futurity and acquire instead the quality of presentness. What I mean is that raininess will be, but is not now being, manifested in my neighbourhood."
31. Whitrow, *op. cit.*, p. 313.
32. *D* iii.134; cp. *Taishō* i.75b–c.
33. Whitrow, *op. cit.*, p. 312.
34. *S* ii.94–7; *Taishō* ii.81c–82a.
35. *A* iv.137; cp. *Taishō* i.682b.
36. C. D. Broad, *Scientific Thought* (London: Routledge & Kegan Paul, 1923), p. 351.
37. As a result of the acceptance of the theory of moments, David Hume reduced causation to mere succession of ideas. His theory of moments is very clearly set out in *A Treatise of Human Nature*, ed. L. A. Selby-Bigge (Oxford: The Clarendon Press, 1888), p. 39 f.
38. Whitrow, *op. cit.*, p. 153.
39. *Dhammapada-aṭṭhakathā* (London: PTS 1906–1914), i.319.
40. *Atthasālinī*, ed. E. Müller (London: PTS, 1897), p. 421.
41. *Sammohavinodanī* (hereafter cited as *VbhA*) ed. A. P. Buddhadatta (London: PTS, 1923), p. 7.
42. *Abhidharmadīpa* (hereafter cited as *Ad*), ed. P. S. Jaini (Patna, K. P. Jayaswal Research Institute, 1959), p. 104.
43. *VbhA* 7.
44. *Sphuṭārthābhidharmakośavyākhyā* of Yaśomitra (hereafter cited as *Sakv*), ed. U. Wogihara (Tokyo: The Publication Association of Abhidharmakośavyākhyā, 1932–1936), p. 33.
45. *VbhA* 25, Rūpaṃ garupariṇāmaṃ dandhanirodhaṃ, arūpaṃ lahupariṇāmaṃ khippanirodhaṃ.
46. Ibid. 25–26, Rūpe dharente yeva soḷasa cittāni uppajjitvā nirujjhanti. Taṃ pana sattarasamena cittena saddhiṃ nirujjhati.
47. *L'Abhidharmakośa de Vasubandhu*, traduction et annotations par Louis de la Vallée Poussin (Paris: Paul Geuthner, 1923–1925), v.52 ff.; *Taishō* xxix.104c; *Ad* 259; Tattvasaṃgraha, ed. E. Krishnamacharya (Baroda: Oriental Institute, 1926), i.504.
48. *Points of Controversy* (translation of *Kathāvatthu*), by S. Z. Aung and Mrs. Rhys Davids (London: PTS, 1915), p. 84 ff.
49. Ibid. p. 95 f.
50. *Sakv* p. 362.
51. Whitrow, *op. cit.*, p. 179, where it is given as a theory formulated by Albert Einstein.
52. *Sarvadarśanasaṃgraha*, ed. V. S. Abhyankar (Poona: Bhandarkar Oriental Research Institute, 1924), p. 36.
53. Chap. xix, Kālaparīkṣā.
54. *MKV* 382
55. *MK* xix.3, tasmāt kālo na vidyate

191

56. Ibid. xix.1.
57. *MKV* 385.
58. *MK* xix.5.
59. See *MK* chapters iv, v, vii, xv, and xviii.
60. Ibid. xxiv.8.
61. *MKV* 493.

John M. Koller On Buddhist views of devouring time

In thinking about Buddhist views of time and temporality it is important to remember that Buddhism is essentially a practical quest aimed at overcoming *dukkha* and not a system or set of systems of metaphysics. In the *Majjhima Nikāya, Sutta* 63, the Buddha responds to Māluṅkyāputta's request for metaphysical theories with the parable of the man wounded by a poisoned arrow, drawing the conclusion that constructing metaphysical systems is not the way to overcome *dukkha*. Referring to his refusal to engage in the metaphysical speculation necessary to answer Māluṅkyāputta's questions about the eternality or finitude of the world, relation between the body and soul, and the possibility of life after death, the Buddha says, "And why, Mālunkyāputta, have I not elucidated thus? Because Mālunkyāputta, this profits not, nor has to do with the fundamentals of religion, nor tends to aversion, absence of passion, cessation, quiescence, the supernatural faculties, supreme wisdom, and nirvana; therefore have I not elucidated it?"[1] Further, in *Sutta* 72 of the *Majjhima Nikāya,* Vaccha, a wandering ascetic, tries to get the Buddha to commit himself to a metaphysical position on these same questions and is told, with respect to each of the suggested metaphysical theories, that the theory ". . . is a jungle, a wilderness, a puppet-show, a writhing, and a fetter, and is coupled with misery, ruin, despair, and agony, and does not tend to aversion, absence of passion, cessation, quiescence, knowledge, supreme wisdom and nirvana."[2]

This point, that not only is metaphysics merely useless but that it is actually harmful to the quest for *nirvāṇa,* made so forcefully by the Buddha in these discourses needs to be kept in mind when discussing Buddhist views of time and temporality, for, as I shall maintain, time is a theoretical construct to explain temporal becoming, and therefore is itself a metaphysical view, the elaboration of which was implicitly discouraged in Buddhism by the Buddha himself.

To the extent this negative attitude toward metaphysics was characteristic of Buddhism, one would not expect to find an elaborate metaphysics of time. By the same reasoning, when metaphysical theories were put forth—such as the views of Dharmatrāta, Ghoṣaka, Buddadeva, and Vasumitra examined by McDermott—one is not surprised to find other Buddhist philosophers such as Śāntarakṣita and Kamalaśīla issuing sharp rejoinders, which as McDermott points out, charge these Sarvāstivādins with having embraced the total existence of everything in a changeless, timeless moment as a result of having taken the *dharmas* of analysis to be ontological existents. This is the root of their "everything-exists theory" (the literal meaning of *sarvāstivāda*), and having made this mistake they—as exemplified by Dharmatrāta—try to account for temporal becoming in terms of changing *appearances.* But having

John M. Koller is Associate Professor of Philosophy at Rensselaer Polytechnic Institute.

already effectively denied change by postulating unchanging being as the basic reality, they get not real, but only apparent, becoming. In effect, they have denied temporal becoming.

Now, since the implicit rejection of temporal becoming found in Sarvāstivāda is obviously at odds with the Buddhist emphasis on becoming and cannot be squared with the centrality of the principle expressing the inner connectedness of temporal becoming, known as *pratītyasamutpāda* within Buddhism, it is considered an erroneous view by Sautrāntikas, Yogācārins, and Mādhyamikas. To come to grips with the question of whether or not the Sarvāstivādins have a mistaken view of time and becoming requires an analysis of these concepts. In the following paragraphs I will develop an analysis of time and temporal becoming which I do not wish to attribute to any historical person or school, but which I feel squares with the already mentioned Buddhist aversion to metaphysics and also with the importance attached to a process or becoming view of existence and the centrality of *pratītyasamutpāda.* If the account seems inspired by Nāgārjuna, I admit such inspiration, but this is not the place to argue the historical question of Nāgārjuna's views on the subject, though I will suggest later that the thrust of this analysis is not at odds with Nāgārjuna's views.

Time is generally understood to have something to do with change, as evident in the common view that changes take place in time. In fact, it has been a historical commonplace to move from the view that changes take place in time to the view that time is a container of changing entities. This, in turn, has led to questions concerning the kind of thing this container is, and whether or not this thing is itself contained by a prior time. As has been done historically—in both East and West—one can continue to generate not only an unlimited number of times as containers for previous times but also a host of philosophical problems in trying to account for the natures of these times, and the relationships between these various times, on the one hand, and between any of these times and changing reality, on the other. However, this is a well-known story to anyone familiar with the history of philosophy, and if, as I believe most Buddhist philosophers do, you view the various historical attempts to take time to be part of the ontological furniture of the universe *as a mistake*, then the important thing is to see the genesis of this mistake.

If we begin with the common view that changes take place in time and that therefore time is, in some sense, a container of change, it is the innocent-sounding phrase "changes take place in time" that we must examine first. The phrase suggests that there are two things—change and time. But as soon as one reflects that the concept of change already involves the notion of time in some sense—for change logically involves succession, which is a time-laden concept—it is obvious that either the concept of time is already contained in the concept of change as a logical feature or part—in which case there is a redundancy in saying that changes take place in time, or else the "time" implicit in change is different than the "time" in which changes take place. If the "time" in which changes occur is the same "time" that is implicit in the concept of change and if that is the only concept of change recognized, it would seem that to take time as a container of change is a mistake. The source of the mistake is the entification of the conceptual elements present in the elucidation of change. The mistake consists in assigning ontological status to features of conceptual construction. On this account it might be said that although change is real, time is not. This, however, is misleading for it suggests that time is understood to be something more than the experienced succession in temporal becoming. If, on the other hand, at least two different senses of time are recognized—one, the temporal becoming or succession involved in change, and the other, the container in which temporal becoming takes place—one is faced with the problem of relationship between these two supposedly different but related temporal concepts. Again, either one or both of these "times" might be thought to be fundamental ontological entities, or else features of the conceptual ordering of experience.

In working toward a resolution of these issues it might be worthwhile to note that apparently everyone agrees that "time," in any of its senses, involves an ordering—an ordering of "nows" and "thens." This starting point does not enable one to escape the charge of circularity, for "then" and "now" are clearly temporal concepts. But it would be quite unreasonable to expect an analysis of time to reduce time to something nontemporal, for while circularity would be avoided, the reduction of the temporal to the nontemporal would be committed. Neither will this starting point resolve the question of whether the ordering involved is a part of reality independently of the workings of the human mind, or whether this ordering is a mental construction placed on a reality that in itself is devoid of such ordering. Since the history of debate between realists and idealists—in both East and West—makes clear that even if this issue is capable of resolution, it certainly has not yet been resolved, it might be best to start from a position that is neutral in this respect. Fortunately such a neutral position is available, for both realist and idealist begin with the admission that human experience reveals certain orderings in its contents. Reality as experienced is shown—by self-conscious inspection of this experience—to contain at least temporal and spatial orderings. The contents of experience reveal that some items are "here" rather than "there," and "then" rather than "now." If this be granted, it would seem that the proper place to begin an analysis of time and temporality is with the terms and relations "now" and "then." These terms correspond to the temporal ordering found in experience, and to provide a rational explanation of these terms and the implied relations, a conceptual system with certain theoretical terms sufficiently powerful to generate a satisfactory explanation is required.

The theoretical term that suggests itself is "time," which means that, for the sake of clarity, some other term is to be used for the experienced "now-then" ordering. The proposal is that we use the term "temporality" to refer to the experienced "now-then," which is not assignable ontologically to either a mental or extramental realm, because it is prior to these categories, and that we use "time" as a theoretical term, to cover the temporal terms and relations as these are understood conceptually.

One of the advantages of this analysis of time and temporality is that it enables us to recognize the universality of temporal experience as well as the particularity of varying concepts of time. Temporal experience is universal because temporality is an aspect or feature of human experience, and all experience contains ordered "nows" and "thens." On the other hand, there are many ways the temporal dimension of experience can be approached conceptually in an attempt to arrive at a theoretical understanding of it. Since, on this analysis, time represents the conceptual understanding and explanation of temporality, there can be as many "times" as there are different theoretical analyses of temporality as an integral feature of experience. Viewing time as a theoretical construct used to represent the interconnections among the temporal relations found in experience (and between these temporal relations and others, for example, spatial) in order to achieve a rational explanation of the temporal dimension of experience, it is reasonable to expect that religious, moral, political, etc. concerns present in the cultural conditioning of the theorist will influence both the sense of which aspects of temporal experience are most important, and, therefore, central to the theory, and the criteria of adequacy for the explanation. In this sense time is a culturally determined construct.

Before making some comparisons between Nāgārjuna's views and the above analysis, it is worth noting the similarity between this analysis and the view expressed by van Fraassen in his recent book on Western views of space and time. After reviewing various problems of the theory of time he says, "Our conclusion is that it is not necessary to say that there is such a thing as time, but that if we do, the best possible answer to the further question what kind of thing it is, is that it is a logical space."[3] By "logical space" he means something similar to what I intend by the characterization "conceptual construct to afford theoretical understanding," as is clear from his remark, "We characterize the notion of *logical space* by saying that a logical space is a certain mathematical construct used to represent certain conceptual interconnections."[4]

This view of time as a conceptual construct or logical space fits in well with Nāgārjuna's views on the subject. His analysis of time in chapter 19 of the *Mūlamadhyamakakārikā* is, as Kalupahana notes, directed primarily at the Sarvāstivādin, who took time to be an ontological container of change and divided the container into three segments: past, present, and future. The argument in chapter 19 that the Sarvāstivādin view that past time, present time, and future time are three ontological entities is fundamentally untenable, is concisely and accurately presented by Kalupahana. However, even though chapter 19, taken by itself, supports Kalupahana's conclusion that Nāgārjuna ". . . employed his dialectic to demonstrate the unreality or non-existence of time," it must be remembered that this conclusion (verse 3, "*tasmāt kālo na vidyate*") follows from the Sarvāstivādin view of time. All Nāgārjuna is denying here is the reality of time *as conceived by the Sarvāstivādins,* that is, time as an ontological reality containing change. It is entirely open for Nāgārjuna to accept that time does exist as a conceptual ordering of temporal experience. Indeed, if one looks to the purpose of the *Mūlamadhyamakakārikā* as a whole, it is hard to deny that this is Nāgārjuna's view, for the purpose of the entire dialectic seems to be to point out that our views or explanations of experience are conceptual constructs, and, therefore, should not be mistaken for the direct experience of reality itself. As Inada points out in the introductory essay prefacing his translation of the *Kārikā,* ". . . the argumentation lodged against all systems, positions or viewpoints (*dṛṣṭi*) by Nāgārjuna is not another way of establishing a standpoint, e.g. relativism, but it is a unique way of calling to attention the myriad and multiphased factors of conditions at play in the immediate concretizing karmaic present which, by the way, is the only locus whereby concourse with reality as such (*yathābūtam*) can be had."[5]

The most important clues to Nāgārjuna's view of time are found neither in chapter 19, devoted to arguments against the Sarvāstivādin view of time, nor in chapter 2, devoted to the temporal notion of "going," but are found in chapter 1, where he examines the conditions that are required for a conceptual understanding of reality. There he points out that understanding and description are possible only when the relational conditions of the experienced reality are determined. But, he argues, there is no way in which the relational conditions of our understanding can be equated with the relational conditions of experienced reality itself, concluding the chapter with the following assertion and skeptical (perhaps rhetorical) question: "Consequently, the effect (i.e., arisen entity) is neither with relational nor without non-relational condition. Since the effect has no existing status, where are the relational and non-relational conditions?"[6]

Now, if it is the case that all concepts and views are conceptual constructions placed on experience, then it follows that the concept of time is also a conceptual construction placed on experience (in this case the temporal dimension thereof). That Nāgārjuna accepts this position that conceptual views are constructs placed on experience seems evident not only in the *Kārikā* but also in his assertion, in verse 20 of the *Vigrahavyāvartanī*, that he has no theories of his own to offer (granted the reason that he offered no theory was his distinction between truth and theory). He does, of course accept *pratītyasamutpāda*, but it can be argued that this is simply to accept the *fact* of a temporal and spatial dimension of experience and not to accept a thesis about the intelligible structure of this dimension. Taken as a thesis about the connectedness experienced in change, *pratītyasamutpāda* is *śūnya*—as are all views or theses. The acceptance of *pratītyasamutpāda* as being the heart of the Buddhist *dharma*, on the other hand, makes clear that there is no rejection of temporality as the experienced succession in change.

With this distinction between time and temporality in mind we can move on to consider the significance of the Jātaka vision quoted in Kalupahana's essay: "Time consumes all beings / including oneself; / the being who consumes time, / cooks the cooker of beings." As pointed out, time here is equated with Māra, the personification of death, making time *the* dreaded evil in life. This is an interesting picture, present in varying images in most religions. Time, in the guise of change, devours all things, and the only paths to salvation are to either find an existence free from the influence of time—which means eventually coming to regard the temporal order as ultimately unreal or else to make one's peace with time and change, in effect adjusting one's lifestyle to "groove" with the fact of temporal becoming as the ultimate reality. Either alternative will enable one to escape the jaws of the monster, Death. The first alternative involves fleeing the realm of the monster, thereby escaping his clutches. The second alternative involves taming the monster, making time one's friend rather than enemy. The Buddhists, for the most part, chose the latter alternative, conquering time, whereas the Vedāntin way consisted in choosing the former alternative, leaving behind the terrible world of time for a peaceful world of permanence.

The choice of either alternative requires an analysis of time, with the Vedāntin having to explain the unreality of time at the ultimate level of reality, despite its apparent dominating reality as temporal becoming, and the Buddhist having to explain the nature of changing existence in such a way that it is clear the temporal conditionedness of existence does not imply *dukkha* when life is lived "properly" (that is, according to the *Dharma*). It is this explanation of the relation between change and *dukkha* that is crucial to the Buddhist philosopher.

When time is presented as the devourer of all things, it can be interpreted in different ways. One way is to take it as a metaphorical reference to the inevitability of temporal succession and the qualitative change found in this succession (for example, succession of birth by death). But it can also be interpreted to represent time as a real entity of some kind—part of the ontological furniture of the universe. In this case there might be an effort to show that the entire realm of entities to which time belongs are nonultimate or merely apparent, positing a realm of being beyond in which time does not exist. But from a Buddhist point of view such an interpretation, and the consequent effort to escape to a becomingless realm, would be a mistake resulting from the failure to understand that time is simply a conceptual construct. Although as McDermott convincingly shows through comparisons with certain Western conceptions of time, as well as citing the Sautrāntika arguments against them, that the Sarvāstivādins did submit to the temptation to entify temporal becoming, still, the main thrust of Buddhism is away from such entification and in the direction of seeing entities of all kinds as constructs of the mind.

If time is a terrible monster (personified as Māra) devouring all things, then *dukkha* cannot be eliminated until Māra itself is conquered or devoured, and so the question is: Does time inevitably devour man, or can man devour time? Since the Buddhist position is that *dukkha* can be eliminated, when *dukkha* is presented in the guise of Māra, the answer is clearly that man *can* devour time. As Kalupahana points out, " . . . the one who has attained enlightenment is able to bring time under his control." How is a person to "consume time" and therefore "cook the cooker" of beings (or, in other words, become enlightened?). Kalupahana gives two important reasons (with which I agree): (1) Eradicate the craving and attachment for existence or nonexistence. This means that the loss of existence in death is nothing to be feared in the least—in fact, logically it cannot be feared, (2) put an end to continued becoming (*bhava*). This means that neither death nor rebirth—with its consequent redeath—are possible.

The answer seems incomplete, however, for the question that nags is "how is it possible to overcome becoming if becoming is an inevitable feature of existence?" Here the distinction made earlier between temporality and time is helpful. Temporality—and in that sense, temporal becoming—is an inevitable feature of existence, and as such can never be overcome. But by the same token temporality is just that, a feature of existence as it is. It is neither evil nor good, but just temporality. It is neither birth nor death, but simply becoming. Time, on the other hand, as the container of becoming, when it is taken to be an ontological container rather than merely a conceptual container, can be taken as terminating and originating becoming (transferring it from the present to past, or from the future to the present), and thereby responsible for the inevitability of birth and death. So understood, time as the determining container of change is *dukkha*. However, when time is understood to be simply a conceptual ordering of temporality, with no real power to originate and terminate becoming, one is freed from time's bondage to an inevitable death. When one transcends the entrapment of concepts and no longer ontologizes conceptual existence, then the conceptual space of time loses its binding power, and *kāla* is "cooked."

1. Henry Clarke Warren, *Buddhism in Translations* (New York: Atheneum, 1963), p. 122.
2. Ibid., p. 124.
3. Bas C. van Fraassen, *An Introduction to the Philosophy of Time and Space* (New York: Random House, 1970), p. 106.
4. Ibid., p. 104.
5. Kenneth K. Inada, *Nāgārjuna: A Translation of his Mūlamadhyamakakārikā with an Introductory Essay* (Tokyo: Hokuseido Press, 1970), p. 18.
6. Ibid., p. 42.

Lewis R. Lancaster

Discussion of time in Mahāyāna texts

In the early Mahāyāna *sūtras*, the discussion of time (*adhvan*) does not mention the term in the singular, only in the plural: the three times of past, future, and present.[1] The problems of the triple time had occupied Buddhists long before the advent of the Mahāyāna texts and such schools as the Dārṣṭāntikas had proposed that the three times exist and are permanent while the conditioned entities which move through them are impermanent. They described their view by giving the analogy of three houses one beside the other. From the first house a man emerges and goes to the second, that is, he leaves the future and enters the present, then he moves from the second house to the third, thereby going from the present to the past.[2] Man is the impermanent and fleeting one while the three houses of time are fixed and stand always ready to receive the constant flow of impermanent things.

Since this idea of permanence and fixed state of the three times belonged to the non-Mahāyāna schools, we could expect to find arguments in the Mahāyāna *sūtras* attacking such positions. However, a careful reading of the earliest *sūtras* from the Mahāyāna shows that they did not directly refer to or attack such doctrines. That is, they did not try to disprove through debate or rhetorical devices the existence of one, two, or three times. Their approach is a positive one and not a defensive stance. The Mahāyāna *sūtras* merely state what has been understood and cognized by the Buddha,[3] it is not presented as a matter to be proved or disproved, but only as a statement of what is. The Buddha as an enlightened one possessed all-knowledge, the supernormal power developed through *samādhi* or trance and in this special state he was able to penetrate and comprehend the nature and essence of the three times.[4] When the triple times were viewed in this special way, they appeared to the Buddha as equals,[5] the same,[6] without distinctions or separations.[7] The times did not oppose one another,[8] for there was nothing in the present which was different or distinct from the future. This being the case, the *sūtras* say, the three divisions of time, the three characteristic marks of time, are limited to the mundane world, to those who lack the insights of the all-knowers[9]; but, on the higher level, the transcendent plane, these marks are shown to be an illusion. Therefore, the Buddha taught that the three times only possess one mark, the mark of lacking any distinguishing characteristics.[10]

Later, some of the Mahāyāna texts elaborated the doctrine that the three times are all equal and the same without distinctions. They reasoned that if the division of time into three parts was an inherently valid and real one, belonging to the very nature of time, then one must be able to delineate clear limits between the past and present or the present and the future.[11]

Lewis R. Lancaster is Professor of Oriental Languages, University of California, Berkeley.

But, say these texts, one cannot discover such limits, for the beginning of time is beyond comprehension and is never determined and the end of time stretches out endlessly without a limit.[12] Since the beginning and end of time can never be established, then neither can the middle of time.[13]

It was recognized that the determination of the sameness of the three times was beyond the capabilities of ordinary man. The *Ta Chih Tu Lun*, commentary of the *Prajñāpāramitā* compiled by Kumārajīva, states that those who do not have all-knowledge will encounter obstacles when they try to achieve a cognition of the three times.[14] Even such famous disciples as Śāriputra and Mañjuśrī were unable to comprehend this sameness fully. Thus, the Buddha has to resort to two methods when teaching about time: (1) When he teaches the penetration and comprehension of the three times without obstacles, this may be called his analytical teaching (*vibhajya-nirdeśa*); (2) But when he teaches that the triple times have not even a single characteristic mark, this is the teaching of limitless emptiness (*ananta-nirdeśa*).[15]

We can assume from this that the teaching, which is part of the process by which one attains special cognition, and the discussion about the resultant experience are two very different procedures.

If the triple times have not even a single distinguishing characteristic, does this mean that the Mahāyāna taught the nonexistence of time? It is never said that time is lacking existence, but only that time is empty (*śūnyatā*)[16] and that it is suchness (*tathatā*),[17] for since it lack any marks, it is the whole reality, the truly universal. But this is not only true for time, it is true of everything, for example, form, *skandhas*, *dharmas* all conditioned things.[18] Saying that the denial of any real characteristic mark is in fact the denial of existence would imply that the Mahāyāna *sūtras* are teaching a doctrine of nihilism, which they explicitly deny.[19]

It is true that the denial of characteristics limited to any one of the three times had implications for the theories of ontology. If no past can be determined, then you cannot say there is a past fire,[20] if no present, then how can you speak of a present fire; and if fire does not exist in the past, present, or future, then in what sense can you say it does exist? The answer is always that fire, men, and *dharmas* exist in a conventional mundane way, but in the transcendent realm, fire is empty of those characteristics which separate it from water, space, fuel, etc.

If the three times cannot be separated, the next question to be handled by these texts was whether one can establish the idea of long time and short time. While we might expect an immediate answer along the same lines as that used with regard to the three times, such is not the case in the *Avataṃsaka-sūtra*. In this text, it is maintained that our universe is but one of thousands of universes or world systems.[21] All of these worlds are not on the same scale, and so our own system is encapsulated within another realm that in expanse is beyond anything we can comprehend. We live, says the *Avataṃsaka-sūtra,* in the realm of Śākyamuni, and if we were to add up all the days and nights of our world system until they totaled a *kalpa,* these countless years would be equal to but one day and one night in the realm of Amitābha. And if one were to stay in Amitābha's realm for a *kalpa* of that time, it would be equal to one day and one night in the next realm of Vajrasaṃhata and one *kalpa* there would equal one day and one night in Dharmaketu's realm, and so on through hundreds of millions of Buddha realms.[22] It is interesting to note that the names for these realms, which reach out beyond our possible understanding, are in part the names of the former Buddhas described in the *Lalitavistara,*[23] where fifty-four names are given as part of the endless list of Buddhas who have existed in the aeons of the past. In the *Avataṃsaka-sūtra,* these Buddhas of the past have been transformed into the dwellers of the realms which stretch out into endless time and space. On the other hand, one can turn around and look at the point of a hair or a grain of sand, and there, the text says, are contained a thousand worlds,[24] small beyond anything we can possibly imagine and one day and one night in our Śākyamuni Buddha realm, we can infer would be a *kalpa* of time in one of these. In this way, we can carry the description out to a point in which we have *kalpas* of time in one world system equal to a trillionth of a second in another.

The result of these descriptions of the realms and the length of time within them, is the negation of any limit, which can be termed "long" or "short." For what is long in one universe is short in another, and any such description or measurement is a mere convention based on our size and relative relationship.

Therefore, the *sūtras* once again bring us back to the emptiness of time, as well as to the difficulty of its comprehension, and absence of characteristic marks.

There is yet a third aspect of time which is not handled by the discussion of the three times or length of time. Man experiences change: he is born, grows old and dies, and all of his possessions eventually crumble and disintegrate. This is seen as the action of time; time the all powerful force in life. In fact, time is more important and more powerful than death, for time touches animate and inanimate objects, it affects all at all times and not just a few who are in any given moment touched by death. This inevitability of time was part of the teaching of the *Atharva Veda,*[25] where time was personified as a horse galloping along with a water jar on his back and the jar was filled to the brim with water, but not a drop fell from the jar, for nothing and no one escapes the clutches of time. While the texts may argue about whether time can be divided into three or two or many, the fact remains that man and all he possesses is destroyed by time. And it is this characteristic that is the most difficult to handle, for it is not a question of mere speculation, it is the most intensely personal and confronting experience of life.

In Mahāyāna, as well as in Hindu Tantric literature Mahākāla, Great Time, became a major deity. It is Mahākāla, the "great howler," who is "beautiful yet ferocious," who shines like the "flame of the sun," with eyes that are "large shooting flames and at the center of them is an endless pool of darkness around which the edges are always flaming."[26] In his left hand he holds a staff, a three-pointed spear; in the right hand a skull bowl with blood and a great sword; his beard and hair are wildly streaming; and around his chest he wears garlands of severed human heads or sometimes skulls; his mouth is bloodied and he has long, sharp fangs. His hips are covered with a tiger's skin. In Tibetan calendars he is often depicted with the days and months of the year and all the creatures of the world caught between his dripping fangs, and he is endlessly consuming everything. In this we can see the aspects of Śiva and even the old Vedic deity Rudra,[27] the destructive life forces.

Little wonder then that Mahākāla, in later Mahāyāna was propitiated as a deity, a protective one, even though in his terrible aspect, he is the great destroyer. But what better protector to have than one who can destroy everything. In Mongolia and Tibet, Mahākāla became the chief of the guardians of the *dharma,*[28] and in one Sādhana we find the phrase: "O, you who tame the wicked beings please protect me, please protect me. Please give, please give, please destroy all (of them) . . . all the wicked ghouls, demons and half-men beasts, please make all of them peaceful."[29]

Is this an intrusion into Buddhism of non-Buddhist material, a tradition that is cut off from the main line of thought and development. The answer must be in the negative. For Mahākāla was the way in which the Buddhist handled the most overwhelming and personally important aspect of time. It is the terrible part of time, its destroying quality which frightens man. Here in the Tantras, the terrible is placated through magic and ritual, and Time the terrible becomes Time the protector. By the conversion of Time the destroyer, the killer with blood dripping from his lips, to the supportive guardian, the characteristic marks of destroyer and protector have been erased and there is no difference between Time in its dual nature. In the same way that the three times were shown to be empty and without definable limits, and as short and long were taught to be mere conventional expressions and not descriptions of reality, so too, the terrible and productive aspects of time are shown to be the same. Thus the major impact of the teaching about time in early Mahāyāna *sūtras* or in the later Tantras appears to be in agreement.

Now the question arises as to how we are to handle such material. Is it true that time has no definable divisions and that such divisions as we might make into past, present, and future, long and short, horrible and appealing, are not real divisions but only conventional expressions? Is time that is marked by having no special characteristic mark, such as present or past, to be considered as "time"? What of the admission by the texts that this material arises not from a reasoned argument or even logical thought processes, but from the special state of mind achieved by the Buddha when he entered *samādhi* or that special trance named "The *Samādhi* in which one sees that the three times are all equal and the same."[30] Are the texts correct in stating that those who lack all-knowledge will not be able to experience directly the three times as being the same? And is this special knowledge of a Buddha or a *bodhisattva* of any worth or of any importance to philosophers?

Nāgārjuna obviously felt that it was possible to take such material, derived from special mental states, and by subjecting it to reasoned arguments, show the validity of its teaching. Was he successful and is it possible for philosophers and logicians of today to do the same?

1. The numerous references to the Chinese texts will be given by *Taishō* document number and page only (hereafter abbreviated *T*). *T* 228–590c; 232–762b; 261–880c; 220 (16)–1102c; 1512–842b. For other references, see F. Edgerton, *Buddhist Hybrid Sanskrit Dictionary* (New Haven, Conn.: Yale University Press, 1953), p. 18; E. Conze, *Materials for a Dictionary of the Prajñāpāramitā-sūtras* (Tokyo: Suzuki Research Institute, 1969), p. 19.

2. *T* 1545–393a; *Kathāvatthu,* ed. A. C. Taylor, (London, PTS, 1964–1967), xv. 3, ix. 12.

3. *T* 228–630c; 234–747c; 1509–255a; 310–291b; *L'Abhidharmakośa de Vasubandhu,* tr. and ann. Louis de la Vallée Poussin (Paris: Paul Geuthner, 1923), II, p. 253.

4. *T* 234–747c; 225–507c; 279–648b; 657–166b.

5. *T* 228–590c; 231–723c; 240–776a.

6. *T* 244–789a; 240–776a; 310–252c and 517c; 257–245c.

7. *T* 234–747c; 231–723c; 244–822c.

8. *T* 220(4)–823b; 220(5)–937c; 240–776a.

9. *T* 310–291b; 228–630c; 234–747c; 1509–337c.

10. *T* 1509–225a; 228–630c; 220(1)–340b.

11. *T* 220(3)–436a–b and 515c.

12. *T* 244–822c; 228–590c; 257–245c.

13. *T* 220(5)–869; see Frederick J. Streng, *Emptiness, a Study in Religious Meaning* (New York: Abingdon Press, 1967), pp. 196 and 205, for a translation of the *Mūlamadhaymakakārikās.*

14. *T* 1509–255a.

15. Ibid.

16. *T* 222–203c.

17. *T* 220(4)–823b; 220(5)–937c.

18. T. R. V. Murti, *The Central Philosophy of Buddhism,* (London, George Allen & Unwin, 1970), pp. 165ff.

19. Ibid., p. 164; *T* 220(6)–1091.

20. *T* 220(1)–340b; 1509–330b and 337c.

21. *T* 279–241a.

22. Ibid., p. 241a.

23. *T* 187–539c.

24. See the discussion of C. C. Cheng, *The Buddhist Teaching of Totality* (University Park, Penn.: Pennsylvania State University Press, 1971), p. 5.

25. *Atharva Veda Samhitā*, tr. W. D. Whitney (New Delhi: Motilal Banarsidass, 1962), see 19:53.

26. These descriptive phrases were taken at random from an unpublished manuscript by William Stablein titled "Mahākāla." Parts of this will be available soon in his dissertation from Columbia University.

27. V. Fausböll, *Indian Mythology according to the Mahābhārata*, Luzac's Oriental Religious Series 1 (London: Luzac and Co., 1903); *Mahābhārata*, tr. P. C. Ray (Calcutta: Bharata Press, 1890), see 7504–7510.

28. Stablein, p. ix.

29. Ibid., pp. 24ff.

30. *T* 1509–306c; 225–507a; 279–684b.

THE BUDDHIST DOCTRINE OF FLUX

Satkari Mookerjee

The Nature of Existence

The whole universe of reals has been classified by the *Naiyāyikas* under two exclusive heads, *viz.*, *kṛtakas* (products or perishable) and *akṛtakas* (non-products or imperishable). The *Vātsīputrīyas*, an independent school of Buddhists, however, have grouped all realities under two classes, *viz.*, *kṣaṇika* (momentary) and *akṣaṇika* (non-momentary). Whatever principle of classification be adopted, the conclusion is inevitable that non-eternal entities must be momentary, as they are perishable by their very nature and constitution. Now, if a thing is perishable by its very nature and consitution, it will perish in the very next moment of its birth independently of the service of an external agent. If, however, it is not constitutionally perishable, it must be imperishable and no amount of external force, that may be brought to bear upon it, can make it cease to exist, as a thing cannot forfeit its own nature and assume that of another and yet continue to remain the same entity as before. And there is no medium between momentary and non-momentary, the two classes embracing the whole universe of thought and reality. To suppose, therefore, that a thing may be perishable by its nature and constitution and yet must be dependent upon an external agent to bring about its destruction, involves a necessary absurdity.

It has been urged that as a thing is seen to perish in a determinate place and time, its destruction must be contingent upon an extraneous cause and so long as this destructive agent does not appear, it will naturally continue to exist. The hypothesis of spontaneous destruction is opposed to experience and hence unacceptable. There is no absurdity in supposing that a thing may be perishable by nature and yet may be dependent on an external cause for its destruction, quite as much as a seed, which, though possessed of a natural aptitude for producing a sprout, is seen to effectuate a sprout subject to its association with water, air, soil, and the like and not independently. Experience also shows that hard metals like copper and the like are liquefied, when impinged upon by the flames of fire, but revert to their pristine condition of hardness when the heat communicated by fire is withdrawn. A jug continues to exist until it is crushed by the stroke of a club. So the dialectic of natural constitution—that if a thing is perishable by its nature it will perish by itself—should be accepted with a qualification, in the light of experience, *viz.*, as subject to action by a destructive agent.

The whole argument of the opponent, however, is vitiated by a misreading of facts. The analogy of the seed is pointless as the seed *per se* is not the cause of the sprout, but the particular seed-entity, vested with sprout-producing efficiency, that emerges in the final stage immediately before the sprout is produced. The hard copper is no firm and obdurate entity but is in continual flux ; and when associated with the subsidiary causes, fire and the like, it gives rise to another distinct entity liquid in nature and, when other circumstances supervene, the liquid moments disappear and hard moments manifest themselves. The theory of an external, destructive agent, on the other hand, gives rise to logical complications. The destructive agent, requisitioned for the destruction of an entity, can be posited if it has any effect on the thing to be destroyed ; but this effect will transpire to be illusory on examination. Well, what can be the nature of this effect ? Is it the production of another entity or non-existence of the previous entity ? On the former alternative, a destructive agent has no useful function, as a thing is brought into existence by its own proper cause, which is the immediate, antecedent entity. And to say that the cause of a succeeding event is the cause of the destruction of the previous entity is to say that destruction is self-caused and spontaneous, which is our position. The second alternative that the destructive agent causes non-existence of the previous entity is equally untenable, as only an entity can be produced and non-existence being produced will be an entity—which is absurd. And if this supposed non-existence is identical with the thing that is produced; the cause of destruction as distinct from the previous entity need not be postulated. Moreover, the destructive agent must be supposed to produce an effect on the thing to be destroyed. And is this effect something distinct from the thing on which it is produced or not distinct ? If distinct, it will not destroy the thing, as there is no relation between the two. On the latter alternative, it is useless as nothing new is produced. Aviddhakarṇa, an old *Naiyāyika*, whose opinions are frequently quoted in the *Tattvasaṁgraha*, but who has been entirely forgotten by the later Brāhminical writers, has taken strong exception to the Buddhist position that destruction is spontaneous. He argues, destruction is neither contemporaneous with, nor antecedent to, an entity, but a subsequent event occurring in the next moment, as the Buddhist too would have it. And so being an event occurring at a determinate point of time it must have a cause and cannot be spontaneous.

Uddyotakara, again, has attacked the Buddhist position in the following arguments : if destruction is uncaused, it will be either non-existent like a barren woman's son or an eternal entity like ether (*ākāśa*), as no medium is possible between the two. If it is non-existent, all entities will be eternal, as they will not be subject to destruction and consequently the conception of perishability of all composite bodies will be an unfounded myth. If it is eternal, it will co-exist with all entities—an absurd position, as existence and non-existence, which is the connotation of destruction, are mutually contradictory. If co-existence is denied, there will be no birth, as eternal destruction will preclude all production.

All the objections, the Buddhist rejoins, proceed from a confusion of the meaning of the word 'destruction!' Now, this word, 'destruction' can have two possible meanings: in the first place, it may mean the fluxional nature of all entities; in the second place, it may connote absolute cessation of existence (*bhāvasvarūpa-nivṛtti*). Destruction in the first sense does not connote any negative idea; it only implies that things are in a state of continual flux, that an entity endures only for a moment, yielding place to another entity emerging into being. So if destruction means the fluxional nature of an entity, it does not militate against our position, as we also admit it to have a cause, but as the cause is inherent in its own constitution and nothing foreign to its nature, we style it uncaused. But this fluxional character is nothing distinct from the entity itself and as such cannot be regarded as a subsequent event in regard to its own self, although there is nothing to prevent it from being conceived as a subsequent event in regard to the immediately preceding entity. Destruction in this sense exists and accordingly the conception of the perishability of composite bodies (*saṁskṛta*) is not an unfounded illusion.

Destruction, in the sense of absolute cessation of existence, is, however, an unreal fiction. Pure negation is an abstract idea and has no existence and so cannot be an event, which means the coming into existence of an entity which was previously non-existent. It is as unreal as a sky-lotus and to affirm existence, previous or subsequent, of it is an absurdity. When we say that there is a cessation of existence, we only mean that a thing passes out of existence and not that non-being exists or occurs. It is a meaningless expression. What we seek to establish is that cessation of existence in the sense of pure non-being cannot be an objective category. So the contention of Uddyotakara that the negation of non-being will entail eternal existence of all entities falls to the ground, because all real beings, fluxional in nature, will pass out of existence in the second moment without any gratuitous help from an external entity. The whole contention of Uddyotakara proceeds on the assumption that negation is an objective category, but, as we have seen, it is only an ideal fiction and not a concrete fact, as the *Nyāyavaiśeṣika* school postulates.

The whole allegation of Uddyotakara, that all uncaused entities are either eternal verities or non-entities and negation being an uncaused fact will be eternal, has no force against the *Sautrāntika* philosopher. The *Sautrāntika* does not admit any eternal, uncaused category. The *Vaibhāṣikas*, however, allege that there are three eternal verities, *viz.*, *ākāśa* (space) *pratisaṅkhyānirodha* (dissociation of the mind from impurities effected by transcendental knowledge) and *apratisaṅkhyānirodha* (non-emergence due to absence of causes).[1] But these *Vaibhāṣikas* are not regarded by us as the true followers of the Buddha. They are grouped along with the other heretical schools of thought, *viz.*, the *Naiyāyikas* and the like. The *Sautrāntikas*, who maintain the doctrine of universal flux, have no place in their scheme of realities for an uncaused category. These so-called eternal verities are ideal fictions (*sāṁvṛtas*), pure and simple. Uddyotakara in fathering this doctrine upon the *Sautrāntikas* only betrays his ignorance of the Buddhist position.[2]

As regards the so-called non-perishable entities such as space, time, God and the like, they are mere fictions of imagination

[1] The import and nature of these three eternal categories of the *Vaibhāṣikas* will be elucidated in the chapter on *Nirvāṇa*.

[2] 'Yaccoktam akāraṇam bhavato dvidhā nityam asacceti, tat parasiddhāntānabhijñatayā, yato nyāyavādinām bauddhānām akāraṇam asadeva ...., ye ca Vaibhāṣikā ākāśādivastu sattvena kalpayanti, te yuṣmatpakṣa eva nikṣiptā na śākyaputrīyā iti na tanmatopanyāso nyāyāt '—Kamalaśila Pañjikā, p. 140, *Tattvasaṁgraha*.

and do not exist as objective realities, as the connotation of reality is causal efficiency (*artha-kriyākāritva*) and no causal efficiency is predicable of them. And if these be real entities, as you claim, they must be momentary existents, as causal efficiency is predicable only of things that are momentary. No other definition of reality except causal efficiency can be logically sound. Let us examine the definitions of reality as proposed by the *Naiyāyikas*. *Sattāsambandha* or *sattāsamavāya* (participation or co-inherence in universal existence) is not a tenable definition, as *samavāya* is a form of relation and all relations are unreal. And even if it is allowed, universality (*sāmānya*), particularity (*viśeṣa*) and co-inhesion (*samavāya*), which do not participate in the universal, will have no existence. Nor is the attribution of a *sui generis* existence to each of them a clever hypothesis, as this means too many different types of existence. Moreover, these tentative definitions are confuted by the following dilemma: Is this *sui generis* existence (*svarūpasattā*) something different from existence as such or not different ? In the former alternative, it will be non-existence and the categories concerned will be unreal. In the latter, the *sui generis* existence will be unmeaning, as there is nothing to differentiate it from existence as such and the categories will be lumped into one. So also with regard to the other categories, *viz.*, substance, attribute and action. If they are identical with existence as such, there is no excuse of their being regarded as separate categories and if they are different, they will have no existence of their own. So we see that the very categories of the *Naiyāyika* are reduced to unreal fictions by his own definition.[1] The poor *Naiyāyika* finds himself

[1] The universal (*sāmānya*) cannot participate in any other universal, as this will lead to infinite regression. The universal too cannot be attached to particularity, as in that case the particular will cease to be particular, if it becomes universal in any form. Co-inherence is regarded as one, invisible, eternal relation obtaining between the universal and the particular, substance and attribute, part and whole. There can be no universal relating to this entity, as the idea of the universal presupposes a number of concrete

in the predicament of defining existence as one that is 'existence,' which amounts to a confession of failure.[1]

But what does demarcate such unreal fictions as a rabbit's horn and the like from things which are real ? Well, it is causal efficiency alone and as these fictions cannot possess any causal efficiency, they must be set down as unreal. An objection has been raised that reality cannot be supposed to consist in causal efficiency, as causal efficiency exists even in such unreal fictions as a sky-lotus and the like. These fictions certainly generate an impression in the mind and thus have causal efficiency in that respect, but they cannot be accepted as real on that account. Moreover, in dreams and illusions, unreal things are seen to have practical efficiency. The false snake in the rope is as much a cause of trepidation as the real one, and sometimes a man is seen to develop all the symptoms of poisoning and on some occasions to die, because he was falsely persuaded that he was bitten by a snake. And a dream-elephant is seen to be as powerful as a real elephant of our wakeful experience. If you make causal efficiency the sole test of reality, you will be painfully obliged to accord reality to those fictions.

The Buddhist replies that predication of causal efficiency relates to an objective reality and does not include subjective fictions. In dreams and illusions the objects that are experienced, are not real, objective facts, but are evolved from the imagination. The contents of these experiences are but the objectified memory-impressions and have no existence, outside the experiencing mind. It will be a sheer perversion of facts to apply to these mental fictions the standard of reality, which belongs to objective facts. Such unreal fictions, as sky-lotus and

individuals sharing in it and as *samavāya* is one, the question of its being a universal cannot arise. See *Kirṇāavali*: vyakter abhedas tulyatvaṁ saṅkaro 'thā' navasthitiḥ | rūpahānir asambandho jātibādhakasaṁgrahaḥ ||

[1] Compare in this connexion the observations of Prof. Mctaggart in his 'Nature of Existence,' Ch. I. Sec. 5.

the like, are purely subjective facts without any objective foundation and as causal efficiency has been postulated as the test of an objective reality, it cannot have any application to these fictitious representations of the imagination. When we deny causal efficiency to these ideal fictions, we deny it in the sense of their being objective realities. All these objections could be enforced if we held with Kumārila and the *Naiyāyikas* that illusions and dreams were conversant about realities.[1] But according to our theory these experiences are purely subjective and are absolutely devoid of any objective reference. Causal efficiency therefore stands unrefuted as the test and definition of reality, as reality connotes real, substantive facts and not subjective fictions.[2]

And causal efficiency is exercisable either in succession or simultaneity and as simultaneity and succession are incompatible with the supposed permanent entity, causal efficiency is restricted to the momentary, fluxional entity alone. One may legitimately enquire: Why is it that practical efficiency cannot be predicated of a non-fluxional, permanent entity? Because it is redargued by the following dilemma: Has your "permanent" power of past and future practical efficiency during its exertion of present practical efficiency or no? If it has such power, it cannot fail to execute the past and future actions exactly as it does its present action, because the execution of an action is the inevitable consequence of such efficiency, which it is conceded to possess. And there is no reason why there should be any delay in the effectuation of such actions as the causal

[1] Kumārila holds that even memory and dream experiences contain an objective reference like perception. The contents of these experiences are real, objective facts, though in dreams and illusions these facts are presented under a wrong spatio-temporal relation. Nothing but an existing fact can become an object of experience and so the objects of dreams and illusions even are real facts though the spatial and temporal relations are perverted, *cf.* "svapnādipratyaye bāhyaṁ sarvathā nahi neṣyate | sarvatrālambanaṁ bāhyam deśakālānyathātmakam ||" *Śloka-vārttika*, p. 242.

[2] *Vide Tattvasaṁgraha*, verses 425-427.

efficiency is present intact. The point at issue can be brought home by the following argument.

That, which has causal efficiency in respect of anything, does execute that thing without fail, as for instance the full assemblage of causes. And this entity has past and future causal efficiency (and should therefore execute the past and future actions without fail). On the second alternative (if the permanent has no such efficiency of past and future agency), it will never do those actions, as exertion of practical efficiency results from power alone. The privation of past and future efficiency in the permanant can be specifically driven home by the following syllogism: What at any time does not do anything, that at that time is incapable of doing it, as for instance, a gravel is unable to produce a sprout. And this "permanent" does not execute its past and future actions during its execution of present action (and consequently does not possess the power for the same).

It is proved beyond doubt that this supposed "permanent" has present practical efficiency, but it does not of a surety possess its past and future efficiency. And as co-existence of efficiency and non-efficiency, two contradictory qualities, is not possible in a single entity, the conclusion is irresistible that the present entity is distinct from the past and the future entity and is thus fluxional. It may be urged that causal efficiency may exist in a thing without the effect being produced and this is confirmed by the fact that the seed in the granary is regarded as the cause of the sprout, though the sprout is not immediately produced. But this objection is based upon a misconception. In ordinary parlance, a remote, possible cause is said to possess causal efficiency. But this is a loose, popular conception and cannot be made the basis of a philosophical enquiry. In reality, however, the cause of the sprout is the peculiar seed-entity that immediately and invariably produces the sprout. The seed in the granary is regarded as the cause of the sprout only in view of a remote possibility. So there is no room for confusion between a real cause, which is immediately and invariably attended with an effect, and a remote possible cause, which can be regarded as a cause only by courtesy.

But the *Naiyāyikas* and other realists demur to accept the position of the Buddhist set forth above. They urge that fluxional cause could be accepted if the invariable concomitance of causal efficiency with momentariness was established. But this is impossible. It is quite plausible that a permanent entity, though it is the sole and sufficient cause, can exercise its causal efficiency only in conjunction with subsidiaries and as these subsidiaries occur in succession, successive execution of past and future actions is not incompetent to a permanent cause. The cause does not independently produce the effect as it develops its causal efficiency only in association with its subsidiaries. The production of the effect is contingent upon the co-presence of the subsidiaries and so does not take place when the set of subsidiaries is absent. The presence and absence of the subsidiaries, however, do not at all affect the real nature of the cause, as the cause is entirely distinct from them.

The co-presence of subsidiaries, the Buddhist observes, is an idle hypothesis. If the permanent develops its causal efficiency on its own account and is not at all assisted by the subsidiaries, the latter become absolutely useless. And if the peculiar effect-producing efficiency, that manifests itself in the last moment, is identical with its past nature, nothing can prevent the production of the effect.[1] If this nature is a different one, you cannot claim the previous entity as the cause. And if you suppose that the cause has not undergone any mutation, production becomes impossible, as its previous inefficiency will persist. But it may be contended that the permanent entity is one of the causes, and not the sole and sufficient cause. It is the entire collocation of causes (*sāmagrī*) that produces the effect and not the cause alone, however powerful it might be. The relation between cause and effect is not one of mutual necessary implication (*anyayoga-vyavaccheda*), but non-separation with one term

[1] *Vide* SBNT., p. 27, 11, 6-9.

lying independent (*ayogavyavaccheda*) as in invariable concomitance (*vyāpti*). Thus, as in *vyāpti*, the *probandum* can exist without the *probans*, though the *probans* cannot, so also a cause can exist independently of the effect, though not the effect. And in this conception of causal relation the popular view and philosophers' estimate do coincide.[1]

Well, we Buddhists, have no quarrel with you on the point that several factors combine to produce a self-same effect. What we contend for is that a permanent cause cannot *ex hypothesi* stand in need of any auxiliary factors. If the invariable efficient or inefficient nature of the permanent continues, there will be either production or non-production of the effect for all times. So there is no logic in the position of the upholders of the permanent entity that it is the full collocation of causes and not a single cause, that is productive of the effect. We have it from experience that several causal factors combine to produce a self-identical effect and we do not challenge this position. But the point at issue is whether the "permanent" undergoes any mutation or not. If there is no mutation, either production or non-production will be inevitable, as indicated above. If,

[1] Tasmād vyāptivat kāryakāraṇabhāvo 'py ekatra anyayogavyavacchedena, anyatra ayoga-vyabacchedenā' va boddhavyaḥ, tathaiva laukikaparīkṣakānāṁ sampratipatteḥ (*op. cit.*, p. 37). *Vyāpti* is the invariable concomitance of the *probans* (middle term) with the *probandum* and this is the very ground and *conditio sine qua non* of all inference. This relation is stated in the major premiss of Aristotelian syllogism, in which the middle term is invariably distributed, though not necessarily the major term, which may be taken in its entire or partial extension according to circumstances. Accordingly *vyāpti* has been spoken of as of two distinct types, to wit (1) *samavyāpti* in which the two terms are co-extensive and (2) *asamavyāpti*, in which the *probandum* is of wider extension than the *probans*. The contention is whether the relation of causality is of necessity one of co-extensive concomitance or may be a relation of unequal extension with one term wider than, and hence independent of, the other. The Buddhist maintains the former view and the *Naiyāyika* affirms the latter possibility with emphasis.

however, the permanent mutates, it ceases to be permanent. And this dilemma is unavoidable. No reliance again can be placed on recognition ((*pratyabhijñā*), on the strength of whose testimony the unchanged identity of the cause could be established. Recognition is an unsafe guide, as we see there is recognition even in the case of growing hair and nails and the like. Apparently therefore the relation of cause and effect is one of mutual necessary implication and not non-separation with one term lying independent, as the *Naiyāyika* affirms. The analogy of *vyāpti* is inapplicable, as *vyāpti* is a relation between two concepts and not entities and as concepts are remotely related to reals, the relation is found to congrue with facts. But the cause, you posit, has a real existence as distinct from conceptual existence.[1] An objection is sometimes raised in this connection that as there is no permanent entity, according to the Buddhist, he cannot have any experience of such, much less can he make it the term of a syllogistic argument. And if he has direct or indirect experience of such permanent entity, he cannot consistently deny his own experience. When he asserts that the "permanent" cannot have causal efficiency, he admits the existence of the permanent and cannot deny it without contradicting himself. The objection is a frivolous one, but will be dwelt on at length in a separate section, because the *Naiyāyikas* have made capital out of this.[2] Suffice it to say here that the

[1] tasmāt sākṣāt kārya-kāraṇa-bhāvāpekṣayā ubhayatrāpy anyayoga-vyavacchedaḥ. vyāptau tu sākṣāt paramparayā kāraṇamātrāpekṣayā kāraṇe vyāpake ayogavyavacchedaḥ kārye vyāpye anyayogavyavacchedaḥ ......vikalpārūḍharūpāpekṣayā vpāptau dvividham avadhāraṇam. SBNT., pp. 38-39.

[2] *Cf.* 'The Nature of Existence:' "It has been objected to this that, *e.g.*, the fourth angle of a triangle must be real, if we can predicate anything of it with truth. And thus any predication of unreality would contradict itself. But this seems to me to be mistaken. In order to make any predication about anything, I must have an idea of that thing, and the idea—the psychical event in my mind—must be real. But a real idea of such an angle does not involve the reality of the angle." P. 1, fn. 2.

permanent in our syllogism is a hypothetical entity and not an experiential fact. What we mean by the "permanent" is this: if the nature of causal efficiency, that is evinced in the subsequent entity, be the same with the nature of the previous entity, or if the inefficient nature of the previous entity be identical with the efficient nature of the subsequent entity, there will be either production or non-production of the effect always. So we do not go beyond our experiential data, as the efficient and the non-efficient momentary entities are real objective facts. What we seek to prove is that there can be no identity between the two entities on pain of either of the undesirable issues, *viz.*, constant production or non-production.

It has been sufficiently proved that a self-sufficient permanent cause can have no need of auxiliaries, which can have no function. If, however, these auxiliaries are supposed really to assist the main cause, they can have a legitimate function and can become necessary. But if they assist, they will produce some supplementation (*atiśaya*) in the causal entity and the question naturally arises as to the nature of its relation to the causal entity. Is this supplementation something distinct or non-distinct from the thing on which it is produced? If it is distinct from the causal entity, then this adventitious supplementation will be the cause and not the non-fluxional entity; for the effect will follow, by concomitance and non-concomitance, the adventitious supplemetation.[1] In this case, causal efficiency will be possible only in the momentary, fluxional entity and not the permanent, which the opponent has sought to prove. If the supplementation is considered to be non-distinct, that is to say, identical with the permanent causal entity, we ask whether the previous inefficient nature continues or ceases to exist On the former alternative, there will be no production, as the previous inefficiency will operate as a bar. On the second

1 "tasmin sati hi kāryāṇāṁ utpādas tadabhāvataḥ | anutpādāt sa evaivaṁ hetutvena vyavasthitaḥ ||" T. S. Kār, p. 400.

alternative, the previous inefficient entity has ceased and a new entity identical with supplementation, designated in Buddhist technology as *Kurvadrūpa* (effect-producing object) comes into being and so the cause becomes fluxional.

The hypothesis of the permanent cause as discharging successive functions in association with successive subsidiaries, has transpired to be illusory. But there may be another alternative, *viz.*, that a permanent entity exerts its several causal efficiencies all at once and not in succession. But this will not stand the following dilemma. This "permanent," endued with the power of producing all its effects simultaneously, either continues to exist or does not continue after production of its effects. On the first alternative there will be production of all its effects just as much at one time as at another. On the second, the expectation of its permanency is as reasonable as expecting a seed, eaten by a mouse, to germinate.[1]

The *Naiyāyika* will perhaps seek shelter under his precious theory of *samavāya* (co-inherence)—a relation, which, they claim, has the miraculous efficiency of harmonising identity with difference. Certainly the subsidiaries produce some supplementation in the permanent causal entity, but the supplementation, though a distinct entity, coinheres in the causal entity and thus becomes a part and parcel of its being. But the question naturally arises that if the supplementation in question is something distinct, how can it have a relation with the basic entity without producing another supplementation. And this second supplementation, too, being a distinct entity, will hang loose and can be connected with the help of another supplementation and so on *ad infinitum*. The co-inherence theory thus transpires to be a dodge to take in the credulous, unenquiring fellows. But the never-ending series of supplementations is not the only difficulty in the theory of successive subsidiaries. There are

[1] dvitīye sthāyitvavṛttyāśā mūṣikabhakṣitabījādāv aṅkurādijanana-prārthanām anuharet. SDS., p. 24.

many-sided regressions in *infinitum*. There will be infinite regressions of all the factors involved in production. Thus, the seed, the subsidiaries, and supplementation are the three necessary conditions of production. We have seen that there will be a never-ending series of supplementations and these supplementations can be produced with the help of subsidiaries. And these subsidiaries can be of help if they produce supplementation in the supplementations themselves—otherwise they will not be required. Thus, there will be an infinite chain of supplementations afforded by the subsidiaries. So with regard to the basal cause and so with regard to the subsidiaries in their mutual relations. It is plain, therefore, that nothing can be explained by relations, as these relations will for ever fall apart and infinite regressions in each and every case will be inevitable. But the theory of flux is wonderfully immune from these difficulties—as it does not posit any relation at all. The factors being momentary units stand self-contained and self-sufficient.

Relations are requisitioned to harmonise permanence with change, but we have seen how they fail. Permanence and change, being mutually contradictory, cannot be made to constitute a harmonious whole even by virtue of these relations, which have been exposed to be hollow devices.

Trilocana,[1] the teacher of Vācaspati Miśra, contends that the whole controversy of the Buddhist turns upon a false basis. The permanent cause is absolutely independent of the subsidiaries and is not at all assisted or benefited by them. It is the effect

[1] **From frequent references to, and quotations of opinions of, Trilocana made by Ratnakīrti in his treatises on '*Apoha*' and '*Kṣaṇabhaṅgasiddhi*' it can be legitimately inferred that Trilocana was an author of repute and he must have written either a commentary or an independent standard work on *Nyāya* philosophy. It is certainly a pity that all his works are lost. That Trilocana profoundly influenced Vācaspati Miśra is not open to doubt, as the latter has recorded his debt to the former in unmistakable language. (*Cf*. Trilocana-gurūnnītamārgānugamanonmukhaiḥ | yathāmānaṁ yathāvastu vyākhyātam idam īdṛśam || Tāt. Ṭ., p. 133.)**

which is so benefited being dependent upon the subsidiaries as it cannot come into being if the set of subsidiaries be absent. For, causal power (*sāmarthya*) is of two kinds: natural and adventitious, the latter consisting in the presence of subsidiaries. There is no logical difficulty, therefore, that the cause does not produce the effect always, as the requisite power constituted by the subsidiaries is lacking. But this is mere shifting of the ground. How can the effect, which is not yet born, have any necessity for the subsidiaries? We could accept this view, however, if the effect could independently come into being. But then the subsidiaries and all that they connote become unavailing. If the effect is independent, how can the seed be the cause? And if the seed is the cause, why should it fail to produce the effect? Nor is it supposable that the effects are perverse and sometimes do not come into being inspite of the causes, as in that case they will not be the effects of those causes. But it may be contended that a particular entity is regarded as the effect of a cause, not because it happens when the cause is there, but because it disappears when the cause disappears. But this interpretation of causal relation is indefensible. Logically we can set down the absence of the effect to the absence of the cause, only if the presence of the effect is dependent upon the presence of the cause. Otherwise the effect will be independent of the cause and the disappearance of the cause will not entail the disappearance of the effect. So the presence of the cause must be invariably followed by the presence of the effect, just as much as the absence of it is followed by the absence of the other. Otherwise the so-called cause will cease to be the cause at all.[1] Nyāyabhūṣaṇa[2] however, contends that the argument, that a

[1] "tadbhāve'pi na bhāvaśced abhāve' bhāvitā kutaḥ |
tadabhāvaprayuktaśca so'bhāva iti tat kutaḥ ||" SBNT., p. 41.

[2] Nyāyabhūṣaṇa is the name of a very old commentary on the Nyāyasāra of Bhāsarvajña and it exercised a very pronounced influence on the later development of Nyāya thought and perhaps created a sub-section of

cause should discharge all its future functions even while it discharges its present function, because the future causal efficiency is present in it at the time, is a case of plain self-contradiction just like the statement—'My mother is barren.' How can the future causal efficiency function in the present? If it did, it would cease to be future efficiency. Certainly causal efficiency for blue cannot result in the production of yellow.

The contention of Nyāyabhūṣaṇa, Ratnakīrti observes, is but a mere jugglery with words. If the permanent cause possesses permanent causal efficiency, why should it function at some future time and not in the immediate present, on the basis of which future efficiency is postulated? The opponent may answer, 'because, we see it actually functioning in the future.' Yes, but as this is incompatible with its permanency, you should regard it as momentary. You cannot suppose that it is the nature of the permanent to function in the future, because such a supposition is logically absurd. A thing is supposed to have a particular nature only when there is logical necessity for such a supposition; and no hypothesis, however convenient, can be accepted if it violates the canons of logic.[1] The Buddhist

thinkers, who were called Bhūṣaṇīyās. See *Bibliography of Nyāya Philosophy* by Principal Gopīnāth Kavirāj and the introduction to *Nyāyasāra* by Dr. S. C. Vidyābhūṣaṇa.

[1] SBNT., pp. 41-42.

References:

T. S., śls. 350-546.

SBNT., pp. 20-53.

It may be interesting to observe in this connection that Mr. Bertrand Russell arrives at the same conclusion that there is no persistence in the world, each entity being momentary and the idea of persistence is only an illusion due to continuity in the series. He takes his cue from the cinematograph and avers that not only the cinema-man, but "The real man too, I believe, however the police may swear to his identity, is really a series of momentary men, each different one from the other, and bound together, not by a numerical identity, but by continuity and certain intrinsic laws. And what applies to men applies equally to tables and chairs,

therefore concludes that as the theory of permanent cause fails to explain facts and on the contrary introduces logical compli-

the sun, moon and stars. Each of these is to be regarded, not as one single persistent entity, but as a series of entities, succeeding each other in time, *and lasting only for a brief period, though probably not for a mere mathematical instant.*" (P. 129.) The Buddhist philosophers long ago anticipated Mr. Bertrand Russell and I am tempted to believe they are more logical and consistent than Mr. Russell. Mr. Russell seems to suffer from a confusion in this respect. His abhorrence for the "infinitesimal," which he borrows from modern mathematical speculations, is responsible for this aberration. Now, moments cannot be finite divisions of time, as this means that there are no moments at all. If a span of time consisting of many smaller divisions be regarded as the unit, the smaller divisions will have no meaning. The *mathematical instant*, of which he speaks, is not an empirical fact but a logical presupposition. Nor does the introduction of the "infinitesimal" re-open the gates of the puzzles of Zeno. The Buddhist philosopher does not admit the reality of motion. Motion is only a "logical construction" or a "symbolic fiction" to quote Mr. Russell's own words. There being no permanence anywhere in the world, no single thing can be in two places. The things are different and distinct. That the "arrow in its flight is truly at rest" (p. 81) is also the finding of the Buddhist philosopher, but only subject to a proviso, *viz.*, that the arrow is not one but many arrows successively appearing in the horizon, which give rise to the illusion of a persistent identity owing to continuity of similar entities. The Buddhist emphasises the aspect of similarity as the cause of the illusion of permanence, which Mr. Russell omits to emphasize. Continuity alone cannot be credited with this capacity for producing illusion, as continuity of dissimilar things does not have this effect. The syllables of a word are quickly uttered, but the quickness of succession does not stand in the way of their being perceived as discrete and distinct entities. So by continuity we must understand uninterrupted succession of similar entities, which should be emphasised for the sake of clarity and precision. The "intrinsic laws" of which Mr. Russell speaks, are regarded by the Buddhists as the law of causality, in the language of the Buddhist, as the law of relative origination (*pratītyasamutpāda*). The superstitions of ages which have clustered round the concept of cause have been smashed into smithereens by the sledgehammer blows of the Buddhist dialectic and it has been formulated in a manner which can be accepted without prejudice to facts. Mr. Russell seems to play into the hands of sceptics, when he declares

cations, which are insurmountable, the tneory of flux should be adopted as it is the happiest possible explanation of the world of reality.

the causal relation to be a mere case of probability. The failure of prophecy, by which he sets so much store, does not go against the law of causality. It is due to imperfect knowledge. The nature of the causal relation will be explained in the third chapter of the present book and to ask for a logical *à priori* explanation will lead to scepticism or idealism, as will be shown in Chapter IV. *Vide Mysticism and Logic.*

RITA GUPTA

THE BUDDHIST DOCTRINE OF MOMENTARINESS AND ITS PRESUPPOSITIONS

Dharmakīrti's argument in Hetubindu

All of us are familiar with the saying, "nāsau munir yasya mataṁ na bhinnaṁ – "none is a sage whose views do not differ from those of others". We find the adage in action in the highly edifying controversy regarding the momentary, or enduring nature of things that raged between the Buddhist and the Nyāya schools of philosophy. In this paper I shall try to highlight the main points around which the wrangle has been carried on by giants on both sides. My analysis in based chiefly on a study of the doctrine of momentariness as presented by Dharmakīrti in his *Hetubindu*.

I

Everything in the phenomenal world, according to the Buddha, is characterised by impermanence. This doctrine of impermanence of everything was later developed by the Buddhist philosophers as the doctrine of momentariness of everything. It was probably Dharmakīrti who, for the first time, presented to us, in a succinct manner, the logical arguments supporting this doctrine. The gradual elaboration and unfolding of his arguments are traceable in the works of Śantarakṣita, Kamalaśīla, Jñānaśrī and Ratnakīrti. I shall, however, confine myself here mainly to an analysis of the fundamental arguments which are contained in the theory as presented in Dharmakīrti's *Hetubindu*.

Buddhist logicians, led by Dharmakīrti, maintain that everything in the phenomenal world is in a flux in the sense that it comes into existence at one moment and goes out of existence at the next. How is it so? According to Dharmakīrti, anything, if it is to be called a really existent thing (as opposed to an unreal thing), must have some causal efficacy (artha-kriyākāritva). To put it more simply, '*to be*', *i.e.*, '*to exist*', *means* '*to do something*'. But, as indicated in the next paragraph, in order to be causally efficacious, a thing must be momentary. Thus, it follows that, according to the Buddhists, whatever exists and thereby has some causal efficacy, must also be momentary.

In support of their premise that everything in the phenomenal world is

Journal of Indian Philosophy 8 (1980) 47–68. 0022–1791/80/0081–0047 $02.20

causally efficacious, and, consequently, momentary, the Buddhists adopt the argument of *reductio ab absurdum* (*prasaṁgānumāna*). If a thing has causal efficacy and is, at the same time, non-momentary, i.e., enduring, then it would have to be characterised by two contradictory predicates. But the co-existence of contradictory properties in a thing is incompatible with the identity of the thing. Hence, for the sake of logical consistency, we must admit that an entity, to be causally effective, must be momentary. This is demonstrated in a more detailed way as follows:

Suppose a non-momentary thing, like a seed, having causal efficacy, produces another thing, viz., a sprout. Now, it can do its work only in two ways, either gradually (*krameṇa*) or instantly (*yugapat*). Let us analyse the first alternative. Let us suppose that the seed at $moment_1$ *is not the cause of the sprout*, but at $moment_2$ the seed becomes, or *is, the cause* of the sprout. Now, since the seed at $moment_2$ is *producer of the sprout*, and since the seed at $moment_1$ is *non-producer of the sprout*, therefore, it follows that the seed of $moment_1$ *must be different* from the seed of $moment_2$; (for, otherwise, we shall have to maintain the absurd position that an identical thing may be simultaneously the seat of two contradictory properties). Therefore, we are forced to admit that, to be causally effective in a gradual way, a thing must be momentary.

Let us now consider the second alternative of the seed producing its effect, the sprout, instantly. (Instances of this are available in such situations as the lock opening the instant the key turns to the required position.) Here we may reasonably ask, after having *finished* its job of producing the sprout, *all at one go*, at a particular moment, say $moment_1$, what is the seed supposed to do at a subsequent $moment_2$? It cannot very well do the same thing that it did at $moment_1$. Nobody can kill a bird that has been killed already! Thus, we have to admit that the seed at $moment_1$ is *producer of the sprout* and at $moment_2$ it is *non-producer of the sprout*. Now, in order to avoid the absurdity of saying that two contradictory properties can belong to one and the same thing, it is obligatory on our part to admit that the seed at $moment_1$ *is different* from the seed at $moment_2$, and that in order to acquire instant causal efficacy a thing must be momentary.

But the Naiyāyikas say that if the Buddhists argued in that way, then they would be guilty of producing an Inconstant Reason (*anaikāntika hetu*).[1] Their Reason, "possession of contradictory qualities (of being *producer* and also *non-producer*)" ('*viruddha-dharmādhyāsa*') is not invariably concomitant ith what is to be proven,[2] "difference (between seed of moment$_1$ and seed f moment$_2$)" ('*bhinnatvaṁ*'). As a matter of fact, it is the *same seed* which as previously existing in the granary, and was *not producer* of the sprout, hich later came to *produce* the sprout in the field when it was assisted by ıxiliary causes like water, earth and sunshine. Therefore, the Buddhists ould be forced to admit that the existence of the seed in the granary re- resents one *stage* of the same seed. Can any one claim that the seed in the eld, which is soon followed by the sprout, is a totally different entity from e seed in the granary?

But the Buddhists reply that they are not guilty of advancing any such efective reasoning as the Naiyāyikas are trying to foist on them. To be onsistent, one has to admit that the seed in the granary is different from the ed in the field which actually produces[3] the sprout. The seed in the granary annot, in strict sense of the term, be said to be the producer of the sprout. he productive power of a thing must be its intrinsic property. That being e case, if the seed in the granary had such a power, then why could it not oduce the sprout even while staying in the granary? Why did it have to epend on the so-called auxiliary conditions?[4] If that seed were never able to oduce the sprout by itself, if it were *necessarily dependent* on the so-called uxiliary conditions' in order to produce, should we not, in all fairness, say at the seed necessarily lacked productive power? Should we not say that e so-called auxiliaries are producing the sprout? Why should we label the ıxiliaries as mere 'helpers'? Therefore, productivity can be ascribed only to ıch a thing which is intrinsically capable of producing its effect, and as ıch produces it immediately without depending on anything else (*akṣepa- iyā-kāritva*). Accordingly, one should be forced to admit that only the *int action* in the last stages of the seed (*antya-bīja* = *kurvad-bīja*), water, ınshine, etc., which is immediately followed by the appearance of the rout, is the *real producer* of the sprout. How could the seed in the granary en be called the producer of the sprout? From all this it would follow that ere is no identity between the seed in the granary (non-productive of the rout) and the seed in the field which actually produces the sprout.

There is no doubt that the seed in the granary appears to the ordinary eople to be the same as the seed in the field that actually gives rise to its fspring. Yet, the logic of their arguments, the Buddhists urge, will reveal to e intelligent people the absolute distinction between the two. The seed is at st existing in the granary. The moment the farmer takes it out and puts it in the pot in order to take it to the field it becomes conjoined with a differ condition, and that causal condition must initiate some change in it. And hence the seed is a different seed. When the seed is placed in the field it becomes related with yet another different condition. The causal potency (that condition must make the seed different from the seed in the pot. Once the field is watered the seed combines with yet another different causal complex consisting of water, sunlight etc. That confluence of causes makes the seed different from the seed in the dry field. The seed underground undergoes all sorts of changes as a result of its conjunction with more and more causal conditions from moment to moment, and in this way the proc of sprouting starts underground. [See *Hetubindu-ṭīkā*, p. 116]. When the process reaches some maturity, the tiny sprout comes out of the earth with which it was covered.

Innumerable metamorphoses happen to the seed underground although the details of the transformation are not visible to us. In the same way, countless changes happen to the seed from the moment of its being taken c of the granary to its being sown in the field though these changes are also not detected by the human eye. Hence, the seed in the granary is entirely different from the seed in the field which (assisted by certain conditions) ultimately brings the sprout to existence. The seed in the granary was produced by a tree. It was competent to generate only a similar seed and therefore went on generating a seed-series in the granary. The seed in the fi which ultimately begot the young plant could do so due to an assemblage c causes that are completely different from the causes attending the seed in t granary. The seed in the granary, which was not associated with earth, wate sunshine, etc., was endowed only with the potency to generate a similar see whereas the seed in the field, getting the contact of earth, water, etc., is capable of setting up the sprout. Hence, the two seeds are endowed with different causal potencies. Each of them, again, owes its origin to different causal conditions. Therefore, for the sake of logical consistency, one has necessarily to admit that the two seeds are different, in spite of the similari in their looks. From all this, it is also evident that a particular seed (*kimcid*) alone (which has been invested with a special capacity, due to its being the locus of various causal influences of different moments) is the matrix of a particular (kasyacit) sprout. The reason is that, that seed alone (and not the seed of the granary) is forthwith followed by the effect, the sprout. [See *Hetubindu*, p. 53. See also *Ṭīkā*, pp. 116–117].

II

The same matter is elucidated by the Buddhists in a more technical way as follows:

All the so-called auxiliary or co-operating causes of any offshoot, according to the Buddhists, are convergent streams of efficient moments. They are called 'creeping causes' (*upasarpaṇapratyaya*) inasmuch as theirs is a 'staccato' movement (since the former moment of such a cause is completely different from the later moment, one cannot be said to 'flow into the other'). At the meeting-point of such streams of efficient causes, a new series, the effect series, begins. [When the series of the moments of the said moisture, heat and seed unite the last moments of each of those series are followed by the first moment of the shoot. See below]. That meeting-point, which has been described in Buddhist philosophy as the locus (āśraya) of such streams of converging, 'creeping causes' (*upasarpaṇādi*), can alone be properly said to be the only capable cause of the effect, since that alone is followed by the advent of the effect. [See *Hetubindu*, p. 53. See also *Ṭīkā*, p. 117]. The ultimate moments of such efficient creeping causes are justly described by Dharmakīrti as "momentary entities which have neither any preceding nor any succeeding stages, and which are incapable of existing in a different manner and in a different place."

[teṣāṁ ca na pūrvaṁ, na paścān na pṛthag-bhāveti samarthān api pūrvā-para-pṛthag-bhāva-bhāvino doṣā nopalīyante see *Hetubindu*, p. 53.]

It is now evident that the Buddhists are not arguing with the help of an 'inconstant' (*vyabhicāri*) Reason. It cannot be said that the *same seed* is the recipient of two contradictory properties of 'fecundity' and 'infecundity', and yet it is an identical seed. The reason is: the last moments of each said series of seed, moisture, heat, etc., which are properly called 'causes', could not, by definition, be said to have *existed before*. The so-called 'former stages' of the seed, moisture, heat, earth, etc., are really the causes of the 'convergence' of the streams of seed-moments, moisture-moments, etc. This 'conflux' is, in its turn, capable of causing the emergence of the effect – the sprout. Hence, the so-called 'preceding stages' of the seed, water, earth, etc., could not be said to be the causes of the genesis of the seedling. (See below).

The Naiyāyikas can still agrue the case. They adroitly bring forth another objection against the Buddhists. It runs as follows:

As is obvious from the above, the Buddhists are reluctant to analyse the causal situation in terms of one main cause and other auxiliary causes merely *helping* the former in its job of production. They insist that the effect is the result of the *conjoint action* of a number of causal factors which are arbitrarily divided as the 'main cause' and its 'helpers'. But the Naiyāyikas point out that, in such a case, the multiplicity of causes should really result in the origin of a plurality of effects. Yet, experience show that, even though a number of causes and conditions may be present at the time of the production of the effect, the resulting effect is of one uniform nature. Does it not prove that the effect is produced by one main cause, which is merely *assisted* in its task by some auxiliary causes? Dharmakīrti meets this objection by pointing out that, in fact, each of the different causes and so-called conditions does indeed make its special contribution to the fact of the appearance of the effect. Take the case of the origination of an earthen pot. *At least* three causes are present here: (i) clay, (ii) the potter and (iii) the thread. Here the clay accounts for the earthenness of the pot, which character distinguishes the pot from things like trees which are not made out of clay. The potter (with his wheel) is responsible for the peculiar shape of the pot which distinguishes it from things lacking such shapes, e.g., the unmanipulated lump of clay. The thread also has its own contribution to make. It separates the earthen pot from the wheel and as such makes it different from the pot which could otherwise have been still attached to the wheel. Hence, it is quite evident that each of the three factors of the causal complex is responsible for one character or the other of the effect. Yet, we easily gloss over the details of the resulting thing, and wrongly think that, since the latter is a single entity like a pot, it could not be the end-product of three equally indispensable, different causes.[5]

One must not, however, conclude, Dharmakīrti reminds the critics, that the multiple conditions produce multiple, *separate* and *unrelated* effects. The various characters of the effect in question do combine to form a unitary effect. The earthen character of the pot is due to the lump of clay; and the particular shape of the pot is derived from the potter. Yet the earthenness of the pot cannot be conceived of as an entity completely different from the particular shape of the pot. Had they been completely different, it would have been possible to perceive that shape of the pot in abstraction, without having to perceive it as the sahpe of an *earthen* pot. In the same way, it would have been possible to perceive the earthenness of the pot in abstraction, without having to perceive the peculiar shape[6] in which the latter happens to be encased. As a matter of fact, the shape and the earthenness of the pot combine to form a unıtary effect.[7] And this explains why, on perceiving the form of the pot, one also perceives the earthenness of the pot, and the knowledge of the earthenness of the pot also brings in its fold the apprehension of the particular visual aspect of the pot.

> ["na ca tayoḥ śakti-viśeṣa-viṣaya-bhede' pi taj-janita-viśeṣa-bhedasya kāryasya svabhāva-bhedaḥ, mṛt-saṁsthānayor aparas-parā'tmatayā saṁsthāna-mṛd-rūpābhyāṁ tayor apratibhāsana-prasaṁgāt. *Hetubindu*, p. 49].

Men may come and men may go but this enlightened duel goes on, full-blooded. The Naiyāyikas bring forward another objection against the Budd-hists: since substance and attributes are two separate categories of being, the Buddhists are bound to admit that the clayness of the pot and its shape are two different entities, each resulting from its own cause, namely, the clay and the potter. [Hence, clayness and the shape really point to the existence of a *multiplicity* in a case which is erroneously believed to be a case of unity.] But the answer to this objection has already been given by Dharmakīrti by pointing out that, if the clayness of the pot and its shape were different (and completely separable) entities, then it would have been possible to perceive the one without the other. On the contrary, Dharmakīrti asks the Naiyāyikas, "Does your supposition, that the clayness of the pot is different from its shape, fare any better?" If the shape were different from the clay, why could the potter not produce them separately? The Naiyāyikas try to hold on to their position by urging that, since substance and quality naturally imply one another, therefore, the potter cannot produce them separately. But, then, Dharmakīrti points out that since substance is the substrate of its quality, and since the substrate and that which inheres in it are *naturally connected*, the role of the potter becomes redundant, here. The clay and the shape, then would themselves have been conjoined intrinsically, without the help of an extrinsic joiner, viz., the potter. But the Naiyāyikas try to get over this difficulty by arguing that although the shape as a quality must always be related to *some substrate* or other, yet what makes the shape a quality fit for being related to a *particular* substance (e.g., the clay of the particular pot) is the potter himself. If the *particular shape* intrinsically had the fitness for being conjoined to the *particular* clay, then the clay of the pot would have acquired the shape of the pot even before the potter exercised his productive activities!

Taking the cue from the opponents, Dharmakīrti urges: We would similarly like to argue that, although the clay could not remain without having some shape or other, and although a particular shape must be the shape of some thing or other, yet what makes the shape the shape of a *particular* thing (i.e., the pot), and what makes the pot have a *particular* shape, is the effort of the potter. It is the potter who makes the shape and the clay of a particular pot fit objects for entering into a special relation, known as the relation of '*tādātmya*' [Stcherbatsky, in his *Buddhist Logic*, vol. II, has translated the word 'tādātmya', misleadingly, as 'identity'. 'Tādātmaya' really stands for 'co-extensiveness', 'integral relationship' and other similar relations.] One can thus easily realise that the earthenness and the form of the pot are not two completely independent and separate entities. They are rather like the two ends of a pencil, or like the genus and the species. Although different, yet they necessarily imply one another. Hence, Dharmakīrti argues, it would not be unfair to say that the pot requires two different causes: clay and the potter. Each of them makes some contribution, though the result, the pot, is one uniform object. The shape of the pot and its clay are, thus, not separately and independently existing entities.

> ["api ca yadi saṁsthānaṁ bhinnaṁ mṛdaḥ, kulālaḥ kiṁ na pṛthak karoti. guṇasya dravya-paratantratvam iti na pṛthak karoti. tat-saṁsthanādhārātmakaṁ yadi svabhāvena tad dravyaṁ tat-saṁsthānaṁ vā tadādheyātmakaṁ, kiṁ kulālāpekṣayeti cet, na tataḥ paraspara-sambandha-yogyatā-pratilambhāt, anyathā vastuna eva yogyatā dharmateti prag api mṛt-piṇḍasya saṁ-sthāna-viśeṣa-sambandha yogyatve sati saṁsthāna-viśeṣeṇa-sambandha prasaṅgaḥ. evam tarhi sā yogyatā mṛddravyasya kulālād bhavatīti nānayoḥ svabhāva-bhedaḥ, bhede hi prāgvat prasajyeta. asti tāvat eka-svabhāvatve' pi kasyacid aneka-pratyayo-pādheya-viśeṣateti. na mṛt-saṁsthānayor eka-svabhāvatva-sād-hānāya nirbandhaḥ". *Hetubindu*, p. 49. See also *Ṭīkā*, pp. 96–98.]

The Naiyāyikas at this point try to hit the ball back into the opponents'

thing throughout the long course of its life history. And, is it not a wildly unjustified demand?

The Buddhist thinkers are not exactly making a demand as conteded above. What they urge is: we shall have to see whether the thing, whose identity is under consideration, still has the *capacity* to produce the thing which it produced before. If it no longer possesses such a capacity, it will not be 'regarded as the identical thing any longer'. Diamond has the capacity to make impression on glass. If a stone, closely resembling diamond in all other respects, nevertheless does not possess the aptitude to cut a piece of glass, how can it be designated as diamond? The distinction of different entities depends on their distinctive causal efficacies. As a result, if a thing is no longer in possession of its creative ability by virtue of which it has once brought about a particular effect, how can it still deserve to be called the same identical thing? If x had produced y at m_1, and if later, at m_2, it lacks this generative capacity, what reasons could we possibly have for regarding it to be the same thing? Thus, what the Buddhist philosophers are really demanding is that the distinction between one thing and another is determined by observing their productive ability. And this demand is, after all, not as unreasonable as it might seem at the first sight.

North Eastern Hill University, Shillong, India

ACKNOWLEDGEMENT

I am indebted to Professor B. K. Matilal for his generous help in the interpretation of some of the difficult passages of the *Hetubindu* and its *Ṭīkā*.

NOTES

1 See *Hetubindu*, pp. 45f. and *Ṭīkā*.

2 'Sādhya'.

3 We must point out that we are using the word 'producer' here in a loose sense. As a matter of fact, the Buddhists say that nothing at all is produced in the real sense of the term. Everything merely comes into existence 'depending' on some condition.

4 *Hetubindu*, p. 45.

5 *Hetubindu*, pp. 47–49.

6 I.e., the shape of the clay pot.

7 What makes it a composite unit is not, however, a particular substract of these qualities. It is rather the particular function which the shape and the earthenness serve

together, e.g., the job of drawing water with untensils of the shape of the pot.

8 "Tatra santānāśrayeṇa, viśeṣotpādanaṁ pratyayānāṁ saha-kriyocyate, na dravyāśrayeṇa". *Hetubindu*, p. 59. See also *Ṭīkā*, pp. 127–130.

9 One must not, however, think of the series as a static thing which had been existing previously, and which came to inherit some specialities as a result of coming into contact with some causal complexes.

BIBLIOGRAPHY

[1] *Dharmakīrtis Hetubinduḥ*, Teil I; Edited by Ernst Steinkellner Wien, 1967.

[2] *Hetubindu ṭīkā* by Arcaṭa Bhaṭṭa as found in *Hetubindu-prakaraṇam*, Gaekward's Oriental Series, No. CXIII, Baroda, 1949.

Discussion of the Buddhist Doctrines of Momentariness and Subjective Idealism in the Nyaya-sutras

By JWALA PRASAD

THERE is a difference of opinion among scholars as regards the exact significance of such *Nyāya-sūtras* as are supposed to refer to the doctrines of the Mādhyamika and the Yogācāra schools of Buddhism. It has also been suggested that probably some of these *sūtras* have been interpolated later on, possibly by Vātsyāyana—the author of the *Nyāya-bhāṣya*. After making a careful study of the *sūtras* in question, however, I have come to the conclusion that some of them, in any case, do not refer to the Buddhist doctrines at all, and form a natural and quite an integral part of the particular sections in which they occur, and that the theory which regards them as later interpolations is not justifiable.

First I propose to consider one such section of the *Nyāya-sūtras*, viz. iii, 2, 10, to iii, 2, 18, which, according to all the commentators beginning with Vātsyāyana, is supposed to contain a refutation of the Buddhist doctrine of momentariness (*kṣaṇika-vāda*). According to Vidyābhūṣaṇa these *sūtras* refer to the doctrine of momentariness, as found in the *Laṅkāvatāra-sūtra*, chap. vi ; and he also holds that *Sūtra*, iii, 2, 10, which forms the main basis for holding this view, has probably been interpolated by Vātsyāyana.[1]

Now improbable as it might appear that none of the many distinguished commentators should have been able to see the points which I am going to raise against this time-honoured view, I cannot help thinking that this particular section does not refer to the Buddhist doctrine of momentariness at all, and that the commentators have simply been carried away by the notions suggested by the term " *kṣaṇikatvād* " in *Sūtra*, iii, 2, 10. Some of the modern

[1] Vidyābhūṣaṇa, *History of Indian Logic*, pp. 120, 121. *Sūtra*, iii, 2, 10, being *Sphaṭike 'py aparāparotpatteḥ kṣaṇikatvād vyaktīnām ahetuḥ*.

scholars have noticed the abruptness and superfluousness of introducing such a topic in the middle of an altogether different discussion, and have, hence, suggested the theory of interpolation. I shall try presently, however, to show that the *Sūtras*, iii, 2, 1, to iii, 2, 17, form one whole section dealing with the transitory nature of cognition (*buddhi*), and that the discussion contained in it refers only to the Sāṃkhya view, according to which the *buddhi* is a permanent and abiding faculty. That these *sūtras* were once looked upon as forming one section and as referring to the topic of the non-permanence of *buddhi* will appear from the concluding section of the *Nyāya-bhāṣya* on *Sūtra*, iii, 2, 17—*iti upapannam anityā buddhir iti* "thus it is proved that *buddhi* is non-eternal". Vardhamāna had noticed this point about the *Bhāṣya*, but he himself regarded these *sūtras* as forming an altogether different section. He says: "Some people have held that this is only a part, and continuation, of the foregoing section, and should not be treated as a separate section; specially because the *Bhāṣya*, at the end of the present section, concludes with the words: 'Thus it is proved that *buddhi* is non-eternal,' from which it is clear that the *Bhāṣya* takes the whole as one section dealing with the non-eternality of *buddhi*. But the fact of the matter is that the subject-matter of the present section is totally different. . ."[1] The *Tātparya* and the *Pariśuddhi* simply explain away this introduction of a discussion of the Buddhist doctrine of momentariness into this section. As has already been pointed out, the chief ground for holding that this section refers to the Buddhist doctrine of *kṣaṇika-vāda* is to be found in the language of *Sūtra*, iii, 2, 10—*sphatike 'py aparāparotpatteḥ kṣaṇikatvād vyaktīnām ahetuḥ*. Now this *sūtra* should normally be regarded as an answer (*uttara-pakṣa*) to one of the preceding *sūtras*, which represent the opponent's view (*pūrva-pakṣa*) from the point of view of the Sāṃkhya, viz. *sphaṭikānyatvābhimānavat tadanyatvābhimānaḥ* "there is a false notion

[1] *Indian Thought*, x, p. 313.

of its being different, like that with regard to the difference pertaining to a rock-crystal"; that is to say, the Sāṃkhya opponent says that *buddhi*, though really one, appears to be diverse, just like a rock-crystal, which also appears to be different because of the reflections of the different colours upon it. It will appear that the *Nyāya-sūcī-nibandha* and the commentators regard this *sūtra* as the end of the section dealing with the non-eternality of *buddhi* "*iti navabhiḥ sūtrair buddhy-anityatā-prakaraṇam*"; and, according to them, an altogether new section begins with the *Sūtra sphaṭike 'py*, etc., which, according to all the commentators, contains an objection to the doctrine of permanence of things from the point of view of the Buddhist, who holds the doctrine of momentariness. The *sūtra* has been translated thus: "In the rock-crystal also, one (rock-crystal) being produced after another, since all the individual things are momentary, there is to be found no reason." The following seven *sūtras* are then supposed to contain a discussion of the doctrine of momentariness between the Buddhist and the Nyāya philosopher. Now I cannot help thinking that this view is the most absurd to hold, and it is so for the following reasons:—

1. It is very unusual and unnatural that at the end of a discussion the author of the *Nyāya-sūtras* should stop with a *sūtra* representing the opponent's view (*pūrva-pakṣa*) and not finish with an answer establishing his own view (*uttara-pakṣa*).

2. It would be curious that the author of the *Nyāya-sūtras*, while trying to establish the non-eternality of *buddhi* as against the Sāṃkhya philosopher, should leave him and the subject under discussion alone, and abruptly usher in a Buddhist, apparently against the Sāṃkhya first, make him say something which is distinctly against the Nyāya view, and then begin to measure swords with him.

3. The *Sūtras*, iii, 2, 10 to iii, 2, 18 are evidently a discussion of the Sāṃkhya view of cause and effect rather than of the

Buddhist doctrine of momentariness. This is clear from the example of the production of curd out of milk, and from the fact that as the *Sūtra* "*na payasaḥ pariṇāmaḥ guṇāntara-prādur-bhāvād*" could not be explained in terms of a discussion between a Nyāya philosopher and the Buddhist, the *Bhāṣya* introduces it with the observation: *atra kaścit parihāram āha* "here someone has offered the following refutation"; and the *Vṛtti* actually says: *saugata-mate sāṃkhyadūṣaṇam upanyasati* "the author points out a defect in the Buddhist doctrine from the point of view of the Sāṃkhya". A study of the *sūtras* in question will easily show that the *sūtra* is not an answer to the Buddhist view, which is, in fact, to be found in none of the *sūtras* in this section, but to the Nyāya view that the effect is different from the cause; for it is said in this *sūtra* that milk, while it becomes curd, is only transformed by the appearance of different qualities. Further, would it not be a curious procedure again that the Nyāya philosopher should introduce a Sāṃkhya, with a view different from his own, to meet his opponent, who, this time, is the Buddhist?

The fact is that a hopeless confusion has been created by the assumption that the *Sūtra sphaṭike 'py*, etc., has reference to the Buddhist doctrine of momentariness,[1] simply because

[1] For considerations of space it is impossible to consider here every *sūtra* in this section, but the main arguments given above should be sufficient to show that the Buddhist doctrine of momentariness is not the theme of these *sūtras*. It is evident that it is the term *kṣaṇikatvād* in the *sūtra* which has suggested the presence of this doctrine here; but it is to be noted that *kṣaṇika* and its derivatives are quite normally used to denote simply "momentary" as apart from the technical sense of the term as found in the Buddhist metaphysics. A very happy example of the use of the word, and that, too, in order to express the momentary nature of cognition (*buddhi*), which forms the subject of discussion in the present context also, is to be found in the Śabara-bhāṣya under *Mīmāṃsā-sūtra*, i, 1, 5, where it is said: *arthaviṣayā hi pratyakṣa-buddhiḥ, buddhy-antara-viṣayā; kṣaṇikā hi sā, na buddhy-antara-kālam-avasthāsyate*. Another text of the *Śloka-vārttika* under *Mīmāṃsā-sūtra*, i, 1, 4, and the *Kāśikā* on the same provide another example of the use of this term in the same kind of context. Speaking about *buddhi*, the *Vārttika* says: *na hi sā kṣaṇam-apy-āste jāyate vā pramātmakam* (i, iv, 54); and the *Kāśikā* explains: *kintu nendriyādivaj jātā satī buddhiḥ kṣaṇamātram apy āste*, etc.

it happens to contain the term *kṣaṇikatvād*. I shall presently offer my own explanation of the *sūtra*, and show that the *Sūtras*, iii, 2, 1, to iii, 2, 17, form one continuous section dealing with the non-eternality of *buddhi*, as against the Sāṃkhya view that it is eternal.

After the Sāṃkhya explanation of the non-simultaneity of cognitions and the non-recognition of an object, as given in the *Sūtras*, iii, 2, 6, and 7, has been refuted by the Nyāya philosopher by means of the assertion contained in the *Sūtra*, iii, 2, 8, *na gatyabhāvāt*, that the explanation given by the Sāṃkhya cannot be true because, according to them, there is no motion in *buddhi*, the follower of the Sāṃkhya says in *Sūtra*, iii, 2, 9 that there is only a semblance of difference (and therefore of diversity) in cognitions like that to be found in the case of a rock-crystal (which, although one, appears to be different according to the reflections on it). After this, I hold that the assertion *hetv-abhāvād*, which has been regarded as a *Nyāya-sūtra* by some, and as only a part of the *Bhāṣya* by others, is really a *Nyāya-sūtra* forming the *uttara-pakṣa* along with the next three *sūtras*, viz. *sphaṭike 'py*, etc. In the *Sūtra*, *na hetv-abhāvād*, it is said that there is no proof that *buddhi* is like a rock-crystal (it is simply an illustration which you give), and in the next *sūtra* then, *sphaṭike 'py aparāparotpatteḥ kṣaṇikatvād vyaktīnām ahetuḥ*, it is further maintained that even the case of a crystal is not in point, since, in it also, because the reflections are produced one after another, the individual reflections are momentary, the main object being to emphasize the fact that the diversity of reflections in a crystal is not a case of semblance, but of real production by the objects reflected into it. The term "*api*" in *sphaṭike 'py* is very significant, and is indicative of the fact that this *sūtra* is a development of an argument begun in a previous *sūtra*, and this we actually find in the *Sūtra*, *na hetv-abhāvād*. The next two *sūtras* also represent the *uttara-pakṣa*: In the *Sūtra*, *niyamahetv-abhāvād yathā-darśanam abhyanujñā* it is said that as there is no reason to support a universal rule (with regard to the permanence or transitoriness of objects), we can admit (the truth or falsity of this character about things) only in accordance with our experience; since, according to the *Nyāya-sūtras*, neither are all the objects necessarily permanent, nor are they necessarily transitory.[1] But, it is pointed out in the next *Sūtra*, *notpatti-vināśa-kāraṇopalabdheḥ*, that in this particular case, it is not right to say that *buddhi* is permanent, because the causes of the production and destruction of cognitions can be perceived.[2] This leads to a discussion of the nature of production by means of the example of curd and milk, which discussion also is evidently one between a follower of the Sāṃkhya and a Nyāya philosopher.

It is rather strange that Vidyābhūṣaṇa should see in the *Sūtra sphaṭike 'py*, etc., an echo of the doctrine of momentariness as found in the *Laṅkāvatāra-sūtra*, chap. vi,[3] when, evidently, the doctrine as defined in this work shows a distinct divergence from the view about the production of individuals contained in the *Nyāya-sūtra* in question. According to Vidyābhūṣaṇa's own quotation and its translation,[4] the author of the *Laṅkāvatāra-sūtra* says, "A momentary thing is that which is inactive, distinct in itself, and not liable to cessation. By calling things momentary I mean that they are not produced; I do not, O fools! say that they are destroyed after being produced."[5] This statement clearly shows that the doctrine of momentariness, as explained here, simply means change, and not production and destruction of things every moment; while in the

[1] Cf. *Nyāya-sūtra*, iv, 1, 28.

[2] Cf. *Ns.*, iii, 2, 24: "Inasmuch as cognition is recognized as non-eternal, its destruction proceeds from another cognition, just like sound."

[3] *History of Indian Logic*, p. 121.

[4] *History of Indian Logic*, p. 246.

[5] *Nirvyāpāraṃ kṣaṇikaṃ viviktaṃ kṣayavarjitam,*
Anutpattiṃ ca dharmāṇāṃ kṣaṇikārthaṃ vadāmy-aham,
Utpattyanantaraṃ bhaṅgaṃ na vai deśemi bāliśāḥ.

Nyāya-sūtra under consideration there is a distinct mention of the production of individuals one after another—*aparāparotpatteḥ*. It will appear that the doctrine that all things are non-eternal, since they have the character of being produced and destroyed, is considered by the author of the *Nyāya-sūtras* in another section beginning with the *Sūtra*, iv, 1, 25, *sarvam anityam utpatti-vināśa-dharmakatvāt*, and that various doctrines relating to eternality, non-eternality and change are dealt with in the Fourth Book of the *Nyāya-sūtras*. Hence the doctrine of momentariness, instead of being introduced in Book III, 2, in the middle of a discussion irrelevant to the subject from the Nyāya point of view, could have been easily introduced in the Fourth Book; and, in fact, the doctrine of non-eternality as found in that Book is not very different from the doctrine of momentariness. Further, it must be remembered that it is the complete destruction and the fresh production of *all* individual things which the author of the *Nyāya-sūtras* objects to. He does admit non-eternality in the case of some kinds of existence, for example, in the case of cognitions themselves.

The other section of the *Nyāya-sūtras* which I propose to consider here is that which consists of *Sūtra*, iv, 2, 26, and the following *sūtras*. According to some, it refers to the Buddhist doctrine of subjective idealism (*vijñāna-vāda*), while according to others, it contains a discussion of the philosophy of the Mādhyamika School (*Śūnya-vāda*). Vidyābhūṣaṇa holds that *Sūtra*, iv, 2, 26, and the next are later interpolations, and refer to the doctrine of *vijñāna-vāda* as found in the *Laṅkāvatāra-sūtra*, chaps. ii and xi.[1] The view that these *sūtras* refer to the *vijñāna-vāda* has been questioned and refuted by Jacobi as against Stcherbatsky, who held this view on the authority of Vācaspati Miśra.[2] *Sūtra*, iv, 2, 26, which is the most important in this section, is: *buddhyā vivecanāt tu bhāvānāṃ yāthātmyānupalabdhis tantvapakarṣaṇe*

[1] *History of Indian Logic*, p. 120.

[2] *Journal of the American Oriental Society*, xxxi (1911).

paṭasadbhāvānupalabdhivat tadanupalabdhiḥ. and an examination of the language of the *sūtra* will show that it certainly does not refer to the doctrine that things cannot be conceived to exist apart from the ideas of them. I shall also presently show that the *sūtra* does not refer to the doctrine of *Śūnya-vāda* either, as Jacobi holds. A faithful translation of the *sūtra* will indicate what it actually means. It may be rendered thus: "And by means of an analysis by intellect (*buddhyā vivecanāt tu*), the true nature of existent things is not cognized (*bhāvānāṃ yāthātmyānupalabdhiḥ*); they cannot be cognized, just as the existence of cloth is not cognized after the threads have been separated from one another." It will appear that Vidyābhūṣaṇa's translation of the *sūtra*, viz. "Things, some say, do not possess a reality if they are separated from our thoughts, just as there is no reality in a web separated from its threads,"[1] is evidently not correct. "*buddhyā vivecanāt*" certainly does not mean here "separated *from* our thoughts", and "*bhāvānāṃ yāthātmyānupalabdhiḥ*" only means "the non-cognition of the true nature of things". The example of threads and cloth clearly shows that what is meant to be asserted in the *sūtra* is that the true nature of the whole cannot be known by analyzing it into parts, which is a distinctly Nyāya view about the nature of the whole. Further, the particle *tu* in "*buddhyā vivecanāt tu*" indicates that the assertion in the *sūtra* is a development of some argument that has gone before; and this is to be found in the preceding *sūtra, anavasthākāritvād*, etc. Thus it will appear that the *Sūtra*, iv, 2, 26, along with iv, 2, 25, instead of representing the Buddhist view, forms the Nyāya answer (*uttara-pakṣa*) to the opponent's view (*pūrva-pakṣa*) contained in *Nyāya-sūtras*, iv, 2, 23 and 24, in which it is said that an atom is not an indivisible whole but an aggregate of infinite parts. In defence of the doctrine of indivisibility of atoms it is said firstly, in iv, 2, 25, that a denial of the doctrine will lead to a regress *ad infinitum*, and secondly, in case it be said that

[1] *Nyāya-sūtras* (*Sacred Books of the Hindus*), p. 133.

an atom can be understood only as something made of parts, it is asserted in iv, 2, 26, that the nature of the whole cannot be known by analyzing it into its parts.[1] Then the following two *sūtras,* iv, 2, 27, and iv, 2, 28, again form the *pūrva-pakṣa.* In the first of these *vyāhatatvād ahetuḥ,* it is said that what has been asserted about the nature of the whole is no ground, because it is vitiated by contradiction; the meaning being that it is contradictory to say that the whole cannot be known by the cognition of its parts; and in the second of these *tadāśrayatvād apṛthag-grahaṇam,* it is further said that the whole is not known apart from its parts, for its existence depends upon them. Then the next *sūtra, pramāṇataś cārthapratipatteḥ,* represents the *uttara-pakṣa,* and asserts that an object is proved to exist, or is known by means of a *pramāṇa,* that is to say, an object as a whole is known by means of the various *pramāṇas*; and this leads to a discussion in the following *sūtras* on the validity and limitations of the *pramāṇas.* It will appear thus that the whole section contains a discussion on the nature of the whole in its relation to the parts, and that *Sūtra,* iv, 2, 26 simply emphasizes the Nyāya view that the true nature of the whole is known independently of its parts, and not by an analysis of its parts, or rather by analyzing it away into its parts.

The explanation of such forced interpretations of the *Nyāya-sūtras* as have been discussed above is to be found in the fact that the commentators were too anxious to make use of anything that they could get hold of in the language of the *sūtras* in order to refute the Buddhist doctrines, which were ever pressing upon them, to pause and consider how far they were justified in doing so.

[1] Compare the arguments contained in *Sūtras,* iv, 2, 7, to iv, 2, 15, especially the opponent's view in iv, 2, 14, where it is said that the perception of things would be possible, just like the perception of a mass of hair by a person of dim vision.

Th. Stcherbatsky

THE THEORY OF INSTANTANEOUS BEING (KṢAṆIKA-VĀDA).

§ 1. The problem stated.

In the preceding chapter the importance has been pointed out which the Buddhists attach to their fundamental principle that there are two, and only two sources of knowledge, the senses and the understanding, and to the fact that they are utterly heterogeneous, so as to be the one the negation of the other. We thus have a sensuous and non-sensuous, or a non-intelligible and an intelligible source of knowledge.

In the opening words of his great treaty Dignaga makes the statement that in strict conformity with this double source of knowledge the external world is also double, it is either the particular or the general; the particular is the object corresponding to sensuous cognition, the general, or universal, is the object corresponding to the understanding or the reason. We thus have a double world, in India just as in Europe, a sensible one and an intelligible one, a *mundus sensibilis* and a *mundus intelligibilis*, a κόσμος αἰσθητός and a κόσμος νοετός. We will now proceed to examine the Buddhist ideas of the one and of the other.

The sensible world consists of *sensibilia* which are but momentary flashes of energy. The perdurable, eternal, pervasive Matter which is imagined as their support or substratum is a fiction of the Sankhyas and other schools. All things without exception are nothing but strings of momentary events. «This their character of being instantaneous, of being split in discrete moments, says Kamalaśīla,[1] pervades everything. By proving this our fundamental thesis alone, we could have repudiated at one single stroke[2] the God (of the theists), the eternal Matter (of the Sānkyas) and all the wealth of (metaphysical) entities imagined by our opponents. To examine them one by one, and to compose elaborate refutations at great length was a perfectly useless trouble, since the same could have been done quite easily.[3] Indeed, no one of our opponents will admit that these entities are instantaneous, that they disappear as soon as they appear, that their essence is to disappear without leaving any trace behind.[4] We, indeed, are perfectly aware that by prooving the instantaneous character of Being in general, these (metaphysical) entities would have been *eo ipso* repudiated. We, therefore, will proceed to expatiate upon the arguments in proof of this theory in order (once more) to repudiate those entities which have already been examined, viz God, Matter (Nature, the Soul as it is established in different schools), up to the (half-permanent) «personality» of the Vātsīputrīya-Buddhists; and in order also to support the repudiation of those (enduring) entities which will be examined in the sequel, viz the Universals, Substance, Quality, Motion, Inherence, up to the (instantaneous) elements existing in «the three times» (as they are admitted by the Sarvāstivāda-Buddhists),[5] the (eternal) Matter as admitted by the Materialists,[6] the eternal Scriptures as admitted by the brahmins.[7] Thus (no vestige of an enduring entity will be left) and the theory of Instantaneous Being will be clearly established. A critical examination of the (supposed) stability of existence contains therefore the final outcome of all Buddhist philosophy». Such is the leading idea of Buddhism — there is no other ultimate reality than separate, instantaneous bits of existence. Not only eternal entities, be it God or be it Matter, are denied reality, because they are assumed to be enduring and eternal, but even the simple stability of empirical objects is something constructed by our imagination. Ultimate reality is instantaneous.

---

1 Cp. TSP., p. 131. 17 ff. (condensed).
2 *eka-prahāreṇa eva.*
3 *svalpa-upāyena.*
4 *niranvaya-nirodha-dharmaka.*
5 *trikāla-anuyāyino bhāvasya* (*dharma-svabhāvasya*), cp. CC., p. 42.
6 Lit. «the four great elements of the Cārvākas».
7 Lit. «the eternal sounds of the Scriptures of the Jaiminīyas».

§ 2. Reality is kinetic.

«It is natural, says the same Kamalaśīla,[1] on the part of a normal human being[2] who is engaged in the pursuit of his daily aims to enquire about the existence or non-existence of everything[3] (he wants)... Not to do it would be abnormal.[4] Therefore, anything a man avails himself of, whether directly or indirectly, in whatsoever a place, at whatsoever a time, is called by him real...[5] Now, we (Buddhists) prove that such (real) things, viz things that are objects of some purposive actions,[6] are instantaneous, (they have a momentary duration). There is no exception to the rule that the capacity of being the object of a purposive action is the essential feature establishing reality. It is a feature conterminous with existence.[7] But a thing cannot be the object of a purposive action and cannot be efficient otherwise than by its last moment. Its former moments cannot overlap the moment of efficiency in order to produce the effect, still less can its future moments produce the preceding effect. «We maintain, says the same author,[8] that an object can produce something only when it has reached the last moment of its existence (which is also its unique real moment), its other moments are non efficient». When a seed is turned into a sprout, this is done by the last moment of the seed, not by those moments when it lay placidly in the granary.[9] One might object that all the preceding moments of the seed are the indirect[10] causes of the sprout. But this is impossible, because if the seed would not change every moment, its nature would be to endure and never to change. If it is said that the moment of the sprout is produced by a «totality» of causes and

---

1 TSP., p. 151. 19 ff.

2 *prekṣavān.*

3 *arthasya (= vastu-mātrasya) astitva-anastitvena vicāraḥ.*

4 *unmattaḥ syāt.*

5 *yad eva padārtha-jātam... tatraiva vastu-vyavasthā*; note the contrast between *padārtha* and *vastu*; among *padārthas* those alone are *vastu* which are efficient. The realists distinguish *svarūpa-sattā* from *sattā-sāmānya*, the Buddhists deny this distinction, cp. SDS., p. 26.

6 *arthā-kriyā-kāri-rūpa.*

7 *sādhyena (=sattayā) vyāpti-siddhiḥ.*

8 Ibid., p. 140. 19.

9 *kuśūlādi-stho na janayati*, ibid.

10 *na mukhyataḥ*, ibid, p. 140. 22; the preceding moments are called *upasarpaṇa-pratyaya*, cp. NK., p. 126.8, 135.8 etc.

conditions,[1] the same applies to every moment, since every moment has its own totality of causes and conditions owing to which it exists. «This our moment (i. e., the moment which we consider to be real) is the moment when an action (i. e., the run of uniform moments) is finished».[2] But an action, in this sense, is never finished, every moment is necessarily followed by a next moment. The break in that motion which constitutes the essence of reality is nothing but the appearance of an outstanding or dissimilar moment.[3] It is outstanding for our practical requirements, because it is natural for us to disregard the uninterrupted change of moments and to take notice of it only when it becomes a new quality, i. e., sufficient to impress a new attitude on our behaviour or on our thought. The identity of the foregoing moments in the existence of a thing consists simply in disregarding their difference.[4] The break in this identity is not a break in their motion, it always is something imagined, it is an integration of moments whose difference we are not able to notice. «The essence of reality is motion», says Šāntirakṣita.[5] Reality indeed is kinetic, the world is a cinema. Causality,[6] i. e., the interdependance of the moments following one another, evokes the illusion of stability or duration, but they are, so to speak, forces or energies[7] flashing into existence without any real enduring substance in them, but also without intervals or with infinitesimally small intervals.[8]

This theory whose main lines are here briefly sketched, and which is supported by a series of arguments to be examined in the sequel of our analysis, is regarded by the Buddhists themselves, as well as by their opponents, as the keystone of the whole of their ontology.

The idea that there is no stability in the external world and that existence is nothing but a flow of external becoming, is familiar to us from the history of Greek philosophy where in the person of Hera-

---

1 *sāmagrī = hetu-kāraṇa-sāmagrī*; the totality of causes and conditions of a thing cannot be distinguished from the thing itself, — *sahakāri-sākalyam na prāpter atiricyate*, Tātp., p. 80.5.

2 AKB ad II.46 — *kriyā-parisamāpti-lakṣaṇa eva eṣo naḥ kṣaṇaḥ;* transl. vol. I, p. 232.

3 *vijātīya-kṣaṇa-utpāda.*

4 *bheda-agraha.*

5 TS., p. 138.9 — *cala-bhāva-svarūpa = kṣaṇika*; TSP., p. 117.17 — *cala = anitya*, cp. ibid., 137.22.

6 TS., p. 1 — *calaḥ pratītya-samutpādaḥ*, cp. TSP., p. 131.12.

7 *saṃskāra.*

8 *nirantara.*

cleitus it marks an episode in its early period, an episode which was soon forgotten in the subsequent development of Greek thought. We find it again in India as the foundation of a system whose roots go back into the VI-th century B. C. But here it is not an episode, it has an incessant development through a variety of vicissitudes, in a series of elaborate systems, and after an agitated life of 15 centuries it forsakes its native soil only to find a new home in other Buddhist countries. Since the same idea reappears in modern European speculation and is even partly supported by modern science, the historian will be interested to gain insight into the arguments by which it was established in India and into the forms in which it has there been shaped.

We are faced in India by two quite different theories of a Universal Flux. The motion representing the world-process is either a continuous motion or it is a discontinuous, although compact,[1] one. The latter consists of an infinity of discrete moments following one another almost without intervals. In the first case the phenomena are nothing but waves or fluctuations[2] standing out upon a back-ground of an eternal, all-pervading, undifferentiated Matter[3] with which they are identical. The Universe represents a *legato* movement.[4] In the second case there is no matter at all, flashes of energy[5] follow one another and produce the illusion of stabilized phenomena. The Universe is then a *staccato* movement. The first view is maintained in the Sānkhya system of philosophy, the second prevails in Buddhism.[6] We have here a case, not quite unfamiliar to the general historian of philosophy, of two contrary philosophical systems both apparently flowing from the same first principle.

The arguments brought forward by the Buddhists are the following ones.

---

1 *sāndratara.*

2 *vṛtti.*

3 *pradhāna.*

4 *pariṇāma-vāda.*

5 *saṃskāra-vāda = sanghāta-vāda.*

6 Both theories are rejected by the Realist; they are very pregnantly formulated by Udayana, Parišuddhi, p. 171—172 — *na tāvat pratikṣaṇa-vartamānatvam Saugata-mata-vad vastunaḥ svarūpotpādaḥ, nāpi Sānkhya-vad vastu-svarūpa-sthairye'pi pariṇati-bheda eva Mīmāṃsakaiḥ svī-kriyate.* It must be added that the Sānkhyas nevertheless deny the visibility of *samavāya* and this fundamental feature distinguishes them also from the Vaišeṣikas and apparently also from the old Yoga school.

§ 3. Argument from the ideality of Time and Space.

The theory of Universal Momentariness implies that every duration in time consists of point-instants following one another, every extension in space consists of point-instants arising in contiguity and simultaneously, every motion consists of these point-instants arising in contiguity and in succession.[1] There is therefore no Time, no Space and no Motion over and above the point-instants of which these imagined entities are constructed by our imagination.

In order to understand the Buddhist conception of Time, of Space and of Motion we must confront them with the divergent conceptions established in the Indian realistic schools. To this method we will be obliged to recur almost at every step of our investigation. We begin with Time and Space.

According to the Indian Realists, Time is a substance. It is one, eternal and all-pervading.[2] Its existence is inferred from the facts of consecution and simultaneity between phenomena. Space is likewise a substance,[3] it is one, eternal and all-embracing. Its existence is inferred from the fact that all extended bodies possess impenetrability, they are beside each other in space. Prašastapāda adds[4] the very interesting remark that Time, Space and Cosmical Ether, being each of them unique in their kind,[5] the names given to them are, as it were, proper names,[6] not general terms.[7] Different times are parts of one and the same time. When Time and Space are represented as divided in many spaces and different times, it is a metaphor. The objects situated in them,[8] but not Space itself and not Time itself, are divided. They are, therefore, «not discursive or what is called general concepts».[9] They are representations produced «by a single object» only.[10]

---

1 *nirantara-kṣaṇa-utpāda.*

2 VS., 2.6 — 9, cp. Prašastp., p. 63.23 ff.

3 VS., 2. 10—16, cp. Prašastp., p. 67.1 ff.

4 p. 58.5 ff.

5 *ekaika.*

6 *paribhāṣikyaḥ sanjñāḥ.*

7 *apara-jāty-abhāve.*

8 *añjasā ekatvepi .. upādhi-bhedān nānātvopacāraḥ.*

9 It is curious that one of the principle arguments of Kant for establishing the unreality of Time and Space is found in an Indian realistic system, without drawing the same conclusion as Kant has done, CPR., p. 25.

10 Cp. N. Kandalī, p. 59.6 — *vyakti - bheda - adhiṣṭhāna.* Kant, CPR., p. 25, has concluded from this fact that time must be an intuition, because «a re-

It is clear that the Indian realists, just as some European rationalists considered Time and Space as two allembracing receptacles containing each of them the entire Universe.

The separate reality of these two receptacles is denied by the Buddhists. Real, we have seen, is a thing possessing a separate efficiency of its own. The receptacles of the things have no separate efficiency.[1] Time and Space cannot be separated from the things that exist in them. Hence they are no separate entities. Owing to our capacity of productive imagination we can take different views of the same object and distinguish between the thing and its receptacle, but this is only imagination. Every point-instant may be viewed as a particle of Time, as a particle of Space and as a sensible quality, but this difference is only a difference of our mental attitude[2] towards that point-instant. The point-instant itself, the ultimate reality cut loose from all imagination is qualityless, timeless and indivisible.

In the first period of its philosophy Buddhism admitted the reality of Space as one of the elements[3] of the universe. It was an empty space imagined as an unchanging,[4] eternal, allembracing element. But when later Buddhists were confronted by Idealism in their own home, they saw that the reality of external objects does not admit of a strict proof, and the reality of a substantial space was then denied. Substantial time[5] was likewise denied, but subtle time, i. e., the moment, the point-instant[6] of efficiency, was not only asserted, it was made, as we shall presently see, the fulcrum on which the whole edifice of reality was made to rest. The notions of substantial time and space were not attacked on the score that they were *a priori* intuitions whose empirical origine it was impossible to conceive, but they were destroyed dialectically on the score that the notions

presentation, which can be produced by a single object only, is an intuition». The Buddhists would never have said that, because for them a single object (*vyakti* = *svalakṣaṇa*) is only the point-instant and the intuition is only the pure sensation (*nirvikalpakam pratyakṣam*) corresponding to its presence.

[1] They are not *artha-kriyā-kārin*.

[2] *kālpanika*; cp. the remarks of the translators of Kathāvatthu, p. 392 ff.

[3] Under the name of *ākāša*, which name denotes in the Nyāya-Vaišeṣica system the Cosmical Ether serving for the propagation of sound. Kamalašīla says, TSP., p. 140.10, that the Vaibhāṣikas, since they admit the reality of this element, do not deserve to be called Buddhists — *na Šākya-putrīyāḥ*.

[4] *asaṃskṛta*.

[5] *sthūlaḥ kālaḥ*, in Kathā-vatthu — *mahakāla*.

[6] *kṣaṇaḥ*=*sūkṣmaḥ kālaḥ*.

of duration and extention as they are used in common life covertly contain contradictions and therefore cannot be accepted as objectively real.

§ 4. Duration and extention are not real.

Indeed, if we assume that a thing, although remaining one, possesses extension and duration, we will be landed in a contradiction, so far we consider reality as efficiency. One real thing cannot exist at the same time in many places, neither can the same reality be real at different times. If that were the case, it would run against the law of contradiction. If a thing is present in one place, it cannot at the same time be present in another place. To be present in another place means not to be present in the former place. Thus to reside in many places means to be and at the time not to be present in a given place. According to the Realists empirical things have a limited real duration. They are produced by the creative power of nature or by human will or by the will of God out of atoms. The atoms combine and form real new unities. These created real unities reside, or inhere, in their *causa materialis*, i. e., in the atoms. Thus we have one real thing simultaneously residing in a multitude of atoms, i. e. in many places. This is impossible. Either is the created unity a fiction and real are only the parts, or the parts are fictions and real is only the ultimate whole. For the Buddhists the parts alone are real, the whole is a fiction,[1] for it were a reality, it would be a reality residing at once in many places, i. e., a reality at once residing and not residing in a given place.[2]

By similar considerations it is proved that a thing can have no duration. If a thing exists at a moment A, it cannot also exist at some moment B, for to exist really at the moment A means not to have any real existence at the moment B or at any other moment. If we thus admit that the same thing continues to exist at the moment B, this could only mean that it at once really exists and

---

[1] Cp. Avayavi-nirākaraṇa by ācārya Aśoka in the «Six Buddhist Tracts» and Tātp., p. 269.3 ff., NK., p. 262.10 ff, N. Kandalī, p. 41.12 ff.

[2] Cp. the words of Leibniz (Extrait d'une lettre 1693) — «extension is nothing but a repetition or a continued multiplicity of that which is spread out, a plurality, continuity and coexistence of parts»; and «in my opinion corporeal substance consists in something quite other than being extended and occupying place»; and «extension is nothing but an abstraction».

does not really exist at the moment A. If a thing could have real duration through several moments, it would represent a real unity existing at once at different times. Either is the enduring unity a fiction and real are only the moments, or the moments are fictions and real is only duration. For the Buddhists the moments alone are real, duration is a fiction, for if it were a reality, it would be a reality existing at different times at once,[1] i. e., existing and at the same time non-existing at a given moment.

Thus it is that ultimate reality for the Buddhist is timeless, spaceless and motionless. But it is timeless not in the sense of an eternal being, spaceless not in the sense of an ubiquitous being, motionless not in the sense of an allembracing motionless whole, but it is timeless, spaceless and motionless in the sense of having no duration, no extension and no movement, it is a mathematical point-instant, the moment of an action's efficiency.

§ 5. Argument from direct perception.

The momentary character of everything existing is further established by arguments from perception and inference. The first of them is an argument from direct perception.[2] That sensation is a momentary flash is proved by introspection. But a momentary sensation is but the reflex of a momentary thing. It cannot seize neither what precedes nor what follows. Just as when we perceive a patch of blue colour in a momentary sensation, we perceive just the thing which corresponds to that sensation, i. e., the blue and not the yellow, even so do we perceive in that sensation just the present moment, not the preceding one, and not the following one. When the existence of a patch of blue is perceived, its non-existence, or absence, is *eo ipso* excluded and hence its existence in the former and in the following moments is also excluded. The present moment alone is seized by sensation. Since all external objects are reducible to sense-data, and the corresponding sensations are always confined to a single moment, it becomes clear that all objects, as far as they affect us, are momentary existences. The duration of the object beyond the moment of sensation cannot be warranted by sensation itself, it is an extension of that sensation, a construction of our imagination. The latter constructs the image of the object, when stimulated by sensation, but sensation alone, pure sensation, points to an instantaneous object.

1 Cp. Tātp., p. 92.13 ff., translated in vol. II, App. I.; cp. NK., p. 125.

2 NK., p. 123. 14 ff; Tātp., p. 92. 15 ff.

§ 6. Recognition does not prove duration.

To this argument the Realist makes the following objection.[1] It is true, says he, that sensation apprehends only a blue coloured surface and that it does not apprehend at that time something different from it. But we cannot go all the length of maintaining that sensation apprehends the precise time of its duration and that this duration is momentary. Sensation itself lasts for more than a moment, it can last for two or three moments. It is not at all proved that it lasts only a single moment, and it is not at all impossible that a thing endures and produces gradually a series of sensations the one after the other.

The Buddhist answers.[2] Let us (for the sake of argument) admit that the momentary character of all existence is not reflected directly in our cognition, (but does duration fare any better? is duration reflected directly?). Yes it is! says the Realist. There is a consecrated fact, the fact of Recognition[3] which proves the stability and duration of things, it is a cognition of the pattern «this is the same crystal gem (which I have seen before»). This judgment, answers the Buddhist, does not at all prove the stability and duration of the crystal, it does not prove that its former condition is quite the same as its present condition. And if this is not proved, nothing lies in the way of our assuming that there is an imperceptible uninterrupted process of change even in the crystal gem. It will then be not an enduring substance, but a change of momentary existencies following one another. Indeed, the judgment «this is that same crystal» is an illicit association of two utterly heterogeneous elements which have nothing in common. The element «this» refers to the present, to a sensation and to a real object. The element «that» refers to the past, to something surviving exclusively in imagination and memory. They are as different as heat and cold. Their unity cannot be created even by the allmighty god Indra! If such things could be identical, there is no reason why the whole of the Universe should not be composed of identical things. Memory whose function is limited to the past cannot grasp the present moment, nor can sensation, whose function is limited to the present, apprehend the past. When there is a discrepancy in the causes, the effect cannot be identical, or else the result would be

---

[1] NK., p. 123. 23 ff.

[2] Ibid., p. 124. 7.

[3] *pratyabhijñā bhagavatī*, cp. the same argument in NS., III. 1. 2.

produced not by the causes, but at haphazard. Memory and sensation have each their respective field of action and their own result, they cannot mix up so as to work the one in the field of the other. Recognition is not to be distinguished from memory, and memory is produced by thought construction, it is not a direct reflex of reality. Therefore the contention of the Realist that recognition proves duration betrays only his desire that it should be so.[1]

§ 7. Arguments from an analysis of the notion of existence.

Although neither immediate perception, nor recognition can prove the stability of the objects of the external world, nevertheless let us, for the sake of argument, says the Buddhist,[2] concede the point and admit that immediate perception apprehends objects representing some stability. However, this perception is falsified. Stability is an illusion,[3] there are cogent arguments [4] against our admitting stability and duration.

The first argument consists in deducing analytically the fact of constant change from the conception of existence. Existence, real existence, we have seen, means efficiency, and efficiency means change. What is absolutely changeless is also absolutely unefficient; what is absolutely unefficient does not exist. For instance, the Cosmical Ether, even in the opinion of those who admit that it is a stuff, it is supposed to be motionless. But for the Buddhists, the motionless is causally unefficient and therefore does not exist. Motionless and unexistent are convertible terms, since there is no other means to prove one's existence than to produce some effect. If something exists without any effect at all, its existence is negligible. The Buddhists conclude that whatsoever does not change, does not exist.

The argument is thrown into the form of the following syllogism.[5]

Major premise. Whatsoever exists is subject to momentary change.

---

1 *manoratha-mātram*, cp. ibid., p. 124. 24.

2 Ibid , p. 127. 7 ff.

3 *samāropita-gocaram akṣaṇikam*, ibid.

4 Ibid., p. 123-34.

5 TS., p. 143. 17 ff.; this syllogism appears in a different form in SDS., p. 26, where it is quoted from Jñāna-śrī, and in NK., p. 127-9.

Example.[1] As, e. g., a jar (whose ultimate reality is but a point-instant of efficiency).

Minor premise.[2] But the Cosmical Ether is supposed to be motionless.

Conclusion. It does not exist.

That all existing objects are changing every moment is proved by a dilemma. Existing means efficient. The question then arises, is this efficiency perdurable or is it momentary? If it is perdurable, then all the moments the object is supposed to last must participate in the production of the effect. But that is impossible. The preceding moments cannot overlap the last moment in order to participate in the production of the effect. Perdurable means static and static means non efficient, i. e., not producing at the time any effect; unefficient means non existing. Every real object is efficient in producing the next following moment of its duration. The object must therefore produce its effect at once or it will never produce it. There is nothing intermediate between being static and not being static. To be static means to be motionless and eternally unchanging,[3] as the Cosmical Ether was supposed to be (by Indian realists as well as by some modern scientists). Not to be static means to move and to change every moment.[4] Things cannot stop and after taking rest begin to move again, as the naive realism of common life and realistic philosophy assumes. There is motion always going on in living reality, but of this motion we notice only some special moments which we stabilize in imagination.

The deduction of momentariness from existence is called an analytical deduction.[5] Indeed, the judgment «existence means efficiency» and «efficiency means change» are analytical, because the predicate is implied in the subject and is elicited by analysis. The same thing which is characterized as existent, can also be characterized as efficient and as changing. The terms existence, efficiency and change are connected by *„existential identity"*,[6] that is to say, they can be without

---

1 The example of Jñānaśrī is *yathā jaladharaḥ*, probably for metrical reasons.

2 The upanaya in NK. is *saṃś ca ... śabdādir* and in Jñānaśrī's formula *santaś ca bhāvā amī*. In the form quoted by Šāntirakṣita and Kamalaśīla the argument is a *prasanga-sādhana*, since the motionless Ether, as well as eternal time and eternal God etc. are assumed to exist by the opponents, they are therefore valid examples only for them.

3 *nitya = apracyuta-anutpanna-sthiraika-svabhāva*, Anekāntaj, f. 2. a. 10.

4 *anitya = prakṛtyā eka-kṣaṇa-sthiti-dharmaka*, ibid.

5 *svabhāvānumāna.*

6 *tādātmya.*

contradiction applied to one and the same point of reality, to a real fact. There are other characteristics which are connected with them by the same tie of Existential Identity, viz «whatsoever has an origin is always changing»,[1] «whatsoever is produced by causes is impermanent»,[2] «whatsoever is variable in dependence on a variation of its causes is subject to momentary change»,[3] «whatsoever is produced by a conscious effort is impermanent»[4] — all these characteristics, although they may have a different extension, are called «existentially identical», because they may without contradiction be applied to one and the same reality. A jar which is produced by the effort of the potter may also be characterized as variable, as a product, as having an origin, as changing, efficient and existent. In this sense the deduction of momentariness is an analytical deduction.

§ 8. Argument from an analysis of the notion of non-existence.

The foregoing argument in favour of the theory of Instantaneous Being was drawn from an analysis of the notion of existence as meaning efficiency. The present one is also analytical,[5] but it is drawn from the opposite notion of Non-existence[6] as meaning Annihilation.[7] What is annihilation to the thing annihilated? Is it the annihilated thing itself or it is something else,[8] a separate unity, being added to a thing in the course of its annihilation? Is the non-existence of a thing something real or is it a mere idea?

Here again in order to understand the Buddhist view we must contrast it with what it is opposed to, we must take into consideration the opinions of the Indian Realists. Just as Time and Space are for them real entities in which the things are residing; existence — something inherent in the existing things; efficiency is something additional to a thing when it becomes efficient; causality — a real relation uniting cause and effect; motion — a reality added to the thing when it

1 NB., III. 12.
2 Ibid., III. 13.
3 Ibid, III. 15.
4 Ibid.
5 *svabhāva-anumāna*.
6 *abhāva*.
7 *vināśa*.
8 *arthāntaram*.

begins to move; a Universal — a reality residing in the particular; the relation of Inherence — a reality residing in the members of that relation, — even so is Non-existence for the Realist something valid and real, it is something over and above the thing which disappears.

The Buddhist denies this, Non-existence cannot exist. He denies ultimate reality to all that set of hypostasized notions. They are for him mere ideas or mere names, some of them even pseudo-ideas. A mere idea, or a mere name, is a name to which nothing separate corresponds, which has no corresponding reality of its own. A pseudo-idea is a word to which nothing at all corresponds, as, e. g., «a flower in the sky». Thus existence is for the Buddhist nothing but a name for the things existing; efficiency is the efficient thing itself; Time and Space are nothing besides the things residing in them; these things again are nothing over and above the point-instants of which they represent an integration; Causality is dependent origination of the things originating, these things themselves are the causes, there is no real causality besides their existence; motion is nothing beyond the moving thing; a Universal is not a reality «residing» in the particular thing, it is a mere idea or a mere name of the thing itself; Inherence is an unreality of a second degree, since it is admitted in order to unite the particular thing with the Universal which itself is nothing but a name. Finally Non-existence or the annihilation of a thing is also a mere name, nothing over and above the thing annihilated.[1]

The controversy between Buddhists and Realists on this subject of Non-existence is a natural outcome of their different conception of reality. For the Buddhist the only reality is the efficient point-instant, all the rest is interpretation and thought-construction. The Realist, on the other hand, distinguishes between 3 categories of «existence»[2] (substance, quality, motion), and 4 categories of valid «meaning»[3] (universals, differentials, inherence and non-existence), which also have objective reality. Non-existence is valid since it is produced by its own causes.[4] The non-existence of a jar, e. g., is produced by the stroke of a hammer. It is not a mere name like a «flower in the sky».[5] But the

---

1 TS., p. 134. 25.

2 *sattā = astitva.*

3 *padārtha = bhāva.*

4 TSP., p. 135. 1, cp. NK., p. 142. 1-2.

5 According to Vātsyāyana, NBh., p. 2, existence and non-existence are two sides of reality. Everything can possess existence and non-existence as well. For this reason the amalgamated Nyāya-Vaiśeṣika school has added a seventh category, non-

Buddhist answers that existence alone can have a cause, non-existence cannot be produced.[1] If we understand by the non-existence of a thing its replacement by another thing,[2] this non-existence will not be something different from the replaced thing itself. If we understand by it its simple non-existence,[3] then its cause will produce nothing and cannot be called a cause. To do nothing means not to do anything; to be a non-producer means not to be a cause. Hence non-existence will have no reality and no validity.

But then, the Realist asks again, what indeed is annihilation to the thing annihilated, is it something or is it nothing? If it were nothing, argues the Realist, the thing would never be annihilated and would continue to exist. It therefore must be something valid. If it is something separate,[4] added to the thing in the course of its annihilation, answers the Buddhist, it will remain separate, allthough added, and the thing will also remain unaffected,[5] notwithstanding the vicinity of such an uncomfortable neighbour. Let the «venerable gentleman»[6] of such a thing remain intact after destruction, retorts the Realist, it will be your «Thing-in-Itself»,[7] a thing deprived of all its general and special properties and efficiencies.[8] In so saying the Realist hints at the Buddhist theory of ultimate reality which is but a bare point-instant. This point, he says, will indeed remain even after the thing be destroyed. «This your realistic non-existence is empty and

existence, to the six categories of the old Vaišeṣika school. But this opinion did not prevail in the realistic camp without strong opposition. Prašastapāda among the Vaišeṣikas and Prabhākara among the Mīmāṃsakas rally in this point to the Buddhists, cp. Prāšast., p. 225. and ŠD, p. 322 ff. Šāntirakṣita, p. 135. 6 ff., simply accuses the realist of assuming that non-existence is an effect, like the plant produced by the seed. But Kamalašīla remarks, p. 135. 16, that this is not quite correct, since the Naiyāyiks and others do not assert that non-existence «exists» like a substance (*dravyādivat*), it is «a meaning» (*padārtha*), but not a substance (*dravya*).

1 TSP., p. 135. 10.

2 Ibid., p. 135. 23.

3 Ibid., 136. 3 ff.; cp. NK. p. 132. 8 ff.

4 TSP., p. 133. 20 ff.; NK., p. 132. 3 ff.

5 NK., p. 139. 15—*asmin (pradhvaṃse) bhinna-mūrtau kim āyātam bhāvasya? na kiṃcit!* The realists who assume real non-existence, real relations, real annihilation are ridiculed by the Buddhist. If these things are real, they say, they should possess separate bodies, then we shall have «non-existence in person» — *vigrahavān abhāvah, vigrahavān sambandhaḥ, bhinna-mūrtir vināšaḥ*.

6 *āyuṣmān bhāvaḥ*, ibid.

7 *svalakṣaṇa*, ibid.

8 *nirasta-samasta-arthakriya*, ibid.

nil, says the Buddhist to the Vaišeṣika, because it is outside the disappearing thing», it has nothing of its own to support it in the external world. «Just the contrary, answers the Vaišeṣika, your non-existence, i. e. nominalistic non-existence, is empty and nil, because it is included in the disappearing thing and does not represent any separate unity by itself».[1] That existence as well as non-existence must be separate unities added to some thing is clear, because there is between them a possessive relation which finds its expression in speech. The Genitive case in the expressions «existence *of* a thing», «non-existence *of* a thing» points to the fact that a thing can possess existence or non-existence. These expressions, answers the Buddhist, are nothing but perverse language, just as the expression «the body *of* a statue», while the statue itself is the body, there is nothing that possesses this body. The Genitive case «of» has here no meaning at all.[2] Existence and non-existence are not different appurtenances of a thing, they are the thing itself.

There are indeed two kinds of annihilation,[3] empirical annihilation called destruction[4] and a transcendental one called evanescence[5] or impermanence.[6] The first is the annihilation of the jar by a stroke of the hammer. The second is, so to speak, the destruction of the jar by time; an imperceptible, infinitely graduated, constant deterioration or impermanence which is the very essence of reality. Šāntirakṣita[7] therefore says «reality itself is called annihilation, viz, that ultimate reality which has the duration of a moment». It is not produced by a cause[8] like the stroke of a hammer; it arises by itself,[9] since it belongs to the essence of reality,[10] reality is impermanent. The fact that the annihilation of a thing always follows upon its previous existence[11] does not apply to such reality.[12] This reality is dynamic[13] in its

---

1 Cp. NBT., transl., p. 83 n. 4.

2 TSP., p. 138. 27, 142. 27 etc.

3 TSP., p. 137. 21, 156. 11.

4 *pradhvaṃša.*

5 *vināša = vinašvaratva.*

6 *anitya = kṣaṇika.*

7 TS., p. 137. 26—*yo hi bhāvaḥ kṣaṇa-sthāyī vināša iti gīyate.*

8 TSP., p. 138.2—*ahetuka*, cp. ibid., p. 133. 13.

9 TS., p. 132. 12; NK, p. 131. 23.

10 *vinašvara-svabhāva=vastu=cala-vastu-svabhāva*, TSP., p. 138. 10.

11 *vastv-anantara-bhāvitva*, ibid., p. 138. 11.

12 *na ... tādṛši=na cala-svarūpe*, ibid., p. 138. 10.

13 *cala-bhāva-svarūpa*, ibid., p. 138. 9.

essence, it is indivisible,[1] it cannot be divided in parts so that non-existence should follow upon existence,[2] its evanescence arises simultaneously with its production,[3] otherwise evanescence would not belong to the very essence of reality.[4] Existence and non-existence are thus different names given to the same thing «just as a donkey and an ass are different names given to the same animal».[5]

§ 9. Šāntirakṣita's formula.

The formulation of the theory of Instantaneous Being as laid down by Šāntirakṣita in the dictum that «the momentary thing represents its own annihilation»[6] is remarkable in the highest degree. It shows us clearly the kind of reality we have to deal with in Buddhist logic. It is evidently not the empirical object that can be called its own annihilation. Nobody will deny that when a jar has been broken to pieces by a stroke of the hammer it has ceased to exist. But beyond this obvious empirical change there is, as stated above, another, never beginning and never stopping, infinitely graduated, constant change, a running transcendental ultimate reality. The creation of the jar out of a clump of clay and its change into potsherds are but new qualities, i. e., outstanding moments in this uninterrupted change. There is nothing perdurable, no static element in this process. An everlasting substantial matter is declared to be pure imagination, just as an everlasting substantial Soul. There is, therefore, as Šāntirakṣita says, in every next moment not the slightest bit left of what has been existent in the former moment. The moments are necessarily discrete, every moment, i. e., every momentary thing is annihilated as soon as it appears, because it does not survive in the next moment. In this sense everything represents its own annihilation. If something of the preceding moment would survive in the next moment, this would mean eternity, because it would survive in the third and following moments just in the same way as it did survive in the second. Static means eternal;[7] if matter exists, it necessarily is eternal, if it

[1] *niraṃša*, ibid., p. 138. 10.

[2] *yena tad-anantara-bhāvitvam asya bhavati*, ibid., p. 138. 11.

[3] *nāšasya tan-niṣpattāv eva niṣpannatvāt*, ibid.

[4] *anyathā .... (cala)-svabhāvam .... na syāt*, ibid., p. 138. 12.

[5] TS., p. 139. 7.

[6] TS., p. 137.26.

[7] *nityatvam = avasthāna-mātram.* Tātp., p. 239. 24; cp. TSP., p. 140.24 — *yady utpāda-anantaram na vinašyet, tadā pašcād api... tad-avasthaḥ (syāt).*

does not exist, being is necessarily instantaneous. As already mentioned above, the first view is advocated in the Sānkhya system, the second in Buddhism. There can be nothing in the middle, there can be no eternal matter with changing qualities, as naive realism and the realistic systems assume. The transcendentalist, on the other hand, assumes that ultimate reality cannot be divided in substance and quality, it must be indivisible and instantaneous.

This kind of annihilation, transcendental annihilation, is not produced by occurrent causes.[1] Since existence itself is constant annihilation, it will go on existing, i. e., being annihilated and changing, without needing in every case any cause of annihilation. The elements of existence are automatically evanescent,[2] they do not want any additional circumstance [3] in order to produce that change which is going on always and by itself.

Just as the totality [4] of causes and conditions of every event is necessary followed by that event, because the totality is present,[5] nothing else is needed, the totality is the event itself,[6] just so everything is evanescent by its nature, no other cause of annihilation or change is needed. Reality has been characterized as efficiency, it can also be characterized as evanescence or annihilation.

§ 10. Change and Annihilation.

The conception of a change[7] is a direct corollary from the conception of annihilation. Having repudiated the realistic view of annihilation, the Buddhist naturally also repudiates the realistic conception of a change. What is the exact meaning of the word «change?» It means, as already mentioned, either that one thing is replaced by another thing, or that the thing remains the same, but its condition, or quality, has changed, i. e., has become another quality. If it means the first, the Buddhist will not object.[8] But since there is a change at every moment, the thing will be at every moment replaced by another thing.

---

1 TSP., p. 140.25 — *kim nāśa-hetunā tasya kṛtam yena vinaśyeta.*

2 *svarasa-vināśinaḥ (sarve dharmāḥ).*

3 Ibid., p. 141.9 — *sarvathā akiṃcit-kara eva nāśa-hetur iti.*

4 *sāmagrī.*

5 TSP., p. 132.17.

6 Cp. Tatp., p. 80.5 — *sahakāri-sākalyam na prāpter atiricyate.*

7 *sthity-anyathātva* or *anyathātva*, cp. TSP., p. 140.25 ff.

8 *siddha-sādhyatā*, ibid., p. 137.23.

If it means the second, then a series of difficulties arise for the Realist. He assumes the existence of real substances along with real qualities. But ultimate reality cannot be so divided,[1] it cannot represent a stable stuff with real moving qualities situated upon it, as though it were a permanent home for passing visitors. This conception of naive realism cannot stand scrutiny. From the two correlative parts one alone must remain as ultimately real. It can be called a substance, but then, it will be a substance without qualities. Or it may be the qualities, but these qualities will be absolute qualities, without belonging to any substance. «Whatsoever exists, says Yašomitra,[2] is a thing», it neither is a quality nor a substance. Reality, existence, thing and momentary thing are synonyms. If qualities are real, they are things. The categories of substance and quality are relative, they therefore do not reflect ultimate reality,[3] they are created by our intellect.

In this denial of a real substance-to-quality relation the Buddhists, as already mentioned, were at one with the Sānkhyas, but on the positive side both schools parted in opposite directions. The Sānkhyas assumed as ultimately real eternal matter alone, which itself is constantly changing, they denied the separate reality of its passing manifestations. The Buddhists, on the contrary, denied the separate reality of the perdurable matter and stuck to the reality of the passing qualities alone, thus converting them into absolute qualities, qualities not belonging to any substance.

Moreover, the Realist must face in regard of the reality of change the same difficulty with which he was confronted in regard of the reality of annihilation.[4] Does change represent something different from the thing changing or is it this thing itself? If it is nothing different, nothing will happen to the thing, the thing will remain as it was, there will be no change. If it is something apart, it will remain apart and there again will be no change. There is no other issue left than to assume that the words «the change of a thing» contain a perverse expression[5] and that in reality, in ultimate reality, there is another thing at every consecutive moment. When brass is changed from a solid into a liquid condition, the realist assumes that the matter is «the same», but its condition

[1] Ibid., p. 134.3.

[2] Cp. CC, p. 26 n., cp. TSP., p. 128. 17 — *vidyamānam = vastu = dravya = dharma.*

[3] *dharma-dharmi-bhāvo... na sad-asad apekṣate.* (Dignāga).

[4] Cp. TSP., p. 141.2 ff.

[5] Ibid., p. 142.27.

is other». The causes producing destruction, fire etc., cannot annihilate the matter, but they destroy its condition and produce a change.[1] The thing desappears not absolutely, but conditionally, in functional dependence upon causes which produce the change. But this is impossible. The thing must either remain or go, it cannot do both at once, changing and remaining. If it has changed, it is not the same.[2] The example of melted brass proves nothing. Melted brass and solid brass are «other» objects.[3]

§ 11. Motion is discontinuous.

Just as existence is not something added to the existing thing, but it is this thing itself, and just as annihilation, evanescence or change are not something real in superaddition to the thing changing or destroyed, but they are the thing itself, — just so is motion nothing additional to the thing, but it is the thing itself. «There is no motion, says Vasabandhu,[4] because of annihilation». Things do not move, they have no time to do it, they disappear as soon as they appear. Momentary things, says Kamalaśīla, cannot displace themselves «because they disappear at that very place at which they have appeared».[5]

This statement, i. e. the statement that there is no motion, that motion is impossible, seems to stand in glaring contradiction with the former statement according to which reality is kinetic, everything is nothing but motion. Indeed when it is maintained that reality is kinetic, it is implied that everything moves and there is no real stability at all; and when it is maintained that there can be no real motion, it follows by implication that reality consists only of things stabilized and endurable. However these two apparently contradictory statements are only two different expressions of the same fact. The so called stability is the stability of one moment only,[6] and the so

---

1 Ibid., p. 140.27 — *anyathātvam kriyate.*

2 Ibid., p. 141.1 — *na hi sa eva anyathā bhavati*; p. 141.9 — *naikasya anyathātvam asti.*

3 Ibid., p.— 141.10 — *na asiddho hetuḥ*, i. e., the *hetu* of the realist is *asiddha.*

4 AK., IV. I — *na gatir nāśāt*; cp. Tātp., p. 383.13 — *karma-upalāpa-nibandhano hy ayam kṣaṇika-vādaḥ.*

5 TSP., p. 232.90 *tasya (kṣaṇikasya) janma-deśa eva cyuteḥ, nāśād, deśāntara-prāpty-asambhavāt.*

6 *eka-kṣaṇa-sthiti.*

called motion is nothing over and above the consecution of these moments arising without interruption in close contiguity the one after the other[1] and thus producing the illusion of a movement. Movement is like a row of lamps sending flashes the one after the other and thus producing the illusion of a moving light. Motion consists of a series of immobilities. «The light of a lamp, says Vasubandhu,[2] is a common metaphorical designation for an uninterrupted production of a series of flashing flames. When this production changes its place, we say that the light has moved, but in reality other flames have appeared in other contiguous places».

Thus the Buddhists by purely speculative methods came to envisage Motion in a way which bears some analogy with modern mathematical physics.

In order better to understand the position of the Buddhists in this problem we must here again, first of all, contrast the Buddhist views with the views of Indian Realists. This will lead us to another distinction, the distinction between motion considered empirically and motion considered transcendentally.

According to the realistic school of the Vaišeṣikas, motion is a reality, it is one of the three things in which the genus Existence inheres, the other two being Substance and Quality.[3] Motion is something different from the thing moving, it consists in the fact that the conjunction of the thing with its place has been destroyed and a new conjunction of it with a new place has been produced. Prašastapāda[4] defines motion as the real non-relative[5] cause, producing the change of position of a particle in space. It is instantaneous in the first moment and persistent, impressed motion or momentum,[6] in the following ones, up to the moment when the body is again at rest. The Vaišeṣikas accept one impressed motion as duration, lasting till the cessation of the motion.[7] For the Naiyāyiks,

---

1 *nirantara-kṣaṇa-utpāda.*

2 AK., IX, cp. my transl. in Soul Theory, p. 938.

3 The highest genus «existence», *sattā*, inheres, according to the Vaišeṣikas (VS., I. 2. 7—8), in things belonging to the categories of substance, quality and motion. The other categories are «meanings» *padārtha*, they have «*Geltung*» which sometimes is called *svarūpa-sattā*, but they do not «exist».

4 Prašastp., p. 290 ff.

5 *anapekṣa*, i. e., not merely relative to rest (?).

6 *saṃskāra.*

7 *bahūni karmāṇi... ekas tu saṃskāro'ntarāle*, ibid., p. 302.11.

on the contrary, impressed motion is also split into momentary motions, each generating the one that succeeds it. In this respect the Nyāya view falls in line with the Buddhist one. But the idea of an absolute moment as a single point-instant of reality was distasteful to all Realists; even in those cases where they accept constant change, they, as has been already mentioned, compose it of three-momentary or six-momentary durations. When a body falls to the ground, the force acting on it is gravity in the first instance and impressed motion in the succeeding moments, but gravity continues to operate.[1] This affords some explanation of the accelerated motion of falling bodies, as will be stated later on.

The Buddhist view is distinguished from these speculations by the fundamental theory which denies the existence of any substance. There is therefore no motion in the things, but the things themselves are motion. When Vasubandhu, therefore, declares that «there is no motion, because of annihilation», it is this realistic idea of a real motion which he denies. Motion exists empirically. If the Realists would simply maintain that this empirical motion has some cause behind it, the Buddhist would not object.[2] But this cause, according to his theory, consists of momentary fulgurations succeding one another in contiguous places without any abiding stuff in them. These flashes arise not out of the same stuff, but, so to speak, out of nothing,[3] since the foregoing flash is totally extinct[4] before the succeeding one arises. «There is, says Kamalašīla,[5] not the slightest bit of some particle of a thing which survives» in the next succeeding moment.

The picture which the Buddhists made themselves of the real condition of the world is best of all elicited in the manner in which

---

1 *ādyam gurutvād, dvitīyādīni tu gurutva-saṃskārābhyām* ibid., p. 304.17. «Why do we not assume one movement in the interval between its beginning and its end»? asks Prašasta, p. 302.11, i. e., why do we not, like the Buddhists and Naiyāyiks, maintain that it is instantaneous? and answers «because of many conjunctions», i. e. motion being by its very definition conjunction-disjunction with a place, there are as many conjunctions as there are places through which, e. g., an arrow passes in its flight. Cp. H. Bergson's idea that such motion is indivisible. According to the Vaišeṣikas motion is infinitely divisible, but the force (*saṃskāra*) or momentum is one.

2 The «existence» of the preceding moment is the cause: *sattaiva vyāpṛtiḥ*, TS. kār. 1772.

3 *niranvaya.*

4 *niruddha.*

5 TSP., p. 183—*na hi svalpiyaso'pi vastv-aṃšasya kasyacid anvayo'sti.*

they tried to explain the phenomemon of accelaration in a falling body[1] or the phenomenon of the rising smoke.[2] They found in these phenomena a striking confirmation of their idea that at every moment of its existence the falling body is really «another» body, because it is differently composed. Its weight is different at every moment. Every material body is a composition of four fundamental elements, which are conventionally called earth, water, fire and wind. Under the name of «earth» the solid element is understood, «water» is the name for the force of cohesion or viscidity, «fire» means temperature, and «wind» means weight or motion. All these elements or forces are present in whatsoever piece of matter, always in the same proportion. If the bodies are sometimes solid and sometimes liquid, sometimes hot and sometimes moving, this depends on the greater amount of intensity[3] in the energy representing the elements, not on its quantitative predominance. That the element of solidity is present in water is proved by its capacity of supporting a ship on its surface. That the «liquid» element is present in fire is proved by the fact that the particles of fire are holding together in a flame. It is clear that the fundamental elements of matter are rather forces or momentary quanta of energy than substantial atoms. They accordingly fall under the category of «cooperators» or «cooperating forces». The fourth element is called «motion», but also «lightness», i. e., weight.[4] Thus every material object is the meeting-point of the forces of repulsion, attraction, heat and weight. When a body falls, its movement in every point is accelarated, i. e., is «another» movement. It is also another weight and another quantum of the force of gravitation. The Buddhist philosopher concludes that the falling body is another body in every consecutive moment of its motion, because the quantum of energy is different in every moment and the material bodies in general are nothing over and above the quanta of energy which enter in their composition.[5]

---

1 AKB., ad 11.46, de la Vallée's transl. I, p. 229—230.

2 Ibid.

3 *utkarṣa*. It thus appears that ancient Indian had something in the kind of a dynamical theory of matter, as opposed to a mechanistic one, cp. below.

4 *laghutva* = *iraṇātmaka*, cp. AKB., ad I. 12.

5 On the motion in a falling body cp. NV., p. 420.

§ 12. Annihilation certain a priori.

Thus the argument which proceeds by an analysis of the notions of non-existence and annihilation leads to the establishment of the theory of momentariness just as the argument drawn from the analysis of the notion of existence as causal efficiency. We have pointed out that both arguments are analityeal, hence the conclusion appears with logical necessity. There is a third argument which differs but very slightly from the second. It starts from the fact that everything necessarily[1] must have an end. There is nothing at all that would have no end. This trivial truth which is known to every body, when minutely examined, cannot mean anything else than that evanescence is the very core of existence. If everything is evanescent, it is always evanescent, a thing cannot be severed from its own essence, there is therefore no duration at all. The evanescence of everything is *a priori* certain.

Thus it is that the momentary character of all existence is something which can be established *a priori*.[2]

Vācaspati-mišra[3] informs us that the early Buddhists deduced the idea of Momentariness by an induction from observation, it was for them an *a posteriori* idea. They at first noticed that such objects, as fire, light, sound, thought, were changing at every moment. A little more attention convinced them that our body is also changing constantly, so that at every consecutive point-instant it is «another» body. Then by a broad generalisation from observation, in an inductive way, they concluded, «just as this our body, so also the crystal gem»; it also is older of a moment in every succeeding point-instant. This way of reasoning was followed by the early Buddhists. But the later Buddhists did not prove momentariness by a generalisation from induction. They had found that annihilation, i. e., an end, was necessary, unavoidable, *a priori* certain, no need of proving it by observation. The realists answered by the following reasoning.[4] «Please, said they to the Buddhists, consider the following dilemma: does the continuity

---

[1] *dhruva-bhāvi* = *avašyam-bhāvi*, NK., pp. 132.14 ff.; Tātp., p. 383.19 ff; TS., p. 132.15 ff; NBT., 11.37.

[2] *a priori* in the sense of non-empirical; literally *a priori* could be translated as *pratyañcaḥ pratyayāḥ*, cp. NK., p. 267.19, *parāñcaḥ* = *a posteriori*, Tātp., p. 84.18.

[3] Tātp., p. 380 ff.

[4] Ibid., 386.14 ff.

of existence of the potsherds necessarily follow upon the continuity of the existence of the jar, or not? If not, then the end of the jar is not at all necessary. We may indeed open our eyes as much as you like, we do not arrive at perceiving the end of the jar otherweise than at the moment of its change into potsherds.[1] Thus the necessary end of the jar is not really proved. Now let us admit that it is (*a priori*) necessary, nevertheless when it really happens, we observe that this necessary end depends upon the stroke of a hammer, that is to say, an adventitious cause, it is not necessary at all. The end is not concomitant with unconditional (*a priori*) necessity, you must prove that it does not depend upon a special circumstance. Therefore, since your proof of momentary change is thus repudiated, you really must admit that the recognition of the same jar in consecutive moments of its existence proves that it is one and the same jar (and not «another» jar in every moment)». But the Buddhist answers, «Whatsoever is not (*a priori*) necessary, depends upon special causes, just as the colour of a cloth depends upon the dye which has been applied; it is not necessary. If all existing things were likewise dependent for their end upon special causes, then we would have empirical objects which never would have an end, we would have eternal empirical objects. But this is impossible. The necessity of an end points to the fact that the things are so born that they go at the same moment as they are born, they go by themselves, without a special cause, they do not continue in the next moment. Thus it is proved that they change at every moment».

§ 13. Momentariness deduced from the law of contradiction.

Whatsoever exists, exists separately [2] from «other» existing things. To exist means to exist separately. What exists really has an existence of its own; to have an existence of its own, means to stand out from among other existing things. This is an analytic proposition, since the notion of «apartness» belongs to the essential features of the notion of «existence».[3] If something is not apart from other existing things, if it has no existence of its own, if its existence coalesces with the existence

---

1 NK., p. 139.21 ff.

2 *sarvam pṛthak*, NS., IV. 1. 36.

3 *bhāva-lakṣaṇa-pṛthaktvāt*, ibid.

of other things, it is a mere name for those other things, or a construction of our imagination. E. g., the whole does not exist separately from its constituent parts, time and space do not exist apart from point-instants, the Soul does not exist apart from mental phenomena, Matter does not exist apart from sense-data etc., etc. Since they are not apart, they do not exist at all.

Now, what is the thing which is really something quite apart from all other existing things, which is something quite unique?[1] It is the mathematical «point-instant».[2] Its only relation to other existents is «otherness». It is numerically other, not qualitatively. Every relation and every quality is something belonging to two realities at least, and therefore something unreal itself, as something having no existence of its own, apart from these two realities.

The formula of this «law of otherness» runs thus. A thing is «other», if united to incompatible properties.[3] Difference of quality involves a difference of the thing, if the qualities are mutually exclusive. Two qualities are not incompatible if the one is under the other, the one a part of the other, e. g. colour and red. But they are incompatible if they are both under the same determinable, as, e. g., red and yellow or, more properly, red and non-red. If the determinable is very remote or if there is no common determinable at all, the incompatibility is still greater.[4] It is obvious that this statement of the law of otherness is but a negative form of the law of contradiction as expressed in European logic by Aristoteles: nothing can possess at the same time, in the same place and in the same respect two mutually exclusive properties. This European formula of the law of contradiction presupposes the existence of the relation of substance and quality, or of «continuants and occurrents». In India we are faced, as mentioned above, by two systems which deny the objective reality of this relation. The Sānkhya admits a continuant only and the Buddhists admit merely the occurrents. A thing is then another thing whenever its determinations are other. These determinations are Time, Space and Quality.[5] A thing is other when its quality is other, e. g., the same thing cannot be at once red and yellow, i. e., red and non-red. It is other when its position in space is other, e. g., the radiance of a jewel in one place and its radiance in another place are two different things.

---

[1] *sarvato vyāvṛtta, trailokya-vyāvṛtta.*

[2] *kṣaṇa = svalakṣaṇa.*

[3] NBT., p. 4—*viruddha-dharma-saṃsargād anyad vastu.*

[4] Cp. below on the law of contradiction and on *apoha.*

[5] *deśa-kāla-ākāra-bhedaś ca viruddha-dharma-saṃsargaḥ.* NBT., ibid.

Since an extended body involves position in at least two points of space, extension is not something ultimately real, in every point the thing is ultimately another thing. The same applies to time. The same thing cannot really exist in two different moments, in every instant it is a different thing.[1] Even the moment of sensation and the moments of a thing's apperception refer, in ultimate reality, to two different things. Their unity in the presentation is a constructed or imagined unity.

Thus every reality is another reality. What is identical or similar is not ultimately real. The real is the unique,[2] the thing in itself, the unrelated thing. All relations are constructed, relation and construction are the same. Ultimate reality is non-constructed, non imagined, non-related reality, the thing as it strictly is in itself, it is the mathematical point-instant.

We will revert to this problem when considering the Indian formula of the laws of Identity and of Contradiction. It is sufficient at present to point out the connection between the law of Contradiction and the theory of Instantaneous Existence. Many philosophers in Europe have laid down the dictum that identity implies difference. A is different from B even if they are identical, and *a fortiori*, when they are only similar. Buddhist philosophy operates with the (transcendental) notion of absolutely dissimilar and non-identical realities which are discrete point-instants.[3] Leibniz's principle that there are no two absolutely identical things in nature, the identity of indiscernibles being resolved in a continuity of qualitative change is, to a certain extent, comparable with the Buddhist view, with that capital difference that the discontinuous, unique and discrete thing is the limit of all continuity and is converted into an absolute ultimate existence of the mathematical point-instant.[4]

---

[1] The example given NBT., p. 4. 6, is evidently chosen with the intention to be approved both by the Buddhist and the Realist, but the real meaning of the Buddhist appears from the remark, ibid., p. 4. 8 ff.

[2] *svalakṣaṇam = paramārtha-sat.*

[3] Cp. below on the history of the idea of *kṣaṇikatva.*

[4] Among modern authors I find the «law of otherness» thoroughly discussed in W. E. Johnson Logic, I. ch. XII. The coincidences with Indian speculations are often striking. But the idea that «the real» must be «one» real, and that real being means one being is already familiar to the schoolmen who maintained that *«ens et unum convertuntur»*; it has been enlarged upon by Leibniz and lead him to the establishment of the ultimate reality of his Monads.

§ 14. Is the point-instant a reality? The differential calculus.

In the preceding exposition it has been sufficiently established that empirical Time and Space are, for the Buddhist, fictions constructed by our understanding on the basis of sensible point-instants which alone are the ultimate reality. Against this theory which reduces the reality to the «this», the «now», the «here», and converts all the rest of our knowledge into imaginative and relative differentiation, the Realists raised the very natural objection that the point-instant itself is no exception to the general rule, since it is also nothing but a construction in thought, a mere name without any corresponding reality. «In assuming, says Uddyotakara[1] to the Buddhist, that time itself is nothing but a name, you evidently also must assume that the shortest time, the time-limit, is likewise nothing but a name». The Buddhist retorts that the shortest time, the mathematical point-instant, is something real, since it is established in science.[2] The astronomer makes it the basis of all his computations. It is an indivisible time particle, it does not contain any parts standing in the relation of antecedence and sequence.[3] The Indian astronomers made a distinction between «time grossly measured»[4] and a «subtle time»,[5] measured with precision. The motion of a thing during a single moment they called instantaneous motion, or the «motion of just that time»,[6] i. e., not of another time, not of another moment. This time is nothing but the differential of a planet's longitude. Such a moment is no reality, says the Realist, it is a mere mathematical convenience.[7] «Just the contrary, says the Buddhist, we maintain that the instantaneousness of being is the ultimately real thing». The only thing in the universe which is a non-construction, a non-fiction, is the sensible point-instant, it is the real basis of all constructions.[8] It is true that it is a reality which cannot be represented in a sensuous image,[9] but this is just because it is

---

1 NV., p. 418. 15.

2 NVTP., p. 387. 1-*jyotir-vidyā-siddha*.

3 *pūrva-apara-bhāga-vikala*. Ibid., cp. NK., p. 127. 12.

4 *sthūla-kāla, kāla-piṇḍa*.

5 *sūkṣma-gatiḥ*.

6 *tat-kālikī gatiḥ*.

7 *sanjñā-mātram*.

8 *vāstavīkṣaṇikatā abhimatā*.

9 *kṣaṇasya (jñānena) prāpayitum aśakyatvāt*, cp. NBT., p. 12. 19 (*prāptiḥ = savikalpakam jñānam*).

not a thought-construction. The absolutely unique point-instant of reality, as it cannot be represented, can also not be named [1] otherwise than by a pronoun «this», «now» etc. Consequently it is not a mere name, it is no name at all, it has no name; ultimate reality is unutterable. What is utterable is always more or less a thought-construction. [2] Thus it is that the mathematical point-instant is a fiction for the Realist and a reality for the Buddhist, and *vice versa* empirical time or «gross time»,[3] «substantial time» [4] is a reality for the Realist and a fiction for the Buddhist. Just as the mathematician constructs his velocities out of differentials, so does the human mind, a natural mathematician, construct duration out of momentary sensations.

That space likewise contains no other ultimate reality than the momentary sensation has already been pointed out. [5] Dharmakīrti says: [6] «an extended form exists in the (real) object not (more) than in its idea. To admit that (the extended body) exists in one (unextended atom) would be a contradiction, and to admit that (the same extended body being one) is present in many (atoms) is an impossibility». The extended body being thus a fiction, there is no other issue left than to admit the ultimate reality of the point-instant.[7]

Whether the honour of having discovered the Differential Calculus must really be attributed to the Hindu astronomers we must leave it for others to decide,[8] but in any case they were unquestionally the discoverers of the mathematical zero. The idea of a mathematical limit, therefore, must have bean familiar to Indian scholars.[9] It is no wonder

[1] TSP., p. 276.

[2] *śabdā vikalpa-yonayaḥ, vikalpāḥ śabda-yonayaḥ* (Dignāga).

[3] *sthūla-kāla.*

[4] *kāla-piṇḍa.*

[5] Cp. above, p. 85 ff.

[6] Cp. NVTT., p. 425. 20—*tasmān nārthe na vijñāne...*

[7] The Thing-in-Itself has been compared with a «Differential of Sensibility» by S. Maimon.

[8] Dr. B. N. Seal asserts it and Mr Spottiswoode, the Royal Astronomer, to whom the facts have been submitted, admitted it with reservations, cp. P. G. Ray's Hindu Chemistry, v. II, p. 160 ff (where Dr. B. N. Seal's article is reprinted from his Positive Sciences of the Hindus).

[9] M. H. Bergson asserts that the world of the mathematician is indeed an instantaneous world, it is also *kṣaṇika* as the world of the Buddhist. He says (Cr. Ev., p. 23—24)—«the world the mathematician deals with is a world that dies and is reborn at every instant, the world which Descartes was thinking of when he spoke of continuous creation». This idea is indeed quite Buddhistic, it sounds as if it were put in sanscrit—*ye bhāvā nirantaram ārabhyanta iti mahāpaṇḍita-śrī-*

that they applied it in the field of general philosophy, they were not the only school to do it.[1]

§ 15. History of the doctrine of Momentariness.

The origin of the theory of Instantaneous Being is most probably pre-Buddhistic.[2] Its vicissitudes in Buddhism are interwoven with the history of different sects. Since the literature of the majority of these sects is lost beyond recovery, we must be content to point out some salient features which will allow us tentatively to draw the main line of its development. We may at present distinguish between 1) the initial form of the doctrine when it was laid down with considerable precision, 2) a series of deviations and fluctuations in the schools of Hīnayāna, 3) a crisis of the doctrine in the schools of Mahāyāna when it seemed to be given up altogether, 4) its reintroduction in the school of Asanga and Vasubandhu, and 5) its final form in the school of Dignāga and Dharmakīrti.

This final form, we have seen, implies that ultimate reality belongs to the mathematical point-instant, to a time-unit which contains no parts standing in the relation of antecedence and sequence or, more precisely, to the infinitesimal differential points of reality, out of which our intellect constructs the empirical world as it appears to our understanding in manifold images. The theory is at that time founded on epistemological investigations. It is then the direct consequence of the theory of two heterogeneous sources of our knowledge, the senses which supply merely the detached point-instants of pure reality and the intellect which constructs of these infinitesimals a manifold and ordered world

At the opposite end of this historical process, at the starting point of Buddhism, we find a theory which is essentially the same, although

---

Dhekaratena vikalpitās, te sarve jyotir-vidyā-prasiddhāḥ pratikṣaṇam utpadyante vinaśyante ca. This being the precise rendering of Bergson's words, sounds like a quotation from an Indian text. It is also noteworthy that one of the synonyms for thought or constructive thought is computation *(sankalana)*. Thus thought, productive imagination and mathematics become closely related, cp. vol. II, p. 292 — *saṁākalayet = vikalpayet = utprekṣeta.*

[1] The Sānkhya-Yoga in this point, as in many others, comes very near to the Buddhist view, cp. Vyāsa on III. 52—*kālo vastu-śūnya-buddhi-nirmāṇaḥ sarva-jñāna-anupātī, kṣaṇas tu vastu-patitaḥ* ...., cp. B. N. Seal, op. cit., p. 80. Vijñāna-bhikṣu points out «time has no real, or objective, existence apart from the «moment», but the latter is real, being identical with the unit of change in phenomena»—*guṇa-pariṇāmasya kṣaṇatva-vacanāt.* Ibid.

[2] Cp. CC., p. 65 ff.

it is then bereft of its epistemological foundation. All reality is split in separate elements which are instantaneous. The theory of momentariness is implied in the pluralistic theory of the separate elements of existence. As soon as Buddhism made its appearance as a theory of elements, it was already a theory of instantaneous elements. Having arisen as a spirited protest against the Monism of the Upanishads[1] and of Sānkhya, it did not stop half the way, it asserted straight off the exclusive reality of the minutest elements of existence.[2] These elements were not mathematical points however, they were momentary sense-data and thought-data, linked together in an individual life only by the laws of causal interdependence. It would have been natural to assume that the Buddhists arrived at this precise formulation gradually, and that the starting point of the development was the general and very human consideration of impermanence as it naturally suggests itself to the mind in common life. However it seems that at the time when the fundamental principles of Buddhism were laid down, the formula «no substance, no duration, no other bliss than in Nirvāṇa» already referred not to simple impermanence, but to the elements of existence whose ultimate reality was confined to the duration of a single moment, two moments being two separate elements.[3]

---

[1] Just as in the history of Vedānta we have here mutual indebtedness. The early Buddhists were influenced by Sānkhya ideas, but later on the Pātañjala-Yogas were very strongly influenced by the formulas of the Sarvāstivādins, cp. my CC., p. 47.

[2] If we accept the highly ingenious suggestion of the late M. E. Senart, that the term *satkāya-dṛṣṭi* is initially a corruption of *satkārya-dṛṣṭi*, we will see that the fundamental tenet of the Sānkhyas becomes a fundamental error for the Buddhists. The Sānkhyas (and Ājīvikas) maintain that everything, although constantly changing, exists eternally, nothing new appears in the world and nothing disappears; the Buddhists, on the contrary, maintain that everything exists instantaneously, it appears out of nothing and reverts at once into nothing, there is no *sub*-stance at all. Both these theories are radical (*ekānta*), they deny the categories of Inherence, Substance and Quality, deny the eternal atoms and maintain infinite divisibility, they are both opposed in these points by the Vaiśeṣikas. The central point at issue seems to have been the problem of Inherence. Vaiśeṣikas, and probably the early Yogas, admitted it, Sānkhyas and Buddhists rejected it, although from opposite sides. The «radical» standpoint of the Buddhists seems to have been their original view. The character of the deviations from it in the schools of the Vatsīputrīyas, Sarvāstivādins, Kāsyapīyas and others clearly shows that the «radical» view of separate and momentary elements lies at the bottom.

[3] CC., p. 38.

Now just in the middle between this initial and the final form of the doctrine it underwent a dangerous crisis.

The school of the Mādhyamikas bluntly denied the reality of the supposed point-instants of existence. Against the theory they appealed to common sense. Who is the man of sense, they thought, who will believe that a real thing can appear, exist and disappear at the same moment.[1] However this denial has no special bearing upon the theory of instantaneousness, since that school declared every separate object and every notion to be dialectical, relative and illusive.

The history of the theory of instantaneous reality during the first period prooves clearly how difficult it is for the human mind to grapple with the idea of pure change, i. e., the idea of a reality in which there is no *sub*-stance at all. The categories of an abiding substance with changing qualities is so deeply rooted in all our habits of thought that we always become reluctant to admit pure change, even when it is urged upon us by logic.

The school of the Vatsīputrīyas were the first among the early schools which admitted the existence of a certain unity between the elements of a living personality. Their position in this problem is highly instructive. They dared not readmit the spiritual substance of a Soul, so strong was the opposition against this idea in Buddhist circles. But they also were reluctant to deny any kind of unity between the separate elements of a personality and admit that the separate elements constituting a personality hold together only by causal laws. They therefore adopted an intermediate course. The personality was declared to be something dialectical, neither identical with its elements, nor different from them. It was not given the reality of an ultimate element, nor was that reality denied altogether.[2] This course of admitting dialectical reality and neglecting the law of contradiction reminds us of the dialectical method very popular among the Jains and consisting in assuming everywhere a double and contradictory real essence. It prooves at the same time that the doctrine of a radical separateness of all elements and their exclusive link in causal laws was anterior to the rise of the school of the Vatsīputrīyas.

Another attack against the theory of absolute change originated in the schools of the Sarvāstivādins and of the Kāšyapīyas. The theory

---

[1] Cp. Candrakīrti in the Madhy. vṛtti., p. 547.

[2] Cp. Vasubandhu's exposition of that theory, AK. IX, transl. in my Soul Theory.

of absolute change implies the idea that only the present exists. The past does not exist, because it exists no more, and the future is not real, because it does not yet exist. To this the Sarvāstivādins objected that the past and the future are real, because the present has its roots in the past and its consequences in the future. The Kāśyapīyas divided the past into a past whose influence has been exhausted and a past whose influence has not yet been exhausted. The second they maintained was real, the first was not real. This theory involved the danger of shifting into the pale of Sānkhya with its permanent stuff and its changing manifestations. In fact some Sarvāstivādins divided the elements in a permanent essence and momentary manifestations.[1] They nevertheless protested against the accusation of drifting into Sānkhya. All elements, they maintained, were instantaneous, they appeared and disappeared just at the same moment.[2]

Vasubandhu informs us[3] that the theory of the Sarvāstivādins was an innovation of the «exegetical literature», i. e., it was introduced by the ābhidharmikas, and it is not found, according to him, in the genuine Discourses of the Buddha. The school of the Sautrāntikas, that is to say, that school which proclaimed on its banner a return to the genuine doctrine of the Discourses, denied therefore the permanent essence of the elements and reestablished the doctrine that reality consists of momentary flashes, that the «elements appear into life out of non-existence and return again into non-existence after having been existent» for a moment only. «When a visual sensation arises, says Buddha in one of his discourses, there is absolutely nothing from which it proceeds, and when it vanishes, nought there is to which it retires».[4] But although arising «out of nothing» the elements are interdependent, i. e., connected by causal laws which evoke an illusion of their stability.

A further deviation from the principle of separate, momentary and equal elements consists in the division of Matter into primary and secondary elements and in the difference established between a central element of pure consciousness as separate from the secondary

1 Cp. Vasubandhu's exposition, transl. in CC., p. 76. ff.; cp. O. Rosenberg, Problems.

2 It is clear that the Sartāstivādins tackled the same problem which occupies our modern Geltungs-philosophie: the past, just as the universal, does not «exist», but it is real, since it is valid (es *gilt*, es *hat Bedeutung*).

3 CC., p. 90.

4 Ibid., p. 85.

elements representing mental phenomena or moral forces. This decidedly was a back door for the categories of substance and quality partly to reenter into their usual position out of which they were ousted by Buddhism at its start.[1] Therefore the division of the momentary elements into primary and secondary did not remain without protest. Vasubandhu informs us that Buddhadeva did not admit neither the central position of pure consciousness among the mental elements of a personality nor the fundamental position of the tangibles among the elements of matter.[2]

The Ceylonese school preserved faithfully the original doctrine, viz, that every element is instantaneous, it cannot last even for two consecutive moments, because nothing survives in the next moment from what existed in the previous one. But in its mediaeval period this school invented a very curious theory according to which the moment of thought was much shorter than the momentary sense-datum.[3] A kind of preestablished harmony was supposed to exist between the moments of the external world and the moments of their cognition, a momentary sense-datum corresponding to 17 thought-moments. In order clearly to apprehend a momentary sense-datum thought must have passed through 17 consecutive stages, from the moment of being evoked out of a subconscious condition up to the moment of reverting into that condition. If the series for some reason were incomplete, the cognition would not attain clearness. These 17 moments are the following ones: 1) subconsciousness,[4] 2—3) first movement of thought and its desappearance[5], 4) choice of one of the 5 senses[6] (doors), 5) the sense chosen,[7] 6) sensation,[8] 7) presentation,[9] 8) its affirmation,[10] 9—15) emotions,[11] 16—17) two moments of reflexion,[12] after which the series corresponding to one moment of the external sense-datum is at an end.

---

1 Cp. my CC., p. 35 ff.

2 Cp. AK., IX, cp. my Soul Theory

3 Abhidhammatthasaṃgaho, IV. 8 (Kosambi ed., p. 18).

4 *atīta-bhavaṃga*

5 *bhavaṃga-calana, bhavaṃga-uccheda.*

6 *pañcadvārāvajjana-cittaṃ.*

7 *cakkhu-viññānaṃ.*

8 *sampaṭicchana-cittaṃ.*

9 *santīraṇa-cittaṃ.*

10 *voṭṭhapana-cittaṃ.*

11 *javanaṃ.*

12 *tadārammaṇaṃ.*

This theory seems to be quite unknown in all other schools. But the fundamental idea of no duration and no substance has evidently guided those who invented it.

In the first period of Mahāyāna the theory of Instantaneous Being lost every importance, since in the empirical plane the school of the Mādhyamikas had nothing to object against naive realism[1] and in regard of the Absolute it admitted only a cognition through mystic intuition.

However the theory of Instantaneous Being was reasserted in the second period of the Mahāyāna, in the school of the Yogācāras, in Buddhist Idealism. This school began by maintaining the reality of thought on the principle of *cogito ergo sum*.[1] The elements of thought were assumed as instantaneous, but the school at the same time aimed at maintaining the reality of the whole without denying the reality of the parts. The ultimate elements were divided in three classes: pure or absolute existence,[2] pure imagination[3] and a contingent reality between them.[4] The first and last class were admitted as two varieties of reality, the second, pure imagination, was declared to be unreal and non-existent. In this threefold division of the elements we have already the germ of that radical discrimination between sensible reality and imaginative thought which became later on, in the school of Dignāga, the foundation stone of his theory of cognition.

But although the theory of Instantaneous Being has been reintroduced by Buddhist Idealism, it did not enjoy an unconditioned sway. Just as in the Hīnayāna period the categories of substance and quality although officially banned, always tended to reappear through some back-door,[5] just so in the idealistic period the notion of a Soul, although it continued to be officially repudiated — Buddhists still remain the champions of Soullessness — nevertheless haunted the domain of Buddhist philosophy and tended to introduce itself in some form or other into the very heart of Buddhism. At first a «store house of consciousness»[6]

---

[1] Cp. above, p. 12.

[2] *pari-niṣpanna.*

[3] *pari-kalpita.*

[4] *para-tantra.*

[5] Cp. CC., p. 35.

[6] *ālaya-vijñāna.* On the rearrangement of the system of the elements of existence by Asanga cp. L. de la Vallée Poussin, Les 75 et les 100 dharmas, Muséon, VI, 2, 178 ff. The system of Asanga includes *ālaya-vijñāna* among the *saṃskṛta* and *tathatā* among the *asaṃskṛta-dharmas.*

Stcherbatsky, I

was imagined to replace the cancelled external reality. All the traces of former deeds and all the germs of future thoughts were stored up in that receptacle. In compliance with Buddhist tradition this consciousness was also assumed as instantaneous, but it was evidently nothing but a Soul in disguise and as such was repudiated in the school of Dignāga and Dharmakīrti.[1] Saint Asanga, the founder of Buddhist Idealism, apparently fluctuated between this theory of a store of consciousness and the mystic idea of the Mādhyamikas, for whom the individual was but a manifestation of the Absolute or of the Cosmical Body of the Buddha. This manifestation under the names of «Buddha's progeny»,[2] «Buddha's seed»,[3] «Buddha's womb»,[4] the «element of Buddhahood»[5] was again nothing but a Soul in disguise corresponding to the *jīva* of the Vedāntins, just as the Cosmical Body of Buddha corresponds to their «Highest Brahma».

In the Sautrāntika-Yogācāra school of Dignāga and Dharmakīrti the theory of Instantaneous Being was finally laid down in the form and with the arguments which have been here examined, but it did not exclude the unity of the elements on another plane, from the stand-point of the highest Absolute, as will be explained later on.

§ 16. Some European parallels.

Leibniz declares in the preface to his Théodicée that one of the famous labyrinths, in which our reason goes astray, consists in the discussion of continuity and of the indivisible points which appear to be its elements. To reconcile the notion of substance as continuous with the contrary notion of discontinuous elements, he devised his theory of Monads which are not extensive, but intensive and perceptive units. Some remarks on the analogies between Leibnizian and Buddhist ideas will be made later on.

The similarity with the views of Heracleitus has already been pointed out. We have also had several occasions to draw the attention of the reader on some remarkable coincidences between them and the views

---

1 Cp. vol. II, p. 329, n.

2 *tathāgata-gotra.*

3 *sarvajña-bīja.*

4 *tathāgata-garbha.*

5 *tathāgata-dhātu.* On this problem as well as on the development of Asangas ideas cp. E. Obermiller's translation of Uttara-tantra.

of a modern philosopher, M. H. Bergson. It will perhaps not be amiss to reconsider this point once more, in order better to understand, by way of a contrast, the Buddhist point of view. There is indeed much similarity in the form in which the idea of an universal flux has taken shape in both systems, but there is also a divergence in the interpretation of this fact. There is an almost complete coincidence in some of the chief arguments used for its establishment, and there is a capital difference in the final aims of both systems.

The final aim of Bergson is to establish a real duration and a real time, he is a realist. The ultimate reality of the Buddhist is beyond our time and beyond our space, he is a transcendentalist.

The arguments for the establishment of the fact of a universal flux of existence are drawn on both sides 1) from introspection, 2) from an analysis of the notion of existence as meaning constant change and 3) from an analysis of the notion of non-existence as being a pseudo-idea.

«What is the precise meaning of the word „exist"», asks Bergson[1] and answers, «we change without ceasing, the state itself is nothing but a change»,[2] «change is far more radical as we are at first inclined to suppose».[3] The permanent substratum of these changes, the Ego, «has no reality»,[4] «there is no essential difference between passing from one state to another and persisting in the same state», it is an «endless flow».[5]

In these words Bergson makes a statement to the effect that 1) there is no Ego, i. e., no permanent substratum for mental phenomena, 2) existence means constant change, what does not change does not exist, 3) these changing states are not connected by a permanent substratum, ergo they are connected only by causal laws, the laws of their consecution and interdependence. The coincidence with the fundamental principles of Buddhist philosophy could not be more complete. Buddhism is called 1) the no-Ego doctrine,[6] 2) the doctrine of impermanence, or of Instantaneous Being,[7] and 3) the doctrine of

---

1 Creative Evolution (London, 1928), p. 1.

2 Ibid., p. 2.

3 Ibid., p. 1.

4 Ibid., p. 4.

5 Ibid., p. 3.

6 *anātma-vāda.*

7 *kṣaṇika-vada.*

Dependent Origination,[1] i. e., the doctrine which substitutes causal laws for the permanent substratum of passing phenomena.

The cause of growing old, continues Bergson,[2] are not the phagocytes, as the realist imagines, it must lie deeper, «properly vital in growing old is the insensible, infinitely graduated, continuance of the change of form in everything existing». «Succession is an undeniable fact even in the material world».[3] The Buddhist, we have seen, also directs his attention to the human body after having noticed the constant change which constitutes the quasi duration of a fire, of sound, of motion or of a thought. The human body is also nothing but constant change. He concludes, «just as the human body, so is also the crystal gem», existence is nothing but constant change; this is a general law, what does not change does not exist, as, e. g., the Cosmical Ether. The reason why our thought converts motion into stability is, according to Bergson, the fact that we are «preoccupied before everything with the necessities of action». Out of that duration which constantly «makes itself or it unmakes itself, but never is something made»[4] «we pluck out these *moments*[5] that interest us»,[6] thought prepares our action upon the things. The Buddhist, we have seen, likewise defines thought as a preparation to purposive action upon things, and reality as a thing, or a point-instant, which experiences this action.

But still more remarkable is the coincidence in the arguments which both the Buddhists and Bergson have drawn in favour of their theories from an analysis of the ideas of non-existence and annihilation. The idea of non-existence is closely related to the problem of the essence of a negative judgment. This problem has been solved in European logic by Ch. Sigwart: negation is but a special kind of affirmation.[7] This is exactly the Buddhist view, as will be shown in a later chapter. Bergson devotes some of his most eloquent pages[8] to the development of this theory. On this occasion he establishes that annihilation is a pseudo-idea, that «we speak of the absence of a thing sought for whenever we find (instead of it) the presence of another

1 *pratītya-samutpāda-vāda.*
2 Ibid., p. 19—20.
3 Ibid., p. 10.
4 Ibid., p. 287.
5 Ital. mine.
6 Ibid., p. 288.
7 Cp. Creative Evolution, pp. 304, 312.
8 Ibid., p. 287—314.

reality».[1] He establishes that annihilation is not something «in superaddition» to a thing, just as production is not something in superaddition to nothing. Bergson even maintains that the nothing contains not less, but more than the something.[2] Is it not the same as Sāntirakṣita declaring that «the thing itself is called annihilation?» [3] Both the Buddhists and Bergson reject as absurd the every day conception of change, of annihilation and motion. Change is not a sudden disaster ushered into the placidly existing thing, neither is annihilation something that supersedes existence, nor motion something added to a thing. Both systems deny the existence of an enduring substance. So far they agree. Bergson's dynamic conception of existence, his idea that existence is constant change, constant motion, motion alone, absolute motion, motion without any stuff that moves [4] — this idea which it is so difficult for our habits of thought to grapple with — is, on its negative side, in its stuff denial, exactly the same as the Buddhist contention. There are, we have seen, on the Indian side three different systems which maintain the theory of constant change; the Sānkhya system which maintains that matter itself is constant change; the Yoga system which maintains the existence of a perdurable stuff along a constant change in its qualities or conditions and the Buddhist system which denies the reality of an eternal matter and reduces reality to mere motion without any background of a stuff.

But here begins the capital divergence between both systems. Bergson compares our cognitive apparatus with a cinematograph [5] which reconstitutes a movement out of momentary stabilized snapshots.[6] This is exactly the Buddhist view. He quotes the opinion of Descartes that existence is continuous new creation.[7] He also quotes the paralogism of Zeno who maintained that «a flying arrow is

[1] Ibid., p. 312.

[2] Ibid., p. 291; and p. 302— «however strange our assertion may seem there is more... in the idea of an object conceived as „not existing", than in the idea of this same object conceived as „existing"». Bergson, p. 290, reproaches philosophers «to have paid little attention to the idea of the nought», but this by no means refers to Indian philosophers. Some **Hegelians** also thought that the Nothing is more than the Something; cp. **Trendelenburg**, Log. Untersuch I. 113.

[3] Cp. above, p. 95.

[4] Cp. especially his lectures on «La perception du changement».

[5] Ibid., p. 322 ff.

[6] Ibid., p. 322, 358.

[7] Ibid., p. 24; cp. above p. 107, n. 9.

motionless, for it cannot have time to move, that is, to occupy at least two successive positions, unless at least two moments are allowed it».[1] Is it not just the same as Vasubandhu telling us that there is no motion, because (in the next moment) the thing is no more?[2] Or Šāntirakṣita telling that there is in the second moment not the slightest bit left of what existed the moment before?[3] But this instantaneousness, according to Bergson, is an artificial construction of our thought. He thinks that every attempt to «reconstitute change out of states» is doomed, because «the proposition that movement is made out of immobilities is absurd».[4] However the Buddhist, we have seen, when challenged to explain the construction of motion out of immobility, points to mathematical astronomy which also constructs the continuity of motion out of an infinite number of immobilities.[5] Our cognitive apparatus is not only a cinematograph, it also is a natural mathematician. The senses, indeed, even if continuity be admitted, can pluck out only instantaneous sensations, and it is the business of the intellect to reconstitute their continuity. Bergson thinks, that if the arrow leaves the point A to fall down in the point B, its movement AB is simple and indecomposable», a single movement is, for him, «entirely a movement between two stops».[6] But for the Buddhists there are no stops at all other than in imagination, the universal motion never stops, what is called a stop in common life is but a moment of change, the so called «production of a dissimilar moment».[7] In short, duration for the Buddhist is a construction, real are the instantaneous sensations, for Bergson, on the contrary, real is duration, the moments are artificial cuts in it.[8]

---

1 Ibid., 325.

2 AK., IV. 1.

3 TS., p. 173.27., cp. TSP., p. 183.12.

4 Op. cit., p. 325.

5 Cp. above, p. 106.

6 Op. cit., p. 326.

7 *vijātīya-kṣaṇa-utpāda*.

8 In order to complete the comparison in this point we ought to have considered the Bergsonian Intuition of the artist with the Buddhist theory of an intelligible, non-sensuous, mystic Intuition of the Saint, but this is a vast subject which deserves separate treatment.

Über den Stand der Indischen Philosophie zur Zeit Mahāvīras und Buddhas

F. O. Schrader

Vorwort.

In der Einleitung zum fünfundvierzigsten Bande der Sacred Books of the East hat Professor Jacobi einige Nachrichten der Jainas über ketzerische Lehren mit analogen buddhistischen Traditionen in Parallele gestellt. Er begründet seinen Versuch mit den Worten: „The records of the Buddhists and Jainas about the philosophical ideas current at the time of the Buddha and Mahāvīra [1]), meagre though they be. are of the greatest importance to the historian of that epoch. For they show us the ground on which, and the materials with which, a religious reformer hat to build his system.“ Dieser Ausspruch brachte mich, nachdem ich schon früher durch Herrn Professor Leumann auf das zu besprechende System der dreihundertdreiundsechzig Darśanas aufmerksam gemacht worden war, auf den Gedanken, nach jinistischen, buddhistischen und wenn möglich auch brahmanischen Quellen eine Schilderung der zu Mahāvīras und Buddhas Zeit besonders vertretenen philosophischen Richtungen zu geben. Zwar musste ich mir sagen, dass zu einem solchen Unternehmen eigentlich die Zeit noch nicht gekommen sei, indem die vollständige Erschliessung der jinistischen Litteratur

1) Dies ist der erste bedeutende Lehrer der noch heute in Indien zahlreich vertretenen Religionsgenossenschaft der Jainas.

voraussichtlich noch manche wichtige Aufschlüsse geben würde. Aber je mehr ich während meines Strassburger Studiums von dieser Litteratur [1]) kennen lernte, um so mehr drängte sich mir die Überzeugung auf, dass, wenn nicht ein unerhörter Zufall uns noch in den Besitz des, speziell von den philosophischen Ansichten handelnden, verloren gegangenen zwölften Anga bringen sollte, kaum irgendwelche Nachrichten zu Tage treten werden, die nicht von unseren Hauptgewährsmännern, Malayagiri und Śīlāṅka, in ihren Kommentaren verwertet worden sind. Und so glaube ich denn, die vorliegende Schrift mit gutem Gewissen der Öffentlichkeit übergeben zu können, nachdem ich zuvor meinem verehrten Lehrer, Herrn Professor Leumann, für die liebenswürdige Unterstützung, die er mir bei der Anfertigung meiner Arbeit zuteil werden liess, meinen wärmsten Dank ausgesprochen habe.

1) Eine Übersicht über dieselbe findet man in Vol. XVI und XVII von Webers Indischen Studien (Leipzig 1883 u. 84).

Inhalt

Bibliographie.

Abhayadeva: Verfasser einer Sthānāṅga-Ṭīkā, q. v.
Ācāra-Ṭīkā: Śīlāṅkas Kommentar zum Ācārāṅga, q. v. Handschriften: Berl. MS. orient. fol. 1694 und fol. 716, zitiert als B und b.
Ācārāṅga: das erste Aṅga des Jaina-Kanons. Herausgegeben zusammen mit Śīlāṅkas Kommentar. Calcutta 1880. Übersetzt i. d. Sacred Books, s. Jacobi.
Aitareya-Brāhmaṇa. Herausg. v. Th. Aufrecht. Bonn 1879.
Ānandagiri. The Śaṅkaravijaya. Calcutta 1868.
Aṅguttara-Nikāya. Ed. by R. Morris. London 1883.
Aśvaghoṣa. The Buddha-Carita. Sanskrit text ed. by E. B. Cowell. Oxford 1893.
The Buddha-Carita. Translated from the Sanskrit by E. B. Cowell. Oxford 1894.
The Fo-Sho-Hing-Tsan-King. Translated by S. Beal. Oxford 1883.
Atharvaśira-Upaniṣad, s. Upaniṣaden.
Atharvaveda-Saṃhitā. With the comment. of Sāyaṇāchārya ed. by Shankar Pandurang Pandit. Bombay 1895.
Beal. Romantic Legend of Sakya Buddha. London 1875.
Bhagavadgītā. Sanscr. et lat., annot. adj. A. G. a Schlegel. Bonnae 1823.
Bhāgavata-Purāṇa. Sanscrit et Français publ. p. Eug. Burnouf. Paris 1840—47.
Bhagavatī: das fünfte Aṅga des Jaina-Kanons. Mit der Ṭīkā des Abhayadeva herausgegeben. Benares 1882.
Bhaṭṭotpala, s. Varāhamihira.
Brahmajāla-Sutta, s. Dīgha-Nikāya.
Bṛhadāranyaka-Upaniṣad, s. Upaniṣaden.
Bṛhat-Saṃhitā, s. Varāhamihira.
Buddhacarita, s. Aśvaghoṣa.
Buddhaghosa, Kommentator des Dīgha-Nikāya, s. Sumaṅgala-Vilāsinī.
Chāndogya-Upaniṣad, s. Upaniṣaden.

Deussen, P. Die Sūtras des Vedānta. Leipzig 1887.
Sechzig Upaniṣads des Veda. Leipzig 1897.
Allgemeine Geschichte der Philosophie I, 1 u. 2. Leipzig 1894 u. 1899.
Dhammapada. Palice et lat. ed. V. Fausböll. Haun 1855.
Dhammasaṅgaṇi. Transl. by Caroline A. F. Rhys Davids. London 1900.
Dīgha-Nikāya. Pali text ed. by T. W. Rhys Davids and I. E. Carpenter. Vol. I. London 1889.
Gauḍapāda, s. Māṇḍūkya-Upaniṣad.
Gommaṭasāra: ein in Gāthās geschriebenes Digambara-Werk dogmatischen Inhaltes. Strassburger Handschrift Nr. 415.
Grimblot. Sept Suttas Palis. Paris 1876.
Harṣakula, s. Sūtrakṛtāṅga.
Hodgson. Essays on the Languages, Literature, and Religion of Nepál and Tibet. London 1874 (reprint).
Hoernle. The Uvāsagadasāo. Calcutta, Bibl. Ind. 1888—90.
Hopkins. The religions of India. Boston 1898.
The great epic of India. New-York 1901.
Jacobi. Jaina Sūtras transl. from Prakṛt. Oxford 1884 and 1895. (Vol. XXII u. XLV der Sacred Books of the East, ed. by F. Max Müller.)
Kāma-Sūtra, s. Vātsyāyana.
Kaṭha-Upaniṣad, s. Upaniṣaden.
Kena-Upaniṣad, s. Upaniṣaden.
Kern. Manual of Indian Buddhism. Strassburg 1896.
Kevaddha-Sutta, s. Dīgha-Nikāya.
Ludwig. Der Rigveda. Prag 1876—88.
Mādhavāchārya. Sarvadarśanasaṃgraha. Calcutta 1858 (Bibl. Ind.).
Mahābhārata. Herausg. mit dem Kommentar des Nīlakaṇṭha. Bombay o. J. (1890).
Translated by Protap Chandra Roy. Calcutta 1886—96.
Mahāparinibbāna-Sutta. Ed. by Childers. Journal of the Royal Asiatic Society, 1874—76.
Mahāvagga: erster Teil des Vinaya-Piṭaka, q. v.
Maitrāyaṇa-Upaniṣad, s. Upaniṣaden.
Majjhima-Nikāya. Ed. by V. Trenckner. Vol. I. London 1888.
Übersetzt von K. E. Neumann („Die Reden Gotamo Buddhos“). Leipzig 1896 fg.
Malayagiri: Verfasser einer Nandī-Ṭīkā, q. v.
Māṇḍūkya-Upaniṣad. Ed. with Kārikās of Gauḍapāda etc. Poona 1890.
Mānava-Dharmaśāstra. Ed. by J. Jolly. London 1887.
Mārkaṇḍeya-Purāṇa. Ed. by K. M. Banerjea. Calcutta 1862.
Milindapañho. Ed. by V. Trenckner. London 1880.
Translated by T. W. Rhys Davids. Sacred Books of the East vol. XXXV, XXXVI.
Müller, Max. The six systems of Indian philosophy. London 1899.

Nandī: ein kanonischer Jaina-Text. Herausg. nebst Malayagiris Kommentar. Calcutta, *saṃvat* 1936.
Nandī-ṭīkā des Malayagiri. Wegen der Ausgabe s. Nandī. Handschrift: Berl. MS. orient. fol. 654.
Nīlakaṇṭha, s. Mahābhārata.
Nṛsiṃhapūrvatāpiny-Upaniṣad, s. Upaniṣaden.
Oldenberg. Buddha, sein Leben, seine Lehre, seine Gemeinde. 3. Aufl. Berlin 1897.
Die Religion des Veda. Berlin 1894.
Puggala-Paññatti. Ed. by R. Morris. London 1883.
Rāmānuja. Śrībhāṣya. Benares 1885 fg. (Pandit, New Series).
Rājavārttika, s. Tattvārtha-Sūtra.
Rigveda. Ed. with Bhāṣya of Sāyaṇāchārya. Bombay 1890—91.
Rhys Davids, Caroline, s. Dhammasaṅgaṇi.
Rhys Davids, T. W. Dialogues of the Buddha. London 1899.
Rockhill. The Life of the Buddha. London 1884.
Sāmaññaphala-Sutta, s. Dīgha-Nikāya.
Saṃyutta-Nikāya. Ed. by L. Feer. London 1884—88.
Śaṅkaravijaya, s. Ānandagiri.
Sarvadarśanasaṃgraha, s. Mādhavāchārya.
Śatapatha Brāhmana. Herausg. von A. Weber. Berlin 1855.
Transl. by J. Eggeling. Sacred Books of the East vol. XII, XXVI, XLI, XLIII.
Śīlāṅka, s. Sūtrakṛtāṅga.
Sumaṅgala-Vilāsinī: Buddhaghosa's comment. on the Dīgha-Nikāya. Pāli text ed. by T. W. Rhys Davids and J. E. Carpenter. Part. I. London 1886.
Sūtrakṛtāṅga: das zweite Aṅga des Jaina-Kanons. Herausgegeben mit der Ṭīkā des Śīlāṅka und der Dīpikā des Harṣakula. Bombay 1880. Übersetzt in den Sacred Books of the East, s. Jacobi.
Sthānāṅga: das dritte Aṅga des Jaina-Kanons. Herausgegeben nebst der Ṭīkā des Abhayadeva. Benares 1880.
Sthānāṅga-Ṭīkā des Abhayadeva. Wegen der Augsabe s. Sthānāṅga. Handschriften: Berl. MS. orient. fol. 1124 und 745, zitiert als B und b.
Śvetāśvatara-Upaniṣad, s. Upaniṣaden.
Tattvārtha-Sūtra, s. Umāsvāti.
Tevijja-Suttanta, s. Dīgha-Nikāya.
Umāsvāti. Tattvārtha-Sūtra. Ein dogmatischer Jaina-Text. Herausgegeben in R. G. Bhandarkar's Report for 1883/84, p. 405 bis 417. Bombay 1887.
Handschriftliche Kommentare: 1) des Siddhasena: Poona Palmblatt-MS. P XIII, 7, zitiert als *P*; Strassbg. MS. 458, zitiert als *S*; Poona Papier-MS. VIII, 595, zitiert als *p*; 2) Haribhadras „Laghuvṛtti": P X 369, zitiert als *π*; 3) Rājavārttika: Strassbg. MS. 366, zitiert als *s*; Poona MS. P XVIII 275, zitiert als *Pr*.

Upanisaden. Neben Deussens Übersetzung (s. Deussen) wurden die elf, die zweiunddreissig und die hundertundacht Upaniṣaden (Bombay 1886, 1895, Poona 1895) benutzt.

Uttarādhyayana: ein kanonischer Jaina-Text. Mit Kommentaren herausg. Calcutta 1880. Übersetzt in den Sacred Books of the East, s. Jacobi.

Varāhamihira. The Bṛhat-Saṃhitā. With the comment. of Bhaṭṭotpala ed. by M. Sudh. Dvivedi. Part. I. Benares 1895.

Vātsyāyana. Kāmasūtram. Übersetzt von Richard Schmidt. 2. Aufl. Leipzig 1900.

Vedāntasāra. Ed. by G. A. Jacob. Bombay 1894.

Vinaya-Piṭaka. Ed. by H. Oldenberg. London 1879—83.

Viṣṇu-Purāṇa. Translated by H. H. Wilson, ed. by Fitzedward Hall. London 1864—1870.

Weber. Indische Litteraturgeschichte. 2. Aufl. Berlin 1876.
Über ein Fragment der Bhagavatī. Berlin 1866—67.

Yājñavalkyas Gesetzbuch. Sanskrit und deutsch herausgegeben von A. F. Stenzler. Berlin 1849.

I. Einleitender und allgemeiner Teil.

Wie dem Inder der Begriff der Geschichte von jeher ein Fremdes war, so hat er auch eine Geschichte der Philosophie im eigentlichen Sinne nicht hervorgebracht, und was mit diesem Namen von Indologen (so von Aufrecht im Catalogus Oxoniensis) gelegentlich bezeichnet wird, ist nichts weiter als eine mehr oder weniger willkürliche Zusammenstellung philosophischer Gedanken oder Gedankensysteme. Selbst Mādhava-Sāyaṇa, der Verfasser des berühmten und in der That bewundernswerten Sarvadarśanasaṃgraha („Übersicht über alle Systeme"), hat von der Leistung seines Werkes kein höheres Bewusstsein als das, „zum Ergötzen der Edlen" aus bunten Blumen einen Kranz geflochten zu haben.[1]) Aber Mādhava geht insofern doch wissenschaftlich zu Werke, als er die Systeme seiner und früherer Zeiten „sorgfältig durchforscht" und in einem gewissen genetischen Zusammenhang darzustellen bemüht ist. Von solchen Versuchen ist das Zeitalter Buddhas noch weit entfernt. In den heiligen Schriften sowohl der Buddhisten wie der Jainas erscheint, wo von der Philosophie im allgemeinen oder von der Stellung der Philosophen zu diesem oder jenem Problem die Rede ist, entweder eine blosse Aufzählung von Schlagworten, die zu jener Zeit gang und gäbe waren — so Majjhimanikāya I, 3, 5: „Ewig ist die Welt", „Zeitlich ist die Welt", „Endlich ist die Welt", „Unendlich ist die Welt"; Sūtrakṛtāṅga I, 1, 4, 6: „Unendlich und ewig ist die Welt", „Endlich (im Raum) und ewig (in der Zeit) ist die Welt" etc. — oder es wird an der Hand eines oder mehrerer solcher Schlagworte ein ganzes System von Denkmöglichkeiten entwickelt, ganz unbekümmert darum, ob diese

1) Sarvadarś. Einleitung Vers 4.

nach Art der lullischen Kunst zu Tage geförderten Ideen in Wirklichkeit irgendwo vertreten waren oder nicht. Sehen wir beispielshalber einmal zu, wie Buddha dazu kommt, zwanzig Arten der *sakkāyadiṭṭhi*[1]), d. h. des Glaubens an eine (dauernde) Wirklichkeit der Individualität[2]) zu statuieren. „Da hält," erklärt der Meister (Majjh. Nik. I, 5, 4), „... ein gewöhnlicher Mensch ... den Körper für das Selbst (1) oder das Selbst für körperhaft (2) oder den Körper für im Selbst enthalten (3) oder das Selbst für im Körper enthalten (4); er hält das Gefühl für das Selbst oder das Selbst für gefühlartig etc. (5—8), die Wahrnehmung für das Selbst etc. (9—12), die *saṅkhārā*[3]) für das Selbst etc. (13—16), das Bewusstsein für das Selbst etc. (17—20)." Mit anderen Worten: die Thatsache, dass von gewissen Denkern der Dualismus von Leib und Seele anerkannt, von anderen geleugnet wurde, dass einige im Körper, andere in der Erkenntnis, wieder andere im Gefühl das eigentlich Wesenhafte sahen[4]), ist für Buddha Grund genug, in vier Variationen jeden der fünf *khandhā* oder Daseinsformen für die möglichen und folglich thatsächlichen[5]) Angelpunkte ontologischer Spekulationen auszugeben. Solcher Art sind nun auch die beiden umfassenderen Übersichten, mit deren Betrachtung und Vergleichung wir unsere Untersuchung über den Stand der indischen Philosophie zu Mahāvīras und Buddhas Zeit am zweckmässigsten beginnen werden, nämlich das jinistische System der dreihundertdreiundsechzig Darśanas und das Brahmajāla Buddhas.

Dem jinistischen Kanon zufolge[6]) giebt es dreihundertdreiundsechzig philosophische Ansichten (darśana), die auf folgende Weise in vier Klassen (vādi-samavasaraṇa) einzuteilen seien:

---

1) sat-kāya-dṛṣṭi. Childers (Pāli Dictionary, sub voce) und sein Gewährsmann Subhūti sind mit ihrer Ableitung des Wortes durchaus im Unrecht gegenüber Burnouf.

2) Im Gegensatz steht die Lehre Buddhas von der momentanen Veränderung aller Dinge.

3) Das Wort *saṅkhāra* bedeutet im obigen Zusammenhang eine Anzahl psychischer Fähigkeiten und Eigenschaften (Überlegung, Gedächtnis, Habsucht, Fröhlichkeit, Stolz etc.), dagegen im weiteren Sinne (vgl. u. a. die letzten Worte Buddhas, Mahāp. 6) jedes gewordene und vergängliche Ding überhaupt.

4) Vgl. Vedāntasāra: Cārvākas tu „Sa vā eṣa puruṣo 'nna-rasa-maya" ....; aparaś cārvākaḥ „Anyo 'ntara ātmā prāṇa-maya" ....; anyas tu cārvākaḥ „Anyo 'ntara ātmā mano-maya" ....; bauddhas tu „Anyo 'ntara ātmā vijñāna-maya" etc. (khaṇḍa 19).

5) Diese beiden Begriffe sind zumal bei den Buddhisten niemals streng geschieden.

6) Sūtrakṛt. I, 12; II, 2, 79; I, 6, 27; I, 10, 17; Sthān. IV, 4, Ed. fol. 316a; Bhag. XXX, 1, Ed. fol. 1837; Nandī Ed. p. 429 fg.; Gommaṭasāra II, 7, 66—85; Sūtrakṛta-niry. 118b—120, Ed. (Sūtrakṛtāṅga) p. 447 fg.; Śīl. ad Āc. I, 1, 1, 3, Ed. p. 14 fg.; Kommentare zu Tattvārtha VIII, 1. Vgl. auch Weber, Ind. Stud. XVII, 75 f., XVI, 259 fg.

1. **Kriyā-vāda.**

jīva ajīva āsrava bandha saṃvara nirjarā puṇya apuṇya mokṣa	sva para	nitya anitya	kāla īśvara ātman niyati svabhāva

9 × 2 × 2 × 5 = **180**

2. **Akriyā-vāda.**

jīva ajīva āsrava bandha saṃvara nirjarā mokṣa	sva para	kāla īśvara ātman niyati svabhāva yadṛcchā

7 × 2 × 6 = **84**

3. **Ajñāna-vāda.**

jīva ajīva āsrava bandha saṃvara nirjarā puṇya apuṇya mokṣa	sattva asattva sadasattva avācyatva sadavācyatva asadavācyatva sadasadavācyatva

9 × 7 = **63**

utpatti	sattva asattva sadasattva avācyatva	1 1 1 1

67

1*

4. Vinaya-vāda.

	sura
	nṛpati
kāya	yati
vāc	jñāti
manas	sthavira
dāna	adhama
	mātṛ
	pitṛ
4 ×	8 = 32

Dieses Schema ist eine Erweiterung der, wahrscheinlich durch das Auftreten Gosālas (s. unten) hervorgerufenen, Jinisten und Buddhisten gleich geläufigen Einteilung aller Philosophen in Kriyā- und Akriyā-vādinas, d. h. solche, die 1. Willensfreiheit, 2. Verantwortlichkeit, 3. Wiederverkörperung anerkannten, und solche, die gegen diese Annahme ganz oder teilweise ablehnend sich verhielten.

Zusatzbemerkung. Von der Lehre Buddhas, mit Rücksicht auf die ich oben das Wort Wiederverkörperung statt der engeren Begriffes Seelenwanderung wähle, habe ich die folgende, der landläufigen Erklärung widersprechende Auffasssung gewonnen.

Wer die Gleichung *aniccam = dukkham = anattā* („Was nicht ewig ist, ist Leid; was Leid ist, ist Nicht-Selbst", Saṃy. Nik. XXX, 1 u. sonst) anerkennt, wird notwendig auch ihre Umkehrung: *niccam = adukkham = attā* gelten lassen. Hieraus folgt, dass Nirvāṇa, als das Leidlose und Ewige, auch das Selbst (Absolute) ist, eine Annahme, in der wir beträchtlich bestärkt werden, wenn wir Aussprüche wie Saṃy. Nik. XXII, 33: „Werft ab, ihr Mönche, was nicht euer ist (yaṃ na tumhākam): .... den Leib, das Gefühl, die Wahrnehmung" etc. oder die immer wiederkehrende Aufforderung an den Erlösungsbedürftigen, bei der Betrachtung eines jeden Daseinselementes sich die Worte zuzurufen: „Das ist nicht mein, das bin ich nicht, nicht ist dies mein Selbst" (Majjh. Nik. I, 3, 2 etc.), ins Auge fassen. Solche Äusserungen sind einfach unverständlich, wenn man sie nicht auf einen metaphysischen Dualismus bezieht: Buddha sieht auf der einen Seite (loka) ein beständiges Werden und Vergehen, eine ununterbrochene Aufeinanderfolge von Erscheinungen, von denen keine, so wenig wie die Zeit selbst, auch nur einen Augenblick beharrt — auf der anderen Seite das absolute Gegenteil, das Unaussprechliche, ewig Gleiche, die Nichtwelt, das Nirvāṇa, das Selbst (attā). Nun wird allerdings an keiner Stelle des gesamten Kanons Nirvāṇa mit dem Selbst identifiziert und andererseits zu unzähligen Malen erklärt, dass in der Welt nirgends ein Selbst zu finden sei. Aber dieser Widerspruch löst sich durch die Thatsache, dass das Wort *attā*, wo immer es begegnet, die substanzielle Individualseele bedeutet,[1]) so dass die Vermutung, Buddha habe mit

1) Auch die von C. Rhys Davids in ihrer Einleitung (p. XXXVI) zum Dhammasaṅgaṇi zitierte Stelle des Majjh. Nik. (I 3, 2) ist, wie aus dem Zusammenhang deutlich ersichtlich, nur eine Verspottung der Ansicht, als ob ein Nichtabsolutes jemals ewig sein könne.

diesem Wort noch einen ganz anderen Sinn verbunden, über den sich zu äussern er nicht für gut fand (s. S. 40, 51, 38), uns unbenommen bleibt. Somit ist die Leugnung des *attā*, d. h. der beharrenden Individualseele, nicht als eine Leugnung der Substanz zu verstehen, sondern nur als eine Verbannung der Substanz aus der Welt des Beschränkten, als die Erkenntnis, dass Sein und Dasein (Substanz und Kausalität) in demselben Sinne wie absolut und relativ einander ausschliessen.

Und ebensowenig wie die Substanz hat Buddha die Seele geleugnet. Nur wich seine Auffassung der letzteren von allem Althergebrachten derartig ab, dass er notwendig seinen Zeitgenossen als ein Seelenleugner erschien. Man vergegenwärtige sich, etwa am Kap. 8 unseres besonderen Teils, die ungemeine Naivität der damaligen Seelentheorieen. Durchweg wurde das Verhältnis von Seele und Körper nach der Analogie des bleibenden Dinges und seiner wechselnden Eigenschaften aufgefasst, ja sogar über Form, Gewicht, Farbe etc. der Seele stellte man Vermutungen an (Sūtrakṛt. II, 1, 15; vgl. unser Kap. 9: Mita-vāda). Solchen kindlichen Anschauungen trat nun Buddha, als konsequenter Herakliteïst, mit der unerhörten Behauptung entgegen, dass es ein Unveränderliches, eine Substanz in der Welt überhaupt nicht gebe, dass alles, was irgendwie Form und Grenzen habe, in beständiger, momentaner Veränderung sei. Hierdurch wurde die Seele in m e t a p h y s i s c h e r Hinsicht dem Körper gleichgestellt, d. h. sie wurde, wie dieser, ein *saṅkhāra* (Gegensatz: *asaṅkhatā dhātu*). Indem nun Buddha von ihr noch alle Funktionen des Bewusstseins (vedanā, saññā, saṅkhārā [vgl. S. 2 Anm. 3], viññāṇa) abtrennte und diese mit dem physischen Körper (rūpa) zu dem Begriff des *puggala* (Individuum) vereinigte, behielt er als die Wurzel des Individuums, als den Charakter, die Individualität, den „Durst" (taṇhā) übrig, d. h. genau das, was Schopenhauer den Willen nennt. Dieser, auf ein bestimmtes Dasein gerichtete, individuelle Lebenstrieb ist das „alter ego" (dutiyā, Sutta-Nipāta 740; s. C. Rhys Davids, Dhammasaṅgaṇi 1059), die „Führerin" (bhava-nettī, Dhammasaṅgaṇi 1059) des Menschen, der „Faden" (sutta, ibid.), der durch all die verschiedenen Existenzen sich fortspinnt, bis er im Nirvāṇa abgeschnitten wird. Sehen wir hierin ein organisches Gebilde, das ebenso in ununterbrochenem Prozess begriffen ist wie der aus den *khandhā* gebildete physisch-psychische Körper, aber diesen überdauert, indem es, der Pflanzenwurzel vergleichbar, jedesmal wenn der *puggala* durch den Tod von ihm abgeschnitten wird (ucchijjhati), mit Naturnotwendigkeit einen neuen *puggala* aus sich hervortreibt, neue *khandhā* um sich sammelt, bis es endlich, wie die Flamme, die keinen Brennstoff mehr erreicht,[1]) spurlos verschwindet

---

1) Für den Buddhisten ist, wie für den Kāla-vādin, der diese Vorstellung aufgebracht haben dürfte (s. hinten S. 25) die ganze Welt in einem ununterbrochenen Verbrennungsprozess begriffen (Dhammapada XI, 1 u. a.), und zweifellos geht der Ausdruck *nirvāṇa* (Erlöschen) auf den Vergleich des Organismus mit der Flamme zurück, wie ihn z. B. Milindapañha II, 2, 1 verwendet, um zu zeigen, inwiefern das Individuum von seiner Geburt bis zu seinem Tod dasselbe geblieben und doch in jedem Augenblick ein anderes geworden ist. Hier ist die Lampe gleichsam der Körper und die Flamme das was wir Seele nennen — ein sehr glückliches Bild, wenn man die Erklärung hinzufügt, dass natürlich auch die Lampe in momentaner, wenn auch unmerklicher Veränderung sich befindet. Dass man ähnlich auch die Wiedergeburt als ein Fortbrennen (Wiederaufleuchten) einer und derselben Flamme sich vorgestellt haben muss, zeigt II, 2, ibid. das Bild von dem als Kind verlobten Mädchen, um das ein zweiter Freier deshalb mit Recht sich zu bewerben glaubt, weil seit der Verlobung Jahre vergangen und das versprochene Kind mit seiner Geliebten nicht identisch sei. „Er mag sagen, was er will," meint der König,

(nibbāti, nirvāti): so haben wir den buddhistischen Seelenbegriff und das, was Buddha berechtigt, in dieser veränderten Form die alte Seelenwanderungslehre beizubehalten. Aber diese Seele ist Wille, Kraft, Aktualität, und nicht, wie in allen vorbuddhistischen Systemen, eine beharrende Substanz (attā), und zwar deshalb nicht, weil sie nach der Ansicht Buddhas als ein beschränktes Wesen (saṅkhāra) vom Absoluten (atta, τὸ ὄν) durch ebendieselbe unermessliche Kluft getrennt ist, die den *puggala* und die übrige Welt von ihm trennt.

Ich weiss, das man gegen diese Auffassung mit Berufung auf den *paṭicca-samuppāda* protestieren wird. Aber ich bezweifle sehr, dass man angesichts der vier heiligen Wahrheiten und überhaupt der unverkennbar zentralen Stellung, die in den Piṭakas die *taṇhā* einnimmt, in dieser, Buddhisten und Nichtbuddhisten gleich rätselhaften Formel etwas anderes sehen darf als eine, dem ältesten Evangelium fremde, nicht sehr glückliche Nachbildung gewisser Evolutionsreihen der heterodoxen Philosophie, und ich sehe vor allem nicht ein, inwiefern der *paṭicca-samuppāda* der obigen Erklärung der *taṇhā* widerspricht. Denn wie die termini *saṅkhārā, viññāna, vedanā* hier offenbar etwas anderes bedeuten als die gleichnamigen *upādāna-kkhandhā*, da ja die letzteren erst mit dem neunten bezw. zehnten Gliede erscheinen, so kann auch die *taṇhā*, weil aus ihr durch *upādāna* das Individuum hervorgeht, unmöglich nur ein Zustand des Individuums sein. Übrigens kann man auch die *taṇhā* als erste Ursache ansehen, wenn man die folgende Erklärung von Vasubandhus Abhidharmakośa gelten lässt, die mir Herr Wogihara aus Tokio nach der chinesischen Übersetzung des Hiouen Thsang mitteilt:

Vergangenheit	1. *avijjā*	vergangene Ursache
	2. *saṅkhārā*	
Gegenwart	3. *viññāna*	gegenwärtige Wirkung
	4. *nāma-rūpa*	
	5. *saḷ-āyatana*	
	6. *phassa*	
	7. *vedanā*	
	8. *taṇhā*	gegenwärtige Ursache
	9. *upādāna*	
	10. *bhava*	
Zukunft	11. *jāti*	zukünftige Wirkung
	12. *jarā-marya* etc.	

Hiernach scheint der *paṭicca-samuppāda* meinem Versuch, die *taṇhā* nicht nur als psychologische, sondern zugleich als metaphysische Kategorie zu fassen, eher günstig als zuwider zu sein.

Indem man [1]) von den Kriyā- bezw. den Akriyā-vādinas diejenigen aussonderte, welche, ohne die Willensfreiheit und Verant-

„dieses erwachsene Mädchen hat doch aus jenem (Kinde) sich entwickelt." „Geradeso, o Grosskönig," entgegnet der Weise, „ist die Persönlichkeit (nāmarūpa), welche stirbt, verschieden von der, die wieder geboren wird. Aber doch ist diese aus jener entstanden (nibbatta) und eben darum von deren Sünden nicht befreit."

1) d. h. die Jainas; für die Buddhisten haben die beiden Wörter immer nur den obigen Sinn, da sie andernfalls zu den Akriyā-vādinas sich hätten rechnen müssen. Nur ein scheinbarer Widerspruch ist es, wenn die Jainas trotz ihrer Einteilung des Kriyā-vāda in hundertundachtzig „Ketzereien" (mithyā-dṛṣṭi) sich selbst für Kriyā-vādinas erklären. Denn „Ketzer" (prāvā-

wortlichkeit[1]) zu bestreiten, das philosophische Wissen (von einer Wiederverkörperung etc.) 1. für belanglos oder 2. für unsicher und schädlich erklärten, und ferner unter Akriyā-vādin oder Nāstika nunmehr den Leugner der Seelensubstanz und (oder) der Verantwortlichkeit und Willensfreiheit verstand, erhielt man vier Klassen von Philosophen, von denen die erste Wissen und Sittlichkeit,[2]) die zweite das blosse Wissen,[3]) die dritte die Ablehnung alles Wissens (Skepsis) und die vierte die blosse Sittlichkeit[4]) für den Weg zum Glück ausgab.[5]) Bei der weiteren Einteilung der ersten drei Klassen ist das Verhältnis der grösseren Systeme: des Theïsmus, Idealismus (īśvara-, ātma-vāda) etc. zu den neun sog. Kategorien (padārthās, tattvāni) der Jaina-Dogmatik: Seele, Nichtseele, Hinströmung, Bindung, Eindämmung, Zerreibung, Gut, Böse, Erlösung[6]) grundlegend. Man dachte sich, dass z. B. der Kāla-vādin jedes einzelne dieser neun Prinzipien als ein unabhängig (svataḥ) oder ein abhängig (parataḥ)[7])

---

duka) ist nach jinistischer Ansicht ein Kriyā-vādin nur dann, wenn er nicht alle neun Kategorien (jīva etc.) und alle fünf Prinzipien (kāla etc., s. S. 13) anerkennt oder, was dasselbe ist, die Absolutheit (ekāntatva) eines Prinzipes behauptet. So wenigstens erklärt uns Śīlāṅka (ad Sūtrakṛt. I, 12, 1 u. 11) das Verhältnis, der freilich hier, um die Jainas als vollkommene *āstikās* erscheinen zu lassen, in der Reihe der fünf *īśvara* und *ātman* durch *purākṛta* und *puruṣakāra* ersetzt. Denn selbstverständlich wurde von den Jainas die Existenz des *ātman* = *brahman* und vor allem die des *īśvara* durchaus negiert. Die Sache mag sich aber verhalten wie sie wolle, jedenfalls geht aus den jinistischen sowohl wie aus den buddhistischen Texten (vgl. bes. Sūtrakṛt. I, 12, 20 u. 21 und Mahāvagga VI, 31) deutlich hervor, dass die Jainas sich offen für Kriyā-vādinas erklärten. Dies gilt jedoch nur für die alte, vom Agnostizismus noch nicht beeinflusste Lehre; der *syādvādin* that sich viel darauf zu gute, weder ein *āstika* noch ein *nāstika* zu sein (vgl. S. 50).

1) Diese beiden Begriffe sind bei Buddhisten und Jainas vereinigt, sonst aber vielfach getrennt: vgl. die Kapitel Kāla-, Svabhāva-, Niyati-vāda und die materialistischen Theorien.

2) vijjā-caraṇam, Sūtrakṛt. I, 12, 11.

3) Akriyā-vādinas tu jñāna-vādinas, Śīlāṅka ad Sūtrakṛt. I, 6.

4) jñāna-kriyābhyām antareṇa, Śīlāṅka ad Sūtrakṛt. I, 12, 1. Wie man sieht, fallen die Buddhisten unter keine dieser Klassen. Sie werden aber, trotz ihrer Hochhaltung der Moral, zu den Akriyā-vādinas gerechnet.

5) Te sarve prāvādukā jainā iva nirvāṇaṃ mokṣam āhuḥ, Harṣakula ad Sūtrakṛt. II, 2, 79. *Nirvāṇa* und *mokṣa* schliessen nicht notwendig die Idee des Jenseits ein: vgl. die letzte Klasse des Brahmajāla (S. 10).

6) Die Übersetzung teilweise nach Deussen, „Die Sūtras des Vedānta" p. 365. *Ajīva* = *pudgala* ist jeder atomische sowohl wie zusammengesetzte Körper (aṇu, skandha), *āsrava* das „Einfliessen" von Karman in die Seele („die interessierte Sinnesthätigkeit", Govindānanda ad Ved. Sūtr. II, 2, 33), *bandha* die Bindung der Seele durch Karman, *saṃvara* die Verhinderung neuen und *nirjarā* die Vernichtung alten Karmans.

7) Die Kommentare geben (offenbar mit Hinblick auf den Syādvāda) folgende Erklärungen dieser Ausdrücke: „Tatra svata iti svenaiva rūpeṇa jīvo'sti na parôpādhy-apekṣayā hrasvatva-dīrghatve iva" (Acārāṭīkā I, 1, 3); „Kathaṃ punaḥ parato' stitvam ātmano 'bhyupagamyate? Na tv etat prasiddham eva. Iha sarva-padārthānāṃ parapadārtha-svarūpâpekṣayā (pararūpâpekṣaḥ,

Existierendes, ferner als ein Ewiges (nitya) oder als ein Zeitliches (anitya) anerkennen oder leugnen oder skeptisch bezweifeln könne. Dies ergab für den Kāla-vāda $9 \times 2 \times 2 \times 3 = 108$ mögliche Sätze[1],) und jede der drei Klassen hätte, wenn man das obige Verfahren ausser auf den Kāla-vāda auch auf die übrigen vier metaphysischen Standpunkte: den Īśvara-vāda etc. anwandte, $9 \times 2 \times 2 \times 5 = 180$ Darśanas umfassen müssen. Aber ein Blick auf unsere Tabelle lehrt, dass nur der Kriyā-vāda 180 Abteilungen hat. Bei der zweiten und der dritten Klasse verfuhr man, sei es um die *yadṛcchā* (s. unten) und die sieben agnostischen termini (S. 46 fg.) in das Schema zu bringen, sei es um die Zahl 363 zu erreichen,[2]) inkonsequent[3]) und erhielt in der oben ersichtlichen Weise 84 Akriyā-vādinas und 67 Ajñāna-vādinas. Was endlich die vierte Klasse betrifft, so handelt es sich hier um Pflichten, die bezüglich des Körpers, der Rede, der Gedanken und des materiellen Besitzes gegen Götter, Könige, Asketen, Verwandte, Greise, Sklaven, Mutter und Vater zu erfüllen sind.

Sehr verschieden von diesem System der dreihundertdreiundsechzig Darśanas ist das „Brahman-Netz", in dem Buddha alle Spekulationen (diṭṭhi-gatāni) gefangen zu haben vorgiebt. Hier (Brahmajālasutta I, 29 fg.) werden in zwei Haupt- mit je fünf Unterklassen zweiundsechzig Ketzer vorgeführt:

I. Pubbanta-kappikā, alle die über den ersten Anfang der Dinge spekulieren. Zu ihnen gehören

1. Sassata-vādino, die Äternalisten[4]), deren Behauptung zufolge die Seele (attā) sowohl wie der Schauplatz ihrer Wanderungen (loko) ewig ist, eine Erkenntnis, zu der die einen durch logische Erwägungen (takko, vīmaṅsā) kommen (4), die anderen, in-

---

Abhayadeva) svarūpa-paricchedo yathā dīrghatvâpekṣayā hrasva-paricchedo hrasvatâpekṣayā ca dīrghatvasyêti (hrasvatv'ādy-apekṣo dīrghatv'ādi-paricchedа, id.). Evam eva cânātmanaḥ (c'ātmanaḥ, id.) stambha-kumbh'ādīn samīkṣya tad-vyatirikte vastuny ātma-buddhiḥ pravartata iti, ato, yad ātmanaḥ svarūpaṃ tat parata evâvadhāryate, na svata iti" (ibid.); „Parata iti parebhyo vyāvṛttena rūpeṇa vidyate khalv ayam ātmē'ty arthaḥ" (Malayagiri).

1) Dieselben sind, den Kommentaren zufolge, nach dem Muster „Asti jīvaḥ svato nityaḥ kālataḥ" zu bilden (?).

2) 363 Städte sind dem König der Sindhu- und Sovīra-Länder unterthan: Bhag. XIII, 6; Utt. Kath. XVIII, 48 (Jacobi, Erzählungen in Mahārāshṭrī, p. 28).

3) Wenn die Kommentatoren den Fortfall von *puṇya apuṇya* und *nitya anitya* bei der zweiten Klasse gelegentlich mit der Bemerkung erklären, dass ja der Akriyā-vāda eine Seele nicht anerkenne, so vergessen sie das Prinzip der Einteilung, nach dem die zweite Klasse eben dieselben Urteile über *jīva, ajīva* etc. nur verneint, die die erste bejaht. Ebensowenig ist einzusehen, warum der Agnostiker sich nicht über *kāla* etc. äussern sollte.

4) Diese Übersetzung und die der beiden folgenden Namen gebe ich nach Rhys Davids (Dialogues of the Buddha), von dem im übrigen meine Erklärung des Brahmajāla nicht abhängig ist, da dieselbe in der obigen Form bereits fertig vorlag, als ich R. D.'s Werk zu Gesicht bekam.

dem sie durch Askese, Meditation etc. 1. ihrer früheren Geburten (in dem gegenwärtigen Kalpa) sich erinnern, 2. zehn Kalpas nebst ihren In- und Evolutionen oder gar 3. deren vierzig überschauen.

2. Ekacca-sassata-vādino, die Semi-Äternalisten, die die Ewigkeit der Existenz auf 1. einen einzigen persönlichen Gott (mahā-brahmā, issaro, nimmātā) oder 2. die über Spiel und Wollust erhabenen Götter oder 3. die über Neid und Feindschaft erhabenen Götter oder 4. alles Geistige (cittan ti vā mano ti vā viññānan ti vā) beschränken.

3. Antânantikā, die Extensionisten. Sie lehren, 1. dass die Welt endlich = begrenzt, 2. dass sie unendlich, 3. dass sie beides zugleich, nämlich nach oben und unten begrenzt, aber in seitlicher Ausdehnung unbegrenzt, 4. dass sie keins von beidem sei.

4. Amarā-vikkhepikā,[1]) d. h. alle, die 1. aus Furcht vor einer falschen Aussage, 2. aus Furcht vor einer sündigen Lust (upādāna), 3. aus Furcht vor einem Disput, 4. aus Trägheit in philosophischen Fragen jede direkte Antwort methodisch (s. S. 46) umgehen.

5. Adhicca-samuppannikā, die das Dasein von Welt und Seele für zufällig erklären, weil ihre Erinnerung nicht bis zum Ursprung derselben zurückreiche (1—3) oder weil ein solcher überhaupt undenkbar sei (4).

II. Aparanta-kappikā, alle die über die Zukunft spekulieren, nämlich

1. Saññi-vādino, die behaupten, dass die Seele nach dem Tode mit Bewusstsein und ewig [2]) fortlebe und dass diese jenseitige Seele 1. körperhaft, 2. körperlos, 3. beides zugleich, 4. keins von beidem, 5. endlich (begrenzt), 6. unendlich, 7. beides zugleich, 8. keins von beidem, 9. einheitlich bewusst, 10. vielheitlich bewusst, 11. beschränkt bewusst, 12. unbeschränkt bewusst,[3]) 13. selig, 14. unselig, 15. beides zugleich, 16. lust- und leidlos sei.

2. Asaññi-vādino, die eine unbewusste ewige Fortdauer nach dem Tode annehmen und die jenseitige Seele für 1. körperhaft, ... (wie oben) ...... 8. unräumlich erklären.

3. Neva-saññi-nâsaññi-vādino, nach deren Lehre die Seele nach dem Tode ein weder bewusstes noch unbewusstes ewiges

---

1) Wegen der Erklärung dieses Namens s. S. 46.

2) arogo = nicco, Buddhaghosa; vgl. Sūtrakṛt. I, 1, 3, 15: siddhā ya te arogā ya.

3) Gogerly übersetzt (Grimblot, Sept Suttas Pālis): „. . . . that it will have one mode . . . . many modes of consciousness, that it will have but a few perceptions, that its perceptions will be boundless.“

Leben habe [1]) und dabei 1. körperhaft, 2. körperlos ..... (wie oben) ...... oder 8. unräumlich sei.

4. Uccheda-vādino, die behaupten, dass durch den Tod das ganze Wesen „abgeschnitten" = zerstört werde (ucchijjhati), aber über das Wann und Wo dieses Ereignisses uneinig sind, indem den einen der Tod des grobstofflichen Leibes (1), anderen der Tod in einer der Himmelswelten (2—3), noch anderen der Tod in einer der vier Arūpa(Nichtform)-Welten (4—7) als das absolute Ende gilt, je nachdem sie nämlich 1. nur eine grobstoffliche Seele, 2. ausserdem eine sinnlich-begehrende, 3. ferner eine gemütartige, 4. ferner eine raumunendliche, 5. ferner eine bewusstseinsunendliche, 6. ferner eine die „Nichtsheit" schauende, endlich 7. ausser den sechs genannten eine weder bewusste noch unbewusste (überbewusste?) Seele annehmen.

5. Diṭṭhadhamma-nibbāna-vādino, die annehmen, dass die höchste Glückseligkeit = Leidlosigkeit (nirvāṇa) schon im Diesseits erreicht werden könne, und als das summum bonum entweder die vollkommene Befriedigung der fünf Sinne (1) oder eines der vier Jhāna (Grade der Ekstase) ansehen (2—5).

Halten wir diese Aufstellung mit der jinistischen zusammen, so ist sofort ersichtlich, dass eine blosse Vergleichung hier gar nichts erreichen kann, indem alle Identifizierungen, die sich etwa vornehmen lassen (I, 2, 1 = īśvara-vādinas, I, 2, 4 = ajñāna-vādinas, I, 2, 5 = yadṛcchā-vādinas), zunächst nur Gleichsetzungen von Namen sind und nur Ansichten betreffen, die ohnehin historisch bezeugt sind. Wir ziehen es daher vor, die Frage, was an den beiden Systemen mehr als blosse Konstruktion ist, für jedes derselben einzeln zu beantworten.

Dass die beiden Hauptabteilungen des Brahmajāla nicht wie Kriyā- und Akriyā-vāda einander ausschliessen, ist ohne weiteres klar. Wer über den Anfang der Dinge spekuliert, wird — von seltenen Ausnahmen abgesehen (adhicca-samuppannikā) — sich nicht versagen können, auch über das letzte Ende (Erlösung) seine Ansicht zu äussern, und dass nicht alle Aparanta-kappikā mit dem Buddhismus den Anfang der Dinge für unerkennbar erklärten, zeigen die vielen brahmanischen Schöpfungstheorien. Der Unterschied wird folglich dahin zu bestimmen sein, dass bei der ersten Klasse die eine, bei der zweiten Klasse die andere Betrachtung das Hauptinteresse in Anspruch nahm. Verdächtig aber bleibt, dass jede Klasse fünf Unterabteilungen hat, und in der That ist durchaus

1) Wie Uddaka Rāmaputta, ein Lehrer Buddhas, zu dieser Ansicht kam, sagt uns Aśvaghoṣa (Buddhacarita XII, 84): „Und da doch Bewusstsein wie Nichtbewusstsein noch gewissermassen körperlich sind (? yasmāc c'ālambane sūkṣme saṃjñā'saṃjñe), schritt er weiter fort zu der Annahme, dass es einen nicht Unbewussten noch Bewussten gebe, und fand hierin seine Ruhe."

nicht einzusehen, warum die Amarā-vikkhepikā nicht ebensogut zur zweiten Klasse gerechnet werden sollten. Sie passen in Wahrheit überhaupt nicht in diese Einteilung. Sodann könnten wir bei II, 1 bis 3 uns wundern, dass nicht nach dem bekannten Schema (+ —, — +, + +, — —) vor dem Neva-saññi-nâsaññi-vāda ein Saññāsaññi-vāda eingeschoben worden ist. Doch ist eine solche Ansicht nirgends bezeugt, wogegen II, 3, das auf den ersten Blick eine blosse Erdichtung scheint, in den Piṭakas Belege findet.[1]) Somit dürfte die Zehnteilung in Ordnung sein. Von den zweiundsechzig Meinungen ferner, die unter die zehn Klassen verteilt sind, beruht wohl ein gutes Drittel wirklich auf Erfindung. Andere, so I, 1, 4, sind so vielfach, z. B. von Sāṃkhyas, Śaivas u. s. w., vertreten, dass es zwecklos ist, über sie in Vermutungen sich zu ergehen, und höchstens die Erklärung Buddhaghosas, dass zu II, 1, 1 u. a. die Ājīvikas[2]) gehörten, hier noch erwähnt zu werden verdient. Betreffs des Restes endlich können wir ausser auf die Vermutung von Rhys Davids, dass bei II, 4, 4 an Āḷāra Kālāma, einen Lehrer Buddhas, zu denken sei,[3]) nur noch auf die folgende Parallele uns beziehen, die zugleich eine Warnung sein mag, bei Aufzählungen wie der gegenwärtigen nicht zu viel auf die Phantasie des Autors zu schieben.

Sūtrakṛt. I, 1, 4, 5—7 ist die Rede von zwei verschiedenen Ansichten über die Welt (loga-vāya), die nämlich einerseits für „unendlich und ewig", von einem andern „kühnen" Philosophen aber für „endlich und ewig" erklärt werde; sodann (V. 7) von der Annahme einer unbegrenzten Erkenntnis, der die Behauptung von der Beschränktheit alles Erkennens gegenüberstände.[4]) Sollte hier nicht eine Beziehung zu den Antânantikā Buddhas (I, 3) vorliegen? und ist nicht die zweite Notiz eine deutliche Bestätigung der Appamāna-saññi- und der Paritta-saññi-vādinas (II, 1, 12 u. 11)?

Viel leichter als aus dem Brahmajāla ist aus dem System der dreihundertdreiundsechzig Darśanas der historische Kern herauszuschälen. Lassen wir alles jinistische Beiwerk bei Seite,

---

1) Majjh. Nik. I, 3, 6 u. 4, 6. Leider erfahren wir nur die nackte Thatsache, dass Uddaka Rāmaputta das Reich des Weder-Bewussten-noch-Unbewussten verkündigte; vgl. aber die vorige Anmerkung.

2) Deren Oberhaupt der berühmte Makkhali Gosāla war; s. S. 35 und S. 36 Anm. 3.

3) Dies ist wohl ein Irrtum. Nach der Stelle, auf die sich R. D. (Dialogues of the Buddha, p. 47 Anm.) bezieht, nämlich Majjh. Nik. I, 164, verkündet Ā. K., genau wie bei Aśvaghoṣa, Buddhacarita XII, 63, das *ākiñcaññ'āyatana*, fiele also im Brahmajāla unter II, 4, 6, falls er ein Uccheda-vādin wäre. Doch ist auch letzteres nicht der Fall, wie die Bemerkung Buddhas, Majjh. Nik. I, 165 über die fragl. Lehre zeigt: „Diese Lehre führt nicht .... zur Erlöschung .... zum Nirvāṇa, sondern nur zur Erscheinung (upapatti) im Reiche der Nichtsheit."

4) „.... iham egesim āhiyam; .... iti dhīro 'tipāsai." Natürlich ist die Rede von zwei Ansichten und nicht, wie der Kommentator glaubt, von nur einer.

so bleiben die Ausdrücke *kāla*, *īśvara*, *ātman*, *niyati*, *svabhāvá*, *yadṛcchā*, die termini des Ajñāna- und die des Vinaya-vāda und endlich die allgemeinen Bezeichnungen Kriyā- und Akriyā-vāda, zu denen wir, mit den letzten beginnend, im einzelnen Folgendes bemerken.

Mit eiserner Konsequenz hatte Makkhali Gosāla sein Prinzip der Gesetzmässigkeit auf alle Erscheinungen auch des psychischen Lebens ausgedehnt und die Freiheit des Willens, vielleicht als erster der indischen Philosophen, direkt in Abrede gestellt. Gegen diese Lehre erhoben im Interesse der Moral Jinisten und Buddhisten den leidenschaftlichsten Widerspruch. Dem N'atthi kammam n'atthi kiriyam n'atthi viriyam (Es giebt kein Werk, keine That, keinen Willen), das in der Schule Gosālas zum wichtigsten Dogma geworden war, schleuderte Mahāvīra ein Atthi uṭṭhāne ti vā kamme ti vā bale ti vā vīrie ti vā purisa-kkāre-parakkame ti vā (Es giebt eine Anstrengung, eine That, eine Kraft, einen Willen, eine Männlichkeit, eine Gewalt)[1]) entgegen, und Buddha gab mit seiner Antwort „Ich verkünde das Handeln, das Schaffen, das Wollen" (Aham... kamma-vādo kiriya-vādo viriya-vādo) zugleich die Erklärung, dass, wie von allen Gewändern ein härenes das schlechteste, so von allen Lehren des Makkhali Lehre die schlechteste sei.[2]) Kein Zweifel, dass dieser Streit mit Gosāla zu der besprochenen Einteilung der Philosophen in Kriyā- und Akriyā-vādinas geführt hat. Und zwar scheinen hierin, nach Mahāvagga VI, 31 zu urteilen, die Jainas den Bauddhas vorangegangen zu sein. Sie bezeichneten als Akriyā-vāda alle Lehren, die irgendwie, z. B. durch die Behauptung der Substanzlosigkeit aller Dinge, die Moral zu gefährden schienen, während für Buddha dieses Wort nur die Leugnung des freien Willens bedeutete, nämlich die Behauptungen, 1. dass die Notwendigkeit, 2. dass Gott, 3. dass der Zufall alles bewirke.[3])

Wir wenden uns zum **Vinaya-vāda**. Unter diesem Namen werden alle Schulen zusammengefasst, die die Lebensführung für wichtiger als das Wissen erklärten. Malayagiri unterscheidet zwei Richtungen: 1. diejenigen, welche durch Gehorsam gegen die Götter, Könige, Eltern u. s. w., durch Glauben, Demut, Mildthätigkeit und 2. die, welche durch Selbstpeinigung (Askese) die Erlösung zu erringen hofften. „Aus der Demut folgt das Wissen, aus dem Wissen das Schauen, aus dem Schauen die gute Sitte, aus den guten Sitten (dem rechten Wandel) die Erlösung, aus der Erlösung grenzenlose Seligkeit" lautet der einzige uns überlieferte Vers.[4])

---

1) Bhagavatī I, 3, 5, Ed. fol. 67a.

2) Aṅguttara-Nikāya III, 135; vgl. Oldenberg, Buddha³ p. 79.

3) sabbaṃ taṃ pubbe kata hetu .... issara-nimmāna-hetu .... ahetu-apaccayā ti. Aṅguttara-Nikāya III, 61, 1.

4) Viṇayā ṇāṇaṃ, ṇāṇāo daṃsaṇaṃ, daṃsaṇāo (daṃsaṇāhi, b) caraṇaṃ ca | caraṇāhiṃto mokkho, mokkhā (mokkhe, a) sokkham aṇābāhaṃ (°vāhaṃ, a) || Ācāra-ṭīkā I, 1, 3.

Ein einziges System ist, nach dem Ausweis der Kommentare, der Ajñāna-vāda oder Agnostizismus, und die Ausdrücke *kāla* (Zeit), *īśvara* (Herr), *ātman* (Selbst), *niyati* (Notwendigkeit), *svabhāva* (Natur) und *yadṛcchā* (Zufall) werden als die metaphysischen Prinzipien von sechs verschiedenen Richtungen erklärt. Diese sieben Ansichten nun werden im Besonderen Teil den Gegenstand unserer Betrachtung bilden. Nach ihrer vielfachen Nennung in den alten Jaina-Texten zu urteilen sowie nach der ausführlichen Besprechung und Widerlegung, die ihnen die Kommentare widmen, müssen sie den Hauptbestand der damaligen heterodoxen (jainafeindlichen) Philosophie gebildet haben, und ihr Ursprung fällt, wie sich zeigen wird, mit der einzigen Ausnahme vielleicht des Niyati-vāda, der damals gerade aufgekommen sein mag (s. oben), sogar in die vorbuddhistische Zeit, so dass höchstens, mit Hinblick auf das Brahmajāla, die Frage noch aufgeworfen werden könnte, ob auch Buddha alle diese Ansichten kannte oder ob etwa dieselben in dem Felde seiner Wirksamkeit gerade nicht vertreten waren. Diese Frage erledigt sich eigentlich schon durch die Thatsache, dass Buddha in derselben Gegend lehrte wie Mahāvīra. Es sind aber auch der Ajñāna-, Īśvara-, Ātma-, Niyati- und Yadṛcchā-vāda in den Piṭakas bezeugt (s. unten: „Besonderer Teil"), und die Bekanntschaft Buddhas mit dem Kāla- und dem Svabhāva-vāda wird durch die Nachrichten der nordbuddhistischen Texte[1]) zusammen mit der, Aṅg. Nik. III, 69, 9, Pugg. Pañ. IV p. 57/58 und sonst sich findenden Aufzählung „kāla-vādī bhūta-vādī attha-vādī dhamma-vādī vinaya-vādī"[2]) wenigstens wahrscheinlich. Denn dass Buddha diese letzten Ausdrücke auf den frommen Mönch bezieht, der „zur rechten Zeit", „in Übereinstimmung mit den Thatsachen" u. s. w. redet, hat genau so wenig zu sagen, wie wenn er in der genannten Stelle des Mahāvagga (VI, 31) sich selbst einen Akiriya- und Uccheda-vādin nennt, weil er das „Nichtthun" der bösen Thaten und die „Ausrottung" der Leidenschaft anempfehle. Allerdings aber ist denkbar, dass die Kommentare, trotz ihrer Bezugnahme auf alte Quellen, diese oder jene Lehre so schildern, wie sie zu ihrer, nicht zu Mahāvīras Zeit, sich darstellte,[3]) und dies ist der Hauptgrund, weswegen wir, wenn irgend möglich,

---

1) So führt in Buddhacarita IX, 47 fg. (vgl. die chinesische Version im Band XIX der Sacred Books of the East und bes. Beal, Romantic Legend p. 166 fg.!) der Mantrin des Königs, um Buddha zur Umkehr zu bewegen, ihm alle Ansichten vor, die eine Selbsterlösung für unmöglich erklären, nämlich den Svabhāva-, Iśvara-, (Ātma-?), Yadṛcchā-, und eine eigentümliche Art von Karma-vāda, und XVIII, 55 fg. äussert sich Buddha auch über den Kāla-vāda. Übrigens sind diese Lehren sogar schon einer Upaniṣad bekannt: s. S. 43.

2) *Bhūta-vādin* ist der Materialist (Cārvāka); zu *artha-vādin* vgl. die *artha-cintakās* (Eudämonisten, Opportunisten) im ersten Kapitel des Kāmasūtra (I, 2); *dharma* ist Religion und *vinaya* Moral (Anstandslehre).

3) In diesem Sinne dürfte z. B. Malayagiris Polemik gegen den Ātma-vāda aufzufassen sein.

die zu besprechenden Anschauungen bis zu ihrem Ursprung bezw. bis zur Zeit der alten Upaniṣaden zurückverfolgen werden.

Als Akriyā- oder Nāstika-vāda rechnen unsere Kommentare ausser dem Yadṛcchā-vāda den Materialismus,[1]) den Buddhismus und das Sāṃkhya. Von diesen dreien werden wir den ersten zusammen mit den ihm verwandten, wenn auch zum Teil als Kriyā-vāda gerechneten atomistischen Theorien in einem besonderen (dem achten) Kapitel behandeln; der Buddhismus aber ist natürlich wie der Jinismus von der gegenwärtigen Arbeit ausgeschlossen, und was das Sāṃkhya betrifft, so bietet das Tripiṭaka nicht eine und der Siddhānta ausser den von Weber besprochenen Namen Saṭṭhitanta und Kāvila,[2]) soviel ich sehe, nur drei Stellen, die mit einiger Sicherheit auf diese Lehre bezogen werden können, nämlich Sūtrakṛt. I, 1, 3, 6: Īsareṇa kaḍe loë, pahāṇāī (pradhān'ādi) tathā'vare, „Von Gott ist die Welt gemacht, sagen die einen, von der Urmaterie u. s. w. die anderen" und Sūtrakṛt. I, 10, 16 und I, 1, 13, wo mit den „kühnen" Philosophen, die eine unthätige Seele (akiriya āyā, akāraü appā) annehmen, doch wohl in der That, wie die Kommentare behaupten, die Sāṃkhyas gemeint sind, da diese Ansicht (akāraka-vāda, akarmaka-vāda, akriyā-vāda), obschon bereits dem ältesten Vedānta eigen, als Hauptcharakteristikum des Sāṃkhya gilt. Nun wird von einem nachchristlichen Autor[3]) unter den Begriffen, die zu Weltursachen hypostasiert wurden, neben *kāla* und *svabhāva* allerdings auch *pradhāna* genannt, und auch die tibetische Übersetzung eines buddhistischen Sanskṛt-Textes[4]) und sogar die Śvetāśvatara-Upaniṣad[5]) hat in diesem Zusammenhang das Wort für „Natur" bezw. den Ausdruck *yoni*; aber dies beweist nicht, dass Buddha und Mahāvīra das Sāṃkhya gekannt haben, und das Schweigen der alten Texte sowohl des Jinismus wie des Buddhismus über diesen Punkt und nicht zum wenigsten der Umstand, dass *pradhāna* und *puruṣa* nicht im System der dreihundertdreiundsechzig Darśanas figurieren, zeugen meines Erachtens wenigstens dafür, dass das Sāṃkhya zu jener Zeit und in jener Gegend, wenn überhaupt eine, nur eine äusserst geringe Rolle gespielt hat. Dies ist einer der Gründe, die mich abhielten, im gegenwärtigen Falle das Mahābhārata zu verwerten. Der andere liegt in der Unmöglichkeit, eine spezielle Darstellung des epischen Sāṃkhya zu geben,

---

1) Natürlich konnte ein *cārvāka* auch *yadṛcchā-vādin* sein; aber ebensowohl ist er als *niyati-vādin* u. s. w. denkbar, weshalb wir, den Kommentaren folgend, diese Anschauung für sich behandeln.

2) Weber, Über ein Fragment der Bhagavati, II, 246—48.

3) Varāhamihira, Bṛhat-saṃhitā I, 7.

4) Bçes pai phrin yig (Suhṛl-lekha) transl. by Heinrich Wenzel, Journ. of the P. T. S. 1886. „The aggregates do not arise from desire (? hdod-rgyal), not from time, not from nature (prakṛti), not from themselves (svabhāvāt), nor from the Lord (īśvara), nor yet are they without cause" (V. 50).

5) s. Kap. 6: Iśvara-vāda.

bevor über die Philosophie des Śāntiparvan überhaupt eine eingehende Untersuchung angestellt worden ist. Zu dieser aber hat Prof. Hopkins in hundert Seiten seines ausgezeichneten Werkes eingestandenermassen erst den Grund gelegt.*)

Endlich müssen wir eine Stelle des Rājavārttika (VIII, 1), eines etwa im achten Jahrhundert geschriebenen, höchst ausführlichen Kommentares zu Umāsvātis Tattvārtha-sūtra, hier anführen, in der als Vertreter der besprochenen vier Samavasaraṇa-Gruppen eine grössere Anzahl von Autoritäten genannt werden. Wir finden zahlreiche Namen von vedischen und nachvedischen Gelehrten; ausserdem mehrere Namen, über die uns die brahmanische Litteratur keine Auskunft giebt. Wir meinen nicht, dass die letzteren ernst zu nehmen sind, noch dass die Einreihung der Namen in das genannte Schema uns irgendwelche wichtige Aufschlüsse erteilen kann, glauben aber deshalb diese Liste dem Leser nicht vorenthalten zu dürfen, weil sie in interessanter Weise zeigt, wie weit ein jinistischer Gelehrter in die brahmanische Litteratur einzudringen vermochte. In diesem Sinne lassen wir die Namen nebst den Varianten (auch denjenigen, die sich bei Siddhasena und Haribhadra finden) und einigen erklärenden Bemerkungen hier folgen.

Kokkula[1] — Kāṃṭheviddhi[2] — Kauśika[3] — Hariśmaśru[4] — Māṃthanika[5] — Romaka[6] — Hārīta[7] [8]Muṇḍ'Âśvalāyan[9]'ādīnāṃ kriyāvāda-dṛṣṭīnām**) aśīti-śataṃ.

Marīcikumāra[10] — [11]Kapil'Olūka[12] — Gārgya[13] — Vyāghrabhūti[14] — Vādvali[15] — Māṭhara[16] — [17]Maudgalyāyan'ādīnām akriyā-vāda-dṛṣṭīnāṃ***) catur-aśītiḥ.

Śākalya[18] — Bāṣkala[19] — Kuthumi[20] — Sātyamugri[21] — Rāṇāyana[22] — Kaṇva[23] — Madhyaṃdina[24] — Mauda[25] — Pippalāda[26] — Bādarāyaṇa[27] — Sviṣṭakṛd[28] — Aitikāyana[29] — Vasu[30] — Jaiminy[31] — ādīnām ajñāni-kudṛṣṭīnāṃ sapta-ṣaṣṭiḥ.

Vasiṣṭha[32] — Parāśara[33] — Jātukarṇa[34] — Vālmīki[35] — Romaharṣaṇi[36] — Satyadatta[37] — Vyās'[38] — Ailāputr'[39] — Aupamanyav'[40] — Endradatt'[41] — Âyaḥsthūṇ'[42] — ādīnāṃ vainayika-dṛṣṭīnāṃ dvātriṃśad. —

1., 2. unbelegt. 3. Lehrer des Yajur-veda; Verfasser von Atharva-sūtras. 4., 5. unbelegt. 6. nur in Romaka-siddhānta, dem Namen eines astronomischen Werkes, erhalten. 7. Lehrername im Aitareya-Āraṇyaka; medizinische Autorität; Verfasser von Dharma-sūtras. 8. Verfasser der Muṇḍa-Upaniṣad? 9. °āścalāyana, *P*; °āślāyana, *S* und *p*; °āślāṃghana, *π*; °āśvala, *s*. Verfasser von Śrauta-sūtras. (Nach der Worttrennung von *S* wäre Muṇḍāśvalāyana nur ein Name.)

10. ein in der Jaina-Legende begegnender philosophierender

*) Great Epic, Preface p. X und Kap. III, „Epic Philosophy".

**) In *S* wird diese Klasse als akriyā-vādinas und die nächste als kriyā-vādinas bezeichnet.

***) Vgl. die vorige Anmerkung.

Asket. 11. der sagenhafte Stifter der Sāṃkhya-Schule. 12. nach Weber (Ind. Lit.[2], 263) = Kaṇāda, dem Gründer des Vaiśeṣika. °ollaka, *P*, *S*, *p*; °olūke, *π*. 13. Lehrer des Sāma-veda, des Atharva-veda, Grammatiker etc. 14. Grammatiker. 15. gemeint ist Vāḍvali; derselbe vermutlich in Mahābh. XIII, 252, wo die Ausgaben Vāduli und Vāhuli bieten. 16. nur bekannt als Name eines weisen Papageis in nordbuddhistischen Erzählungen (übersetzt von Schiefner). 17. Schüler Buddhas, = Pāli Moggalāna.

18., 19. berühmte Veda-Lehrer (Ṛk-saṃhitā). Vaṣkula, *P*; Vaṣula, *S*; Cakula, *p*; Vaśrulaṃ, *π*; Vālkala, *s*; Vatkala, *P*ʳ. 20. Verfasser eines Smṛti-śāstra (Kauthuma = Schule des Sāma-veda). Kuṣumi, *P*. 21. eine im Veda mehrfach erwähnte Autorität. 22. Gründer einer Sāmaveda-Schule. Nārāyaṇa, *s*; Chāṇāyaṇa, *P*ʳ. 23. Ṛgveda-Dichter; Gründer einer Schule des weissen Yajus. Kaṇṭha, *P* u. *P*ʳ; Kava, *S* u. *p*. 24. Gründer der Mādhyaṃdina-Schule des weissen Yajus. Mādhyaṃdina, *s* u. *P*ʳ; Madhyadina, *p*; Madhyaṃdine, *π*. 25., 26. Lehrer des Atharva-veda. Paippalāda, *s* u. *P*ʳ; Pippalyāda, *p*; Piṣpelīda, *π*. 27. Verfasser der Vedānta-sūtras. 28. vermutlich Phantasie-Name, = Agni. 29. fehlerhaft für Aitiśāyana, Lehrer der Karma-mīmāṅsā. 30. Ṛgveda-Dichter. 31. Gründer der Karma-mīmāṅsā.

32. berühmter Ṛgveda-Ṛṣi und -Dichter. 33. Lehrername im weissen Yajus und im Sat. Br.; ältester indischer Astronom. 34. statt Jātūkarṇya, Lehrer des weissen Yajus. 35. Lehrer des schwarzen Yajus; Verfasser des Rāmāyaṇa. 36. fehlerhaft für Romaharṣaṇa oder für Raumaharṣaṇi; gemeint ist der bekannte Erzähler der Purāṇa-Texte. 37. unbekannt. 38. berühmter Veda-Lehrer, Verfasser des Mahābhārata, eines Gesetzbuches etc. 39. °Elāputra, *S*, *p*, *π*. Offenbar hat der Verfasser an den in Jaina-Erzählungen begegnenden Ilāputra gedacht, kaum an den Nāga Elāpatra. 40. Lehrer des Sāma-veda. 41. unbekannt. 42. Lehrer des weissen Yajus. °sthūla, *P*, *S* u. *π*.

II. Besonderer Teil: Die einzelnen Systeme.

1. Kāla-vāda.

„Als Yudhiṣṭhira die Herrschaft wiedererlangt hatte und in einem Enkel seine Stammfolge gesichert sah, da schwelgte er mit seinen (nunmehr) den Weltwächtern vergleichbaren Brüdern im höchsten Glück. Aber während sie so ihrem Heim sich widmeten und sorglos an nichts anderes dachten, ging seinen Gang der unsichtbare Kāla (die Zeit), der ewig unwiderstehliche. Als Vidura sein Kommen gewahrte, sprach er zu Dhṛtarāṣṭra:[1] ‚Schnell, o König, verlass dein Heim! Sieh jenen Schrecken sich nahen, o Herr, vor dem es noch nie einen Schutz gab in der Welt; Kāla ist's, der Erhabene, dem wir alle unterthan. Von ihm ereilt, wird seines Lebens, das ihm so teuer ist, im Augenblick der Mensch beraubt; was helfen dann Schätze, was alle Güter der Welt!'"

Diese Stelle, obwohl einem Texte entnommen, der Kāla nur als magische Kraft Viṣṇus gelten lassen will (Bhāg. Pur. I, 13, 15—19), zeigt sehr deutlich das Motiv, das u. a. besonders dazu geführt haben muss, in der Zeit das absolut höchste Prinzip zu erblicken: es ist die unerbittliche Notwendigkeit, die den Menschen und jede Kreatur aus der Kindheit über das Alter zum Tode leitet, die Erkenntnis des „Sarvaṃ kṣayiṣṇu (Alles ist hinfällig)".[2]) Zunächst auf die organische Welt beschränkt, wurde sie, durch den Hang des Inders

1) dem blindgeborenen Stammherrn der Kauravas, der nach dem Ende des grossen Bhārata-Krieges mit König Yudhiṣṭhira und seinen Brüdern sich aussöhnte und zusammenlebte. Wie jeder Brahmane war er durch das Gesetz des Manu moralisch verpflichtet, die letzten Jahre seines Lebens in der Waldeinsamkeit philosophischen Betrachtungen zu widmen. Er folgte denn auch der Aufforderung Viduras und kam schliesslich mit seinen beiden Frauen durch einen Waldbrand um. S. Mahābhārata XV.

2) Maitrāyaṇa-Upaniṣad I, 4.

2

zum Analogieschluss, schon früh auch auf diejenigen Erscheinungen ausgedehnt, die dem primitiven Denken als unveränderlich und feststehend gelten, auf Erde, Sonne, Gestirne, Götter. „Giebt es doch," klagt die Maitrāyaṇa-Upaniṣad, „Vertrocknung grosser Meere, Einstürzen der Berge, Wanken des Polarsterns, Reissen der Windseile [welche die Sternbilder an den Polarstern binden], Versinken der Erde, Stürzung der Götter aus ihrer Stelle!" [1]) Sah man so die ganze Natur in beständiger Umwandelung begriffen, so konnte man durch die Verwechselung von Bedingung und Ursache wohl darauf verfallen, die Zeit, sei es als persönliche Gottheit, sei es als unpersönlichen Weltgrund, zum Prinzip der Dinge zu machen. Dieser Schritt ist verständlich, wenn auch ohne Parallele in der abendländischen Philosophie.[2]) Rätselhaft aber und ungeheuerlich muss es uns erscheinen, wenn trotz der fortschreitenden Entwickelung des philosophischen Denkens diese Vorstellung sich nicht nur halten, sondern sogar zu einem System ausgestalten und Jahrhunderte lang besonders auf die Religion einen Einfluss ausüben konnte, der im Mahākāla des Sivaïsmus (s. unten) noch heute nachklingt. Vielleicht wird der folgende Versuch einer historischen Skizze des Kāla-vāda (wie diese Anschauung in Indien heisst) einiges Licht auf diese Frage werfen.

Beginnen wir unsere Untersuchung mit dem Ṛ g v e d a, so zeigt sich, dass in dieser frühesten, der Spekulation noch wenig geneigten Periode der indischen Geschichte das abstrahierende Denken noch nicht dazu gelangt war, ein Wort zu bilden, das unserem Zeitbegriff genau entspricht. Es ist die Rede von Lebenszeit, von Tagen, Nächten, Monaten, Jahren, niemals aber von der Zeit als solcher. Den Wechsel der Zeiten erklärte man durch das Rad des Ṛta (etwa = Weltordnung), das mit seinen drei Naben (nabhyāni)[3]), zwölf Speichen (arās) oder Reifen (pradhayas) und dreihundertsechzig Pflöcken (śaṅkavas) im Laufe des Jahres einmal um den Himmel sich dreht.[4]) Das Ṛta ist Satzung (dhāman) des Varuṇa (und Mitra), der ausserdem zusammen mit den Ādityas als sein Hüter (gopā) erscheint. Im übrigen bleibt das Verhältnis dieser Ordnung zu den Göttern im unklaren, ähnlich wie das der Moira bei Homer.[5])

---

1) ibid. I, 7; s. Deussen, Sechzig Upaniṣads des Veda.

2) Bei Pherekydes von Syros ist *Χρόνος* nur einer der weltbildenden Faktoren, nicht absolut höchstes Prinzip.

3) Nach Ludwig („Der Rigveda", V, p. 446) sind die Jahreszeiten: Sommer, Regenzeit, Winter gemeint; Deussen denkt zugleich an Erde, Luftraum und Himmel als die drei ineinander steckenden Naben des Sternenrades („Allgemeine Geschichte der Philosophie" I, 1 p. 108 u. 119).

4) Vgl. bes. Ṛgveda I, 164.

5) Vgl. Oldenberg, „Die Religion des Veda", p. 195 fg. Bemerkenswert ist, dass die Namen zweier Ādityas, nämlich Aṃśa und Bhaga, in ihrer Grundbedeutung („Teil, Anteil") mit griech. *Μοῖρα*, *Αἶσα*, lat. Parca zusammentreffen; vgl. auch avest. baya, aksl. bogŭ, beide = „Gott", sowie aksl. bogatŭ „begütert".

Auf annähernd demselben Standpunkt finden wir die ältere Brāhmaṇa-Litteratur. Zwar ist hier gelegentlich die Rede vom „Vergangenen (, Gegenwärtigen) und Zukünftigen" (Bṛh. Up. III, 8, 3; IV, 4, 15), zwar erscheint bereits das Wort *kāla:* aber das letztere hat, wie das einzige Mal, wo es im Ṛgveda vorkommt (X, 42, 9), immer nur die Bedeutung der bestimmten Zeit (= ved. ṛtu), und wenn statt von der unendlichen Zeit vom unendlichen Jahr oder den unendlichen Jahreszeiten gesprochen (Śat. Br. IV, 3, 1, 7; Ait. Br. IX, 5) oder wenn als die Ursache des Sterbens das Jahr genannt wird (Śat. Br. X, 4, 3, 1), wenn ferner auch solche Stellen, die von einer Entstehung der Zeit reden (Ṛgv. X, 190, 2; Bṛh. Up. I, 2, 5; Śat. Br. XI, 1, 6, 1), dieselbe nicht anders denn als Jahr, *saṃvatsara*, zu bezeichnen wissen, so werden wir annehmen dürfen, dass es auch in der Brāhmaṇa-Periode ein Wort für die Zeit als solche noch nicht gab. Erst die Maitrāyaṇa-Upaniṣad[1]) zeigt das Aufkommen des Wortes *kāla* neben *saṃvatsara*, indem sie einerseits das Jahr nebst Mond, Sternbildern und Planeten aus der „Sonne, die da auch Zeit heisst" hervorgehen lässt, andrerseits die Sonne für die Geburtsstätte der Zeit, d. h. des Jahres, erklärt (sūryo yoniḥ kālasya).

Aber doch enthalten bereits die Brāhmaṇas einen beachtenswerten Ansatz zum Kāla-vāda. Er liegt in der, zumal dem Śatapatha-Brāhmaṇa so geläufigen Gleichsetzung des Jahres mit Prajāpati, dem „Herrn der Geschöpfe", die sich ganz natürlich dadurch erklärt, dass man alles Wachstum der Pflanzenwelt, von der ja auch die Existenz der höheren Organismen abhängt, in erster Linie auf den Wechsel der Jahreszeiten zurückführte. In diesem Sinne erklärt bereits ein spätvedisches Gedicht (Ṛgveda X, 190) das Jahr für den „Herrscher über alles, was die Augen bewegt (viśvasya miṣato vaśī)". Gleichwohl kommt es dem Denker der Brāhmaṇa-Periode so wenig wie den Sängern des Ṛgveda jemals in den Sinn, die Zeit als Absolutum zu fassen. Sie ist dort immer ein Geschaffenes, Gewordenes. So ist sie Bṛh. Up. I, 2, 4 ein Kind des Hungers oder Todes (aśanāyā, mṛtyu) und der Rede (vāc)[2]), Chānd. Up. IV, 15, 5 der Sonne untergeordnet, Bṛh. Up. III, 8, 4 in den Äther (ākāśa) „eingewoben und verwoben", Ṛgveda X, 190 aus dem „wogenden Ocean", d. h. den Urwassern, entsprungen.

Erst der Atharvaveda bietet zwei Hymnen, die mit dieser Auffassung brechen und — zweifelsohne in bewusstem Gegensatz zur vedischen Orthodoxie — die Zeit für das unbedingt Höchste erklären. Hiess es in der erwähnten Stelle des Ṛgveda: „Aus dem wogenden Ocean wurde das Jahr (die Zeit) geboren", so beginnt Atharv. XIX, 54 geradezu mit den Worten: „Aus der Zeit sind die

---

1) die zwar in der Hauptsache wohl nachbuddhistisch ist, aber doch manches Ältere überliefert.

2) des blinden Willens und des Intellektes, in schopenhauerscher Sprache.

2*

Wasser entsprungen (Kālād āpaḥ samabhavan)", und Atharv. XIX, 53 erkühnt sich, die Zeit den Vater Prajāpatis, Träger Brahmans und des Parameṣṭhin, ja den Erzeuger Svayambhūs (des Absoluten) zu nennen. In Anbetracht ihrer Wichtigkeit als erste Repräsentanten des Kāla-vāda lassen wir die beiden Lieder in Prosa-Übersetzung hier folgen, ohne uns indessen auf eine Erklärung aller Einzelheiten einzulassen, da dieselbe nebst einer trefflichen metrischen Wiedergabe im ersten Teil von Deussens Allgemeiner Geschichte der Philosophie zu finden ist (p. 210 fg.).

Atharv. XIX, 53. „Kāla fährt dahin als ein Ross mit sieben Zügeln,[1]) tausendäugig, alterlos, samenreich; weise Seher lenken ihn;[2]) alle Wesen sind seine Räder (1). Sieben Räder zieht jener Kāla nebst sieben Naben; Unsterblichkeit ist die Achse; all diese Wesen (Dinge) offenbarend[3]) eilt Kāla dahin als erster Gott (2). Ein voller Krug ist Kāla zugewiesen; wir sehen ihn ja, wo immer wir sind; er kommt heran[3]) an alle Wesen; Kāla nennt man ihn, der im höchsten Himmel (thront) (3). Er brachte alle Wesen hervor — er schritt hinweg über alle Wesen; als Vater wurde er ihr Sohn; deshalb giebt es keine höhere Macht als ihn (4). Kāla hat jenen Himmel gezeugt, Kāla auch diese Erdenwelten; in Kāla hat das Vergangene und Zukünftige, hat auch das Gegenwärtige Platz[4]) (5). Kāla hat das Wachstum geschaffen; in Kāla glüht die Sonne; in Kāla sind alle Wesen; in Kāla schaut das Auge (6). In Kāla ist der Wille, in Kāla der Hauch, in Kāla der Name beschlossen; es freuen sich Kālas (d. h. des richtigen Zeitpunktes), wenn sie ihn erlangt haben, alle diese Geschöpfe (7). In Kāla ist Tapas, in Kāla das Mächtigste, in Kāla ist Brahman (neutr.) beschlossen; Kāla ist der Herr des Alls, der da Prajāpatis Vater war (8). Von ihm gezeugt, von ihm geboren hat auch das Tad[5]) in ihm nur Bestand; Kāla, zu Brahman geworden, trägt den Parameṣṭhin (Allerhöchsten) (9). Kāla schuf die Geschöpfe, Kāla zu Anfang Prajāpati; Svayambhū und Kaśyapa sind aus Kāla, Tapas aus Kāla geboren worden (10)."

---

1) Vgl. Ṛgveda I, 164, 2a: „Sapta yuñjanti ratham eka-cakram, eko aśvo vahati sapta-nāmā", wo nach Deussen (Allg. Gesch. d. Phil. I, p. 108) 1. die sieben himmlischen Hotar's, 2. das Firmament, 3. die Sonne, 4. die sieben Ādityas gemeint sind.

2) „Nur die Weisen sind Wagenlenker, alle andern Wesen sind die passiven Räder", Deussen.

3) Deussen stellt añjan (2c) und pratyaṅ (3c) als „herwärts" und „wegwärts" in Parallele (sa imā viśvā bhuvanāny añjan; . . . . . . pratyaṅ).

4) „Was war, was sein wird, durch die Zeit
Getrieben muss entfalten sich", Deussen.

Ich ziehe es vor, Sāyaṇa zu folgen.

5) Vgl. Ṛgveda X, 129, 2: „Ānīd avātaṃ svadhayā tad ekam", sowie die Upaniṣad-Formeln „Tat tvam asi", „Tad etad", „Etad vai tad". Unser Autor, der es darauf abgesehen hat, die Brahmanen zu übertrumpfen, sucht alle höchsten Begriffe derselben zusammen, um sie seinem Prinzip unterzuordnen.

Atharv. XIX, 54. „Aus Kāla gingen die Wasser hervor, aus Kāla Brahman (neutr.), Tapas, die Räume; in Kāla geht die Sonne auf, in Kāla geht sie wieder unter[1]) (1). Durch Kāla weht der Wind, durch Kāla ist die Erde gross; der grosse Himmel ist in Kāla beschlossen (2). In Kāla hat Vergangenes und Zukünftiges ein Zauberwort einst geschaffen; aus Kāla sind die Lieder gekommen; der Opferspruch ging aus Kāla hervor (3). In Kāla hat man das Opfer ersonnen, den Göttern zum ewigen Genuss; in Kāla sind Gandharven und Apsaras', in Kāla die Welten gegründet (4). In Kāla ist jener Aṅgiras, ist Atharvan vom Himmel hierher gekommen; diese Welt und die höchste Welt und die heiligen Welten und die heiligen Gesetze (5): alle Welten bezwungen habend durch das göttliche Wort (brahman): so eilt Kāla dahin als höchster Gott (6)."

Wie man sieht, ist es einfach das Prinzip des Werdens, das hier unter dem Namen Kāla als Herr des Weltalls gepriesen wird, ähnlich wie Rohita (Sonnenkraft), Anaḍvah und Vaśā (Zeugungskraft),[2]) und schwerlich hätte Kāla diese Gottheiten überlebt, wäre er nicht zu praktischer Bedeutung gelangt durch seine Verbindung mit der gewaltigen Macht des Fatalismus. Im Mahābhārata, nächst den Veden das älteste Denkmal brahmanischer Kultur, ist dieses Bündnis bereits ein so inniges, dass an vielen Orten *kāla* mit den besonderen Wörtern für Schicksal: *daiva*, *diṣṭa*, *bhāvya*, *bhavitavya* etc. geradezu synonym gebraucht wird. Da aber in anderen Teilen des Riesengedichtes[3]) diese Wörter für sich und mit eigenem Sinn erscheinen, halten wir es für zweckmässig, unserer Betrachtung des epischen Kāla-vāda eine kurze Analyse dieser termini vorauszuschicken, zumal auch die später zu besprechenden Anschauungen des Niyati-, Svabhāva- und Yadṛcchā-vāda dieselbe erfordern.

Im Mahābhārata sind auf Kāla als ihre gemeinsame Bedingung die folgenden Begriffe übertragen worden:

1. Diṣṭa, „das Gewiesene". Dieses Wort erscheint zuerst[4]) in der Bedeutung „Lebensziel", um das dem Menschen erreichbare Alter (von hundert Jahren) zu bezeichnen, dann, im Epos, in dem allgemeinen Sinne des Vorherbestimmten, so VI, 3, 47 in Dhṛtarāṣṭras Äusserung über den Bhārata-Krieg: „Ich glaube, dass dieses längst bestimmt war: ‚Ein Männermorden wird stattfinden'", und I, 228, 22: „Als vorherbestimmt betrachte diesen Untergang des Khāṇḍava

1) Vgl. hiergegen die erwähnte Stelle der Maitrāyaṇa-Upaniṣad (VI, 14): „Die Sonne ist die Wiege der Zeit."

2) Atharvaveda XIII, 2, 39, XIII, 3, 5; IV, 11, 7. 11; X, 10, 30. Vgl. Deussen: Allgemeine Geschichte der Philosophie I, 1, 209 fg.

3) das nach einer beliebten Schätzung 20 × die Ilias umfasst und die Arbeit mehrerer Jahrhunderte repräsentiert.

4) Atharvaveda X, 3, 16, XII, 3, 55: purā diṣṭāt pur' āyuṣaḥ; diṣṭaṃ no tra jarase ni neṣat.

(-Waldes)". *Diṣṭa* ist natürlich auch das menschliche Handeln, wenn es als die Wirkung früheren Karmans gedacht wird (Yad anyad diṣṭa-bhāvasya puruṣasya svayaṃ-kṛtam, V, 77, 10).

2. Daiva, „göttlich", ist zunächst alles, was die Götter, Dämonen oder Naturkräfte wirken, d. h. Kälte, Hitze, Regen, Hunger, Durst und Krankheit[1]) (V, 77, 9; vgl. Atharv. IV, 26, 7) sowohl wie alles Aussergewöhnliche, Erstaunliche, der Erwartung Widersprechende, z. B. die Entführung der Draupadī (III, 273, 6), die auffällige Vergesslichkeit der Feldherrn (VII, 83, 6), die Niederlage des grossen Kaurava-Heeres (VI, 76, 19 fg.: viparītam idaṃ sarvaṃ pratibhāti). Sodann ist *daiva* gleich *diṣṭa*, wenn das Vorherbestimmte als ein Gottgewolltes, und gleich *karman*,[2]) wenn dieses nicht automatisch wirkend, sondern als göttliche Gerechtigkeit gedacht wird. So bezeichnet III, 31, 35 fg. Yudhiṣṭhira die Früchte des *karman* als Geheimnisse der Götter (deva-guhyāni, rakṣyāṇi devānām) und III, 32, 17 heisst es: „Was immer ein Mensch durch göttlichen Ratschluss (daivena vidhinā) als Vorherbestimmtes (diṣṭaṃ nāma) geniesst, das, o Pārtha, wird Schicksal (daivam) genannt" (vgl. VI, 76, 19: daivam atra purātanam).

3. Haṭha. Dieses Wort, dessen Herkunft noch nicht ermittelt ist, wird III, 32, 13 fg. von *diṣṭa*, *daiva*, *pauruṣa* und *svabhāva*[3]) ausdrücklich unterschieden und als die Erlangung des Unvermuteten erklärt[4]), muss also entweder den Zufall oder die unerklärliche Notwendigkeit bezeichnen. Da die beiden Begriffe sich aufs engste berühren, kann es nicht Wunder nehmen, dass überall, wo das Wort begegnet, in der That beide Auslegungen möglich sind (vgl. bes. XII, 32, 12 u. 19; 177, 10 – 12).[5])

4. Bhāvya, bhavitavya, „was eintreffen muss", drückt ganz allgemein, d. h. ohne Rücksicht auf die causa movens, den Begriff des Notwendigen aus.

5. Vidhi, vidhāna, vihita ist das Vorgeschriebene, Angeordnete, mit dem Nebenbegriff des Gesetzmässigen.

---

1) Vgl. Suśr. I, 89, 18 u. II, 396, 9, wo es von den Krankheiten heisst, sie seien daiva-bala-pravṛttāḥ.

2) Vgl. den bekannten Spruch: „Pūrva-janma-kṛtaṃ karma tad daivyam iti kathyate", Hitop. Einl. 32. Dagegen wird in den Dharmaśāstras *daiva* von *pūrvakṛta* (*paurvadaihika*) getrennt, so Manu VII, 166, XI, 47 und Yājñ. I, 348.

3) *diṣṭa* ist hier gleich *daiva* (s. oben), *pauruṣa* das freie Handeln, *svabhāva* die Naturanlage.

4) vgl. Nīlakaṇṭha: Acintitasyātarkitasya ca lābho haṭhaḥ.

5) Lehrreich vor allem ist die Geschichte des Maṅki (XII, 177) von dem Kamel und den beiden Stieren. Hier liegt, wie V. 11 erklärt, ein *kākatālīya* (s. hinten sub Yadṛcchāvāda), d. h. ein reiner Zufall, vor. Dennoch ruft Maṅki aus „Imaṃ paśyata saṃgatyā mama daivam upaplavam!" Man beachte übrigens, dass die Adverbien haṭhena und haṭhāt in der klassischen Litteratur stets „mit Zwang, notgedrungen" bedeuten.

6. Bhāgadheya, „sors", ist der Anteil (auch Plur.: bhāgadheyāni) des Einzelnen am Glück und Unglück der Welt, das alte *bhaga* (S. 18 Anm. 5).

Dass alle diese Begriffe ineinander übergreifen und daher selbst ohne die Vermittelung von Kāla allmählich synonym werden mussten, liegt auf der Hand. Sie werden denn auch von dem späteren Daivapara unterschiedslos für dieselbe Sache verwendet.

Nach dieser Abschweifung schreiten wir nunmehr zur Darstellung des epischen Kāla-vāda, einer insofern nicht leichten Aufgabe, als das Material hierzu über das ganze Epos verstreut ist und folglich den verschiedensten Zeiten angehören kann. Immerhin sind es nur einige Abschnitte, die speziell vom Kāla-vāda handeln, und auf diese wird sich naturgemäss, unter gelegentlicher Heranziehung sporadischer Äusserungen, unsere Darstellung beschränken. Wir meinen die Adhyāyas 223/25, 227/28, 25 (V. 5—16), 28 (V. 18 bis 44) und 33 (V. 14 fg.) des zwölften Buches (Śānti-parvan).

Adhy. 223 bis 225 enthalten eine Unterredung Indras mit dem gefallenen Dämonenfürsten Bali. Letzterer, ehedem mächtiger als die Götter, ist jetzt als Esel verkörpert und muss mit einer leeren Hütte als Wohnung vorlieb nehmen. Dort findet ihn Indra, der gerade auf dem Rücken seines Elephanten Airāvata eine Erdenfahrt macht, und fragt ihn, ob er sich nicht unglücklich fühle. Bali verneint die Frage. „Vergängliches erblicke ich hier, dem Gesetze des Zeitumlaufs Unterworfenes. Deshalb, o Śakra, klage ich nicht. Denn alles dieses hat ja ein Ende (5). Endlich sind auch diese Leiber der Wesen, o Fürst der Götter! Deshalb, o Śakra, klage ich nicht. Habe ich doch nicht verschuldet, was ich leide! (nâparādhād idaṃ mama) (6)" u. s. w. Mit einer ganz ähnlichen Exposition beginnt Adhy. 226, nur dass hier an Stelle des Bali ein anderer Dämonenfürst, Namuci, erscheint und von einer Eselsverkörperung nicht die Rede ist. Adhy. 227 erzählt dann, aber mit grösserer Ausführlichkeit (212 gegen 126 Ślokas), die Geschichte von Indra und Bali noch einmal. Ich denke, dass uns hier in der That, wie Bhīṣma angiebt, eine alte Legende (itihāsaḥ purātanaḥ) vorgetragen wird, und zwar in zwei Versionen, von denen die kürzere und zuerst erzählte die ältere ist.[1]) Was Adhy. 226 betrifft, so ist derselbe meines Erachtens nur durch seine äussere Ähnlichkeit zu diesen Stücken hierher gelangt. Er verkündigt eine Art Prädestinationstheorie und nennt nicht ein einziges Mal das Wort *kāla*, obschon er zum Kāla-vāda nicht eigentlich im Widerspruch steht. Adhy. 25 endlich steht der Ansicht Balis ziemlich nahe, während 28 (Aśmagīta) *kāla* schon unbedenklich mit *bhavitavya*, *diṣṭa* etc. gleichsetzt[2])

---

1) Auf die sektiererischen Stellen der zweiten kommen wir noch zu sprechen.

2) Keine solche Identifikation begegnet in unseren beiden Haupttexten. Auch III, 273, 6 scheint noch einen Unterschied zu machen zwischen *kāla*, *daiva* und *bhavitavya*, und in der mehrfach genannten Erklärung der verschiedenen Schicksalsbegriffe in III, 32 ist gar von *kāla* noch nicht die Rede.

und 33 den Versuch macht, den Kāla-vāda mit der Karman-Theorie in Einklang zu bringen. Nach alle dem scheint es am zweckmässigsten, der folgenden Auseinandersetzung des epischen Kālavāda die Lehre Balis in ihrer älteren Form zu Grunde zu legen und von sonstigem Material nur heranzuziehen, was sich mit ihr widerspruchslos vereinigen lässt.

Beginnen wir mit der Frage nach der Natur von Kāla. Ist Kāla, wie z. B. bei den Jainas[1]), eine Substanz oder nicht, und ist er wirklich das absolut höchste Prinzip oder nur, vergleichbar der Māyā des Vedāntin, eine dem Absoluten auf unerklärliche Weise inhärierende schöpferische Kraft (śakti)? Die zweite Frage zunächst ist mit Nein zu beantworten. Dass im späteren Epos Kāla des öfteren mit Māyā und Prakṛti direkt identificiert wird, kann nicht Wunder nehmen; unser Haupttext aber feiert Kāla in völlig unzweideutiger Weise als den Inbegriff alles Göttlichen: „Dem man durch Laufen nicht entgehen kann, dem man auch stehend nicht entgeht:[2]) ihn wahrzunehmen sind die fünf Sinne nicht genug. [3])Einige nennen ihn Agni, einige Prajāpati; die Jahreszeiten, Monate und Halbmonate, Tage und Nächte, Vormittag, Nachmittag und Mittag wieder andere; den Augenblick auch nennt man ihn. So nennt man mit vielen Namen ihn, der nur einer ist.[3]) Ihn, in dessen Gewalt dieses Weltall ist, erkenne als Zeit!" (224, 51—54)[4]) und auch sonst wird Kāla ausdrücklich als „ohne einen Herrn" (anīśa), „ohne Vater und Mutter" bezeichnet (227, 93; 33, 17). Andererseits zeigt sich, dass diese Theorie über Kāla in abstracto nichts Bestimmtes zu sagen weiss,[5]) sich vielmehr damit begnügt, den Zeitbegriff, sei es in theïstischer oder in pantheïstisch-materialistischer Weise, zu versinnbildlichen. So erscheint die Zeit sowohl als die göttliche Ordnung (vidhir divyaḥ), das ewige Gesetz (dharmaḥ sanātanaḥ), der Lenker und Züchtiger (śāstar), der Schöpfer (dhātar) wie auch als „das furchtbare, geheimnisvolle, stets gegenwärtige, unvergängliche Feuer" (227, 91),[6]) das die Wesen erzeugt

---

1) Dhammo ahammo āgāsaṃ davvam ikkikam āhiyam;
aṇaṃtāni ya davvāṇi kālo puggala-jaṃtavo.
(Gutes, Böses und Raum [Äther] werden für je eine Substanz erklärt, für unzählige Substanzen dagegen Zeit, Körper und Seelen).
Uttarādhyayana XXVIII, 8.

2) Ein Upaniṣad-Gedanke.

3) Vgl. das Puruṣa-Lied des Ṛgveda (I, 164, 46).

4) Hiermit ist der vorhergehende Passus (46—50) nur zu vereinigen, wenn man ihn wie Nīlakaṇṭha versteht (kāl'ākhyaṃ brahma) oder als die Mitteilung einer fremden Meinung auffasst (āhur), die zwar ein unveränderliches Sein annimmt, aber doch alles Geschehen auf Bhagavān-Kāla zurückführt. Endlich wäre es auch denkbar, dass eine spätere Hand hier thätig gewesen ist.

5) Kālaḥ kāle nayati mām „Die Zeit führt mich in der Zeit" (227, 29) ist, soviel ich sehe, die einzige, kaum ernst genommene Äusserung, in der das Kardinalproblem des systematischen Kāla-vāda, das Verhältnis der empirischen zur metaphysischen Zeit, sich zeigt.

6) Ich lese 'kṣare statt kṣare.

und auffrisst (sute cåtti ca prajāḥ, 232, 41; 239, 19), als das grosse Wasser, in dem alles schwimmt, in dem die Menschen wie Blasen entstehen und zerplatzen (27, 30) und zu dem die *svabhāvās* (Naturkräfte) sich wie Strömungen, der *dharma* wie ein Eiland und das Veda-Wissen wie ein Schiff verhalten (236, 13). Aber „wie dieses All versinkt in dem abgrundlosen Zeitocean mit seinen Riesenkrokodilen Alter und Tod, das versteht kein Mensch" (28, 44).

Beliebt vor allem ist hier wie später der Vergleich der Zeit mit dem Feuer. Wie von letzterem die Speise oder das Brennholz, so wird die Welt von der Zeit „gargekocht" und „verbrannt".[1]) Auch Schöpferin ist natürlich die Zeit; doch besteht ihre Thätigkeit als solche nur in dem Vereinigen der unzerstörbaren fünf Elemente: Erde, Licht (jyotir), Äther, Wasser, Wind. Wie bei Empedokles ist offenbar auch hier das physische Geschehen nichts als „Mischung" und „Auflösung von Gemischtem".[2]) Thöricht, heisst es, sei der Mann, der da glaube, er könne töten oder getötet werden; „Verbranntes nur wird wieder verbrannt, Getötetes wieder getötet, längst Vernichtetes wieder vernichtet" (224, 20).

Und wie die Elemente (Materie), so sind auch die Seelen, obwohl nicht von Kāla erschaffen,[3]) dennoch in seiner Gewalt. Ihre Wanderung folgt seiner „göttlichen Ordnung", seinem „ewigen, allgerechten Gesetz" (purāṇaḥ śāśvato dharmaḥ sarva-prāṇabhṛtāṃ samaḥ), das in bestimmtem Wechsel (paryāya-dharmeṇa) jedem Sterblichen das gleiche Mass von Glück und Unglück zu teil werden lässt. „Entstehen und Vergehen...... alles steht fest (pratiṣṭhitam)..... folgt der Regel (vidhānam anuvartate). Sitzen, Liegen, Gehen, Stehen, Essen, Trinken: alles ist dem Menschen durch die Zeit bestimmt (niyatam) (28, 19—21). Aber keine planmässige Weltentwicklung kennt diese Theorie, sondern nur ein beständiges Rollen des Schicksalsrades, eine ewige Wiederkehr aller Dinge. Warte nur, sagt Bali dem spottenden Indra, es kommt eine Zeit, in der wieder eine grosse Schlacht zwischen Göttern und Dämonen stattfinden und mich, wie einstmals, zum Herrscher der Welt machen wird. „Durch den Wechsel (paryāyeṇa) allein bist du zur Śakrawürde gelangt, o Śakra, nicht durch dein Thun" (225 Ende; 227, 28).

Was für die Praxis aus solchen Anschauungen folgt, liegt auf der Hand. Ist es Kāla, der alles vollbringt, vom Grössten bis zum

---

1) Kālaḥ pacati bhūtāni kālaḥ saṃharaṭi prajāḥ
kālaḥ supteṣu jāgarti kalo hi duratikramaḥ.
„Die Zeit bringt die Wesen zur Reife, die Zeit rafft dahin die Geschöpfe, die Zeit wacht über den Schlafenden; der Zeit kann niemand entfliehen" ist der von Späteren bei Nennung des Kāla-vāda unweigerlich zitierte Vers.

2) *Φύσις οὐδενός ἐστιν ἁπάντων*
θνητῶν οὐδέ τις οὐλομένου θανάτοιο τελευτή
ἀλλὰ μόνον μῖξίς τε διάλλαξίς τε μιγέντων.

3) In 223, 7 muss mit *jīvitam* das physische Leben gemeint sein, da eine Ablehnung der individuellen Unsterblichkeit gegen V. 12 desselben Kapitels und gegen die Rahmenerzählung verstösst.

Geringsten, so wird der Weise in sein innerstes Ich[1]) sich zurückziehen und wie ein unbeteiligter Zuschauer das Naturtreiben an sich vorüberziehen lassen. „Unbewegt wie der Himālaya" wird er Glück und Unglück, Sieg und Niederlage mit demselben Gleichmut hinnehmen, stets eingedenk der grossen, „schwer zu gewinnenden" Erkenntnis: „Nicht ich bin der Thäter (Nâhaṃ kartā)".[2]) Hier findet denn auch die den Stoikern vorgeworfene und von ihnen mit Mühe abgelehnte „ignāva ratio" ihren offenen Ausdruck: Niemand, heisst es, habe sich etwas zuzuschreiben, weder im Guten noch im Bösen, und alles Leid rühre lediglich her von der Wahnidee des eigenmächtigen Ich. Da der Handelnde erschaffen und also unfrei sei,[3]) da überhaupt alles von Kāla bewirkt werde: „wer sollte gegen wen sich versündigen können! (kaḥ kasyêhâparādhyati; 139, 49)". „Nicht ich bin der Thäter, nicht du bist der Thäter; Thäter ist stets nur der mächtige (Kāla); was mich zur Reife bringt, gleichwie die Frucht am Baume, das ist jener Kāla" (227, 85). „Kāla ist der Handelnde und der Wandelnde: alles andere ist Nichtursache (sarvam anyad akāraṇam)" (227, 73). Auch Śrī, die Glücksgöttin, wird folgerichtig nur als Begleiterscheinung Kālas gefasst. Sie selbst erklärt (225, 10): „Nicht Dhātar noch Vidhātar[4]) bestimmen mich irgendwie; Kāla allein ist mein Herr, o Śakra," und sie verlässt Bali, in dem sie so viele Jahrhunderte gewohnt, als er, „von der Zeit gedrängt",[5]) den Pfad der Tugend verlässt.

Natürlich hat eine so zweifelhafte Zulassung der Karman-Lehre der Orthodoxie Späterer nicht mehr genügt und allerlei Versuche ins Leben gerufen, *karman* und *kāla* in besseren Einklang zu bringen. So wird XII, 33 Kāla zum Zeugen und Richter der menschlichen Werke (karma-sākṣin) erhoben oder vielmehr erniedrigt und der grosse Bhārata-Krieg, mirabile dictu, für ein blosses Mittel Kālas, die früheren Werke der Krieger zur Reife zu bringen, erklärt, und XIII, 51—56 erscheint der klagenden Mutter eines durch Schlangenbiss umgekommenen Kindes Mṛtyu, der Tod, um die Schuld auf

1) dessen erkennende Thätigkeit ausserhalb des mechanischen Kausalnexus steht und, wie im Sāṃkhya, überhaupt nicht als Thätigkeit gilt.

2) „Ubi nil vales, ibi nil velis," Geulinx. Wie man sieht, ist diese Idee eine ganz natürliche Folge der fatalistischen Weltanschauung und nicht notwendig dem Sāṃkhya entlehnt.

3) Yadi kartā bhavet kartā na kriyeta kadācana;
yasmāt tu kriyate kartā tasmāt kartā'py anīśvaraḥ, [illegible] vgl. 28, 26:
„Was einem bei seiner Geburt bestimmt war, auf d[illegible]cke wandelt er".

4) Vgl. Appendix I, p. 58.

5) kālenôpanipīḍitaḥ, 225, 14; vgl. 223, 1: kāla-daṇḍa-viniṣpiṣtas „vom Stocke der Zeit niedergeschlagen" und 236, 12: kālam abhyudyataṃ paśyen nityam atyantamohanam.

Kāla zu schieben,[1]) worauf dann Kāla erklärt, dass er stets und überall nur durch das Karman des Menschen sich bestimmen lasse.

Hiermit nehmen wir Abschied vom Epos und wenden uns zum systematischen Kāla-vāda. Diese etwas kühne Bezeichnung findet ihre Begründung darin, dass wir aus den durch Malayagiri im Kommentar zur Nandī überlieferten Zitaten auf das derzeitige Vorhandensein eines speziellen Lehrbuches des Kāla-vāda zu schliessen genötigt sind. Leider sind die Nachrichten über dieses System — ausser dem Nandī-Kommentar kommt allein noch die Ācāra-ṭīkā mit einer kurzen Notiz in Betracht — so spärlich, dass man Bestimmteres, zumal über die Durchführung des Prinzips im einzelnen, daraus nicht entnehmen kann. Was sich erkennen lässt, ist dieses: dass man sich abmühte, für die Zeit als Absolutum eine treffende Definition zu finden[2]) und die dabei notwendig sich ergebenden Widersprüche durch allerlei verzweifelte Operationen zu heben suchte. Gegenüber den epischen Vorstellungen ist dies gewiss ein Fortschritt; aber die Beweisführung ist doch noch so naïv, dass man kaum umhin kann, den Ursprung dieser Ideen in eine frühe Zeit zu verlegen, wenn auch die Heftigkeit und verhältnismässige Ausführlichkeit, mit der Malayagiri dieses „kindliche Gerede“ und „Geschwätz eines sinnlos Betrunkenen“ bekämpft, die Vermutung nahe legt, dass man selbst zu seiner Zeit noch solche Argumente vorzubringen gewagt habe. Jedenfalls können wir unter den genannten Verhältnissen dem Gegenstand kaum anders gerecht werden, als wenn wir die Notiz Śīlāṅkas und die erwähnten Zitate — es sind nur zwei — in der Form des Originals hier mitteilen und vorher eine Übersicht geben über die Polemik M.'s, da letztere einen Rückschluss gestatten möchte auf die Natur dieser seltsamen Doktrin, die vollkommen verständlich erst werden wird, wenn wir über die ganze Entwickelung des Zeit- sowie des Raumbegriffes in Indien eine eingehende Darstellung haben.

M. stellt die Alternative, dass die Zeit entweder ein „Einheitliches, Ewiges, Allgegenwärtiges“ oder ein „durch die Sekunden u. s. w. Veränderliches“ sein müsse. Im ersten Falle sei man genötigt, die Priorität und Posteriorität (pūrvatva, aparatva) einer „anderen Zeit“ zuzuschreiben, womit, da ja auch diese zur absoluten Zeit in Beziehung gesetzt werden müsse, ein regressus in infinitum entstände; oder man entschlösse sich mit anderen zur Annahme von „Begleitern“ (sahacāriṇas, *ξυναίτια*),[3]) von denen die Bezeichnungen „früher“ und

---

1) Vgl. XII, 149, 32: „Wisse, o Rechtskundiger, dass ich der Tod bin. In eigener Person bin ich gekommen, um im Auftrage Kālas (kālena codito) dich, o Brahmane, von hier fortzuholen.“

2) Schon die beiden atharvischen Zeithymnen scheinen Vergangenheit, Gegenwart und Zukunft von der absoluten Zeit zu trennen (XIX, 53, 5; 54, 3); vgl. auch S. 24 Anm. 5.

3) Vgl. Sarvadarśanasaṃgraha[1] p. 10 („sahakāriṇas“). Die Denkunmöglichkeit einer aktuellen Substanz führte zur buddhistischen Lehre von der

„später“ auf die Zeit übertragen würden,[1]) was einem circulus vitiosus gleichkäme, indem von der Priorität etc. der Zeit auf die der „Begleiter“ und umgekehrt geschlossen würde. Im zweiten Fall aber müsste, wenn die Zeit alleiniges Erklärungsprinzip alles Geschehens bleiben sollte, in der gleichen Jahres- und Tageszeit überall das Gleiche sich ereignen, was den Thatsachen widerspräche.[2])

Sīlāṅka definiert in der Ācāraṭīkā im Sinne des Kāla-vāda die Zeit wie folgt: „Sie ist übersinnlich; fähig, zugleich die lange und die kurze That zu offenbaren;[3]) die Ursache des Bestehens von Kälte, Hitze und Regen; in den Sekunden, Minuten, Stunden, Nachtwachen, Tagen und Nächten, Halbmonaten, Monaten, Jahreszeiten, Halbjahren, Jahren, Yugas, Kalpas, Palyopamas, Sāgaropamas, Utsarpinis und Avasarpinis[4]) verkörpert; die Form (rūpa) der Thätigkeit aller Dinge u. s. w., der wiederkehrenden, vergangenen, zukünftigen und gegenwärtigen.“

Die beiden Zitate des Nandi-Kommentators endlich lauten: 1. „Ohne die Zeit gäbe es keine gute noch böse Geburt;[5]) was immer geboren wird in der Welt, das hat wahrlich jene zur Ursache. Auch sieht man nicht ausser der Zeit die Bohnenreife, selbst wenn Kessel u. s. w. in der Nähe sind; deshalb ist sie jener zuzuschreiben. Wäre die Zeit nicht, so wären auch Geburt u. s. w. ohne Regel,[6]) da sie durch die blosse Existenz einer von anderen angenommenen Ursache eintreten müssten.[7]) Die Zeit bringt die Dinge zur Reife, die Zeit rafft die Geschöpfe dahin; die Zeit wacht über den Schlafenden; der Zeit kann niemand entfliehen.“ 2. „Was mit der früheren Zeit u. s. w. in Verbindung steht, das hat Teil an der Bezeichnung „früher“ u. s. w.; die Priorität und Posteriorität (aber) kommen von ihrer (der Zeit) Natur, nicht anderswoher.“[8])

Momentvernichtung (s. hinten p. 56) auf der einen, zur vedāntischen Māyā-Theorie auf der andern Seite.

1) „Wie etwa Tribünenbänke schreien (Beifall jauchzen; indem die darauf sitzenden Personen es thun)“ ist M.'s ironische Erklärung.

2) Eine einfachere Widerlegung giebt Ānandagiri im Unterkommentar zur Māṇḍūkyakārikā (II, 24): „Wäre die Zeit ein Einheitliches, so könnte es keine Sekunden u. s w. geben; und ist sie ein Vielheitliches, so kann sie nicht absolut sein.“ Vgl. auch Śaṅkaravijaya 46: 'Kālasya brahmatvam .... atyantam agrāhyam .... tasya janyatva-darśanāt sāvayavatvāt.'

3) yugapac cira-kṣipra-kriyā'bhivyaṅgyo.

4) S. Appendix I, p. 61.

5) ex conj.: garbhavāsa-śubh'ādikam; Ed. u. MS. haben °vāla°.

6) „Kindheit, Knaben-, Jünglings-, Mannes- und Greisenalter: alle diese sind nur denkbar durch die Verteilung bestimmter Zeiten (pratiniyata-kāla-vibhāge).“ M.

7) M. erklärt: „Atha ‚pareṣṭa-hetu-sadbhāva-mātrād‘ iti parābhimata-vanitā-puruṣa-saṃyog'ādi-mātra-rūpa-hetu-sadbhāva-mātrād eva.“

8) „So kommt es,“ sagt M., „dass, weil er mit einer früheren Zeit verbunden war, der König Bharata früher lebte, und Rāma u. s. w. später, da diese mit einer späteren Zeit in Verbindung waren.“

Hierzu möchte ich noch den charakteristischen, von Bhaṭṭotpala im Kommentar zur Bṛhatsaṃhitā (I, 7) überlieferten Vers stellen: „Eine ewige, einheitliche, allgegenwärtige Substanz, das Mass aller Handelnden, (aber selbst) von der Thätigkeit verschieden: so beschreiben die einen die Zeit; als die Bewegung der Sonne, Planeten und Fixsterne andere; vielheitlich durch die Verschiedenheit der Perioden (? āvṛtti-bhedena) wissen die Zeitverständigen (Astronomen) die Zeit."

Der Kāla-vāda hat sich, in der systematischen sowohl wie in der unsystematischen Form, als sehr langlebig erwiesen. Eine wie bedeutende Macht er z. B. noch im sechsten Jahrhundert gebildet haben muss, ersieht man daraus, dass ihn Varāhamihira († 587 p. C.) in dem Eingang seines berühmten Werkes so angesehenen Systemen wie dem Sāṃkhya und dem Vaiśeṣika an die Seite stellt.[1]) Aber nicht sowohl die Philosophie als vielmehr die Religion ist von ihm beeinflusst worden, wie wir am Śivaïsmus und am Viṣṇuïsmus hier noch in Kürze zeigen wollen.

Was zunächst den Śivaïsmus betrifft, so ist seine Verbindung mit dem Kāla-vāda so wenig auffallend, dass man sich vielmehr wundern müsste, wenn er aus demselben kein Kapital geschlagen hätte. Man erwäge die folgenden Beziehungen: 1. Agni wird schon in den Brāhmaṇas von Rudra-Śiva kaum mehr getrennt, und Agni ist, wie wir sahen, das beliebteste Symbol der Zeit; 2. Śiva ist der Zerstörer, „der Gott, der das Töten liebt," schon in der vedischen Zeit (Ait. Br. III, 34), und ebenso früh ist das „Jahr" der Tod (Śat. Br. X, 4, 3, 1); 3. Śiva ist der „Schwarze" = nīla, śyāma, kāla (: κηλίς, cālīgo); kāla aber ist auch das (etymologisch nicht erklärte) Wort für Zeit.[2]) Diese Beziehungen, wenigstens die erste und dritte, müssen bereits dem Autor von Mahābh. XII, 227 vorgeschwebt haben, wenn er V. 80 von dem „Zeitfeuer" und der „Zeitfessel" redet und weiter (V. 81) Bali von Kāla sagen lässt: „Das ist ja der schwarze Mann, den die Welt nicht überwinden kann; vor mir steht er, der Schreckliche, der mich gebunden hat, wie man ein niederes Tier mit einem Strick fesselt."[3]) So ist denn Śiva zum „Grossen Kāla" geworden, und auch seine Gemahlin, die blutdürstige Durgā oder Kālī, ist zum Kāla-vāda in Beziehung getreten, wie u. a. Mārk. Pur. 81, 55 zeigt, wo es von ihr, geradeso

1) Für die Behauptung verschiedener Kommentatoren, dass der Kālāvāda die gewöhnliche Weltanschauung der Astronomen und Astrologen sei, bietet der Śaṅkaravijaya eine Illustration in der Debatte des grossen Vedānta-Lehrers mit dem prahlerischen Kṣapaṇaka (Kap. 27 u. 46). Beachtenswert ist ferner, dass bei Vātsyāyana (Kāmasūtra II, 21) die k ā l a k ā r a ṇ i k ā s auf die Bali-Legende sich berufen, sowie die Erwähnung der k ā l a c i n t a k ā s und k ā l a v i d a s in Gauḍapādas Māṇḍūkyakārikā (I, 8; II, 24).

2) Sollte der Begriff „Zeit" bei *kāla* sich aus dem älteren „der Schwarze, Finstere, Todesgott" entwickelt haben?

3) Ayaṃ sa puruṣaḥ śyāmo lokasya duratikramaḥ;
baddhvā tiṣṭhati māṃ raudraḥ paśuṃ raśanayā yathā.

wie Mahābh. XII, 232, 41 von der Zeit, heisst, dass sie die Welt erschaffe und verzehre.

Weniger in die Augen springend, aber doch unverkennbar ist der Einfluss des Kāla-vāda im Viṣṇuïsmus. Hier werden (Viṣṇu-Pur. I, 2) vier Erscheinungsformen des höchsten Wesens unterschieden: Pradhāna (Urmaterie), Puruṣa (Geist), Vyakta (sichtbare Materie) und Kāla (Zeit), und diese Trennung scheint wenigstens im Viṣṇu-Purāṇa einigermassen durchgeführt. Hingegen im Bhāgavata-Purāṇa, dem bei weitem beliebtesten Textbuch der Viṣṇuïten, lässt Viṣṇu alles durch Kāla ausführen, und es fehlt selbst nicht an Stellen, die Viṣṇu geradezu Kāla nennen oder gar von Kāla wie von einer unabhängigen Macht sprechen (I, 6, 9; 8, 28; 9, 14; 13, 16 fg. etc.). Auch in den späteren Upaniṣaden wird Viṣṇu vielfach geradeso wie Śiva mit Kāla direkt identifiziert.[1])

Als ein Beispiel für die Stellung der brahmanischen Philosophie zum Kāla-vāda sei zum Schluss noch die Maitrāyaṇa-Upaniṣad genannt, die im sechsten Prapāṭhaka offenbar auf eine Vermittelung des neuen Glaubens mit der orthodoxen Upaniṣad-Lehre hinzielt. Man vergleiche: „Wer die Zeit als das Brahman verehrt, vor dem weicht die Zeit weit zurück," „Aus der Zeit entstehen die Wesen, aus der Zeit gewinnen sie Wachstum, in die Zeit kehren sie zurück; die Zeit ist die formlose Form (mūrtir amūrtimān)" (14) mit der unmittelbar folgenden Erklärung: „Zwei Körper wahrlich hat das Brahman: die Zeit und die Nichtzeit. Was da früher ist als die Sonne, das ist die Nichtzeit, die unteilbare; aber was die Sonne und die Gestirne sind,[2]) das ist die Zeit mit Teilen (kālaḥ sakalaḥ)" sowie dem Schlussvers „Die Zeit bringt alle Wesen zur Reife in ihrem grossen Selbst; worin aber die Zeit heranreift, wer den kennt, der ist ein Vedakenner" (15).

2. Svabhāva-vāda.

Dass alle Dinge kraft ihrer eigenen Natur (svabhāva-vaśāt) entständen, ist die Behauptung der Svabhāva-vādinas, und zwar wird, wie uns Śīlāṅka[3]) erklärt, unter *svabhāva* im besonderen verstanden „Die Anlage eines Dinges zu einer seinem Wesen entsprechenden Entwickelung" (vastunaḥ svata eva tathā-pariṇati-bhāvaḥ). „So nämlich," heisst es, „wird aus dem Thon ein Topf, aber keine Matte etc., und aus den Fäden eine Matte, kein Topf etc.", und auch das beliebte Bild von der Mudga-

1) So heisst es Nṛsiṃhapūrv. IV, 3 von Viṣṇu „Der da Nṛsiṃha .... und der da Kāla ist" und ebenso Atharvaśiras 2 von Śiva: „Der da Rudra .... und der Kāla ist."

2) adity'ādyaḥ; „was mit der Sonne anfing", Deussen.

3) Ācāraṭīkā I, 1, 3.

Bohne, die nicht durch Kessel, Brennholz, Zeit[1]) u. s. w., sondern ganz allein durch ihre Natur zur Reife käme, muss wieder herhalten.

Dies ist, nach Mādhava, Bhaṭṭotpala, Śīlāṅka u. a., die Ansicht der Cārvākas, die, geradeso wie die europäischen Materialisten auf die Frage, wie die Mannigfaltigkeit der Welt zustande komme, die wohlfeile Antwort „Von selbst" (svabhāvāt) immer bereit hatten. Dass aber die im Siddhānta genannten Svabhāva-vādinas keine Cārvākas waren, beweist der Umstand, dass sie zu den Kriyā-vādinas gerechnet werden. Sie müssen mindestens die Seelenwanderung anerkannt haben. Wie sie sich jedoch die Seele dachten, wie den Svabhāva, wie das Verhältnis der natura naturans zur natura naturata: diese Fragen können wir leider nicht entscheiden, da unsere Texte uns hier im Stiche lassen. Aber die Widerlegung Malayagiris sowohl wie einige der überlieferten Verse machen den Eindruck, als habe man zum Teil oder in gewisser Hinsicht auf die Vielheit der Naturkräfte zu gunsten eines einzigen, allgegenwärtigen Svabhāva verzichtet, und es ist somit wahrscheinlich, dass wir es hier mit einem Vorläufer jenes nepalesisch-buddhistischen Svabhāva-vāda zu thun haben, über den Hodgson in seinen Essays (London 1874) einige Mitteilungen macht. Es wird daselbst im wesentlichen Folgendes ausgeführt.

Hauptcharakteristika des Svabhāva-vāda sind 1) Leugnung der Immaterialität und 2) Behauptung der unendlichen Vervollkommnungsfähigkeit des Menschen. Die Welt regiert sich selbst durch die *svabhāvās*, d. h. die ihr immanenten, unbewusst zweckthätigen Naturkräfte, und schwankt in gesetzmässigem Wechsel beständig hin und her zwischen *pravṛtti* und *nirvṛtti*,[2]) den Zuständen der zunehmenden Verdichtung und Verdünnung der Materie.[3]) Hiervon weicht die Anschauung der sog. **Prājñika-svābhāvikas** dadurch ab, dass sie die *svabhāvās* als transcendente Prototypen der Erscheinungswelt und in ihrer Vereinheitlichung als höchste

---

1) In einem Kommentar zum Pūja-kāṇḍa der Rakṣā Bhagavatī wird mehrfach von dem „in der Zeit arbeitendem Svabhāva" gesprochen (Hodgson, Essays p. 76).

2) Diese Schreibung beruht wohl auf einem Irrtum. Wir haben pravṛtti und nivṛtti (Entwickelung und Rückbildung); ausserdem nirvṛti, nirvṛtti „Vollendung".

3) Vielleicht liegt diese Meinung auch in dem von Śīlāṅka überlieferten, Bhagavadgītā XIII, 27 nachgebildeten Vers:

Svabhāvataḥ pravṛttānām nivṛttānām svabhāvataḥ |
nâham kartē'ti bhūtānām yaḥ paśyati sa paśyati ||

sowie in den Worten, mit denen Mahābh. XII, 222, 14 (s. S. 32) der Svabhāva-vādin Prahlāda seinen Vortrag an Indra beginnt:

Pravṛttim ca nivṛttim ca bhūtānām yo na budhyate |
tasya stambho bhaved bālyān, nâsti stambho 'nupaśyataḥ ||
Svabhāvāt sampravartante nivartante tathaiva ca |
sarve bhāvās tathā'bhāvāḥ; puruṣârtho na vidyate ||

Gottheit (Yoni, Ādi-prajñā, Ādi-dharma) betrachten.[1]) Beide Klassen von Svābhāvikas aber halten an der Existenz der (feinstofflichen) Individualseele und deren Entwickelung durch unzählige Geburten zur Vollkommenheit der Nirvṛtti fest, sind also, wenn auch als Materialisten, so doch keinesfalls als Cārvākas (ucchedavādinas) anzusehen.[2])

Eine andere Form des Svabhāva-vāda wird uns im zwölften Buch des Mahābhārata vorgeführt. Dort erscheint (Adhy. 222) diese Lehre mit Sāṃkhya-Ideen verquickt: Körperwelt und Svabhāva werden als *vikārās* und *prakṛtiḥ parā* einander gegenübergestellt, und die Behauptung, dass der Ātman Nichtthäter sei, ist auffallend stark betont; alles Handeln, jeder Gedanke, jeder Erfolg, vom kleinsten bis zum grössten (Erlösung) wird ausschliesslich Svabhāva zugeschrieben, so dass der Puruṣa (Ātman) keineswegs, wie im klassischen Sāṃkhya, als conditio sine qua non des Weltprozesses erscheint.[3])

Die Freiheit des Willens ist, nach der einstimmigen Behauptung unserer Kommentatoren, von allen Svabhāva-vādinas entschieden geleugnet worden. „Wer giebt den Dornen ihre Schärfe, wer Wild und Vögeln ihr buntes Gewand? Aus dem Svabhāva ist all dies entsprungen; es giebt keinen freien Willen (kāmacāra); wozu die Anstrengung?!" lässt Sīlāṅka mit Aśvaghoṣa[4] seinen Gegner sagen, und er fügt hinzu: „Wer mit dem Gedanken „Kein Ich ist der Thäter" die Wesen sich entwickeln und zur Ruhe kommen sieht, der sieht die Wahrheit."

3. Niyati-vāda.

Während bei den besprochenen Ansichten die Naturnotwendigkeit, soweit dieselbe Anerkennung findet, nur eine Erscheinungsform des höchsten Prinzips (kāla, svabhāva) ist, wird sie vom Niyati-vādin zu diesem selbst erhoben, und zwar (nach Malayagiri) auf Grund einer Betrachtung über das Verhältnis von Ursache und Wirkung. Letzteres, sagt der Niyati-vādin, wäre ungeregelt, und es gäbe überhaupt keine Ordnung in der Natur (pratiniyata-

---

1) Vgl. die Stellung der platonischen ἰδέαι in Deussens System (Elemente der Metaphysik, p. 121).

2) H. Kern, „Manual of Indian Buddhism" p. 134 Anm. setzt irrtümlich Cārvākas = Materialisten. Es verdient Beachtung, dass auch der Vedāntin und der Sāṃkhyin von der Seele die obige Auffassung hatten, soweit sie dieselbe als wandernde Individualseele betrachteten.

3) Svabhāvāl labhate prajñāṃ, śāṃtim eti svabhāyataḥ |
Svabhāvād eva tat sarvaṃ yat kiṃcid anupaśyasi ‖ (35).
Svabhāvād eva tat sarvam iti me niścitā matiḥ |
ātma-pratiṣṭhā prajñā vā mama nāsti tato 'nyathā ‖ (23).

4) Buddhacarita IX, 52.

rūpa-vyavasthā), wenn es nicht eine transcendente[1] Notwendigkeit gäbe: die Niyati. „Weil alle Dinge in bestimmter Form (niyaten' aiva rūpeṇa) ins Dasein kommen, deshalb sind sie Geschöpfe der Niyati und durchdrungen von ihrer Natur. Wenn irgendwo, irgendwann, irgendwie etwas geschieht, so geschieht es ebendort, ebendann und in eben der Weise mit Notwendigkeit; wer vermöchte sie (die Niyati) von der Hand zu weisen?" lautet der von M. überlieferte Vers, dessen zweiter Teil, nach seiner häufigen Zitierung zu urteilen, das eigentliche Credo des Niyati-vādin bildet [2]).

Aber die Frage nach der Natur der Niyati wird von den verschiedenen Kommentatoren keineswegs in übereinstimmender Weise beantwortet, und dies hat offenbar seinen Grund in der, auch aus M.'s Widerlegung deutlich hervorblickenden Thatsache, dass es verschiedene Richtungen von Niyati-vādinas gab, oder richtiger, dass unter diesem Namen alle Denker zusammengefasst wurden, die, ohne dem Kāla- oder Svabhāva-vāda zu huldigen, einen entschiedenen Determinismus vertraten. So wird erklärlich, dass Abhayadeva (Sthānāṅg, IV, 4, Komment.) die Niyati die durch die Notwendigkeit wirkende Zweckvollzieherin (avaśyatayā .... prayojana-kartrī) nennt, Śīlāṅka (ad Sūtrakṛ. I, 1, 2, 3) sie als das gesetzmässige Zusammentreffen (sva-pariṇāmena .... saṃgatir) erklärt und Nīlakaṇṭha (ad Mahābh. XII, 233, 21) darin das Prinzip der Mīmāṃsakas sieht. Letzteres freilich ist zweifellos ein Irrtum. Denn wenn sich ein durchgehender Zug des Niyati-vāda feststellen lässt, so ist es die Leugnung der moralischen Verantwortlichkeit [3]), verbunden mit der Behauptung, dass jedes Geschehen *sāṃgatika*, d. h. die unausbleibliche Resultante gegebener Verhältnisse sei.

Unter solchen Umständen werden wir auch Gosālas Lehre, obwohl dieselbe eine Verabsolutierung der Niyati zum selbständig thätigen höchsten Prinzip nicht kennt, an dieser Stelle behandeln dürfen, zumal das sonstige Material über den Niyati-vāda ein äusserst geringes und, von den besprochenen Nachrichten abgesehen, auf das Sūtrakṛtāṅga und seine Kommentare beschränkt ist. Immerhin wird es zweckmässig sein, dieses wenige der Betrachtung von Gosālas Lehre vorauszuschicken.

---

1) Die Annahme, dass die Wirkung durch den *svabhāva* der Ursache (kāraṇa śakti) zustande komme, wird abgelehnt.

2) Auch Gommaṭasāra erklärt:
 Jat tu jadā jena jahā jassaya niyameṇa hodi, tat tu tadā
 tena tahā tassa have idi-vādo niyadi-vādo du.

3) Vgl. Sūtrakṛt. I, 12, 1, Ṭīkā, wo *niyati* neben *purākṛta* und *puruṣakāra* als Weltfaktor anerkannt wird (Ansicht der Jainas), ähnlich wie Mahābh. III, 32, 18 fg. u. 34 fg. *haṭha* neben *daiva* = *diṣṭa* und *svabhāva* = *puṃsaḥ prayatna* (pauruṣa) als Quelle der *artha-siddhi* gilt (traidham etan nirucyate).

3

Sūtrakṛt. I, 1, 2, 1—3 liefert mit folgenden Worten das Glaubensbekenntnis eines Niyati-vādin: „Es giebt Einzelseelen (puḍho-jiyā); dieselben empfinden Lust und Leid und wechseln ihren Staud (= wandern). Aber jenes Leid ist nicht ihr eigenes Werk, geschweige denn das eines andern (Agenten wie Kāla, Svabhāva, Karman). Lust nnd Leid, ob himmlisch oder irdisch, geniessen weder als ihr eigenes noch als anderer Werk die Einzelseelen: es ist (vielmehr) ein Notwendiges (saṃgaïaṃ, eigentl. ‚Zusammengetroffenes')" [1]). Hierzu fügt Śīlāṅka den vielzitierten Vers: „Wenn vermöge der Macht der Niyati dem Menschen etwas zuteil werden soll, so muss es geschehen, sei es gut oder böse; keinem wird bei noch so grosser Anstrengung Nichtvorherbestimmtes zuteil, und, was sein soll, kann nicht vernichtet werden." [2])

Eine ebenso breite wie inhaltsarme Schilderung des Niyati-vāda findet sich Sūtrakṛt. II, 1, 29—33. In der Ṭīkā dazu nennt Śīlāṅka die Niyati-vādinas *paraloka-bhīravas* („die sich vor dem Jenseits fürchten") und legt ihnen u. a. folgende Aussprüche in den Mund: „Sehr vernünftig lässt der Niyati-vādin das sichtbare Thun des Menschen (dṛṣṭaṃ puruṣakāram) (als Ursache von Lust und Leid) nicht gelten, sondern nimmt (als solche) die unsichtbare Notwendigkeit (adṛṣṭa-niyati) an." „Durch die Niyati wird man, auch gegen den Willen, das zu thun veranlasst, wodurch man der Kette der Leiden teilhaftig wird." „In der Welt geschieht dem, der an bösem Thun Gefallen findet, kein Leid, wohl aber dem, der das Gute übt, weil eben die Niyati (nicht Karman) dieses herbeiführt."

Als Niyadi-vāda könnte allenfalls auch die in Mahābh. XII, 226 dargelegte Anschauung des Namuci [3]) bezeichnet werden, wofern man nämlich dieselbe wegen der Ausdrücke *śāstar* und *dhātāras* nicht lieber einen konsequenten Theïsmus nennen will. Yathā niyukto 'smi tathā vahāmi „Wie mir bestimmt, so lebe ich dahin" ist das Thema dieses Abschnittes, aus dem als originell der Vergleich des Menschen mit dem bergabwärts fliessenden Wasser hervorgehoben zu werden verdient.

Über die Lehre des Makkhali Gosāla endlich — neben Buddha und Mahāvīra der bedeutendste Tīrthakara seiner Zeit [4])

1) Auch hier scheint die Niyati nicht eigentlich ein metaphysisches Prinzip zu sein, vielmehr an den Begriff des *haṭha* (S. 22) und der *yadṛcchā* (S. 37) zu streifen.

2) Prāptavyo niyati-bal'āśrayeṇa yo'rthaḥ
so 'vaśyaṃ bhavati nṛṇāṃ śubho'śubho vā;
bhūtānāṃ mahati kṛte 'pi hi prayatne
nâbhāvyaṃ bhavati na bhāvino 'sti nāśaḥ.

3) s. oben S. 23.

4) Er war ein Schüler Mahāvīras, bis er durch die drollige Idee der Reanimation (S. 35 Anm. 4) in dessen Ungnade fiel. Über sein Leben und sein tragisches Ende vgl. den interessanten Aufsatz Leumanns in der Wiener Zeitschrift für die Kunde des Morgenl. III p. 329 ff.

— besitzen wir zwei verhältnismässig ausführliche Berichte, einen buddhistischen im Sāmaññaphalasutta und einen jinistischen in der Bhagavatī [1]. Diesen zufolge ist der eigentliche Ausgangspunkt seines Philosophierens die Überzeugung von der ausnahmslosen Gesetzmässigkeit alles Geschehens. Er entwirft ein detailliertes System der Entwickelung = Seelenwanderung (saṃsāra-suddhi): jedes Wesen, versichert er, muss in dem Zeitraum von 8 400 000 Mahākalpas [2]) alle Daseinsmöglichkeiten erschöpfen, bevor es, wie eine Schnur, die sich nicht weiter abwickeln kann, zur Ruhe kommt; es muss siebenmal als Gottheit, siebenmal als unorganisches Wesen, siebenmal als organisches Wesen und endlich (nach Erlangung des höchsten Wissens) siebenmal durch Reanimation [3]), d. h. Körperwechsel innerhalb desselben Lebens [4]), geboren werden, um in feststehender Reihenfolge (aṇupuvvenaṃ) [5]) sämtlicher 600 Arten des dreifachen Karman (That, Rede, Gedanke) in ihren 60 000 Haupt- und 500 000 Unterabteilungen sich zu entledigen [6]). Die letzten Verkörperungen sind die folgenden: als Gottheit im oberen Māṇasuttava; zum vierten Mal als organisches Wesen; als Gottheit im mittleren M.; zum fünften Mal als organisches Wesen; als Gottheit im unteren M.; zum sechsten Mal als organisches Wesen; als Gottheit im Bambhaloga; zum siebenten Mal als organisches Wesen. Mit diesem letzten Leibe erlangt man Allwissenheit (saṃkhāṇa) und wird, wie gesagt, nach siebenmaligem Körpertausch endlich erlöst (sijjhanti bujjhanti), d. h. zu den reinen Geistern versammelt, die, über Lust und Leid erhaben, in einem unbeschreiblichen Jenseits wohnen. Denn die Absorption in Brahman ist bei Gosāla wie bei Mahāvīra einfach deshalb ausgeschlossen, weil es ein höchstes Prinzip nicht giebt.

Auf die sonstigen Einzelheiten des Systems: Einteilung der Menschen in sechs Klassen, des menschlichen Lebens in acht Stadien etc. können wir hier nicht eingehen [7]). Wir bemerken nur noch, dass dasselbe sechs Hauptteile gehabt haben soll: Erlangung, Nichterlangung (lābha, alābha), Lust, Leid, Leben, Tod,

---

1) Die wesentlichen Teile des jinistischen Berichtes sind übersetzt worden von Leumann in Rockhill, „Life of the Buddha“, Appendix I, und von Hoernle im „Uvāsagadasāo“, Appendix I. Eine Übersetzung des Sāmaññaphala-sutta bietet Rhys Davids in seinem „Dialogues of the Buddha“. Obwohl die Berichte einander ergänzen, ist ein in allen Einzelheiten klares Bild des Systems durch sie nicht zu gewinnen.

2) Ein Mahākalpa ist (nach purāṇischer Theorie) = 311 040 000 000 000 Jahre.

3) paüṭṭaparihāre = nigaṇṭhigabbhā (production by grafting, Rhys Davids)?

4) Auf diese Weise bestreitet unser Philosoph, ausser durch seinen Körper mit Gosāla, dem einstigen Schüler Mahāvīras, identisch zu sein, da nämlich vor Jahren die Seele jenes Gosāla der seinigen Platz gemacht habe.

5) „Nach dem Mass bemessen sind Lust und Leid; es giebt nicht Verminderung und Vermehrung.“

6) So nach der Bhagavatī; der Pāli-Text hat kleinere Zahlen.

7) S. bes. Buddhaghosas Kommentar, übersetzt von Hoernle, Uvāsagadasāo, Appendix II.

und schliessen unsere Betrachtung des Niyati-vāda mit einigen Worten über den Determinismus Gosālas.

Dass Gosāla nicht nur von den Jainas bekämpft, sondern auch von Buddha für den schlimmsten aller Irrlehrer erklärt worden ist[1]), hat vor allem seinen Grund in der Hartnäckigkeit, mit der er die Freiheit des Willens und die moralische Verantwortlichkeit in Abrede stellte. Sein Vortrag an Ajātaśatru beginnt mit den Worten: „Nicht Grund noch Ursache, o Grosskönig, giebt es zur Befleckung der Wesen: ohne Grund und Ursache fallen sie in Sünde; nicht Grund noch Ursache giebt es zur Reinigung der Wesen: ohne Grund und Ursache werden sie wieder rein. Nicht ich, nicht du, kein Mensch ist ein (selbständig) Handelnder. Keine Macht, keine Kraft, keine Gewalt, kein Mut vermag (in Wahrheit) etwas auszurichten. Wie Bestimmung, Umstände, Naturanlage sie leiten (niyati-saṅgati-bhāva-pariṇatā), so müssen machtlos, kraftlos, willenlos alle Wesen ohne Ausnahme in den sechs Arten von Geburten Lust und Leid erproben." Aber dies ist kein Fatalismus im Sinne des Kāla-vāda, vielmehr eine blosse Ablehnung des liberum arbitrium indifferentiae, ein Bekenntnis zum Determinismus. Gosāla ist weit entfernt, in quietistischer Resignation die Hände in den Schoss zu legen oder, wie jener Kaśyapa, mit einer Verbeugung vor dem Schicksal zu thun, was er wohl hätte vermeiden können[2]. Für ihn giebt es keine höhere Macht als den Menschen, und er ist überzeugt, dass dieser, unter richtiger Benutzung der Verhältnisse, alles vermag. So kommt es, dass er zwar den moralischen Erfolg von *sīla*, *vata*, *tapa* ausdrücklich leugnet, aber doch die Selbstzucht als Mittel zur Erlangung magischer Kräfte etc. empfiehlt und auch selbst durch sechsmonatliche strenge Askese die Jinaschaft erreicht haben will[3].

4. Yadṛcchā-vāda.

„Diejenigen, welche mit Rücksicht auf den Gang der Ereignisse ein feststehendes Verhältnis von Ursache und Wirkung

---

1) Oldenberg, Buddha[3] p. 79.

2) Sa viditvā'tha bhāryāyās taṃ nirbandhaṃ vikarmaṇi
natvā diṣṭāya rahasi tayā'thôpaviveśa ha. Bhāg. Pur. III, 14, 30.

Auch das Mahābhārata hat Beispiele für eine solche direkte Beeinflussung des Handelns durch die Schicksalsidee, so IX, 1, 7:
Sa daivaṃ balavan matvā bhavitavyaṃ ca Pārthivaḥ
saṃgrāme niścayaṃ kṛtvā punar yuddhāya niryayau.

3) Die Sekte der Ājīvakas, als deren Leiter Gosāla erscheint und die nach dem Zeugnis der Aśoka-Edikte noch im dritten vorchristlichen Jahrhundert eine starke Stellung einnahm und auch später öfter erwähnt wird, soll auf die Askese noch grösseres Gewicht als selbst die Jainas gelegt haben (Rhys Davids, Dialogues of the Buddha: p. 221).

(pratiniyataḥ kārya-kāraṇa-bhāvaḥ) nicht gelten lassen, sondern alles durch den Zufall (yadṛcchā) erklären, heissen Yadṛcchā-vādinas. Sie sagen wie folgt: „Ein geregeltes Verhältnis von Ursache und Wirkung kann es nicht geben, da ein solches, wie aus den folgenden Beispielen ersichtlich, unerweisbar ist (tathā-pramāṇen-āgrahaṇāt). Ein Śālūka (essbare Lotuswurzel) entsteht aus einem Śālūka sowohl wie aus dem Kuhmist; Feuer entsteht aus dem Feuer, doch auch aus dem Reibholz; Rauch aus Rauch, aber auch durch Feuer, Brennholz etc.; aus der Wurzelknolle entsteht die Kadalī sowohl wie aus dem Samenkorn, und ein Schössling etc. kann aus dem Samen nicht weniger wie aus einer Stelle eines Zweiges hervorgehen." [1])

Dies hört sich fast an, [2]) als ob dem Yadṛcchā-vāda die Erkenntnis Humes zu Grunde liegt, dass wir bei jedem Kausalverhältnis in Wahrheit nur ein Nacheinander, nicht ein Durcheinander wahrnehmen, und in der That liesse sich recht wohl verstehen, dass zur Zeit Buddhas, in der ja die Begriffe Substanz und Kausalität und ihr gegenseitiges Verhältnis bereits diskutiert wurden [3]), u. a. diese Entdeckung gemacht worden wäre. Gleichwohl müssen wir auch die naivere Form hier berücksichtigen, in der uns der Yadṛcchā-vāda in der Ācāra-Ṭīkā (I, 1, 3) vorgeführt wird. Daselbst heisst es: „... Das nicht durch eine Absicht bedingte Erlangen eines Dinges heisst Zufall (An-abhisaṃdhi-pūrvikā 'rtha-prāptir yadṛcchā). ... Nicht hat die Krähe die Erkenntnis ‚Auf mich wird die Palmnuss fallen' noch die Palmnuss die Absicht ‚Ich will auf die Krähe fallen', sondern dies geschieht eben zufällig. ... Und so ist nach dem Maxim von der Krähe und der Palmnuss (kākatālīya-nyāya) alles auf Erden: Geburt, Alter, Tod etc. als zufällig anzusehen."

Dass die *yadṛcchā* nicht sowohl ein metaphysisches Prinzip, als vielmehr die Leugnung eines solchen ist, kann nicht zweifelhaft sein und geht überdies aus einem Zitat Malayagiris hervor [4]) sowie aus der Versicherung des letzteren, dass die Yadṛcchā-vādinas sämtlich Akriyā-vādinas seien.

Mit dem Yadṛcchā-vāda in Verbindung zu bringen ist wohl auch der im Suttapiṭaka mehrfach erwähnte Ahetu-vāda („Nicht-

---

1) Malayagiri zur Nandī.

2) Es ist schwer zu glauben, dass der Yadṛcchā-vāda neben dem Kāla-vāda etc., mit denen er regelmässig (einmal auch in der Śvet. Up.) zusammen genannt wird, sich behauptet haben würde, wenn er nur in der naiven, durch die offenkundige Regelmässigkeit des Naturgeschehens auf Schritt und Tritt widerlegten Behauptung bestanden hätte, dass in der Succession der Ereignisse keinerlei Ordnung herrsche.

3) Vgl. unsere Zusatzbemerkung S. 4 fg. Auch an das Wort *paṭicca* = *pratītya* „nachfolgend" sei hier erinnert, das Buddha eigens mit Rücksicht auf seine Kausaltheorie geprägt zu haben scheint: Saṃy. Nik. XII, 67.

4) „Na khalv, anyathā vastu-sadbhāvaṃ paśyanto 'nyathā 'tmānam, prekṣāvantaḥ parikleśayanti."

ursachenlehre") sowie die Ansicht der Adhicca-samuppamikā im zweiten Abschnitt des Brahmajāla-sutta, der zufolge Seele und Welt durch Zufall da sind (Adhicca-samuppanno attā ca loko ca) [1]).

5. Ātma-vāda.

Unter dem Namen Ātma-vāda, auch Ātmâdvaita-vāda, verstehen unsere Kommentatoren jede monistische Metaphysik, die irgendwie auf die Ātman-Lehre der Upaniṣaden zurückgeht oder zurückzugehen scheint, alle Systeme, denen die Welt nicht als Schöpfung eines persönlichen Gottes, sondern entweder als Erscheinung oder „Umwandelung" (pariṇāma) des unpersönlichen höchsten Wesens oder aber als ein scheinbar neben dem letzteren, in Wahrheit überhaupt nicht existierendes „Truggebilde" (vivarta, māyā) gilt. Ich nenne diese Richtungen Pantheïsmus und Akosmismus.

Als Idealismus mag man den Ātma-vāda überhaupt bezeichnen; auf die Māyā-Lehre im besonderen aber sollte man, um einer Verwechselung mit dem, auf ganz anderen Voraussetzungen ruhenden kantischen Idealismus vorzubeugen, diesen Namen nicht anwenden. Setzen wir fest, dass der Gegensatz von Absolutum (Gott) und Welt 1. vom Pantheïsten als der des Dinges zu seinen Eigenschaften und Modi, 2. vom subjektiven Idealisten (Solipsisten) als der des Bewusstseinsträgers zum Bewusstseinsinhalt, 3. vom Transcendentalisten als zwar bestehend, aber schlechterdings unbegreiflich erklärt wird (weil es eine logische Unmöglichkeit ist, dass das Absolute zugleich ein Nichtabsolutes sein oder neben sich haben kann), so werden wir als die Wurzel der Māyā Lehre nicht den (subj.) Idealismus, sondern den Transcendentalismus bezeichnen müssen. Denn nicht durch erkenntnistheoretische Sophistereien [2]), sondern durch die einfache logische Erwägung, dass ausser dem *brahman* nichts sein kann, kommt der Inder dazu, die Welt für unreal (asat, māyā) zu erklären, und nicht die Beschränkung der empirischen Realität auf den Bewusstseinsinhalt eines einzigen Subjektes ist dieser Lehre wesentlich, vielmehr die Behauptung, dass die ganze

1) Vielleicht bezieht sich diese Behauptung nur auf den ersten Anfang, ebenso wie Ed. v. Hartmann (Schelling) die Welt für das „absolut Zufällige" erklärt, ohne doch die Naturnotwendigkeit zu bestreiten.

2) Die metaphysische Frage nach dem Verhältnis des Absoluten zur Welt wird, insofern das erkennende Subjekt als solches mitsamt seinen Anschauungs- und Denkformen eo ipso zur Welt des Bedingten gehört, durch das Erkenntnisproblem überhaupt nicht berührt, und es ist eine blosse Selbsttäuschung des Idealisten, wenn er durch Konstatierung von Elementen apriori oder durch die Leugnung der Vielheit erkennender Subjekte bzw. die Annahme eines „Bewusstseins überhaupt" das fragliche Verhältnis um ein Haar verständlicher gemacht zu haben glaubt. Dem kantischen Idealismus würde ein Śaṅkara wahrscheinlich mit dem *vikalpa* begegnen, ob der „reine Verstand" Erscheinung (māyā) oder Ding an sich (brahman) sei, vielleicht auch mit einem Hinweis auf Māṇḍ.-Kār. IV, 54: „Nicht aus dem Geist entspringt Natur, noch aus Natur der Geist entspringt", da ja Subjekt und Objekt als *māyā* dem absoluten Brahman gleich nahe oder gleich fern ständen.

subjektiv-objektive Welt, weil mit der Idee des Absoluten unvereinbar, ein metaphysisch Nichtseiendes ist. Mit dem sog. subjektiven Idealismus der deutschen Philosophie trifft der Akosmismus nur da zusammen, wo (durch eine μετάβασις aus dem metaphysischen ins erkenntnistheoretische Gebiet) die *māyā* subjektiv, nämlich als Vorstellung, gefasst wird (Solipsismus).

Was von solchen Systemen zur Zeit des aufkommenden Buddhismus bestanden habe, ist eine Frage von eminenter Wichtigkeit, und um so mehr muss man bedauern, dass gerade in diesem Punkte die jinistischen Texte fast ebenso schweigsam sind wie die buddhistischen. Immerhin dürfte es nützlich sein, diese spärlichen Angaben, so wenig sie das Problem definitiv zu lösen vermögen, in Folgendem einmal zusammenzustellen.

Von buddhistischen Texten kommt, da alle anderen Angaben, z. B. des Brahmajāla-sutta, gänzlich unbestimmt und allgemein gehalten sind, allein das Tevijja-suttanta in Betracht. Dort nämlich erklärt der Brahmane Vāseṭṭha dem Buddha, dass, wie viele Wege zu einem Dorfe, so auch viele Wege zur „Gemeinschaft mit Brahman" (brahma-sahavyatāya) führen: „Verschiedene Brahmanen, o Gotama, lehren verschiedene Wege: die Addhariya-Brahmanen, die Tittiriya-Brahmanen, die Chandoka-Brahmanen, die Chandāva-Brahmanen, die Brāhmacariya-Brahmanen [1]). Führen denn alle diese Wege zum Heil? Kann man auf jedem zur Vereinigung mit Brahman gelangen?" Über den Charakter dieser Lehren erfahren wir noch Folgendes: „Diese in den drei Veden bewanderten Brahmanen sagen so: Was wir nicht erkennen, was wir nicht sehen, zur Einigung mit dem führt der Weg, den wir lehren [2]; das ist der rechte Weg" etc. Hieraus ergeben sich zwei wichtige Thatsachen: 1. dass zur Zeit Buddhas und im Bereich seines Wirkens die Upaniṣad-Tradition, so sehr sie zurückgetreten sein mochte [3], keineswegs erloschen war; 2. dass im besonderen das Dogma von der Unerkennbarkeit des Absoluten seine Existenz bewahrt hatte.

Vgl. u. a. Kāṭh. Up. VI, 12: „Nicht mit der Rede, nicht mit dem Denken, nicht mit dem Auge kann man es erreichen; ‚es ist': wie sollte man es anders begreifen?" und das berühmte ‚Wem es ein Unbekanntes ist, dem ist es bekannt; wem es ein Bekanntes ist, der versteht es nicht" (Ken. Up. 11). Wie kommt es, dass diese Lehre im ganzen Tripiṭaka nicht bekämpt, ja, wie es scheint, nicht einmal erwähnt und an dieser einzigen Stelle, die eine Auseinandersetzung mit ihr erwarten lässt („the Buddhist answer to the Upaniṣad theory" nennt Rhys Davids das

1) Rhys Davids (Dialogues of the Buddha p. 303) setzt den vorletzten Namen, den er Chandavā schreibt, in Parenthesen und verbessert den letzten in Bahvṛca. „The Adhvaryu, Taittirīya, Chandoga, and Bahvṛca priests — those skilled in liturgy generally, and in the Yajur, Sāma and Ṛg Vedas respectively — are probably meant."

2) Yaṃ na jānāma yaṃ na passāma, tassa sahavyatāya maggaṃ desema.

3) Unter den sechs gefeierten Häuptern, die im Suttapiṭaka so oft genannt werden, ist kein Vertreter vedischer Lehren!

Suttanta, Dialogues of the Buddha p. 298) von Buddha (ganz im Einklang mit der Methode der Suttantas, ibid.) absichtlich falsch ausgelegt wird, nämlich als ein Streben nach dem Brahman-Himmel? Mir scheint hierfür nur die eine Erklärung möglich, dass Buddhas Begriff des *nirvāna* mit dem des *paramam brahma* sich ausserordentlich nahe berührte, aber nicht vollkommen deckte. Verbirgt sich nämlich — was die Mehrheit unserer Buddhologen bekanntlich leugnet — im Wort *nirvāṇa* der Begriff des Absoluten und ist es, wie Schopenhauer will, die schärfste Formulierung dieses Begriffes, so wird das erwähnte Verhalten Buddhas zur Upaniṣad-Lehre (und zugleich seine Stellung zum Ajñāna-vāda, s. S. 51) auf folgende Weise verständlich.

Nirvāṇa als der absolute Gegensatz zur Welt ist mit dem höchsten Prinzip des Vedānta nicht identisch: es ist nicht reine Geistigkeit (vijñāna-ghana), sondern das absolut Bestimmungslose; es ist nicht höchste Realität (satyasya satyam), sondern das absolut Unvergleichliche: nicht real, nicht irreal, nicht beides zugleich noch zugleich keins von beidem; es ist nicht die Ursache der Welt, weder die materielle noch die bewirkende, sondern der absolute Gegensatz aller Kausalität. Mit anderen Worten: während der Vedāntin es nicht über sich gewinnen kann, sein höchstes Prinzip von allen denkbaren Beziehungen zur Welt zu trennen und somit, ohne es zu wollen und zu ahnen, im Pantheïsmus stecken bleibt, ist Buddha zu der Einsicht gelangt, dass der metaphysische Dualismus von Absolutem und Relativem die letzterreichbare philosophische Erkenntnis ist, dass dieser Gegensatz nur konstatiert, in keiner Weise aber (es sei denn im Yoga) begriffen werden kann.

War, wie ich glaube, dieser Transcendentalismus (der vom subj. Idealismus so weit entfernt ist wie vom Pantheïsmus, s. oben) die Ansicht Buddhas, so liegt auf der Hand, warum er mit demselben nicht hervortrat. Buddha wusste nur allzugut, dass diese Einsicht nicht nur der grossen Menge unerreichbar, sondern selbst dem geschulten Philosophen schwer beizubringen sei[1]), dass seine Lehre, wenn sie ex professo diese Grundlage erhielt, notwendig missverstanden, als *diṭṭhi* (Spekulation, Phantasiegebilde) betrachtet werden und ihres ethischen Charakters verlustig gehen würde. Nicht ein Philosoph, sondern ein Weltheiland wollte er sein. So entschloss er sich, allen metaphysischen Erörterungen prinzipiell aus dem Wege zu gehen und seine Jünger betreffs der letzten Fragen der Philosophie nicht zu Wissenden, sondern zu Gläubigen zu machen (vgl. die zehn *avyākatāni*).

Nun aber ist das Dogma von der Unerkennbarkeit des *braman-ātman* in den Upaniṣaden nicht nur dem Akosmismus, sondern auch dem Pantheïsmus eigen (vgl. z. B. Chānd. Up. VI, 8 fg. die Lehre des Uddālaka Āruṇi) — wie überhaupt daselbst diese beiden Anschauungen noch sozusagen in der Indifferenz sich befinden — so dass wir mit der Frage, ob die eine Ansicht oder die andere oder beide zugleich in der uns interessierenden Zeit vertreten

1) Nicht allein die indische, sondern auch die ganze europäische Philosophie — von der parmenideischen Gleichung $\varepsilon\hat{\iota}\nu\alpha\iota = \nu o\varepsilon\hat{\iota}\nu$ an bis zu Schopenhauers Annahme des raum-, zeit- und kausalitätslosen „Willens", ja bis zur Gegenwart — ist hierfür beweisend. Gerade diejenigen, welche am meisten vom Absoluten reden, z. B. Schelling, sind am wenigsten geneigt, mit diesem Begriffe ernst zu machen. Ich hoffe diesen Punkt, an dem die Bedeutung der indischen Philosophie für die Philosophie überhaupt wie nirgends sonst zum Ausdruck kommt, einmal in einer besonderen Abhandlung zu besprechen.

waren, uns an die jinistischen Texte wenden müssen. Die Antwort scheint zu besagen, dass beide Ansichten ihre Verteidiger hatten, die zweite aber vorherrschte.

Auf den Akosmismus nämlich können wir mit Sicherheit nur Sūtrakṛt. I. 12, 7 beziehen, wo es von einigen Philosophen — nach Śīlāṅka den Śūnya-vādinas — heisst: „Keine Sonne geht auf noch unter, kein Mond nimmt zu oder ab, keine Ströme fliessen, keine Winde wehen: für leer (vaṃjho) erklären sie die ganze Welt". Hierzu käme allenfalls noch die Bemerkung des Sūtrakṛt. II, 6, 47 mit Ārdraka streitenden Ekadaṇḍin, dass der grosse Purisa in allen Wesen ungeteilt (samatta-rūve) enthalten sei [1]).

Für den vedāntischen Pantheïsmus kommt zunächst Sūtrakṛt. I, 1, 1, 9 in Betracht, wo erklärt wird, dass das denkende Prinzip (vinnū) in derselben Weise als Vielheit erscheine wie die Erdmaterie (puḍhavī-thūbhe), vor allem aber das Gleichnis vom weissen Lotus, Sūtrakṛt. II, 1. Hier erscheint neben dem Materialisten, dem Atomisten und dem Deterministen als vierter Ketzer ein Vedāntin (īsara-kāraṇie!?) [2]) mit der Behauptung: „Alle Dinge der Welt haben den Purisa als Erstes und Letztes, sind vom Purisa herbeigeführt, aus dem Purisa entstanden, vom Purisa geoffenbart, mit dem Purisa innig verknüpft, vom Purisa durchdrungen," ein Verhältnis, das im weitern Verlauf als das des Geschwüres oder Unwohlseins zum Leibe, des Ameisenhaufens, Baumes oder Lotus zur Erde, des Wassertümpels oder der Blase zum Wasser erklärt wird.

Zu dieser Auffassung des Ātma-vāda als Pantheïsmus neigt auch Śīlāṅka, wenn er in der Ācāraṭīkā (I, 1. 3) den *ātman* als den Inbegriff alles Werdens (viśva-pariṇati-rūpa) bezeichnet. Freilich rechnet ebenderselbe an einer anderen Stelle (Sūtrakṛt. II, 1, 25—28) auch den Īśvara- und den Vivarta-vāda (Theïsmus und Akosmismus) hierher. Malayagiri hingegen bezeichnet zwar, wie auch Abhayadeva, als Glaubensbekenntnis des Ātma-vādin das bekannte „Puruṣa evêdaṃ sarvam", richtet aber seine ganze scharfsinnige Polemik [3]) ausschliesslich gegen den Akosmismus.

---

1) falls nämlich diese Erklärung richtig ist. Jacobi (Sacred Books of the East XLV p. 418) bevorzugt die andere und übersetzt: „(But we assume) an invisible, great, eternal, imperishable, and indestructible Soul, who excels all other beings in every respect, as the moon excels the stars". Der Text ist:

Avvatta-rūvaṃ purisaṃ mahaṃtaṃ
saṇātaṇaṃ akkhayaṃ avvayaṃ ca;
savvesu bhūtesu vi savvato se
caṃdo va tārāhiṃ samatta-rūve.

2) Śīlāṅka erklärt hier puruṣa, īśvara und ātman als Synonyma.

3) Dieselbe gipfelt in der Alternative, dass die „Täuschung" vom Zweitlosen entweder verschieden sein müsse oder nicht. Beide Annahmen höben das Zweitlose auf.

Gommaṭasāra endlich beschreibt (MS. p. 341) den *ātman* als „ein einziges grosses Selbst, Mensch, Gott, alldurchdringend, in allen Gliedern gleichsam verborgen, vernunftbegabt, eigenschaftslos, das höchste Wesen“ [1]), was auf den Pantheïsmus geradesowohl wie (des „gleichsam“ wegen) auf den Akosmismus sich beziehen kann.

6. Īśvara-vāda.

Das Aufkommen des Theïsmus (Monotheïsmus) in Indien ist insofern von besonderem Interesse, als diese Anschauung verhältnismässig spät und aus dem Ātma-vāda sich entwickelt hat. Den vedischen Hymnen sowie der älteren Brāhmaṇa-Litteratur ist sie noch gänzlich fremd, und erst in jener mittleren Schicht der Upaniṣaden, in der auch Sāṃkhya-Ideen zum ersten Mal erscheinen, beginnt sie hervorzutreten. um im Śivaïsmus und Viṣṇuismus sich dann die dominierende Stellung zu erobern, die ihr bis heute geblieben ist.

Anīśa ātmā, anīso appā „das machtlose Selbst“ wird einstimmig von den jinistischen Erklärern als der Hauptnerv des Theïsmus bezeichnet, und dies ist allerdings wohl als ein Bekenntnis der menschlichen Ohnmacht, vor allem aber, wie am besten die Polemiken der verschiedenen Systeme gegen den Ātma-vāda zeigen, als eine Ablehnung des subjektiven Idealismus zu verstehen, d. h. jener bekannten Upaniṣad-Lehre, der zufolge die Welt aus dem Subjekt des Erkennens, wie die Fäden aus der Spinne oder die Funken aus dem Feuer, hervorgeht. Man wandte hiergegen ein, dass doch niemand sich selbst Leid schaffe, dass die Thatsächlichkeit des Leidens und die Unwissenheit der Kreatur (ajño jantur) die Nichtabsolutheit des „Selbst“ beweise und mithin aller Zwang, den das Ich erfahre, von einem ihm überlegenen Nichtich ausgehen müsse: einem „Herrn“ (īśa) oder „Treiber“ (preritar) der Welt.

Diese Ansicht finden wir als die Grundlage eines Systems zum ersten Mal offen verkündigt in der Śvetāśvatara-Upaniṣad, einem höchst eigenartigen, in schwungvollen Versen abgefassten Werke, das besonders wegen seines eklektischen Charakters sehr schwer zu beurteilen ist. Ich möchte indes das Folgende für sicher halten: 1. dass diese Upaniṣad nicht das Werk eines einzigen Autors ist, vielmehr die ganze Entwickelung einer Schule repräsentiert; 2. dass ihren ursprünglichen Bestand nur die ca. zwölf Verse des ersten Kapitals bilden, in denen die Lehre

---

1) Ekko ceva mahappā puriso devo ya savva-vāvī ya savv'aṅga-ṇigūḍho viya saceyaṇo nigguṇo paramo.

vom dreifachen Brahman erklärt wird; 3. dass der vollendete Theïsmus der späteren Kapitel, der an den Namen des Rudra sich knüpft, aus eben dieser Lehre vom dreifachen Brahman hervorgegangen ist. Versuchen wir, diese Entwickelung näher kennen zu lernen.

Unsere Upaniṣad beginnt nach einigen einleitenden Worten mit einer Aufzählung der herrschenden Weltanschauungen[1]):

Kāḷa-svabhāvo niyatir yadṛcchā
bhūtāni yônih puruṣa iti cintyam.

Von diesen Schlagworten haben wir die ersten vier bereits kennen gelernt; das fünfte bezieht sich auf den Materialismus (S. 52 fg.) und *yonih puruṣa* (Urmaterie, Geist) auf das Sāṃkhya-System[2]. Es folgt dann im zweiten Halbvers die Abweisung dieser Ansichten und des subjektiven Idealismus, mit dem stillschweigenden Hinweis auf die Notwendigkeit eines neuen Systems:

Saṃyoga eṣāṃ na tv, ātma-bhāvād;
ātmā'py anīśaḥ sukha-duḥkha-hetoḥ,

d. h., frei übersetzt[3]: „Diese Begriffe, deren Hypostasierung schon früher als unstatthaft erkannt wurde, sind auch in ihrer Vereinigung zur Grundlage eines einwandfreien Systems nicht hinreichend, da in einem solchen der Begriff des Absoluten (ātman) Platz haben muss. Aber das Absolute mit dem „Selbst" (ātman) zu identifizieren, geht gleichfalls nicht an. Denn das Selbst (die Seele) ist Lust und Leid unterworfen, mithin unfrei." Und jetzt wird die neue Lehre vom dreifachen Brahman (trividhaṃ brahma) entwickelt, deren Grundgedanken die folgenden zu sein scheinen[4]:

1. Durch den Zwang der Wahrnehmungen (bhoktṛ-bhāvāt, eig. das Geniesser-Sein) sind wir genötigt, dem Subjekt (bhoktar, ātman, hara) ein nicht mehr noch minder reales Objekt (bhogya, bhogârtha, pradhāna) gegenüberzusetzen.

2. Da das letztere (die Materie) so wenig wie das erstere (der Geist) selbständig wirken kann, ist zur Erklärung des Geschehens ein höchster Herr (īśa, deva) oder Regierer (preritar, eig.: Treiber) anzunehmen.

3. Das Absolute darf, weil es alles zugleich (viśva-rupa) und kausalitätslos (akartar; vgl. I, 1: Kann Brahman Ursache sein?) ist, weder als Schöpfer noch als Lenker der Welt aufgefasst werden.

---

1) Dass diese Aufzählung älter ist als die der Jainas (s. Einleitung), beweist das Fehlen des *īśvara*, dessen Einführung eben unsere Upaniṣad bezweckt.

2) Es scheint hier bereits der Dualismus des klassischen Sāṃkhya mit seiner Vielheit individueller Geister vorzuliegen, da im zweiten Teile des Verses der *ātman* von den genannten Prinzipien unterschieden wird.

3) Eine wörtliche Übersetzung wäre unverständlich.

4) Die Dispositionslosigkeit der Upaniṣad macht bestimmtere Aussagen unmöglich.

Das Brahman ist also ein dreifaches, insofern es 1. *preritar*, 2. *bhoktar* und 3. *bhogârtha* ist. Es ist aber andererseits, als die Verschmelzung aller Gegensätze, natürlich nur eines. Der Jünger der Wahrheit muss daher die drei Prinzipien sowohl unterscheiden wie als Einheit erkennen lernen:

„Wir sangen euch von jenem höchsten Brahman,
in dem die Dreiheit steht, die ewig feste;
wer sie durchschauet scharfen Blicks, der Weise [1]),
geburtfrei geht er auf im höchsten Brahman" (I, 7).
„Es schweift ein Schwan auf diesem Brahmanrade,
dem weiten Plane alles Seins und Werdens;
verschieden glaubt er sich vom höchsten Lenker,
bis er in ihm Unsterblichkeit gefunden" (I, 6).
„... er wird zum All, wird frei von Thun und Leiden,
wenn er im Brahman jene Dreiheit schaut" (I, 9).

Vorzugsweise aber wird die Erlösung als eine durch die Erkenntnis des *preritar* zu erreichende Gottwerdung gefasst (jñātvā devaṃ mucyate sarvapāśaiḥ), und dies ist der Grund dafür, dass schon in der Śvetāśvatara-Schule selbst die Lehre vom dreifachen Brahman in einen vollkommenen Theïsmus umschlug. Man vergass, dass nach den Voraussetzungen der Lehre jedes der drei Prinzipien vom Absoluten den gleichen Abstand 0 oder ∞ hatte, sah in dem *preritar* gleichsam das Bindeglied von Gott und Welt und eliminierte alsbald den nunmehr unverständlichen Begriff des *paramaṃ brahma* oder vereinigte vielmehr das letztere mit dem *preritar* zu einem einzigen persönlichen Gott (maheśvara), der durch seine Zauberkraft die Welt aus sich hervorgehen lässt. So heisst es denn bereits in unserer Upaniṣad, deren erstes Kapitel nur von der in Brahman ruhenden Dreiheit weiss. zu Anfang des fünften Kapitels, dass zwei Ewigkeiten, Geist und Nichtgeist (Materie) [2]), im „unendlichen" höchsten Brahman enthalten seien, und nur hier und da taucht noch die Idee der Verschiedenheit des persönlichen und des absoluten Gottes auf (III, 7).

Auf diese Weise wurde aus dem stolzen System des *trividhaṃ brahma*, das recht eigentlich den Gipfel der Upaniṣad-Spekulation bildet, die platte Doktrin des Īśvara-vāda. Dieselbe hat natürlich die verschiedensten Formen angenommen: durch ihren unphilosophischen Charakter konnte sie ebenso leicht mit dem Akosmismus

---

1) atrāntaraṃ brahmavido viditvā. Hiermit wird zum ersten Mal die im Sāṃkhya eine so grosse Rolle spielende Forderung der unterscheidenden Erkenntnis ausgesprochen.

2) vidyā'vidye īśate yas tu so 'nyaḥ; vgl. I, 10a: kṣar'ātmānāv īśate deva ekaḥ, wonach die Erklärung Deussens: „Das Nichtwissen, d. h. die in ihm befangene Seele und das Wissen, d. h. die Erlösung" kaum richtig ist.

wie mit pantheïstischen Elementen sich verbinden [1]). Frei von solchen Beimischungen aber ist der von den Jainas überlieferte Theïsmus. Dieser lehrt einen höchsten Herrn, der eine vierfache Vollkommenheit: Allwissenheit, Leidenschaftslosigkeit, Allmacht und Allgüte besitze [2]), alle Dinge erschaffen habe und die „unwissende Kreatur" zur Seligkeit oder zur Verdammnis führe. Wie diese Grundsätze durchgeführt wurden, mag man aus der beigefügten Übersetzung (Appendix II) ersehen.

Selbstverständlich sind auch im Mahābhārata theïstische Ansichten vertreten. Doch scheint mir hier, vom Viṣṇuismus und Śivaismus abgesehen, ein reiner Īśvara-vāda nur in III, 30, dem Glaubensbekenntnis der Draupadī, vorzuliegen, einem Kapitel, das wir auch deshalb nicht übersehen dürfen, weil es zugestandenermassen auf eine alte Sage (itihāsaḥ purātanaḥ) [3]) sich gründet und einen der von Malayagiri zur Charakterisierung des Īśvara-vāda zitierten Verse enthält. Letzterer macht ganz den Eindruck, als ob er der Śvetāśvatara-Schule entstamme [4]). In diesem Kapitel äussert sich der Glaube an die absolute Abhängigkeit des Menschen von Gott, verbunden mit einem kräftigen Zweifel an der Allgerechtigkeit des letzteren. Der Mensch, heisst es, sei niemals sein eigener Herr (ātmâdhīna), er möge thun was er wolle. Von Gott (īśāna), der im Urbeginn den Samen der Welt entsendet habe [5]), werde er gelenkt wie der hölzerne Hampelmann, wie der Ochse am Nasenring, der Vogel an der Schnur. Wenn man ihn auch nicht sehen könne, sei der Herr gleichwohl überall gegenwärtig: wie der Äther durchdringe er die Wesen. Aber nicht wie ein Vater oder eine Mutter walte er über den Geschöpfen: wie ein böser Feind hetze er sie gegeneinander, ihren Sinn bethörend durch seinen Zauber (chadma-kṛtvā, mohayitv'ātma-māyayā). Vereinigend und trennend nach seiner Laune: so spielt der Herr mit den Wesen, wie ein

1) So ruht das Viśiṣṭâdvaita Rāmānujas zwar auf der Trinität von *cit*, *acit* und *paramêśvara*, identifiziert aber den letzteren mit dem pantheistischen *brahman* und erhält auf diese Weise einen Gott, der der Welt immanent und zugleich transcendent ist. In diesem Sinne wird die aus *cit* und *acit* (Geist und Materie) bestehende Welt einerseits geradezu als der Leib Brahmans bezeichnet, andererseits Brahman (unter dem Namen Vāsudeva) als persönlicher Gott verehrt, der aus „Mitleid" die Menschen zu erlösen bestrebt sei. Dies ist vielleicht der merkwürdigste Synkretismus, den die Geschichte der indischen Philosophie aufzuweisen hat.

2) Jñānam apratighaṃ (apratithaṃ, Ed.) yasya vairāgyaṃ ca jagat-pater |
aiśvaryaṃ caiva dharmaś ca sahasiddhaṃ catuṣṭayaṃ ||
Vgl. die Bezeichnung Viṣṇus als caturmūrtidhṛt und caturvyūha.

3) Über den Doppelsinn von itihāsa vgl. Hopkins, Great Epic p. 51.

4) Ajño jantur anīśo 'yam ātmanaḥ sukhaduḥkhayoḥ | īśvara-prerito gacchet svargaṃ narakam eva ca (svargaṃ vā śvabhram eva vā, Malayagiri).

5) purastāc chukram uccaran; Kommentar falsch; vgl. Mahābh. VI, 76, 26:
Atha bhāvyam evaṃ hi Saṃjayaitena sarvathā |
purā dhātrā yathā sṛṣṭaṃ tat tathā naitad anyathā
sowie die vedischen Kosmogonien.

Kind mit seinem Spielzeug." Zwar heisse es, er verteile nur Lohn und Strafe; aber wenn es wahr sei, dass die That dem Thäter folge, so müsste allein den Īśvara die Strafe treffen. „Wenn aber die böse That nicht den Thäter erreicht, so gilt die Macht allein, und ich beklage die Schwachen." Hiermit schliesst die Rede der Draupadī. Die Antwort ihres Gatten (Kap. 31) ist schön, aber wenig überzeugend: Es sei gemein, mit der Tugend Handel zu treiben (dharma-vāṇijyako hīno), das Gute nur um des Lohnes willen zu thun, das Böse nur um der Strafe willen zu meiden. Man solle an die Gerechtigkeit Gottes glauben, wie es die grossen Weisen von jeher gethan hätten. „Der Erfolg der frommen und der bösen Thaten, ihr Ursprung und ihr Ende sind Gottesgeheimnisse (deva-guhyāni), du Schöne!" Die nun folgende Bekehrung der Draupadī ist deutlich als der Zusatz eines vedāntischen Revisors zu erkennen, vor allem an der Versicherung, dass auch Dhātar-Vidhātar der Seelenwanderung unterworfen sei [1].

7. Ajñāna-vāda.

Eine hervorragende Rolle hat zu Mahāvīras und Buddhas Zeiten und noch lange über diese hinaus in Indien der Agnostizismus (Skeptizismus) gespielt. Er scheint den meisten Systemen seinen Stempel aufgedrückt und die Neigung des Inders zu Haarspaltereien auf die Spitze getrieben zu haben. Wann er aufgekommen, lässt sich mit Bestimmtheit nicht sagen. Doch möchte ich glauben, dass der in buddhistischen Texten genannte Sañjaya Belaṭṭhiputta, wenn nicht der Gründer, so doch der erste bedeutendere Vertreter dieser Richtung war. Ihre Anhänger erhielten nach der Amarā, einer schwer zu fangenden Fischart, den bezeichnenden Spitznamen Amarā-vikkhepikā, „wriggling eels" (Max Müller), und ihr Raisonnement ist, zufolge dem Brahmajāla- und dem Sāmaññaphala-sutta dieses: „Fragst du mich, ob es ein Jenseits giebt, so antworte ich: Hätte ich die Überzeugung oder Empfindung [2]), dass es ein Jenseits giebt, so würde ich es dir erklären. So aber kann ich nicht sagen, ob es so oder so, ob anders ist, ob es nicht ist oder ob es nicht nicht-ist. Fragst du mich, ob es kein Jenseits giebt . . . ., ob ein Jenseits zugleich ist und nicht-ist, so antworte ich etc. (wie oben). Mit anderen Worten: die Amarā-vikkhepikā verfochten die Behauptung, dass man von einem Übersinnlichen (Jenseits, Geburt ohne Eltern,

---

1) Umgekehrt behauptet Hopkins (Great Epic, p. 189), dass Draupadī an den vedāntischen Īśvara geglaubt habe und „a later rewriting of the scene mixes up Bhagavat, Īśvara and Prajāpati".

2) iti ce me assa.

Karman, Existenz des Vollendeten nach dem Tode) weder sagen könne, dass es ist, noch dass es nicht ist, noch dass es zugleich ist und nicht ist, noch dass es weder ist noch nicht ist.

Atthi, n'atthi, atthi ca n'atthi ca, n'ev'atthi na n'atti. Der Keim dieser Lehre dürfte in der alten Streitfrage liegen, ob *ātman-brahman* ein Seiendes oder ein Nichtseiendes genannt werden müsse (Chānd. Up. VI, 2; III, 19 u. a.; vgl. Ṛgv. X, 129, 4), ein Streit, der erst in der epischen Zeit allgemein dahin entschieden wurde, dass auf das Absolute keinerlei ontologische Bestimmungen anwendbar seien, dass man es weder seiend noch nichtseiend (weder in noch neben Raum und Zeit existierend, vgl. S. 38) noch seiend-nichtseiend nennen könne (na san na câsat sad-asac ca tan na, Hopkins, Great Epic. p. 118, 121). Hieraus entwickelten dann die Ajñānikas den vierteiligen Satz, dass jede positive wie negative Aussage über ein Sein oder ein gleichzeitiges Sein und Nichtsein vermieden werden müsse, dass man von keinem Transcendenten behaupten könne, dass es ein Seiendes, dass es kein Seiendes, dass es ein Seiendnichtseiendes, dass es kein Seiendnichtseiendes sei. Diese vier Sätze scheinen auch die Jainas als die einfachere und ursprünglichere Form des Saptabhaṅgīnaya (s. hinten) beibehalten zu haben; vgl. Mahābh. XII, 233, 21 u. 239, 6:

„Etad evaṃ ca n'aivam ca na côbhe nânubhe na ca |
karmasthā viṣayaṃ brūyuḥ; sattvasthāḥ samadarśinaḥ",

wo *karmasthā* als *Arhatānāṃ yaugikaṃ nāma* erklärt und *etad evam* auf den ersten, *n'aivaṃ ca* auf den zweiten und vierten, *na côbhe* auf den dritten und siebenten, *nânubhe* auf den fünften und sechsten *bhaṅga* bezogen werden.

Man sollte glauben, dass solche Spitzfindigkeiten nicht mehr zu überbieten seien. Aber die Ajñānikas haben es fertig gebracht, sich auf eine noch höhere Stufe der Abstraktion zu schwingen. Sie machten — zu welcher Zeit, muss einstweilen dahingestellt bleiben — aus den vier Sätzen[1]) sieben, wandten diese sieben auf die bekannten neun Kategorien (jīva, ajīva etc.; S. 7) und vier von ihnen auf eine zehnte Kategorie, die des Entstehens (utpatti), an und erhielten auf diese Weise siebenundsechzig Möglichkeiten der Ablehnung transcendenter Erkenntnis. Und zwar wird die Annahme der sieben *vikalpās* folgendermassen motiviert:[2])

„1. Realität (sattva) kommt einem Dinge zu, insofern man es für sich betrachtet; 2. Irrealität (asattva), insofern man es auf ein anderes bezieht; Realirrealität[3]) (sadasattva), insofern ein Teil eines Topfes oder sonstigen Gegenstandes, z. B. der Hals, nach dem Satz der Realität durch sein Hals-sein etc. real, hingegen hinsichtlich der Rundheit etc. eines andern Teiles des Topfes etc., z. B. des Bodens, oder mit Hinblick auf die Modi[4]) eines andern

---

1) Ete catvāro 'pi vikalpāḥ sakal'ādeśā iti gīyante sakala-vastu-viṣayatvāt, Malayagiri.

2) Abhayadeva ad Sthānāṅg. IV, 4.

3) Diese Wortbildung sowie die folgenden Monstra mögen, mit Rücksicht auf die Notwendigkeit einer genauen Übersetzung, hier ausnahmsweise gestattet sein.

4) *paryāyās*; was gemeint ist, zeigt der folgende *vikalpa*.

Gegenstandes nach dem Satz der Irrealität irreal ist.[1]) 4. Soll nun ein Ding, z. B. ein Topf, als ein ungeteiltes Ganze mit Rücksicht auf die Modi anderer Dinge, wie Matten etc., und zugleich[2]) mit Rücksicht auf die eigenen Modi, wie Trinkgefäss, Lehmklumpen, langer oder runder Hals etc., bezeichnet werden, so liegt, weil man es (in diesem Fall) weder real noch irreal nennen kann, Undefinierbarkeit (avaktavyatva, avācyatva) eben dieses Topfes oder sonstigen Gegenstandes vor. 5. Ist ferner ein Teil eines Topfes oder anderen Gegenstandes, indem man ihn nach dem Satz der Realität bezeichnet, real, hingegen mit Rücksicht auf einen andern Teil, der zugleich durch seine und durch andere Modi bezeichnet wird, weder real noch irreal zu nennen, so handelt es sich um Realundefinierbarkeit (sadavaktavyatva). 6. Ist ein Teil dieses Topfes oder sonstigen Gegenstandes dem Satz der Irrealität zufolge irreal, hingegen mit Rücksicht auf einen andern Teil .... (wie bei 5) .... weder real noch irreal zu nennen, so liegt bei diesem Topfe u. s. w. Irrealundefinierbarkeit (asadavaktavyatva) vor. 7. Ist endlich ein Teil eines Topfes oder andern Gegenstandes dem Satze der Realität zufolge real, hingegen mit Rücksicht auf einen andern Teil dem Satze der Irrealität zufolge irreal, ferner mit Rücksicht auf einen dritten Teil ..... (wie oben) ..... weder real noch irreal zu nennen, so muss diesem Topfe oder andern Gegenstande Realirrealundefinierbarkeit (sadasadavaktavyatva) zugeschrieben werden."

„Von diesen Sätzen sollen der erste, zweite und vierte auf das ganze Ding angewendet werden, die übrigen vier auf Teile des Dinges. Von einigen aber wird auch der dritte Satz als auf das ganze Ding anwendbar bezeichnet, indem nämlich ein Ding als Ganzes hinsichtlich seiner Modi und der anderer Dinge realirreal sei. In diesem Sinne heisst es in der Ācāraṭīkā: ‚Wenn es sich um ein Entstehen (*utpatti*, die zehnte Kategorie, s. oben) handelt, so kommen die letzten drei Sätze nicht in Betracht, da sie nur auf Teile von Dingen (padārthâvayava) anwendbar sind, das Entstehen aber keine Teile hat.'"[3]) Freilich, inwiefern die anderen neun Kategorien „Teile" haben, wird uns von keinem Kommentator erklärt. Ist etwa das fragliche Wort (avayava) hier mit „Art" zu übersetzen?

In ihrer Anwendung auf die Kategorien haben nun die obigen Sätze die folgende Form: „Wer kann sagen, dass es eine Seele

1) „Sadasattvaṃ svarūpa-pararūpābhyāṃ vidyamānâvidyamānatvam", Malayagiri.

2) Hierzu und zum folgenden *vikalpa* vgl. Sarvadarśanasaṃgraha III, ed.[1] p. 41:

Krameṇôbhaya-vāñchāyāṃ prayogaḥ samudāya-bhāk |
Yugapad tad-vivakṣāyāṃ syād avācyam aśaktitaḥ.

3) vgl. Śīlāṅka ad Sūtrakṛt. I, 12, 1: Uttaraṃ bhaṅgaka-trayam utpanna-bhāvâvayavâpekṣam iha bhāvôtpattau na saṃbhavati.

(Materie etc.) giebt (nicht giebt etc.), oder was hat man davon, dieses zu wissen?" „Wer kann sagen, dass das Entstehen real (irreal etc.) ist, und was nützt es, dieses zu wissen?" womit gemeint ist, „dass niemand, der um die Erkenntnis der Seele und anderer übersinnlicher Dinge bemüht ist, es zu einem genauen Wissen bringt, und dass ein solches Wissen überhaupt keinerlei Nutzen verspricht" [1]).

Aus zwei Gründen nämlich hält der Ajñānika das Nichtwissen für das Beste (ajñānam eva śreyas): 1) weil keine Autorität ein Ding vollkommen (restlos) erklären kann; 2) wegen der Unwirksamkeit unwissentlich kontrahierten Karmans [2]). Mit dieser letzten Ansicht, die von den Buddhisten acceptiert, von den Jainas dagegen aufs entschiedenste abgelehnt wurde, hat es folgende Bewandnis:

Ob eine Handlung schlimmes Karman (aśubha-karman) und durch dieses eine „heftige Reife" (dāruṇa-vipāka) erzeugt, hängt, nach der Meinung der Ajñānikas, lediglich ab von der Intensität der Absicht (tīvrâdhyavasāya, manaso'bhiniveśa) und der „Beflecktheit des Geistes" (citta-kāluṣya), aus denen sie hervorging. Lag eine Thätigkeit des Willens (manas) überhaupt nicht vor, sondern nur eine solche des Körpers oder der Rede, so kann Karman nicht haften: es gleicht dann einer Staubschicht auf einer trockenen weissen Mauer: durch den Wind der nächsten besten guten Absicht (śubhâdhyavasāya) wird es gleichsam fortgeblasen [3]). Nun aber sei es, wie das bellum omnium contra omnes der Philosophen deutlich zeige, gerade die Wissenschaft, die durch Erweckung des Eigendünkels und der Disputiersucht wie nichts anderes „Beflecktheit des Geistes" und „Verbohrtheit des Willens" erzeuge. Man müsse ihr deshalb aus dem Wege gehen und frei bekennen, dass man nichts wisse noch wissen könne [4]). Nur durch diese vollkommene Meinungsenthaltung sei Freiheit von Karman, sei Nirvāṇa zu erhoffen. —

Es hat seine guten Gründe, dass kein System von Malayagiri eine so ausführliche Besprechung und Widerlegung erfahren hat wie das der Ajñānikas. Zunächst und vor allem war es die wirkliche Hilflosigkeit dieser Theorie gegenüber, die M. so viele Worte machen liess. Von allen seinen sog. Gegenbeweisen sind nur zwei

1) Ācāraṭīkā I, 1, 3.

2) Ajñānam eva śreyo 'saṃcintyakṛta-karmabandha-vaiphalyāt. Tathā na jñānaṃ kasyâpi kvacid api vastuny asti, pramāṇānām asaṃpūrṇaṃ vastu viṣayatvāt (Ṭīkā zu Bhagavatī 30, 1).

3) Eine Fortbildung dieser Theorie begegnet Sūtrakṛt. I, 1, 2, 25—28. Hier wird auch derjenige von Sünde freigesprochen, der eine Handlung nur beabsichtigt, nicht aber ausführt, oder aus Jähzorn handelt. „Nur durch den Willen oder nur durch den Leib entsteht keine Karman-Fessel; aber wo eigene That, Veranlassung oder Erlaubnis (svayaṃkṛta-kāritânumatayaḥ) vorliegt und dazu ein böser Wille (kliṣṭâdhyavasāya): da bindet Karman" (Śīlāṅka).

4) vgl. die *ἀποχή* der griechischen Skeptiker.

einigermassen stichhaltig: dass die wahre philosophische Einsicht von Voreingenommenheit und Leidenschaft und also vom Saṃsāra befreie und dass man, um sich von der Haltlosigkeit des Agnostizismus zu überzeugen, nur seine Verteidiger zu fragen brauche, ob denn ihre Lehre ein Wissen oder ein Nichtwissen sei [1]).

Wie kommt es aber, dass M., der sonst Punkt für Punkt die Ketzer widerlegt, die von den Jainas bekanntlich bejahte Frage, ob man unwissentlich sündigen könne, in seiner Polemik überhaupt nicht berührt? Wich er in diesem Falle von der orthodoxen Meinung ab? Und wie konnte er es über sich gewinnen, das ganze System der sieben *vikalpās* mit Stillschweigen zu übergehen? Hatte er hier den Häretikern nichts vorzuwerfen?

Was die erste Frage betrifft, so mag in der That M. den Buddhisten, die diesen paradoxesten der jinistischen Glaubenssätze mit Vorliebe angriffen [2]), im stillen recht gegeben haben; das andere Problem aber löst sich durch einen Blick auf jenes berühmte System der sieben Tropen (saptabhaṅgīnaya, syādvāda), das den Jainas zu ihrem bekannten Beinamen der Syādvādines (Relativisten) verholfen hat. Dieee sieben *bhaṅgās* sind nämlich mit den *vikalpās* der Agnostiker in formeller Hinsicht identisch, ausser dass ihnen das Wörtlein *syāt* vorgesetzt ist. Durch letzteres freilich wird nun ihre Anwendung gerade ins Gegenteil umgekehrt. Hatte nämlich der Ajñānika behauptet, dass man von übersinnlichen Dingen nicht Realität, Irrealität etc. aussagen könne, so erklärte jetzt der Syādvādin, dass man ihnen wie überhaupt allen Dingen zwar keine absolute, wohl aber eine relative Realität, Irrealität etc. zuschreiben dürfe und müsse, dass durch die Verbindung des Prädikats mit einem *kathaṃcid* oder *syāt* („in gewisser Hinsicht") jede ontologische Behauptung unangreifbar werde. „Der Syādvāda hat seinen Namen daher, dass er unter unbedingter Aufgabe des Absoluten Behauptungen von beschränkter Geltung aufstellt. Auf das System der sieben Tropen sich stützend, lehrt er die Arten des Anzunehmenden und des Abzulehnenden" [3]).

Es ergiebt sich also die überraschende Thatsache, dass der Saptabhaṅgīnaya, von einem einzigen, freilich dem wichtigsten,

1) Diese Frage werden die Ajñānikas wie ihre griechischen Brüder beantwortet haben: dass nämlich ihre Meinung keine eigentliche Erkenntnis, sondern ein blosses Bekenntnis, eine Meinungsenthaltung sei (s. Windelband, Geschichte der Philosophie² p. 164).

2) vgl. u. a. Feers Aufsatz in den Akten des sechsten Orientalisten-Kongresses (III, 2, p. 69 fg.) sowie Sūtrakṛt. II, 6 das Gespräch Ārdrakas mit dem Buddhisten. Eine wirkliche Begründung der jinistischen Ansicht habe ich nirgends gefunden.

3) Sarvadarśanasaṃgraha¹ p. 42; vgl. Malayagiris Glosse zum Niyativāda: „Das ist es ja eben, wodurch die Jainas auf ihrem Standpunkte glänzen, dass sie durch die Unterscheidung von eigenem und fremdem Sein u. s. w. (svapara-bhāv'ādinā) jedes Ding als ein Relatives betrachten und nicht, wie Euresgleichen, durch die Annahme des Absoluten sich den Blick verfinstern."

Bestandteil abgesehen, durch die Jainas den Agnostikern abgeborgt worden ist, und es fragt sich nur noch, wann die Entlehnung geschah. Für diese Frage fällt zunächst in Betracht, dass im ganzen Siddhānta vom Syādvāda nicht die Rede ist[1]), sodann die auffallend logische Tendenz der Digambara-Schriften. Beide Umstände scheinen darauf hinzudeuten, dass das Auftreten des Syādvāda mit der Verbreitung des Jinismus nach Südindien zusammenhängt. Hier nämlich sahen sich die Jainas zur Auseinandersetzung mit dem (im Norden sehr schwachen[2]) Brahmanentum genötigt, und hier werden sie als Waffe gegen die spitzfindigen Angriffe, die zweifellos von allen Seiten auf sie eindrangen, den allbezwingenden Syādvāda erfunden haben.

Nicht so leicht wie beim Jinismus, ist beim Buddhismus der agnostische Einfluss nachzuweisen. Die Frage, ob der Tathāgata nach dem Tode seiend, nichtseiend etc. sei, gehört zu den Dingen, die der Erhabene prinzipiell nicht erklärt (avyākatāni)[3]). Buddha lässt also in dubio, was der Ajñānika verneint: ob man den Erlösten seiend, nichtseiend etc. nennen dürfe. Zu dieser Stellungnahme können ihn meines Erachtens nur zwei Gründe bewogen haben. Entweder war für ihn Parinirvāṇa = absolute Vernichtung, und nur, um nicht als Lokāyatika und Verächter der Moral dazustehen[4]), gab er dieses nicht zu; oder er hatte sich für seine Person zur Annahme des Absoluten entschieden[5]) und wandte auf dasselbe die gerade hier vorzüglich passenden agnostischen Formeln[6]) nur deshalb nicht an, um nicht mit den Ajñānikas verwechselt und für einen Philosophen gehalten zu werden[7]). Die Entscheidung liefert u. a.[5]) das bekannte Gespräch Buddhas mit Mālunkyaputta (Majjhimanikāya 63). Hier erklärt Buddha, dass er auf die Erörterung des fraglichen Problems[8]) deshalb verzichte, weil die meisten sterben würden, ehe sie die Lösung begriffen hätten und weil er eine Ethik, keine Metaphysik verkünde. Dies passt wahrlich nicht auf das materialistische Nichts, das so vielfach für die Krone der Lehre Buddhas ausgegeben wird, wohl aber, und zwar vortrefflich, auf jenes völlig beziehungslose X, das wir das Absolute nennen. Spätere Buddhisten haben denn auch ruhig die agnostischen Formeln in diesem Sinne

---

1) Die Kommentare sind hier natürlich nicht beweisend.

2) vgl. S. 39 Anm. 3.

3) vgl. u. a. das Poṭṭhapāda-sutta des Dīghanikāya.

4) „Denn die Buddhisten sind verkappte Materialisten". Śīlāṅka ad Sūtrakṛt. I, 12, 4.

5) vgl. S. 4, S. 40, S. 38.

6) Ich meine die vier *sakalādeśās*, vgl. S. 47.

7) Über die verächtliche Bedeutung des Wortes *diṭṭhi* bei Buddha vgl. Rhys Davids, Dialogues of the Buddha, p. XXVI.

8) Es handelt sich um die *avyākatāni* überhaupt.

4*

angewandt[1]), was zugleich mit der buddhistischen Auffassung der Sünde (S. 49) die Jainas dazu geführt haben mag, die Buddhisten für Ajñānikas zu erklären[2]).

8. Materialistische und atomistische Theorien.

1. Die einfachste Art des Materialismus tritt uns Sūtrakṛt. I, 1, 1, 11 u. 12 und II, 1, 15—19 entgegen in dem (von den Kommentatoren so genannten) Tajjīvataccharīra-vāda, der sich mit der Kraft- und Stoff-Lehre unserer Materialisten einigermassen zu decken scheint. Er leugnet die Allseele, erkennt aber Einzelseelen an, die den Umfang der Körper haben und mit diesen entstehen und vergehen. Seele und Leib seien, wenn nicht als identisch, so doch als untrennbar verknüpft anzusehen, da noch niemand die beiden getrennt habe aufweisen können, wie Schwert und Scheide, Zuckersaft und Zuckerrohr, Feuer und Reibholz. Gut und Böse, Himmel und Hölle seien leere Worte; man könne schlagen, brennen und morden, soviel man wolle (ohne dafür eine andere als irdische Strafe gewärtigen zu brauchen[3]).

Diese Lehre erinnert lebhaft an das Übermenschtum Purāṇa Kassapas (Sāmaññaphala-sutta 16—18), mit dem „jener Totschläger" (se hamtā), dem die obigen Ansichten in den Mund gelegt werden[4]), in der That wohl identisch ist, und auch des sagenhaften Pāyāsi-Paesi muss als typischen Vertreters des Tajjīvataccharīra-vāda hier gedacht werden. In einem interessanten Dialog, den uns die Jainas sowohl wie die Buddhisten überliefern, entwickelt der letztere alle möglichen für seine Ansicht beizubringenden Gründe — z. B. dass keiner seiner verstorbenen Freunde das Versprechen, ihn über Himmel und Hölle aufzuklären, eingelöst habe, dass er niemals bei Hinrichtungen eine Seele habe entweichen sehen noch in Leichnamen trotz allen Suchens eine solche gefunden habe etc. — bis er schliesslich zum rechten Glauben (dem Jinismus auf der einen, dem Buddhismus auf der anderen Seite) bekehrt wird[5]).

---

1) vgl. das in Oldenbergs „Buddha" übersetzte Gespräch der Nonne Khemā mit dem König Pasenadi.

2) Śākyā api prāyaśo ajñānikāḥ, Śīlāṅka ad Sūtrakṛt. I, 12, 2.

3) Dass dieser Materialismus die irdische Strafe anerkennt, wird zwar nirgends gesagt (begreiflicherweise, da die Nachrichten darüber aus gegnerischem Munde kommen), ist aber doch wohl aus der Thatsache zu folgern, dass diese Ansicht öffentlich gelehrt, ja sogar dem Staatsoberhaupt vorgetragen wurde.

4) „Taṃ haṇaha khaṇaha ḍahaha payaha ālumpaha pilumpaha sahasā khāreha vipāramusata!" Vgl. auch Sūtrakṛt. II, 1, 24.

5) Die Übersetzung beider Versionen des Dialogs von Prof. Leumann steht in den Akten des sechsten Orientalisten-Kongresses III, 2, p. 469 fg.

2. Denselben Geist wie die obige Theorie atmet die Lehre des Ajita Kesakambalī (Sāmaññaphalasutta 22—24)[1], der alles Lebende für eine Zusammensetzung der vier Elemente: Erde, Wasser, Feuer, Luft (paṭhavī, āpo, tejo, vāyo) erklärt. Auch die Jānakas[2]), angeblich eine buddhistische Sekte, hegen nach Sūtrakṛt. I, 1, 18 die letztgenannte Ansicht[3]).

3. Fünf Elemente, nämlich ausser den genannten der Äther (puḍhavī, āu, teju, vāu, āgāsa), werden von den Bhūtavādinas oder Pañcabhautikas angenommen[4]). Diese Elemente sind unerschaffen, ewig, von nichts abhängig (apurohitā), bilden in ihrer Mischung (samavāya) alle Dinge „bis zum Grashalm herab" und lassen auch das Bewusstsein aus sich hervorgehen[5]).

4. Hierzu fügen als sechstes Element die Seele (āyā, ātman) die Ātmaṣaṣṭha-vādinas, über deren Lehre das Sūtrakṛtāṅga folgendermassen sich äussert: „Es giebt fünf Elemente, sagen einige; und ein sechstes sei die Seele, und Seele und Welt seien ewig. Beide gingen nicht zugrunde, und ein Nichtseiendes könne nicht entstehen; alle Dinge existierten mit Notwendigkeit" (I, 1, 1, 15 u. 16)[6]); „Diese fünf Elemente sind unerschaffen... selbstständig, ewig. Die Seele aber sei ein sechstes (Element), meinen einige; es gäbe keinen Untergang des Seienden und kein Entstehen des Nichtseienden" (II, 1, 22)[7]). Ob dieses, wie Śīlāṅka will, auf

---

1) Über die wörtlichen Anklänge derselben an Sūtrakṛt. II, 1, 15—19 s. Jacobi in den Sacred Books of the East, vol. 45, Introd. p. 24.

2) Jacobi, S. B. 45 p. 238 Anm. 4, bringt dieses Wort in Zusammenhang mit den Ausdrücken Mahā-yāna, Hīna-yāna, was sich aus chronologischen Gründen zu verbieten scheint. Auch Webers Vorschlag, an Anhänger des Videha-Königs Janaka zu denken (Ind. Stud. XVI, p. 259) ist kaum annehmbar.

3) Die vier Elemente werden, freilich nur als subjektive Phänomene, auch von Buddha selbst zugegeben, z. B. im Kevaddhasutta.

4) Sūtrakṛt. I, 1, 1, 7 u. 8 und II, 1, 20—24; die Namen nach Śīlāṅka.

5) „tebbho ego tti āhiyā", Sūtrakṛt. I, 1, 1, 8. Der Ātman ist „einer" im Vergleich zu dem aus vielen Teilen bestehenden Körper. An eine Allseele (s. Jacobi) ist hier gewiss nicht gedacht. — Auch die Lehre von den fünf Skandhas wird als materialistische Theorie im Sūtrakṛt. (I, 1, 1, 17) erwähnt.

6) Saṃti paṃca mahabbhūyā, iham egesi āhiyā |
āya-baṭṭho puṇo āhu, āyā loge ya sāsae[1] ‖ (15).
Uhau[2] ṇa viṇassaṃti, no ya uppajjae asaṃ |
savve vi savvahā bhāvā niyatī-bhāvam āgayā[3] ‖ (16).

Kommentar: 1) Tatr'ātmanaḥ sarva-vyāpitvād amūrtatvāc c'ākāśasyêva śāśvatatvam, pṛthivy-ādīnām ca tadrūpâpracyuter avinaśvaratvam iti; 2) Ubhayata iti nirhetuka-sahetuka-vināśa-dvayena na vinaśyanti ..... yadi vā dvirūpād ātmanaḥ svabhāvāc cetanâcetana-rūpān na vinaśyatîti; 3) niyati-bhāvaṃ nityatvam āgatā(!). — Zu 15 b vgl. übrigens Brahmajālasutta I die Beschreibung des Sassata-vāda: „Sassato attā ca loko ca, vañjho kūṭaṭṭho esikaṭṭhāyiṭṭhito; te ca sattā sandhāvanti saṃsaranti cavanti upapajjanti; atthi tv eva sassati-samaṃ."

7) Ete paṃca mahabbhūyā aṇimmiyā ... sataṃtā sāsatā. Āyā baṭṭhā puṇa ege evam āhu; sato naṭṭhi vināso, asato naṭṭhi saṃbhavo.

Sāṃkhyas und Śaivâdhikāriṇas oder, mit Harṣakula, auf Sāṃkhyas und Vaiśeṣikas zu beziehen ist, lassen wir dahingestellt. Zweifellos aber handelt es sich hier um grobsinnliche Vorstellungen, ähnlich etwa den von Yājñavalkya im Dharmaśāstra (III, 72 fg.) entwickelten [1]) oder denen der Jaina-Embryologie [2]).

5. Endlich muss hier der Saptakāya-vāda des Pakudha Kaccāyana genannt werden (Sāmaññaphalasutta 25—27). Diesem zufolge wird die ganze Welt gebildet durch sieben unerschaffene und unzerstörbare Elemente (kāyās): Erde, Wasser, Feuer, Luft, Lust, Leid [3]) und Seele (paṭhavi, āpo, tejo, vāyo, sukhe, dukkhe, jīva). Da dieselben absolut unveränderlich sind, kann es Tod und Mord in Wahrheit nicht geben. Denn „nur durch den Zwischenraum der sieben Elemente fährt ja das Schwert". Auch die Geistesthätigkeiten beruhen sämtlich nur auf einer Verschiebung der Elemente [4]).

9. Acht Arten von Akriyā-vādinas.

Eine Aufzählung der Akriyā-vādinas [5]) giebt von allen unseren Quellen allein das Sthānāṅga. Aber diese lässt sich dem, in einem früheren Kapitel derselben Schrift gleichfalls genannten Schema der dreihundertdreiundsechzig Darśanas nicht einfügen und scheint überhaupt auf dasselbe keinerlei Rücksicht zu nehmen, indem sie unter akriyā-vādin nicht nur den Leugner der Seele und der sittlichen Weltordnung, sondern den Häretiker schlechthin versteht. Acht Arten von Hauptketzereien werden aufgezählt (ekkā-vādī aṇikka-vādī mita-vādī nimmita-vādī sāya-vādī samuccheda-vādī ṇiyā-vādī ṇasaṃtiparaloga-vādī) und von Abhayadeva wie folgt erklärt.

---

1) „Bei der Verbindung von Mann und Frau, wenn Blut und Samen rein sind, nimmt der Herr die fünf Elemente an, und ist selbst das sechste (pañcadhātu svayaṃ ṣaṣṭha ādatte yugapat prabhuḥ). .... Im ersten Monat ist er eine feuchte Masse, von den Elementen umhüllt, im zweiten Monat ein Fleischgewächs, im dritten mit Gliedern und Sinneswerkzeugen begabt" etc. (ed. Stenzler, p. 97). Vgl. Jacobi, loc. cit. p. 237 Anm. 4.

2) Weber, Ind. Stud. XVI, p. 439.

3) Es sei hier an die Guṇa-Theorie erinnert sowie an die alte, ins vedische Zeitalter zurückreichende Gewohnheit der Inder, *dharma* und *adharma* (gut und böse) als eine Art Substanzen zu betrachten, mit denen die Seele in Berührung kommt.

4) Tattha natthi hantā vā ghātetā vā sotā vā sāvetā vā viññātā vā viññāpetā vā.

5) vgl. Einleitung S. 4 fg. u. S. 12. Ich gebrauche oben das Wort im jinistischen Sinne.

1. **Eka-vāda**. die Lehre von der ausschliesslichen Realität eines Prinzipes. Hierzu gehören: a) der **Ātmâdvaita-vāda** (Akosmismus[1]?); b) der **Puruṣâdvaita-vāda** (subjektiver Idealismus, spiritualistischer Pantheismus?)[2]; c) der **Śabdâdvaita-vāda** oder Panlogismus, demzufolge das göttliche Wort (Vedawort) der Träger aller Dinge ist („Sarvaṃ śabd'ātmakam idam"); d) der **Sāmānya-vāda** oder Universalismus, die Lehre von der metaphysischen Realität des Generischen. Über alle diese Ansichten erfahren wir leider nichts Genaues. Für die ersten beiden werden vier Zitate beigebracht: Brahmabindu-Up. 12 (Eka eva hi bhūt'ātmā etc.), Īśa-Up. 5 (Tad ejati tan n'aijati etc.) und der Vers „Nitya jñāna-vivartto 'yaṃ kṣiti-tejo-jal'ādikaḥ | ātmā tad-ātmakaś cêti saṃgirate[3]) pare punar" (?); zur Erläuterung des Panlogismus wird derselbe Vers aus Bhartṛharis Brahmakāṇḍa angeführt, den Mādhava bei Besprechung der Sphoṭa-Theorie[4]) zitiert: „Brahman ohne Anfang und Ende, der da als des Wortes unvergängliche Wesenheit in der Form von Dingen erscheint, aus dem die Weltschöpfung entspringt"; und über den Sāmānya-vāda erfahren wir nur, dass er alles für eines erkläre „wegen der Einheit des Gemeinsamen", was an das Vaiśeṣika-System erinnert, demzufolge das höchste Genus, Sattā (Existenz), durch Upādhis („Verkleidungen") in Species sich differenziert und durch diese den Substanzen, Qualitäten und „Handlungen" inhäriert.

2. **Aneka-vāda** oder Pluralismus. Unter diesem Namen werden die Gegner der monistischen Systeme, im besonderen die Atomisten und Nominalisten[5]) verstanden.

---

1) s. S. 38 fg.

2) Akriyāvāditā câsya (ekavādinaḥ) sad-bhūtasyâpi tadanyasya nâstîti pratipādanāt **ātmâdvaita-puruṣâdvaita-śabd'ādvait'ādīnam** yuktibhir aghaṭamānānām astitvâbhyupagamāt. Da für die ersten beiden Ansichten die Beispiele (s. unten) zusammen gegeben werden, ist nicht zu erkennen, wodurch sie sich unterscheiden, es sei denn aus der Verbindung des ersten mit den drei folgenden Zitaten: Aparas tv ātmaivâsti nânyad iti pratipannas. Tad uktaṃ: „Puruṣa evêdaṃ" etc. Wahrscheinlich ist A. selbst der Unterschied nicht ganz klar gewesen.

3) saṃgiraṃte, Ba.

4) Schon lange vor der Einführung der Schrift ist in Indien über das Verhältnis der Laute (Buchstaben) zum Wort und des Wortes zu seiner Bedeutung philosophiert worden. Man konstatierte, dass die einzelnen Laute, da sie an sich sinnlos seien und nur momentan existierten, weder für sich noch in ihrer Vereinigung zum Verständnis des Wortsinnes führen könnten und dass deshalb ein *sphoṭa* das letztere vermitteln müsse. „Der *sphoṭa* ist ein von den Buchstaben verschiedenes, durch die Buchstaben offenbartes, zum Verständnis des Sinnes führendes ewiges Wort (nityaḥ śabdaḥ)," Sarvadarś. p. 141.

5) Es wird eine anziehende Aufgabe sein, die Geschichte des Universalienproblems in Indien aufzudecken. Bis jetzt fehlt es hierfür leider an Anhaltspunkten, da die Geschichte des Vaiśeṣika noch in Dunkel gehüllt ist.

3. Mita-vāda, die Lehre von der Begrenztheit alles Seienden. Die Welt ist weder zeitlich noch räumlich unendlich [1]) und auch die Seele nicht allgegenwärtig (wie der Vedānta lehrt), sondern von der Grösse eines Daumengliedes oder eines Hirsekorns.

4. Nirmita-vāda oder Schöpfungslehre. A. beschreibt hier eine an den Sṛṣṭi-vāda der Purāṇen erinnernde Emanationstheorie: Der „undenkbare Ātman" lässt, in urweltlicher Finsternis sich kasteiend, aus seinem Nabel eine goldene Lotusblume und aus dieser den Gott Brahman hervorgehen. Letzterer schafft die acht Weltmütter: Aditi, Diti, Manu, Vinatā, Kadru, Sulasā, Surabhi und Ilā, die dann ihrerseits, je nach ihrer Bestimmung, die Götter, Dämonen, Menschen, Vögel, Schlangen, Gottschlangen (nāgās), Vierfüssler und Pflanzen ins Dasein rufen. Die Verteidiger dieser Ansicht sollen sich auf den teleologischen Beweis stützen: „Die Welt muss einen vernunftbegabten Urheber haben, weil sie, wie der Topf, eine Konstruktion (saṃsthāna) zeigt."

5. Śāta-vāda oder Bequemlichkeitslehre. Diese Theorie wendet sich vornehmlich gegen die Askese mit dem Argument dass ein Gewand, das man mit weissen Fäden webe, nicht rot, sondern weiss werde, dass, mit anderen Worten, irdisches Leid nicht jenseitiges Glück zur Folge haben könne. Wer Lust wolle, müsse lustig sein (Sukh'āsevanāt sukham evêti). A. zitiert hier einen Vers, der die Lebensweise der Buddhisten verspottet [2]), woraus natürlich nicht folgt, dass mit den Śāta-vādinas ursprünglich die Buddhisten gemeint waren.

6. Samuccheda-vāda oder die Lehre von der Momentvernichtung [3]). Dieselbe kommt, indem sie den Begriff der thätigen Substanz als contradictio in adjecto erkennt, zu dem Schlusse, dass man Realität = Aktualität (kriyā-kāritva) setzen und statt der Kausalität ein „momentanes, ursachloses Verschwinden" annehmen müsse [4]).

Dass Kaṇāda seine vierte Kategorie von einem früheren System, eben unserem Sāmānya-vāda, geborgt hat, ist nicht ausgeschlossen. Wie die Jainas über die Universalien dachten, zeigt Abhayadeva mit den Worten: „Denn keineswegs giebt es überhaupt kein Genus, weil in diesem Fall die Erkenntnis eines Nichtgetrennten (Identischen) unmöglich wäre."

1) vgl. die Antânantikā Buddhas (Brahmajālasutta 16—22).

2) vgl. Leumann in W. Z. K. M. 1889, p. 332 Anm.

3) In buddhistischen Texten wird unter Uccheda-vāda stets die Leugnung eines Fortlebens nach dem Tode verstanden. Da jedoch diese Ansicht unter No. 8 (Nasantiparaloka-vāda fällt, haben wir keinen Grund, die Angabe A.'s, dass im gegenwärtigen Falle der Kṣaṇabhaṅga-vāda gemeint sei, zu bezweifeln Vielleicht existierte diese Lehre, so leicht sie aus den Prinzipien Buddhas sich ableiten lässt, doch schon vor dem Auftreten des letzteren (womit natürlich nicht geleugnet werden soll, dass das Sthānaṅga nachbuddhistisch ist).

4) Die Buddhisten werden nicht erwähnt.

7. N i t y a - v ā d a, die Lehre von der Unzerstörbarkeit der Materie. Alles Entstehen und Vergehen ist nur ein Sichtbar- und Unsichtbarwerden, eine Metamorphose (pariṇati) der ewig unvergänglichen Grundstoffe Lehm etc.[1]).

8. N a - s a n t i - p a r a - l o k a - v ā d a, Materialismus. Erlösung, Jenseits und Wiedergeburt werden geleugnet und das Bewusstsein für eine Eigenschaft der Materie (bhūta-dharma) erklärt[2]).

1) vgl. oben S. 53 die Lehre der Ātmaṣaṣṭha-vādinas sowie den Satkārya-vāda der Sāṃkhyas.

2) vgl. die Lehre Bṛhaspatis im Sarvadarśanasamgraha (p. 6 fg.) und die der Bhūta-vādinas oben S. 53, speziell Anm. 5.

Appendix I.

Uber das Zeitrad.

Durch die Philosophie des Kāla-vāda ist die mythologische Vorstellung vom Sternen- und Zeitrad [1]) nicht verdrängt worden. Vielmehr hat diese neben jener sich fortentwickelt, wie die folgenden Beispiele zeigen mögen.

Im Pauṣya-parvan des Mahābhārata wird erzählt, wie dem Brahmanenschüler Uttaṅka ein Paar kostbarer Ohrringe, die er seiner Herrin zu überbringen hatte, vom Schlangenkönig Takṣaka gestohlen wurden. Auf der Verfolgung des letzteren begriffen tritt Uttaṅka durch einen Erdspalt, den ihm Indras Donnerkeil eröffnet hat, in das Reich der Schlangen ein. Nach vergeblichem Bemühen, die Schlangen für sich zu gewinnen, erblickt er plötzlich „zwei Frauen an einem Webstuhl, ein kunstvolles Gewand webend. Und an dem Stuhle waren schwarze und weisse Fäden. Und er sah auch ein Rad mit zwölf Speichen, das von sechs Knaben gedreht wurde. Und einen Mann sah er und ein herrliches Ross." Betend wendet er sich an diese, erhält durch ihre Vermittelung das Geschmeide zurück, kehrt heim und erfährt nun von seinem Lehrer, den er um Erklärung angeht, dass die beiden Frauen Dhātar und Vidhātar („Schöpfer" und „Verteiler") [2]), die schwarzen und

---

1) s. oben S. 18.

2) Natürlich sind weder die Ādityas gemeint noch, wie Nīlakaṇṭha erklärt, Citi und Māyā, sondern entweder der als Doppelperson gedachte schaffende und richtende Gott („Dhātā Īśvaro . . . . . Vidhātā Dharmo", N. ad Mahābh. III, 32, 7) oder die beiden Aśvin, die in dem alten Hymnus Mahābh. I, 3, 55 fg. das Schwarze und das Weisse weben und mit Sonne und Himmel das Zeitrad schaffen (Hopkins, Religions of India, p. 360), oder endlich es handelt sich hier um eine indogermanische Reminiscenz, indem die beiden Frauen (Vergangenheit und Zukunft, Vergehen und Werden?) den Parcen und Nornen sich an die Seite stellen. Im letzten Falle wäre die Erklärung des Lehrers ein Zusatz von

die weissen Fäden die Nächte und die Tage, die sechs Knaben die Jahreszeiten, das Rad das Jahr, der Mann Parjanya (der Regengott) und das Ross Agni (der Feuergott) seien.

Bhāgavata-Purāṇa V, 22, betitelt Jyotiścakra-varṇanam „Beschreibung des Sternenrades", beginnt mit der Frage des Königs Parīkṣit, wie es denn zu verstehen sei, dass die „göttliche Sonne", den Meru [1]) und den Dhruva (Polarstern) zur Rechten lassend, nach links zu den Sternen sich wende — worauf der Weise Śuka die Antwort erteilt: „Gleichwie mit einer in Drehung begriffenen Töpferscheibe die etwa darauf befindlichen Ameisen und sonstigen Tierchen zugleich sich drehen, dennoch aber, da sie ja an verschiedenen Orten (der Scheibe) sind, jedes seine eigene Bahn hat: geradeso laufen, wenn das Zeitrad mit seinen Sternscharen den Dhruva und den Meru von rechts (d. h. ehrerbietig) umwandelt, die auf ihm ruhende Sonne und anderen Planeten mit ihm zugleich herum, indem dieselben gleichwohl ihren eigenen Lauf haben, da sie ja in verschiedenen Bildern und verschiedenen Gruppen sich befinden."

Bhāgavata-Purāṇa V, 23 hat den Titel „Beschreibung der Gestalt Śiśumāras" und lautet (im Auszug) wie folgt: „Śuka sprach: Dreizehn mal hunderttausend Yoyanas entfernt von hier, so wird gesagt, ist des Viṣṇu höchste Stätte, wo der grosse Diener des Erhabenen, Dhruva, der Sohn des Uttānapāda, von Agni, Indra, Prajāpati, Kaśyapa und Dharma, die für die gleiche Zeitdauer vereinigt sind und ihn verehrungsvoll umwandeln, indem sie ihn zur Rechten lassen, für die Dauer eines Kalpa [2]) noch heute wohnt. Seine Macht soll hier beschrieben werden (1). Gleichsam als die feste Stütze der Sternscharen: der Planeten, Nakṣatras u. s. w., die durch die erhabene Zeit, die schlummerlose, unmerkbar dahinwandelnde gedreht werden [3]), vom Īśvara hingestellt, leuchtet er immerdar (2). Gleichwie viele Stück Weidevieh (ākramaṇa-paśavaḥ), die zusammen an einen Pfahl gebunden sind, die drei Tageszeiten über je nach ihrem Stand verschiedene Kreise beschreiben: geradeso wandeln die Sternscharen: Planeten etc., durch äussere und (oder) innere Bande an dieses Zeitrad gefesselt, auf den Polarstern sich stützend, vom Winde getrieben, bis zum Ende des Kalpas im Kreise umher.

---

späterer Hand oder einer der unzähligen lapsus memoriae des Hindu-Homers. Jedenfalls verdient Beachtung, dass in der altindischen sowohl wie in der griechisch-römischen und nordischen Mythologie zur Symbolisierung des Zeitbegriffs das Bild der spinnenden Frau verwendet wird.

1) Ein fabelhafter Berg, aus Gold und Edelsteinen bestehend, um den wie die Blätter der Lotusblume die Kontinente gelagert sind.

2) kalpa-jīvinām ājīvya. 1 Kalpa oder Tag Brahmans = 4 320 000 000 Jahre.

3) graha-nakṣatr'ādīnām animiṣeṇâvyakta-raṃhasā bhagavatā Kālena bhrāmyamāṇānām.

Wie in der Luft Wolken oder Vögel, die einen durch die Kraft des Windes, die anderen durch ihr Karman [1]) gelenkt, sich einherbewegen: so auch wandeln die Lichtscharen den Weg ihres Karman, ohne auf die Erde zu fallen (3). Einige stellen, in der Andacht des erhabenen Vāsudeva (Viṣṇu) versunken, das Lichterheer in der Gestalt eines Śiśumāra [2]) sich vor (4). An der Schwanzspitze dieses Śiśumāra, dessen Kopf nach Süden schaut und dessen Leib ringförmig gekrümmt ist, wird der Polarstern gedacht; die Länge des Schwanzes nehmen Prajāpati, Agni, Indra und Dharma ein; an der Schwanzwurzel sind Dhātar und Vidhātar, an der Hüfte die sieben Ṛṣis. An die rechte Seite des nach Süden gekrümmten Körpers setzt man die nördlichen Sternbilder, an die linke die südlichen, so dass die beiden Seiten des ringförmig gebogenen Śiśumāra gleich viele Teile haben. Auf dem Rücken aber steht Ajavīthī, und aus dem Leibe kommt die Himmelsgaṅgā (Milchstrasse) hervor (5). . . . . (6). An dem oberen Kinnbacken ist Agastya, an dem unteren Yama, im Munde Aṅgāraka, ... die Sonne in der Brust, im Herzen Nārāyaṇa, im Manas der Mond, ... an den Brüsten die beiden Aśvin, ... in allen Gliedern die Kometen, in den Haaren alle Sternscharen (Nebel) (7). — Diese, alle Gottheiten umfassende Form des erhabenen Viṣṇu soll man Tag für Tag in der Dämmerung betrachten und mit den Worten anbeten: „Verehrungsvoll lasst uns gedenken der Welt des Lichtes (der Sterne), des Laufes der Zeit, des Herrn der Weltwächter (? animiṣa), des grossen Geistes“ (8). Wer so den Träger aller Gestirne, die höchsterhabene Dreizeit [3]) verehrt, die das Böse fortscheucht von denen die sie anbeten, oder wer dreimal ihren Namen nennt, dem wird alsbald schwinden, was er zu jener Zeit etwa Böses gethan (9).“

Wenden wir uns zum Schluss zur Jaina-Litteratur, so lernen wir die eigentümliche Verschmelzung kennen, die die indische Lehre vom Zeitrad mit der indisch-europäischen Vorstellung von den vier Weltaltern eingegangen ist [4]). Nachdem aus den zwölf Monaten, die in der vedischen Zeit die Speichen des Rades vorstellten, zwölf Jahrtausende geworden waren [5]), verfiel man auf die Idee, hiernach die Dauer der vier Weltalter zu bestimmen, was folgendermassen geschah:

---

1) „That, Werk, Natur, Charakter“. Nach indischer Auffassung ist alles Thun und Leiden des Individuums die naturgesetzliche Folge seiner früheren Handlungen.

2) eine Art Schildkröte.

3) graha'rkṣa-tārā-mayam ādhidaivikam . . . . . trikālam; *ādhidaivika* eigentl. = „auf die höchste Gottheit (adhidaiva) bezüglich“, was man hier mit Rücksicht auf das Viṣṇu-Purāṇa (I, 2) dahin deuten könnte, dass Kāla zu den vier Erscheinungsformen Viṣṇus gehört.

4) Diese Verschmelzung bespricht Prof. Leumann in einer noch nicht veröffentlichten „Übersicht über die Āvaśyaka-Litteratur“, p. 43.

5) Dieses die einleuchtende Vermutung Leumanns.

Kṛta-yuga („gut") = 400 + 4000 + 400 = 4800 Jahre
Tretā-yuga („gut-schlecht") = 300 + 3000 + 300 = 3600 Jahre
Dvāpara-yuga (schlecht-gut") = 200 + 2000 + 200 = 2400 Jahre
Kali-yūga („schlecht") = 100 + 1000 + 100 = 1200 Jahre
zusammen 12 000 Jahre

wobei die den Tausenden vor- und nachgesetzten Jahrhunderte die Morgen- bezw. Abenddämmerung des betreffenden Zeitalters bedeuten. Diese Vorstellung von den vier Weltaltern und ihrer verschiedenen Daúer übertrugen nun die Jainas, ins Masslose vergrössert, mit nicht sehr grossem Geschick wieder auf das Zeitrad, das auf diese Weise, statt der ursprünglich gleich langen Speichen, zwölf Perioden von sehr verschiedener Länge darstellte, nämlich

1. „best" susama-susamā = 400 000 000 000 000 Sāgaras [1])
2. „gut" susamā = 300 000 000 000 000 "
3. „gut-schlecht" susama-dussamā = 200 000 000 000 000 "
4. „schlecht-gut" dussama-susamā = 100 000 000 000 000 " minus 42 000 Jahre
5. „schlecht" dussamā = 21 000 Jahre
6. „schlechtest" dussama-dussamā = 21 000 Jahre
7. id. id. id.
8. „schlecht" dussamā = 21 000 Jahre

u. s. w. in der umgekehrten Reihenfolge wie oben. Die Speichen 1 bis 6 bilden die ussappiṇī oder aufsteigende, die Speichen 7 bis 12 die osappiṇī oder absteigende Hälfte des in 2 000 000 000 000 000 Sāgaras von Jahren (eine zweimillionstellige Zahl) einmal sich herumdrehenden Zeitrades.

1) Ein Sāgara („Ocean") ist = $8\,400\,000^{19}$ Jahre; s. Weber, „Über ein Fragment der Bhagavatī".

Appendix II.

Eine jinistische Widerlegung des Theïsmus.

Die folgende Uebersetzung soll einen Begriff geben von der Methode unseres Hauptgewährsmanns Malayagiri und zugleich zeigen, wie der gebildete Inder mit dem Christentum sich auseinandersetzt. Denn obwohl unser Autor mit dem Īśvara-vāda natürlich nicht das Christentum meint, steht diese Ansicht der christlichen dennoch in mancher Beziehung so nahe, dass zweifellos der heutige Jaina, um sich gegen das Christentum zu verteidigen, dieselben Argumente ins Feld führen wird, die ihm sein Urahn als Waffen gegen den Īśvara-vāda überliefert. Diese Widerlegung des Theïsmus glaubten wir ferner auch deshalb dem Leser nicht vorenthalten zu dürfen, weil sie eingehender ist als die bereits bekannten und überdies in einer sehr ansprechenden Form sich darbietet, nämlich der des Dialogs. Malayagiri zeigt zuerst durch den Mund des Jaina (J.) die Ansicht des Theïsten (T.), um dann in Rede und Gegenrede die beiden Standpunkte sich messen zu lassen.[1])

J. Die Gottgläubigen (Īśvara-vādinas) behaupten, dass die ganze Welt von einem Herrn erschaffen worden sei, dass dieser Herr vier Eigenschaften habe, nämlich Allwissenheit, Leidenschaftslosigkeit, Allgüte und Allmacht, und dass er es sei, der die Menschen zum Himmel und zur Erlösung führe; oder:

„Allwissenheit, Freiheit von weltlichen Gelüsten, Allmacht und höchste Tugend: das ist des Weltherrn vierfache Vollkommenheit.
Unwissend ist die Kreatur, unfrei durch Leiden und Freuden;
vom Herrn geführt kommt sie zum zum Himmel, der Herr treibt sie zur Hölle.“

1) Der Text ist durch das Streichen von Wiederholungen etc. in der Übersetzung teilweise etwas vereinfacht worden.

. . . . Diese Ansicht verwerfen wir, weil es für das Dasein eines Herrn keinen Beweis giebt.

T.: Allerdings können wir das Dasein eines Herrn beweisen, und zwar durch einen Vernunftschluss (Syllogismus). Wir sagen, dass alles was eine Absicht zum Ausdruck bringt, z. B. ein Beil beim Holzhacken, von einem vernunftbegabten Thäter regiert sein muss. Denn die Beile u. s. w. können doch, da sie keine Vernunft haben, unmöglich von selbst thätig sein. Wäre letzteres der Fall, so würden sie (da dann die Thätigkeit zu ihrer Natur gehörte), ununterbrochen arbeiten, was bekanntlich nicht geschieht. Man ist also zur Annahme genötigt, dass die zweckmässige Thätigkeit einen verständigen Urheber habe. Und da nun die ganze Welt einem Ziel zustrebt, so ergiebt sich als treibende Kraft des Alls der „Herr". Ein weiterer Beweis ist der folgende: Alles was eine bestimmte Form, z. B. Kreisförmigkeit, aufweist, hat einen vernünftigen Urheber. Dies wird durch die Erfahrung an Töpfen etc. bewiesen. Es muss daher auch von Bergen etc. angenommen werden [1]).

J.: Das geben wir nicht zu. Für u n s ist ganze Mannigfaltigkeit der Welt durch das Karman (s. S. 60 Anm. 1) bedingt, indem, wenn Berge wie der Vaitāḍhya oder der Himavat und Länder wie Bharata (sic!), Airāvata, Videha oder andere Inseln zur Freude oder zum Leid der Wesen sich verändern, als Ursache der jeweiligen Veränderung immer nur das Karman der dort wohnenden Lebewesen anzusehen ist. Allbekannt z. B. ist ja, dass, wenn ein rechtschaffener König das Land regiert, durch den Einfluss seines Karman überall Wohlstand sich entwickelt. Das Karman aber ist an die Seele gebunden, und die Seele ist vernunftbegabt, insofern sie Bewusstsein hat. So ist das Regieren einer vernunftbegabten Ursache und das zweckmässige Handeln erklärt, mithin alles in Ordnung.

T.: Keineswegs! Denn wir behaupten, dass ein höchster „Herr" die vernunft- oder verstandbegabte Ursache der Welt sei.

J.: Dann sind eure Beispiele unglücklich gewählt. Denn für die Thätigkeit der Axt und für das Entstehen des Topfes etc. sind, wie wir zeigten, Tischler, Töpfer etc. in jeder Hinsicht genügende Erklärungen.

T.: Aber die Tischler etc. verrichten ihre Thätigkeit nicht von selbst, sondern unter der Leitung eines höchsten Herrn.

J.: Dann muss man annehmen, dass auch jener Herr zu seiner Thätigkeit eines andern (höhern) Herrn bedürfe, dieser wieder eines andern u. s. w., und so ständen wir vor der hoffnungslosen Finsternis eines regressus in infinitum.[2])

---

1) „Die Erde muss einen Schöpfer haben, da sie, wie Töpfe etc., das Aussehen eines Produktes hat" (Sarvadarśanasaṃgraha).

2) Für Nichtindologen sei hier bemerkt, dass dieser wie der folgende logische Ausdruck (circulus vitiosus) eine genaue Übersetzung des entsprechenden Saṃskṛt-Terminus ist.

T.: Aber die Tischler und alle andern Kreaturen sind von Natur unwissende Wesen: darum müssen sie ihre Thätigkeit unter einer Führung verrichten. Der Herr hingegen ist allwissend und braucht darum bei seiner Thätigkeit keinen Führer. Und so liegt kein regressus in infinitum vor.

J.: Aber ein circulus vitiosus! Denn aus dem Postulat der Allwissenheit folgert ihr, dass es ein unwissendes und abhängiges Wesen gebe, während zugleich die angenommene Unselbständigkeit einer unwissenden Kreatur die Allwissenheit (eines Schöpfers) beweisen soll. Ist also die eine Annahme unerwiesen, so muss es auch die andre sein. Ferner: wenn jener Allwissende „leidenschaftslos" ist, zu welchem Zwecke lässt er dann die unwissende Kreatur auf Abwege geraten? Gerechte und vernünftige Herren beteiligen sich bekanntlich nur an guten Werken, nicht auch an bösen. Der aber schafft mehr Böses als Gutes. Wie sollte er da wohl allwissend und leidenschaftslos sein!

T.: Der Erhabene ist allwissend und leidenschaftslos, insofern er den Weg zum rechten Handeln zeigt. Die Menge der Übelthäter aber empfängt von ihm ihre Strafe, und so, indem er sich vom Bösen abwendet und es straft, ist er der Wissende und der Herr.

J.: Auch hierin ist keine Logik, weil auch das Böse schliesslich auf niemand anders als den Herrn zurückzuführen ist. Denn der Mensch ist nicht der Thäter, weil bei ihm die selbständige Thätigkeit im Guten wie im Bösen eben durch seine Unwissenheit ausgeschlossen ist. Mithin, wenn der Herr das Böse thut und dann, nachdem er es bestraft hat, das Gute: wie sollte er da wohl sein Handeln vorher überlegt haben!

T.: Wenn er zum Bösen sich wendet, so thut er es nur mit Rücksicht auf das Karman. Denn nur dann verhängt der Erhabene Böses, wenn er deutlich erkannt hat, dass ein Karman es verlangt. Sein Handeln ist also kein unüberlegtes.

J.: Aber jenes Karman ist doch auch nur sein Werk! sah er die Folgen vorher: warum hat er es geschehen lassen?

T.: Aber er ist ja gar nicht der Anstifter zum Bösen! vielmehr thut er von sich aus nur das Gute, lässt aber dem Übelthäter seine Strafe zu teil werden — gerade so wie es irdische Herrscher, Könige u. s. w., machen, die auch Strafen austeilen, ohne doch ihr Volk zum Bösen zu verleiten.

J.: Dieser Vergleich ist deshalb nicht am Platz, weil andere Herrscher nicht imstande sind, das Böse zu unterdrücken. Haben doch selbst mächtige Könige die Sünden des Denkens, der Zunge und der That nicht überall verhindern können! Jener Erhabene aber soll ja fähig sein, nach Belieben das Gute oder das Böse thun oder nicht thun zu lassen. Wie kommt es also, dass er die bösen Handlungen nicht nur nicht verhindert, sondern im Gegenteil sehr zufrieden ist, sie strafen zu können?

T.: Aber wir behaupten ja gar nicht, dass er das Böse verhindern kann!

J.: Dann hört gefälligst auf, in alle Welt hinauszuposaunen, alles habe der Herr geschaffen.

T.: Wir meinen, dass jener das Gute und das Böse zwar selbst thut, hingegen als „Herr“ Lohn und Strafe austeilt, da er zu deren Genuss selbst nicht fähig ist.

J.: Unglaublich! Jemand soll Gutes und Böses schaffen, nicht aber deren Folgen geniessen können? Man stelle sich einen Koch vor, der seinen Reisbrei nicht selbst kosten kann! Aber lassen wir das einmal auf sich beruhen und halten es ferner für begreiflich, dass der Herr den Tugendhaften z. B. mit der Liebe einer berauschten Götterjungfrau belohnt, so bleibt doch die Frage offen, wie er sich dazu verstehen kann, die böse That durch den Sturz in die Hölle und ähnliche Strafen zu verfolgen. Denn edle und verständige Herrn werden durch das allumfassende Mitleid, das ihre Seele erfüllt, abgehalten, andern Qual zu bereiten.

T.: Zu seiner Unterhaltung macht der Herr es so.

J.: Wenn das wahr wäre: wo bliebe da seine Einsicht! wozu müssen, wenn er sich unterhalten will, alle Wesen den Tod erleiden?

„Wozu denn ein vernünftig Spiel,
Wenn nur das Spiel des Herren Ziel!
Wie kann dem Herren zum Vergnügen
Die Kreatur dem Tod erliegen?“

Übrigens kann nur die Leidenschaft sich zum Spiel eine Welt erschaffen, nicht aber die Wunschlosigkeit. Wie sollte daher der Herr sich mit Spielen abgeben!

T.: Aber wir sagen ja gar nicht, dass er wunschlos sei.

J.: Dann ist er den andern begehrenden Wesen gleichzustellen und weder allwissend noch der Schöpfer der Welt.

T.: Vielmehr ist er zugleich begehrend, allwissend und der Schöpfer der Welt, insofern dieses eben seine Natur ist. Und hier muss jedes weitere Nachfragen aufhören. Denn:

„Warum dies so und anders nicht,
Danach fragt nur ein blöder Wicht.
Dass wohl das Feuer brennen kann,
Doch nicht die Luft, weiss jedermann.“

J.: Das ist Unsinn. Nur bei der sinnlich erkennbaren „Natur“ eines Dinges ist die „Nachfrage“ [1]) unstatthaft. Fragt z. B. jemand: „Wie kommt das Feuer dazu, zu brennen? durch seine Stofflichkeit?

1) Dies ist einer der vielen indischen Kunstausdrücke, denen weder ein Wort der klassischen noch der modernen europäischen Sprachen genau entspricht. Paryanuyoya heisst nämlich nur diejenige Nachfrage, die mit der Absicht des Widerlegens ausgesprochen wird.

warum haben dann nicht andere Stoffe, z. B. die Luft, das gleiche Vermögen?" so ist die Antwort: „Das Brennen ist die sinnlich wahrnehmbare Natur des Feuers. Wie also sollte dasselbe eine ‚Nachfrage' erfordern!" Der Herr hingegen kann als Schöpfer der Welt und Allwissender n i c h t wahrgenommen werden. Deshalb ist, wo es sich um s e i n e Natur handelt, eine Nachfrage unbedingt notwendig. Denn, wollte man auch beim Unsichtbaren die Nachfrage für überflüssig erklären, so könnte jeder Philosoph, dessen Behauptungen von einem andern angefochten werden, sich auf die „Natur" seines Prinzips versteifen und so die Möglichkeit einer ihm gefährlichen Debatte einfach abschneiden. Ferner aber: behauptet man, dass die ganze Welt vom „Herrn" geschaffen sei, so wird man schwerlich bestreiten können, dass auch alle Lehrbücher aller (philosophischen und religiösen) Systeme von ihm ins Dasein gerufen sind. Diese Lehrbücher aber widersprechen einander und sind daher notwendig zum Teil gut, zum Teil trügerisch. Wie kann daher der Herr, wenn er zugleich den wahren und den falschen Weg zeigt, als Autorität gelten!

T.: Aber nicht alle Lehrbücher hat der Herr geschaffen, sondern nur die wahren.

J.: Dann giebt es also Dinge, die nicht vom Herrn erschaffen worden sind, und deine These (der Herr sei der Schöpfer des Alls) wird hinfällig. [Übrigens scheitert die Behauptung, dass es nur einen einzigen, unabhängigen Schöpfer gebe, auch an dem Beispiel des von vielen Menschen, den Baumeistern u. s. w. errichteten Palastes sowie an der Überlegung, dass, wenn jener die ganze Welt schafft, alle andern überflüssig werden, wie es in der Vītarāgastuti heisst:

„‚Einzig und ewig ist der Weltenschöpfer;
Das All durchdringt er, der Mächtige, Wahre':
Von solchen unseligen Irrgedanken
sind Mahāvīras Schüler nicht befangen."

Und an anderer Stelle:

Das wäre nicht ein Meister der Natur,
Der seine Kraft im Grossen übte nur;
Wenn aber a l l e s wird von Gott gemacht,
Wozu sind w i r dann auf die Welt gebracht?][1])

Ferner nehmen wir für ein Gebilde nur dann eine vernünftige Ursache an, wenn wir es vorher einmal durch eine vernünftige Ursache haben entstehen sehen. Man denke an verfallene Tempel, Brunnen etc. Hingegen der Anblick von Abendwolken, Ameisen-

1) Dieser Passus steht nicht im Text, sondern ist aus dem Sarvadarśanasaṃgraha (ed. p. 30 fg.) von mir hierher übernommen worden, da er einen von M. zufällig übergangenen, sonst aber in dem Kampf gegen den Iśvaravāda eine grosse Rolle spielenden Gedanken bringt. Die Wiedergabe des letzten Verses trifft nur den allgemeinen Sinn des im einzelnen nicht ganz klaren Originals.

haufen etc., mag deren Form auch noch so regelmässig sein, nötigt uns keineswegs zur Annahme e i n e s verständigen Urhebers, da wir nämlich einen solchen und sein Verhältnis zu dem fraglichen Gebilde uns nicht vorstellen können. Und ebensowenig können wir aus der Form der Berge etc. unserer Erde auf einen vernunftbegabten Schöpfer schliessen, da wir dieselben von einem solchen nicht haben machen sehen.

T.: Das geben wir nicht zu, weil der Umstand, dass in beiden Fällen dasselbe Wort zur Anwendung kommt,[1]) uns beweist, dass in unserer Annahme eines vernünftigen Urhebers kein Widerspruch liegt. Es ist somit alles in Ordnung.

J.: Durchaus nicht! Denn die Erfahrung lehrt, dass ein Wort, je nach seinem Zusammenhang, Verschiedenes bedeuten kann, so dass, wer aus der Identität des Wortes Identität der Dinge folgert, z. B. aus dem Worte „gaus" (das ursprünglich Rind, in übertragenem Sinne aber auch Himmel, Erde, Mutter, Rede u. a. bedeutet) den Schluss ziehen muss, dass alles, was mit diesem Wort bezeichnet wird, Hörner habe.

T.: Aber diese Annahme widerlegt ja der Sinnenschein, was bei unserer Annahme eines Herrn nicht der Fall ist. Wir sind also im Recht.

J.: Da sieht man, wie wenig ihr mit der logischen Methode vertraut seid! Aus der Thatsache, dass e i n e Annahme durch die sinnliche Wahrnehmung widerlegt wird, folgt doch noch nicht, dass man überall sonst aus der Wortidentität Identität der entsprechenden Dinge folgern darf. Im Gegenteil lehrt uns gerade die sinnliche Wahrnehmung, dass es ein allgemeines und notwendiges Verhältnis von Wortidentität und Dingidentität nicht giebt, und ihr solltet wissen, dass der Syllogismus nicht auf die Abwesenheit eines sinnfälligen Widerspruchs, sondern auf einen (anerkannten) Zusammenhang von Dingen (vyāpti) sich gründet.[2]) Ein solcher Zusammenhang nun ist im gegenwärtigen Falle nicht aufweisbar und eure Behauptung mithin als Fehlschluss erkannt. Gebt ihr das nicht zu, so müsst ihr z. B. folgenden Schluss für unwiderleglich und darum vernünftig erklären: „Alle Thongebilde sind von Töpfern gemacht, z. B. Töpfe; jener Ameisenhaufen besteht aus Thon; also hat ihn ein Töpfer gemacht."

T.: Aber hiergegen spricht doch die „Unsichtbarkeit", da bisher niemand einen Töpfer bei einer solchen Thätigkeit gesehen hat.

J. Und genau so steht es mit eurem Beweis für den „Herrn". Denn wäre wirklich ein „Herr" der Urheber all dieser Dinge, so würde man ihn irgendeinmal irgendwo wahrnehmen. Er wird aber

---

1) Ein *saṃsthāna* „Gebilde" ist sowohl der Tempel wie die Wolke und der Berg.

2) Ein solcher unbestrittener Zusammenhang liegt z. B. in dem Syllogismus „In dem Berg muss Feuer sein, weil er raucht" zwischen Rauch und Feuer vor.

5*

nicht wahrgenommen, weshalb wir eure Annahme für falsch erklären. Und damit genug! —

Malayagiri lebte im vierzehnten Jahrhundert; aber seine Auseinandersetzungen stammen, wie er selbst zugiebt, aus dem Munde der alten Lehrer. Dass der Philosoph seiner Zeit mit der „Lehre vom Herrn" leichter fertig wurde, mag zum Schluss ein Zitat aus dem Sarvadarśanasaṃgraha zeigen. Dort (ed. p. 152) äussert sich Mādhava (um 1330 p. C.) folgendermassen:

„Was aber das Geschrei der Gottgläubigen betrifft, dass ein ‚höchster Herr' aus ‚Liebe'[1]) (die Welt) schaffe, so ist dasselbe jetzt fast verstummt, nachdem man eingesehen hat, dass diese Ansicht dem folgenden Dilemma nicht entgehen kann: ‚Ist jener Herr schon (als Erlöser) thätig, bevor er die Welt schafft oder erst nachher?' Im ersten Falle ist, da es ja noch keine Körper u. s. w. und also auch kein Leid[2]) giebt, nicht ersichtlich, wie er den Wunsch hegen kann, lebende Wesen aus dem Leid zu erlösen; die zweite Annahme aber bewegt sich im Kreise, indem sie aus der Liebe die Schöpfung und aus der Schöpfung die Liebe hervorgehen lässt."

1) *karuṇayā* eig. „aus Mitleid", nämlich zu den (gleich ihm unerschaffenen) Seelen. Selbst das atheïstische Sāṃkhya lehrt, dass die „blinde" Natur nur zum Zweck der Erlösung sich den Seelen offenbare.

2) vgl. Kap. 8 No. 5 (S. 54), bes. Anm. 3.

Druck von G. Kreysing in Leipzig.

TIME AND ETERNITY IN BUDDHISM

by

Shoson Miyamoto

This essay consists of three main parts: linguistic, historical and textual.(1)

I. To introduce the theory of time in Buddhism, let us refer to the Sanskrit and Pāli words signifying "time". There are four of these: *samaya, kāla, kṣaṇa* (*khaṇa*) and *adhvan* (*addhan*). *Samaya* means a coming together, meeting, contract, agreement, opportunity, appointed time or proper time. *Kāla* means time in general, being employed in the term *kāla*-doctrine or *kāla-vāda*, which holds that time ripens or matures all things. In its special meaning kāla signifies appointed or suitable time. It may also mean meal-time or the time of death, since both of these are most critical and serious times in our lives. Death is expressed as *kāla-vata* in Pāli, that is "one has passed his late hour." *Kṣaṇa* also means a moment,

---

(1) The textual part is taken from the author's Doctoral Dissertation: Middle Way thought and Its Historical Development. which was submitted to the Imperial University of Tokyo in 1941 and published in 1944 (Kyoto: Hozokan). Material used here is from pp. 162–192. Originally this fromed the second part of „ Philosophical Studies of the Middle," which was delivered at the Annual Meeting of the Philosophical Society, Imperial University of Tokyo, in 1939 and published in the *Journal of Philosophical Studies* (Nos. 631, 632, 633). Since at that time there was no other essay published on the time concept in Buddhism, these earlier studies represented a new and original contribution by the author. Up to now, in fact, such texts as "The Time of the Sage," "The Pith and Essence" have survived untouched. The subject of "time and the Timeless" has been treated more recently by Dr. Ananda K. Coomaraswamy in his article "*Time and Eternity,*" (Ascona, Switzerland, 1942), pp. 40–41, and again in „ *Time and Eternity in Indian Thought*" by Professor Mircea Eliade of Chicago: the seventh essay in "*Man and Time*" (Eranos Jahrbuch, Bol- lingen Series, XXX, 1951), p. 191.

opportunity, or the moment of fulfillment of purpose. Finally, *adhvan* refers to a stretch or length of space or time. It may mean a road or journey in space and time past, present or future.

Thus, with the exception of *adhvan*, these terms signify the moment of time as something appointed or expected. They are to be compared with *kairos*, the time of purpose measured by quality,

It is quite usual in the history of religions to find the word "time" used in the sense of the moment of fullness of a realization or aim. Among these terms, however, it is the word *samaya*...coming together...which is most frequently employed in the Buddhist scriptures. For instance, almost all of the sutras begin with the words "*Evaṃ maya śrutam: ekasmin samaye Bhagavān Rājagṛhe viharati sma*...etc." In these introductory phrases, the four conditions...time, place, the master and his audience...are posited. The coming together of these four necessarily indicates an auspicious event which happens once for all in the long eons of sacred history. It is the appointed time for the accomplishment of the Bodhisattva's vow (*praṇidhāna*) or firm resolution and striving. which he attains through his untiring acts of meritorious conduct (*Bodhisattva-caryā*). From the standpoint of his audience, it is conceived as an opportunity which may be an "eternal once."

Among all of these kinds of appointed times and opportunities, the most important and auspicious one is the moment of Buddha's enlightenment under the Bodhi tree at Buddhagaya. This single moment of the Great Awakening (*ekakṣaṇābhisambodhi*) is the prototype after which all Buddhist sacred time is patterned. From the attainment of arhatship down to the *satori* of Zen and the single moment of the faith-experience of Shinran (1173-1262), there is no kind of religious time which is not centered upon this first great attainment of Nirvāṇa. This is also true of the Buddhist concept of eternity. Another application of this term *kṣaṇa*-moment is in speaking of the moment of the conversion of sinners.(2) For criminals this moment can be that in which the decisive act is committed which causes one to fall into damnation, but it can also mean the rare moment of one's emergence from hell after expiation and purification. A parable says:

> If there were a yoke with one hole in it floating in the ocean and borne about by the four winds, it would be easier for a one-eyed turtle rising to the surface once in a hundred years to put its head through the hole than for such a being to attain man's estate.

It is clear that this concept of *kṣaṇa*-moment has been accentuated in Buddhist theories of time. Moreover, this has led to the "theory of momentariness" (*kṣaṇika-vāda*) and also to the idea of continuity (*santāna*). The synthetic unification of *kṣaṇa*-momentariness and *santāna*-continuity has been accelerated by the philosophical studies of Adhidharma, completed by the Vijñāna-vāda, the School of Buddhist Idealism, and further developed in the time theory of Fa-tsang (643–712) in the Hua-yen school in China, synthesizing *sūnyatā* (emptiness) thought with the constructive idealist position.

II. The Buddhist view that all things are in a state of flux is well known. But few realize that there were two basically different schools of thought. On the one hand, Theravāda, representing the elders and conservative disciples, tended to be moralistic in practice and analytic in theory. They were called "Abhidharmists," which means scholars of the analytic study of Dharma. They contributed many psychological studies of the body, the mind, and of things and their relationships. But their observations of the details of structures, attributes and relationships were always bound up with a fundamental ethical viewpoint. Among the Abhidharmists, the Theravādins of the Pāli tradition and the Sarvāstivādins of the Sanskrit tradition were the most influential. The Sarvāstivādins' role was especially important

(2) The word *kaṣṇa* or "moment" means the minimal unit of time. But the "theory of momentariness" was a later term of the Abhidharmists, who imputed to *kṣaṇa* not only momentariness but also duration (*sthiti*) and continuity (*santāna*). It must be noted that even the Sarvāstivādins strictly held to the principle of the Middle Way as seen in the Mahāvibhāṣā (Vols. 8, 49, 199, 200), which has been referred to in the author's Middle Way Thought, pp. 298–346.

from the broader viewpoint of the history of Buddhist thought, because they carried out their scholarly achievements amid the attacks and counterattacks not only of many Buddhist achools, but also of several schools of Brahmanic and Non-Brahmanic thought on the continent of India. Moreover, being the largest and most widespread school, it split into many smaller currents of thought. At their headquarters in North India, they were called "orthodox" and "tradional," because the mountainous surroundings of Kashmir tended to keep them conservative. On the contrary, the Gandhāra group, situated along the East-West international highway, became more progressive and their way of thought was naturally quite tolerant and inclusive, as has been shown, for instance, by the examples of Greco-Gandhāra art of that area. The famous systematizers of the Vijñāna Idealist school of Mahāyāna Buddhism, the brothers Asaṅga and Vasubandhu, were reared and educated in this atmosphere and environment of Gandhāra.

The other main school, the Mahāsaṅghikas, representing a young and miscellaneous multitude, avowed claims of religious faith and devotion. To them Buddha was simply a supernatural figure and the Dharma was the Logos of cosmic unity. The Mahāyāna doctrines of *Buddha-kāya* and *Dharmta* had a close connection with these notions. These, then, were the two main opposing schools. The one centered upon the humanity of Buddha and the ethical and psychological analysis of Dharma, while the other tended to worship the mystical figure of Buddha in the way of faith.

One cannot fail to perceive this deep gulf which existed from the earliest phase. The Mahāsaṅghikas simply emphaized the "present" or "now" in life and ignored the past and future, but the conservative analysts evaluated every functional aspect of past, present and future while at the same time substantiating continuity. The contrast was that of direct, intuitive knowledge on the one hand and of discursive on the other.

Now I should like to trace briefly the highlights of the various theories concerning time. First of all, Buddhists opposed the eternalist school, the Kālavādins, who insisted upon absolute time as the first cause and creation of everything, and they also opposed the ideological theories of permanence (*nitya*) and self (*ātman*) of ego-centric Aryan nationalism along with the upper-class ritualistic formalism of the Brahmans.[3] The Buddhist situation can be likened to that of a certain critic who emphasizes the opposing notions, since they hinted at the new ideas of impermanence (*anitya*) and egolessness (*anātman*). This kind of negativistic innovation can be seen as an outgrowth of the times, for with the deeper penetration of Aryan colonization into the heart of India the needs of an ever expanding frontier had to be met. These negative but novel theories shattered the ideology of a closed society and opened the vista of religious truth to the oppressed and underprivileged multitudes. Thus arose a new Aryan universalism including all classes of men and becoming the solid basis of Buddhism as a universal religion. It was out of this same need that the Middle Way principle appeared for the first time in Buddhism.

The time theory of early or primitive Buddhism is identical with that of the Mahāsaṅghikas noted earlier, that is, "the past and future are without existence; the present is the real existent." The analytic Sarvāstivādins (everything-exists-school), however, developed also a realism which held that the self exists (*svabhāva*). Subsequently, they elaborated a theory of the simultaneous formation of past, present and future.[4] Even among the Sarvāstivādins, scholars are found to differ with each other on the discrimination of the present, past and future. Traditionally, it has been said that among the different theories, Vasumitra's condition or situation theory is (*avasthā*) correct. He likens the three kinds of time to three

(3) The Kālavādins' theory is mentioned as the seventeenth of twenty in the Āryadeva's Nirvāna-theories of Hinayāna and other Indian Schools (Nanjio 1260, Taisho 32). See also Louis de la Vallée Poussin, Prasannapadā, 1913, p. 386; Prof. Kenkyo Fuji of Niigata University, "*Time Theory of Nāgārjuna*" (Annual Report of Nihon Butsugakuin, 1940), pp. 182–189; Ananda K. Coomaraswamy, "*Time and Eternity,*" *op. cit.*, 1942, p. 15; Etienne Lamotte, Le Traité de la grande vertu de sagesse de Nāgārjuna (Louvain, 1944), Book I, pp. 76 ff.; Prof. H. Nakamura, Unversity of Tokyo, Early Vedānta Philosophy (Tokyo, 1950), pp. 222–223.

(4) The three periods of time (past, present and future) are called *trayo 'dhvānaḥ* or *tayo addhā*. Nāgārjuna's criticism on time was also based upon this *adhvan*-time.

straws in a lottery or drawing (*vartika, gulika*). The difference is merely one of position or situation, as being put in the "situation of one, of ten, or of a hundred." Vasubandhu, the most representative scholar of Vijñānavāda, enumerated four theories of time.(5) 1) Dharmatrāta says that past, present and future are differentiated by their appearance or existing nature (*bhāva-anyathātva*). But their substane (*dravya*) remains the same, just as a golden vase may change its form Through the process of melting and remolding. Their shapes or appearances may differ from each other, but the substance of *goldness* is always kept as gold. 2) Ghoṣaka says that past, present and future are differentiated by their character (*lakṣaṇānyathātva*). When a thing is united with the character of the past, it is the past, and in like manner, that which is united with the character of the present, and of the future, future. 3) Vasumitra's theory was given above. 4) Buddhadeva says times are differentiated according to their relationships (*anyonyathātva,apeksa*) just as a woman is called "mother" by her child and "daughter" by her parent.

Nāgārjuna, the most representative thinker of early Mahāyana Buddhism and the author of the famous "Verses on the Middle" or Madhyamaka-kārikā, synthesizing two opposing theories by the Middle Way principle, wrote in the nineteenth chapter of his *Criticism on Time* (*Kālaparīkṣa*) as follows:

(1) If because of the past there are future and present,
then future and present must be in the past.

(2) If within the past there were neither future nor present,
then of future and present
How are they caused by the past?

(3) Independent of the past there is no future
nor any present,
therefore these two periods do not. exist.

---

(5) For the four great masters on time among the Sarvāstivādins see: *Mahavibhaṣa*, Vol. 75; S. Miyamoto, Mahāyāna and Hinayāna (Tokyo, 1944), p.21; L. de la Vallée Poussin, L'Abhidharmakośa de Vasubandhu, V, pp. 52–54, 1925.

(4) Because such is the case, we know that the two other periods
and above, between, below, unity, difference...
all such states as these have no existence.

(5) Time standing still cannot be had, and time cannot be had.
If time cannot be had how can one teach time's qualities?

(6) *Because of things there is time,*
Apart from things how can time be?
Even things do not exist,
How much less can time exist?

Nāgārjuna agreed with the Sarvāstivādins' denial of the existence of time, but opposed their concept of entity-realism (*svabhāvavāda*). He drew the conclusion of the non-existence of time from the Madhyamaka standpoint of non-substantiality (*niḥsvabhāvavāda*), which was a restatement of the original Buddhist teaching of non-self.

In the course of time a reaction arose to offset the non-subjectivity among the traditional schools in North India. Diverging streams of thought gradually took shape and even opposing ideas and theories were integrated into a system. The full flowering of this tendency is found in the Vijñāna-vāda, the school of so-called Buddhist Idealism. Its adherents were quite proud of their new theory of the "Vijñāna Middle Way." They criticized the Mādhyamika view of non-substantiantiality and the Prajñāpāramitā teaching on emptiness as the other extreme of the Abhidharma concept of entity-realism. This was a most interesting situation, but a most subtle and delicate affair. First of all, we recall that the Gautama's enlightenment was based upon the Middle way principle. Thus it has been said that whatever Buddha taught was always in the light of this principle. With the rise of Mahāyāna, there appeared the Middle May school (Mādhyamika) of Nāgārjuna, and now, as the final culmination of Indian Mahāyāna Buddhism, the Vijñāna-vāda arises, stating. "Ours is the latest theory, the third sermon, supplementing not only the Buddha's first sermon, but also the second sermon of the Prajñāpārmitā-sūtra and that of Nāgārjuna." While these claims may appear to be antagonistic to each other, one thing is quite clear: *all of these schools claim to be based upon the Middle Way principle.*

The Vijñānavādins, setting up time as a category, and adapting the causation theory of *bīja* or seed, differentiate the present from the past and future. It was really they who conceived of time not only in its momentariness (*kṣaṇika*), but also in its continuity (*santāna*). Fa-tsang, the systematizer of Hua-yen philosophy, synthesized Mādhyamika's Fourfold propositions or *catuḥkoṭikas* and Eight Noes or *aṣṭaviśeṣaṇa-pratiṣedhāḥ*: fourfold non-duality, and the Vijñānavādins' six qualities of seed: 1) momentariness, 2) simultaneous existence with the effect, 3) continuity in flux, 4) determined transmission of moral characteristics, 5) dependence on multiple conditions, 6) fruition of its own effect, in the doctrine of "six qualities of interdependent causation."(6) Hua-yen philosophy centered upon the actuality of a singleness of mind in which the cosmic and creative structure of being and non-being are integrated, and also elaborated on the conventional time divisions by making past, present and future each a threefold category, thus making nine. Since each one of these nine is interdependent with each of the others and since all of them interpenetrate, these nine functions are generalized into one single instant of actuality, resulting in the composition of ten kinds of time altogether. Fa-tsang proposed this so-called "Doctrine of the ten mysteries of harmonious interdependence," expounding thereby his time concept in the theory of "simultaneous appearance in completeness" and in that of "differential formation in the multiple dimensions of ten ages," on the basis of interdependent causation and cosmic unity.(7)

III. Now let us turn to a very old passage which reveals the Buddha's insight into time. It is found in a text called *The Sage of Time*, or

(6) "Yüan-chi yin-mên liu-i fa" (Engi inmon rokugi hō), in Wu-chiang chang (*Gokyō shō*) (Nanjio 1591, Taisho 45, pp. 502–03). S.Miyamoto, Ultimate Middle and Voidness (Tokyo, 1943), pp. 577–583. The author presents in the form of a table and diagram the theoretical development of the synthesis of opposing ideas such as momentariness and continuity, voidness and self-existence, cause and conditions, etc.

haddekaratta (literally, the night of the sage), in the Middle Discourses f the Buddha (Nos. 131~134, M. N.), with equivalents in both Chinese gamas and Pāli Nikāyas:

Do not chase after the past; do not seek for the future.
The past is already no more; the future is not yet.
And see the elements of present in every place,
Without attachment, without moving......yet clearly see and strive in the present.
Do earnestly the task for today; who knows the nearness of death on the morrow?
Truly who can say he will not meet the great army of death?
Such a man of realization, earnestly striving day and night without indolence,
He, surely, is the sage of time, the peaceful one, the steady one.[8]

This Time of the Sage is the realization of the oneness of man with e absolute or Dharma in which one brings his entire being into the stant of the *real present* and strives toward utter selflessness and conse- ent gratefulness to all of life. It is the basis of religious practice and ads to wisdom, enlightenment, and Nirvāṇa.

In one of the scriptures of Jātaka (Hatthipāla, Jātaka, No. 509), there related the incident of Gopāla, who aspired to become a disciple of the

---

7) "Shih hsüan yüan-chi wu-ai fa" (Jū gen engi muge hō) in Wu-chiang chang, *op. cit.* J. Takakusu, The Essentials of Buddhist Philosophy (1947), pp. 120–121, translates as follows: "The theory of co-relation, in which all things have co-existence and simultaneous rise," and "The theory of variously completing ten time-periods creating one entity." Dr.Fung Yu-lan, History of Chinese Philosophy (1953), pp. 349–355, renders these as: "The theory of simultaneous completeness" (*Tung-shih chü-tsu hsiang-yin mên, Dōji gusoku soō mon*), and "The theory of the variable formation of the ten ages" (*Shih-shih chieh-fa i-chang mên, Jisse kakuhō ijō mon*). Mr. Taitetsu Unno has recently sent me his translations of the same terms, as follows: "The theory of simultaneous, co-existent correspondence" and "the theory of disjunctive formation of elements separated in ten time-worlds."

8) Compare Lord Chalmers' translation in Further Dialogues of the Buddha, ed. by Mrs. Rhys Davids, (London: Humphrey Milford, 1927), Vol. II, p. 261.

Buddha. But the King would not hear of this, and urged him to succeed to the crown, Gopāla answers the King: "Oh King, do not speak of tomorrow of things that can be done today. The good must be performed this very day." Gopāla continues, reciting some verses from *The Time of the Sage*:

People idly pass the days, saying:
  Tomorrow I will, the next time I will.
But alas, these thoughts never come again.
  Knowing that they fail to come again,
When good thoughts arise,
  Who among the sages would throw them away?

Shinran (1173~1262), founder of the Shin sect, when ready to take the vow of celibacy at the age of nine, was asked to postpone his initiation ceremony until the following day. He answered:

Like cherry blossoms are the hearts
  That tomorrow think they might
For who can tell but there might be
  A tempest in the night?

A Japanese Zen master, Shoju-Rājin, in his poetic saying, *The One-Day Living of the Sage*, wrote:

Just think of present things,
The past cannot return,
Tomorrow is hidden from us.

Expanding this in his diary, he wrote: "The *most important fact* refers to the heart of the now on this very day. There is no tomorrow for him who neglects this fact. People usually think of the future and make plans, but are unaware of the *exact stroke of the present* (literally, 'hit-target-now')." Not to lose the "*exact stroke of the present*" means to live without being shackled to the present, possessing steadiness and equilibrium.

The *Mahā-sāropama-sutta* (29, M. M.), which includes the *Bhaddekaratta*, or *Time of the Sage*, explains the famous parable of the *Pith* of the Tree. This parable relates how man, originally seeking the pith or core (*sāra*) of the tree, loses sight of his primary objective and becomes attached to the branches and leaves and becomes wrongly shackled to the bark. This is used to trace the path of the disciple who enters the Buddhist Sangha with a fervent aspiration for truth, but after practicing the disciplines and gaining some recognition, drifts into indolence, saying, "I have gained merit, I have become famous, the other disciples are not famous and their powers are insignificant." The Buddha says:

> Monks, it is like a man walking about aiming at the pith, seeking for the pith, looking about for the pith of a great, stable and pithy tree, who passes by the pith itself, passes by the softwood, passes by the bark, passes by the young shoots, and who, having cut down the branches and foliage, might go amay taking them with him and thinking they were the pith.(9)

Even those who are not taken by worldly recognition are equally to be censured. They are proud of their observance of the precepts, saying, "I have observed the precepts. I am a good man. Those priests violated the precepts. They are bad men." This is like mistaking the bark for the pith of the tree. It is only a little better than those who mistake the branches for the pith. The gist of this is the essence of the sutta, *The Night of the Sage*. It says, "Do not be taken by frivolities, but grasp the heart of the matter."

Why is this analysis of time stressed? The Pāli scriptures teach that one must realize enlighenment in the real and immediate present by selflessness and non-attachment. In the suttas it states:

> And what is the reason (for the analysis of time)? The verses of *Bhaddekaratta* say: there is meaning, there is truth, and these become the basis for religious practice. This leads to wisdom, to enlightenment, to Nirvāṇa.

The reason for the stress on the analysis of time is identical with the

(9) Translated by I. B. Horner in The Collection of Middle Length Sayings (London: Luzac and Co., Ltd., 1954. Published for the Pali Text Society), Vol. I, p. 238.

'reason for the stress on the Middle Way theory in the first sermon of Buddha, the Sutta on the Turning of the Wheel of Dharma, and the Ten or Fourteen Indefinites (*avyākata*).

In a sutta in the Anguttara Nikāya there is a explanation to the effect that the past is one extreme, the future is another extreme and the present is the " middle ". (*majjhe, vemajjhe*)' In the *Suttanipāta*, also, this " middle " is applied to the present.

The present is the "middle" between the end-limit (*pubbe ante*) of the past and the beginning-limit (*pacchā*) of the future. The analysis of time is to be free of attachments to these two extremes and yet remain free from attachment to the present.

The two negations of the past and future comprise the analytic method of the Middle Way. It denies the two extremes. The steadiness in the present is the Middle Way analysis applied to itself. Thus, in the analysis of time the spirit of the Middle Way operates. Analysis analyzes the extremes and also itself. Analysis must be " analysis of non-analysis " to be true analysis, and this is identical to the idea that true middle is a non-middle. The theory of the Middle applied spatially is Nirvāṇa, and applied in terms of time is timeless time.

It is interesting to note that although Sakyamuni Buddha was said to have been cognizant of past and future existences, he gave the following advice to Sakuludayi, who was attached to past and future:

> However, Sakuludayi, set aside thoughts of the past; set aside thoughts of the future. I will teach you the truth: this being, that becomes; from the arising of this, that arises; this not becoming, that does not become; from the ceasing of this, that ceases.

Thus he stresses the importance of the standpoint of dharma based upon conditional origination and the insight into the present. Sakyamuni constantly taught the clear and right view of life based upon conditional origination and the necessity of practice based upon this insight. He taught:

> Dharma is a reality of the present, a timeless reality, a reality which openly says come and see; it leads to Nirvāṇa, it is self-evi-

dent to the wise.

This same passage is repeated with reference to Nirvāṇa.

The Buddha, being identified with the Dharma and Nirvāṇa, is non-composite (*asamkhata*), beyond time (*akāliko*, timeless), transcends the aeons (*kappātito vippamutto*) and is not a man of aeons (*akkapiyo*). He is to be in time and samsāra, yet goes beyond time and samsāra.

From the hedonistic standpoint sensual pleasures are the most immediate reality, and such things as ideals and self-improvements are time-consuming. But for those who are intent upon self-improvement and whose thoughts are upon the transiency of life, the standpoint of Dharma is the immediate reality and the pursuit of sensual pleasures is the pursuit of evanescent time.

These two extremes apply to the priesthood and the layman; in the case of Sakyamuni he realized a now guiding spirit in the ideal of a Middle Way between the extremes of courtly luxury and ascetic self-mortification. In the Ágamas the priesthood is considered the second extreme and is related to the third which is the Middle Way principle, and in Mahāyāna the two extremes are negated and the new ideal of Middle Way is advocated.

These two standpoints are interestingly contrasted in a sutta in the Samyutta Nikāya. When the disciple Samiddhi had finished bathing in the hot spring of Rājagaha and was drying himself, a *deva* illuminated the grove of the spring with brilliant light and approached Samiddhi. He spoke in verse to him:

> O bhikku, you beg for alms without enjoying life,
> And while enjoying life you do not beg for alms.
> O bhikku, beg for alms while enjoying life.
> Do not let time pass you by.

And then Samiddhi answers:

> I do not know about your time.
> Time is hidden and it does not appear.
> Therefore I beg for alms without enjoying life.

Time will not pass me by.

At that time the *deva* came down to earth and said;

O bhikku, you renounced the world when very young,

When possessing virility, black hair and youth filled with happiness,

You did not enjoy the pleasures in the first period of life.

O bhikku, enjoy the pleasures of life,

Do not pursue that which extends over time

By throwing away the immediate reality.

And Samiddhi answers;

O friend, I do not throw away the immediate reality and pursue that which extends over time.

O friend, I throw away that which extends over time and pursue the immediate reality.

For, O friend, "Pleasures extend over time, there is much suffering, much pain, and torments increase evermore,

But this Dharma is immediate reality, not extending over time.

It invites you to come and see; it leads to Nirvāṇa, self-evident to the wise man."

Thus the Lord teaches.

The two standpoints in this Samiddhi-sutta are contrasted in another sutta in the *Samyutta* by the voice of *Mara*, the Tempter, enticing a bhikku on the one hand and the figure of a bhikkhu practicing asceticism on the other.

The following selections from the *Suttanipāta* all express the immediate reality which transcends time:

The "Saint" has washed away
all evil, inly bred
or from without; no more
he'll enter time.. like gods
and men, the brood of time. (3. 6. 511)

....

Who outgrows time...to come

or past...by purity
and insight, with Release
from all that springs from sense. (2. 13. 373)

....

Grasping not, grudging not, the saint unmoved
to "high" or "low" or "equal" lays no claim;
timeless, he whirls down grooves of time no more' (4. 10. 860)[10]

Thus it is clear that he who does not chase after the past, pursue the future, or who is not captured by the present and yet perceives clearly the Dharma in the present, truly sees the Buddha.

To prerceive the Dharma in the immediate present and to see the Buddha means to live in the Eternal Now, theTimeless Time. It is what the Zen people refer to as "the ordinary mind is the Way." In the wri. tings of Shinshu this is expressed as: "In Buddhism there is no such thing called tomorrow. You must hurry, hurry the matters concerning the teachings of the Buddha."

Dogen (1200～1253), the founder of Soto Zen, refers to the "present now" in his *Essay on Time* (*Uji*): "Time is not merely transitory. It dwells in its own situation. Time itself does not flow. It looks as if it is over there, but it is now......This is continuity." "Working freely in a manner proper to your own situation...that is your personal time."[11]

In conclusion I would like to say just a few words about my quite obvious omission of any discussion of the subject of eternity in this paper. In Buddhist thought the concept of eternity is closely associated with Nirvāṇa. Moreover, the Buddha declared that silence is more appropriate to the subject of eternity than much talking. One cannot speak of eternity as being relative to time, nor can it be discussed as a subject in itself. Eternity is neither a prolongation of time nor a quantitative concept, but one

---

(10) Page and verse references are to Lord Chalmers, Buddha's Teachings. Vol. XXXVII in the Harvard Oriental Series, ed. C. R. Lanman. Cambridge, Massachusetts: Harvard University Press, 1932.

(11) Dogen's essay on time: see Prof. Reiho Masunaga, The Sōtō Approach to Zen (Tokyo, 1958), pp. 81–90.

which is qualitative. It is approached through Nirvāṇa or through the doctrine of Buddha-kāya. While these are central concepts in Buddhism, they would require much more space for adequate treatment than the scope of this paper allows.

I have also omitted for some of the same reasons a discussion of time in the sense of "chronos"...historical time. History in Buddhist thought is to be conceived as a life history, and model for this kind of time is the Buddha's own life, including his birth, enlightenment, preaching and death. These four events are commemorated in sacred monuments and by pilgrimages of Buddhists everywhere. It is in relation to the Buddha's life history that each individual sees the importance of his own life history. In like manner, as Buddha went from his ascetic life out into the world to preach and teach, so the individual finds his own life meaningful by associating with others in ethical and religious practices. The stupas, inscriptions, sculptured images, and many historical and geographical records of pilgrimages serve to remind him of the one whom he follows and also serve as our clues to the events in the Buddha's own life.

As for the measurement of time as...western time is based upon the units of the second, minute, hour, etc....Buddhist time has for its basic unit the *kṣaṇa*, which equals to one-seventy-fifth of a second,[12] but I am glad to leave this to the scientists to explain.

** This essay was delivered at a panel discussion on the topic "Doctrines of Time and Eternity" held at the Annual Meeting of the National Association of Biblical Instructors at the Union Theological Seminary in New York on Monday, December 29, 1958, "The Hindu Viewpoint" was presented by Swami Akhilananda of The Ramakrishna Vedanta Society; "The Biblical Viewpoint" was presented by Professor Edmund Perry of Northwestern University: and "The Buddhist Viewpoint" was presented by Professor Shoson Miyamoto, visiting professor at th University of Chicago.

(12) 120 *kṣaṇaṣ* = 1 *tatkṣaṇa*; 60 *tatkṣaṇas* = 1 *lava*; 30 *lavas* = 1 *muhurta*; 30 *muhurta* = 1 *ahorātra* (day and night, 24 hours, 648,000 *kṣaṇas*). A *kṣaṇa* equals $\frac{1 \text{ second.}}{75}$

NO TIME, GREAT TIME AND PROFANE TIME IN BUDDHISM

This essay maintains that some important Buddhist texts contribute to a neat formulation of man's most treasured modes of thought: No Time as the source of religion, Great Time as the source of myth, and Profane Time as the source of reason. These three forms of Time are not so named in the Buddhist works. The limitation of data to Indo-Tibetan materials makes possible the addition of an expression "No Time" to the two categories "Great Time" and "Profane Time" utilized by Eliade for worldwide cultural materials, while he marshals the evidence and terminology that facilitate the integration of Eastern and Western spirit.[1] Eliade's ontological interpretation of such modes is well known. The present writer is not thereby released from the obligation to rework the available data according to his understanding of Buddhism. Then—to anticipate the development—without asserting any ontological status for such modes elsewhere in the world, it does appear that in the Buddhist case, in the Indian context, the three modes of thought allude to three modes of being.

There is no claim to involve all of Buddhism in this treatment, although the prevalent Buddhist genesis legend, already studied, will play a significant role.[2] The metaphysical discussion stems

[1]Among the works of Mircea Eliade, the following have been especially important to this paper: *Myths, Dreams and Mysteries* (London, 1960); *The Sacred and the Profane* (New York, 1961).

[2]Alex Wayman, "Buddhist Genesis and the Tantric Tradition," *Oriens Extremus*, 9 (1962): 127-31. The essay also appears in A. Wayman, *Buddhist Tantras* (Samuvel Weiser, New York 1973).

from one celebrated text of Mahāyāna Buddhism—the work called *Madhyānta-vibhāga* which Asaṅga (*ca.* 375-430 A.D.) is held by tradition to have received from the future Buddha Maitreya in the Tuṣitā (a heaven).[3] Asaṅga, a leading exponent of Yogācāra Buddhism, might be the author of the *Madhyānta-vibhāga*, upon which his younger brother (probably half-brother) Vasubandhu wrote a commentary.[4]

Religion, Myth, and Reason in Buddhism

Although the origins of Buddhism have not been fully explained in regard to such modes as "religion," "myth," and "reason," there is little doubt that in its subsequent development, well advanced in the early centuries B.C., Buddhism possessed all these categories of thought.

At the heart of its religion, Mahāyāna Buddhism places the Buddha himself with the body of omniscience called the Dharmakāya ("outside the three worlds"), and adds the two phenomenal bodies called Saṃbhoga-kāya ("at the top of the realm of form") and Nirmāṇa-kāya ("in the realm of desire"). Voidness (*śūnyatā*) means the annihilation of corrupting influences of man's nature, leaving unvoided the Buddha natures. The laws (*dharma*) stem from the void realm of nature (*dharmadhātu*).

Myth in Buddhism includes not only the important genesis legend and the mythical portion of the Buddha's legendary life, but also the extensive literature called the Jātakas ("birth stories"), explained as the illustrious births of the Buddha in his anterior incarnations as a *bodhisattva*, a being striving toward enlightenment while exhibiting exemplary conduct to assist other beings.

The reasoning side of Buddhism played an outstanding role, as the antagonist, in the development of the traditional Hindu schools of philosophy. So well developed is this side of Buddhism that

[3]Alex Wayman, *Analysis of the Śrāvakabhūmi Manuscript* (Berkeley and Los Angeles, 1961), pp. 33-34.

[4]Gadjin M. Nagao, ed., *Madhyāntavibhāga-bhāṣya* (Tokyo, 1964). See also the salient work: Th. Stcherbatsky, *Madhyānta-Vibhanga* ("Discourse on Discrimination between Middle and Extremes"), ascribed to Bodhisattva Maitreya and commented on by Vasubandhu and Sthiramati, translated from the Sanskrit (*Bibliotheca Buddhica*, vol. 30 [Leningrad, 1936]; only the first chapter, with commentary and subcommentary, has been translated herein).

some early Western Orientalists considered Buddhism to be pre-eminently rational.

Creation According to the Madhyānta Vibhāga

Before setting forth the intended structure of three modes of thought, I shall separately treat the rather technical data of the *Madhyānta-vibhāga*, which not only contributes decisively to the present topic but also conveys a rather different picture of the Yogācāra from the way the latter is depicted in current surveys of Indian philosophy.

The *two realities* of the Yogācāra metaphysics are called *abhūta-parikalpa* and *śūnyatā*, here translated respectively as the "Imagination of Unreality" and "Voidness," compatible with Stcherbatsky's respective renditions, the "Universal Constructor of Phenomena" and the "Absolute." The *Madhyānta-vibhāga* states (I, 1):

There was the Imagination of Unreality,
And in it no duality (of subject and object).
There was Voidness in it,
And it was in that (Voidness).[5]

Of the reality called "Imagination of Unreality," what is the "Unreality" (*abhūta*) and what the "Imagination" (*parikalpa*)? The text states (I, 5): "What is imagined is explained as the 'objective thing' (*artha*); what is dependent, as the construction process of unreality; and what is perfect, as the unreality of both (subject and object)."[6] And from the text (I, 3) and Vasubandhu's commentary, we learn that the "Imagination" has its own four characters (*svalakṣaṇa*), called "objective thing" (*artha*), "personal organ" (*sattva*), "self" (*ātman*), and "representation" (*vijñapti*):

Perception was engendered as the projection of (six kinds of) objective things, (five) personal organs, self (=mind), and (six kinds of) representations. The objective thing does not

[5]abhūta-parikalpo 'sti dvayan tatra na vidyate /
śūnyatā vidyate tv atra tasyām api sa vidyate //
[6]kalpitaḥ paratantraś ca pariniṣpanna eva ca /
arthād abhūtakalpāc ca dvayābhāvāc ca deśitaḥ //

belong to it (i.e., perception). Since the former (the objective thing) is unreal, the latter (perception) is also unreal.[7]

The implication is that when the Imagination of Unreality is not so imagining, its four characters are not grouped in subject-object relation, and that when it is so imagining, the "self" approaches the "personal organ," whereupon the "representation" falsely depicts the "objective thing." As with all such ultimate processes, the *modus operandi* of the primordial subject-object emergence is wrapped in mystery. However, it seems to involve an interaction of the "self" and the "personal organ" with Voidness as Dharmadhātu ("realm of Dharma"), which is the material cause.[8]

The reality called "Voidness" has this character (I, 13*a-b*): "the unreality of both (subject and object), and the reality (subjacent) of this unreality."[9] This translation, following Stcherbatsky, is consistent with Yogācāra definitions in other works as typified by two statements, one of which specifies what is voided and the other of which specifies what remains not voided. The following verse (I, 14) clarifies the sense of the "reality (subjacent) of this unreality" by names of Voidness, justified in the next verse (I, 15):

> Thusness (*tathatā*) because not otherwise, True Limit (*bhūtakoṭi*) because not wrong, Attributeless (*animitta*) because the cessation of attributes, Ultimate State (*paramārthatā*) because the domain of the noble ones, the Realm of Dharma (*dharmadhātu*) because having the noble natures (*dharma*).

Verses I, 8-9 and Vasubandhu's commentary portray the Ima-

[7]artha-satvātma-vijñapti-pratibhāsaṃ prajāyate /
vijñānaṃ nāsti cāsyārthas tad-abhāvāt tad apy asat //
Vasubandhu's commentary (Nagao, *Madhyāntavibhāga-bhāṣya*, pp. 18-19) clarifies the word "self" (*ātman*) as the "corrupted mind" (*kliṣṭamanas*) and the six things as objects grasped by the six sense organs (five by the word *sattva*), including mind as the sixth, in terms of six representations (*vijñapti*).

[8]Such an idea is found near the beginning of Asaṅga's *Śrāvakabhūmi*, in a passage for which original Sanskrit is lacking; here it is translated from Tibetan (Derge edition of Tanjur, *Sems tsam*, *Śrāvakabhūmi*, 2b): "However, that seed does not have the characteristics of difference so long as it stays apart from the six sense bases (*ṣaḍāyatana*). That seed has been handed down in lineage from beginningless time and has states obtained through the six sense bases which are attained by means of 'true nature' (*dharmatā*)."

[9]dvayābhāvo hy abhāvasya bhāvaḥ śūnyasya lakṣaṇam.

gination of Unreality in a new role. Since its own characters (*svalakṣaṇa*) had projected the unreal perception, the younger Imagination of Unreality is now precisely that unreal perception of the unreal objective thing:

> Now the Imagination of Unreality was consciousness (of) and mentals, composing the three realms (of desire, of form, and formless). Perception (="consciousness of") sees the objective thing itself; its mentals see modifications of the objective thing. The first one is the foundation-perception (=*ālaya-vijñāna*). The other ones pertain to experience. These are the mentals (namely, feelings, *vedanā*) which enjoy, (ideas, *saṃjñā*) which distinguish, and (motivations, *saṃskāra*) which activate (perception).[10]

That passage covers two stages of the process which the present essay intends to keep separate. They are "consciousness of," which sees the objective thing itself, and mentals, which see modifications of the thing. They are preceded by the atemporal state in which the Imagination of Unreality abides with Voidness deprived of the subject-object relationship.

No Time, the Source of Religion

No Time means the revelation of reality, everywhere, always. Man may or may not intuit the dazzling ultimate. It is *other* than Great Time when nature predicts by omens and man obeys. It is *other* than Profane Time when man predicts by reason and nature obeys.

The story of Buddhist genesis alludes to a mode of being prevailing as "men of the first eon" while the lower receptacle worlds are reevolving after the periodic destruction. These men have bodies made of mind, are self-luminous, feed on joy, and are wherever they wish to be. Their actions have immediate fruition, and so involve No Time.[11]

In the *Madhyānta-vibhāga*, No Time is the mysterious truth of a voidness reality subjacent to the unreality of subject and

[10]abhūtaparikalpaś ca citta-caittās tridhātukāḥ /
tatrārtha-dṛṣṭir vijñānaṃ tad-viśeṣe tu caitasāḥ //
ekam pratyaya-vijñānaṃ dvitīyam aupabhogikaṃ /
upabhoga-pariccheda-prerakās tatra caitasāḥ //

[11]Wayman, "Buddhist Genesis."

object—a reality neither joined to nor separate from the creative center called Imagination of Unreality. This Voidness is the goal to which the noble ones (the elect) aspire, because it has the noble natures, called in other Buddhist texts the "Buddha natures" (*buddhadharma*).

Generally, Buddhist texts referred to this state as Nirvāṇa, more properly "Nirvāṇa without remainder." "Nirvāṇa with remainder" is approximately Great Time. The Mahāyāna "Nirvāṇa without fixed abode" (*apratiṣṭhita-nirvāṇa*) is all three Times.

GREAT TIME, THE SOURCE OF MYTH

Great Time is the marvelous beginning of time in the sense of an interval not always progressing in a continuous line, as does Profane Time, which has an anterior past, a present moment, and a posterior future. The interval of time is colored by a glorious quality, because then is the contact with earth by the hero, walking with erect stature. His fabulous and exemplary adventures need only be recounted in myth to inspire the imagination, and possibly also the conduct of men in later Profane Time, especially men who are close to the soil. The myth of the Buddha's life also begins with this walking, as the child leaves his mother's womb by the right side, takes seven steps toward the north, and announces, "I am at the top of the world. . ."[12] The future Buddha's seven steps are (No Time in) Great Time; his announcement is (No Time in) Profane Time.

> All those examples point to the touching of earth as constituting a symbolic moment which we could call Moment 1, as the preliminary moment to mundane life (in case of infant), to spiritual life (in case of Buddha), to the symbolization of the spiritual life (in case of main body of the rite), to acceptance in marriage (in case of the auspicious bride). At Moment 1, the being is not yet alive, but anticipates the whole future life. Astrologically, at the moment of birth the infant is at the center of the universe, in sympathetic communion with the planets and stars, which indelibly impress the being with a sort of centripetal force.[13]

[12]Cf. Eliade, *Myths, Dreams and Mysteries*, pp. 110-15.

[13]Alex Wayman, "Climactic Times in Indian Mythology and Religion," *History of Religions*, 4 (1965): 310-11.

This place where earth is touched is the Center, of which Eliade frequently speaks.

In the Buddhist story of genesis, on the surface of earth there appeared an earth essence—in the Tantric version called an ambrosia (*amṛta*)—which a greedy being tasted with his finger and then ate mouthfuls of. Other beings followed suit. Thus they became dependent on subtle morsel food and no longer fed on joy. They gradually lost the body made of mind as their bodies became heavier and more substantial. The ones who indulged least proudly retained their beautiful form. The sun, moon, and year became known. Hell beings, beings in the embryonic states, and the gods involved with desire (*kāmāvacāradeva*) still have the subtle kind of food which does not give rise to excrement or urine.[14]

According to the *Madhyānta-vibhāga*, in the beginning the world became inner-outer, or subject-object. That is to say, what was always there in No Time continued just the same. But an imaginary relationship was introduced among the four characters, semi-divine beings as it were, of the Imagination of Unreality. Perhaps in a magic square they projected their own being through Voidness into an Imagination of Unreality the younger. This is first the foundation perception called "basic perception" (*ālaya-vijñāna*) which has as object the objective thing itself. Since as yet there are no modifications (*viśeṣa*) of the objective thing, there is no error (*bhrānti*) or specific illusion. Nevertheless, the objective thing is said to be unreal. The unreality here is the cosmic illusion, the beginning of downfall. The fascinating objective thing conceals in its very freshness the specific illusion that is sure to follow in a subsequent remove of Profane Time. From the beginning, the world was pervaded by delusion (*moha*). It is as the Buddha tells: all constructed things (*saṃskāra*) are suffering. In Great Time, the suffering is of transformation.

Profane Time, the Source of Reason

This is horizontality. Man has nature down where it can be handled. But he believes that his inner knowledge stems from outer happenings. Time now, according to Lévy-Bruhl, is what

[14]Wayman, "Buddhist Genesis."

"our" minds—the minds of us, the "civilized"—take it to be. In his graphic words:

> extending indefinitely in imagination, something like a straight line, always homogeneous by nature, upon which events fall into position, a line on which foresight can arrange them in an unilinear and irreversible series, and on which they must of necessity occur one after the other.[15]

As long as man lives a profane life, his best guide is reason, which is limited and superficial, accompanied by the latest "laws of thought." The remarkable achievements of science fall here. Profane existence proves itself by accumulations such as merchandise and books (religious and secular), and also by desacralized leavings or residues. It is "the rest of life" after Moment 1.

In Buddhist genesis, the beings began to subsist on coarse morsel food, which gave rise to excrement and urine. The distinguishing characteristics of male and female arose, along with sexual desire and relevant acts. Then the idea of "private property" arose with individual rice plots, followed by stealing and consequent violence. Those beings elected a "great chosen one" (*mahāsammata*) to provide security.[16] This shows the emergence of lust and hatred, then private property and the status of ruler and ruled.

The *Madhyānta-vibhāga* alludes to this state of being by "mentals" seeing the modifications of the objective thing. These mentals pertain to experience, and are feelings, ideas, and motivations. They are also called the "evolving perceptions" (*pravṛtti-vijñāna*). This state is full-blown illusion.

Recapitulations

It is a basic feature of Eliade's writings that he denies a purely profane existence. The homogeneity of profane space is interrupted by certain "holy places" dear to the memory of even the profane nonreligious man.[17] While Eliade has not defined the profane life in the terms I have employed above, I see no conflict with his position on this matter. I can therefore go on to agree

[15]Lucien Lévy-Bruhl, *Primitive Mentality* (Boston, 1966), p. 123.
[16]Wayman, "Buddhist Genesis."
[17]So in Eliade, *The Sacred and the Profane*.

with him on this denial of the pure profane. There is no need to repeat here his well-presented justifications. My methods of demonstrating this conclusion are additional. Here there are two kinds of recapitulation—that of childhood and that of the daily life of man.

The Recapitulation in Childhood

In a brief communication[18] I called attention to the Indian theory of life stages, of which the first three are in point now. They are the first year of life under the Moon, the second and third years under Mars, and the fourth through twelfth under Mercury. In the first year—as modern child development study shows—the baby begins with no distinction between himself and his environment, and so is akin to the nondual state of No Time, from which he gradually emerges during the balance of the year. Recently emerged from the primeval waters called the amniotic fluid and still dependent on liquids, the infant is governed by the Moon. For purposes of our correspondences based on Indian classifications, the entire year will be taken conventionally as the "nondual state." About the beginning of the second year, the child starts to walk: this inaugurates the heroic stage of walking on earth. It is a kind of *anabasis*, "advance uphill" (classically used for "military advance"). Also in the next two years the child speaks magic syllables expressing his desires and commanding their fulfillment by parents. Morbid regressions to this state could be called *catabasis*, "retreat to the sea" (classically used for "military retreat"). So the child during those two years is governed by Mars, the commander-in-chief in Indian astrology. This is childhood's type of Great Time. Phylogenetic recapitulation in Profane Time is shown by the last period of childhood, the fourth through the twelfth year, when the lad or girl develops the power of reasoning while playfully dashing hither and yon under the dominion of Mercury. Modern studies show that the child is now a "socialized being" and his games increasingly have rules.[19] The ages assigned to these stages are of course stated with generality and are not meant to deny individual differences.

[18] "The Stages of Life according to Varāhamihira," *Journal of the American Oriental Society*, 83 (1963): 360-61.

[19] Jean Piaget, *Play, Dreams and Imitation in Childhood* (New York, 1962), p. 142.

The Daily Recapitulation

Each day, man's life exhibits modes that disguise the three times. Properly speaking, the disguise is inaugurated by puberty, because the maturation of the sexually differentiated characteristics recalls what in the Buddhist genesis legend inaugurated the last period, corrupted by lust and hatred. In short, dreamless sleep corresponds to No Time, dream to Great Time, and the waking state to Profane Time.

I must stress—and in a similar vein, so does Eliade[20]—that the kind of correspondence referred to in the itemization of recapitulations does not imply identity with the three Times. Indeed, elements in correspondence are both related in some way and differ in some way. No Time, Great Time, and Profane Time each have a universal or shared character. The recapitulations are personal or private. Thus, Great Time is the source of myth as held by a certain society to work out public problems while a dream is a private matter to work out private problems. The dream is also like Great Time in its shortened psychological distance between subject and object, evidenced by the conversion of discursive thinking into nondiscursive imagery, especially in dramatic presentation, and also by its premonitory character (in the sense of showing trends). In contrast, dreaming is mostly inspired by experiences of the waking state, preeminently Profane Time, while Great Time is mostly inspired by No Time. Certain cases of unsuccessful ("unresolved") dreaming even parallel the successful "walking" of Great Time by the striking act of somnambulism. The recapitulations of childhood are more faithful to the three Times (hence the Biblical advice for entering the Kingdom of Heaven). That the third period (ages four through twelve), when the child is allowed to go out and play with other children, establishes Profane Time, is a matter to be justified. Buddhism generally explained that "discursive thought" (*vikalpa*) is the nescience (*avidyā*), or cause of it, that heads the Dependent Origination (*pratītya-samutpāda*) constituting Phenomenal Life (*saṃsāra*). This "discursive thought" is the basis of human reasoning with its rules. But a child playing by itself does not devise rules for games.[21] Therefore, I understand the third period of

[20]Eliade, *Myths, Dreams and Mysteries*, p. 17.
[21]Piaget, *Play, Dreams and Imitation*, p. 142.

childhood to be involved in the parable of the Buddhist Mahāyāna scripture called *Sāgaramatiparipṛcchā:* "Now suppose this boy, being a child, would fall into a pit of night-soil while playing...." It turns out that this "pit of night-soil" is a term for *saṃsāra.*[22]

While the recapitulations in both childhood and daily life are not identical with the three Times, they do share the universal character in a salient feature. That is to say, we can combine the childhood and daily recapitulations to observe that although the child, and then the child becomes an adult, are in aspects of Profane Time, they do indeed still recapitulate all three Times. They do so irrespective of the degree of religious feeling in particular persons, do so irrespective of such rites as baptism, and do so whether or not people indulge in food and sex sacramentally. In every life the "Moment 1" is Great Time, the rest of life Profane Time, but throughout life there are these recapitulations, echoes, and intimations of the Sacred. This is why no person in Profane Time can be utterly dissociated from No Time and Great Time. In this light, an irreligious as well as a religious person may use with sincerity such expressions as the "sanctity of the home."

Breakthroughs

By "breakthrough" I refer to the numinous experience as described by Otto (*Das Heilige*). It is an irrational revelation of overwhelming majesty or of mysterious power. The complete otherness of the revelation makes it appear as a breakthrough from a superior, nonhuman realm. According to the classification utilized above, this breakthrough would be from No Time into Great Time or from No Time into Profane Time. In the Indian context, the first case—overwhelming majesty of No Time in Great Time—is illustrated in the *Bhagavadgītā* by Krishna's revelation of his cosmic form to Arjuna. This is also the *saṃbhogakāya* of the Buddha preaching to the great *bodhisattvas* in the Akaniṣṭha Heaven. The second case—the mysterious power of No Time in Profane Time—is illustrated by the Hindu-Buddhist Act of Truth. This act is done by Sītā in the Hindu epic *Rāmāyaṇa* and there are many examples in Buddhist scriptures. Here the performer declares the truth of his outstanding acts and

[22]The parable is quoted in Jikido Takasaki, *A Study on the Ratnagotravibhaga*(*Uttaratantra*) (Rome, 1966,) pp. 246-47.

commands the gods to produce the desired miracle. The miracle—an incredible event apparently violating "Nature's laws"—is the breakthrough. Ānandagarbha contains this ritual statement in his *Śrīparamādi-ṭīkā:* "He should recite, 'Oh Bhagavat Vajrasattva, just as it is true that all *dharmas* are like a dream, by virtue of that truth may I be allowed to see and be allowed to hear the such-and-such desired dream!' "[23]

Both kinds of breakthrough have been responsible in numerous cases for the striking religious phenomenon of "conversion." In the category of breakthrough I would also place some debatable religious experiences, of more or less sullied character, all for "ego-defense": battlefield trauma, epilepsy, young man in the whorehouse, psychedelic drugs (as indicated by such images of "shattering" as walls breached by sea-water).

Participations

There is also the attempt to ascend to higher states of consciousness as though to live integrally in them, reified as modes of being—a sort of mystical immersion—or at least to be able to get into and out of those states whenever one wishes. Hence we speak of participation in Great Time or in No Time. Success here can be understood as either discovery or verification of spiritual truth, and also as the acquisition of supernormal powers. Eliade writes:

> Upon the plane of the archaic religions, participation in the condition of the "spirits" is what endows the mystics and the magicians with their highest prestige. It is during his ecstasy that the shaman undertakes, *in the spirit*, long and dangerous mystical journeys even up to the highest Heaven to meet the God, or up to the Moon or down into Hell, etc.[24]

Whatever be the truth in these cases, it is the human mind which so asserts it. It is a wonderful feature of Profane Time that it asserts the truth of religion. The higher Times have truth but do not assert it. Great Time should include the Buddhist search

[23] / bcom ldan ḥdas rdo rje sems dpaḥ bden pa gaṅ gis chos thams cad rmi lam dan ḥdra bar mñam paḥi bden pa des bdag ḥdod paḥi rmi lam che ge mo mthoṅ bar mdzod cig / thos par mdzod cig ces brjod par byaḥo / (Kyoto-Tokyo Photographic reprint [1959-61] of *Kanjur-Tanjur*, vol. 72, pp. 305-3).

[24] Eliade, *Myths, Dreams and Mysteries*, p. 95.

for or experience of suffering as a Noble Truth. For this it is necessary to reduce, even to abolish, psychological distance—man's advancing self-awareness in Profane Time that he is differentiated from the object (nature), which curtails a person's empathy with beings located mentally by that person in other groups. This factitious grouping—the castes of India and the world—is the prejudice engendered during the third period of childhood (see "Recapitulations").

Buddhism, in common with Hinduism, believed that by a regular course of conduct, such as restrictions on food and sex activity, and by finding the proper place and there a *guru*, a person (preferably male) could then undertake the somewhat arduous training for *samādhi* and thus ascend to various levels of consciousness, even the highest, the Incomparable Complete Enlightenment of the Buddha. This meditative ascension is usually stated in terms of sensory experience. The attainment of mental calm gradually brings out certain supernormal faculties, such as divine hearing. Eliade points out, "In short, throughout religious history, sensory activity has been used as a means of participating in the sacred and attaining to the divine."[25] In the *bodhisattva* doctrine of Mahāyāna Buddhism this is also stressed. Thus, in Atiśa's *Bodhipathapradīpa* (verses 35-36):

> Just as a bird with unspread wings cannot fly up to the sky, in the same way the one without the power of the supernormal faculties cannot serve the aim of the sentient beings.
>
> The merits of a single day that are due to the supernormal faculties would not occur in a hundred births for one lacking the supernormal faculties.[26]

In that way, those *bodhisattvas* who are called "great beings" (*mahāsattva*) are in Great Time, vastly able to serve the aim of sentient beings by dint of the supernormal faculties.

Extraordinary sensory experience is governed by the second instruction of the Buddhist path, which is arranged in three instructions: (1) morality (*adhiśīla-śikṣa*), (2) concentration (*adhisamādhi-śikṣa*), and (3) insight (*adhiprajñā-śikṣa*).[27] The implication

[25]Eliade, *Myths, Dream and Mysteries*, p. 74.

[26]Manuscript translation from Tibetan by Alex Wayman.

[27]The famous Pāli text, Buddhaghosa's *Visuddhimagga*, is arranged in three parts in accordance with three instructions.

of these instructions is that Buddhism is not seeking to attain Great Time or No Time just for the sake of doing so, or for the sake of gaining a striking experience. The old Buddhist aim was of liberation (No Time) and later came the Bodhisattva ideal (Great Time). Since Great Time had the seed of downfall into Profane Time, the Buddhist rationale of reaching that lofty state is to do it in circumstances whereby the concurrent hypnotic delusion is eliminated. And so it was taught that on top of the mental calming, the fruit of the second instruction, there should be the insight which sees things as they really are (what early Buddhism said) or which sees things arising as in a dream (what later Buddhism said).

The order of instructions places morality as the foundation for both mental calming and insight. This is borne out by the assignment of certain rites to Great Time. Ritual action has this in common with the heroic conduct of Great Time: one has to give up all random action and do things with exactitude in the performance of a ritual, and one has to give up all means and timid acts in order to have heroic conduct. That is to say, they both demand the abandonment of the usual human weaknesses exhibited in Profane Time. These rites have features in common with meditation procedures. I have in mind especially the *maṇḍala* rites of Tibetan Buddhism,[28] which are analogous to steps of meditation. Here one has to select the proper site, remove all the stones, potsherds, and other pains of the soil, and meditatively seize the site by vowing to perform the reviewed rite. In Buddhist meditation one must also find the right meditative object, eliminate gross corruptions from the mind, and seize the meditative object by leaving off the usual mental dashing hither and yon to a multitude of sensory objects.

These meditative procedures—the old ways or the "shortcuts" such as the *Tantras* claim to have—are meant to reach an otherworldly condition. It is here that the myth, especially the genesis legend, serves the function of reminding profane man of that mode of being he has lost and even suggesting how he may return. Then, what does Buddhism have to say about participating in Great Time and No Time as modes of being in the senses

[28]See Ferdinand D. Lessing and Alex Wayman, trans., *Mkhas grub rje's* ("Fundamentals of the Buddhist Tantras"), (The Hague, 1968), pp. 279 ff.

suggested by the genesis legend? It was believed in ancient Buddhism that by advanced meditative techniques one could draw from the physical body a duplicate of it called the "body made of mind" (*manomaya-kāya*), as recorded in the *Dīgha-nikāya:*

> Here a monk creates a body from this (his) body, having form mind-made, with all limbs and parts, not deprived of senses. Just as if a man were to pull out a reed from its sheath, he would know: "This is the sheath, this the reed. The sheath is one thing, the reed is another. It is from the sheath that the reed has been drawn forth."[29]

The *Laṅkāvatāra-sūtra* distinguishes three degrees in development of this "body made of mind": (1) its potential separation during stabilization in the pleasure of *samādhi;* (2) its separation due to reversal of the basis of the evolving perceptions and of the basic perception (*ālayavijñāna*), with a reorientation ("alteration of consciousness") toward *dharmas* (natures); and finally, (3) its becoming a body of the Buddha.[30] The second stage, pervaded by "forbearance of the unoriginated natures" (*anutpattikadharmakṣānti*), means living without terror in Great Time; while the third stage, when the "body made of mind" has been initiated as a Buddha, means living in No Time. These three stages of the "body made of mind" appear to reverse the three downward stages of the Buddhist genesis legend and, by mastering the three Times, to prove the myth.

In addition, there are ancient and modern claims that certain drugs, now called "consciousness expanding" (psychedelic), such as the current LSD—possibly the *soma* of the ancient Vedic cult is in the same category—bring one easily to the experience of Great Time. Drugs that arouse striking sensory images have precisely this *intense mindfulness* (*smṛti*) in common with *yoga*. In the case of drugs, however, the experience is of kaleidoscopic and somewhat distorted images rather than the "one pointedness of mind" (*ekāgratā-citta*) of *samādhi* and is uncontrolled by the subject except for some affective preconditioning ("expectancy").

[29]See Paravahera Vajirañāṇa Mahāthera, *Buddhist Meditation in Theory and Practice* (Colombo, Ceylon, 1962), p. 440; and Mircea Eliade, *Yoga; Immortality and Freedom* (New York, 1958), p. 165.

[30]See Alex Wayman, "Studies in Yama and Māra," *Indo-Iranian Journal*, 3 (1959): 119.

Therefore, these drugs cannot supply the mental calm (*śamatha*) necessary for the supernormal faculties. They seem to amount to at least one of the two extremes rejected by the Buddha in favor of the Middle Path—the extreme of indulgence in a riot of sense images; possibly also they represent the extreme of mortification, of body chemistry.

Indeed, an artist of the visionary type is more likely to live in Great Time than any drug-taker. This is because when perception sees the bare objective thing, that object, as "nature," has the upper hand: being the only thing perceived, it has virtual hypnotic value. Notice the words of Picasso:

> There must be darkness everywhere except on the canvas, so that the painter becomes hypnotized by his own work and paints almost as though he were in a trance.... He must stay as close as possible to his own inner world if he wants to transcend the limitations his reason is always trying to impose on him.[31]

Jung writes consistently: "A great work of art is like a dream; for all its apparent obviousness it does not explain itself and is never unequivocal. A dream never says: 'You ought', or: 'This is the truth.' "[32] The breakdown of formal profane structures through shortened psychological distance can bring types of religious experiences to artists and drug-takers as well as to *yogins*. However, there is no special distinction in reaching Great Time or No Time somehow or other, no matter in how disoriented a manner; for, after all, there are the recapitulations which all of us experience normally without risk.

Conclusion

If one accepts the terminology of three Times associated with three modes of thought and further accepts that these modes of thought allude to modes of being, he can easily grant that there are various ways of reaching or plunging into those modes of being as a veritable transfer or flight of consciousness to a different

[31] Francoise Gilot and Carlton Lake, *Life with Picasso* (New York, 1965), pp. 110-11.

[32] C. G. Jung, *Modern Man in Search of a Soul* (New York, 1933), p. 171.

field or domain, one that is initially strange and possibly frightening. The three Times themselves, and the corresponding procedure used for dealing with them, are a kind of thinking well known from the ancient *Upaniṣads*, on the background of which Buddhism itself arose. The states of Waking, Dream, and Dreamless Sleep are encompassing categories and are themselves included in the Fourth State (Turīya), which seems to be the forerunner of the Mahāyāna "Nirvāṇa without fixed abode."

The use of the categories "No Time," "Great Time," and "Profane Time" for subsuming disparate features of man's development or states of consciousness is not surprising since the mind of man is structurally the same, though given to different "ways of thought"; and, after all, one can select from various sources the particular material that fits into a prearrangement. The formulation would be outstanding if it should prove to fit well with other salient features of man's thought and life which persons at large might cogently adduce as worthy of inclusion in such schema—that is, if it should turn out to be a more convenient description for worthy data than other schematic descriptions in use. This is for others to judge.

Time in Indian and Japanese Thought

HAJIME NAKAMURA*

1 *The Notion of Time in India*

The Indian conception of time is very different from what the Western mind regards as intuitively obvious. In Indian thought, time, like other phenomena, is conceived statically rather than dynamically. It is, of course, recognized that the things of this world are always moving and changing. But the substance of things is seen as basically unchanging, its underlying reality unaffected by the ceaseless flux. The Indian does not concede that we never step into the same river twice; he directs our attention not to the flow of water but to the river itself, the unchanging universal. Indian thought places a high value on universality, and the connection between this, and the static conception of phenomena, is of course not accidental. "The one remains, the many change and flee."

This static conception of time permeates Indian thought. It could hardly fail to do so, for it is present in the very forms of language itself, conditioning all philosophical thinking. In the classical Indian languages, there are no words which corresponded to the concept "to become." The verb formed from the root *bhū* can be translated as both "to become" and "to exist." These two aspects of perceived reality, conceived as antithetical by the Western mind, are not even distinguished. "To become" is merely an aspect of "to exist." The noun *bhava*, formed from the same root, can mean either "being born" or "existing";[1] in other words, to become is to be born. To express the idea of change at all, Indians had to make shift with the words *anyathā bhavati* or *anyathābhāva*—"being otherwise." Becoming is expressed in terms of being, dynamic is seen as a phase of static.

* The author and the editor wish to thank Clara Park of Williamstown, Massachusetts, for her valuable assistance in revising the manuscript.

The point of view permeates the language. The noun, which expresses the more stable and unchanging aspects of a thing, is in Sanskrit more likely to be used than the verb, and correspondingly adjectives are more frequent than adverbs. In classical Sanskrit,[2] indeed, especially in prose writings, it became usual to employ verbal nouns or participles instead of finite verbs. For example, the sentence "Because of the rain, the food appears" is expressed in classical Sanskrit as "Because of the rain, appearance of the food (is possible)." It has been the practice since ancient times to use the participial form instead of the finite verb to express the past tense, and it became a common expression in colloquialism of the later periods.[3] Sanskrit will also use an adjective, which is static in feeling, to express an idea which might take a verb in the languages of the West. The classic Western expression of the sense of flux uses a vivid and specific verb. "All things flow" (πάντα ρει). The corresponding idea is expressed in Sanskrit as *sarvam anityam*, "all existences are impermanent."

We find the same habit of mind conditioning the use of periphrastic forms. The periphrastic perfect, though seldom found in the Vedas, appears frequently in the literature after the Brahmaṇas. "He went" becomes *gamayām cakāra* (literally, "he did going"). Again, the periphrastic future may be used to express future action.[4] For example, the word *gantāsi* (you are the one who goes) is used to express the meaning "you will go," thus directing the attention away from the action to the stable state of the actor.

The primacy of the noun is illustrated in the Sanskrit denominative, a category of verb not found in the classical grammar of the West. For example, the denominative *putrīyati* is formed from the noun *putra* (son) and means "to desire to have a son," and *svāmīyati*, from the noun *svāmin* (master) means "to regard as a master." Generally speaking, the denominative connotes the meaning of "to be . . . ," "to work as . . . ," "to regard as . . . ," "to desire . . . ," but the real emphasis of the word is on the noun.

Similarly, the meaning "to be able to," expressed in Western languages by verbs or auxiliary verbs, is expressed in Sanskrit by an adjective, *śakya*, or an indeclinable, *śakyam*. For example, *na devāsuraiḥ sarvaiḥ śakyaḥ prasahitum yudhi* (*Rāmāyaṇa* II, 86, 11) = *non potest proelio superari a cunctis dis daemonibusque*[5] (he cannot be conquered in battle by all the gods and spirits).

In Sanskrit, then, finite verbs are seldom used; the verb appears mainly as a verbal noun, and the nominal sentence is more often used than the verbal sentence. Usage of the infinitive of the verb is also limited; it is never used as subject[6] or as object. When it seems necessary to use the infinitive as an object, an abstract noun formed from the root of the verb is used instead, thus directing attention from the changing aspect of the action to the unchanging universal: "to appear" does not equal "appearance."

The centrality of the noun is further illustrated by the absence in Sanskrit of the adverbial suffix which is common to all Western languages. Adjectives are converted into adverbs by adding ὡς in Greek, *-ment* in French, *-ly* and *-lich* in English and German. In Sanskrit, however, the accusative case of the adjective is used if it is necessary to modify the verb. Ablative and locative cases of adjectives may also be used adverbially. The adverb itself is not even acknowledged as a part of speech in Sanskrit.

There are other curious illustrations of this tendency to comprehend things through their static aspects. To connect two ideas, Western languages use such conjunctions as *and* or *then*; Sanskrit, in contrast, will express the same idea by adding the demonstrative pronoun *sa* to the subject of the sentence, as if "John runs and jumps" were to be expressed as "John running he jumping." The conjunction emphasizes the separateness of events; the demonstrative focuses on the subject, unchanging through time.

On the whole, then, Western people comprehend action through its changing aspects, while Indians tend to comprehend it attributively. In particular, many Indians consider that action is an unchanging aspect, even an attribute, of existence. Westerners tend to regard action as an active phenomenon while Indians tend to look upon it statically. In the sentence *sabbe saṅkhārā aniccā* (all things are impermanent), a basic idea of Indian Buddhism, *aniccā*, is an adjective. For an Indian, even the statement that "all things of this world are changing and moving" is not, as it was for Heraclitus, the expression of the changing aspects of existences, but the expression of a static and unchanging state.

In Indian philosophy the Absolute is generally explained as a Being beyond all temporal appearances. These exist and change in time; the Absolute, in contrast, is essentially static. In the Upaniṣads, the Absolute is repeatedly expressed as "Imperishable."[7] "Ātman is imperishable for it cannot be destroyed. . . . It is unfettered, it does not suffer, it is not injured."[8] "This is that great unborn Self who is imperishable, incorruptible, eternal, fearless, Brahman."[9] Early Buddhism does not lay emphasis on a metaphysical Absolute as such, but the same habit of mind is found in the principle of *pratītyasamutpāda*, later developed in Mahāyāna Buddhism, which states that nothing can disappear or arise. In Indian thought, as in the Sanskrit language, it is the idea of Being which receives central consideration.

Indian philosophers in general replace the concept of Becoming by three aspects of temporal existence: Appearance, Extinction, and Continuance. All three states are clearly conceived as static. They are referred to early in the Upanisads and are generally accepted by the orthodox schools of Brahmanism and Jainism. Buddhism also designates these as the three aspects of the conditioned or phenomenal being.[10] Other words which are considered equivalent to "becoming" (*vikāra*, *vikriyā*, *pariṇāma*. *vipariṇāma*, etc.) in fact express the specialization of the simple into the complex and should be understood as meaning "evolution" or "development," rather than "becoming." Indian philosophy contains a number of variations on the three basic states, and the Sarvāstivāda school, the most eminent of Abhidharma Buddhist schools, added a fourth, namely *jarā* or "decaying," which was interpreted as "changing to the other" (*anyathā-bhāva, anyathātva*).[11] This might seem to come close to "becoming"; the theory, however, was not accepted by all Buddhist schools, and Decay is no real analogue of Becoming as the idea appears in Western philosophy.

There are evident similarities here to ancient Greek thought, at least in its Platonic and Parmenidean aspects. Plato formulated the antithesis between Being and Becoming; he saw the true essence of reality as consisting of changeless, timeless forms. Geometry, as an investigation of the fixed forms of material bodies in space, was the typical pattern of science in ancient times, and in the physical sciences only statics was developed. Interest in the changing world of phenomena, however, was also an important element in Greek thought; "all things flow" is after all as Greek as Plato's ideal forms. Modern thought has concerned itself increasingly (though not exclusively) with Becoming; kinetics has replaced statics in the center of the physicist's attention, and mathematics has turned to analytics and algebra, in which *variable* quantities are examined. Modern thought is described as "progressive," "dynamic"; the unique contribution of Indian thought, in contrast, can be a kind of rest and joyfulness which may be very welcome to those who are tired of the frantic movement of their culture.

The persistent Indian conception of a transcendent reality as more important than the phenomenal world it underlies and sustains results in a kind of paralysis of the individual's sensitivity to time, if we understand "time" to mean the passage and flow of specific events in our experience. This paralysis manifests itself in a characteristic lack of time concepts which non-Indians regard as common sense. (Indian thought may show an intense preoccupation with other, more metaphysical senses of time; in the Vedic period time was seen as the fundamental principle of the universe, "Time, the steed, [who] runs with seven reins, thousand-eyed, ageless, rich in seed. The seers, thinking holy thoughts, mount him, all the worlds are his wheels. . . . With seven wheels does this Time ride, seven navels has he, immortality is his axle. . . . Time, the first god, now hastens onward"[12] But this is hardly the time in which human beings carry on their common concerns.)

Language, as usual, is where this lack of common-sense concepts is most clearly seen: the Indian people did not have a clear awareness of the discrimination of tense. Although in Sanskrit, as in Greek, there are five kinds of tenses, they are not sharply discriminated in meaning.[13] To indicate past time, the imperfect, perfect, past participle active, aorist and historical present are used almost indiscriminately,[14] and the frequency with which a given tense is used varies not according to meaning but according to historical period. The aorist is often used in the sixth century B.C., for instance, but in classical Sanskrit is no longer common. The discrimination between absolute past and relative past is not clearly made in the ancient Indian language.

In modern Hindustani as well, we find similar linguistic phenomena. The adverb *kal* means both "yesterday" and "tomorrow." *Parson* means "the day after tomorrow" as well as "the day before yesterday"; *atarson* means equally "three days ago" or "three days from now." The meaning of these terms can be determined only through context.

Since the lack of common-sense time concepts is built into the language of India, both ancient and modern, it is not surprising to find it manifested in Indian religion and historiography. The Buddha was born under a tree in the park at Lumbini, attained Enlightenment under a tree at Gaya, and entered Nirvana under a tree at Kusinagara. These three events, according to common-sense notions, must have taken place on different dates, yet they are all celebrated by Indians and South Asiatics on the same Wesak day in May. Indians have not exerted themselves to grasp the concept of time quantitatively, and have never written historical books with accurate dates. According to the Indian world view, the universe, world, and social order are eternal; personal life, however, is only one sample of a succession of lives existing repeatedly in limitless time. If one's life is conceived as infinitely repeated, it becomes meaningless. The idea of the transmigration of souls, the perpetual self-revolution of rebirth, has appeared only occasionally in the West, but in India it is a basic assumption of the common people as well as of philosophers. Passing phenomena, whether the events of the individual life or of more generalized history, have no real significance. It is natural enough that no importance is given to providing them with accurate dates.

We should thus be prepared to find the Indian conception of history very different from our own. Indian books of history are few in number, and these few are tinged with a fantastic and legendary color. They are not products of historical science but rather works of art. Usually they are written in verse. Indians are not satisfied with the simple description of facts in the language of daily use. They beautify the past and try to idealize it. They ignore precise figures, exact sequences of events, and other details of time and place. Far from exerting themselves to give exact sizes of armies, say, or expenditures, they exaggerate astronomically with magnificent and brilliant hyperbole.

As an example, consider the *Mahāvaṃsa*, the most reliable work of history produced in ancient Ceylon. Even this book, though highly informative from the modern historian's point of view, is saturated with a mysterious and legendary atmosphere. For instance, though Mahānāman, the author of the *Mahāvaṃsa*, lived in the fifth century A.D., in an age not too distant from the time of King Duṭṭhagāmaṇī, his descriptions of this greatest of Ceylon's rulers are already full of fantastic elements, and the reader must make a careful distinction between myth and that which is historically true. The histories or "chronicles" of medieval European monks and the biographies of eminent Buddhist monks in China and Japan have a similar style, but the *Mahāvaṃsa* stretches historical truth to an incomparably greater degree.

Another example is Kalhaṇa's *Rājataraṅgiṇī*, the chronicle of a Kashmiri dynasty and one of the best historical works ever written by an Indian. In it Kalhaṇa details the social situation of his time and the activities of the various personages in it with an accuracy that no other Indian book of history has attained. Yet Oldenberg can still describe it in these terms:

> If one removes all the poetic elements from Kalhaṇa's story, and compares it with events of the time, he will find that the account is in essence on a level no higher than that of a more or less accurate article in a newspaper or a cartoon in a political comic paper. The process of formation that this story has undergone is not that of historical thinking but that of poetry—poetry in the Indian sense with its brilliant quality and also with its weakness. And Kalhana himself has a very distinct idea on this point; he feels himself as a poet and he is a poet.[15]

It is worth pointing out that Kalhaṇa scarcely pays heed to causal sequence when considering historical events. His dates are inaccurate and sometimes clearly the products of pure imagination.

The Indians themselves have attached little significance to their books of history; most Indians have been much more interested in religion and poetry than in historical documentation. For the Indians, a minor error in the recitation of the Vedas has been a serious matter. But they have been thoroughly indifferent to the erroneous recording of dates or facts in their books of history.[16] This lack of historical consciousness is distinctly observable in the Buddhist attitude to the rules of their order. In the period after the death of the Buddha, Buddhists had to establish new precepts in order to meet changing social conditions. As some of the new rules were not compatible with the older ones, they hesitated to include them in the traditional books of ordination (*pāṭimokkhas*), and instead attached them to the *pāṭimokkhas* as supplements. Although they would not alter the traditional books, however, they were not afraid to claim the authority of the Buddha's own teaching even for these supplementary precepts of their own creation, completely ignoring the historical facts. Their concern for the proper observance of the precepts was far stronger than their regard for historical accuracy.

This lack of interest in history is very different from what we find in China. The Chinese derive their rules of social conduct from the examples of their ancestors as set down in their books of history. The Indians, on the other hand, gain their principles of behavior from their religious books, and at the same time fables and parables such as the *Pañcatantra* and *Hitopadeśa* contribute toward the diffusion of practical morals into daily life. These books, embodiments of the enduring spirit of folk-tale, present for contemplation eternal paradigms of human experience—paradigms which are by their nature timeless and in that sense, outside history.

The concentration on the universality behind and beyond the variety of concrete phenomena of our experience is in its essence contemplative. Language again provides a key to thought; the meditative character of Indian thought is forcibly illustrated in the concept of causal relations as expressed in the forms of Sanskrit itself. To indicate the causal relation between two notions, *Sanskrit forms a compound which suggests that the natural order of thought is to begin with the effect and trace it back to the cause*. Accordingly, the expression "effect and cause" (*phalahetu*) occurs instead of the familiar "cause and effect." The contemplative attitude thus erases time: one can only speak of "effect and cause" if the effect is already known and both effect and cause present to the contemplative mind *sub specie aeternitatis*. Although the Latin phrase suggests that this habit of thinking is not wholly foreign to the West, the natural order of Western thought is clear: it is to proceed temporally from cause to effect. Even though the relationship is seen, it is seen in time. In Sanskrit, in contrast, many expressions emphasize this meditative view in which progressive phenomena are seen as already complete. *Kāryakāraṇabhāva* means, not "the relation of cause and effect," but of "effect and cause." What would in Western languages appear as the "relation of the knower and the knowable" is in Sanskrit "the relation of the knowable and the knower (*gamyagamakabhāva*)."[17] We find similar reversals of Western order in the "relation of the generated and the generative (*janyajanakabhāva*)"; "the relation of the proved and the prover (*sādhyasādhakabhava*)"; "the relation of the established and the establishing (*vyayasthāpyavyavasthāpakabhāva*)";[18] "the relation of the activated and the activator (*pravartyapravartayitṛtva*)."[19] Each of these expressions appears reversed to Western minds, and even to other Orientals. Accordingly, when scholars translated the original texts into Chinese they changed the word order. Tibetan scholars also understood the causal relationship differently from the Indian; they translated *phalahetu* ("effect and cause") into *rgyu daṇ hbras-bu* ("cause and effect"). This way of thinking, in which the notion of effect is formed first and that of the cause inferred and stated afterward, is retrospective, and is basically different from the approach which starts from the cause. The retrospective, contemplative attitude is in further contrast to the thinking processes of natural science, through which, with the help of inductive and deductive reasoning, the cause of an effect is investigated and ascertained by functional correlation without giving primacy either to cause or effect.

Even when Indians do investigate the relation of two phenomena from cause to effect, they generally do not take the view that a single effect is caused by a single active movement, but prefer to consider that effects are produced by the combination of various causes. Therefore, most Indian thinkers do not employ the term which corresponds to the Aristotelian notion of efficient cause. While *nimitta-kāraṇa* is linguistically the equivalent of *causa efficiens*, it is also used to express the Western notion of *causa occasionalis*. The Sanskrit expression in fact describes a final cause or aim, that is, a teleological relation. And such relations, East and West, are traditional subjects of contemplation.

It would be incorrect to infer from the foregoing that the Indian people have no concept of abstract time. On the contrary, the view of the uncertainty and transiency of life which is at the center of both Buddhism and Jainism demonstrates that they understand from their heartfelt experience the changing phases of the world. Buddhism from the outset emphasized the transience and impermanence of human existence. All things pass away. On account of our fragility we are subject to disease and death. From transience comes suffering. The Buddha asked his disciples: "That which is transient, O monks, is it painful or pleasant?" "Painful O Master!"[20] Our dreams, our hopes, our wishes—all of them will be forgotten as if they had never been. This is a universal principle. "Whatever is subject to origination is subject also to destruction."[21] Necessary and inexorable is the death of all that is born. The difference is only in the degree of duration. Some things may last for years, others for a brief while only. But all must vanish. For the ignoble craving for worldly things must be substituted the noble aspiration for the "incomparable security of Nirvāṇa free from corruption":

O transient are our life's experience!
Their nature 'tis to rise and pass away
They happen in our ken, they cease to be.
O well for us when they are sunk to rest![22]

There is no substance which abides forever. All matter is force; all substance is motion. The state of every individual is unstable, sure to pass away.

In later days the sentiment of impermanence became more peculiarly Indian than Buddhist. Suffering is seen as one with transience. Craving causes suffering since the impermanence of what we crave causes disappointment and sorrow. The Buddhist beatitude lies in our realization that all things are transient and we should not cling to them.

2 The Japanese Attitude Toward Time and Change

Japanese Buddhism also emphasized the transience of the phenomenal world. But the Japanese attitude toward this transience is very different from the Indian. The Japanese disposition is to lay a greater emphasis upon sensible, concrete events, intuitively apprehended, than upon universals. It is in direct contrast to the characteristic Indian reaction to the world of change, which is to reject it in favor of an ultimate reality, a transcendent Absolute in which the mind can find refuge from the ceaseless flux of observed phenomena. The Japanese reaction is rather to accept, even to welcome, the fluidity and impermanence of the phenomenal world.

This way of thinking, far from positing a changeless Absolute, regards the phenomenal world itself as the Absolute and explicitly rejects the recognition of any ultimate reality beyond or above it. What is widely known among post-Meiji philosophers in the last century as the "theory that the phenomenal is actually the real" has deep roots in Japanese tradition.

Master Dōgen, the thirteenth-century thinker who is said to have founded the Sōtō-Zen sect, asserts the transience of things as strongly as any Indian Buddhist. "Time flies more swiftly than an arrow and life is more transient than dew. We cannot call back a single day that has passed." But his emphasis is positive, not negative: "A man may live as the slave of the senses for one hundred years but if he lives one day upholding the Good Law, it will favorably influence his coming life for many years." And Dōgen stresses the primacy of the phenomenal world: "We ought to love and respect this life and this body, since it is through this life and this body that we have the opportunity to practice the Law and make known the power of the Buddha. Accordingly, righteous practice for one day is the Seed of Buddhahood, of the righteous action of All the Buddhas."[23]

What we see and experience is thus recognized as itself the ultimate reality. There is no greater reality, changeless and invisible; there is nothing to be apprehended that is not already exposed to us.[24] For Master Dōgen, impermanence is itself the absolute state, and this impermanence is not to be rejected but to be valued. "Impermanence is the Buddhahood. . . .[25] The impermanence of grass, trees, and forests is verily the Buddhahood. The impermanence of the person's body and mind is verily the Buddhahood. The impermanence of the country and scenery is verily the Buddhahood."[26]

In other places Dōgen says: "Death and life are the very life of the Buddha," and "These mountains, rivers and earth are all the See of Buddhahood." In the Lotus Sūtra, Dōgen finds the same vein of thought: "Concerning the Lotus Sūtra . . . the cry of a monkey is drowned in the sound of a rapid river. [Even] these are preaching this sūtra, this above all." He who attains the purport of this sūtra, says the Master, will discern the preaching of the doctrine even in the voices at an auction sale, for even in the mundane world "our Buddha's voice and form [are] in all the sounds of the rapid river and colors of the ridge."[27]

One is reminded of the words of the Chinese poet Su Tung-p'o: "The voice of the rapids is verily the wide long tongue [of the Buddha]. The color of the mountains is no other than [his] pure chaste body." This way of thinking is Japanese Zen Buddhism. In the words of Master Mujū, "Mountains, rivers, earth, there is not a thing that is not real."[28]

Starting from such a viewpoint, Dōgen gives to some phrases of Indian Buddhist scriptures interpretations that are essentially different from the original meaning. There is a phrase in the *Mahāparinirvāṇa-sūtra* that goes as follows: "He who desires to know the meaning of Buddhahood should survey the time and wait for the occasion to come. If the time comes, the Buddhahood will be revealed of itself."[29] To this concept of Buddhahood as something possible and accessible, Dōgen gives a characteristic twist. He reads the phrase "survey of time" as "make a survey in terms of time," and the phrase "if the time comes" as "the time has already come." His interpretation of the original passage becomes, in this way, something like the following:

> Buddhahood is time. He who wants to know Buddhahood may know it by knowing time as it is revealed to us. And as time is something in which we are already immersed, Buddhahood also is not something that is to be sought in the future but is something that is realized where we are.[30]

We see here Dōgen's effort to free himself from the idealistic viewpoint held by some of the Indian Mahāyāna Buddhists. In Dōgen's unique philosophy of time, "all being is time";[31] the ever-changing, incessant temporal flux is identified with ultimate Being itself.

Again and again Dōgen emphasizes that the true reality is not static but dynamic. "It is a heretical doctrine," says Dōgen, "to think the mind mobile and the essence of things static. It is a heretical doctrine to think that the essence is crystal clear and the appearance changeable."[32] Again, "It is a heretical doctrine to think that in essence water does not run, and the tree does not pass through vicissitude. The Buddha's way consists in the form that exists and the conditions that exist. The bloom of flowers and the fall of leaves are the conditions that exist. And yet unwise people think that in the world of essence there should be no bloom of flowers and no fall of leaves."[33]

Dōgen criticizes the Chinese Zen Buddhist Ta-hui (1089–1163), who taught that mind and essence are not caught up in the world of birth and death. According to Dōgen, Ta-hui was wrong in teaching that "the mind is solely perception and conceptualization, and the essence is pure and tranquil."[34] Here again a static way of thinking is rejected, and this rejection makes Dōgen's emphasis very different from anything which Indian or Chinese Buddhism has prepared us for.

This characteristic willingness to accept the phenomenal world as given and to live contentedly in it is not confined to Buddhism in Japan. It appears in modern Shintoism as well. The founder of the Konkō sect teaches: "Whether alive or dead, you should regard the heaven and earth as your own habitation."[35] And as Dōgen criticized and metamorphosed Chinese Zen, so Jinsai Itō (1627–1705) changed the form of Chinese neo-Confucianism. To Jinsai, the true reality of both earth and heaven is strongly active in a way which we would call evolutionary. Nothing but eternal development exists. Jinsai completely denies what is called death.

The *Book of Changes* (*I Ching*) says, "the great virtue of heaven and earth is called life." It means that living without ceasing is nothing but the way of heaven and earth. And in the way of heaven and earth there is no death, but life, there is no divergence, but convergence. That is because the way of heaven and earth is one with life. Though the bodies of ancestors may perish, their spirits are inherited by their posterity, whose spirits are again inherited by their own posterity. When life thus evolves, without ceasing, into eternity, it may rightly be said that no one dies.[36]

According to Jinsai the world of reality is nothing but change and action, and action is in itself good. "Stillness is the end of motion, while evil is the change of good; and good is a kind of life, while evil is a kind of death. It is not that these two opposites are generated together, but they are all one with life."[37]

Jinsai Itō's younger contemporary Ogiu Sorai, though a rival of Jinsai's, admires the latter's activities as "the supreme knowledge of a thousand years," and denounces the static character of the Chinese School of *Li*. In fact it can be said that all of the characteristically Japanese scholars believe in phenomena as the fundamental mode of existence. They unanimously reject the quietism of the neo-Confucianists of the Sung period.[38]

The way of thinking that recognizes absolute significance in the temporary, phenomenal world seems to be culturally related to the traditional Japanese love of nature. The Japanese love mountains, rivers, flowers, birds, grass and trees, and represent them in the patterns of their kimonos; they are fond of the delicacies of the season, keeping edibles in their natural form as much as possible in cooking. Within the house, flowers are arranged in a vase and dwarf trees are placed in the alcove, flowers and birds are engraved in the transom and painted on the sliding screen, and in the garden miniature mountains, streams and lakes are created. Japanese literature is deeply involved with nature and treats it with warm affection. Typical are the essays in the *Pillow Book* (*Makura no Sōshi*), which describes the beauties of the seasons. The loving concern with the particularities of nature is familiar to us through Japanese art; it is just as marked in Japanese poetry. If the poems on nature were to be removed from the collections of Japanese poems, how many would be left? Haiku, the characteristic Japanese seventeen-syllable short poems, are unthinkable apart from natural objects and the changing seasons, but the differences in attitude are as instructive as the similarities. Here is a poem by Master Dōgen:

Flowers are in spring, cuckoos in summer,
In autumn is the moon, and in winter
The pallid glimmer of snow.

The meaning of the above poem is very close to that of the Chinese verse by Wu-men Hui-k'ai:

A hundred flowers are in spring, in autumn is the moon,
In summer is the cool wind, the snow is in winter;
If nothing is on the mind to afflict a man,
That is his best season.

Similar as the poems are, the Japanese substitution of "cuckoos" for the Chinese "cool wind" has produced an entirely different effect. Both cuckoos and cool wind are sensible phenomena, but while the wind gives the sense of indefinite, remote boundlessness, the cuckoos give an impression that is limited, almost cosy.

An even better example is the poem composed on his deathbed by Ryōkan:

For a memento of my existence
What shall I leave (I need not leave anything)?
Flowers in the spring, cuckoos in the summer
And maple leaves
In the autumn.

"Maple leaves" are felt to be far closer to ourselves than "the moon," which Wu-men chose to associate with autumn. Enjoyment of nature is common to both China and Japan, but whereas the Chinese prefer the boundless and distant, the Japanese prefer the simple and compact. Dōgen took a Spartan attitude toward human desires, but he had a tender heart for seasonal beauties:

The peach blossoms begin
To bloom in the breeze of the spring;
Not a shadow of doubt
On the branches and leaves is left.
Though I know that I shall meet
The autumn moon again,
How sleepless I remain
On this moonlit night.

What is the origin of this tendency of the Japanese to grasp the absolute in terms of the world as it exists in time? Probably in the mildness of the weather, the benign character of the landscape, and the rapid and conspicuous change of seasons. Since Nature appears to be relatively benevolent to man he can love it rather than abhor it. Nature, as it changes in time, is thought of as at one with man, not hostile to him. Man feels congenial to his world, he has no grudge against it. This is at least a partial explanation for what is a basic tendency in Japanese thought.

Whatever its source, this willingness to accept the human being's situation in time has many manifestations in Japanese philosophy. Most of the Buddhist sects in Japan teach that doctrines should always be made "à propos of the time." Later Mahāyāna Buddhism employs the concept of the Three Times, the three periods which follow the demise of Lord Buddha. The first thousand years is called the Period of the Perfect Law, when the religion of the Buddha was genuinely and perfectly practiced. The second thousand years is the Period of the Copied Law, when the religion of the Buddha was practiced only in limiting the practices of the sages and monks of the past. The last period, the Period of the Latter Law, is seen as a time of open degeneration.

These ideas took deep root in Japan. The idea, in particular, of the third, degenerate age penetrated deep into the core of the doctrines of various sects. These admitted that they were in the age of degeneration, but instead of exhorting a return to the Perfect, or even the Copied Law, they claimed that the exigencies of the time should be considered and religious doctrines made suitable to them. The sects even vied in claiming the superiority of their respective sūtras (or doctrines) *because* they were most suited to the corruption of the age. Nichiren, the Buddhist prophet, claimed that one could be saved only by the spiritual power of the Lotus Sūtra, whose gospel he alone was entitled to spread. The corruption of the age is no handicap: "The Adoration of the Lotus of the Perfect Truth shall prevail beyond the coming ages of ten thousand years, nay eternally in the future." It is indeed an advantage:

> Is it not true that one hundred years' training in a heavenly paradise does not compare with one day's work in the earthly world, and that all service to the Truth during the two thousand years of the ages of the Perfect Law and the Copied Law is inferior to that done in the one span of time in the age of the Latter Law? All these differences are due, not to Nichiren's own wisdom, but to the virtues inherent in the times. Flowers bloom in the spring, and fruits are ripe in the autumn; it is hot in summer and cold in winter. Is it not time that makes these differences?[39]

Nichiren here welcomes the processes of time, even if they bring corruption; he sees them as an opportunity for service to the truth. Time provides the opportunity for a turning point from degeneration to regeneration.

Nichiren laid special emphasis upon the particularity and specificity of the truth of humanity. The Japanese unfriendliness for universals is plain in this passage:

> The learning of just one word or one phrase of the Right Law, if only it accords with the time and the propensity of the learner, would lead him to the attainment of the Way. The mastery of a thousand scriptures and ten thousand theories, if they should not accord with the time and the propensity of the one who masters them would lead him nowhere.[40]

Nichiren evaluates doctrines by five standards, all specific in character. These are: the teaching of the sūtra, the spiritual endowments of the learner (what he calls the "propensity"), the country in which the doctrine is practiced, and the temporal order of circumstances affecting the practice of the doctrine. Saichō, an ancient Buddhist teacher, also regarded the time and the country as important factors, but it was Nichiren who established them as basic principles, presented in a clear and distinct form. Such a method of evaluation of religious truth in terms of social and individual particularities, would hardly be found in the Buddhist thought of India or China. It is clear that even where India and Japan have shared a set of religious assumptions, the characteristic national habits of thought have led to entirely different conceptions both of Time and of Ultimate Reality.

Bibliography

This is the bibliography of the articles or the passages reprinted in this Volume. The order of the bibliographical references here is the same as given in the list of the contents.

1. Bareau, André, 'The Notion of Time in Early Buddhism', *East and West* 7, 1957, pp. 353-64. (The Editor)
2. Walleser, M., 'Die Zeit', *Die philosophische Grundlage des älteren Buddhismus*, Heidelberg, 1925, pp. 123-33.
3. Sasaki, Genjun H., 'The Time Concept in Abhidharma', *Proceedings of the 26th International Congress of Orientalists*, New Delhi, 1964, pp. 471-80. (The Publisher)
4. Mus, Paul, 'La notion de temps réversible dans la mythologie bouddhique', *Annuaire de l'École pratique des Hautes-Études*, section des sciences religieuses. XIX- XX, 1939, pp. 5-38.
5. la Vallée Poussin, Louis de, 'Notes sur le 'moment' ou kṣaṇa des bouddhistes', *Rocznik Orientalistyczny* 8, 1932, pp. 1-9.
6. la Vallée Poussin, Louis de, 'La controverse de temps et du pudgala dans le Vijñānakāya', *Études Asiatiques (École française d'Extrême-Orient)*, 1925, pp. 343-76.
7. Stcherbatsky, Th., 'Vasubandhu on the Fundamental Principle of the Sarvāstivāda School', *The Central Conception of Buddhism and the Meaning of the Word "Dharma"*, Royal Asiatique Society, London, 1923. pp. 76-91.
8. la Vallée Poussin, Louis de, L'Abhidharmakośa de Vasubandhu Chapter V, Paul Geuthner, Paris, 1925, pp. 50-66.
9. la Vallée Poussin, Louis de, 'Documents d'Abhidharma: la controverse du temps', *Mélanges chinois bouddhiques* 5, 1937, pp. 7-158.
10. Keith, A.B., 'The Doctrine of Reality (The Nature of Time)', *Buddhist Philosophy in India and Ceylon*, Oxford University Press, 1923, pp. 163-68.

11. Schayer, Stanislaw, *Contributions to the Problem of Time in Indian Philosophy*, Krakow, 1938. (The Publisher)

12. Jha, G.N. (tr.), 'Examination of the doctrine of 'Traikālya'– Things continuing to exist during three points of Time', *The Tattvasaṃgraha of Śāntarakṣita with the Commentary of Kamalaśīla*, Oriental Institute, Baroda, 1939, Vol. II, pp. 861-86.

13. McDermott, A. Charlene, 'The Sautrāntika arguments against the traikālyavāda in the light of the contemporary tense revolution', *Philosophy East and West* 24, 1974, pp. 193-200. (The Editor)

14. Williams, Paul M., 'Buddhadeva and Temporali ty', *Journal of Indian Philosophy* 4, 1977, pp. 279- 94. (The Publisher)

15. McGovern, W.M., 'Cosmic Synthesis', *A Manual of Buddhist Philosophy*, London, 1923, pp. 43-48.

16. Stcherbatsky, Th., 'Le temps (kāla)', *La théorie de la connaissance et la logique chez les bouddhistes tardifs*, Librarie Orientaliste Paul Geuthner, Paris, 1926, pp. 12-39.

17. Inada, Kenneth K., 'Time and temporality- A Buddhist approach', *Philosophy East and West 24*, 1974, pp. 171-79. (The Editor)

18. Kalupahana, David J., 'The Buddhist conception of time and temporality', *Philosophy East and West* 24, 1974, pp. 181-91. (The Editor)

19. Koller, John M., 'On Buddhist view of devouring time', *Philosophy East and West* 24, 1974, pp. 201-8. (The Editor)

20. Lancaster, Lewis R., 'Discussion of time in Mahāyāna texts', *Philoso phy East and West* 24, 1974, pp. 209-14. (The Editor)

21. Mookerjee, Satkari, 'The Buddhist Doctrine of Flux (The Nature of Existence)', *The Buddhist Philosophy of Universal Flux*, University of Calcutta, 1935, pp. 1- 19.

22. Gupta, Rita, 'The Buddhist Doctrine of Momen tariness and its Pre-suppositions: Dharmakīrti's – Arguments in Hetubindu', *Journal of Indian Philosophy* 8, 1980, pp. 47-68. (The Publisher)

23. Prasad, Jwala, 'Discussion of the Buddhist Doctrine of Momentariness and Subjective Idealism in the Nyāya-sūtras', *Journal of the Royal Asiatic Society*, 1930, pp. 31-39.

24. Stcherbatsky, Th., 'The Theory of Instantaneous Being (Kṣaṇabhaṅga-vāda)', *Buddhist Logic*, Dover Publications, New York, 1962, (First published by the Academy of sciences of the USSR, Leningrad, 1930), pp. 79- 118.

25. Schrader, F.O., *Über den Stand der indis chen Philosophie zur Zeit Mahāvīras und Buddhas*, Leipzig, 1902.

26. Miyamoto, Shoson, 'Time and Eternity in Bud dhism', *Journal of Indian and Buddhist Studies* 7, no. 2, 1959, pp. 31-41. (The Editor).

27. Wayman, Alex, 'No Time, Great Time, and Profane Time in Buddhism', *Buddhist Insight* (Essays by Alex Wayman), Motilal Banarsidass, Delhi, 1989, pp. 269-85. (The author and the Publisher)

28. Nakamura, Hajime, 'Time in Indian and Japanese Thought', *The Voices of Time*, edited by J.T. Fraser, New York, G. Braziller, 1966, pp. 77-85. (The Editor)